West's Law School Advisory Board

IDEAS OF THE FIRST AMENDMENT

By

Vincent Blasi
Corliss Lamont Professor of Civil Liberties
Columbia Law School and
James Madison Distinguished Professor of Law
University of Virginia

AMERICAN CASEBOOK SERIES®

THOMSON
WEST™

Mat #40417208

610 Opperman Drive
P.O. Box 64526
St. Paul, MN 55164–0526
1–800–328–9352

Printed in the United States of America

ISBN-13: 978–0–314–16361–5
ISBN-10: 0–314–16361–1

TEXT IS PRINTED ON 10% POST CONSUMER RECYCLED PAPER

To Nancy,
who asks all the right questions,
and cares about the answers.

*

Preface

This book is as much about doctrinal ideas of First Amendment law as it is about philosophical ideas concerning the political and moral principle of freedom of speech. It is designed to facilitate a course in which the central project is to examine and answer such questions as: (1) Should it make an important difference whether the method of regulating speech is "prior," as with licensing requirements and injunctions, or "subsequent," as with criminal and civil sanctions? (2) Why, if at all, should regulations of speech that turn on the viewpoint expressed by the speaker be considered far more problematic than regulations that are "viewpoint neutral" in form but nevertheless highly speech-restrictive in their impact? (3) Should speech that is likely to cause harm in a short time frame and by means of a direct causal sequence be more subject to prohibition than speech the predicted consequences of which are delayed and contingent yet eventually very damaging? (4) Should only speech that conveys opinions, grievances, proposals, and observations of a political nature be accorded protection under the First Amendment? Or do the best reasons for a strong free speech principle apply as well to other expressive, communicative, or inquisitive endeavors such as artistic expression, scientific inquiry, and personal criticism? Does "the freedom of speech" extend to communications that are integral to, or that may even in themselves constitute, commercial transactions or discriminatory practices? Does the First Amendment imply a right to express oneself by means of symbolic conduct? A right not to reveal one's beliefs or political associations? A right to capture the (at least momentary) attention of unwilling audiences? In short, what counts as a First Amendment activity? (5) Ought reasons for regulating speech that are "paternalistic" in character, designed to protect audiences from their own susceptibilities, be categorically disallowed? (6) Is it ever permissible to limit the speech of some participants in public debate in order to prevent them from drowning out the voices of others? (7) Should the regulation of speech by means of civil sanctions or the denial of benefits be considered less problematic than the punishment of speech by means of criminal sanctions? (8) Does the First Amendment require that certain publicly-owned spaces and other resources be made available to facilitate speech by private citizens?

It is the thesis of this book that these and no more than three or four additional doctrinal ideas of comparable scope and importance ought to form the spine of an introductory course on the First Amendment. Furthermore, it is the (more original) thesis of this book that such questions are best studied not by examining, necessarily at a breathless pace, snippets of vast numbers of Supreme Court opinions that elaborate three-part tests and ever-proliferating doctrinal subcategories, but rather by engaging some of the greatest writings on the freedom of speech that have been generated in the Anglo-American tradition, and asking how those writings—some political polemics, some judicial opinions—might help one to think about the pivotal doctrinal questions.

A considerable advantage of this approach to the subject is that students can study, indeed *must* study, how some of the finest practitioners of the art of persuasion went about building their arguments. Because the canonical writings are few in number and reprinted virtually unedited, and because their rich arguments are the focal point of the course, the rushed treatment that diminishes too many law school courses can be avoided. The luxury of devoting one or two weeks to a single essay or opinion provides an opportunity to examine in a systematic fashion the different types of arguments that an advocate might employ: from consequences, from commitment, from coherence, from entitlement, from identity, from experience, from necessity, from character, from institutional capacity, from nature, from design, etc. When I teach these materials, I devote classroom time to studying the art of making concessions, anticipating and refuting counter-arguments, choosing illustrations, invoking authority, appealing to common sense and shared experience, delimiting contentions, rationing eloquence, ordering one's arguments, and not overreaching. Ideas of the First Amendment can be, in part, a course in elementary rhetoric—a subject that ought to play a larger role in a legal education than it currently does.

Although the book is not organized along conventional doctrinal lines, most of the leading Supreme Court opinions interpreting the First Amendment are included, each presented in juxtaposition with one of the canonical writings in order to facilitate critical evaluation and interpretation of both. The cumulative effect of using the cases in this way is that virtually all of the traditional doctrinal categories are covered. The book includes cases on: the advocacy of crime or revolution, libel, obscenity and pornography, campaign finance, publishing classified material, flag-burning, prior restraint, compelled speech and association, racial hate speech, on-site abortion protests, immigration and naturalization, broadcast regulation, the right of reply, selective subsidies for speech, labor picketing, commercial advertising, denials of public employment, guilt by association, library internet censorship, face-to-face insults, offensive speech, nude dancing, public demonstrations, and the freedom of expressive associations to practice forms of discrimination that are illegal in other contexts. Two issues that I consider especially basic and instructive, the pledge of allegiance and campaign finance, surface in almost every chapter.

Finally, this book is intended to help aspiring lawyers improve their writing. One of the best ways to become a better writer is to read good writers. The subject of freedom of speech has inspired some memorable prose. Each of the seven thinkers around whom these materials are organized was a great writer; two of them (Milton and Holmes) number among the finest stylists ever to employ the English language. This book puts that prose front and center.

Acknowledgments

So many students and colleagues contributed to this book that I cannot possibly list them all. Three outstanding teachers, Stanley Fish, Kent Greenawalt, and Seana Shiffrin, taught from these materials at various times and gave me the benefit of their experiences. On two occasions, I had the special pleasure of team teaching the course, first with Stanley Fish and later with Seana Shiffrin. Of the many students who offered suggestions that have been incorporated in the book, Micah Schwartzman deserves special mention for coming up with the idea for Chapter Nine. During the final months of preparing the materials for publication, I was aided in countless ways by Nicole Altman, Pallavi Guniganti, and Nathan Johnson. I could not have completed the book without their intelligent, energetic, and wise assistance. I have been fortunate to work at two law schools that encourage pedagogic innovations and facilitate them in every way possible. Among the many persons at Columbia Law School and the University of Virginia School of Law who have supported this project, I want especially to thank Pam Messina, Betty Snow, and Gabriel Soto for assistance (and patience) far beyond the call of duty. My greatest debt by far is to the remarkable students in the nineteen courses on Ideas of the First Amendment that I have taught at Columbia and the University of Virginia since 1992. Their thoughtful papers from those courses continue to educate me; they constitute my most valuable resource in preparing for class. What a privilege it has been to teach such talented and inquisitive students.

Excerpts from the following books and articles appear with the kind permission of the copyright holders or their lawful agents, executors, or successors.

Floyd Abrams, Speaking Freely: Trials of the First Amendment. Copyright 2005 by Floyd Abrams.

Sharon Achinstein, Milton and the Revolutionary Reader. Copyright 1994 by Princeton University Press.

Elizabeth Anderson, Value in Ethics and Economics. Copyright 1993 by Harvard University Press.

C. Edwin Baker, Human Liberty and Freedom of Speech. Copyright 1989 by Oxford University Press.

Jack M. Balkin, Digital Speech and Democratic Culture: A Theory of Freedom of Expression for the Information Society. Copyright 2004 by Jack M. Balkin.

Lance Banning, The Sacred Fire of Liberty: James Madison and the Founding of the Federal Republic. Copyright 1995 by Cornell University Press.

Arthur E. Barker, Milton and the Puritan Dilemma. Copyright 1942 by University of Toronto Press.

Isaiah Berlin, John Stuart Mill and the Ends of Life. Copyright 1969 by Isaiah Berlin. Permission granted by Curtis Brown Group, Ltd.

Lillian R. BeVier, Rehabilitating Public Forum Doctrine: In Defense of Categories. Copyright 1993 by the University of Chicago Press.

Lillian R. BeVier, United States v. American Library Association: Whither First Amendment Doctrine. Copyright 2004 by the University of Chicago Press.

Ashutosh A. Bhagwat, The Story of *Whitney v. California*: The Power of Ideas. Copyright 2004 by Foundation Press.

Vincent Blasi, Free Speech and Good Character: From Milton to Brandeis to the Present. Copyright 2002 by the University of Chicago Press.

Vincent Blasi, Holmes and the Marketplace of Ideas. Copyright 2005 by the University of Chicago Press.

Vincent Blasi, Milton's *Areopagitica* and the Modern First Amendment. Copyright 1996 by Yale Law School.

Vincent Blasi, School Vouchers and Religious Liberty: Seven Questions from Madison's Memorial and Remonstrance. Copyright 2002 by Cornell Law Review.

Vincent Blasi, Six Conservatives in Search of the First Amendment: The Revealing Case of Nude Dancing. Copyright 1992 by the William & Mary Law Review.

Vincent Blasi, The First Amendment and the Ideal of Civic Courage: The Brandeis Opinion in *Whitney v. California.* Copyright 1988 by the William & Mary Law Review.

Vincent Blasi & Seana Shiffrin, The Story of *West Virginia State Bd. of Educ. v. Barnette*: The Pledge of Allegiance and the Freedom of Thought. Copyright 2004 by Foundation Press.

Lee C. Bollinger, The Tolerant Society. Copyright 1986 by Oxford University Press.

Robert H. Bork, Neutral Principles and Some First Amendment Problems. Copyright 1971 by the Indiana Law Journal.

Robert H. Bork, The Tempting of America. Copyright 1990 by Robert H. Bork.

William Bouwsma, Venice and the Defense of Republican Liberty. Copyright 1968 by The University of California Press.

William J. Brennan, Jr., The Supreme Court and the Meiklejohn Interpretation of the First Amendment. Copyright 1965 by the Harvard Law Review Association.

Thomas Corns, John Milton: The Prose Works. Copyright 1998 by Simon & Schuster, Inc.

Robert M. Cover, The Left, The Right, and the First Amendment 1918–28. Copyright 1981 by the Maryland Law Review.

John Patrick Diggins, The Proud Decades: America in War and Peace 1941–1960. Copyright 1988 by John Patrick Diggins.

John Patrick Diggins, The Rise and Fall and the American Left. Copyright 1973 by John Patrick Diggins.

Ronald Dworkin, Freedom's Law: The Moral Reading of the Constitution. Copyright 1996 by Ronald Dworkin.

Frank H. Easterbrook, The State of Madison's Vision of the State: A Public Choice Perspective. Copyright 1994 by the Harvard Law Review Association.

Stanley Elkins & Eric McKitrick, The Age of Federalism. Copyright 1993 by Oxford University Press.

Joseph J. Ellis, Book Review: Founding Brothers. Copyright 1995 by The New Republic.

Stanley Fish, Driving from the Letter: Truth and Indeterminacy in Milton's *Areopagitica*. Copyright 1988 by Stanley Fish.

Owen M. Fiss, Free Speech and Social Structure. Copyright 1986 by Owen M. Fiss.

Eric Foner, The Story of American Freedom. Copyright 1999 by Eric Foner.

Charles Fried, The New First Amendment Jurisprudence: A Threat to Liberty. Copyright 1992 by the University of Chicago Law Review.

Fred W. Friendly, Minnesota Rag. Copyright 1981 by Fred W. Friendly.

Henry J. Friendly, Mr. Justice Brandeis: The Quest for Reason. Copyright 1960 by The University of Pennsylvania Law Review.

Henry Louis Gates, Book Review: Let Them Talk. Copyright 1993 by The New Republic.

Robert W. Gordon ed., The Legacy of Oliver Wendell Holmes, Jr. Copyright 1992 by Stanford University Press.

Kent Greenawalt, Fighting Words: Individuals, Communities and Liberties of Speech. Copyright 1995 by Princeton University Press.

Thomas C. Grey, Holmes and Legal Pragmatism. Copyright 1989 by Thomas C. Grey.

Thomas C. Grey, Holmes, Pragmatism, and Democracy. Copyright 1992 by the Oregon Law Review.

Gerald Gunther, Learned Hand and the Origins of Modern First Amendment Doctrine: Some Fragments of History. Copyright 1975 by Gerald Gunther.

Gerald Gunther, Learned Hand: The Man and the Judge. Copyright 1994 by Usingen Corporation (Alfred A. Knopf).

Learned Hand, Sources of Tolerance. Copyright 1939 by the University of Pennsylvania Law Review.

Thomas W. Hazlett and David W. Sosa, "Chilling" the Internet? Lessons from FCC Regulation of Radio Broadcasting. Copyright 1998 by the Michigan Telecommunications and Technology Law Review.

Christopher Hill, Milton and the English Revolution. Copyright 1977 by Christopher Hill.

John Illo, Areopagiticus Mythic and Real. Copyright 1988 by Taylor & Francis, Inc.

Harry Kalven, Jr., A Worthy Tradition. Copyright 1988 by Jamie Kalven.

Harry Kalven, Jr., The New York Times Case: A Note on the "Central Meaning of the First Amendment." Copyright 1964 by the University of Chicago Press.

N. H. Keeble, Milton and Puritanism. Copyright 2001 by Blackwell Publishing, Ltd.

Christopher Kendrick, Milton: A Study in Ideology and Form. Copyright 1986 by Christopher Kendrick.

Ralph Ketcham, Framed for Posterity: The Enduring Philosophy of the Constitution. Copyright 1993 by the University Press of Kansas.

Ralph Ketcham, James Madison: A Biography. Copyright 1991 by University of Virginia Press.

Charles R. Lawrence III, If He Hollers Let Him Go: Regulating Racist Speech on Campus. Copyright 1990 by Charles R. Lawrence III.

Leonard W. Levy, Emergence of a Free Press. Copyright 1985 by Leonard W. Levy.

Barbara K. Lewalski, The Life of John Milton. Copyright 2000 by Barbara K. Lewalski.

Anthony Lewis, Make No Law: The *Sullivan* Case and the First Amendment. Copyright 1991 by Anthony Lewis.

David Loewenstein, Milton and the Drama of History. Copyright 1990 by Cambridge University Press.

Catharine A. MacKinnon, Only Words. Copyright 1993 by Catharine A. MacKinnon.

Alpheus Thomas Mason, Brandeis: A Free Man's Life. Copyright 1956 by Alpheus Thomas Mason.

Alexander Meiklejohn, Free Speech and Its Relation to Self-Government. Copyright 1948 by Harper & Row. Permission granted by Harper-Collins Inc.

Alexander Meiklejohn, The First Amendment Is an Absolute. Copyright 1961 by the University of Chicago Press.

Alexander Meiklejohn, What Does the First Amendment Mean? Copyright 1953 by the University of Chicago Law Review.

Louis Menand, The Metaphysical Club. Copyright 2001 by Louis Menand.

Sheldon M. Novick, The Unrevised Holmes and Freedom of Expression. Copyright 1992 by the University of Chicago Press.

Michael St. John Packe, The Life of John Stuart Mill. Copyright 1954 by Michael St. John Packe.

J. Max Patrick ed., The Prose of John Milton. Copyright 1967 by Doubleday, a division of Random House, Inc.

Richard Polenberg, Fighting Faiths: The Abrams Case, the Supreme Court, and Free Speech. Copyright 1987 by Richard Polenberg.

Richard A. Posner ed., The Essential Holmes. Copyright 1992 by the University of Chicago Press.

Robert Post, Meiklejohn's Mistake. Copyright 1993 by Robert Post.

Robert Post, Reconciling Theory and Doctrine in First Amendment Jurisprudence. Copyright 2000 by Robert Post.

Robert W. Post, The Constitutional Concept of Public Discourse: Outrageous Opinion, Democratic Deliberation, and *Hustler Magazine v. Falwell*. Copyright 1990 by the Harvard Law Review Association.

David M. Rabban, Free Speech in Its Forgotten Years. Copyright 1997 by Cambridge University Press.

Margaret Jane Radin, Contested Commodities. Copyright 1996 by Harvard University Press.

Jack N. Rakove, James Madison and the Creation of the American Republic. Copyright 1990 by Jack N. Rakove.

Joseph Raz, Liberalism, Scepticism, and Democracy. Copyright 1989 by the Iowa Law Review.

Joseph Raz, Free Expression and Personal Identification. Copyright 1991 by Oxford University Press.

Martin H. Redish, Unlawful Advocacy and Free Speech Theory: Rethinking the Lessons of the McCarthy Era. Copyright 2004 by the University of Cincinnati Law Review.

Richard Rorty, Philosophy and Social Hope. Copyright 1999 by Richard Rorty.

Gary Rosen, American Compact: James Madison and the Problem of Founding. Copyright 1999 by the University Press of Kansas.

John Rumrich, Radical Heterodoxy and Heresy. Copyright 2001 by Blackwell Publishing, Ltd.

Alan Ryan ed., Mill: a Norton Critical Edition. Copyright 1997 by W. W. Norton & Co.

T. M. Scanlon, Jr., Freedom of Expression and Categories of Expression. Copyright 1979 by the University of Pittsburgh Law Review.

Frederick Schauer, Free Speech: A Philosophical Enquiry. Copyright 1982 by Cambridge University Press.

Steven H. Shiffrin, The First Amendment, Democracy, and Romance. Copyright 1990 by Steven H. Shiffrin.

Ernest Sirluck ed., The Complete Prose Works of John Milton, Vol. Two. Copyright 1959 by Yale University Press.

John Skorupski, John Stuart Mill. Copyright 1989 by John Skorupski.

Geoffrey R. Stone, Perilous Times: Free Speech in Wartime. Copyright 2004 by Geoffrey R. Stone.

Geoffrey R. Stone, Autonomy and Distrust. Copyright 1993 by the University of Colorado Law Review.

Philippa Strum, Brandeis: Beyond Progressivism. Copyright 1993 by Philippa Strum.

Philippa Strum, Louis D. Brandeis: Justice for the People. Copyright 1984 by Philippa Strum.

Kathleen M. Sullivan, Free Speech and Unfree Markets. Copyright 1995 by the University of California Los Angeles Law Review.

Kathleen M. Sullivan, Political Money and Freedom of Speech. Copyright 1997 by the University of California Davis Law Review.

Cass R. Sunstein, Deliberative Trouble? Why Groups Go to Extremes. Copyright 2000 by the Yale Law Journal.

Cass Sunstein, Republic.com. Copyright 2001 by Princeton University Press.

William Thomas, Mill. Copyright 1985 by Oxford University Press.

Richard Vernon, John Stuart Mill and Pornography: Beyond the Harm Principle. Copyright 1996 by the University of Chicago Press.

Jeremy Waldron, Mill and the Value of Moral Distress. Copyright 1987 by Blackwell Publishing, Ltd.

Christina E. Wells, Reinvigorating Autonomy: Freedom and Responsibility in the Supreme Court's First Amendment Jurisprudence. Copyright 1997 by the Harvard Civil Rights-Civil Liberties Law Review.

Bernard Williams, Truth and Truthfulness: An Essay in Genealogy. Copyright 2002 by Princeton University Press.

Bernard Wishy, Prefaces to Liberty: Selected Writings of John Stuart Mill. Copyright 1959 by Bernard Wishy.

The Learned Hand correspondence with Oliver Wendell Holmes, Jr., Zechariah Chafee, Jr, Felix Frankfurter, and Elliot Richardson is reproduced by permission of the Harvard Law School and Mr. Jonathan Hand Churchill, literary executor for the Hon. Learned Hand.

*

Summary of Contents

Table of Contents

Chapter Six (Oliver Wendell Holmes)

*

Table of Cases

The principal cases are in bold type. References are to pages.

IDEAS OF THE FIRST AMENDMENT

*

United States Constitution

Amendment One

Congress shall make no law respecting an establishment of religion, or prohibiting the free exercise thereof; or abridging the freedom of speech, or of the press; or the right of the people peaceably to assemble, and to petition the government for a redress of grievances.

*

Chapter One

INTRODUCTION

MINERSVILLE SCHOOL DIST. v. GOBITIS

Supreme Court of the United States, 1940.
310 U.S. 586, 60 S.Ct. 1010, 84 L.Ed. 1375.

Mr. JUSTICE FRANKFURTER delivered the opinion of the Court.

* * *

Lillian Gobitis, aged twelve, and her brother William, aged ten, were expelled from the public schools of Minersville, Pennsylvania, for refusing to salute the national flag as part of a daily school exercise. The local Board of Education required both teachers and pupils to participate in this ceremony. The ceremony is a familiar one. The right hand is placed on the breast and the following pledge recited in unison: "I pledge allegiance to my flag, and to the Republic for which it stands; one nation indivisible, with liberty and justice for all." While the words are spoken, teachers and pupils extend their right hands in salute to the flag. The Gobitis family are affiliated with "Jehovah's Witnesses", for whom the Bible as the Word of God is the supreme authority. The children had been brought up conscientiously to believe that such a gesture of respect for the flag was forbidden by command of scripture.[1]

* * *

We must decide whether the requirement of participation in such a ceremony, exacted from a child who refuses upon sincere religious grounds, infringes without due process of law the liberty guaranteed by the Fourteenth Amendment.

* * *

1. Reliance is especially placed on the following verses from Chapter 20 of Exodus:

"3. Thou shalt have no other gods before me.

"4. Thou shalt not make unto thee any graven image, or any likeness of any thing that is in heaven above, or that is in the earth beneath, or that is in the water under the earth:

"5. Thou shalt not bow down thyself to them, nor serve them: * * * "

In the judicial enforcement of religious freedom we are concerned with a historic concept. See Mr. Justice Cardozo in *Hamilton v. Regents*, 293 U.S. 245, 265, 55 S.Ct. 197, at page 205, 79 L.Ed. 343. The religious liberty which the Constitution protects has never excluded legislation of general scope not directed against doctrinal loyalties of particular sects. Judicial nullification of legislation cannot be justified by attributing to the framers of the Bill of Rights views for which there is no historic warrant. Conscientious scruples have not, in the course of the long struggle for religious toleration, relieved the individual from obedience to a general law not aimed at the promotion or restriction of religious beliefs.-The mere possession of religious convictions which contradict the relevant concerns of a political society does not relieve the citizen from the discharge of political responsibilities. The necessity for this adjustment has again and again been recognized. In a number of situations the exertion of political authority has been sustained, while basic considerations of religious freedom have been left inviolate. *Reynolds v. United States*, 98 U.S. 145; *Davis v. Beason*, 133 U.S. 333; Selective Draft Law Cases, 245 U.S. 366; *Hamilton v. Regents*, 293 U.S. 245. In all these cases the general laws in question, upheld in their application to those who refused obedience from religious conviction, were manifestations of specific powers of government deemed by the legislature essential to secure and maintain that orderly, tranquil, and free society without which religious toleration itself is unattainable. Nor does the freedom of speech assured by Due Process move in a more absolute circle of immunity than that enjoyed by religious freedom. Even if it were assumed that freedom of speech goes beyond the historic concept of full opportunity to utter and to disseminate views, however heretical or offensive to dominant opinion, and includes freedom from conveying what may be deemed an implied but rejected affirmation, the question remains whether school children, like the Gobitis children, must be excused from conduct required of all the other children in the promotion of national cohesion. We are dealing with an interest inferior to none in the hierarchy of legal values. National unity is the basis of national security.

* * *

This Court has had occasion to say that "the flag is the symbol of the nation's power,—the emblem of freedom in its truest, best sense.... it signifies government resting on the consent of the governed; liberty regulated by law; the protection of the weak against the strong; security against the exercise of arbitrary power; and absolute safety for free institutions against foreign aggression." *Halter v. Nebraska*, 205 U.S. 34, 43.

* * *

The influences which help toward a common feeling for the common country are manifold. Some may seem harsh and others no doubt are foolish. Surely, however, the end is legitimate. And the effective means for its attainment are still so uncertain and so unauthenticated by science as to preclude us from putting the widely prevalent belief in flag-saluting beyond the pale of legislative power. It mocks reason and denies our whole history to find in the allowance of a requirement to salute our flag on fitting occasions the seeds of sanction for obeisance to a leader.

The wisdom of training children in patriotic impulses by those compulsions which necessarily pervade so much of the educational process is not for our independent judgment. Even were we convinced of the folly of such a measure, such belief would be no proof of its unconstitutionality. For ourselves, we might be tempted to say that the deepest patriotism is best engendered by giving unfettered scope to the most crochety beliefs. Perhaps it is best, even from the standpoint of those interests which ordinances like the one under review seek to promote, to give to the least popular sect leave from conformities like those here in issue. But the court-room is not the arena for debating issues of educational policy. It is not our province to choose among competing considerations in the subtle process of securing effective loyalty to the traditional ideals of democracy, while respecting at the same time individual idiosyncracies among a people so diversified in racial origins and religious allegiances. So to hold would in effect make us the school board for the country. That authority has not been given to this Court, nor should we assume it.

* * *

Judicial review, itself a limitation on popular government, is a fundamental part of our constitutional scheme. But to the legislature no less than to courts is committed the guardianship of deeply-cherished liberties. *See Missouri, K. & T.R. Co. of Texas v. May*, 194 U.S. 267, 270. Where all the effective means of inducing political changes are left free from interference, education in the abandonment of foolish legislation is itself a training in liberty. To fight out the wise use of legislative authority in the forum of public opinion and before legislative assemblies rather than to transfer such a contest to the judicial arena, serves to vindicate the self-confidence of a free people.[2]

Reversed.

Mr. Justice McReynolds concurs in the result.

Mr. Justice Stone (dissenting).

I think the judgment below should be affirmed.

Two youths, now fifteen and sixteen years of age, are by the judgment of this Court held liable to expulsion from the public schools and to denial of all publicly supported educational privileges because of their refusal to yield to the compulsion of a law which commands their participation in a school ceremony contrary to their religious convictions. They and their father are citizens and have not exhibited by any action

2. It is to be noted that the Congress has not entered the field of legislation here under consideration.

or statement of opinion, any disloyalty to the Government of the United States. They are ready and willing to obey all its laws which do not conflict with what they sincerely believe to be the higher commandments of God. It is not doubted that these convictions are religious, that they are genuine, or that the refusal to yield to the compulsion of the law is in good faith and with all sincerity. It would be a denial of their faith as well as the teachings of most religions to say that children of their age could not have religious convictions.

The law which is thus sustained is unique in the history of Anglo–American legislation. It does more than suppress freedom of speech and more than prohibit the free exercise of religion, which concededly are forbidden by the First Amendment and are violations of the liberty guaranteed by the Fourteenth. For by this law the state seeks to coerce these children to express a sentiment which, as they interpret it, they do not entertain, and which violates their deepest religious convictions.

* * *

The guaranties of civil liberty are but guaranties of freedom of the human mind and spirit and of reasonable freedom and opportunity to express them. They presuppose the right of the individual to hold such opinions as he will and to give them reasonably free expression, and his freedom, and that of the state as well, to teach and persuade others by the communication of ideas. The very essence of the liberty which they guaranty is the freedom of the individual from compulsion as to what he shall think and what he shall say, at least where the compulsion is to bear false witness to his religion. If these guaranties are to have any meaning they must, I think, be deemed to withhold from the state any authority to compel belief or the expression of it where that expression violates religious convictions, whatever may be the legislative view of the desirability of such compulsion.

History teaches us that there have been but few infringements of personal liberty by the state which have not been justified, as they are here, in the name of righteousness and the public good, and few which have not been directed, as they are now, at politically helpless minorities. The framers were not unaware that under the system which they created most governmental curtailments of personal liberty would have the support of a legislative judgment that the public interest would be better served by its curtailment than by its constitutional protection. I cannot conceive that in prescribing, as limitations upon the powers of government, the freedom of the mind and spirit secured by the explicit guaranties of freedom of speech and religion, they intended or rightly could have left any latitude for a legislative judgment that the compulsory expression of belief which violates religious convictions would better serve the public interest than their protection. The Constitution may well elicit expressions of loyalty to it and to the government which it created, but it does not command such expressions or otherwise give any indication that compulsory expressions of loyalty play any such part in our scheme of government as to override the constitutional protection of freedom of speech and religion. And while such expressions of loyalty, when voluntarily given, may promote national unity, it is quite another matter to say that their compulsory expression by children in violation of their own and their parents' religious convictions can be regarded as playing so important a part in our national unity as to leave school boards free to exact it despite the constitutional guarantee of freedom of religion. The very terms of the Bill of Rights preclude, it seems to me, any reconciliation of such compulsions with the constitutional guaranties by a legislative declaration that they are more important to the public welfare than the Bill of Rights.

VINCENT BLASI & SEANA V. SHIFFRIN, THE STORY OF *WEST VIRGINIA STATE BOARD OF EDUCATION v. BARNETTE*: THE PLEDGE OF ALLEGIANCE AND THE FREEDOM OF THOUGHT

in Constitutional Law Stories (M. Dorf ed. 2004).

The Court's ruling upholding the power of the school board to require all children, including the Witnesses, to salute the flag was handed down June 3, 1940, as routed French and British troops were desperately being evacuated from Dunkirk. Many Americans regarded the Witnesses' refusal to recite the pledge as evidence of disloyalty and of their sympathy and even collaboration with the Nazi regime.[40] Fears at the time ran high about a "fifth column," a largely imagined network of domestic spies and enemies. The Witnesses were suspected by some of involvement in such a network. These misguided suspicions were only reinforced as the Witnesses persisted in their refusal to recite the pledge even after *Gobitis* was handed down.

In the weeks following the Supreme Court's decision, there were hundreds of violent attacks against Witnesses and their property, some abetted by local law enforcement officials. In Richwood, West Virginia, a group of American Legion vigilantes, led by a sheriff's deputy, forced several Witnesses to drink large quantities of castor oil, roped them together, then paraded them through the town. Over five hundred taunting citizens followed the procession, which at one point was halted for an impromptu flag salute ceremony and a reading of the American

40. Ironically, the Witnesses viewed the required pledge as an imported mechanism of Nazi oppression aimed particularly at them. Although they misperceived the impetus and historical origins of the pledge, the Witnesses' fears of the Nazis were well grounded. The Nazis outlawed the movement's activities in 1933, and in response the Witnesses refused to deliver the Nazi salute. Approximately 10,000 Jehovah's Witnesses in Germany were sent to concentration camps. *See* J.S. Conway, *The Nazi Persecution of the Churches, 1933–45,* at 196 (1968) ("Foremost among the opponents of Nazism were the Jehovah's Witnesses, of whom a higher proportion (97 per cent) suffered some form of persecution than any of the other churches. No less than a third of the whole following were to lose their lives as a result of their refusal to conform or compromise.") The Witness movement was also banned in Canada and Australia for a short period of years in the 1940s. Witnesses have suffered a variety of forms of persecution in a number of other countries as well, among them Spain, Italy, Greece, Argentina, Egypt and Indonesia.

Legion constitution. Finally, the Witnesses were marched to the edge of town, where they found their automobiles painted with swastikas and graffiti accusing them of being "Hitler's spies" and a "Fifth Column." A Rawlins, Wyoming mob beat up five Witnesses, three men and two women, and burned their cars; in another Wyoming community, a member of the sect was literally tarred and feathered. Two months after the *Gobitis* decision, in August 1940, Albert Walkenhorst was lured from his home in Norfolk, Nebraska, by a group of vigilantes posing as fellow Witnesses and castrated. A month later, near Little Rock, Arkansas, a Jehovah's Witnesses convention ground was assaulted by workers from a federal pipeline project wielding as weapons screwdrivers, pipes, and firearms; two Witnesses were shot and four others were hospitalized.

Although vigilante activity against the Witnesses increased dramatically following the Court's flag salute ruling, there had been disturbing incidents earlier that year. In April of 1940, Walter Chaplinsky, a vociferous Jehovah's Witness preaching in Rochester, New Hampshire, was surrounded by a group of men who scornfully invited him to salute the flag. While one veteran attempted to pummel Chaplinsky, the town marshal looked on, warned the Witness that things were turning ugly, but refused to arrest the assailant. After the marshal left, the assailant returned with a flag and attempted to impale Chaplinsky on the flagpole, eventually pinning him onto a car while other members of the crowd began to beat him. A police officer then arrived, not to detain or disperse members of the mob but to escort Chaplinsky to the police station. En route, the officer and others who joined the escort directed epithets at the hapless Witness. When Chaplinsky responded in kind, calling the marshal who had reappeared "a damn fascist and a racketeer," he was arrested for, and later convicted of, using offensive language in public.

The American Civil Liberties Union collected reports of these assaults. Its records, which were forwarded to the Justice Department, indicated that in 1940 attacks were mounted against nearly 1500 Jehovah's Witnesses in 335 separate incidents in 44 states. After reviewing the files, Justice Department attorneys Victor W. Rotnem and F. G. Folsom, Jr., observed: "Almost without exception, the flag and the flag salute can be found as the percussion cap that sets off these acts." In Litchfield, Illinois, vigilantes pulled Witness Bob Fischer from his car, draped a flag over the hood, and when he refused their demand that he salute the flag, slammed his head against the hood for nearly thirty minutes as the chief of police looked on. One participant later bragged, "We almost beat one guy to death to make him kiss the flag." A Connorsville, Indiana mob went on the attack after the rancorous trial of Witnesses Grace Trent and Lucy McKee for flag desecration, sedition, and riotous conspiracy. The attorney for the defendants, his wife, and several other Witnesses who attended the proceedings were beaten and chased out of town. The behavior of the defendants that provoked the prosecution and the vigilantes' wrath consisted of distributing literature opposing the compulsory pledge of allegiance and refusing to salute a Legionnaire's flag lapel pin. The Boston Globe reported that after the

Witnesses' Kingdom Hall in Kennebunk, Maine was burned, "someone affixed a small American flag to the charred front of the hall." Reporter Beulah Amidon observed a crowd "in an unnamed hamlet in the Deep South" throwing pieces of wood and rubble at a procession of seven Jehovah's Witnesses. When she asked the local sheriff, who was enjoying the spectacle, what had caused the disturbance, he explained that the Witnesses were being run out of town: "They're traitors—the Supreme Court says so. Ain't you heard?"

Questions

1) In his majority opinion in *Gobitis*, Justice Frankfurter adopts a highly deferential standard of judicial review, in large part because "[t]o fight out the wise use of legislative authority in the forum of public opinion and before legislative assemblies rather than to transfer such a contest to the judicial arena, serves to vindicate the self-confidence of a free people." Do the vigilante atrocities that followed in the wake of the Court's decision cast doubt on this claim? Or is the important part of the story, in terms of Justice Frankfurter's preference for political remedies, the role of the Justice Department in bringing the persecution of the Jehovah's Witnesses to public attention? What should we make of the frequent presence of local law enforcement officials among the members of the mobs that attacked the Witnesses for their refusal to salute the flag?

2) In his *Gobitis* dissent, Justice Stone states that the "very essence" of the constitutional guaranties of civil liberty is "the freedom of the individual from compulsion as to what he shall think and what he shall say, at least where the compulsion is to bear false witness to his religion." Did any of the Witness children suffer "compulsion as to what he shall think?" Why the "at least" qualification? Do Justice Stone's reasons for protecting citizens from having to "bear false witness" not apply when the objector's grounds of refusal are moral or political rather than religious?

CHAPLINSKY v. NEW HAMPSHIRE

Supreme Court of the United States, 1942.
315 U.S. 568, 62 S.Ct. 766, 86 L.Ed. 1031.

Mr. JUSTICE MURPHY delivered the opinion of the Court.

Appellant, a member of the sect known as Jehovah's Witnesses, was convicted in the municipal court of Rochester, New Hampshire, for violation of Chapter 378, Section 2, of the Public Laws of New Hampshire: "No person shall address any offensive, derisive or annoying word to any other person who is lawfully in any street or other public place, nor call him by any offensive or derisive name, nor make any noise or exclamation in his presence and hearing with intent to deride, offend or annoy him, or to prevent him from pursuing his lawful business or occupation."

The complaint charged that appellant "with force and arms, in a certain public place in said city of Rochester, to wit, on the public sidewalk on the easterly side of Wakefield Street, near unto the entrance of the City Hall, did unlawfully repeat, the words following, addressed to the complainant, that is to say, 'You are a God damned racketeer' and 'a damned Fascist and the whole government of Rochester are Fascists or agents of Fascists' the same being offensive, derisive and annoying words and names."

Upon appeal there was a trial de novo of appellant before a jury in the Superior Court. He was found guilty and the judgment of conviction was affirmed by the Supreme Court of the State. 91 N.H. 310, 18 A.2d 754.

By motions and exceptions, appellant raised the questions that the statute was invalid under the Fourteenth Amendment of the Constitution of the United States in that it placed an unreasonable restraint on freedom of speech, freedom of the press, and freedom of worship, and because it was vague and indefinite. These contentions were overruled and the case comes here on appeal.

There is no substantial dispute over the facts. Chaplinsky was distributing the literature of his sect on the streets of Rochester on a busy Saturday afternoon. Members of the local citizenry complained to the City Marshal, Bowering, that Chaplinsky was denouncing all religion as a "racket". Bowering told them that Chaplinsky was lawfully engaged, and then warned Chaplinsky that the crowd was getting restless. Some time later a disturbance occurred and the traffic officer on duty at the busy intersection started with Chaplinsky for the police station, but did not inform him that he was under arrest or that he was going to be arrested. On the way they encountered Marshal Bowering who had been advised that a riot was under way and was therefore hurrying to the scene. Bowering repeated his earlier warning to Chaplinsky who then addressed to Bowering the words set forth in the complaint.

Chaplinsky's version of the affair was slightly different. He testified that when he met Bowering, he asked him to arrest the ones responsible for the disturbance. In reply Bowering cursed him and told him to come along. Appellant admitted that he said the words charged in the complaint with the exception of the name of the Deity.

Over appellant's objection the trial court excluded as immaterial testimony relating to appellant's mission "to preach the true facts of the Bible", his treatment at the hands of the crowd, and the alleged neglect of duty on the part of the police. This action was approved by the court below which held that neither provocation nor the truth of the utterance would constitute a defense to the charge.

It is now clear that "Freedom of speech and freedom of the press, which are protected by the First Amendment from infringement by Congress, are among the fundamental personal rights and liberties which are protected by the Fourteenth Amendment from invasion by state action." *Lovell v. City of Griffin*, 303 U.S. 444, 450. Freedom of worship is similarly sheltered. Cantwell v. Connecticut, 310 U.S. 296, 303.

Appellant assails the statute as a violation of all three freedoms, speech, press and worship, but only an attack on the basis of free speech is warranted. The spoken, not the written, word is involved. And we cannot conceive that cursing a public officer is the exercise of religion in any sense of the term. But even if the activities of the appellant which preceded the incident could be viewed as religious in character, and therefore entitled to the protection of the Fourteenth Amendment, they would not cloak him with immunity from the legal consequences for concomitant acts committed in violation of a valid criminal statute. We turn, therefore, to an examination of the statute itself.

Allowing the broadest scope to the language and purpose of the Fourteenth Amendment, it is well understood that the right of free speech is not absolute at all times and under all circumstances. There are certain well-defined and narrowly limited classes of speech, the prevention and punishment of which has never been thought to raise any Constitutional problem. These include the lewd and obscene, the profane, the libelous, and the insulting or "fighting" words—those which by their very utterance inflict injury or tend to incite an immediate breach of the peace. It has been well observed that such utterances are no essential part of any exposition of ideas, and are of such slight social value as a step to truth that any benefit that may be derived from them is clearly outweighed by the social interest in order and morality. "Resort to epithets or personal abuse is not in any proper sense communication of information or opinion safeguarded by the Constitution, and its punishment as a criminal act would raise no question under that instrument." *Cantwell v. Connecticut,* 310 U.S. 296, 309, 310.

The state statute here challenged comes to us authoritatively construed by the highest court of New Hampshire. It has two provisions—the first relates to words or names addressed to another in a public place; the second refers to noises and exclamations. The court (91 N.H. 310, 18 A.2d 757) said: "The two provisions are distinct. One may stand separately from the other. Assuming, without holding, that the second were unconstitutional, the first could stand if constitutional." We accept that construction of severability and limit our consideration to the first provision of the statute.

On the authority of its earlier decisions, the state court declared that the statute's purpose was to preserve the public peace, no words being "forbidden except such as have a direct tendency to cause acts of violence by the person to whom, individually, the remark is addressed."[3] It was further said: "The word 'offensive' is not to be defined in terms of what a particular addressee thinks. * * * The test is what men of common intelligence would understand would be words likely to cause an average addressee to fight. * * * The English language has a number of words and expressions which by general consent are 'fighting words'

3. *State v. Brown,* 68 N.H. 200, 38 A. 731; State v. McConnell, 70 N.H. 294, 47 A. 267.

when said without a disarming smile. * * * Such words, as ordinary men know, are likely to cause a fight. So are threatening, profane or obscene revilings. Derisive and annoying words can be taken as coming within the purview of the statute as heretofore interpreted only when they have this characteristic of plainly tending to excite the addressee to a breach of the peace. * * * The statute, as construed, does no more than prohibit the face-to-face words plainly likely to cause a breach of the peace by the addressee, words whose speaking constitute a breach of the peace by the speaker—including 'classical fighting words', words in current use less 'classical' but equally likely to cause violence, and other disorderly words, including profanity, obscenity and threats."

We are unable to say that the limited scope of the statute as thus construed contravenes the constitutional right of free expression. It is a statute narrowly drawn and limited to define and punish specific conduct lying within the domain of state power, the use in a public place of words likely to cause a breach of the peace. *Cf. Cantwell v. Connecticut*, 310 U.S. 296, 311; *Thornhill v. Alabama*, 310 U.S. 88, 105. This conclusion necessarily disposes of appellant's contention that the statute is so vague and indefinite as to render a conviction there under a violation of due process. A statute punishing verbal acts, carefully drawn so as not unduly to impair liberty of expression, is not too vague for a criminal law. *Cf. Fox v. Washington*, 236 U.S. 273, 277.

Nor can we say that the application of the statute to the facts disclosed by the record substantially or unreasonably impinges upon the privilege of free speech. Argument is unnecessary to demonstrate that the appellations "damn racketeer" and "damn Fascist" are epithets likely to provoke the average person to retaliation, and thereby cause a breach of the peace.

The refusal of the state court to admit evidence of provocation and evidence bearing on the truth or falsity of the utterances is open to no Constitutional objection. Whether the facts sought to be proved by such evidence constitute a defense to the charge or may be shown in mitigation are questions for the state court to determine. Our function is fulfilled by a determination that the challenged statute, on its face and as applied, does not contravene the Fourteenth Amendment.

Affirmed.

KENT GREENAWALT, FIGHTING WORDS: INDIVIDUALS, COMMUNITIES, AND LIBERTIES OF SPEECH

(1995).

What communications do the reasons for free speech cover? Liberal democracies have a great need for free discourse about public affairs, but the reasons for liberty of speech are much broader, extending to all subjects of human concern. They clearly cover general statements of fact, such as "rapid inflation causes social instability," and particular statements of fact, such as "Serbians shelled Sarajevo yesterday." They also cover general and particular assertions of value: "love is the greatest good" and "you should not lie to your friend about your grades." The reasons for free speech also cover stories, works of art, and outbursts of feeling whose aim is to express and illuminate by means other than explicit statements of fact or value.

The reasons for free speech hardly apply to some sorts of communication. Consider two people agreeing to commit a crime. Their words of agreement dominantly represent commitments to action, not assertions of facts or values or expressions of feeling. Their words *change* the normative environment the two people inhabit, creating new obligations and claims. The communications are what I call *situation-altering*; they are much more "action" than "expression." It should come as little surprise that the punishment of ordinary criminal conspiracies has rarely been thought to raise problems of free speech. Orders or commands, offers of agreement, and invitations, such as "just try to hit me," are similar to agreements in their situation-altering character. These also change the normative environment. So do what I call *manipulative threats* and *offers*. Suppose Gertrude tells Claude, "I will give you two thousand dollars if you hire my sister"; or, "I will tell everyone about your time in prison if you do not hire her." Gertrude's comment in either instance sets in play consequences that would not otherwise occur; they are situation-altering.

Hovering between situation-altering utterances and ordinary assertions of fact and value are what I call *weak imperatives*. These weak imperatives are requests and encouragements that do not sharply alter the listener's normative environment, as does a command. If Gertrude says to her distant acquaintance, "Please hire Joseph," or "Beat him up," her immediate aim is to produce action, but she has not created new rights or new obligations, or new consequences of Claude's behavior. Weak imperatives often indicate feelings and reflect beliefs about values and facts, and they cannot always be disentangled from expressions about these matters. Weak imperatives are covered by the reasons for free speech to a greater degree than situation-altering utterances, but they may be prohibited more often than assertions of fact and value.

* * *

The *meaning* of most insults and epithets amounts to mixed assertions of facts and values. Words like "stupid" and "cheating" have fairly definite content. The significance of group epithets is much more vague, but they call to mind whatever "negative" qualities are associated with a group, qualities such as laziness, greed, dishonesty, stupidity, vulgarity. They also indicate a harsh, unfavorable judgment about members of the group.

If insults and group epithets involve assertions of fact and value, does it follow that they are covered by the reasons for freedom of speech? Even if they are covered, their restriction *might* still be warranted because these comments are too dangerous or too misleading; but should we recognize candidly that restriction is an exception to the privilege speakers usually have to choose their own terms to express their views? When insults and group epithets are spoken about people who are not present, they are indeed an extremely crude way to attribute characteristics and render judgments. Many of the broad reasons for free speech clearly apply.

In contrast, when insults and epithets are employed face-to-face, the analysis of their use becomes more complicated. In such encounters, abusive remarks often approximate "ordinary" action more closely and may even amount to situation-altering utterances. At the extreme, social convention might establish that certain insults invite or even "demand" set responses, i.e., calling a man "chicken" to his face might be understood as a challenge to fight. In that event, uttering the insult would be a different way of saying "I challenge you to fight." As chapter 1 explains, such a statement is situation-altering because it changes the normative environment. It grants the listener a privilege to fight, and in some environments may place him under a kind of duty to fight if he is not to be judged a coward. The phrase, "you are chicken," seems to have some fact and value content, attributing cowardice, but if "you are chicken," just happens to be how one invites a fight, the situation-altering aspect matters more than any message about the qualities of the person who is challenged. No insults function widely with this kind of precision in modern western societies, but conventions among various subgroups may approximate this kind of clarity. In settings where a person utters abusive words that are understood by him and his listener to invite a fight, the communication is dominantly situation-altering.

* * *

Abusive words can be deeply wounding to their victims, but is that a proper basis for criminal penalties or civil liability? Much harsh language is a natural part of heated personal exchanges and strong intellectual disagreements. Since few of us are able and inclined to modulate our discourse to the magnitude of a subject, the law must tolerate many words that hurt. The Supreme Court has been right to invalidate criminal provisions that reach broadly to offensive or opprobrious language.

If the use of any words can be punished because they wound the listener, it is only a small subcategory of all injurious words; a category narrowed in terms of the speaker's aims, the way language is used, damage to the listener, or some combination of these criteria. Suppose that four men think that humiliating a Hispanic woman who is standing alone would be "fun." They use their harshest words to insult her gender and ethnic origin, and call her a "whore." Their words wound deeply. Remarks whose dominant object is to hurt and humiliate, not to assert facts or values, have very limited expressive value. Their harm can be serious. Writing of racist remarks, Mari Matsuda said, "The negative effects of hate messages are real and immediate for the victims.

Victims of vicious hate propaganda have experienced physiological symptoms and emotional distress ranging from fear in the gut, rapid pulse rate and difficulty in breathing, nightmares, post-traumatic stress disorder, hypertension, psychosis, and suicide." Viewed alone, verbal behavior aimed dominantly at humiliation should not be constitutionally protected against punishment.

This conclusion fits the actual language of *Chaplinsky*, which speaks of words "which by their very utterance inflict injury *or* tend to incite an immediate breach of the peace." But line-drawing problems are severe. The speaker's motives may be mixed, and separating an intent to humiliate from an honest but vulgar statement of views is often difficult. A general criminal prohibition of abusive words that are designed to hurt and humiliate probably should be judged unconstitutional. However, penalties are proper when, as in my example, someone has *initiated contact* with a person just to harass him or her. Such behavior resembles making harassing telephone calls, an activity that courts have consistently assumed may be punished despite the absence of a danger of immediate violence. Penalties are also proper when abusive language accompanies a clear intent to intimidate someone from exercising legally protected rights.

Questions

1) Is it accurate to characterize a statement by a man who believes he is in police custody, delivered directly to the City Marshal, "You are a God damned racketeer" as "no essential part of any exposition of ideas." What about Chaplinsky's further assertion, "the whole government of Rochester are Fascists or agents of Fascists?" Does the fact that Chaplinsky was aggrieved that the persons who had attacked him were not being arrested bear on whether his remarks should be considered to be within the class of utterances that raise a First Amendment issue when they are the basis for a criminal prosecution?

2) What is the relationship, in the *Chaplinsky* Court's view, between its assertion that fighting words "by their very utterance inflict injury or tend to incite an immediate breach of the peace" and its claim that such words are "of slight social value as a step to truth"?

3) Would it have mattered to the Court if Chaplinsky had not directed his remarks directly to Marshal Bowering? Should it have?

4) Is there any basis in the text of the First Amendment for marking out a class of utterances to which the protections of the constitutional provision categorically do not apply?

WEST VIRGINIA STATE BOARD OF EDUCATION v. BARNETTE

Supreme Court of the United States, 1943.
319 U.S. 624, 63 S.Ct. 1178, 87 L.Ed. 1628.

Mr. JUSTICE JACKSON delivered the opinion of the Court.

Following the decision by this Court on June 3, 1940, in *Minersville School District v. Gobitis*, 310 U.S. 586, the West Virginia legislature amended its statutes to require all schools therein to conduct courses of instruction in history, civics, and in the Constitutions of the United States and of the State "for the purpose of teaching, fostering and perpetuating the ideals, principles and spirit of Americanism, and increasing the knowledge of the organization and machinery of the government." Appellant Board of Education was directed, with advice of the State Superintendent of Schools, to "prescribe the courses of study covering these subjects" for public schools. The Act made it the duty of private, parochial and denominational schools to prescribe courses of study "similar to those required for the public schools."

The Board of Education on January 9, 1942, adopted a resolution containing recitals taken largely from the Court's *Gobitis* opinion and ordering that the salute to the flag become "a regular part of the program of activities in the public schools," that all teachers and pupils "shall be required to participate in the salute honoring the Nation represented by the Flag; provided, however, that refusal to salute the Flag be regarded as an Act of insubordination, and shall be dealt with accordingly."

The resolution originally required the "commonly accepted salute to the Flag" which it defined. Objections to the salute as "being too much like Hitler's" were raised by the Parent and Teachers Association, the Boy and Girl Scouts, the Red Cross, and the Federation of Women's Clubs.[4] Some modification appears to have been made in deference to these objections, but no concession was made to Jehovah's Witnesses.[5] What is now required is the "stiff-arm" salute, the saluter to keep the right hand raised with palm turned up while the following is repeated: "I

4. The National Headquarters of the United States Flag Association takes the position that the extension of the right arm in this salute to the flag is not the Nazi–Fascist salute, "although quite similar to it. In the Pledge to the Flag the right arm is extended and raised, palm Upward, whereas the Nazis extend the arm practically straight to the front (the finger tips being about even with the eyes), palm Downward, and the Fascists do the same except they raise the arm slightly higher." James A. Moss, *The Flag of the United States: Its History and Symbolism* (1914) 108.

5. They have offered in lieu of participating in the flag salute ceremony "periodically and publicly" to give the following pledge:

"I have pledged my unqualified allegiance and devotion to Jehovah, the Almighty God, and to His Kingdom, for which Jesus commands all Christians to pray.

"I respect the flag of the United States and acknowledge it as a symbol of freedom and justice to all.

"I pledge allegiance and obedience to all the laws of the United States that are consistent with God's law, as set forth in the Bible."

pledge allegiance to the Flag of the United States of America and to the Republic for which it stands; one Nation, indivisible, with liberty and justice for all."

Failure to conform is "insubordination" dealt with by expulsion. Readmission is denied by statute until compliance. Meanwhile the expelled child is "unlawfully absent" and may be proceeded against as a delinquent. His parents or guardians are liable to prosecution, and if convicted are subject to fine not exceeding $50 and jail term not exceeding thirty days.

Appellees, citizens of the United States and of West Virginia, brought suit in the United States District Court for themselves and others similarly situated asking its injunction to restrain enforcement of these laws and regulations against Jehovah's Witnesses. The Witnesses are an unincorporated body teaching that the obligation imposed by law of God is superior to that of laws enacted by temporal government. Their religious beliefs include a literal version of Exodus, Chapter 20, verses 4 and 5, which says: "Thou shalt not make unto thee any graven image, or any likeness of anything that is in heaven above, or that is in the earth beneath, or that is in the water under the earth; thou shalt not bow down thyself to them nor serve them." They consider that the flag is an "image" within this command. For this reason they refuse to salute it.

Children of this faith have been expelled from school and are threatened with exclusion for no other cause. Officials threaten to send them to reformatories maintained for criminally inclined juveniles. Parents of such children have been prosecuted and are threatened with prosecutions for causing delinquency.

The Board of Education moved to dismiss the complaint setting forth these facts and alleging that the law and regulations are an unconstitutional denial of religious freedom, and of freedom of speech, and are invalid under the "due process" and "equal protection" clauses of the Fourteenth Amendment to the Federal Constitution. The cause was submitted on the pleadings to a District Court of three judges. It restrained enforcement as to the plaintiffs and those of that class. The Board of Education brought the case here by direct appeal.

This case calls upon us to reconsider a precedent decision, as the Court throughout its history often has been required to do. Before turning to the *Gobitis* case, however, it is desirable to notice certain characteristics by which this controversy is distinguished.

The freedom asserted by these appellees does not bring them into collision with rights asserted by any other individual. It is such conflicts which most frequently require intervention of the State to determine where the rights of one end and those of another begin. But the refusal of these persons to participate in the ceremony does not interfere with or deny rights of others to do so. Nor is there any question in this case that their behavior is peaceable and orderly. The sole conflict is between authority and rights of the individual. The State asserts power to condition access to public education on making a prescribed sign and profession and at the same time to coerce attendance by punishing both parent and child. The latter stand on a right of self-determination in matters that touch individual opinion and personal attitude.

As the present Chief Justice said in dissent in the *Gobitis* case, the State may "require teaching by instruction and study of all in our history and in the structure and organization of our government, including the guaranties of civil liberty which tend to inspire patriotism and love of country." 310 U.S. at page 604. Here, however, we are dealing with a compulsion of students to declare a belief. They are not merely made acquainted with the flag salute so that they may be informed as to what it is or even what it means. The issue here is whether this slow and easily neglected route to aroused loyalties constitutionally may be short-cut by substituting a compulsory salute and slogan. This issue is not prejudiced by the Court's previous holding that where a State, without compelling attendance, extends college facilities to pupils who voluntarily enroll, it may prescribe military training as part of the course without offense to the Constitution. It was held that those who take advantage of its opportunities may not on ground of conscience refuse compliance with such conditions. *Hamilton v. Regents*, 293 U.S. 245. In the present case attendance is not optional. That case is also to be distinguished from the present one because, independently of college privileges or requirements, the State has power to raise militia and impose the duties of service therein upon its citizens.

There is no doubt that, in connection with the pledges, the flag salute is a form of utterance. Symbolism is a primitive but effective way of communicating ideas. The use of an emblem or flag to symbolize some system, idea, institution, or personality, is a short cut from mind to mind. Causes and nations, political parties, lodges and ecclesiastical groups seek to knit the loyalty of their followings to a flag or banner, a color or design. The State announces rank, function, and authority through crowns and maces, uniforms and black robes; the church speaks through the Cross, the Crucifix, the altar and shrine, and clerical raiment. Symbols of State often convey political ideas just as religious symbols come to convey theological ones. Associated with many of these symbols are appropriate gestures of acceptance or respect: a salute, a bowed or bared head, a bended knee. A person gets from a symbol the meaning he puts into it, and what is one man's comfort and inspiration is another's jest and scorn.

Over a decade ago Chief Justice Hughes led this Court in holding that the display of a red flag as a symbol of opposition by peaceful and legal means to organized government was protected by the free speech guaranties of the Constitution. *Stromberg v. California*, 283 U.S. 359. Here it is the State that employs a flag as a symbol of adherence to government as presently organized. It requires the individual to communicate by word and sign his acceptance of the political ideas it thus bespeaks. Objection to this form of communication when coerced is an old one, well known to the framers of the Bill of Rights.[6]

It is also to be noted that the compulsory flag salute and pledge requires affirmation of a belief and an attitude of mind. It is not clear whether the regulation contemplates that pupils forego any contrary convictions of their own and become unwilling converts to the prescribed ceremony or whether it will be acceptable if they simulate assent by words without belief and by a gesture barren of meaning. It is now a commonplace that censorship or suppression of expression of opinion is tolerated by our Constitution only when the expression presents a clear and present danger of action of a kind the State is empowered to prevent and punish. It would seem that involuntary affirmation could be commanded only on even more immediate and urgent grounds than silence. But here the power of compulsion is invoked without any allegation that remaining passive during a flag salute ritual creates a clear and present danger that would justify an effort even to muffle expression. To sustain the compulsory flag salute we are required to say that a Bill of Rights which guards the individual's right to speak his own mind, left it open to public authorities to compel him to utter what is not in his mind.

Whether the First Amendment to the Constitution will permit officials to order observance of ritual of this nature does not depend upon whether as a voluntary exercise we would think it to be good, bad or merely innocuous. Any credo of nationalism is likely to include what some disapprove or to omit what others think essential, and to give off different overtones as it takes on different accents or interpretations.[7] If official power exists to coerce acceptance of any patriotic creed, what it shall contain cannot be decided by courts, but must be largely discretionary with the ordaining authority, whose power to prescribe would no doubt include power to amend. Hence validity of the asserted power to force an American citizen publicly to profess any statement of belief or to engage in any ceremony of assent to one presents questions of power that must be considered independently of any idea we may have as to the utility of the ceremony in question.

Nor does the issue as we see it turn on one's possession of particular religious views or the sincerity with which they are held. While religion supplies appellees' motive for enduring the discomforts of making the issue in this case, many citizens who do not share these religious views hold such a compulsory rite to infringe constitutional liberty of the

6. Early Christians were frequently persecuted for their refusal to participate in ceremonies before the statue of the emperor or other symbol of imperial authority. The story of William Tell's sentence to shoot an apple off his son's head for refusal to salute a bailiff's hat is an ancient one. 21 Encyclopedia Britannica, 14th Ed., 911, 912. The Quakers, William Penn included, suffered punishment rather than uncover their heads in deference to any civil authority. Braithwaite, *The Beginnings of Quakerism* (1912) 200, 229–230, 232, 233, 447, 451; Fox, *Quakers Courageous* (1941) 113.

7. For example: Use of "Republic," if rendered to distinguish our government from a "democracy," or the words "one Nation," if intended to distinguish it from a "federation," open up old and bitter controversies in our political history; "liberty and justice for all," if it must be accepted as descriptive of the present order rather than an ideal, might to some seem an overstatement.

individual. It is not necessary to inquire whether non-conformist beliefs will exempt from the duty to salute unless we first find power to make the salute a legal duty.

The *Gobitis* decision, however, assumed, as did the argument in that case and in this, that power exists in the State to impose the flag salute discipline upon school children in general. The Court only examined and rejected a claim based on religious beliefs of immunity from an unquestioned general rule. The question which underlies the flag salute controversy is whether such a ceremony so touching matters of opinion and political attitude may be imposed upon the individual by official authority under powers committed to any political organization under our Constitution. We examine rather than assume existence of this power and, against this broader definition of issues in this case, re-examine specific grounds assigned for the *Gobitis* decision.

1. It was said that the flag-salute controversy confronted the Court with "the problem which Lincoln cast in memorable dilemma: 'Must a government of necessity be too strong for the liberties of its people, or too weak to maintain its own existence?' and that the answer must be in favor of strength." *Minersville School District v. Gobitis*, supra, 310 U.S. at page 596.

We think these issues may be examined free of pressure or restraint growing out of such considerations.

It may be doubted whether Mr. Lincoln would have thought that the strength of government to maintain itself would be impressively vindicated by our confirming power of the state to expel a handful of children from school. Such oversimplification, so handy in political debate, often lacks the precision necessary to postulates of judicial reasoning. If validly applied to this problem, the utterance cited would resolve every issue of power in favor of those in authority and would require us to override every liberty thought to weaken or delay execution of their policies.

Government of limited power need not be anemic government. Assurance that rights are secure tends to diminish fear and jealousy of strong government, and by making us feel safe to live under it makes for its better support. Without promise of a limiting Bill of Rights it is doubtful if our Constitution could have mustered enough strength to enable its ratification. To enforce those rights today is not to choose weak government over strong government. It is only to adhere as a means of strength to individual freedom of mind in preference to officially disciplined uniformity for which history indicates a disappointing and disastrous end.

The subject now before us exemplifies this principle. Free public education, if faithful to the ideal of secular instruction and political neutrality, will not be partisan or enemy of any class, creed, party, or faction. If it is to impose any ideological discipline, however, each party or denomination must seek to control, or failing that, to weaken the influence of the educational system. Observance of the limitations of the

Constitution will not weaken government in the field appropriate for its exercise.

2. It was also considered in the *Gobitis* case that functions of educational officers in states, counties and school districts were such that to interfere with their authority "would in effect make us the school board for the country." *Id.*, 310 U.S. at page 598.

The Fourteenth Amendment, as now applied to the States, protects the citizen against the State itself and all of its creatures—Boards of Education not excepted. These have, of course, important, delicate, and highly discretionary functions, but none that they may not perform within the limits of the Bill of Rights. That they are educating the young for citizenship is reason for scrupulous protection of Constitutional freedoms of the individual, if we are not to strangle the free mind at its source and teach youth to discount important principles of our government as mere platitudes.

Such Boards are numerous and their territorial jurisdiction often small. But small and local authority may feel less sense of responsibility to the Constitution, and agencies of publicity may be less vigilant in calling it to account. The action of Congress in making flag observance voluntary and respecting the conscience of the objector in a matter so vital as raising the Army contrasts sharply with these local regulations in matters relatively trivial to the welfare of the nation. There are village tyrants as well as village Hampdens, but none who acts under color of law is beyond reach of the Constitution.

3. The *Gobitis* opinion reasoned that this is a field "where courts possess no marked and certainly no controlling competence," that it is committed to the legislatures as well as the courts to guard cherished liberties and that it is constitutionally appropriate to "fight out the wise use of legislative authority in the forum of public opinion and before legislative assemblies rather than to transfer such a contest to the judicial arena," since all the "effective means of inducing political changes are left free." *Id.*, 310 U.S. at page 597, 598, 600.

The very purpose of a Bill of Rights was to withdraw certain subjects from the vicissitudes of political controversy, to place them beyond the reach of majorities and officials and to establish them as legal principles to be applied by the courts. One's right to life, liberty, and property, to free speech, a free press, freedom of worship and assembly, and other fundamental rights may not be submitted to vote; they depend on the outcome of no elections.

In weighing arguments of the parties it is important to distinguish between the due process clause of the Fourteenth Amendment as an instrument for transmitting the principles of the First Amendment and those cases in which it is applied for its own sake. The test of legislation which collides with the Fourteenth Amendment, because it also collides with the principles of the First, is much more definite than the test when only the Fourteenth is involved. Much of the vagueness of the due process clause disappears when the specific prohibitions of the First become its standard. The right of a State to regulate, for example, a public utility may well include, so far as the due process test is concerned, power to impose all of the restrictions which a legislature may have a "rational basis" for adopting. But freedoms of speech and of press, of assembly, and of worship may not be infringed on such slender grounds. They are susceptible of restriction only to prevent grave and immediate danger to interests which the state may lawfully protect. It is important to note that while it is the Fourteenth Amendment which bears directly upon the State it is the more specific limiting principles of the First Amendment that finally govern this case.

Nor does our duty to apply the Bill of Rights to assertions of official authority depend upon our possession of marked competence in the field where the invasion of rights occurs. True, the task of translating the majestic generalities of the Bill of Rights, conceived as part of the pattern of liberal government in the eighteenth century, into concrete restraints on officials dealing with the problems of the twentieth century, is one to disturb self-confidence. These principles grew in soil which also produced a philosophy that the individual was the center of society, that his liberty was attainable through mere absence of governmental restraints, and that government should be entrusted with few controls and only the mildest supervision over men's affairs. We must transplant these rights to a soil in which the laissez-faire concept or principle of non-interference has withered at least as to economic affairs, and social advancements are increasingly sought through closer integration of society and through expanded and strengthened governmental controls. These changed conditions often deprive precedents of reliability and cast us more than we would choose upon our own judgment. But we act in these matters not by authority of our competence but by force of our commissions. We cannot, because of modest estimates of our competence in such specialties as public education, withhold the judgment that history authenticates as the function of this Court when liberty is infringed.

4. Lastly, and this is the very heart of the *Gobitis* opinion, it reasons that "National unity is the basis of national security," that the authorities have "the right to select appropriate means for its attainment," and hence reaches the conclusion that such compulsory measures toward "national unity" are constitutional. *Id.*, 310 U.S. at page 595. Upon the verity of this assumption depends our answer in this case.

National unity as an end which officials may foster by persuasion and example is not in question. The problem is whether under our Constitution compulsion as here employed is a permissible means for its achievement.

Struggles to coerce uniformity of sentiment in support of some end thought essential to their time and country have been waged by many good as well as by evil men. Nationalism is a relatively recent phenomenon but at other times and places the ends have been racial or territorial security, support of a dynasty or regime, and particular plans for saving souls. As first and moderate methods to attain unity have failed, those bent on its accomplishment must resort to an ever-increasing severity. As governmental pressure toward unity becomes greater, so strife becomes more bitter as to whose unity it shall be. Probably no deeper division of our people could proceed from any provocation than from finding it necessary to choose what doctrine and whose program public educational officials shall compel youth to unite in embracing. Ultimate futility of such attempts to compel coherence is the lesson of every such effort from the Roman drive to stamp out Christianity as a disturber of its pagan unity, the Inquisition, as a means to religious and dynastic unity, the Siberian exiles as a means to Russian unity, down to the fast failing efforts of our present totalitarian enemies. Those who begin coercive elimination of dissent soon find themselves exterminating dissenters. Compulsory unification of opinion achieves only the unanimity of the graveyard.

It seems trite but necessary to say that the First Amendment to our Constitution was designed to avoid these ends by avoiding these beginnings. There is no mysticism in the American concept of the State or of the nature or origin of its authority. We set up government by consent of the governed, and the Bill of Rights denies those in power any legal opportunity to coerce that consent. Authority here is to be controlled by public opinion, not public opinion by authority.

The case is made difficult not because the principles of its decision are obscure but because the flag involved is our own. Nevertheless, we apply the limitations of the Constitution with no fear that freedom to be intellectually and spiritually diverse or even contrary will disintegrate the social organization. To believe that patriotism will not flourish if patriotic ceremonies are voluntary and spontaneous instead of a compulsory routine is to make an unflattering estimate of the appeal of our institutions to free minds. We can have intellectual individualism and the rich cultural diversities that we owe to exceptional minds only at the price of occasional eccentricity and abnormal attitudes. When they are so harmless to others or to the State as those we deal with here, the price is not too great. But freedom to differ is not limited to things that do not matter much. That would be a mere shadow of freedom. The test of its substance is the right to differ as to things that touch the heart of the existing order.

If there is any fixed star in our constitutional constellation, it is that no official, high or petty, can prescribe what shall be orthodox in politics, nationalism, religion, or other matters of opinion or force citizens to confess by word or act their faith therein. If there are any circumstances which permit an exception, they do not now occur to us.[8]

8. The Nation may raise armies and compel citizens to give military service. Selective Draft Law Cases (*Arver v. United States*), 245 U.S. 366,. It follows, of course, that those subject to military discipline are under many duties and may not claim many freedoms that we hold inviolable as to those in civilian life.

We think the action of the local authorities in compelling the flag salute and pledge transcends constitutional limitations on their power and invades the sphere of intellect and spirit which it is the purpose of the First Amendment to our Constitution to reserve from all official control.

The decision of this Court in *Minersville School District v. Gobitis* and the holdings of those few per curiam decisions which preceded and foreshadowed it are overruled, and the judgment enjoining enforcement of the West Virginia Regulation is affirmed.

Affirmed.

Mr. JUSTICE ROBERTS and Mr. JUSTICE REED adhere to the views expressed by the Court in *Minersville School District v. Gobitis*, 310 U.S. 586, and are of the opinion that the judgment below should be reversed.

Mr. JUSTICE BLACK and Mr. JUSTICE DOUGLAS, concurring.

We are substantially in agreement with the opinion just read, but since we originally joined with the Court in the *Gobitis* case, it is appropriate that we make a brief statement of reasons for our change of view.

Reluctance to make the Federal Constitution a rigid bar against state regulation of conduct thought inimical to the public welfare was the controlling influence which moved us to consent to the *Gobitis* decision. Long reflection convinced us that although the principle is sound, its application in the particular case was wrong. *Jones v. Opelika*, 316 U.S. 584, 623. We believe that the statute before us fails to accord full scope to the freedom of religion secured to the appellees by the First and Fourteenth Amendments.

The statute requires the appellees to participate in a ceremony aimed at inculcating respect for the flag and for this country. The Jehovah's Witnesses, without any desire to show disrespect for either the flag or the country, interpret the Bible as commanding, at the risk of God's displeasure, that they not go through the form of a pledge of allegiance to any flag. The devoutness of their belief is evidenced by their willingness to suffer persecution and punishment, rather than make the pledge.

No well-ordered society can leave to the individuals an absolute right to make final decisions, unassailable by the State, as to everything they will or will not do. The First Amendment does not go so far. Religious faiths, honestly held, do not free individuals from responsibility to conduct themselves obediently to laws which are either imperatively necessary to protect society as a whole from grave and pressingly imminent dangers or which, without any general prohibition, merely regulate time, place or manner of religious activity. Decision as to the constitutionality of particular laws which strike at the substance of religious tenets and practices must be made be this Court. The duty is a solemn one, and in meeting it we cannot say that a failure, because of religious scruples, to assume a particular physical position and to repeat the words of a patriotic formula creates a grave danger to the nation. Such a statutory exaction is a form of test oath, and the test oath has always been abhorrent in the United States.

Words uttered under coercion are proof of loyalty to nothing but self-interest. Love of country must spring from willing hearts and free minds, inspired by a fair administration of wise laws enacted by the people's elected representatives within the bounds of express constitutional prohibitions. These laws must, to be consistent with the First Amendment, permit the widest toleration of conflicting viewpoints consistent with a society of free men.

Neither our domestic tranquillity in peace nor our martial effort in war depend on compelling little children to participate in a ceremony which ends in nothing for them but a fear of spiritual condemnation. If, as we think, their fears are groundless, time and reason are the proper antidotes for their errors. The ceremonial, when enforced against conscientious objectors, more likely to defeat than to serve its high purpose, is a handy implement for disguised religious persecution. As such, it is inconsistent with our Constitution's plan and purpose.

[A concurring opinion of Mr. JUSTICE MURPHY is omitted.]

Mr. JUSTICE FRANKFURTER, dissenting.

One who belongs to the most vilified and persecuted minority in history is not likely to be insensible to the freedoms guaranteed by our Constitution. Were my purely personal attitude relevant I should wholeheartedly associate myself with the general libertarian views in the Court's opinion, representing as they do the thought and action of a lifetime. But as judges we are neither Jew nor Gentile, neither Catholic nor agnostic. We owe equal attachment to the Constitution and are equally bound by our judicial obligations whether we derive our citizenship from the earliest or the latest immigrants to these shores. As a member of this Court I am not justified in writing my private notions of policy into the Constitution, no matter how deeply I may cherish them or how mischievous I may deem their disregard. The duty of a judge who must decide which of two claims before the Court shall prevail, that of a State to enact and enforce laws within its general competence or that of an individual to refuse obedience because of the demands of his conscience, is not that of the ordinary person. It can never be emphasized too much that one's own opinion about the wisdom or evil of a law should be excluded altogether when one is doing one's duty on the bench. The only opinion of our own even looking in that direction that is material is our opinion whether legislators could in reason have enacted such a law. In the light of all the circumstances, including the history of this question in this Court, it would require more daring than I possess to deny that reasonable legislators could have taken the action which is before us for review. Most unwillingly, therefore, I must differ from my brethren with regard to legislation like this. I cannot bring my mind to believe that the "liberty" secured by the Due Process Clause gives this Court authority to deny to the State of West Virginia the attainment of that which we all recognize as a legitimate legislative end, namely, the promotion of good citizenship, by employment of the means here chosen.

* * *

Under our constitutional system the legislature is charged solely with civil concerns of society. If the avowed or intrinsic legislative purpose is either to promote or to discourage some religious community or creed, it is clearly within the constitutional restrictions imposed on legislatures and cannot stand. But it by no means follows that legislative power is wanting whenever a general non-discriminatory civil regulation in fact touches conscientious scruples or religious beliefs of an individual or a group. Regard for such scruples or beliefs undoubtedly presents one of the most reasonable claims for the exertion of legislative accommodation. It is, of course, beyond our power to rewrite the state's requirement, by providing exemptions for those who do not wish to participate in the flag salute or by making some other accommodations to meet their scruples. That wisdom might suggest the making of such accommodations and that school administration would not find it too difficult to make them and yet maintain the ceremony for those not refusing to conform, is outside our province to suggest. Tact, respect, and generosity toward variant views will always commend themselves to those charged with the duties of legislation so as to achieve a maximum of good will and to require a minimum of unwilling submission to a general law. But the real question is, who is to make such accommodations, the courts or the legislature?

This is no dry, technical matter. It cuts deep into one's conception of the democratic process—it concerns no less the practical differences between the means for making these accommodations that are open to courts and to legislatures. A court can only strike down. It can only say "This or that law is void." It cannot modify or qualify, it cannot make exceptions to a general requirement. And it strikes down not merely for a day. At least the finding of unconstitutionality ought not to have ephemeral significance unless the Constitution is to be reduced to the fugitive importance of mere legislation. When we are dealing with the Constitution of the United States, and more particularly with the great safeguards of the Bill of Rights, we are dealing with principles of liberty and justice "so rooted in the traditions and conscience of our people as to be ranked as fundamental"—something without which "a fair and enlightened system of justice would be impossible". *Palko v. Connecticut*, 302 U.S. 319, 325; *Hurtado v. California*, 110 U.S. 516, 530, 531. If the function of this Court is to be essentially no different from that of a legislature, if the considerations governing constitutional construction are to be substantially those that underlie legislation, then indeed judges should not have life tenure and they should be made directly responsible to the electorate. There have been many but unsuccessful proposals in the last sixty years to amend the Constitution to that end. See Sen. Doc. No. 91, 75th Cong., 1st Sess., pp. 248–51.

Conscientious scruples, all would admit, cannot stand against every legislative compulsion to do positive acts in conflict with such scruples. We have been told that such compulsions override religious scruples only as to major concerns of the state. But the determination of what is major and what is minor itself raises questions of policy. For the way in which men equally guided by reason appraise importance goes to the very heart of policy. Judges should be very diffident in setting their judgment against that of a state in determining what is and what is not a major concern, what means are appropriate to proper ends, and what is the total social cost in striking the balance of imponderables.

What one can say with assurance is that the history out of which grew constitutional provisions for religious equality and the writings of the great exponents of religious freedom—Jefferson, Madison, John Adams, Benjamin Franklin—are totally wanting in justification for a claim by dissidents of exceptional immunity from civic measures of general applicability, measures not in fact disguised assaults upon such dissident views. The great leaders of the American Revolution were determined to remove political support from every religious establishment. They put on an equality the different religious sects—Episcopalians, Presbyterians, Catholics, Baptists, Methodists, Quakers, Huguenots—which, as dissenters, had been under the heel of the various orthodoxies that prevailed in different colonies. So far as the state was concerned, there was to be neither orthodoxy nor heterodoxy. And so Jefferson and those who followed him wrote guaranties of religious freedom into our constitutions. Religious minorities as well as religious majorities were to be equal in the eyes of the political state. But Jefferson and the others also knew that minorities may disrupt society. It never would have occurred to them to write into the Constitution the subordination of the general civil authority of the state to sectarian scruples.

The constitutional protection of religious freedom terminated disabilities, it did not create new privileges. It gave religious equality, not civil immunity. Its essence is freedom from conformity to religious dogma, not freedom from conformity to law because of religious dogma. Religious loyalties may be exercised without hindrance from the state, not the state may not exercise that which except by leave of religious loyalties is within the domain of temporal power. Otherwise each individual could set up his own censor against obedience to laws conscientiously deemed for the public good by those whose business it is to make laws.

The prohibition against any religious establishment by the government placed denominations on an equal footing—it assured freedom from support by the government to any mode of worship and the freedom of individuals to support any mode of worship. Any person may therefore believe or disbelieve what he pleases. He may practice what he will in his own house of worship or publicly within the limits of public order. But the lawmaking authority is not circumscribed by the variety of religious beliefs, otherwise the constitutional guaranty would be not a protection of the free exercise of religion but a denial of the exercise of legislation.

The essence of the religious freedom guaranteed by our Constitution is therefore this: no religion shall either receive the state's support or incur its hostility. Religion is outside the sphere of political government. This does not mean that all matters on which religious organizations or beliefs may pronounce are outside the sphere of government. Were this so, instead of the separation of church and state, there would be the subordination of the state on any matter deemed within the sovereignty of the religious conscience. Much that is the concern of temporal authority affects the spiritual interests of men. But it is not enough to strike down a non-discriminatory law that it may hurt or offend some dissident view. It would be too easy to cite numerous prohibitions and injunctions to which laws run counter if the variant interpretations of the Bible were made the tests of obedience to law. The validity of secular laws cannot be measured by their conformity to religious doctrines. It is only in a theocratic state that ecclesiastical doctrines measure legal right or wrong.

* * *

That which to the majority may seem essential for the welfare of the state may offend the consciences of a minority. But, so long as no inroads are made upon the actual exercise of religion by the minority, to deny the political power of the majority to enact laws concerned with civil matters, simply because they may offend the consciences of a minority, really means that the consciences of a minority are more sacred and more enshrined in the Constitution than the consciences of a majority.

We are told that symbolism is a dramatic but primitive way of communicating ideas. Symbolism is inescapable. Even the most sophisticated live by symbols. But it is not for this Court to make psychological judgments as to the effectiveness of a particular symbol in inculcating concededly indispensable feelings, particularly if the state happens to see fit to utilize the symbol that represents our heritage and our hopes. And surely only flippancy could be responsible for the suggestion that constitutional validity of a requirement to salute our flag implies equal validity of a requirement to salute a dictator. The significance of a symbol lies in what it represents. To reject the swastika does not imply rejection of the Cross. And so it bears repetition to say that it mocks reason and denies our whole history to find in the allowance of a requirement to salute our flag on fitting occasions the seeds of sanction for obeisance to a leader. To deny the power to employ educational symbols is to say that the state's educational system may not stimulate the imagination because this may lead to unwise stimulation.

* * *

The flag salute exercise has no kinship whatever to the oath tests so odious in history. For the oath test was one of the instruments for suppressing heretical beliefs. Saluting the flag suppresses no belief no[r] curbs it. Children and their parents may believe what they please, avow their belief and practice it. It is not even remotely suggested that the requirement for saluting the flag involves the slightest restriction against the fullest opportunity on the part both of the children and of their parents to disavow as publicly as they choose to do so the meaning that others attach to the gesture of salute. All channels of affirmative free expression are open to both children and parents. Had we before us any act of the state putting the slightest curbs upon such free expression, I should not lag behind any member of this Court in striking down such an invasion of the right to freedom of thought and freedom of speech protected by the Constitution.

* * *

Questions

1) What kind of an argument is Justice Jackson making? Does he claim that the right to be free from being made to affirm a political belief and to salute a political symbol derives from a basic personal *entitlement* to control one's declarations of belief? Or does his argument rest on the proposition that such a compelled affirmation is forbidden by the *authority* of the constitutional text? How can a text that guarantees "the freedom of speech" be read to protect the freedom not to speak? Justice Jackson has some strong things to say about the history of regimes that tried to coerce uniformity of belief; is his, then, an argument from *experience?* Or is the *Barnette* opinion ultimately based on a claim about *consequences:* that a deeper, more durable and meaningful patriotism will result if schoolchildren are encouraged to learn about national values free from the coercion of required rote recitation? Whether or not the level of patriotic commitment would increase under the freedom recognized by *Barnette*, could one argue that *consistency* with the principle that political authority derives from the consent of the governed requires that schoolchildren not be coercively indoctrinated in the manner represented by a compulsory flag salute ceremony?

2) The right recognized in *Barnette* is to be free of the obligation to recite the pledge of allegiance in a public school ceremony, not the right to be free of the peer pressures to participate when such a ceremony is held during school hours. In contrast, the right recognized in the Supreme Court's decisions involving school prayer is the right not to have such ceremonies conducted in public schools, even when objecting students are permitted to excuse themselves. Why the difference in the scope of the rights recognized? Why is the Court in *Barnette* not concerned that students who object to reciting the pledge of allegiance will feel enormous peer pressure to participate in the ceremony or, if they resist that pressure, will suffer ostracism or vigilante reprisals?

WOOLEY v. MAYNARD

Supreme Court of the United States, 1977.
430 U.S. 705, 97 S.Ct. 1428, 51 L.Ed.2d 752.

Mr. Chief Justice Burger delivered the opinion of the Court.

The issue on appeal is whether the State of New Hampshire may constitutionally enforce criminal sanctions against persons who cover the motto "Live Free or Die" on passenger vehicle license plates because that motto is repugnant to their moral and religious beliefs.

(1)

Since 1969 New Hampshire has required that noncommercial vehicles bear license plates embossed with the state motto, "Live Free or Die." N.H.Rev.Stat.Ann. § 263:1 (Supp. 1975). Another New Hampshire statute makes it a misdemeanor "knowingly (to obscure) . . . the figures or letters on any number plate." N.H.Rev.Stat.Ann. § 262:27–c (Supp. 1975). The term "letters" in this section has been interpreted by the State's highest court to include the state motto. *State v. Hoskin*, 295 A.2d 454 (1972).

Appellees George Maynard and his wife Maxine are followers of the Jehovah's Witnesses faith. The Maynards consider the New Hampshire State motto to be repugnant to their moral, religious, and political beliefs,[9] and therefore assert it objectionable to disseminate this message by displaying it on their automobiles. Pursuant to these beliefs, the Maynards began early in 1974 to cover up the motto on their license plates.[10]

On November 27, 1974, Mr. Maynard was issued a citation for violating § 262:27–c. On December 6, 1974, he appeared pro se in Lebanon, N. H., District Court to answer the charge. After waiving his right to counsel, he entered a plea of not guilty and proceeded to explain his religious objections to the motto. The state trial judge expressed sympathy for Mr. Maynard's situation, but considered himself bound by the authority of *State v. Hoskin*, supra, to hold Maynard guilty. A $25 fine was imposed, but execution was suspended during "good behavior."

On December 28, 1974, Mr. Maynard was again charged with violating § 262:27–c. He appeared in court on January 31, 1975, and

9. Mr. Maynard described his objection to the state motto:

"(B)y religious training and belief, I believe my 'government' Jehovah's Kingdom offers everlasting life. It would be contrary to that belief to give up my life for the state, even if it meant living in bondage. Although I obey all laws of the State not in conflict with my conscience, this slogan is directly at odds with my deeply held religious convictions.

" . . . I also disagree with the motto on political grounds. I believe that life is more precious than freedom." Affidavit of George Maynard, App. 3.

10. In May or June 1974 Mr. Maynard actually snipped the words "or Die" off the license plates, and then covered the resulting hole, as well as the words "Live Free," with tape. This was done, according to Mr. Maynard, because neighborhood children kept removing the tape. The Maynards have since been issued new license plates, and have disavowed any intention of physically mutilating them.

again chose to represent himself; he was found guilty, fined $50, and sentenced to six months in the Grafton County House of Corrections. The court suspended this jail sentence but ordered Mr. Maynard to also pay the $25 fine for the first offense. Maynard informed the court that, as a matter of conscience, he refused to pay the two fines. The court thereupon sentenced him to jail for a period of 15 days. He has served the full sentence.

* * *

A

We begin with the proposition that the right of freedom of thought protected by the First Amendment against state action includes both the right to speak freely and the right to refrain from speaking at all. See *Board of Education v. Barnette*, 319 U.S. 624, 633–634 (1943); *id.*, at 645 (Murphy, J., concurring). A system which secures the right to proselytize religious, political, and ideological causes must also guarantee the concomitant right to decline to foster such concepts. The right to speak and the right to refrain from speaking are complementary components of the broader concept of "individual freedom of mind." *Id.*, at 637. This is illustrated by the recent case of *Miami Herald Publishing Co. v. Tornillo*, 418 U.S. 241 (1974), where we held unconstitutional a Florida statute placing an affirmative duty upon newspapers to publish the replies of political candidates whom they had criticized. We concluded that such a requirement deprived a newspaper of the fundamental right to decide what to print or omit:

> "Faced with the penalties that would accrue to any newspaper that published news or commentary arguably within the reach of the right-of-access statute, editors might well conclude that the safe course is to avoid controversy. Therefore, under the operation of the Florida statute, political and electoral coverage would be blunted or reduced. Government-enforced right of access inescapably 'dampens the vigor and limits the variety of public debate,' *New York Times Co. v. Sullivan*, 376 U.S. 254, at 279 (1964)." *Id.*, at 257.

The Court in *Barnette*, was faced with a state statute which required public school students to participate in daily public ceremonies by honoring the flag both with words and traditional salute gestures. In overruling its prior decision in *Minersville District v. Gobitis*, 310 U.S. 586 (1940), the Court held that "a ceremony so touching matters of opinion and political attitude may [not] be imposed upon the individual by official authority under powers committed to any political organization under our Constitution." 319 U.S., at 636. Compelling the affirmative act of a flag salute involved a more serious infringement upon personal liberties than the passive act of carrying the state motto on a license plate, but the difference is essentially one of degree. Here, as in *Barnette*, we are faced with a state measure which forces an individual, as part of his daily life indeed constantly while his automobile is in public view to be an instrument for fostering public adherence to an ideological point of view he finds unacceptable. In doing so, the State "invades the sphere of intellect and spirit which it is the purpose of the First Amendment to our Constitution to reserve from all official control." *Id.*, at 642.

New Hampshire's statute in effect requires that appellees use their private property as a "mobile billboard" for the State's ideological message or suffer a penalty, as Maynard already has. As a condition to driving an automobile a virtual necessity for most Americans the Maynards must display "Live Free or Die" to hundreds of people each day.[11] The fact that most individuals agree with the thrust of New Hampshire's motto is not the test; most Americans also find the flag salute acceptable. The First Amendment protects the right of individuals to hold a point of view different from the majority and to refuse to foster, in the way New Hampshire commands, an idea they find morally objectionable.

B

Identifying the Maynards' interests as implicating First Amendment protections does not end our inquiry however. We must also determine whether the State's countervailing interest is sufficiently compelling to justify requiring appellees to display the state motto on their license plates. *See, e. g., United States v. O'Brien*, 391 U.S. 367, 376–377 (1968). The two interests advanced by the State are that display of the motto (1) facilitates the identification of passenger vehicles,[12] and (2) promotes appreciation of history, individualism, and state pride.

The State first points out that passenger vehicles, but not commercial, trailer, or other vehicles are required to display the state motto. Thus, the argument proceeds, officers of the law are more easily able to determine whether passenger vehicles are carrying the proper plates. However, the record here reveals that New Hampshire passenger license plates normally consist of a specific configuration of letters and numbers, which makes them readily distinguishable from other types of plates, even without reference to the state motto. Even were we to credit the State's reasons and "even though the governmental purpose be legitimate and substantial, that purpose cannot be pursued by means that broadly stifle fundamental personal liberties when the end can be more narrowly achieved. The breadth of legislative abridgment must be viewed in the light of less drastic means for achieving the same basic purpose." *Shelton v. Tucker*, 364 U.S. 479, 488 (1960).

11. Some States require that certain documents bear the seal of the State or some other official stamp for purposes of recordation. Such seal might contain, albeit obscurely, a symbol or motto having political or philosophical implications. The purpose of such seal, however, is not to advertise the message it bears but simply to authenticate the document by showing the authority of its origin.

12. The Chief of Police of Lebanon, N. H., testified that "enforcement of the motor vehicle laws is facilitated by the State Motto appearing on noncommercial license plates, the benefits being the ease of distinguishing New Hampshire license plates from those of similar colors of other states and the ease of discovering misuse of license plates, for instance, the use of a 'trailer' license plate on a non-commercial vehicle." Brief for Appellants 20.

The State's second claimed interest is not ideologically neutral. The State is seeking to communicate to others an official view as to proper appreciation of history, state pride, and individualism. Of course, the State may legitimately pursue such interests in any number of ways. However, where the State's interest is to disseminate an ideology, no matter how acceptable to some, such interest cannot outweigh an individual's First Amendment right to avoid becoming the courier for such message.

We conclude that the State of New Hampshire may not require appellees to display the state motto[13] upon their vehicle license plates; and, accordingly, we affirm the judgment of the District Court.

Affirmed.

* * *

Mr. Justice Rehnquist, with whom Mr. Justice Blackmun joins, dissenting.

* * *

The State has simply required that all noncommercial automobiles bear license tags with the state motto, "Live Free or Die." Appellees have not been forced to affirm or reject that motto; they are simply required by the State, under its police power, to carry a state auto license tag for identification and registration purposes.

[T]he Court relies almost solely on *Board of Education v. Barnette*, 319 U.S. 624 (1943). The Court cites *Barnette* for the proposition that there is a constitutional right, in some cases, to "refrain from speaking." What the Court does not demonstrate is that there is any "speech" or "speaking" in the context of this case. The Court also relies upon the "right to decline to foster (religious, political, and ideological) concepts," ibid., and treats the state law in this case as if it were forcing appellees to proselytize, or to advocate an ideological point of view. But this begs the question. The issue, unconfronted by the Court, is whether appellees, in displaying, as they are required to do, state license tags, the format of which is known to all as having been prescribed by the State, would be considered to be advocating political or ideological views.

The Court recognizes, as it must, that this case substantially differs from *Barnette*, in which schoolchildren were forced to recite the pledge of allegiance while giving the flag salute. However, the Court states "the difference is essentially one of degree." But having recognized the rather obvious differences between these two cases, the Court does not explain why the same result should obtain. The Court suggests that the test is

13. It has been suggested that today's holding will be read as sanctioning the obliteration of the national motto, "In God We Trust" from United States coins and currency. That question is not before us today but we note that currency, which is passed from hand to hand, differs in significant respects from an automobile, which is readily associated with its operator. Currency is generally carried in a purse or pocket and need not be displayed to the public. The bearer of currency is thus not required to publicly advertise the national motto.

whether the individual is forced "to be an instrument for fostering public adherence to an ideological point of view he finds unacceptable." Ibid. But, once again, these are merely conclusory words, barren of analysis. For example, were New Hampshire to erect a multitude of billboards, each proclaiming "Live Free or Die," and tax all citizens for the cost of erection and maintenance, clearly the message would be "fostered" by the individual citizen-taxpayers and just as clearly those individuals would be "instruments" in that communication. Certainly, however, that case would not fall within the ambit of *Barnette*. In that case, as in this case, there is no affirmation of belief. For First Amendment principles to be implicated, the State must place the citizen in the position of either apparently to, or actually "asserting as true" the message. This was the focus of *Barnette*, and clearly distinguishes this case from that one.

In holding that the New Hampshire statute does not run afoul of our holding in *Barnette*, the New Hampshire Supreme Court in *Hoskin, supra*, 295 A.2d, at 457, aptly articulated why there is no required affirmation of belief in this case:

> "The defendants' membership in a class of persons required to display plates bearing the State motto carries no implication and is subject to no requirement that they endorse that motto or profess to adopt it as matter of belief."

As found by the New Hampshire Supreme Court in *Hoskin*, there is nothing in state law which precludes appellees from displaying their disagreement with the state motto as long as the methods used do not obscure the license plates. Thus appellees could place on their bumper a conspicuous bumper sticker explaining in no uncertain terms that they do not profess the motto "Live Free or Die" and that they violently disagree with the connotations of that motto. Since any implication that they affirm the motto can be so easily displaced, I cannot agree that the state statutory system for motor vehicle identification and tourist promotion may be invalidated under the fiction that appellees are unconstitutionally forced to affirm, or profess belief in, the state motto.

The logic of the Court's opinion leads to startling, and I believe totally unacceptable, results. For example, the mottoes "In God We Trust" and "E Pluribus Unum" appear on the coin and currency of the United States. I cannot imagine that the statutes, see 18 U.S.C. §§ 331 and 333, proscribing defacement of United States currency impinge upon the First Amendment rights of an atheist. The fact that an atheist carries and uses United States currency does not, in any meaningful sense, convey any affirmation of belief on his part in the motto "In God We Trust." Similarly, there is no affirmation of belief involved in the display of state license tags upon the private automobiles involved here.

I would reverse the judgment of the District Court.

[An opinion dissenting in part by JUSTICE WHITE, joined in part by JUSTICES REHNQUIST and BLACKMUN, is omitted.]

Question

Is *Wooley v. Maynard* a proper application of the *Barnette* principle? Would any fellow motorist viewing Maynard's vehicle assume that the slogan on his license plate represented his own views? If not, is the right not to speak that is at issue in the case simply the right not to be the unwilling carrier of the state's message? What is the basis for that right? Is it violated whenever the official currency contains state messages: "In God We Trust" "Novus Ordo Seclorum" "E Pluribus Unum"? If someone were to claim that the dollar bill of the United States violates the First Amendment, could *Wooley* be distinguished? Observe that Justice Rehnquist raises this challenge in his dissent but the majority opinion is silent on the matter.

ADDITIONAL READINGS

Gobitis and Barnette

Irving Dilliard, "The Flag Salute Cases," in John A. Garraty ed., Quarrels That Have Shaped the Constitution (rev. ed. 1987)

Robert A. Ferguson, The Judicial Opinion as Literary Genre, 2 Yale J. L. & Humanities 201 (1990)

Abner S. Greene, The Pledge of Allegiance Problem, 64 Fordham L. Rev. 451 (1995)

Peter Irons, The Courage of Their Convictions, Ch.1 (1988)

David R. Manwaring, Render Unto Caesar: The Flag Salute Controversy (1962)

Shawn Francis Peters, Judging Jehovah's Witnesses: Religious Persecution and the Dawn of the Rights Revolution (2000)

Steven D. Smith, *Barnette's* Big Blunder, 78 Chgo.–Kent L. Rev. 625 (2003)

Chaplinsky

Comment, The Epitome of an Insult, A Constitutional Approach to Designated Fighting Words, 72 U. Chi. L. Rev. 385 (2005)

Note, The Fighting Words Doctrine, 93 Colum. L. Rev. 1527 (1993)

Note, The Demise of the Chaplinsky Fighting Words Doctrine, 106 Harv. L. Rev. 1129 (1993)

Wooley

Randall P. Bezanson, Speaking Through Others' Voices: Authorship, Originality and Free Speech, 38 Wake Forest L. Rev. 983 (2003)

Leora Harpaz, Justice Jackson's Flag Salute Legacy: The Supreme Court Struggles to Protect Intellectual Individualism, 64 Tex. L. Rev. 817 (1986)

Seana V. Shiffrin, What Is Really Wrong With Compelled Association? 99 Nw. U. L. Rev. 839 (2005)

Chapter Two

JOHN MILTON

WILLIAM BOUWSMA, VENICE AND THE DEFENSE OF REPUBLICAN LIBERTY: RENAISSANCE VALUES IN THE AGE OF THE COUNTER–REFORMATION

(1968).

The crucial difference between ... the medieval vision and that of the Renaissance, was an utterly different conception of the general nature of order; every other difference between them can be related to this. To put the matter in its simplest terms: in the medieval vision of reality, every dimension of the universe and every aspect of human existence were seen as part of an objective and cosmic system of order. But the Renaissance mind perceived nothing of the sort. Unable and frequently little caring to find coherence in the universe as a whole, it discerned only such limited and transient patterns of order as could be devised by man himself. Furthermore, the medieval vision identified a definite pattern in the universal order. All things appeared to be arranged in a hierarchy of complexity and value, an arrangement whose basis was ideal and therefore utterly static. In this conception some things were unalterably higher and therefore better, others were lower and thus inferior. But in the Renaissance vision there was no such hierarchy, and instead of stasis it saw merely, though often reluctantly, the incessant flux of things. The medieval vision attributed reality only to what was general and could therefore be related to the universal system. The Renaissance vision, sure only of the particular, located reality there. The medieval vision of reality, as a system comprehending all things, was closed; the Renaissance vision, comprehending very little and uncertain that anything had its definite place, was open.

This description evidently contrasts ideal types, and accounts of such a kind are always likely to approach caricature. Nevertheless, what I have here represented as the "medieval vision" is useful to explain systematic descriptions of feudalism (if less so to expose how feudalism worked), to illuminate the major purposes of at least some schoolmen, and to understand the elaborate justifications of medieval theocracy. It may also be observed here that by the sixteenth century many expositions of the medieval position were hardly more nuanced than my own sketch of it, though they were often developed at great length. I am not aiming, however, for novelty; I wish here only to provide a brief preliminary for some comment on issues that fundamentally concerned the thinkers of the Renaissance.

Implicit in the medieval vision is a remarkable confidence in the intellectual capacities of man. It assumed not only the existence of a universal order but also a substantial capacity in the human mind to grasp this order. The intellectual optimism in this position is particularly notable; in an important sense medieval culture took a far higher view of some human capacities than did that of the Renaissance. Furthermore, the medieval position tended to identify man with his intellect, and his ability to apprehend the pattern of universal order was closely related to the ultimate purpose of human existence. By contemplating its perfect structure and ascending its stages, man could, with his mind, rise from what was good to what was better, and finally approach and seek to unite himself intellectually with what was best. Contemplation was thus the noblest of pursuits, the highest path of existence; activity in the world of men and particular things was not only inferior but could chiefly be justified only by its contribution to something superior to itself. Augustine might be cited on this point: "The active life is necessary not for its own sake but as preparation for contemplation."[5] The value attached to contemplation also led to contempt for the concrete and particular, which in this perspective evidently derived its "reality" only from participation in the general structure of things. Truth depended on first principles, not on immediate perceptions, and practice on theory rather than the reverse. Experience had little or no independent existence; it was required to conform to theory, not to determine it. That experience often failed to meet this obligation only proved its inferiority to the essential dimension of reality.

This general conception of reality was reflected in a characteristic political model that was almost the converse of the political model of the Renaissance. The essential feature of the medieval political ideal was its denial of the legitimacy of the particular, the autonomous, and the secular. Hence it rejected the propriety of such independent political entities as have been the primary subject of modern political discourse; it was concerned rather with the social (as well as spiritual) unity of all Christians in a single body, the *ecclesia* or *respublica christiana,* terms often used interchangeably. According to James of Viterbo, no community but the church could be considered a *vera respublica* since only the church could supply, in their true meaning, the benefits of government. The church alone was in direct contact with the ultimate source of all benefit, and nothing could be more clear than that the church was one.

And like the larger dimensions of reality, the *respublica christiana* was necessarily organized as a hierarchical system in which lower ends were subordinated to higher, and inferior powers to superior; authority

5. *Contra Faustum Manichaeum,* Ch. 53.

in the entire structure descended from above. Its systematic character meant that the clergy were superior to the laity and gave an ultimate supremacy, in temporal as in spiritual matters (since the former ranked lower in the hierarchy of values), to the pope. And as subordinate members of a universal system men could be seen to have no right to govern themselves, and states no right to determine their separate courses of action. Self-determination, in this view, could only appear, in the deepest sense, as a violation of the very structure of reality, and political duty appeared to consist only in patient submission and obedience. Man, in this system, was always and necessarily a subject; he could not be a citizen. Thus the ideal had important ethical implications.

Political responsibility in this conception could only seem relatively contemptible, at best an ancillary necessity. It was clearly better for any man, if he could, to leave it to such baser sorts as were incapable of rising to higher things, and himself to withdraw from the confusing and generally meaningless particularity of daily life to abide in the realm of the general and the unchanging. Related to this attitude was a substantial indifference to history, which was concerned with the inferior realm of change, from which (at best) general truths of a low and practical character could only occasionally be abstracted; there are no historians among the great ancients gathered around the fire in Dante's Limbo. The medieval conception of reality found expression not in historical compositions but in magnificent architectonic systems of thought, final answers in as final a form as possible to perennial questions, designed rather to close than to continue discussion.

I am describing here a great vision rather than an actuality, and it will be unnecessary to discuss either its complex origins (more hellenistic than specifically Christian) or the long effort of the papacy to translate it into a reality, although it may be observed that this effort was not so successful as has often been supposed. Its earlier protagonists were largely content to enunciate the ideal and to demand the world's conformity; the notion that the ideal had generally achieved acceptance would have required concrete political and historical evidence and a species of discourse which these men rarely found congenial. The historical claim came, on the whole, later, and largely during the period with which this book is concerned.

The spiritual leaders of the *respublica christiana* made, nevertheless, a considerable effort to impose their lofty conception on the refractory world; and to promote it they devised several techniques destined for particular importance, not only directly and practically during earlier episodes in the elaboration of the theocratic ideal but also because they stimulated the elaboration of a new political consciousness from the fourteenth century onward. These techniques included the excommunication of rulers, usually accompanied by a formal declaration of deposition; the release of subjects from obedience together with the encouragement of revolt as a sacred duty; and the interdiction of an entire political community as a means of bringing public pressure to bear on its government. Often used in combination, these devices gave a cutting edge to the spiritual sword. They were the instruments by which the superior spiritual authority enforced its will against the lesser members of the body politic. Their use implemented the general claim to sovereignty over the entire *respublica christiana;* submission to them implied the acceptance of this claim by the temporal power. As a primary means for imposing theoretical requirements on political practice, the spiritual weapons wielded by popes were bound to provoke crises and thereby to stimulate reflection about the nature of human society and its organization. They had therefore a considerable role in developing the characteristic political attitudes of the Renaissance, particularly for Venice.

The antithesis of the *respublica christiana* was the Renaissance republic, a phenomenon whose importance for the remarkable achievements of Italy during the fourteenth, fifteenth, and sixteenth centuries has received some emphasis from modern scholars. But the relation between republicanism and Renaissance culture was recognized long ago. Thus, toward the end of the sixteenth century, Giovanni Botero discussed it in an unusually general way; but he did so, as he generally sought to do in other connections, because it had already become a familiar sentiment. In the extended section on Venice in his *Relationi universali* Botero wrote:

> From good government derive all those good qualities in subjects that belong to civil and virtuous life, every means for doing good things, all the arts both of peace and war, of acquiring and saving, all polite customs, all noble manners, every honored form of politeness. For this reason free cities of great size surpass those that are subject to princes, at once in magnificence of buildings and in beauty of streets and squares, in multitude of people, in variety of arts, in refinement of manners, and in every kind of polity [*politia*] and humanity. Venice and Genoa prove it, and Florence and Siena did so in their time.

It had early become a commonplace that republican freedom made better men, supplied better government, and nourished a more brilliant culture than other kinds of government.

To appreciate the significance of the Renaissance republic, it is necessary to emphasize, however, that (like the *respublica christiana*) it was not simply a political construction; it rested, as an ideal, on specific assumptions, and it pointed to a set of general attitudes. Republicanism was intimately connected with powerful convictions about the nature of man that bore directly on his capacity to apprehend the structure of reality, though perhaps not so immediately with positive beliefs about its ultimate nature, a point on which republicanism was likely to be agnostic. The belief that a republic was the form of government most appropriate to the human condition, and therefore best suited to bring out the full potentialities of man, as Botero suggested, was thus a reflection of fundamental attitudes to experience as a whole.

Republicanism, to put the matter in its simplest terms, did not identify the essence of man with his intellect. It tended rather (though such modes of thought were not altogether congenial to it) to find man's essence in his will. Republicanism lacked, therefore, the confidence implicit in the medieval vision in the power of the human reason to grasp general patterns of order to which every element in creation, and notably man himself, must conform. It saw no absolute structure in the nature of things, no clear gradations of ultimate value, no ground for classifying some elements in the universe as higher and others as lower, no reason accessible to man for affirming that reality consisted of a system of unchanging forms and that the fluidity of common experience could be dismissed as meaningless. It accepted inconsistency, contradiction, and paradox as insurmountable.

The historical significance of Renaissance humanism lies in the fact that it reflected this set of essentially skeptical attitudes. Instead of attempting to coordinate classical texts into a system, it rejected the possibility of systematic knowledge in favor of a kind of intellectual pluralism. Renaissance humanism recognized that men filled various roles in society or had, in their personal lives, a variety of needs which might require a variety of intellectual postures. Humanistic culture was unsystematic and eclectic; it was prepared to range among alternative positions and to select whichever seemed appropriate to a particular set of circumstances. And a professional humanist was simply a man who made appropriate attitudes available for the use of others. From this standpoint it seems to make little difference whether a rhetorician employed by a government, like Salutati or Bruni, actually believed personally in what he wrote on its behalf. The attitude toward the nature of truth implied by his profession was itself utterly at odds with the systematic mentality attached to the medieval vision of reality. A man who believed one thing but wrote another, for whatever purpose, or who supplied an argument for one occasion utterly inconsistent with what he provided for another, was, against this background, perhaps a more striking phenomenon than one who simply deviated from traditional views on particular issues. And it is particularly significant that the profession of rhetoric seems to have involved no great burden on the conscience.

A skeptical, antisystematic position generally characterized the great Florentines who first brought republican political discourse to a high level of articulation, although hints of it may be discovered (along with entirely contrary tendencies) at least as early as Petrarch and Salutati. Machiavelli and Guicciardini, the latter more consistently, rejected the abstract and general for the concrete and particular, the theoretical for the empirical. They did so from their understanding of the nature of man and in a spirit of profound disillusionment with the consequences of relying on the generalizing intellect. "Philosophers and theologians and all those who investigate the supernatural and the invisible," declared Guicciardini, "say thousands of insane things. As a matter of fact, men are in the dark about such matters, and their investigation has served and serves more to exercise the intellect than to find truth." But the objection went beyond metaphysics to all general statements. The difficulty with any generalization was that it was all too likely to take on a life and a power of its own, to attempt to control the details it had been intended only to summarize, in effect (to paraphrase Walter Ullmann) to transform an ascending into a descending theme of intellectual authority. This is the meaning of Machiavelli's conviction that "in general men deceive themselves a great deal, in specific things not so much," on the basis of which he praised the Romans for their wisdom in disregarding a general principle of whose abstract truth they had been fully persuaded.

From this perspective the life men lived, in contrast to an uncontrolled speculation about life in general, appeared to consist of discrete moments in particular situations; for all practical purposes (in the literal sense) this was the true nature of reality. Hence Guicciardini's sweeping prescription:

> It is a great error to speak of things of the world absolutely and indiscriminately and to deal with them, as it were, by the book. In nearly all things one must make distinctions and exceptions because of differences in their circumstances. These circumstances are not covered by one and the same rule. Nor can these distinctions and exceptions be found written in books. They must be taught by discretion.

From a strictly intellectual point of view republicanism may thus appear deeply pessimistic, and its dim view of man's generalizing intellect was often extended to his capacity for virtue. But what republicanism yielded in this area it sometimes made up for in others. It assumed the existence of a wide range of positive values in the nonintellectual dimensions of human experience: in the infinite variety of the material world of place and time, in the various dimensions of the emotional life, in problems of moral choice, in creative expression, in the struggle (albeit so often tragic) between man and his destiny. And since it did not conceive of man primarily as an intellectual being, it freed him to engage in the active life as the mode of existence best suited to his complex nature. Social responsibility was valuable not only for society but for individual men as well because it meant exposure to a broad range of experiences.

Renaissance republicanism adapted this vision of man to politics; it tried to solve the problem of adjustment to a reality that was, in any general or ultimate sense, beyond human grasp. For the heart of republicanism, as Botero seems to have recognized, was the claim to liberty; and liberty meant the rejection of subordination. A true republic was in the first place a particular power, not a participant in a universal system directed by some superior authority; and it claimed the right to determine its own policies simply on the basis of its particular interest. Nor was its internal structure, in the medieval sense, systematic. It was directed not to a single end from above, by a prince, but by a body of citizens, who somehow represented the community and its interests, and who were related to one another by a principle very different from that of hierarchy.

* * *

Constitutions, in this tradition, were seen to serve a variety of important functions. For Machiavelli only a sound constitution could solve the problem posed by man's mortality; good institutions survived the men who made them. They could also strengthen states against external attack and thus enable men to control their own destiny; by its internal structure, over which it has substantial power, a state could resist those perils over which it has none. Above all, a constitutional polity served to restrain those special interests in the state which, if allowed to act unchecked, would destroy it; a constitution was thus the best guardian of freedom. In looking back on the history of Florence, therefore, Machiavelli concluded that such greatness as she had achieved had resulted from the civil and military institutions "by which the Florentines established their liberty." Conversely, he attributed all tribulations of the Republic to her constitutional defects. As he makes a Florentine patriot observe, "The laws, the statutes, the methods of government here always have been and now are managed not as required by free government but as required by the ambition of the dominant faction." Instead of coordinating the various interests in the state, the Florentine constitution had strengthened some at the expense of others; but the point was that it ought to and could have been better devised.

The ideal represented by Machiavelli is thus one of balance and pluralism. It recognizes political value in the various components of a society, and it aims to allow each to make its specific contribution to the governance of the whole. The theory of the mixed constitution, adapted from the ancients and destined for so prominent a place in later political discourse, was attractive to the republicans of the Renaissance precisely because it seemed to express this ideal. Thus Machiavelli saw clearly that leadership was essential to a republic, which must somehow provide for strong executive authority and prompt action to meet any crisis; but at the same time it had to be restrained by constitutional means from subverting the republic. Only the nobility could supply qualities of valor and generosity, but its characteristic ambition had also to be kept in check. The people, finally, were devoted to liberty and equality; but since these were not the only political virtues, and could indeed degenerate through excess, this group too required control. Ideally, therefore, each of the three elements in political life would not only make a peculiar contribution to the whole but would also help to keep the other two within bounds.

It should again be apparent that the principle of order in this conception is not that of hierarchy but the idea of dynamic equilibrium. The mixed constitution thus occupies much the same place in the structure of internal politics as the balance of power in international affairs; its principle of operation is identical. The hierarchical ideal applied to internal politics, on the other hand, would seem from this point of view to spell disaster. For Machiavelli the rise of any of the three components of a well-ordered polity above the others would not only reduce their capacity to contribute those qualities which they alone could give to political life, but also by its own excesses stimulate a reaction to the opposite extreme. The result could only be that contrasting forms of government, each excessive and defective in its own way, would succeed each other in a constant and disorderly alternation. This truth had been tragically illustrated, he believed, by the history of Florence.

But reality, as the Renaissance understood it, was not only particularized and ungraded; it was also fluid and subject to change. Mutability in this conception was not merely illusory and meaningless; it was a part of the true nature of things, insofar as men could apprehend them in this life. Change had to be acknowledged, reckoned on, adapted to, and provided for. Balance in external affairs and constitutional processes to solve domestic problems may thus be seen as devices to manage the omnipresent possibility of change in the realm of politics.

J. MAX PATRICK, INTRODUCTION

in The Prose of John Milton (J. Max Patrick ed. 1967).

Resourcefulness, industry, and marriage to Sarah Jeffrey (who possessed both virtue and wealth), enabled John Milton senior to overcome the rigidities of the English social system. He derived from an undistinguished Roman Catholic Oxfordshire family, became an Anglican, went to London (probably as a musician), rose to some prominence in the business world as a scrivener engaged in legal and financial affairs, and gained social status as a gentleman by acquiring a coat of arms. He also won some recognition as a composer: his eight-part choral work for the King of Poland has not survived, but his hymns are still sung in the Church of England. He brought up his children, Anne, John, and Christopher, in a cultured, comfortable, pious, tolerant London household, encouraging John to become an Anglican priest and Christopher to enter the field of law.

The future poet was born on December 9, 1608, five years after James I succeeded Queen Elizabeth I, eight years before the deaths of Shakespeare and Cervantes. Like the royal family, Milton senior had his sons tutored by a Scot—Thomas Young. In 1620, the year when the Pilgrims settled New Plymouth, twelve-year-old John entered St. Paul's School. There he received an admirable humanistic education which greatly influenced the program of studies later propounded in *Of Education.* In 1625 Charles I came to the throne and, at a somewhat older age than was customary, John enrolled in Christ's College, Cambridge. A disagreement with his tutor led to his rustication or temporary expulsion, but he returned, displayed his virtuosity in the Prolusions or Academic Exercises which he published in his old age, and received his B.A. in 1629, two years before the death of John Donne.

By this time Milton had composed a number of short poems in Latin and English. In 1634 his *Mask* (better known as *Comus*) entertained the aristocratic Bridgewater family; it was published without his name and without Henry Lawes' music for it, about three years later. *Lycidas,* a pastoral elegy occasioned by the drowning of a college acquaintance, was printed in a volume of poems in memory of Edward King.

About 1638 Milton went on a tour of France and Italy but did not reach Greece, as he had intended, because of the social, political, economic, and religious crisis in England. Tensions had become acute on a political level between king and parliament and, inside the Church of England, between conservatives who felt that the Reformation had gone far enough—or too far—and others, loosely called "Puritans," who wanted forms of faith and worship more Protestant than those established by law. These oppositions were exacerbated by problems of inflation, taxation, obsolete institutions and vested interests, increasing population, and the advance of capitalism.

"Puritan," as ordinarily understood today, is a misleading term to apply to Milton senior or either of his sons. They were a moderate Church of England family; the boys attended a school whose services were Anglican; and John subscribed to the Thirty–Nine Articles when he entered Christ's College. If the Miltons sang psalms, they also warbled madrigals; and their home was frequented by musicians, many of them Roman Catholics and Royalists. Indeed, Christopher Milton supported the king and the established church and ultimately became a Roman Catholic judge under James II. Art and literature were regarded with favor in the Milton home; and the fact that John somehow managed to get a poem of tribute to Shakespeare into the second folio suggests the broad and up-to-date cultural interests of his family. Nor should it be forgotten that John wrote and never disowned poems honoring the Anglican bishop, Joseph Andrewes, and the Roman Catholic Marchioness of Winchester. Indeed, had John died in 1640, he would probably have been classed with Robert Herrick, George Herbert, and Abraham Cowley as an Anglican poet who wrote charming masques for the aristocracy, memorialized a young man who would have become a Church of England pastor, composed a number of excellent elegiac poems, and celebrated festivals of the Anglican church year. The urbane seriousness of *L'Allegro* and *Il Penseroso* can hardly be called puritanical.

Even the Milton who wrote the prose works in the present collection cannot unreservedly be called a Puritan: *Protestant* is a more apt term. Like the more advanced Anglicans and unlike many, probably most, of the Presbyterians, Baptists, and Congregationalists of the revolutionary period, Milton rejected the Calvinistic doctrine of predestination and believed in free will. His teachings on divorce horrified most Christians of all kinds. And had he published *Christian Doctrine,* its heresies would likewise have shocked most Englishmen of his times. On the other hand, Protestants in general, including High Anglicans, have found his epics and *Samson Agonistes* to be Christian, not distinctively Puritan, poems.

The same cannot be said for some of his prose tracts. Certainly he opposed episcopacy—government of the church by a hierarchy of bishops who claimed and exercised powers beyond what the Bible (as interpreted by Milton) seemed to justify, powers such as the exclusive right to ordain priests. Indeed, Milton rejected the doctrine of apostolic succession and regarded bishops as no more than presbyters (ministers or priests). He regarded the bishops' assumption and exercise of control over preaching, publication, doctrine, ritual, and interpretation of the Bible as a tyranny, one based on what he viewed as man-made traditions, worldliness, self-interest, alliance with secular powers, and either ignorance or deliberate falsification of what Holy Scripture and Right Reason teach. He felt that the bishops and their supporters were not only hindering but preventing the continued reformation of God's church in England. In Milton's opinion, God had shown special favor to his Englishmen when Wycliffe initiated the movement toward Scripture-based Protestantism. Under the Tudors, papal power in England had been broken and doctrinal and administrative reforms had gone a long way to remove "Popery" from English religion. Nevertheless, it seemed obvious to Milton that despite what he believed to be the finger of God pointing to the removal of episcopacy, the Reformation had remained incomplete in England and lagged behind what was accomplished in other Protestant countries. In attacking the bishops, Milton took what seemed to be the most obvious step toward freeing religion from man-imposed tyranny.

Milton did not initiate the attack on the prelates. Archbishop Laud, who had tried to regularize the Church of England in what seemed to Milton a step backward to Romanism, was impeached in 1640, the year of the Root and Branch Petition against government of the church by bishops. Taking these as a cue for literary action, Milton published *Of Reformation, Of Prelatical Episcopacy,* and *Animadversions upon the Remonstrants Defence* in 1641, and *The Reason of Church–Government* and *An Apology against a Pamphlet,* in 1642, all in the cause of religious liberty.

Meanwhile he had set up a household of his own and partly occupied himself with teaching. Among his few pupils were John and Edward Phillips, sons of his sister Anne. This activity brought in some money, but Milton lived chiefly on wealth derived from his father. For example, he held a mortgage against some land owned by Richard Powell of Oxfordshire. The Powells and Miltons were old friends and had long been involved in such transactions. It is, accordingly, not improbable that John made the acquaintance of Richard's daughter Mary and chose her as his possible bride long before 1642, when he won her hand. They were married about May, when he was thirty-three and she was little more than half his age. Though women grew to responsible maturity earlier in those days, this teen-age girl seems to have had some difficulty in adjusting to a household that included the Phillips boys and offered less gaiety and social activities than she was accustomed to. On the other hand, when Milton consented to her visiting her father's home, about July 1642, there was apparently no severe tension between them, for he confidently expected her return and was surprised when she did not come back. External factors probably made the crucial difference: the civil war erupted; the Powells were Royalists; and Milton's anti-prelatical tracts had identified him with the rebels. Prospects for a parliamentary success may have looked slim when viewed from Oxfordshire; and the Powells may well have decided that the prudent course was to avoid identification with the losing side. On the other hand, if the Royalists lost, the marriage tie would still hold good, and the Powells perhaps presumed on what eventually happened—that Milton's good nature and decency would lead him to take back a repentant wife who put the blame on her mother. Moreover, the Powells were in royalist territory, and communications and travel to parliamentary London were difficult and dangerous.

Milton tried to get Mary to return, but not to the heroic extent of disguising himself and penetrating into enemy territory to reclaim her. Instead, within a year of her failure to return, he made that return somewhat difficult by publishing *The Doctrine and Discipline of Divorce* in August 1643, following it with an enlarged edition six months later, and with three other tracts, *The Judgement of Martin Bucer* (August 1644) and *Tetrachordon* and *Colasterion* (March 1645): all of them urged that divorce be allowed for incompatibility, their central point being that the essence of Christian marriage lies in the rational and spiritual union of what is highest in humanity, thus distinguishing it from animals. He thought that a couple who are joined contractually and carnally but lack higher marital love and are naturally incompatible in mind and temperament should not be forced by church or state to remain yoked. He advocated that if a couple made a sincere effort over a reasonable period of time to iron out difficulties and find harmony and companionship, it should be recognized that there had never been a true marriage. The greater part of Milton's tracts on the subject tried to demonstrate that such views were in accord with the Bible.

Inasmuch as remarkably little is known about Milton's personal relationship with his wife and his attitude toward her, it is unfair to them to assume that they were seriously and permanently incompatible or that he was embittered by this experience through-out his life. What is obvious is that their few months together after the marriage did not amount to a sincere effort to find harmony over a reasonable period of time. There is no evidence that they did not find compatibility after her return. Mary remained with him till her death and bore him several children. It is also noteworthy that the experience did not stop Milton from entering upon two subsequent marriages.

The divorce tracts had a larger purpose than private aims. Milton regarded them as part of a program for religious, domestic, and political freedom in which he successively attacked the tyranny of bishops, the oppression of canon law as it persisted in the regulations governing marriage and divorce, and the tyranny of kings and state-controlled religion. All were aspects of his effort to continue the Reformation. His tractate *Of Education* (June 1644) dealt with another aspect of domestic freedom and was part of his larger attack against the tyrannies of custom, tradition, and thought control. Throughout his writings he particularly opposed the domination of education, theology, and thinking by the Schoolmen—the divines and philosophers in the degenerated tradition of medieval scholasticism. Their methods and Milton's earliest attacks on them are discussed below in the section on Milton's *Prolusions.*

Having attacked the bishops, Milton recognized that what he regarded as tyranny was still repugnant when its powers were merely transferred to, and exercised by others. So he continued to attack abuses of authority, institutions which enabled them, and doctrines and traditions which supported them. Thus his divorce pamphlets attacked canon law, the courts and institutions to which its powers had been transmitted, and, above all, the doctrines and customs which prevented the establishment of what he believed to be a better discipline of marriage and divorce. Criticisms of the enslaving force of custom are reiterant in his tracts. They may also be viewed as part of a struggle over the means of controlling men's ideas and actions—the pulpit, the press, and educational institutions. Traditionally these had largely been controlled by the church—that is, ultimately by the bishops, though the ecclesiastics were themselves often subject to state control.

In 1640, the eve of the civil war, when those symbols of secular and ecclesiastical tyranny Laud and Strafford were being impeached, the system of censorship, which was largely under the bishops' control, had broken down. Thus the printing presses were opened to those who, like Milton, wanted to advance the Reformation in England. But in 1643 the Long Parliament instituted a system whereby books, pamphlets, newspapers, and even posters could not be published legally without a license of approval obtained prior to publication from any one of a small group of officials appointed for that purpose. This put a major means of influencing men's ideas into the hands of mediocre men and those who appointed them.

What most disturbed Milton was that such censorship would prevent a free discussion and search for truth among the adherents of Bible-based Protestantism. He was not unwilling to curb Roman Catholics and Anglicans to the extent that they held church tradition as an authority complementary to Holy Scripture; for in Milton's judgment, traditions, when not clearly grounded on the Bible, were man-made and violated what he interpreted as scriptural injunctions against adding one jot or tittle to the completeness of God's Word. In short, he saw this Licensing Order as an effort to prevent the Reformation from continuing beyond what Calvin and other Protestant reformers had taught. And in Milton's view, although man should not add to what the Bible taught as necessary to salvation, Christians were nevertheless obliged to study and discuss it; for by so doing they could discover new riches and insights, could clarify what was previously not fully or properly understood, and could thus continue to advance the Reformation. Thus his title to the first divorce tract proclaimed that he had restored the doctrine and discipline of divorce "From the Bondage of Canon Law, and Other Mistakes, to the True Meaning of Scripture." By preventing publication of such truth-discovering tracts, Parliament, instead of furthering the Reformation, was stopping it and acting as tyrannically as the bishops and the monarchy.

Accordingly Milton composed *Areopagitica,* his most famous and most influential pamphlet. In it he made a powerful case against prepublication censorship, though he granted that if books, authors, and printers broke known laws (against libel, blasphemy, and the like), the books could be destroyed and those responsible for them punished. Perhaps the most powerful—certainly the most characteristic—of his numerous arguments was that, even as prelatical tyranny could prevent men from exercising their highest and distinctive rationality, and even as yoking an incompatible man and woman denied them the harmonious union of their highest human faculties, so censorship was an attempt to stifle man's essential rationality, thus thwarting his proper humanity.

In 1645 Milton also published his *Poems . . . both English and Latin, Compos'd at Several Times;* and it was in that year that he received Mary back as his wife. In 1646 their daughter Anne was born.

Meanwhile, on the national scene, the army was remodeled, King Charles surrendered to the Scots, the first civil war came to an end, the abolition of episcopacy was completed, and Presbyterianism was officially decreed but imperfectly established in England. In 1647 Milton's father died, and in the next year another daughter, Mary, was born. The king escaped and, in 1648, made a treaty with the Scots, with the result that the second civil war began. When the Royalists had been defeated and a republican Commonwealth established, Milton, who had been tutoring, writing a history of Britain, and otherwise engaged in private studies, took the occasion of Charles I's beheading to publish *The Tenure of Kings and Magistrates* (February 1649), in which he justified the overthrow of tyrants and denounced the Presbyterians for having turned from advancing the Revolution in the first civil war to supporting Charles in the second. Having denounced ecclesiastics and their laws and practices for thwarting men's responsible exercise of choice and reason and discussion, and having condemned censorship which prevented the right use of humanity's distinctive powers, and having inveighed against education and customs which warp healthy development of those powers, Milton now asserted that any ruler who arrogates himself above the human condition and derogates his subjects to the status of beasts or vermin thereby forfeits not only his claim to rule but also his right to live.

In 1650 second editions of *The Tenure* and *Eikonoklastes* appeared, Oliver Cromwell succeeded Lord Fairfax as commander of the armed forces and defeated the Scots at Dunbar, and Milton was kept busy writing letters of state to foreign powers in his capacity as Secretary for Foreign Tongues. But in answer to a royalist apology for Charles I, he managed to find time to write *Pro Populo Anglicano Defensio* (February

1651), which later became known as his "First Defense of the English People." Since it was intended for an international audience, it was written in Latin. Meanwhile, personal afflictions bore heavy on Milton: in 1652 he became completely blind; and, although this misfortune was alleviated by the birth of a son in 1651, it was followed in the next year not only by the death of the infant John but by the deaths of his wife Mary and daughter Deborah.

Considering that his light was spent, that it was a kind of death to hide his talent, but that an omnipotent God had no need of man's services, Milton recognized that men who only stand and wait also serve Him through their obedience and through their refusal to lie down under the burden of affliction. Accordingly he stood ready to perform whatever providence indicated, whenever and however his talents were called upon. After Oliver Cromwell became Lord Protector in 1653, Milton continued to perform his duties as Secretary; as such, he had some share in the negotiations that ended the first Anglo–Dutch war (1652–54). Moreover, in May 1654, he published his "Second Defense of the English People," *Pro Populo Anglicano Defensio Secunda,* a reply to an apology for Charles I which Milton believed to be the work of Alexander More, though its author was in fact Pierre du Moulin. *Pro Populo* is now read chiefly for the autobiographical passages and the account of Oliver Cromwell, which are printed below. Milton followed it, in August 1655, with his "Third Defense," *Pro se Defensio,* in which he answered his detractors. In 1656 he married Katherine Woodcock, who bore him a daughter in the following year. But both the mother and little Katherine died in 1658.

Also in 1658 Richard Cromwell succeeded his father. Milton took the occasion to publish, in February and August, complementary tracts against the evils of state-controlled religion and a nationally supported clergy. The times were turbulent, but with great flexibility, as governments changed from Protector to Rump Parliament to army and re-restored Rump, Milton continued his work as Secretary for Foreign Tongues and did what little he could to prevent restoration of the monarchy. To this end he published *The Readie and Easie Way to Establish a Free Commonwealth* in March 1660, revising it for a second edition about April. But his advocacy of a self-perpetuating senate on the Venetian model was ineffective.

The restoration of Charles II in 1660 meant that Milton's life and property were in danger; for he had been a major propagandist in justifying the execution of the new king's father. But thanks to influential friends and his blindness, he was spared. After the Act of Oblivion he was allowed to return to the obscurity of private life.

Though this enforced retirement faced him with many difficulties, it was fortunate for English poetry. Over many years Milton had planned to write on the fall of man; indeed, he wrote part of a drama on the theme before he decided to couch it as an epic. Because he believed that God had given the English an exceptional opportunity to lead an ever-advancing reformation of church and state, he had gladly served both his God and his country. But Englishmen failed to use their opportunity properly; and, as a result, he turned to a task which was difficult for one whose hopes and efforts had been frustrated by the Restoration—the task of justifying the ways of God and asserting his eternal providence—a providence which took account even of the Restoration.

Gradually Milton adjusted himself to life in defeat. In 1663 he married Elizabeth Minshull, who was much his younger: she survived him into the eighteenth century. The plague of 1665 drove them to take refuge in Chalfont St. Giles; and it was there that Milton allowed his friend Thomas Ellwood to read a manuscript of *Paradise Lost.* Publication was delayed by the Great Fire of 1666. The first edition, in ten books, appeared in 1667 and was followed in 1671 by *Paradise Regain'd,* accompanied by *Samson Agonistes.*

Meanwhile he published a number of prose works he had probably written in whole or part previously: *Accidence Commenc't Grammar* (June 1669) was followed by *The History of Britain* (1670) and a treatise on the art of logic, *Artis Logicae Plenior Institutio* (1672—the year of the first production of William Wycherley's *The Country Wife*). A newly written tract, *Of True Religion,* reached print about May 1673; and in the autumn of that year the second edition of *Poems* was accompanied by *Of Education.* Publication of the familiar letters and college prolusions in May 1674 was followed in July by the second edition of *Paradise Lost,* in twelve books, and by Milton's death which probably occurred on November 8. He was buried, as his father had been before him, with Church of England rites in the chancel of the Church of St. Giles in Cripplegate.

N. H. KEEBLE, MILTON AND PURITANISM

in A Companion to Milton (Thomas N. Corns ed. 2001).

THE "AMBIGUOUS ILL-MADE WORD"

The term "puritan" became current during the 1560s as a pejorative nickname for Protestants who, dissatisfied with the Elizabethan settlement of the church by the Act of Uniformity of 1559, would have subscribed to the contention of the *Admonition to Parliament* of 1572 that "we in England are so fare off, from having a church rightly reformed, accordying to the prescript of Gods worde, that as yet we are not come to the outwarde face of the same." Puritans were distinguishable by their dissatisfaction with the rites and ceremonies of the Elizabethan church and by their desire to continue the process of Protestant reformation, halted in mid-career in England, they believed, in the compromise of an established church which retained government by bishops and a liturgy still modelled on that of Rome. They never, however, belonged to a single sect or constituted a clearly defined group within or without the episcopal Church of England. Drawing on native Lollard traditions which, despite sustained persecution, had survived in popular culture since the early fifteenth century, and fired by the zeal of exiles who, having fled during the reign of the Roman Catholic Queen

Mary (1553–8), now returned inspired by their experience of the reformed practices of Jean Calvin (1509–64) at Geneva and Johann Bullinger (1504–75) at Zurich, puritanism had no one founder, no single recognized leader and no agreed policy. It embraced many forms and degrees of discontent with the *via media* of the Elizabethan church, from refusing to observe some of its rituals and ceremonial practices (such as, for ministers, wearing a surplice or, for worshippers, kneeling to receive the sacrament), to a refusal to attend the parish church and a rejection of the validity of episcopal orders. To realize their aspirations, puritans came to propose a variety of alternative models of church government and also, as they came into conflict with ecclesiastical institutions and the state authorities which supported those institutions, a variety of alternative constitutional political models.

The term "puritan" is hence capacious and vague. Its scope has been much debated by modern historians who have sought to limit its connotations, but they are hampered by the looseness of its use in the seventeenth century. This was fully recognized at the time: "the detested odious name of Puritan," remarked the anonymous *Discourse Concerning Puritans* (1641), probably the work of Henry Parker, so "dilates itself" in ecclesiastical, political and moral senses that its "vast circumference" encompasses a multitude of meanings; it is "an ambiguous ill-made word," agreed the eminent puritan divine Richard Baxter. In a much cited chapter on "The Definition of a Puritan" the modern historian Christopher Hill collected together a great many such citations illustrating the varied and conflicting senses of the word and the frustration of contemporaries with its elusiveness.

Nevertheless, while it is impossible to offer a precise definition of puritanism in ecclesiological, doctrinal or political terms, there is not, in practice, much difficulty in recognizing the puritan spirit. While it manifested itself in a variety of ecclesiastical, theological and constitutional positions, its defining characteristic was a dissatisfaction with the present realization of Christian ideals and a consequent determination to reform practices and institutions. Its various strategies and platforms shared a desire to recover for individuals and for congregations the purity of doctrine, the simplicity of worship, the commitment of ministry and the integrity of faith which (it was believed) had characterized the early, or "primitive", church of the first three centuries after Christ, before the growth of the ascendancy of Rome over western Christendom led (so it was held) to the corruption of the Christian Gospel and church. For all the revolutionary impetus of its politics, puritanism is hence marked by the backward glance, by a constant longing to return not only to the days of the early church, but even to the purity and innocence of Eden: the prospect of paradise regained haunts its imagination. Its moral and spiritual effort was directed to living as though "strangers and pilgrims on the earth", natives of "a better country, that is, an heavenly" (Hebrews 11: 13, 16). It was this repudiation of the world which led to characterizations of the puritan as a fanatic killjoy like Shakespeare's Malvolio in *Twelfth Night.*

* * *

Since the culture of the time identified the well-being of the nation with uniform religious practice, any form of dissent or noncompliance was rigorously punished, by fines, imprisonment, mutilation or even (for persistent offenders) exile. For the greater part of its history, puritanism was in conflict with the law of the land and puritans were subject to various punitive legal measures and to persecution. The exception was the brief period during the 1640s and 1650s when men of puritan conviction gained political power. The loss of that power with the restoration of the Stuart monarchy in 1660 led to a period of sustained and determined persecution intended finally to suppress all dissident opinion. The attempt failed. The acceptance of toleration as a religious and civil duty was perhaps the most significant cultural development of the seventeenth century. It was a development driven by the courageous determination of generations of puritans not to submit their consciences to the dictates of ecclesiastical or state power. This resolution is nowhere more evident than in Milton's life and writing. He is a central figure in the cultural history of puritanism, a man whose life was shaped by commitment to its religious and political cause, whose writings were occasioned by their demands and whose creativity was inspired by their ideals. To read Milton is to know what it was to be a puritan.

Milton and Puritan Ecclesiology

The ecclesiastical history of puritanism is marked by the promulgation of, controversy over and rivalry among a succession of models of Reformed church government. Presbyterianism was the aim of the majority of early puritans, led by such Cambridge men as Walter Travers (*c.* 1584–1635) and Thomas Cartwright (1535–1603). This aspiration survived to become the official policy of the Long Parliament which, having abolished episcopacy in January 1643, summoned the Westminster Assembly of Divines in September 1643 to advise on a new church settlement. However, despite the publication of the Assembly's series of classic Presbyterian formularies—*Directory of Church-Government* (1644), *Directory of Public Worship* (1645), *Confession of Faith* (1648) and *Larger and Shorter Catechism* (1648)—its efforts were frustrated by opposition from within the puritan movement itself. The polity known originally as "Independency", but in New England and subsequently in England as "congregationalism" was, under the patronage of Oliver Cromwell (1599–1658), successfully championed by the New Model Army with its watch-cry of "Liberty of Conscience".

While Presbyterians continued to think, like the episcopalians, in terms of a parish-based national church with a hierarchical government and a legally enforceable uniformity of belief and practice (with rigorous punishment of dissenters), Independency was based upon the autonomy of each separate congregation. Such congregations gathered themselves under ministers whom they elected and they ran their affairs in ways which were markedly democratic. While different churches might associate together, this system imposed upon no one church or region authority over the others, nor did it recognize a ministerial hierarchy.

* * *

Milton, by his own account, was "destin'd of a child" for a career in the church, but, convinced by the lordly high-handedness of the bishops (as it appeared to him) that "tyranny had invaded the Church", he refused to "subscribe slave" to secure ordination and so found himself, in a memorable phrase, "Church-outed by the Prelats." As it appears in a rhetorically charged polemical tract (*The Reason of Church–Government,* 1642), this passage may not be biographically reliable, but its accuracy matters less than the fact that Milton clearly wished to claim for himself a classic puritan's progress. He had been sufficiently conservative to write, in 1626, poems commemorating such pillars of the Jacobean church as Lancelot Andrewes, Bishop of Winchester ("Elegy III") and Nicholas Felton, Bishop of Ely ("*In Obitum Praesulis Eliensis*"); but by 1637, when he wrote "Lycidas", there is a distinctly puritan edge to the scorn with which, in the voice of St Peter, he derides those ministers who "for their bellies sake, / Creep and intrude, and climb into the fold" while "The hungry sheep look up, and are not fed" (lines 114–15, 125). Outrage at such neglect of its pastoral duty was what fuelled puritan discontent with the Caroline church. When, a few years later, Milton returned from his continental tour in order to commit himself to the oppositional cause, it was this scorn which animated his first prose writings in the service of the Revolution. In a series of vituperative antiprelatical tracts (that is, tracts written against episcopacy) published in 1641–2 he excoriated the bishops: Andrewes was now a target of mockery.

In January 1643 the Long Parliament did abolish episcopacy, and convened the Westminster Assembly of Divines to advise on a national church settlement. It is a curiosity of Milton's antiprelatical tracts that, while they have a very great deal to say about bishops, and none of it good, they have almost nothing to say about what church polity should replace them. Hence, while Milton may be supposed in 1641–2 to have had Presbyterian sympathies, there is no evidence in him of any firm Presbyterian commitment, or even of much interest in ecclesiology *per se.* It is the prospect of the corrupt and tyrannical exercise of power which animates his writing, as it would do throughout his life. Before very long, he discerned this abuse in Presbyterians no less than in episcopalians. In *Areopagitica* (1644) he registered his disappointment at the determination of the Long Parliament, the majority of whose members were Presbyterians, to re-impose censorship and to stifle debate. Presbyterianism, it appeared, was quite as determined to outlaw dissent from its views as the episcopalians had been to enforce compliance with theirs. Of this, Milton had first-hand experience. He was deeply affected by the savagery of the response to his divorce tracts of 1643–5, three of them addressed to the Long Parliament and the first also to the Westminster Assembly. He was attacked in print by William Prynne, a leading lawyer and MP, and by Robert Baillie, a Scottish Presbyterian commissioner at the Westminster Assembly, and he found himself among the heretics and fanatics berated in Edwards's *Gangraena* (1646) as a libertine "divorcer". In two poems of 1646 (not published until 1673) Milton reacted bitterly to this outcry. In Sonnet XII he protested that he "id but prompt the age to quit their clogs" (line 1) and, denying the authority of "shallow Edwards and Scotch What-d'ye-call" to determine the limits of tolerable opinion, he concluded his extended sonnet "On the New Forcers of Conscience under the Long Parliament" with resounding alliterative condemnation: "New *Presbyter* is but old *Priest* writ large" (lines 12, 20).

Thereafter, Milton is to be counted among the Independents. It had been for "crowding free consciences and Christian liberties into canons and precepts of men" that he had condemned the "Prelaticall tradition" in *Areopagitica* (1644), and for "the liberty to know, to utter, and to argue freely according to conscience, above all liberties" that he had argued passionately in that tract. The uncompromising resolution with which Milton privileged conscience above all external authorities may have been unusual (though not unique: George Fox is his equal in this), but its general bias is distinctive of the individualism of puritanism. Inwardness and experiential immediacy are everywhere preferred in Milton. Throughout his writings there runs an authentically puritan opposition between the hollowness of habitual compliance with external forms and the integrity of inner commitment. The hypocrisy which Milton stigmatized in such phrases as "a grosse conforming stupidity", "this iron yoke of outward conformity", "the ghost of a linnen decency", "the gripe of custom," was conceived as the single most serious obstacle to the spiritual life, whose highest virtue he took to be sincerity. It is as the "Spirit, that dost prefer / Before all temples the upright heart and pure" that Milton characterizes the God whom he invokes at the opening of *Paradise Lost* (I. 17–18). It is with the sincerity of extemporary prayer, "and other rites / Observing none", that Adam and Eve address God before retiring for the night (IV. 736–7). Above all, it is the attainment of an experiential "paradise within thee, happier far" than the material bliss of Eden that Michael recommends to Adam, and *Paradise Lost* to its readers in the fallen world (XII. 587).

VINCENT BLASI, THE ELLIOT LECTURE: MILTON'S *AREOPAGITICA* AND THE MODERN FIRST AMENDMENT

Yale Law School Occasional Papers, Series Two (1996).

When King Charles I was forced by financial exigencies to convene the Long Parliament in November of 1640, he set in motion a political dynamic that led to civil war less than two years later and his own beheading within the decade. One of the first actions of the new

Parliament was to abolish the Court of Star Chamber, the infamous offshoot of the King's Privy Council which had served as the principal forum for calling to account political opponents, religious dissenters, and those who defied crown-granted monopolies of the printing trade. The abolition of Star Chamber meant, in effect, suspension of the licensing system that had been in operation for over a century, a regulatory hiatus that was more a byproduct of the attack on royal prerogative than a deliberate policy in favor of a free press.

The immediate result was a flourishing of political and religious ideas the likes of which England had never before experienced. Tudor and early Stuart licensing had been variable though sometimes draconian, often corrupt, and usually porous. The elimination in 1641 of the institutions of press control caused a dramatic increase in both the volume of advocacy and the range of views expressed. By one count, the number of pamphlets published during the year 1640 was 22; in 1642 it was 1,966.

In this atmosphere of excited disputation among antiroyalist factions, King Charles raised his standard at Nottingham in August of 1642. Civil war was at hand. The royalist prospect was by no means bleak. Throughout the year 1642, as various schemes for accommodation failed, about two-fifths of the House of Commons and most of the Lords chose to side with the King. The early skirmishes of the war were indecisive. In mid–1643 the parliamentary armies suffered serious setbacks. Those who believed the parliamentary cause to be the work of divine providence began to have doubts.

Concerned both about disunity in its own ranks and the effectiveness of Crown propaganda, Parliament in June of 1643 decided to reinstate government control over printing. A small number of master printers was authorized to operate presses. Those who held printing patents were enlisted, through their trade organization the Stationers' Company, to search out and bring to justice all who printed without a license. The economic self-interest of monopoly privilege was thus united with the demand for religious and political conformity.

Specialized licensers were appointed to examine writings in specified categories. Four censors were named, for example, to scrutinize law books, three for books of philosophy and history, one for "mathematics, almanacks, and prognostications." Parliament served as the enforcement agency, usually through its committees. Not only miscreant authors and printers but also licensers who had been too permissive were subject to imprisonment.

During the period of low military morale when the Licensing Order was enacted, the leaders of Parliament decided they could no longer postpone coming to grips with the volatile religious issues they had to that point shrewdly kept off the agenda for fear of dividing the antiroyalist coalition. Now, however, they needed a Scottish alliance. In return for lending their military resources to the parliamentary cause, the Scots wanted a religious settlement in England along strict Presbyterian lines, a prospect that drew mixed reviews among the rank and file in Parliament. Though many members considered themselves Presbyterians, most were unsympathetic to the severe Calvinist theology and the theocratic subordination of secular institutions that were features of Scottish Presbyterianism.

In the hope of generating a mutually acceptable religious settlement, Parliament created the Westminster Assembly, a convocation of 120 English clerics, thirty laymen from the Lords and Commons, and eight Scottish representatives. Debate in the Assembly proceeded continuously for months at a high level of piety and prolixity. Intense and bitter disagreements persisted, however, on such issues as congregational autonomy and toleration. The fierce disputes within the Assembly spilled over into the House of Commons, the pulpits, the army camps, and the streets, and generated some notable essays on the subject of religious toleration. Several of these were published in violation of the Licensing Order of 1643.

For more than two years, John Milton did not participate in these fundamental debates. True, in 1641, at the age of thirty-two, he did put on hold his carefully prepared career as a poet and joined in the pamphlet warfare that swirled around him, sacrificing what he termed his "calm and pleasing solitariness" to embark in "a troubled sea of noises and hoarse disputes." He became a controversialist, however, only to attack the pretensions, ignorance, venality, and laziness of the Anglican bishops. The five pamphlets he devoted to that worthy cause certainly display a poison pen and a capacity for animus, but show no deep interest in the theological questions that were tearing apart the Westminster Assembly and the wider Puritan nation. Once the Church of England was disestablished and its bishops expelled from the House of Lords, Milton turned his attention instead to an issue of small general but immense personal concern: the legitimate grounds of divorce.

In Oxford in the summer of 1642 he had met and quickly married the vivacious, attractive teen-age daughter of one of his father's debtors. Mary Powell, seventeen years Milton's junior, was accustomed to a large household and an active social life. She seems to have had little in common with her studious, devout, and brilliant husband. Her family was royalist. After a month or so of living with Milton in London, she deserted him and rejoined her parents. War broke out shortly thereafter, and Mary remained in the royalist stronghold of Oxford for the next three years.

This was a shattering experience for a man of Milton's pride and idealism, particularly because an important strain of Puritan theology viewed marital love as a manifestation of the love of God. Although his wife eventually returned and bore four children by him (dying in childbirth with the last), Milton's travail prompted him to examine whether a marriage could properly be terminated for incompatibility alone, without the adultery required by law and almost everyone's understanding of the Scriptures. James Holly Hanford nicely summarizes the thesis of Milton's 1643 pamphlet *The Doctrine and Discipline of Divorce:*

> His main plea is that incompatibility of temper is a more vital impediment to the higher objects of marriage than any other, and that the will of the parties should therefore be admitted as decisive for the continuance or dissolution of the bond.... The principle is in perfect accord with Milton's whole philosophy. It was because he thought nobly of marriage as a spiritual rather than a merely physical union that he resented the common idea that it was dissoluble only on physical grounds. The idea of an external compulsion, binding two human beings together when mutual love and sympathy had departed, was repellent to his reason and excited him to eloquent and passionate denunciation.

In the course of his divorce analysis, developed over the next two years in a much expanded second edition as well as three subsequent tracts, Milton produced arguments concerning the nature of truth, the grip of custom, and the principle of consent that he would draw upon in his later polemics, including *Areopagitica.*

The immediate consequence of his effort, however, was to mark him in the eyes of English and Scottish Presbyterians as a dangerous radical with licentious sympathies. One minister went so far as to make these accusations the subject of a sermon preached before the House of Commons. The boldness and singularity of Milton's views on divorce cannot be denied, but the sexual innuendo was manifestly unfair and deeply hurtful to him. Whatever else one might wish to accuse Milton of, a lack of personal discipline or an affinity for others who succumb to their impulses is surely wide of the mark. His views on divorce derived from his idealism and sense of Christian duty, not any form of libertinism. The calumny that his divorce pamphlets engendered almost certainly contributed to Milton's conclusion, at the heart of *Areopagitica,* that the newly ascendant Presbyterians in the Westminster Assembly and Parliament were as bigoted and potentially oppressive as the hated Anglican hierarchy whose overthrow had been the first priority of the Puritan revolution. As he later put it in a sonnet: "New Presbyter is but Old Priest writ large."

Milton apparently tried to get *The Doctrine and Discipline of Divorce* licensed for publication. When approval was denied, he published his tract in defiance of the law. Only one of his subsequent divorce pamphlets appeared with a licenser's imprimatur. It is possible that his experience with the censor prompted his polemic against licensing. It is also possible that he wrote *Areopagitica* at the behest of the journeymen printers of the City of London. This politically active group, with whom Milton was in contact, saw its livelihood threatened by the prospect of strict enforcement of the Licensing Order for the benefit of the limited number of master printers favored by Parliament with monopoly privileges. The argument of *Areopagitica* seems to reflect both of these influences, as well as Milton's growing interest in church-state relations and toleration.

JOHN MILTON, AREOPAGITICA: A SPEECH FOR THE LIBERTY OF UNLICENSED PRINTING TO THE PARLIAMENT OF ENGLAND*

(1644).

This is true liberty, when free-born men,
Having to advise the public, may speak free,
Which he who can, and will, deserves high praise;
Who neither can, nor will, may hold his peace:
What can be juster in a state than this?

Euripides, *The Suppliants*

* * *

Lords and Commons, there can no greater testimony appear, than when your prudent spirit acknowledges and obeys the voice of reason from what quarter soever it be heard speaking; and renders ye as willing to repeal any Act of your own setting forth, as any set forth by your predecessors.

If ye be thus resolved, as it were injury to think ye were not, I know not what should withhold me from presenting ye with a fit instance wherein to show both that love of truth which ye eminently profess, and that uprightness of your judgment which is not wont to be partial to yourselves; by judging over again that

Order which ye have ordained to regulate printing:—that no book, pamphlet, or paper shall be henceforth printed, unless the same be first approved and licensed by such, or at least one of such, as shall be thereto appointed. For that part which preserves justly every man's copy[1] to himself, or provides for the poor, I touch not, only wish they be not made pretences to abuse and persecute honest and painful[2] men, who offend not in either of these particulars. But that other clause of licensing books, which we thought had died with his brother quadragesimal[3] and matrimonial[4] when the prelates expired, I shall now attend with such a homily, as shall lay before ye, first the inventors of it to be those whom ye will be loath to own; next what is to be thought in general of reading, whatever sort the books be; and that this Order avails nothing to the suppressing of scandalous, seditious, and libellous books, which were mainly intended to be suppressed. Last, that it will be primely to the discouragement of all learning, and the stop of truth, not only by

* Annotations by Merritt Y. Hughes from *Milton: Prose Selections* (Odyssey Press, 1947).

1. *copy:* copyright.

2. *painful:* diligent, willing to take pains.

3. *quadragesimal:* pertaining to the forty days of Lent. The Puritans had relaxed the traditional, Anglican restrictions on diet during Lent.

4. Milton approved Parliament's act in securing the "civil liberty of marriage; transferring ratifying and registering of marriage to the civil magistrates."

disexercising and blunting our abilities in what we know already, but by hindering and cropping the discovery that might be yet further made both in religious and civil wisdom.

I deny not, but that it is of greatest concernment in the Church and Commonwealth, to have a vigilant eye how books demean themselves as well as men; and thereafter to confine, imprison, and do sharpest justice on them as malefactors. For books are not absolutely dead things, but do contain a potency of life in them to be as active as that soul was whose progeny they are; nay, they do preserve as in a vial the purest efficacy and extraction of that living intellect that bred them. I know they are as lively, and as vigorously productive, as those fabulous dragon's teeth; and being sown up and down, may chance to spring up armed men.[5] And yet, on the other hand, unless wariness be used, as good almost kill a man as kill a good book. Who kills a man kills a reasonable creature, God's image; but he who destroys a good book, kills reason itself, kills the image of God, as it were in the eye. Many a man lives a burden to the earth; but a good book is the precious life-blood of a master spirit, embalmed and treasured up on purpose to a life beyond life. "Tis true, no age can restore a life, whereof perhaps there is no great loss; and revolutions of ages do not oft recover the loss of a rejected truth, for the want of which whole nations fare the worse."

We should be wary therefore what persecution we raise against the living labours of public men, how we spill that seasoned life of man, preserved and stored up in books; since we see a kind of homicide may be thus committed, sometimes a martyrdom, and if it extend to the whole impression, a kind of massacre; whereof the execution ends not in the slaying of an elemental life, but strikes at that ethereal and fifth essence,[6] the breath of reason itself, slays an immortality rather than a life. But lest I should be condemned of introducing license, while I oppose licensing, I refuse not the pains to be so much historical, as will serve to show what hath been done by ancient and famous commonwealths against this disorder, till the very time that this project of licensing crept out of the Inquisition,[7] was catched up by our prelates, and hath caught some of our presbyters.

In Athens, where books and wits were ever busier than in any other part of Greece, I find but only two sorts of writings which the magistrate cared to take notice of; those either blasphemous and atheistical, or

5. In *Metamorphoses* III, 95–126, Ovid relates the sowing of the teeth of the dragon which was killed by Cadmus, king of Thebes. The planted teeth instantly sprang up as armed men, who instantly attacked one another and within an hour were almost all slain.

6. *Quintessence:* Latin, *quinta essentia.* The "fifth essence" of ancient and medieval philosophy, supposed to be the substance of which the heavenly bodies were composed, and to be ... latent in all things, the extraction of it by distillation or other methods being one of the great objects of alchemy.

7. Milton referred not only to the Spanish Inquisition which was instituted in Spain in 1480 and took some strong measures against heresy in Holland in the sixteenth century, but also to the whole inquisitorial movement which was first instituted by the Council of Toulouse in 1229.

libellous. Thus the books of Protagoras[8] were by the judges of Areopagus[9] commanded to be burnt, and himself banished the territory for a discourse begun with his confessing not to know whether there were gods, or whether not. And against defaming, it was decreed that none should be traduced by name, as was the manner of Vetus Comoedia,[10] whereby we may guess how they censured libelling. And this course was quick enough, as Cicero[11] writes, to quell both the desperate wits of other atheists, and the open way of defaming, as the event showed. Of other sects and opinions, though tending to voluptuousness, and the denying of divine Providence, they took no heed.

Therefore we do not read that either Epicurus,[12] or that libertine school of Cyrene,[13] or what the Cynic impudence uttered,[14] was ever questioned by the laws. Neither is it recorded that the writings of those old comedians were suppressed, though the acting of them were forbid; and that Plato commended the reading of Aristophanes, the loosest of them all, to his royal scholar Dionysius, is commonly known, and may be excused, if holy Chrysostom,[15] as is reported, nightly studied so much the same author and had the art to cleanse a scurrilous vehemence into the style of a rousing sermon.

* * *

Thus much may give us light after what sort books were prohibited among the Greeks.

The Romans also, for many ages trained up only to a military roughness resembling most the Lacedaemonian guise, knew of learning little but what their twelve Tables, and the Pontific College with their

8. Protagoras (?480–411 B.C.) of Abdera, in Thrace, was the first of the great sophists or professional teachers of rhetoric. In 411 he was impeached for a theological treatise which began by disclaiming all knowledge on his part as to whether or not the Gods exixted. The book was burned and Protagoras is said to have been banished from Athens.

9. "Scorners or Despisers of the gods," wrote Thomas Heywood in *The Hierarchie of the blessed Angells* (1635), p. 32, "were convented before the Aeropagitae; and being convicted, their goods were sold at a publique out-cry and their irreligions grauen upon pillars, to make their persons odible."

10. *Vetus Comoedia:* in the Old Comedy of Athens, says Gilbert Norwood in *Greek Comedy* (1931), p. 28, "we know certainly of but one law restraining" comic freedom of personal reference, and that "endured from 440–39 til 438–7, less than three years."

11. The reference is to Cicero's treatise On the Nature of Gods I, xxiii, where the punishment of Protagoras is regarded as having done much to repress open atheism, "inasmuch as even doubt" of the existence of the gods "was punished."

12. Epicurus taught that the gods existed, but in no way concerned themselves about human affairs.

13. The life of the founder of the Cyrenaic school, Aristippus, as told by Diogenes Laertius, contains many scandalous stories of libertinism.

14. The stories of Diogenes' search in open daylight with a lantern for an honest man, and of his contempt for Alexander's invitation to live at court in preference to his tub or shack, illustrate the severity and unconventionality of the Cynics, whose most famous representative he was. They made virtue rigorously the sole object of life.

15. An interest in Aristophanes on the part of John Chrysostom (347–407 A.D.), the "golden mouthed" bishop of Constantinople, would seem noteworthy to Puritans who honored him most because (according to Socrates Scholasticus, *Ecclesiastical History* VI, xvi) he was banished from his see for opposing the idolatrous honor paid to the empress Eudoxia and the "common playes and showes" that she approved.

augurs and flamens[16] taught them in religion and law; so unacquainted with other learning, that when Carneades[17] and Critolaus,[18] with the Stoic Diogenes,[19] coming ambassadors to Rome, took thereby occasion to give the city a taste of their philosophy, they were suspected for seducers by no less a man than Cato[20] the Censor, who moved it in the Senate to dismiss them speedily, and to banish all such Attic babblers out of Italy. But Scipio[21] and others of the noblest senators withstood him and his old Sabine austerity; honoured and admired the men; and the censor himself at last, in his old age, fell to the study of that whereof before he was so scrupulous. And yet at the same time Naevius[22] and Plautus,[23] the first Latin comedians, had filled the city with all the borrowed scenes of Menander[24] and Philemon.[25] Then began to be considered there also what was to be done to libellous books and authors; for Naevius was quickly cast into prison for his unbridled pen, and released by the tribunes upon his recantation; we read also that libels were burnt, and the makers punished by Augustus.[26] The like severity, no doubt, was used, if aught were impiously written against their esteemed gods. Except in these two points, how the world went in books, the magistrate kept no reckoning.

And therefore Lucretius[27] without impeachment versifies his Epicurism to Memmius, and had the honour to be set forth the second time by

16. The Pontific College went back to the most revered of the half-legendary Roman Kings, Numa, and its president, the Pontifex Maximus, was the greatest religious dignitary in republican Rome. The flamens were priests subordinate to the *pontifices,* and the angurs, whose business it was to consult the omens before public acts such as battles, treaties and holidays, composed another priestly college.

17. Carneades (?213–129 B.C.), the founder of the Third or New Academy at Athens, was a skeptic and an opponent of Stoicism. In 155 B.C. he was sent from Athens to Rome with Diogenes and Critolaus to protest against a fine which had been assessed against the Athenians for destroying Oropus. In Rome he shocked public opinion by first defending and then attacking the principle of justice in two formal addresses.

18. Critolaus was the head of the Peripatetic of Aristotelian School of philosophy in Athens in the middle of the second century B.C.

19. Diogenes succeeded Zeno as head of the Stoic School at Athens. He must not be confused with Diogenes the Cynic.

20. The elder Cato (?234–149 B.C.) was Censor in 184, and was a proverbial exemplar of the primitive and rather philistine Roman virtues.

21. Scipio the Younger (?185–129 B.C.), who captured Carthage in 146, was friendly with Terence and Polybius and other writers. In Cicero's dialogue *On Friendship* his geniality and his esteem for the virtues that Cato practiced on his Sabine farm were familiar to every schoolboy.

22. Naevius produced the first of his satiric plays about 235 B.C. He was imprisoned for attacking Scipio the younger and the aristocratic party in his plays and obliged to recant. He died in exile in Utica ?202 B.C.

23. Plautus (?254–184 B.C.) was the most popular of Roman writers of comedy.

24. Menander (342–291 B.C.) wrote over one hundred comedies, the surviving portions of seven of which are almost our only representation of the Athenian New Comedy, upon which Plautus' plays were modelled.

25. Philemon (?361–263 B.C.) was a rival of Menander. Only a few short fragments of his plays survive, but two of them are suggested as sources which Plautus followed closely in his *Mercator* and *Trinummus.*

26. In the *Annals,* I, Ixxii, Tacitus says that Augustus was so disturbed by the insolent libels of Cassius Severus against the most illustrious men and women in Rome that he became concerned for the enactment of a law against libel.

27. Lucretius' *De rerum natura* was dedicated to Gaius Memmius Gemellus, who was praetor in 58 B.C. The great poem

Cicero, so great a father of the Commonwealth; although himself disputes against that opinion in his own writings. Nor was the satirical sharpness or naked plainness of Lucilius,[28] or Catullus,[29] or Flaccus,[30] by any order prohibited. And for matters of state, the story of Titus Livius,[31] though it extolled that part[32] which Pompey held, was not therefore suppressed by Octavius Caesar of the other faction. But that Naso[33] was by him banished in his old age, for the wanton poems of his youth, was but a mere covert of state over some secret cause: and besides, the books were neither banished nor called in. From hence we shall meet with little else but tyranny in the Roman empire, that we may not marvel, if not so often bad as good books were silenced. I shall therefore deem to have been large enough, in producing what among the ancients was punishable to write; save only which, all other arguments were free to treat on.

By this time the emperors were become Christians, whose discipline in this point I do not find to have been more severe than what was formerly in practice. The books of those whom they took to be grand heretics[34] were examined, refuted, and condemned in the general Councils;[35] and not till then were prohibited, or burnt, by authority of the emperor. As for the writings of heathen authors, unless they were plain invectives against Christianity, as those of Porphyrius[36] and Proclus,[37] they met with no interdict that can be cited, till about the year 400, in a Carthaginian Council,[38] wherein bishops themselves were forbid to read the books of Gentiles, but heresies they might read: while others long before them, on the contrary, scrupled more the books of heretics than of Gentiles. And that the primitive Councils and bishops were wont only to declare what books were not commendable, passing no further, but leaving it to each one's conscience to read or to lay by, till after the year 800, is observed already by Padre Paolo,[39] the great unmasker of the Trentine Council.[40]

frankly defends the Epicurean views about the gods and about the mortality of the soul.

28. Lucilius (148–103 B.C.) is usually recognized as the founder of Roman satire.

29. Among the vivid lyrics of Catullus (87–47? B.C.) were some lampoons of Caesar and his partisans.

30. Quintus Horatius Flaccus (Horace, 65–8 B.C.) hardly challenged censorship of any kind by his *Satires*.

31. Titus Livius (59 B.C.–17 A.D.) wrote a history of Rome from the founding of the city to the death of Drusus in 9 A.D.

32. *part:* party or faction

33. *Naso*: Ovid (Publius Ovidius Naso) was banished to Tomi near the mouth of the Danube; tradition says less on account of his licentious poems than for an intrigue with the granddaughter of the Emperor Augustus, Julia. He died at Tomi in 18 A.D.

34. "Heresy," said Milton in *Of True Religion,* "is in the will and choice professedly against scripture; error is against the will, in misunderstanding the scripture."

35. The first general council of the Church was held in Nicara in Bithynia in 325A.D.

36. Porphyry (233–305? A.D.) is said to have been a pupil of Origen in his youth and to have turned against Christianity after coming under the influence of Plotinus in Rome. His book against Christianity was publicly destroyed by order of the emperor Theodosius.

37. Proclus (412–485 A.D.), some of whose Neoplatonic books were read with interest in the Renaissance, was an implacable enemy of Christianity.

38. Milton refers to the fourth Council of Carthage, which met in 398 A.D.

39. Padre Paolo or Pietro Sarpi (1552–1623) was a leader in the challenge of the Venetians to the authority of the popes. Milton refers to his *History of the Council of Trent,* which was turned into English in 1620 by Nathaniel Brent.

40. The Council of Trent in the Tyrol met at frequent intervals between 13 De-

After which time the Popes of Rome, engrossing what they pleased of political rule into their own hands, extended their dominion over men's eyes, as they had before over their judgments, burning and prohibiting to be read what they fancied not; yet sparing in their censures, and the books not many which they so dealt with: till Martin V.,[41] by his bull, not only prohibited, but was the first that excommunicated the reading of heretical books; for about that time Wickliffe and Huss, growing terrible, were they who first drove the Papal Court to a stricter policy of prohibiting. Which course Leo X[42] and his successors followed, until the Council of Trent and the Spanish Inquisition engendering together brought forth, or perfected, those Catalogues and expurging Indexes, that rake through the entrails of many an old good author, with a violation worse than any could be offered to his tomb. Nor did they stay in matters heretical, but any subject that was not to their palate, they either condemned in a Prohibition, or had it straight into the new purgatory of an index.

To fill up the measure of encroachment, their last invention was to ordain that no book, pamphlet, or paper should be printed (as if St. Peter had bequeathed them the keys of the press also out of Paradise) unless it were approved and licensed under the hands of two or three glutton friars. For example:

> Let the Chancellor Cini be pleased to see if in this present work be contained aught that may withstand the printing.
>
> VINCENT RABBATTA, Vicar of Florence.
>
> I have seen this present work, and find nothing athwart the Catholic faith and good manners: in witness whereof I have given, etc.
>
> NICOLO GINI, Chancellor of Florence.
>
> Attending the precedent relation, it is allowed that this present work of Davanzati may be printed.
>
> VINCENT RABBATTA, etc.
>
> It may be printed, July 15.
>
> FRIAR SIMON MOMPEI D'AMELIA,
> Chancellor of the Holy Office in Florence.

Sure they have a conceit, if he of the bottomless pit had not long since broke prison, that this quadruple exorcism would bar him down. I fear their next design will be to get into their custody the licensing of that

cember, 1545 and 4 Dec, 1563, and ended its efforts to reconcile Catholic and Protestant Europe by reaffirming most of the great positions and doctrines of Catholicism.

41. Martin V (Otto Colonna) was Pope from 1417 to 1431.

42. Leo X (Giovanni dei Medici) was Pope from 1513 to 1521.

which they say Claudius intended, but went not through with.[43] Vouchsafe to see another of their forms, the Roman stamp:

> Imprimatur, If it seem good to the reverend Master of the Holy Palace.
>
> BELCASTRO, Vicegerent.
>
> Imprimatur, Friar Nicolo Rodolphi, Master of the Holy Palace.

Sometimes five Imprimaturs are seen together dialogue-wise in the piazza of one title-page, complimenting and ducking each to other with their shaven reverences, whether the author, who stands by in perplexity at the foot of his epistle, shall to the press or to the sponge. These are the pretty responsories,[44] these are the dear antiphonies,[45] that so bewitched of late our prelates and their chaplains with the goodly echo they made; and besotted us to the gay imitation of a lordly Imprimatur,[46] one from Lambeth House,[47] another from the west end of Paul's;[48] so apishly Romanizing, that the word of command still was set down in Latin; as if the learned grammatical pen that wrote it would cast no ink without Latin; or perhaps, as they thought, because no vulgar tongue was worthy to express the pure conceit of an Imprimatur, but rather, as I hope, for that our English, the language of men ever famous and foremost in the achievements of liberty, will not easily find servile letters enow to spell such a dictatory presumption English.

And thus ye have the inventors and the original of book-licensing ripped up and drawn as lineally as any pedigree. We have it not, that can be heard of, from any ancient state, or polity or church; nor by any statute left us by our ancestors elder or later; nor from the modern custom of any reformed city or church abroad, but from the most antichristian council and the most tyrannous inquisition that ever inquired. Till then books were ever as freely admitted into the world as any other birth; the issue of the brain was no more stifled than the issue of the womb: no envious Juno[49] sat cross-legged over the nativity of any man's

43. [According to Caius Suetonius Tranquillus, *The History of the Twelve Caesars, Emperors of Rome,* the emperor Tiberius Claudius "being told of a modest person who had like'd to have killed himself with retention, had thoughts once of publishing an Edict, whereby he would make it lawful to break wind at the Table, and to ease themselves of any flatulency in any place whatsoever."]

44. *responsories:* sections of the Psalms sung interspersed between readings from the missal in the mass.

45. *antiphonies:* hymns or anthems sung in responsive parts by two choirs.

46. *Imprimatur:* "let it be printed," the order stamped on manuscripts which are permitted by ecclesiastical authority to be sent to the press. "To the sponge"—meaning, to have the contents wiped off—has been applied to manuscripts unworthy of publication since Suetonius helped to popularize the expression in the *Life of Augustus,* 2, 85.

47. *Lambeth House:* Lambeth Palace, still the official residence of the Archbishop of Canterbury on the south bank of the Thames, in Southwark, London.

48. *Paul's:* St. Paul's Cathedral in London, the headquarters of the Bishop of London, who traditionally took a leading part in the licensing of books.

49. In *Metamorphoses* IX, 285–319, Ovid tells the story of Juno's cruelty to Alcmena in placing the goddess of childbirth cross-legged beside her, muttering charms to prevent her delivery of the infant Hercules. On the seventh night of labor the wit of Alcmena's maid tricked the cross-

intellectual offspring; but if it proved a monster, who denies, but that it was justly burnt, or sunk into the sea? But that a book, in worse condition than a peccant soul, should be to stand before a jury ere it be born to the world, and undergo yet in darkness the judgment of Radamanth[50] and his colleagues, ere it can pass the ferry backward into light, was never heard before, till that mysterious iniquity, provoked and troubled at the first entrance of Reformation, sought out new limbos[51] and new hells wherein they might include our books also within the number of their damned. And this was the rare morsel so officiously snatched up, and so ill-favouredly imitated by our inquisiturient bishops, and the attendant minorites[52] their chaplains. That ye like not now these most certain authors of this licensing order, and that all sinister intention was far distant from your thoughts, when ye were importuned the passing it, all men who know the integrity of your actions, and how ye honour truth, will clear ye readily.

But some will say, what though the inventors were bad, the thing for all that may be good? It may so; yet if that thing be no such deep invention, but obvious, and easy for any man to light on, and yet best and wisest commonwealths through all ages and occasions have forborne to use it, and falsest seducers and oppressors of men were the first who took it up, and to no other purpose but to obstruct and hinder the first approach of Reformation; I am of those who believe it will be a harder alchemy than Lullius[53] ever knew, to sublimate[54] any good use out of such an invention. Yet this only is what I request to gain from this reason, that it may be held a dangerous and suspicious fruit, as certainly it deserves, for the tree that bore it, until I can dissect one by one the properties it has. But I have first to finish, as was propounded, what is to be thought in general of reading books, whatever sort they be, and whether be more the benefit or the harm that thence proceeds.

* * *

"To the pure, all things are pure";[55] not only meats and drinks, but all kind of knowledge whether of good or evil; the knowledge cannot defile, nor consequently the books, if the will and conscience be not defiled.

legged goddess into rising and so breaking the charm that closed her mistress's womb.

50. Rhadamanthus, a legendary king of Crete, was appointed by Zeus to judge the souls of the dead, together with Minos and Aeacus, stripping every soul naked of every corporal covering so as to look it through and through.

51. *limbos:* regions adjoining hell, such as the *limbus puerorum,* or limbo of babes, and *limbus patrum,* or limbo of the patriarchs who were delivered after the crucifixion, when Christ harrowed hell.

52. *minorities:* Franciscans, who had been known in England, from their grey habits, as Grey Friars. They were traditionally the humblest of all the monastic orders.

53. *Lullius:* Raymond Lully (1234?–1315) was traditionally better known for his writings on alchemy and medicine than he was for the missionary ardor that took him to north Africa three times and finally ended his life by martyrdom in Mauretania.

54. *sublimate:* in alchemy, to transform a base into a precious metal.

55. Titus i, 15.

For books are as meats and viands are; some of good, some of evil substance; and yet God, in that unapocryphal vision, said without exception, "rise, Peter, kill and eat", leaving the choice to each man's discretion. Wholesome meats to a vitiated stomach differ little or nothing from unwholesome; and best books to a naughty mind are not unappliable to occasions of evil. Bad meats will scarce breed good nourishment in the healthiest concoction; but herein the difference is of bad books, that they to a discreet and judicious reader serve in many respects to discover, to confute, to forewarn, and to illustrate. Whereof what better witness can ye expect I should produce, than one of your own now sitting in Parliament, the chief of learned men reputed in this land, Mr. Selden;[56] whose volume of natural and national laws proves, not only by great authorities brought together, but by exquisite reasons and theorems almost mathematically demonstrative, that all opinions, yea errors, known, read, and collated, are of main service and assistance toward the speedy attainment of what is truest. I conceive, therefore, that when God did enlarge the universal diet of man's body, saving ever the rules of temperance, he then also, as before, left arbitrary the dieting and repasting of our minds; as wherein every mature man might have to exercise his own leading capacity.

How great a virtue is temperance, how much of moment through the whole life of man! Yet God commits the managing so great a trust, without particular law or prescription, wholly to the demeanour of every grown man. And therefore when he himself tabled the Jews from heaven, that omer,[57] which was every man's daily portion of manna, is computed to have been more than might have well sufficed the heartiest feeder thrice as many meals. For those actions which enter into a man, rather than issue out of him, and therefore defile not, God uses not to captivate under a perpetual childhood of prescription, but trusts him with the gift of reason to be his own chooser; there were but little work left for preaching, if law and compulsion should grow so fast upon those things which heretofore were governed only by exhortation. Solomon[58] informs us, that much reading is a weariness to the flesh; but neither he nor other inspired author tells us that such or such reading is unlawful: yet certainly had God thought good to limit us herein, it had been much more expedient to have told us what was unlawful than what was wearisome. As for the burning of those Ephesian books by St. Paul's converts;[59] 'tis replied the books were magic, the Syriac so renders them. It was a private act, a voluntary act, and leaves us to a voluntary imitation: the men in remorse burnt those books which were their own;

56. John Selden (1584–1654) had published his *De Jure Naturali et Gentium* in 1640.

57. The *omer* was the measure of manna which Moses was commanded in Exodus xvi, 16, to ration to the Israelites daily. The account lays stress on the abundance of the supply.

58. Ecclesiastes xii, 12. Mark vii, 15: "There is nothing from without a man, that entering into him can defile him: but the things which come out of him, those are they that defile the man."

59. The story is found in Acts xix, 19.

the magistrate by this example is not appointed; these men practised the books, another might perhaps have read them in some sort usefully.

Good and evil we know in the field of this world grow up together almost inseparably; and the knowledge of good is so involved and interwoven with the knowledge of evil, and in so many cunning resemblances hardly to be discerned, that those confused seeds which were imposed upon Psyche[60] as an incessant labour to cull out, and sort asunder, were not more intermixed. It was from out the rind of one apple tasted, that the knowledge of good and evil, as two twins cleaving together, leaped forth into the world. And perhaps this is that doom which Adam fell into of knowing good and evil, that is to say of knowing good by evil. As therefore the state of man now is; what wisdom can there be to choose, what continence to forbear without the knowledge of evil? He that can apprehend and consider vice with all her baits and seeming pleasures, and yet abstain, and yet distinguish, and yet prefer that which is truly better, he is the true warfaring[61] Christian.

I cannot praise a fugitive and cloistered virtue, unexercised and unbreathed, that never sallies out and sees her adversary but slinks out of the race, where that immortal garland[62] is to be run for, not without dust and heat. Assuredly we bring not innocence into the world, we bring impurity much rather;[63] that which purifies us is trial, and trial is by what is contrary. That virtue therefore which is but a youngling in the contemplation of evil, and knows not the utmost that vice promises to her followers, and rejects it, is but a blank[64] virtue, not a pure; her whiteness is but an excremental[65] whiteness. Which was the reason why our sage and serious poet Spenser, whom I dare be known to think a better teacher than Scotus[66] or Aquinas,[67] describing true temperance

60. Milton would know the story of Psyche best in *The Golden Ass* of Aupleius IV–VI. Anger because Psyche has won Cupid's love makes Venus doom her to sort the various kinds of grain out of a vast, mixed pile, but the work is done for her by the sympathetic ants.

61. *wayfaring,* the reading of the first edition, has the weight of priority, but *warfaring* is suggested by the fact that the entire passage seems to echo Lactantius' repeated stress in *Institutes* III, xxix; V, vii; and VI, *passim* upon a Christian ethnic "ex quo fit ut virtus nulla sit, si *adversarius desit.*" In three extant copies of the first edition of *Aeropagitica* the "y" in *Wayfaring* is changed to "r" in a hand that may be Milton's.

62. *that:* like the Latin *ille,* the word is used to refer to something well known. Milton is perhaps thinking of that prize for which St. Paul described himself as pressing forward in Philippians iii, 14, or of the crown of righteousness in II Timothy iv, 8, or of the crown of life that is promised in James, I, 12, to him "that endureth temptation" and "is tried."

63. In *Christian Doctrine* I, xi, Milton's belief in the doctrine of original sin is explicit. It is "common to all men" and is "that which our first parents, and in them all their posterity committed."

64. *blank:* pale or colorless.

65. *excremental:* excrescential, external.

66. John Duns Scotus (1265?–1308), the Subtle Doctor in the Scholastic tradition, was born in Scotland but taught at Paris and Oxford and died in Cologne. He was a Franciscan, and in several important ways his teaching was opposed to that of his great Dominican predecessor, St. Thomas. The prejudice against Scholastic logic which Milton illustrates here was responsible for the quite unfair development of the word dunce from Duns Scotus' name.

67. St. Thomas Aquinas (1225?–1274), the Seraphic Doctor, in his *Summa Theologiae* left the greatest monument of Scholastic thought, and in his *Summa contra Gen-*

under the person of Guion, brings him in with his palmer through the cave of Mammon, and the bower of earthly bliss, that he might see and know, and yet abstain. Since therefore the knowledge and survey of vice is in this world so necessary to the constituting of human virtue, and the scanning of error to the confirmation of truth, how can we more safely, and with less danger, scout into the regions of sin and falsity than by reading all manner of tractates and hearing all manner of reason? And this is the benefit which may be had of books promiscuously read.

But of the harm that may result hence three kinds are usually reckoned. First, is feared the infection that may spread; but then all human learning and controversy in religious points must remove out of the world, yea the Bible itself; for that ofttimes relates blasphemy not nicely,[68] it describes the carnal sense of wicked men not unelegantly, it brings in holiest men passionately murmuring against Providence through all the arguments of Epicurus;[69] in other great disputes it answers dubiously and darkly to the common reader. And ask a Talmudist[70] what ails the modesty of his marginal Keri,[71] that Moses and all the prophets cannot persuade him to pronounce the textual Chetiv. For these causes we all know the Bible itself put by the Papist must be next removed, as Clement of Alexandria,[72] and that Eusebian[73] book of Evangelic preparation, transmitting our ears through a hoard of heathenish obscenities to receive the Gospel. Who finds not that Irenaeus,[74] Epiphanius,[75] Jerome, and others discover more heresies than they well confute, and that oft for heresy which is the truer opinion?

Nor boots it to say for these, and all the heathen writers of greatest infection, if it must be thought so, with whom is bound up the life of human learning, that they writ in an unknown tongue, so long as we are sure those languages are known as well to the worst of men, who are

tiles, the greatest medieval compendium of Christian doctrine.

68. *nicely:* delicately.

69. Solomon's thought in Ecclesiastes was often compared with Epicurus' qualified advice to "eat, drink, and be merry."

70. *Talmudist:* a scholar in the oral tradition which grew up about the Books of Moses and codified their legal and ritualistic elements

71. *Keri:* what is read, opposed to *Chetiv:* what is written.

72. Clement of Alexandria (?150–? A.D.) was the first of the great Fathers of the Church to bring an intimate knowledge of Greek philosophy and religion to the enrichment as well as the defense of Christianity.

73. Eusebius' *PreparatioEvangelica* is well described by Milton's words in the text. Many patristic books exhibited the worst features of pagan thought and religious practice to turn their readers to Christianity.

74. Ireneas (140?–202? A.D.) became Bishop of Lyons in 177. He wrote *Against Heresies* to combat Gnosticism.

75. Milton may have been interested in the *Panarion* or general refutation of heresies which was written by Epiphanius (315–403), who became Bishop of Constantia in Cyprus in 367. He was certainly familiar with Socrates' story in the *Ecclesiastical History* VI, ix and xiii, or Epiphanius' quarrel with John, Bishop of Constantinople, and of his seeming prostitution of his position as a controversialist in a struggle for power. He died at sea on his way home from Constantinople, in fulfillment, Socrates suggests, of John's curse upon him. His position in the Arian controversy once led one of his opponents to charge "that he thought of God basely and abjectly, attributing to him the forme or shape of man"—a fact that would certainly have interested Milton.

both most able and most diligent to instil the poison they suck, first into the courts of princes, acquainting them with the choicest delights and criticisms of sin.[76] As perhaps did that Petronius[77] whom Nero called his Arbiter, the master of his revels; and the notorious ribald of Arezzo,[78] dreaded and yet dear to the Italian courtiers. I name not him for posterity's sake, whom Henry VIII named in merriment his vicar of hell. By which compendious way all the contagion that foreign books can infuse will find a passage to the people far easier and shorter than an Indian voyage, though it could be sailed either by the north of Cathay eastward, or of Canada westward, while our Spanish licensing gags the English press never so severely.

But on the other side that infection which is from books of controversy in religion is more doubtful and dangerous to the learned than to the ignorant; and yet those books must be permitted untouched by the licenser. It will be hard to instance where any ignorant man hath been ever seduced by papistical book in English, unless it were commended and expounded to him by some of that clergy: and indeed all such tractates, whether false or true, are as the prophecy of Isaiah was to the eunuch, not to be understood without a guide. But of our priests and doctors how many have been corrupted by studying the comments of Jesuits and Sorbonists, and how fast they could transfuse that corruption into the people, our experience is both late and sad. It is not forgot, since the acute and distinct Arminius[79] was perverted merely by the perusing of a nameless discourse written at Delft, which at first he took in hand to confute.

Seeing, therefore, that those books, and those in great abundance, which are likeliest to taint both life and doctrine, cannot be suppressed without the fall of learning and of all ability in disputation, and that these books of either sort are most and soonest catching to the learned, from whom to the common people whatever is heretical or dissolute may quickly be conveyed, and that evil manners are as perfectly learnt without books a thousand other ways which cannot be stopped, and evil doctrine not with books can propagate, except a teacher guide, which he might also do without writing, and so beyond prohibiting, I am not able to unfold, how this cautelous[80] enterprise of licensing can be exempted from the number of vain and impossible attempts. And he who were

76. *criticisms:* critical refinements—here of an elegant connoisseur of the pleasures of vice.

77. Gaius Petronius was called by Tacitus (*Annals* XVI, xvii) *arbiter elegantiarum* or a kind of unofficial director of entertainments at the court of the emperor Nero. Milton was thinking of the witty indecencies of the famous surviving fragment of his *Satiricon,* known as *Trimalchio's Dinner.*

78. Pietro Aretino (1492–1557), by practicing a kind of magnificent literary blackmail and by exploiting the aristocratic taste for indecency, achieved banishment from Rome as well as from Arezzo, won a European reputation, and left some revealing records of his times behind him.

79. The allusion to Arminius (1560–1609), the Dutch opponent of the extreme Calvinistic belief about Predestination, shows that Milton was hardly in sympathy with him at this time. Arminius was Professor of Theology at Leyden, and was said to have been persuaded against Calvin's position by the writing of one or more obscure Dutch clergymen to whom he was asked, in his official capacity, to reply.

80. *cautelous:* tricky.

pleasantly disposed could not well avoid to liken it to the exploit of that gallant man who thought to pound up the crows by shutting his park gate.

Besides another inconvenience, if learned men be the first receivers out of books and dispreaders both of vice and error, how shall the licensers themselves be confided in, unless we can confer upon them, or they assume to themselves above all others in the land, the grace of infallibility and uncorruptedness? And again, if it be true that a wise man, like a good refiner, can gather gold out of the drossiest volume, and that a fool will be a fool with the best book, yea or without book; there is no reason that we should deprive a wise man of any advantage to his wisdom, while we seek to restrain from a fool, that which being strained will be no hindrance to his folly. For if there should be so much exactness always used to keep that from him which is unfit for his reading, we should in the judgment of Aristotle[81] not only, but of Solomon[82] and of our Saviour,[83] not vouchsafe him good precepts, and by consequence not willingly admit him to good books; as being certain that a wise man will make better use of an idle pamphlet, than a fool will do of sacred Scripture.

"Tis next alleged we must not expose ourselves to temptations without necessity, and next to that, not employ our time in vain things. To both these objections one answer will serve, out of the grounds already laid, that to all men such books are not temptations, nor vanities, but useful drugs and materials wherewith to temper and compose effective and strong medicines, which man's life cannot want.[84] The rest, as children and childish men, who have not the art to qualify[85] and prepare these working minerals, well may be exhorted to forbear, but hindered forcibly they cannot be by all the licensing that Sainted Inquisition could ever yet contrive. Which is what I promised to deliver next: that this order of licensing conduces nothing to the end for which it was framed; and hath almost prevented[86] me by being clear already while thus much hath been explaining. See the ingenuity[87] of Truth, who, when she gets a free and willing hand, opens herself faster than the pace of method and discourse can overtake her."

It was the task which I began with, to show that no nation, or well-instituted state, if they valued books at all, did ever use this way of licensing; and it might be answered, that this is a piece of prudence lately discovered. To which I return, that as it was a thing slight and

81. In the *Nicomachean Ethics* X, viii, 3, Aristotle acknowledges, in closing his great work, that discourses on ethics have no effect on ordinary mankind and can inspire virtue only in men of generous temperament.

82. Wisdom is before him that hath understanding; but the eyes of a fool are in the ends of the earth. (Prov. xvii, 24.)

83. "Give not that which is holy unto dogs, neither cast ye your pearls before swine." (Matt. vii, 6.)

84. *want:* do without, lack.

85. *qualify:* fix the quality or nature of a drug by proper compounding.

86. *prevented:* anticipated or "got ahead of "another person in arriving somewhere, or—as here—in doing something.

87. *ingenuity:* ingenuousness, liberality.

obvious to think on, so if it had been difficult to find out, there wanted not among them long since who suggested such a course; which they not following, leave us a pattern of their judgment that it was not the rest knowing, but the not approving, which was the cause of their not using it.

Plato, a man of high authority, indeed, but least of all for his Commonwealth, in the book of his Laws, which no city ever yet received, fed his fancy by making many edicts to his airy burgomasters, which they who otherwise admire him wish had been rather buried and excused in the genial cups of an Academic night sitting.[88] By which laws he seems to tolerate no kind of learning but by unalterable decree, consisting most of practical traditions, to the attainment whereof a library of smaller bulk than his own Dialogues would be abundant. And there also enacts, that no poet should so much as read to any private man what he had written, until the judges and law-keepers had seen it, and allowed it. But that Plato meant this law peculiarly to that commonwealth which he had imagined, and to no other, is evident. Why was he not else a lawgiver to himself, but a transgressor, and to be expelled by his own magistrates; both for the wanton epigrams and dialogues which he made, and his perpetual reading of Sophron Mimus and Aristophanes, books of grossest infamy, and also for commending the latter of them, though he were the malicious libeller of his chief friends, to be read by the tyrant Dionysius, who had little need of such trash to spend his time on? But that he knew this licensing of poems had reference and dependence to many other provisos there set down in his fancied republic, which in this world could have no place: and so neither he himself, nor any magistrate or city, ever imitated that course, which, taken apart from those other collateral injunctions, must needs be vain and fruitless. For if they fell upon one kind of strictness, unless their care were equal to regulate all other things of like aptness to corrupt the mind, that single endeavour they knew would be but a fond labour;[89] to shut and fortify one gate against corruption, and be necessitated to leave others round about wide open.

If we think to regulate printing, thereby to rectify manners, we must regulate all recreation and pastimes, all that is delightful to man. No music must be heard, no song be set or sung, but what is grave and Doric. There must be licensing dancers, that no gesture, motion, or deportment be taught our youth but what by their allowance shall be thought honest;[90] for such Plato was provided of.[91] It will ask more than the work of twenty licensers to examine all the lutes, the violins, and the guitars in every house; they must not be suffered to prattle as they do,

88. *i.e.*, forgotten, after being tossed out for discussion by Plato's friends as some unrecorded symposium in the Academy.

89. *fond:* ineffective, foolish.

90. *honest:* honorable, decent.

91. The passage in the *Laws* (800–802) which Milton has in mind provides that a selection from the countless existing songs of the Greeks shall be made by mature judges—men not under fifty—to make sure that the ideal city for which he is legislating shall have no music or poetry which does not rightly praise the gods and the great dead.

but must be licensed what they may say. And who shall silence all the airs and madrigals that whisper softness in chambers? The windows also, and the balconies must be thought on; there are shrewd[92] books, with dangerous frontispieces,[93] set to sale; who shall prohibit them, shall twenty licensers? The villages also must have their visitors[94] to inquire what lectures[95] the bagpipe and the rebeck[96] reads, even to the ballatry[97] and the gamut of every municipal fiddler, for these are the countryman's Arcadias,[98] and his Monte Mayors.

Next, what more national corruption, for which England hears ill[99] abroad, than household gluttony: who shall be the rectors of our daily rioting? And what shall be done to inhibit the multitudes that frequent those houses where drunkenness is sold and harboured? Our garments also should be referred to the licensing of some more sober workmasters to see them cut into a less wanton garb. Who shall regulate all the mixed conversation[100] of our youth, male and female together, as is the fashion of this country? Who shall still appoint what shall be discoursed, what presumed, and no further? Lastly, who shall forbid and separate all idle resort, all evil company? These things will be, and must be; but how they shall be least hurtful, how least enticing, herein consists the grave and governing wisdom of a state.

To sequester out of the world into Atlantic and Utopian[101] polities, which never can be drawn into use, will not mend our condition; but to ordain wisely as in this world of evil, in the midst whereof God hath placed us unavoidably. Nor is it Plato's licensing of books will do this, which necessarily pulls along with it so many other kinds of licensing, as will make us all both ridiculous and weary, and yet frustrate; but those unwritten, or at least unconstraining, laws of virtuous education, religious and civil nurture, which Plato there mentions as the bonds and ligaments of the commonwealth,[102] the pillars and the sustainers of every written statute; these they be which will bear chief sway in such matters as these, when all licensing will be easily eluded. Impunity and remissness, for certain, are the bane of a commonwealth; but here the great art

92. *shrewd:* mischievous, wicked.

93. *frontispieces:* fronts or decorated pages at the beginning.

94. *visitors:* inspectors. The term was hateful because it was applied to the officials whom Archbishop Laud had sent throughout England to see that parish clergy conformed to this regulation of the services.

95. *lectures:* addresses, particularly of the kind that were popular among the Puritans and were forbidden or discouraged by the bishops.

96. *rebeck:* a simple fiddle, originally with only two strings.

97. *ballatry:* balladry. Such stuff as Autolycus exhibits in A Winter's Tale, IV, iv, 262–330.

98. Sir Philip Sidney's *Arcadia,* and perhaps also that of the Italian, Sannazaro, and the *Diana Enamorada* of the Portuguese, Jorge de Montemayor (1520?–1561).

99. *hears ill:* hears unfavorably mentioned. The idiom is Greek.

100. *conversation:* social intercourse.

101. As he has condemned the strict social regulation of Plato's *Republic* and *Laws,* Milton now objects to the same aspect of the *Utopia* of Sir Thomas More and of Sir Francis Bacon's *New Atlantis.* The "sequester" one's self in such speculative commonwealths is mere escapism.

102. Milton is thinking of the passage in the *Republic* IV, 424–33, where Plato makes sound education the basis of social order.

lies, to discern in what the law is to bid restraint and punishment, and in what things persuasion only is to work.

If every action, which is good or evil in man at ripe years, were to be under pittance[103] and prescription and compulsion, what were virtue but a name, what praise could be then due to well-doing, what gramercy[104] to be sober, just, or continent? Many there be that complain of divine Providence for suffering Adam to transgress; foolish tongues! When God gave him reason, he gave him freedom to choose, for reason is but choosing;[105] he had been else a mere artificial Adam, such an Adam as he is in the motions.[106] We ourselves esteem not of that obedience, or love, or gift, which is of force: God therefore left him free, set before him a provoking object, ever almost in his eyes; herein consisted his merit, herein the right of his reward, the praise of his abstinence. Wherefore did he create passions within us, pleasures round about us, but that these rightly tempered are the very ingredients of virtue?

They are not skilful considerers of human things, who imagine to remove sin by removing the matter of sin; for, besides that it is a huge heap increasing under the very act of diminishing, though some part of it may for a time be withdrawn from some persons, it cannot from all, in such a universal thing as books are; and when this is done, yet the sin remains entire. Though ye take from a covetous man all his treasure, he has yet one jewel left, ye cannot bereave him of his covetousness. Banish all objects of lust, shut up all youth into the severest discipline that can be exercised in any hermitage, ye cannot make them chaste, that came not hither so; such great care and wisdom is required to the right managing of this point. Suppose we could expel sin by this means; look how much we thus expel of sin, so much we expel of virtue: for the matter of them both is the same; remove that, and ye remove them both alike.

This justifies the high providence of God, who, though he command us temperance, justice, continence, yet pours out before us, even to a profuseness, all desirable things, and gives us minds that can wander beyond all limit and satiety. Why should we then affect a rigour contrary to the manner of God and of nature, by abridging or scanting those means, which books freely permitted are, both to the trial of virtue and the exercise of truth? It would be better done, to learn that the law must needs be frivolous, which goes to restrain things, uncertainly and yet equally working to good and to evil. And were I the chooser, a dream of well-doing should be preferred before many times as much the forcible hindrance of evil-doing. For God sure esteems the growth and completing of one virtuous person more than the restraint of ten vicious.

103. *pittance:* ration, allowance. Originally, the word was applied to a monk's portion of food.

104. *gramercy:* thanks.

105. Milton put this definition dogmatically because he expected his readers to recognize it as Aristotle's in the *Nicomachean Ethics* III, ii, 6.

106. *motions:* puppet shows.

And albeit whatever thing we hear or see, sitting, walking, travelling, or conversing, may be fitly called our book, and is of the same effect that writings are, yet grant the thing to be prohibited were only books, it appears that this Order hitherto[107] is far insufficient to the end which it intends. Do we not see, not once or oftener, but weekly, that continued court-libel against the Parliament and City, printed, as the wet sheets can witness, and dispersed among us, for all that licensing can do? Yet this is the prime service a man would think, wherein this Order should give proof of itself. If it were executed, you'll say. But certain, if execution be remiss or blindfold now, and in this particular, what will it be hereafter and in other books? If then the Order shall not be vain and frustrate, behold a new labour, Lords and Commons, ye must repeal and proscribe all scandalous and unlicensed books already printed and divulged[108]; after ye have drawn them up into a list, that all may know which are condemned, and which not; and ordain that no foreign books be delivered out of custody, till they have been read over. This office will require the whole time of not a few overseers, and those no vulgar men. There be also books which are partly useful and excellent, partly culpable and pernicious; this work will ask as many more officials, to make expurgations and expunctions,[109] that the commonwealth of learning be not damnified. In fine, when the multitude of books increase upon their hands, ye must be fain to catalogue all those printers who are found frequently offending, and forbid the importation of their whole suspected typography. In a word, that this your Order may be exact and not deficient, ye must reform it perfectly according to the model of Trent and Seville, which I know ye abhor to do.

Yet though ye should condescend to this, which God forbid, the Order still would be but fruitless and defective to that end whereto ye meant it. If to prevent sects and schisms, who is so unread or so uncatechized in story, that hath not heard of many sects refusing books as a hindrance, and preserving their doctrine unmixed for many ages, only by unwritten traditions? The Christian faith, for that was once a schism, is not unknown to have spread all over Asia, ere any Gospel or Epistle was seen in writing. If the amendment of manners be aimed at, look into Italy and Spain, whether those places be one scruple the better, the honester, the wiser, the chaster, since all the inquisitional rigour that hath been executed upon books.

Another reason, whereby to make it plain that this Order will miss the end it seeks, consider by the quality which ought to be in every licenser. It cannot be denied but that he who is made judge to sit upon the birth or death of books, whether they may be wafted into this world or not, had need to be a man above the common measure, both studious, learned, and judicious; there may be else no mean mistakes in the

107. The *Mercurius Aulicus* or *Court Mercury,* published while King Charles had his headquarters at Oxford.

108. *divulged:* publicly distributed, made generally available.

109. *expunctions:* expungings, excisions by the censor.

censure of what is passable or not; which is also no mean injury. If he be of such worth as behooves him, there cannot be a more tedious and unpleasing journey-work,[110] a greater loss of time levied upon his head, than to be made the perpetual reader of unchosen books and pamphlets, ofttimes huge volumes. There is no book that is acceptable unless at certain seasons; but to be enjoined the reading of that at all times, and in a hand scarce legible, whereof three pages would not down at any time in the fairest print, is an imposition which I cannot believe how he that values time and his own studies, or is but of a sensible[111] nostril, should be able to endure. In this one thing I crave leave of the present licensers to be pardoned for so thinking; who doubtless took this office up, looking on it through their obedience to the Parliament, whose command perhaps made all things seem easy and unlaborious to them; but that this short trial hath wearied them out already, their own expressions and excuses to them who make so many journeys to solicit their licence are testimony enough. Seeing therefore those who now possess the employment by all evident signs wish themselves well rid of it; and that no man of worth, none that is not a plain unthrift of his own hours, is ever likely to succeed them, except he mean to put himself to the salary of a press corrector; we may easily foresee what kind of licensers we are to expect hereafter, either ignorant, imperious, and remiss, or basely pecuniary. This is what I had to show, wherein this Order cannot conduce to that end whereof it bears the intention.

I lastly proceed from the no good it can do, to the manifest hurt it causes, in being first the greatest discouragement and affront that can be offered to learning, and to learned men.

It was the complaint and lamentation of prelates, upon every least breath of a motion to remove pluralities, and distribute more equally Church revenues, that then all learning would be for ever dashed and discouraged. But as for that opinion, I never found cause to think that the tenth part of learning stood or fell with the clergy: nor could I ever but hold it for a sordid and unworthy speech of any churchman who had a competency left him. If therefore ye be loath to dishearten utterly and discontent, not the mercenary crew of false pretenders to learning, but the free and ingenuous sort of such as evidently were born to study, and love learning for itself, not for lucre or any other end but the service of God and of truth, and perhaps that lasting fame and perpetuity of praise which God and good men have consented shall be the reward of those whose published labours advance the good of mankind; then know that, so far to distrust the judgment and the honesty of one who hath but a common repute in learning, and never yet offended, as not to count him fit to print his mind without a tutor and examiner, lest he should drop a schism, or something of corruption, is the greatest displeasure and indignity to a free and knowing spirit that can be put upon him.

110. *journey-work:* work by the day, or work by a journeyman or day-laborer.

111. *sensible:* sensitive

What advantage is it to be a man, over it is to be a boy at school, if we have only escaped the ferula[112] to come under the fescue of an Imprimatur; if serious and elaborate writings, as if they were no more than the theme of a grammar-lad under his pedagogue, must not be uttered without the cursory eyes of a temporizing and extemporizing licenser? He who is not trusted with his own actions, his drift not being known to be evil, and standing to the hazard of law and penalty, has no great argument to think himself reputed in the Commonwealth wherein he was born for other than a fool or a foreigner. When a man writes to the world, he summons up all his reason and deliberation to assist him; he searches, meditates, is industrious, and likely consults and confers with his judicious friends; after all which done he takes himself to be informed in what he writes, as well as any that writ before him. If, in this the most consummate act of his fidelity and ripeness, no years, no industry, no former proof of his abilities can bring him to that state of maturity, as not to be still mistrusted and suspected, unless he carry all his considerate diligence, all his midnight watchings and expense of Palladian[113] oil, to the hasty view of an unleisured licenser, perhaps much his younger, perhaps his inferior in judgment, perhaps one who never knew the labour of bookwriting, and if he be not repulsed or slighted, must appear in print like a puny[114] with his guardian, and his censor's hand on the back of his title to be his bail and surety that he is no idiot or seducer, it cannot be but a dishonour and derogation to the author, to the book, to the privilege and dignity of learning.

And what if the author shall be one so copious of fancy, as to have many things well worth the adding come into his mind after licensing, while the book is yet under the press, which not seldom happens to the best and diligentest writers; and that perhaps a dozen times in one book? The printer dares not go beyond his licensed copy; so often then must the author trudge to his leave-giver, that those his new insertions may be viewed; and many a jaunt will be made, ere that licenser, for it must be the same man, can either be found, or found at leisure; meanwhile either the press must stand still, which is no small damage, or the author lose his accuratest thoughts, and send the book forth worse than he had made it, which to a diligent writer is the greatest melancholy and vexation that can befall.

And how can a man teach with authority, which is the life of teaching; how can he be a doctor in his book as he ought to be, or else had better be silent, whenas all he teaches, all he delivers, is but under the tuition, under the correction of his patriarchal[115] licenser to blot or alter what precisely accords not with the hidebound humour which he

112. *ferula:* a schoolmaster's rod. The fescue is usually defined as a pointer.

113. *Palladian:* pertaining to Pallas Athene. The oil of the olive tree which was sacred to her, when burned by an author, might be regarded as no less her gift than the wisdom which she was supposed to give to her devotees.

114. *puny:* a child, a person under the legal age of majority.

115. *Patriarchal* seems to be used in the technical, ecclesiastical sense, of a patriarch or prelate in charge of a patriarchate—roughly equivalent to an archbishopric.

calls his judgment? When every acute reader, upon the first sight of a pedantic licence, will be ready with these like words to ding the book a quoit's distance from him: I hate a pupil teacher, I endure not an instructor that comes to me under the wardship of an overseeing fist. I know nothing of the licenser, but that I have his own hand here for his arrogance; who shall warrant me his judgment? The State, sir, replies the stationer,[116] but has a quick return: The State shall be my governors, but not my critics; they may be mistaken in the choice of a licenser, as easily as this licenser may be mistaken in an author; this is some common stuff; and he might add from Sir Francis Bacon,[117] "that such authorized books are but the language of the times." For though a licenser should happen to be judicious more than ordinary, which will be a great jeopardy of the next succession, yet his very office and his commission enjoins him to let pass nothing but what is vulgarly received already.

Nay, which is more lamentable, if the work of any deceased author, though never so famous in his lifetime and even to this day, come to their hands for licence to be printed, or reprinted, if there be found in his book one sentence of a venturous edge, uttered in the height of zeal (and who knows whether it might not be the dictate of a divine spirit?) yet not suiting with every low decrepit humour of their own, though it were Knox[118] himself, the reformer of a kingdom, that spake it, they will not pardon him their dash: the sense of that great man shall to all posterity be lost, for the fearfulness or the presumptuous rashness of a perfunctory licenser. And to what an author this violence hath been lately done, and in what book of greatest consequence to be faithfully published, I could now instance, but shall forbear till a more convenient season.[119]

Yet if these things be not resented seriously and timely by them who have the remedy in their power, but that such iron-moulds[120] as these shall have authority to gnaw out the choicest periods of exquisitest books, and to commit such a treacherous fraud against the orphan remainders of worthiest men after death, the more sorrow will belong to that hapless race of men, whose misfortune it is to have understanding. Henceforth let no man care to learn, or care to be more than worldly-wise; for certainly in higher matters to be ignorant and slothful, to be a common steadfast dunce, will be the only pleasant life, and only in request.

116. The Stationers' Company was the official organization of London printers and publishers.

117. Milton is quoting from Bacon's An *Advertisement touching the Controversies of the Church of England,* from which he quotes again below.

118. John Knox (1505–1572), the strongest leader of the Presbyterians in Scotland and the uncompromising opponent of Mary, Queen of Scots.

119. As the unidentified author, White suggested either Sir Edward Coke (1552–1634), whose *Institutes* were published with some mutilation by Parliament's authority, or John Knox (1505–1572), whose *History* suffered mutilation in the edition published in 1644.

120. *iron moulds:* "A spot or discoloration on cloth etc. caused by iron-rust or ink-stain."

And it is a particular disesteem of every knowing person alive, and most injurious to the written labours and monuments of the dead, so to me it seems an undervaluing and vilifying of the whole nation. I cannot set so light by all the invention,[121] the art, the wit, the grave and solid judgment which is in England, as that it can be comprehended in any twenty capacities how good soever, much less that it should not pass except their superintendence be over it, except it be sifted and strained with their strainers, that it should be uncurrent without their manual stamp. Truth and understanding are not such wares as to be monopolized[122] and traded in by tickets[123] and statutes and standards. We must not think to make a staple commodity of all the knowledge in the land, to mark and licence it like our broadcloth and our woolpacks. What is it but a servitude like that imposed by the Philistines,[124] not to be allowed the sharpening of our own axes and coulters,[125] but we must repair from all quarters to twenty licensing forges? Had anyone written and divulged erroneous things and scandalous to honest life, misusing and forfeiting the esteem had of his reason among men, if after conviction this only censure were adjudged him that he should never henceforth write but what were first examined by an appointed officer, whose hand should be annexed to pass his credit for him that now he might be safely read; it could not be apprehended less than a disgraceful punishment. Whence to include the whole nation, and those that never yet thus offended, under such a diffident[126] and suspectful prohibition, may plainly be understood what a disparagement it is. So much the more, whenas debtors and delinquents may walk abroad without a keeper, but unoffensive books must not stir forth without a visible jailer in their title.

Nor is it to the common people less than a reproach; for if we be so jealous[127] over them, as that we dare not trust them with an English pamphlet, what do we but censure them for a giddy, vicious, and ungrounded people; in such a sick and weak state of faith and discretion, as to be able to take nothing down but through the pipe[128] of a licenser? That this is care or love of them, we cannot pretend, whenas, in those popish places where the laity are most hated and despised, the same strictness is used over them. Wisdom we cannot call it, because it stops but one breach of licence, nor that neither: whenas those corruptions, which it seeks to prevent, break in faster at other doors which cannot be shut.

121. *invention:* creative power, the writer's talent for finding what to say and how to say it.

122. Monopolies in various commodities had been granted to several of Elizabeth's courtiers and increased in James I's reign, until in 1624 they were abolished, except as patents permitted them on new inventions.

123. *tickets:* official warrants or permissions of any kind.

124. When the Philistines disarmed the Israelites and forbade them to have forges, "all the Israelites went down to the Philistines, to sharpen every man his share, and his coulter, and his ax." (I Sam, xiii, 20.)

125. *coulter:* the iron "foot" or point of the plough.

126. *diffident:* lacking in confidence, suspicious.

127. *jealous:* suspiciously watchful.

128. *pipe:* a tube for taking medicine.

And in conclusion it reflects to the disrepute of our ministers also, of whose labours we should hope better, and of the proficiency which their flock reaps by them, than that after all this light of the Gospel which is, and is to be, and all this continual preaching, they should still be frequented with such an unprincipled, unedified and laic[129] rabble, as that the whiff of every new pamphlet should stagger them out of their catechism and Christian walking. This may have much reason to discourage the ministers when such a low conceit is had of all their exhortations, and the benefiting of their hearers, as that they are not thought fit to be turned loose to three sheets of paper without a licenser; that all the sermons, all the lectures preached, printed, vented in such numbers, and such volumes, as have now well nigh made all other books unsaleable, should not be armour enough against one single Enchiridion,[130] without the castle of St. Angelo[131] of an Imprimatur.

And lest some should persuade ye, Lords and Commons, that these arguments of learned men's discouragement at this your Order are mere flourishes, and not real, I could recount what I have seen and heard in other countries, where this kind of inquisition tyrannizes; when I have sat among their learned men, for that honour I had, and been counted happy to be born in such a place of philosophic freedom, as they supposed England was, while themselves did nothing but bemoan the servile condition into which learning amongst them was brought; that this was it which had damped the glory of Italian wits; that nothing had been there written now these many years but flattery and fustian. There it was that I found and visited the famous Galileo,[132] grown old, a prisoner to the Inquisition, for thinking in astronomy otherwise than the Franciscan and Dominican licensers thought. And though I knew that England then was groaning loudest under the prelatical yoke, nevertheless I took it as a pledge of future happiness, that other nations were so persuaded of her liberty. Yet was it beyond my hope that those worthies were then breathing in her air, who should be her leaders to such a deliverance, as shall never be forgotten by any revolution of time that this world hath to finish. When that was once begun, it was as little in my fear that what words of complaint I heard among learned men of other parts uttered against the Inquisition, the same I should hear by as learned men at home, uttered in time of Parliament against an order of licensing; and that so generally that, when I had disclosed myself a companion of their discontent, I might say, if without envy, that he whom an honest quaestorship had endeared to the Sicilians was not

129. *laic:* belonging to the laity. One of the grievances of the Puritans against Laud was his apparent increasing of the prestige of the clergy at the expense of the laity in the English church.

130. *enchiridion:* a manual or small hand-book.

131. The castle of St. Angelo, on the left bank of the Tiber in Rome, was built in 136 A.D. by the emperor Hadrian and was used as an imperial mausoleum for nearly a century. In Milton's time it was the papal prison.

132. Galileo (1564–1642) was in prison near Florence when Milton visited there in 1638–9. Although he was the prisoner of the Inquisition from the publication of his evidence for the Copernican theory in 1632 until his death, he was not entirely inaccessible to visitors.

more by them importuned against Verres,[133] than the favourable opinion which I had among many who honour ye, and are known and respected by ye, loaded me with entreaties and persuasions, that I would not despair to lay together that which just reason should bring into my mind, toward the removal of an undeserved thraldom upon learning. That this is not therefore the disburdening of a particular fancy, but the common grievance of all those who had prepared their minds and studies above the vulgar pitch to advance truth in others, and from others to entertain it, thus much may satisfy.

And in their name I shall for neither friend nor foe conceal what the general murmur is; that if it come to inquisitioning again and licensing, and that we are so timorous of ourselves, and so suspicious of all men, as to fear each book and the shaking of every leaf, before we know what the contents are; if some who but of late were little better than silenced from preaching,[134] shall come now to silence us from reading, except what they please, it cannot be guessed what is intended by some but a second tyranny over learning: and will soon put it out of controversy, that bishops and presbyters are the same to us, both name and thing. That those evils of prelaty, which before from five or six and twenty sees[135] were distributively charged upon the whole people, will now light wholly upon learning, is not obscure to us: whenas now the pastor of a small unlearned parish on the sudden shall be exalted archbishop over a large diocese[136] of books, and yet not remove, but keep his other cure too, a mystical[137] pluralist. He who but of late cried down the sole ordination of every novice Bachelor of Art, and denied sole jurisdiction over the simplest parishioner, shall now at home in his private chair assume both these over worthiest and excellentest books and ablest authors that write them.

This is not, ye Covenants[138] and Protestations[139] that we have made! this is not to put down prelaty; this is but to chop an episcopacy; this is but to translate the Palace Metropolitan[140] from one kind of dominion into another; this is but an old canonical[141] sleight of commuting our

133. While serving as quaestor in Sicily in 75 B.C., Cicero won such confidence that the Sicilians asked him to prosecute Gaius Verres for his extortions there as praetor in 73–1. After taking less than two months to collect evidence, Cicero virtually won his case and drove Verres into exile by the first of his orations against him.

134. The Presbyterian clergy and their supporters in Parliament.

135. *sees:* the seats of headquarters of bishops.

136. *diocese:* the province or territory administered by a bishop.

137. *mystical:* (probably in this case) mysterious or strange.

138. On 28 February, 1638, the Scots signed their National Covenant in Edinburgh and consolidated their resistance to Charles's effort to impose episcopacy on the Scottish Presbyterian church. The Solemn League and Covenant which Parliament finally ratified with the Scots in September, 1643, secured Scottish military aid against Charles for Parliament at the price of an engagement that the English church should become essentially Presbyterian.

139. In May, 1641, when Charles planned to use the army to overawe Parliament, the members agreed on a Protestation asserting civil liberties, parliamentary freedom, etc.

140. *metropolitan*: pertaining to an archbishop or to his power or property.

141. *canonical:* pertaining to Canon Law or lawyers.

penance. To startle thus betimes at a mere unlicensed pamphlet will after a while be afraid of every conventicle, and a while after will make a conventicle[142] of every Christian meeting. But I am certain that a State governed by the rules of justice and fortitude, or a Church built and founded upon the rock of faith and true knowledge, cannot be so pusillanimous. While things are yet not constituted in religion, that freedom of writing should be restrained by a discipline imitated from the prelates and learnt by them from the Inquisition, to shut us up all again into the breast of a licenser, must needs give cause of doubt and discouragement to all learned and religious men.

Who cannot but discern the fineness[143] of this politic drift, and who are the contrivers; that while bishops were to be baited down,[144] then all presses might be open; it was the people's birthright and privilege in time of Parliament, it was the breaking forth of light. But now, the bishops abrogated and voided[145] out of the Church, as if our Reformation sought no more but to make room for others into their seats under another name, the episcopal arts begin to bud again, the cruse[146] of truth must run no more oil, liberty of printing must be enthralled again under a prelatical commission of twenty, the privilege of the people nullified, and, which is worse, the freedom of learning must groan again, and to her old fetters: all this the Parliament yet sitting. Although their own late arguments and defences against the prelates might remember them,[147] that this obstructing violence meets for the most part with an event utterly opposite to the end which it drives at: instead of suppressing sects and schisms, it raises them and invests them with a reputation. The punishing of wits enhances their authority, saith the Viscount St. Albans;[148] and a forbidden writing is thought to be a certain spark of truth that flies up in the faces of them who seek to tread it out. This Order, therefore, may prove a nursing-mother[149] to sects, but I shall easily show how it will be a step-dame to Truth: and first by disenabling us to the maintenance of what is known already.

Well knows he who uses to consider, that our faith and knowledge thrives by exercise, as well as our limbs and complexion.[150] Truth is compared in Scripture to a streaming fountain;[151] if her waters flow not in a perpetual progression, they sicken into a muddy pool of conformity and tradition. A man may be a heretic in the truth;[152] and if he believe

142. *conventicle:* a religious meeting of any of the independent sects whose services were forbidden

143. *fineness:* subtlety, cleverness.

144. *baited down*: i.e., like bears in the sport of bear-baiting.

145. *voided:* emptied out, expelled.

146. Milton was thinking of the widow's inexhaustible cruse of oil. I Kings xvii, 12.

147. *remember:* remind.

148. *Viscount St. Albans:* Bacon.

149. "And kings shall be thy nursing fathers, and their queens thy nursing mothers." (Isa. xlix, 23.)

150. *complexion:* the balance of "humors" in the body, on which an individual's health and character were understood to depend.

151. Psalms lxxxv, ii.

152. Cf. Milton's definition of heresy in *Of True Religion* as "a religion taken up and believed from the traditions of men" and his contrast there of "implicit faith" with "unimplicit truth."

things only because his pastor says so, or the Assembly[153] so determines, without knowing other reason, though his belief be true, yet the very truth he holds becomes his heresy.

There is not any burden that some would gladlier post off to another than the charge and care of their religion. There be—who knows not that there be?—of Protestants and professors[154] who live and die in as arrant an implicit faith as any lay Papist of Loretto.[155] A wealthy man, addicted to his pleasure and to his profits, finds religion to be a traffic so entangled, and of so many piddling accounts, that of all mysteries[156] he cannot skill[157] to keep a stock going upon that trade. What should he do? fain he would have the name to be religious, fain he would bear up with his neighbours in that. What does he therefore, but resolves to give over toiling, and to find himself out some factor,[158] to whose care and credit he may commit the whole managing of his religious affairs; some divine of note and estimation that must be. To him he adheres, resigns the whole warehouse of his religion, with all the locks and keys, into his custody; and indeed makes the very person of that man his religion; esteems his associating with him a sufficient evidence and commendatory of his own piety. So that a man may say his religion is now no more within himself, but is become a dividual[159] movable, and goes and comes near him, according as that good man frequents the house. He entertains him, gives him gifts, feasts him, lodges him; his religion comes home at night, prays, is liberally supped, and sumptuously laid to sleep; rises, is saluted, and after the malmsey,[160] or some well-spiced brewage, and better breakfasted than he whose morning appetite would have gladly fed on green figs between Bethany and Jerusalem,[161] his religion walks abroad at eight, and leaves his kind entertainer in the shop trading all day without his religion.

Another sort there be who, when they hear that all things shall be ordered, all things regulated and settled, nothing written but what passes through the custom-house of certain publicans[162] that have the tonnaging and poundaging[163] of all free-spoken truth, will straight give themselves up into your hands, make 'em and cut 'em out what religion ye please: there be delights, there be recreations and jolly pastimes that

153. The Assembly of Divines, then sitting at Westminister, was prevailingly Presbyterian.

154. *professors:* persons professing religious (and presumably Protestant) faith.

155. Since 1294, when the veneration of the Italian shrine at Loretto, near Ancona, began in recognition of the translation there by angels of the house where Christ was born, the popularity of the shrine has attested Catholic faith.

156. *mysteries:* trades, skills—in the sense in which the term was applied to the trades which were organized into guilds.

157. *skill:* contrive.

158. *factor:* agent.

159. *dividual:* separable.

160. *malmsey:* a strong, sweet wine.

161. Riding from Bethany on his way to Jerusalem, Christ "was hungry: And seeing a fig tree afar off. . . . he came, if haply he might find anything thereon: and . . . found nothing but leaves." (Mark xi, 12–3.)

162. *publicans:* tax-gatherers.

163. Tonnage and poundage were a form of excise taxes traditionally granted to the king by Parliament, but disputed in 1641, when "the tonnage and poundage act declared the taking of all such duties without the consent of Parliament illegal."

will fetch the day about from sun to sun, and rock the tedious year as in a delightful dream. What need they torture their heads with that which others have taken so strictly and so unalterably into their own purveying? These are the fruits which a dull ease and cessation of our knowledge will bring forth among the people. How goodly and how to be wished were such an obedient unanimity as this, what a fine conformity would it starch us all into! Doubtless a staunch and solid piece of framework, as any January could freeze together.

Nor much better will be the consequence even among the clergy themselves. It is no new thing never heard of before, for a parochial minister, who has his reward and is at his Hercules' pillars[164] in a warm benefice, to be easily inclinable, if he have nothing else that may rouse up his studies, to finish his circuit in an English Concordance and a topic folio, the gatherings and savings of a sober graduateship, a Harmony[165] and a Catena;[166] treading the constant round of certain common doctrinal heads, attended with their uses, motives, marks, and means, out of which, as out of an alphabet, or sol-fa, by forming and transforming, joining and disjoining variously, a little bookcraft, and two hours' meditation, might furnish him unspeakably to the performance of more than a weekly charge of sermoning: not to reckon up the infinite helps of interlinearies,[167] breviaries, synopses, and other loitering gear. But as for the multitude of sermons ready printed and piled up, on every text that is not difficult, our London trading St. Thomas[168] in his vestry,[169] and add to boot St. Martin and St. Hugh, have not within their hallowed limits more vendible ware of all sorts ready made: so that penury he never need fear of pulpit provision, having where so plenteously to refresh his magazine. But if his rear and flanks be not impaled,[170] if his back door be not secured by the rigid licenser, but that a bold book may now and then issue forth and give the assault to some of his old collections in their trenches, it will concern him then to keep waking, to stand in watch, to set good guards and sentinels about his received opinions, to walk the round and counter-round with his fellow inspectors, fearing lest any of his flock be seduced, who also then would be better instructed, better exercised and disciplined. And God send[171] that the fear of this diligence, which must then be used, do not make us affect the laziness of a licensing Church.

164. *Hercules pillars:* Gibraltar and the promontory opposite to it, which in the ancient world represented the final limit of at least ordinary travel or ambition.

165. *harmony:* a simple treatise bringing divergent scripture narratives, such as those in the four gospels, into harmony with one another

166. *catena:* (in Latin) chain. The term was applied to complications as various as St. Thomas Aquinas' Catena Aurea and the Golden Chaine of William Perkins.

167. interlinearies: interlinear commentaries on scripture.

168. St. Thomas, etc. The identification of the London churches intended are not clear, but the three spots indicated evidently bounded the book-selling district in the city.

169. *vestry:* wardrobe or dressing room for the clergy in a church. The implication seems to be that this vestry served as a shop, or that an adjacent shop was called the vestry

170. *impaled:* protected.

171. *send,* the reading of the original, has been emended by some editors to *fend: i.e.,* prevent, forfend.

For if we be sure we are in the right, and do not hold the truth guiltily, which becomes not, if we ourselves condemn not our own weak and frivolous teaching, and the people for an untaught and irreligious gadding rout, what can be more fair than when a man judicious, learned, and of a conscience, for aught we know, as good as theirs that taught us what we know, shall not privily from house to house, which is more dangerous, but openly by writing publish to the world what his opinion is, what his reasons, and wherefore that which is now thought cannot be sound? Christ urged[172] it as wherewith to justify himself, that he preached in public; yet writing is more public than preaching; and more easy to refutation, if need be, there being so many whose business and profession merely it is to be the champions of truth; which if they neglect, what can be imputed but their sloth, or unability?

Thus much we are hindered and disinured[173] by this course of licensing, toward the true knowledge of what we seem to know. For how much it hurts and hinders the licensers themselves in the calling of their ministry, more than any secular employment, if they will discharge that office as they ought, so that of necessity they must neglect either the one duty or the other, I insist not, because it is a particular, but leave it to their own conscience, how they will decide it there.

There is yet behind of what I purposed to lay open, the incredible loss and detriment that this plot of licensing puts us to; more than if some enemy at sea should stop up all our havens and ports and creeks, it hinders and retards the importation of our richest merchandise, truth;[174] nay, it was first established and put in practice by Antichristian malice and mystery on set purpose to extinguish, if it were possible, the light of Reformation, and to settle falsehood; little differing from that policy wherewith the Turk upholds his Alcoran,[175] by the prohibition of printing. 'Tis not denied, but gladly confessed, we are to send our thanks and vows to Heaven louder than most of nations, for that great measure of truth which we enjoy, especially in those main points between us and the Pope, with his appurtenances the prelates: but he who thinks we are to pitch our tent here, and have attained the utmost prospect of reformation that the mortal glass[176] wherein we contemplate can show us, till we come to beatific vision, that man by this very opinion declares that he is yet far short of truth.

Truth indeed came once into the world with her divine Master, and was a perfect shape most glorious to look on: but when he ascended, and

172. Questioned by the high priest, "Jesus answered him, I spake openly to the world; . . . in secret have I said nothing." (John xviii, 20.)

173. *disinured*: diverted from a customary practice, or one to which habit has become injured.

174. Perhaps an allusion to the pearl of great price in Christ's parable of the merchant who sold everything for that single purchase (Matt, xiii, 46)—or to the "trade, nor for gold, silver, jewels, nor for silks, nor for spices, nor for any other commodity of matter, but only for God's first creature, which was *Light,*" which Bacon describes his New Atlanteans as maintaining.

175. *Alcoran:* The *Koran* or sacred book of the Mohammedans.

176. *glass:* mirror. Perhaps an illusion to I Corinthians xiii, 12: "For now we see through (or *in*) a glass, darkly; but then, face to face."

his Apostles after him were laid asleep, then straight arose a wicked race of deceivers, who, as that story goes of the Egyptian Typhon[177] with his conspirators, how they dealt with the good Osiris, took the virgin Truth, hewed her lovely form into a thousand pieces, and scattered them to the four winds. From that time ever since, the sad friends of Truth, such as durst appear, imitating the careful search that Isis made for the mangled body of Osiris, went up and down gathering up limb by limb, still as they could find them. We have not yet found them all, Lords and Commons, nor ever shall do, till her Master's second coming; he shall bring together every joint and member, and shall mould them into an immortal feature of loveliness and perfection. Suffer not these licensing prohibitions to stand at every place of opportunity, forbidding and disturbing them that continue seeking, that continue to do our obsequies[178] to the torn body of our martyred saint.

We boast our light; but if we look not wisely on the sun itself, it smites us into darkness. Who can discern those planets that are oft combust,[179] and those stars of brightest magnitude that rise and set with the sun, until the opposite motion of their orbs bring them to such a place in the firmament, where they may be seen evening or morning? The light which we have gained was given us, not to be ever staring on, but by it to discover onward things more remote from our knowledge. It is not the unfrocking of a priest, the unmitring of a bishop, and the removing him from off the presbyterian shoulders, that will make us a happy nation. No, if other things as great in the Church, and in the rule of life both economical and political, be not looked into and reformed, we have looked so long upon the blaze that Zuinglius and Calvin hath beaconed up to us, that we are stark blind. There be who perpetually complain of schisms and sects, and make it such a calamity that any man dissents from their maxims. 'Tis their own pride and ignorance which causes the disturbing, who neither will hear with meekness, nor can convince; yet all must be suppressed which is not found in their Syntagma.[180] They are the troublers, they are the dividers of unity, who neglect and permit not others to unite those dissevered pieces which are yet wanting to the body of Truth. To be still searching what we know not by what we know, still closing up truth to truth as we find it (for all her body is homogeneal and proportional), this is the golden rule in theology as well as in arithmetic, and makes up the best harmony in a Church; not the forced and outward union of cold, and neutral, and inwardly divided minds.

Lords and Commons of England! consider what nation it is whereof ye are, and whereof ye are the governors: a nation not slow and dull, but

177. Milton's public was familiar with Plutarch's *Isis* and *Osiris*, where the myth is interpreted as a symbol of the ceaseless assembly by Isis of the divine truth which is continually mangled and scattered by Typhon.

178. *obsequies:* acts of veneration or of worship.

179. *combust:* burnt up. The term was technically applied in astrology to any planet approaching within eight and a half degrees of the sun.

180. *syntagma:* collection, systematic compilation.

of a quick, ingenious and piercing spirit, acute to invent, subtle and sinewy to discourse, not beneath the reach of any point the highest that human capacity can soar to. Therefore the studies of learning in her deepest sciences have been so ancient and so eminent among us, that writers of good antiquity and ablest judgment have been persuaded that even the school of Pythagoras and the Persian wisdom took beginning from the old philosophy of this island. And that wise and civil Roman, Julius Agricola,[181] who governed once here for Caesar, preferred the natural wits of Britain before the laboured studies of the French. Nor is it for nothing that the grave and frugal Transylvanian[182] sends out yearly from as far as the mountainous borders of Russia, and beyond the Hercynian wilderness,[183] not their youth, but their staid men, to learn our language and our theologic arts.

Yet that which is above all this, the favour and the love of Heaven, we have great argument to think in a peculiar manner propitious and propending[184] towards us. Why else was this nation chosen before any other, that out of her, as out of Sion,[185] should be proclaimed and sounded forth the first tidings and trumpet of Reformation to all Europe? And had it not been the obstinate perverseness of our prelates against the divine and admirable spirit of Wickliff, to suppress him as a schismatic and innovator, perhaps neither the Bohemian Huns and Jerome,[186] no nor the name of Luther or of Calvin, had been ever known: the glory of reforming all our neighbours had been completely ours. But now, as our obdurate clergy have with violence demeaned[187] the matter, we are become hitherto the latest and the backwardest scholars, of whom

God offered to have made us the teachers. Now once again by all concurrence of signs, and by the general instinct of holy and devout men, as they daily and solemnly express their thoughts, God is decreeing to begin some new and great period in his Church, even to the reforming of Reformation itself: what does he then but reveal himself to his servants, and as his manner is, first to his Englishmen?[188] I say, as his manner is,

181. Julius Agricola (37–93 A.D.) was proconsul in Britain from 78 to 85, and under him the Roman conquest was consolidated. In the *Life of Agrippa* his son-in-law, Tacitus, says that he educated the sons of the chiefs in the liberal arts so successfully that those who had recently despised the language of the Romans were soon anxious to become eloquent in it.

182. From 1535 until 1689 Transylvania was independent, and in the seventeenth century it was aggressively Protestant. In May 1655, after the massacre of the Waldensians in Piedmont, Milton, as Secretary to the Council of State, wrote cordially to the Transylvanian prince about the joint action that Cromwell was proposing between England and several continental states.

183. Hales points out that the name *Hercynian* survives in that of the Harz (mountains), but the ancient writers applied it vaguely to most of the mountains in the south and center of Germany.

184. *propending:* inclining.

185. *Sion:* Mount Zion in Jerusalem, used to represent Jerusalem itself.

186. Jerome of Prague (d. 1416), a strong supporter of Huss, studied and read Wycliffe's work at Oxford in 1398, and later became a devoted, though not perfectly loyal, supporter of Huss in Bohemia. He was burned at the stake.

187. *demeaned:* conducted, handled.

188. Milton is speaking of the popular faith expressed by Hugh Peters when he said in the Whitehall debates that "God seems to call for something at our hands about religion, and that only because we are Englishmen."

first to us, though we mark not the method of his counsels, and are unworthy.

Behold now this vast city: a city of refuge, the mansion house of liberty, encompassed and surrounded with his protection; the shop of war hath not there more anvils and hammers waking, to fashion out the plates[189] and instruments of armed justice in defence of beleaguered truth, than there be pens and heads there, sitting by their studious lamps, musing, searching, revolving new notions and ideas wherewith to present, as with their homage and their fealty, the approaching Reformation: others as fast reading, trying all things, assenting to the force of reason and convincement. What could a man require more from a nation so pliant and so prone to seek after knowledge? What wants there to such a towardly and pregnant soil, but wise and faithful labourers, to make a knowing people, a nation of prophets, of sages, and of worthies? We reckon more than five months yet to harvest; there need not be five weeks; had we but eyes to lift up, the fields are white already.[190]

Where there is much desire to learn, there of necessity will be much arguing, much writing, many opinions; for opinion in good men is but knowledge in the making. Under these fantastic terrors of sect and schism, we wrong the earnest and zealous thirst after knowledge and understanding which God hath stirred up in this city. What some lament of, we rather should rejoice at, should rather praise this pious forwardness among men, to reassume the ill-deputed care of their religion into their own hands again. A little generous prudence, a little forbearance of one another, and some grain of charity might win all these diligences to join, and unite in one general and brotherly search after truth; could we but forgo this prelatical tradition of crowding free consciences and Christian liberties into canons and precepts of men. I doubt not, if some great and worthy stranger should come among us, wise to discern the mould and temper of a people, and how to govern it, observing the high hopes and aims, the diligent alacrity of our extended thoughts and reasonings in the pursuance of truth and freedom, but that he would cry out as Pyrrhus[191] did, admiring the

Roman docility and courage: If such were my Epirots, I would not despair the greatest design that could be attempted, to make a Church or kingdom happy.

Yet these are the men cried out against for schismatics and sectaries; as if, while the temple[192] of the Lord was building, some cutting, some squaring the marble, others hewing the cedars, there should be a sort of irrational men who could not consider there must be many

189. *plates:* armor of plate mail.

190. Milton paraphrases Christ's words to the disciples whom he sent to preach to the Jews. (John iv, 35.)

191. Pyrrhus (318–272 B.C.), King of Epirus, is said by Florus (*Epitome de gestis Romanorum* I, 18) to have paid this tribute to Roman discipline after his victory over Valerius Laevinus at Heraclea in 280 B.C.

192. The stones for Solomon's temple were all shaped exactly for their positions at the quarry. (I Kings vi, 7; but cf. the longer account in II Chronicles ii, 5–9.)

schisms[193] and many dissections made in the quarry and in the timber, ere the house of God can be built. And when every stone is laid artfully together, it cannot be united into a continuity, it can but be contiguous in this world; neither can every piece of the building be of one form; nay rather the perfection consists in this, that, out of many moderate varieties and brotherly dissimilitudes that are not vastly disproportional, arises the goodly and the graceful symmetry that commends the whole pile and structure.

Let us therefore be more considerate builders, more wise in spiritual architecture, when great reformation is expected. For now the time seems come, wherein Moses the great prophet may sit in heaven rejoicing to see that memorable and glorious wish of his fulfilled, when not only our seventy elders, but all the Lord's people, are become prophets. No marvel then though some men, and some good men too perhaps, but young in goodness, as Joshua[194] then was, envy them. They fret, and out of their own weakness are in agony, lest these divisions and subdivisions will undo us. The adversary again applauds, and waits the hour: when they have branched themselves out, saith he, small enough into parties and partitions, then will be our time. Fool! he sees not the firm root, out of which we all grow, though into branches: nor will beware until he see our small divided maniples[195] cutting through at every angle of his ill-united and unwieldy brigade. And that we are to hope better of all these supposed sects and schisms, and that we shall not need that solicitude, honest perhaps, though over-timorous, of them that vex in this behalf, but shall laugh in the end at those malicious applauders of our differences, I have these reasons to persuade me.

First, when a city shall be as it were besieged and blocked about, her navigable river infested, inroads and incursions round, defiance[196] and battle oft rumoured to be marching up even to her walls and suburb trenches, that then the people, or the greater part, more than at other times, wholly taken up with the study of highest and most important matters to be reformed, should be disputing, reasoning, reading, inventing, discoursing, even to a rarity and admiration, things not before discoursed or written of, argues first a singular goodwill, contentedness and confidence in your prudent foresight and safe government, Lords and Commons; and from thence derives itself to a gallant bravery and well-grounded contempt of their enemies, as if there were no small number of as great spirits among us, as his was, who when Rome was nigh besieged by Hannibal,[197] being in the city, bought that piece of

193. Milton puns on the literal meaning of *schism,* cutting or division.

194. When Joshua was still one of Moses' "young men," he protested against certain prophets in the camp. "And Moses said unto him, Enviest thou for my sake? Would God that all the Lord's people were prophets." (Num. xi, 29).

195. *maniple:* a small company or unit of Roman soldiers.

196. Milton was thinking of the situation after the battle of Edgehill in October, 1643, when the Royalists advanced to the London suburbs, which had been fortified during the preceeding summer.

197. Livy's *History* (XXVI, xi) tells the story of the damaging effect on the morale of Hannibal's Carthaginians who were besieging Rome when it was reported that the field where he had his headquarters had

ground at no cheap rate, whereon Hannibal himself encamped his own regiment.

Next, it is a lively and cheerful presage of our happy success and victory. For as in a body, when the blood is fresh, the spirits pure and vigorous, not only to vital but to rational faculties, and those in the acutest and the pertest operations of wit and subtlety, it argues in what good plight and constitution the body is; so when the cheerfulness of the people is so sprightly up, as that it has not only wherewith to guard well its own freedom and safety, but to spare, and to bestow upon the solidest and sublimest points of controversy and new invention, it betokens us not degenerated, nor drooping to a fatal decay, but casting off the old and wrinkled skin of corruption to outlive these pangs and wax young again, entering the glorious ways of truth and prosperous virtue, destined to become great and honourable in these latter ages. Methinks I see in my mind a noble and puissant nation rousing herself like a strong man after sleep, and shaking her invincible locks: methinks I see her as an eagle mewing[198] her mighty youth, and kindling her undazzled eyes at the full midday beam; purging and unscaling her long-abused sight at the fountain itself of heavenly radiance; while the whole noise of timorous and flocking birds, with those also that love the twilight, flutter about, amazed at what she means, and in their envious gabble would prognosticate a year of sects and schisms.

What would ye do then? should ye suppress all this flowery crop of knowledge and new light sprung up and yet springing daily in this city? Should ye set an oligarchy of twenty engrossers[199] over it, to bring a famine upon our minds again, when we shall know nothing but what is measured to us by their bushel? Believe it, Lords and Commons, they who counsel ye to such a suppressing do as good as bid ye suppress yourselves; and I will soon show how. If it be desired to know the immediate cause of all this free writing and free speaking, there cannot be assigned a truer than your own mild and free and humane government. It is the liberty, Lords and Commons, which your own valorous and happy counsels have purchased us, liberty which is the nurse of all great wits; this is that which hath rarefied and enlightened our spirits like the influence of heaven;[200] this is that which hath enfranchised, enlarged and lifted up our apprehensions, degrees above themselves.

Ye cannot make us now less capable, less knowing, less eagerly pursuing of the truth, unless ye first make yourselves, that made us so, less the lovers, less the founders of our true liberty. We can grow ignorant again, brutish, formal and slavish, as ye found us; but you then must first become that which ye cannot be, oppressive, arbitrary and

just been sold at "*an unreduced price*" inside Rome.

198. [*mewing*: renewing by moulting].

199. *engrossers:* persons attempting to "corner" a market.

200. Milton probably thought in astrological terms, as he did in describing the Union of Adam and Eve:

> . . . all Heav'n
> And happy Constellations on that hour
> Shed their selectest influence.
> (P.L. VIII, 511–3.)

tyrannous, as they were from whom ye have freed us. That our hearts are now more capacious, our thoughts more erected to the search and expectation of greatest and exactest things, is the issue of your own virtue propagated in us; ye cannot suppress that, unless ye reinforce an abrogated and merciless law, that fathers may dispatch at will their own children. And who shall then stick closest to ye, and excite others? not he who takes up arms for coat and conduct,[201] and his four nobles[202] of Danegelt.[203] Although I dispraise not the defence of just immunities, yet love my peace better, if that were all. Give me the liberty to know, to utter, and to argue freely according to conscience, above all liberties.

What would be best advised, then, if it be found so hurtful and so unequal[204] to suppress opinions for the newness or the unsuitableness to a customary acceptance, will not be my task to say. I only shall repeat what I have learned from one of your own honourable number, a right noble and pious lord, who, had he not sacrificed his life and fortunes to the Church and Commonwealth, we had not now missed and bewailed a worthy and undoubted patron of this argument. Ye know him, I am sure; yet I for honour's sake, and may it be eternal to him, shall name him, the Lord Brook.[205] He writing of episcopacy, and by the way treating of sects and schisms, left ye his vote,[206] or rather now the last words of his dying charge, which I know will ever be of dear and honoured regard with ye, so full of meekness and breathing charity, that next to his last testament, who bequeathed love and peace to his disciples,[207] I cannot call to mind where I have read or heard words more mild and peaceful. He there exhorts us to hear with patience and humility those, however they be miscalled, that desire to live purely, in such a use of God's ordinances, as the best guidance of their conscience gives them, and to tolerate them, though in some disconformity to ourselves. The book itself will tell us more at large, being published to the world, and dedicated to the Parliament by him who, both for his life and for his death, deserves that what advice he left be not laid by without perusal.

And now the time in special is, by privilege to write and speak what may help to the further discussing of matters in agitation. The temple of Janus[208] with his two controversial faces might now not unsignificantly be set open. And though all the winds of doctrine were let loose to play

201. *coat and conduct:* an obsolete tax, originally levied to pay for clothing and transporting feudal troops in the king's service, and revived by Charles I in his effort to obtain funds without a parliamentary grant.

202. *noble:* a coin worth about six shillings and eight pence.

203. *Danegelt:* originally, the money secured by taxation in England to buy off the Danish invaders of the Saxon kingdoms. Under the Norman kings it was established as a tax on land. King Charles's lawyers appealed to it in Hampden's case.

204. *unequal:* unjust, inequitable.

205. *Lord Brooke:* In the Latin sense of the word *patron* (*patronus*) Milton was thinking of Brooke as the advocate or oratorical champion of his cause.

206. *vote:* solemn wish.

207. John xiv, 27.

208. Janus, the ancient Italian deity of gates and doors, had a sacred gateway in the Roman Forum which was always open in time of war—probably because it was supposed to make the armies that departed through it fortunate. In peace it was kept closed.

upon the earth, so Truth be in the field, we do injuriously, by licensing and prohibiting, to misdoubt her strength. Let her and Falsehood grapple; who ever knew Truth put to the worse, in a free and open encounter? Her confuting[209] is the best and surest suppressing. He who hears what praying there is for light and clearer knowledge to be sent down among us, would think of other matters to be constituted beyond the discipline of Geneva, framed and fabricked[210] already to our hands. Yet when the new light which we beg for shines in upon us, there be who envy and oppose, if it come not first in at their casements. What a collusion is this, whenas we are exhorted by the wise man to use diligence, to seek for wisdom as for hidden treasures[211] early and late, that another order shall enjoin us to know nothing but by statute? When a man hath been labouring the hardest labour in the deep mines of knowledge, hath furnished out his findings in all their equipage: drawn forth his reasons as it were a battle ranged: scattered and defeated all objections in his way; calls out his adversary into the plain, offers him the advantage of wind and sun, if he please, only that he may try the matter by dint of argument: for his opponents then to skulk, to lay ambushments, to keep a narrow bridge of licensing where the challenger should pass, though it be valour enough in soldiership, is but weakness and cowardice in the wars of Truth.

For who knows not that Truth is strong, next to the Almighty? She needs no policies, nor stratagems, nor licensings to make her victorious; those are the shifts and the defences that error uses against her power. Give her but room, and do not bind her when she sleeps, for then she speaks not true, as the old Proteus[212] did, who spake oracles only when he was caught and bound, but then rather she turns herself into all shapes, except her own, and perhaps tunes her voice according to the time, as Micaiah[213] did before Ahab, until she be adjured into her own likeness. Yet is it not impossible that she may have more shapes than one. What else is all that rank of things indifferent, wherein Truth may be on this side or on the other, without being unlike herself? What but a vain shadow else is the abolition of those ordinances, that hand-writing nailed to the cross?[214] What great purchase is this Christian liberty which Paul so often boasts of?[215] His doctrine is, that he who eats or eats not, regards a day or regards it not, may do either to the Lord.[216] How many other things might be tolerated in peace, and left to conscience, had we but charity, and were it not the chief stronghold of our hypocrisy to be ever judging one another?

209. *her: i.e.,* of her, in an objective sense. The reference is to Falsehood.

210. *fabricked:* fabricated.

211. Proverbs viii, II.

212. The myth of Proteus' prophetic power goes back to the *Odyssey* IV, 384–93.

213. For a time Micaiah, the prophet of God, agreed with the four hundred pagan prophets who gave Ahab the advice which led him into an attack on Ramoth–Gilead in which he lost his life. When he was adjured to speak the truth, he warned Ahab that the other prophets were inspired by "a lying spirit." (I Kings xxii, 23.)

214. "Blotting out the handwriting of ordinances that was against us, ... and took it out of the way, nailing it to his cross." (Col. ii, 14.)

215. *E.g.* in Galatians v, I.

216. A paraphrase of Romans xiv, 6.

I fear yet this iron yoke of outward conformity hath left a slavish print upon our necks; the ghost of a linen decency yet haunts us. We stumble and are impatient at the least dividing of one visible congregation from another, though it be not in fundamentals; and through our forwardness to suppress, and our backwardness to recover any enthralled piece of truth out of the grip of custom, we care not to keep truth separated from truth, which is the fiercest rent and disunion of all. We do not see that, while we still affect by all means a rigid external formality, we may as soon fall again into a gross conforming stupidity, a stark and dead congealment of wood and hay and stubble,[217] forced and frozen together, which is more to the sudden degenerating of a Church than many subdichotomies of petty schisms.

Not that I can think well of every light separation, or that all in a Church is to be expected gold and silver and precious stones: it is not possible for man to sever the wheat from the tares,[218] the good fish from the other fry; that must be the Angels' ministry at the end of mortal things. Yet if all cannot be of one mind—as who looks they should be?—this doubtless is more wholesome, more prudent, and more Christian, that many be tolerated, rather than all compelled. I mean not tolerated popery, and open superstition, which, as it extirpates all religions and civil supremacies, so itself should be extirpate, provided first that all charitable and compassionate means be used to win and regain the weak and the misled: that also which is impious or evil absolutely either against faith or manners no law can possibly permit, that intends not to unlaw itself: but those neighbouring differences, or rather indifferences, are what I speak of, whether in some point of doctrine or of discipline, which, though they may be many, yet need not interrupt the unity of spirit, if we could but find among us the bond of peace.[219]

In the meanwhile if any one would write, and bring his helpful hand to the slow-moving Reformation which we labour under, if Truth have spoken to him before others, or but seemed at least to speak, who hath so bejesuited us that we should trouble that man with asking license to do so worthy a deed? and not consider this, that if it come to prohibiting, there is not aught more likely to be prohibited than truth itself; whose first appearance to our eyes, bleared and dimmed with prejudice and custom, is more unsightly and unplausible than many errors, even as the person is of many a great man slight and contemptuous to see to.[220] And what do they tell us vainly of new opinions, when this very opinion of theirs, that none must be heard but whom they like, is the worst and newest opinion of all others; and is the chief cause why sects and schisms do so much abound, and true knowledge is kept at distance from us; besides yet a greater danger which is in it.

217. "Now if any man build upon this foundation gold, silver, precious stones, wood, hay, stubble." (I Cor. iii, 12.)

218. This is the lesson of the parable of the tares and the wheat in Matthew xiii, 24–30

219. An echo of Ephesians iv, 3.

220. *to see to:* to look at.

For when God shakes a kingdom[221] with strong and healthful commotions to a general reforming, 'tis not untrue that many sectaries and false teachers are then busiest in seducing; but yet more true it is, that God then raises to his own work men of rare abilities, and more than common industry, not only to look back and revise what hath been taught heretofore, but to gain further and go on some new enlightened steps in the discovery of truth. For such is the order of God's enlightening his Church, to dispense and deal out by degrees his beam, so as our earthly eyes may best sustain it.

Neither is God appointed[222] and confined, where and out of what place these his chosen shall be first heard to speak; for he sees not as man sees, chooses not as man chooses, lest we should devote ourselves again to set places, and assemblies, and outward callings of men; planting our faith one while in the old Convocation[223] house, and another while in the Chapel at Westminster; when all the faith and religion that shall be there canonized[224] is not sufficient without plain convincement, and the charity of patient instruction to supple the least bruise of conscience, to edify the meanest Christian, who desires to walk in the Spirit, and not in the letter of human trust, for all the number of voices that can be there made; no, though Harry VII himself there, with all his liege tombs about him, should lend them voices from the dead, to swell their number.

And if the men be erroneous who appear to be the leading schismatics, what withholds us but our sloth, our self-will, and distrust in the right cause, that we do not give them gentle meetings and gentle dismissions, that we debate not and examine the matter thoroughly with liberal and frequent audience; if not for their sakes, yet for our own? seeing no man who hath tasted learning, but will confess the many ways of profiting by those who, not contented with stale receipts, are able to manage and set forth new positions to the world. And were they but as the dust and cinders of our feet, so long as in that notion they may yet serve to polish and brighten the armoury of Truth, even for that respect they were not utterly to be cast away. But if they be of those whom God hath fitted for the special use of these times with eminent and ample gifts, and those perhaps neither among the priests nor among the Pharisees,[225] and we in the haste of a precipitant zeal shall make no distinction, but resolve to stop their mouths, because we fear they come with new and dangerous opinions, as we commonly forejudge them ere

221. "And I will shake all nations, and the desire of all nations shall come." (Hag. ii, 7.)

222. *appointed:* bound by prescription.

223. The Chapter-house at Westminister was the meeting-place of Laud's Convocations, while the Assembly of Divines at Westminister was meeting in Henry VII's chapel.

224. *canonized:* formulated in canons, given the force of ecclesiastical law. *The Longer and Shorter Catechisms* are the best known of the results of the long sittings of the Westminister Assembly.

225. Milton thought of the traditional skill of the Hebrew Pharisees in law and of their unwillingness to meet Christ as an equal in their many encounters with him.

we understand them; no less than woe to us, while, thinking thus to defend the Gospel, we are found the persecutors.

There have been not a few since the beginning of this Parliament,[226] both of the presbytery and others, who by their unlicensed books, to the contempt of an Imprimatur, first broke that triple ice clung about our hearts, and taught the people to see day: I hope that none of those were the persuaders to renew upon us this bondage which they themselves have wrought so much good by contemning. But if neither the check that Moses gave to young Joshua, nor the countermand which our Saviour gave to young John,[227] who was so ready to prohibit those whom he thought unlicensed, be not enough to admonish our elders how unacceptable to God their testy mood of prohibiting is; if neither their own remembrance what evil hath abounded in the Church by this set of licensing, and what good they themselves have begun by transgressing it, be not enough, but that they will persuade and execute the most Dominican part of the Inquisition over us, and are already with one foot in the stirrup so active at suppressing, it would be no unequal distribution in the first place to suppress the suppressors themselves: whom the change of their condition hath puffed up, more than their late experience of harder times hath made wise.

And as for regulating the press, let no man think to have the honour of advising ye better than yourselves have done in that Order published next before this, "that no book be printed, unless the printer's and the author's name, or at least the printer's, be registered." Those which otherwise come forth, if they be found mischievous and libellous, the fire and the executioner will be the timeliest and the most effectual remedy that man's prevention can use. For this authentic Spanish policy of licensing books, if I have said aught, will prove the most unlicensed book itself within a short while; and was the immediate image of a Star Chamber decree to that purpose made in those very times when that Court did the rest of those her pious works, for which she is now fallen from the stars with Lucifer. Whereby ye may guess what kind of state prudence, what love of the people, what care of religion or good manners there was at the contriving, although with singular hypocrisy it pretended to bind books to their good behaviour. And how it got the upper hand of your precedent Order so well constituted before, if we may believe those men whose profession gives them cause to inquire most, it may be doubted there was in it the fraud of some old patentees and monopolizers in the trade of bookselling; who under pretence of the poor in their Company not to be defrauded, and the just retaining of each man his several copy, which God forbid should be gainsaid, brought divers

226. *this Parliament:* the Long Parliament, which first assembled on 3 November, 1640. Milton thought of England as embarking under its guidance upon an enterprise more heroic than the first ventures of men on the sea, for which Horace said that hearts strengthened by *aes triplex* (triple brass) were needed.

227. When John reported having seen a man casting out devils in Jesus' name, "Jesus said unto him, Forbid him not, for he that is not against us is for us." (Luke ix, 50.)

glossing colours to the House, which were indeed but colours, and serving to no end except it be to exercise a superiority over their neighbours; men who do not therefore labour in an honest profession to which learning is indebted, that they should be made other men's vassals. Another end is thought was aimed at by some of them in procuring by petition this Order, that, having power in their hands, malignant books might the easier scape abroad, as the event shows.

But of these sophisms and elenchs[228] of merchandise I skill not. This I know, that errors in a good government and in a bad are equally almost incident; for what magistrate may not be misinformed, and much the sooner, if liberty of printing be reduced into the power of a few? But to redress willingly and speedily what hath been erred,[229] and in highest authority to esteem a plain advertisement[230] more than others have done a sumptuous bride, is a virtue (honoured Lords and Commons) answerable to your highest actions, and whereof none can participate but greatest and wisest men.

Questions

1) What kind of an argument is Milton making? Does he make his case primarily by advancing a claim about the *consequences* of licensing? Or is he asserting that the Licensing Order is contrary to the *design* of the English commonwealth or divine providence? Or does he claim that the licensing of books and pamphlets violates a *commitment* or fails to exhibit *consistency* with the basic tenets and practices of the Parliamentary regime? Or is his point that the distrust and servility inherent in licensing weakens the *character* of the English people? Or does he assert that writers have a natural *entitlement* to publish without first obtaining official permission?

2) What is Milton's view about the nature of truth and the human capacity to know it? How does that view inform his understanding of the value of dissenting speech?

3) Milton repeatedly employs metaphors of dynamism, vitality, rigidity, sloth, decay, and regeneration. How do these figures advance his argument?

4) How does the ideal of unity (and the risk of disorder) figure in Milton's argument?

5) Contemporary theorists tend to emphasize three rationales for a robust freedom of speech: a) speech facilitates the search for truth; b) speech is

228. *elench:* "a fallacious answer to a sophistical question."

229. *what hath been erred:* what mistakes have been made. Milton's construction is a Latinism.

230. *advertisement:* intimation, notification.

essential to democratic self-government; c) speech is an integral aspect of human autonomy. Does Milton's argument fall under one of these heads? Does he make points that suggest a wholly different rationale?

6) What controversial assumptions does Milton make about human nature? How much does his argument depend on those assumptions?

7) To what extent does Milton's argument rest on controversial assumptions associated with Protestant theology? Does he say anything interesting that a non-Protestant (Catholic, Jew, Muslim, atheist, agnostic) can agree with that bears on the propriety of toleration?

8) Does Milton concede that the publishing of evil ideas sometimes can cause serious harm? How, if at all, does he take account of this possibility? Does he undertake a systematic "cost-benefit" analysis of the effects of unlicensed printing? Even if not, does Milton offer any astute observations or judgments that might contribute to such an analysis?

9) Is this an argument only about *religious* toleration or does Milton also advocate political toleration? Are the reasons for political toleration the same as for religious toleration?

10) Is this exclusively an argument against regulating printing by licensing (what is now called prior restraint) or does Milton's critique apply also to other forms of speech regulation such as criminal prosecution?

11) Milton criticizes the Licensing Order on the ground that it reflects distrust of authors and their audiences. What is his reason for assuming that persons who write pamphlets that challenge prevailing ideas deserve to be trusted? Why does he think that their audiences should be trusted? Is his call for such trust based on empirical suppositions? Moral? Political? Religious?

JOHN MILTON, THE DOCTRINE AND DISCIPLINE OF DIVORCE

(1643).

If it were seriously askt, and it would be no untimely question, Renowned Parlament, select Assembly, who of all Teachers and Maisters that have ever taught, hath drawn the most Disciples after him, both in Religion, and in manners, it might bee not untruly answer'd, Custome. Though vertue be commended for the most perswasive in her *Theory;* and Conscience in the plain demonstration of the spirit, finds most evincing, yet whether it be the secret of divine will, or the originall blindnesse we are born in, so it happ'ns for the most part, that Custome still is silently receiv'd for the best instructer.

SAMUEL JOHNSON, THE LIVES OF THE POETS

(1779).

Milton's republicanism was, I am afraid, founded in an envious hatred of greatness and a sullen desire of independence, in petulance impatient of control and pride disdainful of superiority. He hated monarchs in the state and prelates in the church, for he hated all whom he was required to obey. It is to be suspected that his predominant desire was to destroy rather than establish, and that he felt not so much the love of liberty as repugnance to authority.

SHARON ACHINSTEIN, MILTON AND THE REVOLUTIONARY READER

(1994).

Who was reading these pamphlets and ephemera? This question is tricky, since evidence of readership is hard to come by. More people could read than could write in seventeenth-century England, so the most humble, but avid, readers left no written record of their reading habits. There were, of course, economic limitations to readership; yet pamphlets and ballads were often consumed in public, shared, or passed around from one person to another. Richard Brathwaite and many others complained about the wide circulation of the ballads from the city into the country, "till at last they grow so common there too, as every poor milk-maid can chant and chirp it under her cow." Evidence from booksellers' stock is slim, since bookshop owners rarely took note of such low literature. But we can estimate who might have been reading them from taking note of literacy and bookselling figures for the period. Historians have estimated that 30 percent of adult males could read; the figures were considerably higher in London, where 60 percent of adult males were literate. Press runs for an individual pamphlet would range from 500 to 1,500 copies, and the number of almanacs produced annually for the Stationers' Company in the 1660s ran between 300,000 to 400,000, or one for every four families. The typical cost of a pamphlet or chapbook was cheap, 2*d.*–6*d.*; some of the pamphlets I treat here went into more than one edition. There was a steady market in popular wares such as ballads, and fierce fights broke out among printers throughout the period over copyrights for such golden eggs.

The writers of the civil war period differed from their forbears, however, in their conceptions about their audience and also in their intentions toward politically engaging that audience. Civil war pamphleteers adapted literary conventions and seized upon the popular audience for a new end: to fight a war over opinions, specifically *political* opinions. The Protestant and Catholic literature of the sixteenth century had inaugurated the widespread use of print for polemical purposes, and in the seventeenth century, this medium found political and social avenues to add to the religious ones. As Samuel Hartlib wrote in 1641, "the art of Printing will so spread knowledge that the common people, knowing their own rights and liberties will not be governed by way of oppression." The political pamphleteers of the 1640s conceived of their audience more broadly than had those writing before. With the exception of sermons, prior political writing had achieved limited visibility, since it was written in an oblique style, in secret, or had been smuggled into England from the Continent. The writers had addressed specific elites; the Marprelate tracts, for example, addressed the clergy, and anti-Spanish pamphlets were written in the 1620s for king, court, and clergy (Sir Simonds D'Ewes read them and noted that the king had, too). Yet the nonpolitical writings in the vernacular tradition—the jestbooks, almanacs, and "penny merriments"—could attract a wide audience. In this period, the elite and the popular audiences merged, and political writings were addressed to the public as a whole, and intended to rouse that public into action.

Another key difference was that the earlier pamphleteers wrote under strained conditions, as exceptions to the general rule of political silence. The yearly output of presses prior to the civil war period was small since the printing industry was closely regulated by the governing board of the Stationers' Company, then in the tight reigns of Crown and church. In the 1640s, the output of the press exploded to the thousands. This quantitative difference produced a new degree of audience saturation; forty pamphlets could reach more readers than could four. Few in London at the time of the civil wars could ignore or miss the phenomenon of the pamphlets.

BARBARA K. LEWALSKI, THE LIFE OF JOHN MILTON: A CRITICAL BIOGRAPHY

(2000).

The title, alluding to the written oration presented by Isocrates to the Ecclesia or popular assembly of Athens on the subject of the powers exercised by the Areopagus, the Court of the Wise, identifies Milton's tract as a deliberative oration. He self-consciously takes on the role of the Greek orator Isocrates, "who from his private house wrote that discourse to the Parlament of *Athens*, that perswades them to change the forme of *Democraty* which was then establisht." Addressing his tract to the "High Court of Parlament," Milton offers to advise them as to "what might be done better" to advance the public good and promote liberty, making here his most overt and artful claim to the role of citizen-adviser to the state. His terms import the ethos of Athenian democracy, hinting that London has become a new Athens, a center of vibrant political and cultural life; in Milton's "speech" we hear echoes of Pericles's funeral oration celebrating Athenian democracy. But Milton expects his literate reader to recognize that his proposals for reform stand in direct opposition to those of Isocrates and Plato because they are based on a different ethics and politics. Isocrates proposed that the Areopagus reform Athenian morals by reinstating censorship over citizens' activities, and Plato proposed in the *Republic* and the *Laws* to banish most literature lest it corrupt a virtuous citizenry. Milton insists that only reading of all kinds, forcing the continuous, free, and active choice between good and evil, will allow the good to advance in virtue and truth to vanquish error, thereby producing rational citizens with a developed Protestant conscience and a classical sense of civic duty. Milton may be the first to address directly the issue of how to construct a liberty-loving republican citizenry who will support radical reform. *Areopagitica* validates and defends the emerging public sphere, the marketplace of ideas open to ordinary citizens, that was being created in revolutionary England by the deluge of pamphlets and newsbooks.

In this tract Milton does not speak of himself as a poet, but he embodies that role throughout, in a poetic style vibrant with striking images and figures, little allegories, small narratives. Often these derive from epic and romance. Milton constructs citizen-readers and writers who are engaged in "Wars of Truth," which involve combat and danger, heroic adventures and trials, constant struggles, difficult quests, and which stimulate intellectual energy and cultural vibrancy. Moreover, as David Norbrook observes, the allusive, literary character of this tract and its sublimity of style give the lie to royalist claims that the revolution's democratizing impulses will level and degrade culture. On his title page Milton includes an epigraph taken from Euripides's *The Suppliant Women*, identifying his own "speech" to the English parliament with Theseus's speech defending Athenian democracy and its freedom of speech against Theban tyranny:

> This is true Liberty when free born men
> Having to advise the public may speak free,
> Which he who can, and will, deserv's high praise,
> Who neither can nor will, may hold his peace;
> What can be juster in a State than this?

Milton saw his self-image as a virtuous and learned citizen-author compromised by prior censorship, which undermines the autonomy and authority that role demands.

At this auspicious, reforming moment Milton again claims the role of prophet: "When God shakes a Kingdome with strong and healthfull commotions to a generall reforming," he calls "men of rare abilities," like Milton, to discover new truths. Now, however, Milton does not see himself as a solitary voice crying in the wilderness as in the divorce tracts, but as a participant in a lively, though widely dispersed, scholarly community. Even when London was under siege such men—including, he implies, himself—were "disputing, reasoning, reading, inventing, discoursing, ev'n to a rarity, and admiration," things not before discourst or writt'n of London is also a prophetic milieu: Milton portrays it as a City of Refuge (Numbers 35:11–24) in an England that is becoming a Nation of Prophets (Numbers 11:29), thereby fulfilling Moses' desire that "not only our sev'nty Elders, but all the Lords people are become Prophets." These texts may carry millenarian overtones, but Milton no longer seems to think that Christ's Second Coming is imminent: his focus is on the transformations needed now. And, as always for Milton, the mode of prophecy is not sudden supernatural illumination but painstaking scholarship and authorship:

> Behold now this vast City; a City of refuge, the mansion-house of liberty ... there be pens and heads there, sitting by their studious lamps, musing, searching, revolving new notions and ideas wherewith to present, as with their homage and their fealty the approaching Reformation: others as fast reading, trying all things, assenting to the force of reason and convincement.... What wants there ... but wise and faithfull labourers, to make a knowing people, a Nation of Prophets, of Sages, and of Worthies.

These resonant Hebraic images figure England as a New Israel that eschews uniformity for a higher unity. City and nation are made up of many men studying and writing in their private chambers but through their books actively engaging with one another—a sharp iconographic contrast to the royalist figure of the body politic as one man with body and limbs subservient to the monarchical head, or to the later Hobbesian figure of the sovereign containing all other bodies. Similarly, the church is figured in terms of building the Lord's Temple, a process requiring "many schisms and many dissections made in the quarry and in the timber," so that the stones are laid artfully together, "contiguous" but not cemented.

Then, taking on the voice of the poet-prophet as he did in *Of Reformation* and *Animadversions*, Milton envisions England under the metaphors of the awakening Samson or an eagle renewed to youth and power:

> Methinks I see in my mind a noble and puissant Nation rousing herself like a strong man after sleep, and shaking her invincible locks: Methinks I see her as an Eagle muing her mighty youth, and kindling her undazl'd eyes at the full midday beam; purging and unscaling her long abused sight at the fountain it self of heav'nly radiance.

In ringing, vehement tones, Milton proclaims in this tract his own need and right to participate in the national and religious renewal: "Give me the liberty to know, to utter, and to argue freely according to conscience, above all liberties."

DAVID LOEWENSTEIN, MILTON AND THE DRAMA OF HISTORY

(1990).

THE CITY OF REFUGE AND THE TEMPLE OF GOD

Milton's visions of the great city of refuge and the temple of God are likewise both highly expressive of his historical consciousness, revealing its crucial interconnection with his figurative discourse. These metaphorical passages, figurative expressions of Milton's radicalism, suggest that the historical process remains progressive and dynamic only when reformation permits, paradoxically, both union and conflict within the godly nation. The city of refuge passage—a vision of thriving London itself—is one of the most vivid representations of dynamic historical renovation in Milton's revolutionary prose works.

Just preceding this vision, Milton includes a prophetic passage proclaiming a new vital era of history:

> Now once again by all concurrence of signs, and by the generall instinct of holy and devout men . . . God is decreeing to begin some new and great period in his Church, ev'n to the reforming of Reformation it self: what does he then but reveal Himself to his servants, and as his manner is, first to his English-men.

One of the essential history lessons Adam learns at the end of *Paradise Lost* is that, in postlapsarian ages, God will reveal "his presence" in "many a sign" (XI. 351); indeed, Milton's visionary sense of history in *Areopagitica* reveals that the signs of God's dramatic presence now appear to the elect, warfaring Englishmen. Milton's passage emphasizes his keen awareness of great historical forces working themselves out in his age: the vast, teeming city of refuge is thus both a sign and illustration of God's active presence in history.

This depiction of London is essentially a vision of the godly nation in microcosm, engaged in a kind of perpetual ideological warfare:

> the shop of warre hath not there more anvils and hammers waking, to fashion out the plates and instruments of armed Justice in defence of beleaguer'd Truth, then there be pens and heads there, sitting by their studious lamps, musing, searching, revolving new notions and idea's wherewith to present, as with their homage and their fealty the approaching Reformation: others as fast reading, trying all things, assenting to the force of reason and convincement.

The "shop of warre" suggests that the godly people must not only challenge and refashion traditional religious and political authorities, but also keep the process of reformation in continual revolutionary activity. Rather than allowing themselves to degenerate into a state of "dull ease," the people "should be disputing, reasoning, reading, inventing, discoursing, ev'n to a rarity, and admiration." Such debates among revolutionary Puritans might well concern, as they did in the remarkable Army Debates held at Whitehall in the late 1640s, the relation of the historical and prophetic significance of Scripture to the present politics of reformation and government. What emerges again and again in *Areopagitica* is Milton's sense of the resurgent, almost tangible energy of the regenerate body politic, an energy created and sustained by the dynamics of perpetual ideological disagreement and combativeness.

Milton's portrayal of the teeming city preparing itself for war is therefore both literal (a reflection of the increasing evidence of civil war in and around London which had, in 1643, undergone a vast scheme of military fortification and defense) and symbolic—a powerful expression of Milton's dynamic vision of social transformation in history. The passage suggests that ideological confrontation and combativeness within political and religious spheres generate more and more intellectual energy, activity, and progress: "Where there is much desire to learn, there of necessity will be much arguing, much writing, many opinions; for opinion in good men is but knowledge in the making" (II, 554). Milton's emphasis here is clearly upon "knowledge in the making," upon process rather than static completion.

ARTHUR E. BARKER, MILTON AND THE PURITAN DILEMMA

(1942).

The *Areopagitica* was a defence of those who could bring "a helpful hand to the slow-moving reformation which we labour under" because truth had spoken to them "before others." Among these was to be numbered the author of *The Doctrine and Discipline of Divorce,* to whom the new *Ordinance for Printing* of June 14, 1643, seemed a disastrous renunciation of assistance. From the point of view of the Presbyterians, the restraint of printing through ministerial licensers served as a necessary protection for the reformation, now no longer attacking but entrenching itself through the Assembly and Parliament. It provided a barrier against the counter-attacks of the routed prelatists and against the clamouring extremists who threatened to undermine the one right discipline before it could be established. Milton's attack on the ordinance consequently indicates the extent to which his view of reformation had been clarified and transformed as a result of the condemnation of his opinions on divorce.

The anti-episcopal pamphlets had called for a reformation not "slow-moving" but "speedy and vehement." By 1644, Milton had come to see that it was not to be happily completed merely by "the unfrocking of a priest, the unmitring of a bishop, and the removing him from off the presbyterian shoulders"; for his own experience of Presbyterian reaction seemed to show that there were deeper sources of "this working mystery of ignorance and ecclesiastical thraldom which under new shapes and disguises begins afresh to grow upon us." Apparently Christ is not after all "ready at the door"; nor will it avail to think in terms of "Atlantic and Utopian polities which never can be drawn into use." The world is at best a place of mingled good and evil, the New Jerusalem a heavenly city. Reformation is not to be achieved at a blow and immediately upon the downfall of Babylon. Though it may be plain that episcopacy is antichristian, truth is not everywhere so imperatively obvious. It requires laborious and skilful gatherers, and even they may discover that their labours do not immediately persuade.

In Milton's second group of pamphlets the emphasis is not on reformation and divine prescript but on liberty and free reasoning. Instead of a rebuilding according to the clearly revealed pattern, reformation becomes a progressive search for truth. Thanks is to be given "for that great measure of truth" already enjoyed; but it is not to be taken for granted (as apparently by the Assembly) that "we are to pitch our tent here, and have attained the utmost prospect of reformation that the mortal glass wherein we contemplate can show us, till we come to beatific vision. . . ." In the anti-episcopal pamphlets the cloudiness of that glass had served to explain the corrupt stubbornness of episcopacy, and to demonstrate the necessity for setting divine prescript above depraved human wisdom. It now serves to demonstrate the danger of mistaking human error for divine truth, and to prove the need for unrestricted discussion of doubtful matters. Christ brought truth back to the world, and it is revealed in Scripture; but man is not yet in full possession of the truth revealed.

> Truth indeed came once into the world with her divine master, and was a perfect shape most glorious to look on; but when he ascended and his apostles after him were laid asleep, then straight arose a wicked race of deceivers who, as that story goes of the Egyptian Typhon with his conspirators, how they dealt with the good Osiris, took the virgin Truth, hewed her lovely form into a thousand pieces, and scattered them to the four winds. From that time ever since, the sad friends of Truth, such as durst appear, imitating the careful search that Isis made for the mangled body of Osiris, went up and down gathering up limb by limb still as they could find them. We have not yet found them all, Lords and Commons, nor ever shall do till her master's second coming; he shall bring together every joint and member, and shall mould them into an immortal feature of loveliness and perfection.

The divinely perfect truth of the Gospel, its sudden corruption, the return of perfection with the second coming, these ideas had found a place in the anti-episcopal pamphlets. But when Digby and Falkland had urged moderation because of man's uncertainty and the dangers of the appeal to *jus divinum,* Milton had proclaimed the certainty of the one right discipline.

The *Areopagitica* marks a significant change in the emphasis of his thought. Scripture remains for him the revelation of the divine will. But in 1641 he had thought of history as the record of the church's progressive degeneracy, and of the downfall of episcopacy as the effect of a sudden divine intervention, the prelude perhaps to the second coming. He now thinks of the future as a progression from truth to truth which will terminate only when the divine pattern is at length completely imparted to man at Christ's return. He begins to look, not backward with the orthodox Puritans to the express command of God, but forward. To that extent he becomes less the reformer than the revolutionary, especially since the achievement of the perfect pattern—though finally possible only with divine assistance—requires the human activity of "free reasoning."

This development in Milton's thinking reflects a similar development in English Puritanism. The idea of the progressiveness of reformation and the search for truth was profoundly important in the toleration controversy because it made possible a theory of liberty without destroying the fundamental assumption that all ultimate truth was enshrined, though obscurely, in Scripture.

VINCENT BLASI, THE ELLIOT LECTURE: MILTON'S *AREOPAGITICA* AND THE MODERN FIRST AMENDMENT

Yale Law School Occasional Papers: Series Two (1996).

We must not try to secularize Milton. Religious conviction was central to his thought and to that of his audience. And I do not mean the type of rationalistic, latitudinarian religious conviction that may explain the tolerationist positions of later thinkers such as Jefferson and Madison, and perhaps even John Locke. Milton read the Bible (in Hebrew and Greek) for several hours every day. He wrote an ambitious theological treatise. When his political world lay in ruins at the Stuart Restoration, a regression welcomed by the very English people in whom he had once placed so much trust, Milton's undespairing response was to complete the Christian epic for which he is best known, to "assert eternal providence, and justify the ways of God to men." Those of us who do not share his profound theological convictions may be able to profit from some features of his thought, and perhaps even employ them for our own purposes. But such a venture in intellectual scavenging must be undertaken with caution and awareness.

Let me specify three significant ideas in *Areopagitica*—the list could be much longer—that a modern reader might be tempted to draw upon in fashioning a secular argument for the freedom of speech but would be wrong to do so. In each instance, the meaning of the idea and the source of its appeal in Milton's day was so much a function of its religious underpinnings that the secular counterpart can draw no sustenance from Milton's thought.

One idea is that truth is strong and will prevail without the help of the censor's coercive assistance. This is the point of the famous "winds of doctrine" passage with its striking, if unfortunate, wrestling metaphor. Elsewhere in the tract Milton proclaims that truth "needs no policies, nor stratagems, nor licensings to make her victorious; those are the shifts and the defenses that error uses against her power." Surely his assertion regarding the likely consequences of freedom was an important part of his case, but we must realize that Milton's sweeping generalization about the strength of truth was not offered in the spirit of empirical demonstration, nor even of didactic history. Milton was simply affirming, once again, his faith in divine providence.

"For who knows not," he says, "that Truth is strong, next to the Almighty." He concedes that in turbulent times "false teachers are then busiest in seducing." Not to worry: "God then raises to his own work men of rare abilities and more than common industry . . . to go on some new enlightened steps in the discovery of truth." Even the limits of human understanding he attributes to the divine plan: "for such is the order of God's enlightening his church, to dispense and deal out by degrees his beam, so as our earthly eyes may best sustain it." Truth in Milton's cosmos is destined to prevail in due time, for a reason that can have no secular analogue.

A second feature of Milton's thought that First Amendment votaries have no business using concerns what may be the most significant step in any truth-based argument for the freedom of speech. This is the claim that the endeavor of seeking to know the truth—or to put it in less grandiose terms, to improve one's understanding—has special priority. Modern liberals are often challenged on this point, and some have not resisted the urge to enlist Milton in their defense. Several of the most eloquent passages of the *Areopagitica* exalt the importance and dignity of learning. With his absurd yet endearing exuberance at full throttle, Milton describes authors as "laboring the hardest labor in the deep mines of knowledge." He asserts that "a good book is the precious life-blood of a master spirit embalmed and treasured up on purpose to a life beyond life." He calls truth "our richest merchandise." Nor is Milton's admiration for truth seekers confined to rare persons with unusual gifts like his own. In the London of 1644, he exults, "all the Lord's people are become prophets." He plays the patriotism card in a revealing way. "England," he says, "is a nation ... prone to seek after knowledge," a "nation ... acute to invent, subtle and sinewy to discourse."

Like his faith in the strength of truth, Milton's belief in the priority of truth seeking derived from his theology. The great project that summoned the matchless talents of the English people was, in his words, "the reforming of Reformation itself." Recall his picture of London, the "mansion house of liberty" with its citizens "sitting by their studious lamps, musing, searching, revolving new notions and ideas." In the very same sentence, Milton specifies why these energetic thinkers are so hard at work: "to present, as with their homage and their fealty, the approaching Reformation." Individually no less than collectively, the virtue of "fearless scouting into the regions of sin and falsity" is to discover God's will and to do God's work, to achieve salvation, to run "for that immortal garland," to experience the spiritual struggle of "the true warfaring Christian."

I do not claim that Milton's prodigious intellectual curiosity had no secular dimension. He was a man of the Renaissance as well as the Reformation. The finest Latinist in England, he knew Virgil and Ovid almost by heart. His interest in the astronomical discoveries of his age was keen and even finds expression in the pages of *Paradise Lost.* He wrote a lengthy history of England and a brief history of Russia.

But much as Milton valued many forms of secular knowledge, the argument of *Areopagitica* is for a purposive liberty: the Christian Liberty of the Puritan saint searching after God's partially revealed truth. Milton was a Christian perfectionist, not a utilitarian. "God sure esteems the growth and completing of one virtuous person," he says, "more than the restraint of ten vicious." That is why for Milton the search for understanding is not to be balanced against the material harms it may cause—harms he fully acknowledges.

A third idea in Milton that has achieved some undeserved modern currency is that exposure to falsity is conducive to the appreciation of truth. Erroneous opinions he characterizes as "dust and cinders" that "may yet serve to polish and brighten the armory of truth." A "discreet and judicious" reader can use bad books "to discover, to confute, to forewarn, and to illustrate." More than two hundred years after Milton wrote, John Stuart Mill was to build his *Essay On Liberty* around a secular reformulation of these notions.

I have no doubt of the validity of this line of argument. In fact, I regard as possibly the two most important pages I have ever read the passage in *On Liberty* in which Mill argues, from Cicero, that a person should strive to understand his opponents' ideas with greater imagination and sympathy than he devotes to knowing his own. If every advocate and every scholar would only reread those pages before entering the lists, the world would be a better place.

The thought is magnificent, but it is not Milton's. However important falsity may be to the search for truth, or foolishness to the search for wisdom, or exaggeration to the search for accuracy, or radicalism to the search for moderation, Milton's argument in *Areopagitica* provides scant reason for a secular appreciation of uncongenial ideas. For Milton was not in pursuit of either capacious sensibility or dialectical facility, though in fact he possessed both. What he valued was the ability to resist temptation. Self-discipline in the service of God, an integral component of Christian Liberty, is for him the overriding objective of the freedom he urges upon the English nation. "That which purifies us is trial," he says, "and trial is by what is contrary." "[B]ooks freely permitted" are means, he asserts, "both to the trial of virtue and the exercise of truth." That is why "the high providence of God . . . gives us minds that can wander beyond all limit and satiety." "Trial" and "exercise"—the imagery is physical, even martial. Milton's concern here is Christian discipline and fortitude, not intellectual curiosity.

I could, if necessary, demonstrate further how thoroughly Milton's conception of truth is bound up in his religious conviction—how, for example, his emphasis on the fallibility of human judgment, rooted in the fallen condition of postlapsarian man, has little in common with modern skepticism, or how his temperamental respect for radical, seemingly bizarre ideas derived from his belief that in millennial times the Word of God can emanate from the most unlikely sources. My principal point should be clear: Those parts of Milton's argument in *Areopagitica* that rest heavily on his claims and assumptions regarding truth—its nature, its strength, its function, its importance—cannot rightly be employed to make the secular case for the freedom of speech. Furthermore, the limits Milton recognized to the principle of toleration, so much a product of his view of truth, cannot inform the modern project of defining the boundaries of expressive freedom.

So what is left? Can the *Areopagitica* help us at all as we struggle to interpret the modern First Amendment? I think so.

"If it were seriously asked," begins Milton's pamphlet *The Doctrine and Discipline of Divorce*, "and it would be no untimely question ... who of all teachers and masters that have ever taught have drawn the most disciples after him, both in religion and in manners, it might be not untruly answered Custom." Were Milton pressed to name the second most esteemed teacher through the ages, almost certainly he would have said Authority. *Areopagitica* is about more than religious truth: Milton's case for free expression depends in no small degree on his observation, repeated throughout the tract in a variety of figurations, that vitality is the defining quality of a political community, and that vitality cannot be maintained—stagnation will inevitably set in—if the prescriptions of Custom and Authority are allowed to go unchallenged. Milton's theology may be dated, or at least unconvincing to most moderns, but his grasp of political dynamics should command our attention.

Milton is often thought of as a dreamer, but he valued highly the art of shrewd observation. He was a close student and admirer of Machiavelli and adopted the Florentine as his mentor on the subject of how to write history. The *Areopagitica* is couched in the argot of political realism: "to sequester out of the world in Atlantic and Utopian polities which can never be drawn into use will not mend our condition," Milton states. Instead, he urges his countrymen to "ordain wisely ... in this world of evil." In Book VIII of *Paradise Lost*, the angel Raphael counsels Adam: "be lowly wise ... Dream not of other worlds."

The lowly wisdom of *Areopagitica* is considerable. Milton insists, for example, that the policy of licensing cannot be assessed without taking into account the capacities, incentives, working conditions, loyalties, and temperaments of the persons who will serve as licensers. "There cannot be," he says, "a more tedious and unpleasing journey-work, a greater loss of time levied upon [a man's] head, than to be made the perpetual reader of unchosen books and pamphlets, ofttimes huge volumes ... and in a hand scarce legible, whereof three pages would not down at any time in the fairest print." With such a job description, "we may easily foresee what kind of licensers we are to expect hereafter, either ignorant, imperious, and remiss, or basely pecuniary."

Milton asserts the inevitable futility of censorship and notes the pressure for more severe measures that such futility begets. Each failed regulatory venture will lead, he predicts, to additional such attempts "as will make us all both ridiculous and weary, and yet frustrate." Moreover, the effort to suppress dissident speakers often backfires, for as Bacon remarked, the "punishing of wits enhances their authority."

Still another practical feature of licensing he identifies is how responsibility for the censorial decision is often divided and accountability thereby evaded—a problem, we might believe, that also plagues the modern administrative state. "Sometimes," Milton says, "five imprimaturs are seen together dialogue-wise in the piazza of one title-page complementing and ducking each to other with their shaven reverences, whether the author, who stands by in perplexity at the foot of his epistle, shall to the press or to the sponge." This metaphor employs Catholic allusions—elsewhere he describes licensers as "glutton friars"—and so might be read to state only a particular grievance. It is important to the argument in *Areopagitica,* however, that Milton accuses the new Presbyterian censors of being as overweening and unaccountable, as "puffed up" as he puts it, as their precursors in Rome, Madrid, and Canterbury. "The episcopal arts begin to bud again," he laments, sounding like no one so much as Lord Acton.

Milton's observations concerning the corruptions of power deserve to be as numbingly familiar as they now are. No less valid, though less commonly acknowledged in the free speech controversies of our day, is his point that public order, public morality, and mutual respect among citizens cannot be achieved by coercive legislation alone. Effective control of evil and disorder, says Milton, must depend heavily on "those unwritten, or at least unconstraining laws of virtuous education, religious and civil nurture." These, as Plato recognized, are "the bonds and ligaments of the commonwealth, the pillars and sustainers of every written statute." A government that looks down upon its citizens, that dares "not trust them with an English pamphlet," will see those bonds and ligaments atrophy. The new Parliamentary censorship Milton calls a reproach to the common people, treating them as "giddy, vicious, and ungrounded ... in such a sick and weak state of faith and discretion as to be able to take nothing down but through the pipe of a licenser."

Some modern critics might respond that whether or not the people on the streets of London in 1644 were indeed "an unprincipled, unedified laic rabble" likely to stagger at "the whiff of every new pamphlet," as Milton berates the Presbyterian censors for assuming, the targets of today's demagogues answer well to that description. Never before, such critics might add, have the technologies of mass communication made the susceptibilities of audiences so dangerous. These objections have some force, I do not doubt. We must remember, however, that this is exactly the argument that gripped the regulators of Milton's day. Then the new technology of mass communication was the unlicensed pamphlet, printed in bulk, in the vernacular, no longer confined to abstruse theological disquisitions. The new audience consisted of Hobbes' masterless men, many of them previously illiterate sectaries apparently receptive to the most disruptive religious and civil nostrums. The guardians of public order doubted whether a war could be fought and the Reformation completed if the masses were subject to such unscrupulous manipulation. Milton believed, on the other hand, that the war could be won and the Reformation advanced only by permitting the unsettling free thinking to flourish.

* * *

In building an argument for free speech that emphasizes strength of character, distrust of authority and convention, and the danger of stagnation, Milton offers good reasons to believe in free speech even in a world suffused with irrationality and injustice and destined to remain so. To find in Milton wisdom that can help us give meaning to the modern First Amendment, we need not turn him into a skeptic or a democrat. It is enough that we appreciate him for what he was: a gifted and courageous writer, sympathetic to an aristocracy of merit, who explained in unforgettable prose how the freedom of speech can serve as a powerful force against rigidity and abuse. Milton has little to teach us about truth or democracy but much to teach us about corruption, accountability, character, and vitality.

STANLEY FISH, DRIVING FROM THE LETTER: TRUTH AND INDETERMINACY IN MILTON'S *AREOPAGITICA*

in Re–Membering Milton (Mary Nyquist & Margaret W. Ferguson ed. 1988).

Banish All Objects of Lust

Some years ago, a very literate professor of law with more than a casual interest in the First Amendment confessed himself surprised when I reminded him that in the *Areopagitica* Milton excludes Catholics and some others from his plea for general toleration. He hadn't remembered it that way and had always thought of Milton as an exemplary spokesman for free speech and free expression. Of course, he isn't alone. As John Illo points out, Milton's tract has almost always been read as a classic liberal plea for "complete liberty." "The preponderance of English scholarship," Illo writes, "has drawn Milton into its own liberal centre, which claims a Western and ultimately an Attic heritage of universal freedom." This is especially true in the modern day, when the *Areopagitica* (through an irony its author would have understood but not appreciated) has become a basic text supporting the ethic of disinterested inquiry, and Milton the revolutionary has become a man with the ability "to look at social issues without using the glasses of sectarian theology, which is . . . very rare in this passionate time." The writer here is Harold Laski, one of many contributors to a volume marking the three hundredth anniversary of the publication of *Areopagitica* and titled, significantly, *Freedom of Expression*. In this volume, Milton is not only the apostle of unrestrained freedom (precisely the *accusation* leveled at him by his contemporaries), he is also and "above all, a Humanist—the greatest representative in England of that movement which had abandoned the dogmatism of the middle ages and was seeking for a natural or empirical basis for its beliefs." The same encomiast declares of the *Areopagitica,* "there is no encroachment on 'the liberty to know, to utter and to argue freely' which it does not . . . oppose," apparently forgetting the encroachments that the tract itself urges. And when Mulk Raj Arnand expresses the wish that the "great passage about the value of a book" be inscribed on the luggage labels of students in India, so that "the consciences of the Customs authorities at Bombay will be touched," he seems not to realize (or seems, again, to have forgotten) that in the sentence which introduces that very passage, Milton affirms the right of the Commonwealth to keep "a vigilant eye how Bookes demeane themselves" and "thereafter to confine, imprison, and do sharpest justice on them as malefactors." Only the Dean of St. Paul's, W. R. Matthews, is apparently aware of the fact that "Milton's conception of the nature of tolerable books was limited." "It appears," he says gently, "that many who have not recently read his book have an exaggerated notion of what he urges as reasonable liberty."

That "many," as Illo reminds us, would seem to include almost the whole body of Milton scholars. There have of course been exceptions: Illo himself, writing from the left, and Willmoore Kendall, writing from the right, have argued for a Milton less generous in his ecumenism, a Milton who is not above acts of exclusion and sharp judgment. And Ernest Sirluck has given us a pragmatically political Milton who in the *Areopagitica* argues in several directions at once, hoping thereby to please the several constituencies whose support would be necessary for the revoking of the act of 1643. But by and large, in the writings and minds of most men and women, the *Areopagitica* remains what it was for those who celebrated it in 1944, and one is not surprised to find this ringing statement at the conclusion of the entry for the tract in the *Milton Encyclopedia:* "*Areop.* has long been loved by learned and literate men . . . [for] its ability . . . to inspire almost all people to a sense of the sanctity of free expression."

In what follows, I would like to continue in the direction indicated by the work of Illo and Kendall and advance a series of theses even more radical (at least in terms of received opinion) than theirs. Specifically, I will argue that Milton is finally, and in a profound way, not against licensing, and that he has almost no interest at all in the "freedom of the press" as an abstract or absolute good (and, indeed, does not unambiguously value freedom at all); and that his attitude toward books is informed by none of the reverence that presumably led the builders of the New York Public Library to have this sentence from the tract preside over their catalogue room: "A goode Booke is the precious life-blood of a master spirit, imbalm'd and treasur'd up on purpose to a life beyond life."

Let us begin with that sentence and with the famous paragraph from which it comes:

> I deny not, but that it is of greatest concernment in the Church and Commonwealth, to have a vigilant eye how Bookes demeane themselves, as well as men; and thereafter to confine, imprison, and do sharpest justice on them as malefactors: For Books are not absolutely dead things, but doe contain a potencie of life in them to be as active as that soule was whose progeny they are: nay they do preserve as in a violl the purest efficacy and extraction of that living intellect that bred them. I know they are as lively, and as vigorously productive, as those fabulous Dragons teeth; and being sown up and down, may chance to spring up armed men. And yet on the other

> hand unlesse warinesse be us'd, as good almost kill a Man as kill a good Book; who kills a Man kills a reasonable creature, Gods Image; but hee who destroyes a good Booke, kills reason it selfe, kills the Image of God, as it were in the eye. Many a man lives a burden to the Earth; but a good Booke is the pretious life-blood of a master spirit, imbalm'd and treasur'd up on purpose to a life beyond life. 'Tis true, no age can restore a life, whereof perhaps there is no great losse; and revolutions of ages doe not oft recover the losse of a rejected truth, for the want of which whole Nations fare the worse. We should be wary therefore what persecution we raise against the living labours of publick men, how we spill that season'd life of man preserv'd and stor'd up in Books; since we see a kinde of homicide may be thus committed, sometimes a martyrdome, and if it extend to the whole impression, a kinde of massacre, whereof the execution ends not in the slaying of an elementall life, but strikes at that ethereall and fift essence, the breath of reason it selfe, slaies an immortality rather than a life. But lest I should be condemn'd of introducing licence, while I oppose Licencing, I refuse not the paines to be so much Historicall, as will serve to shew what hath been done by ancient and famous Commonwealths, against this disorder, till the very time that this project of licencing crept out of the *Inquisition,* was catcht up by our Prelates, and hath caught some of our Presbyters.

The first thing to say about this passage is that, detached from the literary idealism it apparently breathes, it is decidedly *un*-Miltonic; first because it locates value and truth in a physical object, and second because the reverence it apparently recommends toward that object is dangerously close to, if not absolutely identical with, worship. The passage seems, in a word, to encourage idolatry, and that is exactly the purpose to which it has been often put when it has been cited as a central "scripture" in the "religion" of the book (the religion, that is, of humanism). This, however, is not Milton's religion. The center of his theology is the doctrine of the inner light, and his entire career can be viewed as an exercise in vigilance in which he repeatedly detects in this or that political or social or ecclesiastical program one more attempt to substitute for the authority of the inner light the false authority of some external and imposed rule. In practical and operational terms, this means that he rejects the claim of any prefabricated or ready-made formulation to contain or identify what is true and valuable, and insists on referring all questions of truth and value to the standard written by the spirit of God in the fleshly tables of the regenerate heart.

It is in this spirit (a word precisely intended) that Milton makes a series of related arguments in the *Apology* (written only a year and a half before the *Areopagitica*). He rejects set prayers in favor of "those free and unimpos'd expressions which from a sincere heart unbidden come into the outward gesture"; he rejects the rules of rhetoric and composition in favor of the "true eloquence" that inheres naturally in the speech of one who is "possest with a fervent desire to know good things, and with the dearest charity to infuse the knowledge of them into others"; he rejects any criticism of his own style that would measure it by some external decorum, and claims as a justification for his bitter vituperative and even obscene words the spirit of zeal that moves him ("there may be a sanctifi'd bitternesse against the enemies of truth"); and he insists that a true poem can be written (and by implication read) only by one who is himself "a composition and pattern of the best and honourablest things; not presuming to sing high praises of heroic men . . . unless he have in himselfe the experience and the practice of all that which is praise-worthy." We might be encouraged by this last assertion to assume that "that which is praise-worthy" or "best and honourablest" could be independently specified, but the phrase "in himselfe" insists on the internality both of those excellences and of the judgment authorized to identify them. In this and every other sentence in the *Apology,* Milton is continually alert to the danger of reifying some external form into the repository of truth and value; and it is the entire business of the tract to neutralize that danger, especially when the form it takes is superficially (another word precisely intended) attractive.

In the first edition of *The Doctrine and Discipline of Divorce* (published in 1643), the form of the danger is no less than the Bible itself. Milton's scorn in this tract is directed at those who believe that the essence of the law is to be found in its letter, in the actual words of the text; these he calls "extreme literalist[s]" and "letter bound" men: they display an "obstinate *literality*" and an "*alphabetical* servility," and have made the text into "a transcendent command" that is "above the worship of God and the good of man." "Wee cannot," Milton thunders, "safely assent to any precept written in the Bible, but as charity commends it to us," and charity is an attribute not of the text, which, like anything else, can be "congeal'd into a stony rigor," but of the interpreter. "The way to get a sure undoubted knowledge of things,", Milton advises (following Saint Paul), is not to confine oneself to "textual restrictions," but "to hold that for truth, which accords most with charity;" and it is with the rule of charity as an interpretive key that Milton proceeds to set aside the apparent meaning of Christ's words touching divorce in favor of the meaning dictated by a charity whose precepts he knows because they are written in his heart. This refusal to equate wisdom and truth with what is written in a book, even if the book is the Bible, will later lead him in the *Christian Doctrine* to reject the authority of the Ten Commandments because he follows the Pauline rule that "whatever is not in accordance with faith, is sin"—which is something quite different, he points out, from holding that "whatever is not in accordance with the ten commandments is sin." And later still, this fierce anti-literalism turns into an even fiercer anti-literaryism as the Christ of *Paradise Regained* declares that the reading of books is "wearisome" and that he "who reads / Incessantly, and to his reading brings not / A spirit and judgment equal or superior, / (And what he brings, what needs he elsewhere seek), / Uncertain and unsettl'd still remains, / Deep verst in books and shallow in himself."

If we return from this brief excursion into Milton's other writings (and additional examples could have easily been adduced) to the *Areopagitica,* the paragraph that offers so extravagant a praise of books looks very curious indeed. First of all, the notion that the essence of mind can be "stored up" in a "violl" sounds less like Milton than like Comus when he offers his magic potion to the Lady with the claim that "one sip of this / Will bathe the drooping spirits in delight / Beyond the bliss of dreams. Be wise and taste." (The Lady, you will recall, is nourished by the "something holy" that "lodges in that breast," something she carries within her and not in her hand, like a cup or a book.) It is also strange to hear Milton asserting that the spirit of a man can be abstracted from the conditions of its daily exercise, and that the truth which finds expression in varied and "unbidden" outward gestures can be so perfectly captured in one of those gestures that it can be "preserved" (in amber, as it were) between the covers of a book. And it is stranger still to find Milton displaying what he himself would describe as a papist idolatry of relics when he exalts the dead letter of a physical object ("imbalm'd" and "preserv'd" indeed) above the living labors of faithful men, and dismisses as "no great losse" the truth that perishes with a life, reserving for the loss of an "impression" or edition the vocabulary of homicide and massacre. It is almost as if he were writing an early draft of the sonnet on the Waldensians and had decided to begin that poem not with "Avenge O Lord thy slaughtered saints" but with "Avenge O Lord thy slaughtered books."

I do not, however, want to rest my case for the falseness of this passage on what Milton had previously written or on what he would later write. My best evidence comes from those places in the *Areopagitica* itself where Milton gives voice to sentiments that undermine (if they do not flatly contradict) any argument for the sanctity of books. Consider, for example, a sentence, some thirteen pages further on in the tract, that begins, "Banish all objects of lust." The phrase "objects of lust" is ambiguous between two readings; it can mean "banish all lustful objects"—that is, all objects that have, as a special property, the capacity to provoke lust; or it can mean banish all objects to which an already existing lust can attach itself. The attraction of the first reading is that it specifies a course of action that can be followed—"Let's get rid of these lust-provoking objects"—while in the second reading the recommended course of action is self-defeating because it would require the banishing of everything.

As it turns out, however, the second reading is the correct one: "Banish all objects of lust, shut up all youth into the severest discipline that can be exercis'd in any hermitage, ye cannot make them chaste that came not hither so." That is to say, chastity is a property not of objects but of persons; and one can neither protect it nor promote it by removing objects from the world. Indeed, even if one went to the impossible lengths of removing all objects, the flourishing of lust and other sins would continue unabated, for, "Though ye take from a covetous man all his treasure, he has yet one jewell left, yet cannot bereave him of his covetousnesse"; and with that "covetousnesse" as the driving force of his very being, such a man will populate the world—even if it is only the inner world of his imagination—with the objects of his desire, with the objects of lust.

It is easy to see how this line of reasoning fits into the case against licensing: insofar as licensing is urged as a means of combating sin, it is, as Milton says, "far insufficient to the end which it intends," because sin does not reside in the objects licensing would remove. But, curiously, if this is a strong argument against licensing (and it is so strong that Milton makes it at least six times), it is equally strong as an argument against the alternative to licensing, the free and unconstrained publishing of books. For it follows that if men and not books are the source of sin, then men and not books are the source of virtue; and if sin will not be diminished by removing its external occasion, then virtue will not be protected by preserving its external representation. If the banishing of books will not eradicate sin, then neither will it prevent the flourishing of virtue; for as conditions of the will rather than of the world, both sin and virtue are independent of the materials on which they happen to operate.

In short, the argument against licensing, which has always been read as an argument *for* books, is really an argument that renders books beside the point: books are no more going to save you than they are going to corrupt you; by denying their potency in one direction, Milton necessarily denies their potency in the other and undercuts the extravagant claims he himself makes in the passage with which we began. Whatever books are, they cannot be what he says they are in those ringing sentences—the preservers of truth, the life-blood of a master spirit, the image of God.

We Bring Impurity Much Rather

Why then does he say it? It will be the business of this chapter to answer that question, and we can begin by noting that at least on the local level he says it *in order* to move away from it. As the prose reaches the rapturous height of calling books an "ethereall and fift essence" and "the breath of reason itself," and seems about to take off into the empyrean, Milton suddenly applies the brakes: "But lest I should be condemn'd of introducing licence, while I oppose Licensing." As it turns out this rhetorical flourish looks forward to the historical digression of the succeeding paragraph, but for a moment it also refers backward to the license Milton has himself committed in transforming books—which are, after all, only objects—into the means and vehicle of grace. The moment passes quickly, almost before it has registered, but it is enough, I think, to cast the shadow of a qualification on what has just been said, a qualification we carry with us as we move into the brief history of "what hath been done by ancient and famous Commonwealths, against this disorder."

By "this disorder," Milton means license, the supposed harm that follows from allowing books to be "as freely admitted into the World as any other birth." It is this liberal practice, Milton tells us, that characterized the societies he is about to survey; and one would expect the point of the ensuing history to be that in these "ancient and famous Commonwealths" the absence of licensing would have as one of its effects the flourishing of virtue. Indeed, this is a directed expectation, given the praise of books as the privileged containers ("violls") of truth and reason, but it is an expectation that is disappointed by a history that never achieves so sharp a focus. Milton begins with what one would think would be his strongest example—the city of Athens, "where Books and wits were ever busier than in any other part of *Greece*;" but rather than celebrating the benefits of this "busyness," he turns immediately to the measures taken by the Athenians to curtail it, and finds "only two sorts of writings which the Magistrate car'd to take notice of; those either blasphemous ... or Libellous." The tonal instability of this section is established immediately by "car'd to take notice of" which hesitates between an expression of approval for the magistrate's restraint and the suggestion that if he had been properly vigilant, he would have taken notice of *more.* That suggestion is given an additional half-life when Milton lists the "sects and opinions" of which the magistrate "tooke no heed" and characterizes them in ways that are strongly judgmental: they are in general "tending to voluptuousnesse" and include "that libertine school of *Cyrene*" and "what the *Cynick* impudence utter'd" and "*Aristophanes* the loosest of them all."

When the survey turns from Greece to Rome the double argument continues, as Milton simultaneously reports on the restraint exercised by magistrates who decline to license and describes the fruits of that restraint (or, more precisely, absence of restraint) in terms that call into question its wisdom. Is it, after all, a good or a bad thing that the "naked plainness" of Lucilius and Catullus and the "wanton" poems of Ovid are allowed to do their work unchecked? This question is never asked in so many words, but Milton's judgmental vocabulary is continually implying it; and, moreover, there is nothing to counter the question on the other side, no instancing of books whose publication is casually related to a virtuous result. The only books Milton ever mentions are those that were allowed to appear despite the fact that they were impious or impudent or scurrilous or loose; it is this fact (established ever so casually but with a cumulative force) that dominates the history Milton surveys, a history which therefore makes the rather narrow and negative point that in a number of societies—some good, some bad, some cultured, some brutish—the absence of prepublication licensing doesn't seem to have made very much difference at all.

Significantly, the lack of a difference goes in both directions: not only is it the case that what Milton will later call "promiscuous reading" did no particular harm; neither, at least on the evidence offered here, did it do any particular good. It seems in fact a "thing indifferent" not correlated in any observable way with the moral status of a commonwealth; and if licensing is thus indifferently related to the production or protection of virtue, so also are books, and the entire history becomes discontinuous with the encomium that introduces it. Rather than providing concrete instances of the extent to which truth and reason are preserved in books, this brief and rather ragged sketch says nothing at all of truth and reason and does not encourage us to draw any conclusion from the fact that until the Inquisition "Books were ... freely admitted into the World"—except the disturbing conclusion, implicit in Milton's judgmental asides, that if *he* had been in a position of authority, that freedom would have been severely restricted.

It is only after the history has been concluded that Milton takes up the question it might have been expected to answer: "what is to be thought in generall of reading Books, ... and whether be more the benefit, or the harm that thence proceeds?" Earlier, when it seemed that what was or was not *in* books was going to be the issue, this would have been just the right question, and one would have had every confidence that it would be answered by a demonstration that the benefit far outweighed the harm, especially since it is through books (or at least it is so asserted) that man has access to "reason itselfe" and the "Image of God." Now, however, in the wake of the inconclusive account of Greek and Roman practice, the question sounds oddly, as if it were posed by someone who hadn't yet realized that the agenda it assumes—the agenda of separating the bad from the good in books—has more or less been abandoned. Nevertheless, that someone pushes on, and offers as a first defense of books the political argument that "heathen learning" is necessary if Christians are to be able to defend themselves against the attack of their pagan enemies. If this sounds reasonable, it also sounds weak, at least in the context of the much stronger claims that have already been made. (It is also an argument with which Satan tempts Christ in *Paradise Regained.*) It is further weakened, at least as a straightforward defense, by the example that is adduced to support it: Jerome's dream of having been whipped by an angel for reading Cicero. Milton attributes the dream to the "politick drift" of "the Divell," who presumably wished to deprive Jerome of Cicero's wisdom; and he adds that "had an Angel bin his discipliner," Jerome would have been more properly chastised not for "grave *Cicero*" but "for scurill Plautus whome he confesses to have bin reading not long before." But if the intention here is to defend the free reading of pagan books, it is hardly furthered by the phrase "scurill Plautus," which (like similar phrases in the history) suggests not freedom but the need for more restraints than are present in Jerome's dream, whoever was its inspirer. Once again the *Areopagitica* displays a curious inability to settle down and to pursue unambiguously the line of argument that was so strongly promised when books were the object of an apparently unqualified praise.

But then, almost before we know it, the tract takes a decisive turn and apparently stabilizes (at least for the moment) when Milton counters Jerome's dream with a vision reported by Dionysius Alexandrinus as he was debating with himself whether or not it was lawful to "venture ...

among" the "defiling volumes" of "hereticks." Milton identifies this second vision as one "sent from God," who speaks to Dionysius in these words: "Read any books what ever come to thy hands, for thou art sufficient both to judge aright, and to examine each matter." This "revelation," as Milton terms it, decides the issue by dissolving it, by transferring the question of value from books, of whatever kind, to Dionysius, who is "sufficient" in the strong sense of *self*-sufficient, capable by virtue (literally) of what is already in him of turning all that he reads into good. Lest we miss the point, Milton drives it home by supplementing Dionysius' citation from Thessalonians ("Prove all things, hold fast that which is good") with "another remarkable saying of the same Author: To the pure all things are pure," which is then immediately and powerfully glossed: "not only meats and drinks, but all kinde of knowledge whether of good or evil; the knowledge cannot defile, nor consequently the books, if the will and conscience be not defil'd." In this declaration Dionysius' anxiety about "defiling volumes" is countered by simply denying that volumes defile; indeed, in this respect books are even more "things indifferent" than meats, for while "bad meats will scarce breed good nourishment in the healthiest concoction," bad books "to a ... judicious Reader serve ... to discover, to confute, to forwarn, and to illustrate." Of course, by the end of this sentence, there are no bad books, in the sense of books that can in and of themselves do harm; for all books, once they enter into the heart of the judicious reader, become the occasion and means by which that judiciousness is exercised and extended. But by the same reasoning, neither are there any good books, in the sense of books that can in and of themselves produce wisdom; for as Milton says within a few pages, if "a wise man like a good refiner can gather gold out of the drossiest volume, ... a fool will be a fool with the best book, yea or without book." The logic of this is inescapable and certainly supports the conclusion that licensing will bring no benefits, since the absence of what we keep from a fool "will be no hindrance to his folly;" but it also supports the corollary conclusion that whatever we make available to a wise man will not be essential to his wisdom, for he will be wise with any book, "yea or without book."

At this point the argument of the *Areopagitica* seems simply to have reversed itself. Where at first the question to be answered was whether the power in books will work for good or evil (a question directly related to the case for and against prepublication licensing), by the time Milton declares that all things are pure to the pure the issue is no longer what is or is not in books, but what is or is not in persons; and consequently it has become a matter of indifference as to whether or not books are licensed, since, at least by the arguments that have so far been marshaled, the flourishing of *either* good or evil does not depend on books. From here, there is a straight line to the sentence that begins "banish all objects of lust" (a recommendation that makes sense only if books are the source either of lust or of virtue) and ends by asserting that "ye cannot make them chaste that came not hither so."

But if the new point of the *Areopagitica* is that men and not books are the repository of purity, then it is a point that barely survives its own introduction; for within a page of saying that all things are pure to the pure, Milton also says that "we bring not innocence into the world, we bring impurity much rather," and by saying this he immediately problematizes what had for a moment seemed to be a resolution (or a dissolution) of the dilemma initially posed, to license or not to license. After all, it isn't much help to observe that purity is a condition of the heart and therefore independent of external pressures and stimuli, if all of our hearts enter the world in a condition of impurity. This impurity is one of the reasons licensing must be numbered among the "vain and impossible attempts" ("how shall the licensers themselves be confided in unlesse we can confer upon them, or they assume to themselves above all others ... the grace of infallibility and uncorruptednesse?"), but it is also a reason for something close to despair, since it leaves mysterious the process by which purity or even its near approximation can be achieved. If licensing is "far insufficient to the end which it intends," both because the "end" is not an external but an internal state and because we enter life *already* fallen from that state, then it would seem that licensing's insufficiency is general and that there is *nothing* we can do "to repair the ruins of our first parents." If purity can be found neither in books, where it first seemed to reside, nor in naturally pure hearts, where the argument next seemed to place it, then it cannot be found anywhere.

That in fact turns out to be the right conclusion, but with a difference that redeems its negativity; for in the very same sentence that proclaims our congenital impurity Milton introduces us to its remedy: "Assuredly we bring not innocence into the world, we bring impurity much rather: that which purifies us is triall and triall is by what is contrary." If virtue is not to be found anywhere—either in a book or in an object, or even in a heart—it is because it must be *made,* and it can be made only by sharpening it against the many whetstones provided by the world, by "what is contrary." Not only does this give a positive direction to an argument that has for a while emphasized only what cannot be done and what will not succeed; it also reanimates the question of licensing and makes it once again weighty. For if the emergence of virtue depends on the availability of materials against which it can be exercised, then it follows that the more materials the better—which means, in turn, the more books there are, the better; and that is why, after the tract has unfolded almost half its length, Milton can finally offer a coherent and noncontradictory argument against licensing: anyone who thinks that he can "remove sin by removing the matter of sin" is mistaken, because sin is a feature not of the outer but of the inner landscape and can be removed (if that is the word) only when that landscape is transformed; and since that transformation can be accomplished only by a continual exercise of the faculty of judgment, it is crucial that the judgment be supplied with occasions for its exercise. Although licensing is offered as a way of promoting virtue, it will operate to eliminate the conditions of virtue's growth by removing the materials on which growth can feed: "look how much we thus expell of sin, so much we expell of vertue; for the matter of them is both the same"; we cannot, therefore, afford to abridge or scant "those means, which books freely permitted are, both to the triall of vertue and to the exercise of truth." Once again, then, books are declared to be absolutely essential to the maintenance of truth and virtue—not, however, because truth and virtue reside in books (as they were said to so many paragraphs ago), but because it is by (the indifferent) means of books that men and women can make themselves into the simulacra of what no book could ever contain.

But this may seem a long way around the barn. If Milton had wanted to tell us (as he now tells us) that books are "necessary to the constituting of human vertue"—as opposed to being the very essence of virtue—why didn't he just come right out and say so in the first place? Why go through the indirect route of first glorifying books excessively and then demonstrating that they cannot possibly be the repository of glory, but can only play an instrumental role in its emergence? The question is its own answer once one realizes that it amounts to asking: Why didn't he simply hand over the truth he wished us to have? To have done so, or rather to claim to have done so, would have been to claim for the *Areopagitica* the very capacity it denies to all other books: the capacity of being the repository of what no book can contain, because it can be written only in the fleshly tables of the heart. In short, if the *Areopagitica* is to be faithful to the lesson it teaches, it cannot teach that lesson directly; rather, it must offer itself as the occasion for the trial and exercise that are necessary to the constituting of human virtue. It must become an instrument in what Milton will later call "knowledge in the making."

The tract performs this self-effacing office in two related ways. First it continually comments on its own inability to capture the truth that informs it. In the very first paragraph, Milton reports that he is in the grip of a "power" within him that simply will not respect the decorums of the formal oration; and as a result he finds himself speaking with a "passion" one does not usually find in a preface. A few pages later he makes a valiant attempt to monitor and control his discourse by "laying before" his readers the order of his arguments, but soon after he has concluded his inconclusive history he finds himself in danger of departing from that order and he catches himself up: "But I have first to finish, as was propounded." He then gets himself back on track and is apparently proceeding according to plan, when suddenly he finds that he is already in the midst of making a point that was to have come later—finds, as he puts it, that the truth has prevented or anticipated him "by being clear already while thus much hath bin explaining." In other words, he has been surprised by truth, and in response he exclaims, "See the ingenuity of Truth, who when she gets a free and willing hand, opens herself faster than the pace of method and discours can overtake her."

The image here is one that will loom larger and larger: it is of a truth that is always running ahead of any attempt to apprehend it, a truth that repeatedly slips away from one's grasp, spills out of one's formulations, and escapes the nets that for a moment promise to catch it. Here that net is the tract itself, which is at this moment disqualifying itself as a vehicle of the truth it wants to convey; but at the same time and by the very same process, it is playing its part in the fashioning of another vehicle, one more able to bear the inscription of the Holy Ghost's pen. That vehicle is the heart of the reader, who is the direct beneficiary of the *Areopagitica*'s failure, or, to be more precise, of Milton's strategy. That strategy is one we have been tracking from the beginning of this chapter: it involves encouraging the reader to a premature act of concluding or understanding, which is then undone or upset by the introduction of a new and complicating perspective. As we have seen, this happens not once but repeatedly, as the reader is first allowed to assume that the point at issue is the purity or impurity to be found in books, and then is told that the content of books (or any other object) is a thing indifferent relative to the purity or impurity already in persons, and finally (or is it finally?) is reminded that all persons are congenitally impure ("we bring impurity much rather") and that therefore the problem must be entirely rethought. The result is, of course, disorienting, but it is also salutary, for in the process of being disoriented the reader is provoked to just the kind of labor and exercise that is necessary to the constitution of his or her own virtue. Thus, by continually defaulting on its promise—the promise of separating the true from the false—the *Areopagitica* offers itself as a means by which its readers can realize that promise in their very activities. In this way, the tract becomes at once an emblem and a casualty of the lesson it teaches: the lesson that truth is not the property of any external form, even of a form that proclaims this very truth.

Pitching Our Tents Here

It is a strategy supremely pedagogical, and one that Milton both describes and names within the year in *Tetrachordon,* as he turns his attention to the manner of Christ's teaching. Milton is particularly struck by Christ's habit of breaking the external, written law in order to fulfill the law of charity; and he compares Christ's actions with the gnomic form of his precepts, and finds that both have the advantage of preventing his followers from too easily identifying the way of virtue with a portable and mechanical rule. "Therefore it is," says Milton, "that the most evangelick precepts are given us in proverbiall formes, to drive us from the letter, though we love ever to be sticking there." By "letter" Milton means any prefabricated, external, and codified packaging of the truth, any identification of the truth with a piece of the world or a piece of behavior or a piece of language that may or may not be its local expression. The opposite of the letter is spirit; and it is the nature of spirit always to resist any attempt to circumscribe or delineate it. Spirit or the law of love is a disposition or orientation of the human heart, an orientation that can take many forms—of action, writing, thought—but cannot be equated with any one of them. To mistake a possible manifestation of the spirit for the spirit itself is to have literalized it and to have made that manifestation into an idol, just as Eve does when, in the first effect of the original sin, she worships a tree. Of course most versions of idolatry are less obviously absurd than Eve's, and since all idolatry presents the opportunity of substituting some easy formula (such as the Ten Commandments) for the strenuous life of following the spirit, it is a persuasive and powerful human temptation—which is why we love ever to be sticking to the letter, and why, too, we must always be driven from it.

In the *Areopagitica* we are continually being driven from the letter, first from the quite literal letter of books, and then from the letter as represented by the history of Athens and Rome, and then from the letter of a comforting, but finally too comforting, Scripture ("to the pure all things are pure"). Of course all of these letters, along with others that could be instanced, are provided by the *Areopagitica* itself, which also provides the arguments that make them momentarily attractive; so that one of the letters the tract is driving us from is itself, as we are not allowed the comfort and false security of sticking to or with any of the formulations it presents in what is finally a self-canceling sequence. By saying you won't find it there—in books, in history, in verses of Scripture—the *Areopagitica* is also saying you won't find it *here*—in the pages of this tract—and finally saying that you won't find it at all, because you can only become it, which is what the tract in its small and self-sacrificing way is helping you to do.

It is a help the need for which is self-replenishing. That is, driving from the letter is a strategy that can have no end, for each time it succeeds it generates the conditions that once again make it necessary: the very act of demonstrating that truth and virtue do not reside "here" will always have the side effect of suggesting that they will instead be found "there"; and at that moment, "there" becomes a new letter from which we must then be driven. The only positive lesson the *Areopagitica* teaches (a lesson it also exemplifies) is the lesson that we can never stop, and it receives a particularly powerful (although of course not definitive) formulation when Milton declares that "he who thinks we are to pitch our tents here and have attain'd the utmost prospect of reformation that the mortall glasse wherein we contemplate, can shew us, till we come to *beatific* vision, that man by this very opinion declares, that he is yet farre short of Truth." By "here" Milton means both the present state of human knowledge and understanding and this particular moment in his own tract. Whatever place or object or condition holds out the possibility of rest and attainment has at that moment become a letter, the occasion for idolatry (and for self-worship, since the temptation is to be satisfied with what one can see by looking in the mirror of one's present opinion rather than to be drawn forward by the future prospect that is not so much disclosed as promised by another "mortall glass," the newly discovered telescope).

As this sentence shows, one of those occasions can even be the Reformation, which for Milton is not a turning back of the clock to some prior state of apostolic purity, but a life-long response to an exhortation with which no one of us can ever comply: "be ye perfect." Although the letter of that exhortation can never be adhered to, one can adhere to its spirit by always looking beyond the prospect one has attained. Those who think of the Reformation as a finite program or agenda—as a series of steps at the end of which the job will have been done and the goal accomplished—make exactly the same mistake that is made by the proponents of licensing: they think that the issues of the moral life, of the attempt to align oneself with the will of God and with truth, can be settled once and for all by a single action (and the point holds even if the action has several steps). The would-be licensers think that the moral life will be perfected when the landscape has been cleared of all objects of lust; the reformers think that the moral life will be perfected when, in accordance with the precepts of Zwingli and Calvin, we have divested ourselves of some of the trappings of popery. In their different ways, both groups bring about "a dull ease and cessation of our knowledge" and "starch us" into as "stanch and solid peece of frame-work, as any January could freeze together." The "laziness of a licensing Church" is also the laziness of a church that is "ever staring on" the light given us by the early reformers, and does not receive that light as a beacon inviting us always "to discover onward things more remote from our [present] knowledge." Licensing and the premature closure of a weak Reformation are alike forms of a single temptation: the temptation to substitute for the innumerable and inconclusive acts that make up the process by which the self is refined and purified some *external* form of purification that can be mechanically applied. It is a temptation felt by every one of Milton's heroes (even the young Jesus of *Paradise Regained*), and it is a temptation that Milton makes the readers of *Areopagitica* feel again and again as he beckons us forward in the name of a truth that always escapes his formulations and our straining apprehensions.

This pattern of seeking and *not* finding is most spectacularly displayed in those passages in which the nature of truth is the overt subject. As we first come upon it, the assertion that a "man may be the heretick in the truth" seems available to a comfortable reading in which an independent truth can be held by a man in one of two ways: either with personal conviction or simply on the strength of what someone else—a pastor, a pope—had told him. Only the first kind of holding is authentic, and as for someone who does the other, "the very truth he holds becomes his heresie." But if the logic of this distinction is pursued, the very notion of a truth that one can hold either rightly or wrongly is problematized; for on the one hand a truth that has not been internalized is no longer the truth, and is merely an empty letter, while on the other a truth sincerely held cannot be given a literal form such that it can be said that someone else is not really holding "it." There is no "it" that is detachable from the holding or being held, and therefore no real sense can be given to the phrase "heretick in the truth." Insofar as it seems for a moment to have a sense, it is itself one more letter—one more invitation to premature closure—from which we must be driven.

We are driven from it again in a sequence that begins with a famous question: "Who ever knew Truth put to the wors in a free and open encounter?" Here truth and falsehood are imagined as opposing armies—clearly distinguishable—that meet on a battlefield. But as the military image is developed, its configurations change; suddenly truth is no longer a property of one of the contending forces, but is rather what will emerge when the reasons of one adversary prove themselves superior to the reasons of the other. Rather than being a participant in the battle, truth is now the name of its outcome; the distinguishability of truth from falsehood is not something with which we begin, but something we must achieve by marching out "into the plain" and trying "the matter by dint of argument."

Truth, in short, has receded from our view, but the rhetoric of the passage still allows us to assume that she will once again come into focus if only we allow "the wars of truth" to continue without prior restraint. The point is made by a comparison of truth with Proteus, the notorious shape shifter and emblem of deception. Proteus, Milton reminds us, would appear in his own shape only when he was bound; but in the case of truth it is exactly the reverse: if you bind or constrain her, "she turns herself into all shapes, except her own." The moral is clear: "give her but room," allow those who claim to know her to contend in the field, and she will soon be discernible.

But that moral becomes unavailable with the very next sentence: "Yet is it not impossible that she may have more shapes than one." But if she has more shapes than one, then she has no shape and is exactly like Proteus—a figure who escapes every attempt to bind her, even when that attempt takes the form of a carefully staged battle at the end of which she is to emerge. The notion of a battle, which seemed at the beginning of this passage to promise an eventual cessation to our labors, now delivers the same inconclusiveness we have met so many times before; and when Milton concludes this sequence by declaring that "Truth may be on this side, or on the other, without being unlike her self," the reflexive pronoun is an almost mocking reminder that the object of our quest has never more escaped us than when we think to have it in view, and is *always* unlike herself.

That object is held out as a lure and a temptation in still another passage, perhaps the most famous of all. It begins with a sad tale. Once upon a time, "Truth indeed came ... into the world ... and was a perfect shape, most glorious to look on"; but then "a wicked race of deceivers ... hewd her lovely form into a thousand pieces." One might say, then, that truth has receded from this story before it even begins; but all, it would seem, is not lost, for the dismemberment of truth has left us with a definite task—the task of "gathering up limb by limb," still as we can find them, the pieces of her body. "We have not yet found them all,'' says Milton, an observation that would seem preliminary to one more exhortation to continue in our search and not to pitch our tents here. But then he adds something much more devastating in its apparent finality: ''nor ever shall doe, till her Masters second comming.''

This is at once the low point and the high point of the tract for the readers who wish to derive from it an understanding of their situation and of the possibilities that situation offers for achieving genuine knowledge. It is a low point because it denies the possibility of ever achieving knowledge and thereby renders the search pointless, of no more efficacy than licensing; but it is the high point if we are able to apply the lesson the *Areopagitica* has repeatedly taught—the lesson that knowledge and truth are not measurable or containable entities, properties of this or that object, characteristics of this or that state, but *modes of being,* inward dispositions, conditions of a heart always yearning for new revelations. In the context of that lesson the fact that we will never succeed in finding every limb and member loses its poignancy; because in the very act of searching, of exercising our judgments and faculties in the manner the tract at once urges and provokes, we are in the process of transforming ourselves into that which we vainly seek. The search is futile only if we conceive of it as a search for something external to us, as a kind of giant jigsaw puzzle made up of precut and prefabricated pieces; but if we think of the search as the vehicle by means of which our knowledge is ''in the making'' and our virtue is in the constituting, then it is always and already succeeding even when, as in this story, it is forever failing. We will indeed never find all the pieces of truth, but if we nevertheless persist in our efforts, when Christ finally does come to ''bring together every joynt and member'' each of us shall be one of them.

The moral, then, is not ''Seek and ye shall find,'' but ''Seek and ye shall become.'' And what we shall become, in a curious Miltonic way, is a licenser, someone who is continually exercising a censorious judgment of the kind that Milton displays when he casually stigmatizes much of Greek and Roman literature as loose or impious or scurrilous. This is the judgment not of one who is free of constraints but of one whose inner constraints are so powerful that they issue immediately and without reflection in acts of discrimination and censure. Ironically it is only by permitting what licensing would banish—the continual flow of opinions, arguments, reasons, agendas—that the end of licensing—the fostering of truth—can be accomplished; accomplished not by the external means that licensing would provide, but by making ourselves into the repository of the very values that licensing misidentifies when it finds them in a world free of defiling books. Books are no more the subject of the *Areopagitica* than is free speech; both are subordinate to the process they make possible, the process of endless and proliferating interpretations whose goal is not the clarification of truth, but the making of us into members of her incorporate body so that we can be finally what the Christ of *Paradise Regained* is said already to be: a living oracle (*PR,* I, 460).

To be a living oracle is to be a totally unified being, one whose "heart / Contains of good, wise, just, the perfect shape" (*PR,* III, 10–11). This, however, is the condition only of Christ; all other men exist at a distance from that which would make them whole, exist in that state of seeking and searching which for Milton marks at once the deficiency and the glory of this vale of tears. Like the moment of mortality, the moment of the *Areopagitica* is situated between two absent unities, one always and already lost, the other to be realized only in the absorption of those consciousnesses that now yearn for it. Although truth "indeed came once into her divine Master and was a perfect shape most glorious to look on," she has long since withdrawn, leaving us to the delusive attraction of those many shapes that would compel us in her name; and although she shall one day be reassembled "into an immortall feature of loveliness and perfection," that day is ever deferred and is only projected that much more into the future each time its dawning is prematurely proclaimed.

Meanwhile, man lives in the gap. Indeed, he *is* the gap, a being defined negatively by the union which perpetually escapes him, and which, once achieved, will mark the cessation of his separateness, his end, in two senses. The impurity we bring into the world is the impurity of difference, of not being one with God; yet it is because of that impurity that difference must not be denied or lamented but embraced; for given the condition in which we all labor—the condition of inevitable fallibility—any unity we might achieve would be a false unity, a conformity not with truth but with some temporally limited project that has solicited our idolatrous worship. The temptation of idolatry, of surrendering ourselves to the totalizing claims of some ephemeral agenda, can be resisted only by the relentless multiplication of that which signifies our lack, the relentless multiplication of difference. We will be "wise in spirituall architecture" only if we build with dissimilar—disunified—materials: "there must be many schisms and many dissections made in the quarry and in the timber, ere the house of God can be built."

This allows us for a moment to assume that in time the house of God will in fact be built, but this is exactly like the assumption, so often encouraged, that the truth will finally emerge, and it is immediately disappointed: "And when every stone is laid artfully together, it cannot be united into a continuity, it can but be contiguous in this world." The first half of this sentence increases the expectation that the second half will report an eventual triumph (when every stone is laid artfully together, the building will be complete), but the triumph is, as it has been so many times before, deferred, and we are left with more of the same—that is, with more difference, with side-by-side (in space and time) efforts which do not cohere except insofar as they signify, in a variety of ways, their own insufficiency and incompleteness. It is an incompleteness that must be at once lamented and protected; lamented because it is the sign of our distance from bliss, protected because as such a sign it is a perpetual reminder that bliss awaits us in a union we can achieve (precisely the wrong word) only when we are absorbed by another into a structure not made by human hands.

ERNEST SIRLUCK, INTRODUCTION

in The Complete Prose Works of John Milton,
Volume Two (Ernest Sirluck ed. 1959).

The tactics, then, may be defined fairly clearly. They consist of what may be called a negative and a positive maneuver. The negative maneuver is to define the opposition as restrictively as the most favorable reading of the situation will permit; then to isolate it; and finally to discredit it. The positive maneuver is to construct a coalition from all available elements, each appealed to on grounds of both principle and interest; and then to depict this coalition as being the nation. Milton's faith in these tactics may be judged from the fact that, with astonishingly little modification, they dominated the whole of his subsequent polemic.

The Limits of Toleration

The extent of the toleration Milton recommends is consistent with these tactics. He is careful not to jeopardize his appeal to the Erastians and other conservatives by letting them wonder whether he is demanding a general toleration; they are assured that he is only speaking of "those neighboring differences, or rather indifferences ... which ... need not interrupt *the unity of Spirit.*" At the same time, he has no intention of imperilling the existing tolerationist coalition by menacing specific sects with exclusion. His toleration is limited on the left in a way which few would think directed at themselves: "that ... which is impious or evil absolutely either against faith or maners no law can possibly permit." (We are reminded of the deliberately coalitionist language, a few days later, of *A Paraenetick,* asking "liberty ... for every way not scandalous.")

Milton is more precise about his limits on the right: "I mean not tolerated Popery, and open superstition, which as it extirpats all religions and civill supremacies, so it self should be extirpat, provided first that all charitable and compassionat means be us'd to win and regain the weak and the misled." Virtually everyone in 1644 who stopped short of general toleration excluded Roman Catholicism. Some Independents who, in the first enthusiasm of the new policy, included Roman Catholicism in their toleration, soon found it a tactical necessity to draw back. But Milton is more severe than was tactically necessary. Some who denied Roman Catholics the public practice of their religion nevertheless forbade the magistrate to inquire into their consciences. Milton's use of the word "open" may seem to raise the possibility that he shared this position, but it would be hard to argue this. Not only does he not make the distinction between belief and practice, but he speaks of "extirpating" Popery—hardly the word one would choose if one meant only to forbid public practice. Rather, Milton's phrase, "Popery, and open superstition," appears to cover the two aspects of Roman Catholicism which, in his opinion, render it intolerable: allegiance to the pope and what he thinks patent or "open" superstition.

If Milton was harsher toward Roman Catholicism than was tactically necessary, what were his reasons?

Partly his view that "it extirpats all . . . civill supremacies." In the seventeenth century the Roman Catholic church's claim to prescriptive authority over the conduct of the believer, even in his capacity of citizen, was very widely considered a standing subversion, or threat of subversion, of national sovereignty. Milton's first two entries under *Subditus* in his Commonplace Book are examples of the voiding by the Vatican of the allegiance of subjects to their kings; and at the end of his life he spells out a final time the argument implied in his quick phrase here: "The Pope . . . pretends right to Kingdoms and States, and especially to this of *England,* Thrones and Unthrones Kings, and absolves the people from their obedience to them."[5] Many of the tolerationists of 1644 excepted Roman Catholics on this ground, nor was the view peculiar to Puritans. Writing three years after the *Areopagitica,* Jeremy Taylor took the same ground:

> Such Doctrines as these, The Pope may dispence with all oathes taken to God or man: He may absolve Subjects from their Allegiance to their naturall Prince: Faith is not to be kept with Hereticks, Hereticall Princes may be slaine by their Subjects. These Propositions are so deprest, and doe so immediately communicate with matter, and the interests of men, that they are of the same consideration with matters of fact, and are to be handled accordingly.[6]

Even Locke, nearly half a century later, made the same point. After denouncing as "opposite to the Civil Right of the Community" the doctrines that "Dominion is founded in Grace" and that "Kings excommunicated forfeit their Crowns and Kingdoms," he concludes: "That Church can have no right to be tolerated by the Magistrate, which is constituted upon such a bottom, that all those who enter into it, do thereby, *ipso facto,* deliver themselves up to the Protection and Service of another Prince. For by this means the Magistrate would give way to the settling of a forrein Jurisdiction in his own Country."[7]

But it was first "as it extirpats all religions" that Milton would extirpate Roman Catholicism. He does not mean by this charge merely that Roman Catholicism declares all other creeds false; in some sense this would apply to all churches, and would scarcely form a basis for excluding Roman Catholicism while admitting the rest. To recover Milton's meaning here we must return to the source from which everything in the *Areopagitica* ultimately derives, Milton's conception of truth. Truth is absolute, and susceptible of being absolutely known. Once, by miracle, it was so known. Since then, malice has obscured and

5. *Of True Religion* (1673).

6. *A Discourse of the Liberty of Prophesying* (1647), p. 253.

7. *A Letter Concerning Toleration* (1689), pp. 46–47.

distorted much of it. The followers of truth, however, have labored in its recovery.

> Truth indeed came once into the world with her divine Master, and was a perfect shape most glorious to look on: but when he ascended, and his Apostles after him were laid asleep, then strait arose a wicked race of deceivers, who ... took the virgin Truth, hewed her lovely form into a thousand pieces, and scatter'd them to the four winds. From that time ever since, the sad friends of Truth ... went up and down gathering up limb by limb still as they could find them.

What must be emphasized is that although the truth is now known only in part, this part is absolutely known. But what is this truth? Milton, writing for an audience quick to take—and subscribe—his meaning when he gives thanks for "that great measure of truth which we enjoy, especially in those main points between us and the Pope," does not trouble to explain; we may, for explication, conveniently turn a second time to the final summary of his case against Roman Catholicism. "True Religion is the true Worship and Service of God, learnt and believed from the Word of God only.... He hath Reveal'd and taught it us in the holy Scriptures ... with strictest command to reject all other traditions or additions whatsoever."[9] The truth Milton gives thanks for, then, is that in matters of religion, Scripture is absolutely and solely authoritative. ... But he thought it the essence of Roman Catholicism to deny this proposition, and to erect a second, equivalent, and in fact superior (because interpretative) authority: the traditions of the church (or, as he would say, of men). This was to subordinate the basis of all "True Religion" to the inventions of men—"to extirpat all religions."

We may think Milton's proscription of Roman Catholicism unnecessarily severe, but we cannot think it inconsistent with the principles upon which he based his plea for toleration. He demands toleration of religious diversity not primarily because truth is relative (although he enlarged the area in which this was so) but because it is incomplete, and only toleration will permit the further recovery of its parts. But this is a rationale which implies a precondition: "To be still searching what we know not, by what we know, still closing up truth to truth as we find it (for all her body is *homogeneal,* and proportionall) this is the golden rule in *Theology.*" "By what we know"—but the fundamental thing "we know" is, for Milton, precisely what Roman Catholicism denies. Hence it cannot claim the protection of the tolerationist argument, and self-defense requires its proscription.

THOMAS N. CORNS, JOHN MILTON: THE PROSE WORKS

(1998).

Milton agrees, then, that a line must be drawn to exclude the unacceptable from the press, but disagrees where the line should be

9. *Of True Religion* (1673), p. 4.

drawn. It is not absolutely clear whether "Popery, and open superstition" simply means Catholicism and *its* superstitious practices or whether it means Catholicism and *other* superstitious practices (such as Laudian ceremonialism). Because Catholicism asserts the preeminence of the rule of the Pope over the civil government of nations, it is a threat to the autonomy of those nations. Because, through agencies of the Counter–Reformation such as the Inquisition, Catholicism suppresses Protestantism where it can and thus (in Milton's view) all godliness, it should itself be suppressed. In the same way, opinions that are "impious or evil," presumably ones condemned by a wide consensus of Protestant opinion, need not be tolerated. Earlier in the tract, Milton expressed the view that the primary organ of royalist propaganda, the newspaper *Mercurius Aulicus,* already subject to an ineffectual ban, should be suppressed. As Milton puts it early in the tract, "I deny not, but that it is of greatest concernment ... to have a vigilant eye how Bookes demeane themselves, as well as men; and thereafter to confine, imprison, and do sharpest justice on them as malefactors."

Milton has been accused of falling somewhat short of the liberal ideal. Such issues, though, are rarely simple. London was the capital of a state at war; it was unreasonable that the other side should be free to disseminate its version of events, and the suppression of *Mercurius Aulicus* was no more than the equivalent of radio jamming. Currently, legislation in the United Kingdom forbids the distribution of material intended to incite racial abuse; the line may be drawn differently, but it is still drawn. The history of the Weimar Republic shows all too vividly the fate of a liberal regime too tolerant of its enemies.

But the problem with *Areopagitica* is not that it limits toleration but that it bases some of its case on a cluster of arguments that point to complete toleration. Milton seeks to define behavior that is meritorious in God's sight in terms of resistance to temptation. If Christians are not exposed to arguments that tempt them into heretical belief or behavior, then they do not earn the reward belonging to those who are rested and who stand firm:

> He that can apprehend and consider vice with all her baits and seeming pleasures, and yet abstain, and yet distinguish, and yet prefer that which is truly better, he is the true warfaring Christian. I cannot praise a fugitive and cloister'd vertue, unexercis'd & unbreath'd, that never sallies out and sees her adversary, but slinks out of the race, where that immortall garland is to be run for, not without dust and heat. Assuredly we bring not innocence into the world, we bring impurity much rather: that which purifies us is triall, and triall is by what is contrary. That vertue therefore which is but a youngling in the contemplation of evill, and knows not the utmost that vice promises to her followers, and rejects it, is but a blank vertue, not a pure; her whitenesse is but an excrementall whitenesse.

Fine words, but the contemplation of evil in its most extreme, for a seventeenth-century Protestant, most surely included contemplation of Catholicism, with its seductive theology of indulgence and saintly mediation and its promise of salvation standing open to all, its comforting rituals, and astonishingly beautiful art and architecture. "Popery" has to be tolerated to know "the utmost that vice promises to her followers." Again, godliness is something to be arrived at through the spiritual exercise of confronting its opposite, and the more powerful the opponent, the greater the spiritual advantage: why not then engagement with Catholicism?

Again, at his most eloquent, he asserts:

> though all the windes of doctrin were let loose to play upon the earth, so Truth be in the field, we do injuriously by licencing and prohibiting to misdoubt her strength. Let her and Falshood grapple; who ever knew Truth put to the wors, in a free and open encounter. Her confuting is the best and surest suppressing.

"Free and open encounter" may suggest that, in circumstances where Truth is not freely disseminated, Falsehood should also be suppressed. But such circumstances need scarcely apply in Civil War London, for *Mercurius Aulicus* was matched by any number of pro-Parliament newsbooks and journals, and the mighty Westminster Assembly of Divines stood ready to respond to Catholic doctrine. So if Truth does indeed always beat Falsehood in a fair fight, why then should there be legislation to suppress Catholicism and royalist propaganda? "Confuting is the best ... suppressing." Again, "To the pure all things are pure, not only meats and drinks, but all kinde of knowledge whether of good or evill; the knowledge cannot defile, nor consequently the books, if the will and conscience be not defil'd." Why not the knowledge, then, of subtle Catholic theology or the claims of the royalist propaganda machine?

CHRISTOPHER HILL, MILTON AND THE ENGLISH REVOLUTION

(1977).

It is difficult to be patient with those critics, innocent of historical knowledge, who tut-tut at Milton's refusal of toleration for Roman Catholics, suggesting that he failed to understand the logic of his own *Areopagitica.* Milton knew very well what he was doing, and it is evidence of the complete change in the politico-religious atmosphere since his day that this still has to be explained. Milton, like Marvell, regarded popery not primarily as a religion—that might have been tolerated—but as "a priestly despotism under the cloak of religion", which "extirpates all religious and civil supremacies". He saw it as "a Roman principality", the outward arm of the Italian potentate whom he regarded as Antichrist, leader of a potential Spanish or French fifth column in England. Milton early wrote Latin poems to celebrate England's escape on Guy Fawkes Day; and what he saw in Italy did not change his belief in the existence of an international Catholic plot aiming at total suppression of free discussion. Milton swallowed whole the stories of Irish massacres of English Protestants, and himself subscribed to the suppression of the Irish revolt. He would not be at all surprised when a papal nuncio headed the Irish rebels. The Irish were "an accursed race", Royalist support for whom was "criminal madness."

Milton further regarded Roman Catholic worship as idolatry, and therefore as one of the most grievous sins described in the Bible, the main offence of the chosen people, against which they had to be warned again and again. Popish (and Laudian) idolatry subordinated the dignity of man to the sanctity of material things, whether they were the bread and wine of the sacrament or consecrated churches. "When all our fathers worshipped stocks and stones" was his summary dismissal of the Catholic Middle Ages. Milton knew that idolatry was a sin to which too many of the common people were addicted. He also believed that popery, even more than prelacy, encouraged laxness and corruption, since through "easy confession, easy absolution, pardons, indulgences, masses" a man could "buy out his peace with money which he cannot with repentance". It was the negation of that strenuous self-discipline which Milton thought fundamental to Christian liberty. In view of popish idolatry, freedom of worship for papists, if allowed, would pander to all that was worst, least rational, most backward-looking, most lax, in natural man. Popery, because of its refusal to accept the fundamental status of the Bible and conscience, could not be met on equal terms. By insistence on implicit faith, Rome "forfeits her Christian liberty". For these reasons, political and cultural as well as religious, Milton in common with many other Englishmen felt that although Roman Catholics might be allowed liberty of conscience in secret, "for just reason of state" they must not be permitted "the public and scandalous use" of worship.

Here Milton represented the normal English Protestant attitude, shared by liberals from Hooker through Selden to Locke. More in need of explanation than Milton's position is that of those eccentric tolerationists who would have been prepared to extend liberty of worship to Catholics—Roger Williams, Richard Overton, William Walwyn, Colonel John Jubbes. None of them was a practical politician in the sense that Milton was, nor was ever associated with any government. Their views would have made this impossible. Sir Henry Vane, who may privately have favoured toleration for Catholics, did nothing in his public capacity to achieve this end. We may admire the consistency in charity of Williams, Walwyn, Overton and Jubbes; to contemporaries they must have seemed, in this respect, totally unrealistic. (I speak only of tolerationists on the radical wing of the Parliamentarians: no explanation is needed for those Laudians who favoured liberty of conscience for papists for exactly the same political reasons as led Milton and his like to oppose it.) Nor did Milton urge the extension of toleration to Jews, as Roger Williams and Oliver Cromwell were prepared to do. A radical like

William Erbery was prepared for toleration to Jews and Turks, but not to papists.

In *Areopagitica* Milton advocated limitations on publishing: the Commonwealth should "have a vigilant eye how books demean themselves as well as men; and thereafter to confine, imprison and do sharpest justice on them as malefactors". He recommended abolition of licensing in advance of publication, not the abolition of laws preventing publication of that "which is impious or evil absolutely, either against faith or manners." It is possible—though I could not prove this—that Milton is here making tactical concessions to those whose views were more conservative than his own. This seems to me more plausible than the suggestion that *Areopagitica* is a party-line document, "a rationale of revolutionary censorship", "a militant and exclusivist revolutionary pamphlet", which scholars have misinterpreted. We should be grateful to John Illo for reminding us that Milton was indeed a revolutionary, not a nineteenth-century liberal. He did not "misunderstand" the logic of his own argument, as liberal scholars have plaintively suggested. On the contrary: Milton was facing not only the tactical problem of how to preserve the greatest possible unity among the opponents of intolerance, but also the difficulties resulting from the shock of new light breaking on "eyes bleared and dimmed with prejudice and custom": the problem of how to establish liberty before all men were educated up to it. His tolerance, like Cromwell's, was limited to those with "the root of the matter" in them. Milton and Cromwell would have thought it was necessarily so limited, since to extend toleration to the intolerant would have defeated its fundamental object—the establishment of a better society.

The proponents of unfreedom—Rome, Charles I, the Presbyterians—were prepared to use violence to prevent the establishment of what Milton, and posterity, regarded as necessary freedoms. Milton's policy of toleration to the left, toleration of nearly all Protestants, could have been a very wide toleration; if it excluded the advocates of intolerance ("to suppress the suppressors"), it would have excluded only those whose views had in the past been widely propagated. New ideas came from the radical Protestant left, and could do so only given the liberty of printing which Milton advocated so warmly. Milton's tolerance had its limits, but it is not quite fair to sneer at him as if he were a twentieth-century fellow traveller who had learnt nothing from the career of Joseph Stalin.

JOHN ILLO, AREOPAGITICUS MYTHIC AND REAL

11 Prose Studies 3 (1988).

Anthony Lewis, not a Milton scholar but a lawyer and senior columnist for The *New York Times,* presents a general opinion in 1987, one that relies upon and is in accord with established scholarly Milton opinion:

> Three hundred years ago John Milton thundered against the English censorship of the time: laws requiring official approval before

any manuscript was published. His view was embraced in our First Amendment.

Here is Leo Miller, a Milton scholar, presenting a similar opinion in the same newspaper, in reply to my corrective letter on Anthony Lewis' misunderstanding, and plainly falsifying, for Milton, as even apologists like Sirluck assert, did *not* advocate separation of church and state:

> Marking our Constitution's bicentennial, we remember Milton as an advocate not only of free speech but also of separation of church and state.

More responsible scholarship and criticism has begun to defend or explain the ambiguity and intolerance of the *Areopagitica,* recognizing what has been there to be seen for three centuries. Two principal arguments have been used to preserve the libertarian *Areopagitica,* the tactical and the necessitarian.

The tactical argument is that Milton included the provisions for control or censorship so that an intolerant Parliament would listen to his larger libertarian purpose, a kind of practical concession or compromise that Milton didn't really mean. Leo Miller uses the argument, as does Christopher Hill, though each also uses the necessitarian. The tactical argument is perilous, for it puts much of Milton's work under a shadow of uncertainty. If Milton didn't mean parts of the *Areopagitica,* what of the other prose works, and how can we know when he is writing his belief and when not? Yet the argument, for all its dangers, might be correct. If it is, then the *Areopagitica* is unusual if not unique in Milton's work, for he is not tactical when he presents strong and heterodox or unpopular positions, in the divorce tracts, or the antiprelatical or anti-monarchic tracts. Nor, of course, was Milton's supposed libertarianism as heterodox as some have thought, or nearly as thoroughgoing as that of contemporaries like Walwyn and Williams. If the *Areopagitica* is really libertarian and democratic, and the illibertarian passages not seriously intended, then it is in disharmony with the rest of Milton's work and life. He is never a democrat in our sense of the word, always an elitist or aristocrat. A Jeffersonian Milton, which is what many not only of journalists and the laity but of scholars and critics have imagined they see in the *Areopagitica,* would be an anomaly. But we need not try to dispose of the tactical argument, for Milton disposed of it ten years later in the *Second Defense,* when there was no need to be tactical:

> I wrote ... *Areopagitica,* on the liberty of the press, so that the determination of true and false, of what should be published and what should be suppressed, might not be under control of ... unlearned men of mediocre judgment.

Milton did not conceal his discriminatory purpose in 1654, or in 1644. The myth of the libertarian *Areopagitica* is not of Milton's making.

The necessitarian argument was elaborated by Ernest Sirluck in the Yale edition (1959); it had been suggested earlier, as by Ernest Myers in 1898:

> Milton's *Areopagitica* . . . is a demand for liberty for innovations to approve themselves if they can, though he too always regarded the Roman Church as rendering exceptional precautions needful.

There are two peculiar deficiencies of the necessitarian argument, one in inconsistency or internal contradiction, the other a deceptive selectivity or deliberate evasion.

The argument is that Milton's Protestant toleration required intolerance of Catholicism because Catholicism was a closed system and a subversive polity. To preserve openness of inquiry, it is argued, inquiry had to stop short at Catholicism. To protect freedom of the press, freedom of the press had to be denied to Catholics. The principle of preserving freedom of the press by denying it, of preserving freedom of inquiry by restricting it, is not confined to Milton scholarship. Sirluck wrote at the end of a decade of denial of freedom to American Communists and other Marxists, freedom not only of publication but of person, for many were imprisoned, not because of any alleged criminal act except that of being members of a Party, their convictions under the Alien Registration Act—the Smith Act—consistently upheld by an intimidated Supreme Court until 1957. For the sake of democratic freedom and First Amendment rights, it was argued, Communists and others had to be deprived of those rights. Sirluck's casual dismissal of the rights of Catholics in Milton's England is an application of the principle endorsed by many a liberal in the 1950s. In the same year as Sirluck's defence of the illiberal *Areopagitica,* 1959, a liberal author, George Spicer, wrote:

> There seemed to be little doubt, however, that the Court, in affirming these convictions, had narrowed the scope of protection of freedom of speech and assembly under the First Amendment. It so interpreted the clear and present danger test as to leave Congress largely free from the restrictions of the First Amendment in meeting the Communist problem. If the effect of this were confined to Communist Party cases, there would be nothing to deplore but it would be naive to anticipate such a happy result.

Apparently neither man can understand how odious, in 1644 or in 1954, is the persecution of a class or category of humans, or the abrogation of their rights, or guilt by association. It rejects the individual worth of humans, obliterates the individual in the group while punishing him or her within the group. As it suppresses his or her voice, it prevents all outside the condemned group from hearing the voice, though any human's voice may be a revelation of truth to any other human. But once encased in myth the scholar like any other person may turn values upside down. The evident, wide and bitter intolerance of Milton is not regretted, even when acknowledged, or it is declared not to be intolerance. American political society has since corrected itself in this regard, and Communists and Socialist Workers are now free to walk the streets as other humans, to run for political office, and to publish their newspapers. Milton scholarship, however, remains apologetic of Milton's intolerance of Catholics, though they were only 1 per cent of the English population, and hardly the political threat that apologists pretend. Milton's intolerance here was spiritual or didactic rather than social or political.

Christopher Hill is even more assertive in his justification of Milton's detestation and intolerance of Catholics, and he finds it

> difficult to be patient with those critics, innocent of historical knowledge, who tut-tut at Milton's refusal of toleration for Roman Catholics, suggesting that he failed to understand the logic of his own *Areopagitica.* Milton knew very well what he was doing, and it is evidence of the complete change in the politico-religious atmosphere since his day that this still has to be explained.

The second sentence, at least in part, is correct, but what also has to be explained is the supposed libertarianism of Milton when, as Hill must acknowledge, some of Milton's contemporaries favoured toleration of Catholics, and of Turks and Jews. Hill tries to explain by asserting that Milton was a "practical politician," though another politician rather more practical than Milton, Oliver Cromwell, extended toleration to Jews, something Milton never urged or considered. As for Milton's practicality in politics, it is a sad and doubtful matter, if we judge it by his publications.

The *Areopagitica* had no effect, and was never reprinted in Milton's lifetime. Why should it be? Before it was transformed by myth, who could know whether it was for or against freedom of the press, for or against governmental control of the press? In 1644 *The Bloudy Tenent of Persecution* was publicly burned and immediately went into a second edition. The *Areopagitica* was ignored. Vehemently anti-Catholic, it was not included in the *Index Librorum Prohibitorum,* though the less offensive *Literae Pseudo-senatus Anglicanae* was. The *Doctrine and Discipline of Divorce* had an early second edition, for it at least said something unequivocal and on a subject always interesting to everyone, but it was hardly practical, for it did not consider the means by which reform might be effected, or whether divorce should be granted by bodies other than Parliament, as by the courts. Nor is there much practicality in the *Areopagitica,* for Milton never tells us by whom or by what mechanism books will be "found to be" "mischievous or libellous," "erroneous and scandalous," or adjudged "impious or evil" or superstitious, or how popish books will be prevented from being published. He speaks of "an appointed officer," but who will appoint Milton's Mrs. Grundy? He wishes away the examining commission of the 1643 Order, but apparently would replace it with an equivalent agency—must replace it if his controls and sanctions on publishing are to be effectual. Milton's sense of the practical is not the strongest element of his genius. The antiprelatical and antimonarchic tracts were not political proposals but responses to already developing positions and events. *The Ready and Easy Way* is as grotesque for its impracticality as for its oligarchic repressiveness. Such tracts, to Milton, projected or demonstrated "things so plain, so rational" that he wondered how anyone could question them.

Alas, for Hill's notion of Milton as practical politician, they were plain and rational to Milton and few besides, and the isolated or eccentric thinker, even if he is right, is hardly a practical politician.

Hill is so intent on preserving the myth of the *Areopagitica* that he can write, as a leading historian of the seventeenth century, that Roger Williams was not "a practical politician in the sense that Milton was, nor was ever associated with any government." The reader stares in disbelief. While Milton was writing *Comus,* Williams, who was only about four years older than Milton, was appointed full minister in Salem, Massachusetts Bay Colony, in defiance of the General Court. While Milton was writing Latin elegies at Horton, Williams was working for a more democratic church in the Colony, defending the Indian tribes against the land claims of the Royal Charter, and the poorer settlers against the Massachusetts oligarchy. While Milton was writing *Lycidas,* Williams, having been banished from Massachusetts, had founded and was helping to organize and govern a new colony at Providence. While Milton was teaching Latin conjugations to his nephews, Williams was resisting the encroachment of the Massachusetts Colony, and, having returned to England, circumvented his powerful Colonial neighbour and secured a patent for the Providence Plantation, from a Presbyterian Parliament that was not sympathetic to him. When Milton was writing the intolerant *Areopagitica,* Williams, in England, was writing the tolerant *Bloudy Tenent of Persecution,* and yet Milton was virtually without experience in government or politics, and therefore, on Hill's premise, free to defend complete freedom. It was Williams who was the tolerationist, after a decade of church and state politics, and after having founded a colony in New England and organized its government, and secured a patent against formidable opposition. Hill's premise that remoteness from practical politics and government is a condition of greater tolerance is disproved in this instance. At least for one with the soul of Roger Williams, to know men in political society is to recognize their need and right to freedom. What better way to understand the self-righteousness and self-justification of persecutors, as related in Chapter XI of *The Bloudy Tenent,* than to have experienced them, as Williams had in the Massachusetts Bay Colony? Milton's remoteness from practical political experience fostered in him not tolerance but doctrinaire intolerance. The tolerant Williams was "never associated with any government"? He established a government, and a colony that would become one of the original thirteen United States! Hill's performance—he is impatient, remember, with those who are innocent of historical knowledge—is a striking illustration of the effects of myth on scholarship.

Questions

1) Does Milton argue that Catholic writings ought to be subject to licensing? If so, what procedure of prior submission and administrative evaluation would he approve? Suppose a writer believed that his work was not "Catholic" in its theology or politics but his critics disagreed. In the

regime proposed by Milton, could such a writer be punished for publishing without a license?

2) When Milton says "I mean not tolerated popery and open superstition," does he mean that Catholics should be permitted to practice their religion discreetly? What practical consequence does he have in mind when he says about denying toleration to Catholics: "provided first that all charitable and compassionate means be used to win and regain the weak and the misled?"

3) How might a defender of Milton answer Professor Corns's point that someone who rests his case for toleration on the claim that knowledge and spiritual strength are acquired by confronting opposing ideas and temptations—"that which purifies us is trial, and trial is by what is contrary"—cannot consistently exclude Catholic ideas from the regime of toleration?

4) One reason that Milton gives for not tolerating Catholic writings is that "popery ... extirpates all religions and civil supremacies." Does he contend that only tolerant religions and political philosophies are entitled to his proposed regime of toleration? Only religions and political philosophies that do not seek to overthrow the current parliamentary regime? If so, does Milton's argument lend support to the militant anti-communists who claimed during the McCarthy Era that Communist Party members and "fellow travelers" should not be able to invoke First Amendment rights because of their presumed lack of commitment to the principle of freedom of speech?

JOHN RUMRICH, RADICAL HETERODOXY AND HERESY

in A Companion to Milton (Thomas N. Corns ed., 2001).

We have noted that Milton composed *Areopagitica* partly in response to the outcry over his divorce tracts and the subsequent drive to license books. The divorce tracts also prepared the way for memorable political arguments that came at the end of the 1640s, against the divine right of kings and their absolute authority over their subjects. As Milton remarks in *The Doctrine and Discipline of Divorce,* "he who marries, intends as little to conspire his owne ruine, as he that swears Allegiance: and as a whole people is in proportion to an ill Government, so is one man to an ill mariage." The connection was recognized at the Restoration and used to mock Milton, for example in Tatham's *Character of the Rump*: "by his will [he] would shake off his governors as he doth his wives, four in a fortnight." As Tatham rightly understood, Milton held that the people enjoy the right to divorce themselves from a tyrannical king, a right that many Presbyterians denied. Some indeed went so far as to argue that a subject people should endure the tyrannies of a Nero rather than rebel against a divinely sanctioned potentate.

The prose works Milton published in the 1640s thus track his increasing divergence from the Presbyterian orthodoxy with which he had allied himself early in the decade—an orthodoxy itself deemed heterodox under the episcopal system. Although subsequent generations would draw inspiration from them, these writings had precious little impact at the time. True, the bishops were undone, but only temporarily. Marriage law long remained unchanged, despite Milton's arguments for divorce. *Areopagitica,* composed as if it were an oration before Parliament, failed to persuade its members to repeal the Licensing Order. Also generally ignored was *The Tenure of Kings and Magistrates*; but at least its publication on 13 February 1649, two weeks after Charles's execution, drew the attention of the new government. Shortly thereafter, Milton was appointed its Secretary for Foreign Tongues, the Commonwealth's voice in Europe. In this role Milton at last made his mark.

Shortly after Charles's trial and execution, the reigning intellectual heavyweight of mid-seventeenth-century Europe, the celebrated Claudius Salmasius, was hired to condemn the English regicides. He produced a massive Latin tract, *Defensio Regia pro Carolo Primo* ("Defence of Kings on Behalf of Charles I"), which portrayed the beheading of the Lord's anointed as an unspeakable crime that would inevitably bring God's wrath down on the English. Charged with replying quickly, Milton, virtually unknown in Europe, composed a light-footed, point-by-point refutation in superb neoclassical Latin, replete with devastating satiric abuse. *Pro Populo Anglicano Defensio* ("Defence of the English People") immediately exalted Milton's continental reputation and as late as 1753 was deemed Milton's "most celebrated work in prose." As Isaac Disraeli later remarked, "all Europe took a part in the paper-war of these two great men", a paper-war in which "the answer of Milton ... perfectly massacred Salmasius."

During the early 1650s counterattacks and renewed Miltonic defences ensued. In them Milton pushes the trope of the warrior for truth and liberty prominent in *Areopagitica* even further, portraying himself as a heroic champion, triumphant before all of Europe:

> I have in the *First Defence* spoken out and shall in the *Second* speak again to the entire assembly and council of all the most influential men, cities, and nations everywhere ... It is the renewed cultivation of freedom and civic life that I disseminate throughout cities, kingdoms, and nations. But not entirely unknown, nor perhaps unwelcome, shall I return if I am he who disposed of the contentious satellite of tyrants [Salmasius], hitherto deemed unconquerable, both in the view of most men and in his own opinion. When he with insults was attacking us and our battle array, and our leaders looked first of all to me, I met him in single combat and plunged into his reviling throat this pen, the weapon of his own choice.

If the 1650s was the decade in which Milton's warriorlike authorial spirit finally became apparent to an admiring world, it was also the decade of his greatest losses. The strain of composing the reply to

Salmasius cost him what little was left of his already failing eyesight, a loss his enemies counted as a sign of divine displeasure at his impiety. In 1652 his troubled first marriage ended when Mary Powell succumbed to complications after the birth of her third daughter, Deborah. Their son, John, less than a year old, died a few months later. His wife, his only son, his sight—all gone in the same year. His second wife, Katherine Woodcock, whom he married in 1656 and with whom he seems finally to have found happiness, died only two years after their marriage, also because of complications from childbirth, so terribly dangerous to women at that period. By the end of the 1650s, in short, he was fast approaching old age as a lonely, blind, twice-widowed father of three daughters, and after the death of Cromwell in 1658 also endured the rapid disintegration of the English Commonwealth he had laboured so intensely to defend. In the first half of the 1650s, Milton proclaimed his own heroism and authorial integrity. It is for us to recognize the more remarkable display of these qualities in the decade's latter years.

In the end, the authorial capital he had accumulated defending the English people was squandered in repeated, futile publications that argued in favour of establishing a republic governed by an elected representative body. The one-time champion of the English people pleaded with his countrymen not to restore the monarchy, though he seems to have foreseen that his arguments would go unheeded: "Thus much I should perhaps have said, though I were sure I should have spoken only to trees and stones; and had none to cry to, but with the Prophet, *O earth, earth, earth!* to tell the very soil it self, what her perverse inhabitants are deaf to." As the Restoration loomed, Milton's fame was quickly translated into calumny, and he became an object of scorn and insult among the people he had defended. Derided as a "blind guide", he was mocked for having "scribbled [his] eyes out" to no effect, berated for having "thrown [his] dirty outrage on the memory of a murdered Prince as if the Hangman were but [his] usher." Royalist Roger L'Estrange commented that Milton had "resolved one great question, by evidencing that devils may indue human shape"; or, allowing that Milton might indeed be human, observed that he gave "every man a horror for mankind when he considers [Milton is] of the race." Another writer, congratulating Charles II on his return and condemning the regicides *en masse* for "destestable, execrable murder, . . . never-before-paralleled nor ever-sufficiently-to-be-lamented-and-abhorred villainies", pauses to single out one culprit by name: "this Murder . . . and these Villainies, were defended, nay extolled and commended, by one Mr. John Milton, [who] did . . . bespatter the white robes of your Royal father's spotless life . . . with the dirty filth of his satirical pen."

It would be difficult to overstate the desire for bloody vengeance among some royalists at the Restoration, or the narrowness of Milton's escape from it. On the anniversary of Charles's execution in 1661, the corpse of Cromwell, dead three years, was disinterred and hoisted at Tyburn alongside those of his son-in-law Henry Ireton (d. 1651) and John Bradshaw. (d. 1659). As reported in a contemporary newspaper account, the punishment of their corpses followed the same general protocol as that observed with living victims: "they were drawn upon sledges to Tyburn. All the way . . . the universal outcry and curses of the people went along with them. When the three carcasses were at Tyburn, they were pulled out of their coffins, and hanged at the several angles of that triple tree,—where they hung till the sun was set; after which they were taken down, and their heads cut off, and their loathsome trunks thrown into a deep hole under the gallows." The carcasses' heads were then fixed on poles by the common hangman and set atop Westminster Hall, where they remained for many years.

Even more extreme punishment was eagerly anticipated by some for Milton, and was indeed inflicted on those regicides who lacked the sense to flee or die before the Restoration. John Egerton, Viscount Brackley, who in his youth had played the part of the elder brother in Milton's *Comus,* inscribed his opinion of Milton's deserts on the title page of *Pro Populo Anglicano Defensio*: "Liber igni, Author furcâ, dignissimi", which is to say, "The book is most deserving of burning, the author the gallows." How charming is divine philosophy! Not all the circling gallows birds were so austere and humourless. Derisively contemplating Milton's execution, John Tatham in 1660 wrote that "he is so much an enemy to usual practices that I believe, when he is condemned to travel to Tyburn in a cart, he will petition for the favour to be the first man that ever was driven in a wheelbarrow." Standard procedure, illustrated by the ritual abuse of the three corpses, called for the convict to be drawn from the Tower on a hurdle or in a cart through the city of London to Tyburn and then subjected to the rest of the usual sentence, which I quote here to give some sense of what Milton risked by staying in London and writing antimonarchical pamphlets to the bitter end: "there to be hanged till he should be half dead; that then he should be cut down alive, his privy parts cut off, his belly ripped, his bowels burnt, his four quarters set up over the four gates of the city, and his head upon London bridge." This was the spectacularly allegorical sentence carved into the flesh of Englishmen convicted of treason up until the nineteenth century. As the regicides' penman, Milton's body presented an obvious surface for inscribing this sentence. Though theories abound, no one has ever been able to explain just how he managed to survive unscathed to complete and publish the poems for which he is now chiefly remembered. *Paradise Lost* was maybe half finished in 1660 and not published until 1667; *Paradise Regained* and *Samson Agonistes* were not published until 1671.

Zagorin observes that "in exposing his antimonarchical opinions so outspokenly at such a moment, [Milton] stood virtually alone." Many others associated with the regicides prudently fled the country. John Dryden, who keened in verse on the occasion of Cromwell's death in 1658, wrote poetry celebrating the arrival of Charles II in London in 1660. Those who claim that Milton did not genuinely advocate free speech, except perhaps as the victim of ideological delusion, or that his ideal of liberty evinces false consciousness, must consider his stubborn behaviour as the Restoration approached foolhardy, if not suicidal. It was, on the other hand, authentically Protestant behaviour. Orwell in 1946 traced the bourgeois heritage of intellectual liberty and integrity to the Protestant tradition and specifically cites Milton before offering this observation on heresy: a heretic—political, moral, religious, or aesthetic—was one who refused to outrage his own conscience. His outlook was summed up in the words of the Revivalist hymn:

'Dare to be a Daniel
'Dare to stand alone;
'Dare to have a purpose firm,
'Dare to make it known.'

By 1660 Milton had dared all of the above under circumstances seemingly designed to expose the slightest vacillation. He was heretical to the core.

NEAR v. MINNESOTA

Supreme Court of the United States, 1931.
283 U.S. 697, 51 S.Ct. 625, 75 L.Ed. 1357.

Mr. Chief Justice Hughes delivered the opinion of the Court.

Chapter 285 of the Session Laws of Minnesota for the year 1925 provides for the abatement, as a public nuisance, of a "malicious, scandalous and defamatory newspaper, magazine or other periodical."

* * *

Section 2 provides that, whenever any such nuisance is committed or exists, the county attorney of any county where any such periodical is published or circulated, or, in case of his failure or refusal to proceed upon written request in good faith of a reputable citizen, the Attorney General, or, upon like failure or refusal of the latter, any citizen of the county, may maintain an action in the district court of the county in the name of the state to enjoin perpetually the persons committing or maintaining any such nuisance from further committing or maintaining it.

* * *

Under this statute (section 1, clause (b)), the county attorney of Hennepin county brought this action to enjoin the publication of what was described as a "malicious, scandalous and defamatory newspaper, magazine or other periodical," known as The Saturday Press, published by the defendants in the city of Minneapolis. The complaint alleged that the defendants, on September 24, 1927, and on eight subsequent dates in October and November, 1927, published and circulated editions of that periodical which were "largely devoted to malicious, scandalous and defamatory articles" concerning Charles G. Davis, Frank W. Brunskill, the Minneapolis Tribune, the Minneapolis Journal, Melvin C. Passolt, George E. Leach, the Jewish Race, the members of the grand jury of Hennepin county impaneled in November, 1927, and then holding office, and other persons, as more fully appeared in exhibits annexed to the complaint, consisting of copies of the articles described and constituting 327 pages of the record. While the complaint did not so allege, it appears from the briefs of both parties that Charles G. Davis was a special law enforcement officer employed by a civic organization, that George E. Leach was mayor of Minneapolis, that Frank W. Brunskill was its chief of police, and that Floyd B. Olson, the relator in this action, was county attorney.

Without attempting to summarize the contents of the voluminous exhibits attached to the complaint, we deem it sufficient to say that the articles charged, in substance, that a Jewish gangster was in control of gambling, bootlegging, and racketeering in Minneapolis, and that law enforcing officers and agencies were not energetically performing their duties. Most of the charges were directed against the chief of police; he was charged with gross neglect of duty, illicit relations with gangsters, and with participation in graft. The county attorney was charged with knowing the existing conditions and with failure to take adequate measures to remedy them. The mayor was accused of inefficiency and dereliction. One member of the grand jury was stated to be in sympathy with the gangsters. A special grand jury and a special prosecutor were demanded to deal with the situation in general, and, in particular, to investigate an attempt to assassinate one Guilford, one of the original defendants, who, it appears from the articles, was shot by gangsters after the first issue of the periodical had been published. There is no question but that the articles made serious accusations against the public officers named and others in connection with the prevalence of crimes and the failure to expose and punish them.

* * *

If we cut through mere details of procedure, the operation and effect of the statute in substance is that public authorities may bring the owner or publisher of a newspaper or periodical before a judge upon a charge of conducting a business of publishing scandalous and defamatory matter-in particular that the matter consists of charges against public officers of official dereliction-and, unless the owner or publisher is able and disposed to bring competent evidence to satisfy the judge that the charges are true and are published with good motives and for justifiable ends, his newspaper or periodical is suppressed and further publication is made punishable as a contempt. This is of the essence of censorship.

The question is whether a statute authorizing such proceedings in restraint of publication is consistent with the conception of the liberty of the press as historically conceived and guaranteed. In determining the extent of the constitutional protection, it has been generally, if not universally, considered that it is the chief purpose of the guaranty to prevent previous restraints upon publication. The struggle in England, directed against the legislative power of the licenser, resulted in renunciation of the censorship of the press. The liberty deemed to be established was thus described by Blackstone: "The liberty of the press is indeed essential to the nature of a free state; but this consists in laying no previous restraints upon publications, and not in freedom from censure for criminal matter when published. Every freeman has an undoubted right to lay what sentiments he pleases before the public; to forbid this, is to destroy the freedom of the press; but if he publishes what is improper, mischievous or illegal, he must take the consequence of his own temerity." 4 Bl. Com. 151, 152. See Story on the Constitution, §§ 1884, 1889. The distinction was early pointed out between the extent of the freedom with respect to censorship under our constitutional system and that enjoyed in England. Here, as Madison said, 'the great and essential rights of the people are secured against legislative as well as against executive ambition. They are secured, not by laws paramount to prerogative, but by constitutions paramount to laws. This security of the freedom of the press requires that it should be exempt not only from previous restraint by the Executive, as in Great Britain, but from legislative restraint also.'

* * *

The objection has also been made that the principle as to immunity from previous restraint is stated too broadly, if every such restraint is deemed to be prohibited. That is undoubtedly true; the protection even as to previous restraint is not absolutely unlimited. But the limitation has been recognized only in exceptional cases: "When a nation is at war many things that might be said in time of peace are such a hindrance to its effort that their utterance will not be endured so long as men fight and that no Court could regard them as protected by any constitutional right." *Schenck v. United States*, 249 U.S. 47, 52. No one would question but that a government might prevent actual obstruction to its recruiting service or the publication of the sailing dates of transports or the number and location of troops. On similar grounds, the primary requirements of decency may be enforced against obscene publications. The security of the community life may be protected against incitements to acts of violence and the overthrow by force of orderly government. The constitutional guaranty of free speech does not "protect a man from an injunction against uttering words that may have all the effect of force. *Gompers v. Buck Stove & Range Co.*, 221 U.S. 418, 439." *Schenck v. United States, supra.* These limitations are not applicable here. Nor are we now concerned with questions as to the extent of authority to prevent publications in order to protect private rights according to principles governing the exercise of jurisdiction of courts of equity.

The exceptional nature of its limitations places in a strong light the general conception that liberty of the press, historically considered and taken up by the Federal Constitution, has meant, principally although not exclusively, immunity from previous restraints or censorship. The conception of the liberty of the press in this country has broadened with the exigencies of the colonial period and with the efforts to secure freedom from oppressive administration. That liberty was especially cherished for the immunity it afforded from previous restraint of the publication of censure of public officers and charges of official misconduct.

* * *

The fact that for approximately one hundred and fifty years there has been almost an entire absence of attempts to impose previous restraints upon publications relating to the malfeasance of public officers is significant of the deep-seated conviction that such restraints would violate constitutional right. Public officers, whose character and conduct remain open to debate and free discussion in the press, find their remedies for false accusations in actions under libel laws providing for redress and punishment, and not in proceedings to restrain the publication of newspapers and periodicals. The general principle that the constitutional guaranty of the liberty of the press gives immunity from previous restraints has been approved in many decisions under the provisions of state constitutions.

The importance of this immunity has not lessened. While reckless assaults upon public men, and efforts to bring obloquy upon those who are endeavoring faithfully to discharge official duties, exert a baleful influence and deserve the severest condemnation in public opinion, it cannot be said that this abuse is greater, and it is believed to be less, than that which characterized the period in which our institutions took shape. Meanwhile, the administration of government has become more complex, the opportunities for malfeasance and corruption have multiplied, crime has grown to most serious proportions, and the danger of its protection by unfaithful officials and of the impairment of the fundamental security of life and property by criminal alliances and official neglect, emphasizes the primary need of a vigilant and courageous press, especially in great cities. The fact that the liberty of the press may be abused by miscreant purveyors of scandal does not make any the less necessary the immunity of the press from previous restraint in dealing with official misconduct. Subsequent punishment for such abuses as may exist is the appropriate remedy, consistent with constitutional privilege.

* * *

Judgment reversed.

Mr. Justice Butler (dissenting).

The decision of the Court in this case declares Minnesota and every other state powerless to restrain by injunction the business of publishing and circulating among the people malicious, scandalous, and defamatory periodicals that in due course of judicial procedure has been adjudged to be a public nuisance. It gives to freedom of the press a meaning and a scope not heretofore recognized, and construes "liberty" in the due process clause of the Fourteenth Amendment to put upon the states a federal restriction that is without precedent.

* * *

The Court quotes Blackstone in support of its condemnation of the statute as imposing a previous restraint upon publication. But the previous restraints referred to by him subjected the press to the arbitrary will of an administrative officer.

* * *

The Minnesota statute does not operate as a previous restraint on publication within the proper meaning of that phrase. It does not authorize administrative control in advance such as was formerly exercised by the licensers and censors, but prescribes a remedy to be enforced by a suit in equity. In this case there was previous publication made in the course of the business of regularly producing malicious, scandalous, and defamatory periodicals. The business and publications unquestionably constitute an abuse of the right of free press. The statute denounces the things done as a nuisance on the ground, as stated by the state Supreme Court, that they threaten morals, peace, and good order. There is no question of the power of the state to denounce such transgressions. The restraint authorized is only in respect of continuing to do what has been duly adjudged to constitute a nuisance. The controlling words are: "All persons guilty of such nuisance may be enjoined, as hereinafter provided. * * * Whenever any such nuisance is committed * * * an action in the name of the State" may be brought "to perpetually enjoin the person or persons committing, conducting or maintaining any such nuisance, from further committing, conducting, or maintaining any such nuisance." * * * The court may make its order and judgment permanently enjoining * * * defendants found guilty * * * from further committing or continuing the acts prohibited hereby, and in and by such judgment, such nuisance may be wholly abated. * * * There is nothing in the statute purporting to prohibit publications that have not been adjudged to constitute a nuisance. It is fanciful to suggest similarity between the granting or enforcement of the decree authorized by this statute to prevent further publication of malicious, scandalous, and defamatory articles and the previous restraint upon the press by licensers as referred to by Blackstone and described in the history of the times to which he alludes.

* * *

The judgment should be affirmed.

Mr. JUSTICE VAN DEVANTER, Mr. JUSTICE MCREYNOLDS, and Mr. JUSTICE SUTHERLAND concur in this opinion.

Questions

1) Which of Milton's arguments against the licensing of books and pamphlets also apply to the regulation of speech by means of a judicial injunction? Which do not?

2) Do licensing requirements and injunctions have a common core of shared objectionable features such that regulation "in advance" by either means

of "prior restraint" should be especially disfavored in comparison with alternative methods of regulation such as criminal sanctions and civil liability awards? Doesn't the impact on speech depend mainly on the severity of the sanction rather than whether the form of the restraint is "prior" or "subsequent?"

3) What is the doctrinal significance of Chief Justice Hughes's observation in *Near v. Minnesota* that the liberty of the press historically "was especially cherished for the immunity it afforded from previous restraint of the publication of censure of public officers and charges of official misconduct?" Would the case have been decided differently had the newspaper subject to the Minnesota nuisance injunction not been publishing scandalous assertions about official corruption in the Twin Cities? Do Milton's arguments against licensing apply with less force when the writings subject to censorship are not about the conduct of government officials?

Additional Readings

Milton generally

Thomas Corns, ed., A Companion to Milton (2001)

Dennis Danielson ed., The Cambridge Companion to Milton (1989)

Stanley Fish, How Milton Works (2001)

William Haller, Liberty and Reformation in the Puritan Revolution (1955)

David Loewenstein & James Grantham Turner ed., Politics, Poetics, and Hermeneutics in Milton's Prose (1990)

Areopagitica

Lana Cable, Carnal Rhetoric: Milton's Iconoclasm and the Poetics of Desire, ch. 4 (1995)

Paul M. Dowling, Polite Wisdom: Heathen Rhetoric in Milton's *Areopagitica* (1995)

John X. Evans, Imagery as Argument in Milton's *Areopagitica*, 8 Texas Studies in Literature and Language 192 (1966)

William Kolbrener, Milton's Warring Angels: A Study of Critical Engagements, ch. 1 (1997)

Thomas Kranidas, Polarity and Structure in Milton's *Areopagitica*, 14 English Literary Renaissance 175 (1984)

Eric Nelson, "True Liberty": Isocrates and Milton's *Areopagitica*, 40 Milton Studies 201 (2001)

David Norbrook, *Areopagitica*, Censorship, and the Early Modern Public Sphere, in The Administration of Aesthetics (Richard Burt ed. 1994)

Nigel Smith, *Areopagitica*: Voicing Contexts 1643–5, in Politics, Poetics, and Hermeneutics in Milton's Prose (David Loewenstein and James Grantham Turner ed. 1990)

Blair Worden, Milton's Republicanism and the Tyranny of Heaven, in Machiavelli and Republicanism (Gisela Bock, Quentin Skinner, and Maurizio Viroli eds. 1991)

Juanita Whitaker, "The Wars of Truth": Wisdom and Strength in *Areopagitica*, 9 Milton Studies 185 (1976)

Near v. Minnesota and prior restraint

Fred W. Friendly, Minnesota Rag: The Dramatic Story of the Landmark Supreme Court Case That Gave New Meaning to Freedom of the Press (1981)

Stephen R. Barnett, The Puzzle of Prior Restraint, 29 Stan. L. Rev. 539 (1977)

Vincent Blasi, Toward a Theory of Prior Restraint: The Central Linkage, 66 Minn. L. Rev. 11 (1981)

Thomas I. Emerson, The Doctrine of Prior Restraint, 20 Law & Contemp. Probs. 648 (1955)

John Calvin Jeffries, Jr., Rethinking Prior Restraint, 92 Yale L. J. 409 (1983)

Michael I. Meyerson, The Neglected History of the Prior Restraint Doctrine, 34 Ind. L. Rev. 295 (2001)

Martin H. Redish, The Proper Role of Prior Restraint Doctrine in First Amendment Theory, 70 Va. L. Rev. 53 (1984)

Marin Scordato, Distinction Without a Difference: A Reappraisal of the Doctrine of Prior Restraint, 68 N.C. L. Rev. 1 (1989)

Chapter Three

JAMES MADISON

JOSEPH J. ELLIS, FOUNDING BROTHERS

Review of THE REPUBLIC OF LETTERS: THE CORRESPONDENCE BETWEEN THOMAS JEFFERSON AND JAMES MADISON 1776–1826, EDITED BY JAMES MORTON SMITH

The New Republic, January 30, 1995.

Perhaps all heroes are conveyed to posterity as singular and solitary beings. In the case of Thomas Jefferson, however, the splendor of his isolation seems an essential aspect of his reputation. Jefferson's ultimate act of solitary creation was, of course, the drafting of the Declaration of Independence in June 1776. Sitting in a Windsor chair with his lap-desk and a quill pen, he wrote the magic words of American history. President John Kennedy conjured up this solitary image of Jefferson in his often-quoted remark to the Nobel laureates invited to the White House in 1962: it was, Kennedy observed, "the most extraordinary collection of talents that has ever been gathered at the White House, with the possible exception when Thomas Jefferson dined alone."

James Morton Smith's magisterial collection of the complete correspondence between Jefferson and James Madison should prompt some spirited revisions of the popular imagery. Instead of a mystical loner always gazing presciently into the middle distance, we should now imagine Jefferson standing beside a diminutive fellow Virginian, a confidante who is forever whispering wisdom into his ear and silently editing all his speeches and writings. Indeed, John Quincy Adams long ago hinted at the collaborative character of all things Jeffersonian:

> Mr. Madison was the intimate, confidential and devoted friend of Mr. Jefferson, and the mutual influence of these two mighty minds upon each other is a phenomenon, like the invisible and mysterious movements of the magnet in the physical world, and in which the sagacity of the future historian may discover the solution of much of our national history not otherwise easily accountable.

The special relationship between Jefferson and Madison became a human version of the principle of checks and balances. Jefferson was the visionary idealist; Madison, the canny realist. Together, they created an ideological whole greater than the sum of its parts, and it became the foundation of the liberal tradition in American politics.

* * *

In some very big ways, however, the two patriarchs were sufficiently different in temperament and in the central thrusts of their political thinking to make one wonder just how the partnership endured with such apparent serenity. Granted, they both began their careers as opponents of British power over the Colonies and retained a strong hatred of English imperial arrogance throughout their lives. Both regarded the Federalists, especially the Hamiltonians, as Anglophiles with aristocratic tendencies that represented a betrayal of the republican faith. Both feared concentrations of political power at the federal level, most graphically illustrated by Adams's Alien and Sedition Acts. Both misjudged the capacity of American commerce to influence English and French policy toward American nationhood and suffered the failure of the disastrous embargo of 1807 as a result. Beneath these areas of obvious agreement, however, lay several fundamental differences of opinion about the true meaning of the American Revolution.

The most famous exchange in the correspondence dramatizes these differences quite nicely. In 1789 an excited Jefferson presented Madison with a newfound political principle, the doctrine that "the earth belongs to the living." This bizarre but characteristically Jeffersonian idea was rooted in his aversion to any and all forms of overt coercion, to include the influence of past laws or inherited debts. "We seem not to have perceived," he explained to Madison, "that, by the law of nature, one generation is to another as one independent nation is to another." He produced elaborate calculations to show that, on average, a generation lasted about nineteen years, which meant that all debts, laws, even constitutions, should expire after that time.

Madison complimented Jefferson on his "interesting reflections," then proceeded to demolish the entire notion of generational sovereignty by observing that generational cohorts do not come into the world as discrete aggregates. There is a seamless web of arrivals and departures, along with an analogous web of obligatory connections between past and present generations that are not only unavoidable but also essential for the continuation of civilized society. Jefferson clung to the idea, which was really a fantasy, for the rest of his life; it satisfied some deep craving in his imagination for a world of perfect freedom and independence. (And, given his perpetual and eventually tragic indebtedness, it had economic attraction as well.) But he never put it forward to Madison or anyone else as a serious legislative proposal.

A similar exchange occurred at almost the same time, when Madison sent Jefferson a lengthy analysis of the arguments over the recently drafted Constitution, explaining in great detail the beauty of overlapping jurisdiction between federal and state power and the important role government must play in protecting individual rights. Jefferson wrote back to register his worries about a strong executive. "I own I am not a friend to a very energetic government," he concluded, noting that "after all, it is my principle that the will of the Majority shall always prevail." Since Madison's whole point was that majority rule was the chief threat to individual liberty in the American republic, and that therefore the main task of the new Constitution was to restrain popular majorities rather than release them, the two friends were occupying opposite ends of a great political divide. When Madison sent Jefferson a copy of the *Federalist Papers* to amplify his explanation, Jefferson acknowledged that "it has rectified me in several points." But the truth was that Jefferson found it impossible to think about the powers of government in positive ways, or to believe that popular majorities should ever threaten individual rights. Madison's entire emphasis on balance was at odds with Jefferson's commitment to liberation.

The list of rather stunning disagreements could go on. Although they collaborated in writing the Kentucky and Virginia Resolutions in 1798, agreeing that the Sedition Act was an unwarranted and unconstitutional abuse of federal power. Madison was careful to blur the question of state versus federal authority. Jefferson, on the other hand, denied the federal government any jurisdiction over domestic affairs within the states and sanctioned the right of states to overturn or "nullify" federal laws in terms that Southern secessionists later found immensely helpful. Madison came to the rescue again, excusing Jefferson's states' rights argument as an unfortunate outburst of Jeffersonian excess, and suggesting that, when it came down to the question of the Framers' intent, his credentials were far superior.

The role of the Supreme Court generated the same kind of division. Jefferson despised John Marshall because his rulings enlarged the power of a handful of nonelected judges. "The judiciary of the United States," he wrote in 1820, "is the subtle corps of sappers and miners constantly working under ground to undermine the foundation of our confederated republic." Whenever a landmark constitutional decision was necessary, Jefferson thought it should be put to a democratic vote. Madison considered such a course impractical, unwise and, once again, at odds with the original intent of the Framers.

The Jefferson who comes through in this correspondence is more a political visionary or dreamer than a thinker. The animating impulse of his vision was an instinctive hostility to government, indeed to all forms of authority outside the self. The Jeffersonian cast of mind was moralistic and melodramatic, tending to divide the world into moral dichotomies: liberty versus tyranny; virtue versus corruption; the people versus government. The Declaration of Independence, with its exaltation of American rights and indictment of English wrongs, accurately represented the primal categories of his political system. His abiding appeal is less to our minds than to our imaginations and expectations.

Madison, on the other hand, was every inch a realistic political thinker with an affinity for paradox. Madisonian thought rejected simple polarities in favor of multiple sources of power. If Jefferson's favorite

European philosophers were French, Madison's were Scottish. (Adams's were English.) The Madisonian goal was not personal liberation so much as social stability, which he tended to regard as a product of countervailing forces that government must attempt to orchestrate. Federalist No. 10, with its diagnosis of interacting and off-setting factions within an extended republic, captured the essence of his political wisdom. Madison is more of an acquired taste than Jefferson, but unquestionably the sharper and deeper political thinker.

From the very beginning, then, the American liberal tradition has been an inherently hybrid creature. At the level of mainstream politics, the Jeffersonian side of the legacy has dominated in the same way that Jefferson dominated the relationship with Madison. The seductive simplicities and the eerie optimism of Jefferson's dream are more accessible to a mass audience and also enjoy the incalculable advantage of telling us what we want to hear. Youthful radicals rediscovered the romantic utopianism in the 1960s. Ronald Reagan mastered its idiom and rhetoric with equivalent authenticity in the 1980s. It is the core expression of America's will to believe.

The Madisonian side of the liberal legacy is more prosaic and legalistic. It tells us what we need to know rather than what we want to hear; how republican institutions actually work rather than the ideals toward which they aspire. The Madisonian tradition is more compelling to scholars, jurists and thoughtful journalists than to the larger public. In a sense, it performs the same function that Madison performed for Jefferson; namely, to discipline democratic excesses, edit down great expectations and consolidate gains after a spasm of liberal reform. Or, as Robert Frost put it, the dream of Jefferson was the youthful dream of unabashed and uncomplicated personal freedom and independence; but the dream of Madison was more satisfying to the elders: "It was a dream of a new land to fulfill with people in self-control." Something there was in Jefferson that didn't love that wall, while Madison thought that good fences make good neighbors.

By bringing these letters together for the first time, this comprehensive edition of the Jefferson–Madison correspondence invites such speculations. Not that James Morton Smith would agree with most of mine. To his everlasting credit, Smith's extensive introductions to each section of the correspondence provide a sufficient scholarly context for general readers to understand the issues at stake and reach their own conclusions. Some will surely prefer to interpret the exchange as a gift-package from the past, a reminder of the way it was back when giants walked the earth and American statesmen actually wrote literate and thoughtful letters. Others will want to read the dialogue as an instructive commentary on the strange birth of the liberal tradition in America, particularly intriguing and revealing for those of us in late-liberal America who are wondering whether the tradition has a future.

STANLEY ELKINS & ERIC McKITRICK, THE AGE OF FEDERALISM

(1993).

From the most constructive period of Madison's career, that spanning roughly the decade between 1780 and 1790, there remains a picture of the man that has become more or less traditional. It is the picture of the modest conciliator, the statesman of compromise. James Madison comes to us as the man of sagacity and intelligence, of great learning in the realms of history and political science, who nevertheless does not insist upon himself. He is the quiet builder, mindful of other men's ideas and feelings, willing both to channel their energies and to allow them the credit. He is self-effacing, resourceful, and tireless, his accomplishments being due in no small part simply to his willingness to remain at work long after others had gone to bed. It is thus James Madison who, almost in spite of himself, emerges as the chief architect of the United States Constitution.

There is only one aspect of this picture that does not belong. But add a touch or two, and even with all the rest remaining the whole effect is somehow altered. James Madison was not really a compromiser. He was a revolutionary; his ideological presuppositions, down deep, were immovable; despite all appearances to the contrary, he was one of the most stubborn and willful men of his time. In what to him was fundamental, he was quietly, implacably determined to have his way.

From the present distance, one penetrates the essential Madison just so far. But watching him always with reference to certain fixed points in his personality and career does help us around some of the paradoxes. Probably the most important of such points is the man's almost paralyzing shyness. All his other attributes—some of them quite incongruous, such as his ambition, his talent, his tenacity, and his intellectual authority—had somehow to be arranged about and adjusted to this, in the course of his development and growth. This process of psychic adjustment had some intriguing by-products. He managed to have his talents recognized at an early age, even though it was not until he was thirty that he could bring himself to take the floor at a public gathering. Personal references in his correspondence are maddeningly few, and when in later life he arranged his papers for eventual publication (not to occur until after his death), he appears to have systematically suppressed virtually everything of a "private" nature, though it is not likely that such material had ever really abounded in the first place. For this and other reasons, James Madison's humanity is harder to reconstruct than that of any comparable leader of his time.

Ideas were of consuming importance to him, and some of the most striking ones in the history of American constitutional thought are his. But pride of authorship in the ordinary sense was something he learned to renounce very early, if indeed he ever had it. The cause, the idea, was the vital thing, and time after time he would attribute an origin to someone else rather than claim it for himself, which made for a special kind of delicacy in a man not otherwise given to large gestures of open generosity. Anonymity was far more comfortable than the glare of the limelight. "Madison," as one writer has put it, "was made small enough (five foot six) and sufficiently diffident as not to excite the suspicion of men that he would be in competition with them for anything...." He could go to some lengths to assist in the saving of face, and he had a well-developed sense of how to achieve the measures he sought without making other men angry. And yet this flexibility, as we shall see, was hardly unlimited. It must in any case be remembered that everything he did was done by a man both timid *and* stubborn.

In addition to his extreme personal diffidence, there is a related element in the *modus operandi* of James Madison that is important for an understanding of his career as a whole. Unprepared to confront his environment alone, through direct force of personality—as many men of his time, such as Patrick Henry, could and did do—James Madison always functioned, when he did so effectively, under some kind of "cover." As a rule it was only in the setting of the committee, rather than that of the forum, that he could have an operative public self. The rule had few exceptions. Even the Constitutional Convention, which was the peak point of Madison's career, was in many ways a kind of closed committee, whose actual proceedings were not made public for more than fifty years and then only when he himself chose to do it. Then there was another form of "cover" that Madison maintained in constant repair. He would enter upon no question of policy or law without the most massive prior preparation, which meant that he would almost always know at least twice as much about it as anyone else present. So it is not so much the image of a man, but of the man's knowledge and intelligence with a life of their own, that has left its impress upon history. The "cover" principle even operated, in an odd sort of way, in the sphere of his social relations. Depending on the witness, accounts of Madison's social presence could vary between the most perplexing extremes. One might find him charming; another could think him a "gloomy stiff creature." It was Margaret Bayard Smith who may have hit it closest: "this entertaining, interesting and communicative personage, had a single stranger or indifferent person been present, would have been mute, cold and repulsive."

James Madison was born in 1751 and grew up at Montpelier, a plantation in the Virginia piedmont near the Rapidan, an upper branch of the Rappahannock. Of his forbears he wrote, "They were planters and among the respectable though not the most opulent class." Nevertheless his father, Colonel James Madison—county lieutenant, justice of the peace, large landowner, and vestryman of St. Thomas Parish—was probably the most important man in Orange County. Colonel Madison, who did not have all the learning he would have liked, was determined that his son should receive the best education available. James junior attended a preparatory school at Dunkirk in King and Queen County conducted by the able Scottish pedagogue Donald Robertson. There, and later through a season of tutoring at home, he studied Latin, Greek, French, Spanish, logic, mathematics, and geography, and developed an interest in political philosophy through the reading of Montesquieu and Locke. He entered the College of New Jersey at Princeton in 1769 and completed the course of four years in a little over two. He received the bachelor's degree in September 1771.

Princeton, in addition to its high intellectual élan during the years Madison attended, was already penetrated by an all-but-open republicanism, and the college vibrated with revolutionary sentiments as time went on. Such sentiments were shared, and even abetted, by the president. John Witherspoon was a burly, vigorous, and irrepressible Presbyterian cleric recently arrived from Scotland, where the most advanced ideas of the age in moral and political philosophy were being generated. "The Doctor," as Witherspoon was fondly known to his students, would himself be a signer of the Declaration of Independence and a member of the Continental Congress. In 1770, when the merchants of New York went back on their agreement to maintain non-importation, a copy of their self-justifying letter to the Philadelphia merchants was burned at Princeton in the college yard by the public hangman, hired for the purpose by the students, "all of them appearing in their black Gowns & the bell Tolling."

Though both law and theology were among Madison's many intellectual interests, neither the bar nor the ministry seems ever to have been seriously considered by him as a career, in view of his weak voice and personal shyness. Of the latter failing he was apparently quite conscious, judging from the frequent entries in his youthful commonplace book on timid men and their behavior, culled from the maxims of Cardinal de Retz and others. At Princeton he was among the founding members of the American Whig Society. Little is known of the early activities and purposes of American Whig and its rival society, Cliosophic, except for the so-called paper wars between them, but in these James Madison first found a vehicle of public expression which did not constrain him. Members of each society wrote lampooning ditties about those of the other; these satires would then be read in open hall by a designated spokesman before the entire student body, while the actual authors—notable among whom was Madison—remained anonymous. Madison's verses were a bit on the ribald side, which somewhat relieves the picture we have inherited of him as a man of no wit. Among Madison's fellow Whigs were Hugh Henry Brackenridge, William Bradford, and Philip Freneau; Aaron Burr was a Clio. At commencement, each graduate was expected to deliver an oration. Madison, though a shining student and well enough at the time, could not do it, and was excused. Upon his return home he suffered a breakdown in the form of epileptoid hysteria, an ailment connected with "overstudy, daydreaming, hypochondria and a sense of physical inferiority," and among whose victims, as Breuer and Freud later wrote, "one may meet persons of the clearest intellects, the strongest wills, greatest principles, and of the subtlest minds." For a time Madison kept his friend Bradford in a state of some alarm with letters gloomily predicting his own early death, but seems to have recovered himself through exercise and by temporarily easing up on his reading. Within a year he was back in health.

Early in 1774 five or six Baptists were jailed in Culpeper County for preaching without licenses, and this drew from James Madison an exceptional flare-up of feeling, plus his first words and acts of a public nature. "I have neither patience to hear talk or think of any thing relative to this matter," he wrote to Bradford, "for I have squabbled and scolded abused and ridiculed so long about it, to so little purpose that I am without common patience." It is not clear precisely what he did, but he seems to have exerted some influence on behalf of the dissenters, and the Baptists were to support him in his home district from that time on. The approach of the Revolution in effect opened to the twenty-three-year-old Madison his true career. "On the commencement of the dispute with Great Britain," he later wrote in his "Autobiography" (characteristically referring to himself in the third person), "he entered with the prevailing zeal into the American Cause. . . ." This seems to have occurred to some extent under his father's aegis. At the meeting of freeholders which chose James junior as a member of the Orange County Committee of Safety in 1774, Colonel Madison was elected chairman. Father and son were likewise elected to the Convention of 1776 which was to devise a new government for Virginia. During the adoption of the Declaration of Rights at that convention, the young man once again put himself on record for religious liberty. In committee, he succeeded in having George Mason's article on that point amended from a guarantee of "toleration" to the more ample "free exercise" of religion. He was defeated for a seat in the newly constituted House of Delegates, presumably because he refused to treat the voters to liquor. But his talents were already sufficiently evident to the members of the House that they elected him to the Council of State, where he served under the first two elected Governors of Virginia, Patrick Henry and Thomas Jefferson. Late in 1779 he was chosen to go to the Continental Congress, where he remained until October 1783. By the time he left, his biographer says, he had made himself "the acknowledged leader in every activity that bulwarked independence and pointed toward a strong, firm national union of the states."

Madison's preeminence in Congress came not primarily from speechmaking but from his tireless committee work and the writing of letters, instructions, and reports. He was directly concerned with a range of business that included defense, military finance, revenue, commerce, diplomacy, and western lands. The very intensity with which he committed himself to this work, rarely missing a day's session, made it virtually inevitable that he should also commit himself in the course of it to a broad continental view of the Revolution which had little room for narrow sectional or local interests. It was during this period that he first met Alexander Hamilton, who entered Congress in 1782. The two saw eye to eye on almost everything, and quickly became friends and allies.

Side by side with Madison's nationalism grew a bitterness toward England which was greatly intensified by the British campaign in the South. "Negroes, Horses, Tobacco & c," he wrote to Philip Mazzei, "not the standards and arms of their antagonists, are the trophies which display their success." His reaction to these depredations, says Irving Brant, "deepened an Anglophobia which ruled his mind and emotions for years to come." Madison's mind, whose judicious and rational side may be the more prominent, is nevertheless not at all comprehensible unless this anglophobia is seen as a significant force in its workings.

Still, it is principally to Madison's nationalism that one looks for the energy which propelled his actions from the end of the Revolution through the framing and ratification of the Federal Constitution—through two more terms in the Virginia Assembly, membership in the abortive Annapolis Convention, a return to Congress, a seat at Philadelphia in 1787, and another in the ratifying convention of Virginia in 1788.

Madison's great contribution to the Philadelphia Convention consisted not of compromises—these were for the most part worked out by others—but rather of a master theory and a master plan. The theory—to be known as "Federalism"—was one which rationalized a large republic in the face of the prevailing idea that only small ones could function; it was also one which justified a strong central government in the face of fears in the several states that central power meant tyranny. The plan—to be known as the "Virginia Plan"—specified a series of key arrangements which to Madison were indispensable if Federalism was to work. Most of them were enacted, thanks in great part to the persistence of Madison himself. Two of them, however, were not, despite Madison's every effort to save them. Stubbornly opposed to state encroachments on national power, he resisted state equality in either branch of the national legislature. When the great compromise was reported whereby representation in the lower house was made proportionate to population and that in the Senate made equal, Madison, according to his own words, "was not only fixed in his opposition to the report of the committee but was prepared for any event that might follow a negative of it." It was only with deep disgust that he finally gave in. The other provision he had his heart set on but lost was a sweeping veto by the national government on all state laws. The authority of the federal judiciary was not in his view an adequate substitute. Yet most of Madison's views on national supremacy were in fact embodied in the completed Constitution, even though the powers of the national government would have been still greater if he had fully had his way.

The following year he and Hamilton, with the assistance of John Jay, defended the work of the Convention and the logic of the Constitution in *The Federalist*. In Madison's case it was logical that the thoughts that went into these papers, and into the work he had done at Philadelphia, should have received a fair portion of their shape from Madison's prior intellectual experience.

The Princeton of Madison's day furnished nine delegates to the Federal Convention—more than any other college, and one more than the combined total of Princeton's two closest competitors. For Madison the choice of Princeton, rather than the more convenient William and Mary, was itself that of an at-least-partially prepared mind. Madison's initial revolutionary impulses had already taken the form of strong opposition to the Anglican establishment in Virginia and to the movement in England for sending a bishop to America. Though the Madisons themselves were Anglicans, both father and son seem to have been suspicious enough of Church of England influence at William and Mary that they preferred Presbyterian Princeton, already known for libertarian sentiments and already "talking as if she was to be a bulwark against Episcopacy." Religious liberty was insisted upon there, and the subject was frequently debated. A major premise of Madison's Federalist Number 10—that a multiplicity of interests may function as a guarantee of political stability and against majority despotism—had grown very logically out of Madison's earliest responses to the ecclesiastical situation in Virginia and to his own peculiar determination all through the 1770s and 1780s to pull down the Anglican Church's privileged position there. "If the Church of England had been the established and general Religion in all the Northern Colonies as it has been among us here," he wrote to William Bradford early in 1774, ". . . it is clear to me that slavery and Subjection might and would have been gradually insinuated among us." The shape of the thought is that of Voltaire, whom Madison and his fellow-students read at Princeton. He was fond of quoting Voltaire's quip that if only one sect were allowed in England, "despotism might be apprehended; if two only, they would seek to cut each other's throats; but as there are at least thirty, they live together in peace and happiness."

Enlightenment thought was accessible not only at Princeton but at colleges and academies everywhere in the colonies: the works of Locke and Montesquieu, Vattel and Burlamaqui, even Rousseau and Voltaire, were more or less basic equipment for anyone intellectually concerned with public questions. But the setting at Princeton still seems to have contained a certain extra something, and many writers have tried to account for the special vitality of that setting during the period at which James Madison and his contemporaries studied there. Various elements appear to have intersected in a felicitous way to produce it. The prestige of the college had risen vastly with the trustees' success in persuading the distinguished Witherspoon to take over its leadership, and the excitement generated by Witherspoon's vigorous reorganizing was still new when the young Madison first arrived less than a year later.

It was of considerable importance, moreover, that Witherspoon was fresh from Scotland and that Edinburgh, where he had been trained, was then the most vital intellectual center of the English-speaking world. The English universities of that same period, placidly mired under Establishment control and whose chief professional product was candidates for the Anglican clergy, were moribund. The Scottish universities, on the other hand, were full of energy. It was energy of a contentious and restless sort, and the restlessness was a feature of Scottish society as a whole, in which there were many strains. For a very poor country, the Union of 1707 had opened the way for an economic development which would at least be complementary to, rather than competitive with, that of England, but the advance of prosperity that resulted from it was by no means quickly or evenly achieved. Meanwhile Scots showed themselves willing to talk, at least, about remedies for almost anything. They both considered and achieved reforms in land tenure and agriculture, developed Scottish commerce, and made scientific advances in industry. They discussed electoral reform endlessly, though with fewer results. Even the frequent spasms of emigration (mostly to America) and the Jacobite rebellions of 1715 and 1745 reflected tensions that were salutary as well as disruptive. There was great popular enthusiasm for education. An act of 1696 had provided for the establishment of a school in every parish, as a result of which the Scots in the eighteenth century developed a better system of education than that of any country in Europe. Scottish boys with talent but no money could find their way into the universities to an extent unthinkable in England. The universities themselves catered to a range of intense professional ambition, in public law, science, and medicine as well as theology, and one of their unique features was unofficial student debating societies to whose meetings professors came only on invitation, and in which contention was heated and vigorous. Moreover, the cultural tension between England and Scotland, replete with both attractions and repulsions, imparted still another special element to Scottish intellectual life. On the one hand, English dissenters and nonconformists were welcome at Glasgow and Edinburgh but not at Oxford and Cambridge; on the other hand, the Scot who ventured into the literary world of London was never allowed to forget his provincialism. In conservative eighteenth-century England, the mentality of the outsider—of opposition, of criticism, of reform, of the "Country party"—had few formal or stable vehicles of expression. In Scotland, all this was more or less institutionalized in the universities.

Such, in short, was the setting of the "Scottish Renaissance" of the eighteenth century. It produced a formidable group of luminaries: David Hume, Adam Smith, Francis Hutcheson, Thomas Reid, Adam Ferguson, John Miller, William Robertson, and Lord Kames. They were contemporaries, all knew each other, and all were known to John Witherspoon by the time he left Scotland in 1768 to take up his new station in America.

What Witherspoon gave to his students, and what made him the greatest teacher of his day in America, did not primarily consist in creating bonds of discipleship. He did something better; he brought them the news of ideas, a good many of which, as it happened, he had little use for. In their own management of ideas, however, Witherspoon by his personal example encouraged them, almost in spite of himself, to be selective. Intellectually he was pugnacious, dogmatic, and arbitrary. One of his favorite targets was the moral philosophy of Francis Hutcheson, which he saw as deplorably superficial. On the other hand, the political dimension of Hutcheson's moral system included the first specific discussion of the conditions under which colonies and mother country ought to separate—a doctrine which Witherspoon fully endorsed in both thought and deed. In his lectures on moral philosophy he thundered against David Hume as an "infidel"; in his lectures on eloquence Hume became "sagacious" and possessed of "great reach and accuracy of judgment in matters of criticism." It seems to have been a working principle with Witherspoon that if persons suspected a thing of being pernicious, "they ought to acquaint themselves with it; they must know what it is, if they mean to shew that it is false." His list of what the students ought to read embraces the choicest works of the Enlightenment, pernicious or otherwise. The evidence suggests, moreover, that all, or nearly all, were devoured by the young Madison.

James Madison's theory of the extended republic and of the nature of political man is probably seen in its most compressed form in Federalist Number 10. The assumptions behind it, the particular spirit of inquiry implicit in it, and even certain of its leading ideas—as Douglass Adair has shown—take on additional meaning when viewed with reference to the special edge given to Enlightenment thought by the Scots. The "utopianism" of Enlightenment thinking amounted to more than mere constructs of reason. It had little room, on the other hand, for assumptions such as those of Burke that governments and constitutions were the product of slow organic growth, and that changes in them could only occur in the same way. Nor, at the same time, did it have much in common with one of the central beliefs of nineteenth-century Romanticism, that all discourse on matters of government and society must take for its starting point the unique character and needs of a given people and a given national state. The political philosophers of the Enlightenment tended to be universal planners; they made endless projections into the future. But they also insisted that such projections be based not simply on reason but on experience and evidence, and herein lay both a certain freedom and a certain psychological protection. Behind an attitude of "realism"—a kind of *a priori* skepticism toward any proposed system, and a judicious pessimism about most aspects of human nature—they felt free to inquire into the ways whereby people might still predict, plan, and promote their own progress.

In Scotland this state of mind was brought to a focus probably sharper than occurred anywhere else. It has been conceded that the Scots—Hume, Smith, and Ferguson in particular—are as entitled as any to be called the founders of empirical social science. A basic premise they all shared was that the behavior of people in society occurs in patterns that are more or less uniform in virtually all times and places, and that human nature itself is not subject to very great change. A dependable science of politics and government, with principles of predictability that are applicable anywhere, is therefore possible if those principles are based on experience and observation. It further follows that the materials of experience are to be found in the study of history—the history both of ancient republics and of modern states. (It was for such reasons that John Witherspoon first introduced history to the curriculum at Princeton.) State-making and the forming of commonwealths must thus be guided by the scientific reading of history's lessons—bearing always in mind, of course, that those lessons might be read in more than one way.

Douglass Adair has pictured James Madison writing the Tenth Federalist with the *Essays* of David Hume lying open on his table. There are certainly parallelisms that make this plausible. Hume in 1752 had hoped that an opportunity might some day be afforded for reducing to practice the "Idea of a Perfect Commonwealth," "either by a dissolution of some old government, or by the combination of men to form a new one, in some distant part of the world." Madison in 1788 was justifying in theory, with Hume's assistance, what he had just helped to bring about in practice. Both assumed that among the worst of all perils in a free government was that of faction. A great inspiration for Madison was Hume's insistence that such perils were more easily controlled in a large republic than in a small one, despite Montesquieu's widely believed doctrine that only small states were governable as republics. Each took for granted that factions and parties—they used the terms more or less interchangeably—were evil. A faction, according to Madison, was any group, a majority or minority in the commonwealth, actuated by some "passion, or . . . interest" adverse to the public good or to the rights of the whole. The designs of a minority faction might be thwarted by the republican principle of majority rule. But where was the remedy if the faction should embrace a majority?

The causes of faction, Madison asserted, are "sown in the nature of man." Like Hume, he allowed that there could be any number of occasions for forming factions and all manner of differences—of class, religion, property, and what not—on which they might be based. There has been some conjecture by modern writers as to just what sorts of divisions Madision thought most susceptible to faction. But whatever the answer may be, of one thing he seems to be certain: if factions are not formed on one pretext they will be formed on some other. Men commit aggressions upon one another because—tautology though it may be—it is in man's nature to be aggressive. And yet the remedy for faction is not to remove its causes, because that is impossible; nor is it to take away the liberty without which factions cannot be formed, since to take away liberty is to take away all. Such a cure would be "worse than the disease." The true remedy is not to strike at the causes, but to control the effects.

Small republics, said Hume in the "Idea of a Perfect Commonwealth," are "frail and uncertain," because the close habitation of the people makes them more susceptible to sudden currents of popular passion and facilitates the formation of tyrannical majority factions. Hume then declared that

> in a large government, which is modelled with masterly skill, there is compass and room enough to refine the democracy, from the lower

people ... to the higher magistrates, who direct all the movements. At the same time, the parts are so distant and remote, that it is very difficult, either by intrigue, prejudice, or passion, to hurry them into any measures against the public interest.

It was just such a government as this, Madison thought, that had in fact been formed in America, and it was under just such a government, he argued, that the rights of all would be most secure. In this large and extended republic, there would be a wider choice of representatives, a "greater variety of parties" which would prevent any one party's "being able to outnumber and oppress the rest"; and although "factious leaders may kindle a flame within their particular States, [they] will be unable to spread a general conflagration through the other States...." And so, he concluded, "in the extent and proper structure of the Union ... we behold a Republican remedy for the diseases most incident to Republican government."

The Tenth Federalist was the first of the series that Madison wrote, and it represented the compressed essence of several years' reading and thought as developed in more diffuse form through his correspondence, in the two papers he had written prior to the Convention, "Vices of the Political System of the United States" and "On Ancient and Modern Confederacies," and in the speeches he had made in the Convention itself. Among the ways in which the Tenth Federalist has been read in modern times is as an outline for "brokerage politics," the arts of compromise, the "politics of privacy." Yet in fact such a realm hardly existed in 1789, certainly not for James Madison. The philosopher, the system-builder, is not the man most likely to be found playing the role of compromise broker for other men's "private opportunities," and even less for other men's systems. The "politics of privacy" had virtually no room for the choices and opportunities of a James Madison, because he could not have them in the sense that ordinary men could. His most valued private choices could not be private at all. They were made in the realm of ideas and systems; his opportunity was the public good. He was, when Fisher Ames first observed him in 1789, wholly a public man: he "was bred to it, and has no other profession." He could thus have no clear way of perceiving when those choices might—to use his own definition—become strongly, even dangerously, "factious."

Madison and his friend Hamilton might agree on the structure of the republic, on the extent of its powers, on its need for a strong Executive and a generous revenue, and even on its need to coerce the states. And yet on the republic's character, its moral texture, the face it presented to the rest of the world—matters that almost defied thought—the two could never agree, though they did not as yet know it. The moral weather of James Madison's republic must never be tainted by the least shadow of dependence on Great Britain. This was fundamental; he could go no deeper. And though he may have been thinking thoughts of continental breadth, the eyes through which he saw his republic were still, with all said and done, those of a Virginian.

VINCENT BLASI, SCHOOL VOUCHERS AND RELIGIOUS LIBERTY: SEVEN QUESTIONS FROM MADISON'S MEMORIAL AND REMONSTRANCE

87 Cornell L. Rev. 783 (2002).

In the immediate aftermath of the Revolutionary War, many upstanding citizens of the fledgling state of Virginia were not pleased. They were, in fact, appalled by the decline they perceived in the state of public morals. Newspaper editorials, sermons, and speeches in public assemblies resounded with references to the recent upsurge in gambling, whoring, cockfighting, and public drunkenness. That such departures from the straight and narrow are not uncommon in postwar periods, following all the social dislocations of military mobilization, was no consolation to Virginians eager to show a doubting world that government by the people could work.

The root of the problem, in the view of many, was that the churches of the new commonwealth no longer enjoyed the influence or support they had taken for granted during the colonial period. In particular, the Episcopalian Church, formerly the colony's established Church of England, was suffering. Many of its splendid edifices had been damaged in the fighting; fully half of its clergy were now exiled or discredited former tories. Those ministers who remained were having trouble eliciting sufficient voluntary contributions from congregations unaccustomed to that method of ecclesiastical support.

Into this breach leaped that eloquent opportunist, Patrick Henry. He sponsored in the Virginia Assembly a daring proposal to reinvigorate the public morality. His plan was to harness the fiscal powers of the state in the service of religious teaching, all to the end of civic virtue. A "General Assessment" would be instituted in the form of a property surtax. In contrast to the traditional use of the taxing power to support a single, preferred religion, Henry's proposal permitted each taxpayer to specify which Christian denomination should receive his payment. Those who did not wish to support a church could direct their assessment to a proposed common school fund. The bill provided that a record be kept of each taxpayer's choice of recipient, to be posted in the county courthouse, "there to remain for the inspection of all concerned." Revenues would then be distributed in accordance with these taxpayer directions. Churches could use their allotments to pay for the salaries of their clergy, to provide places of divine worship, and to "none other use whatsoever."[7]

7. The bill contained one explicit exception to this restriction on how the funds could be used: "except in the denominations of Quakers and Menonists, who may receive what is collected from their members, and place it in their general fund, to be disposed of in a manner which they shall think best calculated to promote their particular mode of worship." *Id.* The Quakers and Menonists had no clergy or church buildings so the General Assessment would have been of little or no benefit to them

One member of the Virginia Assembly took particular exception to Henry's proposal, the representative from Orange County, James Madison. Despite his relative youth, by 1784 Madison had a well-formulated position and some hard-earned political savvy regarding the sensitive issue of church-state relations. Eight years earlier he had helped to draft and steer to enactment the religious liberty clause of the new Virginia Constitution. Madison viewed the General Assessment as a patent violation of that constitutional commitment and a profound threat to Virginia's experiment in republican government. He devoted the ensuing year to the cause of defeating Henry's proposal: first by convincing the legislature to postpone action on the measure until after the next election, then by organizing an appeal to the voters to elect assembly candidates who would oppose the General Assessment, and finally by engineering its defeat at the subsequent legislative session. In the course of this campaign, Madison wrote a succinct polemic, the *Memorial and Remonstrance Against Religious Assessments*, which constitutes the most powerful and influential statement of his views on the subject of religious liberty.

THE PROPOSED GENERAL ASSESSMENT

(1784).

WHEREAS the general diffusion of Christian knowledge hath a natural tendency to correct the morals of men, restrain their vices, and preserve the peace of society, which cannot be effected without a competent provision for learned teachers, who may be thereby enabled to devote their time and attention to the duty of instructing such citizens, as from their circumstances and want of education, cannot otherwise attain such knowledge; and it is judged that such provision may be made by the Legislature, without counteracting the liberal principle heretofore adopted and intended to be preserved by abolishing all distinctions of preeminence amongst the different societies or communities of Christians;

Be it therefore enacted by the General Assembly, That for the support of Christian teachers, per centum on the amount, or in the pound on the amount, or in the pound on the sum payable for tax on the property within this Commonwealth, is hereby assessed, and shall be paid by every person chargeable with the said tax at the time the same shall become due; and the Sheriffs of the several Counties shall have power to levy and collect the same in the same manner and under the like restrictions and limitations, as are or may be prescribed by the laws for raising the revenues of this State.

And be it enacted, That for every sum so paid, the Sheriff or Collector shall give a receipt, expressing therein to what society of

absent such an exception. With the exception, however, they were free to use tax-generated funds for proselytizing expenses, something the other sects were not free to do.

Christians the person from whom he may receive the same shall direct the money to be paid, keeping a distinct account thereof in his books.

* * *

And be it further enacted, That the money to be raised by virtue of this act, shall be by the Vestries, Elders, or Directors of each religious society, appropriated to a provision for a Minister or Teacher of the Gospel of their denomination, or the providing places of divine worship, and to none other use whatsoever; except in the denominations of Quakers and Menonists, who may receive what is collected from their members, and place it in their general fund, to be disposed of in a manner which they shall think best calculated to promote their particular mode of worship.

And be it enacted, That all sums which at the time of payment to the Sheriff or Collector may not be appropriated by the person paying the same, shall be accounted for with the Court in manner as by this Act is directed; and after deducting for his collection, the Sheriff shall pay the amount thereof (upon account certified by the Court to the Auditors of Public Accounts, and by them to the Treasurer) into the Public Treasury, to be disposed of under the direction of the General Assembly, for the encouragement of seminaries of learning within the Counties whence such sums shall arise, and to no other use or purpose whatsoever.

JAMES MADISON, A MEMORIAL AND REMONSTRANCE

(1785).

We the subscribers, citizens of the said Commonwealth, having taken into serious consideration, a Bill printed by order of the last Session of General Assembly, entitled "A Bill establishing a provision for Teachers of the Christian Religion," and conceiving that the same if finally armed with the sanctions of a law, will be a dangerous abuse of power, are bound as faithful members of a free State to remonstrate against it, and to declare the reasons by which we are determined. We remonstrate against the said Bill,

1. Because we hold it for a fundamental and undeniable truth, "that Religion or the duty which we owe to our Creator and the manner of discharging it, can be directed only by reason and conviction, not by force or violence." The Religion then of every man must be left to the conviction and conscience of every man; and it is the right of every man to exercise it as these may dictate. This right is in its nature an unalienable right. It is unalienable, because the opinions of men, depending only on the evidence contemplated by their own minds cannot follow the dictates of other men: It is unalienable also, because what is here a right towards men, is a duty towards the Creator. It is the duty of every man to render to the Creator such homage and such only as he believes to be acceptable to him. This duty is precedent, both in order of time and

in degree of obligation, to the claims of Civil Society. Before any man can be considered as a member of Civil Society, he must be considered as a subject of the Governour of the Universe: And if a member of Civil Society, who enters into any subordinate Association, must always do it with a reservation of his duty to the General Authority; much more must every man who becomes a member of any particular Civil Society, do it with a saving of his allegiance to the Universal Sovereign. We maintain therefore that in matters of Religion, no man's right is abridged by the institution of Civil Society and that Religion is wholly exempt from its cognizance. True it is, that no other rule exists, by which any question which may divide a Society, can be ultimately determined, but the will of the majority; but it is also true that the majority may trespass on the rights of the minority.

2. Because if Religion be exempt from the authority of the Society at large, still less can it be subject to that of the Legislative Body. The latter are but the creatures and vicegerents of the former. Their jurisdiction is both derivative and limited: it is limited with regard to the coordinate departments, more necessarily is it limited with regard to the constituents. The preservation of a free Government requires not merely, that the metes and bounds which separate each department of power be invariably maintained; but more especially that neither of them be suffered to overleap the great Barrier which defends the rights of the people. The Rulers who are guilty of such an encroachment, exceed the commission from which they derive their authority, and are Tyrants. The People who submit to it are governed by laws made neither by themselves nor by an authority derived from them, and are slaves.

3. Because it is proper to take alarm at the first experiment on our liberties. We hold this prudent jealousy to be the first duty of Citizens, and one of the noblest characteristics of the late Revolution. The free men of America did not wait till usurped power had strengthened itself by exercise, and entangled the question in precedents. They saw all the consequences in the principle, and they avoided the consequences by denying the principle. We revere this lesson too much soon to forget it. Who does not see that the same authority which can establish Christianity, in exclusion of all other Religions, may establish with the same ease any particular sect of Christians, in exclusion of all other Sects? that the same authority which can force a citizen to contribute three pence only of his property for the support of any one establishment, may force him to conform to any other establishment in all cases whatsoever?

4. Because the Bill violates that equality which ought to be the basis of every law, and which is more indispensible, in proportion as the validity or expediency of any law is more liable to be impeached. If "all men are by nature equally free and independent," all men are to be considered as entering into Society on equal conditions; as relinquishing no more, and therefore retaining no less, one than another, of their natural rights. Above all are they to be considered as retaining an "*equal* title to the free exercise of Religion according to the dictates of Conscience." Whilst we assert for ourselves a freedom to embrace, to profess

and to observe the Religion which we believe to be of divine origin, we cannot deny an equal freedom to those whose minds have not yet yielded to the evidence which has convinced us. If this freedom be abused, it is an offence against God, not against man: To God, therefore, not to man, must an account of it be rendered. As the Bill violates equality by subjecting some to peculiar burdens, so it violates the same principle, by granting to others peculiar exemptions. Are the Quakers and Menonists the only sects who think a compulsive support of their Religions unnecessary and unwarrantable? Can their piety alone be entrusted with the care of public worship? Ought their Religions to be endowed above all others with extraordinary privileges by which proselytes may be enticed from all others? We think too favorably of the justice and good sense of these denominations to believe that they either covet pre-eminences over their fellow citizens or that they will be seduced by them from the common opposition to the measure.

5. Because the Bill implies either that the Civil Magistrate is a competent Judge of Religious Truth; or that he may employ Religion as an engine of Civil policy. The first is an arrogant pretension falsified by the contradictory opinions of Rulers in all ages, and throughout the world: the second an unhallowed perversion of the means of salvation.

6. Because the establishment proposed by the Bill is not requisite for the support of the Christian Religion. To say that it is, is a contradiction to the Christian Religion itself, for every page of it disavows a dependence on the powers of this world: it is a contradiction to fact; for it is known that this Religion both existed and flourished, not only without the support of human laws, but in spite of every opposition from them, and not only during the period of miraculous aid, but long after it had been left to its own evidence and the ordinary care of Providence. Nay, it is a contradiction in terms; for a Religion not invented by human policy, must have pre-existed and been supported, before it was established by human policy. It is moreover to weaken in those who profess this Religion a pious confidence in its innate excellence and the patronage of its Author; and to foster in those who still reject it, a suspicion that its friends are too conscious of its fallacies to trust it to its own merits.

7. Because experience witnesseth that ecclesiastical establishments, instead of maintaining the purity and efficacy of Religion, have had a contrary operation. During almost fifteen centuries has the legal establishment of Christianity been on trial. What have been its fruits? More or less in all places, pride and indolence in the Clergy, ignorance and servility in the laity, in both, superstition, bigotry and persecution. Enquire of the Teachers of Christianity for the ages in which it appeared in its greatest lustre; those of every sect, point to the ages prior to its incorporation with Civil policy. Propose a restoration of this primitive State in which its Teachers depended on the voluntary rewards of their flocks, many of them predict its downfall. On which Side ought their testimony to have greatest weight, when for or when against their interest?

8. Because the establishment in question is not necessary for the support of Civil Government. If it be urged as necessary for the support of Civil Government only as it is a means of supporting Religion, and it be not necessary for the latter purpose, it cannot be necessary for the former. If Religion be not within the cognizance of Civil Government how can its legal establishment be necessary to Civil Government? What influence in fact have ecclesiastical establishments had on Civil Society? In some instances they have been seen to erect a spiritual tyranny on the ruins of the Civil authority; in many instances they have been seen upholding the thrones of political tyranny: in no instance have they been seen the guardians of the liberties of the people. Rulers who wished to subvert the public liberty, may have found an established Clergy convenient auxiliaries. A just Government instituted to secure & perpetuate it needs them not. Such a Government will be best supported by protecting every Citizen in the enjoyment of his Religion with the same equal hand which protects his person and his property; by neither invading the equal rights of any Sect, nor suffering any Sect to invade those of another.

9. Because the proposed establishment is a departure from that generous policy, which, offering an Asylum to the persecuted and oppressed of every Nation and Religion, promised a lustre to our country, and an accession to the number of its citizens. What a melancholy mark is the Bill of sudden degeneracy? Instead of holding forth an Asylum to the persecuted, it is itself a signal of persecution. It degrades from the equal rank of Citizens all those whose opinions in Religion do not bend to those of the Legislative authority. Distant as it may be in its present form from the Inquisition, it differs from it only in degree. The one is the first step, the other the last in the career of intolerance. The magnanimous sufferer under this cruel scourge in foreign Regions, must view the Bill as a Beacon on our Coast, warning him to seek some other haven, where liberty and philanthropy in their due extent, may offer a more certain repose from his Troubles.

10. Because it will have a like tendency to banish our Citizens. The allurements presented by other situations are every day thinning their number. To superadd a fresh motive to emigration by revoking the liberty which they now enjoy, would be the same species of folly which has dishonoured and depopulated flourishing kingdoms.

11. Because it will destroy that moderation and harmony which the forbearance of our laws to intermeddle with Religion has produced among its several sects. Torrents of blood have been spilt in the old world, by vain attempts of the secular arm, to extinguish Religious discord, by proscribing all difference in Religious opinion. Time has at length revealed the true remedy. Every relaxation of narrow and rigorous policy, wherever it has been tried, has been found to assuage the disease. The American Theatre has exhibited proofs that equal and compleat liberty, if it does not wholly eradicate it, sufficiently destroys its malignant influence on the health and prosperity of the State. If with the salutary effects of this system under our own eyes, we begin to

contract the bounds of Religious freedom, we know no name that will too severely reproach our folly. At least let warning be taken at the first fruits of the threatened innovation. The very appearance of the Bill has transformed "that Christian forbearance, love and charity," which of late mutually prevailed, into animosities and jealousies, which may not soon be appeased. What mischiefs may not be dreaded, should this enemy to the public quiet be armed with the force of a law?

12. Because the policy of the Bill is adverse to the diffusion of the light of Christianity. The first wish of those who enjoy this precious gift ought to be that it may be imparted to the whole race of mankind. Compare the number of those who have as yet received it with the number still remaining under the dominion of false Religions; and how small is the former! Does the policy of the Bill tend to lessen the disproportion? No; it at once discourages those who are strangers to the light of revelation from coming into the Region of it; and countenances by example the nations who continue in darkness, in shutting out those who might convey it to them. Instead of Levelling as far as possible, every obstacle to the victorious progress of Truth, the Bill with an ignoble and unchristian timidity would circumscribe it with a wall of defence against the encroachments of error.

13. Because attempts to enforce by legal sanctions, acts obnoxious to so great a proportion of Citizens, tend to enervate the laws in general, and to slacken the bands of Society. If it be difficult to execute any law which is not generally deemed necessary or salutary, what must be the case, where it is deemed invalid and dangerous? And what may be the effect of so striking an example of impotency in the Government, on its general authority?

14. Because a measure of such singular magnitude and delicacy ought not to be imposed, without the clearest evidence that it is called for by a majority of citizens, and no satisfactory method is yet proposed by which the voice of the majority in this case may be determined, or its influence secured. "The people of the respective counties are indeed requested to signify their opinion respecting the adoption of the Bill to the next Session of Assembly." But the representation must be made equal, before the voice either of the Representatives or of the Counties will be that of the people. Our hope is that neither of the former will, after due consideration, espouse the dangerous principle of the Bill. Should the event disappoint us, it will still leave us in full confidence, that a fair appeal to the latter will reverse the sentence against our liberties.

15. Because finally, "the equal right of every citizen to the free exercise of his Religion according to the dictates of conscience" is held by the same tenure with all our other rights. If we recur to its origin, it is equally the gift of nature; if we weigh its importance, it cannot be less dear to us; if we consult the "Declaration of those rights which pertain to the good people of Virginia, as the basis and foundation of Government," it is enumerated with equal solemnity, or rather studied empha-

sis. Either then, we must say, that the Will of the Legislature is the only measure of their authority; and that in the plenitude of this authority, they may sweep away all our fundamental rights; or, that they are bound to leave this particular right untouched and sacred: Either we must say, that they may controul the freedom of the press, may abolish the Trial by Jury, may swallow up the Executive and Judiciary Powers of the State; nay that they may despoil us of our very right of suffrage, and erect themselves into an independent and hereditary Assembly or, we must say, that they have no authority to enact into law the Bill under consideration. We the Subscribers say, that the General Assembly of this Commonwealth have no such authority: And that no effort may be omitted on our part against so dangerous an usurpation, we oppose to it, this remonstrance; earnestly praying, as we are in duty bound, that the Supreme Lawgiver of the Universe, by illuminating those to whom it is addressed, may on the one hand, turn their Councils from every act which would affront his holy prerogative, or violate the trust committed to them: and on the other, guide them into every measure which may be worthy of his blessing, may redound to their own praise, and may establish more firmly the liberties, the prosperity and the happiness of the Commonwealth.

RALPH KETCHAM, JAMES MADISON: A BIOGRAPHY

(1990).

George Mason had the "Remonstrance" printed in Alexandria, and hundreds of copies were circulated throughout the state. In August, Madison reported candidly to Jefferson: "The opposition to the general assessment gains ground. At the instance of some of its adversaries I drew up the remonstrance herewith inclosed. It has been sent thro' the medium of confidential persons in a number of the upper Counties, and I am told will be pretty extensively signed. The Presbyterian clergy, have at length espoused the side of the opposition, being moved either by a fear of their laity or a jealousy of the Episcopalians. The mutual hatred of these sects has been much inflamed by the late Act incorporating the latter. I am far from being sorry for it, as a coalition between them could alone endanger our religious rights, and a tendency to such an event has been suspected."

Madison must have been confidently jubilant as he took his seat in the Assembly that fall: "The table was loaded with petitions and remonstrances from all parts against interposition of the Legislature in matters of Religion." A Presbyterian convention had petitioned for a law establishing religious freedom, and Baptists and Methodists declaimed against a religious tax. The assessment bill of the previous session died silently, and Madison quickly proposed adoption of Jefferson's eloquent "Bill for Establishing Religious Freedom." After its enactment, Madison wrote its author that "I flatter myself [we] have in this country extinguished forever the ambitious hope of making laws for the human mind." Of all his accomplishments as a legislator, Madison took greatest pleasure and pride in this victory.

THE STATUTE OF VIRGINIA FOR RELIGIOUS FREEDOM

Drafted by Thomas Jefferson in 1777 and adopted by the General Assembly in 1786

Whereas almighty God hath created the mind free; that all attempts to influence it by temporal punishments or burthens, or by civil incapacitations, tend only to beget habits of hypocrisy and meanness, and are a departure from the plan of the Holy author of our religion, who being Lord both of body and mind, yet chose not to propagate it by coercions on either, as was in his Almighty power to do; that the impious presumption of legislators and rulers, civil as well as ecclesiastical, who being themselves but fallible and uninspired men, have assumed dominion over the faith of others, setting up their own opinions and modes of thinking as the only true and infallible, and as such endeavouring to impose them on others, hath established and maintained false religions over the greatest part of the world, and through all time; that to compel a man to furnish contributions of money for the propagation of opinions which he disbelieves, is sinful and tyrannical; that even the forcing him to support this or that teacher of his own religious persuasion, is depriving him of the comfortable liberty of giving his contributions to the particular pastor, whose morals he would make his pattern, and whose powers he feels most persuasive to righteousness, and is withdrawing from the ministry those temporary rewards, which proceeding from an approbation of their personal conduct, are an additional incitement to earnest and unremitting labours for the instruction of mankind; that our civil rights have no dependence on our religious opinions, any more than our opinions in physics or geometry; that therefore the proscribing any citizen as unworthy the public confidence by laying upon him an incapacity of being called to offices of trust and emolument, unless he profess or renounce this or that religious opinion, is depriving him injuriously of those privileges and advantages to which in common with his fellow-citizens he has a natural right; that it tends only to corrupt the principles of that religion it is meant to encourage, by bribing with a monopoly of worldly honours and emoluments, those who will externally profess and conform to it; that though indeed these are criminal who do not withstand such temptation, yet neither are those innocent who lay the bait in their way; that to suffer the civil magistrate to intrude his powers into the field of opinion, and to restrain the profession or propagation of principles on supposition of their ill tendency, is a dangerous fallacy, which at once destroys all religious liberty, because he being of course judge of that tendency will make his opinions the rule of judgment, and approve or condemn the sentiments of others only as they shall square with or differ from his own; that it is time enough for the rightful purposes of civil government, for its officers to interfere when principles break out into overt acts against peace and good order; and finally, that truth is great and will prevail if left to herself, that she is the proper and sufficient antagonist to error, and has nothing to fear from the conflict, unless by human interposition disarmed of her natural weapons, free argument and debate, errors ceasing to be dangerous when it is permitted freely to contradict them:

Be it enacted by the General Assembly, That no man shall be compelled to frequent or support any religious worship, place, or ministry whatsoever, nor shall be enforced, restrained, molested, or burthened in his body or goods, nor shall otherwise suffer on account of his religious opinions or belief; but that all men shall be free to profess, and by argument to maintain, their opinion in matters of religion, and that the same shall in no way diminish, enlarge, or affect their civil capacities.

And though we well know that this assembly elected by the people for the ordinary purposes of legislation only, have no power to restrain the acts of succeeding assemblies, constituted with powers equal to our own, and that therefore to declare this act to be irrevocable would be of no effect in law; yet we are free to declare, and do declare, that the rights hereby asserted are of the natural rights of mankind, and that if any act shall be hereafter passed to repeal the present, or to narrow its operation, such act will be an infringement of natural right.

GARY ROSEN, AMERICAN COMPACT: JAMES MADISON AND THE PROBLEM OF FOUNDING

(1999).

The opening and closing sections of the "Memorial and Remonstrance" are its most philosophical parts; they deal directly with the social compact's essential backdrop—the condition of human beings outside of government. They also begin to describe the relationship between "nature's God," invoked by Madison in *The Federalist*, and God the Creator, the more traditional formulation that he employs in this earlier writing. By examining these rival understandings of God, we can see what sort of transcendent ground, if any, he considered necessary to maintain the claims of the social compact.

Leaving aside for a moment the specific polemical intent of the first several paragraphs of the "Memorial and Remonstrance," what is immediately apparent is their dependence on the terms of the social compact. In the opening paragraph, Madison uses "civil society," as in *The Federalist*, to describe the initial stage of the social compact. Whereas the formation of civil society seemed before to be associated with the law of nature and the importunings of necessity, here it appears to be a much more deliberate affair. Civil society is something that one "becomes a member of." It is established by "institution," which imposes a duty on its members, not to government (which is presumably still in the offing) but to what Madison calls "the General Authority." This obligation is rather severe, requiring that a member of civil society reserve his ultimate allegiance for the General Authority regardless of "any subordinate Association" that he might enter into. Only at this point is there a glimmer of the urgency that Madison attaches to civil society and its ends in *The Federalist.*

* * *

The fourth paragraph of the "Memorial and Remonstrance" affirms Article I of the Virginia Declaration of Rights in its assertion that "all men are by nature equally free and independent." Accordingly, Madison can speak of their "natural rights," that is, the liberties that they enjoy in their "free and independent" condition. He goes on to describe the implications of this equality, not for the state of nature but for the civil society that emerges from it. If he were instead to consider the insecurity and uncertainty that such natural equality promotes in the prepolitical condition, he would draw into question his own argument about the primacy of religious duty and remind the attentive reader of the social compact's great purposes. Madison avoids this pitfall by discussing the degree to which natural equality must be maintained in the institutions that *succeed* the state of nature: "all men are to be considered as entering into Society on equal conditions; as relinquishing no more, and therefore retaining no less, one than another, of their natural rights." For Madison, as for his contractarian predecessors, natural liberty is incompatible with political association. It must be modified in order for men to come together in a single community. Natural rights must be transformed into civil rights.

First, however, there are what we might call the intermediate rights of civil society. These fall somewhere between the unregulated equality of natural rights and the carefully defined civil rights of a particular constitution. These intermediate rights include, on the one hand, an equal say in the establishment of a form of government and, on the other, a claim to that government's impartial protection. The latter right is the very purpose of the social compact, while the former provides some assurance, though no guarantee, that it will be respected. Madison alludes to both in concluding his discussion of civil society's jurisdiction: "no other rule exists, by which any question which may divide a Society, can be ultimately determined, but the will of the majority; but it is also true that the majority may trespass on the rights of the minority."

In embryonic form, this is the problem Madison addresses in *Federalist* 10: how to combine majoritarianism with impartiality. In this context, however, he is not speaking of *government* by majority so much as *constitution making* by majority; other "rules" do exist by which a government might decide a divisive question. That the discussion still concerns civil society and its "General Authority" is confirmed by the account of legislative power that Madison offers in the next paragraph. Having established that religion is outside the province of "Society at large," he writes that it is all the more beyond the reach of members of "the Legislative Body," who are "but the creatures and vicegerents of the former."

Madison's use of "creatures" is worth noting, since it follows a section whose theme is the duty incumbent on human beings toward their Creator. The word emphasizes the government's dependence on the people and the derivative nature of its authority, but it also suggests a parallel between the people and God. God's creatures imitate the divine by creating the constitution under which their legislators act, "the great Barrier which defends the rights of the people." As Madison sees it, a constitution represents the chief advantage of entering civil society. It does for individuals what they once had to do for themselves: it "defends" their rights.

But these are not the rights of nature. They are civil rights, rights whose standing derives from their place in a form of government. As Madison enumerates them at the end of the "Memorial and Remonstrance," they include freedom of the press, trial by jury, and the suffrage. As the specific rights by which the more general rights of nature and civil society are made operative, they allow the people to delegate the task of self-defense to "an authority derived from them," to establish a "commission" under which their most fundamental needs will be tended to by their "creatures." The constant anxiety of the state of nature is replaced by a "prudent jealousy," which works to ensure that the terms of the commission are obeyed and that "Rulers" are not "guilty of encroachment." Under such an arrangement, the "first duty of Citizens" is "to take alarm at the first experiment on [their] liberties." Vigilance with respect to one's civil rights comes to take the place of the much more onerous superintendence of one's natural rights.

The right of conscience occupies a peculiar place in this scheme. At times, Madison maintains its similarity to other fundamental rights, insisting that they are all held "by the same tenure," by which he seems to mean some combination of natural origin and constitutional enshrinement. But religious liberty does not come into existence with civil society or government, as do trial by jury or freedom of the press. It antedates the social compact and is unmodified by it. Madison contends "that in matters of Religion, no man's right is abridged by the institution of Civil Society and that Religion is wholly exempt from its cognizance." This immunity, as we have seen, comes from a theologico-political principle that asserts the superiority of religion over politics: "It is the duty of every man to render the Creator such homage and such only as he believes to be acceptable to him. This duty is precedent, both in order of time and in degree of obligation, to the claims of Civil Society."

LANCE BANNING, THE SACRED FIRE OF LIBERTY: JAMES MADISON AND THE FOUNDING OF THE FEDERAL REPUBLIC

(1995).

"True it is," Madison's Memorial had said, that the majority must rule in a republic, "but it is also true that the majority may trespass on the rights of the minority." True it also seemed to be—and never more apparently than in the 1785 assembly—that the will of the majority could be repeatedly at odds with honor or the public good. With every legislative session, Madison had felt increasingly dishonored and revolted by poorly drafted, fluctuating laws. Since his return from Congress, he had struggled unsuccessfully for a revision of Virginia's constitution, lost as often as he won on federal issues, and crafted several state reforms to see them gutted in succeeding sessions. By the spring of 1786, as his attention turned toward the Annapolis Convention, his disgust was equaled only by his fears. For every year had also seen a tide of legislative measures, threatened or enacted, that attempted to combat the current economic troubles by preventing creditors from pressing for their dues or by depriving both the state and federal governments of revenues required in order to perform their duties.

Virginia, it is true, had managed to avoid the most objectionable measures of the postwar years: paper money, postwar confiscations, and laws preventing citizens (though not their British creditors) from suing for recovery of debts. To Madison, however, the escape seemed narrow and increasingly in doubt, nor was it any consolation to a man of continental vision that the malady seemed national in scope. Throughout America, he was beginning to conclude, the "multiplicity," the "mutability," and the "injustice" of provincial laws were calling into question "the fundamental principle of republican government, that the majority who rule in such governments are the safest guardians both of public good and of private rights." The framers of the early revolutionary constitutions, he soon observed, had thought that "a provision for the rights of persons" (that is, for republican self-government) would "include of itself" protection for the rights of property and for the other liberties that individuals had not surrendered to the state. Every year, however, was producing rising doubts that this assumption was correct. "What we once thought the calumny of the enemies of republican governments," he would tell the Constitutional Convention, "is undoubtably true": wherever "a majority are united by a common interest or passion, the rights of the minority are in danger"; the rule of the majority was not assuring a consistent preference for the well-considered interest of the public as a whole.

For Madison, it must be recognized, this was a painful, difficult admission: an insight reached in sorrow, not in triumph. Indeed, whenever he discussed the errors of the early Revolution, Madison consistently referred to the mistakes that "we" had made, to misconceptions he had shared. It was not, he knew, that early revolutionary thinkers had naively thought that a majority could do no wrong. Educated in a culture that idealized the English constitution, revolutionaries had expected individuals to differ, clash, and take advantage of one another, especially if they were rulers. Heirs to British thinking, which insisted on a balanced mixture of the powers of the one, the many, and the few, most early revolutionaries had conceded that a sound and lasting government demanded qualities that they could not associate with representative assemblies: unity, consistency, and wisdom, as well as a reflection of majority desires. Therefore, all the states had instituted complex governments, and most of them had tried, by various expedients, to make the upper house of legislature balance the lower. Many revolutionary leaders still expected that a second legislative house would act as the protector of the few against the many. Bills of rights and written constitutions—most of them insisting on a rigid separation of executive and legislative powers—were intended to assure additional protection for the rights of all.

Nevertheless, in all the early revolutionary constitutions, overwhelming power had been trusted to the lower houses—and thus to the majorities who chose them. When the new state governments were formed, a decade of confrontation with the British had resulted in a revolutionary new insistence on an active and continuous relationship between legitimate authority and popular consent, as well as in a newly literal insistence on inherent, equal rights. The confrontation with a central government that the colonials could not control had taught them that the wielders of authority respond primarily to those to whom they owe their places, those with whom they share a fundamental unity of interests. Throughout the colonies, the governmental branches most immediately responsive to the people had been valiant in the defense of liberty, as had the people "out of doors." Meanwhile, the persistent threat from Britain had destroyed the former trust in English institutions, laying the essential groundwork for the democratic argument that liberation from the tyranny of lords and kings would free America to institute new governments that would be free from the enduring differences and unavoidable corruptions that now appeared inherent in a mixed regime. Even in democracies, of course, individuals would still be equal *only* in their rights, not in their material possessions or their talents. Differences of interest or opinion would continue to result in disagreements and collisions. Nevertheless, the very crux of the republican departure from the English or colonial tradition was the bold new faith that in societies without hereditary ranks, no individual or group could have an interest *permanently* different from the well-considered interest of the whole. By 1776, theory and experience had joined to make it easy to conclude that governments derived entirely from the people, governments reconstituted in a manner that would make the rulers continuously responsible to the ruled, would necessarily pursue the people's interests and defend the people's private rights. Theory and experience had joined to make it difficult to see how the majority—the greater number of the equals who composed republican societies—could wish for anything except the public good, which was their own. Therefore, all the revolutionary states provided for an annual election of the lower house, and most provided for the annual election of their senates and executives as well. Massachusetts, followed by New Hampshire after 1784, was the only state to grant its governor a legislative veto (although New York provided for a governor who was to be a member of a council with this power). And in all the states the upper houses were invariably inclined—or, like Virginia's, constitutionally obliged—to let the lower houses take the lead in writing legislation. In other words, in all the states but two, a relatively ineffective senate was the only institutional restraint on lower houses, chosen yearly by the people.

In the circumstances of the middle eighties, as the people struggled with depression, these arrangements proved a recipe for conflict and a formula for fluctuating laws. Yet only long experience with a disturbing train of measures could compel convinced republicans to reexamine the assumptions that were at their base, for the idea that the majority itself could constitute a faction—"a number of citizens . . . who are united and actuated by some common impulse of passion, or of interest, adverse to the rights of other citizens, or to the permanent and aggregate interests of the community"—could force consistent thinkers to conclude that they might have to choose between their liberal and their republican commitments, neither one of which could be relinquished.

For Madison, the troubling legislative measures and repeated disappointments of the postwar years precipitated just this sort of crisis. With many others, he had come to be increasingly concerned with legislation that infringed the rights of contract or prevented governments from meeting contracts of their own: paper money, stay laws, moratoriums on taxes, and the rest. More than many others, Madison was troubled also by the "multiplicity" and "mutability" of laws. Not only did his ordered mind rebel against these constant fluctuations, but he also sensed that constant changes, like repeated interferences with private contracts, undermined the certainty and trust that bound societies together. In all of his experience, moreover, nothing had disturbed him quite so much as the demand for an assessment to support religion. He had always known that individuals are selfish, that majorities can be mistaken, and that people may pursue their personal, immediate desires at the expense of other people's interests or a more enlightened understanding of their own. Still, the threat of the assessment showed him with a clarity that nothing else had shown that declarations of inherent rights were flimsy barriers to rulers who could fairly claim to speak for the majority itself. And none of his preceding disappointments had presented him with such compelling proof that his convictions could not tolerate a democratic version of the rule that might makes right.

Thus, as he departed for Annapolis, Virginia's legislative leader was entrapped in a profoundly agonizing reexamination of his early revolutionary suppositions. Madison was deeply dedicated to the revolutionary principle that governments derive their just authority from popular consent and must remain responsive to the people. He was deeply dedicated, too, to "justice," by which he meant equality before the laws, security for every individual in what was properly his own, and scrupulous respect by governments for the inherent rights that governments were instituted to preserve. But in the aftermath of recent struggles in the state assembly, he was finding it extremely difficult to reconcile his libertarian with his majoritarian commitments, though he could not abandon either. Though there were many signs that popular majorities were threatening inherent rights, he still believed that rulers who escaped from their dependence on the people were a greater danger still.

The seed of a solution, hindsight may suggest, was present in a corner of his mind. The rights of conscience, his Memorial had said, are "held by the same tenure with all our other rights"; the power that could threaten these could threaten all the others. If this was so, however, then it might be so, as well, that the conditions which had guarded liberty of conscience might protect all other liberties as well. Indeed, in every free society, he soon would write, "the security for civil rights must be the same as for religious rights. It consists in the one case in the multiplicity of interests and, in the other, in the multiplicity of sects." If the Presbyterians and the Episcopalians had been able to cement their tentative alliance, nothing, Madison observed, could have defeated the general assessment. Jealousies between the sects had done what no appeal to principle could have accomplished by itself. And differences among the many more denominations of a vastly larger, federal republic might afford increased security for other rights as well.

THOMAS HOBBES, LEVIATHAN

(1651).

Private Judgement of Good and Evil

I observe the *diseases* of a commonwealth that proceed from the poison of seditious doctrines, whereof one is: *That every private man is judge of good and evil actions.* This is true in the condition of mere nature, where there are no civil laws, and also under civil government, in such cases as are not determined by the law. But otherwise, it is manifest that the measure of good and evil actions is the civil law, and the judge the legislator, who is always representative of the commonwealth. From this false doctrine men are disposed to debate with themselves, and dispute the commands of the commonwealth, and afterwards to obey or disobey them, as in their private judgments they shall think fit. Whereby the commonwealth is distracted and *weakened.*

Erroneous conscience

Another doctrine repugnant to civil society is that *whatsoever a man does against his conscience is sin;* and it dependeth on the presumption of making himself judge of good and evil. For a man's conscience and his judgment is the same thing; and as the judgment, so also the conscience may be erroneous. Therefore, though he that is subject to no civil law sinneth in all he does against his conscience, because he has no other rule to follow but his own reason, yet it is not so with him that lives in a commonwealth, because the law is the public conscience, by which he hath already undertaken to be guided. Otherwise, in such diversity as there is of private consciences, which are but private opinions, the commonwealth must needs be distracted, and no man dare to obey the sovereign power farther than it shall seem good in his own eyes.

Subjects are to be taught, not to affect change of Government

And (to descend to particulars) the people are to be taught, first, that they ought not to be in love with any form of government they see in their neighbour nations, more than with their own, nor (whatsoever present prosperity they behold in nations that are otherwise governed than they) to desire change. For the prosperity of a people ruled by an aristocratical or democratical assembly cometh not from aristocracy, nor from democracy, but from the obedience and concord of the subjects; nor do the people flourish in a monarchy because one man has the right to rule them, but because they obey him. Take away, in any kind of state, the obedience (and consequently the concord of the people) and they shall not only not flourish, but in short time be dissolved. And they that go about by disobedience, to do no more than reform the commonwealth, shall find they do thereby destroy it, like the foolish daughters of *Peleus* (in the fable) which, desiring to renew the youth of their decrepit father, did by the counsel of *Medea* cut him in pieces and boil him, together with strange herbs, but made not of him a new man. This desire of change is like the breach of the first of God's commandments; for there God says *Non habebis Deos alienos*, Thou shalt not have the Gods of other nations, and in another place, concerning *kings*, that they are *Gods*.

Nor adhere (against the Sovereign) to Popular men

Secondly, they are to be taught that they ought not to be led with admiration of the virtue of any of their fellow subjects, how high soever he stand, nor how conspicuously soever he shine in the commonwealth, nor of any assembly (except the sovereign assembly), so as to defer to them any obedience or honour appropriate to the sovereign only, whom (in their particular stations) they represent, nor to receive any influence from them but such as is conveyed by them from the sovereign authority. For that sovereign cannot be imagined to love his people as he ought that is not jealous of them, but suffers them by the flattery of popular men to be seduced from their loyalty, as they have often been (not only secretly, but openly), so as to proclaim marriage with them *in facie Ecclesiae* [in the presence of the Church] by preachers and by publishing the same in the open streets, which may fitly be compared to the violation of the second of the ten commandments.

Nor to Dispute the Sovereign Power

Thirdly, in consequence to this they ought to be informed how great a fault it is to speak evil of the sovereign representative (whether one man or an assembly of men), or to argue and dispute his power, or any way to use his name irreverently, whereby he may be brought into contempt with his people, and their obedience (in which the safety of the commonwealth consisteth) slackened.

JOHN LOCKE, THE SECOND TREATISE OF GOVERNMENT

(1690).

§ 22. The reason why men enter into society is the preservation of their property; and the end why they choose and authorize a legislative is, that there may be laws made, and rules set, as guards and fences to the properties of all the members of the society: to limit the power, and moderate the dominion, of every part and member of the society: for since it can never be supposed to be the will of the society that the legislative should have a power to destroy that which every one designs to secure by entering into society, and for which the people submitted themselves to legislators of their own making; whenever the legislators endeavour to take away and destroy the property of the people, or to reduce them to slavery under arbitrary power, they put themselves into a state of war with the people, who are thereupon absolved from any farther obedience, and are left to the common refuge, which God hath provided for all men, against force and violence. Whensoever therefore the legislative shall transgress this fundamental rule of society; and either by ambition, fear, folly, or corruption, endeavour to grasp themselves, or put into the hands of any other, an absolute power over the lives, liberties, and estates of the people; by this breach of trust they forfeit the power the people had put into their hands for quite contrary ends, and it devolves to the people, who have a right to resume their original liberty, and, by the establishment of a new legislative, (such as they shall think fit) provide for their own safety and security, which is the end for which they are in society. What I have said here, concerning the legislative in general, holds true also concerning the supreme executor, who having a double trust put in him, both to have a part in the legislative, and the supreme execution of the law, acts against both, when he goes about to set up his own arbitrary will as the law of the society. He acts also contrary to his trust, when he either employs the force, treasure, and offices of the society to corrupt the representatives, and gain them to his purposes; or openly pre-engages the electors, and prescribes to their choice, such, whom he has, by solicitations, threats, promises, or otherwise, won to his designs; and employs them to bring in such, who have promised beforehand what to vote, and what to enact. Thus to regulate candidates and electors, and new-model the ways of election, what is it but to cut up the government by the roots, and poison the very fountain of public security? for the people having reserved to themselves the choice of their representatives, as the fence to their properties, could do it for no other end, but that they might always be freely chosen, and so chosen, freely act, and advise, as the necessity of the commonwealth and the public good should, upon examination and mature debate, be judged to require. This, those who give their votes before they hear the debate, and have weighed the reasons on all sides, are not capable of doing. To prepare such an assembly as this, and endeavour to set up the declared abettors of his own will, for the true representatives of the people, and the law-makers of the society, is certainly as great a breach of trust, and as perfect a declaration of a design to subvert the government, as is possible to be met with. To which if one shall add rewards and punishments visibly employed to the same end, and all the arts of perverted law made use of, to take off and destroy all that stand in the way of such a design, and will not comply and consent to betray the liberties of their country, it will be past doubt what is doing. What power they ought to have in the society, who thus employ it contrary to the trust that went along with it in its first institution, is easy to determine; and one cannot but see, that he, who has once attempted any such thing as this, cannot any longer be trusted.

RALPH KETCHAM, JAMES MADISON: A BIOGRAPHY

(1971).

Like Jefferson and Franklin, Madison rested his political thought on the moral standards of John Locke's *Second Treatise on Civil Government*—primarily that reason requires all men be esteemed free and equal. By this Madison understood that to regard man, or any group of men, a priori, as "unfree," was immoral—that is, could not be defended rationally. There was nothing about the "nature" of any men that could be grounds for depriving them of freedom or that could entitle one man to rule another. A man could become fully human only insofar as he was free. Likewise, there was nothing in the nature of men that conferred upon some of them special privileges. Considered rationally, men were equal in rights and in the esteem to which they were entitled on earth and in heaven. When Madison spoke of man in a state of nature he meant simply to express a moral requirement that men ought to be free and equal. He meant to deny the immemorial traditions of government that some men were "by nature" slaves or subjects, that classification of men into unequal orders was both just and inevitable, that obedience was the only duty in government of the mass of men, and that social order required the subjugation of man to authoritarian control.

Madison did not need to suppose that in some primeval age, before the rise of unjust social institutions or tyrannical governments, a society had once existed where all men had enjoyed the full freedom and equality of the state of nature. The concept "state of nature" was moral or normative, describing the condition that ought to be, rather than historical, having reference to a society which might once have existed. Nor did Madison use the terms "free" and "equal" in any absolute or literal sense. He knew perfectly well that any society, especially a complex, civilized one, imposed many legitimate, unavoidable limitations on the right of a man to do as he pleased. Furthermore, since men obviously were unequal in talents and abilities, they would necessarily differ in their achievements in life. The moral imperative of equality required, for example, not that Isaac Newton and his stablekeeper be equal in fame or wisdom or wealth, but rather that one could not justly rule the other and that each had the same "natural" right to life, liberty, and the pursuit of happiness. When Madison spoke of the natural rights of freedom and equality he had in mind ideals, or standards, in terms of which societies and governments could be judged and toward which men should aspire.

In applying these moral imperatives, Madison and other men of reason on both sides of the Atlantic insisted, to begin with, that the state existed to protect and expand freedom and equality of opportunity, and that the surest way to prevent betrayal of this purpose was to rest the powers of government on the consent of the governed. This concept did not always mean in Madison's day, as it might seem to do in the twentieth century, universal suffrage or the elimination of such unrepublican features as a house of lords or a hereditary monarch. Rather, it meant, in the English Whig formulation following Locke, which Madison knew by heart, that there had to be a powerful *portion* of the government responsive to the people, ordinarily through a legislative body composed of their elected representatives. The antiroyalist sentiment of the American Revolution, and the absence of a hereditary nobility in the United States, caused American theorists to lay aside Lockean formulations that the people might consent to hereditary forms, but Madison and most of his colleagues in nation building continued to accept Whiggish limitations on the subsequently hallowed dictum of "one man, one vote," and to work earnestly at "refinements" in government capable of restraining the majority. The essence of consent for Madison was to insure that the government could not ignore or oppose ultimately the will and interests of the people being governed; this was *his* hallowed "republican principle," to which all just governments had to conform. Madison's chief purpose as a political theorist and statesman was to find the mechanisms that would provide such insurance while maintaining order and virtue in government.

Also implied in the doctrine of consent was the right of national independence. Locke had scored the injustice of domination by conquest, the clearest and most complete denial of freedom and equality. The harsh rule of alien armies, wherein some were absolute masters and others abject slaves, was in the political literature of the Age of Reason always the prime example of injustice and denial of the rights of man. When the resistance to British oppression in North America became a movement for independence and a war to expel occupying armies, the sense of connection between natural rights and nationhood increased immensely. Then, as a means to realize both national independence and the principle of consent, the natural-rights theorists insisted on the right of revolution. They reasoned that since government existed to nourish and insure freedom and equality, and indeed had no other purpose, when it betrayed those obligations it lost its legitimate authority and in a sense annulled itself, leaving the people free to replace it. The right of revolution, in fact, was inseparable from the insistence that government, far from being an absolute or divine institution recognizing no superior authority, was subordinate to certain purposes or principles, which those being governed could discern and judge for themselves. A divergence between the acts of government and rationally discoverable natural rights required that the government be changed or abolished.

To give effect to "the republican principle" within a nation, Madison asserted that the freedom least subject to social restraint was freedom of expression, including the rights to believe, speak, and write according to one's own lights. Without these rights, so often denied by allegedly legitimate governments, freedom meant very little. Put positively, man could not be the kind of being Enlightenment philosophers insisted he should or might be without these opportunities of expression. To give further reality to freedom, Madison also considered certain personal immunities sanctioned in English law to be natural rights—trial by jury, confrontation of witnesses, freedom from general warrants, seizures, excessive bail, and cruel punishments, a guarantee of habeas corpus, and subjugation of armies to civil control. Though freedom meant more than these things, the arbitrary, oppressive acts of the Stuarts, Bourbons, and other mighty rulers around the globe made it clear to Madison that substantial success in achieving them would bring mankind immeasurably closer to the moral imperatives.

Madison normally assumed or implied these fundamentals. He seldom discussed them explicitly or argued for them as opposed to other basic principles. They were the sentiments John Adams said were "hackneyed in Congress" in 1774, 1775, and 1776 and which Jefferson said, explaining his objective in drafting the Declaration of Independence, were "an expression of the American mind" at that time. The authority of the Declaration, Jefferson wrote, rested "on the harmonizing sentiments of the day, whether expressed in conversation, in letters, printed essays, or the elementary books of public right, as Aristotle, Cicero, Locke, Sidney, etc." These sentiments guided Madison's efforts to frame, ratify, execute, and expound a free government for the United States.

As a realist and as a practical politician, Madison sought to give meaning to the moral requirements of the natural-rights doctrine in a way relevant to the actual character of man and the society in which he lived. In understanding the nature of man, Madison followed John Locke's *Essay concerning Human Understanding*, which, by insisting that sensory impressions were the sole source of human knowledge, emphasized the diversity of mankind. Each human being was the product of a unique pattern of sense impressions, and therefore in some measure different from other humans. Since this limitless variety resulted from the very nature of the human mind, the life of man had to be organized in ways permitting expression of this diversity. To do otherwise would impose an unjust contradiction on human society. Hence the emphasis on freedom in the thought of Locke and all those who followed him. Furthermore, since, as Locke had put it, after describing the inclination of men to cherish or value different things, "men may choose differently, and yet all choose right," a good society had to be tolerant, flexible, receptive to change, open. Privilege and hierarchy arbitrarily restraining the choices, opportunities, and inclinations of any person were inadmissible. In accepting Lockean espistemology and its understanding of the diversity of mankind, Madison in fact accepted the essential foundation of an open society and the burden, as a theorist of government, of blending variety, change, and uncertainty with more fixed and orderly political concepts.

Madison's political experience confirmed this diversity. He saw the good and bad sides of human nature and all the infinite gradations that could exist between the extremes. The contrast between the benign religious freedom of Pennsylvania and the persecuting bigotry of Virginia had led him to favor liberty of conscience. During the revolution he had experience with both patriots and knaves. In seeking to correct the weaknesses in the Union, he had suffered the opposition of such perversely selfish men as those who dominated the Rhode Island legislature, and he had enjoyed the support of the men gathered in Philadelphia in the summer of 1787, whom he thought "pure in their Motives, ... [and] devoted to the object committed to them." Near the end of his life, reflecting on over half a century of experience with public affairs, Madison observed that "some gentlemen, consulting the purity and generosity of their own minds, without averting to the lessons of experience, would find a security against [tyranny and malice] in our social feelings; in a respect for character; in the dictates of the monitor within.... But man is known to be a selfish, as well as a social being. Respect for character, though often a salutary restraint, is but too often overruled by other motives.... We all know that conscience is not a sufficient safeguard; and besides, that conscience itself may be deluded; may be misled ... into acts which an enlightened conscience would forbid." Such was the diverse nature of man.

Madison insisted, as he remarked during the Federal Convention, that in framing governments, "we must not shut our eyes to the nature of man, nor to the light of experience." Following Locke's empirical method, he studied as fully and carefully as he could the experience of mankind recorded in the histories of his day. From these books, and from the generalizations of philosophers from Aristotle to David Hume, Madison absorbed a sober view of human history. The record was generally one of war, tyranny, violence, stupidity, and corruption, with distressingly few instances of peace, prosperity, and enlightenment. The thought of Machiavelli, Calvin, and Hobbes, known to, though largely rejected by, Madison, helped keep him in mind of human depravity. Unlike some Enlightenment thinkers, who emphasized human goodness to the point of blaming all evil on social conditions, Madison sought always to recognize and take into account the limitations of human nature.

LEONARD W. LEVY, EMERGENCE OF A FREE PRESS

(1985).

Neither freedom of speech nor freedom of press could become a civil liberty until people believed that the truth of their opinions, especially their religious opinions, was relative rather than absolute; until kings and parliaments felt sufficiently strong and stable to be able to ignore political criticism; and until the people considered themselves as the source of sovereignty, the masters rather than the servants of the government. There could be no toleration of dissent when Catholics, Anglicans, and Puritans profoundly believed that the precise shade of belief that each respectively professed must be established as England's only true religion and that all be compelled to accept it for their own salvation as well as for the good of God and the nation. Heresy and nonconformity, severely prosecuted as crimes from the time the Inquisition arrived in England, continued to be crimes after the nationalization of the church under Henry VIII. Whether Catholics or Protestants, or Anglicans or Puritans, controlled the government, the compulsion of conscience for the sake of uniformity necessitated restraints on freedom of speech and press regarding religion. The Reformation, moreover, by making the monarch the head of the established church, converted every religious question into a political one and suffused government policies with religious overtones. As a result, nonconformity and heresy became virtually indistinguishable from sedition and treason. Criticism of the church affected the state and vice versa. Not only did that make criticism dangerous; it made it necessarily wrong when emanating from inferior subjects against their masters. The danger was particularly great for several centuries following the emergence of the national state, when the life of the monarch was in jeopardy, the peace and security of the state precarious. Freedom of religious and political expression was feared as a means of triggering conspiracies, internal disorders, wars, revolutions, or some other disastrous train of events that might pull down church and state.

Just as many torts or private wrongs became crimes, or offenses against the king's peace, so too certain libels became the objects of criminal retribution. As early as 1275 Parliament outlawed "any slanderous News . . . or *false* News or Tales where by discord or occasion of discord or slander may grow between the King and his people or the great men of the Realm . . . " Parliament re-enacted the statute in 1379 for the prevention of the "subversion and destruction of the said realm" by means of false speech. The king's council, which later became the Court of Star Chamber, meted out punishment. These were the earliest statutes making dangerous utterances a crime, and together with the ecclesiastical laws against heresy, blasphemy, and other religious crimes intensified the long history of suppression of opinions deemed pernicious.

The invention of printing, of course, magnified the danger of such opinions. The Crown claimed an authority to control printing presses as a right of prerogative. Henry VIII took over a system for the censorship of heretical manuscripts, long established by the English church and approved by Parliament, and soon applied it to writings on any subject. The manuscript of any work intended for publication had to be submitted to royal officials empowered to censor objectionable passages and to approve or deny a license for the printing of the work. Anything published without an *imprimatur* was criminal. Under Elizabeth the government elaborated the system of prior restraints upon the press, dividing the administration of the complex licensing system among three Crown agencies: the Stationers' Company, a guild of master publishers chartered to monopolize the presses and vested with extraordinary powers of search and seizure; the Court of High Commission, the highest ecclesiastical tribunal, which controlled the Stationers' Company and did the actual licensing; and the Court of Star Chamber which issued decrees defining criminal matter and shared with the Court of High Commission jurisdiction over the trial of offenders. The agencies for enforcement changed during the Puritan Revolution, but the licensing system continued. Under the Restoration, the system was based principally on an act of Parliament, rather than royal prerogative; it continued until 1694.[7] But the expiration of the system at that time did not remotely mean that the press had become free. It remained subject to the restraints of the common law, so-called because it was the law shared in common throughout the realm to distinguish it from local law. The common law was a national or centralized body of non-statutory ("unwritten") and uncodified law devised mainly by the king's royal courts of record in London, especially the Court of Common Pleas (civil jurisdiction) and the Court of King's Bench (criminal jurisdiction), and applied in a supposedly uniform manner by royal judges who served everywhere in the realm.

One might publish without a license, but he did so at the peril of being punished for libel. The point of departure for the modern law of criminal libels was Sir Edward Coke's report of *De Libellis Famosis*, a Star Chamber case of 1606, in which the following propositions were stated. A libel against a private person might be punished criminally on the theory that it provokes revenge and therefore tends, however remotely, to a breach of the peace. But a libel against a government official comprises an even greater offense "for it concerns not only the breach of the peace, but also the scandal of government . . ."[9] The medieval statutes fixed the falsity of the libel as the essence of the crime, but the Star Chamber ruled in 1606 that truth or falsity was not material, because a true statement that damages the reputation of the government or an official is the more dangerous to the public peace. The Star Chamber also ruled that the common law courts possessed concurrent

7. For an excellent discussion of the licensing system from its origins in England to its demise in 1694, see Frederick S. Siebert, *Freedom of the Press in England, 1476–1776* (Urbana, 1952), chaps. 2–3, 6–12.

9. *De Libellis Famosis*, 3 Coke's *Reports* 254 (1606). See Sir James Fitzjames Stephen, *A History of the Criminal Law of England* (London, 1883, 3 vols.), 2:304–5.

jurisdiction over criminal libels. After Parliament abolished the Star Chamber in 1642, the common-law courts had exclusive jurisdiction and applied Star Chamber doctrines in libel prosecutions.

Four major classes of criminal libel emerged from subsequent decisions in the common-law courts. Blasphemous libel or defamation of religion, together with laws against heresy and the establishment of a state church, made freedom of religious expression a risk. The law of obscene libel protected public morality but crimped literary, artistic, and other forms of personal expression. The law of private libel protected individual reputations by making possible civil suits for damages; but the state could prosecute a gross private libel to prevent supposed bad tendencies toward breach of the peace. The use of the criminal law to avenge the defamation of a person made the libel, in such a case, to be known as a "criminal libel," although the same term referred collectively to four classes of libel. Thus criminal libel was a redundant subcategory of the broad offense of criminal libel.

By far the most repressive class of libel was seditious libel. It can be defined in a quite elaborate and technical manner in order to take into account the malicious or criminal intent of the accused, the bad tendency of his remarks, and their truth or falsity. But the crime has never been satisfactorily or consistently defined, the necessary result of its inherent vagueness. Seditious libel has always been an accordion-like concept, expandable or contractable at the whim of judges. Judged by actual prosecutions, the crime consisted of defaming or contemning or ridiculing the government: its form, constitution, officers, laws, conduct, or policies, to the jeopardy of the public peace. In effect, any malicious criticism about the government that could be construed to have the bad tendency of lowering it in the public's esteem, holding it up to contempt or hatred, or of disturbing the peace was seditious libel, exposing the speaker or writer to criminal prosecution. Words damaging to the government that tended, however remotely, to cause a breach of the peace, constituted seditious libel according to the courts, but such reasoning explained nothing because *every* crime theoretically breached the king's peace. Criticism of the government that went too far, not the tendency of the words to breach the peace, distinguished the crime of seditious libel, although loose judicial language sometimes suggested otherwise. Loose language invariably characterized the crime, because the government always alleged that the defendant spoke or wrote maliciously, falsely, scandalously, scurrilously, and seditiously, or some combination thereof.

Sergeant William Hawkins, whose chapter on libels in his influential treatise of 1716 became a standard authority, declared,

> Nor can there be any doubt but that a writing which defames a private person only is as much a libel as that which defames persons entrusted in a public capacity, in as much as it manifestly tends to create ill blood, and to cause a disturbance of the public peace; however, it is certain that it is a very high aggravation of a libel that

it tends to scandalize the government, by reflecting on those who are entrusted with the administration of public affairs, which does not only endanger the public peace, as all other libels do, by stirring up the parties immediately concerned in it to acts of revenge, but also has a direct tendency to breed in the people a dislike of their governors, and incline them to faction and sedition.

The fact that seditious libel was a crime did not make criticism of the government illegal or even risky. By the early eighteenth century, partisanship and polemics characterized the English press. The press teemed with seditious libels, according to judicial standards, but suffered little from prosecutions. As a matter of practice it was remarkably free and unrestrained; prosecutions tended to be selective and exemplary. Judicial standards probably did not coincide with popular ones; juries sometimes rebelled against judicial instructions, refusing to return verdicts of guilty. Moreover, libelous writers frequently had the protection of powerful factional leaders.

Chief Justice John Holt in *Tuchin's Case* (1704) explained the rationale underlying the concept of seditious libel: "a reflection on the government" must be punished because, "If people should not be called to account for possessing the people with an ill opinion of the government, no government can subsist. For it is very necessary for all governments that the people should have a good opinion of it. And nothing can be worse to any government than to endeavour to procure animosities as to the management of it; this has always been looked upon as a crime, and no government can be safe without it."[13]

Through the seventeenth century, certain seditious libels that could be construed as revealing an intention to "compass" or imagine the death of the king were punished as treason. In 1663 William Twyn, for printing a book that endorsed the right of revolution, was held to have compassed the king's death; Twyn was sentenced to be hanged, cut down while still alive, and then emasculated, disemboweled, quartered, and beheaded—the standard punishment for treason. Algernon Sidney also paid the penalty for treason; his offense was the writing of an unpublished treatise on government discovered in his study. Treason as a purely verbal crime, unconnected with some overt act beyond the words themselves, died out after the execution of John Matthews in 1720, convicted under a special statute rather than at common law. Utterances once held to be treasonable became wholly assimilated within the concept of seditious libel. As a lesser crime or misdemeanor, seditious libel merited less severe punishment: imprisonment, fines, the pillory, and whipping.

But prosecution for seditious libel became the government's principal instrument for controlling the press. According to Frederick S.

13. *Rex v. Tuchin*, in Thomas Bayly Howell, comp., *A Complete Collection of State Trials to 1783*, continued by T. J. Howell to 1820 (London, 1816–28, 34 vols.), 14:1095, 1128 (1704), quoted in Stephen, *History of the Criminal Law in England*, 2:318.

Siebert's excellent study of freedom of the press in England, "convictions for seditious libel ran into the hundreds" in both the seventeenth and eighteenth centuries. That probably exaggerated the number of eighteenth-century convictions for seditious libel. Of the period 1700–1730, Siebert said, "Only occasionally was it necessary for the government to crack the whip of seditious libel to remind printers and publishers of their proper function." Of the period 1730–60, he said, it "witnessed the beginning of the revolt of juries and the failure of prosecutions...." A conviction in 1754 he described as "the first to be obtained from a London jury in twenty-seven years." A wide disparity existed between the number of informations filed for seditious libel and the actual number of prosecutions; there was also a disparity between the number of prosecutions and the actual number of convictions. The number of informations undoubtedly "ran into the hundreds." Being arrested, called into court, and forced to pay costs on the dismissal of the information could have an intimidating effect even if the prosecution proceeded no further. In other words, trials, let alone convictions, were not necessary for the law of seditious libel to operate oppressively. One prosecutorial trick was to charge a person with seditious libel, persuade him to leave the country in order to avoid trial, and then outlaw him if he left, thereby preventing his return.

The procedure in prosecuting a seditious libel was extremely objectionable to libertarian theorists, more so than the fact that the accused could be punished for words alone. From 1662 until a century later the secretary of state possessed the power of ferreting out seditious libels by issuing warrants that authorized a search of the homes and offices of all suspects and the arrest of anyone on the mere suspicion of being implicated in the writing, publishing, or circulation of such libels. General warrants, the use of which was severely restricted in felony cases, were employed promiscuously in cases of seditious libel, a misdemeanor. Search, seizure, and arrest were used to harass anti-administration writers and editors against whom the evidence might not warrant a trial. But the government did not remain restricted to trying only those indicted or presented by a grand jury. Alternatively, the attorney-general might proceed against all misdemeanors by an information, that is, by determining the libelous character of a publication, bringing it to the attention of the Court of the King's Bench, and securing a warrant for the arrest and trial of the offender. Prosecuting by information rather than by indictment bypassed the Englishman's beloved institution, the grand jury, which in felony cases stood between him and the government.

At the trial of a seditious libel, the defendant was not even judged by his peers in any meaningful way. Despite the ambiguity of earlier practice, judges in the eighteenth century permitted juries to decide only the fact of the publication. That is, the only question that the jury passed upon was whether the defendant did or did not publish the remarks charged against him and whether they carried the innuendo as alleged. The judges reserved exclusively for themselves as a matter of law the decision on the crucial question whether the defendant's remarks were seditious because maliciously intended and of a bad tendency. In 1731 in the case of *Rex* v. *Francklin*, for example, Chief Justice Thomas Raymond said in his charge to the jury that

> . . . in this information for libel there are three things to be considered, whereof two by you the jury, and one by the court. The first thing under your consideration is whether the defendant Mr. Francklin is guilty of the publication of this Craftsman or not? The second is, whether the expressions in that letter refer to his present majesty and his principal officers and ministers of state, and are applicable to them or not? . . . But then there is a third thing, to wit, whether these defamatory expressions amount to a libel or not? This does not belong to the office of the jury, but to the office of the Court; because it is a matter of law, and not of fact; . . . and there is redress to be had in another place if either of the parties are not satisfied; for we are not to invade one another's province, as is now of late a notion among some people who ought to know better.[21]

The judges also refused to permit the defendant to plead the truth as a defense. Indeed, they proceeded on the theory that the truth of a libel made it even worse because it was more provocative, thereby increasing the tendency to breach of the peace or exacerbating the scandal against the government. As a result of these rules applicable to criminal or crown libels, a man might be arrested on a general warrant, prosecuted on an information without the consent of a grand jury, and convicted for his political opinions by judges appointed by the government he had aspersed.

Thus the disappearance of the prior restraints that had been imposed by the licensing system until 1694 did not meaningfully free the press. Theoretically one might say or print what he pleased, but he was responsible to the common law for allegedly malicious, scurrilous, scandalous, or derogatory utterances which supposedly tended towards the contempt, ridicule, hatred, scorn, or disrepute of other persons, religion, government, or morality. Blackstone, the oracle of the common law in the minds of the American Framers, summarized the law of Crown libels as follows:

> Where blasphemous, immoral, treasonable, schismatical, seditious, or scandalous libels are punished by the English law . . . the liberty of the press, properly understood, is by no means infringed or violated. The *liberty of the press* is indeed essential to the nature of a free state; but this consists in laying no *previous* restraints upon publications, and not in freedom from censure for criminal matter when published. Every freeman has an undoubted right to lay what sentiments he pleases before the public: to forbid this is to destroy the freedom of the press: but if he publishes what is improper, mischievous, or illegal, he must take the consequences of his own temerity. . . . But to punish (as the law does at present) any danger-

21. Howell, *State Trials*, 17:626, 671, 672.

> ous or offensive writings, which, when published, shall on a fair and impartial trial be adjudged of a pernicious tendency, is necessary for the preservation of peace and good order, a government and religion, the only solid foundations of civil liberty. Thus the will of individuals is still left free; the abuse only of that free-will is the object of legal punishment. Neither is any restraint hereby laid upon freedom of thought or enquiry: liberty of private sentiment is still left; the disseminating, or making public, of bad sentiments, destructive of the ends of society, is the crime which society corrects.[24]

Samuel Johnson believed the law too liberal. "It seems not more reasonable," he complained, "to leave the right of printing unrestrained, because writers may be afterwards restrained, than it would be to sleep with doors unbolted, because by our laws, we can hang a thief."

The common law's definition of freedom of the press meant merely the absence of censorship in advance of publication. But the presence of punishment afterwards, for "bad sentiments," oral or published, had an effect similar to a law authorizing previous restraints. A man who may be whipped and jailed for what he says or prints is not likely to feel free to express his opinions even if he does not need a government license to do so. The common-law definition of freedom of the press left the press at the mercy of the Crown's prosecutors and judges. Freedom of discussion and the law of libel simply conflicted; the first could not conceptually coexist with the second.

* * *

The Zenger case originated in a power struggle between New York's governor, William Cosby, and the political faction led by Lewis Morris, who determined to check Cosby's arrogant, mendacious, and illegal regime. Soon after his arrival in New York in the summer of 1732, the royal governor antagonized the local establishment. Rip Van Dam, a leading merchant who was the senior member of the Council, had acted as governor until Cosby arrived. Cosby demanded half the salary that the Council voted for Van Dam. When Van Dam refused to pay, Cosby sued him in the provincial supreme court, after first authorizing its judges to sit as a court of equity, which functioned without a jury. Chief Justice Lewis Morris accepted the arguments of Van Dam's lawyers, James Alexander and William Smith, that an equity court created solely by the governor was illegal, but the other two judges, James DeLancey and Frederick Philipse, supported the governor. Cosby fired Morris and elevated DeLancey to the chief justiceship, without the Council's consent. DeLancey's commission authorized his court to determine both civil and criminal cases. By contrast, in England the judges of the King's Bench, the supreme criminal court, possessed no civil jurisdiction, and the judges of the highest civil court, the Court of Common Pleas, exercised no criminal jurisdiction. Moreover, judges traditionally held

24. Sir William Blackstone, *Commentaries on the Laws of England* (London, 1765–69), book 4, chap. II, 151–152.

office during "good behavior," but Cosby had appointed DeLancey and Philipse to serve at his "pleasure."

Morris, a nabob of New York, joined forces with Van Dam, Alexander and Smith, his two lawyers, Philip Livingston, and Cadwallader Colden, the colony's scientist-politician, and formed a "Popular Party" to challenge the judicial commissions, expose the arbitrary malfeasance of the governor, and regain political power. But the opposition faction needed a voice to shape and mobilize public opinion. Cosby controlled the sole newspaper of the province, the *New-York Gazette*, run by William Bradford, "The King's Printer." The solution was the founding of an opposition newspaper. Thus the *New-York Weekly Journal*, printed by John Peter Zenger, originated as a propaganda vehicle for the Morris faction. Zenger himself, a poorly educated German immigrant, was neither the editor nor writer of his paper; he was merely the printer and had scant understanding of politics or of the opinions that filled the columns of his newspaper. In effect James Alexander was the managing editor and chief editorial writer; Morris, Smith, and Colden, as well as Alexander, posing as pseudonymous readers, contributed letters to the editor scalding the governor and his appointees as villains who had no respect for law, liberty, or private property. Even the advertisements in the newspaper ridiculed the Cosbyites.

The *Weekly Journal* also published extracts from Whig theorists, chief among them John Trenchard and Thomas Gordon, the authors of *Cato's Letters: Or Essays on Liberty, Civil and Religious.* Zenger's paper, as the first independent and truly free press in America, engaging weekly in the dangerous practice of opposing the administration of the province, needed a theory to legitimate its editorial practices. The reading public as well as Crown officers had to be educated. *Cato's Letters* served to castigate Cosby, to broadcast Whig theory, and to rationalize freedom of the press.

In the second issue of the newspaper, in late 1733, Alexander wrote the first of several essays in which he developed a libertarian theory of freedom of the press to justify the newspaper's actual practice of that freedom. At the same time Alexander excoriated Cosby by innuendo. Explaining why freedom of the press was a necessary part of the British constitution, Alexander observed that some people believed that might made right, and "if such an over grown Criminal, or an impudent Monster in Iniquity, cannot immediately be come at by ordinary Justice, let him yet receive the lash of satire, let the glaring truth of his ill administration ... render his actions odious to all honest minds." Two months later the *Weekly Journal* referred to a governor who had turned "rogue."

Cosby decided to stop Zenger's press by imprisoning the printer for his seditious libels. Chief Justice DeLancey failed, however, to convince a grand jury to indict, and he failed again nine months later in October 1734, despite a strong charge on the meaning and dangers of seditious libel. Cosby's Council then urged the Assembly to concur in an order that certain issues of Zenger's newspaper be burned by the common hangman, that a reward be offered for the authors of the libels, and that the printer be prosecuted. The Assembly refused, as did the city's Court of Quarter Sessions. The Council then commanded the sheriff to see to the burning of the papers. On November 17, 1735, Zenger was imprisoned on a warrant issued by the Council charging him with having published "several seditious libels ... tending to raise factions ... among the people ... inflaming their minds with contempt of His Majesty's government, and greatly disturbing the peace thereof."

Although Zenger had the best lawyers in the colony, James Alexander and William Smith, they could not prevent the chief justice from setting bail impossibly high, thus keeping his prisoner in jail. In January 1735 DeLancey failed for a third time to obtain a grand jury indictment. Richard Bradley, the attorney general, then charged Zenger by an information for having published "false, scandalous, malicious, and seditious" libels. That is, on his authority as prosecutor, the attorney general bypassed the grand jury system and singlehandedly preferred charges, an "information" against Zenger before the court, which then ordered a trial. Prosecution by information was legal, though unpopular. Fortunately for Zenger, Bradley's information contained the word "false," which ultimately proved to be the key to his defense. Zenger's lawyers, knowing that a court consisting of DeLancey and Philipse was biased against their client, challenged the legality of the commissions of the judges. DeLancey, outraged, summarily disbarred Alexander and Smith. In their place he appointed a young but able lawyer, John Chambers, to defend Zenger. Chambers, although an opponent of the Morris faction, pleaded Zenger not guilty and diligently challenged prejudiced jurors. The original panel of jurors included Cosby appointees, enemies of Morris, and Cosby's "baker, tailor, shoemaker, candlemaker, joiner, etc." DeLancey, confident that the prosecutor could easily prove that Zenger had published the libels, supported Chambers's motions, with the result that a neutral jury was impaneled to try the case. Meanwhile, as Zenger spent nine months in prison awaiting his trial, his wife tended his press and Alexander supervised the continued publication of the *Weekly Journal.*

August 4, 1735, was the day of the trial. After the attorney general opened the prosecution's case, Andrew Hamilton of Philadelphia surprised the court when he rose in the audience and introduced himself as Zenger's counsel. Chambers yielded. James Alexander had engaged Hamilton, an old friend, to defend the printer and in so doing obtained the services of a man reputed to be the best advocate in America. Hamilton had been attorney general of Pennsylvania and at the time of the trial was speaker of the Pennsylvania Assembly. His case was ready-made for him, because Alexander had prepared a masterful brief.

Hamilton opened the defense with Alexander's daring gambit of confessing Zenger's responsibility for the allegedly libelous articles. Hamilton added, however, that Zenger had a right to publish the truth. The attorney general, believing that the confession virtually awarded the verdict to the prosecution, accurately declared that because Zenger had admitted the publications, "the jury must find a verdict for the King, for supposing they were true ... the law says their being true is an aggravation of the crime." Hamilton disagreed; for the publications to be libelous, he argued, they must be false. Bradley, thinking to impress the jury, reviewed the publications against the governor, concluding that they stirred up sedition and disturbance of the peace by disquieting the minds of the people. Hamilton insisted, however, that the charges against Zenger included the word "false," without proof of which no libel existed; only if the Crown proved the falsehood would he concede the libel. When the Crown attorney refused to offer such proof, on ground that he was not obliged to do so, Hamilton shrewdly offered to prove that the alleged libels were true, knowing that if he persuaded the jury, Cosby in effect would have been convicted. Accordingly the chief justice swiftly intervened: "You cannot be admitted, Mr. Hamilton, to give the truth of a libel in evidence," because it was a libel even if true. "The law was clear," DeLancey correctly stated, "that you cannot justify a libel," and for the second time he quoted Sergeant William Hawkins's authoritative book, *Pleas of the Crown*, in support of his ruling.

Hamilton retorted that the court's law derived from the tyrannical Court of Star Chamber, long since dead, to the good fortune of English liberty; he squeezed precedents to buttress his view of the law that it permitted truth as a defense to a charge of libel. Hamilton could not satisfy DeLancey, because the great legal luminaries of England—Coke, Hale, Holt, and Hawkins—had proved that the common-law courts perpetuated and accepted Star Chamber doctrine. Nevertheless, Hamilton managed to exploit the doubt in the minds of the jurors whether the law made good sense. Mercilessly Hamilton scored the doctrine that truth aggravated a libel; were the jurors supposed to believe that "truth is a greater sin than falsehood"?

When DeLancey stopped Hamilton from arguing further that truth was a defense to a charge of libel, Hamilton necessarily abandoned his reliance on Alexander's brief and shifted his strategy. "Then, gentlemen of the jury," he declared, "it is to you we must now appeal for witnesses to the truth of the facts ... and are denied the liberty to prove." Boldly he played to the jury over the head of the court, concocting an argument that was destined to survive first in public opinion and ultimately in the law itself. He reminded the jurors that as citizens of New York, they knew the facts concerning the supposed libels about the governor's administration. The facts, he declared, were "notoriously known to be true." When a difference arose as to whether Zenger's words should be understood as malicious, seditious, and tending to breach the peace, DeLancey remarked that those who had to judge would understand the words properly. Hamilton told the jurors that they, not the court, were the judges; if they did not understand the words to be false, the publications were not criminal. DeLancey then ruled that the jury's only task was "to find that Zenger printed and published those papers, and leave it to the Court to judge whether they are libelous ... it is in the nature of a special verdict where the jury leave the matter of law to the Court."

Hamilton, addressing the jury, then launched into an argument of several hours. The court's rule, he said, "renders juries useless," a result he again traced to rulings of the "terrible Court of Star Chamber." A free people, having a sense of justice, knew when a governor abused power. They would protect the innocent from him because they were not obliged "to support a governor who goes about to destroy a province . . . or their privileges." Legal restraints on the right of freemen to protest extended only to "what is false." Hamilton admitted that although truth alone could excuse complaints about a bad administration, "nothing ought to excuse a man who raises a false charge or accusation, even against a private person, and that no manner of allowance ought to be made to him who does so against a public magistrate." The attorney general, Hamilton reminded the jury, regarded government as above criticism and insisted that licentiousness could not be tolerated, because it brought rulers into popular contempt. Hamilton did not disagree except that he did not regard truth as licentious. He called attention to the fact that government officials who abused power caused injustice and oppression, thereby deserving the contempt of the people. Thus, if the jury believed that Zenger had published the truth, the verdict should be in his favor.

Hamilton knew that the law was against him and that Zenger was guilty as a matter of law. So he had used the jury as a court of public opinion and turned the case into a trial of Cosby. Hamilton's best defense turned out to be an aggressive assault. Summoning his forensic gifts, he then turned his case into one that would endure as long as people cherished liberty and trusted juries. Ascending the heights of eloquence, he declared in his peroration that Zenger's was not a "small" case:

> . . . the question before the Court and you gentlemen of the jury is not of small nor private concern, it is not the cause of a poor printer, nor of New York alone, which you are now trying. No! It may in its consequences affect every freeman that lives under a British government on the main of America. It is the best cause. It is the cause of liberty; and I make no doubt but that your upright conduct this day will not only entitle you to the love and esteem of your fellow citizens; but every man who prefers freedom to a life of slavery will bless and honor you as men who have baffled the attempt of tyranny; and by an impartial and uncorrupt verdict, have laid a noble foundation for securing to ourselves, our posterity, and our neighbors that to which nature and the laws of our country have given us a right—the liberty—both of exposing and opposing arbitrary power (in these parts of the world, at least) by speaking and writing truth.

Although both the attorney general and chief justice again reminded the jury that scandalous reflection on the government that stirred popular odium was a crime, Hamilton got in a parting shot. He apologized for having been carried away in the cause of freedom. The jury had heard enough. After withdrawing "a short time," they returned a general verdict of not guilty, "upon which there were three huzzas in the hall, which was crowded with people." Zenger left the courtroom a free man.

Within a couple of years, Cosby was dead, Lewis Morris was speaker of the Assembly, and Zenger, prosperous from government contracts, printed an establishment newspaper whose seditious fires were banked. The report of Zenger's trial, however, was enormously popular, in England even more than in America. It had an undeniable attraction for printers, lawyers, and politicians, who quoted it or excerpted it or republished it when it suited their causes. In England, however, it had no noticeable effect. In America its effect was significant even though it had no impact on the law; a jury's verdict does not alter law. But common-law prosecutions petered out after Zenger's case.

ANTHONY LEWIS, MAKE NO LAW

(1991).

"Perhaps it is a universal truth that the loss of liberty at home is to be charged to provisions against danger, real or pretended, from abroad."

James Madison made that perceptive observation in a letter to Vice President Jefferson on May 13, 1798. Its truth has been demonstrated again and again in American history as politicians used the fear of foreign ideology and power to justify the suppression of freedom. The fear that prevailed when Madison wrote was fear of France.

France had supported the American colonies in their war with Great Britain. But gratitude for that help gave way to growing alarm as the French Revolution of 1789 was followed by the Terror and the guillotine. Americans, especially those of conservative bent, came to see France as the home of a malevolent ideology that it would try to send across the Atlantic. Then came war between France and Britain. The United States proclaimed its neutrality, but in Jay's Treaty of 1794 it accepted Britain's claim of the right to seize neutral vessels carrying cargo for France. As a result, in 1796 French warships began attacking American merchant ships bound for Britain.

Anti–French feeling was brought to a boil in April 1798 by the XYZ affair. Talleyrand, the French foreign minister, refused to receive a special American diplomatic mission sent to Paris to try to ease relations. Three agents of Talleyrand demanded a large payment as the price of opening negotiations. The Americans rejected the demand and went home, sending a dispatch ahead to President Adams on what had happened. Adams informed Congress of the business in a message that concealed the names of the offending French agents by referring to them as X, Y and Z. Adams quoted Y as saying that France did not fear the U.

S. diplomats' breaking off their mission because "the French party in America" would soon repair the breach.

Adams's supporters in Congress and the country used "the French party in America" as a reference to the President's political opponents, Jefferson and his supporters. Political parties were just beginning to be formed then. The Framers of the Constitution had not envisaged this development; they provided for the President to be chosen not by popular election but by an august Electoral College. The first choice, Washington, was inevitable. But thereafter forces began to form behind Washington's Vice President, Adams, and his Secretary of State, Jefferson. The election of 1796, after Washington's two terms, was close, Adams defeating Jefferson by 71 electoral votes to 66. As runner-up, Jefferson became Vice President. (The present system of presidential/vice presidential tickets was introduced by the Twelfth Amendment to the Constitution in 1804.)

The Adams supporters were the Federalist party. The Jeffersonians, ancestors of the modern Democratic party, called themselves Republicans or Democratic Republicans. Two hundred years later, it is not so easy to see why the two parties fought each other so bitterly. Both included signers of the Declaration of Independence and delegates to the Constitutional Convention. Alexander Hamilton, one of the authors of the Federalist Papers, the great exposition of the Constitution, was a Federalist; his principal co-author, Madison, was a Republican. But the differences were passionately felt, as the use of the damning phrase "the French party" indicates. The Federalists tended to be the propertied class, more concerned about order in society; they wanted a strong federal government and felt close to Britain. The Republicans spoke, often in populist voice, for farmers and the less affluent; they were suspicious of federal power. Of course those generalities yielded to circumstance: When Jefferson became president, he was by no means timid in the assertion of federal power. But at the time, each saw the other in exaggerated terms. To Republicans, the Federalists favored centralized authority and English manners so much that they really wanted to introduce a monarchy. To Federalists, Republicans were Jacobins who if they took office would install a French-style terror. Abigail Adams, the President's wife, wrote a friend in 1798 that the French party—the Republicans—were busy all over the country "sowing the seeds of vice, irreligion, corruption and sedition."

It was in this atmosphere of bitterness and suspicion that the Sedition Act of 1798 became law. The Federalists controlled both Houses of Congress as well as the presidency, but they saw the Republicans gaining politically. They believed they could arrest that trend by silencing critics of the government, especially in the Republican press, and they made the suppression of criticism a partisan cause. A sedition bill was proposed by the Senate in June 1798 and was approved by a straight party-line vote on July 4: a date evidently chosen by its backers to identify it as patriotic legislation. The House passed its version on July 10; the Republican members had managed to add a clause providing that the law expire on March 3, 1801, when the President's term of office ended. Adams signed the bill into law on July 14.

The Sedition Act made it a crime, punishable by up to two years in prison and a fine of two thousand dollars, to "write, print, utter or publish ... any false, scandalous and malicious writing or writings against the government of the United States, or either house of the Congress ... or the President ... with intent to defame ... or to bring them, or either of them, into contempt or disrepute; or to excite against them, or either or any of them, the hatred of the good people of the United States." The act punished abuse of Congress or the President, but it strikingly omitted Vice President Jefferson from its protection.

The act punished political criticism only if it was "false, scandalous and malicious," and only if the author intended to defame. Those provisions were described by the Federalists as ameliorations of the common-law crime of seditious libel, against which truth was no defense. But though they seemed to promise much, in fact they were of little or no use to those who were charged with sedition under the act. The federal courts, its judges all appointed by Federalist presidents, interpreted the requirement of falsity to make the defendant bear the burden of proving the truth; a critical statement was presumed to be false unless the defendant could prove it true in all respects. The courts applied this rigorous requirement even to statements of mere opinion. If an editor wrote that government policy was headed for disaster, he had to prove the prediction true—which of course he could not. Malice was also presumed, and intent to defame was inferred from publication of words that had a "bad tendency"—the ancient test of seditious libel at common law. Another supposedly liberalizing feature of the statute was that it let the jury decide issues of both fact and law. But here again judges charged juries in a way that left them nothing to decide except whether the accused had published the statement complained of. Moreover, modern research suggests that federal judges and marshals packed juries in Sedition Act cases with Federalists.

The Federalists of 1798 were hardly unique in practicing the politics of fear. There have been repeated examples of what Richard Hofstadter called "the paranoid style in American politics." In the twentieth century Congress passed many laws branding as infamous anyone, citizen or would-be visitor to America, who was suspected of the faintest Communist taint; for forty years politicians won votes by charging their opponents with being soft on communism. The Sedition Act was a product of such zealotry and political calculation. Many Federalists probably believed that their opponents were dangerous radicals who would ruin the country, and this belief was compounded by a royalist assumption that those who were in power had a right to remain there. Speaking for the Sedition Bill in the House, Representative John Allen of Connecticut said: "Let gentlemen look at certain papers printed in this city [Philadelphia, then the seat of government] and elsewhere, and ask themselves whether an unwarrantable and dangerous combination does not exist to overturn and ruin the Government by publishing the most shameless falsehoods." Allen said the critical newspapers printed statements that the Government was hostile to the country's welfare and "ought, therefore, to be displaced, and that the people ought to raise an *insurrection* against the Government." Allen slid easily from criticism of the government to insurrection. The Republican papers were certainly hostile in their criticism, but their aim was to displace the Federalist administration not by insurrection but by means of the ballot box.

A Republican from Pennsylvania, Albert Gallatin, who was later Jefferson's brilliant Secretary of the Treasury, told the House: "This bill and its supporters suppose, in fact, that whoever dislikes the measures of [the] Administration and of a temporary majority in Congress, and shall, either by speaking or writing, express his disapprobation and his want of confidence in the men now in power, is seditious, is an enemy, not of [the] Administration, but of the Constitution, and is liable to punishment." Gallatin concluded that the bill was only a weapon used by a party in power in order "to perpetuate their authority and preserve their present places."

At the end of the debate the House turned to the constitutionality of the bill. Republicans argued that it was beyond the power of Congress and therefore unconstitutional for two reasons. First, the original Constitution had granted no power to the federal government over the press. (Some of the Framers had made this point in arguing that a Bill of Rights with protection of the press was unnecessary.) Second, the speech and press clauses of the First Amendment specifically denied Congress the right to pass such legislation. The Federalists replied that a power to prevent seditious attacks in the press was a necessary incident of any government and hence was within the clause of the Constitution enabling Congress to pass all "necessary and proper" measures to carry out its granted authority. Further, relying on Blackstone, they argued that the First Amendment's "freedom of the press" meant only freedom from prior restraints.

Gallatin and Representative John Nicholas made considered speeches against the bill's constitutionality. Gallatin ridiculed the Blackstonian view of press freedom, saying it was "preposterous to say, that to punish a certain act was not an abridgment of the liberty of doing that act." Gallatin made the further ingenious argument that the Blackstone theory was "absurd" as applied to the free speech clause of the First Amendment. If "freedom" meant only freedom from prior restraint, he asked, how could a government apply prior restraints to men speaking? The free speech clause would have to have been designed to deprive Congress of "a power to seal the mouths or to cut the tongues of the citizens of the Union," for those "were the only means by which previous restraints could be laid on the freedom of speech." Nicholas rejected as inconsistent with freedom any attempt to distinguish truth from falsity in speech, or liberty from license—distinctions that the Federalists had emphasized in their defense of the bill. Any vigorous political criticism would be charged with falsehood, Nicholas said, and printers "would be afraid of publishing the truth, as, though true, it might not always be in their power to establish the truth to the satisfaction of a court." In this passage Nicholas anticipated an important element in the theory of free speech as it developed in the twentieth century: that in true freedom there must be room for error.

Early in 1799 Republicans in the House moved to repeal the Sedition Act. The proposal was rejected in committee and by a party-line vote in the House. But John Nicholas wrote a minority committee report that further developed the idea of free speech. The thinking behind the Sedition Act, he said, was derived from Great Britain, which had a very different system of government. "The King is hereditary, and according to the theory of their Government, can do no wrong. Public officers are his representatives, and derive some portion of his inviolability." They therefore receive "a different sort of respect," Nicholas said, "from that which is proper in our Government, where the officers of Government are the servants of the people, are amenable to them, and liable to be turned out of office at periodical elections."

But the most important voice heard in protest of the Sedition Act was Madison's. After passage of the act, he and Jefferson decided to try to arouse opposition to it in the state legislatures. They acted in secret, for fear that they would be prosecuted under the act—a Father of the Constitution and the Vice President of the United States! Jefferson drafted a resolution that went to the Kentucky Legislature and was approved there in November. It made the argument of federalism—that the Constitution reserved to the states any power to legislate on the press. The Virginia legislature approved resolutions drafted by Madison making the argument that freedom of speech and of the press were the essential guardians of a republican political system. The Virginia Resolutions protested against "the palpable and alarming infractions of the Constitution" in the Sedition Act. It exercised, the resolutions said, "a power not delegated by the Constitution, but, on the contrary, expressly and positively forbidden by one of the amendments thereto—a power which, more than any other, ought to produce universal alarm, because it is leveled against the right of freely examining public characters and measures, and of free communication among the people thereon, which has ever been justly deemed the only effectual guardian of every other right."

That phrase of Madison's, the "right of freely examining public characters and measures," echoed down the decades as the premise of the American political system—the Madisonian premise. Madison expanded on the idea in a Report on the Virginia Resolutions that he wrote in late 1799 and that the Virginia legislature approved in January 1800. Under the United States Constitution, he said, "The people, not the government, possess the absolute sovereignty." That was "altogether different" from Britain—the point Nicholas had made. "Is it not natural and necessary, under such different circumstances, that a different degree of freedom in the use of the press should be contemplated?" In America, Madison continued, "the press has exerted a freedom in canvassing the merits and measures of public men, of every description, which has not been confined to the strict limits of the common law. On this footing the freedom of the press has stood; on this foundation it yet stands."

The Virginia Resolutions and Madison's Report are landmarks in the history of free speech and a free press in the United States. But there was another view in Virginia at the time: a minority report of the House of Delegates, supporting the Sedition Act. According to Albert J. Beveridge, author of the standard life of Chief Justice John Marshall, Marshall wrote the minority report. He had been elected to Congress as a Federalist in April 1799. Marshall wrote:

> To contend that there does not exist a power to punish writings coming within the description of this [Sedition] law, would be to assert the inability of our nation to preserve its own peace, and to protect themselves from the attempts of wicked citizens, who incapable of quiet themselves, are incessantly employed in devising means to disturb the public repose. Government is instituted and preserved for the general happiness and safety; the people therefore are interested in its preservation, and have a right to adopt measures for its security, as well against secret plots as open hostility. But government cannot be thus secured, if, by falsehood and malicious slander, it is to be deprived of the confidence and affection of the people.
>
> It is in vain to urge that truth will prevail, and that slander, when detected, recoils on the calumniator. The experience of the world, and our own experience, prove that a continued course of defamation will at length sully the fairest reputation, and will throw suspicion on the purest conduct. Although the calumnies of the factious and discontented may not poison the minds of a majority of the citizens, yet they will infect a very considerable number, and prompt them to deeds destructive of the public peace, and dangerous to the general safety. This the people have a right to prevent; and therefore, in all the nations of the earth, where presses are known some corrective of their licentiousness has been deemed indispensable.

The Marshall report was a fascinating expression of the political premises that underlay the Sedition Act. It saw government as a fragile creature that had to be protected from "wicked citizens." There could hardly be a sharper contrast to Jefferson's belief that democratic government requires the acceptance of risk and change. Or to Madison's view that the people are sovereign and hence entitled to say what they choose about those whom they appoint temporarily to govern. To Marshall, the government was sovereign, and entitled to preserve itself. It was a very English view.

As for the First Amendment, Marshall construed it in an ingenious way to argue that the Sedition Act did not violate its guarantee of press freedom. The same First Amendment, he noted, said, "Congress shall make no law respecting an establishment of religion." But when the amendment came to the press, he said, "the word *respecting* is dropt, and Congress is only restrained from passing any law abridging its liberty." Thus, he argued, the establishment clause was an absolute bar; but the press clause merely prohibited abridgment of what was then understood as "the freedom of the press." Marshall went on to define that freedom in extremely narrow terms—as Blackstone had, no more. "In fact," he wrote in the minority report, "the liberty of the press is a term which has a definite signification completely understood. It signifies a liberty to publish, free from previous restraint, ... but not the liberty of spreading with impunity false and malicious slanders, which may destroy the peace and mangle the reputation of an individual or of a community." (As a reading of the intention of those who framed the First Amendment, Marshall's point about the word "respecting" was dubious. The Framers wanted to bar Congress from either establishing a national church or ordering states that had established churches to disestablish them; the neutral word "respecting" was designed to keep Congress from acting one way or the other. But Marshall was writing as a politician, not as the great judicial interpreter of the Constitution that he became.)

The significance of the Sedition Act was made clear by the prosecutions brought under it. The most complete modern account, *Freedom's Fetters*, by James Morton Smith, says fourteen men were charged with violating the act during its brief life. They included the editors and owners of the leading Republican newspapers, the Philadelphia *Aurora*, Boston *Independent Chronicle*, New York *Argus*, Baltimore *American* and Richmond *Examiner*. Two other New York State papers, the *Time Piece* and the Mount Pleasant *Register*, ceased publication because of Sedition Act prosecutions. The New London, Connecticut, *Bee* suspended publication from April to August 1800 because its editor, Charles Holt, was serving a sentence for sedition. Most of the cases came to trial in the year 1800, and that was not an accident. President Adams's Secretary of State, Timothy Pickering, encouraged Sedition Act prosecutions, and he planned cases to silence the important Jeffersonian newspapers during the election contest of 1800 between Adams and Jefferson.

The first Sedition Act prosecution was brought not against an editor but against a Republican member of the House of Representatives, Matthew Lyon of Vermont. He was indicted for writing a letter to the editor that was published by the Vermont *Journal* of Windsor, Vermont. Lyon said he would gladly support a government that worked for the happiness of the people but could not be the "humble advocate" of an executive engaged in "a continual grasp for power, in an unbounded thirst for ridiculous pomp, foolish adulation, and selfish avarice...." The indictment charged that those words were a criminal libel on President Adams, "scurrilous, feigned, false, scandalous, seditious and malicious." At the trial the presiding judge was Justice William Paterson of the Supreme Court. (The justices all did extra duty as trial judges in those days, riding a judicial circuit on horseback.) Justice Paterson charged the jury that all it had to decide was whether Lyon's statement could have been made "with any other intent than that of making odious or contemptible the President and government, and bringing them both into disrepute. If you find such is the case, the offense is made out, and you must render a verdict of guilty." The jury convicted Lyon, and he was sentenced to four months in prison, with a fine of $1,000 and court costs of $60.96. Lyon was reelected to Congress while in prison. His jail term was due to expire on February 9, 1799, but he had no money to pay the fine or court costs, and failing payment would have to remain incarcerated. But leading Republicans around the country contributed to a fund for him, Senator Stevens T. Mason of Virginia brought the money in gold to Vermont, and Lyon was released to a triumphal parade in his honor. He returned to Congress a hero, the prosecution having badly misfired.

An even more extreme example of the uses of the Sedition Act was the prosecution of David Brown, a wandering orator—really a vagabond—who traveled around Massachusetts between 1796 and 1798 denouncing the government for land speculation and, latterly, for the Sedition Act and companion measures against aliens. After he spoke in Dedham in 1798, citizens raised a liberty pole with a sign saying: "No Stamp Act, No Sedition, No Alien Bills, No Land Tax; downfall to the Tyrants of America, peace and retirement to the President, Long Live the Vice–President and the Minority; May moral virtue be the basis of civil government." Brown was charged under the Sedition Act for inspiring the erection of the liberty pole. In a trial before the most infamously partisan Federalist on the bench, Justice Samuel Chase of the Supreme Court, sitting on circuit in Massachusetts, Brown pleaded guilty. Justice Chase sentenced him to eighteen months in prison and a fine of $480, saying he imposed the severe sentence because of Brown's "vicious industry" in circulating "his disorganizing doctrines and impudent falsehoods, and the very alarming and dangerous excesses to which he attempted to incite the uninformed part of the community." When his prison term expired in December 1800, Brown could not pay the fine. He remained in prison until Jefferson became President on March 4, 1801, and pardoned all the victims of the Sedition Act.

James T. Callender, a political pamphleteer whose invective infuriated the Federalists, was indicted for sedition in Virginia. He was accused for passages in a book, published as the campaign of 1800 was getting under way, that called Adams a "hoary headed incendiary" and told voters, "Take your choice, then, between Adams, war and beggary, and Jefferson, peace and competency." (The New York Federalist, Harry Croswell, was prosecuted for common-law seditious libel in 1803 for writing that Jefferson had paid Callender to publish those statements.) Justice Chase presided over the grand jury that indicted Callender, and then over the trial. He baited Callender's lawyers and dismissed their arguments so cavalierly that they resigned from the case. The jury, composed entirely of Federalists, convicted Callender, and Justice Chase sentenced him to a prison term of nine months and a $200 fine. Callender stayed in prison until the Sedition Act expired, but that did not silence him. He wrote articles from prison for Virginia newspapers during the election campaign, and he attacked Justice Chase as a judge who acted like a prosecutor. The Callender case was the most celebrated of the Sedition Act prosecutions, and once again it backfired on the Federalists. Republicans published the transcript of Callender's trial, and it became popular evidence of a Federalist inclination to tyranny.

The constitutionality of the Sedition Act was never tested in the Supreme Court because the law expired before a case could reach there. But it should be noted that three of the six men who sat on the Court in 1800, Justices Chase, Paterson and Bushrod Washington, had presided at Sedition Act trials without intimating any constitutional qualms.

As a political tactic, the Sedition Act was a disaster. It aroused popular outrage, becoming a campaign issue itself in the election of 1800 and contributing to Jefferson's defeat of Adams. The Federalists also lost control of Congress in that election, and they soon disappeared as a party. But the act did make an inadvertent contribution, an important one, to the American system of government. It made large numbers of Americans appreciate the importance of free speech and freedom of the press in a democracy: the Madisonian premise. Whether or not the authors of the First Amendment intended it to eliminate the crime of seditious libel, ten years later the weight of opinion, informed and popular, was that such a crime was inconsistent with the American constitutional system.

Jefferson quickly pardoned all those who had been convicted under the Sedition Act. He gave his reasons in a letter to Abigail Adams in 1804. (Despite their bitter enmity before the election of 1800 Jefferson had a long and happy correspondence with both John and Abigail Adams. The two men were intimate friends until they died—on the same day, July 4, 1826, the fiftieth anniversary of the Declaration of Independence.) Jefferson wrote Mrs. Adams:

> I discharged every person under punishment or prosecution under the Sedition Law, because I considered, and now consider, that law to be a nullity, as absolute and palpable as if Congress had ordered us to fall down and worship a golden image; and that it was as much my duty to arrest its execution in every stage, as it would have been to have rescued from the fiery furnace those who should have been cast into it for refusing to worship the image.

It has often been said that Congress remitted the fines of those convicted under the act, but there was no general repayment. Many years later, in 1840, Congress did vote to refund to the heirs of Representative Matthew Lyon the $1,000 fine and $60.96 in court costs, plus interest. One other refund statute, passed in 1850, repaid with interest a $400 fine imposed on Dr. Thomas Cooper, a Pennsylvania pamphleteer, who before his death in 1839 exacted a promise from his wife to keep demanding repayment.

GEOFFREY R. STONE, PERILOUS TIMES: FREE SPEECH IN WARTIME

(2004).

To understand the Sedition Act of 1798, it is essential to appreciate the Federalist view of "the freedom of speech." In short, the Federalists had little faith in free and open debate. As Congressman James A. Bayard observed, confidence that truth prevails over falsehood is "a fine moral sentiment, but our limited knowledge of events [does not] verify it." Federalists believed that the common man was easily manipulated and misled. They feared that even one Jacobin could "alarm a whole country with ridiculous fears of government." The Federalist *Philadelphia Gazette* warned that if "the alarm is caught by the weak," it will soon be "spread by the foolish" like a "contagious disease."

After witnessing the violent aftereffects of the French Revolution, Federalists had no doubt of both the power and the danger of public opinion. Congressman John Allen recounted that "at the commencement of the Revolution in France, those loud and enthusiastic advocates for liberty and equality took special care to occupy and command all the presses." The Jacobins understood that the press was especially potent in holding sway over "the poor, the ignorant, the passionate, and the vicious." "Over all these classes," Allen noted, "the freedom of the press shed its baneful effects," and "the virtuous, the pacific, and the rich, were their victims."

Judge Alexander Addison warned his Federalist colleagues that "speech, writing and printing are the great directors of public opinion, and public opinion is the great director of human action." "Give to any set of men the command of the press," and you "give them the command of the country." It was thus essential for the Federalists to control the Republican press to ensure that "the high priests of Jacobinism" did not lead the people astray.

To the Federalists, these dangers were not theoretical. They saw the Republican press as dishonest, abusive, and utterly irresponsible. As early as 1796, Abigail Adams, who rarely failed to act as her husband's eyes and ears, condemned Republican newspapers as "the offspring of faction and nursed by sedition." Federalists characterized Republican newspapers as pestilent compilers of slander, calumny, and falsehood. Their entire mission, the Federalists charged, was to deceive the public. The *Albany Centinel* accused Republicans of propagating nothing but "lies and liars, as a hot day breeds maggots or musketoes."

Alexander Hamilton took it to be a maxim of the Jacobins that "no character, however upright, is a match for constantly reiterated attacks, however false." "The public mind," he explained, "fatigued" by the struggle to resist "the calumnies which eternally assail it," eventually embraces "the opinion that a person so often accused cannot be entirely innocent." Federalists worried that constant attacks on the reputations of public officials would drive "our wisest and best public officers ... from their stations" and that their successors would be obscure and venal men "without virtue or talents." President Adams complained that the Republican press went to "all lengths of profligacy, falsehood and malignity in defaming our government," and demanded that the "misrepresentations which have misled so many citizens ... must be discountenanced by authority."

There was some merit to these concerns. The most prominent of the Republican newspapers, the *Aurora*, was edited by Benjamin Franklin Bache of Philadelphia. The grandson of Ben Franklin, Bache, who had been raised by his grandfather in Paris, was well educated, temperamental, and self-righteous. At a time of scurrilous journalism, Bache was a master of the art. He once described President Adams as "blind, bald, crippled, toothless [and] querulous," and he accused even the revered George Washington of reveling in neomonarchical ceremony, dipping into the public treasury, and incompetent soldiering.

Bache proclaimed that if ever a nation has been "debauched by a man, the American Nation has been debauched by Washington." At various times, he referred to Washington's manner, carriage, and clothing as "apish," "monarchical," "pompous," and "tawdry." When Washington stepped down as president—in part to escape Bache's unrelenting attacks—Bache castigated him as "the source of all the misfortunes of our country." In January 1797, Washington complained that the *Aurora* had assailed him with "malignant industry and persevering falsehoods" in order to "weaken, if not destroy, the confidence of the Public." Bache's motives were not entirely base. He believed in a polity based on principle, not men, and felt a responsibility to bring even George Washington down to human scale.

Republicans applauded Bache as a fervent advocate for the public good; Federalists despised him as a seditious scoundrel and accused him of being Talleyrand's agent. In 1797, Bache was physically assaulted by a young Federalist, who was later rewarded with a government position. A year later, a mob of drunken Federalists attacked Bache's home and terrorized his wife and children. In June 1798, even before passage of the Sedition Act, the Federalists had Bache arrested and charged with "libeling the President & the Executive Government," without even bothering to specify the publications in question.

Venom was not the exclusive province of Republicans. The most prominent Federalist paper, the *Gazette of the United States*, announced that its mission was to oppose the "the raging madness of Jacobinism." Its editor, John Fenno, characterized critics of the Adams administration as "dismal cacklers," "propagators of calumny," and the "worst and basest of men." William Cobbett, who edited the Federalist *Porcupine's Gazette*, exceeded all others in the art of vilification. He once accused Bache of being an "abandoned liar" and suggested that he be dealt with like "a Turk, a Jew, a Jacobin, or a Dog."

AN ACT CONCERNING ALIENS

1 Stat. 570, June 25, 1798.

Section 1. *Be it enacted by the Senate and House of Representatives of the United States of America in Congress assembled,* That it shall be lawful for the President of the United States at any time during the continuance of this act, to *order* all such *aliens* as he shall judge dangerous to the peace and safety of the United States, or shall have reasonable grounds to suspect are concerned in any treasonable or secret machinations against the government thereof, to depart out of the territory of the United States, within such time as shall be expressed in such order.... And in case any alien, so ordered to depart, shall be found at large within the United States after the time limited in such order for his departure, and not having obtained a *license* from the President to reside therein, or having obtained such *license* shall not have conformed thereto, every such alien shall, on conviction thereof, be imprisoned for a term not exceeding three years, and shall never after be admitted to become a citizen of the United States....

AN ACT IN ADDITION TO THE ACT, ENTITLED "AN ACT FOR THE PUNISHMENT OF CERTAIN CRIMES AGAINST THE UNITED STATES"

1 Stat. 596, July 14, 1798.

Sec. 2. *And be it further enacted,* That if any person shall write, print, utter or publish, or shall cause to procure to be written, printed, uttered or published, or shall knowingly and willingly assist or aid in writing, printing, uttering or publishing any false, scandalous and malicious writing or writings against the government of the United States, or either house of the Congress of the United States, or the President of the United States, with intent to defame the said government, or either house of the said Congress, or the said President, or to bring them, or either of them, into contempt or disrepute; or to excite against them, or either or any of them, the hatred of the good people of the United States, or to stir up sedition within the United States, or to excite any unlawful combinations therein, for opposing or resisting any law of the United States, or any act of the President of the United States, done in pursuance of any such law, or of the powers in him vested by the constitution of the United States, or to resist, oppose, or defeat any such law or act, or to aid, encourage or abet any hostile designs of any foreign nation against the United States, their people or government, then such person, being thereof convicted before any court of the United States having jurisdiction thereof, shall be punished by a fine not exceeding two thousand dollars, and by imprisonment not exceeding two years.

Sec. 3. *And be it further enacted and declared,* That if any person shall be prosecuted under this act, for the writing or publishing any libel aforesaid, it shall be lawful for the defendant, upon the trial of the cause, to give in evidence in his defence, the truth of the matter contained in the publication charged as a libel. And the jury who shall try the cause, shall have a right to determine the law and the fact, under the direction of the court, as in other cases.

JAMES MADISON, REPORT ON THE VIRGINIA RESOLUTIONS

(1799–1800).

The next point which the resolution requires to be proved is, that the power over the press, exercised by the Sedition Act, is positively forbidden by one of the amendments to the Constitution.

The amendment stands in these words: "Congress shall make no law respecting an establishment of religion, or prohibiting the free exercise thereof, or abridging the freedom of speech, or of the press, or of the right of the people peaceably to assemble, and to petition the government for a redress of grievances."

In the attempts to vindicate the Sedition Act, it has been contended, 1. That the "freedom of the press" is to be determined by the meaning of these terms in the common law; 2. That the article supposes the power over the press to be in Congress, and prohibits them only from abridging the freedom allowed to it by the common law.

Although it will be shown, on examining the second of these positions, that the amendment is a denial to Congress of all power over the press, it may not be useless to make the following observations on the first of them:—

It is deemed to be a sound opinion that the Sedition Act, in its definition of some of the crimes created, is an abridgment of the freedom of publication, recognized by principles of the common law in England.

The freedom of the press, under the common law, is, in the defences of the Sedition Act, made to consist in an exemption from all previous restraint on printed publications, by persons authorized to inspect or prohibit them. It appears to the committee that this idea of the freedom of the press can never be admitted to be the American idea of it; since a law inflicting penalties on printed publications would have a similar effect with a law authorizing a previous restraint on them. It would seem a mockery to say that no laws should be passed preventing publications from being made, but that laws might be passed for punishing them in case they should be made.

The essential difference between the British government and the American constitutions will place this subject in the clearest light.

In the British government, the danger of encroachments on the rights of the people is understood to be confined to the executive magistrate. The representatives of the people in the legislature are not only exempt themselves from distrust, but are considered as sufficient guardians of the rights of their constituents against the danger from the executive. Hence it is a principle, that the Parliament is unlimited in its power; or, in their own language, is omnipotent. Hence, too, all the ramparts for protecting the rights of the people,—such as their Magna Charta, their bill of rights, &c., —are not reared against the Parliament, but against the royal prerogative. They are merely legislative precautions against executive usurpation. Under such a government as this, an exemption of the press from previous restraint by licensers appointed by the king, is all the freedom that can be secured to it.

In the United States, the case is altogether different. The people, not the government, possess the absolute sovereignty. The legislature, no less than the executive, is under limitations of power. Encroachments are regarded as possible from the one as well as from the other. Hence, in the United States, the great and essential rights of the people are secured against legislative as well as executive ambition. They are secured, not by laws paramount to prerogative, but by constitutions paramount to laws. This security of the freedom of the press requires that it should be exempt, not only from previous restraint of the executive, as in Great Britain but from legislative restraint also; and this exemption, to be effectual must be an exemption, not only from the previous inspection of licensers, but from the subsequent penalty of laws.

The state of the press, therefore, under the common law, cannot, in this point of view, be the standard of its freedom in the United States.

But there is another view under which it may be necessary to consider this subject. It may be alleged that, although the security for the freedom of the press be different in Great Britain and in this country,—being a legal security only in the former, and a constitutional security in the latter,—and although there may be a further difference, in an extension of the freedom of the press, here, beyond an exemption from previous restraint, to an exemption from subsequent penalties also,—yet the actual legal freedom of the press, under the common law, must determine the degree of freedom which is meant by the terms, and which is constitutionally secured against both previous and subsequent restraints.

The committee are not unaware of the difficulty of all general questions, which may turn on the proper boundary between the liberty and licentiousness of the press. They will leave it, therefore, for consideration only, how far the difference between the nature of the British government, and the nature of the American government, and the practice under the latter, may show the degree of rigor in the former to be inapplicable to, and not obligatory in, the latter.

The nature of governments elective, limited, and responsible, in all their branches, may well be supposed to require a greater freedom of animadversion, than might be tolerated by the genius of such a government as that of Great Britain. In the latter, it is a maxim, that the king—an hereditary, not a responsible magistrate—can do no wrong; and that the legislature, which, in two thirds of its composition, is also hereditary, not responsible, can do what it pleases. In the United States, the executive magistrates are not held to be infallible, nor the legislatures to be omnipotent; and both, being elective, are both responsible. Is it not natural and necessary, under such different circumstances, that a different degree of freedom in the use of the press should be contemplated?

Is not such an inference favored by what is observable in Great Britain itself? Notwithstanding the general doctrine of the common law, on the subject of the press, and the occasional punishment of those who use it with a freedom offensive to the government, it is well known that, with respect to the responsible measures of the government, where the reasons operating here become applicable there, the freedom exercised by the press, and protected by public opinion, far exceeds the limits prescribed by the ordinary rules of law. The ministry, who are responsible to impeachment, are at all times animadverted on, by the press, with peculiar freedom; and during the elections for the House of Commons, the other responsible part of the government, the press is employed with as little reserve towards the candidates.

The practice in America must be entitled to much more respect. In every state, probably, in the Union, the press has exerted a freedom in canvassing the merits and measures of public men, of every description, which has not been confined to the strict limits of the common law. On this footing the freedom of the press has stood; on this foundation it yet stands; and it will not be a breach, either of truth or of candor, to say that no persons or presses are in the habit of more unrestrained animadversions on the proceedings and functionaries of the state governments than the persons and presses most zealous in vindicating the act of Congress for punishing similar animadversions on the government of the United States.

The last remark will not be understood as claiming for the state governments an immunity greater than they have heretofore enjoyed. Some degree of abuse is inseparable from the proper use of every thing; and in no instance is this more true than in that of the press. It has accordingly been decided, by the practice of the states, that it is better to leave a few of its noxious branches to their luxuriant growth, than, by pruning them away, to injure the vigor of those yielding the proper fruits. And can the wisdom of this policy be doubted by any one who reflects that to the press alone, checkered as it is with abuses, the world is indebted for all the triumphs which have been gained by reason and humanity over error and oppression; who reflects that to the same beneficent source the United States owe much of the lights which conducted them to the rank of a free and independent nation and which have improved their political system into a shape so auspicious to their happiness? Had Sedition Acts, forbidding every publication that might bring the constituted agents into contempt or disrepute, or that might excite the hatred of the people against the authors of unjust or pernicious measures, been uniformly enforced against the press, might not the United States have been languishing, at this day, under the infirmities of a sickly Confederation? Might they not, possibly, be miserable colonies, groaning under a foreign yoke?

To these observations one fact will be added, which demonstrates that the common law cannot be admitted as the universal expositor of American terms, which may be the same with those contained in that law. The freedom of conscience, and of religion, is found in the same instrument which asserts the freedom of the press. It will never be admitted that the meaning of the former, in the common law of England, is to limit their meaning in the United States.

Whatever weight may be allowed to these considerations, the committee do not, however, by any means intend to rest the question on them. They contend that the article of the amendment, instead of supposing in Congress a power that might be exercised over the press, provided its freedom was not abridged, meant a positive denial to Congress of any power whatever on the subject.

To demonstrate that this was the true object of the article, it will be sufficient to recall the circumstances which led to it, and to refer to the explanation accompanying the article.

When the Constitution was under the discussions which preceded its ratification, it is well known that great apprehensions were expressed by many, lest the omission of some positive exception, from the powers delegated, of certain rights, and of the freedom of the press particularly, might expose them to danger of being drawn, by construction, within some of the powers vested in Congress; more especially of the power to make all laws necessary and proper for carrying their other powers into execution. In reply to this objection, it was invariably urged to be a fundamental and characteristic principle of the Constitution, that all powers not given by it were reserved; that no powers were given beyond those enumerated in the Constitution, and such as were fairly incident to them; that the power over the rights in question, and particularly over the press, was neither among the enumerated powers, nor incident to any of them: and consequently that an exercise of any such power would be manifest usurpation. It is painful to remark how much the arguments now employed in behalf of the Sedition Act, are at variance with the reasoning which then justified the Constitution, and invited its ratification.

From this posture of the subject resulted the interesting question, in so many of the conventions, whether the doubts and dangers ascribed to the Constitution should be removed by any amendments previous to the ratification, or be postponed, in confidence that, as far as they might be proper, they would be introduced in the form provided by the Constitution. The latter course was adopted; and in most of the states, ratifications were followed by the propositions and instructions for rendering the Constitution more explicit, and more safe to the rights not meant to be delegated by it. Among those rights, the freedom of the press, in most instances, is particularly and emphatically mentioned. The firm and very pointed manner in which it is asserted in the proceedings of the Convention of this state will hereafter be seen.

In pursuance of the wishes thus expressed, the first Congress that assembled under the Constitution proposed certain amendments, which have since, by the necessary ratifications, been made a part of it; among which amendments is the article containing, among other prohibitions on the Congress, an express declaration that they should make no law abridging the freedom of the press.

Without tracing farther the evidence on this subject, it would seem scarcely possible to doubt that no power whatever over the press was supposed to be delegated by the Constitution, as it originally stood, and that the amendment was intended as a positive and absolute reservation of it.

But the evidence is still stronger. The proposition of amendments made by Congress is introduced in the following terms:—

"The conventions of a number of the states having; at the time of their adopting the Constitution, expressed a desire, in order to prevent misconstruction or abuse of its powers, that further declaratory and restrictive clauses should be added; and as extending the ground of public confidence in the government will best insure the beneficent ends of its institutions."

Here is the most satisfactory and authentic proof that the several amendments proposed were to be considered as either declaratory or restrictive, and, whether the one or the other, as corresponding with the desire expressed by a number of the states, and as extending the ground of public confidence in the government.

Under any other construction of the amendment relating to the press, than that it declared the press to be wholly exempt from the power of Congress, the amendment could neither be said to correspond with the desire expressed by a number of the states, nor be calculated to extend the ground of public confidence in the government.

Nay, more; the construction employed to justify the Sedition Act would exhibit a phenomenon without a parallel in the political world. It would exhibit a number of respectable states, as denying, first, that any power over the press was delegated by the Constitution; as proposing, next, that an amendment to it should explicitly declare that no such power was delegated; and, finally, as concurring in an amendment actually recognizing or delegating such a power.

Is, then, the federal government, it will be asked, destitute of every authority for restraining the licentiousness of the press, and for shielding itself against the libellous attacks which may be made on those who administer it?

The Constitution alone can answer this question. If no such power be expressly delegated, and if it be not both necessary and proper to carry into execution an express power; above all, if it be expressly forbidden, by a declaratory amendment to the Constitution,—the answer must be, that the federal government is destitute of all such authority.

And might it not be asked, in turn, whether it is not more probable, under all the circumstances which have been reviewed, that the authority should be withheld by the Constitution, than that it should be left to a vague and violent construction, whilst so much pains were bestowed in enumerating other powers, and so many less important powers are included in the enumeration?

Might it not be likewise asked, whether the anxious circumspection which dictated so many peculiar limitations on the general authority would be unlikely to exempt the press altogether from that authority? The peculiar magnitude of some of the powers necessarily committed to the federal government; the peculiar duration required for the functions of some of its departments; the peculiar distance of the seat of its proceedings from the great body of its constituents; and the peculiar difficulty of circulating an adequate knowledge of them through any other channel;—will not these considerations, some or other of which produced other exceptions from the powers of ordinary governments, altogether, account for the policy of binding the hands of the federal government from touching the channel which alone can give efficacy to its responsibility to its constituents, and of leaving those who administer it to a remedy, for their injured reputations, under the same laws, and in the same tribunals, which protect their lives, their liberties, and their properties?

But the question does not turn either on the wisdom of the Constitution or on the policy which gave rise to its particular organization. It turns on the actual meaning of the instrument, by which it has appeared that a power over the press is clearly excluded from the number of powers delegated to the federal government.

And, in the opinion of the committee, well may it be said, as the resolution concludes with saying, that the unconstitutional power exercised over the press by the Sedition Act ought, "more than any other, to produce universal alarm; because it is levelled against that right of freely examining public characters and measures, and of free communication among the people thereon, which has ever been justly deemed the only effectual guardian of every other right."

Without scrutinizing minutely into all the provisions of the Sedition Act, it will be sufficient to cite so much of section 2d as follows:—"And be it further enacted, that if any shall write, print, utter, or publish, or shall cause or procure to be written, printed, uttered, or published, or shall knowingly and willingly assist or aid in writing, printing, uttering, or publishing, any false, scandalous, and malicious writing or writings against the government of the United States, or either house of the Congress of the United States, with an intent to defame the said government, or either house of the said Congress, or the President, or to bring them or either of them into contempt or disrepute, or to excite against them, or either or any of them, the hatred of the good people of the United States, &c.,—then such persons, being thereof convicted before any court of the United States having jurisdiction thereof, shall be punished by a fine not exceeding two thousand dollars, and by imprisonment not exceeding two years."

On this part of the act, the following observations present themselves:—

1. The Constitution supposes that the President, the Congress, and each of its Houses, may not discharge their trusts, either from defect of judgment or other causes. Hence they are all made responsible to their constituents, at the returning periods of elections; and the President, who is singly intrusted with very great powers, is, as a further guard, subjected to an intermediate impeachment.

2. Should it happen, as the Constitution supposes it may happen, that either of these branches of the government may not have duly discharged its trust, it is natural and proper, that, according to the cause and degree of their faults, they should be brought into contempt or disrepute, and incur the hatred of the people.

3. Whether it has, in any case, happened that the proceedings of either or all of those branches evince such a violation of duty as to justify a contempt, a disrepute, or hatred among the people, can only be determined by a free examination thereof, and a free communication among the people thereon.

4. Whenever it may have actually happened that proceedings of this sort are chargeable on all or either of the branches of the government, it is the duty, as well as the right, of intelligent and faithful citizens to discuss and promulgate them freely—as well to control them by the censorship of the public opinion, as to promote a remedy according to the rules of the Constitution. And it cannot be avoided that those who are to apply the remedy must feel, in some degree, a contempt or hatred against the transgressing party.

5. As the act was passed on July 14, 1798, and is to be in force until March 3, 1801, it was of course that, during its continuance, two elections of the entire House of Representatives, an election of a part of the Senate, and an election of a President, were to take place.

6. That, consequently, during all these elections,—intended, by the Constitution, to preserve the purity or to purge the faults of the administration,—the great remedial rights of the people were to be exercised, and the responsibility of their public agents to be screened, under the penalties of this act.

May it not be asked of every intelligent friend to the liberties of his country, whether the power exercised in such an act as this ought not to produce great and universal alarm? Whether a rigid execution of such an act, in time past, would not have repressed that information and communication among the people which is indispensable to the just exercise of their electoral rights? And whether such an act, if made perpetual, and enforced with rigor, would not, in time to come, either destroy our free system of government, or prepare a convulsion that might prove equally fatal to it?

In answer to such questions, it has been pleaded that the writings and publications forbidden by the act are those only which are false and malicious, and intended to defame; and merit is claimed for the privilege allowed to authors to justify, by proving the truth of their publications, and for the limitations to which the sentence of fine and imprisonment is subjected.

To those who concurred in the act, under the extraordinary belief that the option lay between the passing of such an act, and leaving in force the common law of libels, which punishes truth equally with falsehood, and submits fine and imprisonment to the indefinite discretion of the court, the merit of good intentions ought surely not to be refused. A like merit may perhaps be due for the discontinuance of the corporal punishment, which the common law also leaves to the discretion of the court. This merit of intention, however, would have been greater, if the several mitigations had not been limited to so short a period; and the apparent inconsistency would have been avoided, between justifying the act, at one time, by contrasting it with the rigors of the common law otherwise in force; and at another time, by appealing to the nature of the crisis as requiring the temporary rigor exerted by the act.

But, whatever may have been the meritorious intentions of all or any who contributed to the Sedition Act, a very few reflections will prove that its baleful tendency is little diminished by the privilege of giving in evidence the truth of the matter contained in political writings.

In the first place, where simple and naked facts alone are in question, there is sufficient difficulty in some cases, and sufficient trouble and vexation in all, in meeting a prosecution from the government with the full and formal proof necessary in a court of law.

But in the next place, it must be obvious to the plainest minds, that opinions and inferences, and conjectural observations, are not only in many cases inseparable from the facts, but may often be more the objects of the prosecution than the facts themselves; or may even be altogether abstracted from particular facts; and that opinion, and inferences, and conjectural observations, cannot be subjects of that kind of proof which appertains to facts, before a court of law.

Again: it is no less obvious that the intent to defame, or bring into contempt, or disrepute, or hatred,—which is made a condition of the offence created by the act,—cannot prevent its pernicious influence on the freedom of the press. For, omitting the inquiry, how far the malice of the intent is an inference of the law from the mere publication, it is manifestly impossible to punish the intent to bring those who administer the government into disrepute or contempt, without striking at the right of freely discussing public characters and measures; because those who engage in such discussions must expect and intend to excite these unfavorable sentiments, so far as they may be thought to be deserved. To prohibit the intent to excite those unfavorable sentiments against those who administer the government, is equivalent to a prohibition of the actual excitement of them; and to prohibit the actual excitement of them is equivalent to a prohibition of discussions having that tendency and effect; which, again, is equivalent to a protection of those who administer the government, if they should at any time deserve the contempt or hatred of the people, against being exposed to it, by free animadversions on their characters and conduct. Nor can there be a doubt, if those in public trust be shielded by penal laws from such strictures of the press as may expose them to contempt, or disrepute, or hatred, where they may deserve it, that, in exact proportion as they may deserve to be exposed, will be the certainty and criminality of the intent to expose them, and the vigilance of prosecuting and punishing it; nor a doubt that a government thus intrenched in penal statutes against the just and natural effects of a culpable administration, will easily evade the responsibility which is essential to a faithful discharge of its duty.

Let it be recollected, lastly, that the right of electing the members of the government constitutes more particularly the essence of a free and responsible government. The value and efficacy of this right depends on the knowledge of the comparative merits and demerits of the candidates for public trust, and on the equal freedom, consequently, of examining and discussing these merits and demerits of the candidates respectively. It has been seen that a number of important elections will take place while the act is in force, although it should not be continued beyond the term to which it is limited. Should there happen, then, as is extremely probable in relation to some one or other of the branches of the government, to be competitions between those who are, and those who are not, members of the government, what will be the situations of the competitors? Not equal; because the characters of the former will be covered by the Sedition Act from animadversions exposing them to disrepute among the people, whilst the latter may be exposed to the contempt and hatred of the people without a violation of the act. What will be the situation of the people? Not free; because they will be compelled to make their election between competitors whose pretensions they are not permitted by the act equally to examine, to discuss, and to ascertain. And from both these situations will not those in power derive an undue advantage for continuing themselves in it: which, by impairing the right of election, endangers the blessings of the government founded on it?

It is with justice, therefore, that the General Assembly have affirmed, in the resolution, as well that the right of freely examining public characters and measures, and of communication thereon, is the only effectual guardian of every other right, as that this particular right is levelled at by the power exercised in the Sedition Act.

The resolution *next* in order is as follows:—

> That this state having, by its Convention, which ratified the Federal Constitution, expressly declared that, among other essential rights, "the liberty of conscience and of the press cannot be can-

celled, abridged, restrained, or modified, by any authority of the United States"; and, from its extreme anxiety to guard these rights from every possible attack of sophistry and ambition, having, with other states, recommended an amendment for that purpose, which amendment was in due time annexed to the Constitution; it would mark a reproachful inconsistency, and criminal degeneracy, if an indifference were now shown to the most palpable violation of one of the rights thus declared and secured, and to the establishment of a precedent which may be fatal to the other.

To place this resolution in its just light, it will be necessary to recur to the act of ratification by Virginia, which stands in the ensuing form:—

> We, the delegates of the people of Virginia, duly elected in pursuance of a recommendation from the General Assembly, and now met in Convention, having fully and freely investigated and discussed the proceedings of the Federal Convention, and being prepared, as well as the most mature deliberation hath enabled us, to decide thereon,—DO, in the name and in behalf of the people of Virginia, declare and make known, that the powers granted under the Constitution, being derived from the people of the United States, may be resumed by them whensoever the same shall be perverted to their injury or oppression; and that every power not granted thereby remains with them, and at their will. That, therefore, no right of any denomination can be cancelled, abridged, restrained, or modified, by the Congress, by the Senate or the House of Representatives, acting in any capacity, by the President, or any department or officer of the United States, except in those instances in which power is given by the Constitution for those purposes; and that, among other essential rights, the liberty of conscience and of the press cannot be cancelled, abridged, restrained, or modified, by any authority of the United States.

Here is an express and solemn declaration by the Convention of the state, that they ratified the Constitution in the sense that no right of any denomination can be cancelled, abridged, restrained, or modified, by the government of the United States, or any part of it, except in those instances in which power is given by the Constitution; and in the sense, particularly, "that among other essential rights, the liberty of conscience and freedom of the press cannot be cancelled, abridged, restrained, or modified, by any authority of the United States."

Words could not well express, in a fuller or more forcible manner, the understanding of the Convention, that the liberty of conscience and freedom of the press were *equally* and *completely* exempted from all authority whatever of the United States.

Under an anxiety to guard more effectually these rights against every possible danger, the Convention, after ratifying the Constitution, proceeded to prefix to certain amendments proposed by them, a declaration of rights, in which are two articles providing, the one for the liberty of conscience, the other for the freedom of speech and of the press.

Similar recommendations having proceeded from a number of other states; and Congress, as has been seen, having, in consequence thereof, and with a view to extend the ground of public confidence, proposed, among other declaratory and restrictive clauses, a clause expressly securing the liberty of conscience and of the press; and Virginia having concurred in the ratifications which made them a part of the Constitution,—it will remain with a candid public to decide whether it would not mark an inconsistency and degeneracy, if an indifference were now shown to a palpable violation of one of those rights—the freedom of the press; and to a precedent, therein, which may be fatal to the other—the free exercise of religion.

That the precedent established by the violation of the former of these rights may, as is affirmed by the resolution, be fatal to the latter, appears to be demonstrable by a comparison of the grounds on which they respectively rest, and from the scope of reasoning by which the power of the former has been vindicated.

First, Both of these rights, the liberty of conscience, and of the press, rest equally on the original ground of not being delegated by the Constitution, and consequently withheld from the government. Any construction, therefore, that would attack this original security for the one, must have the like effect on the other.

Secondly, They are both equally secured by the supplement to the Constitution, being both included in the same amendment, made at the same time and by the same authority. Any construction or argument, then, which would turn the amendment into a grant or acknowledgment of power, with respect to the press, might be equally applied to the freedom of religion.

Thirdly, If it be admitted that the extent of the freedom of the press, secured by the amendment, is to be measured by the common law on this subject, the same authority may be resorted to for the standard which is to fix the extent of the "free exercise of religion." It cannot be necessary to say what this standard would be—whether the common law be taken solely as the unwritten, or as varied by the written law of England.

Fourthly, If the words and phrases in the amendment are to be considered as chosen with a studied discrimination, which yields an argument for a power over the press, under the limitation that its freedom be not abridged, the same argument results from the same consideration, for a power over the exercise of religion, under the limitation that its freedom be not prohibited.

For, if Congress may regulate the freedom of the press, provided they do not abridge it, because it is said only, "they shall not abridge it," and is not said "they shall make no law respecting it," the analogy of reasoning is conclusive, that Congress may *regulate,* and even *abridge,* the free exercise of religion, provided they do not *prohibit* it; because it is said only "they shall not prohibit it;" and is *not* said, "they shall make no law *respecting,* or no law *abridging* it."

The General Assembly were governed by the clearest reason, then, in considering the Sedition Act, which legislates on the freedom of the press, as establishing a precedent that may be fatal to the liberty of conscience; and it will be the duty of all, in proportion as they value the security of the latter, to take the alarm at every encroachment on the former.

Questions

1) What kind of an argument is Madison making? From *consequences*? From the *authority* of constitutional text and history? From the lessons of *experience*? From the *design* of the American government?

2) How, if at all, does Madison's argument in the *Virginia Report* build on ideas he developed in the *Memorial and Remonstrance*?

3) Madison was arguing against a form of subsequent punishment, a criminal statute; Milton was arguing against a form of prior restraint, an administrative licensing system. Apart from that difference, how does Madison's argument differ from Milton's in terms of (a) assumptions about human nature and (b) the value ascribed to dissenting speech. Is Madison's argument less "instrumentalist" (in the sense that speech is valued for what it leads to rather than as something intrinsically valuable) than Milton's? More instrumentalist?

4) Does Madison's argument depend on a strong theory of rights? That is, in order for there to be a notion of abuse by government officials, does Madison need the idea that all citizens, or even "the people" as an entity, possess specified rights that can be violated by government? Should someone who is skeptical about the concept of rights but who believes strongly in democracy on a more participatory model find Madison's argument persuasive?

5) Does Madison base his argument on a highly contestable theory of representation? Specifically, to what extent does his argument depend on his strongly held notion that "the people of the nation" constitute the seat of sovereignty, to whom both the state governments and the federal government are accountable?

6) Is Madison too unwilling to try to regulate abuses of the press? Shouldn't he try harder to come up with definitions and institutional checks that would allow certain abuses to be regulated without necessarily leading to excessive authority in government to silence the press?

7) Is it really true that the proper response to officials who transgress their authorized powers is "hatred?"

8) Does Madison's argument apply to censorship by the states? Or is Madison's absolutism wholly a function of his claims about the limited authority of the federal government?

THE FEDERALIST, NUMBER TEN (MADISON)

(1788)

Among the numerous advantages promised by a well-constructed Union, none deserves to be more accurately developed than its tendency to break and control the violence of faction. The friend of popular governments never finds himself so much alarmed for their character and fate, as when he contemplates their propensity to this dangerous vice. He will not fail, therefore, to set a due value on any plan which, without violating the principles to which he is attached, provides a proper cure for it. The instability, injustice, and confusion introduced into the public councils, have, in truth, been the mortal diseases under which popular governments have everywhere perished; as they continue to be the favorite and fruitful topics from which the adversaries to liberty derive their most specious declamations. The valuable improvements made by the American constitutions on the popular models, both ancient and modern, cannot certainly be too much admired; but it would be an unwarrantable partiality, to contend that they have as effectually obviated the danger on this side, as was wished and expected. Complaints are everywhere heard from our most considerate and virtuous citizens, equally the friends of public and private faith, and of public and personal liberty, that our governments are too unstable, that the public good is disregarded in the conflicts of rival parties, and that measures are too often decided, not according to the rules of justice and the rights of the minor party, but by the superior force of an interested and overbearing majority. However anxiously we may wish that these complaints had no foundation, the evidence, of known facts will not permit us to deny that they are in some degree true. It will be found, indeed on a candid review of our situation, that some of the distresses under which we labor have been erroneously charged on the operation of our governments; but it will be found, at the same time, that other causes will not alone account for many of our heaviest misfortunes; and, particularly, for that prevailing and increasing distrust of public engagements, and alarm for private rights, which are echoed from one end of the continent to the other. These must be chiefly, if not wholly, effects of the unsteadiness and injustice with which a factious spirit has tainted our public administrations.

By a faction, I understand a number of citizens, whether amounting to a majority or a minority of the whole, who are united and actuated by some common impulse of passion, or of interest, adverse to the rights of other citizens, or to the permanent and aggregate interests of the community.

There are two methods of curing the mischiefs of faction: the one, by removing its causes; the other, by controlling its effects.

There are again two methods of removing the causes of faction: the one, by destroying the liberty which is essential to its existence; the other, by giving to every citizen the same opinions, the same passions, and the same interests.

It could never be more truly said than of the first remedy, that it was worse than the disease. Liberty is to faction what air is to fire, an aliment without which it instantly expires. But it could not be less folly to abolish liberty, which is essential to political life, because it nourishes faction, than it would be to wish the annihilation of air, which is essential to animal life, because it imparts to fire its destructive agency.

The second expedient is as impracticable as the first would be unwise. As long as the reason of man continues fallible, and he is at liberty to exercise it, different opinions will be formed. As long as the connection subsists between his reason and his self-love, his opinions and his passions will have a reciprocal influence on each other; and the former will be objects to which the latter will attach themselves. The diversity in the faculties of men, from which the rights of property originate, is not less an insuperable obstacle to a uniformity of interests. The protection of these faculties is the first object of government. From the protection of different and unequal faculties of acquiring property, the possession of different degrees and kinds of property immediately results; and from the influence of these on the sentiments and views of the respective proprietors, ensues a division of the society into different interests and parties.

The latent causes of faction are thus sown in the nature of man; and we see them everywhere brought into different degrees of activity, according to the different circumstances of civil society. A zeal for different opinions concerning religion, concerning government, and many other points, as well of speculation as of practice; an attachment to different leaders ambitiously contending for preeminence and power; or to persons of other descriptions whose fortunes have been interesting to the human passions, have, in turn, divided mankind into parties, inflamed them with mutual animosity, and rendered them much more disposed to vex and oppress each other than to co-operate for their common good. So strong is this propensity of mankind to fall into mutual animosities, that where no substantial occasion presents itself, the most frivolous and fanciful distinctions have been sufficient to kindle their unfriendly passions and excite their most violent conflicts. But the most common and durable source of factions has been the various and unequal distribution of property. Those who hold and those who are without property have ever formed distinct interests in society. Those who are creditors, and those who are debtors, fall under a like discrimination. A landed interest, a manufacturing interest, a mercantile interest, a moneyed interest, with many lesser interests, grow up of necessity in civilized nations, and divide them into different classes, actuated by different sentiments and views. The regulation of these various and interfering interests forms the principal task of modern legislation, and involves the spirit of party and faction in the necessary and ordinary operations of the government.

No man is allowed to be a judge in his own cause, because his interest would certainly bias his judgment, and, not improbably, corrupt his integrity. With equal, nay with greater reason, a body of men are unfit to be both judges and parties at the same time; yet what are many of the most important acts of legislation, but so many judicial determinations, not indeed concerning the rights of single persons, but concerning the rights of large bodies of citizens? And what are the different classes of legislators but advocates and parties to the causes which they determine? Is a law proposed concerning private debts? It is a question to which the creditors are parties on one side and the debtors on the other. Justice ought to hold the balance between them. Yet the parties are, and must be, themselves the judges; and the most numerous party, or, in other words, the most powerful faction must be expected to prevail. Shall domestic manufactures be encouraged, and in what degree, by restrictions on foreign manufactures? are questions which would be differently decided by the landed and the manufacturing classes, and probably by neither with a sole regard to justice and the public good. The apportionment of taxes on the various descriptions of property is an act which seems to require the most exact impartiality; yet there is, perhaps, no legislative act in which greater opportunity and temptation are given to a predominant party to trample on the rules of justice. Every shilling with which they overburden the inferior number, is a shilling saved to their own pockets.

It is in vain to say that enlightened statesmen will be able to adjust these clashing interests, and render them all subservient to the public good. Enlightened statesmen will not always be at the helm. Nor, in many cases, can such an adjustment be made at all without taking into view indirect and remote considerations, which will rarely prevail over the immediate interest which one party may find in disregarding the rights of another or the good of the whole.

The inference to which we are brought is, that the *causes* of faction cannot be removed, and that relief is only to be sought in the means of controlling its *effects*.

If a faction consists of less than a majority, relief is supplied by the republican principle, which enables the majority to defeat its sinister views by regular vote. It may clog the administration; it may convulse the society; but it will be unable to execute and mask its violence under the forms of the Constitution. When a majority is included in a faction, the form of popular government, on the other hand, enables it to sacrifice to its ruling passion or interest both the public good and the rights of other citizens. To secure the public good and private rights against the danger of such a faction, and at the same time to preserve the spirit and the form of popular government, is then the great object to which our inquiries are directed. Let me add that it is the great desideratum by which this form of government can be rescued from the opprobrium under which it has so long labored, and be recommended to the esteem and adoption of mankind.

By what means is this object attainable? Evidently by one of two only. Either the existence of the same passion or interest in a majority at the same time must be prevented, or the majority, having such coexistent passion or interest, must be rendered, by their number and local situation, unable to concert and carry into effect schemes of oppression. If the impulse and the opportunity be suffered to coincide, we well know that neither moral nor religious motives can be relied on as an adequate control. They are not found to be such on the injustice and violence of individuals, and lose their efficacy in proportion to the number combined together, that is, in proportion as their efficacy becomes needful.

From this view of the subject it may be concluded that a pure democracy, by which I mean a society consisting of a small number of citizens, who assemble and administer the government in person, can admit of no cure for the mischiefs of faction. A common passion or interest will, in almost every case, be felt by a majority of the whole; a communication and concert result from the form of government itself; and there is nothing to check the inducements to sacrifice the weaker party or an obnoxious individual. Hence it is that such democracies have ever been spectacles of turbulence and contention; have ever been found incompatible with personal security or the rights of property; and have in general been as short in their lives as they have been violent in their deaths. Theoretic politicians, who have patronized this species of government, have erroneously supposed that by reducing mankind to a perfect equality in their political rights, they would, at the same time, be perfectly equalized and assimilated in their possessions, their opinions, and their passions.

A republic, by which I mean a government in which the scheme of representation takes place, opens a different prospect, and promises the cure for which we are seeking. Let us examine the points in which it varies from pure democracy, and we shall comprehend both the nature of the cure and the efficacy which it must derive from the Union.

The two great points of difference between a democracy and a republic are: first, the delegation of the government, in the latter, to a small number of citizens elected by the rest; secondly, the greater number of citizens, and greater sphere of country, over which the latter may be extended.

The effect of the first difference is, on the one hand, to refine and enlarge the public views, by passing them through the medium of a chosen body of citizens, whose wisdom may best discern the true interest of their country, and whose patriotism and love of justice will be least likely to sacrifice it to temporary or partial considerations. Under such a regulation, it may well happen that the public voice, pronounced by the representatives of the people, will be more consonant to the public good than if pronounced by the people themselves, convened for the purpose. On the other hand, the effect may be inverted. Men of factious tempers, of local prejudices, or of sinister designs, may, by intrigue, by corruption, or by other means, first obtain the suffrages, and then betray the interests, of the people. The question resulting is, whether small or extensive republics are more favorable to the election of proper guardians of the public weal; and it is clearly decided in favor of the latter by two obvious considerations:

In the first place, it is to be remarked that, however small the republic may be, the representatives must be raised to a certain number, in order to guard against the cabals of a few; and that, however large it may be, they must be limited to a certain number, in order to guard against the confusion of a multitude. Hence, the number of representatives in the two cases not being in proportion to that of the two constituents, and being proportionally greater in the small republic, it follows that, if the proportion of fit characters be not less in the large than in the small republic, the former will present a greater option, and consequently a greater probability of a fit choice.

In the next place, as each representative will be chosen by a greater number of citizens in the large than in the small republic, it will be more difficult for unworthy candidates to practice with success the vicious arts by which elections are too often carried; and the suffrages of the people being more free, will be more likely to centre in men who possess the most attractive merit and the most diffusive and established characters.

It must be confessed that in this, as in most other cases, there is a mean, on both sides of which inconveniences will be found to lie. By enlarging too much the number of electors, you render the representatives too little acquainted with all their local circumstances and lesser interests; as by reducing it too much, you render him unduly attached to these, and too little fit to comprehend and pursue great and national objects. The federal Constitution forms a happy combination in this respect; the great and aggregate interests being referred to the national, the local and particular to the State legislatures.

The other point of difference is, the greater number of citizens and extent of territory which may be brought within the compass of republican than of democratic government; and it is this circumstance principally which renders factious combinations less to be dreaded in the former than in the latter. The smaller the society, the fewer probably will be the distinct parties and interests composing it; the fewer the distinct parties and interests, the more frequently will a majority be found of the same party; and the smaller the number of individuals composing a majority, and the smaller the compass within which they are placed, the more easily will they concert and execute their plans of oppression. Extend the sphere, and you take in a greater variety of parties and interests; you make it less probable that a majority of the whole will have a common motive to invade the rights of other citizens; or if such a common motive exists, it will be more difficult for all who feel it to discover their own strength, and to act in unison with each other. Besides other impediments, it may be remarked that, where there is a consciousness of unjust or dishonorable purposes, communication is always checked by distrust in proportion to the number whose concurrence is necessary.

Hence, it clearly appears, that the same advantage which a republic has over a democracy, in controlling the effects of faction, is enjoyed by a large over a small republic—is enjoyed by the Union over the States composing it. Does the advantage consist in the substitution of representatives whose enlightened views and virtuous sentiments render them superior to local prejudices and schemes of injustice? It will not be denied that the representation of the Union will be most likely to possess these requisite endowments. Does it consist in the greater security afforded by a greater variety of parties, against the event of any one party being able to outnumber and oppress the rest? In an equal degree does the increased variety of parties comprised within the Union, increase this security. Does it, in fine, consist in the greater obstacles opposed to the concert and accomplishment of the secret wishes of an unjust and interested majority? Here, again, the extent of the Union gives it the most palpable advantage.

The influence of factious leaders may kindle a flame within their particular States, but will be unable to spread a general conflagration through the other States. A religious sect may degenerate into a political faction in a part of the Confederacy; but the variety of sects dispersed over the entire face of it must secure the national councils against any danger from that source. A rage for paper money, for an abolition of debts, for an equal division of property, or for any other improper or wicked project, will be less apt to pervade the whole body of the Union than a particular member of it; in the same proportion as such a malady is more likely to taint a particular county or district, than an entire State.

In the extent and proper structure of the Union, therefore, we behold a republican remedy for the diseases most incident to republican government. And according to the degree of pleasure and pride we feel in being republicans, ought to be our zeal in cherishing the spirit and supporting the character of Federalists. PUBLIUS

THE FEDERALIST, NUMBER FIFTY-ONE (MADISON)

(1788)

TO THE PEOPLE OF THE STATE OF NEW YORK

To what expedient, then, shall we finally resort, for maintaining in practice the necessary partition of power among the several departments, as laid down in the Constitution? The only answer that can be given is, that as all these exterior provisions are found to be inadequate, the defect must be supplied, by so contriving the interior structure of the government as that its several constituent parts may, by their mutual relations, be the means of keeping each other in their proper places.

* * *

But the great security against a gradual concentration of the several powers in the same department, consists in giving to those who administer each department the necessary constitutional means and personal motives to resist encroachments of the others. The provision for defense must in this, as in all other cases, be made commensurate to the danger of attack. Ambition must be made to counteract ambition. The interest of the man must be connected with the constitutional rights of the place. It may be a reflection on human nature, that such devices should be necessary to control the abuses of government. But what is government itself, but the greatest of all reflections on human nature? If men were angels, no government would be necessary. If angels were to govern men, neither external nor internal controls on government would be necessary. In framing a government which is to be administered by men over men, the great difficulty lies in this: you must first enable the government to control the governed; and in the next place oblige it to control itself. A dependence on the people is, no doubt, the primary control on the government; but experience has taught mankind the necessity of auxiliary precautions.

This policy of supplying, by opposite and rival interests, the defect of better motives, might be traced through the whole system of human affairs, private as well as public. We see it particularly displayed in all the subordinate distributions of power, where the constant aim is to divide and arrange the several offices in such a manner as that each may be a check on the other—that the private interest of every individual may be a sentinel over the public rights. These inventions of prudence cannot be less requisite in the distribution of the supreme powers of the State.

* * *

It is of great importance in a republic not only to guard the society against the oppression of its rulers, but to guard one part of the society against the injustice of the other part. Different interests necessarily exist in different classes of citizens. If a majority be united by a common interest, the rights of the minority will be insecure. There are but two methods of providing against this evil: the one by creating a will in the community independent of the majority—that is, of the society itself; the other, by comprehending in the society so many separate descriptions of citizens as will render an unjust combination of a majority of the whole very improbable, if not impracticable. The first method prevails in all governments possessing an hereditary or self-appointed authority. This, at best, is but a precarious security; because a power independent of the society may as well espouse the unjust views of the major, as the rightful interests of the minor party, and may possibly be turned against both parties. The second method will be exemplified in the federal republic of the United States. Whilst all authority in it will be derived from and dependent on the society, the society itself will be broken into so many parts, interests, and classes of citizens, that the rights of individuals, or of the minority, will be in little danger from interested combinations of the majority. In a free government the security for civil rights must be the same as that for religious rights. It consists in the one case in the multiplicity of interests, and in the other in the multiplicity of sects. The degree of security in both cases will depend on the number of interests and sects; and this may be presumed to depend on the extent of country and number of people comprehended under the same government. This view of the subject must particularly recommend a proper federal system to all the sincere and considerate friends of republican government, since it shows that in exact proportion as the territory of the Union may be formed into more circumscribed Confederacies, or States oppressive combinations of a majority will be facilitated: the best security, under the republican forms, for the rights of every class of citizens, will be diminished; and consequently the stability and independence of some member of the government, the only other security, must be proportionately increased. Justice is the end of government. It is the end of civil society. It ever has been and ever will be pursued until it be obtained, or until liberty be lost in the pursuit. In a society under the forms of which the stronger faction can readily unite and oppress the weaker, anarchy may as truly be said to reign as in a state of nature, where the weaker individual is not secured against the violence of the stronger; and as, in the latter state, even the stronger individuals are prompted, by the uncertainty of their condition, to submit to a government which may protect the weak as well as themselves; so, in the former state, will the more powerful factions or parties be gradually induced, by a like motive, to wish for a government which will protect all parties, the weaker as well as the more powerful. It can be little doubted that if the State of Rhode Island was separated from the Confederacy and left to itself, the insecurity of rights under the popular form of government within such narrow limits would be displayed by such reiterated oppressions of factious majorities that some power altogether independent of the people would soon be called for by the voice of the very factions whose misrule had proved the necessity of it. In the extended republic of the United States, and among the great variety of interests, parties, and sects which it embraces, a coalition of a majority of the whole society could seldom take place on any other principles than those of justice and the general good; whilst there being thus less danger to a minor from the will of a major party, there must be less pretext, also, to provide for the security of the former, by introducing into the government a will not dependent on the latter, or, in other words, a will independent of the society itself. It is no less certain that it is important, notwithstanding the contrary opinions which have been entertained, that the larger the society, provided it lie within a practical sphere, the more duly capable it will be of self-government. And happily for the *republican cause*, the practicable sphere may be carried to a very great extent, by a judicious modification and mixture of the *federal principle*. PUBLIUS

JAMES MADISON, SPEECH TO THE VIRGINIA RATIFYING CONVENTION

June 20, 1788.

I have observed, that gentlemen suppose, that the general legislature will do every mischief they possibly can, and that they will omit to do every thing good which they are authorised to do. If this were a reasonable supposition, their objections would be good. I consider it reasonable to conclude, that they will as readily do their duty, as deviate from it: Nor do I go on the grounds mentioned by gentlemen on the other side—that we are to place unlimited confidence in them, and expect nothing but the most exalted integrity and sublime virtue. But I go on this great republican principle, that the people will have virtue and intelligence to select men of virtue and wisdom. Is there no virtue among us? If there be not, we are in a wretched situation. No theoretical checks—no form of government can render us secure. To suppose that any form of government will secure liberty or happiness without any virtue in the people, is a chimerical idea. If there be sufficient virtue and intelligence in the community, it will be exercised in the selection of these men. So that we do not depend on their virtue, or put confidence in our rulers, but in the people who are to choose them.

JAMES MADISON TO THOMAS JEFFERSON

Oct. 17, 1788.

Dear Sir,—The little pamphlet herewith inclosed will give you a collective view of the alterations which have been proposed [by the State Conventions] for the new Constitution. Various and numerous as they appear, they certainly omit many of the true grounds of opposition. The articles relating to Treaties, to paper money, and to contracts, created more enemies than all the errors in the system, positive and negative, put together.

It is true, nevertheless, that not a few, particularly in Virginia, have contended for the proposed alterations from the most honorable and patriotic motives; and that among the advocates for the Constitution there are some who wish for further guards to public liberty and individual rights. As far as these may consist of a constitutional declaration of the most essential rights, it is probable they will be added; though there are many who think such addition unnecessary, and not a few who think it misplaced in such a Constitution. There is scarce any point on which the party in opposition is so much divided as to its importance and its propriety. My own opinion has always been in favor of a bill of rights, provided it be so framed as not to imply powers not meant to be included in the enumeration. At the same time, I have never thought the omission a material defect, nor been anxious to supply it even by *subsequent* amendment, for any other reason than that it is anxiously desired by others. I have favored it because I supposed it might be of use, and, if properly executed, could not be of disservice.

I have not viewed it in an important light—1. Because I conceive that in a certain degree, though not in the extent argued by Mr. Wilson, the rights in question are reserved by the manner in which the federal powers are granted. 2. Because there is great reason to fear that a positive declaration of some of the most essential rights could not be obtained in the requisite latitude. I am sure that the rights of conscience in particular, if submitted to public definition, would be narrowed much more than they are likely ever to be by an assumed power. One of the objections in New England was, that the Constitution, by prohibiting religious tests, opened a door for Jews, Turks, and infidels. 3. Because the limited powers of the federal Government, and the jealousy of the subordinate Governments, afford a security which has not existed in the case of the State Governments, and exists in no other. 4. Because experience proves the inefficacy of a bill of rights on those occasions when its controul is most needed. Repeated violations of these parchment barriers have been committed by overbearing majorities in every State.

In Virginia, I have seen the bill of rights violated in every instance where it has been opposed to a popular current. Notwithstanding the explicit provision contained in that instrument for the rights of conscience, it is well known that a religious establishment would have taken place in that State, if the Legislative majority had found, as they expected, a majority of the people in favor of the measure; and I am persuaded that if a majority of the people were now of one sect, the measure would still take place, and on narrower ground than was then proposed, notwithstanding the additional obstacle which the law has since created.

Wherever the real power in a Government lies, there is the danger of oppression. In our Governments the real power lies in the majority of the community, and the invasion of private rights is *chiefly* to be apprehended, not from acts of Government contrary to the sense of its constituents, but from acts in which the Government is the mere instrument of the major number of the Constituents. This is a truth of great importance, but not yet sufficiently attended to; and is probably more strongly impressed on my mind by facts and reflections suggested by them than on yours, which has contemplated abuses of power issuing from a very different quarter. Wherever there is an interest and power to do wrong, wrong will generally be done, and not less readily by a powerful and interested party than by a powerful and interested prince. The difference, so far as it relates to the superiority of republics over monarchies, lies in the less degree of probability that interest may prompt abuses of power in the former than in the latter; and in the security in the former against an oppression of more than the smaller part of the Society, whereas, in the latter, it may be extended in a manner to the whole.

The difference, so far as it relates to the point in question—the efficacy of a bill of rights in controuling abuses of power—lies in this: that in a monarchy the latent force of the nation is superior to that of the Sovereign, and a solemn charter of popular rights must have a great effect as a standard for trying the validity of public acts, and a signal for rousing and uniting the superior force of the community; whereas, in a popular Government, the political and physical power may be considered as vested in the same hands, that is, in a majority of the people, and, consequently, the tyrannical will of the Sovereign is not to be controuled by the dread of an appeal to any other force within the community.

What use, then, it may be asked, can a bill of rights serve in popular Governments? I answer, the two following, which, though less essential than in other Governments, sufficiently recommend the precaution: 1. The political truths declared in that solemn manner acquire by degrees the character of fundamental maxims of free Government, and as they become incorporated with the National sentiment, counteract the impulses of interest and passion. 2. Although it be generally true, as above stated, that the danger of oppression lies in the interested majorities of the people rather than in usurped acts of the Government, yet there may be occasions on which the evil may spring from the latter source; and on such, a bill of rights will be a good ground for an appeal to the sense of the community. Perhaps, too, there may be a certain degree of danger that a succession of artful and ambitious rulers may, by gradual and well-timed advances, finally erect an independent Government on the subversion of liberty. Should this danger exist at all, it is prudent to guard against it, especially when the precaution can do no injury.

At the same time, I must own that I see no tendency in our Governments to danger on that side. It has been remarked that there is a tendency in *all* Governments to an augmentation of power at the expense of liberty. But the remark, as usually understood, does not appear to me well founded. Power, when it has attained a certain degree of energy and independence, goes on generally to further degrees. But when below that degree, the direct tendency is to further degrees of relaxation, until the abuses of liberty beget a sudden transition to an undue degree of power. With this explanation the remark may be true; and in the latter sense only is it, in my opinion, applicable to the existing Governments in America. It is a melancholy reflection that liberty should be equally exposed to danger whether the Government have too much or too little power, and that the line which divides these extremes should be so inaccurately defined by experience.

Supposing a bill of rights to be proper, the articles which ought to compose it admit of much discussion. I am inclined to think that *absolute* restrictions in cases that are doubtful, or where emergencies may overrule them, ought to be avoided. The restrictions, however strongly marked on paper, will never be regarded when opposed to the decided sense of the public; and after repeated violations, in extraordinary cases will lose even their ordinary efficacy. Should a Rebellion or insurrection alarm the people as well as the Government, and a suspension of the Habeas Corpus be dictated by the alarm, no written prohibitions on earth would prevent the measure. Should an army in time of peace be gradually established in our neighborhood by Britain or Spain, declarations on paper would have as little effect in preventing a standing force for the public safety. The best security against these evils is to remove the pretext for them.

JAMES MADISON, SPEECH TO THE UNITED STATES HOUSE OF REPRESENTATIVES

introducing the proposed Bill of Rights, June 8, 1789

I wish, also, in revising the Constitution, we may throw into that section, which interdicts the abuse of certain powers in the State Legislatures, some other provisions of equal, if not greater importance than those already made. The words, "No State shall pass any bill of attainder, *ex post facto* law," & c., were wise and proper restrictions in the Constitution. I think there is more danger of those powers being abused by the State Governments than by the Government of the United States. The same may be said of other powers which they possess, if not controlled by the general principle, that laws are unconstitutional which infringe the rights of the community. I should, therefore, wish to extend this interdiction, and add, as I have stated in the 5th resolution, that no State shall violate the equal right of conscience, freedom of the press, or trial by jury in criminal cases; because it is proper that every Government should be disarmed of powers which trench upon those particular rights. I know, in some of the State constitutions, the power of the Government is controlled by such a declaration; but others are not. I cannot see any reason against obtaining even a double security on those points; and nothing can give a more sincere proof of the attachment of those who opposed this Constitution to these great and important rights, than to see them join in obtaining the security I have now proposed; because it must be admitted, on all hands, that the State Governments are as liable to attack these invaluable privileges as the General Government is, and therefore ought to be as cautiously guarded against.

LANCE BANNING, THE SACRED FIRE OF LIBERTY: JAMES MADISON AND THE FOUNDING OF THE FEDERAL REPUBLIC

(1985).

If Madison had had his way entirely, the Bill of Rights would have been different in significant respects from the amendments that were finally approved. The alterations would have been incorporated in the body of the Constitution, not tacked onto its end. Madison believed that it would be more logical to interweave amendments with the text: that this would make the charter more accessible to ordinary understandings, and possibly that it would render the amendments as authoritative as the rest. Roger Sherman, on the other hand, insisted that the Constitution, as originally approved, had been the highest sovereign action of the people and should not be alloyed with amendments based on the lesser authority of Congress and the states. Sherman's motion to append the changes rather than incorporate them in the text was defeated when he first proposed it; but, as Madison lamented, the plan of interweaving the amendments proved a victim, in the end, "to *a few* who knew their concurrence to be necessary to the dispatch if not the success of the business."

If Madison had had his way, the Constitution would have opened with a declaration—

> That all power is originally vested in and consequently derived from the people.
>
> That government is instituted and ought to be exercised for the benefit of the people; which consists in the enjoyment of life and liberty, with the right of acquiring and using property, and generally of pursuing and obtaining happiness and safety.
>
> That the people have an indubitable, unalienable, and indefeasible right to reform and change their government whenever it be found adverse or inadequate to the purposes of its institution.

Adoption of this language would have meant, of course, that it would never have been doubted that the fundamental principles of the Declaration of Independence (or of the Virginia Declaration of Rights, from which it was taken) are part of the Federal Constitution, along with the specific liberties which it protects. But Madison conceded in his June 8 speech that it might not be "absolutely necessary" to insert these "truths" at the beginning of the Constitution, and others were determined to restrict the alterations to as few as their proponents could accept.

* * *

In 1788, Madison undoubtedly anticipated that the greatest dangers to the Union and the Revolution would result from state attachments, state encroachments, and majority abuses. He discounted, even as he recognized, the possibility of federal encroachments. He also underestimated—though, again, he certainly acknowledged—how difficult it soon would seem to keep the people actively engaged in federal concerns and thus to keep the government from favoring minorities at their expense. But when we clearly understand how much of what he disagreed with in the new administration's course was what he thought the federal government was never meant to be involved in (or the opposite of policies that nearly everyone believed that it had been created to pursue), his shift of course—concerning popular involvement *and* concerning local rights—will seem a good deal less abrupt and less substantial than his enemies believed. Modern scholarship has privileged the Hamiltonian interpretation of the Constitution, although the Federalists of 1788 were not a single-minded movement. Nevertheless, from Madison's perspective—and perhaps on a dispassionate consideration of the facts—Madison was absolutely right to say that he "deserted Colonel Hamilton, or rather Colonel H. deserted me ... from his wishing to ... administer the

Government . . . into what he thought it ought to be, while, on my part, I endeavored to make it conform to the Constitution as understood by the Convention that produced and recommended it and particularly by the state conventions that *adopted* it." Doubtless, Madison confused the people's understanding with his own; but doubtless, also, we ourselves will certainly mistake James Madison if we do not perceive how earnestly he took the Constitution as the people's act, accepted federal features of the system as essential to preserve the Revolution, and intended to assure that federal officials would remain responsive to the people's will.

Madison was not, of course, a democrat by current definitions of that word. His concept of the people usually excluded large proportions of the population. In addition, he decidedly did not believe that the immediate and unenlightened inclinations of majorities of people should be put into effect without resistance. But this was not because he valued order and protection for the rights of property above all else, although he was in fact quite deeply dedicated to protecting both these things. It was because he knew that *every* kind of right could be endangered by majorities of people, especially when heated passions were involved. He may have been, for modern tastes, a markedly conservative defender of republican self-government. This is quite apparent if we weigh him on a modern scale. But we should not forget that what he was committed to conserving were the most profoundly revolutionary institutions and convictions of his time.

Madison's commitment to the people's rule may not have been as eloquent, as unreserved, or as incautious as Jefferson's or Thomas Paine's or that of some of his opponents in the ratification struggle (who, however, were resisting a proposal that would place substantial federal powers, for the first time, in the hands of the immediate representatives of the voters). His was not the sort of democratic faith attractive to the radical imagination, in his own time or in ours. For all of this, however, Madison was very much a democrat by eighteenth-century standards—and even by some tests that many of the most self-righteous modern democrats would fail. Like Jefferson, who used this term, while Madison did not, he clearly hoped that "natural aristocrats" would rule, not any Dick or Jane who might as well be chosen by blind chance. (Most founders were "elitists" in this sense.) But "natural aristocracy," the two Virginians thought, should rest exclusively on merit and the people's recognition, not on wealth, or birth, or formal educational attainments. Moreover, the "aristocrats" who led should never, as they saw it, cease attending to the people's needs and will. Madison was certainly as firm if not as eloquent a spokesman for political equality as either Jefferson or Paine, and this does not exhaust the senses in which he was thoroughly entitled to this label. However much he feared an unrestrained, self-interested, and passionate majority of people, Madison was also adamant that once the proper checks had been imposed and passing passions had been cooled, the will of the majority must rule.

RALPH KETCHAM, FRAMED FOR POSTERITY: THE ENDURING PHILOSOPHY OF THE CONSTITUTION

(1993).

Reflecting his conviction that "what may be called a bill of rights" should be seen as part and parcel of a larger pattern of government, Madison had at first proposed that the amendments be inserted at eight different places in the original text, especially in Article I, Section 9, where other restrictions on the federal government already existed. Madison did not object when others proposed adding the amendments as a separate package at the end of the Constitution, but his impulse remained to focus attention as much as possible on a viable frame and structure of government. Furthermore, Madison's support for a bill of rights, though entirely sincere in substance, continued to be phrased in tactical terms: it would fulfill the "campaign promises" of himself and other federalists, it might help persuade North Carolina and Rhode Island to come into the union, and it would "kill the opposition everywhere, and by putting an end to the disaffection to the government itself, enable the administration to venture on measures not otherwise safe." In another irony, Madison's chief concern, even in proposing limitations on government to protect natural rights, was to *strengthen* its support and thus its power to act on behalf of the public good.

Madison's original phrasing of what became the First Amendment further revealed his preoccupation with the public rather than the personal or private character of the five freedoms of religion, speech, press, assembly, and petition. He had at first stated these rights in three separate paragraphs, beginning with one on religion: "the Civil rights of none shall be abridged on account of religious belief or worship, nor shall any national religion be established, nor shall the full and equal rights of conscience be in any manner, or on any pretext, infringed." Two things are notable about this proposal. First, the emphasis on not abridging civil rights, rights related to government, and on not having a national religion has clear reference to the "good health" of the processes of government. These religious rights, that is, are necessary to conduct the public business freely and fairly as well as to protect individual liberty of conscience. Second, the last part of the sentence is Madison's effort to state as fully, clearly, and categorically as possible the rights of conscience, not to limit that right by using inadequate language to protect it, as Madison had worried might happen. Although the final phrasing of the religion clause of the First Amendment is also categorical and perhaps more felicitous, it lacks, but without intending to deny, the explicitness on public aspects in Madison's original proposal.

The second paragraph of Madison's "first amendment proposals" reads "the people shall not be deprived or abridged of their right to speak, to write, or to publish their sentiments; and the freedom of the press, as one of the great bulwarks of liberty, shall be inviolable," while the third reads "the people shall not be restrained from *peaceably assembling and consulting for their common good*, nor from applying to the legislature by petitions, or remonstrances for redress of their grievances [emphasis added]." Throughout, when examined closely, Madison's words (themselves culled from the amendments proposed by state ratifying conventions) have an unmistakable public orientation or purpose beyond their obvious attention to personal rights. The image in the emphasized phrase is that of citizens gathering together to discuss the public business, the very essence of self-government. Furthermore, the petitioning is to address legislators to initiate a dialogue over grievances against the government—a dialogue that eighteenth-century usage required the legislature continue by responding to the petition. (Recall that one of the complaints in the Declaration of Independence was the failure of British authorities to respond to petitions.) Thinking of the press as a "bulwark of liberty" also echoes a contemporary understanding that freedom of the press was vital to ensure true freedom by having the means available for a full discussion of public policy. Even speaking, writing, and publishing "sentiments" has particular reference to deliberations on public affairs.

An early draft of what would become the First Amendment, in the hand of Representative Roger Sherman of Connecticut and probably written before Madison's three paragraphs, both embodied Madison's public emphasis and rested "the first amendment freedoms" directly on a natural-rights, higher-law foundation:

> The people have certain natural rights which are retained by them when they enter into Society. Such are the rights of Conscience in matters of religion; of acquiring property, and of pursuing happiness and Safety; of Speaking, writing, and publishing their Sentiments with decency and freedom; of peaceably assembling to consult their common good, and of applying to Government by petition or remonstrance for redress of grievances. Of these rights therefore they shall not be deprived by the Government of the United States.

Each of the terse, compressed parts of the first amendment, then, derived from more elaborate phrases that had a more explicit orientation toward public expression, a right by the people to have full access to the process of "assembling and consulting for their common good." Since the changes in organization and wording were made largely in committee where no record of discussions survive, we cannot be sure why they were made. The recorded debates in the full House of Representatives and the private correspondence of Madison and others, though, reveal no significant controversies or intentions of substantial change in the altered phraseology. Since Madison's main concern was to gain support for the Constitution from those whose objection was the absence of a bill of rights, he was probably willing to go along with more generally acceptable wording. And doubtless the more forceful eloquence of the single sentence attracted some. In any case, far from the revisions being an attempt to change the substance of Madison's original proposals, it seems apparent that their clearer public meaning simply made explicit what remains implicit in the intent of the First Amendment as adopted.

Questions

1) Is there any connection between what Madison says in *Federalist No. 10* and what he says in the *Virginia Report*?

2) In *Federalist No. 10* Madison seeks to "break and control the violence of faction." Why twelve years later did he think that an unqualified freedom of the press would serve that objective? In his day, almost all newspapers were founded and controlled by political parties. In 1799, Madison's most immediate objection to the Sedition Act was that it was a bald attempt by the Federalist Party to jail the most prominent Jeffersonian editors of opposition newspapers leading up to the election of 1800. Shouldn't someone who is concerned about political factions be concerned about defamatory writings, designed to stir up hatred, in party newspapers?

3) In his letter to Jefferson of October 17, 1788, Madison counsels against "absolute restrictions" in a bill of rights. He observes: "The restrictions, however strongly marked on paper, will never be regarded when opposed to the decided sense of the public; and after repeated violations, in extraordinary cases will lose even their ordinary efficacy." Is this statement consistent with his argument in the *Virginia Report*?

JAMES MADISON, PUBLIC OPINION

The National Gazette, December 19, 1791.

Public opinion sets bounds to every government, and is the real sovereign in every free one.

As there are cases where the public opinion must be obeyed by the government; so there are cases, where not being fixed, it may be influenced by the government. This distinction, if kept in view, would prevent or decide many debates on the respect due from the government to the sentiments of the people.

In proportion as government is influenced by opinion, it must be so, by whatever influences opinion. This decides the question concerning a *Constitutional Declaration of Rights,* which requires an influence on government, by becoming a part of the public opinion.

The larger a country, the less easy for its real opinion to be ascertained, and the less difficult to be counterfeited; when ascertained or presumed, the more respectable it is in the eyes of individuals. This is favorable to the authority of government. For the same reason, the more extensive a country, the more insignificant is each individual in his own eyes. This may be unfavorable to liberty.

Whatever facilitates a general intercourse of sentiments, as good roads, domestic commerce, a free press, and particularly a *circulation of newspapers through the entire body of the people,* and *Representatives going from, and returning among every part of them,* is equivalent to a contraction of territorial limits, and is favorable to liberty, where these may be too extensive.

JAMES MADISON, PARTIES

The National Gazette, January 23, 1792.

In every political society, parties are unavoidable. A difference of interests, real or supposed, is the most natural and fruitful source of them. The great object should be to combat the evil: 1. By establishing a political equality among all. 2. By withholding *unnecessary* opportunities from a few, to increase the inequality of property, by an immoderate, and especially an unmerited, accumulation of riches. 3. By the silent operation of laws, which, without violating the rights of property, reduce extreme wealth towards a state of mediocrity, and raise extreme indigence towards a state of comfort. 4. By abstaining from measures which operate differently on different interests, and particularly such as favor one interest at the expence of another. 5. By making one party a check on the other, so far as the existence of parties cannot be prevented, nor their views accommodated. If this is not the language of reason, it is that of republicanism.

In all political societies, different interests and parties arise out of the nature of things, and the great art of politicians lies in making them checks and balances to each other. Let us then increase these *natural distinctions* by favoring an inequality of property; and let us add to them *artificial distinctions,* by establishing *kings,* and *nobles,* and *plebeians.* We shall then have the more checks to oppose to each other: we shall then have the more scales and the more weights to perfect and maintain the equilibrium. This is as little the voice of reason, as it is that of republicanism.

From the expediency, in politics, of making natural parties, mutual checks on each other, to infer the propriety of creating artificial parties, in order to form them into mutual checks, is not less absurd than it would be in ethics, to say, that new vices ought to be promoted, where they would counteract each other, because this use may be made of existing vices.

JAMES MADISON, PROPERTY

The National Gazette, March 29, 1792.

This term in its particular application means "that dominion which one man claims and exercises over the external things of the world, in exclusion of every other individual."

In its larger and juster meaning, it embraces every thing to which a man may attach a value and have a right; and *which leaves to every one else the like advantage.*

In the former sense, a man's land, or merchandize, or money is called his property.

In the latter sense, a man has a property in his opinions and the free communication of them.

He has a property of peculiar value in his religious opinions, and in the profession and practice dictated by them.

He has a property very dear to him in the safety and liberty of his person.

He has an equal property in the free use of his faculties and free choice of the objects on which to employ them.

In a word, as a man is said to have a right to his property, he may be equally said to have a property in his rights.

Where an excess of power prevails, property of no sort is duly respected. No man is safe in his opinions, his person, his faculties, or his possessions.

Where there is an excess of liberty, the effect is the same, tho' from an opposite cause.

Government is instituted to protect property of every sort; as well that which lies in the various rights of individuals, as that which the term particularly expresses. This being the end of government, that alone is a *just* government, which *impartially* secures to every man, whatever is his *own.*

According to this standard of merit, the praise of affording a just security to property, should be sparingly bestowed on a government which, however scrupulously guarding the possessions of individuals, does not protect them in the enjoyment and communication of their opinions, in which they have an equal, and in the estimation of some, a more valuable property.

More sparingly should this praise be allowed to a government, where a man's religious rights are violated by penalties, or fettered by tests, or taxed by a hierarchy. Conscience is the most sacred of all property; other property depending in part on positive law, the exercise of that, being a natural and unalienable right. To guard a man's house as his castle, to pay public and enforce private debts with the most exact faith, can give no title to invade a man's conscience which is more sacred than his castle, or to withhold from it that debt of protection, for which the public faith is pledged, by the very nature and original conditions of the social pact.

* * *

If the United States mean to obtain or deserve the full praise due to wise and just governments, they will equally respect the rights of property, and the property in rights: they will rival the government that most sacredly guards the former; and by repelling its example in violating the latter, will make themselves a pattern to that and all other governments.

FRANK H. EASTERBROOK, THE STATE OF MADISON'S VISION OF THE STATE: A PUBLIC CHOICE PERSPECTIVE

107 Harv. L. Rev. 1328 (1994).

I. MADISON'S VISION OF FACTION

What is faction, and how is it to be brought under control? Answering these questions is Madison's task in The Federalist No. 10, with echoes in No. 51.

Faction, according to The Federalist No. 10, is "a number of citizens, whether amounting to a majority or minority of the whole, who are united and actuated by some common impulse of passion, or of interest, adverse to the rights of other citizens, or to the permanent and aggregate interests of the community." Self-interested voting is a scourge of all republics, breeding contention, oppression, local favoritism, and beggar-thy-neighbor policies. It has brought down efforts at democracy around the globe, and throughout history. It must be conquered—yet, Madison thought, it cannot and must not be conquered.

Faction is strong. People care more about themselves than about others. Although self-interest often should dominate (it leads to Adam Smith's Invisible Hand, with benefits for all), self-love dominates even when people know intellectually that virtuous conduct would be better. When the conflict between self and virtue is irreconcilable, cognitive dissonance leads people to conclude that civic virtue and personal ends coincide. Once this mental transformation occurs, people are impervious to rational argument. Faction's power thus does not depend on cynicism. Not only the factions themselves but also those who serve their interests in legislatures come to believe that their goals are aligned with the public's interest. Interest groups that seek to enlarge their influence would not support cynics for election to public office. Cynics are expensive and unreliable, for sale to the highest bidder. A faction therefore offers its support to persons whose ideals overlap the group's interest. Thus:

> As long as the reason of man continues fallible, and he is at liberty to exercise it, different opinions will be formed. As long as the connection subsists between his reason and his self-love, his opinions and his passions will have a reciprocal influence on each other; and the former will be objects to which the latter will attach themselves.

Faction is not only strong but also beneficial, and therefore must be tolerated. The division of labor is a boon, yet also a source of faction. "A landed interest, a manufacturing interest, a mercantile interest, a moneyed interest, with many lesser interests, grow up of necessity in civilized nations, and divide them into different classes, actuated by different sentiments and views." To have prosperity we need separation of function. Religion and other ingredients of moral life also ensure faction. Differences are to be treasured, are a hallmark of freedom, are an objective of our government. Yet they are faction and in the end may destroy our government.

How can we escape this fate? We do not want to extinguish the differences we cherish, and if we wished to do so we could not without eliminating the role of the governed in public choice—without bringing about the tyranny this republic was established to avoid. Mitigation rather than elimination, then, must be the objective. Madison and his colleagues in the Constitutional Convention sought to check the power of faction by two routes: indirect democracy and the fragmentation of the electoral base.

A. *Indirect Decisionmaking*

Direct democracy will fall victim to faction—not to mention to the passions that led the Athenian jury of five hundred to condemn Socrates—for direct democracy encourages people to vote their own preferences. "[A] pure democracy, by which I mean a society consisting of a small number of citizens, who assemble and administer the government in person, can admit of no cure for the mischiefs of faction." Even voters who begin with the public interest at heart encounter a serious obstacle to voting in the public interest: the probability that any one person's vote will alter the outcome of the election is so small that it does not make sense to invest a lot of time in studying the issues and voting. Rational ignorance among voters, coupled with the self-interest that prevails in default of a strong countervailing force, hinders achievement of the public interest under direct democracy.

Government by elected representatives may solve these problems, for a representative's self-interest is not at stake in the vast majority of votes, and in any event, is not identical to the interests of the constituents. Mediating among many factions, the representative answers to none. Representatives therefore have a larger portion of virtue, especially as their fewness permits selection from among the best in society. In modern terms, Madison's argument is that representatives, as agents who toil in a distant capital, escape effective supervision by their principals in the electorate. The people will elect the person, not the policy, because they have no other real choice; and worthy persons will vote in worthy ways. Agency slack—in private life, a cost of management that corporations strive to curtail—is a boon in government. And the representatives, being fewer in number than the electorate as a whole, are more apt to conclude that their votes do matter and therefore to make the effort necessary to choose wisely.

B. *Fragmentation of the Electoral Base*

Elections from different states with different factions dilute the power of faction. Merchants may dominate in Pennsylvania and tobacco growers in North Carolina, but neither dominates in the larger republic:

> Extend the sphere and you take in a greater variety of parties and interests; you make it less probable that a majority of the whole will have a common motive to invade the rights of other citizens; or if such a common motive exists, it will be more difficult for all who feel it to discover their own strength and to act in unison with each other.

Diversity within the population, which is a source of faction locally, thus provides security in a larger jurisdiction. Fragmentation is to be pursued in a thoroughgoing manner: different state qualifications for voting, different districts for officials to represent (portions of states for members of the House, whole states for senators, the entire nation for the President); different electors (the people for members of the House, state legislatures for senators, the electoral college for the President); different tenures for officeholders (from two years for members of the House to life for judges).

The constitutional plan elaborated in The Federalist Nos. 10 and 51 thus reflects a careful design of political institutions that can bend self-interest to the public good. Adam Smith believed that competition in markets would bend self-interest to the public good. Madison's diagnosis and prescription are the same. Smith lauded competition among producers of private goods and services; Madison sought to promote competition among suppliers of public services. The effort to cope with and even exploit rather than deny the effects of self-love, coupled with a belief that the design of political institutions matters a great deal, make Madison the progenitor of modern public choice theory.

Madison's elaboration of the constitutional plan is the best piece of political philosophy penned on this side of the Atlantic. Recognizing the simultaneous terror, inevitability, and desirability of faction, and proposing conquest by division (the strategy of faction itself), is genius. Madison also anticipates, without quite articulating, the point that a plurality of jurisdictions checks the power of faction even at the local level. Although each local government may control immovable assets (principally land), its ability to take any other step is constrained by exit—in other words, by competition with other jurisdictions. A federal republic strengthens this competition by facilitating movement of assets and persons. Public schools may be the government's tools, but you can shop for the government you prefer!

Dilution of interests through representation, and the inclusion of opposing interests, blunt the power of faction at all levels: locally because states become parts of a common market, and nationally because constituencies are diffuse and terms vary. We can therefore cherish differences in taste, religion, and so on without falling under majority sway. This is Madison's constitutional legacy to us: a vision of the state as attractive today as it was two centuries ago.

II. The State of Madison's Vision

Despite the genius of Madison's plan, his predictions about the relation between the national government and faction have not come true—and not just in the structural, formal sense on which Professor Lawson elaborates in this Symposium. Private interest legislation is common today, much more so than in 1787, and more common at the national level than among the states—the opposite of Madison's belief about what would happen. This predictive failure can be explained as the result of a variety of factors well known to public choice theory: limits on representatives' freedom from factions' influence; increased specialization in production; free rider obstacles to political participation; the considerable advantages to interest groups of obtaining national legislation; and the failure of collective virtue.

A. Limited Agency Space for Representatives

Improved and cheaper forms of communication and transportation have decreased the distance between representatives and their constituents, and thus between representatives and their constituent factions. As communication and transportation costs fall, groups can both unite for common benefit and monitor the conduct of representatives. High-tech gerrymandering matches representatives to stable groups and undermines the constitutional provision of short terms for representatives; today, members of the House have longer average tenure than senators, in part because districts may be gerrymandered but states may not. "Gerrymandering" is perhaps a loaded word; abandon it and the fact remains that there is widespread support for drawing districts so as to unite rather than disperse voters who share characteristics that influence their preferences for public activity. The combination of rapid communication and the ability to link representatives with districts defined by some common feature of the constituents binds public actors more closely to private interests. Indeed, these effects are so strong that some students of the subject believe that no agency space remains—that one may understand the voting of public officials solely by reference to their constituents' economic interests. Those who object to this conclusion do not do so on the ground that representatives retain substantial discretion; rather, the defense is that representatives retain some discretion, so that a few votes may be explained by their ideology rather than by their voters' private interests. All participants in this discourse agree that Madison's vision of a national legislature in which most members, most of the time, look to "the public good" rather than to the clamor of private interests, has not been realized.

Congress itself has developed a structure that reduces agency space. Members serve on committees, which as gatekeepers to the floor and as the principal drafting institutions are highly visible to factions. Interest groups can monitor the behavior of a few committee members much more closely than they can track all members of Congress. The small size of committees also permits the concentration of rewards, whether campaign contributions or other forms of political support. Once assigned to a committee, members rarely lose their places, and leadership on committees depends largely on seniority. These features enable committee members and factions to deal with one another on an enduring basis.

What is true of committees in Congress holds as well for the apparatus Congress creates to administer laws. Interest groups can monitor agencies readily and assure delivery of deals bought and paid for. For example, the Administrative Procedure Act (APA), hailed by many on "good government" grounds because it exposes agency action to public view and invites input, is anti-Madisonian. Extended rulemaking procedures and numerous oversight hearings in Congress reduce agency space and therefore augment the relative power of faction.

B. *Increased Division of Labor*

Improved communication and transportation have fed the growth of more, and more powerful, interest groups. Cheap transportation and communication mean a larger market. Although a larger market decreases the power of states by making exit easier, it also increases the division of labor. More specialization enhances productivity but also produces more—and more powerful—interest groups. Recall that Madison defined faction as a group with a special interest, something shared by its members but not by the general public. Greater specialization in production means more factions, and these factions will be more cohesive, for reasons developed immediately below.

C. *The Free Rider Problem*

The gravest obstacle to faction is free riding. People who could influence legislators, if they tried, need a good reason to try. If other persons similarly situated will do the job, any particular member of the group can sit on the sidelines and reap the benefits without incurring the costs. As the group grows in size, free riding becomes first serious and then intractable—unless a solution can be found. Factions in Madison's time were large and not particularly cohesive. Madison spoke of the "landed interest" and the "manufacturing interest." Overcoming free riding is easier when the group is small, cohesive (ideally, when dropouts are impossible), able to target large benefits on each member and to exclude non-members from sharing in these benefits, and able to spread the costs widely so that the costs do not stir up opposition.

A group prevails if its free riding problem is less serious than that afflicting its rivals. In many ways the most powerful groups are those that the conventional wisdom treats as powerless: for example, minorities that have limited agendas and from which dropping out is not an option; and dairy farmers who are small in number and whose upbringing and way of life make dropping out of the group very costly. Gains per person are larger in small, cohesive factions. If a faction is organized for reasons other than influencing the government—if it is defined by race or a similar characteristic, for example, or if it has a function in industry—it is more costly to leave or take a free ride, and it is also cheaper to add lobbying to existing activities. A more elaborate division of labor means more small factions, defined by economic characteristics that make dropout costly, which means more cohesive, and thus more effective, political action.

Madison, however, feared and designed the federal government to avoid capture by majority factions. "If a faction consists of less than a majority, relief is supplied by the republican principle, which enables the majority to defeat its sinister views by regular vote." In The Federalist No. 51 Madison describes the constitutional structure as one that:

> by comprehending in the society so many separate descriptions of citizens ... will render an unjust combination of a majority of the whole very improbable, if not impracticable.... [In the United States,] society itself will be broken into so many parts, interests and classes of citizens, that the rights of individuals, or of the minority, will be in little danger from interested combinations of the majority.... The degree of security ... will depend on the number of interests and sects.

Madison recognized that the structure of this society would produce interests and sects in profusion, but he did not appreciate how easy it would become to organize these groups from coast to coast. Coalitions of small factions—an unprovided-for case—turn out to be the real threat in the United States.

D. *The Greater Gains in Influencing National Legislation*

The prevalence and prominence of interest groups in national politics today can also be explained in part by the greater gains promised by national, as opposed to state or local, legislation and regulation. Although, as Madison observed, the national government is the hardest to capture—there are more contending interests, many with powerful reasons to resist factions' demands—there are also greater gains in sight. No state could effectively regulate the price of labor or the cost of automobiles. People and factories can move too easily, and the Constitution denies states the power to erect tariffs at their borders. Because it is much more costly to emigrate from the United States than to move to another state, the national government has much more potential power, which creates a reason for factions to concentrate their efforts there.

The value of factious legislation at the national level has risen with the government's increasing command of resources. The Sixteenth Amendment, which authorizes an income tax without apportionment among the states, gives the national government control of whatever portion of the economy it wishes to command. This makes it the prime target for faction. The Seventeenth Amendment cuts down the potential constraints on influencing national legislation by removing from state legislatures the power to select United States Senators.

Many proponents of national legislation argue that movement between states blocks state governments from taking effective action. Environmental law is an obvious candidate: pollution does not respect state borders, so national law designed to stifle the effects of people and goods moving to new states is common. The ineffectiveness of purely local measures was the explicit justification of the national minimum wage law, both in Congress and in the Supreme Court. Thus the competition among jurisdictions that Madison saw as a faction-stifling benefit of the national confederation now is seen as undesirable because of its very tendency to frustrate legislation. There has of course been a change in the objectives of factions; in Madison's time the fear was "[a] rage for paper money[!] , for an abolition of debts, for an equal division of property, or for any other improper or wicked project." But when national legislators share interest groups' goals, the Madisonian barricades to "wicked projects" begin to appear wicked themselves and are more readily disparaged—and disregarded.

Factions strive mightily to suppress the power of exit. National legislation is ideal for this purpose. There is no reason to conclude that the federal government is less vulnerable to faction once the factors that created agency space, in which virtuous legislators could operate, have fallen. The national government will enact fewer private-interest laws than the aggregate of state and local governments, but the public interest costs of each such law will be greater.

E. The Failure to Agree on the Common Weal

Finally, there is a more fundamental explanation for the failure of Madison's predictions regarding the interplay between public and private interest in national government. The core of Madisonian resistance—the common weal to be found and implemented by virtuous legislators—turns out to be empty. It is not simply that Rousseau's concept of general will is hollow. It is that there is no virtuous way to aggregate private wills into collective decisions. People of good will have no common ground around which to rally! They have their own conceptions of the public interest but no way to insist that the collective choice necessarily reflect their views. We are doomed by the logic of majority voting to aggregate private preferences rather than to find a common public good.

Question

Do the observations of Judge Easterbrook regarding the possible obsolescence of important elements of Madison's political theory bear on the contemporary value of Madison's arguments concerning freedom of the press and political accountability?

STANLEY ELKINS & ERIC McKITRICK, THE AGE OF FEDERALISM

(1993).

The Sedition Act of 1798 and its by-products may serve as yet another test of the strikingly divergent states of mind in which the Federalists and the Republicans faced their political future.

This measure—which made it a crime to utter or publish "any false, scandalous, and malicious writing or writings against the government of the United States, or the President of the United States, with intent to defame ... or to bring them into contempt or disrepute"—has of course been much written about, most notably during the present century. The considerable wave of interest that arose in the 1950s over the entire subject of civil liberty produced among other things a view of the Sedition Act and the ensuing prosecutions under it which tended to picture the entire episode as a kind of lapse: an aberration, a betrayal of a libertarian tradition already established and in fact clearly embodied in the Bill of Rights. The governing assumption was that the English common law of seditious libel had been intentionally superseded by the First Amendment of the Constitution, for practical purposes removing all restraints upon freedom of the press, and that the Sedition Act, being "merely declaratory" of the English common law, was therefore unconstitutional.

Subsequent writers have questioned such a view as being an unduly telescoped and present-minded reading both of the Framers' intentions and of the historical development of libertarian thought and practice in America. There is no evidence, they assert, that the First Amendment was designed to abolish the English common law of seditious libel; there is indeed reason to infer that the Framers took for granted the federal courts' jurisdiction over common-law crimes unless otherwise specified by federal statute. It could even be said that the Sedition Act was more than "merely declaratory" of the English common law; it represented a distinct liberalization of English common-law practice, allowing as the new law did for the truth of a statement to be accepted as a defense, for the jury rather than the judge to determine whether a statement was libelous, and for the prosecution's obligation to prove malicious intent. Thomas Jefferson himself, amid the initial Republican attack on the law, certainly did not deny the principle of seditious libel. He rather asserted that the federal government was not empowered with jurisdiction over that particular crime, such jurisdiction being reserved to the states. Several years later in fact, Jefferson as President was to intimate to the Governor of Pennsylvania that "a few prosecutions" of the licentious "tory presses" of that state and others "would have a wholesome effect in restoring the[ir] integrity." It would in reality take time before the problem of seditious libel was fully grasped, there being no settled theory ready to be laid hold of for opposition to the Alien and Sedition Laws of 1798. The most notable immediate protest came, of course, with the Virginia and Kentucky Resolutions of that same year, the principal message of which was a compact theory of government and the obligation to resist centralized tyranny. The first contributions to a specifically libertarian doctrine would be made not by Jefferson but by such other Republican theorists as Gallatin, Madison, Tunis Wortman, and John Nicholas. These men began pointing out that "truth" was no real protection for freedom of the press, there being no clear way of separating truth from falsehood, and that the "no prior restraints" doctrine of the common law was not an adequate protection either, since the press could hardly be free even without prior censorship if a writer could be punished afterward for something he had already said.

Yet it may well be that the idea of civil liberty—civil liberty as counted then, or destined ultimately, among the self-evident and inalienable rights—is not the only key to why the Sedition Act should have raised such an uproar, and why it should have served as the point of departure for an eventual new way of thinking about the whole question of seditious libel. Another key, and perhaps a better one, is the relationship between the press and the state of political practice in America as it had evolved by the final two or three years of the eighteenth century. Along with the sheer proliferation of newspapers that had occurred in the 1790s went the taking for granted that a fair amount of free and easy language toward public figures was tolerable, and by no means all of it had to be respectful. So whatever the law might or might not say, the typical printer could be secure in knowing that public opinion allowed a very wide latitude for the press, and that grand juries were seldom likely to indict, or petit juries convict, for such a crime as seditious libel.

Such was the environment in which the Republican interest was taking shape as an organized opposition. Accordingly the freedom of the Republican press to pass judgment on officeholders—openly, aggressively, even abusively—was essential to the party's survival. In short, the very concept of seditious libel was flatly incompatible with party politics. The Republicans, if only by instinct and after the fact, were beginning to understand this, while the Federalists still had little or no inkling of it. Parties, in any modern sense, cannot function at all under such a principle, and parties by now—though nobody could yet admit it without some discomfort—were there. It might even be said that the Federalists now, in all their distracted movements, were doing something more than moving against "sedition"—more, even, than striking at their political opposition in the hope of suppressing it. Whether they knew it or not—perhaps nobody entirely knew it—they were striking out furiously at parties in general, in a desperate effort to turn back the clock.

To turn back the clock. This thought might well need some drawing out. Could it be that in the very fashioning of the Constitution itself, the Federalists of 1787 had done much the same thing as they were doing now, even though they might then have gone about it in rather a different spirit, and with a significantly higher degree of confidence? In devising the checks and balances of their "constitution against parties" (to use Richard Hofstadter's phrase) the Federalists in their role as founding statesmen had done their utmost to leave as little room in the structure of government for the growth and activity of parties as possible. In this of course they were acting in accordance with convictions still generally shared, and deeply embedded in the tradition of civic humanism that had shaped the value-system of eighteenth-century Anglo-American political discourse.

But the Federalists, who at that time still had no less a person than James Madison as their leading spokesman, appear to have had rather more in mind than "curing"—as Madison put it in the Tenth Federalist—"the mischiefs of faction." Back of this aim was something more comprehensive still, a profound anxiety over whether the right sort of men—men of enlightenment and virtue—would be chosen to occupy the seats of responsibility in the republic's new government. This concern too took its form from the same system of traditional civic humanist values, already threatened, as they saw it, by aggressive new forces afoot in American society that needed to be contained. And here too it was Madison who spoke for the Federalists, on behalf not of the new forces but of the old values.

Gordon Wood has suggested very persuasively that the Federalists, and Madison in particular, as they went about their work in the late 1780s were much more troubled over the irresponsibility and small-mindedness of the state legislatures in the years immediately following the Revolution than they were over the deficiencies of the Articles of Confederation. What most offended them were such short-sighted actions as paper money laws, debtor relief laws, local tariffs, tax postponements, and a tendency to beat down court reforms and similar undertakings intended for the larger public benefit, all amid a babel of contending local demands, selfish private and parochial interests, and the pushing and shoving demagoguery of popular politics. Some general remedy seemed imperative. The Revolution itself had called such conditions into being. The extensive demands in food and military supplies generated by the eight-year war effort, and the newly mobilized entrepreneurial energies that went into supplying them, had effected immense transformations in American social and economic life, most significantly at the local level. The expansion and differentiation of internal trade had created a new acquisitiveness, new appetites, new habits of lending, borrowing, and consumption—whole new patterns of expectation—on a markedly higher plane of diversity and profusion than had been there before. "The Federalists in the 1780s," according to Professor Wood, "had a glimpse of what America was to become—a scrambling business society dominated by the pecuniary interests of ordinary people—and they did not like what they saw. The wholesale pursuit of private interest and private luxury were, they thought, undermining America's capacity for republican government." Moreover, just as the society was becoming more broadly entrepreneurial, so also was it becoming more broadly and diversely political; questionable types who had previously tended to stay "in their place" were now elbowing their way more and more into local and state politics. It was the convergence, indeed the inseparability, of these two tendencies that most Federalists had in mind when they spoke of "faction."

Madison in *The Federalist* was inclined to see the terms "party" and "faction" as more or less interchangeable. But equally interchangeable, or at most barely distinguishable, were "faction" and "interest." There are, he announced, interests everywhere: debtors and creditors, "a landed interest, a moneyed interest, with many lesser interests"; they form themselves into contending parties and factions, full of "unfriendly passions" and "mutual animosity," and are "much more disposed to vex and oppress each other than to cooperate for their common good." The violence of faction (amid which "the public good is disregarded") distracts the harmony of the well-ordered republic, and the greatest danger of all is that of one such faction, through sinister arts and secret cabals, forming itself into a majority force thereupon able to oppress the entire community.

The great object of the Tenth Federalist, as everyone knows, is to show that although the "*causes* of faction cannot be removed" without suppressing liberty itself, means may still be found for "controlling its *effects,*" and they are more likely to exist in a large republic than in a small one. In a large and extended republic Madison discerns three great advantages. One is "a greater variety of parties, against the event of any one party being able to outnumber and oppress the rest"; another is the obstacles afforded by space and distance against concerting and accomplishing "the secret wishes of an unjust and interested majority." But the greatest advantage consists in the widened electoral districts out of which may be chosen *men of the right sort:* "representatives whose enlightened views and virtuous sentiments render them superior to local prejudices and to schemes of injustice." This principle—men of the right sort—comes close to holding the key to the entire Federalist idea.

The Tenth Federalist has often in modern times been read as a theory of broker politics in a pluralist national state, but such a reading had best be taken as an anachronism. There is reason to doubt that this was at all the function Madison had in mind for his men of "enlightened views and virtuous sentiments." Such men were seen by him—and doubtless by all who called themselves Federalists, then or later—not as agents for the lateral mediation of private interests but rather as spirits of detachment able to see well beyond, and well above, such partial interests in the light of a higher public good. They were men apart, gentlemen who by birth, breeding, refinement, and independent circumstances were endowed with a special wideness of vision and were thus peculiarly fitted to dedicate talent and wisdom to disinterested public service.

James Madison himself, to be sure, was to form political connections in the course of the dozen years subsequent to his writing of the Tenth Federalist that would have the effect of attenuating, for him, certain of that paper's central assertions. But for the Federalists of 1800 this image—that of men of "enlightened views and virtuous sentiments"—had become an obsession. It applied to none other than themselves, a beleaguered company whose robes of authority were being smirched by the advancing forces of insolence, vulgarity, disorder, self-interest, faction, and demagoguery. And it was against these forces that the Federalists, with their sedition law, were now blindly striking back.

JACK N. RAKOVE, JAMES MADISON AND THE CREATION OF THE AMERICAN REPUBLIC

(1990).

The Sedition Act of 1798 was the critical element of the Federalist war program. Its provisions subjected to criminal prosecution anyone who wrote, spoke, or published "any false, scandalous and malicious writing" against any member or branch of the federal government. Federalists argued that the act merely put in statutory form the common law doctrine of seditious libel, which made excessive criticism of the government a potentially criminal act. (Indeed, the Act reformed existing law by allowing defendants to invoke the truth of a statement as a defense against the charge of sedition.) Republicans replied that the Act clearly violated the First Amendment to the Constitution, which barred Congress from making laws "abridging the freedom of speech, or of the press." The Federalists' reliance on English practice marked one more effort to corrupt the free government of the United States with monarchical principles. The Republicans also objected to several other laws Congress adopted in 1798. The most notable, the Alien Act, authorized the President to deport any alien he deemed dangerous to the national security.

The controversy over the Sedition Act forced Americans to consider the meaning of freedom of speech and the press far more carefully than they had while adopting the Bill of Rights only a few years earlier. But the deeper understanding of these principles that emerged *after* 1798 was won at a high cost. For President Adams and his party regarded the Sedition Act not as a mere deterrent to be used in extreme cases, but as a handy club to beat their critics into submission. The administration prosecuted offenders vigorously, and a judiciary that was Federalist to a man upheld the convictions. And just in case the Sedition Act prove unequal to the task, some Federalists were prepared to go even further. The new provisional army was placed under the nominal command of the retired Washington. But its real leader was Hamilton, his second in command; and the *eminence grise* of the Federalist party was itching for an excuse to march the troops through the Republican strongholds of Virginia.

In reaction to this intense Federalist effort, Jefferson and Madison moved toward more radical positions in the fall of 1798. Time and again since 1793, Madison had ruefully pondered the advantages that the executive branch enjoyed in foreign affairs. "The Constitution supposes, what the history of all government demonstrates, that the executive is the branch of power most interested in war, and most prone to it," he wrote in April 1798. "It has, accordingly, with studied care, vested the question of war" in Congress. But in practice the President could often force Congress to support his unilateral actions. The people were as easily gulled as their representatives. "The management of foreign relations appears to be the most susceptible of abuse of all the trusts committed to a government," Madison observed, "because they can be concealed or disclosed . . . as will best suit particular views; and because the body of the people are less capable of judging, and are more under the influence of prejudices, on that branch of their affairs, than of any other."

But with both Congress and public opinion under the sway of the war fever of 1798, and the administration using the Sedition Act to rein in its critics, where were Republicans to turn? The surprising answer to which Jefferson and Madison were driven was the state legislatures. After conferring at Montpelier in early July and again at Monticello in October, the two men agreed on the general strategy of having the legislatures of Virginia and Kentucky—both controlled by Republicans—denounce the Alien and Sedition Acts as unconstitutional. In the fall, they drafted resolutions—Jefferson for Kentucky, Madison for Virginia—which trusted lieutenants introduced in the two assemblies.

The idea of encouraging state legislatures to take stands on national issues was not radical, given their role in the election of the Senate. What was radical was the stand that Jefferson and Madison asked them to take. Both men agreed in their fundamental view of the Constitution as a compact among the states vesting certain limited powers in a national government. "In case of a dangerous, palpable, and dangerous exercise of other powers not granted by this compact," the states retained some right to protect their own authority and the liberties of their citizens against the abuse of federal power.

But in explaining how this protection would be provided, the two men's positions diverged. Jefferson spoke of the right of a state to "nullify" illegitimate federal acts, implying that it could *legally* prevent the execution of an unconstitutional law. Madison more cautiously declared that the states could "interpose for arresting the progress of the evil." This seemed to suggest that the states should act *politically* to rouse broad opposition to acts of federal usurpation, presumably by approving resolutions that would call either Congress or the people back to their senses and the proper meaning of the Constitution.

That meaning, Madison thought, was to be "limited by the plain sense and intention" of the Constitution as the original "parties" to the "compact" had understood it. But in developing his arguments against the Alien and Sedition Acts, he could not ignore the changes that had taken place in his own thinking since the late 1780s. Then his entire analysis of the vices of the Confederation had presumed that the states would always prefer their own narrow interests to the general good of the Union. He had similarly felt that liberty would face its greatest dangers not from arbitrary acts of government but from the interests of the popular majorities it represented. And bills of rights, he had also concluded, would provide only a weak defense against majorities bent on pursuing their own ends.

Experience had since proved these expectations wrong, and Madison adjusted his thinking accordingly. Whether one regarded the Federalists as an aristocratic clique who had somehow seized power or a factious majority manipulating public opinion, they had clearly breached the defensive lines of the Constitution's scheme of separated powers. With the Federalists dominating every branch of the national government, Madison now understood that the independent existence of the states had advantages he had overlooked in 1787, if only by providing the Republicans safe havens where they could regroup and plan future operations.

Yet Madison did not have to cross uncharted ground to occupy the positions that he took in 1798. In *Federalist* 46, for example, he had surveyed the various ways in which the states could counter efforts by the federal government "to extend its power beyond its due limits." And in his exchanges with Jefferson on the issue of amendments, he had conceded that a bill of rights could provide "good ground for an appeal to the sense of the community" in case "usurped acts of the government" threatened liberty. Privately he had doubted whether either the states or a bill of rights would be needed to resist "encroachments" from the national government. But it is a mark of the brilliance of his original analysis of the Constitution that he could revive points he had once made more for purposes of argument than from conviction and apply them to events he had not foreseen.

Madison knew how far he had come since 1789, and he knew the dangerous conclusions to which the positions of 1798 led. That is why, in January 1799, he asked Jefferson to consider whether the Kentucky resolutions did not go too far by implying that a state legislature could nullify any act of Congress that it found objectionable. That was a formula not for opposition but for disunion—and disunion was the absolute evil Madison could never imagine, even though Jefferson, in an inspired moment in August 1799, hinted it might prove necessary. Madison was quick to argue that so gloomy a conclusion was premature, and Jefferson, again accepting his friend's tutoring, drew back.

The true challenge, as Madison saw it, was to recapture the national government from its Federalist masters. Well into 1799, that challenge seemed more than the Republicans could surmount. With American ships sweeping French privateers from the Atlantic coast and the West Indies, war fever remained high throughout the country. John Adams had never been so popular, while Federalist candidates ran well in the elections for the Sixth Congress, even winning eight of Virginia's nineteen seats in the House. Nor did Madison and Jefferson find much to cheer in the reaction that the Virginia and Kentucky resolves evoked from other legislatures. None was willing to endorse the Republican position, much less join a united campaign to repeal the detested legislation.

These developments brought Madison's brief retirement from public office to an end. Accepting election to the autumn 1799 session of the Virginia assembly, Madison, though weakened by dysentery, poured his labors into the preparation of a report justifying the resolutions of 1798.

If nothing else, Madison and Jefferson hoped this report would serve as a campaign document for the coming presidential election.

THOMAS JEFFERSON, FIRST INAUGURAL ADDRESS

Mar. 4, 1801.

During the contest of opinion through which we have passed the animation of discussions and of exertions has sometimes worn an aspect which might impose on strangers unused to think freely and to speak and to write what they think; but this being now decided by the voice of the nation, announced according to the rules of the Constitution, all will, of course, arrange themselves under the will of the law, and unite in common efforts for the common good. All, too, will bear in mind this sacred principle, that though the will of the majority is in all cases to prevail, that will to be rightful must be reasonable; that the minority possesses their equal rights, which equal law must protect, and to violate would be oppression. Let us, then, fellow citizens, unite with one heart and one mind. Let us restore to social intercourse that harmony and affection without which liberty and even life itself are but dreary things. And let us reflect that, having banished from our land that religious intolerance under which mankind so long bled and suffered, we have yet gained little if we countenance a political intolerance as despotic, as wicked, and capable of as bitter and bloody persecutions. During the throes and convulsions of the ancient world, during the agonizing spasms of infuriated man, seeking through blood and slaughter his long-lost liberty, it was not wonderful that the agitation of the billows should reach even this distant and peaceful shore; that this should be more felt and feared by some and less by others, and should divide opinions as to measures of safety. But every difference of opinion is not a difference of principle. We have called by different names brethren of the same principle. We are all Republicans, we are all Federalists. If there be any among us who would wish to dissolve this Union or to change its republican form, let them stand undisturbed as monuments of the safety with which error of opinion may be tolerated where reason is left free to combat it. I know, indeed, that some honest men fear that a republican government cannot be strong, that this government is not strong enough; but would the honest patriot, in the full tide of successful experiment, abandon a government which has so far kept us free and firm on the theoretic and visionary fear that this government, the world's best hope, may by possibility want energy to preserve itself? I trust not. I believe this, on the contrary, the strongest government on earth. I believe it the only one where every man, at the call of the law, would fly to the standard of the law, and would meet invasions of the public order as his own personal concern.

NEW YORK TIMES v. SULLIVAN

ORAL ARGUMENT

January 6, 1964.

On the question whether under the First Amendment the traditional rule of strict liability for defamation can be applied to an action brought by a public official against a critic of his official conduct, the following exchange occurred during the argument of Professor Herbert Wechsler, counsel for the New York Times. Wechsler maintained that the First Amendment requires that such a critic be granted absolute immunity from civil actions for defamation:

JUSTICE BRENNAN: "How far does this go, Mr. Wechsler? As long as the criticism is addressed to official conduct?"

WECHSLER: "Yes."

JUSTICE BRENNAN: "Are there any limits whatever which take it outside the protection of the First Amendment?"

WECHSLER: "Well, if I take my instruction from James Madison, I would have to say that within any references that Madison made I can see no toying with limits or with exclusions."

JUSTICE BRENNAN: "You say, then, the First Amendment gives it, in effect, an absolute privilege to criticize . . . "

WECHSLER: "The proposition is that the First Amendment was precisely designed to do away with seditious libel, and seditious libel was the punishment of criticism of the Government and criticism of officials."

JUSTICE GOLDBERG: "And this applies not only to newspapers but to anybody?"

WECHSLER: "Exactly; of course."

JUSTICE GOLDBERG: "In other words, you are not arguing here for a special rule that applies to newspapers?"

WECHSLER: "Certainly not . . . "

JUSTICE STEWART: "Your argument would be the same . . . if The New York Times or anybody else had accused this official of taking a bribe?"

WECHSLER: "Certainly."

JUSTICE STEWART: "Or buying his office?"

WECHSLER: "Certainly. Of course, in the historic period in which Madison was writing, charges of bribery were common, and it was this type of press freedom that he saw in the First Amendment."

JUSTICE WHITE: "Mr. Wechsler, we don't have here a case of deliberate falsehood."

WECHSLER: "No."

NEW YORK TIMES CO. v. SULLIVAN

Supreme Court of the United States, 1964.
376 U.S. 254, 84 S.Ct. 710, 11 L.Ed.2d 686.

MR. JUSTICE BRENNAN delivered the opinion of the Court.

We are required in this case to determine for the first time the extent to which the constitutional protections for speech and press limit a State's power to award damages in a libel action brought by a public official against critics of his official conduct.

* * *

The general proposition that freedom of expression upon public questions is secured by the First Amendment has long been settled by our decisions. The constitutional safeguard, we have said, "was fashioned to assure unfettered interchange of ideas for the bringing about of political and social changes desired by the people." *Roth v. United States*, 354 U.S. 476, 484. "The maintenance of the opportunity for free political discussion to the end that government may be responsive to the will of the people and that changes may be obtained by lawful means, an opportunity essential to the security of the Republic, is a fundamental principle of our constitutional system." *Stromberg v. California*, 283 U.S. 359, 369. "(I)t is a prized American privilege to speak one's mind, although not always with perfect good taste, on all public institutions," *Bridges v. California*, 314 U.S. 252, 270, and this opportunity is to be afforded for "vigorous advocacy" no less than "abstract discussion." *N.A.A.C.P. v. Button*, 371 U.S. 415, 429. The First Amendment, said Judge Learned Hand, "presupposes that right conclusions are more likely to be gathered out of a multitude of tongues, than through any kind of authoritative selection. To many this is, and always will be, folly; but we have staked upon it our all." *United States v. Associated Press*, 52 F.Supp. 362, 372 (D.C.S.D.N.Y.1943). Mr. Justice Brandeis, in his concurring opinion in *Whitney v. California*, 274 U.S. 357, 375–376, gave the principle its classic formulation:

> "Those who won our independence believed * * * that public discussion is a political duty; and that this should be a fundamental principle of the American government. They recognized the risks to which all human institutions are subject. But they knew that order cannot be secured merely through fear of punishment for its infraction; that it is hazardous to discourage thought, * * * hope and imagination; that fear breeds repression; that repression breeds hate; that hate menaces stable government; that the path of safety lies in the opportunity to discuss freely supposed grievances and proposed remedies; and that the fitting remedy for evil counsels is good ones. Believing in the power of reason as applied through public discussion, they eschewed silence coerced by law—the argument of force in its worst form. Recognizing the occasional tyrannies

of governing majorities, they amended the Constitution so that free speech and assembly should be guaranteed."

Thus we consider this case against the background of a profound national commitment to the principle that debate on public issues should be uninhibited, robust, and wide-open, and that it may well include vehement, caustic, and sometimes unpleasantly sharp attacks on government and public officials. See *Terminiello v. Chicago*, 337 U.S. 1, 4; *De Jonge v. Oregon*, 299 U.S. 353, 365. The present advertisement, as an expression of grievance and protest on one of the major public issues of our time, would seem clearly to qualify for the constitutional protection. The question is whether it forfeits that protection by the falsity of some of its factual statements and by its alleged defamation of respondent.

Authoritative interpretations of the First Amendment guarantees have consistently refused to recognize an exception for any test of truth—whether administered by judges, juries, or administrative officials—and especially one that puts the burden of proving truth on the speaker. *Cf. Speiser v. Randall*, 357 U.S. 513, 525–526. The constitutional protection does not turn upon "the truth, popularity, or social utility of the ideas and beliefs which are offered." *N.A.A.C.P. v. Button*, 371 U.S. 415, 445. As Madison said, "Some degree of abuse is inseparable from the proper use of every thing; and in no instance is this more true than in that of the press." 4 Elliot's Debates on the Federal Constitution (1876), p. 571. In *Cantwell v. Connecticut*, 310 U.S. 296, 310, the Court declared:

> "In the realm of religious faith, and in that of political belief, sharp differences arise. In both fields the tenets of one man may seem the rankest error to his neighbor. To persuade others to his own point of view, the pleader, as we know, at times, resorts to exaggeration, to vilification of men who have been, or are, prominent in church or state, and even to false statement. But the people of this nation have ordained in the light of history, that, in spite of the probability of excesses and abuses, these liberties are, in the long view, essential to enlightened opinion and right conduct on the part of the citizens of a democracy."

That erroneous statement is inevitable in free debate, and that it must be protected if the freedoms of expression are to have the "breathing space" that they "need * * * to survive," *N.A.A.C.P. v. Button*, 371 U.S. 415, 433, was also recognized by the Court of Appeals for the District of Columbia Circuit in *Sweeney v. Patterson*, 76 U.S.App.D.C. 23, 24, 128 F.2d 457, 458 (1942). Judge Edgerton spoke for a unanimous court which affirmed the dismissal of a Congressman's libel suit based upon a newspaper article charging him with anti-Semitism in opposing a judicial appointment. He said:

> "Cases which impose liability for erroneous reports of the political conduct of officials reflect the obsolete doctrine that the governed must not criticize their governors. * * * The interest of the public here outweighs the interest of appellant or any other individual. The

protection of the public requires not merely discussion, but information. Political conduct and views which some respectable people approve, and others condemn, are constantly imputed to Congressmen. Errors of fact, particularly in regard to a man's mental states and processes, are inevitable. * * * Whatever is added to the field of libel is taken from the field of free debate."[1]

Injury to official reputation error affords no more warrant for repressing speech that would otherwise be free than does factual error. Where judicial officers are involved, this Court has held that concern for the dignity and reputation of the courts does not justify the punishment as criminal contempt of criticism of the judge or his decision. *Bridges v. California*, 314 U.S. 252. This is true even though the utterance contains "half-truths" and "misinformation." *Pennekamp v. Florida*, 328 U.S. 331, 342, 343, n. 5, 345. Such repression can be justified, if at all, only by a clear and present danger of the obstruction of justice. See also *Craig v. Harney*, 331 U.S. 367; *Wood v. Georgia*, 370 U.S. 375. If judges are to be treated as "men of fortitude, able to thrive in a hardy climate," *Craig v. Harney*, supra, 331 U.S., at 376, surely the same must be true of other government officials, such as elected city commissioners. Criticism of their official conduct does not lose its constitutional protection merely because it is effective criticism and hence diminishes their official reputations.

If neither factual error nor defamatory content suffices to remove the constitutional shield from criticism of official conduct, the combination of the two elements is no less inadequate. This is the lesson to be drawn from the great controversy over the Sedition Act of 1798, 1 Stat. 596, which first crystallized a national awareness of the central meaning of the First Amendment. See Levy, *Legacy of Suppression* (1960), at 258 et seq.; Smith, *Freedom's Fetters* (1956), at 426, 431 and *passim*. That statute made it a crime, punishable by a $5,000 fine and five years in prison, "if any person shall write, print, utter or publish * * * any false, scandalous and malicious writing or writings against the government of the United States, or either house of the Congress * * *, or the President * * *, with intent to defame * * * or to bring them, or either of them, into contempt or disrepute; or to excite against them, or either or any of them, the hatred of the good people of the United States." The Act allowed the defendant the defense of truth, and provided that the jury were to be judges both of the law and the facts. Despite these qualifications, the Act was vigorously condemned as unconstitutional in an attack joined in by Jefferson and Madison. In the famous Virginia Resolutions of 1798, the General Assembly of Virginia resolved that it

1. *See also* Mill, *On Liberty* (Oxford: Blackwell, 1947), at 47:

"* * * (T)o argue sophistically, to suppress facts or arguments, to misstate the elements of the case, or misrepresent the opposite opinion * * * all this, even to the most aggravated degree, is so continually done in perfect good faith, by persons who are not considered, and in many other respects may not deserve to be considered, ignorant or incompetent, that it is rarely possible, on adequate grounds, conscientiously to stamp the misrepresentation as morally culpable; and still less could law presume to interfere with this kind of controversial misconduct."

> "doth particularly protest against the palpable and alarming infractions of the Constitution, in the two late cases of the 'Alien and Sedition Acts,' passed at the last session of Congress * * *. (The Sedition Act) exercises * * * a power not delegated by the Constitution, but, on the contrary, expressly and positively forbidden by one of the amendments thereto—a power which, more than any other, ought to produce universal alarm, because it is levelled against the right of freely examining public characters and measures, and of free communication among the people thereon, which has ever been justly deemed the only effectual guardian of every other right." 4 Elliot's *Debates*, *supra*, pp. 553–554.

Madison prepared the Report in support of the protest. His premise was that the Constitution created a form of government under which "The people, not the government, possess the absolute sovereignty." The structure of the government dispersed power in reflection of the people's distrust of concentrated power, and of power itself at all levels. This form of government was "altogether different" from the British form, under which the Crown was sovereign and the people were subjects. "Is it not natural and necessary, under such different circumstances," he asked, "that a different degree of freedom in the use of the press should be contemplated?" *Id.*, pp. 569–570. Earlier, in a debate in the House of Representatives, Madison had said: "If we advert to the nature of Republican Government, we shall find that the censorial power is in the people over the Government, and not in the Government over the people." 4 Annals of Congress, p. 934 (1794). Of the exercise of that power by the press, his Report said: "In every state, probably, in the Union, the press has exerted a freedom in canvassing the merits and measures of public men, of every description, which has not been confined to the strict limits of the common law. On this footing the freedom of the press has stood; on this foundation it yet stands * * *." 4 Elliot's Debates, supra, p. 570. The right of free public discussion of the stewardship of public officials was thus, in Madison's view, a fundamental principle of the American form of government.[2]

Although the Sedition Act was never tested in this Court,[3] the attack upon its validity has carried the day in the court of history. Fines levied

2. The Report on the Virginia Resolutions further stated:

"(I)t is manifestly impossible to punish the intent to bring those who administer the government into disrepute or contempt, without striking at the right of freely discussing public characters and measures; * * * which, again, is equivalent to a protection of those who administer the government, if they should at any time deserve the contempt or hatred of the people, against being exposed to it, by free animadversions on their characters and conduct. Nor can there be a doubt * * * that a government thus intrenched in penal statutes against the just and natural effects of a culpable administration, will easily evade the responsibility which is essential to a faithful discharge of its duty.

"Let it be recollected, lastly, that the right of electing the members of the government constitutes more particularly the essence of a free and responsible government. The value and efficacy of this right depends on the knowledge of the comparative merits and demerits of the candidates for public trust, and on the equal freedom, consequently, of examining and discussing these merits and demerits of the candidates respectively." 4 Elliot's *Debates*, *supra*, p. 575.

3. The Act expired by its terms in 1801.

in its prosecution were repaid by Act of Congress on the ground that it was unconstitutional. *See, e.g.*, Act of July 4, 1840, c. 45, 6 Stat. 802, accompanied by H.R.Rep.No. 86, 26th Cong., 1st Sess. (1840). Calhoun, reporting to the Senate on February 4, 1836, assumed that its invalidity was a matter "which no one now doubts." Report with Senate bill No. 122, 24th Cong., 1st Sess., p. 3. Jefferson, as President, pardoned those who had been convicted and sentenced under the Act and remitted their fines, stating: "I discharged every person under punishment or prosecution under the sedition law, because I considered, and now consider, that law to be a nullity, as absolute and as palpable as if Congress had ordered us to fall down and worship a golden image." Letter to Mrs. Adams, July 22, 1804, 4 Jefferson's Works (Washington ed.), pp. 555, 556. The invalidity of the Act has also been assumed by Justices of this Court. See Holmes, J., dissenting and joined by Brandeis, J., in *Abrams v. United States*, 250 U.S. 616, 630; Jackson, J., dissenting in *Beauharnais v. Illinois*, 343 U.S. 250, 288–289; Douglas, *The Right of the People* (1958), p. 47. See also Cooley, *Constitutional Limitations* (8th ed., Carrington, 1927), pp. 899–900; Chafee, *Free Speech in the United States* (1942), pp. 27–28. These views reflect a broad consensus that the Act, because of the restraint it imposed upon criticism of government and public officials, was inconsistent with the First Amendment.

There is no force in respondent's argument that the constitutional limitations implicit in the history of the Sedition Act apply only to Congress and not to the States. It is true that the First Amendment was originally addressed only to action by the Federal Government, and that Jefferson, for one, while denying the power of Congress "to controul the freedom of the press," recognized such a power in the States. See the 1804 Letter to Abigail Adams quoted in *Dennis v. United States*, 341 U.S. 494, 522, n. 4, (concurring opinion). But this distinction was eliminated with the adoption of the Fourteenth Amendment and the application to the States of the First Amendment's restrictions. *See, e.g., Gitlow v. New York*, 268 U.S. 652, 666; *Schneider v. State*, 308 U.S. 147, 160; *Bridges v. California*, 314 U.S. 252, 268; *Edwards v. South Carolina*, 372 U.S. 229, 235.

What a State may not constitutionally bring about by means of a criminal statute is likewise beyond the reach of its civil law of libel. The fear of damage awards under a rule such as that invoked by the Alabama courts here may be markedly more inhibiting than the fear of prosecution under a criminal statute. *See City of Chicago v. Tribune Co*, 139 N.E. 86, 90 (1923).

The state rule of law is not saved by its allowance of the defense of truth. A defense for erroneous statements honestly made is no less essential here than was the requirement of proof of guilty knowledge which, in *Smith v. California*, 361 U.S. 147, we held indispensable to a valid conviction of a bookseller for possessing obscene writings for sale.

* * *

A rule compelling the critic of official conduct to guarantee the truth of all his factual assertions—and to do so on pain of libel judgments virtually unlimited in amount—leads to a comparable "self-censorship." Allowance of the defense of truth, with the burden of proving it on the defendant, does not mean that only false speech will be deterred.[19] Even courts accepting this defense as an adequate safeguard have recognized the difficulties of adducing legal proofs that the alleged libel was true in all its factual particulars. See, e.g., *Post Publishing Co. v. Hallam*, 59 F. 530, 540 (C.A.6th Cir. 1893); see also Noel, Defamation of Public Officers and Candidates, 49 Col.L.Rev. 875, 892 (1949). Under such a rule, would-be critics of official conduct may be deterred from voicing their criticism, even though it is believed to be true and even though it is in fact true, because of doubt whether it can be proved in court or fear of the expense of having to do so. They tend to make only statements which "steer far wider of the unlawful zone." *Speiser v. Randall, supra*, 357 U.S., at 526. The rule thus dampens the vigor and limits the variety of public debate. It is inconsistent with the First and Fourteenth Amendments.

The constitutional guarantees require, we think, a federal rule that prohibits a public official from recovering damages for a defamatory falsehood relating to his official conduct unless he proves that the statement was made with 'actual malice'—that is, with knowledge that it was false or with reckless disregard of whether it was false or not.

* * *

[Concurring opinions by JUSTICES BLACK and GOLDBERG are omitted.]

HARRY KALVEN, JR., THE NEW YORK TIMES CASE: A NOTE ON "THE CENTRAL MEANING OF THE FIRST AMENDMENT"

1964 Supreme Court Review 191.

If I am right, the Times case represents a happy revolution of free-speech doctrine. Or, to put the matter differently, analysis of free-speech issues should hereafter begin with the significant issue of seditious libel and defamation of government by its critics rather than with the sterile example of a man falsely yelling fire in a crowded theater.

* * *

The concept of seditious libel strikes at the very heart of democracy. Political freedom ends when government can use its powers and its courts to silence its critics. My point is not the tepid one that there should be leeway for criticism of the government. It is rather that defamation of the government is an impossible notion for a democracy. In brief, I suggest, that the presence or absence in the law of the concept

19. Even a false statement may be deemed to make a valuable contribution to public debate, since it brings about "the clearer perception and livelier impression of truth, produced by its collision with error." Mill, On Liberty (Oxford: Blackwell, 1947), at 15; see also Milton, Areopagitica, in Prose Works (Yale, 1959), Vol. II, at 561.

of seditious libel defines the society. A society may or may not treat obscenity or contempt by publication as legal offenses without altering its basic nature. If, however, it make seditious libel an offense, it is not a free society no matter what its other characteristics.

* * *

The Court did not simply, in the face of an awkward history, definitively put to rest the status of the Sedition Act. More important, it found in the controversy over seditious libel the clue to "the central meaning of the First Amendment." The choice of language was unusually apt. The Amendment has a "central meaning"—a core of protection of speech without which democracy cannot function, without which, in Madison's phrase, "the censorial power" would be in the Government over the people and not "in the people over the Government." This is not the whole meaning of the Amendment. There are other freedoms protected by it. But at the center there is no doubt what speech is being protected and no doubt why it is being protected. The theory of the freedom of speech clause was put right side up for the first time.

FLOYD ABRAMS, SPEAKING FREELY: TRIALS OF THE FIRST AMENDMENT

(2005).

Toward the end of 1971, three cases came before the Supreme Court that raised novel issues [concerning the freedom of the press.] Did journalists actually have any First Amendment right not to disclose their confidential sources? If so, under what circumstances would such a right be applied?

When the Supreme Court decided to resolve these issues by agreeing to hear one of the cases, *Branzburg v. Hayes*, James C. Goodale, general counsel of the *New York Times*, persuaded representatives of other large publications and broadcasters–including the *Chicago Sun–Times*, the *Chicago Daily News*, and the Associated Press, as well as the three major television networks, ABC, NBC, and CBS—to write a single brief seeking to persuade the Court to grant First Amendment protection to journalists regarding their sources.

* * *

After many telephone conferences that I (on behalf of NBC), Goodale (on behalf of the *Times*), and a number of other lawyers representing other media entities participated in, we agreed to approach three scholars. Two of them were legendary, and the third had already broken out of the academic pack and been recognized as an original and highly creative scholar. Professor Paul Freund of the Harvard Law School was the nation's most renowned (and, so it seemed, most quoted) constitutional scholar, but he was too busy working on a manuscript to take the task on. Professor Herbert Wechsler of Columbia Law School was a constitutional scholar of enormous distinction who had represented the

New York Times in 1964 in the most significant First Amendment case of its era, *New York Times v. Sullivan*, which rewrote American libel law to ensure that First Amendment interests were protected. He, too, was unavailable.

We turned next to my choice, [my former professor at Yale Law School Alexander] Bickel, the youngest of the three scholars, who was on sabbatical leave at Stanford in 1971.

* * *

Born in Rumania, Bickel had emigrated to the United States with his family when he was fourteen, speaking little or no English. By the time I saw him enter our seminar in constitutional law, he was thirty-one and already the stuff of student legend–an honored graduate of Harvard Law School, former clerk to Justice Frankfurter, and author of a forthcoming book featuring previously unpublished drafts of opinions of Justice Brandeis. He was a formidable presence in the classroom, demanding and often irascible. His English not only was perfect but seemed specially crafted to deflate our (and all too often my) intellectual pretensions.

Bickel took particular joy in attacking the class's liberal judicial heroes, Justices Hugo Black and William O. Douglas, jurists who had engaged in an ongoing ideological conflict on the Court with Justice Frankfurter.

* * *

I had no idea how Bickel would react when I called him; and after listening carefully to my description of the case and what we wanted from him, he made two comments. First, he reminded me that he was "no First Amendment voluptuary." I knew that well—I would have described myself in similar terms when I was in law school—and chose not to tell him that that was one of the reasons we were calling him in the first place.

Second, he said in a more relaxed tone, "I assume that you are not calling me to ask me to be your law clerk on this brief?"

"No," I said. He would write the brief, I would assist him and we could surely work out any areas of disagreement jointly. He agreed.

For months we worked together by telephone. Bickel wrote a first draft of the brief in California while I provided him from New York with whatever legal backup he asked for. On June 14, 1971, I hosted a lunch at the University Club to introduce Goodale, other lawyers representing the press, and a number of journalists, including *New York Times* national editor Gene Roberts, to Professor Bickel.

* * *

The day before the lunch, a Sunday, the *Times* had published on its front page an article under a deliberately understated and rather bland headline that read:

VIETNAM ARCHIVE: PENTAGON STUDY TRACES
3 DECADES OF GROWING U.S. INVOLVEMENT

What followed on page one and on three full pages later in the newspaper was a description of what the article, in its first line, described as a "massive study of how the United States went to war in Indochina, conducted by the Pentagon three years ago," a study that "demonstrated that four administrations progressively developed a sense of commitment to a non-Communist Vietnam, a readiness to fight the North to protect the South, and an ultimate frustration with the effort—to a much greater extent than their public statements acknowledged at the time." Based as it was on the three-thousand-page-long top secret analysis offered by the study—soon to become known as the Pentagon Papers—and four thousand pages of equally highly classified documents accompanying the analysis, the *Times*'s article of June 13 and a second one a day later seemed to set the stage for a cosmic legal clash between the newspaper and the government.

At our lunch, Bickel warned the lawyers and journalists who were present that while we likely had four votes in the case involving confidential sources, it would be a difficult task to pick up the needed fifth vote.[4] As regards the *Times*'s ongoing publication of the Pentagon Papers, however, we both offered kudos on the story and reassurance that the government would likely not mount a legal challenge to the *Times*'s publication. "That's one," Bickel affirmed, "that you can't lose." Both of us were free with advice to Goodale and Gene Roberts about the articles. The government would not likely be so foolish, we told them, as to seek to restrain the *Times* from publishing since (in language both of us used) "we have never had a prior restraint on the publication of news in our country's history." Supremely confident of our views, as only lawyers without clients are, we told the representatives of the *Times* that if the government went to court, the newspaper would obviously win.

That night, my world changed. Shortly after one a.m. Goodale awakened me with a telephone call to my home. I barely knew him—we had met personally only twice before—and could barely make out what he was saying. The government had demanded that the *Times* cease publication of portions of the Pentagon Papers, he explained. Of course, the newspaper would not do that, he said. The *Times*'s regular counsel at Lord, Day, & Lord, however, had refused to represent the newspaper. As Bickel was in town, and he and I had spoken so persuasively at lunch about the right of the *Times* to publish, would I and my firm join with Bickel in representing the *Times*?

It was all like a dream—the most cheering, fulfilling, and delightful dream imaginable. Except that it all seemed unimaginable. Was I really going to represent the *New York Times* against Richard Nixon's adminis-

4. He was right. The vote was 5–4 against the press, with the critical fifth vote of Justice Lewis Powell separately explained by him in a concurring opinion that was so murky that it remains a subject of dispute to this day.

tration? Was I really going to do so in collaboration with Alexander Bickel, my own professor from Yale?

I spoke quickly. Of course I'd be glad to take on the case, I told Goodale, but I would need my firm's approval before I could do so. Since it was the middle of the night, I couldn't obtain the authorization until the following day. Why didn't I simply go with Bickel to my office immediately, I suggested, and work through the night? I would get back to Goodale in the morning to confirm that we would accept the case.

I picked Bickel up in a taxi and we sped to my office. We came to the Pentagon Papers with a good deal of knowledge of applicable law but none at all of the turmoil at the *Times* that preceded the decision to publish them, or that within the government that had preceded its decision to challenge the *Times*. In fact, we knew almost nothing about the documents themselves.

* * *

The Pentagon Papers had been initiated in 1967 with a decision by Secretary of Defense Robert S. McNamara unique in the history of warfare. In the midst of the United States' seemingly endless involvement in Vietnam, McNamara ordered a historical "study" of the conflict. The secretary, by this point dubious about the American role in the war, wanted answers to fundamental questions about the nature of the struggle. The study, McNamara insisted, should be "encyclopedic and objective." It was expected to require the labor of six full-time professionals and three months to complete. In fact, by the time thirty-six scholars finished the task eighteen months later, a new secretary of defense, Clark M. Clifford, was in place.

The study was ultimately severely attacked. Critics on the left, such as Professor Noam Chomsky, of the Massachusetts Institute of Technology, would charge that it reflected the "pro-Government bias" of its authors. At the other end of the political spectrum, Henry Kissinger, in his memoirs, described it as "selective" and "one-sided," reflecting the antiwar point of view. Some historians, noting the the study had been based entirely upon sources such as the Department of Defense and the Central Intelligence Agency, complained about the lack of White House participation. And since no interviews were permitted of the participants in the war's decision-making process, the result was fairly described by Leslie H. Gelb, director of the Study Task Force that prepared the Pentagon Papers, later the Times national security correspondent and then the director of the Council on Foreign Relations, as "not so much a documentary history as a history based solely on documents—checked and rechecked with antlike diligence."

Whatever its limitations as history, the Pentagon Papers, which covered the decades from World War II to 1968, amply fulfilled the mandate to be encyclopedic. Its seven thousand pages contained a total of 2.5 million words and weighed sixty pounds. The text was thoughtful, often persuasive, inevitably debatable. The supporting documents were devastating, demonstrating an extraordinary level of governmental duplicity based upon an unprecedented source—the very files of the government itself.

On August 7, 1964, both houses of Congress, at the urging of the Johnson administration, had passed a resolution endorsing "all necessary measures to repel any armed attack against the forces of the United States and to prevent any further aggression." As the Pentagon Papers documents revealed, the administration had long sought the added powers conferred by that kind of resolution, and President Johnson had seized upon one particular incident—the allegedly "unprovoked" attack on an American ship in Vietnam's Tonkin Gulf—as the means to get the measure through Congress. He had not shared the true nature of this desire with Congress, nor had he shared with it the fact that prior to the Tonkin incident, American soldiers had been engaged in clandestine warfare against the North Vietnamese.

From other documents, the reader could trace the path of increased American involvement in Vietnam—and of repeated government deception about it. Some of the material revealed in the Papers had been previously reported; some of it had not. But in many instances the documents themselves proved the truth of what had only been alleged. The Truman administration, for example, had "directly involved" the United States in Vietnam by giving military aid to France in her war against the Vietminh. The Eisenhower administration's efforts to rescue South Vietnam from a Communist takeover had played an important role in the final breakdown of the 1954 Geneva accords. The Kennedy administration had turned minor American involvement in Vietnam into a "broad commitment." The Johnson administration had consistently dissembled about American military plans and activities in the nation.

Such revelations, however, had never been intended for public eyes. When the study was delivered to Secretary Clifford on January 15, 1969, it carried a top secret classification. It was filed away, and the war continued to drag on—a circumstance that one of the study's authors, Daniel Ellsberg, soon came to consider intolerable.

A former Marine, and later a consultant in the departments of Defense and State, Ellsberg had started out as a fervent supporter of an American role in the Vietnam War. While assigned there from 1965 to 1967, though, he came to conclude that there was no hope of American success, and upon his return he became increasingly radicalized and increasingly distressed that the newly elected administration was not taking what he viewed as its opportunity to extricate the United States from the folly—and, he would conclude, its criminal conduct—in Vietnam.

As a consultant at the Rand Corporation, a California defense research organization, Ellsberg had access to one of the fifteen copies of the study. Starting in 1969, he tried to interest congressional committees in subpoenaing the study. When all such efforts failed, Ellsberg made a copy of the study available to Neil Sheehan, a *New York Times* reporter.

For three months, in complete secrecy, a team of Times journalists pored over the text, checking it for accuracy and deciding if any portions of the materials could compromise national security. While the *Times* did not have the three most sensitive volumes of the Pentagon Papers—the so-called "negotiating" volumes, dealing with efforts until 1968 to resolve the war diplomatically—what it did have nonetheless presented the newspaper with a soul-wrenching set of decisions.

A century earlier, in the summer of 1871, the *Times* had printed another set of secret internal government documents; in that instance, it had exposed the criminal transgressions of the Tweed Ring in New York City. This time, the stakes were much higher. On the face of it, this sober, respectable paper had to decide whether or not it was going to print top secret documents that dealt with a war in which the nation was still engaged.

The debate within the *Times* was long, exhaustive, and acrimonious. Some disputes were tactical in nature. Should it print any of the classified documents themselves or only portions of the commentary? Should it publish everything in one day (as Goodale urged) to avoid even the risk of a prior restraint, or publish according to its own schedule (as Abe Rosenthal, the newspaper's executive editor, insisted)? Other questions required deeper analysis of the role of journalism in a free society. What should the role of a newspaper be during wartime? When should highly classified documents be published? Executives, editors, reporters, and attorneys argued over the meaning of patriotism and journalistic ethics and over the risks that publication, or nonpublication, of the Papers held for the profession and for the *Times* itself. At one point, Rosenthal, who personally supported the nation's war effort but whose sense of journalistic commitment ultimately led him to be the indispensable journalistic advocate of publication within the newspaper, seriously considered resigning if the *Times* did not publish. At another, James Reston, the *Times*'s legendary Washington columnist, who had won three Pulitzer Prizes and had directed the *Times*'s Washington bureau, and who was (as I would shortly learn) a man of the most extraordinary connections throughout the world, threatened to publish the Pentagon Papers himself in his own newspaper—the tiny *Vineyard Gazette*, on Martha's Vineyard—if the *Times* did not publish.

But the *Times* was, at its core, an establishment newspaper, one that ten years earlier would likely have agreed with the observation Chief Justice Warren Burger later made in the Pentagon Papers case itself that "one of the basic and simple duties of every citizen with respect to the discovery or possession of secret government documents" was "to report forthwith to responsible public officers." For a newspaper that had become a national institution, the decision to publish extensive portions, during wartime, of highly classified documents was a painful one. But for the fact that the journalists and editors of the paper had been lied to so often by the government about the war, the outcome might well have been different.

Another reason why the decision to publish was so difficult was that the *Times* had received the sternest warnings from its own outside counsel about the legal consequences of doing so. For over six decades the paper had been represented by the venerable New York law firm of Lord, Day, & Lord. Lewis J. Loeb, the firm's partner who had advised the Times since 1929, and his senior partner Herbert Brownell, formerly the attorney general under President Eisenhower, had informed the newspaper that its publication of the Pentagon Papers would violate the Espionage Act. Likewise, The *Times*'s publisher, Arthur O. Sulzberger, was advised by them that he could well be jailed as a result of publishing the top secret documents in the paper's possession. Brownell went so far as to announce to Sulzberger (who, as James Reston later wrote, was not amused to hear it) that his father and grandfather, both of whom had been publishers of the *Times*, would never have considered such a course of action. Brownell and Loeb's view was staunchly opposed by Goodale, the *Times*'s general counsel and himself a former associate at Lord, Day, & Lord. Goodale had reviewed the case law independently, prepared legal memoranda rejecting the counsel of Lord, Day & Lord, and repeatedly, at considerable personal risk, urged the *Times* to publish.

Eventually, Sulzberger, then in London, rejecting the views of some of his colleagues in senior management as well as the dire warnings of his outside counsel, made the call to accept the risks of publication rather than those of silence. On Sunday, June 13, the Times published the first in a series of seven articles about the Pentagon Papers. In retrospect, the decision may seem obvious, but it was by no means an easy one at the time, and it remains one for which Sulzberger deserves enormous credit.

* * *

Michael Hess, the chief of the Civil Division of the United States Attorney's Office in Manhattan, was phoning. I stepped out of the room to take the call, and Hess told me that the government was going to court seeking a temporary restraining order barring the *Times* from further publication of the Pentagon Papers and that it would be appearing shortly before federal judge Murray Gurfein. I spoke briefly with Hess, thinking as I did that while my litigation experience was sound and my First Amendment knowledge substantial, I had never even seen an argument before the Supreme Court. As for Bickel, I surmised correctly that he had never appeared in *any* court as counsel. It was a sobering thought. Here, I thought, was a landmark case, an enormous threat to the press and, more broadly, to the First Amendment, being litigated by an academic with no courtroom experience, accompanied by a lawyer who had never even watched a Supreme Court argument. I hoped the thought would not occur to the executives, lawyers, and journalists at the *Times*.

At noon Bickel, Goodale, and I appeared before Judge Gurfein. New cases were assigned at random, and chance had sent this particular one to a judge so new that it was literally the first one he was deciding.

(Years later, another judge sworn in on the same day as Judge Gurfein, Lawrence Pierce, told me that every night since that day in June 1971 when Gurfein drew the Pentagon Papers case, he got down on his knees to thank God that it had not happened to him.)

When we entered Judge Gurfein's courtroom he greeted us grimly. We had checked on him in the brief time before we left for court and learned that he was one of "Tom Dewey's boys," a former prosecutor in New York who had worked as a lawyer with former New York governor and two-time Republican presidential candidate Dewey, and then at the Nuremberg war-crime trials. We also learned that he had a significant background in military intelligence, which we knew would likely prove to be an important factor. But would it make him more hostile to the *Times*'s conduct or more inclined to be skeptical of the government's case?

* * *

When we finally put our papers in on June 17, we included affidavits not only from Sulzberger and various *Times* reporters but from diplomats and historians such as Theodore Sorenson, James MacGregor Burns, Francis Plimpton, Eric F. Goldman, and Barbara Tuchman. And we included an extraordinary affidavit from Max Frankel, which answered many of the questions that my partner Bill Hegarty, who would handle the cross-examination of witnesses at the June 18 hearing, and I had repeatedly asked him. If the material was secret (and classified top secret), how could we justify the paper's decision to publish it? How does the paper decide what sort of "secret" material to print? Why does it print such material at all?

Frankel explained inside Washington to outsiders in a new way. "A small and specialized corps of reporters and a few hundred American officials regularly make use of classified, secret, and top secret information," he wrote. They did it in "a cooperative, competitive, antagonistic and arcane relationship." Without such use of "secrets," Frankel wrote, "there could be no adequate diplomatic, military, and political reporting of the kind our people take for granted." The fourteen-page long document described a sort of reality that generally went undisclosed:

> Presidents make "secret" decisions only to reveal them for the purposes of frightening an adversary nation, wooing a friendly electorate, protecting their reputations. The military services conduct "secret" research in weaponry only to reveal it for the purpose of enhancing their budgets, appearing superior or inferior to a foreign army, gaining the vote of a congressman or the favor of a contractor. The Navy uses secret information to run down the weaponry of the Air Force. The Army passes on secret information to prove its superiority to the Marine Corps. High officials of the government reveal secrets in the search for support of their policies, or to help sabotage the plans and policies of rival departments. Middle-rank officials of government reveal secrets so as to attract the attention of their superiors or to lobby against the orders of

> those superiors. Though not the only vehicle for this traffic in secrets—the Congress is always eager to provide a forum—the press is probably the most important.

Frankel's affidavit was a tour de force, one worthy of publication on its own. Filled with examples of the inner workings of the previously "secret" relationship between the press and those in government, it offered a view that could not only countenance the publication of much classified material but affirm it.

* * *

On Friday, June 18, after Bickel, Hegarty, and I spent another sleepless night in our office, Judge Gurfein conducted a full hearing on the merits of the issues before him. The hearing went well, in large part because of the stellar performances of both Bickel and Hegarty. Hegarty's withering cross-examination of the government's witnesses (all conducted without preparation, since we did not know who they would be or what they would say) left little doubt that while there might be something of a diplomatic flap as a result of publication, the government could offer little to no proof of any genuine military harm it would cause. The key events of the day occurred in a session of the court that was closed, so that the government could make its case that national security interests of the highest order would be compromised by continued publication and by the use of classified information in doing so. Only counsel, witnesses, and Max Frankel (who was present to assist Hegarty in the cross-examination of government witnesses) were permitted to attend. By the end of the long day, we felt good about our chances.

The critical witness was Vice Admiral Francis J. Blouin, depute chief of naval operations for plans and policy. In his direct examination, he had spoken broadly of the harm continued publication would do:

> Q: Do you have present information available which would indicate to you whether the public disclosure of the contents of that study would compromise the military or defense plans of the United States or its intelligence operations?
>
> A: I don't think it would be an overstatement to say that I think it would be a disaster to publish all of these other documents, let alone the ones that have already been published.
>
> Q: Are you also in a position to explain to the Court how past publication by the *New York Times* and the stories which appeared earlier this week have already compromised the intelligence operations of the United States?
>
> A: I would rather not get into detail because I think with the broad experience I have in the field that I can detect things in there that perhaps, as you noted yourself earlier, the ordinary layman would not detect, but that I think as a matter of fact any intelligence organization will derive a great deal of benefit from the articles that have already been published and there is even more juicy material in the other volumes.

In the closed session it quickly became clear that his objections were so far-reaching and would affect so much of what routinely was published in the press that the government's reliance on his testimony asserting that particular portions of the Pentagon Papers could not be published was all but impossible. He referred to material that it "would be just better not to make public." He regretted that our withdrawal plans from Vietnam had been announced publicly by President Nixon, and concluded ruefully: "We just about live by the open book." He conceded that "maybe I am oversensitive," and that his conclusion that the documents "are packed with highly sensitive material, not only straight military, but in the military-political field," rested on "just the quick look I took at these documents." More generally, as he reviewed articles already published in the *Times*, he said, "each article gave me the shivers." When the Court suggested to Blouin that much of what he objected to seeing published was in fact public knowledge, having been repeatedly revealed not only in numerous news reports but in memoirs and other books, the admiral could only reply: "I deplore much of what I read."

Throughout the hearing Judge Gurfein constantly urged the government witnesses to supply him with specific examples of material that would be dangerous to publish. A striking instance occurred in a late-afternoon colloquy between Gurfein and Dennis James Doolin, deputy secretary of defense for international security affairs, who was called by the government to testify as to the propriety of classifying the Pentagon Papers as top secret. Near the end of Doolin's cross-examination, Gurfein asked him: "I will give you one more chance, in this sense. Is there anything you would like to add to your testimony for the enlightenment of the court tying in with more specificity these dangers to security you mentioned arising from incidents that happened between 1945 and 1968 and that appear in these studies?" Doolin replied by alluding to an earlier reference to Thai operations in Laos, which it was the policy of the Thai government to deny (falsely), and on which the United States officially had no comment. Doolin went on: "I might add, Your Honor, that I called ... the Pentagon at lunch and we asked that members of my staff go through the study again looking for one of these, but I didn't have time to come up with a list of, a lengthy list of, specifics." This testimony was offered by the official who over a period of six months, according to his testimony, had reviewed the classified study and recommended to Secretary of Defense Melvin Laird that it not be released, and who had also reviewed the documents since.

The most specific Doolin could get was to suggest what he called "an impact in terms of human intelligence" resulting from revealing to others that we had information and were "reading their traffic." No indication was made whether others were in fact already aware of our intelligence efforts, or how they could benefit in the present from knowledge of what we were doing at the time the documents originated, which at the latest was mid–1968 and for the most part was much earlier, even as long ago as two decades.

The very fact of disclosure—the gross fact of a breach of security, presumably, the disclosure of *any* confidential document—"could have an impact," Doolin insisted, on countries like New Zealand and Thailand, which maintained forces in Vietnam. Publication of the Papers might cause them to accelerate their own withdrawal and thus impede our Vietnamization program. The Australians had already expressed, Doolin said, "their concern, great concern," and at another point he added that the Australian prime minister had said he was "appalled." But all the possible ramifications were plainly surmise, and as Doolin went on, Judge Gurfein gave every indication that he was losing respect for the seriousness of the government case.

Doolin also testified that the United States had been using other governments as intermediaries in attempting to negotiate the release of American prisoners held in North Vietnam, and that such governments would now refuse to undertake confidential missions on our behalf, knowing that perhaps in the future their communications with us might be revealed. This general point, obviously speculative but possibly accurate, recurred in the testimony of other witnesses as well. Bickel orally and Hegarty in the brief he later wrote about it conceded that this argument might have some substance, but not enough to overcome the First Amendment right to publish, especially because confidential diplomatic communications are in due course almost inevitably disclosed, whether in memoirs, other historical writings, or newspaper reports, and they are indeed often made public quite contemporaneously.

Asked to be more specific concerning his fears that other governments would now refuse to be intermediaries in our efforts to release prisoners held in North Vietnam, Doolin said that he thought that the Swedish government would be unlikely to help us further. Asked whether there was any communication with the Swedish government in the documents in issue in the case that would support his contention, Doolin answered, "To the best of my knowledge, no."

Doolin approached any degree of specificity in only two other instances. The documents contained references, he said, "to certain SEATO operational plans, Plan 5 in particular, which is still in existence." In fact, nowhere in the record was there any indication of the original date of the plan, or an explanation of how a plan at least three years old could, while "still in existence," be considered current, so that its revelation would benefit an enemy or potential enemy, given the obvious enormous changes that had been taking place in the military posture of the United States and its allies in Southeast Asia. Nor, again, was there any indication that these plans, while no doubt classified, were not so general as to be obvious, or so old and frequently bruited about as to be familiar.

Doolin's remaining attempt at specificity was to suggest that studies of the value of bombing targets in North Vietnam dating back not just three but four, five, or more years remained of interest and should not be revealed, because "some of them are still targets." When Gurfein remarked that he could not follow why it should still be of interest what targets were selected some years back, Doolin could only reply: "Again, Your Honor, I am trying to be helpful, you have to look at all this in the context of totality of the study, in terms of the decision process taking you into it, in terms of what we did in points of time as we went up in terms of our involvement, and it just gives the other side frankly one hell of a jump ahead."

In our sealed brief later submitted to the court, we argued that while Doolin was the government witness who exhibited the most familiarity with the documents in issue in the case, nothing in his testimony came close to meeting the demanding tests established in First Amendment case law to justify a prior restraint.

By this point in the case, all the lawyers—and sometimes Judge Gurfein himself—were referring to the Supreme Court's leading decision on prior restraint, the 1931 ruling in *Near v. Minnesota*, in a sort of shorthand. *Near* had struck down as unconstitutional a Minnesota statute that permitted injunctions against publications that were "malicious, scandalous, and defamatory." While Chief Justice Charles Evans Hughes's opinion emphasized that "the chief purpose" of the First Amendment was "to prevent previous restraints on publication," he did offer a few examples of what prior restraints *would* be allowed. "No one would question," he wrote, "but that a government might prevent the publication of the sailing dates of transports or the number and location of troops."

All sides quickly compressed the *Near* language into a single question critical to our case: was there an example of material in the Pentagon Papers akin to revelation of details about a "transport"? Or, as we distilled it still further, "Where's the troopship?"

* * *

[Judge Gurfein denied the government's petition to enjoin further publication of the Pentagon Papers but was reversed by the Second Circuit. When the case reached the Supreme Court, the government's position was argued by Solicitor General Erwin Griswold, former dean of the Harvard Law School. Professor Bickel delivered the oral argument for the *New York Times* and the other newspapers subject to injunction.]

Probably the highlight of Griswold's argument, at least for our side, was his clash with Justice Hugo Black. Black had long espoused the view that the First Amendment was an absolute and that when the framers had stated in the First Amendment that "Congress shall make no law ... abridging the freedom of speech or of the press," it meant *no* law at all. While that view had never been shared by a majority of the Court, it remained Black's strongly, almost religiously held belief. Griswold, however, took issue with Black's reading of the amendment: "Now Mr. Justice," he said, looking at Black, "your construction of that is well known, and I certainly respect it. You say that 'no law' means 'no law,' and that should be obvious. I can only say, Mr. Justice, that to me it is equally obvious that 'no law' does not mean 'no law,' and I would seek to persuade the Court that that is true."

This was probably the least persuasive challenge to Justice Black's views ever publicly expressed, and Black listened to it with evident delight. Bickel, who himself had no use for First Amendment absolutism, could have made a more nuanced argument far more gracefully and persuasively. If textual support was required from the language of the First Amendment itself, it would be far easier to maintain that the word "abridging" has considerable room for interpretation, or even (as Justice Scalia has argued) that the words "*the* freedom of speech" must be interpreted historically and not as we might otherwise read it today. The one approach that Griswold should not have taken was the very one he did: arguing that "no law" does not mean "no law."

* * *

Bickel's most critical answers, which were central to winning the case, came in response to a hypothetical question put by Justice Stewart:

> Q: Mr. Bickel, it is understandably and inevitably true that in a case like this, particularly when so many of the facts are under seal, it is necessary to speak in abstract terms, but let me give you a hypothetical case. Let us assume that when the members of the Court go back and open up this sealed record we find something there that absolutely convinces us that its disclosure would result in the sentencing to death of 100 young men whose only offense had been that they were 19 years old and had low draft numbers. What should we do?
>
> A: Mr. Justice, I wish there were a statute that covered it.
>
> Q: Well there is not. We agree, or you submit, and I am asking in this case what should we do.
>
> A: I am addressing a case of which I am as confident as I can be of anything that Your Honor will not find that when you get back to your chambers. It is a hard case. I think it would make bad separation of powers law. But it is almost impossible to resist the inclination not to let the information be published, of course.

Justice Stewart pursued Bickel anew:

> Q: As you know, and I am sure you do know, the concern that this Court has term after term with people who have been convicted and sentenced to death, convicted of extremely serious crimes in capital cases, and I am posing you a case where the disclosure of something in these files would result in the deaths of people who are guilty of nothing.
>
> A: You are posing me a case, of course, Mr. Justice, in which that element of my attempted definition which refers to the chain of causation—

Q: I suppose in a great big global picture this is not a national threat. There are at least 25 Americans killed in Vietnam every week these days.

A: No, sir, but I meant it is a case in which the chain of causation between the act of publication and the feared event, the death of these 100 young men, is obvious, direct, immediate.

Q: That is what I am assuming in my hypothetical case.

A: I would only say as to that that it is a case in which in the absence of a statute, I suppose most of us would say——

Q: You would say the Constitution requires that it be published, and that these men die, is that it?

A: No. I am afraid that my inclinations to humanity overcome the somewhat more abstract devotion to the First Amendment in a case of that sort.

There was much criticism of that answer in the civil liberties community and considerable concern expressed about it by post-argument *Times* journalists. The American Civil Liberties Union filed a rare postargument brief disowning Bickel's response and urging that the only danger that could justify a prior restraint would be to the nation itself, and not to some small subset of its population. In the years that have passed since the Pentagon Papers case, I have occasionally tried to formulate an answer that would fall somewhere between Bickel's and that of the ACLU. But looking back on it, I cannot escape the conclusion that Bickel's response was a required one. For when the tally was taken and we won by a 6–3 vote—"our" four plus justices Stewart and White—our victory was so tenuous that any slight change in the judicial calibration of the case might have deprived us of the additional votes we so desperately needed.

NEW YORK TIMES CO. v. UNITED STATES

Supreme Court of the United States, 1971.
403 U.S. 713, 91 S.Ct. 2140, 29 L.Ed.2d 822.

PER CURIAM.

We granted certiorari in these cases in which the United States seeks to enjoin the New York Times and the Washington Post from publishing the contents of a classified study entitled "History of U.S. Decision–Making Process on Viet Nam Policy."

"Any system of prior restraints of expression comes to this Court bearing a heavy presumption against its constitutional validity." *Bantam Books, Inc. v. Sullivan*, 372 U.S. 58, 70 (1963); see also *Near v. Minnesota ex rel. Olson*, 283 U.S. 697 (1931). The Government "thus carries a heavy burden of showing justification for the imposition of such a restraint." *Organization for a Better Austin v. Keefe*, 402 U.S. 415, 419 (1971). The District Court for the Southern District of New York in the *New York Times* case, 328 F.Supp. 324, and the District Court for the

District of Columbia and the Court of Appeals for the District of Columbia Circuit, 446 F.2d 1327, in the *Washington Post* case held that the Government had not met that burden. We agree.

The judgment of the Court of Appeals for the District of Columbia Circuit is therefore affirmed. The order of the Court of Appeals for the Second Circuit is reversed, 444 F.2d 544, and the case is remanded with directions to enter a judgment affirming the judgment of the District Court for the Southern District of New York. The stays entered June 25, 1971, by the Court are vacated. The judgments shall issue forthwith.

So ordered.

* * *

MR. JUSTICE BLACK, with whom MR. JUSTICE DOUGLAS joins, concurring.

I adhere to the view that the Government's case against the Washington Post should have been dismissed and that the injunction against the New York Times should have been vacated without oral argument when the cases were first presented to this Court. I believe that every moment's continuance of the injunctions against these newspapers amounts to a flagrant, indefensible, and continuing violation of the First Amendment. Furthermore, after oral argument, I agree completely that we must affirm the judgment of the Court of Appeals for the District of Columbia Circuit and reverse the judgment of the Court of Appeals for the Second Circuit for the reasons stated by my Brothers Douglas and Brennan. In my view it is unfortunate that some of my Brethren are apparently willing to hold that the publication of news may sometimes be enjoined. Such a holding would make a shambles of the First Amendment.

Our Government was launched in 1789 with the adoption of the Constitution. The Bill of Rights, including the First Amendment, followed in 1791. Now, for the first time in the 182 years since the founding of the Republic, the federal courts are asked to hold that the First Amendment does not mean what it says, but rather means that the Government can halt the publication of current news of vital importance to the people of this country.

In seeking injunctions against these newspapers and in its presentation to the Court, the Executive Branch seems to have forgotten the essential purpose and history of the First Amendment. When the Constitution was adopted, many people strongly opposed it because the document contained no Bill of Rights to safeguard certain basic freedoms.[5] They especially feared that the new powers granted to a central government might be interpreted to permit the government to curtail freedom

5. In introducing the Bill of Rights in the House of Representatives, Madison said: "(B)ut I believe that the great mass of the people who opposed (the Constitution), disliked it because it did not contain effectual provisions against the encroachments on particular rights * * *." 1 Annals of Cong. 433. Congressman Goodhue added: "(I)t is the wish of many of our constituents, that something should be added to the Constitution, to secure in a stronger manner their liberties from the inroads of power." *Id.*, at 426.

of religion, press, assembly, and speech. In response to an overwhelming public clamor, James Madison offered a series of amendments to satisfy citizens that these great liberties would remain safe and beyond the power of government to abridge. Madison proposed what later became the First Amendment in three parts, two of which are set out below, and one of which proclaimed: "The people shall not be deprived or abridged of their right to speak, to write, or to publish their sentiments; and the freedom of the press, as one of the great bulwarks of liberty, shall be inviolable."[6] The amendments were offered to curtail and restrict the general powers granted to the Executive, Legislative, and Judicial Branches two years before in the original Constitution. The Bill of Rights changed the original Constitution into a new charter under which no branch of government could abridge the people's freedoms of press, speech, religion, and assembly. Yet the Solicitor General argues and some members of the Court appear to agree that the general powers of the Government adopted in the original Constitution should be interpreted to limit and restrict the specific and emphatic guarantees of the Bill of Rights adopted later. I can imagine no greater perversion of history. Madison and the other Framers of the First Amendment, able men that they were, wrote in language they earnestly believed could never be misunderstood: 'Congress shall make no law * * * abridging the freedom * * * of the press * * *.' Both the history and language of the First Amendment support the view that the press must be left free to publish news, whatever the source, without censorship, injunctions, or prior restraints.

In the First Amendment the Founding Fathers gave the free press the protection it must have to fulfill its essential role in our democracy. The press was to serve the governed, not the governors. The Government's power to censor the press was abolished so that the press would remain forever free to censure the Government. The press was protected so that it could bare the secrets of government and inform the people. Only a free and unrestrained press can effectively expose deception in government. And paramount among the responsibilities of a free press is the duty to prevent any part of the government from deceiving the people and sending them off to distant lands to die of foreign fevers and foreign shot and shell. In my view, far from deserving condemnation for their courageous reporting, the New York Times, the Washington Post, and other newspapers should be commended for serving the purpose that the Founding Fathers saw so clearly. In revealing the workings of government that led to the Vietnam war, the newspapers nobly did precisely that which the Founders hoped and trusted they would do.

6. The other parts were:

"The civil rights of none shall be abridged on account of religious belief or worship, nor shall any national religion be established, nor shall the full and equal rights of conscience be in any manner, or on any pretext, infringed."

"The people shall not be restrained from peaceably assembling and consulting for their common good; nor from applying to the Legislature by petitions, or remonstrances, for redress of their grievances." 1 Annals of Cong. 434.

The Government's case here is based on premises entirely different from those that guided the Framers of the First Amendment. The Solicitor General has carefully and emphatically stated:

> "Now, Mr. Justice (Black), your construction of * * * (the First Amendment) is well known, and I certainly respect it. You say that no law means no law, and that should be obvious. I can only say, Mr. Justice, that to me it is equally obvious that 'no law' does not mean 'no law', and I would seek to persuade the Court that that is true. * * * (T)here are other parts of the Constitution that grant powers and responsibilities to the Executive, and * * * the First Amendment was not intended to make it impossible for the Executive to function or to protect the security of the United States."[7]

And the Government argues in its brief that in spite of the First Amendment, "[t]he authority of the Executive Department to protect the nation against publication of information whose disclosure would endanger the national security stems from two interrelated sources: the constitutional power of the President over the conduct of foreign affairs and his authority as Commander-in-Chief."[8]

In other words, we are asked to hold that despite the First Amendment's emphatic command, the Executive Branch, the Congress, and the Judiciary can make laws enjoining publication of current news and abridging freedom of the press in the name of "national security." The Government does not even attempt to rely on any act of Congress. Instead it makes the bold and dangerously farreaching contention that the courts should take it upon themselves to "make" a law abridging freedom of the press in the name of equity, presidential power and national security, even when the representatives of the people in Congress have adhered to the command of the First Amendment and refused to make such a law.[9] See concurring opinion of Mr. Justice Douglas, *post*, at 2145. To find that the President has "inherent power" to halt the publication of news by resort to the courts would wipe out the First Amendment and destroy the fundamental liberty and security of the very people the Government hopes to make "secure." No one can read the history of the adoption of the First Amendment without being convinced beyond any doubt that it was injunctions like those sought here that Madison and his collaborators intended to outlaw in this Nation for all time.

The word "security" is a broad, vague generality whose contours should not be invoked to abrogate the fundamental law embodied in the

7. Tr. of Oral Arg. 76.

8. Brief for the United States 13–14.

9. Compare the views of the Solicitor General with those of James Madison, the author of the First Amendment. When speaking of the Bill of Rights in the House of Representatives, Madison said: "If they (the first ten amendments) are incorporated into the Constitution, independent tribunals of justice will consider themselves in a peculiar manner the guardians of those rights; they will be an impenetrable bulwark against every assumption of power in the Legislative or Executive; they will be naturally led to resist every encroachment upon rights expressly stipulated for in the Constitution by the declaration of rights." 1 Annals of Cong. 439.

First Amendment. The guarding of military and diplomatic secrets at the expense of informed representative government provides no real security for our Republic. The Framers of the First Amendment, fully aware of both the need to defend a new nation and the abuses of the English and Colonial Governments, sought to give this new society strength and security by providing that freedom of speech, press, religion, and assembly should not be abridged. This thought was eloquently expressed in 1937 by Mr. Chief Justice Hughes—great man and great Chief Justice that he was—when the Court held a man could not be punished for attending a meeting run by Communists.

> "The greater the importance of safeguarding the community from incitements to the overthrow of our institutions by force and violence, the more imperative is the need to preserve inviolate the constitutional rights of free speech, free press and free assembly in order to maintain the opportunity for free political discussion, to the end that government may be responsive to the will of the people and that changes, if desired, may be obtained by peaceful means. Therein lies the security of the Republic, the very foundation of constitutional government."[10]

* * *

MR. JUSTICE STEWART, with whom MR. JUSTICE WHITE joins, concurring.

* * *

Undoubtedly Congress has the power to enact specific and appropriate criminal laws to protect government property and preserve government secrets. Congress has passed such laws, and several of them are of very colorable relevance to the apparent circumstances of these cases. And if a criminal prosecution is instituted, it will be the responsibility of the courts to decide the applicability of the criminal law under which the charge is brought. Moreover, if Congress should pass a specific law authorizing civil proceedings in this field, the courts would likewise have the duty to decide the constitutionality of such a law as well as its applicability to the facts proved.

But in the cases before us we are asked neither to construe specific regulations nor to apply specific laws. We are asked, instead, to perform a function that the Constitution gave to the Executive, not the Judiciary. We are asked, quite simply, to prevent the publication by two newspapers of material that the Executive Branch insists should not, in the national interest, be published. I am convinced that the Executive is correct with respect to some of the documents involved. But I cannot say that disclosure of any of them will surely result in direct, immediate, and irreparable damage to our Nation or its people. That being so, there can under the First Amendment be but one judicial resolution of the issues before us. I join the judgments of the Court.

10. De Jonge v. Oregon, 299 U.S. 353, 365.

MR. JUSTICE BLACKMUN, dissenting.

* * *

Each provision of the Constitution is important, and I cannot subscribe to a doctrine of unlimited absolutism for the First Amendment at the cost of downgrading other provisions. First Amendment absolutism has never commanded a majority of this Court. See, for example, *Near v. Minnesota, ex rel. Olson*, 283 U.S. 697, 708 (1931), and *Schenck v. United States*, 249 U.S. 47, 52 (1919). What is needed here is a weighing, upon properly developed standards, of the broad right of the press to print and of the very narrow right of the Government to prevent. Such standards are not yet developed. The parties here are in disagreement as to what those standards should be. But even the newspapers concede that there are situations where restraint is in order and is constitutional. Mr. Justice Holmes gave us a suggestion when he said in *Schenck*,

> "It is a question of proximity and degree. When a nation is at war many things that might be said in time of peace are such a hindrance to its effort that their utterance will not be endured so long as men fight and that no Court could regard them as protected by any constitutional right." 249 U.S., at 52.

I therefore would remand these cases to be developed expeditiously, of course, but on a schedule permitting the orderly presentation of evidence from both sides, with the use of discovery, if necessary, as authorized by the rules, and with the preparation of briefs, oral argument, and court opinions of a quality better than has been seen to this point. In making this last statement, I criticize no lawyer or judge. I know from past personal experience the agony of time pressure in the preparation of litigation. But these cases and the issues involved and the courts, including this one, deserve better than has been produced thus far.

It may well be that if these cases were allowed to develop as they should be developed, and to be tried as lawyers should try them and as courts should hear them, free of pressure and panic and sensationalism, other light would be shed on the situation and contrary considerations, for me, might prevail. But that is not the present posture of the litigation.

The Court, however, decides the cases today the other way. I therefore add one final comment.

I strongly urge, and sincerely hope, that these two newspapers will be fully aware of their ultimate responsibilities to the United States of America. Judge Wilkey, dissenting in the District of Columbia case, after a review of only the affidavits before his court (the basic papers had not then been made available by either party), concluded that there were a number of examples of documents that, if in the possession of the Post, and if published, "could clearly result in great harm to the nation," and he defined "harm" to mean "the death of soldiers, the destruction of alliances, the greatly increased difficulty of negotiation with our enemies, the inability of our diplomats to negotiate * * *." I, for one, have now been able to give at least some cursory study not only to the affidavits, but to the material itself. I regret to say that from this examination I fear that Judge Wilkey's statements have possible foundation. I therefore share his concern. I hope that damage has not already been done. If, however, damage has been done, and if, with the Court's action today, these newspapers proceed to publish the critical documents and there results therefrom "the death of soldiers, the destruction of alliances, the greatly increased difficulty of negotiation with our enemies, the inability of our diplomats to negotiate," to which list I might add the factors of prolongation of the war and of further delay in the freeing of United States prisoners, then the Nation's people will know where the responsibility for these sad consequences rests.

[Each justice submitted either a concurring (six justices) or a dissenting (three justices) opinion. The six other opinions are omitted.]

THE INTELLIGENCE IDENTITIES PROTECTION ACT

(1999).

§ 421. PROTECTION OF IDENTITIES OF CERTAIN UNITED STATES UNDERCOVER INTELLIGENCE OFFICERS, AGENTS, INFORMANTS, AND SOURCES

(a) Disclosure of information by persons having or having had access to classified information that identifies covert agent

Whoever, having or having had authorized access to classified information that identifies a covert agent, intentionally discloses any information identifying such covert agent to any individual not authorized to receive classified information, knowing that the information disclosed so identifies such covert agent and that the United States is taking affirmative measures to conceal such covert agent's intelligence relationship to the United States, shall be fined under Title 18 or imprisoned not more than ten years, or both.

(b) Disclosure of information by persons who learn identity of covert agents as result of having access to classified information

Whoever, as a result of having authorized access to classified information, learns the identity of a covert agent and intentionally discloses any information identifying such covert agent to any individual not authorized to receive classified information, knowing that the information disclosed so identifies such covert agent and that the United States is taking affirmative measures to conceal such covert agent's intelligence relationship to the United States, shall be fined under Title 18 or imprisoned not more than five years, or both.

(c) Disclosure of information by persons in course of pattern of activities intended to identify and expose covert agents

Whoever, in the course of a pattern of activities intended to identify and expose covert agents and with reason to believe that such activities would impair or impede the foreign intelligence activities of the United States, discloses any information that identifies an individual as a covert agent to any individual not authorized to receive classified information, knowing that the information disclosed so identifies such individual and that the United States is taking affirmative measures to conceal such individual's classified intelligence relationship to the United States, shall be fined under Title 18 or imprisoned not more than three years, or both.

Questions

1) Does Madison's argument in the *Virginia Report* support Justice Black's claim in *New York Times v. United States* that with the passage of the First Amendment the "press was protected so that it could bare the secrets of government and inform the people?" How might one find in the First Amendment an unqualified right to criticize "public characters and measures" so as to make officials accountable to the electorate but no right to reveal classified documents for the purpose of promoting government accountability?

2) Does Justice Black's opinion in *New York Times v. United States* suggest that, had he been presented with a case raising the issue, he would have held the Intelligence Identities Protection Act to be a violation of the First Amendment? Is it possible to agree with what Justice Black says in *New York Times v. United States* and nevertheless believe that the federal government possesses the authority to punish persons who reveal the names of undercover intelligence agents? Does Madison's argument provide any basis for distinguishing the two cases?

BUCKLEY v. VALEO

Supreme Court of the United States, 1976.
424 U.S. 1, 96 S.Ct. 612, 46 L.Ed.2d 659.

[PER CURIAM.]

* * *

1. The $1,000 Limitation on Expenditures "Relative to a Clearly Identified Candidate"

Section 608(e)(1) provides that "(n)o person may make any expenditure ... relative to a clearly identified candidate during a calendar year which, when added to all other expenditures made by such person during the year advocating the election or defeat of such candidate, exceeds $1,000."[45] The plain effect of § 608(e)(1) is to prohibit all individuals,

45. The same broad definition of "person" applicable to the contribution limitations governs the meaning of "person" in § 608(e)(1). The statute provides some limited exceptions through various exclusions from the otherwise comprehensive definition of "expenditure." See § 591(f). The most important exclusions are: (1) "any

who are neither candidates nor owners of institutional press facilities, and all groups, except political parties and campaign organizations, from voicing their views "relative to a clearly identified candidate" through means that entail aggregate expenditures of more than $1,000 during a calendar year.

* * *

[T]he First Amendment right to " 'speak one's mind ... on all public institutions' " includes the right to engage in " 'vigorous advocacy' no less than 'abstract discussion.' " *New York Times Co. v. Sullivan*, 376 U.S., at 269, quoting *Bridges v. California*, 314 U.S. 252, 270 (1941), and *NAACP v. Button*, 371 U.S., at 429. Advocacy of the election or defeat of candidates for federal office is no less entitled to protection under the First Amendment than the discussion of political policy generally or advocacy of the passage or defeat of legislation.

It is argued, however, that the ancillary governmental interest in equalizing the relative ability of individuals and groups to influence the outcome of elections serves to justify the limitation on express advocacy of the election or defeat of candidates imposed by s 608(e)(1)'s expenditure ceiling. But the concept that government may restrict the speech of some elements of our society in order to enhance the relative voice of others is wholly foreign to the First Amendment, which was designed "to secure 'the widest possible dissemination of information from diverse and antagonistic sources,' " and " 'to assure unfettered interchange of ideas for the bringing about of political and social changes desired by the people.' " *New York Times Co. v. Sullivan, supra*, 376 U.S., at 266, 269, quoting *Associated Press v. United States*, 326 U.S. 1, 20 (1945) and *Roth v. United States*, 354 U.S., at 484. The First Amendment's protection against governmental abridgment of free expression cannot properly be made to depend on a person's financial ability to engage in public discussion.

* * *

2. Limitation on Expenditures by Candidates from Personal or Family Resources

The Act also sets limits on expenditures by a candidate "from his personal funds, or the personal funds of his immediate family, in connection with his campaigns during any calendar year." § 608(a)(1). These ceilings vary from $50,000 for Presidential or Vice Presidential

news story, commentary, or editorial distributed through the facilities of any broadcasting station, newspaper, magazine, or other periodical publication, unless such facilities are owned or controlled by any political party, political committee, or candidate," § 591(f)(4)(A), and (2) "any communication by any membership organization or corporation to its members or stockholders, if such membership organization or corporation is not organized primarily for the purpose of influencing the nomination for election, or election, of any person to Federal office," § 591(f)(4)(C). In addition, the Act sets substantially higher limits for personal expenditures by a candidate in connection with his own campaign, § 608(a), expenditures by national and state committees of political parties that succeed in placing a candidate on the ballot, §§ 591(i), 608(f), and total campaign expenditures by candidates, § 608(c).

candidates to $35,000 for senatorial candidates, and $25,000 for most candidates for the House of Representatives.

The ceiling on personal expenditures by candidates on their own behalf, like the limitations on independent expenditures contained in § 608(e)(1), imposes a substantial restraint on the ability of persons to engage in protected First Amendment expression. The candidate, no less than any other person, has a First Amendment right to engage in the discussion of public issues and vigorously and tirelessly to advocate his own election and the election of other candidates. Indeed, it is of particular importance that candidates have the unfettered opportunity to make their views known so that the electorate may intelligently evaluate the candidates' personal qualities and their positions on vital public issues before choosing among them on election day. Mr. Justice Brandeis' observation that in our country "public discussion is a political duty," *Whitney v. California*, 274 U.S. 357, 375 (1927) (concurring opinion), applies with special force to candidates for public office. Section 608(a)'s ceiling on personal expenditures by a candidate in furtherance of his own candidacy thus clearly and directly interferes with constitutionally protected freedoms.

The primary governmental interest served by the Act the prevention of actual and apparent corruption of the political process does not support the limitation on the candidate's expenditure of his own personal funds.

* * *

3. Limitations on Campaign Expenditures

Section 608(c) places limitations on overall campaign expenditures by candidates seeking nomination for election and election to federal office. Presidential candidates may spend $10,000,000 in seeking nomination for office and an additional $20,000,000 in the general election campaign. §§ 608(c)(1)(A), (B). The ceiling on senatorial campaigns is pegged to the size of the voting-age population of the State with minimum dollar amounts applicable to campaigns in States with small populations. In senatorial primary elections, the limit is the greater of eight cents multiplied by the voting-age population or $100,000, and in the general election the limit is increased to 12 cents multiplied by the voting-age population or $150,000. §§ 608(c)(1)(C), (D). The Act imposes blanket $70,000 limitations on both primary campaigns and general election campaigns for the House of Representatives with the exception that the senatorial ceiling applies to campaigns in States entitled to only one Representative. §§ 608(c)(1)(C)-(E). These ceilings are to be adjusted upwards at the beginning of each calendar year by the average percentage rise in the consumer price index for the 12 preceding months. § 608(d).

No governmental interest that has been suggested is sufficient to justify the restriction on the quantity of political expression imposed by § 608(c)'s campaign expenditure limitations. The major evil associated with rapidly increasing campaign expenditures is the danger of candidate dependence on large contributions. The interest in alleviating the corrupting influence of large contributions is served by the Act's contribution limitations and disclosure provisions rather than by § 608(c)'s campaign expenditure ceilings. The Court of Appeals' assertion that the expenditure restrictions are necessary to reduce the incentive to circumvent direct contribution limits is not persuasive.

* * *

The interest in equalizing the financial resources of candidates competing for federal office is no more convincing a justification for restricting the scope of federal election campaigns. Given the limitation on the size of outside contributions, the financial resources available to a candidate's campaign, like the number of volunteers recruited, will normally vary with the size and intensity of the candidate's support. There is nothing invidious, improper, or unhealthy in permitting such funds to be spent to carry the candidate's message to the electorate. Moreover, the equalization of permissible campaign expenditures might serve not to equalize the opportunities of all candidates, but to handicap a candidate who lacked substantial name recognition or exposure of his views before the start of the campaign.

The campaign expenditure ceilings appear to be designed primarily to serve the governmental interests in reducing the allegedly skyrocketing costs of political campaigns. Appellees and the Court of Appeals stressed statistics indicating that spending for federal election campaigns increased almost 300% Between 1952 and 1972 in comparison with a 57.6% rise in the consumer price index during the same period. Appellants respond that during these years the rise in campaign spending lagged behind the percentage increase in total expenditures for commercial advertising and the size of the gross national product. In any event, the mere growth in the cost of federal election campaigns in and of itself provides no basis for governmental restrictions on the quantity of campaign spending and the resulting limitation on the scope of federal campaigns. The First Amendment denies government the power to determine that spending to promote one's political views is wasteful, excessive, or unwise. In the free society ordained by our Constitution it is not the government, but the people individually as citizens and candidates and collectively as associations and political committees who must retain control over the quantity and range of debate on public issues in a political campaign.[65]

* * *

65. For the reasons discussed in Part III, *infra*, Congress may engage in public financing of election campaigns and may condition acceptance of public funds on an agreement by the candidate to abide by specified expenditure limitations. Just as a candidate may voluntarily limit the size of the contributions he chooses to accept, he may decide to forgo private fundraising and accept public funding.

KATHLEEN M. SULLIVAN, POLITICAL MONEY AND FREEDOM OF SPEECH

30 U.C. Davis L. Rev. 663 (1997).

I. The Law of Political Money

In our political system, political campaigns are generally funded with private money—the candidates' own resources plus contributions of individuals, political parties, and organized groups. The presidential campaign is an exception, funded publicly since the 1976 campaign. In our system, candidates also communicate primarily through entities that are privately owned—the print and electronic press that provide candidates free news coverage and opportunities for paid political advertisements. One could imagine alternate systems, such as public funding of parties and candidate elections or public ownership of the communications media, but such systems are not our own, nor likely to be our own any time soon.

In the 1976 *Buckley* decision, the Court held that restrictions on political spending implicate freedom of speech. Invalidating some portions of the post-Watergate amendments to the Federal Elections Campaign Act but upholding others, the Court held that contributions to a candidate could constitutionally be limited, but expenditures could not, except as a condition of receiving public funds. Thus, after *Buckley*, candidates may spend all they want, unless they are presidential candidates who have taken public money; so may political parties, individuals, and organized groups such as political action committees (PACs)—as long as they act independently of the candidate. But direct donations to a candidate's campaign may be limited in amount. Under current federal law, an individual is limited in each election to contributing one thousand dollars to a candidate, five thousand dollars to a PAC, and twenty thousand dollars to a national party, and must keep the grand total to twenty-five thousand dollars. PACs may give only five thousand dollars to a candidate, five thousand dollars to another PAC, and fifteen thousand dollars to a national party. Political parties, too, face spending limits when they contribute to the campaigns of their candidates, though these are higher than those for PACs.

The split regime of *Buckley* thus authorizes government to limit the supply of political money, but forbids it to limit demand. Why the distinction? Contributions, the Court said, implicate lesser speech interests; they merely facilitate or associate the contributor with speech. They also raise the specter of "corruption" or the appearance of corruption—that is, the danger of a quid pro quo. Expenditures, the Court said, are more directly expressive, and involve no corruption—a candidate cannot corrupt herself, and those who spend independently of the candidate's campaign cannot reasonably expect a pay-back. Nor, held the Court, could spending limits be justified by the alternative rationale of equalizing political speaking power, because that rationale, the Court said, is "wholly foreign to the First Amendment." Thus, the Court held, the only way government may bring about political expenditure limits is through a quid pro quo of its own: government may induce a candidate to accept expenditure limits in exchange for public subsidies.

Various cogent criticisms have been leveled at the contribution/expenditure distinction. First, both contributions and expenditures may equally express political opinions. As Justice Thomas wrote last summer:

> Whether an individual donates money to a candidate or group who will use it to promote the candidate or whether the individual spends the money to promote the candidate himself, the individual seeks to engage in political expression and to associate with like-minded persons. A contribution is simply an indirect expenditure.[17]

This argues for protecting both expenditures and contributions alike. Second, an "independent" expenditure may inspire just as much gratitude by the candidate as a direct contribution. This argues for regulating them both alike. Finally, it has been objected, it is unclear why expenditure limits may be induced with carrots if they may not be compelled with sticks. This argues for precluding private expenditure limits even as a condition of public subsidies.

These inconsistencies arise from the *Buckley* Court's attempt to solve an analogical crisis by splitting the difference. *Buckley* involved nothing less than a choice between two of our most powerful traditions: equality in the realm of democratic polity, and liberty in the realm of political speech. The Court had to decide whether outlays of political money more resemble voting, on the one hand, or political debate, on the other. The norm in voting is equality: one person, one vote. The norm in political speech is negative liberty: freedom of exchange, against a backdrop of unequal distribution of resources (it has been said that freedom of the press belongs to those who own one). Faced with the question of which regime ought to govern regulation of political money, the Court in effect chose a little of both. It treated campaign contributions as more like voting, where individual efforts may be equalized, and campaign expenditures as more like speech, where they may not.

II. Leading Reform Proposals

Currently on the table are three types of reform proposals to impose new restrictions on political money. One advocates further limiting campaign contributions. The second proposes more conditioning of benefits upon corresponding "voluntary" limits on private spending. The third would place outright restrictions on campaign expenditures. The first two seek to operate within the *Buckley* framework; the third would overrule *Buckley* in part.

The first type of reform proposal would "close loopholes" in the existing regulatory scheme by extending the reach of contribution limits. For example, there are currently no restrictions on contribution "bun-

17. [Colorado Republican Fed. Campaign Comm. v. FEC, 518 U.S. 604, 638 (1996)].

dling" by intermediaries. One political entrepreneur may collect several individual contributions of one thousand dollars each and turn over the entire sum to the candidate, PAC, or party—taking political credit for a much larger amount than she personally could have contributed. Some reform proposals, such as McCain–Feingold, would treat such "bundled" contributions as contributions by the intermediary, and therefore subject to the otherwise applicable contribution limits. In other words, no more bundling.

Other such proposals would impose contribution limits on so-called "soft money"—those sums that now may be given without limit by individuals, PACs, and even corporations and labor unions (who are forbidden to give directly to candidates) to political parties for purposes of grass-roots "party-building" activities. Since the 1988 campaign, use of soft money to finance de facto campaign advertisements has proliferated. Advertisements celebrating one's party, its stand on issues, or the accomplishments of its leadership, after all, do serve to build party loyalty; but to the untutored eye, they may be difficult to distinguish from campaign ads. The same is true of soft money ads attacking the other party. The amount of soft money raised by the two major parties combined has increased from $89 million in 1992 to $107 million in 1994 to roughly $250 million in 1996. Some reform proposals, again including McCain–Feingold, would limit soft money contributions. The Democratic National Committee has announced its intention to limit annual soft money contributions from an individual, corporation, or union to one hundred thousand dollars, and President Clinton said that the Democratic Party would stop taking any soft money if the Republicans would do the same.

Would such new contribution limits be constitutional under the *Buckley* regime? Any limit on party expenditures of soft money would likely be struck down by the current Court in light of its recent decision that political parties may make unlimited independent expenditures on behalf of a particular candidate.[25] But limits on contributions, under *Buckley*, are another matter. The Court has previously upheld ceilings on individual contributions to PACs on the ground that such restrictions prevent end runs around limits on contributions to candidates.[26] Bundling and soft money contribution limits might be defended along similar lines, although they also raise novel and questionable burdens on the right of association.

The second category of reform proposal would find new means to use public funds or other public benefits to induce candidates to agree to "voluntary" spending limits—a practice that *Buckley* held constitutional, at least as to full public financing of presidential campaigns. Extending

25. See Colorado Republican Campaign Comm. v. FEC, 518 U.S. 604 (1996) (invalidating limits on independent expenditures by political parties).

26. See California Med. Ass'n v. FEC, 453 U.S. 182, 197–98 (1981) (upholding $5000 limit on contributions to multi-candidate committees because without such limits, contribution limits upheld in Buckley "could be easily evaded").

full public funding with attached spending limits from presidential to congressional campaigns would be the most obvious version of such reform, but is probably politically infeasible. Some proposals seek to offer smaller carrots, including ones that would not directly incur public expense. For example, the McCain–Feingold Senate bill would extract from broadcasters free and discounted broadcast time. The bill would in turn give the time, as well as postage discounts, to those Senate candidates who complied with specified spending limits.[28] California's Proposition 208 would give free space in the ballot statement and allow higher contributions to candidates who adopted spending limits.[29]

Such proposals too raise First Amendment questions despite the public funding ruling in *Buckley*. For example, while a private funding ban might reasonably further the goal of full public financing of an election—in order to level the playing field—it is hardly clear that private spending limits are equally justified by the relatively trivial communications subsidies proposed in these bills. And of course, the broadcasters might object to the extraction of "free" air time as an unconstitutional compulsion of speech.[30]

The third, most dramatic type of proposal would overrule the expenditure holding in *Buckley* and permit spending limits outright. Since the current Court seems quite uninterested in overruling Buckley, the most plausible vehicle for such a reform would be some type of constitutional amendment. Most advocates of such a reform support an amendment authorizing Congress to reimpose expenditure limits as under the pre-*Buckley* status quo, while leaving the authority to impose contribution limits intact.

III. The Political Theory of Campaign Finance Reform, or the Supposed Seven Deadly Sins of Political Money

What political theory supports arguments for campaign finance reform? Arguments for greater limits on political contributions and expenditures typically suggest that any claims for individual liberty to

28. See S. 25, SS 101–104 (setting forth benefits for political candidates who limit their campaign expenditures).

29. See Cal. Gov't Code § 85600 (West Supp. 1997). Section 85600 was enacted by the California Political Reform Act of 1996, Proposition 208.

30. Compelled carriage of unwanted speech normally triggers strict First Amendment scrutiny. See Pacific Gas & Elec. Co. v. Public Utils. Comm'n, 475 U.S. 1, 20–21 (1986) (invalidating forced inclusion of environmentalist statements in public utility's billing envelope). The Court does not apply strict scrutiny where the government's reason for the compulsion bears no relation to the content of the compelled speech. See Turner Broadcasting Sys., Inc. v. FCC, 512 U.S. 622, 641–42 (1994) (reviewing content-neutral law requiring cable operators to carry unwanted broadcast stations under intermediate scrutiny). Broadcasters, however, have been held subject to compelled carriage requirements that would be unconstitutional if applied to non-broadcast speakers. Compare Red Lion Broadcasting Co. v. FCC, 395 U.S. 367, 400–01 (1969) (upholding mandatory reply obligations applicable to broadcasters), with Miami Herald Pub. Co. v. Tornillo, 418 U.S. 241, 256 (1974) (invalidating mandatory reply obligations applicable to newspapers). With the obsolescence of the spectrum scarcity argument on which Red Lion was premised, it is unclear whether broadcasters would have a compelled-speech objection to the extraction of free or discounted air time for candidates as a condition of their receipt of public licenses.

spend political money ought yield to an overriding interest in a well-functioning democracy. But what is meant by democracy here? The answer is surprisingly complex; several distinct arguments that democracy requires campaign finance limits are often lumped together. I will try to disaggregate them and critically assess each one. The reformers might be said to have identified seven, separate, supposedly deadly sins of unregulated political money.

A. *Political Inequality in Voting*

The first argument for campaign finance limits is that they further individual rights to political equality among voters in an election. This argument starts from the principle of formal equality of suffrage embodied in the one person, one vote rule that emerged from the reapportionment cases.[31] Each citizen is entitled to an equal formal opportunity, ex ante, to influence the outcome of an election. Moreover, each person's vote is inalienable; it may not be traded to others for their use, nor delegated to agents. Literal vote-buying is regarded as a paradigm instance of undemocratic conduct. We no longer countenance gifts of turkeys or bottles of liquor to voters on election day, nor the counting of dead souls. These qualities of voting distinguish the electoral sphere from the marketplace, where goods and services, unlike votes, are fungible, commensurable, and tradeable.

Reformers often proceed from the premise of equal suffrage in elections to the conclusion that equalization of speaking power in electoral campaigns is similarly justifiable in furtherance of democracy. The most radical of such proposals would bar expenditures of private campaign funds altogether, and limit candidates to spending public funds allocated to each voter equally in the form of vouchers that could be used solely for election-related speech. The principle here would be one person, one vote, one dollar.

More commonly, however, the analogy to voting is meant to be suggestive, not literal; few go so far as to say that campaign finance limits are constitutionally compelled, as equipopulous districts are. Nor do most advocates of campaign finance reform argue for literal equality in electoral expenditures; the asserted right to equal political influence on the outcome of electoral campaigns is usually depicted as aspirational. But reformers argue that the goal of equal citizen participation in elections at least helps to justify campaign finance limits as constitutionally permissible. On this view, campaign finance amounts to a kind of shadow election, and unequal campaign outlays amount to a kind of metaphysical gerrymander by which some votes count more than others in that shadow election.

Such arguments from formal equality of the franchise to campaign finance restrictions, however, often fail to articulate a crucial intermedi-

31. See Reynolds v. Sims, 377 U.S. 533, 561–68 (1964) (holding that state's legislative apportionment scheme violates Equal Protection Clause); Baker v. Carr, 369 U.S. 186, 208–37 (1962) (concluding that such claims of equal protection violations are justiciable).

ate step: that political finance sufficiently resembles voting as to be regulable by the equality norms that govern voting. There is an alternative possibility: that political finance more resembles political speech than voting. That is the analogy drawn by the *Buckley* Court, at least with respect to expenditures. The choice of analogy is crucial. In the formal realm of voting—like other formal governmental settings, such as legislative committee hearings and trials in court—speech may be constrained in the interest of the governmental function in question. For example, at a town meeting, *Robert's Rules of Order* govern to ensure that orderly discussion may take place; at a trial, witnesses testify not to all they know but to what they are asked about, subject to rules of evidence and the constraints of relevant rights of the parties. Likewise, one voter does not get ten votes merely because he feels passionately about a candidate or issue.

By contrast, in the informal realm of political speech—the kind that goes on continuously between elections as well as during them—conventional First Amendment principles generally preclude a norm of equality of influence. Political speakers generally have equal rights to be free of government censorship, but not to command the attention of other listeners. Under virtually any theory of the justification for free speech, legislative restrictions on political speech may not be predicated on the ground that the political speaker will have too great a communicative impact, or his competitor too little. Conventional First Amendment norms of individualism, relativism, and antipaternalism preclude any such affirmative equality of influence—not only as an end-state but even as an aspiration. Indeed, such equality of participation as speakers in political debate is foreign even under the more collectivist approach to political speech outlined by Alexander Meiklejohn, who famously noted that the First Amendment "does not require that, on every occasion, every citizen shall take part in public debate.... What is essential is not that everyone shall speak, but that everything worth saying shall be said."[35]

A few perceptive reform advocates have noticed this problem and sought to fill in the missing step—the analogy between political finance and voting that would make equality norms relevant to both. For example, Ronald Dworkin, who largely accepts arguments for unfettered political speech in other contexts, rests his argument for campaign finance limits on the proposition that the right to equal participation as voters must be understood to entail a corollary right to equal participation as advocates in the electoral campaigns that precede and determine the vote:

> Citizens play two roles in a democracy. As voters they are, collectively, the final referees or judges of political contests. But they also participate, as individuals, in the contests they collectively judge:

35. Alexander Meiklejohn, Free Speech and Its Relation to Self-Government 25 (1948).

> they are candidates, supporters, and political activists; they lobby and demonstrate for and against government measures, and they consult and argue about them with their fellow citizens.... (W)hen wealth is unfairly distributed and money dominates politics, ... though individual citizens may be equal in their vote and their freedom to hear the candidates they wish to hear, they are not equal in their own ability to command the attention of others for their own candidates, interests, and convictions.[36]

In other words, formal equality of voting power implies a corollary right to equality in the opportunity to speak out in politics—at least in the particular subset of political speech that is made in connection with electoral campaigns.

But what are the boundaries of an electoral campaign? Dworkin does not suggest that equalization of speaking power is a satisfactory justification for limitations of political speech in other contexts. Yet his own examples belie any easy distinction between the formal realm of electoral discourse, which he would regulate, and the informal realm of ongoing political discourse, which he presumably would not. For example, he lists "lobbying" and "demonstrations" as examples of relevant forms of citizen participation. But lobbying and demonstrations could not, without great alteration in ordinary First Amendment understandings, be regulated on the ground that their leaders had amassed too many resources. Further, elections are seamlessly connected to the informal political debates that continue in the periods between them. The more electoral campaign speech is continuous with such ordinary informal political discourse, the less campaign finance resembles voting, and the more it partakes of a realm of inevitable inequality.

The reformers might answer that the equality principle could be confined to speech made expressly by candidates or their committees during formal electoral campaigns, defined by reference to some particular period in relation to elections. But now practical difficulties arise even as analytical difficulties subside. Such an approach would leave unregulated advocacy that redounds to the benefit of candidates by persons, parties, and organizations independent of them. To the extent such independent speech operates as a substitute for express candidate speech—even if an imperfect one—the principle of equality of voter participation advanced by the limits on formal campaign expenditures will be undermined.

An alternate response by reformers might be to question conventional First Amendment principles generally, and to assert political equality as a justification for regulating a wide range of informal political discourse. Such an approach raises large questions that go beyond the topic here. The key point for now is simply that, short of major revision of general First Amendment understandings, campaign finance reform

36. Ronald Dworkin, The Curse of American Politics, N.Y. Rev. Books, Oct. 17, 1996, at 19, 23.

may not be predicated on equality of citizen participation in elections unless electoral speech can be conceptually severed from informal political discourse. But formal campaign speech has so many informal political substitutes that this proposition is difficult to sustain.

B. Distortion

A second argument against unregulated private campaign finance is related to the first, but focuses less on individual rights than on collective consequences. This argument says that the unequal deployment of resources in electoral campaigns causes the wrong people to get elected, distorting the true preferences of voters. Good candidates who cannot surmount the high financial barriers to entry never get to run, and the choice among those who do is influenced by spending power that is not closely correlated to the popularity of the candidate's ideas. On this view, unequal funding leads both candidates and voters to misidentify the electorate's actual preferences and intensities of preference.

The Supreme Court has accepted such an argument as sufficient to justify some administrative burdens on the deployment of political money. In *Austin v. Michigan Chamber of Commerce*,[40] the Court upheld a state requirement that corporations (except nonprofit corporations organized solely for ideological purposes[41]) make political expenditures solely from separate segregated political funds, not from their general treasuries.[42] The Court reasoned that the government's interest in preventing the "distortion" of the apparent strength of political preferences justified such a segregation requirement.[43] A corporation that spent, for political purposes, money raised for investment purposes, would make it appear that there was more enthusiasm for the ideas it backed than was warranted. Funds raised for expressly political purposes and segregated in a separate political fund or corporate PAC, by contrast, would represent a more accurate proxy for the popularity of the ideas they supported.

Campaign finance reformers would extend this antidistortion principle beyond the particular problems of the corporate form at issue in *Austin*. They suggest that the ability to amass political funds in general does not correlate closely with voter preferences. Rather, the unequal distribution of campaign resources leads to misrepresentation of constituents' actual preferences and intensities of preference. The wealthy (or

40. 494 U.S. 652 (1990).

41. See FEC v. Massachusetts Citizens for Life, Inc., 479 U.S. 238, 256–65 (1986) (invalidating funding segregation requirement for ideological corporations formed for political purposes).

42. Similar federal requirements govern corporations and labor unions. Since 1907, corporations have been barred from spending corporate treasury funds in federal election campaigns, and, since 1947, so have labor unions. See 2 U.S.C. § 441b (1994) (prohibiting use of general funds). Thus, separate political funds are their only vehicle for contribution. See *Id.* (allowing use of segregated funds). Since enactment of the 1974 FECA amendments, even government contractors have been permitted to form segregated political funds. See *Id.* § 441c(b) (permitting government contractors to establish and use separate funds).

43. See Austin, 494 U.S. at 657–60 (examining reasons behind state regulation of corporate expenditures).

those who are good at fund-raising) can spend more money on a candidate they care relatively little about than can the poor (or those who are inept at fundraising) on a candidate to whom they are passionately committed. To the extent such "distorted" campaign speech influences voting, candidates will be elected and platforms endorsed that differ from what voters would otherwise choose.

This argument has both practical and conceptual difficulties. First, a candidate's ability to attract funds is at least to some extent an indicator of popularity. Money may flow directly in response to the candidate's ideas or indirectly in response to the candidate's popularity with others as reflected in poll numbers and the like. To the extent that fundraising accurately reflects popularity, the reformers exaggerate the degree of distortion. Second, there are limits to how far private funding can permit a candidate to deviate from positions acceptable to the mass of noncontributing voters: the free press will to some extent correct information provided in the candidate's advertisements, and polls will discipline the candidate to respond to preferences other than those of his wealthiest backers.

A third and deeper problem is that the concept of "distortion" assumes a baseline of "undistorted" voter views and preferences. But whether any such thing exists exogenously to political campaigns is unclear. Popular attitudes about public policy do not exist in nature, but are formed largely in response to cues from political candidates and party leaders. Moreover, the institutional press—itself owned by large corporations commanding disproportionate power and resources—plays a large role in shaping public opinion. Any attempt to equalize campaign spending would still leave untouched any "distortion" from the role of the press.

C. *Corruption, or Political Inequality in Representation*

A third argument for limiting political contributions and expenditures is often made under the heading of fighting political "corruption." This is a misnomer. Properly understood, this argument is a variation on the political inequality argument. But unlike the first argument above, it focuses not on the unequal influence of voters on elections, but on the elected legislators' unequal responsiveness to different citizens once in office. The charge against unregulated political money here is that it makes citizens unequal not in their ability to elect the candidates of their choice, but in their ability to affect legislative outcomes.

The Court in *Buckley* held contribution limits permissible to prevent "corruption" or the appearance of corruption of legislators by contributors of significant sums. Popular rhetoric about political money often employs similar metaphors: polls show substantial majorities who say that Congress is "owned" by special interests or "for sale" to the highest bidder. It is important to note, however, that the "corruption" charged here is not of the Tammany Hall variety. There is no issue of personal inurement; the money is not going into candidates' pockets but into television advertisements, the earnings of paid political consultants, and various other campaign expenses that increase the chances of election or reelection. This is true a fortiori for expenditures made independent of the candidate's campaign.

The claimed harm here is not, as the term "corruption" misleadingly suggests, the improper treatment of public office as an object for market exchange, but a deviation from appropriate norms of democratic representation. Officeholders who are disproportionately beholden to a minority of powerful contributors, advocates of finance limits say, will shirk their responsibilities to their other constituents, altering decisions they otherwise would have made in order to repay past contributions and guarantee them in the future. Thus, properly understood, the "corruption" argument is really a variant on the problem of political equality: unequal outlays of political money create inequality in political representation.

Again, the difficulties with the argument are both practical and conceptual. First, political money is not necessarily very effective in securing political results. The behavior of contributors provides some anecdotal support: Many corporate PACs, to borrow Judge Posner's phrase, are "political hermaphrodites";[50] they give large sums to both major parties. This hedging strategy suggests a weak level of confidence in their ability to obtain results from any particular beneficiary of their contributions.

President Clinton captured the same point at a press conference where he said that he gives major donors an opportunity for "a respectful hearing" but not a "guaranteed result." While this comment might elicit skepticism, the proposition that campaign donations are a relatively unreliable investment has empirical support. Various studies of congressional behavior suggest that contributions do not strongly affect congressional voting patterns, which are for the most part dominated by considerations of party and ideology. Of course, such evidence may be countered by noting that contributors may be repaid in many ways besides formal floor votes—for example, by relatively invisible actions in agenda-setting and drafting in committees. Furthermore, the few votes that are dominated by contributions may occur when there is the greatest divergence between contributors' and other constituents' interests. Still, the case that contributions divert representative responsiveness is at best empirically uncertain, and not a confident basis for limiting political speech.

A second and deeper problem with the "corruption" argument, once it is properly recast as an argument about democratic representation, is conceptual. The argument supposes that official action should respond to the interests of all constituents, or to a notion of the public good apart from the aggregation of interests, but, in any event, not to the interests

50. LaFalce v. Houston, 712 F.2d 292, 294 (7th Cir. 1983), cert. denied, 464 U.S. 1044 (1984).

of a few by virtue of their campaign outlays. But legislators respond disproportionately to the interests of some constituents all the time, depending, for example, on the degree of their organization, the intensity of their interest in particular issues, and their capacity to mobilize votes to punish the legislator who does not act in their interests. On one view of democratic representation, therefore, there is nothing wrong with private interest groups seeking to advance their own ends through electoral mobilization and lobbying, and for representatives to respond to these targeted efforts to win election and reelection. It is at least open to question why attempts to achieve the same ends through amassing campaign money are more suspect, at least in the absence of personal inurement.

But the question whether disproportionate responsiveness to contributors is ultimately consistent with democratic representation need not be answered to see the problem with the reformers' argument. That problem is that selecting one vision of good government is not generally an acceptable justification for limiting speech, as campaign finance limits do. Rather, what constitutes proper representation is itself the most essentially contested question protected by freedom of speech. The ban on seditious libel, the protection of subversive advocacy, and the general hostility to political viewpoint discrimination illustrate that free speech, under current conceptions, protects debates about what constitutes proper self-government from ultimate settlement by legislatures. To be sure, legislatures are often permitted or compelled to select among democratic theories, or to privilege one version of representation over its competitors in setting up the formal institutions of government. "One person, one vote," for example, privileges egalitarian conceptions over various alternatives—such as the inegalitarian representation provided by the United States Senate. But the right to speak—and, it might be added, to petition—includes the right to challenge any provisional settlement a legislature might make of the question of what constitutes appropriate democratic representation.

In other words, the "anticorruption" argument for campaign finance reform claims the superiority of a particular conception of democracy as a ground for limiting speech. As a result, it runs squarely up against the presumptive ban on political viewpoint discrimination. Campaign finance reformers necessarily reject pluralist assumptions about the operation of democracy and would restrict speech in the form of political money to foster either of two alternative political theories. First, they might be thought to favor a Burkean or civic republican view, in which responsiveness to raw constituent preferences of any kind undermines the representative's obligation to deliberate with some detachment about the public good. Alternatively, they might be thought to favor a populist view in which the representative ought be as close as possible to a transparent vehicle for plebiscitary democracy, for the transmission of polling data into policy. Either way, they conceive democracy as something other than the aggregation of self-regarding interests, each of which is free to seek as much representation as possible. But surely the endorsement of civic republicanism or populism—or any other vision of democracy—may not normally serve as a valid justification for limiting speech. Legislators may enforce an official conception of proper self-government through a variety of means, but not by prohibiting nonconforming expression.

Campaign finance reformers might object that, after all, campaign finance limits in no way stop would-be pluralists from advocating pluralism, but only from practicing it. The utterances being silenced are performative, not argumentative. Such a response, however, is in considerable tension with a long tradition of First Amendment protection for symbolic and associative conduct.[58] A further objection might be that this argument extends only to legislative campaign finance reform, and not to a constitutional amendment such as Senator Bradley and others have proposed. That is surely correct, as an amendment could obviously revise the existing First Amendment conceptions on which the argument rests. But, apart from general reasons to tread cautiously in amending the Constitution, it might well be thought especially risky to attempt by amendment to overrule a constitutional decision that is part of the general fabric of First Amendment law, as the anomaly created by the new amendment might well have unanticipated effects on other understandings of free speech.

D. Carpetbagging

A fourth strand of the reform argument is a variant of the third, with special reference to geography. Except in presidential elections, we vote in state or local constituencies. The fundamental unit of representation is geographic. But money travels freely across district and state lines. Thus, political money facilitates metaphysical carpetbagging. Contributions from or expenditures by nonconstituent individuals and groups divert a legislator's representation away from the constituents in his district and toward nonconstituents, whether they are foreign corporations or national lobbies. Various reform proposals seek to limit carpetbagging by localizing funding: McCain–Feingold, for example, would require candidates not only to limit expenditures but also to raise a minimum percentage of contributions from residents of their home state in order to receive public benefits, such as broadcast and postage discounts.

Again, this seeks to decide by legislation a question of what constitutes proper representation. To some, it might be legitimate for a legislator to consider the views of national lobbies. For example, those lobbies might share strong overlapping interests with her own constituents. Or the legislator might conceive her obligation as running to the nation as well as a particular district. For the reasons just given, a privileged theory of what constitutes proper political representation

58. See generally United States v. O'Brien, 391 U.S. 367 (1968) (addressing draft-card burning); NAACP v. Button, 371 U.S. 415 (1963) (addressing constitutionality of Virginia statute limiting litigation rights).

cannot serve as an adequate ground for limitation of speech, for free speech is itself the central vehicle for debating that very question.

E. Diversion of Legislative and Executive Energies

A fifth critique of the current role of political money, made often by politicians themselves and sometimes elaborated as an argument for campaign reform, is that fundraising takes too much of politicians' time. Many think that incumbents spend so much time fundraising that governance has become a part-time job.

This argument supposes a sharp divide between the public activity of governing and the private role of fundraising. But this distinction is hardly clear. The "marketing" involved in fundraising consists principally of conveying and testing response to information about past and future policy positions. How this differs from the standard material of all political campaigning is unclear, and it may well be continuous with governing. If the need for fundraising were eliminated, legislators would still have to nurture their constituencies in various ways between elections. Some might think that nurturing grass roots is a more wholesome activity than nurturing fat cats; but in that case, the diversion of energies problem simply collapses back into the problem of inequality in political representation discussed earlier. To the extent the candidate makes secret promises to PACs or wealthy individuals that would be unpopular with the mass of the electorate, there are strong practical limits to such strategies, such as the danger of press exposure and constituent retaliation.

However serious the problem of incursion on the candidate's time might be, one thing is clear: the split regime of *Buckley* exacerbates it. Contribution limits mean that a candidate has to spend more time chasing a larger number of contributors than she would have to do if contributions could be unlimited in amount. Concern about time, therefore, may involve a tradeoff with concern about disproportionate influence.

F. Quality of Debate

A sixth critique of the unregulated outlay of political money arises on the demand side rather than the supply side. The problem, in a word, is television. Where does all this political money go? The biggest expense is the cost of purchasing advertising time on television (though increasingly, political consultants take a hefty share). The critics regard repetitious, sloganeering spot advertisements as inconsistent with the enlightened rational deliberation appropriate to an advanced democracy. It is not clear what golden age of high-minded debate they hark back to; the antecedent of the spot ad is, after all, the bumper sticker. Nonetheless, these critics clearly aspire to something wiser and better. Ronald Dworkin's lament is representative: "The national political 'debate' is now directed by advertising executives and political consultants and conducted mainly through thirty-second, 'sound bite' television and radio commercials that are negative, witless, and condescending." Political expenditure limits, some suggest, would cut off the supply of oxygen to this spectacle and force candidates into less costly but more informative venues such as written materials and town hall debates.

To the extent this rationale for campaign finance reform is made explicit, it would appear flatly precluded by conventional First Amendment antipaternalism principles. Permitting limitations on speech because it is too vulgar or lowbrow would wipe out a good many pages of U.S. Reports. Surely a judgment that speech is too crass or appeals to base instincts is a far cry from *Robert's Rules of Order* or other principles of ordered liberty consistent with government neutrality toward the content of speech.

In any event, the indirect means of limiting expenditures may not do much to solve this problem. Why not directly ban political advertising on television outright? Then everyone could campaign on smaller budgets. British politicians, for example, are barred from taking out paid spots on the airwaves. But Britain has strong parties and small districts; we have neither. Banning television advertising in our political culture would impair politicians', especially challengers', ability to reach large masses of the electorate. Banning television advertisements might make us more republican, but it is hardly clear that it would make us more democratic. Moreover, the special First Amendment dispensation the Court has shown for broadcast regulation is increasingly tenuous, and has not been extended to other, increasingly competitive media. To be fully effective, a ban on television advertising might have to extend to cable and the internet, where the constitutional plausibility of regulation is even more dubious.

G. Lack of Competitiveness

Finally, a last argument would locate the key problem in current campaign finance practices in the advantage it confers on incumbents over challengers. Here the claim is that a healthy democracy depends on robust political competition and that campaign finance limits are needed to "level the playing field."The reformers contend that unfettered political money confers an anticompetitive advantage upon incumbents. This advantage arises because incumbents participate in current policymaking that affects contributors' interests. Thus, they enjoy considerable fundraising leverage while in office, and indeed, incumbents received on average four times as much in contributions than challengers in the 1996 congressional election. This incumbent advantage, reformers argue, limits turnover and makes challengers less effective at monitoring and checking incumbents' responsiveness. It is no accident that, for such reasons, some prominent supporters of campaign finance reform, such as Republican Senator Fred Thompson of Tennessee, a cosponsor of the McCain–Feingold bill, are also prominent supporters of term limits.

But there is some practical reason to think this argument gets the competitiveness point backwards. Campaign finance limits themselves may help to entrench incumbents in office. Incumbency confers enormous nonfinancial advantages: name recognition, opportunity to deliver benefits, publicity from the free press, and the franking privilege. To offset these advantages, challengers must amass substantial funds. Challengers' lack of prominence may make it more difficult for them to raise funds from large numbers of small donations. They may therefore depend more than incumbents on concentrated aid from parties, ideologically sympathetic PACs, or even wealthy individual private backers. Of course, once again, contribution limits under the split regime of *Buckley* exacerbate the problem, as incumbents are more likely to be able to raise a large number of capped contributions than challengers can.

The effect of regulation or nonregulation on the competitiveness of elections is a difficult empirical question. But any prediction that campaign regulation will increase electoral competitiveness and turnover is, by virtue of its very empirical uncertainty, at least a questionable ground for limiting political speech.

Question

Notice how much Madison's argument in the *Virginia Report* emphasizes the right of suffrage and how he links that right with the First Amendment. Does his argument in this respect have any implications for the question addressed in *Buckley v. Valeo* whether candidates for office have a First Amendment right to spend unlimited amounts of money on their campaigns?

TEXAS v. JOHNSON

Supreme Court of the United States, 1989.
491 U.S. 397, 109 S.Ct. 2533, 105 L.Ed.2d 342.

JUSTICE BRENNAN delivered the opinion of the Court.

After publicly burning an American flag as a means of political protest, Gregory Lee Johnson was convicted of desecrating a flag in violation of Texas law. This case presents the question whether his conviction is consistent with the First Amendment. We hold that it is not.

I

While the Republican National Convention was taking place in Dallas in 1984, respondent Johnson participated in a political demonstration dubbed the "Republican War Chest Tour." As explained in literature distributed by the demonstrators and in speeches made by them, the purpose of this event was to protest the policies of the Reagan administration and of certain Dallas-based corporations. The demonstrators marched through the Dallas streets, chanting political slogans and stopping at several corporate locations to stage "die-ins" intended to dramatize the consequences of nuclear war. On several occasions they spray-painted the walls of buildings and overturned potted plants, but

Johnson himself took no part in such activities. He did, however, accept an American flag handed to him by a fellow protestor who had taken it from a flagpole outside one of the targeted buildings.

The demonstration ended in front of Dallas City Hall, where Johnson unfurled the American flag, doused it with kerosene, and set it on fire. While the flag burned, the protestors chanted: "America, the red, white, and blue, we spit on you." After the demonstrators dispersed, a witness to the flag burning collected the flag's remains and buried them in his backyard. No one was physically injured or threatened with injury, though several witnesses testified that they had been seriously offended by the flag burning.

Of the approximately 100 demonstrators, Johnson alone was charged with a crime. The only criminal offense with which he was charged was the desecration of a venerated object in violation of Tex.Penal Code Ann. § 42.09(a)(3) (1989).[11] After a trial, he was convicted, sentenced to one year in prison, and fined $2,000. The Court of Appeals for the Fifth District of Texas at Dallas affirmed Johnson's conviction, 706 S.W.2d 120 (1986), but the Texas Court of Criminal Appeals reversed, 755 S.W.2d 92 (1988), holding that the State could not, consistent with the First Amendment, punish Johnson for burning the flag in these circumstances.

* * *

The First Amendment literally forbids the abridgment only of "speech," but we have long recognized that its protection does not end at the spoken or written word. While we have rejected "the view that an apparently limitless variety of conduct can be labeled 'speech' whenever the person engaging in the conduct intends thereby to express an idea," *United States v. O'Brien*, [391 U.S. 367, 376 (1968)] we have acknowledged that conduct may be "sufficiently imbued with elements of communication to fall within the scope of the First and Fourteenth Amendments," [*Spence v. Washington*, 418 U.S. 405, 409 (1974)].

In deciding whether particular conduct possesses sufficient communicative elements to bring the First Amendment into play, we have asked whether "[a]n intent to convey a particularized message was present, and [whether] the likelihood was great that the message would be understood by those who viewed it." 418 U.S., at 410–411. Hence, we have recognized the expressive nature of students' wearing of black armbands to protest American military involvement in Vietnam, *Tinker*

11. Texas Penal Code Ann. § 42.09 (1989) provides in full:

"§ 42.09. Desecration of Venerated Object

"(a) A person commits an offense if he intentionally or knowingly desecrates:

"(1) a public monument; "(2) a place of worship or burial; or

"(3) a state or national flag.

"(b) For purposes of this section, 'desecrate' means deface, damage, or otherwise physically mistreat in a way that the actor knows will seriously offend one or more persons likely to observe or discover his action.

"(c) An offense under this section is a Class A misdemeanor."

v. Des Moines Independent Community School Dist., 393 U.S. 503, 505 (1969); of a sit-in by blacks in a "whites only" area to protest segregation, *Brown v. Louisiana,* 383 U.S. 131, 141–142 (1966); of the wearing of American military uniforms in a dramatic presentation criticizing American involvement in Vietnam, *Schacht v. United States,* 398 U.S. 58 (1970); and of picketing about a wide variety of causes, see, *e.g., Food Employees v. Logan Valley Plaza, Inc.,* 391 U.S. 308, 313–314 (1968); *United States v. Grace,* 461 U.S. 171, 176 (1983).

Especially pertinent to this case are our decisions recognizing the communicative nature of conduct relating to flags. Attaching a peace sign to the flag, *Spence, supra,* at 409–410, 94 S.Ct., at 2729–30; refusing to salute the flag, *Barnette,* 319 U.S., at 632; and displaying a red flag, *Stromberg v. California,* 283 U.S. 359, 368–369 (1931), we have held, all may find shelter under the First Amendment. See also *Smith v. Goguen,* 415 U.S. 566, 588 (1974) (White, J., concurring in judgment) (treating flag "contemptuously" by wearing pants with small flag sewn into their seat is expressive conduct). That we have had little difficulty identifying an expressive element in conduct relating to flags should not be surprising. The very purpose of a national flag is to serve as a symbol of our country; it is, one might say, "the one visible manifestation of two hundred years of nationhood." *Id.,* at 603 (Rehnquist, J., dissenting). Thus, we have observed:

> "[T]he flag salute is a form of utterance. Symbolism is a primitive but effective way of communicating ideas. The use of an emblem or flag to symbolize some system, idea, institution, or personality, is a short cut from mind to mind. Causes and nations, political parties, lodges and ecclesiastical groups seek to knit the loyalty of their followings to a flag or banner, a color or design." *Barnette, supra,* at 632. Pregnant with expressive content, the flag as readily signifies this Nation as does the combination of letters found in "America."

* * *

If there is a bedrock principle underlying the First Amendment, it is that the government may not prohibit the expression of an idea simply because society finds the idea itself offensive or disagreeable.

We have not recognized an exception to this principle even where our flag has been involved. In *Street v. New York,* 394 U.S. 576 (1969), we held that a State may not criminally punish a person for uttering words critical of the flag. Rejecting the argument that the conviction could be sustained on the ground that Street had "failed to show the respect for our national symbol which may properly be demanded of every citizen," we concluded that "the constitutionally guaranteed 'freedom to be intellectually ... diverse or even contrary,' and the 'right to differ as to things that touch the heart of the existing order,' encompass the freedom to express publicly one's opinions about our flag, including those opinions which are defiant or contemptuous." *Id.,* at 593, quoting *Barnette,* 319 U.S., at 642. Nor may the government, we have held, compel conduct that would evince respect for the flag. "To sustain the compulsory flag salute we are required to say that a Bill of Rights which guards the individual's right to speak his own mind, left it open to public authorities to compel him to utter what is not in his mind." *Id.,* at 634.

In holding in *Barnette* that the Constitution did not leave this course open to the government, Justice Jackson described one of our society's defining principles in words deserving of their frequent repetition: "If there is any fixed star in our constitutional constellation, it is that no official, high or petty, can prescribe what shall be orthodox in politics, nationalism, religion, or other matters of opinion or force citizens to confess by word or act their faith therein." *Id.,* at 642. In *Spence,* we held that the same interest asserted by Texas here was insufficient to support a criminal conviction under a flag-misuse statute for the taping of a peace sign to an American flag. "Given the protected character of [Spence's] expression and in light of the fact that no interest the State may have in preserving the physical integrity of a privately owned flag was significantly impaired on these facts," we held, "the conviction must be invalidated." 418 U.S., at 415. See also *Goguen, supra,* 415 U.S., at 588 (White, J., concurring in judgment) (to convict person who had sewn a flag onto the seat of his pants for "contemptuous" treatment of the flag would be "[t]o convict not to protect the physical integrity or to protect against acts interfering with the proper use of the flag, but to punish for communicating ideas unacceptable to the controlling majority in the legislature").

In short, nothing in our precedents suggests that a State may foster its own view of the flag by prohibiting expressive conduct relating to it. To bring its argument outside our precedents, Texas attempts to convince us that even if its interest in preserving the flag's symbolic role does not allow it to prohibit words or some expressive conduct critical of the flag, it does permit it to forbid the outright destruction of the flag. The State's argument cannot depend here on the distinction between written or spoken words and nonverbal conduct. That distinction, we have shown, is of no moment where the nonverbal conduct is expressive, as it is here, and where the regulation of that conduct is related to expression, as it is here. In addition, both *Barnette* and *Spence* involved expressive conduct, not only verbal communication, and both found that conduct protected.

Texas' focus on the precise nature of Johnson's expression, moreover, misses the point of our prior decisions: their enduring lesson, that the government may not prohibit expression simply because it disagrees with its message, is not dependent on the particular mode in which one chooses to express an idea.[11] If we were to hold that a State may forbid

11. THE CHIEF JUSTICE's dissent appears to believe that Johnson's conduct may be prohibited and, indeed, criminally sanctioned, because "his act ... conveyed nothing that could not have been conveyed and was not conveyed just as forcefully in a dozen different ways." *Post,* at 2553. Not only does this assertion sit uneasily next to the dissent's quite correct reminder that the flag occupies a unique position in our society—which demonstrates that messages conveyed without use of the flag are not "just as forcefu[l]" as those conveyed with it—but it also ignores the fact that, in *Spence, supra,* we "rejected summarily" this very claim. See 418 U.S., at 411, n. 4.

flag burning wherever it is likely to endanger the flag's symbolic role, but allow it wherever burning a flag promotes that role—as where, for example, a person ceremoniously burns a dirty flag—we would be saying that when it comes to impairing the flag's physical integrity, the flag itself may be used as a symbol—as a substitute for the written or spoken word or a "short cut from mind to mind"—only in one direction. We would be permitting a State to "prescribe what shall be orthodox" by saying that one may burn the flag to convey one's attitude toward it and its referents only if one does not endanger the flag's representation of nationhood and national unity.

* * *

It is not the State's ends, but its means, to which we object. It cannot be gainsaid that there is a special place reserved for the flag in this Nation, and thus we do not doubt that the government has a legitimate interest in making efforts to "preserv[e] the national flag as an unalloyed symbol of our country." *Spence,* 418 U.S., at 412. We reject the suggestion, urged at oral argument by counsel for Johnson, that the government lacks "any state interest whatsoever" in regulating the manner in which the flag may be displayed. Tr. of Oral Arg. 38. Congress has, for example, enacted precatory regulations describing the proper treatment of the flag, see 36 U.S.C. § § 173–177, and we cast no doubt on the legitimacy of its interest in making such recommendations. To say that the government has an interest in encouraging proper treatment of the flag, however, is not to say that it may criminally punish a person for burning a flag as a means of political protest. "National unity as an end which officials may foster by persuasion and example is not in question. The problem is whether under our Constitution compulsion as here employed is a permissible means for its achievement." *Barnette,* 319 U.S., at 640.

We are fortified in today's conclusion by our conviction that forbidding criminal punishment for conduct such as Johnson's will not endanger the special role played by our flag or the feelings it inspires. To paraphrase Justice Holmes, we submit that nobody can suppose that this one gesture of an unknown man will change our Nation's attitude towards its flag. See *Abrams v. United States,* 250 U.S. 616, 628 (1919) (Holmes, J., dissenting). Indeed, Texas' argument that the burning of an American flag " 'is an act having a high likelihood to cause a breach of the peace,' " Brief for Petitioner 31, quoting *Sutherland v. DeWulf,* 323 F.Supp. 740, 745 (SD Ill.1971), and its statute's implicit assumption that physical mistreatment of the flag will lead to "serious offense," tend to confirm that the flag's special role is not in danger; if it were, no one would riot or take offense because a flag had been burned.

We are tempted to say, in fact, that the flag's deservedly cherished place in our community will be strengthened, not weakened, by our holding today. Our decision is a reaffirmation of the principles of freedom and inclusiveness that the flag best reflects, and of the conviction that our toleration of criticism such as Johnson's is a sign and source of our strength. Indeed, one of the proudest images of our flag, the one immortalized in our own national anthem, is of the bombardment it survived at Fort McHenry. It is the Nation's resilience, not its rigidity, that Texas sees reflected in the flag—and it is that resilience that we reassert today.

The way to preserve the flag's special role is not to punish those who feel differently about these matters. It is to persuade them that they are wrong. "To courageous, self-reliant men, with confidence in the power of free and fearless reasoning applied through the processes of popular government, no danger flowing from speech can be deemed clear and present, unless the incidence of the evil apprehended is so imminent that it may befall before there is opportunity for full discussion. If there be time to expose through discussion the falsehood and fallacies, to avert the evil by the processes of education, the remedy to be applied is more speech, not enforced silence." *Whitney v. California,* 274 U.S. 357, 377 (1927) (Brandeis, J., concurring). And, precisely because it is our flag that is involved, one's response to the flag burner may exploit the uniquely persuasive power of the flag itself. We can imagine no more appropriate response to burning a flag than waving one's own, no better way to counter a flag burner's message than by saluting the flag that burns, no surer means of preserving the dignity even of the flag that burned than by—as one witness here did—according its remains a respectful burial. We do not consecrate the flag by punishing its desecration, for in doing so we dilute the freedom that this cherished emblem represents.

V

Johnson was convicted for engaging in expressive conduct. The State's interest in preventing breaches of the peace does not support his conviction because Johnson's conduct did not threaten to disturb the peace. Nor does the State's interest in preserving the flag as a symbol of nationhood and national unity justify his criminal conviction for engaging in political expression. The judgment of the Texas Court of Criminal Appeals is therefore

Affirmed.

JUSTICE STEVENS, dissenting.

As the Court analyzes this case, it presents the question whether the State of Texas, or indeed the Federal Government, has the power to prohibit the public desecration of the American flag. The question is unique. In my judgment rules that apply to a host of other symbols, such as state flags, armbands, or various privately promoted emblems of political or commercial identity, are not necessarily controlling. Even if flag burning could be considered just another species of symbolic speech under the logical application of the rules that the Court has developed in its interpretation of the First Amendment in other contexts, this case has an intangible dimension that makes those rules inapplicable.

A country's flag is a symbol of more than "nationhood and national unity. It also signifies the ideas that characterize the society that has chosen that emblem as well as the special history that has animated the growth and power of those ideas. The fleurs-de-lis and the tricolor both symbolized 'nationhood and national unity,' but they had vastly different meanings. The message conveyed by some flags—the swastika, for example—may survive long after it has outlived its usefulness as a symbol of regimented unity in a particular nation."

So it is with the American flag. It is more than a proud symbol of the courage, the determination, and the gifts of nature that transformed 13 fledgling Colonies into a world power. It is a symbol of freedom, of equal opportunity, of religious tolerance, and of good will for other peoples who share our aspirations. The symbol carries its message to dissidents both at home and abroad who may have no interest at all in our national unity or survival.

The value of the flag as a symbol cannot be measured. Even so, I have no doubt that the interest in preserving that value for the future is both significant and legitimate. Conceivably that value will be enhanced by the Court's conclusion that our national commitment to free expression is so strong that even the United States as ultimate guarantor of that freedom is without power to prohibit the desecration of its unique symbol. But I am unpersuaded. The creation of a federal right to post bulletin boards and graffiti on the Washington Monument might enlarge the market for free expression, but at a cost I would not pay. Similarly, in my considered judgment, sanctioning the public desecration of the flag will tarnish its value—both for those who cherish the ideas for which it waves and for those who desire to don the robes of martyrdom by burning it. That tarnish is not justified by the trivial burden on free expression occasioned by requiring that an available, alternative mode of expression—including uttering words critical of the flag, see *Street v. New York,* 394 U.S. 576 (1969)—be employed.

It is appropriate to emphasize certain propositions that are not implicated by this case. The statutory prohibition of flag desecration does not "prescribe what shall be orthodox in politics, nationalism, religion, or other matters of opinion or force citizens to confess by word or act their faith therein." *West Virginia Board of Education v. Barnette,* 319 U.S. 624, 642 (1943). The statute does not compel any conduct or any profession of respect for any idea or any symbol.

Nor does the statute violate "the government's paramount obligation of neutrality in its regulation of protected communication." *Young v. American Mini Theatres, Inc.,* 427 U.S. 50, 70 (1976) (plurality opinion). The content of respondent's message has no relevance whatsoever to the case. The concept of "desecration" does not turn on the substance of the message the actor intends to convey, but rather on whether those who view the *act* will take serious offense. Accordingly, one intending to convey a message of respect for the flag by burning it in a public square might nonetheless be guilty of desecration if he knows that others—perhaps simply because they misperceive the intended message—will be seriously offended. Indeed, even if the actor knows that all possible witnesses will understand that he intends to send a message of respect, he might still be guilty of desecration if he also knows that this understanding does not lessen the offense taken by some of those witnesses. Thus, this is not a case in which the fact that "it is the speaker's opinion that gives offense" provides a special "reason for according it constitutional protection," *FCC v. Pacifica Foundation,* 438 U.S. 726, 745 (1978) (plurality opinion). The case has nothing to do with "disagreeable ideas." It involves disagreeable conduct that, in my opinion, diminishes the value of an important national asset.

The Court is therefore quite wrong in blandly asserting that respondent "was prosecuted for his expression of dissatisfaction with the policies of this country, expression situated at the core of our First Amendment values." Respondent was prosecuted because of the method he chose to express his dissatisfaction with those policies. Had he chosen to spray-paint—or perhaps convey with a motion picture projector—his message of dissatisfaction on the facade of the Lincoln Memorial, there would be no question about the power of the Government to prohibit his means of expression. The prohibition would be supported by the legitimate interest in preserving the quality of an important national asset. Though the asset at stake in this case is intangible, given its unique value, the same interest supports a prohibition on the desecration of the American flag.

The ideas of liberty and equality have been an irresistible force in motivating leaders like Patrick Henry, Susan B. Anthony, and Abraham Lincoln, schoolteachers like Nathan Hale and Booker T. Washington, the Philippine Scouts who fought at Bataan, and the soldiers who scaled the bluff at Omaha Beach. If those ideas are worth fighting for—and our history demonstrates that they are—it cannot be true that the flag that uniquely symbolizes their power is not itself worthy of protection from unnecessary desecration.

I respectfully dissent.

[A concurring opinion by JUSTICE KENNEDY and a dissenting opinion by CHIEF JUSTICE REHNQUIST are omitted.]

Questions

1) How, if at all, does Madison's argument in the *Virginia Report* bear on the dispute over flag burning that was addressed by the Supreme Court in *Texas v. Johnson*?

2) How might Madison's argument help one to think about *West Virginia State Board of Education v. Barnette*?

3) Rank order the following contentions in terms of how much Madison's argument in the *Virginia Report*, as elucidated by other writings of his, supports the First Amendment claim. Use (1) to designate the contention that gains the *most* support from Madison's argument and (4) the *least*.

a) A critic of the official conduct of a public official cannot be held liable for defamation unless she publishes a false statement of fact that injures the reputation of the official and does so with a high degree of awareness of the probable falsity of the factual statement.

b) Government cannot enjoin the publication of classified information, even when it relates to diplomatic or military matters, unless the trier of fact determines that the publication of the information will surely result in direct, immediate, and irreparable damage to the nation or its people.

c) Candidates for elective office are entitled to spend as much money on their campaigns as they can legally raise.

d) A person cannot be punished for desecrating an American flag that he lawfully possesses if he does so as a means of communicating a message to an audience, so long as the act of desecration causes no physical harm other than to the flag itself.

Explain the reasons for your rank ordering, with emphasis on the choices you consider to be the most and least supported by Madison's argument.

Additional Readings

The history of seditious libel

Philip Hamburger, The Development of the Law of Seditious Libel and the Control of the Press, 37 Stan. L. Rev. 661 (1985)

Frederick S. Siebert, Freedom of the Press in England 1476–1776 (1952)

The Zenger case

James Alexander, A Brief Narrative of the Case and Tryal of John Peter Zenger, Printer of the New–York Weekly Journal (Stanley Nider Katz, ed. 1972)

Eben Moglen, Considering *Zenger*: Partisan Politics and the Legal Profession in Provincial New York, 94 Colum. L. Rev. 1495 (1994)

Madison's political thought generally

James T. Kloppenberg, The Virtues of Liberalism, ch. 2 (1998)

Richard K. Mathews, If Men Were Angels: James Madison and the Heartless Empire of Reason (1995)

Drew R. McCoy, The Last of the Fathers: James Madison and the Republican Legacy (1989)

Jennifer Nedelsky, Private Property and the Limits of American Constitutionalism: The Madison Framework and Its Legacy (1990)

Thomas L. Pangle, The Spirit of Modern Republicanism: The Moral Vision of the American Founders and the Philosophy of Locke (1988)

Michael P. Zuckert, The Natural Rights Republic: Studies in the Foundations of the American Political Tradition (1996)

The General Assessment and the Memorial And Remonstrance

Thomas E. Buckley, Church and State in Revolutionary Virginia 1776–1787 (1977)

William Lee Miller, The First Liberty: America's Foundation in Religious Freedom (2d ed. 2003)

The Federalist Papers

Douglass Adair, Fame and the Founding Fathers (1974)

Samuel Beer, To Make a Nation: The Rediscovery of American Federalism, ch. 8–10 (1993)

David Epstein, The Political Theory of the Federalist (1984)

Morton White, Philosophy, The Federalist, and the Constitution (1987)

Gary Wills, Explaining America: The Federalist (1981)

The emergence of political parties

Lance Banning, The Jeffersonian Persuasion: Evolution of a Party Ideology (1978)

Robert M. Chesney, Democratic-Republican Societies, Subversion, and the Limits of Legitimate Dissent in the Early Republic, 82 N.C. L. Rev. 1525 (2004)

Noble E. Cunningham,Jr., The Jeffersonian Republicans: The Formation of Party Organization 1789–1801 (1957)

Richard Hofstadter, The Idea of a Party System (1969)

The Sedition Act controversy

James Morton Smith, Freedom's Fetters: The Alien and Sedition Laws and American Civil Liberties (1956)

The Virginia Report

Walter Berns, Freedom of the Press and the Alien and Sedition Laws: A Reappraisal, 1970 Supreme Court Review 106

William J. Watkins, Jr., Reclaiming the American Revolution: The Kentucky and Virginia Resolutions and Their Legacy (2004)

Madison's theory of rights

Knud Haakonssen, From Natural Rights to the Rights of Man: A European Perspective on American Debates, in A Culture of Rights (Michael J. Lacey and Knud Haakonssen ed. 1991)

Jack N. Rakove, The Madisonian Theory of Rights, 31 Wm & Mary L. Rev. 245 (1990)

New York Times v. Sullivan

Richard Epstein, Was *New York Times v. Sullivan Wrong*? 53 U. Chi. L. Rev. 782 (1986)

Anthony Lewis, *New York Times v. Sullivan* Reconsidered: Time to Return to the Central Meaning of the First Amendment, 83 Colum. L. Rev. 603 (1983)

Melville Nimmer, The Right to Speak from *Times* to *Time*: First Amendment Theory Applied to Libel and Misapplied to Privacy, 56 Calif. L. Rev. 935 (1968)

The Pentagon Papers case

David Rudenstine, The Day the Presses Stopped: A History of the Pentagon Papers Case (1996)

The Intelligence Identities Protection Act

Note, The Constitutionality of the Intelligence Identities Protection Act, 83 Colum. L. Rev. 727 (1983)

Campaign finance regulation

Lillian R. BeVier, Money and Politics: A Perspective on the First Amendment and Campaign Finance Reform, 73 Calif. L. Rev. 1045 (1985)

Richard A. Briffault, McConnell v. FEC and the Transformation of Campaign Finance Law, 3 Election L. J. 147 (2004)

Bradley A. Smith, Faulty Assumptions and Undemocratic Consequences of Campaign Finance Reform, 105 Yale L.J. 1049 (1996)

Symposium on Campaign Finance Reform, 94 Colum. L. Rev. 1125 (1994)

Flagburning

Kent Greenawalt, Fighting Words: Individuals, Communities, and Liberties of Speech, ch. 3 (1995)

Frank I. Michelman, Saving Old Glory: On Constitutional Iconography, 42 Stan. L. Rev. 1337 (1990)

Chapter Four

JOHN STUART MILL

BERNARD WISHY, INTRODUCTION

in Prefaces to Liberty: Selected Writings of John Stuart Mill (Bernard Wishy ed. 1959).

The story of Mill's career is inseparable from an account of the ceaseless reforming ferment of his age. Even to sketch Mill's life, one must try to explain what is sometimes called "the Victorian mind"—a bold phrase that, properly used, encompasses the most contradictory moral and intellectual tendencies. A full biography would have to deal as much with the life work of the other principal Victorian writers and European intellectuals of the time as with Mill's own ideas. Some of the important facts about his private life, however, can be separated from discussion of the spirit of his age and the development of his political ideas.

Mill was born in London in 1806. His father was James Mill, then a writer for periodicals, but after 1819 an assistant to the Examiner of Correspondence for the East India Company. He was also an important democratic reformer of the first third of the nineteenth century. John Mill, in his *Autobiography,* does not mention his mother even in connection with his birth. One gathers from other sources that she was, in the stock phrase, a good and kind woman, but completely pushed aside by her husband. James Mill might as well have been the only source of John's existence, for he was the dominating influence in his son's early life.

From all accounts, the child was an intellectual prodigy. Even considering the father's great effort to train his son to be a model of intellectual clarity and scholarliness, John's childhood achievements must ultimately be traced to his extraordinary natural gifts. The father kept the boy at home, close to his side, and laid out for him a systematic course of studies starting with the classics and arithmetic. In this age of soft pedagogics, we are stunned at a child reading Greek at three and Latin at eight. Yet John Mill speaks well of this early start in intellectual life. What is really upsetting about this famous father and son was the absence of spontaneous love and uncalculated tenderness in their relationship. Later in life John would bitterly regret his arid childhood and youth under his father's impatient taunts and demanding supervision. He would resent the affront to his emotions, to his "moral sentiments," and to his imagination implicit in his father's concentration on intellectual analysis. James Mill was not a cruel man; he was simply too self-disciplined and hostile to expressions of feeling to be able to show warmth and affection for his boy. Correction and catechism rather than loving concern were his usual habits with the child. John, as a result, was deeply devoted to his father but could not really love him.

What food for imagination there was in John's early years came from his books of history and biography and from those poets for whom James Mill had use. These books seem to have brought John the excitement and relief of belonging to "the other culture"—the land of imagination—of whose valuable place in education Lionel Trilling has spoken so well.

While John was still an infant, his father met the great philosopher Jeremy Bentham. From that time forward James Mill was the center of the various reform movements sponsored by Bentham's followers. Bentham had proposed that the archaic English law and chaotic public administration be made more rational, that they be based not on fictional justifications but on what he considered a scientific reckoning of pleasures and pains. Government was to aim at securing the greatest happiness for the greatest number; the test of all private and public actions was general happiness, not religious truth or abstract right. The Benthamites' attack on social abuses through the steps of investigation, propaganda, reform legislation, efficient administration, and honest inspection laid the basis for modern English political practice. Such work took up much of the public life of both Mills, and it was John Mill who helped give this influential philosophy its name, Utilitarianism.

The younger Mill's formal studies were supplemented by close acquaintance with the Benthamite world. He knew intimately Bentham himself and the brilliant economist, David Ricardo, among others. By the age of twelve Mill moved from the classics to the study of formal philosophy and economics. At fourteen he traveled abroad to France to live with Bentham's brother and to continue his education. At fifteen, back in London and anticipating a career at the bar, he studied law with the future great jurist and Benthamite, John Austin. At about the same time, he was introduced to the study of psychology. Recalling this awesome course of studies, Mill tells us that Sundays were not exceptions and that play with other children was frowned on. Yet sympathy for him should not obscure his intellectual achievement. Although this boyhood constantly at lessons helped bring on a severe neurotic condition at about the age of twenty, it also produced what was potentially one of the finest minds of the age.

In 1822, at about the age of seventeen, Mill became his father's assistant at the East India Company. The job, he claimed, gave him a strong sense of practical affairs and was a relief from intellectual labors.

By 1856 he had worked his way up to the second highest position in the organization. The famous books, the many pamphlets, the constant letters to the newspapers and journals, the reports, the book reviews—all those earlier writings for which Mill is remembered—were products of off-hours and spare moments, which, fortunately, were ample. From the very beginning of his clerkship, Mill was also writing, organizing, and campaigning for reform. Benthamism, he tells us, became his "religion" and the democratic reform of English society and government his principal objective. Study groups, editorial work, and debating societies were started before he was twenty. All this time, he continued his constant reading and devouring of ideas; the toll on his emotions was prohibitive.

In the fall of 1826, while in "a dull state of nerves," Mill asked himself: "Suppose that all your objects in life were realized; that all the changes in institutions and opinions which you are looking forward to could be completely effected at this very instant: would this be a great joy and happiness to you?" When he found himself answering "No," everything he had been taught to esteem collapsed. (Mill seems to have identified strongly with his father before his "mental crisis." Beyond that we can say very little about his unconscious mind.) The passages in the *Autobiography* describing his unhappiness are deeply moving. Mill believed that neither his friends nor his father could begin to understand his troubled state of mind, let alone counsel him. His description of what was wrong comes down to the starvation of his feelings. He first turned, as he had as a boy, to "the other culture," to "those memorials of past nobleness and greatness from which I had hitherto drawn strength and animation." These failed. Sentence after sentence in Mill's description of 1826–27 mentions "pleasure," only to note its absence in his life. His passions could no longer be satisfied by his goals.

Just as suddenly as this severe depression came on him, it lifted. Reading a moving passage in a book about the death of a father and the succession of his son to his powers, Mill began to weep. The tears helped him to recover; from that moment his burden grew lighter, and gradually the clouds withdrew. He decided that he could not live directly for the happiness of others (the Benthamite creed) or even deliberately for his own happiness. He looked instead for those goals in life that he found brought him happiness as a by-product. Mill's start on steady reading in the poetry of Wordsworth and Byron was a deliberate attempt to fulfill his sensual needs directly. These palliatives were helpful for the next four years, but they soon assumed second place to the influence of his future wife, Mrs. Harriet Taylor.

For the man called by Gladstone the "saint of rationalism," Mill's private life was extraordinarily marked by recurrent rebellions of his nonrational nature. Most powerful rationalists, however, are suppressed romantics. The boy's love of the splendor and glory of the ancient world, his delight in natural scenery, his great attraction to poetry, his "mental crisis"—all suggest that his passions demanded more than merely to serve his intellect and the great Benthamite cause of "utility." His relations with Mrs. Taylor intensified his pleasures in poetry and in the "cultivation of the feelings."

Mrs. Taylor had a "rich and powerful" nature; she was married to a well-to-do, admirable merchant. Mill was twenty-five when they met in 1830; Mrs. Taylor was a little younger. They quickly developed what Mill called "my most valuable friendship"; and for nearly twenty years Mr. Taylor made no moves toward divorce as the couple became deep friends and collaborators. Almost from the beginning Mill seems to have been in love with her and, soon, Mrs. Taylor with him. Yet such was the nature of the friendship that there is little reason to believe that the pair ever became lovers before marriage. The very fact that Mrs. Taylor was already married might have been attractive to Mill, saving him from accepting the sexual responsibilities of marriage. Nevertheless, as Mill and Mrs. Taylor gradually became linked together in the public eye, her husband's situation became impossible. Mrs. Taylor eventually separated from her husband; she continued to see him and to travel with him, but lived alone until Taylor died. Two years later, in 1851, she and Mill (then 45) were married.

Whatever the hidden and mixed motives that kept them together, there can be no doubt that the match was ideal and the marriage supremely happy. Harriet's sudden death in Avignon, in the south of France, in 1858 was a stunning blow to Mill and perhaps accounts for his elaborate praise of her virtues in his later works. What scholars cannot yet agree on is her precise intellectual influence on Mill. Although he extolls her virtues and her contributions to his writings, Mill says that she produced no revolution in his thought. She confirmed and strengthened his tendencies away from abstractions and rigid system toward a greater respect for the complexity of fact and an awareness of the attractions of competing intellectual possibilities. He alleges that she made him more skeptical about generalizations. She seems also to have stood somewhere behind such specific changes as Mill's lessened enthusiasm for democracy and his conversion to a quasi-socialism.

In 1858, the same year Harriet died, the East India Company was dissolved. Mill then chose to use all his time for his writing. For the next fifteen years, except for a three year service in Parliament, he was producing most of the major works in politics and philosophy for which he is remembered. He also maintained a large flow of letters, reviews, and articles. His worldwide reputation as a sensitive liberal intellectual had by now become so much the public mark of the man that George Eliot, the great novelist, expressed fears that he might lose his intellectual independence when he was nominated by the Liberals for Parliament in 1865.

His parliamentary career was, however, a fine and unusual one. He refused to run unless he were allowed to ignore party lines after election. Once in the House of Commons, he brought his great gifts into constant, although at first unpopular, use. His speech in favor of extending the suffrage to the working classes was called epochal, and he helped prevent working class violence, perhaps even revolution, during the agitation for wider suffrage in 1866. He also pushed along many of the Liberal reforms of the next few years and led what was in effect a filibuster against a government bill to close public parks to political meetings; the bill was not passed, and the now famous area for debating unpopular opinions in Hyde Park, London, was assured. Mill also introduced in Parliament for the first time provisions for proportional representation and votes for women.

Despite this record, Mill had made many Liberal and Tory enemies, and he was not re-elected. From 1868 on, he spent much time in Avignon in the company of his stepdaughter, Helen Taylor, who tried to take her mother's place as Mill's critic. Although he finished a number of essays, including the *Autobiography,* the only major piece he saw through publication was *The Subjection of Women,* an attack on those prejudices and laws that, in his opinion had kept Harriet Taylor from the public eminence he thought she deserved.

Mill died suddenly in May 1873 and was buried with his wife at Avignon.

Had Mill taken stock of England before he died, he would have noticed great changes in his lifetime. By extremely hard work and good luck, the English had created what was in effect a new civilization. Despite widespread misery and glaring social inequalities, England was a healthier, more democratic, and more humane society. Factory and city, although still grim and heartbreaking, had taught men new routines that promised future wealth and leisure. Conscious attempts to improve urban life were being made all over England. Police, fire service, better public and private sanitation, and street lighting were appearing everywhere. Free elementary education for all children was spreading and a national education act was passed by Parliament in 1870. Oxford and Cambridge had revised their curricula, had dropped their religious barriers, and were entering one of those brilliant ages that are recurrent in the history of great universities. Many new colleges, universities, and technical schools had also been founded. Religious tests for voting and for seats in Parliament had been removed.

Amid grave fears that democracy would prove a disaster, the urban working class had been given the right to vote in 1867. The modern party system, civil service, and dignified parliamentary procedure were well established. The corruption of public life had declined remarkably; indeed, administration had become so honest that English observers of the United States (then in the throes of the Grant administration scandals) seemed to assume that England had never known anything but a scrupulous regard for the general good among its political leaders and royal family. In short, by 1873, England had squeaked through to the beginning of modernity without social revolution. The middle-class reformers of John Stuart Mill's youth had achieved most of their principal objectives.

EUGENE AUGUST, JOHN STUART MILL: A MIND AT LARGE

(1975).

The meeting of Bentham and James Mill set up shock waves that reverberated down the century, but the immediate repercussions were felt in the fragile Mill household. Having concluded in disgust that his wife was as empty-headed as she was pretty, James installed himself as Bentham's lieutenant and heir-apparent, and spent considerable time away from home. His keen disappointment with his wife as intellectual companion could hardly have escaped the notice of wide-eyed little John, and may help to explain his own quest for a woman he considered his intellectual compeer. The domestic situation further deteriorated under the strain of increasing family size. In all, James fathered nine children—an alarming total for a man acquainted with the gloomy population prophet Thomas Malthus.

Bentham helped when he could. On the grounds of his house at No. 2 Queen Square Place was a cottage once occupied by no less a personage than John Milton. Into this shrine he shunted the Mills in 1810, but its general dankness soon drove them to higher ground at Newington Green.

WILLIAM THOMAS, MILL

(1985).

With the completion of the *Principles of Political Economy* the main elements in Mill's mature philosophy were fixed. His writings in the last phase of his life, from his marriage in 1851 to his death in 1873, elaborate themes he had sketched before 1850. Had he written nothing after the *Principles,* he might have been remembered as a solid theorist who after some uncertain forays into politics and literature had buried his youthful radicalism in two heavy works of philosophy and economics in conscious abandonment of any hope of acquiring a political following. In fact, his fame rests very largely on what he wrote in his last years, and the popular idea of him as the "saint of rationalism", the lonely and ascetic critic of Victorian complacency and convention, derives from On *Liberty* (1859), *Representative Government* (1861), and *The Subjection of Women* (1869). But for these works, it is quite likely that Mill would no longer be read outside the universities. Through them he became a household word. As they are the culmination of the earliest political thinking, we must first ask what makes them stand out from his earlier work.

Two major events helped produce a change of tone to something more urgent and polemical. The first was the French Revolution of 1848 and its aftermath, the shortlived Second Republic. For Mill this was not just a local event in a foreign country. France for him had, since his boyhood visit, been the country of his ideals, where social philosophy was more advanced and its opponents more readily identified than they were in England, where everything was befogged by compromise and goodwill. When Mill uses a phrase like "the best writers on the Continent" he almost always means French writers. So when the French Revolution broke out in February 1848 he became very excited, predicting that a French republic would have the effect of republicanizing all Europe "and England itself probably before we die." He admired the constitution of the Second Republic and defended it as "a digest of the elementary doctrines of representative democracy." While it flourished, he thought little of his own country. "The whole problem of modern society . . . will be worked out, as I have long thought it would, in France and nowhere else." And he added, "As for England, it is dead, vapid, left quite behind by all the questions now rising." Louis Napoleon's *coup d 'etat* in December 1852 was therefore a shock, the more so as it enlisted the peasantry and the mass of the middle classes against the liberal writers and theorists Mill so much admired. Thereafter Napoleon was for Mill the epitome of wickedness, "the most dangerous enemy of the future of humanity." More important, the sort of alliance which he represented, of brutal power, frightened respectability and mass ignorance, had to be held out as a warning to contemporaries. Mill had always disliked the Catholic Church; but now his remarks on the lower classes became sharper and more contemptuous; while the middle classes, reproached in the *Principles* for their heartless hedonism, are henceforth castigated for their mental complacency as well.

The other event was Mill's marriage to Harriet Taylor in April 1851. During their long friendship they had considered they were victims of the institution of marriage. Rumours that they were the objects of gossip only gave them a sense of superiority to the narrow standards of society around them. When John Taylor died in 1849, their own principles did not require them to marry, but they did, preserving their consistency with an enhanced contempt for the insipidity of ordinary society, and making up for the company they missed by saying they were above it. Not that they flouted the canons of respectability. Harriet in particular was deeply sensitive to any hint that her connection with Mill had been improper, and she laid a ban on any she suspected of gossip.

> Tocqueville is a notable specimen of the class which includes such people as the Sterlings, Romillys, Carlyles, Austins—the gentility class—weak in morals, narrow in intellect, timid, infinitely conceited, and gossiping. There are very few men in this country who can seem other than more or less respectable puppets to us.

The list, as Mill's biographer notes, included "almost every man Mill had ever liked." Mill's upbringing and education had given him an "instinct of closeness" and an idiom which it had taken him years of effort to turn into a style accessible to a wide readership. His marriage, instead of widening his circle further, probably increased his sense of isolation and confirmed his highly intellectual view of human life. Once he had felt that, while he had the intellect, others had the emotion without which intellect remained ineffective. Now he had both, and the consciousness made him much more complacent about his heritage, and much less receptive to correction from outside.

The extent of Harriet's influence on Mill has been much debated. Some writers treat his claim that some of his later works were their joint productions as literally true. Others, contrasting his magisterial clarity with her breathless, unpunctuated letters have claimed that she merely gave him back his own measured and qualified views in a more opinionated and dogmatic form. Probably a definitive conclusion is not possible. But one effect of her influence is fairly clear. She made him recast his entire conception of social justice. He was led by her feminism to see the major division in society to be not that of the labouring classes and their masters, but simply that of women and men. The dominion of men over women, he came to feel, was the last vestige of "the system of right founded on might"; women were "the subject-class ..., in a chronic state of bribery and intimidation combined." So the old division of society into the oppressors and oppressed was given a new lease of life and the political imagery of radical agitation revamped to fit the battle of the sexes. Mill recovered a motive for engaging in polemic, this time with the advantage of an established reputation as a philosopher and economist, whose scientific caution was beyond dispute.

Illness gave urgency to what he had to say. Mill had caught tuberculosis from his father and he seems to have given it to his wife. It was a common disease in Victorian England and it was thought to be fatal. Under its threat both showed great courage. The thought that most oppressed them was that they had works still to write which death might cut short. So they planned a series of essays to say what they had to say in a condensed form.... The essays were to be prefaced by "the Life," or what became the *Autobiography,* in which she wanted him to use his reputation to tell the world the truth about their relationship. In the event, Mill recovered his health with an extraordinary journey through France, Italy, and Greece, while Harriet's condition grew rapidly worse. The essay project was not completed. The only one which they were able to finish jointly before her death in 1858 was *On Liberty,* which Mill published the following year with a dedication to her memory. Their collaboration makes it in tone and manner quite unlike his other works.

These background factors explain *On Liberty's* desperate urgency of tone. It is much more condensed than most of his works. It compares in style with the finest of the essays of his prime, deploying a complex argument in clear, calm prose, varied by passages of plangent eloquence. It is in itself a striking example of one of Mill's themes, the need to consider the opposing point of view. In fact Mill sometimes sets out objections to his case more eloquently than he puts the case itself, which may account for the fact that his critics often borrow their points from him. But the central principle, that we are justified in interfering with an individual's actions if they are harming others, but not if we merely wish to do him good, is so forcibly and memorably argued that it has passed into the public philosophy of all the great Western democracies.

ALAN RYAN, INTRODUCTION

in Mill: A Norton Critical Edition (Alan Ryan ed. 1997).

On Liberty is Mill's best-known work. Unusual among his works, it is a manifesto for a single idea: "The object of this Essay is to assert one very simple principle as entitled to govern absolutely the dealings of society with the individual in the way of compulsion and control, whether the means used by physical force in the form of legal penalties, or the moral coercion of public opinion. That principle is, that the sole end for which mankind are warranted, individually or collectively, in interfering with the liberty of any of their number, is self-protection." It was written with a degree of passion unusual in Mill's other writings, and it has aroused passionate responses in its readers; some have felt it to be a noble piece of work but too demanding for ordinary mortals, others have felt it to be out of touch with the society it depicts, a work that pours kerosene on a bonfire, one whose influence has mostly been for the worse. Those academic commentators who have restrained their political emotions while keeping their critical capacities intact have generally been very puzzled by the connection between *On Liberty* and *Utilitarianism.* On the face of it, a Utilitarian should favor whatever interference with liberty does the most good; certainly, he should not favor an "absolute" prohibition on certain sorts of interference in advance of any inquiry into the good they might do. That Mill presumably knew this as well as anyone else makes their relationship all the more puzzling. Mill was in no doubt that *On Liberty* was to be a major part of his intellectual legacy. Exactly what sparked off the idea of writing it is slightly mysterious, however. This is a pity because it would be interesting to have a more precise knowledge of Mill's target. The essay itself has echoes of almost everything that Mill cared for: it attacks the hold of custom on human thinking as A *System of Logic* did; it urges reformers not to allow their benevolence to lead them to create a "nanny" society and thus sacrifice individuality and spontaneity, as the essays "Bentham" and "Coleridge," and the essays on Tocqueville's *Democracy in America* had done; it espouses a doctrine of progress that appears once more in *Representative Government;* and Tocqueville's fear that a democracy might become a society of "industrious sheep" animates the whole work and provides its coda. A thinker who is mentioned only once in the text, but who seems to have been present in Mill's mind throughout was Auguste Comte; Mill's attack on the "liberticide" implications of Comte's plans for the Positivist utopia culminated in his *Auguste Comte and Positivism* in 1865, but it was in his mind from the early 1850s. *On Liberty* was thus an essay attacking not only conservatives but misguided progressives. It was also addressed to himself. Mill, too, wanted social, political, and economic reform for the sake of human happiness and had the intellectual's usual conviction that he knew what would promote that happiness. So it was to himself as well as others that he addressed the demand that they recognize their fallibility, that they acknowledge the autonomy of other persons and their right to conduct their own lives in their own way.

* * *

Last, there should be no blinking at the fierceness of the demands that *On Liberty* makes on us. Mill did not urge us to do our own thing. Mill urged us to find the best and make that our own thing. It is, as has often been said, a defence of "aristocratic liberalism." It defends the right of the ordinary person to do as he or she chooses so long as nobody is harmed thereby, but the ultimate goal is less happiness than a life lived to the full. That is why it is so difficult to attach the usual labels to the essay; Mill is not quite a defender of classical ideals or quite a romantic, he is hostile to self-abnegation but not to self-discipline, he is hostile to those aspects of Christianity that encourage resignation but not to those that encourage the ambition to perfect our characters. He is as distinctive as the author of such a work should be.

JOHN SKORUPSKI, JOHN STUART MILL

(1989).

Mill's essay *On Liberty* gathers together the ruling preoccupations of a lifetime: individuality as one of the elements of well-being, liberty of thought and discussion, the limits to the authority of society over the individual. He described it in his *Autobiography* as

> a kind of philosophic textbook of a single truth, which the changes progressively taking place in modern society bring out into ever stronger relief: the importance, to man and society, of a large variety in types of character, and of giving full freedom to human nature to expand itself in innumerable and conflicting directions.

The lesson, he conceded, might seem unnecessary in a period "decidedly favourable to the development of new opinions". But he thought his time a time of transition, with the openness of such times. New orthodoxies would come to dominate social opinion, the more surely in a democratic and equal state. "It is then that the teachings of the *Liberty* will have their greatest value".

Much of what is most passionately felt in Mill's political philosophy is threaded on this strand—the idea of a society of human beings fully and variously developed, morally vigorous, self-determining. He epitomises the liberalism which achieved its clearest statement and purest influence in the heyday of the nineteenth century—between the Napoleonic period and the growth of big business, socialism and empire. But he deepens and broadens it into a system of thought which fuses maturity of historical and psychological insight with firm philosophical groundings. Liberalism found its philosopher in Mill: only someone with his particular range of intellectual qualities, and his steadfast clarity of character, could have driven so many windows onto its innermost commitments.

This classical liberalism of the nineteenth century was born—as Mill was, and as de Tocqueville was—in that century's early years, and matured in its first three decades. They were decades in which rational radicals were learning lessons from the excesses of Jacobinism in the French Revolution, and of Bonapartism after it; both seemed to them to be rooted in fallacies associated with the idea of popular sovereignty. They were also the decades of Romantic reaction against eighteenth-century enlightenment, bringing an unusual depth of debate about the relations between nature and history, civil society, the state, the self.

The liberal of this period consequently tempers ideals with an understanding of the dilemmas they create. He views democracy with some ambivalence. He is committed to equality of moral status, to the responsibility of each individual; so he must in principle support democratic government—"political" liberty—support it at least as an aspiration. However he pre-eminently cherishes "civil" liberty; he wishes, that is to say, to limit the authority of government—and not only of government but of society as such—over the individual. And he believes that the need to do so is particularly pressing under democratic government; he sees clearly the potential tension between political and civil liberty, between the "liberty of the ancients" and "the liberty of the moderns". Precisely this tension is at the centre of *On Liberty.*

Liberty of thought and discussion, the other main topic of the essay, gives rise to another—*the* other—liberal dilemma. The ideal of moral equality among self-determining individuals implies unrestricted liberty of criticism. At once, however, other elements in the liberal's scheme of priorities pull towards or away from it. Pulling away from it is his awareness that society needs beliefs and institutions which provide an enduring rallying point of allegiance and inspiration. How to reconcile legitimation and continuity with total liberty to criticise all sources of legitimation? Pulling towards it, on the other hand, is his fear of the pressure towards stagnant conformism, the bending and stunting of human potentialities, incessantly exerted by a democratic and equal state. Against this pressure he wishes to guarantee freedom of original and critical thought. But pulling away from it again is his fear of democracy's disregard for the authority of intelligence and balanced judgement; its tendency to bring representative mediocrity, or the politics of simple-minded causes, into unhealthy influence.

All these dangers could operate simultaneously. It could be that modern democracy chronically risks falling into a cycle of periods of cultural stagnation—Mill's "Chinese stationariness"—interrupted by brief phases of undiscriminating assault on its vital traditions and institutions: dominated in both phases by the intellectually second-rate but socially and politically effective.

These questions were all much in Mill's mind. After more than a century of social change it may seem clear that he greatly underestimated the pace of technical and scientific change, and the creative dynamism it would produce; nevertheless the questions remain central for liberal democracy still. No single text affords a complete picture of Mill's views on them; the essay *On Liberty*, which we are concerned with in this chapter, constitutes only a small part of his writings on politics. I am not implying that it diverges from the overall emphasis of these other writings—it is a careful statement of Mill's settled opinions. It deserves its prominence in political philosophy because it contains the philosophic essentials of Mill's liberalism; still it is directed to a particular audience, and emphasises those points which Mill thought it salutary to emphasise to that audience. It was written not for a period of crisis but for a period of normality, and hence responds to Mill's analysis of the normal or chronic dangers of an equal and democratic state. But when, for example, we read Mill's defence of liberty of expression we should not imagine that we are dealing with the opinions of someone to whom the dangers of an unchecked babble of critical voices had never occurred. Mill thought hard about those dangers, about the tensions between liberty of discussion, and authority and allegiance, and that fact must be remembered when we consider that his most extended discussion of the matter comes down so unambiguously for liberty of expression.

JOHN STUART MILL, ON LIBERTY

(1859).

CHAPTER I

INTRODUCTORY

The subject of this Essay is not the so-called Liberty of the Will, so unfortunately opposed to the misnamed doctrine of Philosophical Necessity; but Civil, or Social Liberty: the nature and limits of the power which can be legitimately exercised by society over the individual. A question seldom stated, and hardly ever discussed, in general terms, but which profoundly influences the practical controversies of the age by its latent presence, and is likely soon to make itself recognized as the vital question of the future. It is so far from being new, that, in a certain sense, it has divided mankind, almost from the remotest ages, but in the stage of progress into which the more civilized portions of the species have now entered, it presents itself under new conditions, and requires a different and more fundamental treatment.

The struggle between Liberty and Authority is the most conspicuous feature in the portions of history with which we are earliest familiar, particularly in that of Greece, Rome, and England. But in old times this contest was between subjects, or some classes of subjects, and the government. By liberty, was meant protection against the tyranny of the political rulers. The rulers were conceived (except in some of the popular governments of Greece) as in a necessarily antagonistic position to the people whom they ruled. They consisted of a governing One, or a governing tribe or caste, who derived their authority from inheritance or conquest; who, at all events, did not hold it at the pleasure of the governed, and whose supremacy men did not venture, perhaps did not desire, to contest, whatever precautions might be taken against its oppressive exercise. Their power was regarded as necessary, but also as highly dangerous; as a weapon which they would attempt to use against their subjects, no less than against external enemies. To prevent the weaker members of the community from being preyed upon by innumerable vultures, it was needful that there should be an animal of prey stronger than the rest, commissioned to keep them down. But as the king of the vultures would be no less bent upon preying upon the flock than any of the minor harpies, it was indispensable to be in a perpetual attitude of defence against his beak and claws. The aim, therefore, of patriots, was to set limits to the power which the ruler should be suffered to exercise over the community; and this limitation was what they meant by liberty. It was attempted in two ways. First, by obtaining a recognition of certain immunities, called political liberties or rights, which it was to be regarded as a breach of duty in the ruler to infringe, and which, if he did infringe, specific resistance, or general rebellion, was held to be justifiable. A second, and generally a later expedient, was the establishment of constitutional checks; by which the consent of the community, or of a body of some sort supposed to represent its interests, was made a necessary condition to some of the more important acts of the governing power. To the first of these modes of limitation, the ruling power, in most European countries, was compelled, more or less, to submit. It was not so with the second; and to attain this, or when already in some degree possessed, to attain it more completely, became everywhere the principal object of the lovers of liberty. And so long as mankind were content to combat one enemy by another, and to be ruled by a master, on condition of being guaranteed more or less efficaciously against his tyranny, they did not carry their aspirations beyond this point.

A time, however, came in the progress of human affairs, when men ceased to think it a necessity of nature that their governors should be an independent power, opposed in interest to themselves. It appeared to them much better that the various magistrates of the State should be their tenants or delegates, revocable at their pleasure. In that way alone, it seemed, could they have complete security that the powers of government would never be abused to their disadvantage. By degrees, this new demand for elective and temporary rulers became the prominent object of the exertions of the popular party, wherever any such party existed; and superseded, to a considerable extent, the previous efforts to limit the power of rulers. As the struggle proceeded for making the ruling power emanate from the periodical choice of the ruled, some persons began to think that too much importance had been attached to the limitation of the power itself. That (it might seem) was a resource against rulers whose interests were habitually opposed to those of the people. What was now wanted was, that the rulers should be identified with the people; that their interest and will should be the interest and will of the nation. The nation did not need to be protected against its own will. There was no fear of its tyrannizing over itself. Let the rulers be effectually responsible to it, promptly removable by it, and it could afford to trust them with power of which it could itself dictate the use to be made. Their power was but the nation's own power, concentrated, and in a form convenient for exercise. This mode of thought, or rather perhaps of feeling, was common among the last generation of European liberalism, in the Continental section of which, it still apparently predominates. Those who admit any limit to what a government may do, except in the case of such governments as they think ought not to exist, stand out as brilliant exceptions among the political thinkers of the Continent. A similar tone of sentiment might by this time have been prevalent in our own country, if the circumstances which for a time encouraged it had continued unaltered.

But, in political and philosophical theories, as well as in persons, success discloses faults and infirmities which failure might have concealed from observation. The notion, that the people have no need to limit their power over themselves, might seem axiomatic, when popular government was a thing only dreamed about, or read of as having existed at some distant period of the past. Neither was that notion necessarily disturbed by such temporary aberrations as those of the French Revolution, the worst of which were the work of an usurping few, and which, in any case, belonged, not to the permanent working of popular institutions, but to a sudden and convulsive outbreak against monarchical and aristocratic despotism. In time, however, a democratic republic came to occupy a large portion of the earth's surface, and made itself felt as one of the most powerful members of the community of nations; and elective and responsible government became subject to the observations and criticisms which wait upon a great existing fact. It was now perceived that such phrases as "self-government," and "the power of the people over themselves," do not express the true state of the case. The "people" who exercise the power, are not always the same people with those over whom it is exercised, and the "self-government" spoken of, is not the government of each by himself, but of each by all the rest. The will of the people, moreover, practically means, the will of the most numerous or the most active part of the people; the majority, or those who succeed in making themselves accepted as the majority; the people, consequently, may desire to oppress a part of their number; and precautions are as much needed against this, as against any other abuse of power. The limitation, therefore, of the power of government over individuals, loses none of its importance when the holders of power are regularly accountable to the community, that is, to the strongest party therein. This view of things, recommending itself equally to the intelligence of thinkers and to the inclination of those important classes in European society to whose real or supposed interests democracy is adverse, has had no difficulty in establishing itself; and in political speculations "the tyranny of the majority" is now generally included among the evils against which society requires to be on its guard.

Like other tyrannies, the tyranny of the majority was at first, and is still vulgarly, held in dread, chiefly as operating through the acts of the public authorities. But reflecting persons perceived that when society is itself the tyrant—society collectively, over the separate individuals who compose it—its means of tyrannizing are not restricted to the acts which it may do by the hands of its political functionaries. Society can and does execute its own mandates: and if it issues wrong mandates instead of right, or any mandates at all in things with which it ought not to meddle, it practises a social tyranny more formidable than many kinds of political oppression, since, though not usually upheld by such extreme penalties, it leaves fewer means of escape, penetrating much more deeply into the details of life, and enslaving the soul itself. Protection, therefore, against the tyranny of the magistrate is not enough; there needs protection also against the tyranny of the prevailing opinion and feeling; against the tendency of society to impose, by other means than civil penalties, its own ideas and practices as rules of conduct on those who dissent from them; to fetter the development, and, if possible, prevent the formation, of any individuality not in harmony with its ways, and compel all characters to fashion themselves upon the model of its own. There is a limit to the legitimate interference of collective opinion with individual independence; and to find that limit, and maintain it against encroachment, is as indispensable to a good condition of human affairs, as protection against political despotism.

But though this proposition is not likely to be contested in general terms, the practical question, where to place the limit—how to make the fitting adjustment between individual independence and social control—is a subject on which nearly everything remains to be done. All that makes existence valuable to any one, depends on the enforcement of restraints upon the actions of other people. Some rules of conduct, therefore, must be imposed, by law in the first place, and by opinion on many things which are not fit subjects for the operation of law. What these rules should be, is the principal question in human affairs; but if we except a few of the most obvious cases, it is one of those which least progress has been made in resolving. No two ages, and scarcely any two countries, have decided it alike; and the decision of one age or country is a wonder to another. Yet the people of any given age and country no more suspect any difficulty in it, than if it were a subject on which mankind had always been agreed. The rules which obtain among themselves appear to them self-evident and self-justifying. This all but universal illusion is one of the examples of the magical influence of custom, which is not only, as the proverb says a second nature, but is continually mistaken for the first. The effect of custom, in preventing any misgiving respecting the rules of conduct which mankind impose on one another, is all the more complete because the subject is one on which it is not generally considered necessary that reasons should be given, either by one person to others, or by each to himself. People are accustomed to believe and have been encouraged in the belief by some who aspire to the character of philosophers, that their feelings, on subjects of this nature, are better than reasons, and render reasons unnecessary. The practical principle which guides them to their opinions on the regulation of human conduct, is the feeling in each person's mind that everybody should be required to act as he, and those with whom he sympathizes, would like them to act. No one, indeed, acknowledges to himself that his standard of judgment is his own liking; but an opinion on a point of conduct, not supported by reasons, can only count as one person's preference; and if the reasons, when given, are a mere appeal to a similar preference felt by other people, it is still only many people's liking instead of one. To an ordinary man, however, his own preference, thus supported, is not only a perfectly satisfactory reason, but the only one he generally has for any of his notions of morality, taste, or propriety, which are not expressly written in his religious creed; and his chief guide in the interpretation even of that. Men's opinions, accordingly, on what is laudable or blameable, are affected by all the multifarious causes which influence their wishes in regard to the conduct of others, and which are as numerous as those which determine their wishes on any other subject. Sometimes their reason—at other times their prejudices or superstitions: often their social affections, not seldom their anti-social ones, their envy or jealousy, their arrogance or contemptuousness: but most commonly, their desires or fears for themselves—their legitimate or illegitimate self-interest. Wherever there is an ascendant class, a large portion of the morality of the country emanates from its class interests, and its feelings of class superiority. The morality between Spartans and Helots, between planters and negroes, between princes and subjects, between nobles and roturiers, between men and women, has been for the most part the creation of these class interests and feelings: and the sentiments thus generated, react in turn upon the moral feelings of the members of the ascendant class, in their relations among themselves. Where, on the other hand, a class, formerly ascendant, has lost its ascendency, or where its ascendency is unpopular, the prevailing moral sentiments frequently bear the impress of an impatient dislike of superiority. Another grand determining principle of the rules of conduct, both in act and forbearance which have been enforced by law or opinion, has been the servility of mankind towards the supposed preferences or aversions of their temporal masters, or of their gods. This servility though essentially selfish, is not hypocrisy; it gives rise to perfectly genuine sentiments of abhorrence; it made men burn magicians and heretics. Among so many baser influences, the general and obvious interests of society have of course had a share, and a large one, in the direction of the moral sentiments: less, however, as a matter of reason, and on their own account, than as a consequence of the sympathies and antipathies which grew out of them: and sympathies and antipathies which had little or nothing to do with the interests of society, have made themselves felt in the establishment of moralities with quite as great force.

The likings and dislikings of society, or of some powerful portion of it, are thus the main thing which has practically determined the rules laid down for general observance, under the penalties of law or opinion. And in general, those who have been in advance of society in thought and feeling, have left this condition of things unassailed in principle, however they may have come into conflict with it in some of its details.

They have occupied themselves rather in inquiring what things society ought to like or dislike, than in questioning whether its likings or dislikings should be a law to individuals. They preferred endeavouring to alter the feelings of mankind on the particular points on which they were themselves heretical, rather than make common cause in defence of freedom, with heretics generally. The only case in which the higher ground has been taken on principle and maintained with consistency, by any but an individual here and there, is that of religious belief: a case instructive in many ways, and not least so as forming a most striking instance of the fallibility of what is called the moral sense: for the *odium theologicum*, in a sincere bigot, is one of the most unequivocal cases of moral feeling. Those who first broke the yoke of what called itself the Universal Church, were in general as little willing to permit difference of religious opinion as that church itself. But when the heat of the conflict was over, without giving a complete victory to any party, and each church or sect was reduced to limit its hopes to retaining possession of the ground it already occupied; minorities, seeing that they had no chance of becoming majorities, were under the necessity of pleading to those whom they could not convert, for permission to differ. It is accordingly on this battle-field, almost solely, that the rights of the individual against society have been asserted on broad grounds of principle, and the claim of society to exercise authority over dissentients openly controverted. The great writers to whom the world owes what religious liberty it possesses, have mostly asserted freedom of conscience as an indefeasible right, and denied absolutely that a human being is accountable to others for his religious belief. Yet so natural to mankind is intolerance in whatever they really care about, that religious freedom has hardly anywhere been practically realized, except where religious indifference, which dislikes to have its peace disturbed by theological quarrels, has added its weight to the scale. In the minds of almost all religious persons, even in the most tolerant countries, the duty of toleration is admitted with tacit reserves. One person will bear with dissent in matters of church government, but not of dogma; another can tolerate everybody, short of a Papist or an Unitarian; another, every one who believes in revealed religion; a few extend their charity a little further, but stop at the belief in a God and in a future state. Wherever the sentiment of the majority is still genuine and intense, it is found to have abated little of its claim to be obeyed.

In England, from the peculiar circumstances of our political history, though the yoke of opinion is perhaps heavier, that of law is lighter, than in most other countries of Europe; and there is considerable jealousy of direct interference, by the legislative or the executive power with private conduct; not so much from any just regard for the independence of the individual, as from the still subsisting habit of looking on the government as representing an opposite interest to the public. The majority have not yet learnt to feel the power of the government their power, or its opinions their opinions. When they do so, individual liberty will probably be as much exposed to invasion from the government, as it already is from public opinion. But, as yet, there is a considerable amount of feeling ready to be called forth against any attempt of the law to control individuals in things in which they have not hitherto been accustomed to be controlled by it; and this with very little discrimination as to whether the matter is, or is not, within the legitimate sphere of legal control; insomuch that the feeling, highly salutary on the whole, is perhaps quite as often misplaced as well grounded in the particular instances of its application.

There is, in fact, no recognized principle by which the propriety or impropriety of government interference is customarily tested. People decide according to their personal preferences. Some, whenever they see any good to be done, or evil to be remedied, would willingly instigate the government to undertake the business; while others prefer to bear almost any amount of social evil, rather than add one to the departments of human interests amenable to governmental control. And men range themselves on one or the other side in any particular case, according to this general direction of their sentiments; or according to the degree of interest which they feel in the particular thing which it is proposed that the government should do; or according to the belief they entertain that the government would, or would not, do it in the manner they prefer; but very rarely on account of any opinion to which they consistently adhere, as to what things are fit to be done by a government. And it seems to me that, in consequence of this absence of rule or principle, one side is at present as often wrong as the other; the interference of government is, with about equal frequency, improperly invoked and improperly condemned.

The object of this Essay is to assert one very simple principle, as entitled to govern absolutely the dealings of society with the individual in the way of compulsion and control, whether the means used be physical force in the form of legal penalties, or the moral coercion of public opinion. That principle is, that the sole end for which mankind are warranted, individually or collectively in interfering with the liberty of action of any of their number, is self-protection. That the only purpose for which power can be rightfully exercised over any member of a civilized community, against his will, is to prevent harm to others. His own good, either physical or moral, is not a sufficient warrant. He cannot rightfully be compelled to do or forbear because it will be better for him to do so, because it will make him happier, because, in the opinions of others, to do so would be wise, or even right. These are good reasons for remonstrating with him, or reasoning with him, or persuading him, or entreating him, but not for compelling him, or visiting him with any evil, in case he do otherwise. To justify that, the conduct from which it is desired to deter him must be calculated to produce evil to some one else. The only part of the conduct of any one, for which he is amenable to society, is that which concerns others. In the part which merely concerns himself, his independence is, of right, absolute. Over himself, over his own body and mind, the individual is sovereign.

* * *

It is proper to state that I forego any advantage which could be derived to my argument from the idea of abstract right as a thing independent of utility. I regard utility as the ultimate appeal on all ethical questions; but it must be utility in the largest sense, grounded on the permanent interests of man as a progressive being. Those interests, I contend, authorize the subjection of individual spontaneity to external control, only in respect to those actions of each, which concern the interest of other people. If any one does an act hurtful to others, there is a prima facie case for punishing him, by law, or, where legal penalties are not safely applicable, by general disapprobation. There are also many positive acts for the benefit of others, which he may rightfully be compelled to perform; such as, to give evidence in a court of justice; to bear his fair share in the common defence, or in any other joint work necessary to the interest of the society of which he enjoys the protection; and to perform certain acts of individual beneficence, such as saving a fellow-creature's life, or interposing to protect the defenceless against ill-usage, things which whenever it is obviously a man's duty to do, he may rightfully be made responsible to society for not doing. A person may cause evil to others not only by his actions but by his inaction, and in neither case he is justly accountable to them for the injury.

* * *

But there is a sphere of action in which society, as distinguished from the individual, has, if any, only an indirect interest; comprehending all that portion of a person's life and conduct which affects only himself, or, if it also affects others, only with their free, voluntary, and undeceived consent and participation. When I say only himself, I mean directly, and in the first instance: for whatever affects himself, may affect others through himself; and the objection which may be grounded on this contingency, will receive consideration in the sequel. This, then, is the appropriate region of human liberty. It comprises, first, the inward domain of consciousness; demanding liberty of conscience, in the most comprehensive sense; liberty of thought and feeling; absolute freedom of opinion and sentiment on all subjects, practical or speculative, scientific, moral, or theological. The liberty of expressing and publishing opinions may seem to fall under a different principle, since it belongs to that part of the conduct of an individual which concerns other people; but, being almost of as much importance as the liberty of thought itself, and resting in great part on the same reasons, is practically inseparable from it. Secondly, the principle requires liberty of tastes and pursuits; of framing the plan of our life to suit our own character; of doing as we like, subject to such consequences as may follow; without impediment from our fellow-creatures, so long as what we do does not harm them even though they should think our conduct foolish, perverse, or wrong. Thirdly, from this liberty of each individual, follows the liberty, within the same limits, of combination among individuals; freedom to unite, for any purpose not involving harm to others: the persons combining being supposed to be of full age, and not forced or deceived.

No society in which these liberties are not, on the whole, respected, is free, whatever may be its form of government; and none is completely free in which they do not exist absolute and unqualified. The only freedom which deserves the name, is that of pursuing our own good in our own way, so long as we do not attempt to deprive others of theirs, or impede their efforts to obtain it. Each is the proper guardian of his own health, whether bodily, or mental or spiritual. Mankind are greater gainers by suffering each other to live as seems good to themselves, than by compelling each to live as seems good to the rest.

* * *

Chapter II

Of the Liberty of Thought and Discussion

The time, it is to be hoped, is gone by when any defence would be necessary of the "liberty of the press" as one of the securities against corrupt or tyrannical government. No argument, we may suppose, can now be needed, against permitting a legislature or an executive, not identified in interest with the people, to prescribe opinions to them, and determine what doctrines or what arguments they shall be allowed to hear. This aspect of the question, besides, has been so often and so triumphantly enforced by preceding writers, that it needs not be specially insisted on in this place. Though the law of England, on the subject of the press, is as servile to this day as it was in the time of the Tudors, there is little danger of its being actually put in force against political discussion, except during some temporary panic, when fear of insurrection drives ministers and judges from their propriety;[1] and, speaking generally, it is not, in constitutional countries, to be apprehended that the government, whether completely responsible to the people or not,

1. These words had scarcely been written, when, as if to give them an emphatic contradiction, occurred the Government Press Prosecutions of 1858. That ill-judged interference with the liberty of public discussion has not, however, induced me to alter a single word in the text, nor has it at all weakened my conviction that, moments of panic excepted, the era of pains and penalties far political discussion has, in our own country, passed away. For, in the first place, the prosecutions were not persisted in; and in the second, they were never, properly speaking, political prosecutions. The offence charged was not that of criticizing institutions, or the acts or persons of rulers, but of circulating what was deemed an immoral doctrine, the lawfulness of Tyrannicide.

If the arguments of the present chapter are of any validity, there ought to exist the fullest liberty of professing and discussing, as a matter of ethical conviction, any doctrine, however immoral it may be considered. It would, therefore, be irrelevant and out of place to examine here, whether the doctrine of Tyrannicide deserves that title. I shall content myself with saying, that the subject has been at all times one of the open questions of morals, that the act of a private citizen in striking down a criminal, who, by raising himself above the law, has placed himself beyond the reach of legal punishment or control, has been accounted by whole nations, and by some of the best and wisest of men, not a crime, but an act of exalted virtue and that, right or wrong, it is not of the nature of assassination but of civil war. As such, I hold that the instigation to it, in a specific case, may be a proper subject of punishment, but only if an overt act has followed, and at least a probable connection can be established between the act and the instigation. Even then it is not a foreign government, but the very government assailed, which alone, in the exercise of self-defence, can legitimately punish attacks directed against its own existence.

will often attempt to control the expression of opinion, except when in doing so it makes itself the organ of the general intolerance of the public. Let us suppose, therefore, that the government is entirely at one with the people, and never thinks of exerting any power of coercion unless in agreement with what it conceives to be their voice. But I deny the right of the people to exercise such coercion, either by themselves or by their government. The power itself is illegitimate. The best government has no more title to it than the worst. It is as noxious, or more noxious, when exerted in accordance with public opinion, than when in opposition to it. If all mankind minus one, were of one opinion, and only one person were of the contrary opinion, mankind would be no more justified in silencing that one person, than he, if he had the power, would be justified in silencing mankind. Were an opinion a personal possession of no value except to the owner; if to be obstructed in the enjoyment of it were simply a private injury, it would make some difference whether the injury was inflicted only on a few persons or on many. But the peculiar evil of silencing the expression of an opinion is, that it is robbing the human race; posterity as well as the existing generation; those who dissent from the opinion, still more than those who hold it. If the opinion is right, they are deprived of the opportunity of exchanging error for truth: if wrong, they lose, what is almost as great a benefit, the clearer perception and livelier impression of truth, produced by its collision with error.

It is necessary to consider separately these two hypotheses, each of which has a distinct branch of the argument corresponding to it. We can never be sure that the opinion we are endeavouring to stifle is a false opinion; and if we were sure, stifling it would be an evil still.

First: the opinion which it is attempted to suppress by authority may possibly be true. Those who desire to suppress it, of course deny its truth; but they are not infallible. They have no authority to decide the question for all mankind, and exclude every other person from the means of judging. To refuse a hearing to an opinion, because they are sure that it is false, is to assume that their certainty is the same thing as absolute certainty. All silencing of discussion is an assumption of infallibility. Its condemnation may be allowed to rest on this common argument, not the worse for being common.

Unfortunately for the good sense of mankind, the fact of their fallibility is far from carrying the weight in their practical judgment, which is always allowed to it in theory; for while every one well knows himself to be fallible, few think it necessary to take any precautions against their own fallibility, or admit the supposition that any opinion of which they feel very certain, may be one of the examples of the error to which they acknowledge themselves to be liable. Absolute princes, or others who are accustomed to unlimited deference, usually feel this complete confidence in their own opinions on nearly all subjects. People more happily situated, who sometimes hear their opinions disputed, and are not wholly unused to be set right when they are wrong, place the same unbounded reliance only on such of their opinions as are shared by all who surround them, or to whom they habitually defer: for in proportion to a man's want of confidence in his own solitary judgment, does he usually repose, with implicit trust, on the infallibility of "the world" in general. And the world, to each individual, means the part of it with which he comes in contact; his party, his sect, his church, his class of society: the man may be called, by comparison, almost liberal and large-minded to whom it means anything so comprehensive as his own country or his own age. Nor is his faith in this collective authority at all shaken by his being aware that other ages, countries, sects, churches, classes, and parties have thought, and even now think, the exact reverse. He devolves upon his own world the responsibility of being in the right against the dissentient worlds of other people; and it never troubles him that mere accident has decided which of these numerous worlds is the object of his reliance, and that the same causes which make him a Churchman in London, would have made him a Buddhist or a Confucian in Pekin. Yet it is as evident in itself as any amount of argument can make it, that ages are no more infallible than individuals; every age having held many opinions which subsequent ages have deemed not only false but absurd; and it is as certain that many opinions, now general, will be rejected by future ages, as it is that many, once general, are rejected by the present.

The objection likely to be made to this argument, would probably take some such form as the following. There is no greater assumption of infallibility in forbidding the propagation of error, than in any other thing which is done by public authority on its own judgment and responsibility. Judgment is given to men that they may use it. Because it may be used erroneously, are men to be told that they ought not to use it at all? To prohibit what they think pernicious, is not claiming exemption from error, but fulfilling the duty incumbent on them, although fallible, of acting on their conscientious conviction. If we were never to act on our opinions, because those opinions may be wrong, we should leave all our interests uncared for, and all our duties unperformed. An objection which applies to all conduct can be no valid objection to any conduct in particular.

It is the duty of governments, and of individuals, to form the truest opinions they can; to form them carefully, and never impose them upon others unless they are quite sure of being right. But when they are sure (such reasoners may say), it is not conscientiousness but cowardice to shrink from acting on their opinions, and allow doctrines which they honestly think dangerous to the welfare of mankind, either in this life or in another, to be scattered abroad without restraint, because other people, in less enlightened times, have persecuted opinions now believed to be true. Let us take care, it may be said, not to make the same mistake: but governments and nations have made mistakes in other things, which are not denied to be fit subjects for the exercise of authority: they have laid on bad taxes, made unjust wars. Ought we therefore to lay on no taxes, and, under whatever provocation, make no wars? Men, and governments, must act to the best of their ability. There is no such thing as absolute certainty, but there is assurance sufficient for the purposes of human life. We may, and must, assume our opinion to be true for the guidance of our own conduct: and it is assuming no more when we forbid bad men to pervert society by the propagation of opinions which we regard as false and pernicious.

I answer, that it is assuming very much more. There is the greatest difference between presuming an opinion to be true, because, with every opportunity for contesting it, it has not been refuted, and assuming its truth for the purpose of not permitting its refutation. Complete liberty of contradicting and disproving our opinion, is the very condition which justifies us in assuming its truth for purposes of action; and on no other terms can a being with human faculties have any rational assurance of being right.

When we consider either the history of opinion, or the ordinary conduct of human life, to what is it to be ascribed that the one and the other are no worse than they are? Not certainly to the inherent force of the human understanding; for, on any matter not self-evident, there are ninety-nine persons totally incapable of judging of it, for one who is capable; and the capacity of the hundredth person is only comparative; for the majority of the eminent men of every past generation held many opinions now known to be erroneous, and did or approved numerous things which no one will now justify. Why is it, then, that there is on the whole a preponderance among mankind of rational opinions and rational conduct? If there really is this preponderance—which there must be, unless human affairs are, and have always been, in an almost desperate state—it is owing to a quality of the human mind, the source of everything respectable in man, either as an intellectual or as a moral being, namely, that his errors are corrigible. He is capable of rectifying his mistakes by discussion and experience. Not by experience alone. There must be discussion, to show how experience is to be interpreted. Wrong opinions and practices gradually yield to fact and argument: but facts and arguments, to produce any effect on the mind, must be brought before it. Very few facts are able to tell their own story, without comments to bring out their meaning. The whole strength and value, then, of human judgment, depending on the one property, that it can be set right when it is wrong, reliance can be placed on it only when the means of setting it right are kept constantly at hand. In the case of any person whose judgment is really deserving of confidence, how has it become so? Because he has kept his mind open to criticism of his opinions and conduct. Because it has been his practice to listen to all that could be said against him; to profit by as much of it as was just, and expound to himself, and upon occasion to others, the fallacy of what was fallacious. Because he has felt, that the only way in which a human being can make some approach to knowing the whole of a subject, is by hearing what can be said about it by persons of every variety of opinion, and studying all modes in which it can be looked at by every character of mind. No wise man ever acquired his wisdom in any mode but this; nor is it in the nature of human intellect to become wise in any other manner. The steady habit of correcting and completing his own opinion by collating it with those of others, so far from causing doubt and hesitation in carrying it into practice, is the only stable foundation for a just reliance on it: for, being cognizant of all that can, at least obviously, be said against him, and having taken up his position against all gainsayers knowing that he has sought for objections and difficulties, instead of avoiding them, and has shut out no light which can be thrown upon the subject from any quarter—he has a right to think his judgment better than that of any person, or any multitude, who have not gone through a similar process.

It is not too much to require that what the wisest of mankind, those who are best entitled to trust their own judgment, find necessary to warrant their relying on it, should be submitted to by that miscellaneous collection of a few wise and many foolish individuals, called the public. The most intolerant of churches, the Roman Catholic Church, even at the canonization of a saint, admits, and listens patiently to, a "devil's advocate." The holiest of men, it appears, cannot be admitted to posthumous honors, until all that the devil could say against him is known and weighed. If even the Newtonian philosophy were not permitted to be questioned, mankind could not feel as complete assurance of its truth as they now do. The beliefs which we have most warrant for, have no safeguard to rest on, but a standing invitation to the whole world to prove them unfounded. If the challenge is not accepted, or is accepted and the attempt fails, we are far enough from certainty still; but we have done the best that the existing state of human reason admits of; we have neglected nothing that could give the truth a chance of reaching us: if the lists are kept open, we may hope that if there be a better truth, it will be found when the human mind is capable of receiving it; and in the meantime we may rely on having attained such approach to truth, as is possible in our own day. This is the amount of certainty attainable by a fallible being, and this the sole way of attaining it.

Strange it is, that men should admit the validity of the arguments for free discussion, but object to their being "pushed to an extreme;" not seeing that unless the reasons are good for an extreme case, they are not good for any case. Strange that they should imagine that they are not assuming infallibility when they acknowledge that there should be free discussion on all subjects which can possibly be doubtful, but think that some particular principle or doctrine should be forbidden to be questioned because it is so certain, that is, because they are certain that it is certain. To call any proposition certain, while there is any one who would deny its certainty if permitted, but who is not permitted, is to assume that we ourselves, and those who agree with us, are the judges of certainty, and judges without hearing the other side.

In the present age—which has been described as "destitute of faith, but terrified at scepticism,"—in which people feel sure, not so much that their opinions are true, as that they should not know what to do without them—the claims of an opinion to be protected from public attack are rested not so much on its truth, as on its importance to society. There are, it is alleged, certain beliefs, so useful, not to say indispensable to well-being, that it is as much the duty of governments to uphold those beliefs, as to protect any other of the interests of society. In a case of such necessity, and so directly in the line of their duty, something less than infallibility may, it is maintained, warrant, and even bind, governments, to act on their own opinion, confirmed by the general opinion of mankind. It is also often argued, and still oftener thought, that none but bad men would desire to weaken these salutary beliefs; and there can be nothing wrong, it is thought, in restraining bad men, and prohibiting what only such men would wish to practise. This mode of thinking makes the justification of restraints on discussion not a question of the truth of doctrines, but of their usefulness; and flatters itself by that means to escape the responsibility of claiming to be an infallible judge of opinions. But those who thus satisfy themselves, do not perceive that the assumption of infallibility is merely shifted from one point to another. The usefulness of an opinion is itself matter of opinion: as disputable, as open to discussion and requiring discussion as much, as the opinion itself. There is the same need of an infallible judge of opinions to decide an opinion to be noxious, as to decide it to be false, unless the opinion condemned has full opportunity of defending itself. And it will not do to say that the heretic may be allowed to maintain the utility or harmlessness of his opinion, though forbidden to maintain its truth. The truth of an opinion is part of its utility. If we would know whether or not it is desirable that a proposition should be believed, is it possible to exclude the consideration of whether or not it is true? In the opinion, not of bad men, but of the best men, no belief which is contrary to truth can be really useful: and can you prevent such men from urging that plea, when they are charged with culpability for denying some doctrine which they are told is useful, but which they believe to be false? Those who are on the side of received opinions, never fail to take all possible advantage of this plea; you do not find them handling the question of utility as if it could be completely abstracted from that of truth: on the contrary, it is, above all, because their doctrine is "the truth," that the knowledge or the belief of it is held to be so indispensable. There can be no fair discussion of the question of usefulness, when an argument so vital may be employed on one side, but not on the other. And in point of fact, when law or public feeling do not permit the truth of an opinion to be disputed, they are just as little tolerant of a denial of its usefulness. The utmost they allow is an extenuation of its absolute necessity or of the positive guilt of rejecting it.

In order more fully to illustrate the mischief of denying a hearing to opinions because we, in our own judgment, have condemned them, it will be desirable to fix down the discussion to a concrete case; and I choose, by preference, the cases which are least favourable to me—in which the argument against freedom of opinion, both on the score of truth and on that of utility, is considered the strongest. Let the opinions impugned be the belief in a God and in a future state, or any of the commonly received doctrines of morality. To fight the battle on such ground, gives a great advantage to an unfair antagonist; since he will be sure to say (and many who have no desire to be unfair will say it internally), Are these the doctrines which you do not deem sufficiently certain to be taken under the protection of law? Is the belief in a God one of the opinions, to feel sure of which, you hold to be assuming infallibility? But I must be permitted to observe, that it is not the feeling sure of a doctrine (be it what it may) which I call an assumption of infallibility. It is the undertaking to decide that question for others, without allowing them to hear what can be said on the contrary side. And I denounce and reprobate this pretension not the less, if put forth on the side of my most solemn convictions. However positive any one's persuasion may be, not only of the falsity, but of the pernicious consequences—not only of the pernicious consequences, but (to adopt expressions which I altogether condemn) the immorality and impiety of an opinion; yet if, in pursuance of that private judgment, though backed by the public judgment of his country or his contemporaries, he prevents the opinion from being heard in its defence, he assumes infallibility. And so far from the assumption being less objectionable or less dangerous because the opinion is called immoral or impious, this is the case of all others in which it is most fatal. These are exactly the occasions on which the men of one generation commit those dreadful mistakes which excite the astonishment and horror of posterity. It is among such that we find the instances memorable in history, when the arm of the law has been employed to root out the best men and the noblest doctrines; with deplorable success as to the men, though some of the doctrines have survived to be (as if in mockery) invoked, in defence of similar conduct towards those who dissent from them, or from their received interpretation.

Mankind can hardly be too often reminded, that there was once a man named Socrates, between whom and the legal authorities and public opinion of his time, there took place a memorable collision. Born in an age and country abounding in individual greatness, this man has been handed down to us by those who best knew both him and the age, as the most virtuous man in it; while we know him as the head and prototype of all subsequent teachers of virtue, the source equally of the lofty inspiration of Plato and the judicious utilitarianism of Aristotle, "*i maestri di color che sanno*," the two headsprings of ethical as of all other philosophy. This acknowledged master of all the eminent thinkers who have since lived—whose fame, still growing after more than two thousand years, all but outweighs the whole remainder of the names which make his native city illustrious—was put to death by his countrymen, after a judicial conviction, for impiety and immorality. Impiety, in denying the gods recognized by the State; indeed his accuser asserted (see the "Apologia") that he believed in no gods at all. Immorality, in being, by his doctrines and instructions, a "corrupter of youth." Of these charges the tribunal, there is every ground for believing, honestly found him guilty, and condemned the man who probably of all then born had deserved best of mankind, to be put to death as a criminal.

To pass from this to the only other instance of judicial iniquity, the mention of which, after the condemnation of Socrates, would not be an anti-climax: the event which took place on Calvary rather more than eighteen hundred years ago. The man who left on the memory of those who witnessed his life and conversation, such an impression of his moral grandeur, that eighteen subsequent centuries have done homage to him as the Almighty in person, was ignominiously put to death, as what? As a blasphemer. Men did not merely mistake their benefactor; they mistook him for the exact contrary of what he was, and treated him as that prodigy of impiety, which they themselves are now held to be, for their treatment of him. The feelings with which mankind now regard these lamentable transactions, especially the latter of the two, render them extremely unjust in their judgment of the unhappy actors. These were, to all appearance, not bad men—not worse than men most commonly are, but rather the contrary; men who possessed in a full, or somewhat more than a full measure, the religious, moral, and patriotic feelings of their time and people: the very kind of men who, in all times, our own included, have every chance of passing through life blameless and respected. The high-priest who rent his garments when the words were pronounced, which, according to all the ideas of his country, constituted the blackest guilt, was in all probability quite as sincere in his horror and indignation, as the generality of respectable and pious men now are in the religious and moral sentiments they profess; and most of those who now shudder at his conduct, if they had lived in his time and been born Jews, would have acted precisely as he did. Orthodox Christians who are tempted to think that those who stoned to death the first martyrs must have been worse men than they themselves are, ought to remember that one of those persecutors was Saint Paul.

Let us add one more example, the most striking of all, if the impressiveness of an error is measured by the wisdom and virtue of him who falls into it. If ever any one, possessed of power, had grounds for thinking himself the best and most enlightened among his contemporaries, it was the Emperor Marcus Aurelius. Absolute monarch of the whole civilized world, he preserved through life not only the most unblemished justice, but what was less to be expected from his Stoical breeding, the tenderest heart. The few failings which are attributed to him, were all on the side of indulgence: while his writings, the highest ethical product of the ancient mind, differ scarcely perceptibly, if they differ at all, from the most characteristic teachings of Christ. This man, a better Christian in all but the dogmatic sense of the word, than almost any of the ostensibly Christian sovereigns who have since reigned, persecuted Christianity. Placed at the summit of all the previous attainments of humanity, with an open, unfettered intellect, and a character which led him of himself to embody in his moral writings the Christian ideal, he yet failed to see that Christianity was to be a good and not an evil to the world, with his duties to which he was so deeply penetrated. Existing society he knew to be in a deplorable state. But such as it was, he saw or thought he saw, that it was held together and prevented from being worse, by belief and reverence of the received divinities. As a ruler of mankind, he deemed it his duty not to suffer society to fall in pieces; and saw not how, if its existing ties were removed, any others could be formed which could again knit it together. The new religion openly aimed at dissolving these ties: unless, therefore, it was his duty to adopt that religion, it seemed to be his duty to put it down. Inasmuch then as the theology of Christianity did not appear to him true or of divine origin; inasmuch as this strange history of a crucified God was not credible to him, and a system which purported to rest entirely upon a foundation to him so wholly unbelievable, could not be foreseen by him to be that renovating agency which, after all abatements, it has in fact proved to be; the gentlest and most amiable of philosophers and rulers, under a solemn sense of duty, authorized the persecution of Christianity. To my mind this is one of the most tragical facts in all history. It is a bitter thought, how different a thing the Christianity of the world might have been, if the Christian faith had been adopted as the religion of the empire under the auspices of Marcus Aurelius instead of those of Constantine. But it would be equally unjust to him and false to truth, to deny, that no one plea which can be urged for punishing anti-Christian teaching, was wanting to Marcus Aurelius for punishing, as he did, the propagation of Christianity. No Christian more firmly believes that Atheism is false, and tends to the dissolution of society, than Marcus Aurelius believed the same things of Christianity; he who, of all men then living, might have been thought the most capable of appreciating it. Unless any one who approves of punishment for the promulgation of opinions, flatters himself that he is a wiser and better man than Marcus Aurelius—more deeply versed in the wisdom of his time, more elevated in his intellect above it—more earnest in his search for truth, or more single-minded in his devotion to it when found;—let him abstain from that assumption of the joint infallibility of himself and the multitude, which the great Antoninus made with so unfortunate a result.

Aware of the impossibility of defending the use of punishment for restraining irreligious opinions, by any argument which will not justify Marcus Antoninus, the enemies of religious freedom, when hard pressed, occasionally accept this consequence, and say, with Dr. Johnson, that the persecutors of Christianity were in the right; that persecution is an ordeal through which truth ought to pass, and always passes successfully, legal penalties being, in the end, powerless against truth, though sometimes beneficially effective against mischievous errors. This is a form of the argument for religious intolerance, sufficiently remarkable not to be passed without notice.

A theory which maintains that truth may justifiably be persecuted because persecution cannot possibly do it any harm, cannot be charged with being intentionally hostile to the reception of new truths; but we cannot commend the generosity of its dealing with the persons to whom mankind are indebted for them. To discover to the world something which deeply concerns it, and of which it was previously ignorant; to prove to it that it had been mistaken on some vital point of temporal or spiritual interest, is as important a service as a human being can render to his fellow-creatures, and in certain cases, as in those of the early Christians and of the Reformers, those who think with Dr. Johnson believe it to have been the most precious gift which could be bestowed on mankind. That the authors of such splendid benefits should be requited by martyrdom; that their reward should be to be dealt with as the vilest of criminals, is not, upon this theory, a deplorable error and misfortune, for which humanity should mourn in sackcloth and ashes, but the normal and justifiable state of things. The propounder of a new truth, according to this doctrine, should stand, as stood, in the legislation of the Locrians, the proposer of a new law, with a halter round his neck, to be instantly tightened if the public assembly did not, on hearing his reasons, then and there adopt his proposition. People who defend this mode of treating benefactors, can not be supposed to set much value on the benefit; and I believe this view of the subject is mostly confined to the sort of persons who think that new truths may have been desirable once, but that we have had enough of them now.

But, indeed, the dictum that truth always triumphs over persecution, is one of those pleasant falsehoods which men repeat after one another till they pass into commonplaces, but which all experience refutes. History teems with instances of truth put down by persecution. If not suppressed forever, it may be thrown back for centuries. To speak only of religious opinions: the Reformation broke out at least twenty times before Luther, and was put down. Arnold of Brescia was put down. Fra Dolcino was put down. Savonarola was put down. The Albigeois were put down. The Vaudois were put down. The Lollards were put down. The Hussites were put down. Even after the era of Luther, wherever persecution was persisted in, it was successful. In Spain, Italy, Flanders, the Austrian empire, Protestantism was rooted out; and, most likely, would have been so in England, had Queen Mary lived, or Queen Elizabeth died. Persecution has always succeeded, save where the heretics were too strong a party to be effectually persecuted. No reasonable person can doubt that Christianity might have been extirpated in the Roman empire. It spread, and became predominant, because the persecutions were only occasional, lasting but a short time, and separated by long intervals of almost undisturbed propagandism. It is a piece of idle sentimentality that truth, merely as truth, has any inherent power denied to error, of prevailing against the dungeon and the stake. Men are not more zealous for truth than they often are for error, and a sufficient application of legal or even of social penalties will generally succeed in stopping the propagation of either. The real advantage which truth has, consists in this, that when an opinion is true, it may be extinguished once, twice, or many times, but in the course of ages there will generally be found persons to rediscover it, until some one of its reappearances falls on a time when from favourable circumstances it escapes persecution until it has made such head as to withstand all subsequent attempts to suppress it.

It will be said, that we do not now put to death the introducers of new opinions: we are not like our fathers who slew the prophets, we even build sepulchres to them. It is true we no longer put heretics to death; and the amount of penal infliction which modern feeling would probably tolerate, even against the most obnoxious opinions, is not sufficient to extirpate them. But let us not flatter ourselves that we are yet free from the stain even of legal persecution. Penalties for opinion, or at least for its expression, still exist by law; and their enforcement is not, even in these times, so unexampled as to make it at all incredible that they may some day be revived in full force. In the year 1857, at the summer assizes of the county of Cornwall, an unfortunate man,[2] said to be of unexceptionable conduct in all relations of life, was sentenced to twenty-one months imprisonment, for uttering, and writing on a gate, some offensive words concerning Christianity. Within a month of the same time, at the Old Bailey, two persons, on two separate occasions,[3] were rejected as jurymen, and one of them grossly insulted by the judge and one of the counsel, because they honestly declared that they had no theological belief; and a third, a foreigner,[4] for the same reason, was denied justice against a thief. This refusal of redress took place in virtue of the legal doctrine, that no person can be allowed to give evidence in a court of justice, who does not profess belief in a God (any god is sufficient) and in a future state; which is equivalent to declaring such persons to be outlaws, excluded from the protection of the tribunals; who may not only be robbed or assaulted with impunity, if no one but themselves, or persons of similar opinions, be present, but any one else may be robbed or assaulted with impunity, if the proof of the fact depends on their evidence. The assumption on which this is grounded, is that the oath is worthless, of a person who does not believe in a future state; a proposition which betokens much ignorance of history in those who assent to it (since it is historically true that a large proportion of infidels in all ages have been persons of distinguished integrity and honor); and would be maintained by no one who had the smallest conception how many of the persons in greatest repute with the world, both for virtues and for attainments, are well known, at least to their intimates, to be unbelievers. The rule, besides, is suicidal, and cuts away its own foundation. Under pretence that atheists must be liars, it admits the testimony of all atheists who are willing to lie, and rejects only those who brave the obloquy of publicly confessing a detested creed rather than affirm a falsehood. A rule thus self-convicted of absurdity so far as regards its professed purpose, can be kept in force only as a badge of hatred, a relic of persecution; a persecution, too, having the peculiarity that the qualification for undergoing it is the being clearly proved not to deserve it. The rule, and the theory it implies, are hardly less insulting to believers than to infidels. For if he who does not believe in a future

2. Thomas Pooley, Bodmin Assizes, July 31, 1857. In December following, he received a free pardon from the Crown.

3. George Jacob Holyoake, August 17, 1857; Edward Truelove, July, 1857.

4. Baron de Gleichen, Marlborough Street Police Court, August 4, 1857.

state necessarily lies, it follows that they who do believe are only prevented from lying, if prevented they are, by the fear of hell. We will not do the authors and abettors of the rule the injury of supposing, that the conception which they have formed of Christian virtue is drawn from their own consciousness.

These, indeed, are but rags and remnants of persecution, and may be thought to be not so much an indication of the wish to persecute, as an example of that very frequent infirmity of English minds, which makes them take a preposterous pleasure in the assertion of a bad principle, when they are no longer bad enough to desire to carry it really into practice. But unhappily there is no security in the state of the public mind, that the suspension of worse forms of legal persecution, which has lasted for about the space of a generation, will continue. In this age the quiet surface of routine is as often ruffled by attempts to resuscitate past evils, as to introduce new benefits. What is boasted of at the present time as the revival of religion, is always, in narrow and uncultivated minds, at least as much the revival of bigotry; and where there is the strongest permanent leaven of intolerance in the feelings of a people, which at all times abides in the middle classes of this country, it needs but little to provoke them into actively persecuting those whom they have never ceased to think proper objects of persecution.[5] For it is this—it is the opinions men entertain, and the feelings they cherish, respecting those who disown the beliefs they deem important, which makes this country not a place of mental freedom. For a long time past, the chief mischief of the legal penalties is that they strengthen the social stigma. It is that stigma which is really effective, and so effective is it, that the profession of opinions which are under the ban of society is much less common in England, than is, in many other countries, the avowal of those which incur risk of judicial punishment. In respect to all persons but those whose pecuniary circumstances make them independent of the good will of other people, opinion, on this subject, is as efficacious as law;

5. Ample warning may be drawn from the large infusion of the passions of a persecutor, which mingled with the general display of the worst parts of our national character on the occasion of the Sepoy insurrection. The ravings of fanatics or charlatans from the pulpit may be unworthy of notice; but the heads of the Evangelical party have announced as their principle, for the government of Hindoos and Mahomedans, that no schools be supported by public money in which the Bible is not taught, and by necessary consequence that no public employment be given to any but real or pretended Christians. An Under–Secretary of State, in a speech delivered to his constituents on the 12th of November, 1857, is reported to have said: "Toleration of their faith" (the faith of a hundred millions of British subjects), "the superstition which they called religion, by the British Government, had had the effect of retarding the ascendency of the British name, and preventing the salutary growth of Christianity.... Toleration was the great cornerstone of the religious liberties of this country; but do not let them abuse that precious word toleration. As he understood it, it meant the complete liberty to all, freedom of worship, among Christians, who worshipped upon the same foundation. It meant toleration of all sects and denominations of Christians who believed in the one mediation." I desire to call attention to the fact, that a man who has been deemed fit to fill a high office in the government of this country, under a liberal Ministry, maintains the doctrine that all who do not believe in the divinity of Christ are beyond the pale of toleration. Who, after this imbecile display, can indulge the illusion that religious persecution has passed away, never to return?

men might as well be imprisoned, as excluded from the means of earning their bread. Those whose bread is already secured, and who desire no favors from men in power, or from bodies of men, or from the public, have nothing to fear from the open avowal of any opinions, but to be ill-thought of and ill-spoken of, and this it ought not to require a very heroic mould to enable them to bear. There is no room for any appeal ad misericordiam in behalf of such persons. But though we do not now inflict so much evil on those who think differently from us, as it was formerly our custom to do, it may be that we do ourselves as much evil as ever by our treatment of them. Socrates was put to death, but the Socratic philosophy rose like the sun in heaven, and spread its illumination over the whole intellectual firmament. Christians were cast to the lions, but the Christian Church grew up a stately and spreading tree, overtopping the older and less vigorous growths, and stifling them by its shade. Our merely social intolerance, kills no one, roots out no opinions, but induces men to disguise them, or to abstain from any active effort for their diffusion. With us, heretical opinions do not perceptibly gain or even lose, ground in each decade or generation; they never blaze out far and wide, but continue to smoulder in the narrow circles of thinking and studious persons among whom they originate, without ever lighting up the general affairs of mankind with either a true or a deceptive light. And thus is kept up a state of things very satisfactory to some minds, because, without the unpleasant process of fining or imprisoning anybody, it maintains all prevailing opinions outwardly undisturbed, while it does not absolutely interdict the exercise of reason by dissentients afflicted with the malady of thought. A convenient plan for having peace in the intellectual world, and keeping all things going on therein very much as they do already. But the price paid for this sort of intellectual pacification, is the sacrifice of the entire moral courage of the human mind. A state of things in which a large portion of the most active and inquiring intellects find it advisable to keep the genuine principles and grounds of their convictions within their own breasts, and attempt, in what they address to the public, to fit as much as they can of their own conclusions to premises which they have internally renounced, cannot send forth the open, fearless characters, and logical, consistent intellects who once adorned the thinking world. The sort of men who can be looked for under it, are either mere conformers to commonplace, or time-servers for truth whose arguments on all great subjects are meant for their hearers, and are not those which have convinced themselves. Those who avoid this alternative, do so by narrowing their thoughts and interests to things which can be spoken of without venturing within the region of principles, that is, to small practical matters, which would come right of themselves, if but the minds of mankind were strengthened and enlarged, and which will never be made effectually right until then; while that which would strengthen and enlarge men's minds, free and daring speculation on the highest subjects, is abandoned.

Those in whose eyes this reticence on the part of heretics is no evil, should consider in the first place, that in consequence of it there is never any fair and thorough discussion of heretical opinions; and that such of them as could not stand such a discussion, though they may be prevented from spreading, do not disappear. But it is not the minds of heretics that are deteriorated most, by the ban placed on all inquiry which does not end in the orthodox conclusions. The greatest harm done is to those who are not heretics, and whose whole mental development is cramped, and their reason cowed, by the fear of heresy. Who can compute what the world loses in the multitude of promising intellects combined with timid characters, who dare not follow out any bold, vigorous, independent train of thought, lest it should land them in something which would admit of being considered irreligious or immoral? Among them we may occasionally see some man of deep conscientiousness, and subtile and refined understanding, who spends a life in sophisticating with an intellect which he cannot silence, and exhausts the resources of ingenuity in attempting to reconcile the promptings of his conscience and reason with orthodoxy, which yet he does not, perhaps, to the end succeed in doing. No one can be a great thinker who does not recognize, that as a thinker it is his first duty to follow his intellect to whatever conclusions it may lead. Truth gains more even by the errors of one who, with due study and preparation, thinks for himself, than by the true opinions of those who only hold them because they do not suffer themselves to think. Not that it is solely, or chiefly, to form great thinkers, that freedom of thinking is required. On the contrary, it is as much, and even more indispensable, to enable average human beings to attain the mental stature which they are capable of. There have been, and may again be, great individual thinkers, in a general atmosphere of mental slavery. But there never has been, nor ever will be, in that atmosphere, an intellectually active people. Where any people has made a temporary approach to such a character, it has been because the dread of heterodox speculation was for a time suspended. Where there is a tacit convention that principles are not to be disputed; where the discussion of the greatest questions which can occupy humanity is considered to be closed, we cannot hope to find that generally high scale of mental activity which has made some periods of history so remarkable. Never when controversy avoided the subjects which are large and important enough to kindle enthusiasm, was the mind of a people stirred up from its foundations, and the impulse given which raised even persons of the most ordinary intellect to something of the dignity of thinking beings. Of such we have had an example in the condition of Europe during the times immediately following the Reformation; another, though limited to the Continent and to a more cultivated class, in the speculative movement of the latter half of the eighteenth century; and a third, of still briefer duration, in the intellectual fermentation of Germany during the Goethian and Fichtean period. These periods differed widely in the particular opinions which they developed; but were alike in this, that during all three the yoke of authority was broken. In each, an old mental despotism had been thrown off, and no new one had yet taken its place. The impulse given at these three periods has made Europe what it now is. Every single improvement which has taken place either in the human mind or in institutions, may be traced distinctly to one or other of them. Appearances have for some time indicated that all three impulses are well-nigh spent; and we can expect no fresh start, until we again assert our mental freedom.

Let us now pass to the second division of the argument, and dismissing the Supposition that any of the received opinions may be false, let us assume them to be true, and examine into the worth of the manner in which they are likely to be held, when their truth is not freely and openly canvassed. However unwillingly a person who has a strong opinion may admit the possibility that his opinion may be false, he ought to be moved by the consideration that however true it may be, if it is not fully, frequently, and fearlessly discussed, it will be held as a dead dogma, not a living truth.

There is a class of persons (happily not quite so numerous as formerly) who think it enough if a person assents undoubtingly to what they think true, though he has no knowledge whatever of the grounds of the opinion, and could not make a tenable defence of it against the most superficial objections. Such persons, if they can once get their creed taught from authority, naturally think that no good, and some harm, comes of its being allowed to be questioned. Where their influence prevails, they make it nearly impossible for the received opinion to be rejected wisely and considerately, though it may still be rejected rashly and ignorantly; for to shut out discussion entirely is seldom possible, and when it once gets in, beliefs not grounded on conviction are apt to give way before the slightest semblance of an argument. Waiving, however, this possibility—assuming that the true opinion abides in the mind, but abides as a prejudice, a belief independent of, and proof against, argument—this is not the way in which truth ought to be held by a rational being. This is not knowing the truth. Truth, thus held, is but one superstition the more, accidentally clinging to the words which enunciate a truth.

If the intellect and judgment of mankind ought to be cultivated, a thing which Protestants at least do not deny, on what can these faculties be more appropriately exercised by any one, than on the things which concern him so much that it is considered necessary for him to hold opinions on them? If the cultivation of the understanding consists in one thing more than in another, it is surely in learning the grounds of one's own opinions. Whatever people believe, on subjects on which it is of the first importance to believe rightly, they ought to be able to defend against at least the common objections. But, some one may say, "Let them be taught the grounds of their opinions. It does not follow that opinions must be merely parroted because they are never heard controverted. Persons who learn geometry do not simply commit the theorems to memory, but understand and learn likewise the demonstrations; and it would be absurd to say that they remain ignorant of the grounds of geometrical truths, because they never hear any one deny, and attempt to disprove them." Undoubtedly: and such teaching suffices on a subject like mathematics, where there is nothing at all to be said on the wrong side of the question. The peculiarity of the evidence of mathematical truths is, that all the argument is on one side. There are no objections, and no answers to objections. But on every subject on which difference of opinion is possible, the truth depends on a balance to be struck between two sets of conflicting reasons. Even in natural philosophy, there is always some other explanation possible of the same facts; some geocentric theory instead of heliocentric, some phlogiston instead of oxygen; and it has to be shown why that other theory cannot be the true one: and until this is shown and until we know how it is shown, we do not understand the grounds of our opinion. But when we turn to subjects infinitely more complicated, to morals, religion, politics, social relations, and the business of life, three-fourths of the arguments for every disputed opinion consist in dispelling the appearances which favor some opinion different from it. The greatest orator, save one, of antiquity, has left it on record that he always studied his adversary's case with as great, if not with still greater, intensity than even his own. What Cicero practised as the means of forensic success, requires to be imitated by all who study any subject in order to arrive at the truth. He who knows only his own side of the case, knows little of that. His reasons may be good, and no one may have been able to refute them. But if he is equally unable to refute the reasons on the opposite side; if he does not so much as know what they are, he has no ground for preferring either opinion. The rational position for him would be suspension of judgment, and unless he contents himself with that, he is either led by authority, or adopts, like the generality of the world, the side to which he feels most inclination. Nor is it enough that he should hear the arguments of adversaries from his own teachers, presented as they state them, and accompanied by what they offer as refutations. This is not the way to do justice to the arguments, or bring them into real contact with his own mind. He must be able to hear them from persons who actually believe them; who defend them in earnest, and do their very utmost for them. He must know them in their most plausible and persuasive form; he must feel the whole force of the difficulty which the true view of the subject has to encounter and dispose of, else he will never really possess himself of the portion of truth which meets and removes that difficulty. Ninety-nine in a hundred of what are called educated men are in this condition, even of those who can argue fluently for their opinions. Their conclusion may be true, but it might be false for anything they know: they have never thrown themselves into the mental position of those who think differently from them, and considered what such persons may have to say; and consequently they do not, in any proper sense of the word, know the doctrine which they themselves profess. They do not know those parts of it which explain and justify the remainder; the considerations which show that a fact which seemingly conflicts with another is reconcilable with it, or that, of two apparently strong reasons, one and not the other ought to be preferred. All that part of the truth which turns the scale, and decides the judgment of a completely informed mind, they are strangers to; nor is it ever really known, but to those who have attended equally and impartially to both sides, and endeavored to see the reasons of both in the strongest light. So essential is this discipline to a real understanding of moral and human subjects, that if opponents of all important truths do not exist, it is indispensable to imagine them and supply them with the strongest arguments which the most skilful devil's advocate can conjure up.

To abate the force of these considerations, an enemy of free discussion may be supposed to say, that there is no necessity for mankind in general to know and understand all that can be said against or for their opinions by philosophers and theologians. That it is not needful for common men to be able to expose all the misstatements or fallacies of an ingenious opponent. That it is enough if there is always somebody capable of answering them, so that nothing likely to mislead uninstructed persons remains unrefuted. That simple minds, having been taught the obvious grounds of the truths inculcated on them, may trust to authority for the rest, and being aware that they have neither knowledge nor talent to resolve every difficulty which can be raised, may repose in the assurance that all those which have been raised have been or can be answered, by those who are specially trained to the task.

Conceding to this view of the subject the utmost that can be claimed for it by those most easily satisfied with the amount of understanding of truth which ought to accompany the belief of it; even so, the argument for free discussion is no way weakened. For even this doctrine acknowledges that mankind ought to have a rational assurance that all objections have been satisfactorily answered; and how are they to be answered if that which requires to be answered is not spoken? or how can the answer be known to be satisfactory, if the objectors have no opportunity of showing that it is unsatisfactory? If not the public, at least the philosophers and theologians who are to resolve the difficulties, must make themselves familiar with those difficulties in their most puzzling form; and this cannot be accomplished unless they are freely stated, and placed in the most advantageous light which they admit of. The Catholic Church has its own way of dealing with this embarrassing problem. It makes a broad separation between those who can be permitted to receive its doctrines on conviction, and those who must accept them on trust. Neither, indeed, are allowed any choice as to what they will accept; but the clergy, such at least as can be fully confided in, may admissibly and meritoriously make themselves acquainted with the arguments of opponents, in order to answer them, and may, therefore, read heretical books; the laity, not unless by special permission, hard to be obtained. This discipline recognizes a knowledge of the enemy's case as beneficial to the teachers, but finds means, consistent with this, of denying it to the rest of the world: thus giving to the elite more mental culture, though not more mental freedom, than it allows to the mass. By this device it succeeds in obtaining the kind of mental superiority which its purposes require; for though culture without freedom never made a large and liberal mind, it can make a clever *nisi prius* advocate of a cause. But in countries professing Protestantism, this resource is denied; since Protestants hold, at least in theory, that the responsibility for the choice of a religion must be borne by each for himself, and cannot be thrown off upon teachers. Besides, in the present state of the world, it is practically impossible that writings which are read by the instructed can be kept from the uninstructed. If the teachers of mankind are to be cognizant of all that they ought to know, everything must be free to be written and published without restraint.

If, however, the mischievous operation of the absence of free discussion, when the received opinions are true, were confined to leaving men ignorant of the grounds of those opinions, it might be thought that this, if an intellectual, is no moral evil, and does not affect the worth of the opinions, regarded in their influence on the character. The fact, however, is, that not only the grounds of the opinion are forgotten in the absence of discussion, but too often the meaning of the opinion itself. The words which convey it, cease to suggest ideas, or suggest only a small portion of those they were originally employed to communicate. Instead of a vivid conception and a living belief, there remain only a few phrases retained by rote; or, if any part, the shell and husk only of the meaning is retained, the finer essence being lost. The great chapter in human history which this fact occupies and fills, cannot be too earnestly studied and meditated on.

It is illustrated in the experience of almost all ethical doctrines and religious creeds. They are all full of meaning and vitality to those who originate them, and to the direct disciples of the originators. Their meaning continues to be felt in undiminished strength, and is perhaps brought out into even fuller consciousness, so long as the struggle lasts to give the doctrine or creed an ascendency over other creeds. At last it either prevails, and becomes the general opinion, or its progress stops; it keeps possession of the ground it has gained, but ceases to spread further. When either of these results has become apparent, controversy on the subject flags, and gradually dies away. The doctrine has taken its place, if not as a received opinion, as one of the admitted sects or divisions of opinion: those who hold it have generally inherited, not adopted it; and conversion from one of these doctrines to another, being now an exceptional fact, occupies little place in the thoughts of their professors. Instead of being, as at first, constantly on the alert either to defend themselves against the world, or to bring the world over to them, they have subsided into acquiescence, and neither listen, when they can help it, to arguments against their creed, nor trouble dissentients (if there be such) with arguments in its favor. From this time may usually be dated the decline in the living power of the doctrine. We often hear the teachers of all creeds lamenting the difficulty of keeping up in the minds of believers a lively apprehension of the truth which they nominally recognize, so that it may penetrate the feelings, and acquire a real mastery over the conduct. No such difficulty is complained of while the creed is still fighting for its existence: even the weaker combatants then know and feel what they are fighting for, and the difference between it and other doctrines; and in that period of every creed's existence, not a few persons may be found, who have realized its fundamental principles in all the forms of thought, have weighed and considered them in all their important bearings, and have experienced the full effect on the character, which belief in that creed ought to produce in a mind thoroughly imbued with it. But when it has come to be an hereditary creed, and to be received passively, not actively—when the mind is no longer compelled, in the same degree as at first, to exercise its vital powers on the questions which its belief presents to it, there is a progressive tendency to forget all of the belief except the formularies, or to give it a dull and torpid assent, as if accepting it on trust dispensed with the necessity of realizing it in consciousness, or testing it by personal experience; until it almost ceases to connect itself at all with the inner life of the human being. Then are seen the cases, so frequent in this age of the world as almost to form the majority, in which the creed remains as it were outside the mind, encrusting and petrifying it against all other influences addressed to the higher parts of our nature; manifesting its power by not suffering any fresh and living conviction to get in, but itself doing nothing for the mind or heart, except standing sentinel over them to keep them vacant.

To what an extent doctrines intrinsically fitted to make the deepest impression upon the mind may remain in it as dead beliefs, without being ever realized in the imagination, the feelings, or the understanding, is exemplified by the manner in which the majority of believers hold the doctrines of Christianity. By Christianity I here mean what is accounted such by all churches and sects—the maxims and precepts contained in the New Testament. These are considered sacred, and accepted as laws, by all professing Christians. Yet it is scarcely too much to say that not one Christian in a thousand guides or tests his individual conduct by reference to those laws. The standard to which he does refer it, is the custom of his nation, his class, or his religious profession. He has thus, on the one hand, a collection of ethical maxims, which he believes to have been vouchsafed to him by infallible wisdom as rules for his government; and on the other, a set of every-day judgments and practices, which go a certain length with some of those maxims, not so great a length with others, stand in direct opposition to some, and are, on the whole, a compromise between the Christian creed and the interests and suggestions of worldly life. To the first of these standards he gives his homage; to the other his real allegiance. All Christians believe that the blessed are the poor and humble, and those who are ill-used by the world; that it is easier for a camel to pass through the eye of a needle than for a rich man to enter the kingdom of heaven; that they should judge not, lest they be judged; that they should swear not at all; that they should love their neighbor as themselves; that if one take their cloak, they should give him their coat also; that they should take no thought for the morrow; that if they would be perfect, they should sell all that they have and give it to the poor. They are not insincere when they say that they believe these things. They do believe them, as people believe what they have always heard lauded and never discussed. But in the sense of that living belief which regulates conduct, they believe these doctrines just up to the point to which it is usual to act upon them. The doctrines in their integrity are serviceable to pelt adversaries with; and it is understood that they are to be put forward (when possible) as the reasons for whatever people do that they think laudable. But any one who reminded them that the maxims require an infinity of things which they never even think of doing would gain nothing but to be classed among those very unpopular characters who affect to be better than other people. The doctrines have no hold on ordinary believers—are not a power in their minds. They have an habitual respect for the sound of them, but no feeling which spreads from the words to the things signified, and forces the mind to take them in, and make them conform to the formula. Whenever conduct is concerned, they look round for Mr. A and B to direct them how far to go in obeying Christ.

Now we may be well assured that the case was not thus, but far otherwise, with the early Christians. Had it been thus, Christianity never would have expanded from an obscure sect of the despised Hebrews into the religion of the Roman empire. When their enemies said, "See how these Christians love one another" (a remark not likely to be made by anybody now), they assuredly had a much livelier feeling of the meaning of their creed than they have ever had since. And to this cause, probably, it is chiefly owing that Christianity now makes so little progress in extending its domain, and after eighteen centuries, is still nearly confined to Europeans and the descendants of Europeans. Even with the strictly religious, who are much in earnest about their doctrines, and attach a greater amount of meaning to many of them than people in general, it commonly happens that the part which is thus comparatively active in their minds is that which was made by Calvin, or Knox, or some such person much nearer in character to themselves. The sayings of Christ coexist passively in their minds, producing hardly any effect beyond what is caused by mere listening to words so amiable and bland. There are many reasons, doubtless, why doctrines which are the badge of a sect retain more of their vitality than those common to all recognized sects, and why more pains are taken by teachers to keep their meaning alive; but one reason certainly is, that the peculiar doctrines are more questioned, and have to be oftener defended against open gainsayers. Both teachers and learners go to sleep at their post, as soon as there is no enemy in the field.

The same thing holds true, generally speaking, of all traditional doctrines—those of prudence and knowledge of life, as well as of morals or religion. All languages and literatures are full of general observations on life, both as to what it is, and how to conduct oneself in it; observations which everybody knows, which everybody repeats, or hears with acquiescence, which are received as truisms, yet of which most people first truly learn the meaning, when experience, generally of a painful kind, has made it a reality to them. How often, when smarting under some unforeseen misfortune or disappointment, does a person call to mind some proverb or common saying familiar to him all his life, the meaning of which, if he had ever before felt it as he does now, would have saved him from the calamity. There are indeed reasons for this, other than the absence of discussion: there are many truths of which the full meaning cannot be realized, until personal experience has brought it home. But much more of the meaning even of these would have been understood, and what was understood would have been far more deeply impressed on the mind, if the man had been accustomed to hear it argued pro and con by people who did understand it. The fatal tendency of mankind to leave off thinking about a thing when it is no longer doubtful, is the cause of half their errors. A contemporary author has well spoken of "the deep slumber of a decided opinion."

But what! (it may be asked) Is the absence of unanimity an indispensable condition of true knowledge? Is it necessary that some part of mankind should persist in error, to enable any to realize the truth? Does a belief cease to be real and vital as soon as it is generally received—and is a proposition never thoroughly understood and felt unless some doubt of it remains? As soon as mankind have unanimously accepted a truth, does the truth perish within them? The highest aim and best result of improved intelligence, it has hitherto been thought, is to unite mankind more and more in the acknowledgment of all important truths: and does the intelligence only last as long as it has not achieved its object? Do the fruits of conquest perish by the very completeness of the victory?

I affirm no such thing. As mankind improve, the number of doctrines which are no longer disputed or doubted will be constantly on the increase: and the well-being of mankind may almost be measured by the number and gravity of the truths which have reached the point of being uncontested. The cessation, on one question after another, of serious controversy, is one of the necessary incidents of the consolidation of opinion; a consolidation as salutary in the case of true opinions, as it is dangerous and noxious when the opinions are erroneous. But though this gradual narrowing of the bounds of diversity of opinion is necessary in both senses of the term, being at once inevitable and indispensable, we are not therefore obliged to conclude that all its consequences must be beneficial. The loss of so important an aid to the intelligent and living apprehension of a truth, as is afforded by the necessity of explaining it to, or defending it against, opponents, though not sufficient to outweigh, is no trifling drawback from, the benefit of its universal recognition. Where this advantage can no longer be had, I confess I should like to see the teachers of mankind endeavoring to provide a substitute for it; some contrivance for making the difficulties of the question as present to the learner's consciousness, as if they were pressed upon him by a dissentient champion, eager for his conversion.

But instead of seeking contrivances for this purpose, they have lost those they formerly had. The Socratic dialectics, so magnificently exemplified in the dialogues of Plato, were a contrivance of this description. They were essentially a negative discussion of the great questions of philosophy and life, directed with consummate skill to the purpose of convincing any one who had merely adopted the commonplaces of received opinion, that he did not understand the subject—that he as yet attached no definite meaning to the doctrines he professed; in order that, becoming aware of his ignorance, he might be put in the way to attain a stable belief, resting on a clear apprehension both of the meaning of doctrines and of their evidence. The school disputations of the Middle Ages had a somewhat similar object. They were intended to make sure that the pupil understood his own opinion, and (by necessary correlation) the opinion opposed to it, and could enforce the grounds of the one and confute those of the other. These last-mentioned contests had indeed the incurable defect, that the premises appealed to were taken from authority, not from reason; and, as a discipline to the mind, they were in every respect inferior to the powerful dialectics which formed the intellects of the "*Socratici viri*;" but the modern mind owes far more to both than it is generally willing to admit, and the present modes of education contain nothing which in the smallest degree supplies the place either of the one or of the other. A person who derives all his instruction from teachers or books, even if he escape the besetting temptation of contenting himself with cram, is under no compulsion to hear both sides; accordingly it is far from a frequent accomplishment, even among thinkers, to know both sides; and the weakest part of what everybody says in defence of his opinion, is what he intends as a reply to antagonists. It is the fashion of the present time to disparage negative logic—that which points out weaknesses in theory or errors in practice, without establishing positive truths. Such negative criticism would indeed be poor enough as an ultimate result; but as a means to attaining any positive knowledge or conviction worthy the name, it cannot be valued too highly; and until people are again systematically trained to it, there will be few great thinkers, and a low general average of intellect, in any but the mathematical and physical departments of speculation. On any other subject no one's opinions deserve the name of knowledge, except so far as he has either had forced upon him by others, or gone through of himself, the same mental process which would have been required of him in carrying on an active controversy with opponents. That, therefore, which when absent, it is so indispensable, but so difficult, to create, how worse than absurd is it to forego, when spontaneously offering itself! If there are any persons who contest a received opinion, or who will do so if law or opinion will let them, let us thank them for it, open our minds to listen to them, and rejoice that there is some one to do for us what we otherwise ought, if we have any regard for either the certainty or the vitality of our convictions, to do with much greater labor for ourselves.

It still remains to speak of one of the principal causes which make diversity of opinion advantageous, and will continue to do so until mankind shall have entered a stage of intellectual advancement which at present seems at an incalculable distance. We have hitherto considered only two possibilities: that the received opinion may be false, and some other opinion, consequently, true; or that, the received opinion being true, a conflict with the opposite error is essential to a clear apprehension and deep feeling of its truth. But there is a commoner case than either of these; when the conflicting doctrines, instead of being one true and the other false, share the truth between them; and the nonconforming opinion is needed to supply the remainder of the truth, of which the received doctrine embodies only a part. Popular opinions, on subjects not palpable to sense, are often true, but seldom or never the whole truth. They are a part of the truth; sometimes a greater, sometimes a smaller part, but exaggerated, distorted, and disjoined from the truths by which they ought to be accompanied and limited. Heretical opinions, on the other hand, are generally some of these suppressed and neglected truths, bursting the bonds which kept them down, and either seeking reconciliation with the truth contained in the common opinion, or fronting it as enemies, and setting themselves up, with similar exclusiveness, as the whole truth. The latter case is hitherto the most frequent, as, in the human mind, one-sidedness has always been the rule, and many-sidedness the exception. Hence, even in revolutions of opinion, one part of the truth usually sets while another rises. Even progress, which ought to superadd, for the most part only substitutes one partial and incomplete truth for another; improvement consisting chiefly in this, that the new fragment of truth is more wanted, more adapted to the needs of the time, than that which it displaces. Such being the partial character of prevailing opinions, even when resting on a true foundation; every opinion which embodies somewhat of the portion of truth which the common opinion omits, ought to be considered precious, with whatever amount of error and confusion that truth may be blended. No sober judge of human affairs will feel bound to be indignant because those who force on our notice truths which we should otherwise have overlooked, overlook some of those which we see. Rather, he will think that so long as popular truth is one-sided, it is more desirable than otherwise that unpopular truth should have one-sided asserters too; such being usually the most energetic, and the most likely to compel reluctant attention to the fragment of wisdom which they proclaim as if it were the whole.

Thus, in the eighteenth century, when nearly all the instructed, and all those of the uninstructed who were led by them, were lost in admiration of what is called civilization, and of the marvels of modern science, literature, and philosophy, and while greatly overrating the amount of unlikeness between the men of modern and those of ancient times, indulged the belief that the whole of the difference was in their own favor; with what a salutary shock did the paradoxes of Rousseau explode like bombshells in the midst, dislocating the compact mass of one-sided opinion, and forcing its elements to recombine in a better form and with additional ingredients. Not that the current opinions were on the whole farther from the truth than Rousseau's were; on the contrary, they were nearer to it; they contained more of positive truth, and very much less of error. Nevertheless there lay in Rousseau's doctrine, and has floated down the stream of opinion along with it, a considerable amount of exactly those truths which the popular opinion wanted; and these are the deposit which was left behind when the flood subsided. The superior worth of simplicity of life, the enervating and demoralizing effect of the trammels and hypocrisies of artificial society, are ideas which have never been entirely absent from cultivated minds since Rousseau wrote; and they will in time produce their due effect, though at present needing to be asserted as much as ever, and to be asserted by deeds, for words, on this subject, have nearly exhausted their power.

In politics, again, it is almost a commonplace, that a party of order or stability, and a party of progress or reform, are both necessary elements of a healthy state of political life; until the one or the other shall have so enlarged its mental grasp as to be a party equally of order and of progress, knowing and distinguishing what is fit to be preserved from what ought to be swept away. Each of these modes of thinking derives its utility from the deficiencies of the other; but it is in a great measure the opposition of the other that keeps each within the limits of reason and sanity. Unless opinions favorable to democracy and to aristocracy, to property and to equality, to co-operation and to competition, to luxury and to abstinence, to sociality and individuality, to liberty and discipline, and all the other standing antagonisms of practical life, are expressed with equal freedom, and enforced and defended with equal talent and energy, there is no chance of both elements obtaining their due; one scale is sure to go up, and the other down. Truth, in the great practical concerns of life, is so much a question of the reconciling and combining of opposites, that very few have minds sufficiently capacious and impartial to make the adjustment with an approach to correctness, and it has to be made by the rough process of a struggle between combatants fighting under hostile banners. On any of the great open questions just enumerated, if either of the two opinions has a better claim than the other, not merely to be tolerated, but to be encouraged and countenanced, it is the one which happens at the particular time and place to be in a minority. That is the opinion which, for the time being, represents the neglected interests, the side of human well-being which is in danger of obtaining less than its share. I am aware that there is not, in this country, any intolerance of differences of opinion on most of these topics. They are adduced to show, by admitted and multiplied examples, the universality of the fact, that only through diversity of opinion is there, in the existing state of human intellect, a chance of fair play to all sides of the truth. When there are persons to be found, who form an exception to the apparent unanimity of the world on any subject, even if the world is in the right, it is always probable that dissentients have something worth hearing to say for themselves, and that truth would lose something by their silence.

It may be objected, "But some received principles, especially on the highest and most vital subjects, are more than half-truths. The Christian morality, for instance, is the whole truth on that subject and if any one teaches a morality which varies from it, he is wholly in error." As this is of all cases the most important in practice, none can be fitter to test the general maxim. But before pronouncing what Christian morality is or is not, it would be desirable to decide what is meant by Christian morality. If it means the morality of the New Testament, I wonder that any one who derives his knowledge of this from the book itself, can suppose that it was announced, or intended, as a complete doctrine of morals. The Gospel always refers to a preexisting morality, and confines its precepts to the particulars in which that morality was to be corrected, or superseded by a wider and higher; expressing itself, moreover, in terms most general, often impossible to be interpreted literally, and possessing rather the impressiveness of poetry or eloquence than the precision of legislation. To extract from it a body of ethical doctrine, has never been possible without eking it out from the Old Testament, that is, from a system elaborate indeed, but in many respects barbarous, and intended only for a barbarous people. St. Paul, a declared enemy to this Judaical mode of interpreting the doctrine and filling up the scheme of his Master, equally assumes a preexisting morality, namely, that of the Greeks and Romans; and his advice to Christians is in a great measure a system of accommodation to that; even to the extent of giving an apparent sanction to slavery. What is called Christian, but should rather be termed theological, morality, was not the work of Christ or the Apostles, but is of much later origin, having been gradually built up by the Catholic Church of the first five centuries, and though not implicitly adopted by moderns and Protestants, has been much less modified by them than might have been expected. For the most part, indeed, they have contented themselves with cutting off the additions which had been made to it in the Middle Ages, each sect supplying the place by fresh additions, adapted to its own character and tendencies. That mankind owe a great debt to this morality, and to its early teachers, I should be the last person to deny; but I do not scruple to say of it, that it is, in many important points, incomplete and one-sided, and that unless ideas and feelings, not sanctioned by it, had contributed to the formation of European life and character, human affairs would have been in a worse condition than they now are. Christian morality (so called) has all the characters of a reaction; it is, in great part, a protest against Paganism. Its ideal is negative rather than positive; passive rather than active; Innocence rather than Nobleness; Abstinence from Evil, rather than energetic Pursuit of Good: in its precepts (as has been well said) "thou shalt not" predominates unduly over "thou shalt." In its horror of sensuality, it made an idol of asceticism, which has been gradually compromised away into one of legality. It holds out the hope of heaven and the threat of hell, as the appointed and appropriate motives to a virtuous life: in this falling far below the best of the ancients, and doing what lies in it to give to human morality an essentially selfish character, by disconnecting each man's feelings of duty from the interests of his fellow-creatures, except so far as a self-interested inducement is offered to him for consulting them. It is essentially a doctrine of passive obedience; it inculcates submission to all authorities found established; who indeed are not to be actively obeyed when they command what religion forbids, but who are not to be resisted, far less rebelled against, for any amount of wrong to ourselves. And while, in the morality of the best Pagan nations, duty to the State holds even a disproportionate place, infringing on the just liberty of the individual; in purely Christian ethics that grand department of duty is scarcely noticed or acknowledged. It is in the Koran, not the New Testament, that we read the maxim—"A ruler who appoints any man to an office, when there is in his dominions another man better qualified for it, sins against God and against the State." What little recognition the idea of obligation to the public obtains in modern morality, is derived from Greek and Roman sources, not from Christian; as, even in the morality of private life, whatever exists of magnanimity, high-mindedness, personal dignity, even the sense of honor, is derived from the purely human, not the religious part of our education, and never could have grown out of a standard of ethics in which the only worth, professedly recognized, is that of obedience.

I am as far as any one from pretending that these defects are necessarily inherent in the Christian ethics, in every manner in which it can be conceived, or that the many requisites of a complete moral doctrine which it does not contain, do not admit of being reconciled with it. Far less would I insinuate this of the doctrines and precepts of Christ himself. I believe that the sayings of Christ are all, that I can see any evidence of their having been intended to be; that they are irreconcilable with nothing which a comprehensive morality requires; that everything which is excellent in ethics may be brought within them, with no greater violence to their language than has been done to it by all who have attempted to deduce from them any practical system of conduct whatever. But it is quite consistent with this, to believe that they contain and were meant to contain, only a part of the truth; that many essential elements of the highest morality are among the things which are not provided for, nor intended to be provided for, in the recorded deliverances of the Founder of Christianity, and which have been entirely thrown aside in the system of ethics erected on the basis of those deliverances by the Christian Church. And this being so, I think it a great error to persist in attempting to find in the Christian doctrine that complete rule for our guidance, which its author intended it to sanction and enforce, but only partially to provide. I believe, too, that this narrow theory is becoming a grave practical evil, detracting greatly from the value of the moral training and instruction, which so many well-meaning persons are now at length exerting themselves to promote. I much fear that by attempting to form the mind and feelings on an exclusively religious type, and discarding those secular standards (as for want of a better name they may be called) which heretofore coexisted with and supplemented the Christian ethics, receiving some of its spirit, and infusing into it some of theirs, there will result, and is even now resulting, a low, abject, servile type of character, which, submit itself as it may to what it deems the Supreme Will, is incapable of rising to or sympathizing in the conception of Supreme Goodness. I believe that other ethics than any one which can be evolved from exclusively Christian sources, must exist side by side with Christian ethics to produce the moral regeneration of mankind; and that the Christian system is no exception to the rule that in an imperfect state of the human mind, the interests of truth require a diversity of opinions. It is not necessary that in ceasing to ignore the moral truths not contained in Christianity, men should ignore any of those which it does contain. Such prejudice, or oversight, when it occurs, is altogether an evil; but it is one from which we cannot hope to be always exempt, and must be regarded as the price paid for an inestimable good. The exclusive pretension made by a part of the truth to be the whole, must and ought to be protested against, and if a reactionary impulse should make the protestors unjust in their turn, this one-sidedness, like the other, may be lamented, but must be tolerated. If Christians would teach infidels to be just to Christianity, they should themselves be just to infidelity. It can do truth no service to blink the fact, known to all who have the most ordinary acquaintance with literary history, that a large portion of the noblest and most valuable moral teaching has been the work, not only of men who did not know, but of men who knew and rejected, the Christian faith.

I do not pretend that the most unlimited use of the freedom of enunciating all possible opinions would put an end to the evils of religious or philosophical sectarianism. Every truth which men of narrow capacity are in earnest about, is sure to be asserted, inculcated, and in many ways even acted on, as if no other truth existed in the world, or at all events none that could limit or qualify the first. I acknowledge that the tendency of all opinions to become sectarian is not cured by the freest discussion, but is often heightened and exacerbated thereby; the truth which ought to have been, but was not, seen, being rejected all the more violently because proclaimed by persons regarded as opponents. But it is not on the impassioned partisan, it is on the calmer and more disinterested bystander, that this collision of opinions works its salutary effect. Not the violent conflict between parts of the truth, but the quiet suppression of half of it, is the formidable evil: there is always hope when people are forced to listen to both sides; it is when they attend only to one that errors harden into prejudices, and truth itself ceases to have the effect of truth, by being exaggerated into falsehood. And since there are few mental attributes more rare than that judicial faculty which can sit in intelligent judgment between two sides of a question, of which only one is represented by an advocate before it, truth has no chance but in proportion as every side of it, every opinion which embodies any fraction of the truth, not only finds advocates, but is so advocated as to be listened to.

We have now recognized the necessity to the mental well-being of mankind (on which all their other well-being depends) of freedom of opinion, and freedom of the expression of opinion, on four distinct grounds; which we will now briefly recapitulate.

First, if any opinion is compelled to silence, that opinion may, for aught we can certainly know, be true. To deny this is to assume our own infallibility.

Secondly, though the silenced opinion be an error, it may, and very commonly does, contain a portion of truth; and since the general or prevailing opinion on any object is rarely or never the whole truth, it is only by the collision of adverse opinions that the remainder of the truth has any chance of being supplied.

Thirdly, even if the received opinion be not only true, but the whole truth; unless it is suffered to be, and actually is, vigorously and earnestly contested, it will, by most of those who receive it, be held in the manner of a prejudice, with little comprehension or feeling of its rational grounds. And not only this, but, fourthly, the meaning of the doctrine itself will be in danger of being lost, or enfeebled, and deprived of its vital effect on the character and conduct: the dogma becoming a mere formal profession, inefficacious for good, but cumbering the ground, and preventing the growth of any real and heartfelt conviction, from reason or personal experience.

Before quitting the subject of freedom of opinion, it is fit to take notice of those who say, that the free expression of all opinions should be permitted, on condition that the manner be temperate, and do not pass the bounds of fair discussion. Much might be said on the impossibility of fixing where these supposed bounds are to be placed; for if the test be offence to those whose opinion is attacked, I think experience testifies that this offence is given whenever the attack is telling and powerful, and that every opponent who pushes them hard, and whom they find it difficult to answer, appears to them, if he shows any strong feeling on the subject, an intemperate opponent. But this, though an important consideration in a practical point of view, merges in a more fundamental objection. Undoubtedly the manner of asserting an opinion, even though it be a true one, may be very objectionable, and may justly incur severe censure. But the principal offences of the kind are such as it is mostly impossible, unless by accidental self-betrayal, to bring home to conviction. The gravest of them is, to argue sophistically, to suppress facts or arguments, to misstate the elements of the case, or misrepresent the opposite opinion. But all this, even to the most aggravated degree, is so continually done in perfect good faith, by persons who are not considered, and in many other respects may not deserve to be considered, ignorant or incompetent, that it is rarely possible on adequate grounds conscientiously to stamp the misrepresentation as morally culpable; and still less could law presume to interfere with this kind of controversial misconduct. With regard to what is commonly meant by intemperate discussion, namely, invective, sarcasm, personality, and the like, the denunciation of these weapons would deserve more sympathy if it were ever proposed to interdict them equally to both sides; but it is only desired to restrain the employment of them against the prevailing opinion: against the unprevailing they may not only be used without general disapproval, but will be likely to obtain for him who uses them the praise of honest zeal and righteous indignation. Yet whatever mischief arises from their use, is greatest when they are employed against the comparatively defenceless; and whatever unfair advantage can be derived by any opinion from this mode of asserting it, accrues almost exclusively to received opinions. The worst offence of this kind which can be committed by a polemic, is to stigmatize those who hold the contrary opinion as bad and immoral men. To calumny of this sort, those who hold any unpopular opinion are peculiarly exposed, because they are in general few and uninfluential, and nobody but themselves feels much interest in seeing justice done them; but this weapon is, from the nature of the case, denied to those who attack a prevailing opinion: they can neither use it with safety to themselves, nor if they could, would it do anything but recoil on their own cause. In general, opinions contrary to those commonly received can only obtain a hearing by studied moderation of language, and the most cautious avoidance of unnecessary offence, from which they hardly ever deviate even in a slight degree without losing ground: while unmeasured vituperation employed on the side of the prevailing opinion, really does deter people from professing contrary opinions, and from listening to those who profess them. For the interest, therefore, of truth and justice, it is far more important to restrain this employment of vituperative language than the other; and, for example, if it were necessary to choose, there would be much more need to discourage offensive attacks on infidelity, than on religion. It is, however, obvious that law and authority have no business with restraining either, while opinion ought, in every instance, to determine its verdict by the circumstances of the individual case; condemning every one, on whichever side of the argument he places himself, in whose mode of advocacy either want of candor, or malignity, bigotry or intolerance of feeling manifest themselves, but not inferring these vices from the side which a person takes, though it be the contrary side of the question to our own; and giving merited honor to every one, whatever opinion he may hold, who has calmness to see and honesty to state what his opponents and their opinions really are, exaggerating nothing to their discredit, keeping nothing back which tells, or can be supposed to tell, in their favor. This is the real morality of public discussion; and if often violated, I am happy to think that there are many controversialists who to a great extent observe it, and a still greater number who conscientiously strive towards it.

Chapter III

On Individuality, As One of the Elements of Well-being

Such being the reasons which make it imperative that human beings should be free to form opinions, and to express their opinions without reserve; and such the baneful consequences to the intellectual, and through that to the moral nature of man, unless this liberty is either conceded, or asserted in spite of prohibition; let us next examine whether the same reasons do not require that men should be free to act upon their opinions—to carry these out in their lives, without hindrance, either physical or moral, from their fellow-men, so long as it is at their own risk and peril. This last proviso is of course indispensable. No one pretends that actions should be as free as opinions. On the contrary, even opinions lose their immunity, when the circumstances in which they are expressed are such as to constitute their expression a positive instigation to some mischievous act. An opinion that corn-dealers are starvers of the poor, or that private property is robbery, ought to be unmolested when simply circulated through the press, but may justly incur punishment when delivered orally to an excited mob assembled before the house of a corn-dealer, or when handed about among the same mob in the form of a placard. Acts of whatever kind, which, without justifiable cause, do harm to others, may be, and in the more important cases absolutely require to be, controlled by the unfavorable sentiments, and, when needful, by the active interference of mankind. The liberty of the individual must be thus far limited; he must not make himself a nuisance to other people. But if he refrains from molesting others in what concerns them, and merely acts according to his own inclination and judgment in things which concern himself, the same reasons which show that opinion should be free, prove also that he should be allowed, without molestation, to carry his opinions into practice at his own cost. That mankind are not infallible; that their truths, for the most part, are only half-truths; that unity of opinion, unless resulting from the fullest and freest comparison of opposite opinions, is not desirable, and diversity not an evil, but a good, until mankind are much more capable than at present of recognizing all sides of the truth, are principles applicable to men's modes of action, not less than to their opinions. As it is useful that while mankind are imperfect there should be different opinions, so is it that there should be different experiments of living; that free scope should be given to varieties of character, short of injury to others; and that the worth of different modes of life should be proved practically, when any one thinks fit to try them. It is desirable, in short, that in things which do not primarily concern others, individuality should assert itself. Where, not the person's own character, but the traditions of customs of other people are the rule of conduct, there is wanting one of the principal ingredients of human happiness, and quite the chief ingredient of individual and social progress.

In maintaining this principle, the greatest difficulty to be encountered does not lie in the appreciation of means towards an acknowledged end, but in the indifference of persons in general to the end itself. If it were felt that the free development of individuality is one of the leading essentials of well-being; that it is not only a coordinate element with all that is designated by the terms civilization, instruction, education, culture, but is itself a necessary part and condition of all those things; there would be no danger that liberty should be undervalued, and the adjustment of the boundaries between it and social control would present no extraordinary difficulty. But the evil is, that individual spontaneity is hardly recognized by the common modes of thinking as having any intrinsic worth, or deserving any regard on its own account. The majority, being satisfied with the ways of mankind as they now are (for it is they who make them what they are), cannot comprehend why those ways should not be good enough for everybody; and what is more, spontaneity forms no part of the ideal of the majority of moral and social reformers, but is rather looked on with jealousy, as a troublesome and perhaps rebellious obstruction to the general acceptance of what these reformers, in their own judgment, think would be best for mankind. Few persons, out of Germany, even comprehend the meaning of the doctrine which Wilhelm von Humboldt, so eminent both as a savant and as a politician, made the text of a treatise—that "the end of man, or that which is prescribed by the eternal or immutable dictates of reason, and not suggested by vague and transient desires, is the highest and most harmonious development of his powers to a complete and consistent whole;" that, therefore, the object "towards which every human being must ceaselessly direct his efforts, and on which especially those who design to influence their fellow-men must ever keep their eyes, is the individuality of power and development;" that for this there are two requisites, "freedom, and a variety of situations;" and that from the union of these arise "individual vigor and manifold diversity," which combine themselves in "originality."[2]

* * *

The human faculties of perception, judgment, discriminative feeling, mental activity, and even moral preference, are exercised only in making a choice. He who does anything because it is the custom, makes no choice. He gains no practice either in discerning or in desiring what is best. The mental and moral, like the muscular powers, are improved only by being used. The faculties are called into no exercise by doing a thing merely because others do it, no more than by believing a thing only because others believe it. If the grounds of an opinion are not conclusive to the person's own reason, his reason cannot be strengthened, but is likely to be weakened by his adopting it: and if the inducements to an act are not such as are consentaneous to his own feelings and character (where affection, or the rights of others are not concerned), it is so much done towards rendering his feelings and character inert and torpid, instead of active and energetic.

He who lets the world, or his own portion of it, choose his plan of life for him, has no need of any other faculty than the ape-like one of imitation. He who chooses his plan for himself, employs all his faculties. He must use observation to see, reasoning and judgment to foresee, activity to gather materials for decision, discrimination to decide, and when he has decided, firmness and self-control to hold to his deliberate decision. And these qualities he requires and exercises exactly in proportion as the part of his conduct which he determines according to his own judgment and feelings is a large one. It is possible that he might be guided in some good path, and kept out of harm's way, without any of these things. But what will be his comparative worth as a human being? It really is of importance, not only what men do, but also what manner of men they are that do it. Among the works of man, which human life is

2. The Sphere and Duties of Government, from the German of Baron Wilhelm von Humboldt, pp. 11–13.

rightly employed in perfecting and beautifying, the first in importance surely is man himself. Supposing it were possible to get houses built, corn grown, battles fought, causes tried, and even churches erected and prayers said, by machinery—by automatons in human form—it would be a considerable loss to exchange for these automatons even the men and women who at present inhabit the more civilized parts of the world, and who assuredly are but starved specimens of what nature can and will produce. Human nature is not a machine to be built after a model, and set to do exactly the work prescribed for it, but a tree, which requires to grow and develop itself on all sides, according to the tendency of the inward forces which make it a living thing.

It will probably be conceded that it is desirable people should exercise their understandings, and that an intelligent following of custom, or even occasionally an intelligent deviation from custom, is better than a blind and simply mechanical adhesion to it. To a certain extent it is admitted, that our understanding should be our own: but there is not the same willingness to admit that our desires and impulses should be our own likewise; or that to possess impulses of our own, and of any strength, is anything but a peril and a snare. Yet desires and impulses are as much a part of a perfect human being, as beliefs and restraints: and strong impulses are only perilous when not properly balanced; when one set of aims and inclinations is developed into strength, while others, which ought to coexist with them, remain weak and inactive. It is not because men's desires are strong that they act ill; it is because their consciences are weak. There is no natural connection between strong impulses and a weak conscience. The natural connection is the other way. To say that one person's desires and feelings are stronger and more various than those of another, is merely to say that he has more of the raw material of human nature, and is therefore capable, perhaps of more evil, but certainly of more good. Strong impulses are but another name for energy. Energy may be turned to bad uses; but more good may always be made of an energetic nature, than of an indolent and impassive one. Those who have most natural feeling, are always those whose cultivated feelings may be made the strongest. The same strong susceptibilities which make the personal impulses vivid and powerful, are also the source from whence are generated the most passionate love of virtue, and the sternest self-control. It is through the cultivation of these, that society both does its duty and protects its interests: not by rejecting the stuff of which heroes are made, because it knows not how to make them. A person whose desires and impulses are his own—are the expression of his own nature, as it has been developed and modified by his own culture—is said to have a character. One whose desires and impulses are not his own, has no character, no more than a steam-engine has a character. If, in addition to being his own, his impulses are strong, and are under the government of a strong will, he has an energetic character. Whoever thinks that individuality of desires and impulses should not be encouraged to unfold itself, must maintain that society has no need of strong natures—is not the better for containing many persons who have much character—and that a high general average of energy is not desirable.

In some early states of society, these forces might be, and were, too much ahead of the power which society then possessed of disciplining and controlling them. There has been a time when the element of spontaneity and individuality was in excess, and the social principle had a hard struggle with it. The difficulty then was, to induce men of strong bodies or minds to pay obedience to any rules which required them to control their impulses. To overcome this difficulty, law and discipline, like the Popes struggling against the Emperors, asserted a power over the whole man, claiming to control all his life in order to control his character—which society had not found any other sufficient means of binding. But society has now fairly got the better of individuality; and the danger which threatens human nature is not the excess, but the deficiency, of personal impulses and preferences. Things are vastly changed, since the passions of those who were strong by station or by personal endowment were in a state of habitual rebellion against laws and ordinances, and required to be rigorously chained up to enable the persons within their reach to enjoy any particle of security. In our times, from the highest class of society down to the lowest every one lives as under the eye of a hostile and dreaded censorship. Not only in what concerns others, but in what concerns only themselves, the individual, or the family, do not ask themselves—what do I prefer? or, what would suit my character and disposition? or, what would allow the best and highest in me to have fair play, and enable it to grow and thrive? They ask themselves, what is suitable to my position? what is usually done by persons of my station and pecuniary circumstances? or (worse still) what is usually done by persons of a station and circumstances superior to mine? I do not mean that they choose what is customary, in preference to what suits their own inclination. It does not occur to them to have any inclination, except for what is customary. Thus the mind itself is bowed to the yoke: even in what people do for pleasure, conformity is the first thing thought of; they like in crowds; they exercise choice only among things commonly done: peculiarity of taste, eccentricity of conduct, are shunned equally with crimes: until by dint of not following their own nature, they have no nature to follow: their human capacities are withered and starved: they become incapable of any strong wishes or native pleasures, and are generally without either opinions or feelings of home growth, or properly their own.

* * *

CHAPTER IV

OF THE LIMITS TO THE AUTHORITY OF SOCIETY OVER THE INDIVIDUAL

What, then, is the rightful limit to the sovereignty of the individual over himself? Where does the authority of society begin? How much of human life should be assigned to individuality, and how much to society?

Each will receive its proper share, if each has that which more particularly concerns it. To individuality should belong the part of life in which it is chiefly the individual that is interested; to society, the part which chiefly interests society.

Though society is not founded on a contract, and though no good purpose is answered by inventing a contract in order to deduce social obligations from it, every one who receives the protection of society owes a return for the benefit, and the fact of living in society renders it indispensable that each should be bound to observe a certain line of conduct towards the rest. This conduct consists, first, in not injuring the interests of one another; or rather certain interests, which, either by express legal provision or by tacit understanding, ought to be considered as rights; and secondly, in each person's bearing his share (to be fixed on some equitable principle) of the labors and sacrifices incurred for defending the society or its members from injury and molestation. These conditions society is justified in enforcing, at all costs to those who endeavor to withhold fulfilment. Nor is this all that society may do. The acts of an individual may be hurtful to others, or wanting in due consideration for their welfare, without going the length of violating any of their constituted rights. The offender may then be justly punished by opinion, though not by law. As soon as any part of a person's conduct affects prejudicially the interests of others, society has jurisdiction over it, and the question whether the general welfare will or will not be promoted by interfering with it, becomes open to discussion. But there is no room for entertaining any such question when a person's conduct affects the interests of no persons besides himself, or needs not affect them unless they like (all the persons concerned being of full age, and the ordinary amount of understanding). In all such cases there should be perfect freedom, legal and social, to do the action and stand the consequences.

It would be a great misunderstanding of this doctrine, to suppose that it is one of selfish indifference, which pretends that human beings have no business with each other's conduct in life, and that they should not concern themselves about the well-doing or well-being of one another, unless their own interest is involved. Instead of any diminution, there is need of a great increase of disinterested exertion to promote the good of others. But disinterested benevolence can find other instruments to persuade people to their good, than whips and scourges, either of the literal or the metaphorical sort. I am the last person to undervalue the self-regarding virtues; they are only second in importance, if even second, to the social. It is equally the business of education to cultivate both. But even education works by conviction and persuasion as well as by compulsion, and it is by the former only that, when the period of education is past, the self-regarding virtues should be inculcated. Human beings owe to each other help to distinguish the better from the worse, and encouragement to choose the former and avoid the latter. They should be forever stimulating each other to increased exercise of their higher faculties, and increased direction of their feelings and aims towards wise instead of foolish, elevating instead of degrading, objects and contemplations. But neither one person, nor any number of persons, is warranted in saying to another human creature of ripe years, that he shall not do with his life for his own benefit what he chooses to do with it. He is the person most interested in his own well-being, the interest which any other person, except in cases of strong personal attachment, can have in it, is trifling, compared with that which he himself has; the interest which society has in him individually (except as to his conduct to others) is fractional, and altogether indirect: while, with respect to his own feelings and circumstances, the most ordinary man or woman has means of knowledge immeasurably surpassing those that can be possessed by any one else. The interference of society to overrule his judgment and purposes in what only regards himself, must be grounded on general presumptions; which may be altogether wrong, and even if right, are as likely as not to be misapplied to individual cases, by persons no better acquainted with the circumstances of such cases than those are who look at them merely from without. In this department, therefore, of human affairs, Individuality has its proper field of action. In the conduct of human beings towards one another, it is necessary that general rules should for the most part be observed, in order that people may know what they have to expect; but in each person's own concerns, his individual spontaneity is entitled to free exercise. Considerations to aid his judgment, exhortations to strengthen his will, may be offered to him, even obtruded on him, by others; but he, himself, is the final judge. All errors which he is likely to commit against advice and warning, are far outweighed by the evil of allowing others to constrain him to what they deem his good.

I do not mean that the feelings with which a person is regarded by others, ought not to be in any way affected by his self-regarding qualities or deficiencies. This is neither possible nor desirable. If he is eminent in any of the qualities which conduce to his own good, he is, so far, a proper object of admiration. He is so much the nearer to the ideal perfection of human nature. If he is grossly deficient in those qualities, a sentiment the opposite of admiration will follow. There is a degree of folly, and a degree of what may be called (though the phrase is not unobjectionable) lowness or depravation of taste, which, though it cannot justify doing harm to the person who manifests it, renders him necessarily and properly a subject of distaste, or, in extreme cases, even of contempt: a person could not have the opposite qualities in due strength without entertaining these feelings. Though doing no wrong to any one, a person may so act as to compel us to judge him, and feel to him, as a fool, or as a being of an inferior order: and since this judgment and feeling are a fact which he would prefer to avoid, it is doing him a service to warn him of it beforehand, as of any other disagreeable consequence to which he exposes himself. It would be well, indeed, if this good office were much more freely rendered than the common notions of politeness at present permit, and if one person could honestly point out to another that he thinks him in fault, without being considered unmannerly or presuming.

We have a right, also, in various ways, to act upon our unfavorable opinion of any one, not to the oppression of his individuality, but in the exercise of ours. We are not bound, for example, to seek his society; we have a right to avoid it (though not to parade the avoidance), for we have a right to choose the society most acceptable to us. We have a right, and it may be our duty, to caution others against him, if we think his example or conversation likely to have a pernicious effect on those with whom he associates. We may give others a preference over him in optional good offices, except those which tend to his improvement. In these various modes a person may suffer very severe penalties at the hands of others, for faults which directly concern only himself; but he suffers these penalties only in so far as they are the natural, and, as it were, the spontaneous consequences of the faults themselves, not because they are purposely inflicted on him for the sake of punishment. A person who shows rashness, obstinacy, self-conceit—who cannot live within moderate means—who cannot restrain himself from hurtful indulgences—who pursues animal pleasures at the expense of those of feeling and intellect—must expect to be lowered in the opinion of others, and to have a less share of their favorable sentiments, but of this he has no right to complain, unless he has merited their favor by special excellence in his social relations, and has thus established a title to their good offices, which is not affected by his demerits towards himself.

What I contend for is, that the inconveniences which are strictly inseparable from the unfavorable judgment of others, are the only ones to which a person should ever be subjected for that portion of his conduct and character which concerns his own good, but which does not affect the interests of others in their relations with him. Acts injurious to others require a totally different treatment. Encroachment on their rights; infliction on them of any loss or damage not justified by his own rights; falsehood or duplicity in dealing with them; unfair or ungenerous use of advantages over them; even selfish abstinence from defending them against injury—these are fit objects of moral reprobation, and, in grave cases, of moral retribution and punishment. And not only these acts, but the dispositions which lead to them, are properly immoral, and fit subjects of disapprobation which may rise to abhorrence. Cruelty of disposition; malice and ill-nature; that most anti-social and odious of all passions, envy; dissimulation and insincerity, irascibility on insufficient cause, and resentment disproportioned to the provocation; the love of domineering over others; the desire to engross more than one's share of advantages (the *pleonexia* of the Greeks); the pride which derives gratification from the abasement of others; the egotism which thinks self and its concerns more important than everything else, and decides all doubtful questions in his own favor;—these are moral vices, and constitute a bad and odious moral character: unlike the self-regarding faults previously mentioned, which are not properly immoralities, and to whatever pitch they may be carried, do not constitute wickedness. They may be proofs of any amount of folly, or want of personal dignity and self-respect; but they are only a subject of moral reprobation when they involve a breach of duty to others, for whose sake the individual is bound to have care for himself. What are called duties to ourselves are not socially obligatory, unless circumstances render them at the same time duties to others. The term duty to oneself, when it means anything more than prudence, means self-respect or self-development; and for none of these is any one accountable to his fellow-creatures, because for none of them is it for the good of mankind that he be held accountable to them.

* * *

CHAPTER V

APPLICATIONS

The principles asserted in these pages must be more generally admitted as the basis for discussion of details, before a consistent application of them to all the various departments of government and morals can be attempted with any prospect of advantage. The few observations I propose to make on questions of detail, are designed to illustrate the principles, rather than to follow them out to their consequences. I offer, not so much applications, as specimens of application; which may serve to bring into greater clearness the meaning and limits of the two maxims which together form the entire doctrine of this Essay and to assist the judgment in holding the balance between them, in the cases where it appears doubtful which of them is applicable to the case.

The maxims are, first, that the individual is not accountable to society for his actions, in so far as these concern the interests of no person but himself. Advice, instruction, persuasion, and avoidance by other people, if thought necessary by them for their own good, are the only measures by which society can justifiably express its dislike or disapprobation of his conduct. Secondly, that for such actions as are prejudicial to the interests of others, the individual is accountable, and may be subjected either to social or to legal punishments, if society is of opinion that the one or the other is requisite for its protection.

In the first place, it must by no means be supposed, because damage, or probability of damage, to the interests of others, can alone justify the interference of society, that therefore it always does justify such interference. In many cases, an individual, in pursuing a legitimate object, necessarily and therefore legitimately causes pain or loss to others, or intercepts a good which they had a reasonable hope of obtaining. Such oppositions of interest between individuals often arise from bad social institutions, but are unavoidable while those institutions last; and some would be unavoidable under any institutions. Whoever succeeds in an overcrowded profession, or in a competitive examination; whoever is preferred to another in any contest for an object which both desire, reaps benefit from the loss of others, from their wasted exertion and their disappointment. But it is, by common admission, better for the general interest of mankind, that persons should pursue their objects undeterred by this sort of consequences. In other words, society admits no right, either legal or moral, in the disappointed competitors, to immunity from this kind of suffering; and feels called on to interfere, only when means of success have been employed which it is contrary to the general interest to permit—namely, fraud or treachery, and force.

Again, trade is a social act. Whoever undertakes to sell any description of goods to the public, does what affects the interest of other persons, and of society in general; and thus his conduct, in principle, comes within the jurisdiction of society: accordingly, it was once held to be the duty of governments, in all cases which were considered of importance, to fix prices, and regulate the processes of manufacture. But it is now recognized, though not till after a long struggle, that both the cheapness and the good quality of commodities are most effectually provided for by leaving the producers and sellers perfectly free, under the sole check of equal freedom to the buyers for supplying themselves elsewhere. This is the so-called doctrine of Free Trade, which rests on grounds different from, though equally solid with, the principle of individual liberty asserted in this Essay. Restrictions on trade, or on production for purposes of trade, are indeed restraints; and all restraint, qua restraint, is an evil: but the restraints in question affect only that part of conduct which society is competent to restrain, and are wrong solely because they do not really produce the results which it is desired to produce by them. As the principle of individual liberty is not involved in the doctrine of Free Trade so neither is it in most of the questions which arise respecting the limits of that doctrine: as for example, what amount of public control is admissible for the prevention of fraud by adulteration; how far sanitary precautions, or arrangements to protect work-people employed in dangerous occupations, should be enforced on employers. Such questions involve considerations of liberty, only in so far as leaving people to themselves is always better, *caeteris paribus*, than controlling them: but that they may be legitimately controlled for these ends, is in principle undeniable.

* * *

Again, there are many acts which, being directly injurious only to the agents themselves, ought not to be legally interdicted, but which, if done publicly, are a violation of good manners, and coming thus within the category of offences against others, may rightfully be prohibited. Of this kind are offences against decency; on which it is unnecessary to dwell, the rather as they are only connected indirectly with our subject, the objection to publicity being equally strong in the case of many actions not in themselves condemnable, nor supposed to be so.

There is another question to which an answer must be found, consistent with the principles which have been laid down. In cases of personal conduct supposed to be blameable, but which respect for liberty precludes society from preventing or punishing, because the evil directly resulting falls wholly on the agent; what the agent is free to do, ought other persons to be equally free to counsel or instigate? This question is not free from difficulty. The case of a person who solicits another to do an act, is not strictly a case of self-regarding conduct. To give advice or offer inducements to any one, is a social act, and may therefore, like actions in general which affect others, be supposed amenable to social control. But a little reflection corrects the first impression, by showing that if the case is not strictly within the definition of individual liberty, yet the reasons on which the principle of individual liberty is grounded, are applicable to it. If people must be allowed, in whatever concerns only themselves, to act as seems best to themselves at their own peril, they must equally be free to consult with one another about what is fit to be so done; to exchange opinions, and give and receive suggestions. Whatever it is permitted to do, it must be permitted to advise to do. The question is doubtful, only when the instigator derives a personal benefit from his advice; when he makes it his occupation, for subsistence, or pecuniary gain, to promote what society and the State consider to be an evil. Then, indeed, a new element of complication is introduced; namely, the existence of classes of persons with an interest opposed to what is considered as the public weal, and whose mode of living is grounded on the counteraction of it. Ought this to be interfered with, or not? Fornication, for example, must be tolerated, and so must gambling; but should a person be free to be a pimp, or to keep a gambling-house? The case is one of those which lie on the exact boundary line between two principles, and it is not at once apparent to which of the two it properly belongs. There are arguments on both sides. On the side of toleration it may be said, that the fact of following anything as an occupation, and living or profiting by the practice of it, cannot make that criminal which would otherwise be admissible; that the act should either be consistently permitted or consistently prohibited; that if the principles which we have hitherto defended are true, society has no business, as society, to decide anything to be wrong which concerns only the individual; that it cannot go beyond dissuasion, and that one person should be as free to persuade, as another to dissuade. In opposition to this it may be contended, that although the public, or the State, are not warranted in authoritatively deciding, for purposes of repression or punishment, that such or such conduct affecting only the interests of the individual is good or bad, they are fully justified in assuming, if they regard it as bad, that its being so or not is at least a disputable question: That, this being supposed, they cannot be acting wrongly in endeavoring to exclude the influence of solicitations which are not disinterested, of instigators who cannot possibly be impartial—who have a direct personal interest on one side, and that side the one which the State believes to be wrong, and who confessedly promote it for personal objects only. There can surely, it may be urged, be nothing lost, no sacrifice of good, by so ordering matters that persons shall make their election, either wisely or foolishly, on their own prompting, as free as possible from the arts of persons who stimulate their inclinations for interested purposes of their own.

* * *

A further question is, whether the State while it permits, should nevertheless indirectly discourage conduct which it deems contrary to the best interests of the agent; whether, for example, it should take measures to render the means of drunkenness more costly, or add to the difficulty of procuring them, by limiting the number of the places of sale. On this as on most other practical questions, many distinctions require to be made. To tax stimulants for the sole purpose of making them more difficult to be obtained, is a measure differing only in degree from their entire prohibition; and would be justifiable only if that were justifiable. Every increase of cost is a prohibition, to those whose means do not come up to the augmented price; and to those who do, it is a penalty laid on them for gratifying a particular taste. Their choice of pleasures, and their mode of expending their income, after satisfying their legal and moral obligations to the State and to individuals, are their own concern, and must rest with their own judgment. These considerations may seem at first sight to condemn the selection of stimulants as special subjects of taxation for purposes of revenue. But it must be remembered that taxation for fiscal purposes is absolutely inevitable; that in most countries it is necessary that a considerable part of that taxation should be indirect; that the State, therefore, cannot help imposing penalties, which to some persons may be prohibitory, on the use of some articles of consumption. It is hence the duty of the State to consider, in the imposition of taxes, what commodities the consumers can best spare; and *a fortiori*, to select in preference those of which it deems the use, beyond a very moderate quantity, to be positively injurious. Taxation, therefore, of stimulants, up to the point which produces the largest amount of revenue (supposing that the State needs all the revenue which it yields) is not only admissible, but to be approved of.

* * *

It was pointed out in an early part of this Essay, that the liberty of the individual, in things wherein the individual is alone concerned, implies a corresponding liberty in any number of individuals to regulate by mutual agreement such things as regard them jointly, and regard no persons but themselves. This question presents no difficulty, so long as the will of all the persons implicated remains unaltered; but since that will may change, it is often necessary, even in things in which they alone are concerned, that they should enter into engagements with one another; and when they do, it is fit, as a general rule, that those engagements should be kept. Yet in the laws probably, of every country, this general rule has some exceptions. Not only persons are not held to engagements which violate the rights of third parties, but it is sometimes considered a sufficient reason for releasing them from an engagement, that it is injurious to themselves. In this and most other civilized countries, for example, an engagement by which a person should sell himself, or allow himself to be sold, as a slave, would be null and void; neither enforced by law nor by opinion. The ground for thus limiting his power of voluntarily disposing of his own lot in life, is apparent, and is very clearly seen in this extreme case. The reason for not interfering, unless for the sake of others, with a person's voluntary acts, is consideration for his liberty. His voluntary choice is evidence that what he so chooses is desirable, or at the least endurable, to him, and his good is on the whole best provided for by allowing him to take his own means of pursuing it. But by selling himself for a slave, he abdicates his liberty; he foregoes any future use of it, beyond that single act. He therefore defeats, in his own case, the very purpose which is the justification of allowing him to dispose of himself. He is no longer free; but is thenceforth in a position which has no longer the presumption in its favor, that would be afforded by his voluntarily remaining in it. The principle of freedom cannot require that he should be free not to be free. It is not freedom, to be allowed to alienate his freedom.

* * *

Questions

1) What kind of an argument is Mill making? From *consequences,* like a good utilitarian? Or is his argument, at bottom, based on a *character* ideal? Or perhaps a natural *entitlement* to freedom of thought?

2) What links to Milton? Does Mill add anything significant to Milton's *reasons* for valuing free expression, or does he simply push the Miltonic line of analysis to its logical conclusion (i.e., broader toleration) when Milton was unwilling to do so?

3) How, if at all, does Mill's argument differ from Madison's in terms of (a) what he takes to be the chief threat to the liberty he defends; (b) his assumptions about human nature; and (c) why he believes that dissenting speech is socially valuable? In what respect is Mill's argument more instrumentalist than Madison's? In what respect is it less instrumentalist?

4) Recall Mill's arguments in Chapter Two regarding how the freedom to express opinions promotes the search for truth under three different assumptions concerning the truth or falsity of the unorthodox opinion that society wishes to suppress. Do those arguments depend ultimately on the premise that opinions have some sort of objective truth value? That such truth value is something that fallible human beings can comprehend, or at least make progress toward comprehending? Can someone who believes that the "truth" or "falsity" of *opinions* (in contrast, perhaps, with empirical observations, propositions of logic, and scientific "laws") is exclusively a matter of social construction, cultural determination, and political power embrace *any* significant argument that Mill makes in Chapter Two?

5) Does Mill believe that expressions of opinion never cause harm? Can he concede that sometimes expressions of opinion cause harm and still defend the "absolute freedom" to express opinions? Notice that he describes the "liberty of tastes and pursuits" and the "liberty . . . of combination among individuals" as extending only to endeavors "not involving harm to others." No such qualification accompanies his descrip-

tion of the "freedom of opinion and sentiment on all subjects" and the "liberty of expressing and publishing opinions." So what exactly is Mill's position regarding the relationship between speech and harm? How, if at all, does his corn dealer example clarify his views in this respect?

6) Where exactly does Mill locate the line between non-governmental "coercion" of opinion, presumably by some form of social disapprobation, of which he disapproves, and the robust refutation of unorthodox ideas, a process he celebrates?

7) Does Mill really assume a "rationalistic" society? What does this mean? Does he ignore the force of passion? Of narrow self-interest? Of peer pressure and inertia? Does he overestimate the power of reason? Or is his problem a false ideal: a desire for reason to play a larger role in human affairs than is feasible and/or desirable?

8) Is it true that action is not inhibited by seeing all sides of a question, that deeper inquiry leads to stronger conviction and resolution? Does Mill make this claim?

JOHN STUART MILL, UTILITARIANISM

(1871).

The creed which accepts as the foundation of morals, Utility, or the Greatest Happiness Principle, holds that actions are right in proportion as they tend to promote happiness, wrong as they tend to produce the reverse of happiness. By happiness is intended pleasure, and the absence of pain; by unhappiness, pain, and the privation of pleasure. To give a clear view of the moral standard set up by the theory, much more requires to be said; in particular, what things it includes in the ideas of pain and pleasure; and to what extent this is left an open question.

* * *

Human beings have faculties more elevated than the animal appetites, and when once made conscious of them, do not regard anything as happiness which does not include their gratification. I do not, indeed, consider the Epicureans to have been by any means faultless in drawing out their scheme of consequences from the utilitarian principle. To do this in any sufficient manner, many Stoic, as well as Christian elements require to be included. But there is no known Epicurean theory of life which does not assign to the pleasures of the intellect, of the feelings and imagination, and of the moral sentiments, a much higher value as pleasures than to those of mere sensation. It must be admitted, however, that utilitarian writers in general have placed the superiority of mental over bodily pleasures chiefly in the greater permanency, safety, uncostliness, & c., of the former—that is, in their circumstantial advantages rather than in their intrinsic nature. And on all these points utilitarians have fully proved their case; but they might have taken the other, and, as it may be called, higher ground, with entire consistency. It is quite compatible with the principle of utility to recognise the fact, that some *kinds* of pleasure are more desirable and more valuable than others. It would be absurd that while, in estimating all other things, quality is considered as well as quantity, the estimation of pleasures should be supposed to depend on quantity alone.

If I am asked, what I mean by difference of quality in pleasures, or what makes one pleasure more valuable than another, merely as a pleasure, except its being greater in amount, there is but one possible answer. Of two pleasures, if there be one to which all or almost all who have experience of both give a decided preference, irrespective of any feeling of moral obligation to prefer it, that is the more desirable pleasure. If one of the two is, by those who are competently acquainted with both, placed so far above the other that they prefer it, even though knowing it to be attended with a greater amount of discontent, and would not resign it for any quantity of the other pleasure which their nature is capable of, we are justified in ascribing to the preferred enjoyment a superiority in quality, so far outweighing quantity as to render it, in comparison, of small account.

Now it is an unquestionable fact that those who are equally acquainted with, and equally capable of appreciating and enjoying, both, do give a most marked preference to the manner of existence which employs their higher faculties. Few human creatures would consent to be changed into any of the lower animals, for a promise of the fullest allowance of a beast's pleasures; no intelligent human being would consent to be a fool, no instructed person would be an ignoramus, no person of feeling and conscience would be selfish and base, even though they should be persuaded that the fool, the dunce, or the rascal is better satisfied with his lot than they are with theirs. They would not resign what they possess more than he, for the most complete satisfaction of all the desires which they have in common with him. If they ever fancy they would, it is only in cases of unhappiness so extreme, that to escape from it they would exchange their lot for almost any other, however undesirable in their own eyes. A being of higher faculties requires more to make him happy, is capable probably of more acute suffering, and is certainly accessible to it at more points, than one of an inferior type; but in spite of these liabilities, he can never really wish to sink into what he feels to be a lower grade of existence. We may give what explanation we please of this unwillingness; we may attribute it to pride, a name which is given indiscriminately to some of the most and to some of the least estimable feelings of which mankind are capable; we may refer it to the love of liberty and personal independence, an appeal to which was with the Stoics one of the most effective means for the inculcation of it; to the love of power, or to the love of excitement, both of which do really enter into and contribute to it: but its most appropriate appellation is a sense of dignity, which all human beings possess in one form or other, and in some, though by no means in exact, proportion to their higher faculties, and which is so essential a part of the happiness of those in whom it is strong, that nothing which conflicts with it could be, otherwise than momentarily, an object of desire to them. Whoever supposes that this preference takes place at a sacrifice of happiness—that the superior being, in anything like equal circumstances, is not happier than the inferior—confounds the two very different ideas, of happiness, and content. It is indisputable that the being whose capacities of enjoyment are low, has the greatest chance of having them fully satisfied; and a highly-endowed being will always feel that any happiness which he can look for, as the world is constituted, is imperfect. But he can learn to bear its imperfections, if they are at all bearable; and they will not make him envy the being who is indeed unconscious of the imperfections, but only because he feels not at all the good which those imperfections qualify. It is better to be a human being dissatisfied than a pig satisfied; better to be Socrates dissatisfied than a fool satisfied. And if the fool, or the pig, is of a different opinion, it is because they only know their own side of the question. The other party to the comparison knows both sides.

It may be objected, that many who are capable of the higher pleasures, occasionally, under the influence of temptation, postpone them to the lower. But this is quite compatible with a full appreciation of the intrinsic superiority of the higher. Men often, from infirmity of character, make their election for the nearer good, though they know it to be the less valuable; and this no less when the choice is between two bodily pleasures, than when it is between bodily and mental. They pursue sensual indulgences to the injury of health, though perfectly aware that health is the greater good. It may be further objected, that many who begin with youthful enthusiasm for everything noble, as they advance in years sink into indolence and selfishness. But I do not believe that those who undergo this very common change, voluntarily choose the lower description of pleasures in preference to the higher. I believe that before they devote themselves exclusively to the one, they have already become incapable of the other. Capacity for the nobler feelings is in most natures a very tender plant, easily killed, not only by hostile influences, but by mere want of sustenance; and in the majority of young persons it speedily dies away if the occupations to which their position in life has devoted them, and the society into which it has thrown them, are not favourable to keeping that higher capacity in exercise. Men lose their high aspirations as they lose their intellectual tastes, because they have not time or opportunity for indulging them; and they addict themselves to inferior pleasures, not because they deliberately prefer them, but because they are either the only ones to which they have access, or the only ones which they are any longer capable of enjoying. It may be questioned whether any one who has remained equally susceptible to both classes of pleasures, ever knowingly and calmly preferred the lower; though many, in all ages, have broken down in an ineffectual attempt to combine both.

From this verdict of the only competent judges, I apprehend there can be no appeal. On a question which is the best worth having of two pleasures, or which of two modes of existence is the most grateful to the feelings, apart from its moral attributes and from its consequences, the judgment of those who are qualified by knowledge of both, or, if they differ, that of the majority among them, must be admitted as final.

JOHN STUART MILL, CIVILIZATION—SIGNS OF THE TIMES

The Westminster Review, April, 1836.

This is a reading age; and, precisely because it is so reading an age, any book which is the result of profound meditation is perhaps less likely to be duly and profitably read than at a former period. The world reads too much and too quickly to read well. When books were few, to get through one was a work of time and labor: what was written with thought was read with thought, and with a desire to extract from it as much of the materials of knowledge as possible. But when almost every person who can spell, can and will write, what is to be done? It is difficult to know what to read, except by reading every thing; and so much of the world's business is now transacted through the press, that it is necessary to know what is printed, if we desire to know what is going on. Opinion weighs with so vast a weight in the balance of events, that ideas of no value in themselves are of importance from the mere circumstance that they *are* ideas, and have a *bonâ-fide* existence as such any-where out of Bedlam. (The world, in consequence, gorges itself with intellectual food; and, in order to swallow the more, *bolts* it.) Nothing is now read slowly, or twice over. Books are run through with no less rapidity, and scarcely leave a more durable impression, than a newspaper-article. It is from this, among other causes, that so few books are produced of any value. The lioness in the fable boasted, that, though she produced only one at a birth, that one was a lion; but if each lion only counted for one, and each leveret for one, the advantage would all be on the side of the hare. When every unit is individually weak, it is only multitude that tells. What wonder that the newspapers should carry all before them? A book produces hardly a greater effect than an article, and there can be three hundred and sixty-five of these in one year. He, therefore, who should and would write a book, and write it in the proper manner of writing a book, now dashes down his first hasty thoughts, or what he mistakes for thoughts, in a periodical. And the public is in the predicament of an indolent man, who cannot bring himself to apply his mind vigorously to his own affairs, and over whom, therefore, not he who speaks most wisely, but he who speaks most frequently, obtains the influence.

Question

Do Mill's arguments in *On Liberty* presuppose a higher degree of responsibility, patience, attentiveness, and integrity in argument on the part of the average person, or most persons, than actually obtains? Has the struggle to be heard in modern mass society led to lower standards in this respect? Recall all his talk about mass culture. Are Mill's observations in the essay "Civilization–Signs of the Times" consistent with the assumptions regarding belief formation and persuasion that inform his argument in *On Liberty*?

JOHN STUART MILL, ESSAY ON COLERIDGE

(1840).

The name of Coleridge is one of the few English names of our time which are likely to be oftener pronounced, and to become symbolical of more important things, in proportion as the inward workings of the age manifest themselves more and more in outward facts. Bentham excepted, no Englishman of recent date has left his impress so deeply in the opinions and mental tendencies of those among us who attempt to enlighten their practice by philosophical meditation. If it be true, as Lord Bacon affirms, that a knowledge of the speculative opinions of the men between twenty and thirty years of age is the great source of political prophecy, the existence of Coleridge will show itself by no slight or ambiguous traces in the coming history of our country; for no one has contributed more to shape the opinions of those among its younger men, who can be said to have opinions at all.

The influence of Coleridge, like that of Bentham, extends far beyond those who share in the peculiarities of his religious or philosophical creed. He has been the great awakener in this country of the spirit of philosophy, within the bounds of traditional opinions. He has been, almost as truly as Bentham, "the great questioner of things established;" for a questioner needs not necessarily be an enemy. By Bentham, beyond all others, men have been led to ask themselves, in regard to any ancient or received opinion, Is it true? and by Coleridge, What is the meaning of it? The one took his stand *outside* the received opinion, and surveyed it as an entire stranger to it: the other looked at it from within, and endeavoured to see it with the eyes of a believer in it; to discover by what apparent facts it was at first suggested, and by what appearances it has ever since been rendered continually credible—has seemed, to a succession of persons, to be a faithful interpretation of their experience. Bentham judged a proposition true or false as it accorded or not with the result of his own inquiries; and did not search very curiously into what might be meant by the proposition, when it obviously did not mean what he thought true. With Coleridge, on the contrary, the very fact that any doctrine had been believed by thoughtful men, and received by whole nations or generations of mankind, was part of the problem to be solved, was one of the phenomena to be accounted for. And as Bentham's short and easy method of referring all to the selfish interests of aristocracies, or priests, or lawyers, or some other species of impostors, could not satisfy a man who saw so much farther into the complexities of the human intellect and feelings—he considered the long or extensive prevalence of any opinion as a presumption that it was not altogether a fallacy; that, to its first authors at least, it was the result of a struggle to express in words something which had a reality to them, though perhaps not to many of those who have since received the doctrine by mere tradition. The long duration of a belief, he thought, is at least proof of an adaptation in it to some portion or other of the human mind; and if, on digging down to the root, we do not find, as is generally the case, some truth, we shall find some natural want or requirement of human nature which the doctrine in question is fitted to satisfy: among which wants the instincts of selfishness and of credulity have a place, but by no means an exclusive one. From this difference in the points of view of the two philosophers, and from the too rigid adherence of each to his own, it was to be expected that Bentham should continually miss the truth which is in the traditional opinions, and Coleridge that which is out of them, and at variance with them. But it was also likely that each would find, or show the way to finding, much of what the other missed.

It is hardly possible to speak of Coleridge, and his position among his contemporaries, without reverting to Bentham: they are connected by two of the closest bonds of association—resemblance, and contrast. It would be difficult to find two persons of philosophic eminence more exactly the contrary of one another. Compare their modes of treatment of any subject, and you might fancy them inhabitants of different worlds. They seem to have scarcely a principle or a premise in common. Each of them sees scarcely anything but what the other does not see. Bentham would have regarded Coleridge with a peculiar measure of the good-humoured contempt with which he was accustomed to regard all modes of philosophizing different from his own. Coleridge would probably have made Bentham one of the exceptions to the enlarged and liberal appreciation which (to the credit of *his* mode of philosophizing) he extended to most thinkers of any eminence, from whom he differed. But contraries, as logicians say, are but *quœ in eodem genere maxime distant,* the things which are farthest from one another in the same kind. These two agreed in being the men who, in their age and country, did most to enforce, by precept and example, the necessity of a philosophy. They agreed in making it their occupation to recall opinions to first principles; taking no proposition for granted without examining into the grounds of it, and ascertaining that it possessed the kind and degree of evidence suitable to its nature. They agreed in recognising that sound theory is the only foundation for sound practice, and that whoever despises theory, let him give himself what airs of wisdom he may, is self-convicted of being a quack. If a book were to be compiled containing all the best things ever said on the rule-of-thumb school of political craftsmanship, and on the insufficiency for practical purposes of what the mere practical man calls experience, it is difficult to say whether the collection would be more indebted to the writings of Bentham or of Coleridge. They agreed, too, in perceiving that the groundwork of all other philosophy must be laid in the philosophy of the mind. To lay this foundation deeply and strongly, and to raise a superstructure in accordance with it, were the objects to which their lives were devoted. They employed, indeed, for the most part, different materials; but as the materials of both were real observations, the genuine product of experience—the results will in the end be found not hostile, but supplementary, to one another. Of their methods of philosophizing, the same thing may be said: they were different, yet both were legitimate logical processes. In every respect the two men are each other's "completing counterpart": the strong points of each correspond to the weak points of the other. Whoever could master the premises and combine the methods of both, would possess the entire English philosophy of his age.

MICHAEL ST. JOHN PACKE, THE LIFE OF JOHN STUART MILL

(1954).

Coleridge and Bentham, Mill began, represented the ageless antithesis of order against progress. The two existed by denial of each other, and there was a relation between them. The problem went down to the roots of human knowledge, to the question how the mind grew conscious of the world outside itself. To Coleridge, as to all transcendental philosophers, it seemed that every object of experience, however apparently real, was no more than a symbol calling up the appropriate idea intuitively present in the mind. The Benthamites did not deny the possible existence of realities beyond the reach of human faculties. But the random peopling of the natural world with supernatural essences appeared to them unwarranted and disorderly. They held that the transcendentalists were too ready to proclaim as absolutes things capable of simpler explanation. Intuitions should be kept to an irreducible minimum, to the residue of undemonstrable truths remaining after the processes of reasoning had gone as far as they were able. Given only the human mind itself, they claimed, with its faculties of memory and association, of recording sensations and relating them together, the rest of the universe could be accounted for.

His own position in this much debated controversy was, Mill stated baldly, alongside Locke and Bentham. "We see no ground for believing that anything can be the object of our knowledge except our experience.... We are therefore at issue with Coleridge on the central idea of his philosophy." But he regarded it as a problem incapable of objective determination, the personal inclination of the individual being decided by his temperament. It was a question of the creative mind against the critical, of the imperative against the interrogative mood; and in daily life the common person tended to filch what he required from either side. When reason would not support an impulse, a conviction often did; just as when sentiment grew stale, experience began to count as wisdom. Practical truth was always a reconciliation.

The outcome as he saw it was more important in politics than in philosophy. Was a form of government the symbol of a hidden entity invested with the authority of the infinite, or was it a convention set up by men to be pulled down when it no longer served their purposes? Was the State a leviathan with a propulsion of its own, or was it no more than a free association of the individuals who composed it? Was the fact that a belief had been held by a majority of the human race over a long period, evidence of its intrinsic truth, or might it turn out to be a superstition? Such were the points at issue, and if the answers lay with the intuitionists, then authority was absolute and the individual was its slave.

Not that Coleridge maintained authority to be necessarily perfect. On the contrary, he held that it was frequently distorted, giving, like a twisted mirror, a false reflection of the truth it represented. He too was a reformer. And of the two methods of reform, his and Bentham's, Mill at this time generally favoured that of Coleridge. The Benthamites were unrealistic. They believed that the individual man was infinitely teachable, and an unerring follower of his own interest; that he would therefore speedily learn to identify his own good with that of the community. All government, they thought, was at the best a necessary evil, a temporary restraint pending increased enlightenment. Here, at the heart of their formula, there was a yawning gap. Between the self-interest of the individual and the greatest happiness of the greatest number there was no natural link, and all efforts to convert the one into the other by a system of legislative penalties and rewards must fail. Coleridge sought improvement through a surer means, the continuity of the human craving for tradition and propriety. History, to the Benthamites a dusty record of the crimes and follies of mankind, was to Coleridge an inspiring chronicle of the gradual unfolding of society. He wished to refashion and use what Bentham wanted to destroy. Instead of smashing the hard nut of convention and throwing away the pieces, he desired to discard the shell and to preserve the kernel.

Looking back upon the articles, Mill later felt that in censuring Bentham before full value had been gained from his iconoclasms, he had been inopportune. The more so, seeing that Bentham had made small pretence to philosophy, and was principally concerned with practical abuses. So in the version left to posterity in the *Dissertations and Discussions,* Mill softened the force of his criticism. As for his praise of Coleridge, he let it stand, being, as he said, an error on the favourable side. His object was to show that if Coleridge was blind to the truths excluded by established creeds, Bentham was equally ignorant of the truths which they contained. That though the two systems of thought were violently opposed, they were also complementary. To show, in fact, "that a Tory philosopher cannot be wholly a Tory, but must often be a better Liberal than Liberals themselves, while he is the natural means of rescuing from oblivion truths which Tories have forgotten, and which the prevailing school of Liberalism never knew."

The permanent value of the essays rests upon their exposition of Mill's concept of synthetic truth. For him, truth was no single element, but a gem of many faces, each capable of different, even contradictory appearance. It was impossible to grasp the whole from a single point of view; and, conversely, every honest point of view achieved an aspect of the truth. That any act of vision depends at least as much upon the situation and the circumstances of the seer as upon the object seen, was

Mill's position in philosophy. It was the theme which ran consistently throughout his life and works, the constant factor in the shifting ground of his development. It throws light on his relation with Harriet, not as his flatterer but as his opposite; with Sterling, not as his disciple, but his friend. It explains his disastrous approaches, first to Carlyle and later on to Comte. It explains why his *Review* was a pantechnicon. It was the groundwork of his *Logic,* and the structure of his *Liberty.* It was the reason why he endured criticism and delighted in correction; the secret of his personal charm, and of his reputation. It was in these essays, in his reconciliation of gigantic adversaries, that he best displayed his power of drawing from opposites a truth greater than either of them could attain alone. It was tolerance, not as weakness, but as creative force.

JAMES FITZJAMES STEPHEN, LIBERTY, EQUALITY, FRATERNITY

(1873).

I think that there are innumerable propositions on which a man may have a rational assurance that he is right whether others are or are not at liberty to contradict him, and that although he does not claim infallibility. Every proposition of which we are assured by our own senses, or by evidence which for all practical purposes is as strong as that of our own senses, falls under this head. There are plenty of reasons for not forbidding people to deny the existence of London Bridge and the river Thames, but the fear that the proof of those propositions would be weakened or that the person making the law would claim infallibility is not among the number.

A asserts the opinion that B is a thief. B sues A for libel. A justifies. The jury give a verdict for the plaintiff, with £1,000 damages. This is nearly equivalent to a law forbidding every one, under the penalty of a heavy fine, to express the opinion that in respect of the matters discussed B is a thief. Does this weaken the belief of the world at large in the opinion that in respect of those matters B is not a thief? According to Mr Mill, no one can have a rational assurance upon the subject unless every one is absolutely free to contradict the orthodox opinion. Surely this cannot be so.

The solution seems to be this. The fact that people are forbidden to deny a proposition weakens the force of the inference in its favour to be drawn from their acquiescence in it; but the value of their acquiescence considered as evidence may be very small, and the weight of other evidence, independent of public opinion, may not only be overwhelming, but the circumstances of the case may be such as to be inconsistent with the supposition that any further evidence will ever be forthcoming.

Again, an opinion may be silenced without any assertion on the part of the person who silences it that it is false. It may be suppressed because it is true, or because it is doubtful whether it is true or false, and because it is not considered desirable that it should be discussed. In these cases there is obviously no assumption of infallibility in suppressing it. The old maxim, "the greater the truth the greater the libel," has a true side to it, and when it applies it is obvious that an opinion is silenced without any assumption of infallibility. The opinion that a respectable man of mature years led an immoral life in his youth may be perfectly true, and yet the expression of that opinion may be a crime, if it is not for the public good that it should be expressed.

In cases in which it is obvious that no conclusion at all can be established beyond the reach of doubt, and that men must be contented with probabilities, it may be foolish to prevent discussion and prohibit the expression of any opinion but one, but no assumption of infallibility is involved in so doing. When Henry VIII and Queen Elizabeth silenced to a certain extent both Catholics and Puritans, and sought to confine religious controversy within limits fixed by law, they did not assume themselves to be infallible. What they thought—and it is by no means clear that they were wrong—was that unless religious controversy was kept within bounds there would be a civil war, and they muzzled the disputants accordingly.

There are, in short, two classes of cases to which, as it appears to me, Mr Mill's argument does not apply—cases in which moral certainty is attainable on the evidence, and cases in which it is not attainable on the evidence.

Where moral certainty is attainable on the evidence the suppression of opinion involves no claim to infallibility, but at most a claim to be right in the particular case.

Where moral certainty is not attainable on the evidence the suppression of opinion involves no claim to infallibility, because it does not assert the falsehood of the opinion suppressed.

* * *

The great defect of Mr. Mill's later writings seems to me to be that he has formed too favourable an estimate of human nature. This displays itself in the chapter now under consideration by the tacit assumption which pervades every part of it that the removal of restraints usually tends to invigorate character. Surely the very opposite of this is the truth. Habitual exertion is the greatest of all invigorators of character, and restraint and coercion in one form or another is the great stimulus to exertion. If you wish to destroy originality and vigour of character, no way to do so is so sure as to put a high level of comfort easily within the reach of moderate and commonplace exertion. A life made up of danger, vicissitude, and exposure is the sort of life which produces originality and resource. A soldier or sailor on active service lives in an atmosphere of coercion by the elements, by enemies, by disease, by the discipline to which he is subjected. Is he usually a tamer and less original person than a comfortable London shopkeeper or a man with just such an income as enables him to do exactly as he likes? A young man who is educated and so kept under close and continuous discipline till he is twenty-two or twenty-three years of age will generally have a much more vigorous and more original character than one who is left entirely to his own devices at an age when his mind and his tastes are unformed. Almost every human being requires more or less coercion and restraint as astringents to give him the maximum of power which he is capable of attaining. The maximum attainable in particular cases depends upon something altogether independent of social arrangements—namely, the nature of the human being himself who is subjected to them; and what this is or how it is to be affected are questions which no one has yet answered.

* * *

To me the question whether liberty is a good or a bad thing appears as irrational as the question whether fire is a good or a bad thing? It is both good and bad according to time, place and circumstance, and a complete answer to the question, In what cases is liberty good and in what cases is it bad? would involve not merely a universal history of mankind, but a complete solution of the problems which such a history would offer. I do not believe that the state of our knowledge is such as to enable us to enunciate any "very simple principle as entitled to govern absolutely the dealings of society with the individual in the way of compulsion and control." We must proceed in a far more cautious way, and confine ourselves to such remarks as experience suggests about the advantages and disadvantages of compulsion and liberty respectively in particular cases.

FREDERICK SCHAUER, FREE SPEECH: A PHILOSOPHICAL ENQUIRY

(1982).

To the extent that Mill uses the argument from truth to support an argument for liberty of discussion absolute in strength (although not unlimited in scope), he makes two implicit assumptions. He assumes that all suppression is based on the asserted falsity of the suppressed view. This, however, is simply wrong. Additionally, he assumes that the search for truth is superior to any other social interest. This assumption too is, at the very least, open to question, and it presents a problem to which I shall return. Thus the argument from truth is dispositive *ex necessitate* only if these two assumptions are both true. In fact, they are most likely both false.

For now it is sufficient to note that the absolutism inherent in Mill's principle of free discussion is the weakest point of his argument. But no argument should be rejected merely because its proponent overstates the case, or attributes unnecessary force to the argument. Stripped of the unnecessary absolutism, Mill's argument demands close attention.

Mill focuses our attention on the possibility that truth may lie in the suppressed opinion. If this is so, then a general policy of prohibiting the expression of opinions thought to be false extinguishes *some* knowledge and perpetuates *some* error. As Mill recognizes, however, we can say much the same thing about *acting* on a belief. If any belief might be wrong, then so might any action be wrong. Yet we cannot and do not let recognition of our fallibility paralyse us into inaction. We can function only if we act in accordance with our strongest beliefs, while still acknowledging that we may be in error. Mill responds by assuming a fundamental distinction between holding a belief and acting on a belief, and taking complete liberty of contradiction to be the very condition that allows us to act in accordance with our uncertain beliefs. We act on a belief rationally only if we know it to be the "best" belief available, and we know a belief to be best only if we have heard all the others.

This argument again appears to overstate the case. As Geoffrey Marshall's example of the Flat Earth Society points out, there are ways of establishing rational assurance other than by standing our beliefs next to all the other beliefs. But the more serious objection is that the distinction between holding a belief and acting on a belief is not to the point. The apt distinction is between acting on a belief and *expressing* a belief, and it is this distinction that may well not exist, because expressions of belief (speech) often affect the conduct of others. If there is a risk that people may come to believe and act on opinions thought by others to be false, then suppressing the false belief is one way of acting on the true belief.

Although Mill's argument is too strong, there is value in his observations. We achieve rational confidence in our views, confidence sufficient to justify action, in most instances by comparing those views to others already evaluated. We can sensibly prefer one view to others only by knowing what the others are. Having heard other views, we can have confidence in a view that has survived all currently available attacks. This at least increases the justification for acting on the surviving belief.

On Liberty can be read as assuming that there is some objective truth, even if we are never sure we have found it. As a result, Mill has been criticized by those who reject the notion of objective truth. If we are always uncertain, they say, then we never know if we have identified truth. These critics accuse Mill of inconsistency in saying that we can never be certain, but that we can search for truth. Apart from the fact that these arguments confuse truth with certainty, confuse a state of the world with a state of mind, the arguments are largely irrelevant to the issue at hand. The question is not certainty, but epistemic advance.

This point is brought out in much of the work of Karl Popper. By stressing falsifiability rather than verifiability, and by characterizing the advance of knowledge as the continual process of exposing error, Popper frees the argument from truth from the problem of certainty. The identification of error may not bring us closer to truth, but the identification of an error is still desirable, and the rejection of an erroneous belief is still an epistemic advance. Popper's argument from the identification of error thus parallels Mill's argument from truth. Both share the same core principle—allowing the expression of contrary views is the only rational way of recognizing human fallibility, and making possible the rejection or modification of those of our beliefs that are erroneous.

The Theory and the Reality

Mill, Popper, and their followers have refined the argument from truth by explaining how knowledge is more likely to be gained in a society in which all views can be freely expressed. But they have still neglected the critical question—does truth, when articulated, make itself known? Does truth prevail when placed side-by-side with falsity? Does knowledge triumph over ignorance? Are unsound policies rejected when sound policies are presented? The question is whether the theory accurately portrays reality. It does not follow as a matter of logical entailment that truth will be accepted and falsehood rejected when both are heard. There must be some justification for assuming this to be an accurate description of the process, and such a justification is noticeably absent from all versions of the argument from truth.

The argument from truth may well be the statement of an ideal. Listening to other positions, suspending judgment (if possible) until opposing views are expressed, and considering the possibility that we might be wrong virtually defines, in many contexts, the process of rational thinking. At least it is a substantial component of the definition.[15] Rationality in this sense may not always lead to increased knowledge, and there may at times be better methods of searching for truth. But all academic disciplines presuppose that this type of rationality has value, and it would be difficult to prove this presupposition unwarranted. When such rational thinking can be assumed, maximum freedom of discussion is a desirable goal. In systems of scientific and academic discourse, the argument from truth has substantial validity. Those who occupy positions in these fields may not always think rationally, but we are at least willing to say they should, and are inclined to try to replace those who do not think rationally with those who will.

It is one thing to say that truth is likely to prevail in a select group of individuals trained to think rationally and chosen for that ability. It is quite another to say that the same process works for the public at large. Only if the process is effective throughout society can the argument from truth support a Free Speech Principle to limit government power. We must take the public as it is. A scientist who is irrational can or at least should be replaced. A population with a similar failing cannot be replaced. The extent of reason in society is a fact with which we must work, and it is a fact that a plausible theory must accommodate.

15. Rationality is an enormously complex concept. I use "rational" in the sense of "thinking things through", where that in turn suggests *independent* thinking, rather than accepting arguments merely on blind faith. There is more to rationality than just this. Being rational also involves not having inconsistent views, and not holding views inconsistent with known facts. Moreover, rejecting known falsity is also a sign of rationality, but only when one knows *why* the rejected view is false. And that requires that we hear at least once the arguments in favour of the opposing view.

It is hardly surprising that the search for truth was so central in the writings of Milton, Locke, Voltaire, and Jefferson. They placed their faith in the ability of reason to solve problems and distinguish truth from falsehood. They had confidence in the reasoning power of *all* people, if only that power were allowed to flourish. The argument from truth is very much a child of the Enlightenment, and of the optimistic view of the rationality and perfectibility of humanity it embodied. But the naiveté of the Enlightenment has since been largely discredited by history and by contemporary insights of psychology. People are not nearly so rational as the Enlightenment assumed, and without this assumption the empirical support for the argument from truth evaporates. The most prominent weakness of Popper's *The Open Society and Its Enemies* is the assumption that the populace has the rationality Popper sees in scientific enquiry. It is no easy task to apply *The Logic of Scientific Discovery* to a public often unwilling or unable to be logical.

I do not mean to be taken as saying that falsity, ignorance, or evil have inherent power over truth, knowledge, or goodness. Rather, I mean only to deny the reverse—that truth has inherent ability to gain general acceptance. The argument from truth must demonstrate either that true statements have some intrinsic property that allows their truth to be universally apparent, or that empirical evidence supports the belief that truth will prevail when matched against falsehood. The absence of such a demonstration, in the face of numerous counter-examples, is the most prominent weakness of the argument from truth. History provides too many examples of falsity triumphant over truth to justify the assertion that truth will inevitably prevail. Mill noted that "the dictum that truth always triumphs over persecution is one of those pleasant falsehoods which men repeat after one another till they pass into commonplaces, but which all experience refutes". My point is that, *contra* Mill, the point would be the same if we removed the persecution and instead let truth battle with falsehood rather than the forces of oppression. Mill's assumption that the removal of persecution will allow truth to triumph in all cases is every bit as much a "pleasant falsehood".

Of course we know that falsity at times prevailed over truth only by having finally discovered truth with respect to a particular issue. Thus discussions along this line usually distinguish between the long run and the short run. Those who reject the assumptions of the Enlightenment point to instances in which truth and reason have not prevailed. In response, those who place their faith in the power of reason observe that when erroneous views have at times been accepted they have also been discredited in the long run. But the validity of this response depends on just how long the long run is. If there is no limit to its duration, the assertion that knowledge advances in the long run is both irrefutable and meaningless. Yet if the relevant time period is discrete and observable, history furnishes far too many counter-examples for us to have much confidence in the power of truth consistently to prevail.

The elements of rational thinking that prompt and justify the argument from truth undoubtedly are present at various points in society. Although there is no indication that this capacity to separate truth from error is invariably or even consistently present in the population at large, this is not sufficient completely to reject the argument from truth. Certainly the argument retains validity for select groups in which rationality can be presumed. More importantly, the free expression of all views by the entire population, even if a less than perfectly rational population, assists those who can most effectively separate truth from error. The process of advancing knowledge by offering and evaluating challenges and alternate hypotheses depends in part for its effectiveness on the number and variety of such challenges. Although the public may not be the body to identify most effectively sound policies and true statements, its size and diversity make it the ideal body to *offer* the multitude of ideas that are the fuel of the engine for advancing knowledge. By allowing the freest expression of opinion, we increase the number of alternatives and the number of challenges to received opinion. If some proportion of currently rejected ideas indeed are correct, then increasing the pool of ideas will in all probability increase the total number of correct ideas in circulation, and available to those who can identify them as correct. Any perceived inability of the population at large to discern truth does not necessarily deny to that population a valuable function in the truth-seeking process. But there is no particular reason why the group that offers the hypotheses must be the group that decides which hypotheses to accept and which to reject.

In discussing fallibilist theory, we often forget that it is only *possible* that the received opinion is erroneous, and therefore only *possible* that the rejected opinion is true. When we say that all views should be permitted expression so that knowledge may advance, this necessitates being willing to achieve *some* increase in knowledge at the expense of tolerating a great deal of falsity. In order to locate all the sound ideas, we must listen to many unsound ideas. When we allow the expression of an opinion that is only possibly true, we allow the expression of an opinion that is also possibly, perhaps *probably,* false. If the expression of the opinion in question involves no unpleasant consequences even if it is false, unsound, or useless, then there is a potential benefit at no cost. But it is simply a mistake to say that the expression of false or unsound opinions can never have unpleasant consequences.

The predominant risk is that false views may, despite their falsity, be accepted by the public, who will then act in accordance with those false views. The risk is magnified in those circumstances in which people have seemed particularly disposed towards the acceptance of unsound ideas. One good example is race relations. History has shown us that people unfortunately are much more inclined to be persuaded of the rectitude of oppressing certain races or certain religions than they are likely to accept other unsound and no less palpably wrong views.

Moreover, unpleasant side effects may accompany the expression of erroneous views even when there is no risk of widespread acceptance. By side effects I mean those consequences that are not directly attributable to the *falsity* of the views expressed. People may be offended, violence or disorder may ensue, or reputations may be damaged. It is foolish to suppose that the expression of opinions never causes harm. Generally, but not always, the expression of unsound opinions causes greater harm than the expression of sound opinions. When we allow the expression of an opinion because it is possibly true, we often accept an appreciably higher probability of harm than the probability of the truth of a seemingly false opinion. As a result, the strength of protection of the right to dissent afforded by the argument from fallibilism is directly proportionate to the value placed on the goal of searching for knowledge. There is absolute protection only if the search for knowledge is the transcendent value in society. If the search for knowledge does not have a lexical priority over all other values, the possibility that the rejected view may be correct will often be insufficient to justify allowing it to be expressed—depending, of course, on the evaluation of the harm expected to flow from its dissemination.

Question

Does Mill make a persuasive argument that the justification for censorship depends on a claim of infallibility on the part of the person or institution that decides what speech will be permitted? How might one admit to fallibility and still legitimately assume control over the speech of others? How might a defender of Mill answer the criticisms of James Fitzjames Stephen and Frederick Schauer regarding Mill's contention that would-be regulators of speech necessarily assume their own infallibility?

JOHN STUART MILL, THE SUBJECTION OF WOMEN

(1869).

All causes, social and natural, combine to make it unlikely that women should be collectively rebellious to the power of men. They are so far in a position different from all other subject classes, that their masters require something more from them than actual service. Men do not want solely the obedience of women, they want their sentiments. All men, except the most brutish, desire to have, in the woman most nearly connected with them, not a forced slave but a willing one, not a slave merely, but a favourite. They have therefore put everything in practice to enslave their minds. The masters of all other slaves rely, for maintaining obedience, on fear; either fear of themselves, or religious fears. The masters of women wanted more than simple obedience, and they turned the whole force of education to effect their purpose. All women are brought up from the very earliest years in the belief that their ideal of character is the very opposite to that of men; not self-will, and government by self-control, but submission, and yielding to the control of others. All the moralities tell them that it is the duty of women, and all the current sentimentalities that it is their nature, to live for others; to make complete abnegation of themselves, and to have no life but in their affections. And by their affections are meant the only ones they are allowed to have—those to the men with whom they are connected, or to the children who constitute an additional and indefeasible tie between them and a man. When we put together three things—first, the natural attraction between opposite sexes; secondly, the wife's entire dependence on the husband, every privilege or pleasure she has being either his gift, or depending entirely on his will; and lastly, that the principal object of human pursuit, consideration, and all objects of social ambition, can in general be sought or obtained by her only through him, it would be a miracle if the object of being attractive to men had not become the polar star of feminine education and formation of character. And, this great means of influence over the minds of women having been acquired, an instinct of selfishness made men avail themselves of it to the utmost as a means of holding women in subjection, by representing to them meekness, submissiveness, and resignation of all individual will into the hands of a man, as an essential part of sexual attractiveness. Can it be doubted that any of the other yokes which mankind have succeeded in breaking, would have subsisted till now if the same means had existed, and had been as sedulously used, to bow down their minds to it? If it had been made the object of the life of every young plebeian to find personal favour in the eyes of some patrician, of every young serf with some seigneur; if domestication with him, and a share of his personal affections, had been held out as the prize which they all should look out for, the most gifted and aspiring being able to reckon on the most desirable prizes; and if, when this prize had been obtained, they had been shut out by a wall of brass from all interests not centering in him, all feelings and desires but those which he shared or inculcated; would not serfs and seigneurs, plebeians and patricians, have been as broadly distinguished at this day as men and women are? and would not all but a thinker here and there, have believed the distinction to be a fundamental and unalterable fact in human nature?

The preceding considerations are amply sufficient to show that custom, however universal it may be, affords in this case no presumption, and ought not to create any prejudice, in favour of the arrangements which place women in social and political subjection to men.

RICHARD VERNON, JOHN STUART MILL AND PORNOGRAPHY: BEYOND THE HARM PRINCIPLE

106 Ethics 621 (1996).

For important reasons, liberals resist censorship or even reject it entirely. Suspicion of state power, a sense of the value of privacy, and the importance of open communication to their ideal of transparency—these are perhaps the most basic considerations that incline liberals against censorship. But at the same time, violent and degrading pornography is an affront to many of the other values that liberals are likely to hold. They will not see pornography as a feature of a society in which self-respect flourishes, in which relationships are consensual and not coercive, or in which individual dignity is strongly protected by a scheme of rights. The topic is, then, one especially likely to engage liberals in painful self-reflection, and as an aid to such self-reflection, it is natural that they should turn to the classical writings of their tradition as a way of trying to get clear about the values and priorities essential to it.

On Liberty is of course a natural choice for this purpose: not because it has anything explicit to say about pornography but because it deals prominently with the "silencing" of expression, because it is centrally concerned with the drawing of boundaries, and perhaps, too, because—given the nature of the critique of pornography—it is important that our exemplary liberal text be a consequentialist one. Whatever the underlying reason, two recent contributions to this journal have undertaken to reassess *On Liberty* in the light of the problem of pornography, and they have reached diametrically opposed conclusions. David Dyzenhaus reads *On Liberty* through the lens of *The Subjection of Women.*[1] In the latter text he finds a critique of women's "false consciousness" (to use a shorthand term) and a demand that the "real interest" of women, an interest in achieving autonomy, be pursued by the state, and he finds this demand consistent with Mill's liberalism if we agree to read *On Liberty* in a certain way—essentially, as an argument for protecting people's real interests from harm. Robert Skipper, on the other hand, sees in Dyzenhaus's article a classic slippery-slope problem and argues that the Mill of *On Liberty* would have a shorter way with feminist demands for censorship—he would "slam the door" on them.[2]

This article offers a case for thinking that the arguments of *On Liberty* do permit, or even require, the censorship of violent and degrading pornography. However, it argues that the approaches taken by Dyzenhaus and Skipper are flawed. Despite their conflicting conclusions, their two articles are in agreement on three basic points: that Mill believed in freedom of expression, that he believed in a harm principle as the basis for legislation, and that these two beliefs are in conflict when it comes to the issue of pornography. The difference is that Dyzenhaus thinks that when freedom of expression and the harm principle conflict, the harm principle (subtly interpreted) wins, while Skipper thinks that freedom of expression trumps the harm principle—for if it does not, it is nugatory.

The three points which are shared by these discussions are, I believe, false. Mill did not believe in freedom of expression, he did not employ a "harm principle" in the way in which these (and many other interpreters) suggest, and the issue of pornography is not usefully approached in terms of a collision between expression and harm. Nevertheless, there is a Millian critique of pornography which draws upon other elements in *On Liberty* and in other essays: it draws upon the background features which Mill requires to sustain his principle of liberty.

1. David Dyzenhaus, "John Stuart Mill and the Harm of Pornography," *Ethics* 102 (1992): 534–51.

2. Robert Skipper, "Mill and Pornography," *Ethics* 103 (1993): 726–30.

I

The title of *On Liberty's* second chapter is "Of the Liberty of Thought and Discussion." The word "discussion" is frequently used in the chapter, as is the word "opinion". Mill also speaks of "free discussion," "freedom of opinion," and "liberty of the press." Nowhere does he speak of freedom of expression, and he uses the word "expression" only in the phrase "expression of opinion." "Discussion" and "opinion" are words much narrower than "expression" in their scope of reference. (They are narrower, even, than "speech".) A discussion is a process in which discursive or normative views are advanced and assessed in relation to other views and to evidence. An opinion is a discursive or normative belief which the holder is prepared (if the costs are not too high) to state and defend. "Expression" embraces both discussion and the stating of opinions, and much else too. It embraces, for example, singing, praying, swearing, insulting, advertising, begging, and making puns—to limit oneself to cases of verbal expression alone. Now, surely it is clear that not all arguments in favor of freedom of discussion or opinion are also going to support verbal (or pictorial) expression in general.

There are several reasons why one cannot take discussion or the stating of opinions as proxies, in Mill's argument, for other kinds of expression. The most important is the nature of the familiar extended argument that occupies most of chapter 2. It is an argument about the relation between received opinion and truth. Whether we assume that received opinions are true, false, or partly true, we stand to gain, Mill argues, by permitting them to be criticized without reserve. His argument is plausible only if we suppose that the items exchanged in the critical process are propositions about actual or desirable states of affairs in the world, propositions capable of being accumulated into larger bodies of knowledge. A discussion about pornography might be a useful example. People make assertions about its effects, trying to support these assertions with reference to statistical evidence and to relate the predicted effects to goals, such as equality and security, which they recommend to others; other people criticize the way the statistical evidence is gathered and make claims about the priority of other goals such as privacy or autonomy. All that is a process that could fit Mill's model well, but by no stretch of imagination does pornography itself fit it.

Second, if one takes Mill to be advancing a theory of negative liberty, we might see other forms of expression as protected by Mill's critical model, for it is true that his model does not require the restriction of forms of expression other than opinion. But Mill is not advancing a theory of negative liberty. When he says "All restraint, *qua* restraint, is an evil," he cannot mean that it is evil to employ coercion (a position wholly incompatible with utilitarianism); he must mean that restraint, insofar as it is restraint, involves inflicting pain rather than pleasure on people—that we punish people by fining them, not by giving them money. More important, a negative-freedom position is ruled out by the general structure of Mill's argument. What chapter 2 proposes is a general exemption from the process of weighing and balancing gains and losses which normally precedes legislation; that is what Mill means by calling the liberty of thought and discussion "absolute"—it is not to be put in the balance with other liberties. To justify such an exemption, clearly, positive considerations are required, and, as we have seen, the considerations which Mill gives us support only a limited range of forms of expression. What he offers is not a negative freedom of expression but a positive freedom to discuss.

Third, Mill himself directly indicates that the freedom protected by his main argument falls short of protecting expression in general. Assertions—even true ones—may be made in ways which "justly incur severe censure." Mill mentions two kinds of example: one is "to argue sophistically, to suppress facts or arguments, to misstate the elements of the case, or misrepresent the opposite opinion" and the other is to employ "invective, sarcasm, personality and the like." Mill's case against the legislative prohibition of these two classes of things is interesting and revealing. Sophistical argument is "mostly impossible ... to bring home to conviction" and is often made "in perfect good faith." Of invective, Mill says that "it is obvious" that law has no business trying to restrain it and that its only effective restraint is the "morality of public discussion." So, it is clear that Mill's model of critical discussion does not even protect all forms of discussion: it does not protect sophistical discussion or the unduly aggressive assertion of opinions, for such things detract from, rather than promote, the accumulation of truth. Both things are, of course, protected, but only by side arguments about the impossibility of fair conviction. There is, as it were, a penumbra around truth-promoting discussion, and this penumbra covers forms of discussion which are not truth promoting. But this penumbra does not extend to forms of expression which are not discussion at all—which are not even bad discussion.

II

The second problematic area comprises issues raised by the "harm principle." "Harm principle" is not Mill's coinage, but Joel Feinberg's.[6] Of course, no one could miss what Feinberg had in mind in coining his famous phrase. Mill mentions "harm" prominently near the beginning of *On Liberty,* at the point at which he announces the "principle" that the essay is to defend, and the notion also plays an important role in chapter 4, where Mill discusses the limits of legislation. But if the harm principle is taken to be the principle which Mill uses to determine the scope of legislation—and this is how it is taken by theorists of Mill on pornography, as well as by many other interpreters—then it is a profoundly misleading coinage. Mill does not say that acts which harm others may

6. See Joel Feinberg, *Social Philosophy* (Englewood Cliffs, N.J.: Prentice Hall, 1973), p. 25.

be prohibited while harmless acts may not be, and so his argument is not advanced by elucidations of the meaning of 'harm'.

The principle which Mill defends is, he says, "that the sole end for which mankind are warranted ... in interfering with the liberty of action of any of their number, is self-protection. That the only purpose for which power can be rightfully exercised over any member of a civilised community, is to prevent harm to others. His own good, either physical or moral, is not a sufficient warrant." There are two ways of reading this. The standard way, apparently, is to take it to be announcing a criterion for deciding whether legislation is proper or not. The revised way, proposed here, involves noting that Mill's stress falls heavily on the exclusive aspect of his statement—we cannot impose legislation on you for your own good—and that, as for the inclusive aspect, he speaks of the "end" or "purpose" of the use of power, not of a criterion for it.

The disadvantage of the standard reading is manifest. First of all, immediately after announcing his principle, Mill goes on to devote *On Liberty's* longest chapter to defending an "absolute" liberty to which the issue of harm is irrelevant. It would be entirely consistent with his defense of "the liberty of thought and discussion" to admit that discussion (or even the knowledge that people had certain thoughts) caused terrible harm to others, in some sense of harm which we agree to be significant: perhaps what is said or thought by some makes others incapable of self-respect and, hence, of enjoying meaningful lives. That would not matter, given Mill's argument: there is an overriding argument, in terms of larger social utility, for protecting thought and discussion. Second, if we expect a harm principle to tell us what Mill thinks should and should not be prohibited, we will be bitterly disappointed by what follows in his essay, for no known definition of "harm" captures and excludes the cases which Mill apparently wants to capture and exclude. To take just one example, the English language leaves it open whether we should or should not regard offensiveness as harmful (a point which is, of course, in contention at the moment, given the politics of intercultural relations): does anything in Mill's argument depend on how we resolve this question? It does not, for in the case of some kinds of offensiveness—that caused to one religious group by the practices of another, for example—he refuses to approve of legislation, while in the case of others—such as breaches of "manners"—he supports intervention.

The advantage of the revised reading supported here is that it encompasses much more of the subsequent text of *On Liberty.* It takes the well-known "principle" passage to be stipulating terms of legitimacy for political argument, namely, the kinds of reasons that can properly be given in support of restrictive legislation. Paternalist reasons are excluded, reasons based on harm to others are admitted but are not conclusive without further argument, and the exclusion of limits to discussion becomes intelligible, as part of the background conditions for the process of reasoning itself. The standard reading, in short, makes the text of *On Liberty* largely unintelligible. The revised reading does not.

But that is not the end of the problems for the standard reading. Given the expansive meaning of "harm", the standard reading encounters difficulty in accommodating Mill's liberalism. In some sense, every act or word of mine could harm someone, so how can I enjoy the freedom to act or speak at all? The response to this is the myth of Mill's narrow construal of harm—an inevitable myth, given the need to accommodate both a harm principle and Mill's evident liberalism. Given that Mill wanted to restrict the scope of state action and that he believed that the state should prevent harm, what could be more natural than the conclusion that he wanted to restrict the range of the idea of harm? But what displays the mythical basis of this reading is that Mill did not restrict the range of harm. In chapter 5 of *On Liberty,* he notices several ways in which some people harm others without there being a case for legislative intervention. In trade, people harm each other all the time—they raise people's rents, cut their profit margins, or drive them out of business. Mill also mentions competitive examinations, in which those who win diminish the life chances of those who lose. He unmistakably places these matters within the scope of legislation. If our best economic theory told us that the regulation of trade would make it more efficient, we should regulate. If there were a strong public interest in awarding places in law school to candidates other than those with the highest score, then that is what we should do, on Mill's argument. The reason for not doing either of those things is that, Mill believes, the balance of gains and losses is against them. Whatever we make of Mill's examples and of his conclusions about them, it is plainly not a narrow conception of harm that he is using; it is, if anything, too capacious, for we do not normally think that to deprive someone of an opportunity to which they have no entitlement is to harm them.

III

The third common error (arising from the former two) is to suppose that in the argument of *On Liberty,* expression is to be limited by the harm it causes. This supposition, of course, opens up many difficult questions about what counts as being harmed, kinds of expression, and so on, which Mill leaves unanswered. But they are unanswered because they are not Mill's questions. Even with regard to the expression that he does defend—the expression of opinion—he avoids submitting it to a harm test. In the corn dealer passage, in which he distinguishes between writing an article about the price of corn and inciting a mob with a placard, Mill conceives of incitement as a kind of action. (After describing his example, he goes on at once: "*Acts,* of whatever kind, which . . . do harm to others.") This seems entirely reasonable. Surely we would count giving a verbal order to a firing squad as an action, and expression which likewise is linked intentionally and causally to an occurrence counts as an action too. However, Mill does not discuss with much discrimination the harms caused by protected expression. Since he has protected it, it no longer matters to his case whether or in what sense it causes harm.

The question, then, is not whether a form of expression causes harm, but whether it is protected by Mill's argument. J. C. Rees drew attention to the important role here of Mill's idea of rights.[11] In discussing the "limits to the authority of society" in chapter 4, Mill states that we can be called to account for conduct which "consists in injuring the interests of one another; or rather certain interests, which ... ought to be considered as rights." An explanation of rights is offered in *Utilitarianism:* "To have a right, then, is, I conceive, to have something which society ought to defend me in the possession of. If the objector goes on to ask why it ought, I can give him no other reason than general utility." This is consistent with Mill's justification of the right to express opinion, which is derived from the benefits that it brings to "mankind" and the loss that society in general suffers if the right is denied.

But Mill also indicates that there are liberties other than rights. There are two relevant kinds of "acts injurious to others," one being "encroachment on their rights" and the other "infliction on them of any loss or damage not justified by [one's] own rights." It is important to know, then, when someone suffers loss or injury, whether or not the loss is avoidable without infringing on the actor's rights. If it is avoidable, it should be avoided, and one will have an area of liberty additional to the sphere protected by one's own rights.

These considerations put us in a position, at last, to raise the question of the regulation of pornography in the justifying scheme as Mill structures it. Answering the question requires three steps. The first is to ask whether a strong right is in play—to ask, that is, whether pornography should be protected by considerations of general utility. The second is to ask whether the production and consumption of pornography, if not protected by rights, are inseparably connected with the exercise of some other right. Only then would it be relevant to ask the third question, about the harm that the practice causes. The following sections offer one possible "application," in Mill's term, along these lines.

IV

The first step is easy to accomplish. If there is a serious positive argument for pornography in terms of general utility, it has yet to be constructed. A Bataille-like case built on the liberating power of transgression is all that comes to mind, but that case needs a lot of work before it becomes a serious one. Besides, if successful, it would open the door to much more than the toleration of pornography, since the whole body of criminal law expresses the belief that some transgressions are intolerable. So let us move on at once to the second step, which is more

11. John C. Rees, *John Stuart Mill's "On Liberty"* (Oxford: Clarendon, 1985), pp. 173–74.

problematic. If there is no positive argument for a right to pornography, is it protected by the exercise of other rights?

We can imagine several possibilities here. There could be a covering right—a right to privacy, for example—which has the effect of embracing various practices not themselves directly protected by rights. Or there could be a slippery-slope problem, arising from the fact (or the fear) that it is too difficult to separate the practice in question from other practices that one would not want to punish.

Privacy is, in fact, the only relevant example of a covering right that comes to mind—one can exclude another candidate, a libertarian property right, because it is inconsistent with Mill's whole approach and indeed rules out Mill's line of inquiry. It is certainly dubious that a right to privacy could be extracted from *On Liberty.* As Dyzenhaus points out, Mill treats what is private as the conclusion of an argument rather than a premise for it. There are particular kinds of intrusion by the state that one would want to restrict severely, and some of these might inhibit legislation against the possession of pornography. But it is hard to see how they could inhibit legislation against the production and sale of pornography, which, like all trade, is a social act.

The slippery-slope problem is harder and resists summary treatment. The argument suffers from a general defect, which is that it both asserts and denies that a discrimination can be made. It asserts that we can see a moral difference between A and B, because we know that we want to suppress A but not B; yet, at the same time it denies that the discrimination can be made, since suppressing A will entail suppressing B, too. If we can tell the difference, why can we not express it in legislation? Schauer points out that while we can make the discrimination, it may be that they cannot:[16] that the police and the courts will not reliably separate A from B or that future legislators will wrongly take laws against A as precedents for laws against B. Such considerations would lead us to overprotect or to avoid legislation close to disputed boundaries. It is hard to say in general terms where this leaves the argument for and against the restriction of pornography. The most obvious boundary problem concerns work of artistic merit, the overprotection of which may be the most common basis for the case against antipornography legislation. But surely the boundary cannot be disputed to the extent that all pornography gets to be protected. We can at least draw boundaries with more confidence than we can in, say, proposing to censor literature containing sexist attitudes.

Anxiety about precedential force is harder to assess. To state this potential anxiety as strongly as possible, we may be worried about what happens when states become moralistic and act to suppress anything but the most clearly demonstrable of harms. What else will come within their reach? Worse still, we may be worried about the reflexive impact on

16. Frederick Schauer, "Slippery Slopes," *Harvard Law Review* 99 (1985): 361–83, p. 373.

citizens as they become accustomed to a state which takes their moral lives in hand. Mill, like Tocqueville, was concerned not only about legislative decisions but also about the kind of people who make them and the ways in which character is shaped by politics; it is legitimate to wonder if a state which undertook to suppress pornography would be one which embodied the attitude to government which Mill admired.

V

Those, then, are some of the reservations that one might have. Against these, in the third stage of Mill's decision process, we do have to introduce considerations about harm. Let us assume that the harm arising from pornography is diffuse and that our model of causation contains speculative elements. If we could show direct harm to assignable persons arising from specifiable pornographic items, or even if we could reliably demonstrate harms arising from the pornography industry diffusely, the case would be too easy, and it is doubtful that there would be much debate. At any rate, the assumption made here is that there is a reasonable guess that at least some kinds of pornography play a role in creating a general climate which diminishes the lives of women. What sort of weight can we give this, and what aspect of Mill's argument, in *On Liberty* or elsewhere, can we draw upon?

Mill warns us that the principle of liberty can apply successfully only in certain contexts. It does not apply in the case of children, for example; it did not apply in military societies such as the Greek cities, constantly on the edge of survival and unable to wait for the longterm benefits of freedom; it cannot apply to "barbarians," or, as he alternatively puts it, it requires the context of "a civilized society." What he means by civilization may repay some inquiry. In his essay on that subject, Mill—following many eighteenth-century theorists of civil society—identifies civilization with the division of labor and, hence, with increasing interdependence. As civilization advances, it is increasingly the case that individuals must take satisfaction from collective rather than personal projects and take as their "ideal object" the project of collective self-improvement. However, this process is accompanied by a frightening increase in personal vulnerability. In barbaric or "savage" societies "each person shifts for himself" and "trusts to his own strength and cunning," whereas in a civilized community we depend constantly on each others' self-restraint and conscientiousness. Hence, Mill places enormous weight on personal security, against violations of which, he says, we must be in a state of constant protest.

Security is at risk, of course, from direct and willful (or at least foreseeable) injuries by others, hence, the criminal law. But Mill is clear that civilized society depends on a more diffusely focused responsibility as well, requiring mutual consideration in the most ordinary circumstances of life. We cannot depend on one another without strong expectations about the conduct of others or unless those expectations are generally met. Mill's civilized society is not like Adam Smith's civil (or "great") society, in which strangers are united not by benevolence but by reciprocal interest; nor, on the other hand, is it a face-to-face community in which people have intimate knowledge of one anothers' needs. It is based on reciprocal trust and concern among strangers. That is why we save the man on the unsafe bridge.[19]

It is *The Subjection of Women* that shows the importance of this theme, for its central theme is that sexual inequality is a relic of, precisely, barbarism or of the regime of "strength" which civilization has in general superseded. It is one of "the barbarisms to which men cling longest," which "has not lost the taint of its brutal origin." In one department of life after another, progress has abolished the law of the strongest, leaving the status of women as "a solitary breach" of civilization's "fundamental law." It is "as if a gigantic dolmen, or a vast temple of Jupiter Olympius, occupied the site of St. Paul's and received daily worship." To this relic of barbarism Mill opposes a conception of civilized virtue: "The true virtue of human beings is fitness to live together as equals; claiming nothing for themselves but what they as freely concede to everyone else; regarding command of any kind as an exceptional necessity, and in all cases a temporary one; and preferring, whenever possible, the society of those with whom leading and following can be alternate and reciprocal."

The application of this to the case of pornography is not hard to see. Suppose it were a reasonable guess that pornography is among those things that shore up barbaric inequality and impede the cultivation of the civilized virtues of reciprocity? That would create a powerful case against it, since, as we have seen, those virtues are no mere ideals but actually are preconditions of the principle of liberty itself. The grounds for legislating against pornography would not, in that case, be moralistic ones, but political. Although one might rightly balk at the idea that the state advocated in *On Liberty* had the cultivation of virtue as its direct object, nothing in Mill's discussion prevents that state from defending the moral basis on which its own institutions and practices ultimately rest.

VI

To the claim that pornography is objectionable because it "eroticizes inequality," Skipper objects that there are many other ways of reinforcing inequality, not all of them proper subjects for legislation. "One must wonder about the many other approaches that are at least as effective. Inequality can and has been romanticized, glorified, celebrated, patriotized, totemized, sacralized, proselytized, and aestheticized." Must all such things be banned? That is a good objection. Many of the processes mentioned in this quote would receive protection, as noted above, by covering rights: it does not seem that a liberal state could prosecute a church which sacralized inequality or a Nietzsche interest group which proselytized it. Depending on the kind of inequality in question, the

19. For an illuminating discussion, see Samuel V. La Selva, " 'A Single Truth': Mill on Harm, Paternalism, and Good Samaritanism," *Political Studies* 36 (1988): 486–96.

manner and place in which it was celebrated, and so on, perhaps some of these ways of reinforcing inequality might be prohibited too—we need more detail. But one should respond to Skipper's objection on its own terms. There may be special reasons which apply in the erotic case but not in others. As is well known, erotic attraction is peculiarly inseparable from other drives, generally in ways that are obscure to the subject, and is often associated with feelings of power, powerlessness, or (typically) both at once. The consequence is that equality and transparency in sexual relations are especially elusive goals, so that vulnerability is at its peak. Mill shows little sign of any such concern, favoring sociological rather than psychological explanations of inequality and trusting in institutional solutions. But it would be continuous with his argument to raise the question not just of reciprocity between the sexes but also of sexual reciprocity. If we were persuaded that some kinds of pornography tended diffusely to make such reciprocity even more difficult than it is, the case for its elimination would be attractive. There can be little doubt that modes and sites of emotion resist compartmentalization and that the achievement of Millian virtue involves the whole person.

KINGSLEY INTERNATIONAL PICTURES CORP. v. REGENTS OF THE UNIVERSITY OF THE STATE OF NEW YORK

Supreme Court of the United States, 1959.
360 U.S. 684, 79 S.Ct. 1362, 3 L.Ed.2d 1512.

MR. JUSTICE STEWART delivered the opinion of the Court.

Once again the Court is required to consider the impact of New York's motion picture licensing law upon First Amendment liberties, protected by the Fourteenth Amendment from infringement by the States. *Cf. Joseph Burstyn, Inc., v. Wilson*, 343 U.S. 495.

The New York statute makes it unlawful "to exhibit, or to sell, lease or lend for exhibition at any place of amusement for pay or in connection with any business in the state of New York, any motion picture film or reel (with certain exceptions not relevant here), unless there is at the time in full force and effect a valid license or permit therefor of the education department...." The law provides that a license shall issue "unless such film or a part thereof is obscene, indecent, immoral, inhuman, sacrilegious, or is of such a character that its exhibition would tend to corrupt morals or incite to crime....." A recent statutory amendment provides that, 'the term 'immoral' and the phrase "of such a character that its exhibition would tend to corrupt morals' shall denote a motion picture film or part thereof, the dominant purpose or effect of which is erotic or pornographic; or which portrays acts of sexual immorality, perversion, or lewdness, or which expressly or impliedly presents such acts as desirable, acceptable or proper patterns of behavior."

As the distributor of a motion picture entitled "Lady Chatterley's Lover," the appellant Kingsley submitted that film to the Motion Picture Division of the New York Education Department for a license. Finding three isolated scenes in the film "immoral within the intent of our Law," the Division refused to issue a license until the scenes in question were deleted. The distributor petitioned the Regents of the University of the State of New York for a review of that ruling. The Regents upheld the denial of a license, but on the broader ground that "the whole theme of this motion picture is immoral under said law, for that theme is the presentation of adultery as a desirable, acceptable and proper pattern of behavior."

Kingsley sought judicial review of the Regents' determination. The Appellate Division unanimously annulled the action of the Regents and directed that a license be issued. 165 N.Y.S.2d 681. A sharply divided Court of Appeals, however, reversed the Appellate Division and upheld the Regents' refusal to license the film for exhibition. 175 N.Y.S.2d 39.

The Court of Appeals unanimously and explicitly rejected any notion that the film is obscene. See *Roth v. United States*, 354 U.S. 476. Rather, the court found that the picture as a whole "alluringly portrays adultery as proper behavior." As Chief Judge Conways' prevailing opinion emphasized, therefore, the only portion of the statute involved in this case is that part of §§ 122 and 122—a of the Education Law requiring the denial of a license to motion pictures "which are immoral in that they portray 'acts of sexual immorality * * * as desirable, acceptable or proper patterns of behavior.' " 175 N.Y.S.2d 40. A majority of the Court of Appeals ascribed to that language a precise purpose of the New York Legislature to require the denial of a license to a motion picture "because its subject matter is adultery presented as being right and desirable for certain people under certain circumstances."

We accept the premise that the motion picture here in question can be so characterized. We accept too, as we must, the construction of the New York Legislature's language which the Court of Appeals has put upon it. That construction, we emphasize, gives to the term "sexual immorality" a concept entirely different from the concept embraced in words like "obscenity" or "pornography." Moreover, it is not suggested that the film would itself operate as an incitement to illegal action. Rather, the New York Court of Appeals tells us that the relevant portion of the New York Education Law requires the denial of a license to any motion picture which approvingly portrays an adulterous relationship, quite without reference to the manner of its portrayal.

What New York has done, therefore, is to prevent the exhibition of a motion picture because that picture advocates an idea—that adultery under certain circumstances may be proper behavior. Yet the First Amendment's basic guarantee is of freedom to advocate ideas. The State, quite simply, has thus struck at the very heart of constitutionally protected liberty.

It is contended that the State's action was justified because the motion picture attractively portrays a relationship which is contrary to the moral standards, the religious precepts, and the legal code of its citizenry. This argument misconceives what it is that the Constitution protects. Its guarantee is not confined to the expression of ideas that are conventional or shared by a majority. It protects advocacy of the opinion that adultery may sometimes be proper, no less than advocacy of socialism or the single tax. And in the realm of ideas it protects expression which is eloquent no less than that which is unconvincing.

Advocacy of conduct proscribed by law is not, as Mr. Justice Brandeis long ago pointed out, "a justification for denying free speech where the advocacy falls short of incitement and there is nothing to indicate that the advocacy would be immediately acted on." *Whitney v. California*, 274 U.S. 357, 376 (concurring opinion). "Among free men, the deterrents ordinarily to be applied to prevent crime are education and punishment for violations of the law, not abridgment of the rights of free speech * * *." Id., 274 U.S. at 378.[1]

The inflexible command which the New York Court of Appeals has attributed to the State Legislature thus cuts so close to the core of constitutional freedom as to make it quite needless in this case to examine the periphery. Specifically, there is no occasion to consider the appellant's contention that the State is entirely without power to require films of any kind to be licensed prior to their exhibition. Nor need we here determine whether, despite problems peculiar to motion pictures, the controls which a State may impose upon this medium of expression are precisely coextensive with those allowable for newspapers, books, or individual speech. It is enough for the present case to reaffirm that motion pictures are within the First and Fourteenth Amendments' basic protection. *Joseph Burstyn, Inc. v. Wilson*, 343 U.S. 495.

Reversed.

[Concurring opinions by JUSTICES BLACK, FRANKFURTER, DOUGLAS, CLARK, and HARLAN are omitted.]

Question

Is Richard Vernon correct that Mill's argument for the liberty to express opinions "on all subjects" does not justify the freedom to disseminate pornographic images of nude women? Does Vernon's interpretation imply that Mill's argument does not support the Supreme Court's decision in *Kingsley Pictures Corp. v. Regents*?

AMERICAN BOOKSELLERS ASSOCIATION v. HUDNUT

United States Court of Appeals, Seventh Circuit, 1985.
771 F.2d 323.

EASTERBROOK, CIRCUIT JUDGE.

Indianapolis enacted an ordinance defining "pornography" as a practice that discriminates against women. "Pornography" is to be

1. Thomas Jefferson wrote more than a hundred and fifty years ago, "But we have nothing to fear from the demoralizing reasonings of some, if others are left free to demonstrate their errors. And especially when the law stands ready to punish the first criminal act produced by the false reasoning. These are safer correctives than the conscience of a judge." Letter of Thomas Jefferson to Elijah Boardman, July 3, 1801, Jefferson Papers, Library of Congress, Vol. 115, folio 19761.

redressed through the administrative and judicial methods used for other discrimination. The City's definition of "pornography" is considerably different from "obscenity," which the Supreme Court has held is not protected by the First Amendment.

To be "obscene" under *Miller v. California,* 413 U.S. 15 (1973), "a publication must, taken as a whole, appeal to the prurient interest, must contain patently offensive depictions or descriptions of specified sexual conduct, and on the whole have no serious literary, artistic, political, or scientific value." *Brockett v. Spokane Arcades, Inc.,* 472 U.S. 491 (1985). Offensiveness must be assessed under the standards of the community. Both offensiveness and an appeal to something other than "normal, healthy sexual desires" are essential elements of "obscenity."

"Pornography" under the ordinance is "the graphic sexually explicit subordination of women, whether in pictures or in words, that also includes one or more of the following:

(1) Women are presented as sexual objects who enjoy pain or humiliation; or

(2) Women are presented as sexual objects who experience sexual pleasure in being raped; or

(3) Women are presented as sexual objects tied up or cut up or mutilated or bruised or physically hurt, or as dismembered or truncated or fragmented or severed into body parts; or

(4) Women are presented as being penetrated by objects or animals; or

(5) Women are presented in scenarios of degradation, injury, abasement, torture, shown as filthy or inferior, bleeding, bruised, or hurt in a context that makes these conditions sexual; or

(6) Women are presented as sexual objects for domination, conquest, violation, exploitation, possession, or use, or through postures or positions of servility or submission or display."

The Indianapolis ordinance does not refer to the prurient interest, to offensiveness, or to the standards of the community. It demands attention to particular depictions, not to the work judged as a whole. It is irrelevant under the ordinance whether the work has literary, artistic, political, or scientific value. The City and many amici point to these omissions as virtues. They maintain that pornography influences attitudes, and the statute is a way to alter the socialization of men and women rather than to vindicate community standards of offensiveness. And as one of the principal drafters of the ordinance has asserted, "if a woman is subjected, why should it matter that the work has other value?" Catharine A. MacKinnon, *Pornography, Civil Rights, and Speech,* 20 Harv.Civ.Rts.—Civ.Lib.L.Rev. 1, 21 (1985).

Civil rights groups and feminists have entered this case as amici on both sides. Those supporting the ordinance say that it will play an important role in reducing the tendency of men to view women as sexual objects, a tendency that leads to both unacceptable attitudes and discrimination in the workplace and violence away from it. Those opposing the ordinance point out that much radical feminist literature is explicit and depicts women in ways forbidden by the ordinance and that the ordinance would reopen old battles. It is unclear how Indianapolis would treat works from James Joyce's *Ulysses* to Homer's *Iliad;* both depict women as submissive objects for conquest and domination.

We do not try to balance the arguments for and against an ordinance such as this. The ordinance discriminates on the ground of the content of the speech. Speech treating women in the approved way—in sexual encounters "premised on equality" (MacKinnon, *supra,* at 22)—is lawful no matter how sexually explicit. Speech treating women in the disapproved way—as submissive in matters sexual or as enjoying humiliation—is unlawful no matter how significant the literary, artistic, or political qualities of the work taken as a whole. The state may not ordain preferred viewpoints in this way. The Constitution forbids the state to declare one perspective right and silence opponents.

* * *

The ordinance contains four prohibitions. People may not "traffic" in pornography, "coerce" others into performing in pornographic works, or "force" pornography on anyone. Anyone injured by anyone who has seen or read pornography has a right of action against the maker or seller. Trafficking is defined as "the production, sale, exhibition, or distribution of pornography." [The ordinance] provides that the trafficking paragraph "shall not be construed to make isolated passages or isolated parts actionable."…. [The ordinance also] defines as a prohibited practice the "assault, physical attack, or injury of any woman, man, child, or transsexual in a way that is directly caused by specific pornography."…. It is a complete defense to a trafficking case that all the materials in question were pornography only by virtue of category (6) [which prohibits presenting women as sexual objects for domination, etc.] of the definition of pornography.

* * *

"If there is any fixed star in our constitutional constellation, it is that no official, high or petty, can prescribe what shall be orthodox in politics, nationalism, religion, or other matters of opinion or force citizens to confess by word or act their faith therein." *West Virginia State Board of Education v. Barnette,* 319 U.S. 624, 642 (1943). Under the First Amendment the government must leave to the people the evaluation of ideas. Bald or subtle, an idea is as powerful as the audience allows it to be. A belief may be pernicious—the beliefs of Nazis led to the death of millions, those of the Klan to the repression of millions. A pernicious belief may prevail. Totalitarian governments today rule much of the planet, practicing suppression of billions and spreading dogma that may enslave others. One of the things that separates our society from theirs is our absolute right to propagate opinions that the government finds wrong or even hateful.

* * *

Indianapolis justifies the ordinance on the ground that pornography affects thoughts. Men who see women depicted as subordinate are more likely to treat them so. Pornography is an aspect of dominance. It does not persuade people so much as change them. It works by socializing, by establishing the expected and the permissible. In this view pornography is not an idea; pornography is the injury.

There is much to this perspective. Beliefs are also facts. People often act in accordance with the images and patterns they find around them. People raised in a religion tend to accept the tenets of that religion, often without independent examination. People taught from birth that black people are fit only for slavery rarely rebelled against that creed; beliefs coupled with the self-interest of the masters established a social structure that inflicted great harm while enduring for centuries. Words and images act at the level of the subconscious before they persuade at the level of the conscious. Even the truth has little chance unless a statement fits within the framework of beliefs that may never have been subjected to rational study.

Therefore we accept the premises of this legislation. Depictions of subordination tend to perpetuate subordination. The subordinate status of women in turn leads to affront and lower pay at work, insult and injury at home, battery and rape on the streets.[2] In the language of the legislature, "[p]ornography is central in creating and maintaining sex as a basis of discrimination. Pornography is a systematic practice of exploitation and subordination based on sex which differentially harms women. The bigotry and contempt it produces, with the acts of aggression it fosters, harm women's opportunities for equality and rights [of all kinds]." Indianapolis Code § 16–1(a)(2).

Yet this simply demonstrates the power of pornography as speech. All of these unhappy effects depend on mental intermediation. Pornography affects how people see the world, their fellows, and social relations. If pornography is what pornography does, so is other speech. Hitler's orations affected how some Germans saw Jews. Communism is a world view, not simply a *Manifesto* by Marx and Engels or a set of speeches. Efforts to suppress communist speech in the United States were based on the belief that the public acceptability of such ideas would increase

2. MacKinnon's article collects empirical work that supports this proposition. The social science studies are very difficult to interpret, however, and they conflict. Because much of the effect of speech comes through a process of socialization, it is difficult to measure incremental benefits and injuries caused by particular speech. Several psychologists have found, for example, that those who see violent, sexually explicit films tend to have more violent thoughts. But how often does this lead to actual violence? National commissions on obscenity here, in the United Kingdom, and in Canada have found that it is not possible to demonstrate a direct link between obscenity and rape or exhibitionism. The several opinions in *Miller v. California* discuss the U.S. commission. See also *Report of the Committee on Obscenity and Film Censorship* 61–95 (Home Office, Her Majesty's Stationery Office, 1979); Special Committee on Pornography and Prostitution, 1 *Pornography and Prostitution in Canada* 71–73, 95–103 (Canadian Government Publishing Centre 1985). In saying that we accept the finding that pornography as the ordinance defines it leads to unhappy consequences, we mean only that there is evidence to this effect, that this evidence is consistent with much human experience, and that as judges we must accept the legislative resolution of such disputed empirical questions. See *Gregg v. Georgia,* 428 U.S. 153, 184–87 (1976) (opinion of Stewart, Powell, and Stevens, JJ.).

the likelihood of totalitarian government. Religions affect socialization in the most pervasive way. The opinion in *Wisconsin v. Yoder,* 406 U.S. 205 (1972), shows how a religion can dominate an entire approach to life, governing much more than the relation between the sexes. Many people believe that the existence of television, apart from the content of specific programs, leads to intellectual laziness, to a penchant for violence, to many other ills. The Alien and Sedition Acts passed during the administration of John Adams rested on a sincerely held belief that disrespect for the government leads to social collapse and revolution—a belief with support in the history of many nations. Most governments of the world act on this empirical regularity, suppressing critical speech. In the United States, however, the strength of the support for this belief is irrelevant. Seditious libel is protected speech unless the danger is not only grave but also imminent. See *New York Times Co. v. Sullivan,* 376 U.S. 254 (1964); cf. *Brandenburg v. Ohio, supra; New York Times Co. v. United States,* 403 U.S. 713 (1971).

Racial bigotry, anti-semitism, violence on television, reporters' biases—these and many more influence the culture and shape our socialization. None is directly answerable by more speech, unless that speech too finds its place in the popular culture. Yet all is protected as speech, however insidious. Any other answer leaves the government in control of all of the institutions of culture, the great censor and director of which thoughts are good for us.

Sexual responses often are unthinking responses, and the association of sexual arousal with the subordination of women therefore may have a substantial effect. But almost all cultural stimuli provoke unconscious responses. Religious ceremonies condition their participants. Teachers convey messages by selecting what not to cover; the implicit message about what is off limits or unthinkable may be more powerful than the messages for which they present rational argument. Television scripts contain unarticulated assumptions. People may be conditioned in subtle ways. If the fact that speech plays a role in a process of conditioning were enough to permit governmental regulation, that would be the end of freedom of speech.

* * *

Much of Indianapolis's argument rests on the belief that when speech is "unanswerable," and the metaphor that there is a "marketplace of ideas" does not apply, the First Amendment does not apply either. The metaphor is honored; Milton's *Aeropagitica* and John Stuart Mill's *On Liberty* defend freedom of speech on the ground that the truth will prevail, and many of the most important cases under the First Amendment recite this position. The Framers undoubtedly believed it. As a general matter it is true. But the Constitution does not make the dominance of truth a necessary condition of freedom of speech. To say that it does would be to confuse an outcome of free speech with a necessary condition for the application of the amendment.

A power to limit speech on the ground that truth has not yet prevailed and is not likely to prevail implies the power to declare truth. At some point the government must be able to say (as Indianapolis has said): "We know what the truth is, yet a free exchange of speech has not driven out falsity, so that we must now prohibit falsity." If the government may declare the truth, why wait for the failure of speech? Under the First Amendment, however, there is no such thing as a false idea, *Gertz v. Robert Welch, Inc.,* 418 U.S. 323, 339 (1974), so the government may not restrict speech on the ground that in a free exchange truth is not yet dominant.

At any time, some speech is ahead in the game; the more numerous speakers prevail. Supporters of minority candidates may be forever "excluded" from the political process because their candidates never win, because few people believe their positions. This does not mean that freedom of speech has failed.

* * *

Any rationale we could imagine in support of this ordinance could not be limited to sex discrimination. Free speech has been on balance an ally of those seeking change. Governments that want stasis start by restricting speech. Culture is a powerful force of continuity; Indianapolis paints pornography as part of the culture of power. Change in any complex system ultimately depends on the ability of outsiders to challenge accepted views and the reigning institutions. Without a strong guarantee of freedom of speech, there is no effective right to challenge what is.

* * *

Affirmed.

CATHARINE A. MacKINNON, ONLY WORDS

(1993).

The law against pornography was not designed to see harm to women in the first place. It is further weakened as pornography spreads, expanding into new markets (such as video and computers) and more legitimate forums and making abuse of women more and more invisible as abuse, as that abuse becomes more and more visible as sex. So the Court becomes increasingly *unable to tell* what is pornography and what is not, a failing it laments not as a consequence of the saturation of society by pornography, but as a specifically judicial failure, then finally as an impossibility of line-drawing. The stage is thus set for the transformation of pornography into political speech: the excluded and stigmatized "ideas" we love to hate. Obscured is the way this protects what pornography says and ignores what it does, or, alternatively, protects what pornography says as a means of protecting what it does. Thus can a law develop which prohibits restricting a film because it advocates adultery, but does not even notice a film that is made from a rape.

Nothing in the American law of obscenity is designed to perceive the rape, sexual abuse of children, battering, sexual harassment, prostitution, or sexual murder in pornography. This becomes insulting upon encountering obscenity law's search for harm and failure to find any. The law of child pornography, by contrast—based as it is on the assumption that children are harmed by having sex pictures made of them—applies a test developed in areas of speech other than the sexual: if the harm of speech outweighs its value, it can be restricted by properly targeted means. Given the history of the law of pornography of adult women, it is tempting to regard this as a miracle. Child pornography is not considered the speech of a sexually dissident minority, which it is, advocating "ideas" about children and sex, which it does. Perhaps the fact that boys were used in the film in the test case has something to do with it. The ability to see that child pornography is harmful has everything to do with a visceral sense of the inequality in power between children and adults, yet inequality is never mentioned.

Now, in this context of speech and equality concerns, consider again the judicial opinion on the law Andrea Dworkin and I wrote and Indianapolis passed. This law defines the documented harms pornography does as violations of equality rights and makes them actionable as practices of discrimination, of second-class citizenship. This ordinance allows anyone hurt through pornography to prove its role in their abuse, to recover for the deprivation of their civil rights, and to stop it from continuing. Judicially, this was rendered as censorship of ideas.

In *American Booksellers v. Hudnut,* the Court of Appeals for the Seventh Circuit found that this law violated the First Amendment. It began by recognizing that the harm pornography does is real, conceding that the legislative finding of a causal link was judicially adequate: " . . . we accept the premises of this legislation. Depictions of subordination tend to perpetuate subordination. The subordinate status of women in turn leads to affront and lower pay at work, insult and injury at home, battery and rape on the streets. In the language of the legislature, '[p]ornography is central in creating and maintaining sex as a basis of discrimination.' " Writing for the panel, Judge Easterbrook got, off and on, that "subordination" is something pornography does, not something it just says, and that its active role had to be proven in each case brought under the ordinance. But he kept losing his mental bearings and referring to pornography as an "idea," finally concluding that the harm it does "demonstrates the power of pornography as speech." This is like saying that the more a libel destroys a reputation, the greater is its power as speech. To say that the more harm speech does, the more protected it is, is legally wrong, even in this country.

Implicitly applying the political speech model, Judge Easterbrook said that the law restricted the marketplace of ideas, the speech of outcast dissenters—referring presumably to those poor heads of organized crime families making ten billion dollars a year trafficking women. He said the law discriminated on the basis of point of view, establishing an approved view of what could be said and thought about women and sex. He failed to note at this point that the invalidated causes of action included coercion, force, and assault, rather a far cry from saying and thinking. He reminded us of *Sullivan,* whose most famous dictum is that to flourish, debate must be "uninhibited, robust, and wide-open." Behind his First Amendment facade, women were being transformed into ideas, sexual traffic in whom was protected as if it were a discussion, the men uninhibited and robust, the women wide-open.

Judge Easterbrook did not say this law was not a sex discrimination law, but he gave the state interest it therefore served—opposition to sex inequality—no constitutional weight. He did this by treating it as if it were a group defamation law, holding that no amount of harm of discrimination can outweigh the speech interests of bigots, so long as they say something while doing it.

RONALD DWORKIN, FREEDOM'S LAW: THE MORAL READING OF THE CONSTITUTION

(1996).

People's lives are affected not just by their political environment—not just by what their Presidents and legislators and other public officials do—but even more comprehensively by what we might call their moral environment. How others treat me—and my own sense of identity and self-respect—are determined in part by the mix of social conventions, opinions, tastes, convictions, prejudices, life styles, and cultures that flourish in the community in which I live. Liberals are sometimes accused of thinking that what people say or do or think in private has no impact on anyone except themselves, and that is plainly wrong. Someone to whom religion is of fundamental importance, for example, will obviously lead a very different and perhaps more satisfying life in a community in which most other people share his convictions than in a dominantly secular society of atheists for whom his beliefs are laughable superstitions. A woman who believes that explicit sexual material degrades her will likely lead a very different, and no doubt more satisfying, life among people who also despise pornography than in a community where others, including other women, think it liberating and fun.

Exactly because the moral environment in which we all live is in good part created by others, however, the question of who shall have the power to help shape that environment, and how, is of fundamental importance, though it is often neglected in political theory. Only one answer is consistent with the ideals of political equality: that no one may be prevented from influencing the shared moral environment, through his own private choices, tastes, opinions, and example, just because these tastes or opinions disgust those who have the power to shut him up or lock him up. Of course, the ways in which anyone may exercise that influence must be limited in order to protect the security and interests of others. People may not try to mold the moral climate by intimidating women with sexual demands or by burning a cross on a black family's lawn, or by refusing to hire women or blacks at all, or by making their working conditions so humiliating as to be intolerable.

But we cannot count, among the kinds of interests that may be protected in this way, a right not to be insulted or damaged just by the fact that others have hostile or uncongenial tastes, or that they are free to express or indulge them in private. Recognizing that right would mean denying that some people—those whose tastes these are—have any right to participate in forming the moral environment at all. Of course it should go without saying that no one has a right to *succeed* in influencing others through his own private choices and tastes. Sexists and bigots have no right to live in a community whose ideology or culture is even partially sexist or bigoted: they have no right to any proportional representation for their odious views. In a genuinely egalitarian society, however, those views cannot be locked out, in advance, by criminal or civil law: they must instead be discredited by the disgust, outrage, and ridicule of other people.

MacKinnon's "egalitarian" argument for censorship is important mainly because it reveals the most important reason for resisting her suggestions, and also because it allows us to answer her charge that liberals who oppose her are crypto-pornographers themselves. She thinks that people who defend the right to pornography are acting out of self-interest, not principle—she says she has been driven to the conclusion that "speech *will* be defined so that men can have their pornography." That charge is based on the inadequacy of the conventional explanation, deriving from John Stuart Mill, that pornography must be protected so that truth may emerge. What is actually at stake in the argument about pornography, however, is not society's chance to discover truth, but its commitment to the very ideal of equality that MacKinnon thinks underrated in the American community. Liberals defend pornography, though most of them despise it, in order to defend a conception of the First Amendment that includes, as at least one of its purposes, protecting equality in the processes through which the moral as well as the political environment is formed. First Amendment liberty is not equality's enemy, but the other side of equality's coin.

MacKinnon is right to emphasize the connection between the fight over pornography and the larger, more general and important, argument about the freedom of Americans to say and teach what others think politically incorrect. She and her followers regard freedom of speech and thought as an elitist, inegalitarian ideal that has been of almost no value to women, blacks, and others without power; they say America would be better off if it demoted that ideal as many other nations have. But most of her constituents would be appalled if this denigration of freedom should escape from universities and other communities where their own values about political correctness are now popular and take root in the more general political culture. Local majorities may find homosexual art or feminist theater just as degrading to women as the kind of pornography MacKinnon hates, or radical or separatist black opinion just as inimical to racial justice as crude racist epithets.

That is an old liberal warning—as old as Voltaire—and many people have grown impatient with it. They are willing to take that chance, they say, to advance a program that seems overwhelmingly important now. Their impatience may prove fatal for that program rather than essential to it, however. If we abandon our traditional understanding of equality for a different one that allows a majority to define some people as too corrupt or offensive or radical to join in the informal moral life of the nation, we will have begun a process that ends, as it has in so many other parts of the world, in making equality something to be feared rather than celebrated, a mocking, "correct" euphemism for tyranny.

T.M. SCANLON, JR., FREEDOM OF EXPRESSION AND CATEGORIES OF EXPRESSION

40 U. Pitt. L. Rev. 519, 547–48 (1979).

Earnest treatises on the virtues of a sexually liberated society can be reliably predicted to have no effect on prevailing attitudes towards sex. What is more likely to have such an effect is for people to discover that they find exciting and attractive portrayals of sex which they formerly thought offensive or, vice versa, that they find boring and offensive what they had expected to find exciting and liberating. How can partisans of sexual change be given a fair chance to make this happen except through a relaxation of restrictions on what can be publicly displayed? I do not assume that the factual claims behind this argument are correct. My question rather is, if they were correct what would follow? From the fact that frequent exposure to material previously thought offensive is a likely way to promote a change in people's attitudes, it does not follow that partisans of change are entitled to use this means. Proponents of a change in attitude are not entitled to use just *any* expressive means to effect their aim even if the given means is the only one that would actually have the effect they desire: audience interests must also be considered. It must be asked whether exposure to these means leads to changes in one's tastes and preferences through a process that is, like subliminal advertising, both outside of one's rational control and quite independent of the relevant grounds for preference, or whether, on the contrary, the exposure to such influences is in fact part of the best way to discover what one really has reason to prefer. I think that a crucial question regarding the regulation of pornography and other forms of allegedly corrupting activity lies here.

It is often extremely difficult to distinguish influences whose force is related to relevant grounds for the attitudes they produce from influences that are the work of irrelevant factors. Making this distinction requires, in many cases, a clearer understanding than we have both of the psychological processes through which our attitudes are altered and of the relevant grounds for holding the attitudes in question. The nature of these grounds, in particular, is often a matter of too much controversy to be relied upon in defining a right of freedom of expression. The power to restrict the presentation of "irrelevant influences" seems threatening because it is too easily extended to restrict any expression likely to mislead.

Subliminal advertising is in this respect an unusual case, from which it is hard to generalize. A law against subliminal advertising could be acceptable on first amendment grounds because it could be framed as a prohibition simply of certain techniques—the use of hidden words or images—thus avoiding controversial distinctions between relevant and irrelevant influences. Where we are concerned with the apparent—as opposed to the hidden—content of expression, however, things become more controversial (even though it is true that what is clearly seen or heard may influence us, and be designed to do so, in ways that we are quite unaware of).

Questions

1) How might MacKinnon answer Dworkin's contention that even persons with the most disgusting views deserve the opportunity to participate in molding the moral climate? Could she subscribe to Dworkin's premise regarding the right to participate and nevertheless develop persuasive reasons why the materials and practices that she argues should be civilly actionable are not a legitimate part of an open-ended process of moral development?

2) Do Professor Scanlon's observations offer more support to Professor MacKinnon or to Professor Dworkin?

JEREMY WALDRON, MILL AND THE VALUE OF MORAL DISTRESS

35 Political Studies 310 (1987).

I

In the modern discussion of pornography and obscenity—and in the perennial liberal debates about freedom, toleration, and neutrality—it remains unclear what or how much should be made of the fact that people in one group find the views, the tastes, or the life-style of others in their community *disturbing*. Even if an action (or a book or a film) is not directly harmful, in the sense that it does not actually contribute to the causation of injury, loss, or damage, still it may be perceived as indecent, insulting, degrading, threatening, or distressing in less tangible ways. In the pornography debate, in particular, there is much to be said for the view that politicians and philosophers have concentrated too long on what pornography *does* (what it causes) and too little on what it *is* or what it represents, especially as far as women are concerned. That balance is now gradually being redressed, but further consideration of the issues involved in this shift of concerns is certainly necessary. Undoubtedly one of the main characteristics of pornography (though one which it shares with the best art and literature) is that it *disturbs* us and makes us uneasy. That, I suppose, can be regarded as one of its *effects*, and, to the extent that people do not like being disturbed, to the extent that being disturbed in this way *hurts*, such an effect may be regarded as one of the *harmful* consequences of pornography and therefore as a basis for part of the case in favor of its prohibition. Alternatively, it may be argued that these negative effects accrue only because of moral views and prejudices that are held already by those who suffer from them, and therefore that they provide no distinct basis for prohibition apart from whatever arguments can be constructed out of the moral views and prejudices themselves.

A full consideration of the issues here would involve untangling the various ideas that come together when we talk about a person being *disturbed* by another's behavior: the perception of threat, the perception of insult, the perception of symbol or representation, the vehemence of moral condemnation, the feeling of outrage, the elements of pity, contempt, sublimated guilt, shame, and so on. These need to be distinguished and their connections with one another carefully investigated in order to be able to deal sensitively with the variety of cases that can be accumulated under this general heading. A full consideration would also mean exploring the way in which each of these strands is perceived in the various traditions of liberal and nonliberal argument: we must not assume, for example, that the Kantian argument for toleration and the Millian argument for toleration treat *moral outrage* or *threat* or *perceived insult* in the same way. On the contrary, these elements will be assigned different roles in different arguments, even when those arguments are driving toward substantially the same conclusion. There is, then, a lot to be done before we have anything like a satisfactory account of the relation between the fact that something is disturbing and a proposal that it ought to be prohibited.

My aims in the present chapter are very modest. I want to concentrate on what I shall call the element of moral distress—the fact that someone is distressed because of what he takes to be the immorality or the depravity of another's behavior. (Think, for example, of the distress many citizens experience when they see two men kissing passionately or when they consider what those two get up to in their bedroom at night.) I want to consider the place of this sort of distress, this element of disturbance, in what is perhaps the most influential of the modern liberal arguments for toleration—the argument in John Stuart Mill's essay, *On Liberty*.

If we approach the issue of the social enforcement of ethical and religious standards in terms of Mill's famous Harm Principle—the principle which holds that "the only purpose for which power can be rightfully exercised over any member of a civilized community, against his will, is to prevent harm to others"—we face the following question. Does moral distress of the kind I have mentioned count as *harm* for the purposes of Mill's principle?

Theoretically, at least, the question is an important one. It is true that moral conservatives and perfectionists have not usually relied on the existence of these harms to justify the enforcement of their moral views. From their perspective, that would be a rather sordid and self-interested approach; they prefer to attack the Harm Principle directly rather than squeeze out an interpretation of it congenial to their commitments. Instead, Mill's critics make use of the problem to *discredit* the Harm Principle, and to show the folly of imagining that there can be a sphere of individual morality and immorality which in principle does not affect the interests of other people.[6] The liberal, then, for his part, is interested in the problem not because he imagines that conservatives will try to justify the moralistic use of power on this basis, but because of the implicit challenge posed to the meaning and point of the principle he has invoked to protect individual liberty.

One possible approach that the liberal might take is to concede that moral distress falls within the scope of the Harm Principle, but to insist that it is, on the whole, outweighed by the pain that would be involved in the prohibition of the conduct that occasions it. After all, the fact that one's conduct harms another is, on Mill's account, only a necessary not a sufficient justification for intervention; once harm is established, everything depends on a calculation of the costs and the benefits of preventing it. The point of the Harm Principle is to establish a threshold which must be crossed before utilitarian calculations of that sort are even in order, not to elevate every little incident of harm into a pretext for prohibition. But this approach seems unsatisfactory, from a liberal point of view, for two reasons. First, it makes the case against the enforcement of ethical and religious standards rather more precarious than liberals have usually been willing to concede. On this approach the liberty, for example, of a religious minority will depend on how large the opposing majority is and on the intensity of the popular feeling directed against them. If the majority is very large and the feeling very intense, then the "harm" (to the "interests" of the majority) that could be prevented by persecution might greatly outweigh the harm that persecution would cause. But one's liberal instincts suggest that the case for toleration becomes *more* not less compelling the smaller and less popular the group whose liberty is in question. Second, if we agree that ethical and religious conviction is in part a matter of feeling and that everyone who takes his convictions seriously is to some degree upset when he discovers that others do not share them, it seems odd that the mere existence of moral distress should be sufficient to cross the threshold test established by the Harm Principle. For then what work is the principle doing? What cases of the enforcement of morals could it possibly exclude? The answer is: only those cases which are not really taken seriously by the moralists anyway. That is why I suggest that the problem of morality-dependent harm poses a threat not just to the operation, but to the very coherence, of the Harm Principle. If a moralist's *natural* and *predictable* response to deviance is sufficient to count as his being harmed, then the idea of deploying a *Harm* Principle to limit the enforcement of conventional morals seems hopelessly ill-conceived.

6. This appears to be the intention in R. P. Wolff, *The Poverty of Liberalism* (Boston, 1968), Ch. 1. and in Patrick Devlin. *The Enforcement of Morals* (Oxford, 1965), Ch. 6.

The question of moral distress has been considered many times in the vast literature that has accumulated around Mill's essay. I want to argue that if we approach it in terms of Mill's *arguments* for the Harm Principle, we get an answer which is clear, unequivocal, and surprising: far from providing the basis of an argument for prohibition, moral distress on Mill's account is actually a *positive* feature of deviant actions and life-styles; the outrage and disturbance that deviance evokes is something to be welcomed, nurtured, and encouraged in the free society that Mill is arguing for.

II

Let me begin with one or two comments about methodology and interpretation. The problem of whether moral distress should be regarded as *harm* for the purposes of Mill's principle is not one that can be resolved by a logical analysis of the concept of harm or by looking up "harm" in a dictionary. There is at least one sense of the term in which anyone who is discomforted and distressed by an activity is *eo ipso* harmed by it (he experiences what feels from the inside remarkably like pain), even if there are other narrower senses, which an analytically minded liberal might want to invoke, which do not cover this type of experience. When we are faced, in this way, with rival conceptions of harm, the question is then not what "harm" *really* means, but what reasons of principle there are for preferring one conception to another in the present context. A similar point can be made about the maneuver, common among Mill scholars, which insists that his principle was concerned only with harm to individual *interests*. The concept of interest is also a contested one. There are conceptions in terms of which moral distress has an indubitably adverse effect on one's interests:

> Suppose that Jones is a devout Calvinist or a principled vegetarian. The very presence in his community of a Catholic or a meat-eater may cause him fully as much pain as a blow in the face or theft of his purse.... If the existence of ungodly persons in my community tortures my soul and destroys my sleep, who is to say that my interests are not affected?

And there are, as I shall argue, conceptions in terms of which one's interests should be said to be promoted rather than disserved by the experience of moral distress. Once again, the question is not what "interests" *really* means, but rather what reasons of principle there are for preferring one conception of interests to another in this context.

When we are considering a text like *On Liberty*, we need to remember that a doctrine such as the Harm Principle is not a piece of legislation, and questions posed in jurisprudence and political philosophy about how it is to be understood are not questions of statutory construction. As a pronouncement it has no authority in itself. The principle is presented in Chapter 1 of *On Liberty* as the upshot of an argument which Mill is about to present, and the only meaning or interest it can possibly have for us lies in its relation to that justificatory argument. If we accept, as I think we must, that terms such as "harm" and "interests" (like "power," "liberty," and "law") have no clear or indisputable meaning awaiting our analysis, and that they rather pick out concepts whose nature it is to be contested from different evaluative standpoints, then the question is not simply which is the better conception of harm, but which conception answers more adequately to the purposes for which the concept is deployed. In the context of *On Liberty*, those purposes are established by Mill's *arguments* for freedom of opinion and life-style, that is, by his account of what we have to lose if liberty in those areas is withheld.

III

On Liberty contains several arguments in favor of individual freedom of thought, discussion, and life-style. The most important of these are based on the desirability of what I am going to refer to as *ethical confrontation*—the open clash between earnestly held ideals and opinions about the nature and basis of the good life. Ethical confrontation should be understood to include conflicts on all sorts of issues—moral, philosophical, political, and religious—and to range from verbal debate on the one hand to the demonstration and flaunting of rival life-styles on the other. On Mill's view, the main argument against interference with individual liberty was that it diminished the occasion and opportunity for ethical confrontation in this sense.

Mill's attitude to confrontation was far from nihilistic; he did not take any satanic delight in the prospect of a *bellum omnium contra omnes* in the ethical realm. Although he denied the existence of any *one* solution to the problem of the good life, he certainly believed that there were objectively better and worse solutions. As much as any of his perfectionist critics, he believed that genuine moral progress was possible. But progress, Mill insisted, was certainly not *guaranteed* under modern conditions; he rejected as a "pleasant falsehood" the dictum that truth always triumphs and that the good will come out on top in the end. He saw a real danger that contemporary society might become stuck in a mire of prejudice and mediocrity, a danger of its becoming "another China"—a more worrying analogue to the "stationary society" that he foresaw in the realm of economics.[8] If we want our society to remain progressive, Mill said, we must work at it, and the disappearance of ethical confrontation would be alarming evidence that we were failing in that task.

What contribution does ethical confrontation make to progress? The contribution, on Mill's account, is of two sorts. First, it contributes to the emergence of new and better ideas. Second, it makes an important contribution to the way ideas are held in society.

The first argument depends on a roughly dialectical account of ethical progress. It is a safe assumption that neither the prevailing doctrines in a society (if there are any) nor their main rivals express the

8. J.S. Mill. *Principles of Political Economy* (London, 1965), Book IV, Ch. 6.

whole truth about the human condition and the good life; most current doctrines contain elements of the truth and moral progress is a matter of the development of new doctrines that take up half-truths from here and there, and generate syntheses which have somewhat greater verisimilitude than the views out of which they grew. Mill does not believe that this process of synthesis can be contrived deliberately by any individual moralist acting on his own.

> Truth in the great practical concerns of life is so much a question of the reconciling and combining of opposites that very few have minds sufficiently capacious to make the adjustment with an approach to correctness, and it has to be made by the rough process of a struggle between combatants fighting under hostile banners.

Similarly, brand new ideas do not spring up ready formed in the minds of their proponents; they emerge phoenix-like from "the collision of adverse opinions" in the antagonism of open debate and confrontation.

The second argument concerns not the ideas themselves, but the way they are held. According to Mill, progress is empty and the truth about the good life not worth pursuing, if the views that result are not held in a lively and committed spirit with a full awareness of their meaning and significance for human life and action. When ideas and lifestyles clash in open debate, each is put on its mettle, and its adherents are required continually to reassert and therefore to reexamine the content and grounds of their views. No view, however popular, can afford to take its preeminence for granted in an atmosphere of open controversy; each person will take his view seriously and will be made acutely aware in the course of the debate of all its implications for his life and practice. So, if a given creed has anything to offer, ethical confrontation will bring it out; and if it has darker, hidden implications, those will emerge too in the course of earnest and committed debate about its desirability. Without that challenge, the prevailing view, even if it is the soundest view, is likely to take on the character of an empty prejudice or "a few phrases learned by rote." In this condition, a truth is worthless because it does not inform one's action to any significant extent; the valuable kernel of a half-truth lies hidden behind the blandness of its verbal repetition; and a falsehood poses no real provocative challenge to those who might be capable of refuting it.

Further, Mill was convinced that humans themselves benefit, morally and intellectually, from involvement in ethical confrontation. Partly this is a matter of the development of a certain sort of open-mindedness—the open-mindedness that results when each is intellectually alert to the possibility of criticism and cares passionately about its adequate rebuttal. This is not the so-called open-mindedness of the dilettante—the man who is willing to debate and defend an idea whether he believes it or not. As we shall see, Mill is almost as frightened of that attitude as he is of the dead weight of prejudice. He is looking instead for committed open-mindedness—the openness of a man who is anxious to listen and respond to criticism precisely because he takes his view seriously and is interested in it as a view about the good life or whatever and not just as a verbal habit from which he finds it psychologically difficult to dissociate himself. Partly too it is a matter of the way in which an idea is held and of the effect on a person of full commitment to one view rather than another. Mill seems to be suggesting that, in an environment of confrontation, commitment heightens and alerts the mental faculties, whereas in an atmosphere of conformity we get

> the cases, so frequent in this age of the world as almost to form the majority, in which the creed remains, as it were, outside the mind, incrusting and petrifying it against all other influences addressed to the higher parts of our nature; manifesting its power by not suffering any fresh and living conviction to get in, but itself doing nothing for the mind or heart except standing sentinel over them to keep them vacant.

For these reasons, Mill thinks ethical confrontation is indispensable for genuine moral progress in society. The existence of a plurality of opinions clashing with one another is, he asserted, the only explanation of the progressive character of western civilization to date. But at a time when economic and social forces are making society increasingly homogeneous and the variety of circumstances is diminishing, it becomes even more important not to interfere with what remains of individuality and the clash of ideas that it generates.

So much is this so, that Mill suggests it might be necessary to *manufacture* dissent if it does not offer itself spontaneously. Even in the utopian circumstance of genuine ethical consensus, the lack of intellectual contention and antagonism would be "no trifling drawback" from the universal recognition of the truth. Fortunately, that is not a problem we have to face:

> If there are any persons who contest a received opinion, or who will do so if law or opinion will let them, let us thank them for it, open our minds to listen to them, and rejoice that there is someone to do for us what we otherwise ought, if we have any regard for either the certainty or vitality of our convictions, to do with much greater labour for ourselves.

IV

I do not propose to examine the merits of these arguments. But if there is anything in them at all, then they suggest a striking revaluation of moral offence and distress. Ethical confrontation, we have seen, is a positive good for Mill: it improves people and it promotes progress. But ethical confrontation is not a painless business. It always hurts to be contradicted in debate, if one takes seriously the views one is propounding, and it is distressing to be faced with examples of life-styles which pose a genuine challenge to the validity and grounds of one's own. People are naturally disturbed when they are involved in the collision of opinions. If nobody is disturbed, distressed, or hurt in this way, that is a sign that ethical confrontation is not taking place, and that in turn, as we have seen, is a sign that the intellectual life and progress of our civilization may be grinding to a halt. In those circumstances, we saw that Mill would propose a desperate remedy: we would have to manufacture ethical conflict in order to shake the complacency of accepted views and generate the shock, distress, and disturbance that were missing.

If, on the other hand, widespread moral distress *is* detectable in the community, then far from being a legitimate ground for interference, it is a positive and healthy sign that the processes of ethical confrontation that Mill called for are actually taking place. That a man is morally distressed by another's homosexuality, for example, is for Mill a sign, first, that he takes his own views on sexual ethics seriously, second, that he recognizes now the need to reassert vigorously the grounds of his own convictions, being confronted so dramatically and disturbingly with a case of its denial, and third—if (as is probable) the moral truth about sexual relations is the monopoly neither of his opinion nor its rival—it is a sign that ideas are struggling and clashing with one another in the way that Mill thought most likely to lead to the final emergence of a more balanced and sober truth about human sexuality.

Think what would be entailed by an interpretation which regarded moral distress as sufficient to cross the threshold established by the Harm Principle. What ought to be taken as evidence that freedom of thought and life-style was promoting progress would be invoked instead as a prima facie reason for interfering with that freedom. A sign of vitality would be cited as a necessary condition for legitimately suppressing that vitality. A symptom of progress would be deployed as a justification for acting in a way that would bring progress to a halt. If we assume that Mill took his own arguments seriously, we must say that this cannot have been his view. Since he believed that ethical confrontation was indispensable for moral and social progress, and since he used this as his main argument for individual liberty, it seems odd to suggest that he could have regarded the pain of debate and the distress of moral challenge as reasons for waiving the general ban on interference with personal liberty. Progress through the collision of opinion is the premise of Mill's liberalism. The sensitivity of the opinions involved in these collisions cannot therefore be taken as a basis for arguments justifying the restriction of liberty.

In a recent note, David Gordon has argued that moral distress might count as harm for the purposes of Mill's principle, provided it did not "arise from the holding of false moral views, judged by a correct account of morality."[9] But this account cannot be squared with Mill's arguments either. I shall leave aside the point that this requires the assessor of harm to be already in possession of the moral truth before he can determine which views should be heard in public debate and which life-styles flaunted. For Mill the more important point is that moral distress

9. David Gordon. "Honderich on morality-dependent harm," *Political Studies*, 32 (1984), p. 288.

arising from a correct moral view indicates that the truth is being challenged, the view scrutinized, and therefore the mind of the true believer kept open and alert to the importance of the creed to which he (correctly, on this hypothesis) clings. If moral challenges were to be suppressed because of the sensibilities of those in possession of the truth—indeed if those sensibilities were even to be regarded as a reason for suppression—then the dangers of moral prejudice, intellectual stagnation, and the "incrustation" of the mind, which Mill knew could affect the truth as much as falsehood, would rear their heads again.

For these reasons, the concept of harm in Mill's principle cannot intelligibly be construed in a way that includes moral distress of the kind I have been discussing.

V

If the problem of moral distress is simply the problem of offense and disturbance occasioned by the fact that others hold or practice conceptions of the good that one regards as immoral or depraved, then the points I have just made dispose of it. Sometimes, however, the problem is confused with another one—the problem of the distress occasioned by the *manner* in which a rival conception of the good is expressed. People often say that they are distressed, and some may claim to be harmed, by seeing a life-style they detest *flaunted* or exhibited *aggressively* in front of them. I think Mill's argument has the capacity to deal with this problem also.

The first thing to say is that the good effects of ethical confrontation, on Mill's account, will not accrue unless views are put forward passionately, forcefully, and directly, in a manner that opponents of those views cannot practicably ignore. At the end of Chapter 2 of *On Liberty*, Mill has to deal with the (typically English) suggestion "that the free expression of all opinions should be permitted on condition that the manner be temperate." He is rightly suspicious of any temperateness proviso:

> If the test be offence to those whose opinions are attacked, I think experience testifies that this offence is given whenever the attack is telling and powerful, and that every opponent who pushes them hard, and whom they find it difficult to answer, appears to them, if he shows any strong feeling on the subject, an intemperate opponent.

Intemperance in this sense is as indispensable for progress as the confrontation which it generates, on Mill's account. A "temperate" debate would be one in which views were compared and exchanged in dilettante fashion without any real moral or intellectual engagement on either side.

(In this connection, it is worth noting that when Mill described his father in his *Autobiography*, he cited as a virtue the fact "that he, in a degree once common, but now unusual, threw his feelings into his opinions," and went on:

> Those, who having opinions which they hold to be immensely important, and their contraries to be prodigiously hurtful, have any deep regard for the general good, will necessarily dislike, as a class and in the abstract, those who think wrong what they think right, and right what they think wrong.)

It is a very common error to confuse liberalism with the lack of this strong feeling, but Mill insists that vehemence and toleration are perfectly compatible, and that "none but those who do not care about opinions, will confound this with intolerance."

Mill does concede that "the manner of asserting an opinion ... may be very objectionable and may justly incur severe censure." He has in mind the use of personal invective, sarcasm, vituperative language, and so on. Clearly, these tactics can be distressing, and the distress they occasion adds little to the forcefulness (for Mill's purposes) of the debate or confrontation into which they are introduced. For this reason they are to be condemned and restrained by popular opinion (though Mill is still adamant that "law and authority have no business" in restraining them). He also believes that they are more common tactics on the side of orthodoxy than of heterodoxy and that there is "more need to discourage offensive attacks on infidelity than on religion." For our purposes, the important point is that the distress occasioned by sarcasm and vituperation is not to be regarded as a morality-dependent harm. I can be "harmed" in this sense as much by the sarcastic inculcation of a creed that I am disposed already to believe as by the vituperative objections of an ethical opponent. The harm (if that is what it is) is done by the calculated attack on personality and self-confidence involved in sarcasm and vituperation, not by the attack, however shocking, on the substance of one's views. So Mill's condemnation of this sort of thing, like his later (though, on his own admission, much less well thought out) condemnation of bad manners, adds little to the case for bringing moral distress within the scope of his Harm Principle.

Another suggestion often made in relation to Mill's Harm Principle is that an action may be "harmful" if performed in public even though it would harm no one if it were performed in private. What society generally regards as immorality should be tolerated provided it is practiced in the privacy of one's own bedroom (or wherever) and not brought into the public view. On this account, the public/private distinction is primarily a matter of *geography* rather than a question of the different nature of the moral standards involved.

It is tempting to interpret Mill's distinction between self-regarding and other-regarding actions along similar lines, so that a self-regarding action is paradigmatically an action performed behind closed doors. I think this temptation should be resisted. If moral progress depends, as Mill claims, on struggle and confrontation between opposing views of the good life, the last thing we want is that people should conceal or disguise from others the fact that their opinions or lifestyles are different. The moral, philosophical, and religious confrontation that Mill is calling for must be *public* confrontation between the practicing adherents of rival and antagonistic ethics. Otherwise the benefits to society—not just to the antagonists but also to "the calmer and more dispassionate bystander"—will not be realized. Indeed, one possibility that worries Mill is this—that eccentric, novel, and heretical life-styles might be coerced by public opinion and collective mediocrity back into the purely private lives of those who practice them. In those circumstances, the ideas themselves may survive, but their existence will make little contribution to the general good if, as Mill puts it, "the most active and inquiring intellects find it advisable to keep the general principles and grounds of their convictions within their own breasts." The alternative views will

> never blaze out far and wide; but continue to smoulder in the narrow circles of thinking and studious persons among whom they originate, without ever lighting up the general affairs of mankind with either a true or a deceptive light.

Mill's argument for liberty commits him to the view that such "reticence on the part of heretics" is a social evil, and I think he would regard the modern idea (made popular since the findings of the Wolfenden Report[4]) that we should confine our deviant practices to the privacy of our own bedrooms, and never show them off to our neighbors, with similar disquiet.

When Mill talks, at the beginning of the essay, about a "sphere" of self-regarding action, we must not think of the boundaries of the sphere in quasi-physical terms, as though they were barriers blocking off the awareness of one's action from people liable to be affected by that awareness. (They are not like "transmitter shields" in Bruce Ackerman's "liberal" utopia, allowing anyone to screen out stimuli that he finds distressing.[5] Mill, I think, would be horrified by the suggestion in Ackerman's work that liberalism might involve the physical realization of this intellectual atomism.) Paradoxically, perhaps, the argument for freedom in relation to "self-regarding" actions rests on the hope and the possibility that the progress of moral debate, the struggle between rival views, and therefore (at least indirectly) the course of others' lives, will in fact be affected by those actions.

There is an isolated paragraph in Chapter 5 of *On Liberty* where Mill appears to subscribe to the view that there are some actions, harmless in private, which if done publicly may constitute indecency and therefore be liable to legitimate prohibition. This is a difficult passage to accommodate and one on which Mill, on his own account, found it unnecessary to dwell. He does however make it clear that it is not the deviance or the perceived or actual immorality of the actions in question which makes their public performance indecent; rather it is a matter of the *type* of action that it is. For example, on this view, *all* forms of public copulation might be regarded as indecent, *including* marital sex in the

4. See *Report of the Committee on Homosexual Offences and Prostitution* (London, 1957), esp. para. 62.

5. Bruce Ackerman, *Social Justice in the Liberal State* (New Haven, 1980), pp. 179–80.

missionary position for the sole and only purpose of procreation, not just sodomy, fellatio, masturbation, etc. So if the spectacle of indecency is to be regarded as harmful, the harm involved is not (straightforwardly) moral distress, in the sense with which we are concerned.

Even so, I find this passage the most difficult to reconcile with the overall tendency of Mill's argument. There is, surely, a debate to be had about the merits of public lovemaking; and making love in public would be, on Mill's own account, an important contribution to the initiation or the course of such a debate. If copulation in public were banned on the grounds that it is "bad manners" or offends against public decency, it is difficult to see how people could ever get a real sense of the issues involved in this argument, or even of what their own views actually entailed. The danger here, as I see it, is that the very "despotism of custom" which, according to Mill, is the deadliest enemy of individuality and progress, might creep in under the cover of standards of decency to threaten those values all over again.

For this reason, I think the passage we are considering should charitably be overlooked in our reconstruction of Mill's view. If it is not, even the whole basis of his argument for liberty is called into question. At any rate, this isolated passage apart, it is clear that the argument of *On Liberty* does not license the conclusion that putative immorality should be kept from public view.

VI

I have said that Mill is precluded, by his arguments for liberty, from taking moral distress and offence seriously as a form of harm for the purposes of his Harm Principle. In a recent article, Ted Honderich has suggested that this is incompatible with Mill's underlying utilitarianism. "If Mill is Utilitarian with respect to the proper rules for society, how can he be taken to ignore distress when it happens to be the morality-dependent kind?"[2] After all, no one is denying the reality of this distress, nor does our argument depend at all on the view that those concerned are "putting it on" in order to gain some sort of unfair advantage in the utilitarian calculus. The distress is there, on any account, and Honderich is worried by the suggestion that a self-confessed utilitarian might be disposed not to take it seriously. On Honderich's interpretation, Mill *does* include this distress as a form of harm, and dismisses it (to the extent that he does) only on the basis that it is quantitatively inconsiderable.

This last move, however, will not do. Mill describes societies in which the overwhelming majority are revolted by, say, the sexual, religious, or dietary habits of a few. If moral distress counts at all in utilitarian calculation, then there can be no evident or clear-cut case for tolerating this minority deviance. Since Mill believed that there *was* such

2. Honderich ["On Liberty and morality-dependent harm," Political Studies, 30 (1982) p. 513].

a case for toleration, no matter how strong and widespread the revulsion, he cannot have held the view that Honderich attributes to him.

Actually, Honderich is mistaken about the character of Mill's utilitarian theory. Mill's utilitarianism is not a Benthamite calculus of pleasures and pains, or of satisfactions and dissatisfactions, of all sorts. The value on which liberty is based is certainly utility, on Mill's account, but, as he insists in his introduction to the essay, "it must be utility in the largest sense, grounded on the permanent interests of man as a progressive being." I take it that this passage refers, not merely to the nature of Mill's utilitarian *computations* (for example, taking a long-run rather than a short-run view, etc.), but to the character of his utilitarian *values*—the fundamental values which he thinks will be promoted by his libertarianism. A considerable part of *On Liberty* is devoted to showing what it is for man to be "a progressive being" and what his interests in such a condition are. These are the interests whose promotion Mill's utilitarianism seeks to maximize.

If we accept the arguments about progress in Chapter 2 of *On Liberty* and spontaneity in Chapter 3, it is not then open to us to say that distress or resentment when one's preconceptions are challenged goes against one's interests as a progressive being. A creature who defined his interests—even in part—in terms of being free from the shock and perturbation of ethical debate and being free from anxiety about the grounds or validity of his opinions would be like the satisfied (and no doubt morally complacent) "fool" mentioned in *Utilitarianism.* Mill is adamant, in the latter work, that there is a distinction between *happiness*, understood as the leading value of his ethical system, and mere contentment or satisfaction. By insisting that distress and uneasiness under the impact of ethical confrontation are negative values for Mill, Honderich is driving the theory back toward the very Benthamism that Mill wanted to repudiate.

It is certainly true that Mill wants to argue, in consequentialist fashion, that the benefits of free discussion and of the open struggle between competing conceptions of the good life outweigh the costs of such confrontation. The costs include the bad effects of people believing falsehoods (Mill concedes, with common sense, that "it is dangerous and noxious when opinions are erroneous") and the dangers of people practicing life-styles that are actually depraved. They include also the tendency for religious and philosophical sectarianism to be "heightened and exacerbated" by the freest discussion. (In certain circumstances, where sectarianism may lead to violence, these costs are so great as to outweigh the benefits of liberty.[3]) But, in Mill's calculations at any rate, the costs of freedom do *not* include the distress occasioned by contradiction or the pain and shock of forceful debate. Those are not experiences which a progressive being has a genuine interest in avoiding and they are therefore not negative values or costs in relation to the permanent interests of man as a progressive being.

3. This, I take it, is the force of the "corn dealer" example.

HILL v. COLORADO

Supreme Court of the United States, 2000.
530 U.S. 703, 120 S.Ct. 2480, 147 L.Ed.2d 597.

JUSTICE STEVENS delivered the opinion of the Court.

At issue is the constitutionality of a 1993 Colorado statute that regulates speech-related conduct within 100 feet of the entrance to any health care facility. The specific section of the statute that is challenged, Colo.Rev.Stat. § 18–9–122(3) (1999), makes it unlawful within the regulated areas for any person to "knowingly approach" within eight feet of another person, without that person's consent, "for the purpose of passing a leaflet or handbill to, displaying a sign to, or engaging in oral protest, education, or counseling with such other person...."[4] Although the statute prohibits speakers from approaching unwilling listeners, it does not require a standing speaker to move away from anyone passing by. Nor does it place any restriction on the content of any message that anyone may wish to communicate to anyone else, either inside or outside the regulated areas. It does, however, make it more difficult to give unwanted advice, particularly in the form of a handbill or leaflet, to persons entering or leaving medical facilities.

The question is whether the First Amendment rights of the speaker are abridged by the protection the statute provides for the unwilling listener.

* * *

4. The entire § 18–9–122 reads as follows:

"(1) The general assembly recognizes that access to health care facilities for the purpose of obtaining medical counseling and treatment is imperative for the citizens of this state; that the exercise of a person's right to protest or counsel against certain medical procedures must be balanced against another person's right to obtain medical counseling and treatment in an unobstructed manner; and that preventing the willful obstruction of a person's access to medical counseling and treatment at a health care facility is a matter of statewide concern. The general assembly therefore declares that it is appropriate to enact legislation that prohibits a person from knowingly obstructing another person's entry to or exit from a health care facility.

"(2) A person commits a class 3 misdemeanor if such person knowingly obstructs, detains, hinders, impedes, or blocks another person's entry to or exit from a health care facility.

"(3) No person shall knowingly approach another person within eight feet of such person, unless such other person consents, for the purpose of passing a leaflet or handbill to, displaying a sign to, or engaging in oral protest, education, or counseling with such other person in the public way or sidewalk area within a radius of one hundred feet from any entrance door to a health care facility. Any person who violates this subsection (3) commits a class 3 misdemeanor.

"(4) For the purposes of this section, 'health care facility' means any entity that is licensed, certified, or otherwise authorized or permitted by law to administer medical treatment in this state.

"(5) Nothing in this section shall be construed to prohibit a statutory or home rule city or county or city and county from adopting a law for the control of access to health care facilities that is no less restrictive than the provisions of this section.

"(6) In addition to, and not in lieu of, the penalties set forth in this section, a person who violates the provisions of this section shall be subject to civil liability, as provided in section 13–21–106.7, C.R.S."

II

Before confronting the question whether the Colorado statute reflects an acceptable balance between the constitutionally protected rights of law-abiding speakers and the interests of unwilling listeners, it is appropriate to examine the competing interests at stake. A brief review of both sides of the dispute reveals that each has legitimate and important concerns.

The First Amendment interests of petitioners are clear and undisputed. As a preface to their legal challenge, petitioners emphasize three propositions. First, they accurately explain that the areas protected by the statute encompass all the public ways within 100 feet of every entrance to every health care facility everywhere in the State of Colorado. There is no disagreement on this point, even though the legislative history makes it clear that its enactment was primarily motivated by activities in the vicinity of abortion clinics. Second, they correctly state that their leafletting, sign displays, and oral communications are protected by the First Amendment. The fact that the messages conveyed by those communications may be offensive to their recipients does not deprive them of constitutional protection. Third, the public sidewalks, streets, and ways affected by the statute are "quintessential" public forums for free speech. Finally, although there is debate about the magnitude of the statutory impediment to their ability to communicate effectively with persons in the regulated zones, that ability, particularly the ability to distribute leaflets, is unquestionably lessened by this statute.

On the other hand, petitioners do not challenge the legitimacy of the state interests that the statute is intended to serve. It is a traditional exercise of the States' "police powers to protect the health and safety of their citizens." *Medtronic, Inc. v. Lohr,* 518 U.S. 470, 475 (1996). That interest may justify a special focus on unimpeded access to health care facilities and the avoidance of potential trauma to patients associated with confrontational protests. See *Madsen v. Women's Health Center, Inc.,* 512 U.S. 753 (1994); *NLRB v. Baptist Hospital, Inc.,* 442 U.S. 773 (1979). Moreover, as with every exercise of a State's police powers, rules that provide specific guidance to enforcement authorities serve the interest in evenhanded application of the law. Whether or not those interests justify the particular regulation at issue, they are unquestionably legitimate.

It is also important when conducting this interest analysis to recognize the significant difference between state restrictions on a speaker's right to address a willing audience and those that protect listeners from unwanted communication. This statute deals only with the latter.

The right to free speech, of course, includes the right to attempt to persuade others to change their views, and may not be curtailed simply because the speaker's message may be offensive to his audience. But the protection afforded to offensive messages does not always embrace offensive speech that is so intrusive that the unwilling audience cannot avoid it. *Frisby v. Schultz,* 487 U.S. 474, 487 (1988). Indeed, "[i]t may not be the content of the speech, as much as the deliberate 'verbal or visual assault,' that justifies proscription." *Erznoznik v. Jacksonville,* 422 U.S. 205, 210–211, n. 6 (1975). Even in a public forum, one of the reasons we tolerate a protester's right to wear a jacket expressing his opposition to government policy in vulgar language is because offended viewers can "effectively avoid further bombardment of their sensibilities simply by averting their eyes." *Cohen v. California,* 403 U.S. 15, 21 (1971).

The recognizable privacy interest in avoiding unwanted communication varies widely in different settings. It is far less important when "strolling through Central Park" than when "in the confines of one's own home," or when persons are "powerless to avoid" it. *Id.,* at 21–22, 91 S.Ct. 1780. But even the interest in preserving tranquility in "the Sheep Meadow" portion of Central Park may at times justify official restraints on offensive musical expression. *Ward,* 491 U.S., at 784, 792. More specific to the facts of this case, we have recognized that "[t]he First Amendment does not demand that patients at a medical facility undertake Herculean efforts to escape the cacophony of political protests." *Madsen,* 512 U.S., at 772–773.

The unwilling listener's interest in avoiding unwanted communication has been repeatedly identified in our cases. It is an aspect of the broader "right to be let alone" that one of our wisest Justices characterized as "the most comprehensive of rights and the right most valued by civilized men." *Olmstead v. United States,* 277 U.S. 438, 478 (1928) (Brandeis, J., dissenting).[24] The right to avoid unwelcome speech has special force in the privacy of the home, *Rowan v. United States Post Office Dept.,* 397 U.S. 728, 738 (1970), and its immediate surroundings, *Frisby v. Schultz,* 487 U.S., at 485, but can also be protected in confrontational settings. Thus, this comment on the right to free passage in going to and from work applies equally—or perhaps with greater force—to access to a medical facility:

> "How far may men go in persuasion and communication and still not violate the right of those whom they would influence? In going to and from work, men have a right to as free a passage without obstruction as the streets afford, consistent with the right of others to enjoy the same privilege. We are a social people and the accosting by one of another in an inoffensive way and an offer by one to communicate and discuss information with a view to influencing the other's action are not regarded as aggression or a violation of that other's rights. If, however, the offer is declined, as it may rightfully be, then persistence, importunity, following and dogging become unjustifiable annoyance and obstruction which is likely soon to savor of intimidation. From all of this the person sought to be influenced

24. This common-law "right" is more accurately characterized as an "interest" that States can choose to protect in certain situations. See *Katz v. United States,* 389 U.S. 347, 350–351 (1967).

has a right to be free, and his employer has a right to have him free." *American Steel Foundries v. Tri–City Central Trades Council,* 257 U.S. 184, 204 (1921).

We have since recognized that the "right to persuade" discussed in that case is protected by the First Amendment, *Thornhill v. Alabama,* 310 U.S. 88 (1940), as well as by federal statutes. Yet we have continued to maintain that "no one has a right to press even 'good' ideas on an unwilling recipient." *Rowan,* 397 U.S., at 738. None of our decisions has minimized the enduring importance of "a right to be free" from persistent "importunity, following and dogging" after an offer to communicate has been declined. While the freedom to communicate is substantial, "the right of every person 'to be let alone' must be placed in the scales with the right of others to communicate." *Id.,* at 736. It is that right, as well as the right of "passage without obstruction," that the Colorado statute legitimately seeks to protect. The restrictions imposed by the Colorado statute only apply to communications that interfere with these rights rather than those that involve willing listeners.

The dissenters argue that we depart from precedent by recognizing a "right to avoid unpopular speech in a public forum." We, of course, are not addressing whether there is such a "right." Rather, we are merely noting that our cases have repeatedly recognized the interests of unwilling listeners in situations where "the degree of captivity makes it impractical for the unwilling viewer or auditor to avoid exposure. See *Lehman v.* [*Shaker Heights,* 418 U.S. 298 (1974)]." *Erznoznik,* 422 U.S., at 209. We explained in *Erznoznik* that "[t]his Court has considered analogous issues—pitting the First Amendment rights of speakers against the privacy rights of those who may be unwilling viewers or auditors—in a variety of contexts. Such cases demand delicate balancing." *Id.,* at 208. The dissenters, however, appear to consider recognizing any of the interests of unwilling listeners—let alone balancing those interests against the rights of speakers—to be unconstitutional. Our cases do not support this view.[5]

* * *

The three types of communication regulated by § 18–9–122(3) are the display of signs, leafletting, and oral speech. The 8–foot separation between the speaker and the audience should not have any adverse impact on the readers' ability to read signs displayed by demonstrators. In fact, the separation might actually aid the pedestrians' ability to see the signs by preventing others from surrounding them and impeding

5. Furthermore, whether there is a "right" to avoid unwelcome expression is not before us in this case. The purpose of the Colorado statute is not to protect a potential listener from hearing a particular message. It is to protect those who seek medical treatment from the potential physical and emotional harm suffered when an unwelcome individual delivers a message (whatever its content) by physically approaching an individual at close range, *i.e.,* within eight feet. In offering protection from that harm, while maintaining free access to health clinics, the State pursues interests constitutionally distinct from the freedom from unpopular speech to which Justice Kennedy refers.

their view. Furthermore, the statute places no limitations on the number, size, text, or images of the placards. And, as with all of the restrictions, the 8–foot zone does not affect demonstrators with signs who remain in place.

With respect to oral statements, the distance certainly can make it more difficult for a speaker to be heard, particularly if the level of background noise is high and other speakers are competing for the pedestrian's attention. Notably, the statute places no limitation on the number of speakers or the noise level, including the use of amplification equipment, although we have upheld such restrictions in past cases. See, *e.g., Madsen,* 512 U.S., at 772–773. More significantly, this statute does not suffer from the failings that compelled us to reject the "floating buffer zone" in *Schenck,* 519 U.S., at 377. Unlike the 15–foot zone in *Schenck,* this 8–foot zone allows the speaker to communicate at a "normal conversational distance." *Id.* Additionally, the statute allows the speaker to remain in one place, and other individuals can pass within eight feet of the protester without causing the protester to violate the statute. Finally, here there is a "knowing" requirement that protects speakers "who thought they were keeping pace with the targeted individual" at the proscribed distance from inadvertently violating the statute. *Id.,* at 378, n. 9.

It is also not clear that the statute's restrictions will necessarily impede, rather than assist, the speakers' efforts to communicate their messages. The statute might encourage the most aggressive and vociferous protesters to moderate their confrontational and harassing conduct, and thereby make it easier for thoughtful and law-abiding sidewalk counselors like petitioners to make themselves heard. But whether or not the 8—foot interval is the best possible accommodation of the competing interests at stake, we must accord a measure of deference to the judgment of the Colorado Legislature. See *Madsen,* 512 U.S., at 769–770. Once again, it is worth reiterating that only attempts to address unwilling listeners are affected.

The burden on the ability to distribute handbills is more serious because it seems possible that an 8–foot interval could hinder the ability of a leafletter to deliver handbills to some unwilling recipients. The statute does not, however, prevent a leafletter from simply standing near the path of oncoming pedestrians and proffering his or her material, which the pedestrians can easily accept.[33] And, as in all leafletting situations, pedestrians continue to be free to decline the tender. In *Heffron v. International Soc. for Krishna Consciousness, Inc.,* 452 U.S. 640 (1981), we upheld a state fair regulation that required a religious organization desiring to distribute literature to conduct that activity only at an assigned location—in that case booths. As in this case, the

33. Justice Kennedy states that the statute "forecloses peaceful leafletting." This is not correct. All of the cases he cites in support of his argument involve a total ban on a medium of expression to both willing and unwilling recipients. Nothing in this statute, however, prevents persons from proffering their literature; they simply cannot approach within eight feet of an unwilling recipient.

regulation primarily burdened the distributors' ability to communicate with unwilling readers. We concluded our opinion by emphasizing that the First Amendment protects the right of every citizen to " 'reach the minds of willing listeners and to do so there must be opportunity to win their attention.' *Kovacs v. Cooper,* 336 U.S. 77, 87 (1949)." *Id.,* at 655, 69 S.Ct. 448. The Colorado statute adequately protects those rights.

* * *

Finally, in determining whether a statute is narrowly tailored, we have noted that "[w]e must, of course, take account of the place to which the regulations apply in determining whether these restrictions burden more speech than necessary." *Madsen,* 512 U.S., at 772. States and municipalities plainly have a substantial interest in controlling the activity around certain public and private places. For example, we have recognized the special governmental interests surrounding schools,[34] courthouses,[35] polling places,[36] and private homes.[37] Additionally, we previously have noted the unique concerns that surround health care facilities:

> " 'Hospitals, after all, are not factories or mines or assembly plants. They are hospitals, where human ailments are treated, where patients and relatives alike often are under emotional strain and worry, where pleasing and comforting patients are principal facets of the day's activity, and where the patient and [her] family . . . need a restful, uncluttered, relaxing, and helpful atmosphere.' " *Id.* (quoting *NLRB v. Baptist Hospital, Inc.,* 442 U.S., at 783–784, n. 12).

Persons who are attempting to enter health care facilities—for any purpose—are often in particularly vulnerable physical and emotional conditions. The State of Colorado has responded to its substantial and legitimate interest in protecting these persons from unwanted encounters, confrontations, and even assaults by enacting an exceedingly modest restriction on the speakers' ability to approach.

JUSTICE KENNEDY, however, argues that the statute leaves petitioners without adequate means of communication. This is a considerable overstatement. The statute seeks to protect those who wish to enter health care facilities, many of whom may be under special physical or emotional stress, from close physical approaches by demonstrators. In doing so, the statute takes a prophylactic approach; it forbids all unwelcome demonstrators to come closer than eight feet. We recognize that by doing so, it will sometimes inhibit a demonstrator whose approach in fact would have proved harmless. But the statute's prophylactic aspect is justified by the great difficulty of protecting, say, a pregnant woman from physical harassment with legal rules that focus exclusively on the

34. See *Grayned v. City of Rockford,* 408 U.S. 104, 119 (1972).

35. See *Cox v. Louisiana,* 379 U.S. 559, 562 (1965).

36. See *Burson v. Freeman,* 504 U.S. 191, 206–208 (1992) (plurality opinion); *id.,* at 214–216 (SCALIA, J., concurring in judgment).

37. See *Frisby v. Schultz,* 487 U.S., at 484–485.

individual impact of each instance of behavior, demanding in each case an accurate characterization (as harassing or not harassing) of each individual movement within the 8–foot boundary. Such individualized characterization of each individual movement is often difficult to make accurately. A bright-line prophylactic rule may be the best way to provide protection, and, at the same time, by offering clear guidance and avoiding subjectivity, to protect speech itself.

As we explained above, the 8–foot restriction on an unwanted physical approach leaves ample room to communicate a message through speech. Signs, pictures, and voice itself can cross an 8–foot gap with ease. If the clinics in Colorado resemble those in *Schenck,* demonstrators with leaflets might easily stand on the sidewalk at entrances (without blocking the entrance) and, without physically approaching those who are entering the clinic, peacefully hand them leaflets as they pass by.

Finally, the 8–foot restriction occurs only within 100 feet of a health care facility—the place where the restriction is most needed. The restriction interferes far less with a speaker's ability to communicate than did the total ban on picketing on the sidewalk outside a residence (upheld in *Frisby v. Schultz,* 487 U.S. 474 (1988)), the restriction of leafletting at a fairground to a booth (upheld in *Heffron v. International Soc. for Krishna Consciousness, Inc.,* 452 U.S. 640 (1981)), or the "silence" often required outside a hospital. Special problems that may arise where clinics have particularly wide entrances or are situated within multipurpose office buildings may be worked out as the statute is applied.

* * *

[A concurring opinion of JUSTICE SOUTER, joined by JUSTICE O'CONNOR, JUSTICE GINSBURG, and JUSTICE BREYER, is omitted.]

JUSTICE SCALIA, with whom JUSTICE THOMAS joins, dissenting.

We have consistently held that "the Constitution does not *permit* government to decide which types of otherwise protected speech are sufficiently offensive to require protection *for the unwilling listener or viewer.*" *Erznoznik v. Jacksonville,* 422 U.S. 205, 210 (1975) (emphasis added). And as recently as in *Schenck,* the Court reiterated that "[a]s a general matter, we have indicated that in public debate our own citizens must tolerate insulting, and even outrageous, speech in order to provide adequate breathing space to the freedoms protected by the First Amendment." 519 U.S., at 383.

The Court nonetheless purports to derive from our cases a principle limiting the protection the Constitution affords the speaker's right to direct "offensive messages" at "unwilling" audiences in the public forum. *Ante,* at 2489. There is no such principle. We have upheld limitations on a speaker's exercise of his right to speak on the public streets *when that speech intrudes into the privacy of the home. Frisby,* 487 U.S., at 483, upheld a content-neutral municipal ordinance prohibiting picketing outside a residence or dwelling. The ordinance, we concluded, was justified by, and narrowly tailored to advance, the government's interest in the "protection of residential privacy." *Id.,* at 484. Our opinion rested upon the "unique nature of the home"; "the home," we said, "is different." *Ibid.* The reasoning of the case plainly assumed the *nonexistence* of the right—common law or otherwise—that the Court relies on today, the right to be free from unwanted speech when on the public streets and sidewalks. The home, we noted, was " 'the one retreat to which men and women can repair to escape from the tribulations of their daily pursuits.' " *Ibid.* (quoting *Carey,* 447 U.S., at 471). The limitation on a speaker's right to bombard the home with unwanted messages which we approved in *Frisby*—and in *Rowan v. Post Office Dept.,* 397 U.S. 728 (1970), upon which the Court also relies—was predicated on the fact that " 'we are often "captives" *outside* the sanctuary of the home and subject to objectionable speech.' " *Frisby, supra,* at 484 (quoting *Rowan, supra,* at 738) (emphasis added). As the universally understood state of First Amendment law is described in a leading treatise: "Outside the home, the burden is generally on the observer or listener to avert his eyes or plug his ears against the verbal assaults, lurid advertisements, tawdry books and magazines, and other 'offensive' intrusions which increasingly attend urban life." L. Tribe, American Constitutional Law § 12–19, p. 948 (2d ed.1988). The Court today elevates the abortion clinic to the status of the home.[3]

* * *

JUSTICE KENNEDY, dissenting.

The means of expression at stake here are of controlling importance. Citizens desiring to impart messages to women considering abortions likely do not have resources to use the mainstream media for their message, much less resources to locate women contemplating the option of abortion. Lacking the aid of the government or the media, they seek to resort to the time honored method of leafletting and the display of signs. Nowhere is the speech more important than at the time and place where the act is about to occur. As the named plaintiff, Leila Jeanne Hill, explained, "I engage in a variety of activities designed to impart information to abortion-bound women and their friends and families. . . ." App. 49. "In my many years of sidewalk counseling I have seen a number of [these] women change their minds about aborting their unborn children as a result of my sidewalk counseling, and God's grace." *Id.,* at 51.

When a person is walking at a hurried pace to enter a building, a solicitor who must stand still eight feet away cannot know whether the

3. I do not disagree with the Court that "our cases have repeatedly recognized the interests of unwilling listeners" in locations, such as public conveyances, where " 'the degree of captivity makes it impractical for the unwilling viewer or auditor to avoid exposure,' " *ante,* at 2490 (quoting *Erznoznik v. Jacksonville,* 422 U.S. 205, 209 (1975)). But we have never made the absurd suggestion that a pedestrian is a "captive" of the speaker who seeks to address him on the public sidewalks, where he may simply walk quickly by. *Erznoznik* itself, of course, *invalidated* a prohibition on the showing of films containing nudity on screens visible from the street, noting that "the burden normally falls upon the viewer to 'avoid further bombardment of [his] sensibilities simply by averting [his] eyes.' " *Id.,* at 210–211 (quoting *Cohen v. California,* 403 U.S. 15, 21 (1971).

person can be persuaded to accept the leaflet or not. Merely viewing a picture or brief message on the outside of the leaflet might be critical in the choice to receive it. To solicit by pamphlet is to tender it to the person. The statute ignores this fact. What the statute restricts is one person trying to communicate to another, which ought to be the heart of civilized discourse.

Colorado's excuse, and the Court's excuse, for the serious burden imposed upon the right to leaflet or to discuss is that it occurs at the wrong place. Again, Colorado and the Court have it just backwards. For these protesters the 100–foot zone in which young women enter a building is not just the last place where the message can be communicated. It likely is the only place. It is the location where the Court should expend its utmost effort to vindicate free speech, not to burden or suppress it.

Perhaps the leaflet will contain a picture of an unborn child, a picture the speaker thinks vital to the message. One of the arguments by the proponents of abortion, I had thought, was that a young woman might have been so uninformed that she did not know how to avoid pregnancy. The speakers in this case seek to ask the same uninformed woman, or indeed any woman who is considering an abortion, to understand and to contemplate the nature of the life she carries within her. To restrict the right of the speaker to hand her a leaflet, to hold a sign, or to speak quietly is for the Court to deny the neutrality that must be the first principle of the First Amendment. In this respect I am in full agreement with Justice Scalia's explanation of the insult the Court gives when it tells us these grave moral matters can be discussed just as well through a bullhorn. It would be remiss, moreover, not to observe the profound difference a leaflet can have in a woman's decisionmaking process.

* * *

Question

Does Mill's statement at the beginning of Chapter Three of *On Liberty* that "even opinions lose their immunity when the circumstances in which they are expressed are such as to constitute their expression a positive instigation to some mischievous act" have a bearing on the dispute in *Hill v. Colorado*? Are protestors who assert "orally to an excited mob assembled before the house of a corn-dealer" that corn dealers are starvers of the poor comparable, for the purpose of applying Mill's principle, to the anti-abortion protestors in *Hill?* Does Jeremy Waldron's essay give us a reason to distinguish the two cases? Does his concept of "moral distress" encompass the feared consequences that were invoked to justify the statute in *Hill*?

BEAUHARNAIS v. ILLINOIS

Supreme Court of the United States, 1952.
343 U.S. 250, 72 S.Ct. 725, 96 L.Ed. 919.

MR. JUSTICE FRANKFURTER delivered the opinion of the Court.

The petitioner was convicted upon information in the Municipal Court of Chicago of violating s 224a of Division 1 of the Illinois Criminal

Code, Ill.Rev.Stat.1949, c. 38, § 471. He was fined $200. The section provides:

> It shall be unlawful for any person, firm or corporation to manufacture, sell, or offer for sale, advertise or publish, present or exhibit in any public place in this state any lithograph, moving picture, play, drama or sketch, which publication or exhibition portrays depravity, criminality, unchastity, or lack of virtue of a class of citizens, of any race, color, creed or religion which said publication or exhibition exposes the citizens of any race, color, creed or religion to contempt, derision, or obloquy or which is productive of breach of the peace or riots....

Beauharnais challenged the statute as violating the liberty of speech and of the press guaranteed as against the States by the Due Process Clause of the Fourteenth Amendment, and as too vague, under the restrictions implicit in the same Clause, to support conviction for crime. The Illinois courts rejected these contentions and sustained defendant's conviction. 97 N.E.2d 343. We granted certiorari in view of the serious questions raised concerning the limitations imposed by the Fourteenth Amendment on the power of a State to punish utterances promoting friction among racial and religious groups. 342 U.S. 809

The information, cast generally in the terms of the statute, charged that Beauharnais "did unlawfully * * * exhibit in public places lithographs, which publications portray depravity, criminality, unchastity or lack of virtue of citizens of Negro race and color and which exposes citizens of Illinois of the Negro race and color to contempt, derision, or obloquy...." The lithograph complained of was a leaflet setting forth a petition calling on the Mayor and City Council of Chicago "to halt the further encroachment, harassment and invasion of white people, their property, neighborhoods and persons, by the Negro * * *." Below was a call for "One million self respecting white people in Chicago to unite ...." with the statement added that "If persuasion and the need to prevent the white race from becoming mongrelized by the negro will not unite us, then the aggressions ... rapes, robberies, knives, guns and marijuana of the negro, surely will." This, with more language, similar if not so violent, concluded with an attached application for membership in the White Circle League of America, Inc.

The testimony at the trial was substantially undisputed. From it the jury could find that Beauharnais was president of the White Circle League; that, at a meeting on January 6, 1950, he passed out bundles of the lithographs in question, together with other literature, to volunteers for distribution on downtown Chicago street corners the following day; that he carefully organized that distribution, giving detailed instructions for it; and that the leaflets were in fact distributed on January 7 in accordance with his plan and instructions. The court, together with other charges on burden of proof and the like, told the jury "if you find

. . . that the defendant, Joseph Beauharnais, did * * * manufacture, sell, or offer for sale, advertise or publish, present or exhibit in any public place the lithograph . . . then you are to find the defendant guilty. . . ." He refused to charge the jury, as requested by the defendant, that in order to convict they must find "that the article complained of was likely to produce a clear and present danger of a serious substantive evil that rises for above public inconvenience, annoyance or unrest." Upon this evidence and these instructions, the jury brought in the conviction here for review.

* * *

Illinois did not have to look beyond her own borders or await the tragic experience of the last three decades to conclude that wilful purveyors of falsehood concerning racial and religious groups promote strife and tend powerfully to obstruct the manifold adjustments required for free, ordered life in a metropolitan, polyglot community. From the murder of the abolitionist Lovejoy in 1837 to the Cicero riots of 1951, Illinois has been the scene of exacerbated tension between races, often flaring into violence and destruction. In many of these outbreaks, utterances of the character here in question, so the Illinois legislature could conclude, played a significant part. The law was passed on June 29, 1917, at a time when the State was struggling to assimilate vast numbers of new inhabitants, as yet concentrated in discrete racial or national or religious groups—foreign-born brought to it by the crest of the great wave of immigration, and Negroes attracted by jobs in war plants and the allurements of northern claims. Nine years earlier, in the very city where the legislature sat, what is said to be the first northern race riot had cost the lives of six people, left hundreds of Negroes homeless and shocked citizens into action far beyond the borders of the State. Less than a month before the bill was enacted, East St. Louis had seen a day's rioting, prelude to an out-break, only four days after the bill became law, so bloody that it led to Congressional investigation. A series of bombings had begun which was to culminate two years later in the awful race riot which held Chicago in its grip for seven days in the summer of 1919. Nor has tension and violence between the groups defined in the statute been limited in Illinois to clashes between whites and Negroes.

In the face of this history and its frequent obligato of extreme racial and religious propaganda, we would deny experience to say that the Illinois legislature was without reason in seeking ways to curb false or malicious defamation of racial and religious groups, made in public places and by means calculated to have a powerful emotional impact on those to whom it was presented. "There are limits to the exercise of these liberties (of speech and of the press). The danger in these times from the coercive activities of those who in the delusion of racial or religious conceit would incite violence and breaches of the peace in order to deprive others of their equal right to the exercise of their liberties, is emphasized by events familiar to all. These and other transgressions of those limits the states appropriately may punish."[16] This was the conclusion, again of a unanimous Court, in 1940. *Cantwell v. State of Connecticut, supra*, 310 U.S. at 310.

It may be argued, and weightily, that this legislation will not help matters; that tension and on occasion violence between racial and religious groups must be traced to causes more deeply embedded in our society than the rantings of modern Know–Nothings. Only those lacking responsible humility will have a confident solution for problems as intractable as the frictions attributable to differences of race, color or religion. This being so, it would be out of bounds for the judiciary to deny the legislature a choice of policy, provided it is not unrelated to the problem and not forbidden by some explicit limitation on the State's power. That the legislative remedy might not in practice mitigate the evil, or might itself raise new problems, would only manifest once more the paradox of reform. It is the price to be paid for the trial-and-error inherent in legislative efforts to deal with obstinate social issues.

* * *

We are warned that the choice open to the Illinois legislature here may be abused, that the law may be discriminatorily enforced; prohibiting libel of a creed or of a racial group, we are told, is but a step from prohibiting libel of a political party.[18]

Every power may be abused, but the possibility of abuse is a poor reason for denying Illinois the power to adopt measures against criminal libels sanctioned by centuries of Anglo–American law. "While this Court sits" it retains and exercises authority to nullify action which encroaches on freedom of utterance under the guise of punishing libel.

* * *

MR. JUSTICE BLACK, with whom MR. JUSTICE DOUGLAS concurs, dissenting.

This case is here because Illinois inflicted criminal punishment on Beauharnais for causing the distribution of leaflets in the city of Chicago. The conviction rests on the leaflet's contents, not on the time,

16. The utterances here in question "are not," as a detached student of the problem has noted, "the daily grist of vituperative political debate. Nor do they represent the frothy imaginings of lunatics, or the 'idle' gossip of a country town. Rather, they indicate the systematic avalanche of falsehoods which are circulated concerning the various groups, classes and races which make up the countries of the western world." Riesman, Democracy and Defamation; Control of Group Libel, 42 Col.L.Rev. at 727. Professor Riesman continues: "Such purposeful attacks are nothing new, of course. * * * What is new, however, is the existence of a mobile public opinion as the controlling force in politics, and the systematic manipulation of that opinion by the use of calculated falsehood and vilification." *Id.*, at 728.

18. It deserves emphasis that there is no such attempt in this statute. The rubric "race, color, creed or religion" which describes the type of group, libel of which is punishable, has attained too fixed a meaning to permit political groups to be brought within it. If a statute sought to outlaw libels of political parties, quite different problems not now before us would be raised. For one thing, the whole doctrine of fair comment as indispensable to the democratic political process would come into play. Political parties, like public men, are, as it were, public property.

manner or place of distribution. Beauharnais is head of an organization that opposes amalgamation and favors segregation of white and colored people. After discussion, an assembly of his group decided to petition the mayor and council of Chicago to pass laws for segregation. Volunteer members of the group agreed to stand on street corners, solicit signers to petitions addressed to the city authorities, and distribute leaflets giving information about the group, its beliefs and its plans.

* * *

This Act sets up a system of state censorship which is at war with the kind of free government envisioned by those who forced adoption of our Bill of Rights. The motives behind the state law may have been to do good. But the same can be said about most laws making opinions punishable as crimes. History indicates that urges to do good have led to the burning of books and even to the burning of "witches."

No rationalization on a purely legal level can conceal the fact that state laws like this one present a constant overhanging threat to freedom of speech, press and religion. Today Beauharnais is punished for publicly expressing strong views in favor of segregation. Ironically enough, Beauharnais, convicted of crime in Chicago, would probably be given a hero's reception in many other localities, if not in some parts of Chicago itself. Moreover, the same kind of state law that makes Beauharnais a criminal for advocating segregation in Illinois can be utilized to send people to jail in other states for advocating equality and nonsegregation. What Beauharnais said in his leaflet is mild compared with usual arguments on both sides of racial controversies.

We are told that freedom of petition and discussion are in no danger "while this Court sits." This case raises considerable doubt. Since those who peacefully petition for changes in the law are not to be protected "while this Court sits," who is? I do not agree that the Constitution leaves freedom of petition, assembly, speech, press or worship at the mercy of a case-by-case, day-by-day majority of this Court. I had supposed that our people could rely for their freedom on the Constitution's commands, rather than on the grace of this Court on an individual case basis. To say that a legislative body can, with this Court's approval, make it a crime to petition for and publicly discuss proposed legislation seems as farfetched to me as it would be to say that a valid law could be enacted to punish a candidate for President for telling the people his views. I think the First Amendment, with the Fourteenth, "absolutely" forbids such laws without any "ifs" or "buts" or "whereases." Whatever the danger, if any, in such public discussions, it is a danger the Founders deemed outweighed by the danger incident to the stifling of thought and speech. The Court does not act on this view of the Founders. It calculates what it deems to be the danger of public discussion, holds the scales are tipped on the side of state suppression, and upholds state censorship. This method of decision offers little protection to First Amendment liberties "while this Court sits."

If there be minority groups who hail this holding as their victory, they might consider the possible relevancy of this ancient remark: "Another such victory and I am undone."

CHARLES R. LAWRENCE III, IF HE HOLLERS LET HIM GO: REGULATING RACIST SPEECH ON CAMPUS

1990 Duke Law Journal 431.

UNDERSTANDING THE INJURY INFLICTED BY RACIST SPEECH

There can be no meaningful discussion about how to reconcile our commitment to equality and our commitment to free speech until we acknowledge that racist speech inflicts real harm and that this harm is far from trivial. I should state that more strongly: To engage in a debate about the first amendment and racist speech without a full understanding of the nature and extent of the harm of racist speech risks making the first amendment an instrument of domination rather than a vehicle of liberation. Not everyone has known the experience of being victimized by racist, misogynist, and homophobic speech, and we do not share equally the burden of the societal harm it inflicts. Often we are too quick to say we have heard the victims' cries when we have not; we are too eager to assure ourselves we have experienced the same injury, and therefore we can make the constitutional balance without danger of mismeasurement. For many of us who have fought for the rights of oppressed minorities, it is difficult to accept that—by underestimating the injury from racist speech—we too might be implicated in the vicious words we would never utter. Until we have eradicated racism and sexism and no longer share in the fruits of those forms of domination, we cannot justly strike the balance over the protest of those who are dominated. My plea is simply that we listen to the victims.

Members of my own family were involved in a recent incident at a private school in Wilmington, Delaware, that taught me much about both the nature of the injury racist speech inflicts and the lack of understanding many whites have of that injury.

As a good Quaker school dedicated to a deep commitment to and loving concern for all the members of its community, Wilmington Friends School also had been a haven for white families fleeing the court ordered desegregation of the Wilmington public schools. In recent years, the school strove to meet its commitment to human equality by enrolling a small (but significant) group of minority students and hiring an even smaller number of black faculty and staff. My sister Paula, a gifted, passionate, and dedicated teacher was the principal of the lower school. Her sons attend the high school. My brother-in-law, John, teaches geology at the University of Delaware. He is a strong, quiet, loving man, and he is white. My sister's family had moved to Wilmington shouldering the extra burdens and anxieties borne by an interracial family moving to a town where, not long ago, the defamatory message of segregation graced the doors of bathrooms and restaurants. Within a year they had made their place as well-loved and respected members of the community, particularly the school community, where Paula was viewed as a godsend and my nephews had made many good friends.

In May of their second year in Wilmington, an incident occurred that shook the entire school community but was particularly painful to my sister's family and others who found themselves the objects of hateful speech. In a letter to the school community explaining a decision to expel four students, the school's headmaster described the incident as follows:

> On Sunday evening, May 1, four students in the senior class met by prearrangement to paint the soccer kickboard, a flat rectangular structure, approximately 8 ft. by 25 ft., standing in the midst of the Wilmington Friends School playing fields. They worked for approximately one hour under bright moonlight and then went home.
>
> What confronted students and staff the following morning, depicted on the kickboard, were racist and anti-Semitic slogans and, most disturbing of all, threats of violent assault against one clearly identified member of the senior class. The slogans written on the kickboard included "Save the land, join the Klan," and "Down with Jews"; among the drawings were at least twelve hooded Ku Klux Klansmen, Nazi swastikas, and a burning cross. The most frightening and disturbing depictions, however, were those that threatened violence against one of our senior black students. He was drawn, in cartoon figure, identified by his name, and his initials, and by the name of his mother. Directly to the right of his head was a bullet, and farther to the right was a gun with its barrel directed toward the head. Under the drawing of the student, three Ku Klux Klansmen were depicted, one of whom was saying that the student "dies." Next to the gun was a drawing of a burning cross under which was written "Kill the Tarbaby."

When I visited my sister's family a few days after this incident, the injury they had suffered was evident. The wounds were fresh. My sister, a care-giver by nature and vocation, was clearly in need of care. My nephews were quiet. Their faces betrayed the aftershock of a recently inflicted blow and a newly discovered vulnerability. I knew the pain and scars were no less enduring because the injury had not been physical. And when I talked to my sister, I realized the greatest part of her pain came not from the incident itself but rather from the reaction of white parents who had come to the school in unprecedented numbers to protest the offending students' expulsion. "It was only a prank." "No one was physically attacked." "How can you punish these kids for mere words, mere drawings." Paula's pain was compounded by the failure of these people, with whom she had lived and worked, to recognize that she had been hurt, to understand in even the most limited way the reality of her pain and that of her family.

Many people called the incident "isolated." But black folks know that no racial incident is "isolated" in America. That is what makes the incidents so horrible, so scary. It is the knowledge that they are not the isolated unpopular speech of a dissident few that makes them so frightening. These incidents are manifestations of an ubiquitous and deeply ingrained cultural belief system, an American way of life. Too often in recent months, as I have debated this issue with friends and colleagues, I have heard people speak of the need to protect "offensive" speech. The word offensive is used as if we were speaking of a difference in taste, as if I should learn to be less sensitive to words that"offend" me. I cannot help but believe that those people who speak of offense—those who argue that this speech must go unchecked—do not understand the great difference between offense and injury: They have not known the injury my sister experienced, have not known the fear, vulnerability, and shame experienced by the Wisconsin coeds. There is a great difference between the offensiveness of words that you would rather not hear—because they are labeled dirty, impolite, or personally demeaning—and the injury inflicted by words that remind the world that you are fair game for physical attack, evoke in you all of the millions of cultural lessons regarding your inferiority that you have so painstakingly repressed, and imprint upon you a badge of servitude and subservience for all the world to see. It is instructive that the chief proponents for sanctioning people who inflict these injuries are women and people of color, and there are few among these groups who take the absolutist position that any regulation of this speech is too much.

Again, *Brown v. Board of Education* is a useful case for our analysis. *Brown* is helpful because it articulates the nature of the injury inflicted by the racist message of segregation. When one considers the injuries identified in the Brown decision, it is clear that racist speech causes tangible injury, and it is the kind of injury for which the law commonly provides, and even requires, redress.

Psychic injury is no less an injury than being struck in the face, and it often is far more severe. *Brown* speaks directly to the psychic injury inflicted by racist speech in noting that the symbolic message of segregation affected "the hearts and minds" of Negro children "in a way unlikely ever to be undone." Racial epithets and harassment often cause deep emotional scarring, and feelings of anxiety and fear that pervade every aspect of a victim's life. Many victims of hate propaganda have experienced physiological and emotional symptoms ranging from rapid pulse rate and difficulty in breathing, to nightmares, post-traumatic stress disorder, psychosis and suicide.

A second injury identified in *Brown*, and present in my example, is reputational injury. "[L]ibelous speech was long regarded as a form of personal assault ... that government could vindicate ... without running afoul of the Constitution." Although *New York Times v. Sullivan* and its progeny have subjected much defamatory speech to constitutional scrutiny—on the reasoning that "debate on public issues should be uninhibited, robust and wide-open' " and should not be "chilled' " by the possibility of libel suits—these cases also demonstrate a concern for balancing the public's interest in being fully informed with the competing interest of defamed persons in vindicating their reputation.[119]

Brown is a case about group defamation. The message of segregation was stigmatizing to black children. To be labeled unfit to attend school with white children injured the reputation of black children, thereby foreclosing employment opportunities and the right to be regarded as respected members of the body politic. An extensive discussion on the constitutionality or efficacy of group libel laws is beyond the scope of this essay. However, it will suffice to note that whereas *Beauharnais v. Illinois*,[121] which upheld an Illinois group libel statute, has fallen into ill repute; and is generally considered to have been overruled implicitly by *Sullivan, Brown* remains an instructive case. By identifying the inseparability of discriminatory speech and action in the case of segregation, where the injury is inflicted by the meaning of the message, Brown limits the scope of Sullivan. Brown reflects that racism is a form of subordination that achieves its purposes through group defamation.

The third injury identified in *Brown* is the denial of equal educational opportunity. *Brown* recognized that black children did not have an equal opportunity to learn and participate in the school community if they bore the additional burden of being subjected to the humiliation and psychic assault that accompanies the message of segregation. Uni-

119. *Sullivan* is primarily a case about the unconstitutionality of labeling speech as seditious libel. It is concerned with censorship of criticism of government. The defamation of blacks or other racial minorities, as groups, does not involve criticism of government. Even when a racial epithet is used to attack a public official, the alleged inferiority of the racial group to which he belongs should not be held to be related to his fitness to hold the position. The individual who defames a racial group with racial epithets and stereotyped caricatures is not concerned that he may have "guessed wrong' " in attempting to ascertain the truth. The racial epithet is the expression of a widely held belief. It is invoked as a statement of political belief—not as a statement of fact which may be proven true or erroneous. Moreover, if the *Sullivan* rule protects erroneous speech because of an ultimate concern for the discovery of truth, then the rule's application to racial epithets must be based on an acceptance of the possible "truth" of racism, a position which, happily, most first amendment absolutists are reluctant to embrace. Professor Matsuda argues that "we [[should] accept certain principles as the shared historical legacy of the world community. Racial supremacy is one of the ideas we have collectively and internationally considered and rejected."

But *Sullivan* also held that "the central meaning of the first amendment is the profound national commitment to the principle that debate on public issues should be uninhibited, robust and wide open." 376 U.S. at 270. Some civil libertarians argue that the status and attributes of various racial groups are public issues about which vigorous debate should be encouraged. This proposition is combined with the proposition that there is no such thing as a false idea to argue that *Sullivan* has necessarily overruled Beauharnais v. Illinois, 343 U.S. 250 (1952). But are racial insults ideas? Do they encourage wide-open debate?

The solution might lie in establishing the equivalent of an actual malice requirement. Discussions that attempt to explore an issue of public concern would be protected, but group defamations that intentionally vilify a group or individual for purposes of harassment or intimidation would receive no protection.

121. 343 U.S. 250 (1952).

versity students bear an analogous burden when they are forced to live and work in an environment where, at any moment, they may be subjected to denigrating verbal harassment and assault. The testimony of non-white students about the detrimental effect of racial harassment on their academic performance and social integration in the college community is overwhelming. A similar injury is recognized and addressed in Title VII's requirement that employers maintain a nondiscriminatory (non-hostile) work environment and in federal and state regulations prohibiting sexual harassment on campuses as well as in the work place.

All three of these very tangible, continuing, and often irreparable forms of injury—psychic, reputational, and the denial of equal educational opportunity—must be recognized, accounted for, and balanced against the claim that a regulation aimed at the prevention of these injuries may lead to restrictions on important first amendment liberties.

* * *

The Other Side of the Balance: Does the Suppression of Racial Epithets Weigh for or Against Speech?

In striking a balance, we also must think about what we are weighing on the side of speech. Most blacks—unlike many white civil libertarians—do not have faith in free speech as the most important vehicle for liberation. The first amendment coexisted with slavery, and we still are not sure it will protect us to the same extent that it protects whites. It often is argued that minorities have benefited greatly from first amendment protection and therefore should guard it jealously. We are aware that the struggle for racial equality has relied heavily on the persuasion of peaceful protest protected by the first amendment, but experience also teaches us that our petitions often go unanswered until they disrupt business as usual and require the self-interested attention of those persons in power.

Paradoxically, the disruption that renders this speech effective usually causes it to be considered undeserving of first amendment protection. Note the cruel irony in the news story appearing in the "Newsreel" at the beginning of this Article that describes Stanford President Kennedy's justification for prosecuting students engaged in a peaceful sit-in for violation of the University's Fundamental Standard. While protesting students were punished, the racist behavior the students were protesting went unpunished. This lack of symmetry was justified on the grounds that punishment might violate the bigots' first amendment rights. Once faith in this symmetry is shaken, the absolutist position loses credence. It is difficult for us to believe that we should fight to protect speech rights for racists because that will ensure our own speech rights. Our experience is that the American system of justice has never been symmetrical where race is concerned. No wonder we see equality as a precondition to free speech, and we place more weight on that side of the balance aimed at the removal of the badges and incidents of slavery that continue to flourish in our culture.

Blacks and other people of color are equally skeptical about the absolutist argument that even the most injurious speech must remain unregulated because in an unregulated marketplace of ideas the best ideas will rise to the top and gain acceptance.[132] Our experience tells us the opposite. We have seen too many demagogues elected by appealing to America's racism. We have seen too many good, liberal politicians shy away from the issues that might brand them as too closely allied with us. The American marketplace of ideas was founded with the idea of the racial inferiority of non-whites as one of its chief commodities, and ever since the market opened, racism has remained its most active item in trade.

But it is not just the prevalence and strength of the idea of racism that makes the unregulated marketplace of ideas an untenable paradigm for those individuals who seek full and equal personhood for all. The real problem is that the idea of the racial inferiority of non-whites infects, skews, and disables the operation of the market (like a computer virus, sick cattle, or diseased wheat). Racism is irrational and often unconscious. Our belief in the inferiority of non-whites trumps good ideas that contend with it in the market, often without our even knowing it. In addition, racism makes the words and ideas of blacks and other despised minorities less saleable, regardless of their intrinsic value, in the marketplace of ideas. It also decreases the total amount of speech that enters the market by coercively silencing members of those groups who are its targets.

Racism is an epidemic infecting the marketplace of ideas and rendering it dysfunctional. Racism is ubiquitous. We are all racists. Racism is also irrational. Individuals do not embrace or reject racist beliefs as the result of reasoned deliberation. For the most part, we do not recognize the myriad ways in which the racism pervading our history and culture influences our beliefs. In other words, most of our racism is unconscious.

The disruptive and disabling effect on the market of an idea that is ubiquitous and irrational, but seldom seen or acknowledged, should be apparent. If the community is considering competing ideas about providing food for children, shelter for the homeless, or abortions for pregnant

132. The "marketplace of ideas' " model sees speech as instrumental to democratic self government. It argues that truth (or the best perspectives or solutions) can be discovered through robust debate, free from government interference. In this model, the value of free speech lies not in the liberty interests of individual speakers, but in the societal benefits derived from unimpeded discussion. This theory has its origins in John Stuart Mill's, On Liberty ch. 2 (1859) (S. Collini ed. 1989). Justice Holmes established its place in first amendment jurisprudence in his dissent in Abrams v. United States, 250 U.S. 616 (1919):

> But when men have realized that time has upset many fighting faiths, they may come to believe ... that the best test of truth is the power of the thought to get itself accepted in the competition of the market, and that truth is the only ground upon which their wishes can safely be carried out.

Id. at 630.

women, and the choices made among the proposed solutions are influenced by the idea that some children, families, or women are less deserving of our sympathy because they are not white, then the market is not functioning as either John Stuart Mill or Oliver Wendell Holmes envisioned it. In John Ely's terms there is a "process defect."[141]

Professor Ely coined the term "process defect" in the context of developing a theory to identify instances in which legislative action should be subjected to heightened judicial scrutiny under the equal protection clause. Ely argues that the courts should interfere with the normal majoritarian political process when the defect of prejudice bars groups subject to widespread vilification from participation in the political process and causes governmental decisionmakers to misapprehend the costs and benefits of their actions. This same process defect that excludes vilified groups and misdirects the government operates in the marketplace of ideas. Mill's vision of truth emerging through competition in the marketplace of ideas relies on the ability of members of the body politic to recognize "truth" as serving their interest and to act on that recognition. As such, this vision depends upon the same process that James Madison referred to when he described his vision of a democracy in which the numerous minorities within our society would form coalitions to create majorities with overlapping interests through pluralist wheeling and dealing.[144] Just as the defect of prejudice blinds the white voter to interests that overlap with those of vilified minorities, it also blinds him to the "truth" of an idea or the efficacy of solutions associated with that vilified group. And just as prejudice causes the governmental decisionmakers to misapprehend the costs and benefits of their actions, it also causes all of us to misapprehend the value of ideas in the market.

Prejudice that is unconscious or unacknowledged causes even more distortions in the market. When racism operates at a conscious level, opposing ideas may prevail in open competition for the rational or moral sensibilities of the market participant. But when an individual is unaware of his prejudice, neither reason nor moral persuasion will likely succeed.

Racist speech also distorts the marketplace of ideas by muting or devaluing the speech of blacks and other non-whites. An idea that would be embraced by large numbers of individuals if it were offered by a white individual will be rejected or given less credence because its author belongs to a group demeaned and stigmatized by racist beliefs.

An obvious example of this type of devaluation would be the black political candidate whose ideas go unheard or are rejected by white voters, although voters would embrace the same ideas if they were championed by a white candidate. Racial minorities have the same experiences on a daily basis when they endure the microaggression of

141. See J. Ely, Democracy and Distrust: A Theory of Judicial Review 103–04, 135–79 (1980).

144. The Federalist No. 51, at 323–24 (J. Madison) (C. Rossiter ed. 1961).

having their words doubted, or misinterpreted, or assumed to be without evidentiary support, or when their insights are ignored and then appropriated by whites who are assumed to have been the original authority.

Finally, racist speech decreases the total amount of speech that reaches the market. I noted earlier in this Article the ways in which racist speech is inextricably linked with racist conduct. The primary purpose and effect of the speech/conduct that constitutes white supremacy is the exclusion of non-whites from full participation in the body politic. Sometimes the speech/conduct of racism is direct and obvious. When the Klan burns a cross on the lawn of a black person who joined the NAACP or exercised his right to move to a formerly all-white neighborhood, the effect of this speech does not result from the persuasive power of an idea operating freely in the market. It is a threat, a threat made in the context of a history of lynchings, beatings, and economic reprisals that made good on earlier threats, a threat that silences a potential speaker.[150] The black student who is subjected to racial epithets is likewise threatened and silenced. Certainly she, like the victim of a cross-burning, may be uncommonly brave or foolhardy and ignore the system of violence in which this abusive speech is only a bit player. But it is more likely that we, as a community, will be denied the benefit of many of her thoughts and ideas.

Again MacKinnon's analysis of how first amendment law misconstrues pornography is instructive. She notes that in concerning themselves only with government censorship, first amendment absolutists fail to recognize that whole segments of the population are systematically silenced by powerful private actors. "As a result, [they] cannot grasp that the speech of some silences the speech of others in a way that is not simply a matter of competition for airtime."

HENRY LOUIS GATES, JR., LET THEM TALK

Review of MARI J. MATSUDA, CHARLES R. LAWRENCE III, RICHARD DELGADO, AND KIMBERLE WILLIAMS CRENSHAW, WORDS THAT WOUND: CRITICAL RACE THEORY, ASSAULTIVE SPEECH, AND THE FIRST AMENDMENT

The New Republic, September 20 and 27, 1993.

It is out of respect for the prerogative of "categorization" that critical race theorists root their model of assaultive speech in the Supreme Court opinion of *Chaplinsky v. New Hampshire* (1942), which bequeathed us the "fighting words" doctrine. Chaplinsky was a Jehovah's Witness who was convicted for calling a city marshall a "God

150. When speech directly threatens violence, as in the phrase "your money or your life' " or in the phone call that takes responsibility for the terrorist bomb attack and threatens another, we recognize its inextricability from the accompanying conduct. It is more difficult to recognize the threat when the violence is systemic and need not be directly referenced in the speech, but the threat is just as effective, arguably even more so.

damned racketeer" and "a damned Fascist." The statute he violated forbade one to address "any offensive, derisive or annoying word to any other person" in a public place.

Affirming the conviction, the Court held that "there are certain well-defined and narrowly limited classes of speech, the prevention and punishment of which have never been thought to raise any Constitutional problem." Among them were "the insulting or 'fighting' words—those which by their very utterance inflict injury or tend to incite an immediate breach of the peace." "Such utterances are no essential part of any exposition of ideas," Justice Murphy wrote for the majority, "and are of such slight social value as a step to truth that any benefit that may be derived from them is clearly outweighed by the social interest in order and morality."

The Court's reference to those words "which by their very utterance inflict injury" is especially cherished by the hate-speech movement, for it seems to presage its account of "assaultive speech," or words that wound. In accord with *Chaplinsky*, critical race theorists emphasize the immediate and visceral harms incurred by hate speech. "Many victims of hate propaganda have experienced physiological and emotional symptoms, such as rapid pulse rate and difficulty in breathing," Charles R. Lawrence writes. Mari J. Matsuda has even more alarming findings to report: "Victims of vicious hate propaganda experience physiological symptoms and emotional distress ranging from fear in the gut to rapid pulse rate and difficulty in breathing, nightmares, post-traumatic stress disorder, hypertension, psychosis, and suicide." And Richard Delgado further notes that the psychic injuries incurred by racist speech have additional costs down the road: "The person who is timid, withdrawn, bitter, hypertense, or psychotic will almost certainly fare poorly in employment settings." (As a member of the Harvard faculty, I would venture there are exceptions to this rule.)

But *Chaplinsky* has other useful elements, too. Thus the approach entailed by the Court's conclusion that such words as the Jehovah's Witness uttered "are no essential part of any exposition of ideas" has also been pressed into service. It shows up in the insistence that racist speech has no content, that it is more like a blunt instrument than a vehicle of thought. "The racial invective is experienced as a blow, not a proffered idea," Lawrence writes.

By contrast, the "fighting words" prong of the *Chaplinsky* test—specifying words likely to incite an immediate breach of the peace—has been widely condemned for bias: why should those persons (women, for example) who are less likely to strike back physically be less protected from abuse? For this reason, Lawrence in effect urges an expansion of the fighting words doctrine, arguing that racist speech (which may silence its victims, rather than provoking them to violence) should be understood as the "functional equivalent of fighting words," and thus equally unworthy of First Amendment protection.

The hate speech movement's deployment of *Chaplinsky* is certainly within the pale of standard legal argument; indeed, the carefully drafted speech code adopted by Stanford University explicitly extends only to "fighting words" or symbols, thus wearing its claim to constitutionality on its face. So if *Chaplinsky* can shoulder the legal and ethical burdens placed upon it, the regulationists have a powerful weapon on their side. Can it?

Probably not. To begin with, it's an open question whether *Chaplinsky* remains, as they say, "good law," given that in the fifty years since its promulgation the Supreme Court would never once affirm a conviction for uttering either "fighting words" or words that "by their very utterance inflict injury." Indeed, in part because of its functional desuetude, in part because of the male bias of the "breach of the peace" prong, the editors of the *Harvard Law Review* have recently issued a call for the doctrine's explicit interment. So much for the doctrine's judicial value.

But they also note, as others have, that statutes prohibiting "fighting words" have had discriminatory effects. An apparently not atypical conviction—upheld by the Louisiana state court—was occasioned by the following exchange between a white police officer and the black mother of a young suspect. He: "Get your black ass in the goddamned car." She: "You god damn mother fucking police—I am going to [the Superintendent of Police] about this." No prize for guessing which one was convicted for uttering "fighting words." As the legal scholar Kenneth Karst reports, "[S]tatutes proscribing abusive words are applied to members of racial and political minorities more frequently than can be wholly explained by any special proclivity of those people to speak abusively." So much for the doctrine's political value.

Nor, finally, does the *Chaplinsky*-derived description of assaultive speech as being devoid of political or other ideational content—"experienced as a blow, not a proffered idea," in Lawrence's compelling formulation—survive closer inspection. Consider the incident that, Lawrence tells us, moved him to take up the hate speech cause in the first place. Two white Stanford freshmen had an argument with a black student about Beethoven's ancestry: he claimed, and they denied, that the Flemish–German composer was really of African descent. The next evening, apparently as a satirical commentary, the white students acquired a poster of Beethoven, colored it in with Sambo-like features, and posted it on the door of the student's dorm room at Ujamaa, Stanford's black theme house. Lawrence "experienced the defacement as representative of the university community's racism and not as an exceptional incident in a community in which the absence of racism is the rule"—and the rest is critical-race-theory history.

Now then, is Lawrence's paradigm example of racist hate speech in fact devoid of ideational or political content, as his analysis would suggest? Evidently not, for in their jointly written manifesto for critical race theory, the authors of *Words That Wound* spell out what they believe its message to have been: "The message said, 'This is you. This is you and all of your African–American brothers and sisters. You are all Sambos. It's a joke to think that you could ever be a Beethoven. It's ridiculous to believe that you could ever be anything other than a caricature of real genius.' " The defaced poster would also inspire a lengthy and passionate essay by the legal theorist Patricia J. Williams, an essay that extracts an even more elaborated account of its meaning. This was one picture, clearly, that really was worth a thousand words.

The same paradox surfaces in Richard Delgado's ground-breaking proposal for a tort action to redress racist speech. To define this tort, he must distinguish offensive racist speech from offensive political speech; for in *Cohen v. California* (1971), the Supreme Court decided that a jacket emblazoned with the words "Fuck the Draft" and worn in a courthouse would be protected as political speech, despite its patent offensiveness. Delgado argues that a racial insult, by contrast, "is not political speech; its perpetrator intends not to discover truth or advocate social action, but to injure the victim." It's a curious disjunction, this, between advocacy and injury. For if Delgado and his fellow contributors have a central message to impart, it's that racial insults are profoundly political, part of a larger mechanism of social subordination, and thus in contravention of the spirit of the "equal protection" clause of the Fourteenth Amendment. And the most harmful forms of racist speech are precisely those that combine injury with advocacy—those that are, in short, the most "political."

"Are racial insults ideas?" Lawrence asks. "Do they encourage wideopen debate?" He means the question to be rhetorical, but after reading his work and those of his fellow critical race theorists, who could possibly doubt it?

Even if we finally reject the picture of assaultive speech as empty of political content, along with the other tenets of the *Chaplinsky* doctrine, the hate-speech movement can still link itself to constitutional precedent through the alternative model of defamation. Indeed, I would argue that the defamation model is more central, more weight-bearing in these arguments than the assaultive one. And note that these *are* alternatives, not just different ways of describing the same thing. The "fighting words"/"assaultive speech" paradigm analogizes racist expression to physical assault: at its simplest, it characterizes an act of aggression between two individuals, victim and victimizer. By contrast, the defamation paradigm analogizes racist speech to libel, a dignitary affront. The harm is essentially social: to be defamed is to be defamed in the eyes of other people.

Here, the guiding precedent is Justice Frankfurter's majority opinion in the 1952 case of *Beauharnais v. Illinois*, in which the Court upheld a conviction under an Illinois group libel ordinance. The ordinance was clumsily written, but it essentially prohibited public expression that "portrays depravity, criminality, unchastity, or lack of virtue in a class of citizens of any race, color, creed, or religion," thereby exposing them to "contempt, derision, or obloquy." Mr. Beauharnais ran afoul of the ordinance when he circulated a leaflet that urged whites to unite against the menace posed by their black fellow citizens.

> Preserve and Protect White Neighborhoods! from the constant and continuous invasion, harassment and encroachment by the Negroes.... The white people of Chicago must take advantage of the opportunity to be united. If persuasion and the need to prevent the white race from being mongrelized by the Negro will not unite us, then the aggressions, rapes, robberies, knives, guns, and marijuana of the Negro surely will.

So averred Mr. Beauharnais, and it was the last sentence, specifying the Negro's offenses, that was held to violate the law. In Justice Frankfurter's opinion: "If an utterance directed at an individual may be the object of criminal sanctions we cannot deny to a state power to punish the same utterance directed at a defined group," at least as long as the restriction is related to the peace and well-being of the state.

To be sure, *Beauharnais v. Illinois* has since fallen into judicial disrepute, having been reversed in its particulars by subsequent cases like the celebrated *Sullivan v. New York Times.* Indeed, more widely cited than Justice Frankfurter's opinion is Justice Hugo Black's dissent: "If there be minority groups who hail this holding as their victory, they might consider the possible relevancy of this ancient remark: 'Another such victory and I am undone.' " And yet Frankfurter's claim for the congruence of individual and group libel is not, on the face of it, implausible. One could argue (as MacKinnon does) that this precedent is deserving of revival—or, more elaborately (as Lawrence does), that it was never truly reversed, because the notion of group libel tacitly underlies and sponsors more prestigious Supreme Court precedents.

Thus MacKinnon, in *Only Words,* deplores the celebrated *Sullivan* case for undermining the vitality, and superior virtue, of *Beauharnais v. Illinois.* "This arrangement avoids the rather obvious reality that groups are made up of individuals," she writes. "In reality, libel of groups multiplies rather than avoids the very same damage through reputation which the law of individual libel recognizes when done one at a time, as well as inflicting some of its own.... The idea seems to be that injury to one person is legally actionable, but the same injury to thousands of people is protected speech." Where's the justice in that? MacKinnon would thus revive the state's winning argument in *Beauharnais:* "[P]etitioner cannot gain constitutional protection from the consequence of libel by multiplying victims and identifying them by a collective term." (A similar argument was elaborated in a classic defense of group defamation laws written by none other than David Riesman during his brief career as a law professor.)

And the plausibility of this simple but powerful idea is what has made it so attractive to theorists of hate speech. As Mari J. Matsuda writes movingly:

> When the legal mind understands that reputational interests ... must be balanced against first amendment interests, it recognizes the concrete reality of what happens to people who are defamed. Their lives are changed. Their standing in the community, their opportunities, their self-worth, their free enjoyment of life are limited. Their political capital—their ability to speak and be heard—is diminished. To see this, and yet to fail to see that the very same things happen to the victims of racist speech, is selective vision.

The defamation model plays an even more central role in Lawrence's analysis. He argues that *Brown v. Board of Education,* decided just two years after *Beauharnais,* is best interpreted as a "case about group defamation. The message of segregation was stigmatizing to Black children.... *Brown* reflects the understanding that racism is a form of subordination that achieves its purpose through group defamation." Indeed, Lawrence seems to move close to the position that *all* racism is essentially to be understood as defamation. And he protests that "there has not yet been a satisfactory retraction of the government-sponsored defamation in the slavery clauses, the Dred Scott decision, the Black codes, the segregation statutes, and countless *other group libels*" (italics are mine).

Let's leave aside for the moment Lawrence's intriguing reinterpretation of legal history. What's wrong with the basic claim here, one endorsed by judges and scholars across the ideological spectrum, that group libel is just individual libel multiplied?

As I say, we should grant that the claim has prima facie plausibility. And yet the very case of *Beauharnais* illustrates the attendant difficulties. For while Mr. Beauharnais's racism is everywhere in evidence, it's actually unclear what charge is being made in the one sentence of his leaflet that was found to be libelous. That is, the accusation about the "aggressions" and so forth of the Negro need not obtain about any particular Negro; and nobody claimed that *no* Negro was guilty of such misdeeds as he enumerated. Since the Sedition Act of 1798, truth has been allowed as a defense in American libel law. But the Illinois ordinance nowhere mentions the question of truth or falsity, and we might think it odd, even insulting, if it did. (At his trial, Mr. Beauharnais offered to prove the truth of his allegations by introducing evidence about the higher incidence of crime in black districts; his offer was declined.) And this points us toward the significant disanalogy between group and individual libel.

Start with the notion that individual libel involves the publication of information about someone that is both damaging and false. Charles Lawrence inadvertently directs us to the source of the problem. The racial epithet, he writes, "is invoked as an assault, not as a statement of fact that may be proven true or false." But that suggests that the evaluative judgments that are characteristic of racial invective do not lend themselves to factual verification, and here the comparison with individual libel breaks down. The same problem emerges when Mac-

Kinnon identifies pornography as group defamation whose message is (roughly) that it would be nice if women were available for sexual exploitation; for a proposition of that form may be right or wrong, but it cannot be true or false. The conclusion Lawrence draws is that racist speech is a form of defamation immune from the *Sullivan* rule protecting statements of fact that are later discovered to be erroneous. A more obvious conclusion to reach would be that racist invective isn't best understood as an extension of individual libel at all. You cannot libel someone by saying "I despise you," which seems to be the essential message common to most racial epithets.

Delgado himself, whose essay was published earliest, offers further reasons to reject the defamation model that colleagues like Lawrence, Matsuda, and MacKinnon find so attractive. As he notes: "A third party who learned that a person was the victim of a racial insult, but did not know the victim, would probably conclude that the victim is a member of a particular racial minority. But if this conclusion is true, the victim cannot recover [under defamation law] because no falsehood has occurred. And whether or not the conclusion is true, it is not desirable that the law view membership in a racial minority as damaging to a person's reputation, even if some members of society consider it so."

I think we may fairly conclude, then, that *Beauharnais* is best left undisturbed in its slumbers, and that the model of group libel founders on the flawed analogy to individual libel. "Nigger" (used in the vocative) is not helpfully treated as group libel for the same reason it is not helpfully treated as individual libel. On the categorization front, at least, civil libertarians need not cede critical race theory an inch.

Questions

1) How should Mill think about hate speech of the sort that was at issue in *Beauharnais v. Illinois*? How should he respond to the argument, advanced by Charles Lawrence and others, that hate speech is a threat to free speech because it silences its targets?

2) In modern debates over the regulation of hate speech on college campuses, opponents of so-called speech codes sometimes argue that the more effective response to racist attitudes and practices is community condemnation. These opponents assert that speech codes create martyrs and mute the moral condemnation by creating controversies over lawyerly line-drawing and due process. Is this argument available to one who subscribes to Mill's argument in *On Liberty*?

ISAIAH BERLIN, JOHN STUART MILL AND THE ENDS OF LIFE

in Isaiah Berlin, Four Essays on Liberty (1969).

He praised what his father had praised—rationality, empirical method, democracy, equality, and he attacked what the utilitarians attacked—religion, belief in intuitive and undemonstrable truths and their dogmatic consequences, which, in their view and in his, led to the abandonment of reason, hierarchical societies, vested interests, intolerance of free criticism, prejudice, reaction, injustice, depotism, misery. Yet the emphasis had shifted. James Mill and Bentham had wanted literally nothing but pleasure obtained by whatever means were the most effective. If someone had offered them a medicine which could scientifically be shown to put those who took it into a state of permanent contentment, their premisses would have bound them to accept this as the panacea for all that they thought evil. Provided that the largest possible number of men receive lasting happiness, or even freedom from pain, it should not matter how this is achieved. Bentham and Mill believed in education and legislation as the roads to happiness. But, if a shorter way had been discovered, in the form of pills to swallow, techniques of subliminal suggestion, or other means of conditioning human beings in which our century has made such strides, then, being men of fanatical consistency, they might well have accepted this as a better, because more effective and perhaps less costly, alternative than the means that they had advocated. John Stuart Mill, as he made plain both by his life and by his writings, would have rejected with both hands any such solution. He would have condemned it as degrading the nature of man. For him man differs from animals primarily neither as the possessor of reason, nor as an inventor of tools and methods, but as a being capable of choice, one who is most himself in choosing and not being chosen for; the rider and not the horse; the seeker of ends, and not merely of means, ends that he pursues, each in his own fashion: with the corollary that the more various these fashions, the richer the lives of men become; the larger the field of interplay between individuals, the greater the opportunities of the new and the unexpected; the more numerous the possibilities for altering his own character in some fresh or unexplored direction, the more paths open before each individual, and the wider will be his freedom of action and thought.

In the last analysis, all appearances to the contrary, this is what Mill seems to me to have cared about most of all. He is officially committed to the exclusive pursuit of happiness. He believes deeply in justice, but his voice is most his own when he describes the glories of individual freedom, or denounces whatever seeks to curtail or extinguish it. Bentham, too, unlike his French predecessors who trusted in moral and scientific experts, had laid it down that each man is the best judge of his own happiness. Nevertheless, this principle would remain valid for Bentham even after every living man had swallowed the happiness-inducing pill and society was thereby lifted or reduced to a condition of unbroken and uniform bliss. For Bentham individualism is a psychological datum; for Mill it is an ideal. Mill likes dissent, independence, solitary thinkers, those who defy the establishment. In an article written at the age of seventeen (demanding toleration for a now almost forgotten atheist named Carlyle), he strikes a note which sounds and resounds in his writings throughout the rest of his life:

> Christians, whose reformers perished in the dungeon or at the stake as heretics, as apostates, as blasphemers—Christians, whose religion breathes charity, liberty and mercy in every line ... that they, having gained the power of which they were the victims, should employ it in the self same way ... in vindictive persecution ... is most monstrous.

He remained the champion of heretics, apostates, and blasphemers, of liberty and mercy, for the rest of his life.

His acts were in harmony with his professions. The public policies with which Mill's name was associated as a journalist, a reformer, and a politician, were seldom connected with the typically utilitarian projects advocated by Bentham and successfully realized by many of his disciples: great industrial, financial, educational schemes, reforms of public health or the organization of labour or leisure. The issues to which Mill was dedicated, whether in his published views or his actions, were concerned with something different: the extension of individual freedom, especially freedom of speech: seldom with anything else. When Mill declared that war was better than oppression, or that a revolution that would kill all men with an income of more than £500 per annum might improve things greatly, or that the Emperor Napoleon III of France was the vilest man alive; when he expressed delight at Palmerston's fall over the Bill that sought to make conspiracy against foreign despots a criminal offence in England; when he denounced the Southern States in the American Civil War, or made himself violently unpopular by speaking in the House of Commons in defence of Fenian assassins (and thereby probably saving their lives), or for the rights of women, or of workers, or of colonial peoples, and thereby made himself the most passionate and best-known champion in England of the insulted and the oppressed, it is difficult to suppose that it was not liberty and justice (at whatever cost) but utility (which counts the cost) that were uppermost in his mind. His articles and his political support saved Durham and his Report, when both were in danger of being defeated by the combination of right and left-wing adversaries, and thereby did much to ensure self-government in the British Commonwealth. He helped to destroy the reputation of Governor Eyre who had perpetrated brutalities in Jamaica. He saved the right of public meeting and of free speech in Hyde Park, against a government that wished to destroy it. He wrote and spoke for proportional representation because this alone, in his view, would allow minorities (not necessarily virtuous or rational ones) to make their voices heard. When, to the surprise of radicals, he opposed the dissolution of the East India Company for which he, like his father before him, had worked so devotedly, he did this because he feared the dead hand of the government more than the paternalist and not inhumane rule of the Company's officials. On the other hand he did not oppose state intervention as such; he welcomed it in education or labour legislation because he thought that without it the weakest would be enslaved and crushed; and because it would increase the range of choices for the great majority of men, even if it restrained some. What is common to all these causes is not any direct connexion they might have with the "greater happiness" principle but the fact that they turn on the issue of human rights—that is to say, of liberty and toleration.

I do not, of course, mean to suggest that there was no such connexion in Mill's own mind. He often seems to advocate freedom on the ground that without it the truth cannot be discovered—we cannot perform those experiments either in thought or "in living" which alone reveal to us new, unthought-of ways of maximizing pleasure and minimizing pain—the only ultimate source of value. Freedom, then, is valuable as a means, not as an end. But when we ask what Mill meant either by pleasure or by happiness, the answer is far from clear. Whatever happiness may be, it is, according to Mill, not what Bentham took it to be: for his conception of human nature is pronounced too narrow and altogether inadequate; he has no imaginative grasp of history or society or individual psychology; he does not understand either what holds, or what should hold, society together—common ideals, loyalties, national character; he is not aware of honour, dignity, self-culture, or the love of beauty, order, power, action; he understands only the "business" aspects of life. Are these goals, which Mill rightly regards as central, so many means to a single universal goal—happiness? Or are they species of it? Mill never clearly tells us. He says that happiness—or utility—is of no use as a criterion of conduct—destroying at one blow the proudest claim, and indeed the central doctrine, of the Benthamite system. "We think", he says in his essay on Bentham (published only after his father's death), "utility or happiness much too complex or indefinite at end to be sought except through the medium of various secondary ends, concerning which there may be, and often is, agreement among persons who differ in the ultimate standard." This is simple and definite enough in Bentham; but Mill rejects his formula because it rests on a false view of human nature. It is "complex and indefinite" in Mill because he packs into it the many diverse (and, perhaps, not always compatible) ends which men in fact pursue for their own sake, and which Bentham had either ignored or falsely classified under the head of pleasure: love, hatred, desire for justice, for action, for freedom, for power, for beauty, for knowledge, for self-sacrifice. In J.S. Mill's writings happiness comes to mean something very like "realization of one's wishes", whatever they may be. This stretches its meaning to the point of vacuity. The letter remains; but the spirit—the old, tough-minded Benthamite view for which happiness, if it was not a clear and concrete criterion of action, was nothing at all, as worthless as the "transcendental" intuitionist moonshine it was meant to replace—the true utilitarian spirit—has fled. Mill does indeed add that "when two or more of the secondary principles conflict, direct appeal to some first principle becomes necessary"; this principle is utility; but he gives no indication how this notion, drained of its old, materialistic but intelligible content, is to be applied. It is this tendency of Mill's to escape into what Bentham called "vague generality" that leads one to ask what, in fact, was Mill's real scale of values as shown in his writings and actions. If his life and the causes he advocated are any evidence, then it seems clear that in public life the highest values for him—whether or not he calls them "secondary ends"—were individual liberty, variety, and justice. If challenged about variety Mill would have defended it on the ground that without a sufficient degree of it many, at present wholly unforeseeable, forms of human happiness (or satisfaction, or fulfilment, or higher levels of life—however the degrees of these were to be determined and compared) would be left unknown, untried, unrealized; among them happier lives than any yet experienced. This is his thesis and he chooses to call it utilitarianism. But if anyone were to argue that a given, actual or attainable, social arrangement yielded enough happiness—that given the virtually impassable limitations of the nature of men and their environment (e.g., the very high improbability of men's becoming immortal or growing as tall as Everest) it were better to concentrate on the best that we have, since change would, in all empirical likelihood, lead to lowering of general happiness, and should therefore be avoided, we may be sure that Mill would have rejected this argument out of hand. He was committed to the answer that we can never tell (until we have tried) where greater truth or happiness (or any other form of experience) may lie. Finality is therefore in principle impossible: all solutions must be tentative and provisional. This is the voice of a disciple of both Saint–Simon and Constant or Humboldt. It runs directly counter to traditional—that is, eighteenth-century—utilitarianism, which rested on the view that there exists an unalterable nature of things, and answers to social, as to other, problems, can, at least in principle, be scientifically discovered once and for all. It is this perhaps, that, despite his fear of ignorant and irrational democracy and consequent craving for government by the enlightened and the expert (and insistence, early and late in his life, on the importance of objects of common, even uncritical, worship) checked his Saint–Simonism, turned him against Comte, and preserved him from the elitist tendency of his Fabian disciples.

There was a spontaneous and uncalculating idealism in his mind and his actions that was wholly alien to the dispassionate and penetrating irony of Bentham, or the vain and stubborn rationalism of James Mill. He tells us that his father's educational methods had turned him into a desiccated calculating machine, not too far removed from the popular image of the inhuman utilitarian philosopher; his very awareness of this makes one wonder whether it can ever have been wholly true. Despite the solemn bald head, the black clothes, the grave expression, the measured phrases, the total lack of humour, Mill's life is an unceasing revolt against his father's outlook and ideals, the greater for being subterranean and unacknowledged.

Mill had scarcely any prophetic gift. Unlike his contemporaries, Marx, Burckhardt, Tocqueville, he had no vision of what the twentieth century would bring, neither of the political and social consequences of industrialization, nor of the discovery of the strength of irrational and unconscious factors in human behaviour, nor of the terrifying techniques to which this knowledge has led and is leading. The transformation of society which has resulted—the rise of dominant secular ideologies and the wars between them, the awakening of Africa and Asia, the peculiar combination of nationalism and socialism in our day—these were outside Mill's horizon. But if he was not sensitive to the contours of the future, he was acutely aware of the destructive factors at work in his own world. He detested and feared standardization. He perceived that in the name of philanthropy, democracy, and equality a society was being created in which human objectives were artificially made narrower and smaller and the majority of men were being converted, to use his admired friend Tocqueville's phrase, into mere "industrious sheep", in which, in his own words, "collective mediocrity" was gradually strangling originality and individual gifts. He was against what have been called "organization men", a class of persons to whom Bentham could have had in principle no rational objection. He knew, feared, and hated timidity, mildness, natural conformity, lack of interest in human issues. This was common ground between him and his friend, his suspicious and disloyal friend, Thomas Carlyle. Above all he was on his guard against those who, for the sake of being left in peace to cultivate their gardens, were ready to sell their fundamental human right to self-government in the public spheres of life; these characteristics of our lives today he would have recognized with horror. He took human solidarity for granted, perhaps altogether too much for granted. He did not fear the isolation of individuals or groups, the factors that make for the alienation and disintegration of individuals and societies. He was preoccupied with the opposite evils of socialization and uniformity.[2] He longed for the widest variety of human life and character. He saw that this could not be obtained without protecting individuals from each other, and, above all, from the terrible weight of social pressure; this led to his insistent and persistent demands for toleration.

Toleration, Professor Butterfield has told us in his own lecture in this series, implies a certain disrespect. I tolerate your absurd beliefs and your foolish acts, though I know them to be absurd and foolish. Mill would, I think, have agreed. He believed that to hold an opinion deeply is to throw our feelings into it. He once declared that when we deeply care, we must dislike those who hold the opposite views. He preferred this to cold temperaments and opinions. He asked us not necessarily to respect the views of others—very far from it—only to try to understand and tolerate them; only tolerate; disapprove, think ill of, if need be mock or despise, but tolerate; for without conviction, without some antipathetic feeling, there was, he thought, no deep conviction; and without deep conviction there were no ends of life, and then the awful abyss on the

2. He did not seem to look on socialism, which under the influence of Mrs Taylor he advocated in the *Political Economy* and later, as a danger to individual liberty in the way in which democracy, for example, might be so. This is not the place to examine the very peculiar relationship of Mill's socialist to his individualist convictions, Despite his socialist professions, none of the socialist leaders of his time—neither Louis Blanc nor Proudhon nor Lassalle nor Herzen—not to speak of Marx, appears to have regarded him even as a fellow traveller. He was to them the very embodiment of a mild reformist liberal or bourgeois radical. Only the Fabians claimed him as an ancestor.

edge of which he had himself once stood would yawn before us. But without tolerance the conditions for rational criticism, rational condemnation, are destroyed. He therefore pleads for reason and toleration at all costs. To understand is not necessarily to forgive. We may argue, attack, reject, condemn with passion and hatred. But we may not suppress or stifle: for that is to destroy the bad and the good, and is tantamount to collective moral and intellectual suicide. Sceptical respect for the opinions of our opponents seems to him preferable to indifference or cynicism. But even these attitudes are less harmful than intolerance, or an imposed orthodoxy which kills rational discussion. This is Mill's faith. It obtained its classical formulation in the tract on Liberty, which he began writing in 1855 in collaboration with his wife, who, after his father, was the dominant figure in his life. Until his dying day he believed her to be endowed with a genius vastly superior to his own. He published the essay after her death in 1859 without those improvements which he was sure that her unique gifts would have brought to it. It is this event that I venture to invite you to celebrate today.

II

I shall not impose upon your patience by giving you an abstract of Mill's argument. I should like to remind you only of those salient ideas to which Mill attached the greatest importance—beliefs which his opponents attacked in his lifetime, and attack even more vehemently today. These propositions are still far from self-evident; time has not turned them to platitudes; they are not even now undisputed assumptions of a civilized outlook. Let me attempt to consider them briefly.

Men want to curtail the liberties of other men, either (*a*) because they wish to impose their power on others; or (*b*) because they want conformity—they do not wish to think differently from others, or others to think differently from themselves; or, finally, (*c*) because they believe that to the question of how one should live there can be (as with any genuine question) one true answer and one only; this answer is discoverable by means of reason, or intuition, or direct revelation, or a form of life or "unity of theory and practice"; its authority is identifiable with one of these avenues to final knowledge; all deviation from it is error which imperils human salvation; this justifies legislation against, or even extirpation of, those who lead away from the truth, whatever their character or intentions. Mill dismisses the first two motives as being irrational, since they stake out no intellectually argued claim, and are therefore incapable of being answered by rational argument. The only motive which he is prepared to take seriously is the last, namely, that if the true ends of life can be discovered, those who oppose these truths are spreading pernicious falsehood, and must be repressed. To this he replies that men are not infallible; that the supposedly pernicious view might turn out to be true after all; that those who killed Socrates and Christ sincerely believed them to be purveyors of wicked falsehoods, and were themselves men as worthy of respect as any to be found today; that Marcus Aurelius, "the gentlest and most amiable of rulers", known as the most enlightened man of his time and one of the noblest, nevertheless authorized the persecution of Christianity as a moral and social danger, and that no argument ever used by any other persecutor had not been equally open to him. We cannot suppose that persecution never kills the truth. "It is a piece of idle sentimentality", Mill observes, "that truth, merely as truth, has any inherent power denied to error, of prevailing against the dungeon and the stake." Persecution is historically only too effective.

> To speak only of religious opinions: the Reformation broke out at least twenty times before Luther, and was put down. Arnold of Brescia was put down. Fra Dolcino was put down. Savonarola was put down. The Albigeois were put down. The Vaudois were put down. The Lollards were put down. The Hussites were put down . . . In Spain, Italy, Flanders, the Austrian Empire, Protestantism was rooted out; and most likely would have been so in England had Queen Mary lived or Queen Elizabeth died . . . No reasonable person can doubt that Christianity might have been extirpated in the Roman Empire.

And if it be said against this that, just because we have erred in the past, it is mere cowardice to refrain from striking down evil when we see it in the present in case we may be mistaken again; or, to put it in another way, that, even if we are not infallible, yet, if we are to live at all, we must make decisions and act, and must do so on nothing better than probability, according to our lights, with constant risk of error; for all living involves risk, and what alternative have we? Mill answers that "There is the greatest difference between presuming an opinion to be true, because with every opportunity for contesting it, it has not been refuted, and assuming its truth for the purpose of not permitting its refutation". You can indeed stop "bad men from perverting society with false or pernicious views", but only if you give men liberty to deny that what you yourself call bad, or pernicious, or perverted, or false, is such; otherwise your conviction is founded on mere dogma and is not rational, and cannot be analysed or altered in the light of any new facts and ideas. Without infallibility how can truth emerge save in discussion? There is no *a priori* road towards it; a new experience, a new argument, can in principle always alter our views, no matter how strongly held. To shut doors is to blind yourself to the truth deliberately, to condemn yourself to incorrigible error.

Mill had a strong and subtle brain and his arguments are never negligible. But it is, in this case, plain that his conclusion only follows from premisses which he does not make explicit. He was an empiricist; that is, he believed that no truths are—or could be—rationally established, except on the evidence of observation. New observations could in principle always upset a conclusion founded on earlier ones. He believed this rule to be true of the laws of physics, even of the laws of logic and mathematics; how much more, therefore, in "ideological" fields where no scientific certainty prevailed—in ethics, politics, religion, history, the entire field of human affairs, where only probability reigns; here, unless full liberty of opinion and argument is permitted, nothing can ever be rationally established. But those who disagree with him, and believe in intuited truths, in principle not corrigible by experience, will disregard this argument. Mill can write them off as obscurantists, dogmatists, irrationalists. Yet something more is needed than mere contemptuous dismissal if their views, more powerful today perhaps than even in Mill's own century, are to be rationally contested. Again, it may well be that without full freedom of discussion the truth cannot emerge. But this may be only a necessary, not a sufficient, condition of its discovery; the truth may, for all our efforts, remain at the bottom of a well, and in the meantime the worse cause may win, and do enormous damage to mankind. Is it so clear that we must permit opinions advocating, say, race hatred to be uttered freely, because Milton has said that "though all the winds of doctrine are let loose upon the earth ... whoever knew truth put to the worse in a free and open encounter?" because "the truth must always prevail in a fair fight with falsehood"? These are brave and optimistic judgments, but how good is the empirical evidence for them today? Are demagogues and liars, scoundrels and blind fanatics, always, in liberal societies, stopped in time, or refuted in the end? How high a price is it right to pay for the great boon of freedom of discussion? A very high one, no doubt; but is it limitless? And if not, who shall say what sacrifice is, or is not, too great? Mill goes on to say that an opinion believed to be false may yet be partially true; for there is no absolute truth, only different roads towards it; the suppression of an apparent falsehood may also suppress what is true in it, to the loss of mankind. This argument, again, will not tell with those who believe that absolute truth is discoverable once and for all, whether by metaphysical or theological argument, or by some direct insight, or by leading a certain kind of life, or, as Mill's own mentors believed, by scientific or empirical methods.

His argument is plausible only on the assumption which, whether he knew it or not, Mill all too obviously made, that human knowledge was in principle never complete, and always fallible; that there was no single, universally visible, truth; that each man, each nation, each civilization might take its own road towards its own goal, not necessarily harmonious with those of others; that men are altered, and the truths in which they believe are altered, by new experiences and their own actions—what he calls "experiments in living"; that consequently the conviction, common to Aristotelians and a good many Christian scholastics and atheistical materialists alike, that there exists a basic knowable human nature, one and the same, at all times, in all places, in all men—static, unchanging substance underneath the altering appearances, with permanent needs, dictated by a single, discoverable goal, or pattern of goals, the same for all mankind—is mistaken; and so, too, is the notion that is bound up with it, of a single true doctrine carrying salvation to all men everywhere, contained in natural law, or the revelation of a sacred book, or the insight of a man of genius, or the natural wisdom of ordinary men, or the calculations made by an elite of utilitarian scientists set up to govern mankind.

Mill—bravely for a professed utilitarian—observes that the human (that is the social) sciences are too confused and uncertain to be properly called sciences at all—there are in them no valid generalizations, no laws, and therefore no predictions or rules of action can properly be deduced from them. He honoured the memory of his father, whose whole philosophy was based on the opposite assumption; he respected Auguste Comte, and subsidized Herbert Spencer, both of whom claimed to have laid the foundations for just such a science of society. Yet his own half-articulate assumption contradicts this. Mill believes that man is spontaneous, that he has freedom of choice, that he moulds his own character, that as a result of the interplay of men with nature and with other men something novel continually arises, and that this novelty is precisely what is most characteristic and most human in men. Because Mill's entire view of human nature turns out to rest not on the notion of the repetition of an identical pattern, but on his perception of human lives as subject to perpetual incompleteness, self-transformation, and novelty, his words are today alive and relevant to our own problems; whereas the works of James Mill, and of Buckle and Comte and Spencer, remain huge half-forgotten hulks in the river of nineteenth-century thought. He does not demand or predict ideal conditions for the final solution of human problems or for obtaining universal agreement on all crucial issues. He assumes that finality is impossible, and implies that it is undesirable too. He does not demonstrate this. Rigour in argument is not among his accomplishments. Yet it is this belief, which undermines the foundations on which Helvétius, Bentham, and James Mill built their doctrines—a system never formally repudiated by him—that gives his case both its plausibility and its humanity.

His remaining arguments are weaker still. He says that unless it is contested, truth is liable to degenerate into dogma or prejudice; men would no longer feel it as a living truth; opposition is needed to keep it alive. "Both teachers and learners go to sleep at their post, as soon as there is no enemy in the field", overcome as they are by "the deep slumber of a decided opinion." So deeply did Mill believe this, that he declared that if there were no genuine dissenters, we had an obligation to invent arguments against ourselves, in order to keep ourselves in a state of intellectual fitness. This resembles nothing so much as Hegel's argument for war as keeping human society from stagnation. Yet if the truth about human affairs were in principle demonstrable, as it is, say, in arithmetic, the invention of false propositions in order to be knocked down would scarcely be needed to preserve our understanding of it. What Mill seems really to be asking for is diversity of opinion for its own sake. He speaks of the need for "fair play to all sides of the truth"—a phrase that a man would scarcely employ if he believed in simple, complete truths as the earlier utilitarians did; and he makes use of bad arguments to conceal this scepticism, perhaps even from himself. "In an imperfect state of the human mind", he says, "the interests of the truth require a diversity of opinions." Or again, "Do we really accept the logic of the persecutors [and say] we may persecute others because we are right, and they may not persecute us because they are wrong?" Catholics, Protestants, Jews, Muslims have all justified persecution by this argument in their day; and on their premisses there may be nothing logically amiss with it. It is these premisses that Mill rejects, and rejects not, it seems to me, as a result of a chain of reasoning, but because he believes—even if he never, so far as I know, admits this explicitly—that there are no final truths not corrigible by experience, at any rate in what is now called the ideological sphere—that of value judgements and of general outlook and attitude to life. Yet within this framework of ideas and values, despite all the stress on the value of "experiments in living" and what they may reveal, Mill is ready to stake a very great deal on the truth of his convictions about what he thinks to be the deepest and most permanent interests of men. Although his reasons are drawn from experience and not *a priori* knowledge, the propositions themselves are very like those defended on metaphysical grounds by the traditional upholders of the doctrine of natural rights. Mill believes in liberty, that is, the rigid limitation of the right to coerce, because he is sure that men cannot develop and flourish and become fully human unless they are left free from interference by other men within a certain minimum area of their lives, which he regards as—or wishes to make—inviolable. This is his view of what men are, and therefore of their basic moral and intellectual needs, and he formulates his conclusions in the celebrated maxims according to which "The individual is not accountable to society for his actions, in so far as these concern the interests of no person but himself," and that

> The only reason for which power can be rightfully exercised over any member of a civilised community against his will is to prevent harm to others. His own good, either physical or moral, is not a sufficient warrant. He cannot rightfully be compelled to do or to forbear . . . because in the opinion of others to do so would be wise or even right.

This is Mill's profession of faith, and the ultimate basis of political liberalism, and therefore the proper target of attack—both on psychological and moral (and social) grounds—by its opponents during Mill's lifetime and after. Carlyle reacted with characteristic fury in a letter to his brother Alexander: "As if it were a sin to control or coerce into better methods human swine in any way . . . Ach Gott in Himmel!"

Milder and more rational critics have not failed to point out that the limits of private and public domain are difficult to demarcate, that anything a man does could, in principle, frustrate others; that no man is an island; that the social and the individual aspects of human beings often cannot, in practice, be disentangled. Mill was told that when men look upon forms of worship in which other men persist as being not merely "abominable" in themselves, but as an offence to them or to their God, they may be irrational and bigoted, but they are not necessarily lying; and that when he asks rhetorically why Muslims should not forbid the eating of pork to everyone, since they are genuinely disgusted by it, the answer, on utilitarian premisses, is by no means self-evident. It might be argued that there is no *a priori* reason for supposing that most men would not be happier—if that is the goal—in a wholly socialized world where private life and personal freedom are reduced to vanishing point, that in Mill's individualist order; and that whether this is so or not is a matter for experimental verification. Mill constantly protests against the fact that social and legal rules are too often determined merely by "the likings and dislikings of society", and correctly points out that these are often irrational or are founded on ignorance. But if damage to others is what concerns him most (as he professes), then the fact that their resistance to this or that belief is instinctive, or intuitive, or founded on no rational ground, does not make it the less painful, and, to that extent, damaging to them. Why should rational men be entitled to the satisfaction of their ends more than the irrational? Why not the irrational, if the greatest happiness of the greatest number (and the greatest number are seldom rational) is the sole justified purpose of action? Only a competent social psychologist can tell what will make a given society happiest. If happiness is the sole criterion, then human sacrifice, or the burning of witches, at times when such practices had strong public feeling behind them, did doubtless, in their day, contribute to the happiness of the majority. If there is no other moral criterion, then the question whether the slaughter of innocent old women (together with the ignorance and prejudice which made this acceptable) or the advance in knowledge and rationality (which ended such abominations but robbed men of comforting illusions)—which of these yielded a higher balance of happiness is only a matter of actuarial calculation. Mill paid no attention to such considerations: nothing could go more violently against all that he felt and believed. At the centre of Mill's thought and feeling lies, not his utilitarianism, nor the concern about enlightenment, nor about dividing the private from the public domain—for he himself at times concedes that the state may invade the private domain, in order to promote education, hygiene, or social security or justice—but his passionate belief that men are made human by their capacity for choice—choice of evil and good equally. Fallibility, the right to err, as a corollary of the capacity for self-improvement; distrust of symmetry and finality as enemies of freedom—these are the principles which Mill never abandons. He is acutely aware of the many-sidedness of the truth and of the irreducible complexity of life, which rules out the very possibility of any simple solution, or the idea of a final answer to any concrete problem. Greatly daring, and without looking back at the stem intellectual puritanism in which he was brought up, he preaches the necessity of understanding and gaining illumination from doctrines that are incompatible with one another—say those of Coleridge and Bentham; he explained in his autobiography the need to understand and learn from both.

III

Kant once remarked that "out of the crooked timber of humanity no straight thing was ever made". Mill believed this deeply. This, and his almost Hegelian distrust of simple models and of cut-and-dried formulae to cover complex, contradictory, and changing situations, made him a very hesitant and uncertain adherent of organized parties and programmes. Despite his father's advocacy, despite Mrs. Taylor's passionate faith in the ultimate solution of all social evils by some great institutional change (in her case that of socialism), he could not rest in the notion of a clearly discernible final goal, because he saw that men differed and evolved, not merely as a result of natural causes, but also because of what they themselves did to alter their own characters, at times in unintended ways. This alone makes their conduct unpredictable, and renders laws or theories, whether inspired by analogies with mechanics or with biology, nevertheless incapable of embracing the complexity and qualitative properties of even an individual character, let alone of a group of men. Hence the imposition of any such construction upon a living society is bound, in his favourite words of warning, to dwarf, maim, cramp, wither the human faculties.

His greatest break with his father was brought about by this conviction: by his belief (which he never explicitly admitted) that particular predicaments required each its own specific treatment; that the application of correct judgement, in curing a social malady, mattered at least as much as knowledge of the laws of anatomy or pharmacology. He was a British empiricist and not a French rationalist, or a German metaphysician, sensitive to day-to-day play of circumstances, differences of "climate", as well as to the individual nature of each case, as Helvétius or Saint–Simon or Fichte, concerned as they were with the *grandes lignes* of development, were not. Hence his unceasing anxiety, as great as Tocqueville's and greater than Montesquieu's, to preserve variety, to keep doors open to change, to resist the dangers of social pressure, and above all his hatred of the human pack in full cry against a victim, his desire to protect dissidents and heretics as such. The whole burden of his charge against the "progressives" (he means utilitarians and perhaps socialists) is that, as a rule, they do no more than try to alter social opinion in order to make it more favourable to this or that scheme or reform, instead of assailing the monstrous principle itself which says that social opinion "should be a law for individuals."

Mill's overmastering desire for variety and individuality for their own sake emerges in many shapes. He notes that "Mankind are greater gainers by suffering each other to live as seems good to themselves, than by compelling each to live as seems good to the rest"—a truism which, he declares, "stands opposed to the general tendency of existing opinion and practice". At other times he speaks in sharper terms. He remarks that

> it is the habit of our time to desire nothing strongly. Its ideal of character is to be without any marked character; to maim by compression, like a Chinese lady's foot, every part of human nature which stands out prominently, and tends to make the person markedly dissimilar in outline to commonplace humanity.

And again:

> The greatness of England is now all collective; individually small, we only appear capable of anything great by combining; and with this our moral and religious philanthropists are perfectly content. But it was men of another stamp that made England what it has been; and men of another stamp will be needed to prevent its decline.

The tone of this, if not the content, would have shocked Bentham; so indeed would this bitter echo of Tocqueville:

> Comparatively speaking, they now read the same things, listen to the same things, see the same things, go to the same places, have their hopes and fears directed to the same objects, have the same rights and liberties and the same means of asserting them ... All the political changes of the age promote it, since they all tend to raise the low and lower the high. Every extension of education promotes it, because education brings people under common influences. Improvement in the means of communication promotes it ... Increase of commerce and manufacture promotes it ... The ascendancy of public opinion ... forms so great a mass of influence hostile to individuality (p. 98) [that] in this age the mere example of non-conformity, the mere refusal to bend the knee to custom, is itself a service.

We have come to such a pass that mere differences, resistance for its own sake, protest as such, is now enough. Conformity, and the intolerance which is its offensive and defensive arm, are for Mill always detestable, and peculiarly horrifying in an age which thinks itself enlightened; in which, nevertheless, a man can be sent to prison for twenty-one months for atheism; jurymen are rejected and foreigners denied justice because they hold no recognized religious beliefs; no public money is given for Hindu or Muslim schools because an "imbecile display" is made by an Under–Secretary, who declares that toleration is desirable only among Christians but not for unbelievers. It is no better when workers employ "moral police" to prevent some members of their trade union being paid higher wages earned by superior skill or industry than the wages paid to those who lack these attributes. Such conduct is even more loathsome when it interferes with private relations between individuals. He declared that "what any person might freely do with respect to sexual relations" should be deemed to be an unimportant and purely private matter which concerns no one but themselves; that to have held any human being responsible to other people, and to the world, for the fact itself (apart from such of its consequences as the birth of children, which clearly created duties which should be socially enforced) would one day be thought one of the superstitions and barbarisms of the infancy of the human race. The same seemed to him to apply to the enforcement of temperance or Sabbath observance, or any of the matters on which "intrusively pious members of society should be told to mind their own business." No doubt the gossip to which Mill was exposed during his relationship with Mrs. Taylor before his marriage to her—the relationship which Carlyle mocked at as platonic—made him peculiarly sensitive to this form of social persecution. But it is of a piece with his deepest and most permanent convictions.

Mill's suspicion of democracy as the only just, and yet potentially the most oppressive, form of government, springs from the same roots. He wondered uneasily whether centralization of authority and the inevitable dependence of each on all and "surveillance of each by all" would not end by grinding all down into "a tame uniformity of thought, dealings and actions", and produce "automatons in human form" and "liberticide". Tocqueville had written pessimistically about the moral and intellectual effects of democracy in America. Mill agreed. He said that even if such power did not destroy, it prevented existence; it compressed, enervated, extinguished, and stupefied a people; and turned them into a flock of "timid and industrious animals of whom the government is a shepherd". Yet the only cure for this, as Tocqueville himself maintained (it may be a little half-heartedly), is more democracy, which can alone educate a sufficient number of individuals to independence, resistance, and strength. Men's disposition to impose their own views on others is so strong that, in Mill's view, only want of power restricts it; this power is growing; hence unless further barriers are erected it will increase, leading to a proliferation of "conformers, time servers, hyprocrites, created by silencing opinion", and finally to a society where timidity has killed independent thought, and men confine themselves to safe subjects. Yet if we make the barriers too high, and do not interfere with opinion at all, will this not end, as Burke or the Hegelians have warned in the dissolution of the social texture, atomization of society—anarchy? To this Mill replies that "the inconvenience arising from conduct which neither violates specific duty to the public, nor hurts any assignable individual, is one which society can afford to bear for the sake of the greater good of human freedom." This is tantamount to saying that if society, despite the need for social cohesion, has itself failed to educate its citizens to be civilized men, it has no right to punish them for irritating others, or being misfits, or not conforming to some standard which the majority accepts. A smooth and harmonious society could perhaps be created, at any rate for a time, but it would be purchased at too high a price. Plato saw correctly that if a frictionless society is to emerge the poets must be driven out; what horrifies those who revolt against this policy is not so much the expulsion of the fantasy-mongering poets as such, but the underlying desire for an end to variety, movement, individuality of any kind; a craving for a fixed pattern of life and thought, timeless, changeless, and uniform. Without the right of protest, and the capacity for it, there is for Mill no justice, there are no ends worth pursuing.

> If all mankind minus one were of one opinion, and only one person were of a contrary opinion, mankind would be no more justified in silencing that one person than he, if he had the power, would be justified in silencing mankind.

In his lecture in this series, to which I have already referred, Sir Richard Livingstone, whose sympathy with Mill is not in doubt, charges him with attributing too much rationality to human beings: the ideal of untrammelled freedom may be the right of those who have reached the maturity of their faculties, but of how many men today, or at most times, is this true? Surely Mill asks far too much and is far too optimistic? There is certainly an important sense in which Sir Richard is right: Mill was no prophet. Many social developments caused him grief, but he had no inkling of the mounting strength of the irrational forces that have moulded the history of the twentieth century. Burckhardt and Marx, Pareto and Freud, were more sensitive to the deeper currents of their own times, and saw a good deal more deeply into the springs of individual and social behaviour. But I know of no evidence that Mill overestimated the enlightenment of his own age, or that he supposed that the majority of men of his own time were mature or rational or likely soon to become so. What he did see before him was the spectacle of some men, civilized by any standards, who were kept down, or discriminated against, or persecuted by prejudice, stupidity, "collective mediocrity"; he saw such men deprived of what he regarded as their most essential rights, and he protested. He believed that all human progress, all human greatness and virtue and freedom, depended chiefly on the preservation of such men and the clearing of paths before them. But he did not want them appointed Platonic Guardians. He thought that others like them could be educated, and, when they were educated, would be entitled to make choices, and that these choices must not, within certain limits, be blocked or directed by others. He did not merely advocate education and forget the freedom to which it would entitle the educated (as communists have), or press for total freedom of choice, and forget that without adequate education it would lead to chaos and, as a reaction to it, a new slavery (as anarchists do). He demanded both. But he did not think that this process would be rapid, or easy, or universal; he was on the whole a pessimistic man, and consequently at once defended and distrusted democracy, for which he has been duly attacked, and is still sharply criticized. Sir Richard has observed that Mill was acutely conscious of the circumstances of his age, and saw no further than that. This seems to me a just comment. The disease of Victorian England was claustrophobia—there was a sense of suffocation, and the best and most gifted men of the period, Mill and Carlyle, Nietzsche and Ibsen, men both of the left and of the right—demanded more air and more light. The mass neurosis of our age is agoraphobia; men are terrified of disintegration and of too little direction: they ask, like Hobbes's masterless men in a state of nature, for walls to keep out the raging ocean, for order, security, organization, clear and recognizable authority, and are alarmed by the prospect of too much freedom, which leaves them lost in a vast, friendless vacuum, a desert without paths or landmarks or goals. Our situation is different from that of the nineteenth century, and so are our problems: the area of irrationality is seen to be vaster and more complex than any that Mill had dreamed of. Mill's psychology has become antiquated and grows more so with every discovery that is made. He is justly criticized for paying too much attention to purely spiritual obstacles to the fruitful use of freedom—lack of moral and intellectual light; and too little (although nothing like as little as his detractors have maintained) to poverty, disease, and their causes, and to the common sources and the interaction of both, and for concentrating too narrowly on freedom of thought and expression. All this is true. Yet what solutions have we found, with all our new technological and psychological knowledge and great new powers, save the ancient prescription advocated by the creators of humanism—Erasmus and Spinoza, Locke and Montesquieu, Lessing and Diderot—reason, education, self-knowledge, responsibility—above all, self-knowledge? What other hope is there for men, or has there ever been?

IV

Mill's ideal is not original. It is an attempt to fuse rationalism and romanticism: the aim of Goethe and Wilhelm Humboldt, a rich, spontaneous, many-sided, fearless, free, and yet rational, self-directed character. Mill notes that Europeans owe much to "plurality of paths." From sheer differences and disagreements sprang toleration, variety, humanity. In a sudden outburst of anti-egalitarian feeling, he praises the Middle Ages because men were then more individual and more responsible: men died for ideas, and women were equal to men. "The poor Middle Ages, its Papacy, its chivalry, its feudality, under what hands did they perish? Under that of the attorney, and fraudulent bankrupt, the false coiner." This is the language not of a philosophical radical, but of Burke, or Carlyle, or Chesterton. In his passion for the colour and the texture of life Mill has forgotten his list of martyrs, he has forgotten the teachings of his father, of Bentham, or Condorcet. He remembers only Coleridge, only the horrors of a levelling, middle-class society—the grey, conformist, congregation that worships the wicked principle that "it is the absolute social right of every individual that every other individual should act in every respect exactly as he ought" or, worse still, "that it is one man's duty that another should be religious", for "God not only abominates the acts of the misbeliever, but will not hold us guiltless if we leave them unmolested." These are the shibboleths of Victorian England, and if that is its conception of social justice, it were better dead. In a similar, earlier moment of acute indignation with the self-righteous defences of the exploitation of the poor, Mill had expressed his enthusiasm for revolution and slaughter, since justice was more precious than life. He was twenty-five years old when he wrote that. A quarter of a century later, he declared that a civilization which had not the inner strength to resist barbarism had better succumb. This may not be the voice of Kant, but it is not that of utilitarianism; rather that of Rousseau or Mazzini.

But Mill seldom continues in this tone. His solution is not revolutionary. If human life is to be made tolerable, information must be centralized and power disseminated. If everyone knows as much as possible, and has not too much power, then we may yet avoid a state which "dwarfs its men", in which "there is the absolute rule of the head of the executive over a congregation of isolated individuals, all equals but all slaves''. With small men ''no great thing can really be accomplished.'' There is a terrible danger in creeds and forms of life which ''compress'', ''stunt'', ''dwarf'' men. The acute consciousness in our day of the dehumanizing effect of mass culture; of the destruction of genuine purposes, both individual and communal, by the treatment of men as irrational creatures to be deluded and manipulated by the media of mass advertising, and mass communication—and so ''alienated'' from the basic purposes of human beings by being left exposed to the play of the forces of nature interacting with human ignorance, vice, stupidity, tradition, and above all self-deception and institutional blindness—all this was as deeply and painfully felt by Mill as by Ruskin or William Morris. In this matter he differs from them only in his clearer awareness of the dilemma created by the simultaneous needs for individual self-expression and for human community. It is on this theme that the tract on Liberty was composed. ''It is to be feared'', Mill added gloomily, ''that the teachings'' of his essay ''will retain their value for a long time.''

It was, I think, Bertrand Russell—Mill's godson—who remarked somewhere that the deepest convictions of philosophers are seldom contained in their formal arguments: fundamental beliefs, comprehensive views of life, are like citadels which must be guarded against the enemy. Philosophers expend their intellectual power in arguments against actual and possible objections to their doctrines, and although the reasons they find, and the logic that they use, may be complex, ingenious, and formidable, they are defensive weapons; the inner fortress itself—the vision of life for the sake of which the war is being waged—will, as a rule, turn out to be relatively simple and unsophisticated. Mill's defence of his position in the tract on Liberty is not, as has often been pointed out, of the highest intellectual quality: most of his arguments can be turned against him; certainly none is conclusive, or such as would convince a determined or unsympathetic opponent. From the days of James Stephen, whose powerful attack on Mill's position appeared in the year of Mill's death, to the conservatives and socialists and authoritarians and totalitarians of our day, the critics of Mill have, on the whole, exceeded the number of his defenders. Nevertheless, the inner citadel—the central thesis—has stood the test. It may need elaboration or qualification, but it is still the clearest, most candid, persuasive, and moving exposition of the point of view of those who desire an open and tolerant society. The reason for this is not merely the honesty of Mill's mind, or the moral and intellectual charm of his prose, but the fact that he is saying something true and important about some of the most fundamental characteristics and aspirations of human beings. Mill is not merely uttering a string of clear propositions (each of which, viewed by itself, is of doubtful plausibility) connected by such logical links as he can supply. He perceived something profound and essential about the destructive effect of man's most successful efforts at self-improvement in modern society; about the unintended consequences of modern democracy, and the fallaciousness and practical dangers of the theories by which some of the worst of these consequences were (and still are) defended. That is why, despite the weakness of the argument, the loose ends, the dated examples, the touch of the finishing governess that Disraeli so maliciously noted, despite the total lack of that boldness of conception which only men of original genius possess, his essay educated his generation, and is controversial still. Mill's central propositions are not truisms, they are not at all self-evident. They are statements of a position which has been resisted and rejected by the modern descendants of his most notable contemporaries, Marx, Carlyle, Dostoevsky, Newman, Comte, and they are still assailed because they are still contemporary. The *Essay on Liberty* deals with specific social issues in terms of examples drawn from genuine and disturbing issues of its day, and its principles and conclusions are alive in part because they spring from acute moral crises in a man's life, and thereafter from a life spent in working for concrete causes and taking genuine—and therefore at times dangerous—decisions. Mill looked at the questions that puzzled him directly, and not through spectacles provided by any orthodoxy. His revolt against his father's education, his bold avowal of the values of Coleridge and the Romantics was the liberating act that dashed these spectacles to the ground. From these half-truths, too, he liberated himself in turn, and became a thinker in his own right. For this reason, while Spencer and Comte, Taine and Buckle—even Carlyle and Ruskin, figures who loomed very large in their generation—are fast receding into (or have been swallowed by) the shadows of the past, Mill himself remains real.

One of the symptoms of this kind of three-dimensional, rounded, authentic quality is that we feel sure that we can tell where he would have stood on the issues of our own day. Can anyone doubt what position he would have taken on the Dreyfus case, or the Boer War, or fascism, or communism? Or, for that matter, on Munich, or Suez, or Budapest, or Apartheid, or colonialism, or the Wolfenden report? Can we be so certain with regard to other eminent Victorian moralists? Carlyle or Ruskin or Dickens? or even Kingsley or Wilberforce or Newman? Surely that alone is some evidence of the permanence of the issues with which Mill dealt and the degree of his insight into them.

V

Mill is usually represented as a just and high-souled Victorian school-master, honourable, sensitive, humane, but "sober, censorious and sad"; something of a goose, something of a prig, a good and noble man, but bleak, sententious, and desiccated; a waxwork among other waxworks in an age now dead and gone and stiff with such effigies. His autobiography—one of the most moving accounts of a human life—modifies this impression. Mill was certainly an intellectual, and was well aware, and not at all ashamed, of this fact. He knew that his main interest lay in general ideas in a society largely distrustful of them: "the English", he wrote to his friend d'Eichthal, "invariably mistrust the most evident truths if he who propounds them is suspected of having general ideas". He was excited by ideas and wanted them to be as interesting as possible. He admired the French for respecting intellectuals as the English did not. He noted that there was a good deal of talk in England about the march of intellect at home, but he remained sceptical. He wondered whether "our march of intellect be not rather a march towards doing without intellect, and supplying our deficiency in giants by the united effort of the constantly increasing multitude of dwarfs". The word "dwarfs", and the fear of smallness, pervades all his writings.

Because he believed in the importance of ideas, he was prepared to change his own if others could convince him of their inadequacy, or when a new vision was revealed to him, as it was by Coleridge or Saint-Simon, or, as he believed, by the transcendent genius of Mrs Taylor. He liked criticism for its own sake. He detested adulation, even praise of his own work. He attacked dogmatism in others and was genuinely free from it himself. Despite the efforts of his father and his mentors, he retained an unusually open mind, and his "still and cold appearance" and "the head that reasons as a great steam engine works" were united (to quote his friend Stirling) with a "warm, upright and really lofty soul" and a touching and pure-hearted readiness to learn from anyone, at any time. He lacked vanity and cared little for his reputation, and therefore did not cling to consistency for its own sake, nor to his own personal dignity, if a human issue was at stake. He was loyal to movements, to causes, and to parties, but could not be prevailed upon to support them at the price of saying what he did not think to be true. A characteristic instance of this is his attitude to religion. His father brought him up in the strictest and narrowest atheist dogma. He rebelled against it. He embraced no recognized faith, but he did not dismiss religion, as the French encyclopaedists or the Benthamites had done, as a tissue of childish fantasies and emotions, comforting illusions, mystical gibberish and deliberate lies. He held that the existence of God was possible, indeed probable, but unproven, but that if God was good he could not be omnipotent, since he permitted evil to exist. He would not hear of a being at once wholly good and omnipotent whose nature defied the canons of human logic, since he rejected belief in mysteries as mere attempts to evade agonizing issues. If he did not understand (this must have happened often), he did not pretend to understand. Although he was prepared to fight for the rights of others to hold a faith detached from logic, he rejected it himself. He revered Christ as the best man who ever lived, and regarded theism as a noble, though to him unintelligible, set of beliefs. He regarded immortality as possible, but rated its probability very low. He was, in fact, a Victorian agnostic who was uncomfortable with atheism and regarded religion as something that was exclusively the individual's own affair. When he was invited to stand for parliament, to which he was duly elected, he declared that he was prepared to answer any questions that the electors of Westminster might choose to put to him, save those on his religious views. This was not cowardice—his behaviour throughout the election was so candid and imprudently fearless, that someone remarked that on Mill's platform God Almighty Himself could not expect to be elected. His reason was that a man had an indefeasible right to keep his private life to himself and to fight for this right, if need be. When, at a later date, his stepdaughter Helen Taylor and others upbraided him for not aligning himself more firmly with the atheists, and accused him of temporizing and shilly-shallying, he remained unshaken. His doubts were his own property: no one was entitled to extort a confession of faith from him, unless it could be shown that his silence harmed others; since this could not be shown, he saw no reason for publicly committing himself. Like Acton after him, he regarded liberty and religious toleration as the indispensable protection of all true religion, and the distinction made by the Church between spiritual and temporal realms as one of the great achievements of Christianity, inasmuch as it had made possible freedom of opinion. This last he valued beyond all things, and he defended Bradlaugh passionately, although, and because, he did not agree with his opinions.

He was the teacher of a generation, of a nation, but still no more than a teacher, not a creator or an innovator. He is known for no lasting discovery or invention. He made scarcely any significant advance in logic or philosophy or economics or political thought. Yet his range, and his capacity for applying ideas to fields in which they would bear fruit was unexampled. He was not original, yet he transformed the structure of the human knowledge of his age.

Because he had an exceptionally honest, open, and civilized mind, which found natural expression in lucid and admirable prose; because he combined an unswerving pursuit of the truth with the belief that its house had many mansions, so that even "one-eyed men like Bentham might see what men with normal vision would not" because, despite his inhibited emotions and his overdeveloped intellect, despite his humourless, cerebral, solemn character, his conception of man was deeper, and his vision of history and life wider and less simple than that of his utilitarian predecessors or liberal followers, he has emerged as a major political thinker in our own day. He broke with the pseudoscientific model, inherited from the classical world and the age of reason, of a determined human nature, endowed at all times, everywhere, with the same unaltering needs, emotions, motives, responding differently only to differences of situation and stimulus, or evolving according to some unaltering pattern. For this he substituted (not altogether consciously) the image of man as creative, incapable of self-completion, and therefore never wholly predictable: fallible, a complex combination of opposites, some reconcilable, others incapable of being resolved or harmonized; unable to cease from his search for truth, happiness, novelty, freedom, but with no guarantee, theological or logical or scientific, of being able to attain them: a free, imperfect being, capable of determining his own destiny in circumstances favourable to the development of his reason and his gifts. He was tormented by the problem of free will, and found no better solution for it than anyone else, although at times he thought he had solved it. He believed that it is neither rational thought, nor domination over nature, but freedom to choose and to experiment that distinguishes men from the rest of nature; of all his ideas it is this view that has ensured his lasting fame. By freedom he meant a condition in which men were not prevented from choosing both the object and the manner of their worship. For him only a society in which this condition was realized could be called fully human. No man deserves commemoration by this Council more than Mill, for it was created to serve an ideal which he regarded as more precious than life itself.

Additional Readings

Mill

Frederick Berger, Happiness, Justice, and Freedom: The Moral and Political Philosophy of John Stuart Mill (1984)

Karl Britton, John Stuart Mill: Life and Philosophy (1969)

Gerald Dworkin ed., Mill's *On Liberty*: Critical Essays (1997)

John Gray, Mill on Liberty: A Defence (2d ed. 1996)

Joseph Hamburger, Intellectuals in Politics: John Stuart Mill and the Philosophic Radicals (1965)

F. A. Hayek, John Stuart Mill and Harriet Taylor: Their Correspondence and Subsequent Marriage (1951)

Gertrude Himmelfarb, On Liberty and Liberalism: The Case of J. S. Mill (1974)

George Kateb, A Reading of *On Liberty*, in John Stuart Mill, On Liberty (David Bromwich & George Kateb eds. 2003)

J.C. Rees, John Stuart Mill's *On Liberty* (1985)

Alan Ryan, J. S. Mill (1975)

Alan Ryan, The Philosophy of John Stuart Mill (2d ed. 1987)

Ten Chin Liew, Was Mill a Liberal? (2004)

Jeremy Waldron, Mill as a Critic of Culture and Society, in John Stuart Mill, On Liberty (David Bromwich & George Kateb eds. 2003)

Obscenity and pornography

Harry Clor, Obscenity and Public Morality (1969)

David Cole, Playing by Pornography's Rules: The Regulation of Sexual Expression, 143 U. Pa. L. Rev. 111 (1994)

David Dyzenhaus, John Stuart Mill and the Harm of Pornography, 102 Ethics 534 (1992)

Jennifer Hornsby and Rae Langton, Free Speech and Illocution, 4 Legal Theory 21 (1998)

Harry Kalven, Jr., Metaphysics of the Law of Obscenity, 1960 Supreme Court Review 1

Catharine A. MacKinnon, Pornography, Civil Rights, and Speech, 20 Harv. Civ. Rts–Civ. Lib. L. Rev. 1 (1985)

Catharine A. MacKinnon, Sex Equality, ch. 10 (2001)

Frederick Schauer, Speech and "Speech:–Obscenity" and "Obscenity": An Exercise in the Interpretation of Constitutional Language, 67 Georgetown. L.J. 899 (1979)

Cass R. Sunstein, Pornography and the First Amendment, 1986 Duke L. J. 589

Robert Skipper, Mill and Pornography 103 Ethics 726 (1993)

Hill v. Colorado and anti-abortion protests

Alan Brownstein, Rules of Engagement for Cultural Wars: Regulating Conduct, Unprotected Speech, and Protected Expression in Anti-abortion Protests, 29 UC Davis L. Rev. 553, 1163 (1996)

William E. Lee, The Unwilling Listener: *Hill v. Colorado's* Chilling Effect on Unorthodox Speech, 35 UC Davis L. Rev. 387 (2002)

Note, The Impermeable Life: Unsolicited Communications in the Marketplace of Ideas, 118 Harv. L. Rev. 1314 (2005)

Racial hate speech

Thomas C. Grey, How to Write a Speech Code Without Really Trying: Reflections on the Stanford Experience, 29 UC Davis L. Rev. 891 (1996)

Alon Harel, Bigotry, Pornography, and the First Amendment, 65 S. Cal. L. Rev. 1887 (1992)

Robert C. Post, Racist Speech, Democracy, and the First Amendment, 32 Wm. & Mary L. Rev. 267 (1991)

Michel Rosenfeld, Hate Speech in Constitutional Jurisprudence: A Comparative Analysis, 24 Cardozo L. Rev. 1523 (2003)

Alexander Tsesis, Regulating Intimidating Speech, 41 Harv. J. of Legis. 389 (2004)

James Weinstein, Hate Speech, Pornography, and the Radical Attack on Free Speech Doctrine (1999)

Isaiah Berlin

John Gray, Isaiah Berlin (1996)

Richard Wollheim, John Stuart Mill and Isaiah Berlin, in The Idea of Freedom (Alan Ryan ed. 1979)

Chapter Five

LEARNED HAND

DAVID M. RABBAN, FREE SPEECH IN ITS FORGOTTEN YEARS

(1997).

The free speech controversies during and after World War I did not spring from a void. Disputes over free speech had previously arisen in an enormous variety of contexts, ranging from political, labor, and sexual radicalism to commercial advertising and election reform. Judges, law professors, officials at all levels of government, activists, social thinkers, and diverse members of the general public addressed free speech issues throughout the decades before the war. Legislation affecting speech preceded the Espionage Act, legal decisions preceded *Schenck*, scholarship preceded Chafee, and defense organizations preceded the ACLU.

Within the wide range of views about free speech articulated before the war, two traditions stand out. A pervasive judicial hostility to virtually all free speech claims contrasted sharply with a comprehensive defense by libertarian radicals of broad protection for almost every expression. Judges in both federal and state courts overwhelmingly invoked the alleged "bad tendency" of speech to deny claims of abridgment in numerous doctrinal settings, such as libel, contempt of court, obscenity, and breach of the peace. Many judges relied on William Blackstone's eighteenth-century commentaries on the English common law of free speech. Some, including Justice Holmes in an important 1907 decision for the Supreme Court,[4] limited the First Amendment and analogous provisions of state constitutions to the English prohibition against prior restraints on speech. The criticism of these decisions by eminent legal scholars had no apparent impact on the courts. At the opposite end of the ideological spectrum from the judiciary was the long American tradition of libertarian radicalism that originated before the Civil War in individualist anarchism, radical abolitionism, free thought, and free love. Prompted by their underlying commitment to the right of individual autonomy in all aspects of life, libertarian radicals maintained

4. Patterson v. Colorado, 205 U.S. 454 (1907).

that speech on virtually any subject should be protected from legal regulation by the state.

My investigation of the prewar period made me realize that developments during and immediately after World War I did not spontaneously create the modern era of free speech. Instead, these developments rapidly obscured the libertarian radical tradition and transformed judicial interpretation of the First Amendment. The impact of the war and its aftermath on progressives lies at the core of this process and reveals a decisive turning point in the history of American liberalism. In brief, World War I transformed many progressives into civil libertarians.

Before World War I, most progressives challenged traditional conceptions of individual rights protected by the Constitution. They identified constitutional rights with the excessive individualism to which they attributed the destructive inequality and division they saw throughout American society. Judicial recognition of these rights, they pointed out, blocked necessary social reform through positive state action. Property and liberty of contract—individual constitutional rights that the Supreme Court increasingly invoked to invalidate reform legislation—dominated the progressive attack on rights. But progressives were not sympathetic to other assertions of individual constitutional rights, including claims based on the First Amendment.

The emphasis by progressives on social harmony similarly limited their conception of free speech. Progressives often appreciated free speech, and even dissent, as qualities that a democratic society should nurture. But many reacted against dissent that was not directed toward positive social reconstruction. Progressives often saw no value in speech that expressed the structural inevitability of class conflict or that denied the feasibility of ultimate social unity.

World War I brought to the surface these latent but important views about free speech that had been embedded in the prior scholarship of progressive intellectuals. Most progressives supported the war. They often treated pacifists with impatience or even hostility, a reaction most dramatically illustrated by a series of essays John Dewey published in *The New Republic* soon after the United States entered the war in 1917. Dewey, who was the leading public intellectual in the country, emphasized the social importance of widespread critical inquiry more than most progressives. Yet he criticized pacifist opposition to the war as a failure to seize its democratic possibilities and ridiculed dissenters for invoking "early Victorian platitudes" about "the sanctity of individual rights."[5]

The failure of World War I "to make the world safe for democracy," combined with the widespread repression of speech during and after the war, forced many progressives, including Dewey, to reconsider both their prewar faith in a benevolent state and their corresponding aversion to constitutional rights. They retained their belief that property and liberty rights should not block progressive social and economic legislation. They

5. John Dewey, Conscription of Thought (1917), reprinted in 10 John Dewey, The Middle Works 1899–1924, at 276, 279 (Jo Ann Boydston ed., 1980).

also came to recognize, however, the state as a constant threat to civil liberties, and they emphasized the centrality of constitutional free speech to the democratic themes that they had elaborated before the war. This combination of views became the core of New Deal constitutional ideology in the 1930s.

The progressives who became postwar civil libertarians developed a conception of free speech that differed significantly from defenses that prevailed before the war. Reflecting the lingering impact of their earlier views, the postwar civil libertarians based their emerging concern about free speech on its contribution to democracy rather than on its status as a natural right of autonomous individuals. They stressed the social benefits derived from freedom of political expression and essentially ignored the many other free speech issues that libertarian radicals, legal scholars, and other commentators addressed before the war. The actual circumstances that transformed progressives into civil libertarians, especially the severe repression of antiwar and postwar radical speech, reinforced their intellectual predisposition to focus on the protection of political expression.

* * *

Before the war, people asserted limitations on speech that have few defenders today. They frequently maintained that the public owners of property had the same rights as their private counterparts to exclude speakers. Many asserted that free speech did not extend to views that were unpatriotic or that expressed class hatred. Most people assumed that the First Amendment did not apply to the states, and Justice Holmes was far from the only person who understood it as nothing more than the transposition of Blackstone's views on free speech into the United States Constitution. The Supreme Court was not alone in refusing to recognize movies as a form of expression covered by the First Amendment. By contrast, other prewar conceptions of speech were much broader than views asserted today. Serious scholars and lawyers maintained that the First Amendment only allows punishment of speech that actually produces an illegal act. Current uses of individual autonomy as a justification for protecting speech are much more narrow than the conception of autonomy held by libertarian radicals before the war. The prewar libertarian radicals viewed free speech as one of a connected set of fundamental rights to personal autonomy that could not be regulated by the state. These rights covered such diverse subjects as marriage, smoking, medical licensing, and many other activities that most people today would consider unrelated to speech.

* * *

The already familiar contrast between the prewar libertarian radicals and the postwar civil libertarians illustrates how social thought influenced positions on free speech. The underlying libertarian commitment to personal autonomy in every aspect of life translated into a strong defense of free speech on all subjects as an individual right beyond state control. The underlying progressive commitment to reforming American society, by contrast, translated after World War I into a belated defense of dissenting political speech as a vital social interest in a democracy.

PALLAVI GUNIGANTI, LEARNED HAND: A SKEPTICAL LIFE

I beseech ye in the bowels of Christ, think it possible ye may be mistaken.

—Oliver Cromwell to the Scottish army before the Battle of Dunbar.

[I would like to have that written] over the portals of every church, every courthouse and at every crossroads in the nation. It seems to me that if we are to be saved it must be through skepticism.

—Learned Hand

Billings Learned Hand was born on January 27, 1872 in Albany, New York to a legal-minded family. His grandfather Augustus Hand was an Associate Justice of the New York Supreme Court 1847–1855 and a delegate to the 1868 Democratic National Convention, and all three of his sons became attorneys. Learned Hand's father, Samuel Hand, received a gubernatorial appointment to the Court of Appeals, New York's highest state court, in 1878. Shortly thereafter, however, he lost his office due to a Republican political victory. Both the father and grandfather were successful practitioners as well. Learned Hand's elder cousin, Augustus Noble Hand, a childhood companion and lifelong friend, preceded him to Harvard College and followed him to both the U.S. District Court for the Southern District of New York and the U.S. Court of Appeals for the Second Circuit.

At Harvard, Hand majored in philosophy under a faculty that included William James and George Santayana. He edited the Harvard *Advocate* and was the orator for the class of 1893. His Class Day speech emphasized the importance of broad knowledge as well as the accomplishment of practical goals: "Our professorship of things in general must not be forgotten, but it must not be a professorship of nothing in particular." Hand himself, however, "was perfectly indeterminate" on what to do next. "I thought of sticking to philosophy, but my cousin had moved along to the law school, and there were so many lawyers in the family—so I went, too." He remained at Harvard for his master's and law degrees, assisted in editing a then-new publication, the *Harvard Law Review*, and graduated with honors in 1896. After graduation, he dropped Billings entirely as his first name, deciding that it was "vastly formidable" and "pompous," and thereafter used Learned, his mother's maiden name.

He was restless in his career as a lawyer: first a clerk in one Albany law office, then a partner at a different Albany firm, then a managing clerk for a New York City firm, then a member of another New York firm. After the intellectual ferment of Harvard at the end of the nineteenth century, "many times I felt like putting a gun to my head," he said. "Nothing but foreclosures, mortgages, settlement of estates. Everything was petty and formal. Nobody wanted to get *behind* a problem." His cousin Augustus explained that Hand "had a speculative train of thought, and thinking based to a considerable extent on precedent did not particularly interest him." Hand instead directed his mental energies toward articles for the *Harvard Law Review* on a range of topics: "Restitution or Unjust Enrichment," "Historical and Practical Considerations Regarding Expert Testimony," "Due Process of Law and the Eight–Hour Day" (a response to *Lochner*) and "The Commodities Clause and the Fifth Amendment."

His father-in-law, Frederick Fincke, unintentionally sparked Hand's interest in a federal judgeship, but counseled on monetary grounds against Hand's actually pursuing the position. "It looks like quitting to me to take the same [salary] plus some alleged honor, rather than fight it out & reach infinitely higher rewards." However, once Hand made it clear that he wanted the judgeship on its own merits, because it was better suited to his mind, Fincke did his best to pull the political strings that would help his son-in-law receive the appointment. In February 1909, Congress authorized the new judgeship, and in April President William Howard Taft rescued Hand from the practice of law by appointing him to the Federal District Court for Southern New York.

The recommendations of Taft's Attorney General, George W. Wickersham, and influential New York attorney Charles C. Burlingham were based more on Hand's personality and merit than on his politics; Hand subsequently supported Theodore Roosevelt against Taft in the 1912 election. Despite doubts about Roosevelt's personal character, Hand agreed with his opposition to the *Lochner* Court, as well as his plan to regulate business and increase legal protections for the underprivileged. The judge and the former president both thought that the judiciary was abusing its power in overturning states' reformist regulations, but Hand thought the solution was in judges' imposing more restraint on themselves. He and other moderate progressives, to say nothing of conservative Republicans, saw Roosevelt's proposal of voter referendums on controversial decisions as destructive of the judicial branch's independence from political pressure. The split in the Republican Party—with Taft as the official candidate and Roosevelt running as the Bull Moose candidate—led to Democrat Woodrow Wilson's winning the White House.

Hand compounded his political ingratitude by standing as a candidate himself on the Progressive ticket for Chief Judge of the New York Court of Appeals, the same court on which his Democratic father had so briefly won a seat. "I knew this: we had to break away from the Hanna thing—the control of the nation by big business," he later explained. Hand did no campaigning and said that he ran only because "it was necessary for someone to be knocked down." He was defeated and never ventured into politics again, but this one failed step into politics is popularly thought to have cost Hand a seat on the U.S. Supreme Court.

President Taft later became Chief Justice Taft and the Grand Old Party was possessed of an elephant-like memory. When Hand was considered for the vacancy left by Justice Pitney's resignation in 1922, Taft wrote to fellow Republican Warren Harding,

> There is a United States District Judge of proper age, Learned Hand. He is an able Judge and a hard worker. I appointed him on Wickersham's recommendation, but he turned out to be a wild Roosevelt man and a progressive, and though on the bench, he went into the campaign. If promoted to our Bench, he would most certainly herd with Brandeis and be a dissenter. I think it would be risking too much to appoint him.

A progressive mindset was clear in Hand even before the Roosevelt–Taft clash. Not having been appointed for his political connections, he was reluctant to follow the established system of political patronage in granting appointments as receivers for insolvency cases to lawyers who asked for them as a partisan favor. Hand tried to appoint on merit, and pressed for reform of the system without success. Long-winded and obfuscating trial lawyers also annoyed him. He once addressed the City Bar Association on the subject of "The Deficiencies of Trial to Reach the Heart of the Matter." He pleaded for lawyers to exercise self-restraint, a "change in heart in ourselves" rather than "formal changes." In anonymous essays for *The New Republic*, Hand discussed issues of judicial power and social reform, and when the Supreme Court overturned laws that protected union members' ability to be employed, he accused the justices of being biased in favor of their own economic class. As Hand noted in an essay for the *Harvard Law Review*, such a bias might have been permitted when all power was held by the same homogeneous group. But with the increase of popular participation in political life, judges—not subject to direct popular control—must exercise self-restraint so their own beliefs would not be imposed as societal values.

One of Hand's first engagements with a First Amendment case was in *United States v. Kennerley*, in which a novel in the realist style of Theodore Dreiser—about a young working woman in New York City whose virtue is corrupted—was accused of being obscene. Hand felt compelled to follow the well-established precedent of having such works considered in isolated pieces rather than as a whole, and at the standard of the most susceptible reader instead of the community at large. He ruled the novel to be obscene under this rule, but added in his opinion:

> I hope it is not improper for me to say that the rule as laid down, however consonant it may be with mid-Victorian morals, does not seem to me to answer to the understanding and morality of the present time . . . I question whether in the end men will regard that as obscene which is honestly relevant to the adequate expression of innocent ideas . . . To put thought in leash to the average conscience of the time is perhaps tolerable, but to fetter it by the necessities of the lowest and least capable seems a fatal policy.

His belief that a variety of preferences must be given as much room to play themselves out as is compatible with organized society extended even to his marital life. Required to be in New York City for his judicial duties, and enjoying its intellectual opportunities, Hand had little time with his wife Frances, who loved the countryside for its beauty and the friends she had there. Rather than attempt to claim any husbandly right of command, he wrote to her (their long separations produced extensive correspondence), "I do believe I have come to see the right you have to follow your way, and I think I have learned not to trammel you as I did in the early years."

Hand had occasionally read *The Masses* and knew its editor Max Eastman from Eastman's work for women's suffrage, a cause in which Frances took interest. This slight acquaintance sufficed for Eastman to ask Hand in 1916 for a letter defending *The Masses'* right to be sold on the newsstands. Hand obliged, though his advocacy failed to convince Ward & Gow to distribute the publication. The judge made clear to Eastman that he did not agree with his politics, but thought it necessary that men think critically, something that Eastman apparently could inspire them to do. When the *Masses* case came before Hand, he wrote in a letter to Frances that he thought the editors "had not done anything which could possibly be illegal, though, of course, their bias is clear enough. I should think that in fairness I should be obliged to protect them," though "my decision would go against [the government], and then whoop-la your little man is in the mud, assuming he is not there anyway." Nonetheless,

> I must do the right as I see it and the thing I am most anxious about is that I shall succeed in giving a decision absolutely devoid of any such considerations [as the prospect of promotion]. There are times when the old bunk about an independent and fearless judiciary means a good deal. This is one of them; and if I have limitations of judgment, I may have to suffer for it, but I want to be sure that these are the only limitations and that I have none of character.

Judge Hand's decision in *Masses Publishing Co. v. Patten* was quickly overturned by the Second Circuit Court of Appeals, and repeated attempts at prosecution of the *Masses* editors, while unsuccessful in convicting them, discouraged them from further publication. His unpopular decision in *Masses* contributed to his being passed over for promotion to the court that had reversed him. Nevertheless, Hand he continued to argue for his narrow construction of the Espionage Act.

The New York court had many citizenship cases, and the statutory requirement that a person prove a nebulously-defined good moral character before being naturalized troubled Judge Hand. A government attorney once argued that a thirty-nine-year-old bachelor who had admitted having sexual relations with unmarried women was disqualified for citizenship due to this breach of conventional morality. When the attorney said to the judge that he surely would not want his daughter to marry such a man, Hand retorted, "I wouldn't want her to marry a man of thirty-nine who hadn't had the impulse!"

When President Calvin Coolidge began to make nominations for the Circuit Courts of Appeals, even Taft thought Hand a good candidate (as the circuit courts rarely dealt with claims about economic due process), and Attorney General Harlan Fiske Stone recommended him. His appointment to the Second Circuit in 1924 had little opposition, and despite his avowals of not being a Republican, the Republican-controlled Senate confirmed him unanimously. The very man who had first overruled Hand's decision in the *Masses* case, Charles M. Hough, swore Hand into office. The senior judge was a lifelong conservative Republican who disliked reformers, but he and Hand became close friends despite—or perhaps partly because of—their political differences. After Hough's death, his widow told Hand, "He often said that you made him *think* as almost no one else did." When Hough criticized Holmes's dissent in *Gitlow v. New York* as "conscienceless & easy going sufferance of 'imperial jaw' from every kind of social vermin," Hand replied, "I had rather lose any right but that of the right to talk."

However, Hand felt himself to be bound by Second Circuit and even more strongly by Supreme Court precedent. The case of *Gitlow v. Kiely* (Benjamin Gitlow had been pardoned by the governor and returned to Communist activity), like *Masses* involving a postmaster's ban of an allegedly revolutionary magazine, came before Hand in April 1931. He voted along with the rest of the Second Circuit to uphold the ban, despite his own belief that Gitlow's First Amendment rights had been violated. He would have liked to have criticized the Supreme Court in dictum, but he knew that his colleagues would not concur, and Hand preferred to keep the peace when little was to be gained from expressing disagreement.

Hand constantly questioned himself, a tendency that he thought both neurotic and necessary. "What are the values? Do you know? Believe me, I do not," he suddenly would say to his law clerk during the discussion of a case. Clerking for Hand was not only mentally but physically challenging; thinking aloud, the judge would outline the general pattern of his decision and ask questions while both he and the clerk strode in opposite directions back and forth across his office. Attentive to detail, he kept a compass, magnifying glass and complete set of maps of the waters adjacent to New York City to aid in admiralty cases, and when lawyers before his court talked in broad generalizations like "those eternal principles of justice," he would shout "Rubbish!"

Though he was well known in the legal profession, Hand's fame did not spread to the laity until "I Am an American Day," May 21, 1944, when he swore in one hundred fifty thousand new citizens before a million and a half people, the largest crowd ever gathered in Central Park. His speech that day, "The Spirit of Liberty," created an avalanche of attention. It reiterated his lifelong inclination to skepticism: "The spirit of liberty is the spirit which is not too sure that it is right. The spirit of liberty is the spirit which seeks to understand the minds of other men and women. The spirit of liberty is the spirit which weighs their interests alongside its own without bias." Or as he said in less stirring rhetoric to a group of lawyers:

> We were wrong in supposing that native intelligence or stupidity have much to do with the workings of democracy or the gift of liberty. It is a question of the habit, so hard to acquire, of detachment in forming beliefs, in the end [a question] of a character of a people, not of its brains. A group of pretty dull men can manage fairly well, if they be disposed to suspend judgment where they do not know the facts, but nothing—I think you will agree—is more exasperating than a group of clever disputants each concealing behind his front of argument determined and uncompromising convictions which no evidence can touch.

He applied this uncertainty to himself, as well. Late in life, he told a friend, "If I were to do it over again, I think perhaps I would be a physicist—open new vistas, move in step with the world. You know, I used to hope that I might be able to garner a harvest of wisdom. That has turned out to be a mistake, for I cannot see much further into the tangle of life than I could fifty years ago. I'm less disappointed than I should have thought. Indeed, there is solace in a companionship where all are groping their way equally in the same fog."

Though Learned Hand had become one of the foremost judges in America long before, the case for which many law students best know him today did not come until 1947. *U.S. v. Carroll Towing* concerned civil tort liability in a dispute alleging damage after a boat-owner's failure to adequately secure his vessel at harbor. He set forth his famous calculus of whether an alleged tortfeasor should have taken a particular precaution thus:

> [T]he owner's duty, as in other similar situations, to provide against resulting injuries is a function of three variables: (1) The probability that she will break away; (2) the gravity of the resulting injury, if she does; (3) the burden of adequate precautions. Possibly it serves to bring this notion into relief to state it in algebraic . . . terms: if the probability be called P; the injury, L; and the burden, B; liability depends upon whether B is less than L multiplied by P: i.e., whether B is less than PL.

This type of mathematical thinking has been expanded by the law and economics school into many other areas. Hand himself used a similar formulation in deciding *Dennis v. United States,* in which he upheld criminal convictions of the leaders of the Communist Party of the United States: "In each case [courts] must ask whether the gravity of the 'evil,' discounted by its improbability, justifies such invasion of free speech as is necessary to avoid the danger." The Supreme Court's affirmation quoted Hand and said, "We adopt this statement of the rule."

Hand retired from regular active service on the Second Circuit in 1951. This appears to have freed him to speak out against McCarthyism.

Though never a Communist sympathizer—he ascribed the pro-Soviet attitudes among many on the left to "the relief of finding something which will take the place of the 'intolerable labor of thought' ... It all comes down, I believe, to whether we have the guts to face the Universe with a consciousness that it is a perpetual question-mark"—he saw the virulent anti-Communism of the early 1950s as a great danger to the Republic.

> [M]y friends, will you not agree that any society which begins to be doubtful of itself; in which one man looks at another and says: "He may be a traitor," in which that spirit has disappeared which says: "I will not accept that, I will not believe that—I will demand proof. I will not say of my brother that he may be a traitor," but I will say, "Produce what you have. I will judge it fairly, and if he is, he shall pay the penalties; but I will not take it on rumor. I will not take it on hearsay. I will remember that what has brought us up from savagery is a loyalty to truth, and truth cannot emerge unless it is subjected to the utmost scrutiny."

At the same time, he hesitated to accept invitations for the express purpose of denouncing McCarthy, concerned that such public statements might have an improper influence on the Cold War cases that came before him as he continued to participate as a judge.

The distinction between "regular active service" and Hand's "retirement" was not much visible in any decrease of work, but it did have some consequence for his law clerks. Ronald Dworkin, who clerked for Hand in 1957–58, recounts how he once asked a young woman whom he had just begun dating to come along with him while he dropped off a memorandum at Hand's house, thinking it would be a short detour on the way to dinner. But Hand invited them inside, made them drinks and talked to the young woman about everything from art history to the Supreme Court. When they left after almost two hours, she asked Dworkin, "If I see more of you, do I get to see more of him?" At the end of his clerkship with Hand, Dworkin asked for a month's paid vacation, a common practice at the time, in order to go on his honeymoon with the same woman. The judge told him that he did not approve of paid vacations for clerks because of the cost imposed on the public, and thought they were particularly inappropriate for the clerk of a judge who technically had retired. A few days after the end of the clerkship, Dworkin and the woman were married. For their wedding present, Hand wrote the couple a personal check for a month's salary.

The Second Circuit itself became a source of concern to Hand toward the end of his career. Two of the judges with whom he had long served, Thomas Swan and his cousin Augustus Hand, both retired in 1953. Their replacements were highly satisfactory, especially the estimable John Marshall Harlan, who went on to have a much admired career as a Justice of the United States Supreme Court. Other proposed successors, however, were of more questionable ability. Hand worried that the kind of political patronage that he had fought unsuccessfully in the progressive years would put judges on his court who would lower its reputation. Nor did the Supreme Court itself escape his criticism. In his Holmes Lectures at Harvard Law School, given in 1958 when he was 86, Hand questioned the Warren Court's frequent holdings invalidating legislative accommodations. In particular, his challenge to the Court's reasoning in *Brown v. Board of Education* produced a contentious exchange of letters between Hand and his longtime correspondent Justice Frankfurter.

By this time, Judge Hand's back pain and (needless) concerns about failing mental powers began to concern him. Taking Holmes as his model, he felt compelled to go on as long as he could, and despite feeling "more and more crippled and less and less useful . . . strange to say, I still prefer not to cash it [in] while I don't have to." Even as his back condition degenerated to the point of requiring a wheelchair, he continued to work and produce opinions that Frankfurter declared to be up to the Hand standard. In July 1961, he suffered two heart attacks. He died on August 18, 1961.

GERALD GUNTHER, LEARNED HAND: THE MAN AND THE JUDGE

(1994).

Learned Hand's most significant work during his early New York City years was the writing of a fifteen-page essay entitled "Due Process of Law and the Eight–Hour Day." Published in the May 1908 issue of the *Harvard Law Review*, the article was a response to a landmark decision by the Supreme Court in 1905, *Lochner v. New York*, a ruling that initiated three decades during which the Court intensively scrutinized and frequently struck down state and federal economic legislation. The name of the case still provides the colloquial label for those decades: the power wielded by the justices during "the *Lochner* era," when the Court engaged in "Lochnerizing" and frequently invalidated popularly supported laws, ultimately provoked public wrath. Hand's strong criticism of the ruling and the kind of judicial behavior it represented was one of the first published attacks on the decision, and one of the most trenchant. His analysis devastated the economic and jurisprudential underpinnings of the ruling and the reign of judicial supremacy—in his view, the abuse of judicial power—that *Lochner* initiated.

Hand's attack on *Lochner*, published in the nation's most widely read professional journal not long after his first, unsuccessful try for a judge-ship, made him more visible, in New York and beyond. But ambition was not his prime motive. Rather, he was eager to elaborate a position on the proper role of the Supreme Court that he had first absorbed in James Bradley Thayer's classes at Harvard Law School, one that he believed in very deeply for the rest of his life. Hand's essay was not only a cutting critique of the legal justifications for the Court's behavior but also a sharp economic and political commentary, unusually blunt for the stately pages of the *Harvard Law Review*.

Lochner v. New York was a 5–4 decision holding unconstitutional a New York law that prohibited the employment of bakery workers for more than ten hours a day or sixty hours a week. The constitutional obstacle to the law, according to the *Lochner* majority, was the due-process provision of the Fourteenth Amendment, which bars any state from depriving "any person of life, liberty, or property without due process of law." The fate of the New York law struck down in *Lochner* was far less important than the approach that the Court's ruling signified: *Lochner* indicated that the justices would review very carefully, and would not hesitate to invalidate, many economic regulations, including the new worker-protective provisions that legislatures were beginning to adopt (decades after they had become commonplace in Europe). Hand's attack on *Lochner* presciently identified the harms that would flow from this judicial attitude, both in the obstruction of the popular will and in the abuse of judicial power.

Lochner was the first Supreme Court decision invalidating a law aiding workers on the ground that it violated due process, but the battle over the proper judicial role in applying due-process standards had raged since the ratification of the Fourteenth Amendment in 1868. "Due process" in its traditional meaning imposed very little restraint on legislatures; historically, it required only that laws be applied through fair procedures. In 1873, soon after the Fourteenth Amendment was adopted, a narrowly divided Court adhered to that narrow interpretation: it set its face strongly against using the due-process clause to establish the Court as "a perpetual censor upon all legislation ... with authority to nullify such as it did not approve." But by the end of the century, this judicial self-restraint began to break down. Instead, the Court began to hint that in due-process cases it would be prepared to consider arguments not only on the fairness of the procedures invoked but also on the substantive merits of the law itself, on the question of whether it was "reasonable" or whether it interfered excessively with basic rights.

When Hand was a law student in the mid–1890s, the Court had not yet struck down a single law on such "substantive due-process" grounds. But Professor Thayer spent much of Hand's constitutional-law course warning about the threatening cloud on the horizon—the risk that the justices would abuse their power and read their political and economic biases into the Constitution. In 1897, some of Thayer's forebodings came true. The Court, in its first major effort to delineate the "liberty" protected by the due-process clause, interpreted it very broadly. Most important, the justices held that "liberty" included a wide range of economic rights, including the right of the individual "to pursue any livelihood or avocation, and for that purpose to enter into all contracts which may be proper, necessary and essential to his carrying out [his] purposes." This identification of the "liberty of contract" as a fundamental right protected by due process planted the seed for the Court's anti-government-regulation, pro-laissez-faire approach of the *Lochner* era. But not until 1905, in *Lochner* itself, did the Court use its newfound power to strike down an economic-reform law.

The *Lochner* majority sounded modest enough, purporting to inquire only into the rationality of New York's law protecting bakery workers. But in fact the *Lochner* decision went much further, demanding a far stronger justification than mere "reasonableness" before it would permit government to interfere with the free economic market. The majority's new "censorship" of regulatory laws rested on its ill-concealed hostility toward the trend to regulate employer-employee relations for the latter's protection. As the *Lochner* majority opinion put it, the Court would not stand idly by while the individual rights of autonomous employees and employers to contract with one another on whatever terms they pleased were placed "at the mercy of legislative majorities." If laws such as New York's were upheld, it insisted, then "[n]ot only the hours of employés, but the hours of employers, could be regulated and doctors, lawyers, scientists, all professional men, as well as athletes and artisans, could be forbidden to fatigue their brains and bodies by prolonged hours of exercise.... [T]here would seem to be no length to which legislation of this nature might not go." And, the majority opinion added, "We do not believe in the soundness of the views which uphold this law." To the *Lochner* Court, simply, laws restricting the hours "in which grown and intelligent men may labor" were "mere meddlesome interferences with the rights of the individual."

Many of Hand's objections were initially voiced in the two dissenting opinions in *Lochner*, by Justice Oliver Wendell Holmes, Jr., and the first Justice John Marshall Harlan, but Hand articulated them more fully and broadly. One argument in defense of New York's law was that it would promote the health of bakery employees: this was the focus of Justice Harlan's dissent, which argued that reasonable people had long advocated restrictions on working hours and that legislatures around the world had in fact enacted such laws; he insisted that the existence of such a body of opinion and legislation precluded the Court from branding the law as "irrational." A different argument addressed the economic welfare of the bakery workers, claiming that the law was justifiable as an effort to redress the inequalities in bargaining power between employers and employees. This argument, the core of Justice Holmes's famous dissent, challenged the claim that any attempt by the state to redress economic inequalities was illegitimate. Holmes argued that the *Lochner* majority was engaged in a raw exercise of judicial power. "This case is decided upon an economic theory which a large part of the country does not entertain," he contended. Whether the Court agreed or not with the increasingly popular views supporting economic regulation had "nothing to do with the right of the majority to embody their opinions in law." In an especially well known passage, Holmes added:

> The Fourteenth Amendment does not enact Mr. Herbert Spencer's Social Statics.... [A] constitution is not intended to embody a particular economic theory, whether of paternalism and the organic relation of a citizen to the State or of *laissez faire*. It is made for

> people of fundamentally differing views, and the accident of our finding certain opinions natural and familiar or novel and even shocking ought not to conclude our judgment upon the question whether statutes embodying them conflict with the Constitution.... I think that the word liberty in the Fourteenth Amendment is perverted when it is held to prevent the natural outcome of a dominant opinion, unless it can be said that a rational and fair man necessarily would admit that the statute proposed would infringe fundamental principles as they have been understood by the traditions of our people and our law. It does not need research to show that no such sweeping condemnation can be passed upon the statute before us.

By 1908, when Hand wrote his article, the Court had reinforced its *Lochner* ruling with two similar decisions whose implications he also condemned. He emphatically agreed with Holmes's contention that the majority had "perverted" due process in *Lochner* and its progeny; indeed, he went beyond Holmes in narrowing the function of courts in cases claiming due-process violations. And his forceful conclusion made clear his disagreement with the *Lochner* majority:

> The question for the courts is not whether the problems have been wisely answered, but whether they can be answered at all, or whether they are taboo. So far as concerns laws limiting the hours of work, the present position seems quite untenable.

The decisive factor, he insisted, was that reasonable persons differed about the economic merits of such laws, and this threw "the whole matter open for exclusive consideration, and for exclusive determination, by the legislature, unless the Court is to step out of the role of interpreter of the Constitution and to decide the question itself as another legislature." Not only was free-market economic theory too amorphous and controversial to be an adequate guide; more important, the very attempt to evaluate the wisdom of protective laws was simply beyond the competence of the judges:

> In short, the whole matter is yet to such an extent experimental that no one can with justice apply to the concrete problems the yardstick of abstract economic theory. We do not know, and we cannot for a long time learn, what are the total results of such "meddlesome interference with the rights of the individual." ... The only way in which the right, or the wrong, of the matter may be shown, is by experiment; and the legislature, with its paraphernalia of committee and commission, is the only public representative really fitted to experiment. That the legislature may be moved by faction, and without justice, is very true, but so may even the court. There is an inevitable bias upon such vital questions in all men, and the courts are certainly recruited from a class which has its proper bias, like the rest.

Hand's clear implication that the justices in the *Lochner* majority were reading their economic biases into the Constitution went further than most commentators were willing to go. But Hand had the youthful courage to speak out. A fervent plea for judicial restraint, a strong endorsement of legislative power to engage in experimentation, a sharp attack on exercises of judicial authority in the *Lochner* mode—these were Hand's central themes.

Hand set forth his supporting arguments succinctly and lucidly. In a passage revealing his deep convictions about the dangers of permitting judges to consider the wisdom or expediency of challenged laws, he stated:

> Whether it be wise or not that there should be a third camera with a final veto upon legislation with whose economic or political expediency it totally disagrees, is a political question of the highest importance. In particular it is questionable whether such a power can endure in a democratic state, while the court retains the irresponsibility of a life tenure, and while its decisions can be reversed only by the cumbersome process of a change of the federal Constitution.... [I]f the court is to retain the absolute right to pass ... on the expediency of statutes passed by the legislature, the difficulty is inherent and in the end it may demand some change, either in the court or in the Constitution.

The risk, in short, was that the *Lochner* philosophy allowed unelected, politically unaccountable judges to decide whether a particular legislative purpose was or was not legitimate. Courts, Hand argued, were not super-legislatures: they exceeded their legitimate powers unless they deferred to elected legislatures on debatable issues.

JOHN PATRICK DIGGINS, THE RISE AND FALL OF THE AMERICAN LEFT

(1973).

> When I was up at Columbia University, one of the most unforgettable and most glamorous experiences I recall in my student life was the first lecture I heard by Max Eastman before the Socialist Study Club. He came before us then as the fair-haired apostle of the new poetry, the knight errant of a new and rebellious generation, the man who was making his dreams come true—as poet, as thinker, as editor, as teacher, as psychologist, as philosopher, as a yea-sayer of the joy and adventure of living in the fullest and richest sense of the word. Even then Max was already a glamorous, exciting figure in the world of letters and in the world of adventure. Life was bursting in all its radiance all around him. For him existence was a fight, a song, a revolution, a poem, an affirmation.
>
> Lincoln Schuster to Victor Gollancz, 1936

> The fiddles are tuning as it were all over America.
>
> John Butler Yeats, 1912

THE GREENWICH VILLAGE REBELLION

Unlike other American Lefts, the first Left of the twentieth century was born in a mood of unparalleled optimism. "One's first strong impression," recalled Malcolm Cowley, "is one of the bustle and hopefulness that filled the early years from 1911–1916.... Everywhere new institutions were being founded—magazines, clubs, little theatres, art or free-love or single-tax colonies, experimental schools, picture galleries. Everywhere was a sense of comradeship and immense potentialities for change." The new intellectuals' open-air habitat was Manhattan's Greenwich Village, which Floyd Dell, the chronicler of Village life, called "a moral health resort"; their spiritual home was Twenty-three Fifth Avenue, Mabel Dodge's notorious apartment, where anyone and everyone who had a plan to remake the world was welcomed: "Socialists, Trade–Unionists, Anarchists, Suffragists, Poets, Relations, Lawyers, Murderers, 'Old Friends,' Psychoanalysts, I.W.W.'s, Single Taxers, Birth–Controlists, Newspapermen, Artists, Modern–Artists, Clubwomen, Women's-Place-is-in-the-Home Women, Clergymen, and just plain men all met there" to experience "freedom" and exchange "opinions."

Dell caught the atmosphere of 1912 when, responding to the poet Edna St. Vincent Millay, he labeled it the "Lyric Year." The period seemed an intellectual saturnalia in which everything was possible and nothing prohibited, a joyous springtime in which, Mabel Dodge recalled, "barriers went down and people reached each other who had never been in touch before." The mood of America's "New Renaissance" was supremely lyrical, an outpouring of emotions and creative energy that had long been repressed. Responding to the thrilling labor strikes that spread from Lawrence, Massachusetts, to Ludlow, Colorado, the literary Left saw itself as the "music-makers" and "movers and shakers" of a revolutionary culture that aimed to break down the dualism between contemplative life and active life. This poetic passion for releasing the emotions and at the same time unifying thought, feeling, and action gave the first Left its distinctive lyrical style and tone. "Our eyes trained for every seeing," wrote Eastman in 1913, "our ears catching the first murmur of a new experience, we ran after the world in our eagerness, not to learn about it, but to taste the flavor of its being." No wonder Eastman could define himself as "the American lyrical Socialist—a child of Walt Whitman reared by Karl Marx."

The Lyrical radicals went further than any previous generation in attempting to fuse politics and art. Whereas Emerson and Thoreau had looked upon collective action with disdain, the young intellectuals embraced it with delight. Whereas the transcendentalists had believed politics the realm of opinion and poetry the realm of truth, the new cultural rebellion denied all dichotomies.

The Lyrical Left rejected Yeats's contention that poetry and politics, imagination and truth, private vision and public life must inevitably be in eternal opposition. Rather, the appeal of the prewar Left was its all-encompassing "integration of conflicting values ... : politics, poetry, and science; justice, beauty, and knowledge." The lyrical impulse to synthesize influenced even the sober-minded Walter Lippmann; in *A Preface to Politics* (1913), he sought to humanize government, to elevate it from "routine" procedures and stale formulas so that "the ideals of human feelings" would "place politics among the genuine, creative activities of men." Making man the measure of politics, Lippmann realized, "amounts to saying that the goal of action is in its final analysis aesthetic and not moral—a quality of feeling instead of a conformity to rule."

The young intellectuals cheerfully presided over the death of the "genteel tradition" as they attacked its Victorian standards, its polite manners and haut-bourgeois tastes, its Puritan heritage and decorous Brahmin literature, and, above all, its condescending certainty that it had found ultimate truth and absolute value. Forsaking the traditional quest for permanent truth and value, the young intellectuals embarked upon a life that embraced change and flux, a new life that had to be experienced before it could be analyzed. Their odyssey often brought them to Bergson, James, Nietzsche, Freud, and D. H. Lawrence, heralds of the antirationalist power of intuition, desire, will, dream, and instinct. Proclaiming a new ethic of gaiety and sensuality, the Lyrical rebels proudly declared themselves to be reckless and irresponsible. "A feeling of power that translates itself into duty is no fun," advised Mabel Dodge, who believed that "consciousness is more important than heroism or than any given ethical or political point of view, and I believe it more desirable to be ignoble and know it than to be noble and not know it." The "superb modern healthiness" of Dostoevsky, announced Randolph Bourne, is his ability to draw no "dividing line between the normal and the abnormal, or even between the sane and insane." Despite the cult of irresponsibility, many intellectuals who had been brought up in a religious environment carried with them the heritage against which they rebelled. Their passion for social justice, their quest for love and friendship, and their thirst for aesthetic experience reflected the internalized values of their Protestant backgrounds. If they rejected the capitalist ethos of striving to make good, many retained the religious ethic of striving to *be* good. In essence, theirs was a Christian culture without Christianity. Even so pagan a libertine as Mabel Dodge could, between taking John Reed as a lover and peyote as an offering, admit in a moment of doubt. "Finally I believed the lack to be in myself when I found myself perpetually unassuaged—and, I thought, only religion will fill me, someday I will find God." But God was dead, and no one knew this better than the generation of 1913.

Although a certain sense of orthodox values and a vague spiritual hunger lingered on, with the collapse of religious beliefs the young intellectuals tried to find meaning and fulfillment in culture, sex, or politics—in many cases all three. Some turned to radical politics for a surrogate religion. For Max Eastman, Marxism would put an end to spiritual anguish: "I need no longer extinguish my dream with my knowledge. I need never again cry out: 'I wish I believed in the Son of

God and his second coming.' " Until 1917, when the Bolshevik Revolution challenged evolutionary democratic socialism, the Lyrical Left's radicalism drew on British Fabian and Guild socialism as well as on Marxism. The Left's socialism was also an outgrowth of a self-conscious youth culture that, at Harvard and Columbia especially, gave the blasé high school graduate the option of radical activism or *Kulturpessimismus.* Students debated socialism in classrooms, fraternities, and at the meetings of the Intercollegiate Socialist Society, where wealthy young scions from the Ivy League listened to Jack London, the golden-boy dropout who was becoming America's first millionaire novelist, lecture on the beauties of the social revolution.

Socialism appealed to intellectuals for diverse reasons. Eastman saw socialism both as a science and as an aesthetic liberation that would bring forth a life of creative leisure. The whimsical playboy John Reed hoped that struggling for socialism would overcome the *mauvaise foi* that plagued him and other middle-class intellectuals: "My happiness is built on the misery of others ... that fact poisons me, disturbs my serenity, and makes me write propaganda when I would rather play." Lippmann, precocious social philosopher and leading figure in the Harvard Socialist Club, considered socialism the only alternative to the corruption of Tammany Hall and the power of big business. Yet it is significant that Lippmann, one of the first American intellectuals to see the relevance to politics of the new irrationalist psychology, was also one of the first of the Lyrical Left to have reservations about socialism. Convinced that any political movement must be built upon a realistic theory of human nature, Lippmann found socialism wanting in two respects: its idolization of the masses ignored the widespread visceral need for heroic leaders, and its faith in the inevitable polarization of classes scarcely took into account the complexity of America's multiclass structure. At the same time, Lippmann rejected the argument of Walling's *Progressivism and After*, that the transition to socialism would be gradual, proceeding from the state capitalism of the industrialists to the progressive reforms of the middle class. Dismissing Walling's reasoning as an expression of the "American Dream," Lippmann believed that socialism could be achieved, if at all, only by organized pressure from the lower classes. That conviction attracted him to the IWW. Although the Wobblies scorned political activity, ignored the probability that the state would not disappear after capitalism, and seemed not to realize that workers' syndicates could exploit consumers as much as industrialists could, Lippmann still believed the IWW possessed tremendous potential because, unlike all other radical movements, "it has practiced actual solidarity." Lippmann refrained from glorifying the IWW, which he regarded as capable of only "insurrection," but he could agree with Eastman that it was "the only genuinely *proletarian* or revolutionary organization that ever existed in America."

The first twentieth-century American Left advertised itself in two different publications, the *New Review* and the *Masses.* The former reflected its sober mind and the latter its soaring spirit. In the *New*

Review the Left debated the basic issues facing socialism, carried symposia on the feminist movement, and explored the relatively new field of Negro history. But this sophisticated theoretical journal was overshadowed by the *Masses*, perhaps the heartiest journal in the history of American radicalism. Free of doctrinal strain, the *Masses* gave radicalism a well-needed lift of laughter. Satirical but not cynical, audacious but not self-righteous, it was animated by eight passions: "fun, truth, beauty, realism, freedom, peace, feminism, revolution." Its masthead promised the *Masses* would please no one and delight everyone:

> A REVOLUTIONARY AND NOT A REFORM MAGAZINE: A MAGAZINE WITH A SENSE OF HUMOR AND NO RESPECT FOR THE RESPECTABLE: FRANK, ARROGANT, IMPERTINENT, SEARCHING FOR THE TRUE CAUSES: A MAGAZINE DIRECTED AGAINST RIGIDITY AND DOGMA WHEREVER IT IS FOUND: PRINTING WHAT IS TOO NAKED OR TRUE FOR A MONEY–MAKING PRESS: A MAGAZINE WHOSE FINAL POLICY IS TO DO AS IT PLEASES AND CONCILIATE NOBODY, NOT EVEN ITS READERS.

Edited by Eastman with the help of Dell and Reed, the *Masses* featured young poets and novelists, reputable journalists, and talented artists and cartoonists who depicted the foibles of the rich and the frustrations of the poor. The breezy combination of bohemianism and radicalism was too much for the stolid labor Left and the old-time socialists like W.J. Ghent, who complained of the *Masses*, "It is peculiarly the product of the restless metropolitan coteries who devote themselves to the cult of Something Else; who are ever seeking the bubble Novelty even at the door of Bedlam." One wit wondered how the *Masses* ever expected to reach the masses:

> They draw nude women for the *Masses*
> Thick, fat, ungainly lasses—
> How does that help the working classes?

Socialist attacks failed to dampen the confident bravado of the Lyrical Left, which did its best to help the lower classes by raising funds for striking coal and textile workers, by publicizing the plight of immigrants and blacks, and by speaking truth to power. What would undermine its optimism was the subsequent challenge of historic events.

War and the State

The first challenge to the ideals of the Left came with the outbreak of the First World War in August 1914. From the establishment of the First International in 1864 to Trotsky's attempt to start a Fourth International in 1939, the ideal of an international working-class community loomed as the great hope of the Left. In the years before the war, when the ideal seemed close to realization, American radicals assumed that European workers had achieved the political strength and maturity to oppose war and declare their solidarity with the Second International. When war came, however, most socialist parliamentarians approved military budgets in their respective governments, while workers responded to the call of nationalism. Radicals had earlier been able to mount antiwar demonstrations, but once war was declared there were no mass protests, no general strikes, no worldwide labor boycotts. The proletariat marched off to battle with the rest of the human race.

In December 1914 the American SP issued a manifesto condemning the war, announcing its neutrality, and declaring it the "supreme duty" of socialists to rededicate themselves to the "imperishable principles of international socialism." The manifesto created bitter inner-party debate. To moderates like Hillquit and Spargo the crisis of European socialism made it clear that workers ultimately placed their country before their class and that, thus, the concept of proletarian internationalism was a "frail wand." The more militant Marxists, like Louis Fraina and Louis Boudin, however, now began to trace the origins of the war to imperialism, an exercise that enabled them to sustain some faith in the misguided masses and to suggest that a new International, purged of all prowar elements, could be organized. The majority of socialist intellectuals and labor leaders changed their positions for various reasons. Some shifted to intervention because of a simple concern for national security; others feared that a Prussianized, imperialistic Germany presented a threat to democracy and the Left; still others believed that the war might hasten the coming of socialism as the government nationalized industry. For three years the Left continued to debate the nature and consequences of the war. By April 1917, when President Wilson went before Congress to ask for a declaration of war, most leading socialist writers had already advocated U.S. intervention. Despite the defection of intellectual luminaries like Walling, London, Simons, and Upton Sinclair, the SP convention issued another antiwar resolution the day after Wilson's address to Congress. The resolution, approved by three-fourths of the delegates, had the support of political leaders like Debs, Hillquit, and Berger. The SP's courageous action proved to be a short-run triumph and a long-run disaster. Shortly afterwards the SP increased its membership by more than 12,000, and in various municipal elections in June socialist candidates gained new support from antiwar voters. But ultimately the SP suffered a psychic wound as members began to accuse one another of class betrayal or national treason. The prowar socialist Charles E. Russell thought his former comrades "should be driven out of the country," and the millionaire socialist J. G. Phelps Stokes suggested they be "shot at once without an hour's delay."

Though the government did not go that far, it went far enough. In June 1917 Congress passed the Espionage Act (supplemented in 1918 by the Sedition Act), which forbade all obstruction of the war effort. Immediately the U.S. Post Office denied mailing privileges to socialist publications, and while editors tried vainly to fight their case in court, the government moved against the SP itself. Before the war was over, almost every major SP official had been indicted for antiwar activity. Enraged mobs had also cracked down on radical dissent everywhere. Throughout the country IWW headquarters were raided. In Oklahoma, Wobblies were rounded up and tarred and feathered; in Arizona they were packed into cattle cars and abandoned in the desert; and in Montana, Frank Little, a crippled IWW leader, was kidnapped and hanged from a railway trestle. The repression bore down heavily on antiwar liberals as well. At Columbia University three professors were fired for having criticized U.S. intervention, whereupon the eminent historian Charles Beard resigned in protest. Watching this affair, the Columbia graduate Randolph Bourne visited one of the dismissed professors, his friend Harold C. Dana.

> "And now that you have been expelled, Harry, will you make the scandal?"
>
> "Certainly not," Dr. Dana said. "I've given my word as a gentleman."
>
> "That's the trouble," Bourne replied with a wide grin. "You look upon all this as a gentlemen's quarrel. You lack Homeric anger."

Gentlemen scholars were not the only ones who disappointed the Lyrical Left. Everywhere the intellectual community seemed to be capitulating. Isadora Duncan, who once symbolized the liberating joys of the body, was now performing patriotic dances in the Metropolitan Opera House. Former *Masses* contributors had gone to work for the Committee on Public Information, Wilson's official propaganda agency; honored intellectuals like Veblen, Dewey, and the former socialist Lippmann had also come out strongly in support of America's entry into the war.

The *Masses* staff continued to oppose the war while the government prosecuted its editors for sedition and conspiracy to obstruct enlistment. During the trial in fall 1917, Eastman spoke eloquently about socialism, civil liberties, and the errors of U.S. foreign policy as another indicted staff member, the artist Art Young, impressed the jury by dozing off at the defendants' table. When his counsel awakened him, he opened his eyes, yawned, reached for his pad, and sketched a cartoon of himself napping, which he entitled "Art Young on Trial for His Life."

Eastman drew on the pulpit-oratory talents he had learned from his minister parents. In his summing up, an extemporaneous three-hour speech later distributed as a pamphlet, he told the jury, "I was brought up with the utmost love for the character and the beauty of the teachings of Jesus of Nazareth, and I count Him much nearer in His faith and His influence to the message of the Socialists than to the message of any other political body of men." Socialists are also good citizens, he said, and by no means unpatriotic; indeed, they believe in "liberty and democracy exactly in the same way" as Jefferson and the "rest of the true revolutionary fathers." Although his thoughts were on events in revolutionary Russia, Eastman knew socialism had no chance in America unless it could be rendered compatible with some cherished native conceits. His speech made a memorable impression on younger radicals in the courtroom and perhaps on a few solid citizens in the jury box. The jury could reach no verdict and the government dropped the case now that the *Masses* had ceased circulating.

MASSES PUB. CO. v. PATTEN

Southern District of New York, 1917.
244 F. 535.

* * *

The plaintiff applies for a preliminary injunction against the postmaster of New York to forbid his refusal to accept its magazine in the mails under the following circumstances: The plaintiff is a publishing company in the city of New York engaged in the production of a monthly revolutionary journal called "The Masses," containing both text and cartoons, each issue of which is ready for the mails during the first ten days of the preceding month. In July, 1917, the postmaster of New York, acting upon the direction of the Postmaster General, advised the plaintiff that the August number to which he had had access would be denied the mails under the Espionage Act of June 15, 1917. Though professing willingness to excerpt from the number any particular matter which was objectionable in the opinion of the Postmaster General, the plaintiff was unable to learn any specification of objection, and thereupon filed this bill, and now applies for a preliminary injunction upon a statement of the facts.

Upon return of the rule to show cause the defendant, while objecting generally that the whole purport of the number was in violation of the law, since it tended to produce a violation of the law, to encourage the enemies of the United States, and to hamper the government in the conduct of the war, specified four cartoons and four pieces of text as especially falling within sections 1 and 2 of title 12 of the act and by the reference of section 1 as within section 3 of title 1. These sections are quoted in the margin.[1]

The four cartoons are entitled respectively, "Liberty Bell," "Conscription," "Making the World Safe for Capitalism," "Congress and Big

1. TITLE I.

Espionage.

Sec. 3. Whoever, when the United States is at war, shall willfully make or convey false reports or false statements with intent to interfere with the operation or success of the military or naval forces of the United States or to promote the success of its enemies and whoever when the United States is at war, shall willfully cause or attempt to cause insubordination, disloyalty, mutiny, or refusal of duty, in the military or naval forces of the United States, or shall willfully obstruct the recruiting or enlistment service of the United States, to the injury of the service or of the United States, shall be punished by a fine of not more than $10,000 or imprisonment for not more than twenty years, or both.

TITLE XII.

Use of Mails.

Section 1. Every letter, writing, circular, postal card, picture, print, engraving, photograph, newspaper, pamphlet, book, or other publication, matter or thing, of any kind, in violation of any of the provisions of this act is hereby declared to be nonmailable matter and shall not be conveyed in the mails or delivered from any post office or by any letter carrier: Provided, that nothing in this act shall be so construed as to authorize any person other than an employe of the dead letter office, duly authorized there to, or other person upon a search warrant authorized by law, to open any letter not addressed to himself,

Sec. 2. Every letter, writing, circular, postal card, picture, print, engraving, photograph, newspaper, pamphlet, book, or other publication, matter or thing, of any kind, containing any matter advocating or urging treason, insurrection, or forcible resistance to any law of the United States, is hereby declared to be nonmailable.

Business." The first is a picture of the Liberty Bell broken in fragments. The obvious implication, taking the cartoon in its context with the number as a whole, is that the origin, purposes, and conduct of the war have already destroyed the liberties of the country. It is a fair inference that the draft law is an especial instance of the violation of the liberty and fundamental rights of any free people.

The second cartoon shows a cannon to the mouth of which is bound the naked figure of a youth, to the wheel that of a woman, marked "Democracy," and upon the carriage that of a man, marked "Labor." On the ground kneels a draped woman marked "Motherhood" in a posture of desperation, while her infant lies on the ground. The import of this cartoon is obviously that conscription is the destruction of youth, democracy, and labor, and the desolation of the family. No one can dispute that it was intended to rouse detestation for the draft law.

The third cartoon represents a Russian workman symbolizing the Workmen's and Soldiers' Council, seated at a table, studying a paper entitled, "Plan for a Genuine Democracy." At one side Senator Root furtively approaches the figure with a noose marked "Advice," apparently prepared to throw it over the head of the workman, while behind him stands Mr. Charles E. Russell, the Socialist member of the Russian Commission, in a posture of assent. On the other side a minatory figure of Japan appears through a door carrying a raised sword, marked "Threat," while behind him follows a conventional John Bull, stirring him up to action. The import again is unambiguous and undisputed. The Russian is being ensnared and bullied by the United States and its Allies into a continuance of the war for purposes prejudicial to true democracy.

The fourth and last cartoon presents a collection of pursy magnates standing about a table on which lies a map, entitled "War Plans." At the door enters an apologetic person, hat in hand, diffidently standing at the threshold, while one of the magnates warns him to keep off. The legend at the bottom runs as follows: "Congress: 'Excuse me, gentlemen, where do I come in?' " Big Business: "Run along, now. We got through with you when you declared war for us." It is not necessary to expatiate upon the import of this cartoon.

The four pieces of text are annexed to the end of this report as addenda, A, B, C, and D. After that part of B so set forth, the article continues, showing the hardships and maltreatment of a number of English conscientious objectors, partly from excerpts out of their letters, partly from reports of what they endured. These statements show much brutality in the treatment of these persons.

The challenged text, omitting the excerpts just mentioned, total about one page out of a total of 28. Throughout the rest are sprinkled other texts designed to arouse animosity to the draft and to the war, and criticisms of the President's consistency in favoring the declaration of war.

The defendant attaches to its papers as well copies of the June and July numbers of The Masses and a number of Mother Earth, a magazine edited by Emma Goldman and Alexander Berkman, recently convicted in this court for a conspiracy to resist the draft. The earlier copies of The Masses contain inflammatory articles upon the war and conscription in revolutionary vein, some of which go to the extent of counseling those subject to conscription to resist. This case does not concern them except in so far as the defendant's position is correct that in the interpretation of the August number the purpose of the writers may be inferred from what preceded, and that an audience addressed in the earlier numbers would put upon the later number a significance beyond what the contents would naturally bear if it stood alone. It is not necessary for a determination of this case to set forth in detail the contents of these numbers. The copy of Mother Earth also need not be referred to.

Gilbert E. Roe, of New York City, for plaintiff.

Earl B. Barnes, of New York City, for defendant.

LEARNED HAND, District Judge (after stating the facts as above).

[1] It is well settled that this court has jurisdiction to review the act of the postmaster. If it appears that his proposed official course is outside of the authority conferred upon him by law, the court cannot escape the duty of so deciding, just as in the case of any other administrative officer. However, again, as in the case of other such officers, the postmaster's decision is final if there be any dispute of fact upon which his decision may rest, and even where it must turn upon a point of law, it has a strong presumption of validity. In this case there is no dispute of fact which the plaintiff can successfully challenge except the meaning of the words and pictures in the magazine. As to these the query must be: What is the extreme latitude of the interpretation which must be placed upon them, and whether that extremity certainly falls outside any of the provisions of the act of June 15, 1917. Unless this be true, the decision of the postmaster must stand. It will be necessary, first, to interpret the law, and, next, the words and pictures.

It must be remembered at the outset, and the distinction is of critical consequence throughout, that no question arises touching the war powers of Congress. It may be that Congress may forbid the mails to any matter which tends to discourage the successful prosecution of the war. It may be that the fundamental personal rights of the individual must stand in abeyance, even including the right of the freedom of the press, though that is not here in question. It may be that the peril of war, which goes to the very existence of the state, justifies any measure of compulsion, any measure of suppression, which Congress deems necessary to its safety, the liberties of each being in subjection to the liberties of all. *The Legal Tender Cases*, 12 Wall, 457. It may be that under the war power Congress may mobilize every resource of men and materials, without impediment or limitation, since the power includes all means which are the practice of nations in war. It would indeed not be necessary, perhaps in ordinary cases it would not be appropriate, even to allude to such putative incidents of the war power, but it is of great consequence at the present time with accuracy to define the exact scope of the question at bar, that no implication may arise as to any limitation upon the absolute and uncontrolled nature of that power. Here is presented solely the question of how far Congress after much discussion has up to the present time seen fit to exercise a power which may extend to measures not yet even considered, but necessary to the existence of the state as such. Every one agrees that the exercise of such power, however wide it may be, rests in Congress alone, at least subject to such martial law as may rest with the President within the sphere of military operations, however broadly that may be defined. The defendant's authority is based upon the act of Congress, and the intention of that act is the single measure of that authority. If Congress has omitted repressive measures necessary to the safety of the nation and success of its great enterprise, the responsibility rests upon Congress and with it the power to remedy that omission.

Coming to the act itself, it is conceded that the defendant's only direct authority arises from title 12 of the act, Secs. 1 and 2. His position is that under section 1 any writing which by its utterance would infringe any of the provisions of other titles in the act becomes nonmailable. I may accept that assumption for the sake of argument and turn directly to section 3 of title 1, which the plaintiff is said to violate. That section contains three provisions. The first is, in substance, that no one shall make any false statements with intent to interfere with the operation or success of the military or naval forces of the United States or to promote the success of its enemies. The defendant says that the cartoons and text of the magazine, constituting, as they certainly do, a virulent attack upon the war and those laws which have been enacted to assist its prosecution, may interfere with the success of the military forces of the United States. That such utterances may have the effect so ascribed to them is unhappily true; publications of this kind enervate public feeling at home which is their chief purpose, and encourage the success of the enemies of the United States abroad, to which they are generally indifferent. Dissension within a country is a high source of comfort and assistance to its enemies; the least intimation of it they seize upon with jubilation. There cannot be the slightest question of the mischievous effects of such agitation upon the success of the national project, or of the correctness of the defendant's position.

All this, however, is beside the question whether such an attack is a willfully false statement. That phrase properly includes only a statement of fact which the utterer knows to be false, and it cannot be maintained that any of these statements are of fact, or that the plaintiff believes them to be false. They are all within the range of opinion and of criticism; they are all certainly believed to be true by the utterer. As such they fall within the scope of that right to criticize either by temperate reasoning, or by immoderate and indecent invective, which is normally the privilege of the individual in countries dependent upon the free expression of opinion as the ultimate source of authority. The argument may be trivial in substance, and violent and perverse in manner, but so long as it is confined to abuse of existing policies or laws, it is impossible to class it as a false statement of facts of the kind here in question. To modify this provision, so clearly intended to prevent the spreading of false rumors which may embarrass the military, into the prohibition of any kind of propaganda, honest or vicious, is to disregard the meaning of the language, established by legal construction and common use, and to raise it into a means of suppressing intemperate and inflammatory public discussion, which was surely not its purpose.

The next phrase relied upon is that which forbids any one from willfully causing insubordination, disloyalty, mutiny, or refusal of duty in the military or naval forces of the United States. The defendant's position is that to arouse discontent and disaffection among the people with the prosecution of the war and with the draft tends to promote a mutinous and insubordinate temper among the troops. This, too, is true; men who become satisfied that they are engaged in an enterprise dictated by the unconscionable selfishness of the rich, and effectuated by a tyrannous disregard for the will of those who must suffer and die, will be more prone to insubordination than those who have faith in the cause and acquiesce in the means. Yet to interpret the word "cause" so broadly would, as before, involve necessarily as a consequence the suppression of all hostile criticism, and of all opinion except what encouraged and supported the existing policies, or which fell within the range of temperate argument. It would contradict the normal assumption of democratic government that the suppression of hostile criticism does not turn upon the justice of its substance or the decency and propriety of its temper. Assuming that the power to repress such opinion may rest in Congress in the throes of a struggle for the very existence of the state, its exercise is so contrary to the use and wont of our people that only the clearest expression of such a power justifies the conclusion that it was intended.

The defendant's position, therefore, in so far as it involves the suppression of the free utterance of abuse and criticism of the existing law, or of the policies of the war, is not, in my judgment, supported by the language of the statute. Yet there has always been a recognized limit to such expressions, incident indeed to the existence of any compulsive power of the state itself. One may not counsel or advise others to violate the law as it stands. Words are not only the keys of persuasion, but the triggers of action, and those which have no purport but to counsel the violation of law cannot by any latitude of interpretation be a part of that public opinion which is the final source of government in a democratic state. The defendant asserts not only that the magazine indirectly through its propaganda leads to a disintegration of loyalty and a disobedience of law, but that in addition it counsels and advises resistance to existing law, especially to the draft. The consideration of this aspect of the case more properly arises under the third phrase of section 3, which forbids any willful obstruction of the recruiting or enlistment service of the United States, but, as the defendant urges that the magazine falls within each phrase, it is as well to take it up now. To counsel or advise a man to an act is to urge upon him either that it is his interest or his duty to do it. While, of course, this may be accomplished as well by indirection as expressly, since words carry the meaning that they impart, the definition is exhaustive, I think, and I shall use it. Political agitation, by the passions it arouses or the convictions it engenders, may in fact stimulate men to the violation of law. Detestation of existing policies is easily transformed into forcible resistance of the authority which puts them in execution, and it would be folly to disregard the causal relation between the two. Yet to assimilate agitation, legitimate as such, with direct incitement to violent resistance, is to disregard the tolerance of all methods of political agitation which in normal times is a safeguard of free government. The distinction is not a scholastic subterfuge, but a hard-bought acquisition in the fight for freedom, and the purpose to disregard it must be evident when the power exists. If one stops short of urging upon others that it is their duty or their interest to resist the law, it seems to me one should not be held to have attempted to cause its violation. If that be not the test, I can see no escape from the conclusion that under this section every political agitation which can be shown to be apt to create a seditious temper is illegal. I am confident that by such language Congress had no such revolutionary purpose in view.

It seems to me, however, quite plain that none of the language and none of the cartoons in this paper can be thought directly to counsel or advise insubordination or mutiny, without a violation of their meaning quite beyond any tolerable understanding. I come, therefore, to the third phrase of the section, which forbids any one from willfully obstructing the recruiting or enlistment service of the United States. I am not prepared to assent to the plaintiff's position that this only refers to acts other than words, nor that the act thus defined must be shown to have been successful. One may obstruct without preventing, and the mere obstruction is an injury to the service; for it throws impediments in its way. Here again, however, since the question is of the expression of opinion, I construe the sentence, so far as it restrains public utterance, as I have construed the other two, and as therefore limited to the direct advocacy of resistance to the recruiting and enlistment service. If so, the inquiry is narrowed to the question whether any of the challenged matter may be said to advocate resistance to the draft, taking the meaning of the words with the utmost latitude which they can bear.

As to the cartoons it seems to me quite clear that they do not fall within such a test. Certainly the nearest is that entitled "Conscription," and the most that can be said of that is that it may breed such animosity to the draft as will promote resistance and strengthen the determination of those disposed to be recalcitrant. There is no intimation that, however hateful the draft may be, one is in duty bound to resist it, certainly none that such resistance is to one's interest. I cannot, therefore, even with the limitations which surround the power of the court, assent to the assertion that any of the cartoons violate the act.

The text offers more embarrassment. The poem to Emma Goldman and Alexander Berkman, at most, goes no further than to say that they are martyrs in the cause of love among nations. Such a sentiment holds them up to admiration, and hence their conduct to possible emulation.

The paragraph in which the editor offers to receive funds for their appeal also expresses admiration for them, but goes no further. The paragraphs upon conscientious objectors are of the same kind. They go no further than to express high admiration for those who have held and are holding out for their convictions even to the extent of resisting the law. It is plain enough that the paper has the fullest sympathy for these people, that it admires their courage, and that it presumptively approves their conduct. Indeed, in the earlier numbers and before the draft went into effect the editor urged resistance. Since I must interpret the language in the most hostile sense, it is fair to suppose, therefore, that these passages go as far as to say:

> "These men and women are heroes and worthy of a freeman's admiration. We approve their conduct; we will help to secure them their legal rights. They are working for the betterment of mankind through their obdurate consciences."

Moreover, these passages, it must be remembered, occur in a magazine which attacks with the utmost violence the draft and the war. That such comments have a tendency to arouse emulation in others is clear enough, but that they counsel others to follow these examples is not so plain. Literally at least they do not, and while, as I have said, the words are to be taken, not literally, but according to their full import, the literal meaning is the starting point for interpretation. One may admire and approve the course of a hero without feeling any duty to follow him. There is not the least implied intimation in these words that others are under a duty to follow. The most that can be said is that, if others do follow, they will get the same admiration and the same approval. Now, there is surely an appreciable distance between esteem and emulation; and unless there is here some advocacy of such emulation, I cannot see how the passages can be said to fall within the law. If they do, it would follow that, while one might express admiration and approval for the Quakers or any established sect which is excused from the draft, one could not legally express the same admiration and approval for others who entertain the same conviction, but do not happen to belong to the society of Friends. It cannot be that the law means to curtail such expressions merely, because the convictions of the class within the draft are stronger than their sense of obedience to the law. There is ample evidence in history that the Quaker is as recalcitrant to legal compulsion as any man; his obstinacy has been regarded in the act, but his disposition is as disobedient as that of any other conscientious objector. Surely, if the draft had not excepted Quakers, it would be too strong a doctrine to say that any who openly admire their fortitude or even approved their conduct was willfully obstructing the draft.

When the question is of a statute constituting a crime, it seems to me that there should be more definite evidence of the act. The question before me is quite the same as what would arise upon a motion to dismiss an indictment at the close of the proof: Could any reasonable man say, not that the indirect result of the language might be to arouse a seditious disposition, for that would not be enough, but that the language directly advocated resistance to the draft? I cannot think that upon such language any verdict would stand. Of course, the language of the statute cannot have one meaning in an indictment and another when the case comes up here, because by hypothesis, if this paper is nonmailable under section 3 of title 1, its editors have committed a crime in uttering it.

After the foregoing discussion it is hardly necessary to speak of section 2 of title 12. The plaintiff insists that refusal to comply with the provisions of the draft cannot be classed as forcible resistance; that such a refusal is, at most, only inaction, the neglect of an affirmative duty even to the extent of submitting to imprisonment. It may be plausibly contended that by forcible resistance Congress meant more than passive resistance, but even if this be not true, the result is the same, because, so construed, the section goes no further than the last phrase of section 3 of title 1 as I have construed it here. What was therefore said upon that section will serve here.

The defendant's action was based, as I understand it, not so much upon the narrow question whether these four passages actually advocated resistance, though that point was distinctly raised, as upon the doctrine that the general tenor and animus of the paper as a whole were subversive to authority and seditious in effect. I cannot accept this test under the law as it stands at present. The tradition of English-speaking freedom has depended in no small part upon the merely procedural requirement that the state point with exactness to just that conduct which violates the law. It is difficult and often impossible to meet the charge that one's general ethos is treasonable; such a latitude for construction implies a personal latitude in administration which contradicts the normal assumption that law shall be embodied in general propositions capable of some measure of definition. The whole crux of this case turns indeed upon this thesis. I make no question of the power of Congress to establish a personal censorship of the press under the war power; that question, as I have already said, does not arise. I am quite satisfied that it has not as yet chosen to create one, and with the greatest deference it does not seem to me that anything here challenged can be illegal upon any other assumption.

Finally, the question arises as to how far the earlier numbers of the paper should be considered. The theory is that the August number covertly refers to the explicit counsel of resistance in the numbers of June and July. A priori such a reference might legitimately incorporate the earlier expressions; I do not doubt that the memory of those expressions may in fact remain in the minds of readers and that they may be revived by the sympathy and accord with conscientious objectors expressed in the August number. Yet the plaintiff is still entitled to ask, whatever the results of its past utterance may be, that some words be pointed out which by some reference fairly inferable from the words themselves relate back to earlier and more explicit statements. I think there are no words in the four passages which admit of such an interpretation.

It follows that the plaintiff is entitled to the usual preliminary injunction.

A.

A Question.

Often I wish we had a continuing census bureau to which we might apply, and have a census taken with classifications of our own choosing. I would like to know to-day, how many men and women there are in America who admire the self-reliance and sacrifice of those who are resisting the conscription law on the ground that they believe it violates the sacred rights and liberties of man. How many of the American population are in accord with the American press when it speaks of the arrest of these men of genuine courage as a "round-up of slackers"? Are there none to whom this picture of the American republic adopting towards its citizens the attitude of a rider toward cattle is appalling? I recall the Essays of Emerson, the Poems of Walt Whitman, which sounded a call never heard before in the world's literature, for erect and insuppressible individuality, the courage of solitary faith and heroic assertion of self. It was America's contribution to the ideals of man. It painted the quality of her culture for those in the old world who loved her. It was a revolt of the aspiring mind against that instinctive running with custom and the support of numbers, which is an hereditary frailty of our nerves. It was a determination to worship and to love, in the living and laughing present, the same heroisms that we love when we look back so seriously over the past.

I wonder if the number is few to whom this high resolve was the distinction of our American idealism, and who feel inclined to bow their heads to those who are going to jail under the whip of the state, because they will not do what they do not believe in doing. Perhaps there are enough of us, if we make ourselves heard in voice and letter, to modify this ritual of contempt in the daily press, and induce the American government to undertake the imprisonment of heroic young men with a certain sorrowful dignity that will be new in the world.

B.

A Tribute.

Emma Goldman and Alexander Berkman
Are in prison,
Although the night is tremblingly beautiful
And the sound of water climbs down the rocks
And the breath of the night air moves through multitudes and multitudes of leaves
That love to waste themselves for the sake of the summer.
Emma Goldman and Alexander Berkman
Are in prison tonight,
But they have made themselves elemental forces,
Like the water that climbs down the rocks;
Like the wind in the leaves;

Like the gentle night that holds us;
They are working on our destinies;
They are forging the love of the nations;
Tonight they lie in prison.

C.

Conscientious Objectors.

We publish below a number of letters written last year from English prisons by conscientious objectors. It is as yet uncertain what treatment the United States government will mete out to its thousands of conscientious objectors, but we believe that our protestors against government tyranny will be as steadfast as their English comrades. It is not by any means as certain that they will be as polite to their guards and tormentors, but we hope they will remember that these are acting under official compulsion and not as free men.

Some discussion has arisen as to whether those whose objection to participating in war is not embodied in a religious formula have the right to call their objection a "conscientious" one. We believe that this old-fashioned term is, however, one that fits their case. There are some laws which the individual feels that he cannot obey, and which he will suffer any punishment, even that of death, rather than recognize as having authority over him. This fundamental stubbornness of the free soul, against which all the powers of the state are helpless, constitutes a conscientious objection, whatever its original sources may be in political or social opinion. It remains to be demonstrated that a political disapproval of this war can express itself in the same heroic firmness that has in England upheld the Christian objectors to war as murder. We recommend to all who intend to stick it out to the end, a thorough reading of the cases which follow, so that they may be prepared for what is at least rather likely to happen to them.

D.

Friends of American Freedom.

Alexander Berkman and Emma Goldman have been arrested, charged with advocating in their paper, Mother Earth, that those liable to the military draft, who do not believe in the war, should refuse to register. That they would be arrested, on some charge, and subjected to bitter prosecution, has been inevitable ever since they appeared as the spokesmen of a working class protest against the plans of American militarism. Whatever you may think of the practicability of such a protest, you must, with their friends, pay tribute of admiration for their courage and devotion.

Alexander Berkman is one of the few men whose character and intelligence ever stood firm through a quarter of a lifetime in prison. Emma Goldman has followed her extreme ideal of liberty for 30 years, up and down, in better places and worse than the federal penitentiary. They can both endure what befalls them. They have more resources in their souls, perhaps, as they have the support of a more absolute faith, than we have who admire them. But let us give them every chance for acquittal that the constitution of the times allow. Let us give them every chance to state their faith. The Masses will receive funds for this purpose.

Questions

1) What kind of an argument is Hand making?

2) How exactly does Hand's test differ from Mill's? Is there a difference between "direct advocacy of law violation" and "positive instigation to a mischievous act?"

3) Both Hand and Madison base their arguments for the protection of political criticism on the implications of the theory of sovereignty to which the nation is committed. Does Hand add anything to Madison's argument, or differ from Madison in premises, priorities, or derivations?

4) Exactly how much of an improvement is Hand's test, compared with a danger test, in terms of yielding predictable outcomes? For example, look at the difference of opinion regarding the meaning of the cartoon, "CONSCRIPTION." Is this just an atypical example?

5) How can Hand protect "intemperate invective" but not protect direct advocacy of lawbreaking?

6) Does Hand's rationale for protecting "hostile criticism" deriving from its role in legitimating government provide enough direction for designing a standard and deciding hard cases? Or is it the case that the concepts of "democracy," "consent of the governed," and "limited government" are so indeterminate that legal doctrines with resolving power cannot be derived therefrom?

7) Can we defend Hand's standard on the ground not that it expresses an important theoretical distinction, but rather that it offers the best place to draw a bright line? Is it permissible to be "arbitrary" in this manner so long as the standard provides maximum security—a safe harbor, so to speak—for a core of protected speech?

8) Should we read the *Masses* opinion as indicating that Hand would uphold broad powers of censorship under the War Power? Or should the unflattering way that he characterizes the rationale for censorship under the War Power be read to indicate that if pushed to decide the issue he would not give Congress extensive power to override the principle of freedom of speech? More generally, is it preferable to suspend the principle of freedom of speech in a time of declared war, or instead to

consider war just another one of the consequences that must be taken into account?

WILLIAM SHAKESPEARE, JULIUS CAESAR

Act III

Cassius. I blame you not for praising Caesar so;
But what compact mean you to have with us?
Will you be pricked in number of our friends,
Or shall we on, and not depend on you?

Antony. Therefore I took your hands, but was indeed
Swayed from the point by looking down on Caesar.
Friends am I with you all, and love you all,
Upon this hope, that you shall give me reasons
Why, and wherein, Caesar was dangerous.

Brutus. Or else were this a savage spectacle.
Our reasons are so full of good regard
That were you, Antony, the son of Caesar,
You should be satisfied.

Antony. That's all I seek;
And am moreover suitor that I may
Produce his body to the market place,
And in the pulpit, as becomes a friend,
Speak in the order of his funeral.

Brutus. You shall, Mark Antony.

Cassius. Brutus, a word with you.
[*Aside to Brutus*] You know not what you do; do not consent
That Antony speak in his funeral.
Know you how much the people may be moved
By that which he will utter?

Brutus. By your pardon:
I will myself into the pulpit first,
And show the reason of our Caesar's death.
What Antony shall speak, I will protest
He speaks by leave and by permission,
And that we are contented Caesar shall
Have all true rites and lawful ceremonies.
It shall advantage more than do us wrong.

Cassius. I know not what may fall; I like it not.

Brutus. Mark Antony, here, take you Caesar's body.
You shall not in your funeral speech blame us,
But speak all good you can devise of Caesar,
And say you do't by our permission;
Else shall you not have any hand at all
About his funeral. And you shall speak

In the same pulpit whereto I am going,
After my speech is ended.

Antony. Be it so;
I do desire no more.

Brutus. Prepare the body then, and follow us.
Exeunt. Manet Antony.

Antony. O pardon me, thou bleeding piece of earth,
That I am meek and gentle with these butchers!
Thou art the ruins of the noblest man
That ever lived in the tide of times.
Woe to the hand that shed this costly blood!
Over thy wounds now do I prophesy
(Which like dumb mouths do ope their ruby lips
To beg the voice and utterance of my tongue),
A curse shall light upon the limbs of men;
Domestic fury and fierce civil strife
Shall cumber all the parts of Italy;
Blood and destruction shall be so in use,
And dreadful objects so familiar,
That mothers shall but smile when they behold
Their infants quartered with the hands of war,
All pity choked with custom of fell deeds;
And Caesar's spirit, ranging for revenge,
With Atè by his side come hot from hell,
Shall in these confines with a monarch's voice
Cry "Havoc," and let slip the dogs of war,
That this foul deed shall smell above the earth
With carrion men, groaning for burial.

[Scene II. *The Forum.*]

Enter Brutus and goes into the pulpit, and Cassius, with the Plebeians.

Plebeians. We will be satisfied! Let us be satisfied!

Brutus. Then follow me, and give me audience, friends.
Cassius, go you into the other street
And part the numbers.
Those that will hear me speak, let "em stay here;
Those that will follow Cassius, go with him;
And public reasons shall be renderèd
Of Caesar's death."

First Plebeian I will hear Brutus speak.

Second Plebeian. I will hear Cassius, and compare their reasons,
When severally we hear them renderèd.

[*Exit Cassius, with some of the Plebeians.*]

Third Plebeian. The noble Brutus is ascended. Silence!

Brutus. Be patient till the last.

Romans, countrymen, and lovers, hear me for my cause, and be silent, that you may hear. Believe me for mine honor, and have respect to mine honor, that you may believe. Censure me in your wisdom, and awake your senses, that you may the better judge. If there be any in this assembly, any dear friend of Caesar's, to him I say that Brutus' love to Caesar was no less than his. If then that friend demand why Brutus rose against Caesar, this is my answer: Not that I loved Caesar less, but that I loved Rome more. Had you rather Caesar were living, and die all slaves, than that Caesar were dead, to live all free men? As Caesar loved me, I weep for him; as he was fortunate, I rejoice at it; as he was valiant, I honor him; but, as he was ambitious, I slew him. There is tears, for his love; joy, for his fortune; honor, for his valor; and death, for his ambition. Who is here so base, that would be a bondman? If any, speak; for him have I offended. Who is here so rude, that would not be a Roman? If any, speak; for him have I offended. Who is here so vile, that will not love his country? If any, speak; for him have I offended. I pause for a reply.

All. None, Brutus, none!

Brutus. Then none have I offended. I have done no more to Caesar than you shall do to Brutus. The question of his death is enrolled in the Capitol; his glory not extenuated, wherein he was worthy, nor his offenses enforced, for which he suffered death.

Enter Mark Antony, with Caesar's body.

Here comes his body, mourned by Mark Antony, who, though he had no hand in his death, shall receive the benefit of his dying, a place in the commonwealth, as which of you shall not? With this I depart, that, as I slew my best lover for the good of Rome, I have the same dagger for myself, when it shall please my country to need my death.

All. Live, Brutus! Live, live!

First Plebeian. Bring him with triumph home unto his house.

Second Plebeian. Give him a statue with his ancestors.

Third Plebeian. Let him be Caesar.

Fourth Plebeian. Caesar's better parts
Shall be crowned in Brutus.

First Plebeian. We'll bring him to his house with shouts and clamors.

Brutus. My countrymen—

Second Plebeian. Peace! Silence! Brutus speaks.

First Plebeian. Peace, ho!

Brutus. Good countrymen, let me depart alone,
And, for my sake, stay here with Antony.
Do grace to Caesar's corpse, and grace his speech

Tending to Caesar's glories, which Mark Antony
By our permission, is allowed to make.
I do entreat you, not a man depart,
Save I alone, till Antony have spoke.

Exit.

First Plebeian. Stay, ho! And let us hear Mark Antony.

Third Plebeian. Let him go up into the public chair; We'll hear him. Noble Antony, go up.

Antony. For Brutus' sake, I am beholding to you.

Fourth Plebeian. What does he say of Brutus?

Third Plebeian. He says, for Brutus' sake,
He finds himself beholding to us all.

Fourth Plebeian. "Twere best he speak no harm of Brutus here!"

First Plebeian. This Caesar was a tyrant.

Third Plebeian. Nay, that's certain.
We are blest that Rome is rid of him.

Second Plebeian. Peace! Let us hear what Antony can say.

Antony. You gentle Romans—
All. Peace, ho! Let us hear him.
Antony. Friends, Romans, countrymen, lend me your ears;
I come to bury Caesar, not to praise him.
The evil that men do lives after them,
The good is oft interrèd with their bones;
So let it be with Caesar. The noble Brutus
Hath told you Caesar was ambitious.
If it were so, it was a grievous fault,
And grievously hath Caesar answered it.
Here, under leave of Brutus and the rest
(For Brutus is an honorable man,
So are they all, all honorable men),
Come I to speak in Caesar's funeral.
He was my friend, faithful and just to me;
But Brutus says he was ambitious,
And Brutus is an honorable man.
He hath brought many captives home to Rome,
Whose ransoms did the general coffers fill;
Did this in Caesar seem ambitious?
When that the poor have cried, Caesar hath wept;
Ambition should be made of sterner stuff.
Yet Brutus says he was ambitious;
And Brutus is an honorable man.
You all did see that on the Lupercal
I thrice presented him a kingly crown,
Which he did thrice refuse. Was this ambition?
Yet Brutus says he was ambitious;

And sure he is an honorableman.
I speak not to disprove what Brutus spoke,
But here I am to speak what I do know.
You all did love him once, not without cause;
What cause withholds you then to mourn for him?
O judgment, thou art fled to brutish beasts,
And men have lost their reason! Bear with me;
My heart is in the coffin there with Caesar,
And I must pause till it come back to me.

First Plebeian. Methinks there is much reason in his sayings.

Second Plebeian. If thou consider rightly of the matter, Caesar has had great wrong.

Third Plebeian. Has he, masters?
I fear there will a worse come in his place.

Fourth Plebeian. Marked ye his words? He would not take the crown,
Therefore "tis certain he was not ambitious."

First Plebeian. If it be found so, some will dear abide it.

Second Plebeian. Poor soul, his eyes are red as fire with weeping.

Third Plebeian. There's not a nobler man in Rome than Antony.

Fourth Plebeian. Now mark him, he begins again to speak.

Antony. But yesterday the word of Caesar might
Have stood against the world; now lies he there,
And none so poor to do him reverence.
O masters! If I were disposed to stir
Your hearts and minds to mutiny and rage,
I should do Brutus wrong and Cassius wrong,
Who, you all know, are honorable men.
I will not do them wrong; I rather choose
To wrong the dead, to wrong myself and you,
Than I will wrong such honorable men.
But here's a parchment with the seal of Caesar;
I found it in his closet; 'tis his will.
Let but the commons hear this testament,
Which, pardon me, I do not mean to read,
And they would go and kiss dead Caesar's wounds,
And dip their napkins in his sacred blood;
Yea, beg a hair of him for memory,
And dying, mention it within their wills,
Bequeathing it as a rich legacy
Unto their issue.

Fourth Plebeian. We'll hear the will; read it, Mark Antony.

All. The will, the will! We will hear Caesar's will!

Antony. Have patience, gentle friends, I must not read it.
It is not meet you know how Caesar loved you.
You are not wood, you are not stones, but men;

And being men, hearing the will of Caesar,
It will inflame you, it will make you mad.
'Tis good you know not that you are his heirs;
For if you should, O, what would come of it?

Fourth Plebeian. Read the will! We'll hear it, Antony!
You shall read us the will, Caesar's will!

Antony. Will you be patient? Will you stay awhile?
I have o'ershot myself to tell you of it.
I fear I wrong the honorable men
Whose daggers have stabbed Caesar; I do fear it.

Fourth Plebeian. They were traitors. Honorable men!

All. The will! The testament!

Second Plebeian. They were villains, murderers! The will! Read the will!

Antony. You will compel me then to read the will?
Then make a ring about the corpse of Caesar,
And let me show you him that made the will.
Shall I descend? And will you give me leave?

All. Come down.

Second Plebeian. Descend. [*Antony comes down.*]

Third Plebeian. You shall have leave.

Fourth Plebeian. A ring! Stand round.

First Plebeian. Stand from the hearse, stand from the body!

Second Plebeian. Room for Antony, most noble Antony!

Antony. Nay, press not so upon me; stand far off.

All. Stand back! Room! Bear back.

Antony. If you have tears, prepare to shed them now.
You all do know this mantle; I remember
The first time ever Caesar put it on:
'Twas on a summer's evening, in his tent,
That day he overcame the Nervii.
Look, in this place ran Cassius' dagger through;
See what a rent the envious Casca made;
Through this the well-belovèd Brutus stabbed,
And as he plucked his cursèd steel away,
Mark how the blood of Caesar followed it,
As rushing out of doors, to be resolved
If Brutus so unkindly knocked, or no;
For Brutus, as you know, was Caesar's angel.
Judge, O you gods, how dearly Caesar loved him!
This was the most unkindest cut of all;
For when the noble Caesar saw him stab,
Ingratitude, more strong than traitors' arms,
Quite vanquished him. Then burst his mighty heart;

And, in his mantle muffling up his face,
Even at the base of Pompey's statue
(Which all the while ran blood) great Caesar fell.
O, what a fall was there, my countrymen!
Then I, and you, and all of us fell down,
Whilst bloody treason flourished over us.
O, now you weep, and I perceive you feel
The dint of pity; these are gracious drops.
Kind souls, what weep you when you but behold
Our Caesar's vesture wounded? Look you here,
Here is himself, marred as you see with traitors.

First Plebeian. O piteous spectacle!

Second Plebeian. O noble Caesar!

Third Plebeian. O woeful day!

Fourth Plebeian. O traitors, villains!

First Plebeian. O most bloody sight!

Second Plebeian. We will be revenged.

[*All.*] Revenge! About! Seek! Burn! Fire! Kill! Slay! Let not a traitor live!

Antony. Stay, countrymen.

First Plebeian. Peace there! Hear the noble Antony.

Second Plebeian. We'll hear him, we'll follow him, we'll die with him!

Antony. Good friends, sweet friends, let me not stir you up
To such a sudden flood of mutiny.
They that have done this deed are honorable.
What private griefs they have, alas, I know not,
That made them do it. They are wise and honorable,
And will, no doubt, with reasons answer you.
I come not, friends, to steal away your hearts;
I am no orator, as Brutus is;
But (as you know me all) a plain blunt man
That love my friend, and that they know full well
That gave me public leave to speak of him.
For I have neither writ, nor words, nor worth,
Action, nor utterance, nor the power of speech
To stir men's blood; I only speak right on.
I tell you that which you yourselves do know,
Show you sweet Caesar's wounds, poor poor dumb
mouths,
And bid them speak for me. But were I Brutus,
And Brutus Antony, there were an Antony
Would ruffle up your spirits, and put a tongue
In every wound of Caesar that should move
The stones of Rome to rise and mutiny.

All. We'll mutiny.

First Plebeian. We'll burn the house of Brutus.

Third Plebeian. Away, then! Come, seek the conspirators.

Antony. Yet hear me, countrymen. Yet hear me speak.

All. Peace, ho! Hear Antony, most noble Antony!

Antony. Why, friends, you go to do you know not what:
Wherein hath Caesar thus deserved your loves?
Alas, you know not; I must tell you then:
You have forgot the will I told you of.

All. Most true, the will! Let's stay and hear the will.

Antony. Here is the will, and under Caesar's seal.
To every Roman citizen he gives,
To every several man, seventy-five drachmas.

Second Plebeian. Most noble Caesar! We'll revenge his death!

Third Plebeian. O royal Caesar!

Antony. Hear me with patience.

All. Peace, ho!

Antony. Moreover, he hath left you all his walks,
His private arbors, and new-planted orchards,
On this side Tiber; he hath left them you,
And to your heirs forever: common pleasures,
To walk abroad and recreate yourselves.
Here was a Caesar! When comes such another?

First Plebeian. Never, never! Come, away, away!
We'll burn his body in the holy place,
And with the brands fire the traitors' houses.
Take up the body.

Second Plebeian. Go fetch fire.

Third Plebeian. Pluck down benches.

Fourth Plebeian. Pluck down forms, windows, anything!

Exeunt Plebeians [*with the body*].

Antony. Now let it work: Mischief, thou art afoot, Take thou what course thou wilt.

MARTIN LUTHER KING, JR., LETTER FROM BIRMINGHAM JAIL

(1963).

We have waited for more than 340 years for our constitutional and God-given rights. The nations of Asia and Africa are moving with jetlike speed toward gaining political independence, but we still creep at horse-and-buggy pace toward gaining a cup of coffee at a lunch counter. Perhaps it is easy for those who have never felt the stinging darts of segregation to say, "Wait." But when you have seen vicious mobs lynch your mothers and fathers at will and drown your sisters and brothers at whim; when you have seen hate-filled policemen curse, kick and even kill your black brothers and sisters; when you see the vast majority of your twenty million Negro brothers smothering in an airtight cage of poverty in the midst of an affluent society; when you suddenly find your tongue twisted and your speech stammering as you seek to explain to your six-year-old daughter why she can't go to the public amusement park that has just been advertised on television, and see tears welling up in her eyes when she is told that Funtown is closed to colored children, and see ominous clouds of inferiority beginning to form in her little mental sky, and see her beginning to distort her personality by developing an unconscious bitterness toward white people; when you have to concoct an answer for a five-year-old son who is asking: "Daddy, why do white people treat colored people so mean?"; when you take a cross-country drive and find it necessary to sleep night after night in the uncomfortable corners of your automobile because no motel will accept you; when you are humiliated day in and day out by nagging signs reading "white" and "colored"; when your first name becomes "nigger," your middle name becomes "boy" (however old you are) and your last name becomes "John," and your wife and mother are never given the respected title "Mrs."; when you are harried by day and haunted by night by the fact that you are a Negro, living constantly at tiptoe stance, never quite knowing what to expect next, and are plagued with inner fears and outer resentments; when you are forever fighting a degenerating sense of "nobodiness"—then you will understand why we find it difficult to wait. There comes a time when the cup of endurance runs over, and men are no longer willing to be plunged into the abyss of despair. I hope, sirs, you can understand our legitimate and unavoidable impatience.

You express a great deal of anxiety over our willingness to break laws. This is certainly a legitimate concern. Since we so diligently urge people to obey the Supreme Court's decision of 1954 outlawing segregation in the public schools, at first glance it may seem rather paradoxical for us consciously to break laws. One may well ask: "How can you advocate breaking some laws and obeying others?" The answer lies in the fact that there are two types of laws: just and unjust. I would be the first to advocate obeying just laws. One has not only a legal but a moral responsibility to obey just laws. Conversely, one has a moral responsibility to disobey unjust laws. I would agree with St. Augustine that "an unjust law is no law at all."

Now, what is the difference between the two? How does one determine whether a law is just or unjust? A just law is a man-made code that squares with the moral law or the law of God. An unjust law is a code that is out of harmony with the moral law. To put it in the terms of St. Thomas Aquinas: An unjust law is a human law that is not rooted in eternal law and natural law. Any law that uplifts human personality is just. Any law that degrades human personality is unjust. All segregation statutes are unjust because segregation distorts the soul and damages the personality. It gives the segregator a false sense of superiority and the segregated a false sense of inferiority. Segregation, to use the terminology of the Jewish philosopher Martin Buber, substitutes an "I-it" relationship for an "I-thou" relationship and ends up relegating persons to the status of things. Hence segregation is not only politically, economically and sociologically unsound, it is morally wrong and sinful. Paul Tillich has said that sin is separation. Is not segregation an existential expression of man's tragic separation, his awful estrangement, his terrible sinfulness? Thus it is that I can urge men to obey the 1954 decision of the Supreme Court, for it is morally right; and I can urge them to disobey segregation ordinances, for they are morally wrong.

Let us consider a more concrete example of just and unjust laws. An unjust law is a code that a numerical or power majority group compels a minority group to obey but does not make binding on itself. This is *difference* made legal. By the same token, a just law is a code that a majority compels a minority to follow and that it is willing to follow itself. This is *sameness* made legal.

Let me give another explanation. A law is unjust if it is inflicted on a minority that, as a result of being denied the right to vote, had no part in enacting or devising the law. Who can say that the legislature of Alabama which set up that state's segregation laws was democratically elected? Throughout Alabama all sorts of devious methods are used to prevent Negroes from becoming registered voters, and there are some counties in which, even though Negroes constitute a majority of the population, not a single Negro is registered. Can any law enacted under such circumstances be considered democratically structured?

Sometimes a law is just on its face and unjust in its application. For instance, I have been arrested on a charge of parading without a permit. Now, there is nothing wrong in having an ordinance which requires a permit for a parade. But such an ordinance becomes unjust when it is used to maintain segregation and to deny citizens the First–Amendment privilege of peaceful assembly and protest.

I hope you are able to see the distinction I am trying to point out. In no sense do I advocate evading or defying the law, as would the rabid segregationist. That would lead to anarchy. One who breaks an unjust law must do so openly, lovingly, and with a willingness to accept the penalty. I submit that an individual who breaks a law that conscience tells him is unjust, and who willingly accepts the penalty of imprisonment in order to arouse the conscience of the community over its injustice, is in reality expressing the highest respect for law.

Question

Under Hand's test, could Marc Anthony be punished for his funeral oration? Could Martin Luther King be punished for his "Letter From Birmingham Jail?" Do these applications cast doubt on the propriety of Hand's test?

MASSES PUB. CO. v. PATTEN

Circuit Court of Appeals, Second Circuit, 1917.
246 F. 24.

ROGERS, CIRCUIT JUDGE.

* * *

The District Judge thought no crime had been committed, and that the magazine was therefore mailable, because the publication did not in so many words directly advise or counsel a violation of the act. He declared that:

"If one stops short of urging upon others that it is their duty or their interest to resist the law, it seems to me one should not be held to have attempted to cause its violation. If that be not the test, I can see no escape from the conclusion that under this section every political agitation which can be shown to be apt to create a seditious temper is illegal. I am confident that, by such language, Congress had no such revolutionary purpose in view."

This court does not agree that such is the law. If the natural and reasonable effect of what is said is to encourage resistance to a law, and the words are used in an endeavor to persuade to resistance, it is immaterial that the duty to resist is not mentioned, or the interest of the persons addressed in resistance is not suggested. That one may willfully obstruct the enlistment service, without advising in direct language against enlistments, and without stating that to refrain from enlistment is a duty or in one's interest, seems to us too plain for controversy. To obstruct the recruiting or enlistment service, within the meaning of the statute, it is not necessary that there should be a physical obstruction. Anything which impedes, hinders, retards, restrains, or puts an obstacle in the way of recruiting is sufficient. In granting the stay of the injunction until this case could be heard in this court upon the appeal Judge Hough declared that:

"It is at least arguable whether there can be any more direct incitement to action than to hold up to admiration those who do act. Oratio obliqua has always been preferred by rhetoricians to oratio recta; the Beatitudes have for some centuries been considered highly hortatory, though they do not contain the injunction, 'Go thou and do likewise.' "

With this statement we fully agree. Moreover, it is not necessary that an incitement to crime must be direct. At common law the 'counseling' which constituted one an accessory before the fact might be indirect. See Wharton's Criminal Law (11th Ed.) Sec. 266. Bishop lays down the rule thus:

"Every man is responsible criminally for what of wrong flows directly from his corrupt intentions. * * * If he awoke into action an indiscriminate power, he is responsible. If he gave directions vaguely and incautiously, and the person receiving them acted according to what he might have foreseen would be the understanding, he is responsible." 1 Bishop on Criminal Law, Sec. 641.

And in *Regina v. Sharpe*, 3 Cox's C.C. 288, it is laid down that:

"He who inflames people's minds and induces them by violent means, to accomplish an illegal object, is himself a rioter, though he take no part in the riot."

* * *

The order granting the preliminary injunction is reversed.

UNITED STATES v. NEARING

Southern District of New York, 1918.
252 Fed. 223.

LEARNED HAND, DISTRICT JUDGE

* * *

That the author of words may in fact be the cause of the commission of crime by others is a trite enough observation. Any discussion of existing laws, designed to show that they are mistaken in means, or unjust in policy, may have that result. Every one knows that the obligation of law in the minds of many men depends altogether upon their approval of its purposes, and that to arouse their disapproval is to terminate their obedience. Indeed, there are few whose allegiance to any given law is not modified by their opinion of its justice, and the measure of whose obedience does not turn in some degree upon that factor.

At common law the utterer of written or spoken words is not criminally liable merely because he knows they will reach those who will find in them the excuse for criminal acts. On the contrary, the rule has always been that, to establish criminal responsibility, the words uttered must amount to counsel or advice or command to commit the forbidden acts, and this is the classic form of expression. 4 Blackstone, 36, 37. Of course, the counsel or advice need not be explicit, since the meaning of words comprises what their hearers understand them to convey. Yet the terms, "counsel" or "advice" have a content which can be determined objectively, and do not depend upon the subjective intent of their author. I tried unsuccessfully in *Masses Pub. Co. v. Patten* (D.C.), 244 Fed. 535, to suggest an analysis of what is included in those terms, and shall not attempt it again. It is enough here merely to suggest that they must have limits determined by the character of the words themselves. That there may be language, as, for instance, Mark Antony's funeral oration, which can in fact counsel violence while it even expressly discountenances it, is true enough; but that raises only the situation, familiar enough everywhere in the law, and already mentioned, of the actual meaning of words to their hearers.

Now, there is nothing in the pamphlet in question which can, as I read it, be understood to constitute any counsel or advice or command to obstruct the draft or to become insubordinate. At least, if it be the pleader's purpose to allege that they reached persons who so understood them, and that the defendants knew of this likelihood, that must be especially alleged. Taken with any interpretation which they can fairly bear, they remain entirely within the range of discussion, and at common law would not, I think, subject their author to criminal responsibility for the results, no matter what his intent.

Whatever may be the rule at common law, I understand [the Second Circuit's decision in] *Masses Pub. Co. v. Patten*, 246 Fed. 24, to lay down an added measure of criminal liability under this statute to the utterance of words which may cause insubordination, or may obstruct the enlistment service. In that case, it is true, there is language which, taken broadly, can be made to mean that the author is liable if he merely knows that his words will so result. This I can hardly think can have been the significance of the decision, since, as I have already shown, the inevitable consequence would be to imperil any discussion of public matters. It certainly was not the purpose of that case to do so, or indeed to insist that the style or manner of the discussion must measure with any standard of taste or temperance. Such a result would be foreign to the whole history of the subject. The test as laid down in that case was, I think, this: That though in the form of public discussion words, which might not themselves amount to advice or counsel to violate the law, would nevertheless make their author criminally responsible if they were in fact the cause of the results forbidden, and if they were uttered with the specific intent of producing those results. In short, the test was made, not objective only, but in part subjective, as is indeed often the case in the definition of crime. At least this is as I understand that case, and it is in this sense that the rule was applied in the trial of the first indictment against the Masses Publishing Company, which was the direct result of the decision of the Circuit Court of Appeals.

* * *

HARRY KALVEN, JR., A WORTHY TRADITION

(1988).

The Holmes Legacy

If the intellectual history starts with Judge Hand's opinion in *Masses* in 1917, the Supreme Court history starts with Justice Holmes's opinion in *Schenck v. United States,* decided on March 3, 1919. For our purposes, *Schenck* is best read, not only against *Masses,* but also together with *Debs v. United States*, decided one week later, on March 10, 1919.

Both *Schenck* and *Debs* arose out of Socialist Party opposition to the war and to conscription. Schenck, a party official, had participated in the preparation and distribution of a leaflet to men who were awaiting induction into the armed forces. Eugene Debs, a nationally prominent leader of the party, had addressed a general audience at a Socialist convention. Both were convicted under the Espionage Act for their communications. Schenck was sentenced to six months; Debs, who a year later, while in prison, was to poll almost a million votes as the Socialist candidate for President, was sentenced to ten years. Both convictions were affirmed unanimously by a Supreme Court which numbered among its members Justices Holmes and Brandeis. And both opinions were written by Justice Holmes.

By modern standards the *Schenck* leaflet is startlingly mild. One side simply presented an argument that conscription violated the involuntary servitude prohibition of the Thirteenth Amendment. It contained references to "venal capitalist newspapers," "gang politicians," and "monstrous wrongs against humanity." The action words were:

> . . . join the Socialist Party in its campaign for the repeal of the Conscription Act. Write to your congressman. . . . You have a right to demand the repeal of any law. Exercise your rights of free speech, peaceful assemblage and petitioning the government for a redress of grievances. . . . sign a petition to congress for the repeal of the Conscription Act. Help us wipe out this stain upon the Constitution!

The other side of the leaflet was a bit more militant. Headed "Assert Your Rights," it argued that officials acted unconstitutionally if they refused to "recognize your right to assert your opposition to the draft." Its most strongly worded sentence—"Will you let cunning politicians and a mercenary capitalist press wrongly and untruthfully mould your thoughts?"—was followed by this: "Do not forget your right to elect officials who are opposed to conscription." For this communication, Schenck and another Party official were convicted of conspiracy to cause "insubordination" in the armed forces and to "obstruct" the recruiting and enlistment services.

Prior to *Schenck* there had been some controversy over whether the First Amendment stood for anything more that the abolition of prior restraints, the Blackstonian definition of freedom of speech. It is the unqualified, if little heralded, achievement of Justice Holmes's opinion to establish that the Amendment applies to subsequent as well as prior restraints. He disposes of the matter in a single sentence: "It may well be that the prohibition of laws abridging the freedom of speech is not confined to previous restraints, although to prevent them may have been the main purpose, as intimated in *Patterson v. Colorado.*"

The opinion then proceeds to the defendants' challenge under the First Amendment to the subsequent restraint imposed in the case at hand:

> We admit that in many places and in ordinary times the defendants in saying all that was said in the circular would have been within their constitutional rights. But the character of every act depends upon the circumstances in which it is done. The most stringent protection of free speech would not protect a man in falsely shouting fire in a theater and causing a panic. It does not even protect a man from an injunction against uttering words that may have all the

> effect of force. The question in every case is whether the words used are used in such circumstances and are of such a nature as to create a clear and present danger that they will bring about the substantive evils that Congress has a right to prevent. It is a question of proximity and degree. When a nation is at war many things that might be said in time of peace are such a hindrance to its effort that their utterance will not be endured so long as men fight and that no court could regard them as protected by any constitutional right. It seems to be admitted that if an actual obstruction of the recruiting service were proved, liability for words that produced that effect might be enforced. The statute of 1917, in [section] 4 punishes conspiracies to obstruct as well as actual obstruction. If the act (speaking, or circulating a paper,) its tendency and the intent with which it is done are the same, we perceive no ground for saying that success alone warrants making the act a crime. *Goldman v. United States.* Indeed that case might be said to dispose of the present contention if the precedent covers all *media concludendi.* But as the right to free speech was not referred to specially, we have thought fit to add a few words.

This passage invites a number of reactions. First, there is the casualness of the tone. Holmes tells us that *Goldman,* a decision affirming the convictions of Emma Goldman and Alexander Berkman for conspiring to violate the Selective Draft Act, is dispositive of the case before him. He is merely adding "a few words" about free speech.

Second, the clear and present danger formula is announced as a premise to support the conviction, not to impeach it. Apparently the *Schenck* leaflet presented a clear and present danger within Holmes's meaning of the words. Also, there is the unnoticed puzzle that, if this is the test, then Schenck could scarcely have been tried under it; surely this is not what the jury was asked to decide.

Third, Holmes makes no effort to limit the statute. He holds that success is not necessary for a conviction and that it is sufficient if the speech be made with the intent and have the tendency to cause obstruction. Then he is willing to infer the "intent" and the "tendency" from the mere distribution of the leaflet to those eligible for the draft:

> Of course the document would not have been sent unless it had been intended to have some effect, and we do not see what effect it could be expected to have upon persons subject to the draft except to influence them to obstruct the carrying of it out.

This would be a questionable exercise with respect to any statute, but it is especially disturbing in the First Amendment area, and it stands in striking contrast to Judge Hand's effort to give a narrow construction to the same provisions of the Espionage Act.

Finally, the concern expressed by Hand for preserving to the uttermost the possibilities of political criticism is, to my ear, altogether missing. Holmes verges on saying that any serious criticism of the war and the draft sent to men who are eligible for service would violate the statute. The fundamental poverty of his analysis is that he treats the problem of political speech as he might any crime. And even this is too generous an assessment, I am afraid, for he does not accord such speech the care in analysis and the stringency of standards he would have applied to, say, a solicitation to arson.

Schenck—and perhaps even Holmes himself—are best remembered for the example of the man "falsely shouting fire" in a crowded theater. Judge Hand said in *Masses* that "words are not only the keys of persuasion, but the triggers of action." Justice Holmes makes the same point by means of the "fire" example, an image which was to catch the fancy of the culture. But the example has long seemed to me trivial and misleading. It is as if the only conceivable controversy over speech policy were with an adversary who asserts that *all* use of words is absolutely immunized under the First Amendment. The "fire" example then triumphantly impeaches this massive major premise. Beyond that, it adds nothing to our understanding. If the point were that *only* speech which is a comparable "trigger of action" could be regulated, the example might prove a stirring way of drawing the line at incitement, but it is abundantly clear that Justice Holmes is not comparing Schenck's leaflet to the shouting of "fire." Moreover, because the example is so wholly apolitical, it lacks the requisite complexity for dealing with any serious speech problem likely to confront the legal system. The man shouting "fire" does not offer premises resembling those underlying radical political rhetoric—premises that constitute criticism of government.

Another important aspect of the *Schenck* opinion is the premise about the impact of wartime upon political tolerance: "In ordinary times" the leaflet would have been constitutionally protected, but "when a nation is at war many things that might be said in time of peace are such a hindrance to its effort that their utterance will not be endured so long as men fight." Does Holmes mean, as the result in *Schenck* suggests, that when a nation is at war public morale is so delicate a matter that seditious libel cannot be permitted? Judge Hand too had considered the impact of speech during wartime but had concluded that the American tradition of freedom of dissent required that the statute be construed so as to permit speech which generated detestation of the war. Perhaps Justice Holmes was making Hand's point that the war powers of Congress might permit legislation that censored utterances damaging to morale, if Congress made its intention to do so sufficiently explicit, that in a showdown the war powers might limit the prohibitions of the First Amendment. But if so, he selected a notably cryptic way of presenting a complex issue.

Above all, *Schenck* bequeaths the principle of clear and present danger as a condition for censorship. There is, of course, a kinship between this principle and the one announced by Judge Hand in *Masses*. Yet the distance between the two analyses is considerable. Undoubtedly it would be forcing matters to assert that Holmes ignores the words, while Hand ignores the surrounding circumstances. Nevertheless, there remains a key difference between them. Hand would require as a threshold test that the state point to words of incitement. He is acutely aware that any less stringent test will foreclose too much serious dissent. Holmes in *Schenck* appears to ignore this countervalue altogether; his approach is rooted in an appraisal of the surrounding circumstances rather than of the words used. If we push the two approaches to their extremes, the coverages crisscross in the minority of instances in which they do not overlap. Under the Holmes approach, speech which contained no concrete advocacy of action might be reached, if the danger was deemed great enough. His application of the principle to the *Schenck* facts underscores this difficulty. By contrast, the Hand approach might fail to reach speech which was imminently dangerous but cleverly worded; and it might also fail to protect speech which was militantly worded but not in fact dangerous. Each would leave some political speech unprotected. My own feeling is that the Hand approach serves to interpose a weightier barrier against the state's impulse in times of tension to intercept serious radical criticism because it is dangerous. In any event, it is important to note that *Brandenburg* carefully combines the two approaches. It draws the line at "advocacy directed to inciting or producing imminent lawless action" *and* "likely to incite or produce such action."

Although the American traditions of political and intellectual tolerance are enormously indebted to Justice Holmes for the contributions his pen and prestige are to make during the next decade, the awkward fact is that the legal tradition gets off to a limping start with his opinion in *Schenck*. This impression deepens when we look at his opinion a week later in *Debs*.

In *Debs* the communication is not addressed to a special audience of men awaiting the draft as in *Schenck*, but to a general audience at a public meeting; and this time there are even fewer direct action words. The dominant theme of Debs's speech was the growth of socialism and a prophecy of its ultimate success. In passing he expressed sympathy and strong admiration for several "loyal comrades" who had been convicted of obstructing the draft and of aiding others in failing to register. He indicted war on general socialist grounds, stating that "the master class has always declared the war and the subject class has always fought the battles ... the working class, who furnish the corpses, have never yet had a voice in declaring the peace." He concluded with the exhortation: "Don't worry about the charge of treason to your masters; but be concerned about the treason that involves yourselves." Further, during the trial he addressed the jury, professing his innocence and declaring: "I have been accused of obstructing the war. I admit it. Gentlemen, I abhor war. I would oppose the war if I stood alone."

Debs was convicted under the "insubordination" and "obstruction" provisions of the Espionage Act and was sentenced to a prison term of ten years. There should, of course, be no special immunity for political leaders, but the imprisoning—for ten years—of a man who has run for President four times for the offense of making a public speech is so alien to American expectations that it clamors for a close look by the Court at the premises supporting so startling a conclusion.

The stage was thus set for the first great Supreme Court opinion exploring the First Amendment. But the chief issues with which the brief Holmes opinion deals are the admission of two items into evidence: the record of the convictions of various persons Debs had named with admiration; and an Anti–War Proclamation adopted by the party on another occasion and not mentioned by Debs in his speech. Justice Holmes finds it possible to connect both of these items with the case against Debs. He dismisses the free speech issue curtly:

> The chief defenses upon which the defendant seemed willing to rely were the denial that we have dealt with and that based upon the First Amendment to the Constitution, disposed of in *Schenck v. United States.*

Later there is this further sentence:

> We should add that the jury were most carefully instructed that they could not find the defendant guilty for advocacy of any of his opinions unless the words used had as their natural tendency and reasonably probable effect to obstruct the recruiting service, etc., and unless the defendant had the specific intent to do so in his mind.

That is all Holmes has to say. He does not devote even a sentence to the circumstance that the special audience of *Schenck* is no longer present, that he is dealing with a speech to the general public. The jury instruction quoted with apparent approval is keyed to "natural tendency" and "reasonably probable effect." Are these for Holmes synonyms of clear and present danger? Equally troublesome, there is no effort to curb the misunderstanding likely to be aroused by the decision itself. If Eugene Debs can be sent to jail for a public speech, what, if anything, can the ordinary man safely say against the war? Although subsequent World War I cases are to provide close competition, *Debs* marks a low point in the Court's performance in speech cases.

GERALD GUNTHER, LEARNED HAND AND THE ORIGINS OF MODERN FIRST AMENDMENT DOCTRINE: SOME FRAGMENTS OF HISTORY

27 Stan. L. Rev. 719 (1975).

THE CORRESPONDENCE IN CONTEXT

I. The Masses Decision, 1917

A. *The background of Masses.*

The letters printed here span a period of less than 3 years, from the summer of 1918 to the spring of 1921. According to the traditional view of the intellectual history of the first amendment, that brief span is ample to encompass all high points of the formative years: in 1918, the crest of prosecutions under the World War I Espionage Act; in the spring of 1919, the Supreme Court's raising of the banner of the "libertarian" clear and present danger test in *Schenck v. United States*; in the fall of 1919, the elaboration of that standard in Holmes' *Abrams* dissent; at the end of 1920, the publication of the book that was to guide speech-protective thinking for a generation, Zechariah Chafee, Jr.'s *Freedom of Speech*. But these letters cannot be viewed adequately in their historical and legal contexts without reaching back a year earlier, to the summer of 1917, when Learned Hand decided *Masses Publishing Co. v. Patten*. For it was in *Masses* that Hand first articulated the alternative approach to freedom of expression problems that he urged upon Holmes before *Schenck* and that he adhered to throughout these letters, even after Holmes' *Abrams* dissent.

To what extent may Congress suppress criticism of government? For more than a century after the demise of the Sedition Act of 1798, there was little occasion for federal courts to confront that question. But soon after America's entry into World War I, Congress revived the issue by enacting the Espionage Act of 1917. The Act did not purport to prohibit seditious libel in so many words, but its administrators soon sought to achieve that effect. The most important provisions were directed at those who "willfully cause or attempt to cause insubordination, disloyalty, mutiny, or refusal of duty, in the military or naval forces of the United States" and those who "willfully obstruct the recruiting or enlistment service of the United States." And another section declared publications violating those provisions "nonmailable." As Postmaster General Albert Sidney Burleson—and soon, prosecutors—read the statute, criticism of government policies could constitute the prohibited interference with military activities if disruption was the natural and reasonable effect of the dissident speech.

One of the first publications to feel the bite of the new law was Max Eastman's *The Masses*, "a monthly revolutionary journal" with a circulation of over 20,000. Thomas G. Patten, the New York Postmaster, acting under orders of the Postmaster General, notified *The Masses* early in July that its forthcoming issue would be excluded from the mails under the Espionage Act. *The Masses* promptly sought a preliminary injunction against Patten. As a result of that motion, Learned Hand became one of the first judges required to interpret the Act. His decision of July 24, 1917—less than 6 weeks after enactment of the law—granted the injunction.[19]

19. 244 F. 535 (S.D.N.Y.), *rev'd*, 246 F. 24 (2d Cir. 1917).

The Hand Papers reveal that this injunction action was not Learned Hand's first contact with Max Eastman's efforts to combat suppression of his magazine. About a year before the Postmaster General's ban, there was an effort to exclude *The Masses* from newsstands in New York City's subway and elevated stations. A state legislative committee scheduled hearings on that exclusion. Max Eastman asked Learned Hand for a statement opposing that ban; Judge Hand promptly complied.

Eastman wrote Hand that if the Judge would send him a statement "that you believe The Masses ought to be on those stands, it will be the favor of a lifetime." Letter from Max Eastman to Learned Hand, June 26, 1916, on file in the Hand

It was a remarkable decision—remarkable even decades later; especially remarkable given the practical and doctrinal climate of the times, so strikingly inhospitable to dissent. Radicals preaching pacifism, conscientious objection, or worse, were anathema in wartime America. And constitutional interpretation offered no shelter. There was doubt that the first amendment applied to postpublication sanctions: the Supreme Court's sparse announcements had embraced the Blackstonian view that freedom of expression was protected solely against prior restraint.[21] And beyond that niggardly view of the first amendment, many Court statements appeared to give the government virtually total discretion in controlling the mails.[22] Moreover, the Government's arguments for suppressing speech under a statute prohibiting acts such as interference with recruiting reflected the customary legal thinking of the day: punishability of speech turned on its probable effect or tendency, on assessments of causation and consequences; talk of the "natural and reasonable effect of the publication" was a characteristic way of framing the question. Most of those who viewed such a standard as too speech-restrictive did not quarrel with the emphasis on guessing about the consequences of speech. Their rejoinder to arguments about bad tendencies and probable effects was to urge a narrower, closer cause-effect relationship represented by formulations such as "direct and immediate"—or "clear and present danger."

Papers, Box 20, Folder 1, Harvard Law Library, Treasure Room. Hand complied the next day, in a statement akin to some of the views expressed in his judicial opinion a year later. Letter from Learned Hand to Max Eastman, June 27, 1916, on file in the Hand Papers, Box 20, Folder 1, Harvard Law Library, Treasure Room. Hand wrote: "I have your letter of the 26th asking me to say that I think 'The Masses' ought not to be excluded by Ward & Gow from the newsstands. I answer unhesitatingly that I think it ought not. I do not often see your paper, and as you probably can guess, I do not feel sympathy with your approach to the question of social and economic reorganization, or the means by which you seek to bring it about. That I prefer another way, does not blind me to the wisdom of giving you the chance to persuade men of yours. I have never seen anything in 'The Masses' which did not have a sincere and genuine relation to these absolutely legitimate purposes. You will forgive my saying that parts of it have at times been extremely repellant to me, though never what you did yourself, but that in my judgment has nothing to do with this matter. Yours is a way, whether it is a good way or a bad way, of getting men to think and feel about those things on which it is most important that they should think and feel. I can conceive no possible defence for excluding you except either that such matters must not be discussed, or that they must be discussed only in a way which accords with the common standards of taste. One alternative is tyrannous absolutism, the other, tyrannous priggism." I do not know whether Hand's letter was entered into the record of the legislative hearings in 1916, or whether the Judge apprised the parties of the statement when the injunction proceeding came before him a year later.

Max Eastman and Learned Hand met on at least one occasion: Eastman recalled in one of his autobiographical volumes that Judge Hand introduced an Eastman lecture on radicalism before "New York's exclusive woman's club," the Colony Club. M. EASTMAN, ENJOYMENT OF LIVING 481–82 (1948). In the 1920's, Eastman became a leading anti-Stalinist; and in his later years, he joined the staff of *The Reader's Digest.* N.Y. Times, Mar. 26, 1969, at 1, col. 1.

21. *See* especially Justice Holmes' opinion for the Court in Patterson v. Colorado, 205 U.S. 454, 462 (1907).

22. *See, e.g.*, Public Clearing House v. Coyne, 194 U.S. 497 (1904); *In re* Rapier, 143 U.S. 110 (1892); *Ex parte* Jackson, 96 U.S. 727 (1877).

C. The response to Masses.

For Hand, the response to *Masses* was painfully disappointing. As he recalled to Chafee more than 3 years later, "it seemed to meet with practically no professional approval whatever." The most formal indication of that disapproval soon appeared in the official reports." Within 2 weeks of Hand's order, Circuit Judge Charles M. Hough took the unusual step of writing an opinion continuing a stay of Hand's injunction pending appeal. Hough, the widely admired, tough-minded son of a brigadier general, was "never tortured by doubt." He was readily attracted to the Postmaster's position on what Hough called "indirect incitement," and he was openly skeptical of Hand's contrary approach:

> [I]t is at least arguable whether there can be any more direct incitement to action than to hold up to admiration those who do act. Oratio obliqua has always been preferred by rhetoricians to oratio recta; the Beatitudes have for some centuries been considered highly hortatory, though they do not contain the injunction "Go thou and do likewise."[47]

When the case came before the full circuit court of appeals a few months later, the criticism of Hand's position was not limited to its vulnerability as to the Marc Anthony problem. Judge Henry Wade Rogers' opinion reversed Hand's order outright.[48] Rogers did not have a mind as strong and brilliant as Hough's, but his capacities were adequate to reflect the mainstream of contemporary legal thinking. Most of his opinion read like an administrative law essay: he emphasized the broad discretion of the Postmaster General, after recalling the contemporary black-letter law about the virtually unlimited power of Congress to exclude matter from the mails. But Rogers did ultimately reach the problems of the appropriate legal standards governing criticism of national policies and their application to the contents of *The Masses.* These questions seemed to him the easiest ones in the case. He noted Hand's incitement test and replied: "This court does not agree that such is the law. If the natural and reasonable effect of what is said is to encourage resistance to a law, and the words are used in an endeavor to persuade to resistance, it is immaterial that the duty to resist is not mentioned, or the interest of the persons addressed in resistance is not suggested." Nor did he find it "necessary that an incitement to crime must be direct." And so it was easy to conclude "that, considering the natural and reasonable effect of the publication, it was intended willfully to obstruct recruiting; and even though we were not convinced that any such intent existed, and were in doubt concerning it, the case would be governed by the principle that the head of a department of the government in a doubtful case will not be overruled by the courts in a matter which involves his judgment and discretion, and which is within his jurisdiction."

47. 245 F. at 106.

48. Masses Publishing Co. v. Patten, 246 F. 24 (2d Cir. 1917).

The rejection of Hand's position was not limited to official statements from the bench. As Hand wrote to his friend and sometime patron, the distinguished New York lawyer and civic leader Charles C. Burlingham:

> I think all this building, plus Veeder, is against me, although Ward does not commit himself. Gus[58] thinks of it as nothing more than another instance of my natural perversity.

The widespread repudiation of Hand's *Masses* approach may have had a temporary impact on the Judge's career as well as on his personal and professional pride. As he recalled to Chafee later: "The case cost me something, at least at the time. . . ." That "cost" may have been the added shadow cast on Hand's opportunity for promotion to the Second Circuit in 1917.

Yet, despite these frustrations, Learned Hand remained content with and committed to his *Masses* position. As he wrote to Burlingham in October, after reporting his cousin Gus' comment that *Masses* represented "nothing more than an instance of my natural perversity":

> [T]he perversity is there all right and God knows how much my subconscious self, which is no doubt a cross-grained critter, may have been fooling with my cerebral centres, but I never was better satisfied with any piece of work I did in my life. I do not mean that I was pleased with it as a judicial performance, but with the result. There is a bit of it that is arguable, no doubt; in the main outlined [*sic*] I have been very happy to do what I believe was some service to temperateness and sanity.

Learned Hand's self-deprecating remark about pride in "result" rather than "judicial performance" is a characteristic one; but in fact, he took pride in both. As his letters demonstrate, his years of effort to spread the message of his *Masses* opinion had a twofold aim: to heighten sensitivity to the importance of protecting free expression values; and to urge his special doctrinal implementation of that sensitivity. If "result" signifies some progress toward the former goal, surely the "judicial performance" is the source of the lasting strength of the doctrinal approach of *Masses*. It is time to turn to the letters printed in the Appendix to examine in somewhat greater detail Learned Hand's values-cum-doctrine campaign.

II. An Encounter on a Train, Summer 1918

The first round of Hand's campaign was fired a year after *Masses*. The target of this initial volley was Supreme Court Justice Oliver Wendell Holmes; and the aim was not to urge the *Masses* doctrine in detail—no Espionage Act case was yet before the Supreme Court—but to

58. Augustus N. Hand, Learned Hand's cousin and lifelong friend, was a judge of the United States District Court for the Southern District of New York. Three years after Learned Hand's appointment to the Circuit Court of Appeals in 1924, Augustus Hand followed him to the Second Circuit.

persuade Holmes of the importance of special sensitivity to free speech values. It was an eloquent but utterly failing effort.

The first confrontation between Hand and Holmes on issues of free speech was a chance one, brief but revealing. Hand and Holmes shared a train ride from New York City most of the way to Boston, on Wednesday, June 19, 1918. Holmes, at the end of the Supreme Court Term, was on his way to his Beverly Farms, Massachusetts, residence; Hand was travelling to his summer home in Cornish, New Hampshire, across the Connecticut River from Windsor, Vermont. They talked about the majority's right to suppress dissent. Echoes of that conversation are preserved for us because Hand, on brooding about it in New Hampshire, decided he "gave up rather more easily" than he should have and decided to restate his position for Holmes; and Holmes promptly replied.

That exchange—Documents 1 and 2 in the Appendix—reveals that a year after *Masses*, months before *Schenck*, Holmes and Hand were indeed very far apart: Hand argued the case for protecting the dissenter; Holmes disagreed. That was a gap in values all the more remarkable because Hand and Holmes shared a common philosophical outlook in most respects. Neither believed in absolutes or eternal truths; both were skeptics, or at least seemed to be; and both doubted the effectiveness as well as the legitimacy of judicial restraints on majority sentiments. Yet from those premises Hand was able to derive arguments for the protection of minority views, more than a year before Holmes arrived at a parallel conclusion in his *Abrams* dissent.

Appendix

Document No. 1. *Learned Hand to Oliver Wendell Holmes, June 22, 1918*

Windsor, Vermont

June 22, 1918.

Dear Mr. Justice

I gave up rather more easily than I now feel disposed about Tolerance on Wednesday. Here I take my stand. Opinions are at best provisional hypotheses, incompletely tested. The more they are tested, after the tests are well scrutinized, the more assurance we may assume, but they are never absolutes. So we must be tolerant of opposite opinions or varying opinions by the very fact of our incredulity of our own. (This may be left for deductive demonstration in accord with the inexorable rules of formal logic by E.D.W., C.J. U.S.Sup.Ct.).[199]

You say that I strike at the sacred right to kill the other fellow when he disagrees. The horrible possibility silenced me when you said it. Now, I say, "Not at all, kill him for the love of Christ and in the name of God,

199. Chief Justice Edward Douglass White. White's opinions typically had a surface appearance of formal logic but were widely thought to be unsatisfactory. *See, e.g.*, McBain, *Edward Douglass White*, in 10 Dictionary of American Biography, pt. 2, at 96, 97 (rev. ed. 1958): "There was no crystal clarity in his reasoning processes and his sentences were long, labored, and involved."

but always realize that he may be the saint and you the devil. Go your way with a strong right arm and a swift shining sword, in full consciousness that what you kill for, and what you may die for, some smart chap like Laski may write a book and prove is all nonsense." I agree that in practical application there may arise some difficulty, but I am a philosopher and if Man is so poor a creature as not to endure the truth, it is no concern of mine. I didn't make him; let the Galled Jade wince, speaking reverently of course.

I sat under the Bo Tree and these truths were revealed unto me. Tolerance is the twin of Incredulity, but there is no inconsistency in cutting off the heads of as many as you please; that is a natural right. Only, and here we may differ, I do say that you may not cut off heads, (except for limited periods and then only when you want to very much indeed), because the victims insist upon saying things which look against Provisional Hypothesis Number Twenty–Six, the verification of which to date may be found in its proper place in the card catalogue. Generally, I insist, you must allow the possibility that if the heads are spared, other cards may be added under that sub-title which will have, perhaps, an important modification.

All this seems to me so perfectly self-evident, self-explanatory and rigidly applicable to the most complicated situations that I hesitate to linger upon it, lest I should seem tolerant of any different of opinion concerning it.

I greatly enjoyed my good fortune in meeting you on the train.

Faithfully yours,

Learned Hand.

Document No. 2. *Oliver Wendell Holmes to Learned Hand, June 24, 1918*

Beverly Farms, Mass.

June 24, 1918

Dear Hand

Rarely does a letter hit me so exactly where I live as yours, and unless you are spoiling for a fight I agree with it throughout. My only qualification, if any, would be that free speech stands no differently than freedom from vaccination. The occasions would be rarer when you cared enough to stop it but if for any reason you did care enough you wouldn't care a damn for the suggestion that you were acting on a provisional hypothesis and might be wrong. That is the condition of every act. You tempt me to repeat an apologue that I got off to my wife in front of the statue of Garrison on Commonwealth Avenue, Boston, many years ago. I said—If I were an official person I should say nothing shall induce me to do honor to a man who broke the fundamental condition of social life by bidding the very structure of society perish rather than he not have his way—Expressed in terms of morals, to be sure, but still, his way. If I were a son of Garrison I should reply—Fool, not to see that every great reform has seemed to threaten the structure of society,—but that society has not perished, because man is a social animal, and with every turn falls into a new pattern like the Kaleidoscope. If I were a philosopher I should say—Fools both, not to see that you are the two blades (conservative and radical) of the shears that cut out the future. But if I were the ironical man in the back of the philosopher's head I should conclude—Greatest fool of all, Thou—not to see that man's destiny is to fight. Therefore take thy place on the one side or the other, if with the added grace of knowing that the Enemy is as good a man as thou, so much the better, but kill him if thou Canst. All of which seems in accord with you. If I may repeat another chestnut of ancient date and printed in later years—When I say a thing is true I mean that I can't help believing it—and nothing more. But as I observe that the Cosmos is not always limited by my Cant Helps I don't bother about absolute truth or even inquire whether there is such a thing, but define the Truth as the system of my limitations. I may add that as other men are subject to a certain number, not all, of my Cant Helps, intercourse is possible. When I was young I used to define the truth as the majority vote of that nation that can lick all others. So we may define the present war as an inquiry concerning truth. Of course you won't suspect me of thinking with levity on that subject because of my levitical speech. I enjoyed our meeting as much as you possibly could have and should have tried to prolong it to Boston but that I feared my wife would worry.

Sincerely Yours

O. W. Holmes

Document No. 3. *Oliver Wendell Holmes to Learned Hand, Feb. 25, 1919*

Supreme Court of the United States,

Washington, D.C.

Feb. 25, 1919

Dear Judge Hand

Instead of the letter I intended to write to you some new work makes it necessary that I should confine myself to a word. I read your Masses decision—I haven't the details in my mind and will assume for present purposes that I should come to a different result—but I did want to tell you after reading it that I thought that few judges indeed could have put their view with such force or in such admirable form.

Sincerely yours

O. W. Holmes

Document No. 4. *Learned Hand to Oliver Wendell Holmes, (late Mar.)* 1919

JUDGE LEARNED HAND's CHAMBERS

Dear Mr. Justice

I have read Debs v. U.S. and the other case[203] and this is positively my last appearance in the role of liberator. I haven't a doubt that Debs was guilty under any rule conceivably applicable. As to the rule actually laid down my dying words are these, now already fast receding in the seas of forgotten errors, and a crazy Saragossa that would be, wouldn't it? All the mad freaks of past contrivance.

The thing against which the statute aims is positive impediments to raising an army. Speech may create such by its influence on others' conduct. In nature the causal sequence is perfect, but responsibility does not go pari passu. I do not understand that the rule of responsibility for speech has ever been that the result is known as likely to follow. It is not,—I agree it might have been—a question of responsibility dependent upon reasonable forecast, with an excuse when the words, had another possible effect. The responsibility only began when the words were directly an incitement. If I am wrong about that, it is mere matter of history. I confess I have no present access to the history.

Assuming that I am not wrong, then it was a question of extending the responsibility, and that was fairly a matter of better and worse. All I say is, that since the cases actually occur when men are excited and since juries are especially clannish groups,—are they societates perfectae?,—it is very questionable whether the test of motive is not a dangerous test. Juries wont much regard the difference between the probable result of the words and the purposes of the utterer. In any case, unless one is rather set in conformity, it will serve to intimidate,—throw a scare into,—many a man who might moderate the storms of popular feeling. I know it did in 1918.

The rule coupled w. Burleson's[204] legal irresponsibility certainly terrorized some of the press whose voices were much needed.

There, that is all! Absolutely and irrevocably all in saecula saeculorum! I bid a long farewell to my little toy ship which set out quite bravely in the shortest voyage ever made.

I was amused at the Harrison law decision,[205] which showed the vast importance of the sacred doctrine of "Imputation." That means the "Mystery" or "sacrament" of being able to impute to Congress purposes you know they didn't have.

Sincerely yours

L. Hand

203. Frohwerk v. United States, 249 U.S. 204 (1919).

204. Albert Sidney Burleson—Postmaster General of the United States, 1913–1921—was responsible for mail bans such as that challenged in the *Masses* case.

205. *See* United States v. Doremus, 249 U.S. 86 (1919).

Document No. 5. *Oliver Wendell Holmes to Learned Hand, Apr. 3, 1919*

Supreme Court of the United States,
Washington, D.C.

April 3, 1919

Dear Judge Hand

Since your letter came I have been so busy propagating new sophistries & c. that I haven't had time to defend the old ones. And now I am afraid that I don't quite get your point. As to intent under the Espionage Act I believe I have said nothing except to note that under the instructions the jury must be taken to have found that Debs's speech was intended to obstruct and tended to obstruct—and except further that evidence was held admissible as bearing on intent. Even if absence of intent might not be a defence I suppose that the presence of it might be material. Leaving that on one side, you say "the responsibility only began when the words were directly an incitement"—I am afraid I do not know exactly what history you have in mind—but I don't see how you differ from the test as stated by me in *Schenck v. U S* (March 3, 1919). "The question in every case is whether the words used are used in such circumstances and are of such a nature as to create a clear and present danger that they will bring about the substantive evils that Congress has a right to prevent. "It is a question of proximity and degree."—I haven't time even now to recur to your decision but I take it that you agree that words may constitute an obstruction within the statute, even without proof that the obstruction was successful to the point of preventing recruiting. That I at least think plain. So I don't know what the matter is, or how we differ so far as your letter goes. With which I send you my blessing and don't hold you bound by your adieu to this stage.

As to the Harrison Drug Act, (*between ourselves*) I am tickled at every case of that sort as they seem to me to confirm the ground of my dissent in the Child Labor case last term. *Hammer v. Dagenhart*, 247 U.S. 257, 277. Also I think the drug act cases rightly decided. In my opinion Congress may have what ulterior motives they please if the act passed in the immediate aspect is within their powers—though personally, were I a legislator I might think it dishonest to use powers in that way.

Yours sincerely
O. W. Holmes

Document No. 6. *Learned Hand to Oliver Wendell Holmes, Nov. 25, 1919*

JUDGE LEARNED HAND's CHAMBERS

Dear Mr. Justice

I was greatly pleased with your dissent in the *Abrams* case, especially with the close which, if I may say so, was in your very highest vein. I am quite confident that whether it is avowed or not, in the end your views must prevail, after people get over the existing hysteria. It will not be the first time that you have formed the law by a minority opinion. I also agree with enthusiasm with your analysis of motive & intent about which there has been much too meagre discussion in the books. It was with a strong emotion that I read your words, stronger because I had found so little professional support for my own beliefs which would always have been expressed so, had I had the power to express them. I cannot help feeling like thanking you, even though I recall the annoyance it gives me when anyone undertakes to thank me for what I may say in an opinion. I always want to answer, "You fool, *I* didn't do it, it just came that way, quite simply and inevitably. If you thank me, you only show that you haven't the remotest idea of what I am doing." So I shall refrain—expressly anyway.

Meanwhile the merry sport of Red-baiting goes on, and the pack gives tongue more and more shrilly. I really can't get up much sympathy for the victims, but I own to a sense of dismay at the increase in all the symptoms of apparent panic. How far people are getting afraid to speak, who have anything really worth while to say, I don't know, but I am sure that the public generally is becoming rapidly demoralized in all its sense of proportion and toleration. For men who are not cock-sure about everything and especially for those who are not damned cock-sure about anything, the skies have a rather sinister appearance.

Nov. 25, 1919 Faithfully yours

Mr. Justice Holmes Learned Hand

Document No. 7. *Oliver Wendell Holmes to Learned Hand, Nov. 26, 1919*[208]

Supreme Court of the United States,

Washington, D.C.

Nov. 26, 1919

My dear Judge

Your letter gives me the greatest pleasure and I am very much obliged to you for writing to me. Sympathy and agreement always are pleasant but they are much more than that when they come from one that I have learned to think of as I do of you. Accept my thanks.

Ever sincerely yours

Hon. Learned Hand O.W. Holmes

Document No. 8. *Zechariah Chafee, Jr. to Learned Hand, Dec. 2, 1919*

LAW SCHOOL OF HARVARD UNIVERSITY

CAMBRIDGE, MASS.

Judge Learned B. Hand, December 2, 1919.

New York City

Dear Sir,

The Harvard Liberal Club of Boston is anxious to make some public recognition of the stand taken by the two Harvard men on the United

208. Letter from Oliver Wendell Holmes to Learned Hand, Nov. 26, 1919, on file in the Hand Papers, Box 103, Folder 24, Harvard Law Library, Treasure Room.

States Supreme Court on the question of freedom of speech, and a dinner is to be given in their honor on January 12 at the Boston City Club. We should like very much to have you come as the guest of the Liberal Club and be one of the speakers.... Our endeavor is to gather a number of thoughtful speakers who will consider the proper limits of discussion at the present time....

I suppose the *Abrams* decision was the same kind of shock to you that it was to me. At all events Holmes' dissent is bound to win against the unreasoning majority opinion as the years go on, and I console myself occasionally with Browning's "baffled to fight better." If the Circuit Court of Appeals had only sustained you, one of the worst pages in our history might not have been written. I am glad to think of Holmes, Brandeis, and yourself, all Harvard Law School men.

Sincerely,

Zechariah Chafee, Jr.

Document No. 9. *Learned Hand to Zechariah Chafee, Jr., Dec. 3, 1919*

JUDGE LEARNED HAND's CHAMBERS

My dear Mr. Chaffee:

I have your letter of December second. It does not seem likely that I shall be able to get away to Boston at the time you mention, January twelfth, but I should like to do so and I will advise you some time early next month as to what the chances are. I do not think, however, that I had better make a speech. If you are going to have Justices Holmes and Brandeis there, and if they are going to speak, I should hardly feel like adding my mite to their plenitude.

I am not much surprised at the *Abrams* case, although the doctrine laid down seems to be what you so well call the "tendency" doctrine, which seems to me entirely destructive of any genuine freedom. I must say, however, that on the facts it seems to me very questionable whether the decision was not correct. At first, upon reading the opinion, I was quite sure the majority was wrong, but the distinction seems to me pretty tenuous between the purpose to encourage resistance to the United States and merely to prevent the United States from overthrowing the Bolshevik party.

Nevertheless, nothing could be more needed than Justice Holmes's opinion. I am delighted that it appeared. Naturally it is some comfort to find myself not in a judicial minority of one. I think I will look over the case more carefully once again, just for curiosity.

I do not altogether like the way Justice Holmes put the limitation. I myself think it is a little more manageable and quite adequate a distinction to say that there is an absolute and objective test to language. I daresay that it is obstinacy, but I still prefer that which I attempted to state in my first *"Masses"* opinion, rather than to say that the connection between the words used and the evil aimed at should be "immediate and direct."

May I say what great pleasure I had in your article in the June number of the "Review," and that I have heard it highly praised by most competent opinion? I must discount my own pleasure, as you treated me so well, but Graham Wallas and Benjamin Cardozo, both high authorities, have each expressed themselves in high praise of it, and I have no doubt there are many others. I wish I had known half as much as you do about the subject when I wrote my opinion, I could have made it so much better. But you know the conditions under which we have to decide these questions. I sometimes think that I never have learned any law since I left the School, and I am condemned by my own limitations when I come to take up a great subject like this. I think I can also say, without exceeding proper deference, that it would have been a great advantage to us all if, when the final dissent was written, it could have been written with your historical perspective.

Faithfully yours,

Learned Hand

Document No. 10. *Zechariah Chafee, Jr. to Learned Hand, Jan. 6, 1920*

LAW SCHOOL OF HARVARD UNIVERSITY

CAMBRIDGE, MASS.

January 6, 1920

Dear Judge Hand,

... I was very much interested in what you wrote me about Judge Holmes's test and your own, and have been wondering whether it is possible to embrace them both in defining the constitutional limits of speech. Suppose we divide utterance as you do in the Masses case into

(1) political agitation

(2) incitement to resistance to law or violation of law.

If the policy behind the First Amendment is the attainment of truth through discussion, can (2) be excluded from its scope since the inciter wants a smash and not discussion? On the other hand can we say that (1) is protected subject to Holmes's test of "clear and present danger"?

Of course the 1917 Espionage Act, properly construed, did not touch (1) at all.

The broadest possible view (short of absolute license for speech) would be this:—

(1) can never be punished;

(2) can be punished only if it satisfies the danger test. This seems to me the right view as a matter of expediency, but I doubt whether Congress is so closely restricted (apart from Supreme Court deci-

sions on the matter, which show amazing readiness to treat much of (1) as if it were (2), and then smite it even if there is no danger).

Hoping that you can come, I am

Sincerely,

Zechariah Chafee, Jr.

Document No. 11. *Learned Hand to Zechariah Chafee, Jr., Jan. 8, 1920*

JUDGE LEARNED HAND's CHAMBERS

Dear Mr. Chafee:

I am sorry to say that I have got myself tied up in a calendar with cases set every day which will prevent my going to Boston. I ought to have remembered the dinner when I was doing this, but frankly, I did not think of it. . . .[214]

As to the general question to be discussed, I should hardly feel like making a speech. In the first place, I have some doubt about the propriety of a judge's taking sides on such matters anyway. In this especial question it so happens that I have expressed myself officially in opinions which have met with almost unanimous disapproval by other Federal judges, and it seems to me pretty clearly inappropriate that I should take part in what certainly may have the appearance of a protest against those which prevailed. I think I at any rate am disqualified, whether or not the same is to be said of other judges.

My view of the matter is about like this. The State,—you see, I still cling to the old nomenclature,—must regard with disapproval all conduct which tends to produce any violation of its laws. It may, and in my judgment must, permit a great deal of such conduct,—utterances,—notwithstanding their tendency, that is, notwithstanding the probability that it may produce a violation of law. This tolerance, however, depends upon the fact that the utterances in question may have some other result than to produce the evil against which the law is directed. Utterances which can have no other results than to do this may therefore be unconditionally forbidden. It seems to me, I own, that the test of immediacy and directness, while in application it may be about the same as the other I shall suggest is not, strictly speaking, correct; I say this with a genuine diffidence. I prefer a test based upon the nature of the utterance itself. If, taken in its setting, the effect upon the hearers is only to counsel them to violate the law, it is unconditionally illegal. By "counsel" I mean to persuade them that their interest or duty lies in

214. By this time, Chafee had advised Hand that Holmes would not be able to come to the dinner—"I fear that Hamlet is to be left out of the play"—and that Brandeis would probably also be absent. Renewing his urging that Hand attend, Chafee had written: "so I hope very much that you can come, and should especially like to meet you myself. Not only your liberty of the press opinions but technical discussions . . . always make me say, here's the Harvard Law School way of looking at legal problems." Letter from Zechariah Chafee, Jr., to Learned Hand, Dec. 5, 1919, on file in the Hand Papers, Box 15, Folder 26, Harvard Law Library, Treasure Room.

violating the law. It may be that that analysis is inadequate, but it is the only one I have been able to find.

As to other utterances, it appears to me that regardless of their tendency they should be permitted. The reason is that any State which professes to be controlled by public opinion, cannot take sides against any opinion except that which must express itself in the violation of law. On the contrary, it must regard all other expression of opinion as tolerable, if not good. As soon as it does not, it inevitably assumes that one opinion may control in spite of what might become an opposite opinion. It becomes a State based upon some opinion, as against any opinion which may get itself accepted, but it has been indubitably the presupposition of democratic states, however little they have lived up to it.

If so, nothing short of counsel to violate law should be itself illegal. There could be no objection to the rule of the Supreme Court, tendency plus a purpose to produce the evil, even though the words did not come to the objective standard, if one were sure of the result in practical administration. The chance that the State would lose any valuable opinion by suppressing those whose purpose was to produce a violation of law, while they kept on the safe side of counselling it, seems to me much too thin for practical estimate. My own objection to the rule rests in the fact that it exposes all who discuss heated questions to an inquiry before a jury as to their purposes. That inquiry necessarily is of the widest scope and if their general attitude is singular and intransigant, my own belief is that a jury is an insufficient protection. I think it is precisely at those times when alone the freedom of speech becomes important as an institution, that the protection of a jury on such an issue is illusory. The event seems to me to have proved this.

Therefore, to be a real protection to the expression of egregious opinion in times of excitement, I own I cannot see any escape from construing the privilege as absolute, so long as the utterance, objectively regarded, can by any fair construction be held to fall short of counselling violence. That much actually sinister utterance will pass, is undoubtedly true, but the whole institution presupposes a balance of evils. In taking sides I suppose one will range oneself according to one's degree of natural scepticism about opinions in general. For myself I think our chief enemies are Credulity, and his brother Intolerance.

Sincerely yours,

Learned Hand

Document No. 12. *Zechariah Chafee, Jr. to Learned Hand, Oct. 25, 1920*

81 IRVING STREET

CAMBRIDGE

October 25.

My dear Judge Hand,

The time is, I am glad to say, rapidly approaching when my book on Freedom of Speech goes to press. Would you give me the great pleasure of dedicating it to you? It was really your opinion in the Masses case that started me on my work. I feel more and more that it was a staggering task to solve the problem as you did at the very outset of the War, with so few precedents and in such pressure and excitement, and also that if your view had only been followed a living public opinion might have developed in this country on the ultimate purposes of the War, which since the armistice we have fatally lacked. I have spoken of your judgment at length in the body of the book, but I should like to place my opinion of it at the very start.

Sincerely,
Zech Chafee Jr.

Document No. 13. *Learned Hand to Zechariah Chafee, Jr., Oct. 28, 1920*
JUDGE LEARNED HAND's CHAMBERS

New York,
October 28, 1920

Dear Mr. Chafee

Your letter has really thrown me in more embarrassment than I have felt for long, indeed as an old lady would say, I am all upset. That you should select me to dedicate your book to fills me with an unaccountable measure of pleasure. Especially, do I feel this in view of the very slight accord which my opinions ever received from the profession at large. It was indeed scarcely necessary to ask my consent to what I should deem to be a very great honor, but as you have done so, I give it with content and indeed with a sense of great humility. You must know that we who have left the School always look back to it as the "fountain of honor." It is from there that we hope to get approval, and it is by their standards that we wish our work to be judged. It follows that they are likely to be the best judges of its quality.

I cannot conclude without expressing my thanks to you for your kindness and repeating my very genuine sense of the unfitness which I have for the signal honor you mean to give me.

Sincerely yours
Learned Hand

Document No. 14. *Learned Hand to Zechariah Chafee, Jr., Dec. 3, 1920*
JUDGE LEARNED HAND's CHAMBERS

Dear Mr. Chafee

[Chafee had written Hand to say that the book was off the press and on its way to Hand, with its dedication to Hand for his work in the *Masses* case. Chafee had apparently once again praised the *Masses* case in his letter of November 30, which is not preserved. Hand responds:] . . . The case cost me something, at least at the time, and, as you know, it seemed to meet with practically no professional approval whatever. I kept up my hopes till Debs's case and when the whole court affirmed that without laying down anything like what I thought was the rule, I confess I began to wonder whether I had not got some kind of wrong squint on the subject.

Later things turned a little the other way, but your very generous, and, I must believe, exaggerated, recognition of my views has been by far the most whole-hearted support I have ever got. It may interest you to know that when I was suddenly faced with the decision, I looked back with the greatest regret at my wasted days. "Here," I thought, "if you only knew enough, there is a place to state correctly, based on scholarship, what is the right rule. You don't know your job; you don't know anything about the history of the subject, and you must fire off your own funny ideas about what ought or oughtn't to be." If then I could have tapped the resources of the H.L.S. I should have been a happy man. However there was nothing very peculiar in that; I feel it so often, and when a book like Williston comes out, I frankly annex it and seek to learn no more. I dare say yours in its field will take its own stand as a similar authority. I shall surely read it, and if anything occurs to me that seems worth saying I shall take great pleasure in letting you have it.

With renewed thanks and the hope of an early meeting I am

Sincerely yours

December 3, 1920. Learned Hand

Document No. 15. *Learned Hand to Zechariah Chafee, Jr., Jan. 2, 1921,* [Learned Hand's draft]

New York

Jan. 2, 1921

My dear Mr. Chafee

My life here is so full of interruptions that I have only just finished reading "Freedom of Speech" and that too without that chance for a continuous perusal which it deserves, instead of in disconnected snatches now and then. It has more than justified all the hopes I had for it, and it will stand for an indefinite time as the most complete and satisfactory exposition of one of the most baffling subjects in the law. Indeed, how baffling it is I never quite realized till I had been over your pages. I kept feeling,—did I write you so before?—that in writing my own opinion, which you have so kindly noticed, it was well that I knew no more than I did. Like the heathen I was saved by my invincible ignorance, and now that you ask me to suggest any deficiencies in your work I can really do nothing, certainly I can bring nothing that I do not carry from its covers.

As you so often point out, the decision in any given case will depend upon the relative values which the tribunal places on the importance of illumination in general through discussion, and the immediate purpose which is in danger. I doubt whether men will ever succeed at once in feeling intensely the necessity of accomplishing this thing, here and now, and in retaining enough detachment to remember that a precedent is a precedent and that the first taste of blood is often the greatest danger. There will be a few who can at least believe of themselves that they combine the two, but their fellows will always put them in the church of Laodicea, and relatively that is really the place for them—in my judgment the most honorable place of all.[219] In any event the result is that we must be content to worry through with as little inconsistency as possible, making prayerful protestations where we must, and securing heartfelt accord when there is no need for protecting those who talk unpalatably—that is, when they have no chance of success.

I am not wholly in love with Holmesy's test and the reason is this. Once you admit that the matter is one of degree, while you may put it where it genuinely belongs, you so obviously make it a matter of administration, i.e. you give to Tomdickandharry, D.J., so much latitude [here Learned Hand wrote and struck out "as his own fears may require," and continued] that the jig is at once up. Besides their Ineffabilities, the Nine Elder Statesmen, have not shown themselves wholly immune from the "herd instinct" and what seems "immediate and direct" to-day may seem very remote next year even though the circumstances surrounding the utterance be unchanged. I own I should prefer a qualitative formula, hard, conventional, difficult to evade. If it could become sacred by the incrustations of time and precedent it might be made to serve just a little to withhold the torrents of passion to which I suspect democracies will be found more subject than for example the whig autocracy of the 18th century. We know very little yet about enormous aggregations such as our present U.S. How can we catch this fly and preserve it in amber? What sanctified ritualistic phrase shall fix the place where discussion ends and words may ex cathedra be said to have no power to enlighten? You have, I dare say, done well to take what has fallen from Heaven and insist that it is manna rather than to set up any independent solution. "Immediate and direct" is all we have; for God's sake let us not look it in the mouth.

Next as to Uncle Henry Clayton.[220] Did I tell you that I always felt a little responsible? We were glad enough to get anyone who could legally

219. The reference to the "church of Laodicea" may warrant some amplification, both because it may be as obscure to others as it was at first to me, and because it is a charming and apt allusion in describing Learned Hand's courageous, concerned, yet characteristically self-doubting effort to steer a road between immediate societal needs and long-term threats to civil liberties.

The reference is to Chapter 3 of *Revelations. Revelations* 3:14–16 states: "And unto the angel of the church of the Laodiceans write . . . I know thy works, that thou art neither cold nor hot: I would thou wert cold or hot. So then because thou art lukewarm, and neither cold nor hot, I will spue thee out of my mouth."

In the New Testament, that description of "neither cold nor hot" but "lukewarm" is one of condemnation. Hand accepts that description as applicable to his stance—and takes pride in it, for that "neither cold nor hot" position was for him "the most honorable place of all."

220. District Judge Henry D. Clayton—former Congressman from Alabama and author of the Clayton Anti–Trust Act—had presided at the *Abrams* trial. Chafee severely criticized Clayton's conduct of the trial.

sit on a bench, and he was fish because he swam into the net. Then I turned the D. Atty loose on him as usual, and lo! a cause célêbre to the honor of no one. But wasn't it a little *over* irresponsible? I fear I am not free from blame. On the law of that case in the Supreme Court I have reflected a little since reading your article in the H.L.R. and now your chapter, and you have brought me around. At first I was even guilty of what seems to be the universally conceded solecism that the Russian expedition was a part of the war. In that you assure me that only poor Wigmore is with me, respectable enough company usually, but a bit toqué here. Well, will this content you? I am charging the jury vice Uncle Henry and without his racy gift of speech. I say: "you must find that the defendants intended to impede the war, and to do so you must decide either that they had that purpose, which in your places I should find they had not, or that they knew that in stopping the production of munitions till the Russian expedition was given up, the war against Germany would inevitably be impeded. If you think that they understood that they could not stop munitions here without that result, that knowledge is enough special intent under the statute. As to the Russian expedition itself I charge you that while you may not review the wisdom or necessity of including a diversion,—if it was intended to be a diversion, in Siberia, or of the release of Czecho–Slovaks who might be made to fight, the U.S. must show you that it was intended by those who directed it as a part of the war w. Germany, and they have showed nothing whatever about it. They might show it perhaps by calling those who directed it and letting them tell you how it was a part of the war. If they had you would have had to take their word for it, however mistaken as strategy you thought it, unless some one satisfied you that they might not be telling you the truth about their own purposes. As no one has told you anything about it, I must take that phase of it from you."

There, am I orthodox? Does there lurk a heresy somewhere in there? Further, I will not go; "Gott hilfe mich, ich kann nicht anders." I have forgotten whether he "hilfs" or "hilfes" mich. That Uncle Henry is a lazy, violent, ignorant old political hack is true; that he is a rather engaging, worldly wise shrewd old codger by no means devoid of charm, and with some talent for getting under the wire w. the C.C.A. is also true. Amen, he is not coming up again, and he takes his rank with judges of his kidney of the past. You have given him the only immortality he will ever get except from his dishonest Clayton Act. By the way I am doubtful of that severity of taste which left out "Judge Clayton produced the Clayton Act."

Item, Deportations. My God, but I never knew they were like that. That comes of never reading the papers, I suppose. Croly says it was all in his sheet, but at that time I was too mad with their intransigance about the Treaty to do them justice in anything. Your doubts about the constitutionality of any deportation, as distinct from exclusion, law, I think I don't share. On the whole I believe that while the justification for freedom of speech is public enlightenment, historically the "right,"—though I join you in hating the word,—is vested in the speaker constitutionally, and our legislatures can engage ad lib. in obscurantism, provided they don't infringe on an individual who can cry out. Now it is inhuman enough, and it has filled me with loathing to have to recognize it, but it is the fact that if I come here and don't get out my "papers" I stay on sufferance. Quite seriously, I don't think we judges could intervene if they deported all aliens who ate with their knives. After all a court which doesn't recognize the post "as of common right" is not going to strain at gnats like deportations.

But you are quite right only to slide over the constitutional aspect. The law's the thing, and a devilish hateful one. In a recent case I squirmed horribly and finally broke the "head hold" that that damned *Lopez* case[221] had on me, for there was a miserable dishonest ground of deportation which certainly held for aught I could do. Lord, it will go against the grain if I have to let a man be deported for his opinions. But we shall see, we shall see....

Well, you will be glad at last that I have nothing more to say. You have I think done a notably admirable thing,—naturally I am prejudiced,—and you have preserved so excellent a good-humor and so much moderation that the book should have influence now in these less excited times. The work must have been severe and the material hard to get in convenient and condensed form. How did you manage to find the time? That is where you active fellows with jobs who write books puzzle me.

But the thing which is nearest to me is what will be least important to your other readers, that you selected me for a very great honor. I must confess I can't help feeling a little danger in it. It is well and admirable to yield to enthusiasm, but I can't help wondering whether a good many years from now when you are old and I am dead, you may not pick up the book and reading the first page, smile with some amusement and some regret. You really will have nothing personal to regret, even if you would not then think of repeating it, but still if I were there then,—and perhaps I shall come back to plague you for your thoughts, because ghosts have no respect for freedom of opinion,—I should feel a little as though I have passed off on you some false coin. Whatever *you* may come to feel I don't know, but you have made *me* feel very happy, and you have pleased three little girls too, who I am glad to say have never regarded their father hitherto as much more than an elderly man with a

221. Lopez v. Howe, 259 F. 401 (2d Cir. 1919), *appeal dismissed & cert. denied*, 254 U.S. 613 (1920). In *Lopez*, the Second Circuit had broadly interpreted a statutory provision governing the deportation of aliens found to be "advocating or teaching anarchy." Judge Rogers refused to limit the provision to "violent" anarchists and held that it covered "philosophical" anarchists as well: "The fact that he is only a philosophical anarchist, and not an advocate of a resort to force and revolution, makes him, in the opinion of Congress, none the less a dangerous presence.... If the government considers his presence undesirable, because of his advocacy of a doctrine which it regards as inimical to civilization, it must have the power to send him out of the country...." 259 F. at 404.

not wholly reliable amiability, though buttressed with a taste for buffoonery.

Sincerely yours

Learned Hand

Document No. 16. *Zechariah Chafee, Jr., to Learned Hand, Mar. 28, 1921*

LAW SCHOOL OF HARVARD UNIVERSITY,

CAMBRIDGE, MASS.

March 28, 1921

My dear Judge Hand:

.... How far, for the sake of protecting ourselves from an obviously bad man, shall we lay down a general rule which will also include persons whose wickedness is less certain. Of course, when you can put a high board fence around the bad men as you can for murder and many other overt acts, we can handle them very well; but in the sedition cases, the attempt to draw a boundary seems to baffle us all. I agree with you that Holmes' distinction would prove unworkable in many cases. The Jury would go over it rough shod. Thomas Reed Powell feels this even more strongly than I do. Your test is surely easier to apply although our old friend Marc Anthony's speech is continually thrown at me in discussion. After all, we ought to take the best test we can find even though it will sometimes break down, and then prevent its breaking down by using channels outside the law to produce greater tolerance in Judges and jurors and the public at large, so that when the next emergency arises we shall be better prepared....

Yours sincerely,

Zech Chafee Jr.

LEARNED HAND, SOURCES OF TOLERANCE

79 U. Pa. L. Rev. 1 (1930).

Liberty is so much latitude as the powerful choose to accord to the weak. So much perhaps must be admitted for abstract statement; anything short of it appears to lead to inconsistencies. At least no other formula has been devised which will answer. If a community decides that some conduct is prejudicial to itself, and so decides by numbers sufficient to impose its will upon dissenters, I know of no principle which can stay its hand. Perhaps indeed it is no more than a truism to say so; for, when we set ourselves this or that limitation, religion for example, we find that we wince in application. Who can say that the polygamy of the Mormons was not a genuine article of that faith? When we forbade it in the name of our morals, was it not an obvious subterfuge still to insist that we recognized religious freedom? Should we tolerate suttee? If we forbid birth-control in the interest of morals, is it inconceivable that we should tax celibacy? We call that conduct moral about whose effect upon our common interest we have unusually strong convictions. We do not hesitate to impose this upon those who do not share our views; and tolerance ends where faith begins. Plato may have been right about the proper relations of the sexes; we should not allow his experiment to be tried. I do not see how we can set any limits to legitimate coercion beyond those which our forbearance concedes.

And yet, so phrased, we should all agree, I think, that the whole substance of liberty has disappeared. It is intolerable to feel that we are each in the power of the conglomerate conscience of a mass of Babbitts, whose intelligence we do not respect, and whose standards we may detest. Life on their terms would be impossible to endure; of their compunctions we have no guarantee. Who shall deliver us from the body of this death? Certainly there was a meaning in Jefferson's hatred of the interposition of collective pressure, though he extended it to so much of what we now accept as government. We may believe that his emphasis was wrong; that it required a great war eventually to clear away the centrifugal tendencies that underlay it; but shall we not feel with him that it is monstrous to lay open the lives of each to whatever current notions of propriety may ordain? That feeling was the energy that lay back of the first ten amendments to the Constitution, which were really a part of the document itself. Impossible though they be of literal interpretation, like a statute, as counsels of moderation rather than as parts of our constituent law, they represent a mood, an attitude towards life, deep rooted in any enduring society.

Jefferson thought that they could be made to prevail by weakening the central power, but he was too astute an observer to rely upon political device alone. It was in the social, not in the political, constitution of his society that real security lay. For it was impossible to sweep a community of small eighteenth century farmers with mob hysteria. His dislike of cities was in part at any rate because they were subject to just such excesses. He did not, and he could not, see that time was to make rural life as susceptible to moral epidemics as the city mobs which he feared and mistrusted. He set his faith upon isolation and isolation in the end has failed him. The shores are no longer studded with rows of solid columns to break the waves of propaganda; they are not studded with anything whatever, and the waves sweep over them without obstacle and run far up into the land. The question I wish to put before you, which all this introduction is to prepare, is this—which I trust you will forgive me for putting in colloquial form—how far is liberty consistent with the methods of the modern "high-power" salesman? If it is not, what is to be done about it? Being Americans, we are not likely to agree that nothing can.

It has always interested me to read of the observations of those patient anthropologists who associate intimately with our cousin, the chimpanzee. I know a woman who endured the embrace of her son's pet for two hours, lest if disturbed in its caresses it might furiously strangle her. Devotion could scarcely ask more. We may learn much of ourselves from what are now, I believe, called the "conduct patterns" of the anthropoids, but it will not interest me so much as if the study could be of the herds. What I want to know is, why we have become so incurably imitative. I can improvise reasons, but you know how worthless that kind of anthropology is, so I shall spare you. But you will agree about the fact I fancy; you will agree that ideas are as infectious as bacteria and appear to run their course like epidemics. First, there is little immunity; nearly all individuals are susceptible, so that the disease spreads like a prairie fire. Next, a period where the curve of infection, as the pathologists say, remains level; this may last a long time. Last a decline of the curve which, so far as is known, nothing can check. The virus has lost its potency, or some immunity has established itself in a wholly mysterious way.

Ideas, fashions, dogmas, literary, political, scientific, and religious, have a very similar course; they get a currency, spread like wildfire, have their day and thereafter nothing can revive them. Were the old questions ever answered? Has anyone ever proved or disproved the right of secession? Most issues are not decided; their importance passes and they follow after. But in their day they rack the world they infest; men mill about them like a frantic herd: not understanding what their doctrines imply, or whither they lead. To them attach the noblest, and the meanest, motives, indifferent to all but that there is a cause to die for, or to profit by. Such habits are not conducive to the life of reason; that kind of devotion is not the method by which man has raised himself from a savage. Rather by quite another way, by doubt, by trial, by tentative conclusion.

In recent times we have deliberately systematized the production of epidemics in ideas, much as a pathologist experiments with a colony of white mice, who are scarcely less protected. The science of propaganda by no means had its origin in the Great War, but that gave it a greater impetus than ever before. To the advertiser we should look for our best technique. I am told that if I see McCracken's tooth-paste often enough in street cars, on billboards and in shop windows, it makes no difference how determined I may be not to become one of McCracken's customers, I shall buy McCracken's tooth-paste sooner or later, whether I will or no; it is as inevitable as that I shut my eyes when you strike at my face. In much the same way political ideas are spread, and moral too, or for that matter, religious. You know the established way of raising money for the School of Applied and Theoretical Taxidermy. One employs a master mind in group suggestion, with lieutenants and field workers. The possible "prospects" are bombarded with a carefully planned series of what for some unknown reason is called "literature"—leaflets, pictures, pathetic appeals, masterful appeals, appeals to patriotism. Shall American animals suffer the indignity of inadequate stuffing, having themselves given their lives to the cause? Will not you as a loyal American do your bit too; they having made the last supreme sacrifice? Taxidermy is a patriotic duty; are you for taxidermy? If not, you are against it, a taxidermical outlaw at best, at worst a taxidermical Laodicean. Brother, show your colors, join some group, at all costs join, be not a non-joiner, a detestable, lily-livered, half-hearted, supercilious, un-American, whom we would exile if we could and would not pass if he sought entrance.

I submit that a community used to be played on in this way, especially one so large and so homogeneous as we have become, is not a favorable soil for liberty. That plant cannot thrive in such a forcing bed; it is slow growing and needs a more equitable climate. It is the product, not of institutions, but of a temper, of an attitude towards life; of that mood that looks before and after and pines for what is not. It is idle to look to laws, or courts, or principalities, or powers, to secure it. You may write into your constitutions not ten, but fifty, amendments, and it shall not help a farthing, for casuistry will undermine it as casuistry should, if it have no stay but law. It is secure only in that constans et perpetua voluntas suum cuique tribuendi; in that sense of fair play, of give and take, of the uncertainty of human hypothesis, of how changeable and passing are our surest convictions, which has so hard a chance to survive in any times, perhaps especially in our own.

LEARNED HAND TO FELIX FRANKFURTER

June 8, 1951.

I have never felt satisfied that there was not an adequate qualitative distinction, baffling as any rule must become in application. I tried to state it years ago in the *Masses* case but have had to abandon it.

So far as the constitution goes, I cannot see why it should protect any speech which contains "aid[ing], abetting, counsel[ing]" etc., to *violate* any law. If that is mingled with otherwise permissible speech I would leave it to Congress to require the utterer to separate the wheat from the chaff. Holmes was wrong I think when he said that every argument is an "incitement"; that was too loose use of language, for incitement more properly means making yourself a party to the venture: an accessory. Maybe in the end the crux is purpose; I rather think it is; and I am as aware as you can be how unreliable a litmus test that is. Still, we do use it all the time.

LEARNED HAND TO ELLIOT RICHARDSON

Feb. 29, 1952.

I dissent from the whole approach to the problem of Free Speech which the Supreme Court has adopted during the last thirty-five or forty years.... I would make the purpose of the utterer the test of his constitutional protection. Did he seek to bring about a violation of existing law? If he did, I can see no reason why the constitution should protect him, however remote the chance may be of his success.

My reasons may sound didactic and too generalized; but here they are. Every society which promulgates a law means that it shall be obeyed until it is changed, and any society which lays down means by which its laws can be changed makes those means exclusive. ... If so, how in

God's name can an incitement to do what will be unlawful if done, be itself lawful? How do words differ from any other way of bringing about an event? ... Of course, I do not mean that it would be wise to punish all utterances whose purpose is to provoke unlawful conduct. Much of it is much better to ignore; too repressive a policy though in itself lawful may often discourage legitimate and even profitable discourse. But that, I submit, is not a constitutional objection, or at least it ought not to be.

Questions

1) In his letter to Professor Chafee of Jan. 8, 1920, Judge Hand says that "any State which professes to be controlled by public opinion, cannot take sides against any opinion except that which must express itself in the violation of the law. On the contrary, it must regard all other expression of opinion as tolerable, if not good. As soon as it does not, it inevitably assumes that one opinion may control in spite of what may become an opposite opinion. It becomes a State based upon some opinion...." This passage may constitute the first important effort to provide a theoretical foundation for the legal doctrine, which has come to dominate modern First Amendment jurisprudence, that "viewpoint discrimination" is either impermissible per se or at least presumptively invalid. Some modern scholars criticize the Court for embracing too fully and indiscriminately, and placing too much emphasis on, the prohibition on viewpoint discrimination. Does this doctrinal principle necessarily follow from the premise of popular sovereignty, as Hand claims? Are there controversial steps in the syllogism that he asserts?

2) Is Hand analyzing the issue in terms of which test would best serve in periods of unusual political paranoia? Notice his references to "when men are excited" (letter to Holmes, late Mar. 1919), "the existing hysteria.... the symptoms of apparent panic" (letter to Holmes, Nov. 25, 1919), "in times of excitement" (letter to Chafee, Jan. 8, 1920). Can this move be defended? Recall that at the beginning of Chapter Two of *On Liberty*, Mill observes: "Though the law of England, on the subject of the press, is as servile to this day as it was in the time of the Tudors, there is little danger of its actually being put in force against political discussion, except during some temporary panic, when fear of insurrection drives ministers and judges from their propriety...."

3) If Hand's concern is to develop a test that will stand up in stressful times and yet allows for *some* regulation of speech, why not a standard that allows punishment only of the direct advocacy of *immediate* lawless action? Or how about: the direct advocacy of lawless action that is actually followed by such action? In general, it seems a little surprising that Hand was willing to stop short of an overt acts test.

ADDITIONAL READINGS

Hand's life and work

Archibald Cox, Judge Learned Hand and the Interpretation of Statutes, 60 Harv. L. Rev. 370 (1947)

Henry F. Friendly, Learned Hand: An Expression from the Second Circuit, 29 Brooklyn L. Rev. 6 (1962)

Kathryn Griffith, Judge Learned Hand and the Role of the Federal Judiciary (1973)

Learned Hand, The Spirit of Liberty: Papers and Addresses of Learned Hand (1953)

Learned Hand, The Bill of Rights (1964)

Orrin G. Judd, Judge Learned Hand and the Criminal Law, 60 Harv. L. Rev. 405 (1947)

Edward A. Purcell, Jr., Learned Hand: The Jurisprudential Trajectory of an Old Progressive, 43 Buff. L. Rev. 873 (1995)

Charles E. Wyzansky, Jr., Judge Learned Hand's Contribution to Public Law, 60 Harv. L. Rev. 348 (1947)

Masses

Vincent Blasi, Learned Hand and the Self–Government Theory of the First Amendment: *Masses Publishing Co. v. Patten*, 61 U. Colo. L. Rev. 1 (1990)

Zechariah Chafee, Jr., Free Speech in the United States (1941)

Kent Greenawalt, Speech, Crime, and the Uses of Language (1989)

Harry Kalven, Jr, A Worthy Tradition, ch. 10 (1988)

Bernard Schwartz, Holmes v. Hand: Clear and Present Danger or Advocacy of Unlawful Action? 1994 Supreme Court Review 209

Geoffrey R. Stone, Judge Learned Hand and the Espionage Act of 1917: A Mystery Unraveled, 70 U. Chi. L. Rev. 335 (2003)

Chapter Six

OLIVER WENDELL HOLMES

ROBERT W. GORDON, INTRODUCTION: HOLMES'S SHADOW

in The Legacy of Oliver Wendell Holmes, Jr. (Robert W. Gordon ed. 1992).

Oliver Wendell Holmes, Jr., was born in 1841 into the center of Boston legal and literary cultures. His maternal grandfather, Charles Jackson, had been a justice of the Massachusetts Supreme Judicial Court. His father, Dr. Oliver Wendell Holmes, Sr. achieved fame both as a medical researcher and as a man of letters, the author of widely read poems and of *The Autocrat at the Breakfast–Table.* The younger Wendell Holmes attended Harvard College, where he showed a talent for poetry and philosophy and took up the Abolitionist cause. When the Civil War broke out in 1861, Holmes accepted a commission in the Twentieth Massachusetts Volunteers. He was in much of the worst fighting of the war, and was badly wounded three times. Many of his friends and classmates died, some of whom had believed as passionately in the Southern cause as he had in the Northern. The war experience may have laid the foundations of Holmes's aloof detachment, his disengagement from causes and distrust of enthusiasms, and the bleakly skeptical foundations of his general outlook, according to which law and rights were only the systems imposed by force by whatever social groups emerged as dominant in the struggle for existence. From his war service on, he would repeatedly speak of personal and social life in military terms, as a fight carried on by soldiers blindly following incomprehensible orders.

On leaving the army, Holmes chose law as his profession, took his degree from Harvard Law School, and entered private practice in Boston. In 1872 he married Fanny Dixwell. The routines of law practice never much satisfied his philosophical and scholarly curiosity or his consuming ambition to make his reputation as an original legal thinker before the age of forty. He kept up connections with speculative thought through association with a group of thinkers who later became known as the founders of American philosophical pragmatism—Chauncey Wright, Nicholas St. John Green, C. S. Peirce, and (one of Holmes's closest friends in the 1870's) William James—and through friendships with

Henry and Brooks Adams. He took leave from practice to serve as editor of a revision of James Kent's *Commentaries on American Law* (the American equivalent to Blackstone's classic general legal treatise). Holmes used the normally subservient role of editor as an occasion to write compressed synthetic essays on whole fields of common law, ostensibly as mere footnotes to Kent's text. He also signed on as coeditor to the new *American Law Review,* for which he wrote many unsigned articles and reviews on legal theory. "My object in writing these articles," he told a friend, "is to take up from time to time the cardinal principles and conceptions of the law and make a new and more fundamental analysis of them—For the purpose of constructing a new Jurisprudence or New First Book of the law." Most of the major themes of Holmes's mature jurisprudence—the substance of which is discussed at length in the essays in this collection—in fact came together in his book on *The Common Law* (1881), which appeared just short of his fortieth birthday. Though later recognized as a landmark work of legal theory and history, this odd, difficult, confusing, and sometimes dazzling book was largely unappreciated or ignored at the time. On the strength of it, however, Holmes was appointed to a professorship at Harvard Law School. He resigned the professorship after only a year to fill a vacancy on his state's highest court, the Supreme Judicial Court of Massachusetts.

Holmes sat on the Massachusetts court for twenty years (1882–1902), becoming its Chief Justice in 1899. During his tenure there he considered, as he said on looking back, "a thousand cases, many of them on trifling or transitory matters." Few of those cases, it turned out, provided much scope for Holmes's talents as a general theorist and historian of the common law, and even when they did, Holmes proved a cautious judge, usually inclined to decide on narrow grounds rather than on broad ideas of policy. His expressive life in this period was mainly lived outside the court, through frequent trips to England and the intellectual friendships he made there and kept up in correspondence with lawyers and literary men like Sir Frederick Pollock, James Bryce, Leslie Stephen, and his brother Fitzjames. He liked the companionship of women, counted several among his lifelong friends, and on one of his trips to England began a passionate (though mostly epistolary) romance with Clare, Lady Castletown.

In this period Holmes continued to develop the main themes of his jurisprudence—that law embodies the policy preferences, conscious or unconscious, of the dominant forces in the community; that when enacted in legislation, such preferences should be deferred to by the courts unless plainly unconstitutional; that general conceptions such as "liberty" and "property" could not practically resolve such questions as whether competitors or labor unions might be privileged to injure the business of others in pursuit of their own economic advantage; that on such issues and any others on which lines of precedent and policy conflicted, judges had to make policy choices of their own; that policy decisions, though ideally made "scientifically," were necessarily often arbitrary; that, viewed realistically from the standpoint of the practitioner, law was nothing more than predictions what courts would do—and expounded them in some notable articles ("Privilege, Malice, and Intent," 1894), and speeches ("The Path of the Law," 1897). Occasionally his general views percolated through to his judicial opinions. One in particular brought him brief national notoriety: in a case where his court had enjoined peaceful picketing of an antiunion employer, Holmes dissented on the ground that the undoubted injury done to the employer's business by union organizing should be, like competition, privileged as a legitimate form of social struggle.

At the age of 60 Holmes was still mostly unknown outside Massachusetts, save to the handful of international scholars who knew his work in legal theory and history. In 1902 President Theodore Roosevelt appointed him to the United States Supreme Court, where he sat for 30 years. On his retirement from the Court at the age of 90, he was celebrated as few judges have ever been, beloved and revered as a national treasure. He had written another thousand opinions in his characteristically compressed style, so succinct as to be almost gnomic, but lit up by brilliant flashes of aphorism. Mostly he wrote for his Court, but the opinions that made him famous were dissents. About 40 of these dissented from decisions in which the Court had invalidated state regulatory legislation such as protective labor laws, usually on the ground that it deprived persons of "liberty or property without due process of law" in violation of the Fourteenth Amendment to the Constitution. In line with his long-held views that concepts like "liberty" and "property" had controversial and historically shifting meanings, changing with the evolution of ideas and the balance of social power, and that all legislation interfered with liberty or property to some extent so that such concepts were far too general to dictate detailed constitutional restraints, Holmes believed constitutional courts should not interfere with legislative policies unless regulation went to plainly unreasonable extremes.

In many of these cases the outcomes Holmes would have chosen would have had the effect of sustaining Progressive-liberal social legislation; and he was often associated in dissent with the liberal wing of his court, with justices like Louis Brandeis and Harlan Stone. Progressive liberals, delighted to find so powerful and distinguished an ally, especially one so witty in his critique of the "classical" or "formalist" premises underlying the Court majority's conservative jurisprudence, adopted Holmes as their patron saint. He was befriended and almost worshipped by young reformers like Felix Frankfurter, Walter Lippmann, Learned Hand, Jerome Frank and Harold Laski; acknowledged for his intellectual influence by philosophers like John Dewey and Morris R. Cohen and economists like John Commons and Richard T. Ely. His liberal admirers had to forgive or overlook Holmes's undisguised contempt for the actual substance of most liberal reforms and his decisions to sustain highly repressive as well as liberal legislation. But the old judge, who had no children of his own, was greatly warmed by his new friends' praise and attention. They stimulated him to keep up his astonishingly rigorous lifelong project of cosmopolitan self-education in philosophy and literature. They published his collected essays, organized *Festschriften* on his work, quoted his opinions in *The New Republic.* They also very probably influenced the development of his ideas on free speech. In another famous series of dissents, Holmes expounded in memorably majestic language what was for the time (the Red Scares of World War I and after) a remarkably libertarian theory of Constitutional limitations on the power of government to criminalize political dissent as sedition, espionage, or syndicalism.

Holmes retired in 1932, after 50 years on the bench. He died in 1935.

JAMES M. McPHERSON, BATTLE CRY OF FREEDOM: THE CIVIL WAR ERA

(1988).

Jubal Early's 15,000 rebels, after driving David Hunter away from Lynchburg in June, had marched down the Shenandoah Valley and crossed the Potomac on July 6. They bowled over a scratch force of Federals at the Monocacy River east of Frederick on July 9 and marched unopposed toward Washington. This seemed a stunning reversal of the fortunes of war. Northern hopes of capturing Richmond were suddenly replaced by fears for the safety of their own capital. The rebels appeared in front of the Washington defenses five miles north of the White House on July 11. Except for convalescents, militia, and a few odds and ends of army units there were no troops to man them, for Grant had pulled the garrison out for service in Virginia. But the fortifications ringing the capital were immensely strong, and Grant, in response to frantic appeals from the War Department, quickly sent the 6th Corps to Washington. These hardened veterans filed into the works just in time to discourage Early from assaulting them.

During the skirmishing on July 12 a distinguished visitor complete with stovepipe hat appeared at Fort Stevens to witness for the first time the sort of combat into which he had sent a million men over the past three years. Despite warnings, President Lincoln repeatedly stood to peer over the parapet as sharpshooters' bullets whizzed nearby. Out of the corner of his eye a 6th Corps captain—Oliver Wendell Holmes, Jr.—noticed this ungainly civilian popping up. Without recognizing him, Holmes shouted "get down, you damn fool, before you get shot!" Amused by this irreverent command, Lincoln got down and stayed down.

LIVA BAKER, THE JUSTICE FROM BEACON HILL

(1991).

On March 8, 1933, Holmes's ninety-second birthday, a festive lunch with Felix Frankfurter, down from Harvard for the occasion, Holmes's secretary—Donald Hiss that year—and a former secretary, Thomas

Corcoran, marked the event. Hiss had gotten hold of some bootleg champagne, and Holmes drank three or four glasses.

"Young fellow," he told Frankfurter, "I don't want you to misunderstand things; I do not deal with bootleggers but I am open to corruption."

The usual cards, gifts, and telegrams had been coming in all day; there seemed to be no letup, and the telegraph boy was complaining. The court clerk had brought flowers, and Chief Justice Hughes had arrived with his wife shortly after luncheon. At about dusk, America's First Family itself pulled up in front of 1720 I Street, and the new president, Franklin Delano Roosevelt, helped by his son James and his wife, Eleanor, emerged from the car and negotiated the front steps of the red brick house while a crowd gathered to watch. At Frankfurter's instigation, he had interrupted his work on the economic emergency—the banks closed, millions unemployed—to pay a birthday call on the former justice and while away a half hour in the library with him. As the chief executive was about to leave, he turned to Holmes and said:

"Justice, you are the greatest living American. For half the history of the Republic you have seen its greatest events and known its greatest men. What is your advice to me?"

"Mr. President," Holmes replied, "you are in a war; I, too, was in a war. There is only one rule in a war. Form your battalions and fight."

OLIVER WENDELL HOLMES, JR., THE COMMON LAW

(1881).

The life of the law has not been logic: it has been experience. The felt necessities of the time, the prevalent moral and political theories, intuitions of public policy, avowed or unconscious, even the prejudices which judges share with their fellow-men, have had a good deal more to do than the syllogism in determining the rules by which men should be governed. The law embodies the story of a nation's development through many centuries, and it cannot be dealt with as if it contained only the axioms and corollaries of a book of mathematics. In order to know what it is, we must know what it has been, and what it tends to become. We must alternately consult history and existing theories of legislation. But the most difficult labor will be to understand the combination of the two into new products at every stage. The substance of the law at any given time pretty nearly corresponds, so far as it goes, with what is then understood to be convenient; but its form and machinery, and the degree to which it is able to work out desired results, depend very much upon its past.

OLIVER WENDELL HOLMES, JR., THE PATH OF THE LAW

10 Harv. L. Rev. 457 (1897).

The rational study of law is still to a large extent the study of history. History must be a part of the study, because without it we cannot know the precise scope of rules which it is our business to know. It is a part of the rational study, because it is the first step toward an enlightened scepticism, that is, toward a deliberate reconsideration of the worth of those rules. When you get the dragon out of his cave on to the plain and in the daylight, you can count his teeth and claws, and see just what is his strength. But to get him out is only the first step. The next is either to kill him, or to tame him and make him a useful animal. For the rational study of the law the black-letter man may be the man of the present, but the man of the future is the man of statistics and the master of economics.

* * *

To an imagination of any scope the most far-reaching form of power is not money, it is the command of ideas. If you want great examples read Mr. Leslie Stephen's *History of English Thought in the Eighteenth Century,* and see how a hundred years after his death the abstract speculations of Descartes had become a practical force controlling the conduct of men. Read the works of the great German jurists, and see how much more the world is governed today by Kant than by Bonaparte. We cannot all be Descartes or Kant, but we all want happiness. And happiness, I am sure from having known many successful men, cannot be won simply by being counsel for great corporations and having an income of fifty thousand dollars. An intellect great enough to win the prize needs other food beside success. The remoter and more general aspects of the law are those which give it universal interest. It is through them that you not only become a great master in your calling, but connect your subject with the universe and catch an echo of the infinite, a glimpse of its unfathomable process, a hint of the universal law.

LOCHNER v. NEW YORK

Supreme Court of the United States, 1905.
198 U.S. 45, 25 S.Ct. 539, 49 L.Ed. 937.

* * *

MR. JUSTICE HOLMES dissenting:

* * *

This case is decided upon an economic theory which a large part of the country does not entertain. If it were a question whether I agreed with that theory, I should desire to study it further and long before making up my mind. But I do not conceive that to be my duty, because I strongly believe that my agreement or disagreement has nothing to do with the right of a majority to embody their opinions in law. It is settled by various decisions of this court that state constitutions and state laws may regulate life in many ways which we as legislators might think as injudicious, or if you like as tyrannical, as this, and which, equally with this, interfere with the liberty to contract. Sunday laws and usury laws are ancient examples. A more modern one is the prohibition of lotteries. The liberty of the citizen to do as he likes so long as he does not interfere with the liberty of others to do the same, which has been a shibboleth for some well-known writers, is interfered with by school laws, by the Postoffice, by every state or municipal institution which takes his money for purposes thought desirable, whether he likes it or not. The 14th Amendment does not enact Mr. Herbert Spencer's Social Statics.

* * *

OLIVER WENDELL HOLMES, JR., NATURAL LAW

32 Harv. L. Rev. 40 (1918).

It is not enough for the knight of romance that you agree that his lady is a very nice girl—if you do not admit that she is the best that God ever made or will make, you must fight. There is in all men a demand for the superlative, so much so that the poor devil who has no other way of reaching it attains it by getting drunk. It seems to me that this demand is at the bottom of the philosopher's effort to prove that truth is absolute and of the jurist's search for criteria of universal validity which he collects under the head of natural law.

I used to say, when I was young, that truth was the majority vote of that nation that could lick all others. Certainly we may expect that the received opinion about the present war will depend a good deal upon which side wins, (I hope with all my soul it will be mine), and I think that the statement was correct in so far as it implied that our test of truth is a reference to either a present or an imagined future majority in favor of our view. If, as I have suggested elsewhere, the truth may be defined as the system of my (intellectual) limitations, what gives it objectivity is the fact that I find my fellow man to a greater or less extent (never wholly) subject to the same *Can't Helps*. If I think that I am sitting at a table I find that the other persons present agree with me; so if I say that the sum of the angles of a triangle is equal to two right angles. If I am in a minority of one they send for a doctor or lock me up; and I am so far able to transcend the to me convincing testimony of my senses or my reason as to recognize that if I am alone probably something is wrong with my works.

Certitude is not the test of certainty. We have been cock-sure of many things that were not so. If I may quote myself again, property, friendship, and truth have a common root in time. One can not be wrenched from the rocky crevices into which one has grown for many years without feeling that one is attacked in one's life. What we most love and revere generally is determined by early associations. I love granite rocks and barberry bushes, no doubt because with them were my earliest joys that reach back through the past eternity of my life. But while one's experience thus makes certain preferences dogmatic for oneself, recognition of how they came to be so leaves one able to see that others, poor souls, may be equally dogmatic about something else. And this again means scepticism. Not that one's belief or love does not remain. Not that we would not fight and die for it if important—we all, whether we know it or not, are fighting to make the kind of a world that we should like—but that we have learned to recognize that others will fight and die to make a different world, with equal sincerity or belief. Deep-seated preferences can not be argued about—you can not argue a man into liking a glass of beer—and therefore, when differences are sufficiently far reaching, we try to kill the other man rather than let him have his way. But that is perfectly consistent with admitting that, so far as appears, his grounds are just as good as ours.

The jurists who believe in natural law seem to me to be in that naive state of mind that accepts what has been familiar and accepted by them and their neighbors as something that must be accepted by all men everywhere. No doubt it is true that, so far as we can see ahead, some arrangements and the rudiments of familiar institutions seem to be necessary elements in any society that may spring from our own and that would seem to us to be civilized—some form of permanent association between the sexes—some residue of property individually owned—some mode of binding oneself to specified future conduct—at the bottom of all, some protection for the person. But without speculating whether a group is imaginable in which all but the last of these might disappear and the last be subject to qualifications that most of us would abhor, the question remains as to the *Ought* of natural law.

It is true that beliefs and wishes have a transcendental basis in the sense that their foundation is arbitrary. You can not help entertaining and feeling them, and there is an end of it. As an arbitrary fact people wish to live; and we say with various degrees of certainty that they can do so only on certain conditions. To do it they must eat and drink. That necessity is absolute. It is a necessity of less degree but practically general that they should live in society. If they live in society, so far as we can see, there are further conditions. Reason working on experience does tell us, no doubt, that if our wish to live continues, we can do it only on those terms. But that seems to me the whole of the matter. I see no *a priori* duty to live with others and in that way, but simply a statement of what I must do if I wish to remain alive. If I do live with others they tell me that I must do and abstain from doing various things or they will put the screws on to me. I believe that they will, and being of the same mind as to their conduct I not only accept the rules but come in time to accept them with sympathy and emotional affirmation and begin to talk about duties and rights. But for legal purposes a right is only the hypostasis of a prophecy—the imagination of a substance supporting the fact that the public force will be brought to bear upon those who do things said to contravene it—just as we talk of the force of gravitation accounting for the conduct of bodies in space. One phrase adds no more than the other to what we know without it. No doubt behind these legal rights is the fighting will of the subject to maintain them, and the spread of his emotions to the general rules by which they are maintained; but that does not seem to me the same thing as the supposed *a priori* discernment of a duty or the assertion of a preexisting right. A dog will fight for his bone.

The most fundamental of the supposed preexisting rights—the right to life—is sacrificed without a scruple not only in war, but whenever the interest of society, that is, of the predominant power in the community, is thought to demand it. Whether that interest is the interest of mankind in the long run no one can tell, and as, in any event, to those who do not think with Kant and Hegel it is only an interest, the sanctity disappears. I remember a very tender-hearted judge being of opinion that closing a hatch to stop a fire and the destruction of a cargo was justified even if it was known that doing so would stifle a man below. It is idle to illustrate further, because to those who agree with me I am uttering commonplaces and to those who disagree I am ignoring the necessary foundations of thought. The *a priori* men generally call the dissentients superficial. But I do agree with them in believing that one's attitude on these matters is closely connected with one's general attitude toward the universe. Proximately, as has been suggested, it is determined largely by early associations and temperament, coupled with the desire to have an absolute guide. Men to a great extent believe what they want to—although I see in that no basis for a philosophy that tells us what we should want to want.

Now when we come to our attitude toward the universe I do not see any rational ground for demanding the superlative—for being dissatisfied unless we are assured that our truth is cosmic truth, if there is such a thing—that the ultimates of a little creature on this little earth are the last word of the unimaginable whole. If a man sees no reason for believing that significance, consciousness and ideals are more than marks of the finite, that does not justify what has been familiar in French sceptics; getting upon a pedestal and professing to look with haughty scorn upon a world in ruins. The real conclusion is that the part can not swallow the whole—that our categories are not, or may not be, adequate to formulate what we can not know. If we believe that we come out of the universe, not it out of us, we must admit that we do not know what we are talking about when we speak of brute matter. We do know that a certain complex of energies can wag its tail and another can make syllogisms. These are among the powers of the unknown, and if, as maybe, it has still greater powers that we can not understand, as Fabre in his studies of instinct would have us believe, studies that gave Bergson one of the strongest strands for his philosophy and enabled Maeterlinck to make us fancy for a moment that we heard a clang from behind phenomena—if this be true, why should we not be content? Why should we employ the energy that is furnished to us by the cosmos to defy it and shake our fist at the sky? It seems to me silly.

That the universe has in it more than we understand, that the private soldiers have not been told the plan of campaign, or even that there is one, rather than some vaster unthinkable to which every predicate is an impertinence, has no bearing upon our conduct. We still shall fight—all of us because we want to live, some, at least, because we want to realize our spontaneity and prove our powers, for the joy of it, and we may leave to the unknown the supposed final valuation of that which in any event has value to us. It is enough for us that the universe has produced us and has within it, as less than it, all that we believe and love. If we think of our existence not as that of a little god outside, but as that of a ganglion within, we have the infinite behind us. It gives us our only but our adequate significance. A grain of sand has the same, but what competent person supposes that he understands a grain of sand? That is as much beyond our grasp as man. If our imagination is strong enough to accept the vision of ourselves as parts inseverable from the rest, and to extend our final interest beyond the boundary of our skins, it justifies the sacrifice even of our lives for ends outside of ourselves. The motive, to be sure, is the common wants and ideals that we find in man. Philosophy does not furnish motives, but it shows men that they are not fools for doing what they already want to do. It opens to the forlorn hopes on which we throw ourselves away, the vista of the farthest stretch of human thought, the chords of a harmony that breathes from the unknown.

OLIVER WENDELL HOLMES, JR. TO HAROLD J. LASKI

May 12, 1919.

I hated to have to write the *Debs* case and still more those of the other poor devils before us the same day and the week before. I could not see the wisdom of pressing the cases, especially when the fighting was over and I think it quite possible that if I had been on the jury I should have been for acquittal but I cannot doubt that there was evidence warranting a conviction on the disputed issues of fact. Moreover I think the *clauses under consideration* not only were constitutional but were proper enough while the war was on. When people are putting out all their energies in battle I don't think it unreasonable to say we won't have obstacles intentionally put in the way of raising troops—by persuasion any more than by force. But in the main I am for aeration of all effervescing convictions—there is no way so quick for letting them get flat.

RICHARD POLENBERG, FIGHTING FAITHS: THE ABRAMS CASE, THE SUPREME COURT, AND FREE SPEECH

(1987).

The Justice Department and the Sedition Act

The origins of the Sedition Act can be traced to the village of Ashland in Rosebud County, Montana. Only sixty people resided there, about as many as in a single tenement house on East 104th Street. One of them was a man named Ves Hall. A rancher who did not disguise his dislike for the war, Hall allegedly declared in January 1918 "that he would flee to avoid going to the war; that Germany would whip the United States, and he hoped so; . . . and that the United States was only fighting for Wall Street millionaires." Hall apparently reserved some of his choicest invective for Woodrow Wilson, labeling him "a Wall Street tool" and "the crookedest–ever President." Whatever expletive the stenographer deleted, it landed Hall in some "hot and furious saloon arguments" and, before long, helped get him arrested. He was indicted under the Espionage Act of June 15, 1917, which made it a crime for anyone to "willfully make or convey false reports or false statements with intent to interfere with the operation or success" of the armed forces, to "willfully cause or attempt to cause insubordination, disloyalty, mutiny, or refusal of duty" in the armed forces, or to "will-fully obstruct the recruiting or enlistment service of the United States, to the injury of the service of the United States."

Hall's trial began on January 13, 1918, before George M. Bourquin, a resident of Montana for thirty-five years, a state judge since 1904, and United States District Judge since 1912. After a two-week trial Bourquin directed a verdict of acquittal. Even if the jury were to find that Hall had made the statements attributed to him, Bourquin ruled, he would not be guilty. The judge asserted that a person's "beliefs, opinions, and hopes," however wicked, could not be considered false statements within the meaning of the law. Bourquin conceded that actual "slanders of the President and Nation" did, indeed, violate the law, but only insofar as they threatened to interfere with the conduct of the war. The Espionage Act required a "specific intent to commit specific crimes," the judge said, and intent depended on "magnitude and proximity." Hall's statements did not satisfy either criterion, for they were made in a kitchen, at a picnic, and in a saloon where they were less likely to cause interference with the war than a fistfight and, perhaps, "a broken head for the slanderer." Bourquin tried to link the concepts of magnitude and proximity to intent with a simple analogy: "if A shot with a .22 pistol with intent to kill B two or three miles away," the judge observed, "A could not be convicted of attempted murder."

Bourquin added two further qualifications to his stringent interpretation of the Espionage Act. Its reference to "military and naval forces," he said, meant "those organized and in service, not those merely registered and subject to future organization and service." Since there were no soldiers or sailors to be found within hundreds of miles of Rosebud County, Hall's statements did not violate the law. To obtain a conviction for obstructing recruitment, Bourquin added, the government had to demonstrate that some actual obstruction had taken place. "The espionage act does not create the crime of attempting to obstruct, only the crime of actual obstruction, and when causing injury to the service." In Bourquin's view, the Espionage Act was truly intended to punish espionage, not seditious speech. "Congress," he noted, "has not denounced as crimes any mere disloyal utterances, nor any slander or libel of the President or any other officer of the United States."

The decision brought on a tornado of criticism which swept away free speech safeguards. On January 28, the day after Bourquin's ruling, the Governor of Montana declared that its citizens were so outraged they might resort to violence. He summoned the state legislature into special session, and when it met on February 14 he provided the verbal thunder and lightning, reiterating that unless steps were taken to curb sedition the people "may be provoked into becoming a law unto themselves." It took only nine days to pass a criminal syndicalism act that made it a crime "to utter, print, write, or publish any disloyal, profane, scurrilous, contemptuous, or abusive language" about the form of government of the United States, the Constitution, soldiers or sailors, the flag, or the uniform of the Army and Navy; to use language calculated "to incite or inflame resistance" to any duly constituted authority; or to "urge, incite or advocate any curtailment of production" of any vital materiel with intent to hinder the war. Before the storm had subsided, the legislature had impeached a judge who had testified as a character witness for Ves Hall.

Within three months the provisions of the Montana statute would be incorporated, nearly verbatim, into a federal Sedition Act. The Senators from Montana, Henry L. Myers and Thomas J. Walsh, were kept fully informed of events at home, and they soon began to badger the Department of Justice, inquiring first whether Judge Bourquin's ruling could be appealed, and then, when informed it could not be, asking support for additional legislation. The Attorney General, Thomas W. Gregory, had been informed by aides that Bourquin's "occupancy of the bench at this time is a most unfortunate thing for the people of Montana." Late in March, therefore, when Walsh told Gregory that Hall's acquittal made it advisable to amend the Espionage Act "so as to make the escape of those similarly traitorously inclined impossible," the Attorney General replied in a cautious but sympathetic manner. He advised Walsh to have a talk with the responsible officials in the Department's War Emergency Division.

The head of that Division was John Lord O'Brian, and his chief assistant was Alfred Bettman. The two men had much in common. Both were in their mid-forties, graduates of Harvard (O'Brian '96, Bettman '94), and lawyers. Both had practiced law in the cities in which they had grown up, O'Brian in Buffalo and Bettman in Cincinnati, and had then plunged into reform politics. O'Brian had served in the New York State Assembly, held an appointment as United States Attorney for the Western District of New York, and, when war was declared, helped administer the draft as chairman of the appeals board. Bettman, "a person with delicate and refined sensibilities," who was "somewhat retiring and shy in his nature," did not run for office but rather devoted himself to city planning. Calling for a scientific approach to urban problems, he supported a measure enabling cities in Ohio to create planning boards. In 1917, Bettman would recall, "I had such an urge to get into a war job, preferably in the law line, that I could hardly stand it." His friend, O'Brian, provided the opportunity he craved. O'Brian went to the War Emergency Division on October 1, 1917, and Bettman joined him within a month.

Regarding themselves as enlightened liberals, cosmopolitan in outlook, and sensitive to questions of individual liberty, O'Brian and Bettman believed that "freedom of discussion is of the very essence of democracy." Prosecutions under the 1917 Espionage Act, in their view, were constitutionally justifiable as long as they were "not directed at sedition or disloyalty" but at protecting "the orderly execution of the laws relating to the raising of armies." Themselves members of the legal profession, they considered the Department of Justice the most dependable of all government agencies because it "consists of lawyers habituated to weighing facts carefully in their relation to law and having, so to speak, a judicial point of view." Well acquainted with left-wing literature, they were scornful of less knowledgeable officials, especially those in military or naval intelligence, who seemed unable to tell the difference between socialists, communists, and anarchists. American institutions were so sturdy, Bettman thought, that revolutionary doctrines "if permitted to bloom in the open . . . will soon wilt."

At the same time, the two officials, as political realists, were dismayed by the ruling in the Ves Hall case. As O'Brian wrote, Judge Bourquin's unnecessarily strict construction would result in "practically nullifying prosecutions." More dismaying still was the prospect of mob violence against radicals, several incidents of which had recently been reported. A federal law would calm public hysteria, they believed, and also leave the crucial decisions concerning prosecution in the hands of moderate, responsible officials. Bettman and O'Brian probably knew that such a law would claim innocent victims, but, in view of the public's ugly mood, so would the absence of a law. An associate of theirs in the Department of Justice later conceded that the Sedition Act "was hard on the defendants," but saw no viable alternative. "Would it not have been harder on them," he asked rhetorically, "if they had been lynched or tarred and feathered?"

If, as Bettman admitted, "the only excuse" for the Sedition Act was "to allay the public sentiment," this seemed reason enough for the Department of Justice to cooperate with Senator Walsh in drafting the measure. The task of enacting appropriate legislation was greatly simplified because the House of Representatives, on March 4, had passed an amendment, although quite a limited one, to the 1917 Espionage Act. A Liberty Loan drive had been scheduled for April, and so the House, with little discussion, had added a new crime to the existing list: willfully making false statements "with intent to obstruct the sale" of war bonds. This measure then went to the Senate Judiciary Committee, of which Walsh was a member. The Committee rewrote the bill, greatly expanding its scope by incorporating the provisions of the Montana criminal syndicalism act. On April 4 Walsh introduced the Sedition Act—technically, the Senate version of an amendment to the Espionage Act—and, in doing so, asserted that Judge Bourquin's "strained construction" of the earlier statute made enactment necessary.

Someone listening to the statements made on the Senate floor in behalf of the bill might well have concluded that the best of all possible ways to protect freedom of speech was to abridge it. Senators argued, as had officials in the Department of Justice, that the alternative to passing the legislation would be mob violence. Occasionally it was alleged that the reign of terror had already begun, more often that the lawlessness was imminent. Senator Walsh heard from one irate constituent who, on a visit to the West Coast, detected a widespread feeling that "traitors and spies should be shot," and reported "the demand is that some positive action be taken or vigilante committees will be organized and the citizens take it into their own hands." There were, in fact, several instances of vicious beatings and even one ghastly lynching, but there was no evidence to suggest that this brutality was motivated by the government's inability to indict people for seditious speech, or that any such number of indictments would end it.

The opposition came chiefly from Republicans, many of them quite conservative, who feared that the bill could be construed broadly so as to curb their own criticisms of the Wilson administration. Theirs was not a plea for freedom, tolerance, or diversity, much less for respecting the rights of radical dissenters, but rather an argument for exempting their own attacks on the President's policies, however harshly worded, from the strictures of the act. The same Senators who feared that the measure could be used "to suppress free and legitimate discussion by the great mass of the loyal people of this country" did not hesitate to brand a speech by a Socialist candidate for Congress "so disloyal as to border on treason" or to denounce the Wilson administration for coddling spies and saboteurs. The bill's Republican critics were as anxious as its advocates to punish speech that interfered with the war so long as the ground rules were understood: Republican rhetoric was to be considered fair, while radical rhetoric would be declared out of bounds.

But how could one guarantee that these rules would be observed? Joseph I. France, a Maryland Republican, hit upon a possible solution. Employing the language of the state criminal libel laws, he introduced the following amendment: "Nothing in this act shall be construed as limiting the liberty or impairing the right of an individual to publish or speak what is true, with good motives and for justifiable ends." Such a proviso, Republicans believed, would protect loyal but not disloyal speech, for to their way of thinking the former was inherently truthful while the latter manifestly was not. No one expressed this view more clearly than former President Theodore Roosevelt. A bitter critic of the administration, he favored "any legislation, no matter how extreme, that will reach the men who vilify and defame America . . . or who preach sedition directly or indirectly," yet he also defended the people's right "to speak the truth freely of all their public servants, including the President, and to criticize them in the severest terms of truth whenever they come short in their public duty." The Senate narrowly rejected the

France amendment on April 9, but the next day the bill's sponsors, eager to win final approval, withdrew their opposition. The Senate quickly adopted the amendment, and then the Sedition Act, by voice votes.

While a conference committee tried to reconcile the Senate and House versions, the Department of Justice threw its considerable influence behind an effort to have the France amendment deleted. To introduce the element of motive, Bettman informed O'Brian on April 15, would render the act practically useless. Under existing law, "intent" to interfere with the war merely implied that individuals knew, or could be assumed to know, that certain acts were likely to produce certain effects, not that their "motive" or purpose was to produce those results. The act's effectiveness, Bettman observed, depended on "the principle that the motive prompting the propaganda is irrelevant." Otherwise, it would be impossible to move against groups whose propaganda impeded the war effort but which claimed to be acting out of high motives—indeed, in the case of religious pacifists, "out of the highest possible motive." The nightmarish prospects were endless; even socialists said they wanted to promote human happiness, and certainly, Bettman added, "the promotion of human happiness is a good motive." O'Brian summarized these arguments for the House and Senate conferees. "In the field of propaganda," he noted, "especially that dangerous form of propaganda known as pacifism, it would in many cases be very difficult for the prosecution to actually disprove assertions of loyalty and justifiable purpose."

The conference committee did what it was urged to do. On April 22 it reported a version of the Sedition Act which omitted the controversial amendment, a version, France commented bitterly, "altered at the behest and under the direction, as it seems to me, of Mr. John Lord O'Brian of the Department of Justice." On May 4 the Senate voted 48 to 26 to accept the committee's recommendation. The vote divided largely along party lines: 38 Democrats and 10 Republicans favored the measure; 2 Democrats and 24 Republicans opposed it. On May 7 the House approved the measure after an impressive display of magniloquent jabber about "pernicious vermin," "spawn of the lower regions," "poison dark spreaders of revolution," and "white livered rabbits who try to tear down the Army and the Nation under the guise of free speech." The final vote was 293 to 1, with Meyer London, a Socialist from New York, the lone dissenter.

The Sedition Act amended the Espionage Act in a number of significant ways. It was now a crime not only to obstruct, but also to attempt to obstruct, recruitment for the draft, or to "say or do anything" with intent to block the sale of war bonds (although bankers still could offer "bona fide and not disloyal advice" regarding their clients' investment portfolios). Modifying slightly the language used by the Montana legislature, the Sedition Act made it a crime to "willfully utter, print, write, or publish any disloyal, profane, scurrilous, or abusive language" about the United States' form of government, Constitution, military or naval forces, or flag, or about the uniform of the Army and

Navy, or to use any language designed to bring any of these various things "into contempt, scorn, contumely, or disrepute." The act also forbade anyone to "willfully urge, incite, or advocate any curtailment of production in this country of any thing or things ... necessary or essential to the prosecution of the war ... with intent by such curtailment to cripple or hinder the United States in the prosecution of the war." Violations were punishable by a fine not to exceed $10,000, by a prison term of up to twenty years, or both. Finally, the Act augmented the Postmaster General's power. He was already authorized to deny second-class mailing privileges to publications he deemed disloyal; now, "upon evidence satisfactory to him" that individuals were using the mail in violation of the Act, he could stop all their mail deliveries.

* * *

Mollie Steimer was the eldest of six children. Her parents lived in Elizabethport, New Jersey, where her father worked at a low-paying job for the Standard Oil Company. She never forgot his "thin and weary-looking appearance" and, especially, his exhaustion every evening. "How tired he usually comes home from work, and how much so when the day's work lasted fourteen hours! He would just have supper, glance at the newspaper and go to bed. Early in the morning, when all were yet asleep, father rose, took his little bundle and again went to the plant. In this manner of miserable existence the years rolled by. What did this hard laboring man get out of life? Nothing! Absolutely nothing (except suffering)." When she testified at the trial, Steimer could have had no inkling of the twin tragedies that would, the following month, overtake her family. In little more than a week her father died suddenly, and her fourteen-year-old brother, Jack, succumbed to Spanish influenza. Remembering Jack, she had to fight back the tears "which came into my eyes as I thought of that lovable boy, so handsome, so eager to read and to learn, so kind to everybody."

Joining the anarchist movement in January 1917, Steimer later attributed her radical convictions to a number of things: dissatisfaction with her family's poverty-stricken way of life, the bleak prospects that stretched before her in the shirtwaist shops, her reading of such books as Peter Kropotkin's *The Conquest of Bread*, August Bebel's *Women and Socialism*, and Sergei Stepniak's *Underground Russia*, her anger at United States intervention in the Mexican Revolution in 1914, and her opposition to World War I. Yet once, in writing to Emma Goldman, she emphasized another reason, more closely related to an awakening feminist consciousness, for attending anarchist gatherings. From about the age of seventeen, she related, she had attended Goldman's meetings: "I was terribly interested in Birth Control. Not for myself, but for my mother who had 6 children which I considered the greatest misfortune that could befall our family and sought help from such as you and Marguerite [Sanger] to save our house from more babies." As an anarchist, Steimer was distinguished by her uncompromising spirit. Even among men and women who were known, as a group, for their implacable, unyielding ways, she gained a reputation for obstinacy and inflexibility. Whatever others may have thought, Steimer never regarded herself as contumacious. "since I first joined the Fr[eedom] Group, I refused to be a follower," she stated matter-of-factly. "I tried to be myself."

Steimer's courtroom demeanor served notice that, even when standing trial, she would continue to be herself. When the judge entered the chamber, for example, and the bailiff ordered everyone to rise, Steimer kept her seat. One newsman reported, half-wonderingly, half-admiringly, "The marshals in charge of the prisoners are totally at a loss what to do about Mollie when the judge comes in. She resolutely refuses to rise. They could lift her up with one of their little fingers, but content themselves with looking in bewilderment at her silk back and her curly hair and holding their breath till everybody sits down again." Taking the witness stand, she brushed aside the usual formalities. She "refused to take the oath and it was ruled that her testimony should go into the record for what it was worth." Harry Weinberger made the mistake, in asking his first question, of calling her by her first name, a liberty he had not taken in addressing the male defendants. "Mollie, where were you born?" When there was no reply, he rephrased the question. "Miss Steimer, where were you born?" Then he got an answer: "In Russia."

Steimer was considerably less willing than her codefendants to allow Weinberger to lead her through his direct examination. While they answered all his questions about the printing and distribution of the leaflets, she would talk only about her own role, and then only circumspectly. When she admitted distributing the leaflets, Weinberger asked, "Where did you give them out?" "In various places," she replied. When he repeated the question, she admonished him, saying, "I don't think it necessary to mention the places." He insisted. "Now, mention just one or two of those places. That is what I want," and her answer, again, "I don't see the necessity of it." "You leave the necessity to me," Weinberger said, understandably exasperated. "I don't think it necessary to do that," she replied firmly. Henry DeLamar Clayton, finally thinking he had found a common ground with Harry Weinberger, made a rare, fraternal comment: "Well, it is the old adage, maybe, Brother Weinberger, "Convince a woman against her will, she is of the same opinion still." "Ignoring the gibe, Steimer calmly volunteered the information that she had distributed the leaflets 'in places where the most workers were working'. I have been trying to reach masses of people, and it does not matter where or in what places I did that."

Steimer, of course, cooperated fully with Weinberger when it came to eliciting her "intent," that is to say, her reason for distributing the leaflets. Her purpose, she said, was "to call the attention of the workers to the fact that international capitalism seeks to crush the Russian Revolution, that the Allies were acting just as tyrannic, just as cruel as the Germans, by invading a neutral country and assailing those workers who were defending the revolutionary freedom." Disclaiming any sympathy for Germany, for militarism anywhere was always an evil, she insisted that she had only wanted to point out the hypocrisy of the United States government which said it supported the right of national self-determination and yet "sought to crush the Russian Revolution and abolish the present government that the Russian workers established." Since the Bolsheviks represented the producing classes, she argued, "I do uphold the Bolshevik movement." With that Weinberger ended his direct examination.

Miller began his cross-examination by asking Steimer if she was an anarchist. Unwilling to provide the simple "yes" or "no" the prosecutor was looking for, she insisted on explaining what she meant by anarchism. Judge Clayton ruled that she was entitled to offer such an explanation. So Steimer stated, "By anarchism, I understand a new social order, where no group of people shall be in power, or no group of people shall be governed by another group of people. Individual freedom shall prevail in the full sense of the word. Private ownership shall be abolished. Every person shall have an equal opportunity to develop himself well, both mentally and physically. We shall not have to struggle for our daily existence, as we do now. No one shall live on the product of others. Every person shall produce as much as he can, and enjoy as much as he needs—receive according to his needs. Instead of striving to get money, we shall strive towards education, towards knowledge." She added that "the workers of Russia are trying to establish such a system." "They are only trying to?" Miller asked. "Yes," the witness said, "if you should not crush them they would succeed."

Steimer similarly stood her ground when Miller badgered her about her concept of law. The prosecutor asked if she believed in laws, only to have her reply, "Explain to me first what you mean by law." Judge Clayton then decided to take a hand in the proceedings. Did she believe in the law under which she had been indicted? "No, I don't believe in such laws." "And you are trying to defeat that law?" "I am." Miller tried again, with the same result: "Do you believe in any laws?" "Please [tell] me what do you mean by law." "Will you answer the question?" "I will not, unless I know exactly what you mean by your question." When, answering another of the judge's queries, Steimer granted "that the people ought not to kill each other," Clayton asked whether that did not justify passing a law against murder. Steimer, following Kropotkin, insisted that in a just society, where everyone "should be well developed mentally" and "able to enjoy life," crime would vanish. "We would not need any laws to punish, and we would not need any courts." Miller asked, "But at the present time we need some laws?" "Because the system is rotten," she answered.

After listening to Steimer's testimony for a few minutes, Judge Clayton began to argue with her, not about the leaflets whose distribution had led to her arrest, nor even about intervention in Soviet Russia, but about marriage and free love. He asked whether she believed in any of the laws designed to protect public morality. "I do not think the laws which are in existence today do protect morality," she replied. What of the laws regarding marriage, the judge asked. Steimer said that women usually got married for economic reasons, "not because of love," and stayed married for the wrong reasons. "What is the use of a law combining them, when their hearts are not combined any more?" she asked. The judge said, "And when the love grows cold, you think they ought to end the marriage relation; that is your idea?" The witness responded icily, "Well, I do not think that this has anything to do with this trial." The judge agreed, but a few minutes later was again asking Steimer whether she believed in polygamy, or in polyandry, or in free love. Thereupon, Steimer turned the tables on Clayton, and began asking the questions. Noting that laws against infidelity were notorious failures, she continued, "May I ask you . . . do not thousands and thousands of such cases prevail anyhow? You have the law." "People may violate vows," the judge conceded. "They do sometimes, and society is trying to protect itself." "It does not succeed," Steimer commented.

Judge Clayton told Steimer that her answers to these questions would "not affect your guilt or innocence in this case," but defended his asking them on the irrelevant grounds that a belief in polygamy was one of the bases for denying citizenship to an alien. Since Steimer had already admitted to being an anarchist, she was legally subject to deportation, and was surely not going to be applying for citizenship. More likely, Clayton's questions were intended to put the witness, or at least her views, in a ludicrous light. Steimer, however, never wavered. "I believe that two people should combine, only when they love each other, honestly and truly, and not because of any other circumstances." Her unwillingness to exhibit the least deference—indeed, her continued defiance—obviously offended the Alabama patriarch. Later in the trial, when she tried to address the courtroom spectators directly, Clayton barked, "You turn around and address the Court. This is one time, Mollie, when you are brought in touch with a knowledge that there is some authority, even over an anarchistic woman."

His curiosity as to Steimer's view of conjugal bliss and the nuptial bond satisfied, the judge permitted the prosecution and defense to resume their sparring over the issue of intent. When Steimer said she favored a general strike to block intervention in Russia, Miller asked, "Did you include the workers in the ammunition factories in your general word "workers' here?" "Yes," she replied. Weinberger immediately tried to repair the damage. He again asked Steimer whether the purpose of the general strike "was to prevent intervention in Russia" rather than "to interfere in the war against Germany." "The war between Germany and the United States does not concern me," she answered, "because I wish to see militarism throughout the entire world crushed by the workers." Miller returned to the attack, centering on the legal distinction between intent and motive. "If all of these munition workers stopped making munitions, do you think that would hinder the United States in the war with Germany?" All Steimer could say, lamely but truthfully, was, "It did not matter to me."

Once, when Steimer refused to give as specific an answer as District Attorney Miller thought she should, he asked the judge to find her in contempt. Clayton responded, "If I ordered her to jail, that would stop the trial. What good would that do? You will just have to do the best you can, Brother Miller." During the entire trial it was only when a woman was testifying—and being uncooperative!—that Judge Clayton addressed the prosecuting and defense attorneys as "Brother," leading one to suspect that he used the term not merely in its familiar courtroom sense but androcentrically, as if to suggest that menfolk shared a common outlook, which, in the very nature of things, was beyond any woman's comprehension. Although Steimer was arrested, indicted, and tried for expressing views deriving from her anarchism, not her feminism, the fact that she was a woman had a great deal to do with the kind of anarchist she became, with her behavior in the courtroom, and with the response she elicited from the judge.

There was, therefore, a good reason for the New York *Tribune* to term her "the young feminist radical," and an even better reason for Emma Goldman, learning, in prison, of the courtroom proceedings, to write, "Mollie's stand is the most inspiring event in my public career. Young boys have made such a stand before ... But not one girl.... So it was left to a child of 18, a Russian Jewess, to redeem our sex & a great principle at that. My work has not been in vain.... I am supremely happy to know that the ideals which have meant life itself to me, have now found a new champion, one so brave and clear & consistent."

ABRAMS v. UNITED STATES

Supreme Court of the United States, 1919.
250 U.S. 616, 40 S.Ct. 17, 63 L.Ed. 1173.

MR. JUSTICE CLARKE delivered the opinion of the Court.

On a single indictment, containing four counts, the five plaintiffs in error, hereinafter designated the defendants, were convicted of conspiring to violate provisions of the Espionage Act of Congress (section 3, title I), of Act June 15, 1917, c. 30, 40 Stat. 219, as amended by Act May 16, 1918, c. 75, 40 Stat. 553.

Each of the first three counts charged the defendants with conspiring, when the United States was at war with the Imperial Government of Germany, to unlawfully utter, print, write and publish: In the first count, "disloyal, scurrilous and abusive language about the form of government of the United States;" in the second count, language "intended to bring the form of government of the United States into contempt, scorn, contumely, and disrepute;" and in the third count, language "intended to incite, provoke and encourage resistance to the United States in said war." The charge in the fourth count was that the defendants conspired "when the United States was at war with the Imperial German Government, * * * unlawfully and willfully, by utterance, writing, printing and publication to urge, incite and advocate curtailment of production of things and products, to wit, ordnance and ammunition, necessary and essential to the prosecution of the war." The offenses were charged in the language of the act of Congress.

It was charged in each count of the indictment that it was a part of the conspiracy that the defendants would attempt to accomplish their unlawful purpose by printing, writing and distributing in the city of New York many copies of a leaflet or circular, printed in the English language, and of another printed in the Yiddish language, copies of which, properly identified, were attached to the indictment.

All of the five defendants were born in Russia. They were intelligent, had considerable schooling, and at the time they were arrested they had lived in the United States terms varying from five to ten years, but none of them had applied for naturalization. Four of them testified as witnesses in their own behalf, and of these three frankly avowed that they were "rebels," "revolutionists," "anarchists," that they did not believe in government in any form, and they declared that they had no interest whatever in the government of the United States. The fourth defendant testified that he was a "socialist" and believed in "a proper kind of government, not capitalistic," but in his classification the government of the United States was "capitalistic."

It was admitted on the trial that the defendants had united to print and distribute the described circulars and that 5,000 of them had been printed and distributed about the 22d day of August, 1918. The group had a meeting place in New York City, in rooms rented by defendant Abrams, under an assumed name, and there the subject of printing the circulars was discussed about two weeks before the defendants were arrested. The defendant Abrams, although not a printer, on July 27, 1918, purchased the printing outfit with which the circulars were printed, and installed it in a basement room where the work was done at night. The circulars were distributed, some by throwing them from a window of a building where one of the defendants was employed and others secretly, in New York City.

The defendants pleaded "not guilty," and the case of the government consisted in showing the facts we have stated, and in introducing in evidence copies of the two printed circulars attached to the indictment, a sheet entitled "Revolutionists Unite for Action," written by the defendant Lipman, and found on him when he was arrested, and another paper, found at the headquarters of the group, and for which Abrams assumed responsibility.

Thus the conspiracy and the doing of the overt acts charged were largely admitted and were fully established.

On the record thus described it is argued, somewhat faintly, that the acts charged against the defendants were not unlawful because within the protection of that freedom of speech and of the press which is guaranteed by the First Amendment to the Constitution of the United States, and that the entire Espionage Act is unconstitutional because in conflict with that amendment.

This contention is sufficiently discussed and is definitely negatived in *Schenck v. United States* and *Baer v. United States*, 249 U. S. 47 and in *Frohwerk v. United States*, 249 U.S. 204.

The claim chiefly elaborated upon by the defendants in the oral argument and in their brief is that there is no substantial evidence in the record to support the judgment upon the verdict of guilty and that the motion of the defendants for an instructed verdict in their favor was erroneously denied. A question of law is thus presented, which calls for an examination of the record, not for the purpose of weighing conflicting testimony, but only to determine whether there was some evidence, competent and substantial, before the jury, fairly tending to sustain the verdict. We shall not need to consider the sufficiency, under the rule just stated, of the evidence introduced as to all of the counts of the indictment, for, since the sentence imposed did not exceed that which might lawfully have been imposed under any single count, the judgment upon the verdict of the jury must be affirmed if the evidence is sufficient to sustain any one of the counts.

The first of the two articles attached to the indictment is conspicuously headed, "The Hypocrisy of the United States and her Allies." After denouncing President Wilson as a hypocrite and a coward because troops were sent into Russia, it proceeds to assail our government in general, saying:

> "His [the President's] shameful, cowardly silence about the intervention in Russia reveals the hypocrisy of the plutocratic gang in Washington and vicinity."

It continues:

> He [the President] is too much of a coward to come out openly and say: "We capitalistic nations cannot afford to have a proletarian republic in Russia."

Among the capitalistic nations Abrams testified the United States was included.

Growing more inflammatory as it proceeds, the circular culminates in:

> "The Russian Revolution cries: Workers of the World! Awake! Rise! Put down your enemy and mine!"
>
> "Yes friends, there is only one enemy of the workers of the world and that is CAPITALISM."

This is clearly an appeal to the "workers" of this country to arise and put down by force the government of the United States which they characterize as their "hypocritical," "cowardly" and "capitalistic" enemy.

It concludes:

> "Awake! Awake, you Workers of the World!
>
> REVOLUTIONISTS."

The second of the articles was printed in the Yiddish language and in the translation is headed, "Workers—Wake Up." After referring to "his Majesty, Mr. Wilson, and the rest of the gang, dogs of all colors!" it continues: "Workers, Russian emigrants, you who had the least belief in the honesty of *our* government,"—which defendants admitted referred to the United States government—

> "must now throw away all confidence, must spit in the face the false, hypocritic, military propaganda which has fooled you so relentlessly, calling forth your sympathy, your help, to the prosecution of the war."

The purpose of this obviously was to persuade the persons to whom it was addressed to turn a deaf ear to patriotic appeals in behalf of the government of the United States, and to cease to render it assistance in the prosecution of the war.

It goes on:

> "With the money which you have loaned, or are going to loan them, they will make bullets not only for the Germans, but also for the Workers Soviets of Russia. *Workers in the ammunition factories, you are producing bullets, bayonets, cannon, to murder not only the Germans, but also your dearest, best, who are in Russia and are fighting for freedom.*"

It will not do to say, as is now argued, that the only intent of these defendants was to prevent injury to the Russian cause. Men must be held to have intended, and to be accountable for, the effects which their acts were likely to produce. Even if their primary purpose and intent was to aid the cause of the Russian Revolution, the plan of action which they adopted necessarily involved, before it could be realized, defeat of the war program of the United States, for the obvious effect of this appeal, if it should become effective, as they hoped it might, would be to persuade persons of character such as those whom they regarded themselves as addressing, not to aid government loans and not to work in ammunition factories, where their work would produce "bullets, bayonets, cannon" and other munitions of war, the use of which would cause the "murder" of Germans and Russians.

Again, the spirit becomes more bitter as it proceeds to declare that—

> "America and her Allies have betrayed [the Workers]. Their robberish aims are clear to all men. The destruction of the Russian Revolution, that is the politics of the march to Russia."
>
> "*Workers, our reply to the barbaric intervention has to be a general strike! An open challenge* only will let the government know that not only the Russian Worker fights for freedom, but also *here in America lives the spirit of Revolution.*"

This is not an attempt to bring about a change of administration by candid discussion, for no matter what may have incited the outbreak on the part of the defendant anarchists, the manifest purpose of such a publication was to create an attempt to defeat the war plans of the government of the United States, by bringing upon the country the paralysis of a general strike, thereby arresting the production of all munitions and other things essential to the conduct of the war.

This purpose is emphasized in the next paragraph, which reads:

> "Do not let the government scare you with their wild punishment in prisons, hanging and shooting. We must not and will not betray the splendid fighters of Russia. *Workers, up to fight.*"

After more of the same kind, the circular concludes:

> "Woe unto those who will be in the way of progress. Let solidarity live!"

It is signed, "The Rebels."

That the interpretation we have put upon these articles, circulated in the greatest port of our land, from which great numbers of soldiers were at the time taking ship daily, and in which great quantities of war supplies of every kind were at the time being manufactured for transportation overseas, is not only the fair interpretation of them, but that it is the meaning which their authors consciously intended should be conveyed by them to others is further shown by the additional writings found in the meeting place of the defendant group and on the person of one of them. One of these circulars is headed: "Revolutionists! Unite for Action!"

After denouncing the President as "Our Kaiser" and the hypocrisy of the United States and her Allies, this article concludes:

> "socialists, Anarchists, Industrial Workers of the World, Socialists, Labor party men and other revolutionary organizations *Unite for Action* and let us save the Workers" Republic of Russia!"
>
> "*Know you lovers of freedom that in order to save the Russian revolution, we must keep the armies of the allied countries busy at home.*"

Thus was again avowed the purpose to throw the country into a state of revolution, if possible, and to thereby frustrate the military program of the government.

The remaining article, after denouncing the President for what is characterized as hostility to the Russian revolution, continues:

> "We, the toilers of America, who believe in real liberty, shall *pledge ourselves*, in case the United States will participate in that bloody conspiracy against Russia, *to create so great a disturbance that the autocrats of America shall be compelled to keep their armies at home, and not be able to spare any for Russia.*"

It concludes with this definite threat of armed rebellion:

> "If they will use arms against the Russian people to enforce their standard of order, *so will we use arms*, and they shall never see the ruin of the Russian Revolution."

These excerpts sufficiently show, that while the immediate occasion for this particular outbreak of lawlessness, on the part of the defendant alien anarchists, may have been resentment caused by our government sending troops into Russia as a strategic operation against the Germans on the eastern battle front, yet the plain purpose of their propaganda was to excite, at the supreme crisis of the war, disaffection, sedition, riots, and, as they hoped, revolution, in this country for the purpose of embarrassing and if possible defeating the military plans of the government in Europe. A technical distinction may perhaps be taken between disloyal and abusive language applied to the *form* of our government or language intended to bring the *form* of our government into contempt and disrepute, and language of like character and intended to produce like results directed against the President and Congress, the agencies through which that form of government must function in time of war. But it is not necessary to a decision of this case to consider whether such distinction is vital or merely formal, for the language of these circulars was obviously intended to provoke and to encourage resistance to the United States in the war, as the third count runs, and, the defendants, in terms, plainly urged and advocated a resort to a general strike of workers in ammunition factories for the purpose of curtailing the production of ordnance and munitions necessary and essential to the prosecution of the war as is charged in the fourth count. Thus it is clear not only that some evidence but that much persuasive evidence was before the jury tending to prove that the defendants were guilty as charged in both the third and fourth counts of the indictment and under the long established rule of law hereinbefore stated the judgment of the District Court must be

Affirmed.

MR. JUSTICE HOLMES, dissenting.

This indictment is founded wholly upon the publication of two leaflets which I shall describe in a moment. The first count charges a conspiracy pending the war with Germany to publish abusive language about the form of government of the United States, laying the preparation and publishing of the first leaflet as overt acts. The second count charges a conspiracy pending the war to publish language intended to bring the form of government into contempt, laying the preparation and publishing of the two leaflets as overt acts. The third count alleges a conspiracy to encourage resistance to the United States in the same war and to attempt to effectuate the purpose by publishing the same leaflets. The fourth count lays a conspiracy to incite curtailment of production of things necessary to the prosecution of the war and to attempt to accomplish it by publishing the second leaflet to which I have referred.

The first of these leaflets says that the President's cowardly silence about the intervention in Russia reveals the hypocrisy of the plutocratic gang in Washington. It intimates that "German militarism combined with allied capitalism to crush the Russian revolution"—goes on that the tyrants of the world fight each other until they see a common enemy—working class enlightenment, when they combine to crush it; and that now militarism and capitalism combined, though not openly, to crush the Russian revolution. It says that there is only one enemy of the workers of the world and that is capitalism; that it is a crime for workers of

America, etc., to fight the workers' republic of Russia, and ends "Awake! Awake, you workers of the world! Revolutionists." A note adds "It is absurd to call us pro-German. We hate and despise German militarism more than do you hypocritical tyrants. We have more reason for denouncing German militarism than has the coward of the White House."

The other leaflet, headed "Workers—Wake Up," with abusive language says that America together with the Allies will march for Russia to help the Czecko–Slovaks in their struggle against the Bolsheviki, and that this time the hypocrites shall not fool the Russian emigrants and friends of Russia in America. It tells the Russian emigrants that they now must spit in the face of the false military propaganda by which their sympathy and help to the prosecution of the war have been called forth and says that with the money they have lent or are going to lend "they will make bullets not only for the Germans but also for the Workers Soviets of Russia," and further, "Workers in the ammunition factories, you are producing bullets, bayonets, cannon to murder not only the Germans, but also your dearest, best, who are in Russia fighting for freedom." It then appeals to the same Russian emigrants at some length not to consent to the "inquisitionary expedition in Russia," and says that the destruction of the Russian revolution is "the politics of the march on Russia." The leaflet winds up by saying "Workers, our reply to this barbaric intervention has to be a general strike!" and after a few words on the spirit of revolution, exhortations not to be afraid, and some usual tall talk ends "Woe unto those who will be in the way of progress. Let solidarity live! The Rebels."

No argument seems to be necessary to show that these pronunciamentos in no way attack the form of government of the United States, or that they do not support either of the first two counts. What little I have to say about the third count may be postponed until I have considered the fourth. With regard to that it seems too plain to be denied that the suggestion to workers in the ammunition factories that they are producing bullets to murder their dearest, and the further advocacy of a general strike, both in the second leaflet, do urge curtailment of production of things necessary to the prosecution of the war within the meaning of the Act of May 16, 1918, c. 75, 40 Stat. 553, amending section 3 of the earlier Act of 1917 (Comp. St. § 10212c). But to make the conduct criminal that statute requires that it should be "with intent by such curtailment to cripple or hinder the United States in the prosecution of the war." It seems to me that no such intent is proved.

I am aware of course that the word "intent" as vaguely used in ordinary legal discussion means no more than knowledge at the time of the act that the consequences said to be intended will ensue. Even less than that will satisfy the general principle of civil and criminal liability. A man may have to pay damages, may be sent to prison, at common law might be hanged, if at the time of his act he knew facts from which common experience showed that the consequences would follow, whether he individually could foresee them or not. But, when words are used exactly, a deed is not done with intent to produce a consequence unless that consequence is the aim of the deed. It may be obvious, and obvious to the actor, that the consequence will follow, and he may be liable for it even if he regrets it, but he does not do the act with intent to produce it unless the aim to produce it is the proximate motive of the specific act, although there may be some deeper motive behind.

It seems to me that this statute must be taken to use its words in a strict and accurate sense. They would be absurd in any other. A patriot might think that we were wasting money on aeroplanes, or making more cannon of a certain kind than we needed, and might advocate curtailment with success, yet even if it turned out that the curtailment hindered and was thought by other minds to have been obviously likely to hinder the United States in the prosecution of the war, no one would hold such conduct a crime. I admit that my illustration does not answer all that might be said but it is enough to show what I think and to let me pass to a more important aspect of the case. I refer to the First Amendment to the Constitution that Congress shall make no law abridging the freedom of speech.

I never have seen any reason to doubt that the questions of law that alone were before this Court in the cases of *Schenck, Frohwerk,* and *Debs* were rightly decided. I do not doubt for a moment that by the same reasoning that would justify punishing persuasion to murder, the United States constitutionally may punish speech that produces or is intended to produce a clear and imminent danger that it will bring about forthwith certain substantive evils that the United States constitutionally may seek to prevent. The power undoubtedly is greater in time of war than in time of peace because war opens dangers that do not exist at other times.

But as against dangers peculiar to war, as against others, the principle of the right to free speech is always the same. It is only the present danger of immediate evil or an intent to bring it about that warrants Congress in setting a limit to the expression of opinion where private rights are not concerned. Congress certainly cannot forbid all effort to change the mind of the country. Now nobody can suppose that the surreptitious publishing of a silly leaflet by an unknown man, without more, would present any immediate danger that its opinions would hinder the success of the government arms or have any appreciable tendency to do so. Publishing those opinions for the very purpose of obstructing, however, might indicate a greater danger and at any rate would have the quality of an attempt. So I assume that the second leaflet if published for the purposes alleged in the fourth count might be punishable. But it seems pretty clear to me that nothing less than that would bring these papers within the scope of this law. An actual intent in the sense that I have explained is necessary to constitute an attempt, where a further act of the same individual is required to complete the substantive crime, for reasons given in *Swift & Co. v. United States*, 196 U. S. 375, 396. It is necessary where the success of the attempt depends upon others because if that intent is not present the actor's aim may be accomplished without bringing about the evils sought to be checked. An intent to prevent interference with the revolution in Russia might have been satisfied without any hindrance to carrying on the war in which we were engaged.

I do not see how anyone can find the intent required by the statute in any of the defendant's words. The second leaflet is the only one that affords even a foundation for the charge, and there, without invoking the hatred of German militarism expressed in the former one, it is evident from the beginning to the end that the only object of the paper is to help Russia and stop American intervention there against the popular government—not to impede the United States in the war that it was carrying on. To say that two phrases taken literally might import a suggestion of conduct that would have interference with the war as an indirect and probably undesired effect seems to me by no means enough to show an attempt to produce that effect.

I return for a moment to the third count. That charges an intent to provoke resistance to the United States in its war with Germany. Taking the clause in the statute that deals with that in connection with the other elaborate provisions of the Act, I think that resistance to the United States means some forcible act of opposition to some proceeding of the United States in pursuance of the war. I think the intent must be the specific intent that I have described and for the reasons that I have given I think that no such intent was proved or existed in fact. I also think that there is no hint at resistance to the United States as I construe the phrase.

In this case sentences of twenty years imprisonment have been imposed for the publishing of two leaflets that I believe the defendants had as much right to publish as the Government has to publish the Constitution of the United States now vainly invoked by them. Even if I am technically wrong and enough can be squeezed from these poor and puny anonymities to turn the color of legal litmus paper; I will add, even if what I think the necessary intent were shown; the most nominal punishment seems to me all that possible could be inflicted, unless the defendants are to be made to suffer not for what the indictment alleges but for the creed that they avow—a creed that I believe to be the creed of ignorance and immaturity when honestly held, as I see no reason to doubt that it was held here but which, although made the subject of examination at the trial, no one has a right even to consider in dealing with the charges before the Court.

Persecution for the expression of opinions seems to me perfectly logical. If you have no doubt of your premises or your power and want a certain result with all your heart you naturally express your wishes in law and sweep away all opposition. To allow opposition by speech seems to indicate that you think the speech impotent, as when a man says that he has squared the circle, or that you do not care whole-heartedly for the result, or that you doubt either your power or your premises. But when men have realized that time has upset many fighting faiths, they may come to believe even more than they believe the very foundations of their own conduct that the ultimate good desired is better reached by free trade in ideas—that the best test of truth is the power of the thought to get itself accepted in the competition of the market, and that truth is the only ground upon which their wishes safely can be carried out. That at any rate is the theory of our Constitution. It is an experiment, as all life is an experiment. Every year if not every day we have to wager our salvation upon some prophecy based upon imperfect knowledge. While that experiment is part of our system I think that we should be eternally vigilant against attempts to check the expression of opinions that we loathe and believe to be fraught with death, unless they so imminently threaten immediate interference with the lawful and pressing purposes of the law that an immediate check is required to save the country. I wholly disagree with the argument of the Government that the First Amendment left the common law as to seditious libel in force. History seems to me against the notion. I had conceived that the United States through many years had shown its repentance for the Sedition Act of 1798 by repaying fines that it imposed. Only the emergency that makes it immediately dangerous to leave the correction of evil counsels to time warrants making any exception to the sweeping command, "Congress shall make no law abridging the freedom of speech." Of course I am speaking only of expressions of opinion and exhortations, which were all that were uttered here, but I regret that I cannot put into more impressive words my belief that in their conviction upon this indictment the defendants were deprived of their rights under the Constitution of the United States.

MR. JUSTICE BRANDEIS concurs with the foregoing opinion.

Questions

1) In the last paragraph of his *Abrams* dissent, is Holmes making an argument from *experience* ("time has upset many fighting faiths")? An argument from *consequences* ("truth is the only ground upon which their wishes safely can be carried out")? An argument from *authority* ("[t]hat at any rate is the theory of our Constitution")? An argument from *design* ("It is an experiment, as all life is an experiment.")? An argument from *coherence* ("[w]hile that experiment is part of our system")? An argument from *distrust* ("we should be eternally vigilant")? All of the above? Or is this paragraph so peripatetic as to defy classification?

2) How, if at all, does the view of life expressed in his essay *Natural Law* inform the last paragraph of Holmes's *Abrams* dissent?

3) How does Holmes's view of human nature compare with the views of human nature that inform the free speech arguments of Madison and Mill?

4) What is Holmes's attitude toward "the tyranny of the majority," the concern that so animated Madison, Tocqueville, and Mill?

5) What is the connection between the theory spelled out in the last paragraph of Holmes's *Abrams* dissent and his adoption of the clear-and-imminent-danger test? Is Holmes's theory different from the theory articulated by Hand in his *Masses* opinion? Do theoretical differences explain why Holmes embraced a test that turns on the predicted consequences of the speech and Hand a test that turns on the meaning conveyed by the speaker?

6) Does Holmes's argument for protecting speech have more in common with Madison's or Mill's? Would Madison's "absolute" denial of authority to Congress to abridge "the freedom of the press" and "the right of freely examining public characters and measures" extend to the pamphlets disseminated by the defendants in *Abrams*? How would Mill's corn dealer example be analyzed under Holmes's clear-and-imminent danger test? In terms of theoretical underpinnings, is Holmes closer to Madison or Mill?

7) How does Holmes's view of truth—its nature, its priority, its relationship to progress—compare to that of Milton? That of Mill? Is there a tension between Holmes's view of the "best test of truth" and his assertion regarding the importance of truth seeking?

8) What does Holmes mean by the statement in the last paragraph: "that truth is the only ground upon which their wishes safely can be carried out?"

9) What does Holmes mean by "leave the correction of evil counsels to time"? Is this the same as leaving the correction of evil counsels to rational refutation? To an ongoing dialectical process?

10) Does Holmes's observation in the last paragraph concerning the invalidity of the Sedition Act bear any relationship to what he says earlier in the paragraph about truth and experiment?

11) What does Holmes mean at the end of his opinion when he says: "Of course I am speaking only of expressions of opinion and exhortations, which were all that were uttered here"? Does his analysis not apply to defamation? To the publication of classified documents? To pornography? Notice also that in the fifth-to-last paragraph of his opinion, Holmes describes his clear-and-imminent danger test as applicable only "where private rights are not concerned."

SHELDON M. NOVICK, THE UNREVISED HOLMES AND FREEDOM OF EXPRESSION

1991 Supreme Court Review 303.

After the [*Abrams*] case had been discussed in conference, Holmes circulated a memorandum that would be a dissent if the convictions were upheld. The majority were deeply disturbed. In what may be a unique instance, a delegation of three justices called on Holmes at his home and pleaded with him not to publish his dissenting opinion, apparently on the ground that unanimity of the justices was as important during the Red Scare as it had been in wartime. Holmes's wife, Fanny, joined in the plea.

Holmes was not persuaded, and published his dissent.

OLIVER WENDELL HOLMES, JR., THE COMMON LAW

(1881).

Acts should be judged by their tendency under the known circumstances, not by the actual intent which accompanies them.

It may be true that in the region of attempts, as elsewhere, the law began with cases of actual intent, as those cases are the most obvious ones. But it cannot stop with them, unless it attaches more importance to the etymological meaning of the word *attempt* than to the general principles of punishment. Accordingly there is at least color of authority for the proposition that an act is punishable as an attempt, if, supposing it to have produced its natural and probable effect, it would have amounted to a substantive crime.

But such acts are not the only punishable attempts. There is another class in which actual intent is clearly necessary, and the existence of this class as well as the name (attempt) no doubt tends to affect the whole doctrine.

Some acts may be attempts or misdemeanors which could not have effected the crime unless followed by other acts on the part of the wrongdoer. For instance, lighting a match with intent to set fire to a haystack has been held to amount to a criminal attempt to burn it, although the defendant blew out the match on seeing that he was watched. So the purchase of dies for making counterfeit coin is a misdemeanor, although of course the coin would not be counterfeited unless the dies were used.

In such cases the law goes on a new principle, different from that governing most substantive crimes. The reason for punishing any act must generally be to prevent some harm which is foreseen as likely to follow that act under the circumstances in which it is done. In most substantive crimes the ground on which that likelihood stands is the common working of natural causes as shown by experience. But when an act is punished the natural effect of which is not harmful under the circumstances, that ground alone will not suffice. The probability does not exist unless there are grounds for expecting that the act done will be followed by other acts in connection with which its effect will be harmful, although not so otherwise. But as in fact no such acts have followed, it cannot, in general, be assumed, from the mere doing of what has been done, that they would have followed if the actor had not been interrupted. They would not have followed it unless the actor had chosen, and the only way generally available to show that he would have chosen to do them is by showing that he intended to do them when he did what he did. The accompanying intent in that case renders the otherwise innocent act harmful, because it raises a probability that it will be followed by such other acts and events as will all together result in harm. The importance of the intent is not to show that the act was wicked, but to show that it was likely to be followed by hurtful consequences.

GITLOW v. NEW YORK

Supreme Court of the United States, 1925.
268 U.S. 652, 45 S.Ct. 625, 69 L.Ed. 1138.

MR. JUSTICE SANFORD delivered the opinion of the Court.

* * *

The indictment was in two counts. The first charged that the defendant had advocated, advised and taught the duty, necessity and propriety of overthrowing and overturning organized government by force, violence and unlawful means, by certain writings therein set forth entitled "The Left Wing Manifesto"; the second that he had printed, published and knowingly circulated and distributed a certain paper called "The Revolutionary Age," containing the writings set forth in the first count advocating, advising and teaching the doctrine that organized government should be overthrown by force, violence and unlawful means.

* * *

It was admitted that the defendant signed a card subscribing to the Manifesto and Program of the Left Wing, which all applicants were required to sign before being admitted to membership; that he went to different parts of the State to speak to branches of the Socialist Party about the principles of the Left Wing and advocated their adoption; and that he was responsible for the Manifesto as it appeared, that "he knew of the publication, in a general way and he knew of its publication afterwards, and is responsible for the circulation."

There was no evidence of any effect resulting from the publication and circulation of the Manifesto.

No witnesses were offered in behalf of the defendant.

Extracts from the Manifesto are set forth in the margin. Coupled with a review of the rise of Socialism, it condemned the dominant "moderate Socialism" for its recognition of the necessity of the democratic parliamentary state; repudiated its policy of introducing Socialism by legislative measures; and advocated, in plain and unequivocal language, the necessity of accomplishing the "Communist Revolution" by a militant and "revolutionary Socialism," based on "the class struggle" and mobilizing the "power of the proletariat in action," through mass industrial revolts developing into mass political strikes and "revolutionary mass action," for the purpose of conquering and destroying the parliamentary state and establishing in its place, through a "revolutionary dictatorship of the proletariat," the system of Communist Socialism. The then recent strikes in Seattle and Winnipeg were cited as instances of a development already verging on revolutionary action and suggestive of proletarian dictatorship, in which the strike-workers were "trying to usurp the functions of municipal government"; and revolutionary Socialism, it was urged, must use these mass industrial revolts to broaden the strike, make it general and militant, and develop it into mass political strikes and revolutionary mass action for the annihilation of the parliamentary state.

* * *

By enacting the present statute the State has determined, through its legislative body, that utterances advocating the overthrow of organized government by force, violence and unlawful means, are so inimical to the general welfare and involve such danger of substantive evil that they may be penalized in the exercise of its police power. That determination must be given great weight. Every presumption is to be indulged in favor of the validity of the statute. And the case is to be considered "in the light of the principle that the State is primarily the judge of regulations required in the interest of public safety and welfare"; and that its police "statutes may only be declared unconstitutional where they are arbitrary or unreasonable attempts to exercise authority vested in the State in the public interest." *Great Northern Ry. v. Clara City*, 246 U.S. 434, 439. That utterances inciting to the overthrow of organized government by unlawful means, present a sufficient danger of substantive evil to bring their punishment within the range of legislative discretion, is clear. Such utterances, by their very nature, involve danger to the public peace and to the security of the State. They threaten breaches of the peace and ultimate revolution. And the immediate danger is none the less real and substantial, because the effect of a given utterance cannot be accurately foreseen. The State cannot reasonably be required to measure the danger from every such utterance in the nice balance of a jeweler's scale. A single revolutionary spark may kindle a fire that, smouldering for a time, may burst into a sweeping and destructive conflagration. It cannot be said that the State is acting arbitrarily or unreasonably when in the exercise of its judgment as to the measures necessary to protect the public peace and safety, it seeks to extinguish the spark without waiting until it has enkindled the flame or blazed into the conflagration. It cannot reasonably be required to defer the adoption of measures for its own peace and safety until the revolutionary utterances lead to actual disturbances of the public peace or imminent and immediate danger of its own destruction; but it may, in the exercise of its judgment, suppress the threatened danger in its incipiency.

* * *

MR. JUSTICE HOLMES (dissenting).

Mr. JUSTICE BRANDEIS and I are of opinion that this judgment should be reversed. The general principle of free speech, it seems to me, must be taken to be included in the Fourteenth Amendment, in view of the scope that has been given to the word "liberty" as there used, although perhaps it may be accepted with a somewhat larger latitude of interpretation than is allowed to Congress by the sweeping language that governs or ought to govern the laws of the United States. If I am right then I think that the criterion sanctioned by the full Court in *Schenck v. United States* applies:

> "The question in every case is whether the words used are used in such circumstances and are of such a nature as to create a clear and present danger that they will bring about the substantive evils that [the State] has a right to prevent."

It is true that in my opinion this criterion was departed from in *Abrams v. United States* but the convictions that I expressed in that case are too deep for it to be possible for me as yet to believe that it and *Schaefer v. United States*, 251 U. S. 466 have settled the law. If what I think the correct test is applied it is manifest that there was no present danger of an attempt to overthrow the government by force on the part of the admittedly small minority who shared the defendant's views. It is said that this manifesto was more than a theory, that it was an incitement. Every idea is an incitement. It offers itself for belief and if believed it is acted on unless some other belief outweighs it or some failure of energy stifles the movement at its birth. The only difference between the expression of an opinion and an incitement in the narrower sense is the speaker's enthusiasm for the result. Eloquence may set fire to reason. But whatever may be thought of the redundant discourse before us it had no chance of starting a present conflagration. If in the long run the beliefs expressed in proletarian dictatorship are destined to be accepted by the dominant forces of the community, the only meaning of free speech is that they should be given their chance and have their way.

If the publication of this document had been laid as an attempt to induce an uprising against government at once and not at some indefinite time in the future it would have presented a different question. The object would have been one with which the law might deal, subject to the doubt whether there was any danger that the publication could produce any result, or in other words, whether it was not futile and too remote from possible consequences. But the indictment alleges the publication and nothing more.

UNITED STATES v. SCHWIMMER

Supreme Court of the United States, 1929.
279 U.S. 644, 49 S.Ct. 448, 73 L.Ed. 889.

MR. JUSTICE BUTLER delivered the opinion of the Court.

Respondent filed a petition for naturalization in the District Court for the Northern District of Illinois. The court found her unable, without mental reservation, to take the prescribed oath of allegiance, and not attached to the principles of the Constitution of the United States, and not well disposed to the good order and happiness of the same; and it denied her application. The Circuit Court of Appeals reversed the decree, and directed the District Court to grant respondent's petition.

The Naturalization Act of June 29, 1906, requires:

> "He (the applicant for naturalization) shall, before he is admitted to citizenship, declare on oath in open court * * * that he will support and defend the Constitution and laws of the United States against all enemies, foreign and domestic, and bear true faith and allegiance to the same." U. S. C. tit. 8, § 381.

* * *

The record shows that respondent strongly desires to become a citizen. She is a linguist, lecturer, and writer; she is well educated and accustomed to discuss governments and civic affairs. Her testimony should be considered having regard to her interest and disclosed ability correctly to express herself. Her claim at the hearing that she possessed the required qualifications and was willing to take the oath was much impaired by other parts of her testimony. Taken as a whole, it shows that her objection to military service rests on reasons other than mere inability because of her sex and age personally to bear arms. Her expressed willingness to be treated as the government dealt with conscientious objectors who refused to take up arms in the recent war indicates that she deemed herself to belong to that class. The fact that she is an uncompromising pacifist, with no sense of nationalism, but only a cosmic sense of belonging to the human family, justifies belief that she may be opposed to the use of military force as contemplated by our Constitution and laws. And her testimony clearly suggests that she is disposed to exert her power to influence others to such opposition.

A pacifist, in the general sense of the word, is one who seeks to maintain peace and to abolish war. Such purposes are in harmony with the Constitution and policy of our government. But the word is also used and understood to mean one who refuses or is unwilling for any purpose to bear arms because of conscientious considerations and who is disposed to encourage others in such refusal. And one who is without any sense of nationalism is not well bound or held by the ties of affection to any nation or government. Such persons are liable to be incapable of the attachment for and devotion to the principles of our Constitution that are required of aliens seeking naturalization.

* * *

MR. JUSTICE HOLMES, dissenting.

The applicant seems to be a woman of superior character and intelligence, obviously more than ordinarily desirable as a citizen of the United States. It is agreed that she is qualified for citizenship except so far as the views set forth in a statement of facts "may show that the applicant is not attached to the principles of the Constitution of the United States and well disposed to the good order and happiness of the same, and except in so far as the same may show that she cannot take the oath of allegiance without a mental reservation." The views referred to are an extreme opinion in favor of pacifism and a statement that she would not bear arms to defend the Constitution. So far as the adequacy of her oath is concerned I hardly can see how that is affected by the statement, inasmuch as she is a woman over fifty years of age, and would not be allowed to bear arms if she wanted to. And as to the opinion the whole examination of the applicant shows that she holds none of the now-dreaded creeds but thoroughly believes in organized government and prefers that of the United States to any other in the world. Surely it cannot show lack of attachment to the principles of the Constitution that she thinks that it can be improved. I suppose that most intelligent people think that it might be. Her particular improvement looking to the abolition of war seems to me not materially different in its bearing on this case from a wish to establish cabinet government as in England, or a single house, or one term of seven years for the President. To touch a more burning question, only a judge mad with partisanship would exclude because the applicant thought that the Eighteenth Amendment should be repealed.

Of course the fear is that if a war came the applicant would exert activities such as were dealt with in *Schenck v. United States*. But that seems to me unfounded. Her position and motives are wholly different from those of Schenck. She is an optimist and states in strong and, I do not doubt, sincere words her belief that war will disappear and that the impending destiny of mankind is to unite in peaceful leagues. I do not share that optimism nor do I think that a philosophic view of the world would regard war as absurd. But most people who have known it regard it with horror, as a last resort, and even if not yet ready for cosmopolitan efforts, would welcome any practicable combinations that would increase the power on the side of peace. The notion that the applicant's optimistic anticipations would make her a worse citizen is sufficiently answered by her examination which seems to me a better argument for her admission than any that I can offer. Some of her answers might excite popular prejudice, but if there is any principle of the Constitution that more imperatively calls for attachment than any other it is the principle of free thought-not free thought for those who agree with us but freedom for the thought that we hate. I think that we should adhere to that principle with regard to admission into, as well as to life within this country. And recurring to the opinion that bars this applicant's way, I would suggest that the Quakers have done their share to make the country what it is, that many citizens agree with the applicant's belief and that I had not supposed hitherto that we regretted our inability to expel them because they believe more than some of us do in the teachings of the Sermon on the Mount.

MR. JUSTICE BRANDEIS concurs in this opinion.

GERTZ v. ROBERT WELCH, INC.

Supreme Court of the United States, 1974.
418 U.S. 323, 94 S.Ct. 2997, 41 L.Ed.2d 789.

We begin with the common ground. Under the First Amendment there is no such thing as a false idea. However pernicious an opinion may seem, we depend for its correction not on the conscience of judges and juries but on the competition of other ideas.

RICHARD A. POSNER, INTRODUCTION

in The Essential Holmes (Richard A. Posner ed. 1992).

Among the fundamental questions that philosophy worries are questions about the meaning and purpose of human life, including the meaning and purpose of human life in a cosmos from which God has departed. Nietzsche, a contemporary of Holmes, said that God is dead. (Dead *for us:* Nietzsche was making a sociological rather than a metaphysical observation.) God had been killed among the thinking class by physics, geology, the "higher criticism" of the Bible, and the theory of evolution—systems of thought that had undermined Christianity's appeal to the rational intellect—and had been badly wounded among the common people by the growth of security and prosperity, which had shifted people's attention from the next world to this one. Christianity had been the foundation of Western civilization. Its disappearance as a living source of metaphysical certitude and ethical foundations was the crisis of modernity. Holmes agreed; and by the depth and eloquence of his belief he became part of a diverse cast of moderns that includes (in addition to Nietzsche and Holmes) Heidegger, Kafka, Gide, Camus, Sartre, Wittgenstein (in his later work), and, among our own contemporaries, Richard Rorty. All these thinkers have been concerned with the personal and social implications of taking seriously the definite possibility that man is the puny product of an unplanned series of natural shocks having no tincture of the divine, and they have been suspicious of efforts to smuggle in God by the back door (perhaps by renaming him Progress, or Science, or Technology, or History, or the Class Struggle) in order to recreate the certitude and the sense of direction that Christianity had provided. Pragmatism and existentialism are characteristic, and related, manifestations of this influential current in modern thought, the first typically American, the second typically European.

It is no accident that a majority of the persons in my list were not professors of philosophy and that all, even those who were not literary artists, had literary or artistic interests and, with the possible exception of Heidegger, wrote with great distinction (present tense, of course, in the case of Rorty). For when we speak of "the meaning of life" we speak of a topic about which literary artists seem to have more to say than philosophers. When modern secular intellectuals seek consolation for a loss, for aging, for the indifference, immensity, and caprice of the universe, or for the cruelty of man, it is to literature rather than to philosophy that they turn. It should come as no surprise that the most penetrating insights into the philosophical topic that I am calling "the meaning of life" come from individuals who fuse philosophical and literary attributes, writing in a form equally remote from academic philosophizing and imaginative literature: notably Nietzsche and Wittgenstein, but also, though in a minor key, Holmes. It is a matter not of sheathing philosophical analysis in graceful language but of aesthetizing philosophy—of seeing in it the materials for conceiving of a life on the model of a work of art. Holmes, most like Nietzsche in this regard, was, then, a "writer-philosopher."

There are affinities in content as well as in form between these great contemporaries. I shall not explore those here. I have tried to explain how I think Holmes ought to be approached, and the arrangement of materials in this volume is intended to assist the reader in taking that approach. I leave it to the reader to discover what is to be found at the end of the journey. The filaments of his thought are astonishing in their variety (I have touched on a few already). One can find pragmatism, atheism, (nineteenth-century) liberalism, materialism, aestheticism, utilitarianism, militarism, biological, social, and historical Darwinism, skepticism, nihilism, Nietzschean vitalism and "will to power," Calvinism, logical positivism, stoicism, behaviorism, and existentialism, together with the explicit rejection of most of these "isms" and a sheer zest for living that may be the central plank in the Holmesian platform. Whether the elements of his thought coalesce to form a coherent philosophy of life I doubt—because I range Holmes in the ranks of the antiphilosophers—but leave to the reader to decide. What I do not doubt is that the variety of intellectual influences that played upon Holmes's subtle and receptive intellect, together with his power of articulation and the daring with which he brought his intellectual storehouse and rhetorical imagination to bear on his professional tasks, makes Holmes a central figure in the intellectual history of this nation, and one who deserves to be more widely and appreciatively read than he is.

I said "intellectual history *of this nation*"—not of the world, and I want now to explain this qualification. Holmes's thought, and the fundamentals of his literary style, were pretty much fixed by the time *The Common Law* appeared. Indeed, the most famous sentence he ever wrote—"The life of the law has not been logic: it has been experience"—graces the opening paragraph of that book. And in Holmes's formative years America was, intellectually, a province of England. How likely is it, then, that Holmes was an *original* thinker and writer? I think his was a syncretic rather than a profoundly original mind, and that is why I used the word "minor" when comparing him to Nietzsche and Wittgenstein. I suspect that he borrowed greatly and to great advantage from the people he met in England as a young man, notably John Stuart Mill and James Fitzjames Stephen, and that by doing so he helped to make American thought cosmopolitan and (paradoxically) to liberate American jurisprudential thought from slavish adherence to English models. He did more than translate English into American. He enriched where he borrowed; his creative imitation was a species of greatness, like that of Shakespeare though on a much smaller scale.

OLIVER WENDELL HOLMES, JR., INTRODUCTION

in Montesquieu, The Spirit of the Laws (1900).

What proximate test of excellence can be found except correspondence to the actual equilibrium of force in the community—that is, conformity to the wishes of the dominant power? Of course, such conformity may lead to destruction, and it is desirable that the dominant power should be wise. But wise or not, the proximate test of a good government is that the dominant power has its way.

OLIVER WENDELL HOLMES, JR. TO HAROLD J. LASKI

Nov. 7, 1917.

[Barbusse] insists that truth is simple—the implication being that all the complexities of the economists and philosophers are cobwebs woven in paid defence of things as they are. I think this the most ominous and dangerous humbug ever offered to the Crowd. Let the mass of men once believe that, as a religion, and reason is powerless and anything may happen.

OLIVER WENDELL HOLMES, JR. TO HAROLD J. LASKI

April 6, 1920.

Truth is the unanimous consent of mankind to a system of propositions. It is an ideal and as such postulates itself as a thing to be attained, but like other good ideals it is unattainable and therefore may be called absurd. Some ideals, like morality, a system of specific conduct for every situation, would be detestable if attained and therefore the postulate must be conditioned—that it is a thing to be striven for on the tacit understanding that it will not be reached.

OLIVER WENDELL HOLMES, JR. TO SIR FREDERICK POLLOCK

Aug. 30, 1914.

Malthus pleased me immensely—and left me sad. A hundred years ago he busted fallacies that politicians and labor leaders still live on. One thinks that an error exposed is dead, but exposure amounts to nothing when people want to believe.

OLIVER WENDELL HOLMES, JR. TO SIR FREDERICK POLLOCK

Aug. 30, 1929.

If there is anything that has been supposed to be compulsory upon us short of not affirming nonsense I should think it was that every phenomenon must have a cause. Yet I find scientific men suggesting nowadays (*e.g.* Eddington) that there are phenomena for which no causes can be discovered and seemingly believing that they are outside the category of cause and effect. I am far from believing with them, but I am entirely ready to believe it on proof. Chauncey Wright a nearly forgotten philosopher of real merit, taught me when young that I must not say *necessary* about the universe, that we don't know whether anything is necessary or not. So I describe myself as a *bet*tabilitarian. I believe that we can *bet* on the behavior of the universe in its contact with us. We bet we can know what it will be. That leaves a loophole for free will—in the miraculous sense—the creation of a new atom of force, although I don't in the least believe in it. I guess (strict sense) that you think man a more important manifestation than I do. I suppose that such differences depend a good deal on the ultimate make-up of different men and hardly can be argued about. Of course from the human point of view he is important; he hardly would live if he didn't think so. Also I hasten to admit that I don't dare pronounce any fact unimportant that the Cosmos has produced. I only mean that when one thinks coldly I see no reason for attributing to man a significance different in kind from that which belongs to a baboon or to a grain of sand.

THOMAS C. GREY, HOLMES AND LEGAL PRAGMATISM

41 Stan. L. Rev. 787 (1989).

Oliver Wendell Holmes is the great oracle of American legal thought, but as with other oracles his message is subject to much dispute. His admiring readers have mainly stressed Holmes the critic of Langdellian legal formalism, who said the life of the law was not logic but experience. Others, generally less admiring, have focused on Holmes the Social Darwinist, who celebrated the struggle for existence, or Holmes the amoral positivist, who analyzed law from the perspective of a "bad man." In recent years, still others have emphasized yet another Holmes, one whose main achievement as a legal thinker, apart from a few memorable anti-formalistic jurisprudential slogans, was a body of surprisingly abstract and conceptual doctrinal writing. One of the few points on which all commentators agree is Holmes' greatness as a prose stylist. But when combined with the range of competing interpretations of his work, even the brilliance of his prose suggests another unflattering account—Holmes the eclectic aphorist, whose purely literary talent for glittering phrases conceals a muddle of mutually inconsistent ideas.

My thesis is that while there are indeed multiple and apparently clashing strands in Holmes' thought, most of them weave together reasonably well when seen as the jurisprudential development of certain central tenets of American pragmatism. Conflicts do remain when Holmes' work is interpreted from this perspective, but they can be explained by a characteristic paradox—the man was disabled by temperament, by experience, and by the historical context in which he found himself from adequately practicing the pragmatism he so eloquently preached.

Holmes as legal pragmatist is hardly a new idea. His associations with Charles Sanders Peirce and William James, as well as his admiration for John Dewey, have led a number of intellectual historians to count him as an adherent and even a founder of the pragmatist movement. At the same time, legal theorists have associated both his generally empirical and instrumental approach to law, and his specific account of legal rules as predictions of judicial decisions, with familiar pragmatist teachings. But there are serious problems with these standard positions. On the biographical side, while Holmes did express admiration for Dewey, he never made clear what it was that he admired. And his more specific remarks about pragmatism and the other well-known pragmatists were critical, often harshly so. He condemned James' version of pragmatism as "humbug"; and while he apparently knew little of Peirce's ideas, he did not think highly of what he knew. In the end, what Holmes said directly about pragmatism and its exponents does not by itself support placing him in the pragmatist camp.

When we turn from Holmes' direct statements about pragmatism and the pragmatists to his legal thought itself, the difficulty is to identify anything distinctively pragmatist in his writings. He did treat law as a utilitarian instrument for the satisfaction of human desires, but as he said himself, "the judging of law by its effects and results did not have to wait for W[illiam] J[ames]."[1] The English analytical positivists who followed Bentham and Austin had made the instrumental approach to law prominent long before American pragmatism came on the scene. Holmes was certainly one of the important American exponents of English analytical positivism, and his prediction theory is a significant elaboration of that approach to law. But if this were all there were to Holmes, we would add little by calling him a pragmatist.

My suggestion is that we can understand the distinctively pragmatist cast to Holmes' legal thought if we take account of the recent revival and reinterpretation of pragmatism within Anglo–American philosophy. The "neo-pragmatists" reject the long-standing treatment of pragmatism as simply a minor element in the triumphant advance of scientific positivism. In this traditional view, the pragmatists were merely thinkers who anticipated and stated in a confused way some of the ideas later worked out more rigorously by the logical positivists and their successors in the philosophy of science. A parallel view of pragmatism in legal

1. 1 HOLMES–LASKI LETTERS 20 (M. Howe ed. 1953) (letter dated Sept. 15, 1916).

theory would see Holmes, Roscoe Pound, and its other exponents as relatively primitive and confused precursors of the more rigorous and sophisticated form of scientific instrumentalist jurisprudence represented by contemporary law and economics, cost-benefit analysis, and public choice theory.

By contrast, the new philosophical interpretation of pragmatism stresses certain ways in which it departs from and indeed undermines orthodox scientific empiricism, particularly in its focus on human inquiry as a culturally situated form of activity. Much as William James' original formulation of pragmatism sought to mediate between "tough-minded" devotees of science and "tender-minded" religious believers,[2] the neo-pragmatists seek a bridge across the divide that has separated Anglo–American from European philosophy in this century. On one side of this divide, English speakers (and some Austrian helpers) have tended to conceive of philosophy as an enterprise dedicated to exploring the foundations of knowledge through a rigorous account of natural scientific method, with the ultimate aim of extending that method to all areas of human inquiry. On the other side, European philosophy has long stood in an adversary relation to natural science and technology, pursuing the (often quasi-religious) search for meaning, sometimes culminating in a discovery of meaninglessness, through the exploration of culture and lived experience.[3]

This schism matters to legal scholars because it extends beyond philosophy to divide students and theorists of social phenomena more generally, including those who focus upon law. The positivist project of developing "social sciences" modeled on physics, chemistry, and biology has dominated Anglo–American social theory, while the European tendency has been to study society and culture interpretively, as text-analogues to be understood rather than as natural phenomena to be explained. The extension of the European style of theorizing into American intellectual life in recent years has produced sharp divisions between the traditionally dominant positivist approach, and a newer movement toward "hermeneutic" and "post-modernist" modes of thought. This division is evident within legal thought as well, where jurisprudential approaches based upon the economic paradigm of rational choice remain dominant, but are increasingly subject to challenge from approaches that stress the centrality of culture, history, language, ideology, and rhetoric.

The neo-pragmatists' pluralistic conception of inquiry challenges the dominance of natural science in the intellectual life of the English-speaking world, and some traditional positivists see their work as a nihilistic challenge to reason itself. But when compared with other post-

2. WILLIAM JAMES, PRAGMATISM: A NEW NAME FOR SOME OLD WAYS OF THINKING 3–40 (1907).

3. This generalization is meant to characterize the main line of European philosophy since Kant's critiques overthrew the tradition of Cartesian foundational rationalism; the line begins with Hegel, runs through Kierkegaard, Nietzsche, and Dilthey, and encompasses such disparate modern thinkers as Heidegger, Sartre, Gadamer, Ricoeur, and Derrida.

modernist thinkers, the new pragmatists can be seen as still working within the scientific empiricist tradition broadly conceived. They tend to reject both the pervasive relativism and the oppositional stance toward natural science that many European philosophers and social thinkers have adopted, and they accept the spirit of scientific inquiry, in which theory is tested against experience by a reflective and critical community of inquirers. Pragmatists see even natural scientific inquiry as having unavoidably interpretive and culturally conditioned aspects; at the same time they believe that humanistic and explicitly evaluative inquiry can be pursued rationally and with the reasonable hope of progress. In social theory generally, and legal theory more particularly, the pragmatist tendency is to promote trade rather than warfare between normative and descriptive theorists, storytellers and model-builders, interpreters and causal explainers.

Finally, in interpreting the history of pragmatism, the neo-pragmatists have departed from their predecessors by emphasizing Dewey over Peirce and James as the central figure in the movement. Dewey's own focus was not so much on the methods of the natural sciences (as with Peirce) or on the life-situation of the individual (as with James), but more on issues of social theory, politics, and law. It was Dewey who particularly developed the pragmatist critique of the traditional philosophical "quest for certainty", Dewey who particularly undermined the positivist dualisms of subject and object, mind and matter, fact and value, and Dewey who particularly stressed the shaping effect of cultural and historical context on human inquiry. And these are the aspects of pragmatism that have dominated the recent revival.

* * *

Those who would make Holmes a pragmatist have usually had in mind his conception of law as the coercive use of state power through the courts, aimed at the promotion of public welfare or the satisfaction of collective wants. The conception is thought pragmatic because it is at once empirical and instrumental. Descriptively, for Holmes, the law is "what the courts . . . do in fact," and it draws its content largely from "[t]he felt necessities of the time."[23] Prescriptively, legal principles are to be derived from "accurately measured social desires," with these to be approximated, in the absence of a better measuring stick, by "conformity to the wishes of the dominant power" in the community.[24]

While nothing in such a conception of law is inconsistent with pragmatism, the difficulty, mentioned already, is seeing anything distinctively pragmatist in it. As Holmes himself was quite aware, the view of law as regularized coercion and as a means to an end was not new either with him or with those we think of as pragmatists. Beginning more than

23. OLIVER WENDELL HOLMES, The Path of the Law (1897), in COLLECTED LEGAL PAPERS 161, 173 (1920); OLIVER WENDELL HOLMES, THE COMMON LAW 5 (M. Howe ed. 1963) (originally published 1881).

24. OLIVER WENDELL HOLMES, Law in Science and Science in Law (1899), in COLLECTED LEGAL PAPERS 210, 226 (1920); OLIVER WENDELL HOLMES, Montesquieu (1900), in COLLECTED LEGAL PAPERS 250, 258.

a century before pragmatism was first heard of, and continuing throughout a long and immensely influential career, Jeremy Bentham had promoted the idea that law was the use of collective force as a means to human happiness. In this, he was followed by his disciple John Austin, whose theory became the orthodoxy of English analytical jurisprudence while Holmes was a law student. Holmes was a member of the first generation of American lawyers to be much influenced by the utilitarian positivism of the analytical jurists; only in a later generation would such views become dominant, as, in a sense, they remain to this day. Yet there was nothing original to America, nothing derived from James or Peirce, nothing peculiar to pragmatism, in Holmes' often reiterated application of Benthamite slogans to law.

Bentham's instrumentalism applied the post-Enlightenment spirit of scientific positivism to law and politics. Central to this spirit was the conviction that, as Richard Rorty has put it, "natural science—facts about how spatio-temporal things worked—was all the Truth there was." Applied to law, the positivist spirit required that if legal propositions were to have scientific standing, they must be reducible to factual claims. Accordingly Austin, following Bentham's lead, analyzed legal rights and duties in terms of two straightforwardly factual questions: what person or group in society is habitually obeyed, and what has he, she, or it commanded? Under this conception, the determination of what the law is requires no value judgment; the lawyer needs only to identify behavioral regularities and consult the plain meanings of words.

For positivists of the Benthamite persuasion, moral and political evaluation could proceed rationally only if evaluative discourse itself could be reduced to factual terms. Otherwise it was pure rhetoric, "simple nonsense," or "nonsense upon stilts."[29] The only empirical realities available as plausible sources of value judgments were human desires and sensations of pleasure or pain. Thus utilitarianism became the prescriptive corollary of positivism. An action or a law was right to the extent it promoted pleasure or satisfaction, and prevented pain or frustration. Given this starting point, moral questions became in principle issues of fact, which, it was hoped, technical progress would one day reduce to mere matters of measurement. But this day was not yet at hand, and the still immature science of utilitarian ethics or "censorial jurisprudence"—the study of what the law should be—had to be kept strictly separate from "expository jurisprudence," the identification of the positive law that was actually in force.

Much of Holmes' legal thought can be explained in terms of this Victorian scientific positivism—what Holmes himself called "the scientific way of looking at the world." From this outlook followed his legal positivism and a version of utilitarianism tempered by skepticism about the practical possibilities of measuring utility. Not only his functional account of law generally, but also his analysis of lawyer's law as

29. JEREMY BENTHAM, Anarchical Fallacies, in 2 THE WORKS OF JEREMY BENTHAM 489, 501 (1962) (J. Bowring ed. 1838–1843).

prediction, his promotion of an external standard of liability, and his critique of the use of moral terms in legal discourse, all were consistent with a program of reducing vague and value-laden questions to clear and factual ones. These aspects of Holmes' legal thought fit in with the utilitarian analytical jurisprudence of Bentham and Austin—the legal branch of nineteenth-century scientific positivism. But while ideas such as these are consistent with pragmatism, they are in no way distinctive to it.

The founding pragmatists managed to break away from the standard brand of scientific positivism. At the same time, and in an analogous way, Holmes' work in legal theory came to surpass that of his positivist predecessors. The differences between pragmatist and positivist theories of knowledge are, in fact, the background against which one can show that Holmes took legal thought beyond analytical positivism, in a distinctively pragmatist direction.

We can best begin our account where the pragmatists themselves did, with their naturalistic account of human mind and mental activity—"inquiry," in Dewey's encompassing term. The pragmatist view of inquiry represented a major departure from long-standing views of human knowledge. British empiricism and its traditional rival, European rationalism, had implicitly shared a dualistic conception of the human being as a spiritual or immaterial mind somehow lodged in a material body. In its origin, this conception of the mind as metaphysically distinct from the body traces back in Western thought at least to Plato, and over time it became fused with the "soul" of Christian theology. Carrying its multiple philosophical and religious origins with it, the notion of the immaterial but substantial mind-soul or spirit was implanted in the foundations of the developing Western scientific world view by both the rationalist Descartes and the empiricist Locke in the seventeenth century. Through the period of the Enlightenment, Western philosophers, however oriented they were toward science, did not root it out. Even in the work of a nineteenth-century philosophical positivist who came as close to pragmatism as did John Stuart Mill, we find an implicitly dualistic account separating mind from matter, in which human knowledge of an objective, material and external world must somehow be built up from subjective and immaterial impressions and ideas occuring in an internal and intangible mental medium.[32] How this is to be done is the "problem of knowledge," to be solved by the special philosophical sub-discipline of "epistemology"; epistemology in turn is built upon an ontology that divides the world into mind and matter, Descartes' res cogitans and res extensa.

The pragmatist departure from this traditional concept of the mental world seems in large part traceable to the influence of nineteenth-century evolutionary thinking. By locating mankind firmly within the

32. JOHN STUART MILL, A SYSTEM OF LOGIC RATIOCINATIVE AND INDUCTIVE, in 7 COLLECTED WORKS OF JOHN STUART MILL 1, 56–64, 74 (J. M. Robson ed. 1973).

animal kingdom, Darwin made it plausible to treat human mental capacities as evolved functions of natural organisms, arising from simpler forms of animal behavior as a result of their survival-promoting tendencies. As this perspective took hold, the distinction between spirit and nature, or mind and matter, came to seem increasingly arbitrary. If the human being was a biological organism, "mind" and "the mental" could only refer to those workings of the organism that rose above whatever level of complexity had come to be defined as "merely animal."

It is a mistake, however, to overemphasize the place of evolutionary biology in the origins of pragmatism; certain characteristic elements of nineteenth-century social thought were equally important. In reaction to the ahistorical rationalism of the Enlightenment, a wide range of social theorists emphasized and developed the importance in human affairs of cultural evolution, or History with a capital "H." This tendency in social thought, which we may loosely label "historicism," stressed the fundamental character of historical change and cultural variation, and thereby undermined the philosophical search for a single definite set of faculties and categories that constituted "the human understanding."

The collectivist bias of emerging historical, linguistic, and anthropological studies helped undermine the notion of the human being as an individual who, by virtue of the imprisonment of his or her spirit in a carnal body, was a little lower than the angels. In its place arose the idea of humanity as a species that, by virtue of its collective capacity to generate, transmit, and adapt culture by means of language, was a little higher than the apes. This concern with cultural as well as biological evolution provided the pragmatists with an essential safeguard against materialist reductionism, or behaviorism, which attempts to escape the "mind-body problem" by simply reducing to the physical, or even denying the reality of, phenomena traditionally classified as mental or cultural.

These developments in biological and social theory focused philosophers' attention on some of the fundamental difficulties with the traditional accounts of mind. How can a ghostly mind be linked to the material world through the bodily machine that it somehow haunts? How can we have reliable knowledge of an outer physical world if all our experience is made up of mental impressions and ideas projected in some inner and immaterial theater? The acute debates over these questions during the previous two centuries had preoccupied philosophers with what John Dewey called "[t]he alleged discipline of epistemology."

The pragmatist breakthrough was to reject all mind-body dualisms and treat thought or "inquiry" as a mode of the human organism's activity, an adaptive product of biological and cultural evolution. Peirce, the founder of pragmatism, described a belief as a "habit of mind" that enables the organism to cope with some aspect of its environment. When action on a habitual belief does not produce the expected result, the believer experiences the "irritation of doubt." "Inquiry," which Peirce described as "a struggle to attain a state of belief" or "settlement of opinion,'' is supposed to resolve the irritation of doubt in favor of some belief that can once again reliably guide the believer's action. Of course, this new belief, when acted upon, might itself lead to new doubt, thus requiring new inquiry.

Though there were important differences among the leading pragmatists, all of them endorsed this Darwinist-historicist account of human inquiry. They treated ''the mind'' as an evolved mode for coping with the environment, a set of biologically based powers that included the crucial capacity to learn language. Linguistic capacity allowed human mental powers to be vastly augmented and modified along many different paths of cultural development. The pragmatists thus provided an escape from the philosophical paradoxes inherent in the confused conception of the Platonic–Christian–Cartesian–Lockean mind-soul, that hybrid entity with its many and conflicting roles: the locus of personal identity and moral being, the active organ of decision, the seat of creativity and imagination, the passive theater of perception, the storehouse of memory, and the immaterial and indestructible survivor of the body's mortality.

The pragmatists' account of the mind and inquiry was thus thoroughly practical, in two related senses. First, on the side that derived from historicist social thought, they treated thinking as contextual and situated; it came always embodied in practices—habits and patterns of perceiving and conceiving that had developed out of and served to guide activity. Some of these habits and patterns were instinctive, some were learned individually, but those most distinctively human resulted from the capacity for language; they were products of culture, collectively developed and transmitted. Second, on the side that derived from Darwinism, the pragmatists regarded thinking as an adaptive function of an organism, practical in the sense that it was instrumental. It had evolved as a problem-solving capacity, oriented toward survival. In its most developed form, thinking functioned to help resolve, by means of conscious reflection and experimental revision, the real problems and live doubts that arose in the course of acting on unreflective and habitual practices. Holmes himself provided a characteristically compact summary of these two tenets: ''all thought,'' he said, is at once ''social'' and ''on its way to action.''[42]

Whereas older accounts of pragmatism emphasized its instrumentalism, the distinctive feature of recent reinterpretations of pragmatism is to give equal significance to its contextualist thesis—the idea that thought is essentially embedded in a context of social practice. Not only is contextualism no less fundamental to the pragmatists' thought than instrumentalism; it is what most sharply distinguishes them from orthodox scientific positivists. Indeed, development of the contextualist thesis

42. OLIVER WENDELL HOLMES, John Marshall (1901), in COLLECTED LEGAL PAPERS 266, 270 (1920).

led the pragmatists to their most profound philosophical innovation: the rejection of philosophical "foundationalism."

Foundationalism is a long name for the age-old philosopher's dream that knowledge might be grounded in a set of fundamental and indubitable beliefs. For the rationalist tradition descended from Descartes, the cornerstones of knowledge are those rational intuitions that survive as clear and distinct ideas in the face of the thinker's effort at universal doubt. For the empiricist tradition running from Bacon, Hobbes, and Locke to the logical positivism of this century, the foundations of factual knowledge are the bare uninterpreted data delivered to the mind by the senses. The tradition of modern Western epistemology, both rationalist and empiricist, has imagined that knowledge can be securely based only if the inquirer strips away all habitual and conventional ways of thought, and builds a purified structure based on valid inferences from indubitable premises.

The pragmatists' first thesis—that knowledge is essentially contextual, situated in habit and practice—holds that no such zero-based method of inquiry is possible. Peirce stated the point forcefully: No one, he said, can set out to think either by "doubting everything" or by "observing 'the first impressions of sense.' " Rather:

> [T]here is but one state of mind from which you can "set out," namely, the very state of mind in which you actually find yourself at the time you do "set out"—a state in which you are laden with an immense mass of cognition already formed, of which you cannot divest yourself if you would; and who knows whether, if you could, you would not have made all knowledge impossible to yourself?[43]

In a similar vein, James stressed that the individual always begins with "a stock of old opinions." When these are put under strain by some incongruous perception or desire, the individual seeks to escape from the "inward trouble" thus generated by "modifying his previous mass of opinions." But "he saves as much of it as he can, for in this matter of belief we are all extreme conservatives.... The most violent revolutions in an individual's beliefs leave most of his old order standing." Similarly, Dewey stressed the beginning of thought in habit; the human being is in the first instance a creature of habit, not of reason. Only when habit and practice become problematic is there occasion for inquiry, the application of conscious intelligence to a situation. The task of inquiry is not the impossible one of building a purified structure of truths from the ground up, but rather the practical one of making such modifications in the existing body of knowledge as will solve the difficulty at hand. This remains as true for the most abstract theoretical puzzle in mathematics or speculative philosophy as it does for those ordinary problems of daily life in which conscious deliberation originates.

Practices are not only habitual and largely unconscious; they are mainly collective in origin. The pragmatists emphasized the social ori-

43. CHARLES SANDERS PEIRCE, What Pragmatism Is (1905), in 5 COLLECTED PAPERS OF CHARLES SANDERS PEIRCE.

gins of the great mass of settled belief from which inquiry proceeds. We see that practices are collective, when we consider that they are mediated by language, the conventional, collectively constituted, spontaneously evolved, complex communicative structure of meaningful signs that underlies all reflective or conscious thought. Language supplies not only the forms in which thought is represented and conveyed, but much of the stuff of thought itself. Thus, Peirce argued that thought was essentially carried on by means of signs, of which the most important were the conventional signs that constitute language. In fact, in emphasizing the role of language and the collective notion of inquiry, Peirce went so far as to hold that reality itself is simply the object on which the representations of a community of inquirers are destined in the long run to converge.

The pragmatists thus broke not only with the foundationalism of the empiricist tradition, but also with its methodological individualism. They did not regard society as a construct built up out of elementary individuals, each possessing a rich array of pre-social qualities. Rather, they argued, the individual person, the knowing, willing subject of Enlightenment epistemology and political philosophy, is only the late and sophisticated product of a complex cultural development.

This first thesis of pragmatism—the situated, historical, practice-constituted character of human life and thought—is not unique to the pragmatists. It has been a central theme for all those modern philosophers who have broken from the foundationalist tradition in Western thought. The erstwhile logical positivist Otto Neurath captured the essence of anti-foundationalism in a famous metaphor, when he described human inquirers as sailors on a boat that can never come to drydock for repair, so that they must maintain and reconstruct it as they sail, using its own material and what flotsam they come upon. In his later work, Wittgenstein often stressed the social, habitual, and practical basis of all reasoning: "What has to be accepted, the given, is . . . forms of life." And Heidegger held that all beliefs presuppose prejudices—judgments already made, implicit in practice, prior to reflection, largely historical and collective in origin, tacitly accepted, and for the moment unquestioned.

Even before pragmatism as such came on the scene, the concept of human inquiry as essentially situated and historically conditioned was one of the central themes of nineteenth-century social thought. It appears in Hegel, from whom it was taken in a revolutionary direction by Marx. But it was must conspicuous in the Burkean-romantic brand of conservative social theory that in the English-speaking world drew inspiration from the traditional ideology of the common law, and found theoretical expression in Friedrich von Savigny, Sir Henry Maine, James Coolidge Carter, and the other proponents of the historical school of jurisprudence. The leading pragmatists, however, did not share the Burkean conservatism common among so many thinkers who stress the centrality of history and context to human social life. Their analysis grants no special authority to unconscious habit and slowly evolved custom; self-conscious reflection and innovative reason are equally central to their account of inquiry. The pragmatist thesis is that human thought always and necessarily arises in a situated complex of beliefs; on any given occasion, the great mass of these beliefs must be left tacit and simply used, not made explicit and subject to doubt, if thought is to proceed at all. But from this the pragmatists draw no inference that any particular idea or belief should be treated as even presumptively immune from questioning.

Rather, pragmatists treat critical reflection as a natural aspect of thought, an aspect as natural, if not as easy, as following habit. Conscious inquiry arises naturally whenever a person enters a problematic situation, a case in which habitual and unconscious belief produces trouble. And this happens all the time, romantic conservatism notwithstanding. Here we come to the second and more familiar pragmatist thesis: Thought or inquiry is instrumental as well as situated in practice. Reflective, deliberative, even contemplative thinking originates in the practical need to solve real problems.

The pragmatists were not, of course, the first to situate thinking within the experience of everyday life; this insight goes back at least to Aristotle. Their innovation was to move the category of the practical from the periphery to the center in their account of human reason. This reversed the familiar Platonic and Aristotelian ordering in which speculation or theory is the primary and highest form of reason. For pragmatists, the capacity for reason is best suited to practical concerns because it arises from our efforts to deal with those concerns.

Both the traditional ordering of the practical and theoretical, and the pragmatist reversal of that ordering, are illustrated in the origin of the term "pragmatism" itself. Peirce took the word from Kant, who had defined "pragmatic" beliefs as those that were "contingent only," supplying a ground for the actual employment of means to certain actions' even though "another might form a better judgment." The strength of a pragmatic belief was measured by the believer's willingness to bet on it: "sometimes it turns out that a man has persuasion sufficient to be valued at one ducat, but not at ten.... Thus pragmatic belief admits of degrees which, according to the difference of the interests at stake, may be large or small."

In Kant's view, this merely contingent and relative pragmatic type of belief was different in kind from genuine knowledge. Through science, human beings could gain true knowledge of the spatio-temporal natural world of cause and effect; and through reflection on their capacity for deliberation about what to do, they could gain true practical knowledge of the moral realm. But the assessment of the likelihood of attaining an end through given means must remain in the lower category of the pragmatic—mere guesswork. In a transvaluative flip worthy of Nietzsche, Peirce reversed the Kantian hierarchy, and assimilated all human science, speculative philosophy, and moral inquiry into the category of the pragmatic. All judgments—scientific and moral as well as prudential and technical—were contingent, probabilistic, relative to a situation and to the interests of an agent or a community of agents. Thought was no longer to be conceived as something distinct from practice, but rather it simply was practice, or activity, in its deliberative or reflective aspect.

In making this assimilation, the pragmatists took a decisive step beyond orthodox nineteenth-century positivism. Following a tradition as firmly lodged in British empiricism as in European rationalism, positivists had treated philosophy and science not as forms of problem-solving practical reason, but as autonomous, distinctively "mental" activities prior to and independent of practice, aimed at providing an accurate representation of an objective external reality. Rejecting this dualism, the pragmatists applied the utilitarian test of consequences to theories, as well as to rules for action, on the ground that all beliefs were, directly or indirectly action-guiding and, accordingly, should be judged by their efficacy in leading the agent through experience successfully.

The notion of making beliefs, thoughts, or propositions accurately represent external reality played no essential part in the pragmatic account of inquiry. The "externality" of "the world" was the other side of the coin to the "internality" of "the mind"; having rejected the one, the pragmatists had no need for the other. They believed that it sometimes made sense to speak of ideas or propositions as copying or representing facts, but representational accuracy was not a general criterion for evaluating either ordinary beliefs or scientific theories. The general criterion was success in helping people cope with the world.

Holmes understood this feature of pragmatism and appreciated its originality; in one of his few bits of grudging praise for James' version of pragmatism, he acknowledged that his old friend had "made a valuable contribution in pointing out that ideas were not necessarily faint pictures of original experience. . . ." He himself often invoked this pragmatist insight into the instrumental character of thought, most notably in the words of his *Gitlow* dissent: "Every idea is an incitement. It offers itself for belief and if believed it is acted on. . . ."[68]

A corollary of pragmatism, derived from the tenets that thought is always both situated and instrumental, is a kind of perspectivism. Because new beliefs emerge out of a complex of already existing beliefs that can never be made fully conscious and explicit, all useful beliefs may not ultimately prove commensurable with each other. Furthermore, because inquiry is at root an instrument to guide action (including the action of further inquiry), its products are subject to revision as the ends sought in action change. This double relativity of situation and purpose implies a tentative attitude toward all beliefs, including especially those "theoretical" and "fundamental" ones to which we are most likely to attribute permanent and universal validity. The pragmatist recognizes that the best account of a phenomenon (such as law) from one angle, for one purpose, at one time, might not serve as well from another perspec-

68. Gitlow v. New York, 268 U.S. 652, 673 (1925).

tive, rooted in another temporal context, and aimed at different goals. In its mature version, as Dewey stated it, pragmatism rejects the assumption that there must exist a comprehensive and final account of "reality" that, if attained, would bring the process of scientific and philosophical inquiry to a close.

Question

Does the complex relationship of Holmes's thought to that of the American pragmatists and European existentialists, as sketched by Judge Posner and Professor Grey, shed any light on the *Abrams* dissent?

RICHARD RORTY, PHILOSOPHY AND SOCIAL HOPE

(1999).

The suggestion that everything we say and do and believe is a matter of fulfilling human needs and interests might seem simply a way of formulating the secularism of the Enlightenment—a way of saying that human beings are on their own, and have no supernatural light to guide them to the Truth. But of course the Enlightenment replaced the idea of such supernatural guidance with the idea of a quasi-divine faculty called "reason". It is this idea which American pragmatists and post-Nietzschean European philosophers are attacking. What seems most shocking about their criticisms of this idea is not their description of natural science as an attempt to manage reality rather than to represent it: Rather, it is their description of moral choice as always a matter of compromise between competing goods, rather than as a choice between the absolutely right and the absolutely wrong.

Controversies between foundationalists and antifoundationalists on the theory of knowledge look like the sort of merely scholastic quarrels which can safely be left to the philosophy professors. But quarrels about the character of moral choice look more important. We stake our sense of who we are on the outcome of such choices. So we do not like to be told that our choices are between alternative goods rather than between good and evil. When philosophy professors start saying that there is nothing either absolutely wrong or absolutely right, the topic of relativism begins to get interesting. The debates between the pragmatists and their opponents, or the Nietzscheans and theirs, begin to look too important to be left to philosophy professors. Everybody wants to get in on the act.

This is why philosophers like myself find ourselves denounced in magazines and newspapers which one might have thought oblivious of our existence. These denunciations claim that unless the youth is raised to believe in moral absolutes, and in objective truth, civilization is doomed. Unless the younger generation has the same attachment to firm moral principles as we have, these magazine and newspaper articles say, the struggle for human freedom and human decency will be over. When we philosophy teachers read this sort of article, we find ourselves being told that we have enormous power over the future of mankind. For all it will take to overturn centuries of moral progress, these articles suggest, is a generation which accepts the doctrines of moral relativism, accepts the views common to Nietzsche and Dewey.

Dewey and Nietzsche of course disagreed about a lot of things. Nietzsche thought of the happy, prosperous masses who would inhabit Dewey's social democratic utopia as "the last men", worthless creatures incapable of greatness. Nietzsche was as instinctively antidemocratic in his politics as Dewey was instinctively democratic. But the two men agree not only on the nature of knowledge but on the nature of moral choice. Dewey said that every evil is a rejected good. William James said that every human need has a prima facie right to be gratified, and the only reason for refusing to gratify it is that it conflicts with another human need. Nietzsche would have entirely agreed. He would have phrased this point in terms of competition between bearers of the will to power, whereas James and Dewey would have found the term "power", with its sadistic overtones, a bit misleading. But these three philosophers made identical criticisms of Enlightenment, and specifically Kantian, attempts to view moral principles as the product of a special faculty called "reason". They all thought that such attempts were disingenuous attempts to keep something like God alive in the midst of a secular culture.

Critics of moral relativism think that unless there is something absolute, something which shares God's implacable refusal to yield to human weakness, we have no reason to go on resisting evil. If evil is merely a lesser good, if all moral choice is a compromise between conflicting goods, then, they say, there is no point in moral struggle. The lives of those who have died resisting injustice become pointless. But to us pragmatists moral struggle is continuous with the struggle for existence, and no sharp break divides the unjust from the imprudent, the evil from the inexpedient. What matters for pragmatists is devising ways of diminishing human suffering and increasing human equality, increasing the ability of all human children to start life with an equal chance of happiness. This goal is not written in the stars, and is no more an expression of what Kant called "pure practical reason" than it is of the Will of God. It is a goal worth dying for, but it does not require backup from supernatural forces.

The pragmatist view of what opponents of pragmatism call "firm moral principles" is that such principles are abbreviations of past practices—way of summing up the habits of the ancestors we most admire. For example, Mill's greater-happiness principle and Kant's categorical imperative are ways of reminding ourselves of certain social customs—those of certain parts of the Christian West, the culture which has been, at least in words if not in deeds, more egalitarian than any other. The Christian doctrine that all members of the species are brothers and sisters is the religious way of saying what Mill and Kant said in non-religious terms: that considerations of family membership, sex, race, religious creed and the like should not prevent us from trying to do unto others as we would have them do to us—should not prevent us from thinking of them as people like ourselves, deserving the respect which we ourselves hope to enjoy.

But there are other firm moral principles than those which epitomize egalitarianism. One such principle is that dishonour brought to a woman of one's family must be paid for with blood. Another is that it would be better to have no son than to have one who is homosexual. Those of us who would like to put a stop to the blood feuds and the gaybashing produced by these firm moral principles call such principles "prejudices" rather than "insights". It would be nice if philosophers could give us assurance that the principles which we approve of, like Mill's and Kant's, are "rational" in a way that the principles of the blood-revengers and the gaybashers are not. But to say that they are more rational is just another way of saying that they are more universalistic—that they treat the differences between women of one's own family and other women, and the difference between gays and straights, as relatively insignificant. But it is not clear that failure to mention particular groups of people is a mark of rationality.

To see this last point, consider the principle "Thou shalt not kill". This is admirably universal, but is it more or less rational than the principle "Do not kill unless one is a soldier defending his or her country, or is preventing a murder, or is a state executioner, or a merciful practitioner of euthanasia"? I have no idea whether it is more or less rational, and so do not find the term "rational" useful in this area. If I am told that a controversial action which I have taken has to be defended by being subsumed under a universal, rational principle, I may be able to dream up such a principle to fit the occasion, but sometimes I may only be able to say, "Well, it seemed like the best thing to do at the time, all things considered." It is not clear that the latter defence is less rational than some universal-sounding principle which I have dreamed up *ad hoc* to justify my action. It is not clear that all the moral dilemmas to do with population control, the rationing of health care, and the like—should wait upon the formulation of principles for their solution.

As we pragmatists see it, the idea that there must be such a legitimating principle lurking behind every right action amounts to the idea that there is something like a universal, super-national court of law before which we stand. We know that the best societies are those which are governed by laws rather than by the whim of tyrants or mobs. Without the rule of law, we say, human life is turned over to emotion and to violence. This makes us think that there must be a sort of invisible tribunal of reason administering laws which we all, somewhere deep down inside, recognize as binding upon us. Something like this was Kant's understanding of moral obligation. But, once again, the Kantian picture of what human beings are like cannot be reconciled with history or with biology. Both teach us that the development of societies ruled by laws rather than men was a slow, late, fragile, contingent, evolutionary achievement.

Dewey thought that Hegel was right, against Kant, when he insisted that universal moral principles were useful only insofar as they were the outgrowth of the historical development of a particular society—a society whose institutions gave content to the otherwise empty shell of the principle. Recently Michael Walzer, a political philosopher best known for his earlier work *Spheres of Justice*, has come to Hegel's and Dewey's defence. In his more recent book *Thick and Thin*, Walzer argues that we should not think of the customs and institutions of particular societies as accidental accretions around a common core of universal moral rationality, the transcultural moral law. Rather, we should think of the thick set of customs and institutions as prior, and as what commands moral allegiance. The thin morality which can be abstracted out of the various thick moralities is not made up of the commandments of a universally shared human faculty called "reason". Such thin resemblances between these thick moralities as may exist are contingent, as contingent as the resemblances between the adaptive organs of diverse biological species.

Someone who adopts the anti-Kantian stance common to Hegel, Dewey and Walzer and is asked to defend the thick morality of the society with which she identifies herself will not be able to do so by talking about the rationality of her moral views. Rather, she will have to talk about the various concrete advantages of her society's practices over those of other societies. Discussion of the relative advantages of different thick moralities will, obviously, be as inconclusive as discussion of the relative superiority of a beloved book or person over another person's beloved book or person.

The idea of a universally shared source of truth called "reason" or "human nature" is, for us pragmatists, just the idea that such discussion *ought* to be capable of being made conclusive. We see this idea as a misleading way of expressing the hope, which we share, that the human race as a whole should gradually come together in a global community, a community which incorporates most of the thick morality of the European industrialized democracies. It is misleading because it suggests that the aspiration to such a community is somehow built into every member of the biological species. This seems to us pragmatists like the suggestion that the aspiration to be an anaconda is somehow built into all reptiles, or that the aspiration to be an anthropoid is somehow built into all mammals. This is why we pragmatists see the charge of relativism as simply the charge that we see luck where our critics insist on seeing destiny. We think that the utopian world community envisaged by the Charter of the United Nations and the Helsinki Declaration of Human Rights is no more the *destiny* of humanity than is an atomic holocaust or the replacement of democratic governments by feuding warlords. If either of the latter is what the future holds, our species will have been unlucky, but it will not have been irrational. It will not have failed to live up to its moral obligations. It will simply have missed a chance to be happy.

I do not know how to argue the question of whether it is better to see human beings in this biologistic way or to see them in a way more like Plato's or Kant's. So I do not know how to give anything like a conclusive argument for the view which my critics call "relativism" and which I prefer to call "antifoundationalism" or "antidualism". It is certainly not enough for my side to appeal to Darwin and ask our opponents how they can avoid an appeal to the supernatural. That way of stating the issue begs many questions. It is certainly not enough for my opponents to say that a biologistic view strips human beings of their dignity and their self-respect. That too begs most of the questions at issue. I suspect that all that either side can do is to restate its case over and over again, in context after context. The controversy between those who see both our species and our society as a lucky accident, and those who find an immanent teleology in both, is too radical to permit of being judged from some neutral standpoint.

KATHLEEN M. SULLIVAN, FREE SPEECH AND UNFREE MARKETS

12 UCLA L Rev 949 (1995).

Consider the two possible ways to bring the constitutional treatment of speech and economic markets into alignment. First, constitutional liberties might be interpreted to mandate deregulation in both the economic marketplace and the marketplace of ideas. In this across-the-board libertarian view, contemporary First Amendment law rests on better political theory than does the law of the Fifth and Fourteenth Amendments. It preserves a capacious sphere for private experiment, in which, in the words of economist Aaron Director, "freedom means . . . responsibility, change, adventure, departure from accepted ways of doing things. It means freedom to choose one's ends as well as means for attaining them."[4] This freedom is as significant in economic as in intellectual life, Director argued, as did his protege, Ronald Coase.[5]

Those who would deregulate both speech and economic markets distrust government equally in both spheres. Richard Epstein, for example, argues that government always has overwhelming temptations toward corruption, given its power to coerce and its power to tax.[6] Rent-seeking by the governing classes is inevitable. Thus, he suggests, we should resurrect something like our current First Amendment law for property rights. After all, he says, there is no reason to suppose that those whom we distrust as self-serving intellectual monopolists when it comes to suppressing dissident leaflets will suddenly turn into "impartial solons" when it comes to enacting trucking regulation or rent control.

4. Aaron Director, The Parity of the Economic Market Place, 7 J.L. & ECON. 1, 8–9 (1964).

5. See R.H. Coase, The Economics of the First Amendment: The Market for Goods and the Market for Ideas, 64 AM. ECON. REV. PROC. 384 (1974).

6. Richard A. Epstein, Property, Speech, and the Politics of Distrust, 59 U. CHI. L. REV. 41 (1992). For a reply to Epstein, see Frank Michelman, Liberties, Fair Values, and Constitutional Method, 59 U. CHI. L. REV. 91 (1992).

On these assumptions, judicial intervention desirably constrains legislators from indulging self-serving incentives to regulate speech, and such constraint should apply equally to economic regulation. Director and Coase view the failure of courts to intervene equally in both spheres as itself explicable in self-interest terms: Courts, where the intellectual class dominates, constrain the rent-seeking of the government classes because they value talk above work, words above widgets. But courts are indifferent to economic regulation despite its greater importance to "the lower orders."[7] As Coase writes,

> Self-esteem leads the intellectuals to magnify the importance of their own market. That others should be regulated seems natural, particularly as many of the intellectuals see themselves as doing the regulating. But self-interest combines with self-esteem to ensure that, while others are regulated, regulation should not apply to them. And so it is possible to live with ... contradictory views about the role of government in these two markets.[8]

In Coase's view, it is "contradictory" to hold that "in the market for goods, government regulation is desirable whereas, in the market for ideas, government regulation is undesirable and should be strictly limited."[9] Coase suggests that this regime ought to be neutralized or perhaps even reversed.

Arguments like Coase's and Epstein's have led some observers to suggest that economic and free speech libertarianism have a deep ideological affinity. Frederick Schauer, for example, has suggested that the by now widely observed "rightward shift in the political center of gravity" of arguments for free speech should come as no surprise.[10] Right-wing rent-seekers will systematically prefer private ordering to regulation, Schauer posits, because they predict that they will enjoy dominance in the private order given their superior access to "economic, social, political, psychological, and cultural" resources—a dominance that, in Schauer's account, speech regulation, like economic regulation, would help to undermine. Advocates of extending free speech libertarianism to the economic sphere would likely defend their preference for private ordering on less instrumental grounds of natural rights or social utility. Whatever its justification, this first response to the existing asymmetry would treat both intellectual and economic exchange as presumptively unregulated markets.

The second possible response to the current asymmetry would take the opposite approach: treat both commercial and intellectual exchange as markets, but permit regulation of both without constitutional impediment. The new speech regulators who take this view suggest that

7. Coase, supra note 19, at 386.

8. Id.

9. Id. at 384.

10. Frederick Schauer, The Political Incidence of the Free Speech Principle, 64 U. COLO. L. REV. 935, 942 (1993). On the rightward drift in free speech advocacy, see J.M. Balkin, Some Realism About Pluralism: Legal Realist Approaches to the First Amendment, 1990 DUKE L.J. 375; Kathleen M. Sullivan, The First Amendment Wars, THE NEW REPUBLIC, Sept. 28, 1992, at 35.

current First Amendment law is an anachronism: If we abandoned laissez-faire in 1937 in the marketplace for goods and services, they say, why maintain faith in the invisible hand in the "marketplace of ideas"? As Cass Sunstein puts it, why not acknowledge that it is time for a "New Deal for speech"?[11]

This argument for greater constitutional latitude for speech regulation has a number of variations.[12] In common, though, the new speech regulators argue that First Amendment law draws the public/private distinction at the wrong boundary. In current law, "censorship" is understood narrowly as the restriction of speech by the government. If Random House rejects my manuscript, that's not censorship but rather market forces, editorial judgment, or just plain taste. Why? The government alone has a monopoly of force. if Random House rejects my manuscript, I can peddle it at Simon & Schuster. On the other hand, if the government bans my novel, I may have to move to France.

The new speech regulators question the view that the worst enemy of speech is government, and conversely, that private entities are entitled to unbridled "editorial" discretion free from government control. They would apply to the First Amendment context insights applied since the New Deal in the economic context by legal realists such as Columbia economist Robert Hale.[13] They observe that the existing distribution of speaking power, like the existing distribution of wealth or income, is not natural or prepolitical, but is rather a product of law. The laws of property, torts, contracts, and crimes, the new speech regulators say, determine who has the wherewithal to speak as well as to bargain. Law determines what legally protected interests your nose shall enjoy against my fist, and so law determines what legally protected interests your eyes and ears, your heart and mind, shall enjoy against my speech.

Because the new speech regulators see "rights" as products of positive law, they do not see government "restrictions" on rights as interventions disturbing a presumptively private order. A prepolitical "free market" does not exist, whether for goods and services or for speech. Government is always everywhere. The choice facing government, in this view, is never a choice between rights on the one hand and government intervention on the other. "Rights" are always threatened by some kind of abridgement: by public abridgement if government acts, or by private abridgement if it does not. Either the state allows A to harm B through inaction, or it protects B from A by limiting A's rights.

11. CASS R. SUNSTEIN, DEMOCRACY AND THE PROBLEM OF FREE SPEECH 16 (1993).

12. See, e.g., CATHARINE A. MACKINNON, ONLY WORDS (1993); MARI J. MATSUDA ET AL., WORDS THAT WOUND: CRITICAL RACE THEORY, ASSAULTIVE SPEECH, AND THE FIRST AMENDMENT (1993); SUNSTEIN, supra note 29; Balkin, supra note 26; Owen M. Fiss, Free Speech and Social Structure, 71 IOWA L. REV. 1405 (1986); Charles R. Lawrence III, If He Hollers Let Him Go: Regulating Racist Speech on Campus, 1990 DUKE L.J. 431; Frederick Schauer, Uncoupling Free Speech, 92 COLUM. L. REV. 1321 (1992).

13. See, e.g., ROBERT L. HALE, FREEDOM THROUGH LAW: PUBLIC CONTROL OF PRIVATE GOVERNING POWER (1952).

Lochner was undermined by such decisions as *Miller v. Schoene*,[14] in which the Court upheld a state law providing for the uncompensated destruction of blighted cedar trees that threatened to infect crops of nearby apples. The Court rejected the claim that the state thus had invaded the cedar owners' property rights, noting that if the state had left the cedars to infect the apples through inaction, it "would have been none the less a choice." Likewise, say the new speech regulators, we should understand that, if the First Amendment is interpreted to forbid liability when A's racist speech causes psychic harm to B, that is "none the less a choice" analogous to leaving the disease-spewing cedar trees in place.

In this view, "rights" are simply provisional statements of policy preferences that we have invested, temporarily, with an extra degree of resistance to the forces of political change. What we make, we can unmake. Minimum wage and maximum hour laws shift worker health costs from worker to employer; so hate speech codes shift hate costs from victim to speaker. If we read the First Amendment to preclude such regulation, the new speech regulators argue, we have simply chosen to leave private harms where they fall.

In the new speech regulators' view, restrictions on speech do not emanate solely or even principally from the state. Some nominally private entities, if unregulated, can wield as much power as government (or even more) over the content and distribution of speech. In this view, for example, corporations, unions, political parties, universities, broadcast media, and organized crime syndicates, to name a few, might have more functional power to shape public discourse than does government, for all its monopoly of force. For example, Fiss, noting that "the social world is largely constituted by entities that partake of both the public and private," argues that some of these entities are both conduit and speaker—private insofar as they speak, but public, and hence regulable, insofar as they are vehicles for the speech of others.

A postmodern close cousin of this portrait of maldistribution in the marketplace for speech emphasizes a broader sort of imbalance. In this view, the distribution of speaking power is determined not so much by the relative power of concrete entities such as corporations and broadcasters, as it is by various cultural forces emanating from multiple sources including, but not limited to, the state. For example, the ambient social power of racism or patriarchy might have the effect of silencing minorities and women. As MacKinnon puts it, this too is censorship, even though it occurs "through official and unofficial privileging of powerful groups and viewpoints" and "through silencing in many forms" other than government control. Hate speech and pornography operate as a kind of cultural unfair trade practice. As MacKinnon writes, "the free speech of men silences the free speech of women," stifling any voice that would talk back.[15]

14. 276 U.S. 272 (1928).

15. CATHERINE A. MACKINNON, FEMINISM UNMODIFIED: DISCOURSES ON LIFE AND LAW 193 (1987).

Many might agree broadly with these accounts of unequal speaking power as a descriptive matter. The new speech regulators' crucial and more controversial normative move is to endorse a catalogue of government regulations of speech that strongly resemble various standard forms of economic regulation, even if they are not always described explicitly in those terms. These arguments for speech regulation, like those for economic regulation, are sometimes allocative and sometimes distributive or paternalist. The allocative arguments suggest that the mix of speech itself—free competition in ideas—is blocked by various market imperfections, and that regulation that appears to limit speech can actually be speech-enhancing. These arguments are parallel to arguments that minimum wage laws or antitrust decrees do not limit economic efficiency but rather facilitate the production decisions that would have resulted had conditions of perfect competition genuinely obtained in the first place. The distributive and paternalist arguments, in contrast, hold that some values, such as equality or public deliberation, trump "allocative efficiency" in the exchange of ideas, and so justify government regulation even if it limits rather than increases the amount or variety of speech that would have been exchanged in the absence of regulation.

To take a few examples, new speech regulators have argued in effect that speech regulation should correct for "market failures," break up speech "monopolies," redistribute relative "speaking power," or protect us from our existing speech "preferences" or "tastes." First, correcting failures in the speech market might include forcing speakers to internalize negative external costs of their speech, or spreading that cost among those indirectly benefited. Frederick Schauer, for example, argues that current First Amendment rules require those harmed by speech to bear disproportionate costs for the benefits derived by the speaker or the rest of us. Thus, free speech operates, in his view, at times as a kind of uncompensated taking for public use. The victim of hate speech, for example, pays her own therapy bills or drops out of school so that the rest of us may "benefit" from the information that race hate is still alive and felt intensely by the speaker. Schauer argues for "uncoupling" the benefit of speech from its costs to the speaker, and looking for ways to "reallocate the costs of free speech protection away from the class of victims and more towards society as a whole."

Second, speech regulation might be modeled on antitrust law. If we force IBM and AT & T into competition, why not permit government trustbusters similarly to break up monopolistic or oligopolistic power over ideas? This antitrust analogy has been urged by new speech regulators, for example, in the context of political campaign finance reform. Stopping rich candidates from buying elections and corporations from spending corporate wealth on politics is, in this view, simply the speech equivalent of the Sherman Act or a cross-ownership prohibition by the FTC. This kind of free speech antitrust law would reject the premise of *Buckley v. Valeo*[16] that "the concept that government may restrict the speech of some elements of our society in order to enhance the relative voice of others is wholly foreign to the First Amendment."

By analogy to antitrust law, speech regulation might also impose obligations on some powerful speakers to share their speaking opportunities with their competitors—despite the usual First Amendment presumption against compulsory carriage of another's speech.[17] Owen Fiss, for example, argues that the Court's decision in *Red Lion Broadcasting Co. v. FCC*[18] ought to be more the rule than the exception. *Red Lion* held that broadcasters could constitutionally be compelled by the FCC's fairness doctrine to carry unwanted speech, as the price of their state-conferred oligopoly power over the airwaves. Fiss would extend this approach to other circumstances of concentrated market power beyond electromagnetic spectrum scarcity.

These antitrust analogies have postmodern close cousins in arguments for regulation of pornography and hate speech. Such regulations operate, in this view, as a form of cultural trustbusting. Speaking power is distorted not only by powerful corporations, unions, political parties, or broadcast media, but also by the ambient power of racism or homophobia, expressed in countless small, unorganized, and even anonymous ways. Promoting competition in this skewed marketplace fairly includes silencing the silencers in order to reduce barriers to entry into public discourse by the silenced. This theory is structurally akin to the losing argument in *Buckley*; it is simply premised on the existence of a more amorphous kind of monopoly. Instead of tuning down the voice of the well-funded candidate in order that competitors may be heard, this variation silences hate in order to permit victims to unthrottle their voices.

Third, those same pornography and hate speech regulations might be described alternatively in redistributive terms. On this account, they are designed to redistribute speaking power for the sake of material equality rather than increased ideological competition or a better mix of speech.

Fourth, some new speech regulators reject the free speech libertarian premise that truth and democracy, like beauty, are best left to the eye of the beholder and endorse a frankly paternalist view. Fiss and Sunstein urge a conception of "deliberative public dialogue" that may require speech inconsistent with existing preferences or tastes. For example, Sunstein endorses content-based regulation of broadcasting in order to increase public awareness about public affairs. Consumers who are deemed misguided or myopic in selecting goods for personal consumption should not be trusted to do any better in choosing among candidates or ideas.

16. 424 U.S. 1 (1976).

17. See, e.g., Pacific Gas & Elec. Co. v. Public Util. Comm'n of Cal., 475 U.S. 1 (1986).

18. 395 U.S. 367 (1969).

In sum, those who advocate a New Deal for speech see the "marketplace of ideas" as analogous to the commercial marketplace. In this respect, they are methodologically similar to their opposite numbers, the libertarians who would more drastically limit government intervention in private orderings in both speech and economic markets.

RED LION BROADCASTING CO. v. FEDERAL COMMUNICATIONS COMMISSION

Supreme Court of the United States, 1969.
395 U.S. 367, 89 S.Ct. 1794, 23 L.Ed.2d 371.

MR. JUSTICE WHITE delivered the opinion of the Court.

The Federal Communications Commission has for many years imposed on radio and television broadcasters the requirement that discussion of public issues be presented on broadcast stations, and that each side of those issues must be given fair coverage. This is known as the fairness doctrine, which originated very early in the history of broadcasting and has maintained its present outlines for some time. It is an obligation whose content has been defined in a long series of FCC rulings in particular cases, and which is distinct from the statutory requirement of § 315 of the Communications Act that equal time be allotted all qualified candidates for public office.

* * *

The broadcasters challenge the fairness doctrine and its specific manifestations in the personal attack and political editorial rules on conventional First Amendment grounds, alleging that the rules abridge their freedom of speech and press. Their contention is that the First Amendment protects their desire to use their allotted frequencies continuously to broadcast whatever they choose, and to exclude whomever they choose from ever using that frequency. No man may be prevented from saying or publishing what he thinks, or from refusing in his speech or other utterances to give equal weight to the views of his opponents. This right, they say, applies equally to broadcasters.

* * *

Although broadcasting is clearly a medium affected by a First Amendment interest, *United States v. Paramount Pictures, Inc.*, 334 U.S. 131, 166 (1948), differences in the characteristics of new media justify differences in the First Amendment standards applied to them. *Joseph Burstyn, Inc. v. Wilson*, 343 U.S. 495, 503 (1952). For example, the ability of new technology to produce sounds more raucous than those of the human voice justifies restrictions on the sound level, and on the hours and places of use, of sound trucks so long as the restrictions are reasonable and applied without discrimination. *Kovacs v. Cooper*, 336 U.S. 77 (1949).

Just as the Government may limit the use of sound-amplifying equipment potentially so noisy that it drowns out civilized private speech, so may the Government limit the use of broadcast equipment. The right of free speech of a broadcaster, the user of a sound truck, or any other individual does not embrace a right to snuff out the free speech of others. *Associated Press v. United States*, 326 U.S. 1, 20 (1945).

* * *

Where there are substantially more individuals who want to broadcast than there are frequencies to allocate, it is idle to posit an unabridgeable First Amendment right to broadcast comparable to the right of every individual to speak, write, or publish. If 100 persons want broadcast licenses but there are only 10 frequencies to allocate, all of them may have the same "right" to a license; but if there is to be any effective communication by radio, only a few can be licensed and the rest must be barred from the airwaves. It would be strange if the First Amendment, aimed at protecting and furthering communications, prevented the Government from making radio communication possible by requiring licenses to broadcast and by limiting the number of licenses so as not to overcrowd the spectrum.

This has been the consistent view of the Court. Congress unquestionably has the power to grant and deny licenses and to eliminate existing stations. *FRC v. Nelson Bros. Bond & Mortgage Co.*, 289 U.S. 266 (1933). No one has a First Amendment right to a license or to monopolize a radio frequency; to deny a station license because "the public interest" requires it "is not a denial of free speech." *National Broadcasting Co. v. United States*, 319 U.S. 190, 227 (1943).

By the same token, as far as the First Amendment is concerned those who are licensed stand no better than those to whom licenses are refused. A license permits broadcasting, but the lisensee has no constitutional right to be the one who holds the license or to monopolize a radio frequency to the exclusion of his fellow citizens. There is nothing in the First Amendment which prevents the Government from requiring a licensee to share his frequency with others and to conduct himself as a proxy or fiduciary with obligations to present those views and voices which are representative of his community and which would otherwise, by necessity, be barred from the airwaves.

This is not to say that the First Amendment is irrelevant to public broadcasting. On the contrary, it has a major role to play as the Congress itself recognized in § 326, which forbids FCC interference with "the right of free speech by means of radio communication." Because of the scarcity of radio frequencies, the Government is permitted to put restraints on licensees in favor of others whose views should be expressed on this unique medium. But the people as a whole retain their interest in free speech by radio and their collective right to have the medium function consistently with the ends and purposes of the First Amendment. It is the right of the viewers and listeners, not the right of the broadcasters, which is paramount. See *FCC v. Sanders Bros. Radio Station*, 309 U.S. 470, 475 (1940); *FCC v. Allentown Broadcasting Corp.*, 349 U.S. 358, 361—362 (1955); 2 Z. Chafee, Government and Mass

Communications 546 (1947). It is the purpose of the First Amendment to preserve an uninhibited marketplace of ideas in which truth will ultimately prevail, rather than to countenance monopolization of that market, whether it be by the Government itself or a private licensee. *Associated Press v. United States*, 326 U.S. 1, 20 (1945); *New York Times Co. v. Sullivan*, 376 U.S. 254, 270 (1964); *Abrams v. United States*, 250 U.S. 616, 630 (1919) (Holmes, J., dissenting). "(S)peech concerning public affairs is more than self-expression; it is the essence of self-government." *Garrison v. Louisiana*, 379 U.S. 64, 74–75 (1964). See Brennan, The Supreme Court and the Meiklejohn Interpretation of the First Amendment, 79 Harv.L.Rev. 1 (1965). It is the right of the public to receive suitable access to social, political, esthetic, moral, and other ideas and experiences which is crucial here. That right may not constitutionally be abridged either by Congress or by the FCC.

* * *

THOMAS W. HAZLETT AND DAVID W. SOSA, "CHILLING" THE INTERNET? LESSONS FROM FCC REGULATION OF RADIO BROADCASTING

4 Mich.Telecom. Tech L. Rev. 35 (1998).

Red Lion: The Rest of the Story

From the Supreme Court's perspective in 1969, the *Red Lion* case began with a feisty octogenarian Reverend John Norris, owner of the Red Lion Broadcasting Company, in Red Lion, Pennsylvania. On November 25, 1964, Norris' station WGCB broadcast a commentary by the Reverend Billy James Hargis, an Oklahoma evangelist preacher. Hargis' "Christian Crusade" was carried on many stations catering to the religious right. During the 15–minute broadcast, Hargis unleashed a scathing 2–minute attack on a liberal journalist, Fred Cook, in response to Cook's recently published book, *Goldwater: Extremist on the Right*. Cook subsequently wrote to several stations that had carried Hargis' program requesting free airtime to respond under the personal attack rules of the Fairness Doctrine.[19] Rev. Norris refused to grant Cook free airtime, though he did offer him access at the same rate paid by Hargis ($7.50 for a quarter-hour). Cook subsequently filed a Fairness Doctrine complaint with the FCC, which ruled that WGCB was obligated to give Cook free airtime. By 1969 the case had found its way to the Supreme Court.

In a landmark decision, the Court upheld the Commission's ruling, ordering WGCB to give Cook free time to respond to the attack. In the

19. The personal attack rules were an addition to the Fairness Doctrine introduced in the 1960s.

majority opinion, Justice Byron White concluded that, "the specific application of the Fairness Doctrine in *Red Lion* ... enhance[s] rather than abridge[s] the freedoms of speech and press protected by the First Amendment."[20] This conclusion of the Court appears to be uninformed of the well-orchestrated campaign by the Democratic National Committee (DNC) to silence pro-Goldwater forces prior to the 1964 presidential elections which had brought this case before them.

In 1962, President Kennedy's policies were under sustained attack from conservative broadcasters across the country. Of particular concern to the President were vocal right-wing opponents of the nuclear test-ban treaty being considered by the Senate at the time. The administration and the DNC seized upon the Fairness Doctrine as a way to counter the "radical right" in their battle to pass the treaty. The Citizens Committee for a Nuclear Test Ban Treaty, which was established and funded by the Democrats, orchestrated a very effective protest campaign against hostile radio editorials, demanding free reply time under the Fairness Doctrine whenever a conservative broadcaster denounced the treaty. Ultimately, the Senate ratified the treaty by a resounding two-thirds majority.

Flush with this success, the DNC and the Kennedy–Johnson Administration decided to extend use of the doctrine to other high-priority legislation and the impending 1964 elections. Democratic Party funding sources were used to establish a professional listening post to monitor right-wing radio. The DNC also prepared a kit explaining "how to demand time under the Fairness Doctrine," which was handed out at conferences. As Bill Ruder, an Assistant Secretary of Commerce under President Kennedy, noted: "Our massive strategy was to use the Fairness Doctrine to challenge and harass right-wing broadcasters in the hope that the challenges would be so costly to them that they would be inhibited and decide it was too expensive to continue."

The Democrats' "fairness" campaign was considered a stunning success by November 1964, when Johnson beat Goldwater in a landslide. The effort had produced 1,035 letters to stations, resulting in 1,678 hours of free airtime.

* * *

Nixon's "Chill"

Soon after the 1968 elections, the Nixon administration adopted a policy of responding to all media reports deemed unfair or inaccurate. Staffers wrote weekly press analyses entitled "Little Lies," which detailed unfavorable media coverage and assigned responsibility for an official response. However, by October, 1969, Nixon's Chief of Staff H.R. Haldeman recognized that the countercriticism campaign was ineffective and they were rapidly falling behind. The administration needed a more targeted approach—what White House aide Jeb Magruder dubbed the "rifle" approach to the media. This strategy, the cornerstone of which

20. 395 U.S. 367, at 375.

was the Fairness Doctrine, was twofold. First, in an attempt to affect network programming, administration staffers used threats of Fairness Doctrine challenges in direct meetings and phone calls with top executives at CBS, NBC and ABC. Second, the Republican National Committee (RNC) initiated a private campaign of direct pressure on broadcasters through Fairness Doctrine complaints and license renewal challenges.

* * *

After five televised speeches by Nixon on Vietnam policy, CBS offered airtime to the Democratic National Committee to respond. Following the first DNC broadcast, the RNC, arguing that the DNC had addressed issues other than Vietnam, demanded time for rebuttal under the Fairness Doctrine. The petition was refused by CBS and the case went before the Commission, which ruled in favor of the RNC. The D.C. Circuit later overturned the FCC's ruling in a blistering opinion, noting that "the [FCC] is functioning in the midst of a fierce political battle, where the stakes are high and the outcome can affect in a very real sense the political future of our nation."[55]

* * *

Extending the "Chill" Beyond Washington Politics

Exploitation of the Fairness Doctrine was not limited to presidents or the major political parties. Many public interest groups used the doctrine to influence the debate on local and regional issues as well as commercial speech. For example, the 1985 FCC proceedings on the Fairness Doctrine recount a battle that ensued over a California referendum on a glass recycling program. The beverage industry prepared an advertising campaign in opposition to the bottle bill. When the bottle bill lobby learned of the advertisements, they wired 500 stations demanding twice the amount of airtime free from any station accepting the commercials. Two-thirds of the stations subsequently refused the bottle industry's ads.

The Fairness Doctrine went beyond public affairs, affecting commercial speech as well. Anti-smoking activists filed a successful fairness complaint against CBS in response to cigarette advertising and the environmental group Friends of the Earth waged a fairness campaign against luxury automobile advertising. The Fairness Doctrine was invoked against advertisements for everything from snowmobiles and trash compactors to Crest toothpaste.

* * *

The FCC Lifts Radio Regulation, 1979–87

By the 1970s, such egregious abuses of the system by both politicians and special interest groups were eroding support for content regulation of radio and television. In the final years of the Carter

55. 454 F.2d at 1027.

administration, the FCC reversed its position on broadcast regulation by arguing for more reliance on marketplace forces and less on content controls. The Commission substantially reduced the burdens on broadcasters with the "Deregulation of Radio" in 1981,[62] which comprised the following:

> Non-entertainment program regulation. The FCC eliminated "guidelines" indicating how much informational programming each station should render to have its license renewed, replacing it with "a generalized obligation for commercial radio stations to offer programming responsive to public issues."
>
> Ascertainment. Elimination of formal documentation of "community needs."
>
> Commercials. Abolition of FCC guidelines on maximum commercial time allowed on radio stations.
>
> Program Logs. Elimination of program logs, to be replaced by "an annual listing of five to ten issues that the licensee covered together with examples of programming offered in response thereto."[63]

* * *

The 1981 deregulation was important because it represented a sea change within the Commission. It now advocated a reliance on marketplace forces to achieve public interest goals, rejecting the viability of regulation. In its 1981 Report and Order implementing the regulatory reforms the Commission stated:

> We believe that, given conditions in the radio industry, it is time to ... permit the discipline of the marketplace to play a more prominent role ... Simply stated, the large number of stations in operation, structural measures, and listenership demand for certain types of program (and for limitations on other types of programming, to wit: commercials) provide an excellent environment in which to move away from the content/conduct type of regulation that may have been necessary for other times, but that is no longer necessary in the context of radio broadcasting to assure operation in the public interest.

* * *

While the 1981 deregulation represented a substantial change in broadcast policy, it left intact the most important form of content control, the Fairness Doctrine. Yet by 1984, the Commission had begun an inquiry into the Fairness Doctrine, questioning its constitutionality and effectiveness. In 1985 the FCC issued a report, concluding, "[W]e no longer believe that the fairness doctrine, as a matter of policy, serves the public interest."[67]

* * *

62. In Matter of Deregulation of Radio, Deregulation of Radio: Report and Order, 84 F.C.C.2d 968 (1981).

63. 84 F.C.C.2d at 971. The Commission lifted the same rules applying to television station licenses in 1984.

67. Fairness Doctrine, 102 F.C.C.2d 142, at 147.

In an extension of the logic behind the 1981 deregulation, the Commission concluded that, "the interest of the public in viewpoint diversity is fully served by the multiplicity of voices in the marketplace today ..." Furthermore, based on the "voluminous factual record," the FCC concluded there was strong evidence that the fairness doctrine "actually inhibits the presentation of controversial issues of public importance ..."

The report concluded that although the first prong was an affirmative obligation to cover controversial issues, the licensees had broad discretion in determining how to comply with the requirement. However, the second prong, which required broadcasters to provide equal access for the presentation of opposing viewpoints, did have a "chilling effect" on controversial speech. This was because any programming on a controversial subject would expose the broadcaster to potential Fairness Doctrine challenges or demands for free air time under the equal access provisions. The Commission summarized the net effect of the doctrine:

> [T]he fairness doctrine in its operation encourages broadcasters to air only the minimal amount of controversial issue programming sufficient to comply with the first prong. By restricting the amount and type of controversial programming aired, a broadcaster minimizes the potentially substantial burdens associated with the second prong of the doctrine while remaining in compliance with the strict letter of its regulatory obligations ... [I]n net effect the fairness doctrine often discourages the presentation of controversial issue programming.[71]

* * *

DID THE FAIRNESS DOCTRINE "WARM" OR "CHILL"?

* * *

A great deal of controversy surrounded the 1981 and 1987 deregulations. Many argued that dropping content rules would drastically reduce the overall supply of informational programming and end balanced coverage of important public issues.[74] Yet, radio has recently enjoyed a resurgence as both an influential medium for the discussion of policy issues and a dynamic business sector. For example, in a major 1993 poll about talk radio, the Times Mirror Center for The People & The Press reported that one in six adults regularly listens to telephone talk shows

71. *Id.* at 160. However, because of uncertainty over the Commission's authority to abolish the Fairness Doctrine, the rule remained in effect until August 1987 when it was finally eliminated. Congress later attempted to codify the fairness doctrine, which would have effectively reimposed the FCC's own regulation. H.R. 1934 / S. 749, 100th Cong., (1987).

74. The FCC received thousands of comments during its 1979–81 proceedings. For example, the ACLU and the National Organization of Women argued that, "consumer satisfaction is not the appropriate criterion for judging performance of radio markets. Rather ... public 'need' as distinguished from public 'want' should be the criterion ..." (84 F.C.C. 2d 968, at 1015). Likewise, the 1987 elimination of the Fairness Doctrine sparked a maelstrom of protest from groups as diverse as the ACLU, Mobil Oil and the NAACP, as well as conservative commentator Pat Buchanan.

about current events, issues and politics. One in four adults had listened to a talk show the day Times Mirror called or the day before, and another quarter said they sometimes listen.

In examining the U.S. radio market over the past two decades, there are three important "events" to consider. First, there is rapid growth in the overall number of radio stations, the bulk of the growth coming in the FM band. FM, which had been long suppressed by FCC policy, finally came into its own in the 1960s (following the FCC's authorization of stereo broadcasting on FM in 1961), and passed AM in listening share in 1979. The increasing number of stations was a function of two interactive forces: public policy (more licenses were supplied by the Commission) and market demand (more stations were economically viable). The second "event" is the 1981 "Deregulation of Radio," and the third is the FCC's abolition of the Fairness Doctrine in August 1987.

One of the advantages of studying radio markets is that stations typically have a distinct format throughout the daily program schedule, and these formats are reported by established industry sources. Hence, published format data can reveal what changes are taking place in radio programming over a given period.

To analyze the effects of content regulation on broadcasters' format choices, we obtained data on radio programming for both AM and FM broadcasters nationwide over the period 1975–1995.

* * *

Econometric analysis of the data suggests that the Commission was correct in its observation that competition between broadcasters was an effective means of delivering public interest outputs. The 1981 deregulation had little effect on the broadcast supply of informational programming. The elimination of the Fairness Doctrine in 1987, however, coincided with a statistically significant change in the structure of the AM radio market. More precisely, after 1987 we see a dramatic increase in the amount of informational programming as the share of news and talk formats rises steadily. Further quantitative analysis also suggests that the repeal of the Fairness Doctrine allowed AM radio to exploit its comparative advantage over FM by substituting talk formats for music.

Fundamentally, the quantitative evidence strongly suggests that repeal of the Fairness Doctrine led to significant increases in informational programming. This outcome is entirely consistent with the FCC's 1985 determination that the doctrine constrained broadcasters by making the presentation of controversial issues economically risky. The marketplace evidence suggests that content controls stifled programming on controversial issues, presumably by increasing the likelihood that a given radio station would be both challenged for not providing adequate access to alternative viewpoints, and forced to grant free air time. Once the doctrine was repealed, broadcasters were free to provide more informational programming, especially on controversial issues, without the fear of Fairness Doctrine challenges. The data show that, in fact, broadcasters provided much more informational programming once the controls were lifted.

CASS R. SUNSTEIN, DELIBERATIVE TROUBLE? WHY GROUPS GO TO EXTREMES

110 Yale L. J. 71 (2000).

Under the "fairness doctrine," now largely abandoned, broadcasters were required to devote time to public issues and to allow an opportunity for opposing views to speak. The second prong of the doctrine was designed to ensure that listeners would not be exposed to any single view. When the FCC abandoned the fairness doctrine, it did so on the ground that this second prong often led broadcasters to avoid controversial issues entirely, and to present views in a way that suggested a bland uniformity. Subsequent research has suggested that the elimination of the fairness doctrine has indeed produced a flowering of controversial substantive programming, frequently with an extreme view of one kind or another; consider talk radio. Typically this is regarded as a story of wonderfully successful deregulation. But from the standpoint of group polarization, things are more complicated. The growth of issues-oriented programming with a strong, often extreme view may create group polarization, and all too many people might be exposed to louder echoes of their own voices, resulting in social fragmentation, enmity, and misunderstanding. Perhaps it is better for people to hear fewer controversial views than for them to hear a single such view stated over and over again.

It is not clear what can be done about this situation. But it certainly makes sense to consider communications initiatives that would ensure that people are exposed to a range of reasonable views, not simply one. This was the original inspiration for the fairness doctrine, and there is reason to encourage media outlets to implement the same goal today.

MIAMI HERALD PUBLISHING CO. v. TORNILLO

Supreme Court of the United States, 1974.
418 U.S. 241, 94 S.Ct. 2831, 41 L.Ed.2d 730.

MR. CHIEF JUSTICE BURGER delivered the opinion of the Court.

The issue in this case is whether a state statute granting a political candidate a right to equal space to reply to criticism and attacks on his record by a newspaper violates the guarantees of a free press.

* * *

The appellee and supporting advocates of an enforceable right of access to the press vigorously argue that government has an obligation to ensure that a wide variety of views reach the public. The contentions of access proponents will be set out in some detail. It is urged that at the time the First Amendment to the Constitution was ratified in 1791 as part of our Bill of Rights the press was broadly representative of the people it was serving. While many of the newspapers were intensely partisan and narrow in their views, the press collectively presented a broad range of opinions to readers. Entry into publishing was inexpensive; pamphlets and books provided meaningful alternatives to the organized press for the expression of unpopular ideas and often treated events and expressed views not covered by conventional newspapers. A true marketplace of ideas existed in which there was relatively easy access to the channels of communication.

Access advocates submit that although newspapers of the present are superficially similar to those of 1791 the press of today is in reality very different from that known in the early years of our national existence. In the past half century a communications revolution has seen the introduction of radio and television into our lives, the promise of a global community through the use of communications satellites, and the spectre of a "wired" nation by means of an expanding cable television network with two-way capabilities. The printed press, it is said, has not escaped the effects of this revolution. Newspapers have become big business and there are far fewer of them to serve a larger literate population. Chains of newspapers, national newspapers, national wire and news services, and one-newspaper towns, are the dominant features of a press that has become noncompetitive and enormously powerful and influential in its capacity to manipulate popular opinion and change the course of events. Major metropolitan newspapers have collaborated to establish news services national in scope. Such national news organizations provide syndicated "interpretive reporting" as well as syndicated features and commentary, all of which can serve as part of the new school of "advocacy journalism."

The elimination of competing newspapers in most of our large cities, and the concentration of control of media that results from the only newspaper's being owned by the same interests which own a television station and a radio station, are important components of this trend toward concentration of control of outlets to inform the public.

The result of these vast changes has been to place in a few hands the power to inform the American people and shape public opinion. Much of the editorial opinion and commentary that is printed is that of syndicated columnists distributed nationwide and, as a result, we are told, on national and world issues there tends to be a homogeneity of editorial opinion, commentary, and interpretive analysis. The abuses of bias and manipulative reportage are, likewise, said to be the result of the vast accumulations of unreviewable power in the modern media empires. In effect, it is claimed, the public has lost any ability to respond or to contribute in a meaningful way to the debate on issues. The monopoly of the means of communication allows for little or no critical analysis of the media except in professional journals of very limited readership.

"This concentration of nationwide news organizations—like other large institutions—has grown increasingly remote from and unresponsive to the popular constituencies on which they depend and which depend on them." Report of the Task Force in Twentieth Century Fund Task Force Report for a National News Council, A Free and Responsive Press 4 (1973).

Appellee cites the report of the Commission on Freedom of the Press, chaired by Robert M. Hutchins, in which it was stated, as long ago as 1947, that "(t)he right of free public expression has . . . lost its earlier reality." Commission on Freedom of the Press, A Free and Responsible Press 15 (1947).

The obvious solution, which was available to dissidents at an earlier time when entry into publishing was relatively inexpensive, today would be to have additional newspapers. But the same economic factors which have caused the disappearance of vast numbers of metropolitan newspapers, have made entry into the marketplace of ideas served by the print media almost impossible. It is urged that the claim of newspapers to be "surrogates for the public" carries with it a concomitant fiduciary obligation to account for that stewardship. From this premise it is reasoned that the only effective way to insure fairness and accuracy and to provide for some accountability is for government to take affirmative action. The First Amendment interest of the public in being informed is said to be in peril because the "marketplace of ideas" is today a monopoly controlled by the owners of the market.

Proponents of enforced access to the press take comfort from language in several of this Court's decisions which suggests that the First Amendment acts as a sword as well as a shield, that it imposes obligations on the owners of the press in addition to protecting the press from government regulation. In *Associated Press v. United States*, 326 U.S. 1, 20 (1945), the Court, in rejecting the argument that the press is immune from the antitrust laws by virtue of the First Amendment, stated:

> "The First Amendment, far from providing an argument against application of the Sherman Act, here provides powerful reasons to the contrary. That Amendment rests on the assumption that the widest possible dissemination of information from diverse and antagonistic sources is essential to the welfare of the public, that a free press is a condition of a free society. Surely a command that the government itself shall not impede the free flow of ideas does not afford non-governmental combinations a refuge if they impose restraints upon that constitutionally guaranteed freedom. Freedom to publish means freedom for all and not for some. Freedom to publish is guaranteed by the Constitution, but freedom to combine to keep others from publishing is not. Freedom of the press from governmental interference under the First Amendment does not sanction repression of that freedom by private interests."

In *New York Times Co. v. Sullivan*, 376 U.S. 254, 270 (1964), the Court spoke of "a profound national commitment to the principle that debate on public issues should be uninhibited, robust, and wide-open." It is argued that the "uninhibited, robust" debate is not "wide-open" but open only to a monopoly in control of the press. Appellee cites the plurality opinion in *Rosenbloom v. Metromedia, Inc.*, 403 U.S. 29, 47, and n.15 (1971), which he suggests seemed to invite experimentation by the State in right-to-access regulation of the press.

Access advocates note that Mr. Justice Douglas a decade ago expressed his deep concern regarding the effects of newspaper monopolies:

> "Where one paper has a monopoly in an area, it seldom presents two sides of an issue. It too often hammers away on one ideological or political line using its monopoly position not to educate people, not to promote debate, but to inculcate in its readers one philosophy, one attitude—and to make money".
>
> "The newspapers that give a variety of views and news that is not slanted or contrived are few indeed. And the problem promises to get worse...." The Great Rights 124–125, 127 (E. Cahn ed. 1963).

They also claim the qualified support of Professor Thomas I. Emerson, who has written that "(a) limited right of access to the press can be safely enforced," although he believes that "(g)overnment measures to encourage a multiplicity of outlets, rather than compelling a few outlets to represent everybody, seems a preferable course of action." T. Emerson, The System of Freedom of Expression 671 (1970).

* * *

However much validity may be found in these arguments, at each point the implementation of a remedy such as an enforceable right of access necessarily calls for some mechanism, either governmental or consensual. If it is governmental coercion, this at once brings about a confrontation with the express provisions of the First Amendment and the judicial gloss on that Amendment developed over the years.

* * *

A responsible press is an undoubtedly desirable goal, but press responsibility is not mandated by the Constitution and like many other virtues it cannot be legislated.

Appellee's argument that the Florida statute does not amount to a restriction of appellant's right to speak because "the statute in question here has not prevented the *Miami Herald* from saying anything it wished" begs the core question. Compelling editors or publishers to publish that which "reason" tells them should not be "published" is what is at issue in this case. The Florida statute operates as a command in the same sense as a statue or regulation forbidding appellant to publish specified matter. Governmental restraint on publishing need not fall into familiar or traditional patterns to be subject to constitutional limitations on governmental powers. *Grosjean v. American Press Co.*,

297 U.S. 233, 244–245 (1936). The Florida statute exacts a penalty on the basis of the content of a newspaper. The first phase of the penalty resulting from the compelled printing of a reply is exacted in terms of the cost in printing and composing time and materials and in taking up space that could be devoted to other material the newspaper may have preferred to print. It is correct, as appellee contends, that a newspaper is not subject to the finite technological limitations of time that confront a broadcaster but it is not correct to say that, as an economic reality, a newspaper can proceed to infinite expansion of its column space to accommodate the replies that a government agency determines or a statute commands the readers should have available.

Faced with the penalties that would accrue to any newspaper that published news or commentary arguably within the reach of the right-of-access statute, editors might well conclude that the safe course is to avoid controversy. Therefore, under the operation of the Florida statute, political and electoral coverage would be blunted or reduced. Government-enforced right of access inescapably "dampens the vigor and limits the variety of public debate," *New York Times Co. v. Sullivan, supra,* 376 U.S., at 279. The Court, in *Mills v. Alabama,* 384 U.S. 214, 218 (1966), stated:

> "[T]here is practically universal agreement that a major purpose of [the First] Amendment was to protect the free discussion of governmental affairs. This of course includes discussions of candidates...."

Even if a newspaper would face no additional costs to comply with a compulsory access law and would not be forced to forgo publication of news or opinion by the inclusion of a reply, the Florida statute fails to clear the barriers of the First Amendment because of its intrusion into the function of editors. A newspaper is more than a passive receptacle or conduit for news, comment, and advertising. The choice of material to go into a newspaper, and the decisions made as to limitations on the size and content of the paper, and treatment of public issues and public officials—whether fair or unfair—constitute the exercise of editorial control and judgment. It has yet to be demonstrated how governmental regulation of this crucial process can be exercised consistent with First Amendment guarantees of a free press as they have evolved to this time. Accordingly, the judgment of the Supreme Court of Florida is reversed.

It is so ordered.

Reversed.

MR. JUSTICE BRENNAN, with whom MR. JUSTICE REHNQUIST joins, concurring.

I join the Court's opinion which, as I understand it, addresses only "right of reply" statutes and implies no view upon the constitutionality of "retraction" statutes affording plaintiffs able to prove defamatory falsehoods a statutory action to require publication of a retraction. See generally Note, Vindication of the Reputation of a Public Official, 80 Harv.L.Rev. 1730, 1739–1747 (1967).

MR. JUSTICE WHITE, concurring.

The Court today holds that the First Amendment bars a State from requiring a newspaper to print the reply of a candidate for public office whose personal character has been criticized by that newspaper's editorials. According to our accepted jurisprudence, the First Amendment erects a virtually insurmountable barrier between government and the print media so far as government tampering, in advance of publication, with news and editorial content is concerned. *New York Times Co. v. United States*, 403 U.S. 713 (1971). A newspaper or magazine is not a public utility subject to "reasonable" governmental regulation in matters affecting the exercise of journalistic judgment as to what shall be printed. Cf. *Mills v. Alabama*, 384 U.S. 214, 220 (1966). We have learned, and continue to learn, from what we view as the unhappy experiences of other nations where government has been allowed to meddle in the internal editorial affairs of newspapers. Regardless of how beneficent-sounding the purposes of controlling the press might be, we prefer "the power of reason as applied through public discussion"[1] and remain intensely skeptical about those measures that would allow government to insinuate itself into the editorial rooms of this Nation's press.

* * *

Questions

1) After *Tornillo*, does Congress have the authority under the First Amendment to require cable television stations to adhere to the standards of fairness that the Court upheld for broadcasters in *Red Lion*?

2) Notice that the Court's opinion in *Tornillo* makes no attempt to distinguish the *Red Lion* precedent. Is that because no convincing reason can be produced for treating broadcasters differently from newspapers so far as the obligation to cover opposing views is concerned?

3) Which decision, *Red Lion* or *Tornillo*, better serves the view of free speech expressed by Holmes's statement "the best test of truth is the power of the thought to get itself accepted in the competition of the market?"

C. EDWIN BAKER, HUMAN LIBERTY AND FREEDOM OF SPEECH

(1989).

The adequacy of the marketplace of ideas must be reconsidered once the assumption of objective truth is replaced with the view that people

1. Whitney v. California, 274 U.S. 357, 375, 47 S.Ct. 641, 648, 71 L.Ed. 1095 (1927) (Brandeis, J., concurring).

individually and collectively choose or create rather than "discover" their perspectives, understandings, and truths. First, it is not clear that the marketplace of ideas is the only, the primary, or the best realm in which to create truth. Do we not, and should we not, create truth by our activities? Second, assuming that speech and debate play a significant role, it is clear that in any process of creation, the conditions of creation will affect the results. The defense of an *unrestricted* marketplace of ideas must either show that it can be expected to lead to the "best" creations (with some criteria for "best") or show that it is itself a proper process in that results are "best" merely because they flow from this process. More generally, the issue becomes: What conditions can we expect to lead to the best choices?

An evaluation of the marketplace may depend on whether different people are advantaged by the choice or creation of the same truth or understanding. Certainly, if a single objective truth exists, its discovery presumably advantages everyone. Thus, assuming public availability of the discovery, it would not matter who made the discovery. Likewise, even if truth is created, as long as a unity of interest exists, differential contributions by various people or groups to its creation may be unimportant. If, instead, groups have divergent interests, the marketplace of ideas (and other activities that might be protected) presumably will lead to the "best" or "proper" or "progressive" understanding *only if* the marketplace favors those groups or interests who should be favored or if it "properly" distributes influence among various people or groups such that optimal compromises are reached. It is not clear that an unregulated marketplace meets either standard. For example, some argue for regulation that would create more or less equal access for all groups to the marketplace. Herbert Marcuse went further and concluded that in present historical circumstances the marketplace of ideas would work properly only if the rich and powerful were completely excluded and access were limited to progressive, leftist elements.

The classic marketplace of ideas theory assumed rationality as well as truth. It relied on reason in two ways. First, the theory assumed that people's reason enables them to comprehend a set reality and test assertions or propositions against that reality. Alternative interpretations of people's relation to the world, for example, those emphasizing people's dependence on "'sense data" rather than direct access to reality, also assume that reason allows people to grasp invariant truths. Second, the classic theory assumed that people use reason to avoid or unmask distortions in perceptions of reality that imbalances in message presentations might otherwise cause. In other words, reason enables people to find the truth that the theory assumes to exist.

Modern social theory also undermines confidence in the marketplace's reliance on assumptions of rationality. Its first reliance is immediately undermined once one rejects the assumption of objective truth.

People cannot use reason to comprehend a set reality because no set reality exists for people to discover. Moreover, modern social theory often rejects reason as the primary determinant of what people conclude to be true. Instead, understanding exists within "language games" or social practices, which seem infinitely various. Our conceptions reflect forms of life rather than reason applied in a metaphorical marketplace of ideas—although speech within this marketplace may be an important, but not necessarily an especially privileged, practice that affects our conceptions.

The sociology of knowledge radicalizes the above point. People's perspectives and understanding are greatly influenced, if not determined, by their experiences and their interests, both of which reflect their different locations in an historically specific socioeconomic structure. Two implications of the sociology of knowledge should be relatively uncontroversial. First, dialogue cannot completely eliminate conflicts and divergences between people's perspectives as long as the social structure causes people to have very different experiences and conflicting interests. Social change—changes in the family, social, economic, or political order—will have greater impact on people's divergent notions of "truth" than will any marketplace of ideas. Second, robust discussion will be insufficient (although not irrelevant) for achieving appropriate understandings since it is at best one determinant of understanding. A progressive development of understanding will depend as much on new experiences and changes in everyday practices as on discussion. Restrictions on experience-generating conduct are just as likely as restrictions on robust debate to stunt this process. Therefore, the goal of advancing truth or better choices does not explain treating the marketplace of ideas as more deserving of constitutional protection than expressive, experience-producing conduct. Any process of progressive development of understanding—the equivalent of the classic model's search for truth—will depend on the existence of a realm in which people can have new or changed experiences. Of course, not all experience-generating conduct can receive constitutional protection. Still, this analysis suggests the desirability of protecting a realm of conduct and everyday activity beyond mere discussion.

The classic model is dependent on rationality in a second way. People must be able to use their rational capacities in order to eliminate distortion caused by the form and frequency of message presentation and to find the core of relevant information or argument. This view of people's reasoning capacities cannot be accepted. It is equally inconsistent with psychoanalytic and behavioral theories. People consistently respond to emotional or "irrational" appeals. "subconscious" repressions, phobias, or desires influence people's assimilation of messages. Stimulus-response mechanisms and processes of selective attention and retention influence understanding or perspectives.

Psychoanalytic considerations emphasize that understanding is a holistic phenomenon that cannot be completely circumscribed by reason and dialogue. Behavioral theory partially explains at the level of the individual what the sociology of knowledge observes at the level of the group—that people maintain particular perspectives even when presented with divergent information. Effective rewards lead people to adopt particular perspectives irrespective of their relation to truth, wisdom, or the progressive interests of humanity. The perspectives that are reinforced will vary depending on the person's social position as well as the stimuli applied. The psychological technique of selective attention and retention, as well as the insights of cognitive dissonance and balance theories, suggest *how* people preserve perspectives consistent with their personal interests.

These psychological insights, extensively relied on by advertisers and propagandists, should eviscerate faith in the ability of the marketplace of ideas to lead to the "best" truths or understandings. Even if some understandings are better than others, there is no reason to expect these to be discovered in the marketplace of ideas. Instead, understandings will depend on the form and quantity of inputs, on the mechanisms by which people process these inputs, and on people's interests and experiences. Without the assurance of rationality as the dominant means by which people evaluate competing viewpoints, robust debate cannot, in itself, be expected to lead to the best perspectives.

Diminished confidence in people's rationality leaves the quality of conclusions reached in robust debate apparently dependent on the quality of inputs or on conditions that would increase confidence in less rational processes. Inputs undoubtedly affect results, No one seriously suggests, however, that the existing distribution of access opportunities is apportioned in accordance with the intelligent or wise contributions each person or group can make to a "best" understanding of the world. Moreover, incredible inequalities of opportunity to use the marketplace also undermine claims that the robust debate provides a "fair" or otherwise justifiable process for regulating the struggle between opposing groups. Reliance on the marketplace of ideas appears improperly biased in favor of presently dominant groups. These groups have greater access to the marketplace. In addition, these dominant groups can legally restrict opportunities for subordinant groups to develop patterns of conduct in which new ideas would appear plausible.

ALEXANDER MEIKLEJOHN, FREE SPEECH AND ITS RELATION TO SELF-GOVERNMENT

(1948).

[T]here is undeniably a genuine, though partial, validity in the dictum that "the best test of truth is the power of the thought to get itself accepted in the competition of the market." It rightly tells us that the only truth which we self-governing men can rely on is that which we win for ourselves in the give and take of public discussion and decision. What we together think at any time is, for us, our truth at that time. And, in the sense in which words are here used, that test of truth is not merely the "best" test. There is no other. But that partial insight has often been interpreted, by the individualism which Mr. Holmes represents, to be a total characterization of the truth-seeking process. And, in that form, it has become, in our American public life, a fruitful source of intellectual irresponsibility and of the errors which irresponsibility brings. We Americans, when thinking in that vein, have taken the "competition of the market" principle to mean that as separate thinkers, we have no obligation to test our thinking, to make sure that it is worthy of a citizen who is one of "the rulers of the nation." That testing is to be done, we believe, not by us, but by "the competition of the market." Each one of us, therefore, feels free to think as he pleases, to believe whatever will serve his own private interests. We think, not as members of the body politic of "We, the People of the United States," but as farmers, as trade-union workers, as employers, as investors. We plan and vote for cotton or beets or silver or steel or wheat. Our ideas belong to the East or the West or the North or the South or the Middle. And our aim, as we debate in those capacities, is not that of finding the truth. The competition of the market will take care of that. Our aim is to "make a case," to win a fight, to make our plea plausible, to keep the pressure on. And the intellectual degradation which that interpretation of truth-testing has brought upon the minds of our people is almost unbelievable. Under its influence, there are no standards for determining the difference between the true and the false. The truth is what a man or an interest or a nation can get away with. That dependence upon intellectual laissez-faire, more than any other single factor, has destroyed the foundations of our national education, has robbed of their meaning such terms as "reasonableness" and "intelligence," and "devotion to the general welfare." It has made intellectual freedom indistinguishable from intellectual license. And to that disastrous end the beautiful words of Mr. Holmes have greatly contributed.

MARGARET JANE RADIN, CONTESTED COMMODITIES

(1996).

THE MARKETPLACE OF IDEAS

Liberal political life is sometimes conceived of in market rhetoric. In this worldview, a Leviathan is needed to overcome coordination problems and seek efficiency; Leviathan's subjects, unruly rent-seeking profit-maximizers, ceaselessly face prisoner's dilemmas and other transaction costs as they try to hold out and free-ride. But more than in the way liberalism itself is sometimes conceived, when it comes to freedom of expression a fabric of market rhetoric has been dominant, at least in the law. In the traditional legal view, freedom of expression protects a "marketplace of ideas." It promotes "free trade in ideas."

Some trace the notion of a marketplace of ideas to Mill's *On Liberty,* although that attribution can be disputed. In its origin the metaphor appealed to the notion of objective truth, which could be pursued most effectively through a marketplace of ideas. It promised that we would converge on the truth through continuing arguments with our opponents. This rhetoric is still prevalent in legal discourse. At the same time, the metaphor has become more skeptical—less committed to the idea that objective truth exists—in the hands of some. In their perspective, one idea is not intrinsically better or worth more than another; each idea's worth is measured only by its level of acceptance on the part of those who receive it. Indeed the value of a "value" is only the acceptance it can gain. The marketplace of ideas metaphor, once a commitment to convergence on objective truth no longer exists, signifies a laissez-faire theory of cultural development, a kind of "cultural drift" theory. Its skepticism—its aura of "Pushpin is as good as poetry"—does resonate with the skeptical reductionism of commodification.

The situation is much more ambiguous with regard to the marketplace of ideas than with regard to the marketplace of economic goods, however. Although much that circulates in the laissez-faire marketplace of ideas is commodified (governed by property and contract), there is also a great deal that is not, that is at least officially in the public domain. In contrast, a laissez-faire marketplace of goods consists entirely of commodified objects. In the contemporary era, the ideology of the laissez-faire market in economic goods has faded, and a broad range of governmental freedom to regulate is generally recognized. Yet, ironically, the ideology of the laissez-faire marketplace remains in full force when it comes to freedom of expression. Standard First Amendment rhetoric still has it that the marketplace of ideas must remain an inviolate laissez-faire realm. Just consider the American Civil Liberties Union's passionate defense of Nazis, Klansmen, and pornographers.

It is unclear why the market ideology has not faded with regard to expression as it has with regard to goods in general. One reason for its staying power may be its ambiguity. Along with the contemporary skeptical connotations of laissez-faire, traces of the original theoretical commitment to end-state truth remain. The notion of (objective) truth is, unlike the notion of intrinsic economic value, something to which we keep returning. Truth may not be some absolute value apart from the debate; but truth may still be conceived to be the end result of unconstrained conversation. In spite of the market rhetoric, then, it may be possible to reconceive the marketplace of ideas in terms of its role in achieving dialogic truth.

At any rate, our situation is that freedom of expression, one of the core commitments of political liberalism, is conceived of primarily in market rhetoric. It is worth pausing to elaborate the metaphor, to reflect on what it means to think of ideas as commodities in a market. How does the power of this metaphor organize the way we understand creation and interaction of ideas?

First, objectification: Ideas are conceptually detached from the individuals who have them, whether those who have them are creators and commentators—in market rhetoric, producers and sellers—or hearers and receivers—in market rhetoric, consumers or buyers. As long as ideas that meet the demand of the audience are produced, it doesn't matter how (if at all) committed to them their producers are, or how (if at all) the ideas are connected with the self-constitution of their producers. Nor does it matter who buys them or how they are connected with the buyers. It is as if buyers—people's minds—could be constituted wholly apart from the ideas that they are willing to buy from time to time. Nor does it matter where the demand comes from or how it is produced: just as in the market for goods, expenditures for advertising and packaging pay off in the marketplace of ideas.

Next, fungibility: Ideas are interchangeable, in the sense that for the purposes of the market, one idea is as good as another. In laissez-faire ideology, it doesn't matter if the market is flooded with ugly, unsafe, and degrading products, so long as people are willing to buy them. The notion of "sound bites" fits into the fungibility aspect of commodification. Moreover, one proponent of a given idea is as good as another; proponents are fungible too. Only if people are willing to buy it does it matter whether an idea is produced, and it doesn't matter who produces it—persons, groups, or corporations; advertising agencies; even the government.

In the marketplace of ideas, the government as idea-producer and disseminator is not functionally or normatively different from other idea-producers and disseminators. When it is understood as speaking, the government is just another speaker in the marketplace because, in laissez-faire ideology, the value of a commodity depends only upon the demand for it by buyers, and not upon who produces it or places it upon the market. Thus, the marketplace of ideas inscribes a public/private distinction, but it is not the one that locates the divide between the state and the free market. Instead it replicates the sovereign/proprietary distinction in the laissez-faire market for goods. When the state is acting in its sovereign capacity, it is supposed to be precluded from interfering with the natural forces of the free market, but when the state is acting as a property owner, it may become a player in the market on the same footing as everyone else.

Next, commensurability: The rhetoric of the marketplace of ideas has not usually explicitly involved commensurability or money equivalence. Paeans to the marketplace of ideas do not usually declaim, "May the idea that commands the highest price win." They do in effect declaim, however, "May the idea that commands the greatest acceptance win," measured by number of adherents and intensity of commitment. This seems to be a thinly veiled commensurability: the value of ideas can be definitively ranked by their level of acceptance. Also, of course, it is evident in practice that ideas as commodities are closely connected with dollars in a number of ways. In a marketplace the value of a commodity depends only on the demand for it, and the demand depends largely on how it is packaged and marketed. Does anyone doubt that as things stand, many ideas are accepted because of packaging and marketing? Or that major political candidates are aptly described as expensively designed, expensively packaged, and expensively marketed products? Media corporations are in the business of selling TV shows and print space to advertisers. Does anyone think it an accident that the news product they produce is not independent of the interests of those advertisers?

Aligned with the reductionist aspect of commensurability, the marketplace of ideas involves a skepticism about values, as noted above. In the marketplace of ideas, the state cannot favor one group's value or expression over another's. In standard First Amendment rhetoric, state action that has an effect on expression must be viewed with intense suspicion unless it is content-neutral. The worst evil is for the state to engage in viewpoint discrimination. Just as the minimal state is supposed to function only to prevent trespass and fraud so the laissez-faire market can work, in the marketplace of ideas, the state as sovereign (though not as speaker) can be only a traffic cop. If there is to be a laissez-faire market in ideas, it cannot be permissible free expression for persons or groups to drown out voices other than their own. Hence restrictions on time, place, and manner are uncontroversial in principle, on the ground of neutrality.

In other words, policing the ideas market, as in any laissez-faire market, involves only preserving competition among producers and sellers and voluntary transactions between sellers and buyers. People may not be coerced or deceived (either by sellers or by the government) into buying ideas. In the ideas market, perfect competition can be pursued by keeping barriers to entry for idea production low (for example, perhaps, by providing education so that the costs of thinking are reduced). If the cost of producing ideas remains low, the supply of them will be high. Domination of the marketplace by one kind of idea—high market share for one producer—is not necessarily a problem. Dominance of one idea need not mean that minds are monopolized in any worrisome sense. If barriers to entry are low, high market share may instead indicate market power resulting from successful product differentiation. That is, demand may be inelastic because of high consumer loyalty to one brand of ideas. Monolithic acceptance of certain ideas need not indicate market failure in the marketplace of ideas.

How do things stand with respect to the marketplace of ideas? Since the New Deal, there has been a disjunction between our level of commitment to the laissez-faire market in ideas versus the market in goods. Paralleling this disjunction is the distinction between speech and conduct that has been salient in the law (and philosophy) of freedom of expression. The goods market represents the realm of acts (conduct) and the ideas market represents the realm of discourse (speech). At least in the post-New Deal era, freedom of expression uses this distinction to mark out its domain. In its stark form, the notion is that a broad range of state regulation of conduct is permissible, whereas state regulation of speech is presumptively impermissible. Only for the realm of conduct has the legal culture mitigated the extreme of commodification (laissez-faire ideology). This means that judges often have to decide in particular cases whether government action is aimed at speech or conduct.

Cases of symbolic speech caused trouble for this model. Such problem cases refined the speech/conduct distinction, at least in theory, to distinguish between the relative importance of the communicative and noncommunicative aspects of people's activities, and/or between state action in which we can appropriately impute a state purpose to affect communication as opposed to state action in which communication is affected only indirectly. I am not sure that these refinements have made great inroads on judges' commonsense acceptance of the stark distinction between speech and conduct. In any case, the refinements also rely on our being able to distinguish clearly between communicative impact and noncommunicative impact, and between state purpose to suppress communicative impact and other state purposes that merely suppress communicative impact indirectly.

Liberal Legal Institutions and Culture-Shaping

The main traditional alternative to a market rhetoric conception of freedom of expression relates to a broadly republican conception of politics. This alternative understanding of freedom of expression gives primacy to political speech. In this view, the purpose of freedom of expression is to foster self-government. Self-government can be narrowly or broadly conceived. If broadly conceived it involves a wide range of activities that foster appropriate self-constitution of persons as well-developed citizens.

In the political conception of freedom of expression, ideas are not conceived of as fungible market commodities. Public debate is not a process of letting the invisible hand validate a direction for the polity. Because it is not, the political conception does not stress content neutrality in the same way as the skeptical marketplace conception. When political expression has primacy, political expression must be distinguished from other kinds. This distinction requires a species of content preference. All that neutrality means in the political conception is that within the class of political speech we don't single out some as preferred and some as not: so that we know were neutral if we give communists and fascists the same speaking rights that we give liberal democrats.

It is obvious that the political conception can be harnessed by conservative statists to curtail protection of important dissenting views or lifestyles, on the ground that they are not relevant to self-government. But it need not be. It could also support a view that the commitment to self-government is vitiated unless there are pervasive cultural commitments to the bases of active citizenship (including education and economic well-being), and that these commitments, among other things, involve the state in duties to foster empowerment of those who have been wrongfully subordinated or excluded. The political conception of freedom of expression, in one guise, supports the view that the commitment to liberal polity is a commitment to protect certain particular values that create, enable, express, and maintain a culture of liberalism.

The political conception of freedom of expression needs to select what is appropriately political, and in doing so it selects specific values that are thought necessary for liberal culture.

A number of recent theories of freedom of expression are more unambiguously committed to a family of liberal theories that are much less skeptical about values than the traditional understanding of the marketplace of ideas in legal culture (at least as I read it). In these theories, liberal institutions shape our culture. The value of freedom of expression is connected to shaping and maintaining a liberal culture with particular characteristics. Debate shifts to the level of what those particular characteristics are or should be; the possibility of a neutral metalevel is denied. This is the way I see, for example, the argument that the law of freedom of expression is designed to create and maintain (against recurrent contradictory tendencies) a cultural character of tolerance. This is also one way to see the argument that freedom of expression ought to protect and encourage (against recurring danger of being crushed by the status quo) "romance" or social destabilization by dissenters who are in some important sense outsiders. One can also see as aimed at liberal culture-shaping the argument that freedom of expression ought to operate to create and maintain the fullest opportunities for self-actualization.

In their frank recognition that liberal culture involves commitment to particular values by the state, these theories call to mind John Dewey (although their proponents are not Deweyans). Dewey thought of freedom of expression as central to developing the kind of culture that can support democracy.

* * *

Thus, according to Dewey, experimental or scientific method as applied to social problems is the method of democracy. In order to make this method part of our social life we require education in its use, and we must use it to create a culture in which free inquiry—the method of "organized intelligence," "the procedure of organized co-operative inquiry"—is featured. The culture that is needed to produce the method of cooperative inquiry is humanistic culture. Thus, for Dewey, "democracy means the belief that humanistic culture *should* prevail." The humanist view of democracy "tells us that we need to examine every one of the phases of human activity"—"culture in general, education, science, art, morals, religion, industry and politics"—to "ascertain what effects it has in release, maturing and fruition of the potentialities of human nature." In the humanist view of democracy, freedom of expression is not a competitive marketplace but rather a cooperative pursuit of human flourishing.

CHRISTOPHER KENDRICK, MILTON: A STUDY IN IDEOLOGY AND FORM

(1986).

The formation of a unified market is a critical development in the transition to capitalism, and under capitalism the market takes on an unwonted importance in the life of the individual: the individual's relation to society comes to be obscurely mediated by the market—governed, that is, by the reified market categories which now take on a dynamic of their own. It is one effect of this reification that the market itself acquires a natural metaphorical power; thus the market apparatus comes to secrete a corresponding ideological apparatus, what will much later be called "the marketplace of ideas," which is not so much an idea as a mental set or structure for the entertainment of ideas. *Areopagitica* is a landmark, in its way, in the formation of this market ideology, and this fact, I think, is how one may account for its continuing ideological force. The essential argument of the treatise is for a free circulation of ideas: "Truth is our most valuable commodity," Milton argues, and it must not be monopolized. But Truth's entrance into the commodity form is an ambivalent one: the whole tract, beginning with the defense of books, might be read as a protest against the commodification of human activity:

> I cannot set so light by all the invention, the art, the wit, the grave and solid judgement which is in England, as that it can be comprehended in any twenty capacities how good soever, much lesse that it should not passe except their superintendence be over it, except it be sifted and strain'd with their strainers, that it should be uncurrant without their manuall stamp. Truth and understanding are not such wares as to be monopoliz'd and traded in by tickets and statutes, and standards. We must not think to make a staple commodity of all the knowledge in the Land, to mark and licence it like our broad cloath, and our wooll packs.

Truth and understanding are not *such* wares. Yet, at least on the literal level, they are wares. In fact, part of Milton's rhetorical strategy is to make all human activities appear in the light of the commodity form. Each sphere of activity is capable of being monopolized, its natural movements bottled up and stapled, and the monopolization of books logically leads to or implies the fetishism of other areas. If books are to be licensed, the third part of Milton's argument goes, then manners, recreation, music, balconies must also be regulated. The regulation of these areas is regarded as a patent impossibility, since they are not really commodities, not really "things" offering themselves to monopoly. Like books, the activities of these areas have a kind of human power that simple wares cannot have. Or so we are left to infer. But this does not change the fact that in being depicted as monopolizable, they have been seen under the aspect of the commodity. And inasmuch as there tends to be an implicit analogy drawn between the naturally deregulated state of such activities and the free movement of commodities on the market, Milton has fetishized these activities, instilling them with the abstract or reified power of the market, in the very process by which he intends to demonstrate their incommensurability with mere "wares." Thus the commodity places its shadowy imprint on much of the imagery in the tract; as a result, market ideology comes to be inscribed most intimately within Milton's argument, and to motivate its very figuration.

BERNARD WILLIAMS, TRUTH AND TRUTHFULNESS: AN ESSAY IN GENEALOGY

(2002).

It is sometimes said that the "marketplace of ideas" can be understood either literally or figuratively. Taken literally, it is presumably an economic market *in* ideas, a set of institutions through which communications expressing ideas are bought and sold—a market in books, newspapers, television programmes, and so on. What is the figurative contrast to this? Let us say that an *idealized* market is a structure in which the success of a given idea is measured not by its being bought but by its being accepted. The competition will be not a commercial interaction between entrepreneurs but an intellectual interaction between people advancing various ideas, and the "market forces" that operate on the ideas will consist of processes that are truth-acquiring relative to the question at hand. Abstracting from particular subject matters, these processes will standardly be such things as careful argument, attention to empirical inquiry, sifting of evidence, and so on. With regard to an idealized market, unlike a commercial one, it will not be a substantive question whether its operation tends to favour the acceptance of the truth, because the model is designed to embody just the processes that will favour the truth. However, the structure should not be idealized too much. We need not assume that the operation of these forces is frictionless, so that investigative investments are necessarily optimized; we should allow for the possibility, which exists in real life, that more time spent in investigating a given question may make it less likely that one will find the truth, not only about other questions but, in some cases, about that very question. The model should be of real people working within a structure that could be socially realized, working in a way that brings about competition between theories, suggestions, and so on (which may or may not be also a competition between people). The substantive question will then be, what actual structures approximate in a reasonable degree to an idealized market. A set of scientific laboratories in communication with one another are a favourable example; it is less clear how far criminal trials under the adversarial system are.

The idea of a free market in ideas as leading to truth has played an important role in the jurisprudence of the United States, and indeed it was first formulated in those terms by Oliver Wendell Holmes in one of the earliest and most influential contributions to First Amendment doctrine. When Holmes said that "the best test of truth is the power of the thought to get itself accepted in the competition of the market," he cannot simply have meant an idealized market, since he was arguing for not regulating certain kinds of speech in the actual social context of political and commercial activity, and the doctrine has been continually invoked ever since in the interest of not interfering with actual markets. The assumption of this approach is that, at least with regard to truths relevant to politics (and that reservation itself raises questions of First Amendment interpretation), the literal commercial market approximates to an idealized market. The trouble is that there is very little reason to accept this assumption. It has been convincingly argued that it is false in terms of economic theory, and at an empirical level the reasons for doubt are very familiar. The literal market generates a high level of noise. Everyone knows that in modern conditions of communication messages compete for attention and cancel each other out, and that they are picked out for reasons that need have nothing to do with their truth. Moreover, the system fails to provide, typically, any structured context for understanding messages. The hearer may know at some level what message each sentence conveys, but not what the messages mean.

In accepting that these are consequences of modern communications, one should not be too impressed by the idea that things used to be better. It is true that there was a time, in the nineteenth and earlier twentieth centuries, when in well-ordered European states and the United States some newspapers gave more space to detailed news and heavy-weight debate of public issues than they do now. But these were far from fully democratic states, and even among people who were fully citizens, such papers did not appeal to everyone. To the extent that they appealed to a narrower section very much engaged in public matters, call it "the political class," there is no reason to think that such a section is less informed now, while it may be that a wider range of people are, if fragmentarily, better informed. However, there is more colour to a different pessimistic belief, that things are going to be worse. In many liberal democracies, and above all in Great Britain, newspapers have increasingly become more and more useless in these respects. In some countries the project of giving intelligible structure to the news and directing attention to public matters has to some extent been sustained by television. This varies very much from place to place, with more suspect *étatisme* in some places and more cringing consumerism in others, but in many countries major TV organizations have retained some sense of responsibility for offering relevant and true information. The international multiplication of TV channels may well reduce that effect. Many channels will offer no news of any sort, and those that do so may well offer either very local or blandly unstructured news.

Moreover, the Internet shows signs of creating for the first time what Marshall McLuhan prophesied as a consequence of television, a global village, something that has the disadvantages both of globalization and of a village. Certainly it does offer some reliable sources of information for those who want it and know what they are looking for, but equally it supports that mainstay of all villages, gossip. It constructs proliferating meeting places for the free and unstructured exchange of messages which bear a variety of claims, fancies, and suspicions, entertaining, superstitious, scandalous, or malign. The chances that many of these messages will be true are low, and the probability that the system itself will help anyone to pick out the true ones is even lower. In this respect, post-modern technology may have returned us dialectically to a transmuted version of the pre-modern world, and the chances of acquiring true beliefs by these means, except for those who already have knowledge to guide them, will be much like those in the Middle Ages. At the same time, the global nature of these conversations makes the situation worse than in a village, where at least you might encounter and perhaps be forced to listen to some people who had different opinions and obsessions. As critics concerned for the future of democratic discussion have pointed out, the Internet makes it easy for large numbers of previously isolated extremists to find each other and talk only among themselves.

The merits of the market as a means of spreading true belief have been exaggerated because liberal historiography tends to treat the spread of expert knowledge itself, in particular the history of natural science, as a triumph of the market over restrictive practices. But this is very misleading. The emergence of scientific inquiry from restrictions exercised by the Church involved a change in the legitimation of belief with respect to physical nature. This change improved truth-discovery, and it involved free scientific inquiry. International scientific inquiry offers an approximation to an idealized market, but it does this only because its actual social structure is in important respects an example of a managed market: it involves such things as an increasingly high entry fee in terms of training, and also, necessarily, a powerful filter against cranks. The orderly management of scientific inquiry implies that the vast majority of suggestions which an uninformed person might mistake for a contribution to science will, quite properly, not be taken seriously and will not find their way to discussion or publication. Very rarely the cranky view turns out to be right, and then the scientists who ignored it are attacked for dogmatism and prejudice. But, they can rightly reply, there was no way of telling in advance that this particular cranky idea was to be taken seriously; the only alternative to their practice of prejudice would be to take seriously all such suggestions, and science would grind to a halt. The point can be generalized. Critics of the marketplace approach to First Amendment doctrine have pointed out that in institutions that are expressly dedicated to finding out the truth, such as universities, research institutes, and courts of law, speech is not at all unregulated. People cannot come in from outside, speak when they feel like it, make endless, irrelevant, or insulting interventions, and so on; they cannot invoke a right to do so, and no-one thinks that things would go better in the direction of truth if they could.

NATIONAL ENDOWMENT FOR THE ARTS v. FINLEY

Supreme Court of the United States, 1998.
524 U.S. 569, 118 S.Ct. 2168, 141 L.Ed.2d 500.

JUSTICE O'CONNOR delivered the opinion of the Court.

The National Foundation on the Arts and the Humanities Act of 1965, as amended in 1990, 104 Stat. 1963, requires the Chairperson of the National Endowment for the Arts (NEA) to ensure that "artistic excellence and artistic merit are the criteria by which [grant] applications are judged, taking into consideration general standards of decency and respect for the diverse beliefs and values of the American public." 20 U.S.C. § 954(d)(1). In this case, we review the Court of Appeals' determination that § 954(d)(1), on its face, impermissibly discriminates on the basis of viewpoint and is void for vagueness under the First and Fifth Amendments. We conclude that § 954(d)(1) is facially valid, as it neither inherently interferes with First Amendment rights nor violates constitutional vagueness principles.

* * *

With the establishment of the NEA in 1965, Congress embarked on a "broadly conceived national policy of support for the ... arts in the United States," see § 953(b), pledging federal funds to "help create and sustain not only a climate encouraging freedom of thought, imagination, and inquiry but also the material conditions facilitating the release of ... creative talent." § 951(7). The enabling statute vests the NEA with substantial discretion to award grants; it identifies only the broadest funding priorities, including "artistic and cultural significance, giving emphasis to American creativity and cultural diversity," "professional excellence," and the encouragement of "public knowledge, education, understanding, and appreciation of the arts." See § § 954(c)(1)-(10).

* * *

Throughout the NEA's history, only a handful of the agency's roughly 100,000 awards have generated formal complaints about misapplied funds or abuse of the public's trust. Two provocative works, however, prompted public controversy in 1989 and led to congressional revaluation of the NEA's funding priorities and efforts to increase oversight of its grant-making procedures. The Institute of Contemporary Art at the University of Pennsylvania had used $30,000 of a visual arts grant it received from the NEA to fund a 1989 retrospective of photographer Robert Mapplethorpe's work. The exhibit, entitled The Perfect Moment, included homoerotic photographs that several Members of Congress condemned as pornographic. Members also denounced artist Andres Serrano's work Piss Christ, a photograph of a crucifix immersed in urine. Serrano had been awarded a $15,000 grant from the Southeast Center for Contemporary Art, an organization that received NEA support.

When considering the NEA's appropriations for fiscal year 1990, Congress reacted to the controversy surrounding the Mapplethorpe and Serrano photographs by eliminating $45,000 from the agency's budget, the precise amount contributed to the two exhibits by NEA grant recipients.

* * *

In the 1990 appropriations bill, Congress also agreed to create an Independent Commission of constitutional law scholars to review the NEA's grant-making procedures and assess the possibility of more focused standards for public arts funding.

* * *

Informed by the Commission's recommendations, and cognizant of pending judicial challenges to the funding limitations in the 1990 appropriations bill, Congress debated several proposals to reform the NEA's grant-making process when it considered the agency's reauthorization in the fall of 1990. The House rejected the Crane Amendment, which would have virtually eliminated the NEA, and the Rohrabacher Amendment, which would have introduced a prohibition on awarding any grants that could be used to "promote, distribute, disseminate, or produce matter that has the purpose or effect of denigrating the beliefs, tenets, or objects of a particular religion" or "of denigrating an individual, or group of individuals, on the basis of race, sex, handicap, or national origin." Ultimately, Congress adopted the Williams/Coleman Amendment, a bipartisan compromise between Members opposing any funding restrictions and those favoring some guidance to the agency. In relevant part, the Amendment became § 954(d)(1), which directs the Chairperson, in establishing procedures to judge the artistic merit of grant applications, to "tak[e] into consideration general standards of decency and respect for the diverse beliefs and values of the American public."*

The NEA has not promulgated any official interpretation of the provision, but in December 1990, the Council unanimously adopted a resolution to implement § 954(d)(1) merely by ensuring that the members of the advisory panels that conduct the initial review of grant applications represent geographic, ethnic, and esthetic diversity. John Frohnmayer, then Chairperson of the NEA, also declared that he would

* Title 20 U.S.C. § 954(d) provides in full that:

"No payment shall be made under this section except upon application therefor which is submitted to the National Endowment for the Arts in accordance with regulations issued and procedures established by the Chairperson. In establishing such regulations and procedures, the Chairperson shall ensure that—

"(1) artistic excellence and artistic merit are the criteria by which applications are judged, taking into consideration general standards of decency and respect for the diverse beliefs and values of the American public; and"

"(2) applications are consistent with the purposes of this section. Such regulations and procedures shall clearly indicate that obscenity is without artistic merit, is not protected speech, and shall not be funded."

"count on [the] procedures" ensuring diverse membership on the peer review panels to fulfill Congress' mandate.

* * *

Respondents raise a facial constitutional challenge to § 954(d)(1), and consequently they confront "a heavy burden" in advancing their claim. Facial invalidation "is, manifestly, strong medicine" that "has been employed by the Court sparingly and only as a last resort." *Broadrick v. Oklahoma,* 413 U.S. 601, 613 (1973). To prevail, respondents must demonstrate a substantial risk that application of the provision will lead to the suppression of speech.

Respondents argue that the provision is a paradigmatic example of viewpoint discrimination because it rejects any artistic speech that either fails to respect mainstream values or offends standards of decency. The premise of respondents' claim is that § 954(d)(1) constrains the agency's ability to fund certain categories of artistic expression. The NEA, however, reads the provision as merely hortatory, and contends that it stops well short of an absolute restriction. Section 954(d)(1) adds "considerations" to the grant-making process; it does not preclude awards to projects that might be deemed "indecent" or "disrespectful," nor place conditions on grants, or even specify that those factors must be given any particular weight in reviewing an application. Indeed, the agency asserts that it has adequately implemented § 954(d)(1) merely by ensuring the representation of various backgrounds and points of view on the advisory panels that analyze grant applications. See Declaration of Randolph McAusland, Deputy Chairman for Programs at the NEA, reprinted in App. 79 (stating that the NEA implements the provision "by ensuring that the peer review panels represent a variety of geographical areas, aesthetic views, professions, areas of expertise, races and ethnic groups, and gender, and include a lay person"). We do not decide whether the NEA's view—that the formulation of diverse advisory panels is sufficient to comply with Congress' command—is in fact a reasonable reading of the statute. It is clear, however, that the text of § 954(d)(1) imposes no categorical requirement. The advisory language stands in sharp contrast to congressional efforts to prohibit the funding of certain classes of speech. When Congress has in fact intended to affirmatively constrain the NEA's grant-making authority, it has done so in no uncertain terms. See § 954(d)(2) ("[O]bscenity is without artistic merit, is not protected speech, and shall not be funded").

Furthermore, like the plain language of § 954(d), the political context surrounding the adoption of the "decency and respect" clause is inconsistent with respondents' assertion that the provision compels the NEA to deny funding on the basis of viewpoint discriminatory criteria. The legislation was a bipartisan proposal introduced as a counterweight to amendments aimed at eliminating the NEA's funding or substantially constraining its grant-making authority. The Independent Commission had cautioned Congress against the adoption of distinct viewpoint-based standards for funding, and the Commission's report suggests that "additional criteria" for selection, if any, should be incorporated as part of the selection process (perhaps as part of a definition of "artistic excellence"), rather than isolated and treated as exogenous considerations. In keeping with that recommendation, the criteria in § 954(d)(1) inform the assessment of artistic merit, but Congress declined to disallow any particular viewpoints.

* * *

If the NEA were to leverage its power to award subsidies on the basis of subjective criteria into a penalty on disfavored viewpoints, then we would confront a different case. We have stated that, even in the provision of subsidies, the Government may not "ai[m] at the suppression of dangerous ideas," *Regan v. Taxation With Representation of Wash.,* 461 U.S. 540, 550 (1983), and if a subsidy were "manipulated" to have a "coercive effect," then relief could be appropriate. See *Arkansas Writers' Project, Inc. v. Ragland,* 481 U.S. 221, 237 (1987) (Scalia, J., dissenting); see also *Leathers v. Medlock,* 499 U.S. 439, 447 (1991) ("[D]ifferential taxation of First Amendment speakers is constitutionally suspect when it threatens to suppress the expression of particular ideas or viewpoints"). In addition, as the NEA itself concedes, a more pressing constitutional question would arise if Government funding resulted in the imposition of a disproportionate burden calculated to drive "certain ideas or viewpoints from the marketplace." *Simon & Schuster, Inc. v. Members of N.Y. State Crime Victims Bd.,* 502 U.S. 105, 116 (1991). Unless § 954(d)(1) is applied in a manner that raises concern about the suppression of disfavored viewpoints, however, we uphold the constitutionality of the provision.

* * *

Finally, although the First Amendment certainly has application in the subsidy context, we note that the Government may allocate competitive funding according to criteria that would be impermissible were direct regulation of speech or a criminal penalty at stake. So long as legislation does not infringe on other constitutionally protected rights, Congress has wide latitude to set spending priorities. See *Regan, supra,* at 549. In the 1990 amendments that incorporated § 954(d)(1), Congress modified the declaration of purpose in the NEA's enabling Act to provide that arts funding should "contribute to public support and confidence in the use of taxpayer funds," and that "[p]ublic funds ... must ultimately serve public purposes the Congress defines." § 951(5). And as we held in *Rust,* Congress may "selectively fund a program to encourage certain activities it believes to be in the public interest, without at the same time funding an alternative program which seeks to deal with the problem in another way." 500 U.S., at 193. In doing so, "the Government has not discriminated on the basis of viewpoint; it has merely chosen to fund one activity to the exclusion of the other." *Ibid.;* see also *Maher v. Roe,* 432 U.S. 464, 475 (1977) ("There is a basic difference between direct state interference with a protected activity and state encouragement of an alternative activity consonant with legislative policy").

* * *

JUSTICE SCALIA, with whom JUSTICE THOMAS joins, concurring in the judgment.

"The operation was a success, but the patient died." What such a procedure is to medicine, the Court's opinion in this case is to law. It sustains the constitutionality of 20 U.S.C. § 954(d)(1) by gutting it. The most avid congressional opponents of the provision could not have asked for more. I write separately because, unlike the Court, I think that § 954(d)(1) must be evaluated as written, rather than as distorted by the agency it was meant to control. By its terms, it establishes content-and viewpoint-based criteria upon which grant applications are to be evaluated. And that is perfectly constitutional.

* * *

The First Amendment reads: "Congress shall make no law ... *abridging* the freedom of speech." U.S. Const., Amdt. 1 (emphasis added). To abridge is "to contract, to diminish; to deprive of." T. Sheridan, A Complete Dictionary of the English Language (6th ed. 1796). With the enactment of § 954(d)(1), Congress did not *abridge* the speech of those who disdain the beliefs and values of the American public, nor did it *abridge* indecent speech. Those who wish to create indecent and disrespectful art are as unconstrained now as they were before the enactment of this statute. *Avant-garde artistes* such as respondents remain entirely free to *epater les bourgeois;*[21] they are merely deprived of the additional satisfaction of having the bourgeoisie taxed to pay for it. It is preposterous to equate the denial of taxpayer subsidy with measures "aimed at the *suppression* of dangerous ideas." *Regan v. Taxation with Representation of Wash.,* 461 U.S. 540, 550 (1983). "The reason that denial of participation in a tax exemption or other subsidy scheme does not necessarily 'infringe' a fundamental right is that—unlike direct restriction or prohibition—such a denial does not, as a general rule, have any significant coercive effect." *Arkansas Writers' Project, Inc. v. Ragland,* 481 U.S. 221, 237 (1987) (Scalia, J., dissenting).

21. Which they do quite well. The *oeuvres d'art* for which the four individual plaintiffs in this case sought funding have been described as follows:

"Finley's controversial show, "We Keep Our Victims Ready," contains three segments. In the second segment, Finley visually recounts a sexual assault by stripping to the waist and smearing chocolate on her breasts and by using profanity to describe the assault. Holly Hughes' monologue "World Without End" is a somewhat graphic recollection of the artist's realization of her lesbianism and reminiscence of her mother's sexuality. John Fleck, in his stage performance "Blessed Are All the Little Fishes," confronts alcoholism and Catholicism. During the course of the performance, Fleck appears dressed as a mermaid, urinates on the stage and creates an altar out of a toilet bowl by putting a photograph of Jesus Christ on the lid. Tim Miller derives his performance "some Golden States" from childhood experiences, from his life as a homosexual, and from the constant threat of AIDS. Miller uses vegetables in his performances to represent sexual symbols.

One might contend, I suppose, that a threat of rejection by the only available source of free money would constitute coercion and hence "abridgment" within the meaning of the First Amendment. I would not agree with such a contention, which would make the NEA the mandatory patron of all art too indecent, too disrespectful, or even too *kitsch* to attract private support. But even if one accepts the contention, it would have no application here. The NEA is far from the sole source of funding for art—even indecent, disrespectful, or just plain bad art. Accordingly, the Government may earmark NEA funds for projects it deems to be in the public interest without thereby abridging speech. *Regan v. Taxation with Representation of Wash., supra,* at 549.

Section 954(d)(1) is no more discriminatory, and no less constitutional, than virtually every other piece of funding legislation enacted by Congress. "The Government can, without violating the Constitution, selectively fund a program to encourage certain activities it believes to be in the public interest, without at the same time funding an alternative program...." *Rust v. Sullivan,* 500 U.S. 173, 193 (1991). As we noted in *Rust,* when Congress chose to establish the National Endowment for Democracy it was not constitutionally required to fund programs encouraging competing philosophies of government—an example of funding discrimination that cuts much closer than this one to the core of *political* speech which is the primary concern of the First Amendment. It takes a particularly high degree of chutzpah for the NEA to contradict this proposition, since the agency itself discriminates—and is required by law to discriminate—in favor of artistic (as opposed to scientific, or political, or theological) expression. Not all the common folk, or even all great minds, for that matter, think that is a good idea. In 1800, when John Marshall told John Adams that a recent immigration of Frenchmen would include talented artists, "Adams denounced all Frenchmen, but most especially "schoolmasters, painters, poets, & C." He warned Marshall that the fine arts were like germs that infected healthy constitutions." J. Ellis, After the Revolution: Profiles of Early American Culture 36 (1979). Surely the NEA itself is nothing less than an institutionalized discrimination against that point of view. Nonetheless, it is constitutional, as is the congressional determination to favor decency and respect for beliefs and values over the opposite because such favoritism does not "abridge" anyone's freedom of speech.

Respondents, relying on *Rosenberger v. Rector and Visitors of Univ. of Va.,* 515 U.S. 819, 833, (1995), argue that viewpoint-based discrimination is impermissible unless the government is the speaker or the government is "disburs[ing] public funds to private entities to convey a governmental message." It is impossible to imagine why that should be so; one would think that directly involving the government itself in the viewpoint discrimination (if it is unconstitutional) would make the situation even worse. Respondents are mistaken. It is the very business of government to favor and disfavor points of view on (in modern times, at least) innumerable subjects—which is the main reason we have decided to elect those who run the government, rather than save money by making their posts hereditary. And it makes not a bit of difference, insofar as either common sense or the Constitution is concerned, whether these officials further their (and, in a democracy, our) favored point of view by achieving it directly (having government-employed artists paint pictures, for example, or government-employed doctors perform abortions); or by advocating it officially (establishing an Office of Art Appreciation, for example, or an Office of Voluntary Population Control); or by giving money to others who achieve or advocate it (funding private art classes, for example, or Planned Parenthood).[22] None of this has anything to do with abridging anyone's speech. *Rosenberger,* as the Court explains, found the viewpoint discrimination unconstitutional, not because funding of "private" speech was involved, but because the government had established a limited public forum—to which the NEA's granting of highly selective (if not highly discriminating) awards bears no resemblance.

The nub of the difference between me and the Court is that I regard the distinction between "abridging" speech and funding it as a fundamental divide, on this side of which the First Amendment is inapplicable. The Court, by contrast, seems to believe that the First Amendment, despite its words, has some ineffable effect upon funding, imposing constraints of an indeterminate nature which it announces (without troubling to enunciate any particular test) are not violated by the statute here—or, more accurately, are not violated by the quite different, emasculated statute that it imagines. "[T]he Government," it says, "may allocate competitive funding according to criteria that would be impermissible were direct regulation of speech or a criminal penalty at stake." The Government, *I* think, may allocate both competitive and noncompetitive funding *ad libitum,* insofar as the First Amendment is concerned.

* * *

JUSTICE SOUTER, dissenting.

The question here is whether the italicized segment of this statute is unconstitutional on its face: "[A]rtistic excellence and artistic merit are the criteria by which applications [for grants from the National Endowment for the Arts (NEA)] are judged, *taking into consideration general standards of decency and respect for the diverse beliefs and values of the American public.*" 20 U.S.C. § 954(d) (emphasis added). It is.

The decency and respect proviso mandates viewpoint-based decisions in the disbursement of Government subsidies, and the Government has wholly failed to explain why the statute should be afforded an exemption from the fundamental rule of the First Amendment that viewpoint discrimination in the exercise of public authority over expressive activity is unconstitutional. The Court's conclusions that the proviso is not

22. I suppose it would be unconstitutional for the government to give money to an organization devoted to the promotion of candidates nominated by the Republican Party—but it would be just as unconstitutional for the government itself to promote candidates nominated by the Republican Party, and I do not think that that unconstitutionality has anything to do with the First Amendment.

viewpoint based, that it is not a regulation, and that the NEA may permissibly engage in viewpoint-based discrimination, are all patently mistaken.

* * *

What if the statute required a panel to apply criteria "taking into consideration the centrality of Christianity to the American cultural experience," or "taking into consideration whether the artist is a communist," or "taking into consideration the political message conveyed by the art," or even "taking into consideration the superiority of the white race"? Would the Court hold these considerations facially constitutional, merely because the statute had no requirement to give them any particular, much less controlling, weight? I assume not. In such instances, the Court would hold that the First Amendment bars the government from considering viewpoint when it decides whether to subsidize private speech, and a statute that mandates the consideration of viewpoint is quite obviously unconstitutional.

* * *

The Government calls attention to the roles of government-as-speaker and government-as-buyer, in which the government is of course entitled to engage in viewpoint discrimination: if the Food and Drug Administration launches an advertising campaign on the subject of smoking, it may condemn the habit without also having to show a cowboy taking a puff on the opposite page;[23] and if the Secretary of Defense wishes to buy a portrait to decorate the Pentagon, he is free to prefer George Washington over George the Third.[24]

The Government freely admits, however, that it neither speaks through the expression subsidized by the NEA,[25] nor buys anything for itself with its NEA grants. On the contrary, believing that "[t]he arts ... reflect the high place accorded by the American people to the nation's rich cultural heritage," § 951(6), and that "[i]t is vital to a democracy ... to provide financial assistance to its artists and the organizations that support their work," § 951(10), the Government acts as a patron, financially underwriting the production of art by private artists and impresarios for independent consumption. Accordingly, the

23. See *Rust v. Sullivan,* 500 U.S. 173, 194 (1991) ("When Congress established a National Endowment for Democracy to encourage other countries to adopt democratic principles, 22 U.S.C. § 4411(b), it was not constitutionally required to fund a program to encourage competing lines of political philosophy such as communism and fascism").

24. On proposing the Public Works Art Project (PWAP), the New Deal program that hired artists to decorate public buildings, President Roosevelt allegedly remarked: "I can't have a lot of young enthusiasts painting Lenin's head on the Justice Building." Quoted in Mankin, Federal Arts Patronage in the New Deal, in America's Commitment to Culture: Government and the Arts 77 (K. Mulcahy & M. Wyszomirski eds.1995). He was buying, and was free to take his choice.

25. Here, the "communicative element inherent in the very act of funding itself," *Rosenberger v. Rector and Visitors of Univ. of Va.,* 515 U.S. 819, 892–893, n. 11 (1995) (Souter, J., dissenting), is an endorsement of the importance of the arts collectively, not an endorsement of the individual message espoused in a given work of art.

Government would have us liberate government-as-patron from First Amendment strictures not by placing it squarely within the categories of government-as-buyer or government-as-speaker, but by recognizing a new category by analogy to those accepted ones. The analogy is, however, a very poor fit, and this patronage falls embarrassingly on the wrong side of the line between government-as-buyer or speaker and government-as-regulator-of-private-speech.

The division is reflected quite clearly in our precedents. Drawing on the notion of government-as-speaker, we held in *Rust v. Sullivan,* 500 U.S. at 194, that the Government was entitled to appropriate public funds for the promotion of particular choices among alternatives offered by health and social service providers (*e.g.,* family planning with, and without, resort to abortion). When the government promotes a particular governmental program, "it is entitled to define the limits of that program," and to dictate the viewpoint expressed by speakers who are paid to participate in it. *Ibid.*[26] But we added the important qualifying language that "[t]his is not to suggest that funding by the Government, even when coupled with the freedom of the fund recipients to speak outside the scope of the Government-funded project, is invariably sufficient to justify Government control over the content of expression." Indeed, outside of the contexts of government-as-buyer and government-as-speaker, we have held time and time again that Congress may not "discriminate invidiously in its subsidies in such a way as to aim at the suppression of ... ideas." *Regan v. Taxation with Representation of Wash.,* 461 U.S. 540, 548 (1983) (internal quotation marks and brackets omitted); see also *Lamb's Chapel,* 508 U.S., at 394 (when the government subsidizes private speech, it may not "favor some viewpoints or ideas at the expense of others"); *Hannegan v. Esquire, Inc.,* 327 U.S. 146, 149 (1946) (the Postmaster General may not deny subsidies to certain periodicals on the ground that they are "morally improper and not for the public welfare and the public good").

Our most thorough statement of these principles is found in the recent case of *Rosenberger v. Rector and Visitors of Univ. of Va.,* 515 U.S. 819 (1995), which held that the University of Virginia could not discriminate on viewpoint in underwriting the speech of student-run publications. We recognized that the government may act on the basis of viewpoint "when the State is the speaker" or when the State "disburses public funds to private entities to convey a governmental message. But we explained that the government may not act on viewpoint when it "does not itself speak or subsidize transmittal of a message it favors but instead expends funds to encourage a diversity of views from private speakers. When the government acts as patron, subsidizing the expression of others, it may not prefer one lawfully stated view over another.

26. In *Rust,* "the government did not create a program to encourage private speech but instead used private speakers to transmit specific information pertaining to its own program. We recognized that when the government appropriates public funds to promote a particular policy of its own it is entitled to say what it wishes." *Rosenberger, supra,* at 833.

Rosenberger controls here. The NEA, like the student activities fund in *Rosenberger,* is a subsidy scheme created to encourage expression of a diversity of views from private speakers. Congress brought the NEA into being to help all Americans "achieve a better understanding of the past, a better analysis of the present, and a better view of the future." § 951(3). The NEA's purpose is to "support new ideas" and "to help create and sustain . . . a climate encouraging freedom of thought, imagination, and inquiry." §§ 951(10), (7); see also S.Rep. No. 300, 89th Cong., 1st Sess., 4 (1965) ("[T]he intent of this act should be the encouragement of free inquiry and expression"); H.R.Rep. No. 99–274, p. 13 (1985) (Committee Report accompanying bill to reauthorize and amend the NEA's governing statute) ("As the Preamble of the act directs, the Endowment['s] programs should be open and richly diverse, reflecting the ferment of ideas which has always made this Nation strong and free"). Given this congressional choice to sustain freedom of expression, *Rosenberger* teaches that the First Amendment forbids decisions based on viewpoint popularity. So long as Congress chooses to subsidize expressive endeavors at large, it has no business requiring the NEA to turn down funding applications of artists and exhibitors who devote their "freedom of thought, imagination, and inquiry" to defying our tastes, our beliefs, or our values. It may not use the NEA's purse to "'suppres[s] . . . dangerous ideas." *Regan v. Taxation with Representation of Wash., supra,* at 548.

The Court says otherwise, claiming to distinguish *Rosenberger* on the ground that the student activities funds in that case were generally available to most applicants, whereas NEA funds are disbursed selectively and competitively to a choice few. But the Court in *Rosenberger* anticipated and specifically rejected just this distinction when it held in no uncertain terms that "[t]he government cannot justify viewpoint discrimination among private speakers on the economic fact of scarcity." 515 U.S., at 835.[27] Scarce money demands choices, of course, but choices "on some acceptable [viewpoint] neutral principle," like artistic excellence and artistic merit;[28] "nothing in our decision[s] indicate[s] that scarcity would give the State the right to exercise viewpoint discrimination that is otherwise impermissible."; see also *Arkansas Ed. Television*

27. The Court's attempt to avoid *Rosenberger* by describing NEA funding in terms of competition, not scarcity, will not work. Competition implies scarcity, without which there is no exclusive prize to compete for; the Court's "competition" is merely a surrogate for "scarcity."

28. While criteria of "artistic excellence and artistic merit" may raise intractable issues about the identification of artistic worth, and could no doubt be used covertly to filter out unwanted ideas, there is nothing inherently viewpoint discriminatory about such merit-based criteria. We have noted before that an esthetic government goal is perfectly legitimate. See *Metromedia, Inc. v. San Diego,* 453 U.S. 490, 507–508 (1981) (plurality opinion). Decency and respect, on the other hand, are inherently and facially viewpoint based, and serve no legitimate and permissible end. The Court's assertion that the mere fact that grants must be awarded according to artistic merit precludes "absolute neutrality" on the part of the NEA, is therefore misdirected. It is not to the point that the Government necessarily makes choices among competing applications, or even that its judgments about artistic quality may be branded as subjective to some greater or lesser degree; the question here is whether the Government may apply patently viewpoint-based criteria in making those choices.

Comm'n v. Forbes, 523 U.S. 666, 676 (1998) (scarcity of air time does not justify viewpoint-based exclusion of candidates from a debate on public television; neutral selection criteria must be employed). If the student activities fund at issue in *Rosenberger* had awarded competitive, merit-based grants to only 50%, or even 5%, of the applicants, on the basis of "journalistic merit taking into consideration the message of the newspaper," it is obvious beyond peradventure that the Court would not have come out differently, leaving the University free to refuse funding after considering a publication's Christian perspective.[29]

* * *

ELIZABETH ANDERSON, VALUE IN ETHICS AND ECONOMICS

(1993).

Civil Society and the Market

Civil society defines a sphere of interaction that ideally is open to all its members on the same terms, independent of their personal relations to others, their social status, or their occupation of government office. Civil society includes markets, profit-making firms, nonprofit institutions such as hospitals and schools, professional associations and labor unions, political parties and action groups, and philanthropic and ideal-based organizations. Although the state may regulate and even fund these institutions, individuals pursue their own purposes in them, which are defined by internal institutional ideals and functions rather than by state fiat. And though individuals may engage in market transactions in their non-market institutional-or role-given capacities, their activities are not and should not be comprehensively governed by market norms. The scope of the market is limited by other roles and institutions in civil society.

The proper relationship of these other institutions to the market raises delicate questions of boundary setting. Consider the status of professionals such as doctors, lawyers, academics, athletes, and artists who sell their services. Excellent performance in professional roles is judged by the standards of goods internal to the practice rather than by external instrumental criteria such as profitability. Academics pursue

29. Justice Scalia suggests that *Rosenberger* turned not on the distinction between government-as-speaker and government-as-facilitator-of-private-speech, but rather on the fact that "the government had established a limited public forum." Leaving aside the proper application of forum analysis to the NEA and its projects, I cannot agree that the holding of *Rosenberger* turned on characterizing its metaphorical forum as public in some degree. Like this case, *Rosenberger* involved viewpoint discrimination, and we have made it clear that such discrimination is impermissible in all forums, even nonpublic ones, *Cornelius v. NAACP Legal Defense & Ed. Fund, Inc.,* 473 U.S. 788, 806 (1985), where, by definition, the government has not made public property generally available to facilitate private speech, *Perry Ed. Assn. v. Perry Local Educators' Assn.,* 460 U.S. 37, 46 (1983) (defining a nonpublic forum as "[p]ublic property which is not by tradition or designation a forum for public communication"). Accordingly, *Rosenberger's* brief allusion to forum analysis was in no way determinative of the Court's holding.

understanding, athletes win games, artists produce aesthetic value, and so forth. Adherence to their defining ideals and goals often involves forgoing opportunities for making money. When professionals sell their services, they enter into market relations that impose norms on their activities which potentially conflict with the norms of excellence internal to their professional roles. The goods internal to these professions become *partially commodified.*

Pluralism does not repudiate such mixed practices. Sphere differentiation should not be confused with complete sphere segregation. The freedom of professionals to sell their services promotes equality of opportunity and autonomy. Achieving excellence in the professions is a full-time activity. If professionals could not be paid for their work, only independently wealthy people would be able to pursue it. Professionals can make a living at what they do by selling their services on the market, seeking private patrons, or obtaining state funding. The market offers some advantages over the other two sources of support. When professional artists and doctors depended on private patrons, their fates were closely tied to the whims and fortunes of one or a few individuals, and they often lose voice over their activities. Reliance on the state can also be dangerous, since one must be careful not to offend the political interests of those in power. The option of marketing one's products or services to the general public can enhance autonomy by restoring voice to self-employed professionals who set their own terms of sale before making contact with their customers.

But the market is no panacea, either. If professionals are employees of profit-making firms, their autonomy can be compromised by the firm's demand to make a profit. Greed can also corrupt self-employed professionals. Artists may pander to public taste rather than challenging it. Lawyers may act merely as hired guns for their clients, harassing those against whom their clients have no genuine legal case. Doctors may perform profitable but medically unwarranted services on ignorant or demanding patients. Some of these dangers can be alleviated through employment by nonprofit organizations, such as museums, hospitals, and universities, whose defining aims are the promotion of goods internal to professional practice. Professional autonomy and integrity are enhanced by differentiation within civil society between profit and nonprofit institutions.

This differentiation can be sustained only if market norms do not wholly govern exchanges of money for professional products or services. Yet some regard market norms as providing the only normatively valid framework for such transactions. This thought lies behind the case for government censorship of the art that it funds. This argument accepts as ethically axiomatic that whoever pays for a good may refuse to pay for any goods that fail to meet her specifications. Hence the National Endowment of the Arts acts within its rights when it refuses to fund art it regards as obscene or politically offensive. The argument views the state as a customer with absolute rights to exit, while it regards state-sponsored art as a mere commodity, the production of which should be purely want-regarding. The same argument would uphold the former policy of the ex-Soviet Union of funding only Lysenkoist genetic theory and of firing scientists who opposed this fraudulent and politically corrupt research program. In general, the state would have the right to fund only public universities and academics whose research and teaching slavishly parroted the party line of state officials, or perhaps the political opinions of the majority of citizens.

If the state should promote citizens' freedom and autonomy, it may not regard itself as a customer with respect to all the projects it funds. Its proper aim in funding projects is not to serve the political interests of the state, the self-interest of its officials, or even the tastes of the majority, but to expand the range of significant opportunities open to its citizens by supporting institutions that enable them to govern themselves by the norms internal to the modes of valuation appropriate to different kinds of goods. Art and science constitute significant domains of human pursuit, each requiring institutions enabling people to regulate their activities in accordance with standards of excellence internal to them. Firms that produce art or science for profit do not fully meet these enabling conditions because they subordinate truth-seeking and aesthetic production to external commercial standards of profitability. Profit and nonprofit art and science institutions that need to charge high prices for access to their products in order to survive exclude all but the wealthy from the opportunities they provide and also mistakenly treat nonrival goods as if they were rivals in consumption. Private philanthropy often undersupplies opportunities to the general public and distorts supply in the interests of snobbery and elitism. State funding of artistic and scientific projects, in which the assignment of grants is determined by peer review rather than by political criteria, can therefore play an irreplaceable role in enhancing the freedom and autonomy of citizens.

Such funding will often result in artistic production that is offensive to public tastes, and scientific theories, such as evolution, that are offensive to popular beliefs. But autonomy is enhanced by providing opportunities for people to learn and grow, even when these opportunities offend, by challenging, their present beliefs and desires. Neither freedom nor autonomy is correctly defined in terms of the satisfaction of given desires or conformity to given beliefs. Both scientific valuation and modern aesthetic appreciation engage a potentiality for self-transcendence, which can be actualized only by permitting experiments that may also fail. The state therefore should recognize the boundary between itself and civil society by not regarding itself as a customer for all the projects it funds.

Questions

1) Proponents of free markets for goods and services point to many different posited advantages of that form of social ordering. These include: low barriers to entry for producers; the nonprescriptive honoring of the revealed preferences of consumers; responsiveness to changing conditions; reduced opportunities for corruption; recognition of the central impor-

tance of the phenomenon of scarcity; the rewarding of innovation, initiative, and risk-taking; the stability associated with the concept of equilibrium, even dynamic equilibrium. Do these advantages have analogies in the realm of ideas?

2) Do ideas have "externalities" (spillover effects), both positive and negative, that are qualitatively and quantitatively different from the externalities that contribute to degrees of "market failure" in the domain of goods and services? If so, does that suggest that Holmes's market metaphor is of limited utility in trying to understand the freedom of speech?

3) Notice that even Milton was concerned about "commodification." Why exactly is the commodification of ideas undesirable? Does Holmes's theory of the First Amendment contribute to the commodification of ideas?

4) Does the concept of the marketplace of ideas imply that government interventions by means of subsidy are as potentially problematic under the First Amendment as government interventions by means of regulation? If not *as* problematic, at least somewhat problematic?

5) Does the concept of the marketplace of ideas imply that viewpoint discrimination by the government is the core First Amendment grievance? How exactly might that follow?

6) Notice that the opinions in *Finley* of Justices O'Connor, Scalia, and Souter all discuss whether the Court's earlier decision in *Rosenberger v. University of Virginia*, which involved the selective subsidization of student publications, governs the case of arts funding by the NEA. Which Justice offers the most convincing analysis of the *Rosenberger* precedent?

VINCENT BLASI, HOLMES AND THE MARKETPLACE OF IDEAS

2004 Supreme Court Review 1.

Holmes never used the phrase "marketplace of ideas." That is a paraphrase supplied by his interpreters. The phrase he actually employed in the *Abrams* opinion, "competition of the market," may suggest a focus on neither the price- and output-determining, utility-maximizing characteristics of markets nor their celebration of discretionary choice, but rather on the harsh fact that economic actors and their products are pitted against one another. This interpretation gains support from Holmes's particular affinity for the work of Malthus, who emphasized scarcity and challenged some of the more ambitious claims of his fellow economists regarding inevitable market self-corrections. Perhaps the key word in Holmes's phrase is not "market" but "competition." In this view, precisely because "truth is the only ground upon which their wishes safely can be carried out," what is needed for ideas is a vibrant, brutal weeding-out process analogous to the function markets for goods and services perform in killing off inefficient enterprises and forcing unproductive workers to be fired. In an unsent letter to Herbert Croly, composed in the year of his Abrams dissent, Holmes said: "in the main I am for aeration of all effervescing convictions—there is no way so quick for letting them get flat."[30] As he put it to John Wu, one of his favorite correspondents in later life: "Every society is founded on the death of men."[31] Every society is also founded, he might have added, on the death of ideas.

Holmes was fascinated by lethal force. As befits a soldier who was seriously wounded at Ball's Bluff, Antietam, and yet again near Fredericksburg, his writings abound with military metaphors and paeans to the dignity of struggle. The centrality of conflict and contest is a recurrent theme in his philosophical musings. Recall his description of life as a "roar of bargain and battle." After his youthful brushes with death and the carnage on a grand scale that he witnessed, it is no wonder that the subject of survival engaged his attention, or that he was intrigued by the discoveries of his fellow Malthusian, Charles Darwin. Holmes considered himself a Darwinist and concentrated his scholarly energies on the question of how law evolves. When Holmes was attending the meetings of the Metaphysical Club during the early 1870s, Chauncey Wright, the group's leader whom Holmes treated as a mentor, was in the midst of an extended, mutually supportive correspondence with Darwin.

A possible difficulty with reading into the market metaphor a Darwinist concern for intellectual adaptation is that Holmes was struck by how resistant to change are the ideas that people hold dear: "One can not be wrenched from the rocky crevices into which one has grown for many years without feeling that one is attacked in one's life."[32] Much as he believed that traditional beliefs regarding population and progress had been disproved by Malthus, Holmes chafed at their resilience: "Malthus pleased me immensely—and left me sad. A hundred years ago he busted fallacies that politicians and labor leaders still live on. One thinks that an error exposed is dead, but exposure amounts to nothing when people want to believe."[33] Holmes may have welcomed the death of ideas but, given his understanding of the psychology of belief formation, one wonders how he could have considered the marketplace of ideas to be the Grim Reaper he sought.

30. See Letter from Holmes to Laski (May 12, 1919), in 1 Holmes–Laski Letters at 204 (cited in note 13).

31. Letter from Holmes to Wu (July 21, 1925), in Max Lerner, ed, The Mind and Faith of Justice Holmes 427–28 (1943).

32. Oliver Wendell Holmes, Jr., Natural Law, 32 Harv. L. Rev. 40 (1918).

33. Letter from Holmes to Pollock (Aug 30, 1914), in 1 Holmes–Pollock Letters at 219. See also Letter from Holmes to Laski (Dec 26, 1917), in 1 Holmes–Laski Letters at 122: ("When I read Malthus I thought he had ripped the guts out of some humbugs—but they are as alive as ever today. Humbugs have no guts—and live all the better without them.").

Actually, the theory of evolution might help to explain why a robust freedom of speech can be extremely valuable even when most individuals remain stubbornly impervious to demonstrably valid refutations of their beliefs. For the engine that drives evolution is not change in the characteristics of individual creatures but rather change over time in the makeup of populations. Natural selection causes the creatures with the most adaptive traits to predominate and those with the least adaptive traits to recede within a population. Applied to the realm of ideas, this selection process causes new entrants to a community who hold more adaptive beliefs to constitute over time a larger proportion of the population. The newcomers with the better-suited ideas arrive due to generational changeover and immigration. As the population changes with the infusion of new persons with different ideas, the pattern of beliefs within the community changes, even if no single individual ever embraces a new idea or discards an old one.

For this dynamic to occur, however, it is essential that the newcomers not simply replicate the preexisting pattern of beliefs. In Darwinist terms, what is needed is variation. To provide that, the newcomers must have the capacity to exercise independent judgment and to form opinions that draw upon experiences different from those that produced the earlier pattern of beliefs. Here is where the freedom of speech comes in. A political regime that discourages and punishes free thought reduces the incidence of variation in the realm of ideas, variation both in the production of new ideas and in the embrace of previously unpopular ideas.

An unregulated marketplace of ideas encourages free thought not so much by determining the equilibrium of the moment as by keeping low the barriers to entry, barriers that take the form not only of coercive sanctions but also social and intellectual peer pressures toward conformity. The sheer proliferation of ideas in a free market complicates perceptions in a manner that helps to weaken such barriers. In addition, the market metaphor makes a statement about the dynamic and chronically incomplete character of understanding and the value of intellectual contest and innovation. Such a statement by the constitutional regime can help to legitimate dissent and discredit demands for orthodoxy, and in that way lend much needed support to newcomers whose heretical notions will almost always engender strong resistance laced with accusations of illegitimacy if not disloyalty.

This demographic account of intellectual evolution assumes that individuals never change their minds about questions that matter to them. That, of course, is an exaggeration. Holmes was impressed by how seldom and slowly people yield to telling criticism, but he never maintained that such resistance is for most persons absolute. When ideas cease to work, whether as guides to conduct or further inquiry, they tend to be abandoned by the individuals whose projects are frustrated as a result. The process takes time and the admission of inefficacy does not come easily for most believers. Much more than rational or empirical refutation in the abstract is required. Usually pressure builds up gradually before it becomes unbearable. But changes of mind do occur, if only rarely, for all but the most refractory zealots. Whether or not it is accurate to call Holmes a pragmatist—a question that has produced a rich literature—he embraced the pragmatist tenet that ideas tend to flourish when they work and wither when they don't. His explicit and extravagant admiration for the writings of John Dewey, though never explained by Holmes in any detail, was very likely because of what Dewey had to say in support of a pragmatist conception of justifiable belief. Holmes said of *Experience and Nature*, Dewey's magnum opus elaborating his theory of knowledge:

> although Dewey's book is incredibly ill written, it seemed to me after several rereadings to have a feeling of intimacy with the inside of the cosmos that I found unequaled. So me-thought God would have spoken had He been inarticulate but keenly desirous to tell you how it was.[34]

The Darwinist/pragmatist strain in Holmes's thought helps to explain how he could have valued the freedom of speech highly, at least by the time of the *Abrams* dissent and thereafter, while nevertheless holding that "beliefs and wishes have a transcendental basis in that their foundation is arbitrary. You can not help entertaining and feeling them, and there is an end of it."[35] Neither demographically driven changes in the pattern of beliefs nor the abandonment of ideas that are not working will occur if people do not take their beliefs seriously. Casual attitudes about belief formation and retention invite conformity, the path of least resistance. Improperly understood, the First Amendment itself can contribute to such dysfunctional conformity. Deprived by the freedom of speech of the comforts of certitude and centralized intellectual authority, people may be tempted to take their beliefs lightly. The market metaphor offers an antidote to this temptation: a powerful image that treats beliefs as significant, even self-defining, and of the highest social priority, all the while being contingent, probabilistic, and tentative. As expounded by Holmes, the market in ideas is not about intellectual gratification and whimsy. It is about important choices with practical consequences under difficult conditions of uncertainty and change. The truths that people come to by free trade in ideas are, remember, "the only ground upon which their wishes safely can be carried out." Conformity, deference to authority, stasis, passivity in the realm of beliefs is not just unfortunate or unwise but dangerous.

The constructive, urgent role that speech can play in the evolution of beliefs under a pragmatist conception of truth insulates Holmes's market metaphor from some of the standard criticisms to which it is subjected. The value of free trade in ideas does not depend on the assumption that there is an objective, perdurable truth to be discovered. It does not depend on the claim that personal beliefs are more or less

34. Letter from Holmes to Pollock (May 15, 1931), in 2 Holmes–Pollock Letters at 287.

35. Holmes, Natural Law, at 41.

independent of the believer's social position, psychological propensities and needs, adventitious experiences, and ideological inheritance. Those assumptions might be implicit in a market metaphor that evoked a finely calibrated measurement of the equilibrium of well-grounded rational beliefs. They are not implicit in Holmes's Darwinist invocation of "the competition of the market."

* * *

In a lecture entitled "The Influence of Darwin on Philosophy," delivered ten years before Holmes's *Abrams* dissent, John Dewey observed:

> The conceptions that had reigned in the philosophy of nature and knowledge for two thousand years, the conceptions that had become the familiar furniture of the mind, rested on the assumption of the superiority of the fixed and final; they rested upon treating change and origin as signs of defect and unreality. In laying hands upon the sacred ark of absolute permanency, in treating the forms that had been regarded as types of fixity and perfection as originating and passing away, the "Origin of Species" introduced a mode of thinking that in the end was bound to transform the logic of knowledge, and hence the treatment of morals, politics, and religion.[150]

What the theory of evolution, the legitimation of fundamental political opposition, and the renunciation of philosophical absolutes all have in common is an emphasis on change. Such emphasis is shared also by free markets. That, I believe, is why Holmes's invocation of all four phenomena in his succinct justification for the freedom of speech is more coherent, and less intellectually peripatetic, than is commonly assumed. A constitutional regime fearful of political entrenchment and dedicated to continual adaptation has every reason to accord high priority to the freedom of speech and to interpret that freedom with reference to the dynamism of free markets. In this regard, the features of markets that merit attention are those that also figure prominently in efficacious governance, scientific inquiry, and natural selection: openness to new ideas and capabilities, thirst for better information, responsiveness to changing conditions, encouragement of innovation and initiative, swift punishment of rigidity, slowness, lack of awareness, or the failure to audit. Whatever their limits and shortcomings, free markets are a powerful force against inertia. So is free speech.

* * *

As Holmes understood the notion, the marketplace of ideas does not offer the prospect of a just distribution of the opportunity to persuade. It does not offer the prospect of wisdom through mass deliberation, nor that of meaningful political participation for all interested citizens. What the marketplace of ideas does offer is a much needed counterweight,

150. John Dewey, The Influence of Darwin on Philosophy, Popular Science Monthly (July 1909), reprinted in The Influence of Darwin on Philosophy and Other Essays 1 (1997).

both conceptual and rhetorical, to illiberal attitudes about authority and change on which the censorial mentality thrives. It honors certain character traits—inquisitiveness, capacity to admit error and to learn from experience, ingenuity, willingness to experiment, resilience—that matter in civic adaptation no less than economic. It devalues deference and discredits certitude, and in the process holds various forms of incumbent authority accountable to standards of performance. It offers a reason to interpret the First Amendment to protect some gestures of opposition and resistance that have nothing to do with dialogue or dialectic. In these respects, Holmes's arresting metaphor serves better as a cultural statement than as a mechanism of social or intellectual ordering. So conceived, it does valuable work.

THOMAS C. GREY, HOLMES, PRAGMATISM, AND DEMOCRACY

71 Ore. L. Rev. 521 (1992)

In the *Abrams* dissent, Holmes did utter the often-quoted formula that the marketplace of ideas supplies the "best test of truth." But in context, the emotional salience of these words is low; Holmes could as well have called the market test the "least bad test of truth." A belief that we would learn the Truth if we had free speech was not what drove Holmes's argument. In his essay Natural Law, he had already published his favorite cynical definition of truth: "the majority vote of that nation that could lick all others."

There was much stronger feeling behind his reminder that "time has upset many fighting faiths," and that "[e]very year if not every day we have to wager our salvation upon some prophecy based upon imperfect knowledge." Today's truth will be thought falsehood tomorrow; we judge and act in conditions of uncertainty—this was one of Holmes's great themes.

But his rhetoric was most forceful in his insistence on our paradoxical commitment to hold in suspense "the very foundations of [our] own conduct," and hence to tolerate views "that we loathe and believe to be fraught with death." Because we can't know what is true, we have to learn to live with what we think is false—which takes training, character, and a stern discipline that must be imposed on the unruly herd by a judicious and unelected elect. An intellectual dose of castor oil is good for the self-satisfied national soul. The old puritan joy at suffering in the cause of virtue lived on in Holmes, a legacy from his Massachusetts ancestors.

The rhetorical center of the *Abrams* dissent reiterated the skeptical premise Holmes had stated in *Lochner*: the Constitution was made "for people of fundamentally different views."[53] What *Abrams* added—that one of the few judicially enforceable super-fundamentals of that constitution was the counter-majoritarian protection of deviant minority opin-

53. Lochner v. New York, 198 U.S. 45, 75–76 (1905) (Holmes, J., dissenting).

ions—was something by no means deducible from this premise. It was majority rule that rested on skepticism about the accessibility of ultimate truth in *Lochner*. In *Abrams,* a similar skepticism was invoked to trump majority rule in the name of free speech. Logically—and Holmes's personal waverings on the free speech issue illustrate this—the skeptical premise could as well have supported the temporary popular majority in the free speech cases. "We judges can't know what is true, so the best, though imperfect, test should be what the majority wants to hear"—so the argument could have run, with equal logic, from the skeptical premise.

In the *Gitlow* dissent, Holmes drew his most explicit link between his judicial protection of free speech and his democratic faith. If the "dominant forces of the community" should come to want "proletarian dictatorship," he wrote, "the only meaning of free speech is that they should be given their chance and have their way."[55] Protection of free discussion, even against the short-term majority, here became an aspect of a long-term commitment to majority rule itself. Again, Holmes offered no argument to justify the presumption in favor of a potential long-term majority over the actual short-term one that had decreed the restriction of speech in question.

And, quite generally, Holmes, in all these famous and eloquent opinions, never did supply an explicit *argument* for preferring either free speech (the possible long-term majority) or democracy (the actual short-term one). His skepticism resonated rhetorically with both commitments for him—in the *Lochner* and *Abrams* dissents respectively—as it has for many readers since. But logically, we must remember, a generalized skepticism has no implications for conduct whatever; it neither supports majority over elite rule, nor freedom of debate over the right of the majority to suppress dissident opinion.

What Holmes did reveal in these opinions was his strong emotional support for democracy, combined with what later emerged as an equally strong support for freedom of speech. Further, he showed that these commitments were bound up for him with his own pervasive skepticism—an attitude he often reiterated, in contexts remote from either democracy or free speech.

Holmes rhetorically demonstrated the strength of his commitments to free speech and democracy by what he was willing to sacrifice to them—capitalism—with his imagined scenario of the majority's embrace of socialist "proletarian dictatorship" in the *Gitlow* opinion. Holmes was a convinced believer in the virtues of a free-market, private-property economy; he had publicly made clear his own lack of sympathy for socialism. And he was inclined to put this view even more pungently in private. Thus, he once wrote to Laski, a good friend and a socialist sympathizer, "I never read a socialist yet from Karl Marx down ... that I didn't think talked drool.... Some essays by the great Webb in Fabian days I thought were slobber, if that is worse than drool."

55. Gitlow v. New York, 268 U.S. 652, 673 (1925) (Holmes, J., dissenting).

It was talk like this that led Yosal Rogat, in his seminal revisionist study, to dissent from the widespread view that Holmes had been led to defer to legislative majorities in constitutional cases by an admirable kind of skeptical humility. "Holmes," said Rogat, "was the least hesitant of men. It is difficult to think of anyone who expressed fewer qualifications or occupied fewer half-way positions."[58] And Holmes, Rogat said, "would tie for last with General DeGaulle" in any humility contest.

Rather than skepticism or humility, Rogat said, it was detachment, lack of emotional involvement, and an attitude of fatalism that led Holmes to defer to legislative majorities. The majority represented the dominant force in the community; as such, it was bound to prevail. What would happen would just plain happen, and Holmes would watch it happen—whether it was war, proletarian revolution, or peaceful progress. And he would watch with spectatorial interest but little real concern. Rogat concluded his powerfully argued indictment: "To a remarkable degree, Holmes simply did not care."

Other revisionist biographers have given Rogat's argument a plausible psychological basis in the young Holmes's grim Civil War experience. A sheltered childhood had scarcely prepared him for three years of combat during which he was wounded three times, twice nearly mortally; saw many of his closest friends killed; and suffered terrible fear, exacerbated by doubts about whether he had fully done his duty. His quite natural psychological defense to this experience, the conjecture goes, was simply to deaden his capacity for emotional involvement.

All this is a useful corrective to the old sentimental view of Holmes as an amiable skeptic and humble aristocratic servant of democracy. But in my view, the revisionist account leaves out too much—both of the human being, and of the deferential judge.

First, the portrayal of Holmes as peculiarly rigid or arrogant in his views confuses his secure willingness to assert and act on his own views with a certainty that they were right—and yet the two are not the same thing. The practical difference shows up in the fact that he was more than usually willing to study arguments that ran against his firm prejudices. For example, at the behest of Laski, Brandeis, and others of his Progressive and Socialist friends, Holmes read much more of the literature of the Left than most people of his political views would have, particularly at his advanced age.

And he even changed his mind on at least one important public question late in life, after hearing the arguments of others—though he didn't acknowledge the change. That at least is how I interpret Holmes's movement on the question of the constitutional status of freedom of speech, from his earlier opinions on the subject to the *Abrams* dissent.

58. [Yosal Rogat, The Judge as Spectator, 31 U. Chi. L. Rev. 213, 251, 253, 255 (1964)].

Finally—and this is most relevant to my subject here—the description of Holmes as a man who "simply did not care" seems to me seriously askew. Holmes was given, especially in his letters, to somewhat melodramatically paradoxical expressions of the form "I can't prove *X,* but I would die for it"; or "men won't agree on *Y,* and if they care enough about it they will soon have to start killing each other." A remark of this sort on free speech—"in which, in the abstract, I have no very enthusiastic belief, though I hope I would die for it"—was chosen to end the fine article on Holmes's First Amendment opinions which Jim O'Fallon edited from a manuscript that Yosal Rogat left behind at his death. Rogat had earlier relied heavily on similar statements to establish his diagnosis of Holmes as suffering from an almost pathologically extreme form of emotional detachment.

I give these remarks of Holmes's a quite different interpretation. When Holmes said he would die or would kill for something, he was expressing, in the pragmatically strongest terms he could find, his *commitment* to it. When he said that he didn't believe in such a view "in the abstract," he meant that he couldn"t support his conviction philosophically, with rational grounds strong enough to match his level of emotional commitment. He called his commitments, what he couldn't help believing, his "can't helps."

What that meant, in pragmatic terms, was that he did not have evidence or rational arguments sufficient in practice to convince other sound people. That is, he was not able to establish that others who disagreed with him on his own fundamentals or "can't helps" were either stupid, mad, or wicked. He frequently and vividly experienced this disjunction between the force of his convictions and the practical power of reason to sustain them; thus "I can't prove *X,* but I would die for it."

Like the revisionists, I also turn to Holmes's formative wartime experience for an explanation. Holmes started the war an abolitionist, one who believed that slavery was an absolute evil. In the war, however, he served with proslavery men whom he came to know—and even, in the shared boredom and terror of war, to love—as courageous comrades, civilized gentlemen, and loyal friends. Many of these men gave their lives to the Union cause, not because they believed it was just, but because local and personal loyalties that ran deeper than reason, and deeper than politics or morals, had drawn them to the fight.

For the rest of his life, Holmes was given to strong endorsement of the ultimate maxim of unreasoned loyalty, "my country, right or wrong"—especially to cosmopolitan interlocutors who would surely not share the sentiment. And in his Memorial Day speech, *The Soldier's Faith,* he gave his most emotionally intense and rhetorically melodramatic celebration of the moral virtue of commitment beyond the bounds of reason:

> [T]here is one thing I do not doubt ... and that is that the faith is true and adorable which leads a soldier to throw away his life in obedience to a blindly accepted duty, in a cause which he little

understands, in a plan of campaign of which he has no notion, under tactics of which he does not see the use.[68]

You may well find that outburst shockingly irrational, dangerously authoritarian, militaristic, even tending toward fascism. When Holmes himself heard the speech criticized as bullying jingoism, he defensively insisted that he had used war as a metaphor for life; that he hated war and was not a militarist, but rather what a later age would call an existentialist. But whether or not that is a persuasive defense, it is very hard to see the author of *The Soldier's Faith* as a man who "simply did not care."

The same is true, though less obviously, of Holmes's gentler expressions of his conviction that the most fundamental springs of human conduct lie below the reach of reason and discussion, in the emotional attachments we form to our fellows and to the places we love. Thus, he wrote that "property, friendship, and truth have a common root in time.... What we most love and revere generally is determined by early associations. I love granite rocks and barberry bushes, no doubt because with them were my earliest joys that reach back through the past eternity of my life."

This, I suggest, is where Holmes got the unexpressed premise to complete his argument for judicial restraint. The belief that the majority should rule was in a sense a matter of blind faith for him, something he was committed to as a soldier of his country—his country, right or wrong. Or, to put it in different terms, and terms I prefer, it was an attachment that had seized him as he had grown up in the soil and in the villages of New England, among the granite rocks and the barberry bushes, and among the town meetings and the Congregational churches in which New England democracy was embodied. In a speech, he once said that we Americans owed to our Puritan heritage "the deepest cause we have to love our country" which was its "democratic spirit," that "instinct ... that makes the American unable to meet his fellow man otherwise than simply as a man."

By now, I hope you can see the connection between Holmes's democratic commitment as I have interpreted it, and Richard Rorty's recent doctrine of the priority of democracy over philosophy. What Rorty says is that we should see ourselves as democrats first, and philosophers second. We should conceive our philosophy not as an unbiased pursuit of the question "what is true?" but rather as a precommitted pursuit of the question "what belief structure serves democracy?"[72]

That, as I understand it, is very much what Holmes did—he experienced constitutional commitment to democracy as a matter of prerational loyalty, without philosophical foundations, and hence immune from

68. Oliver Wendell Holmes, *The Soldier's Faith* (May 30, 1895), *in* THE OCCASIONAL SPEECHES OF JUSTICE OLIVER WENDELL HOLMES 73, 76 (Mark DeWolfe Howe ed., 1962).

72. *See* [Richard Rorty, The Priority of Democracy to Philosophy, in OBJECTIVITY, RELATIVISM, AND TRUTH 183 (1991)].

rationalistic undermining. When Holmes thought about democracy, objections to it always came to his mind. When he thought about other subjects, though, such as the scope and nature of judicial review, the democratic faith was for him an unshakable presupposition. Rorty's championing of solidarity and even ethnocentrism as the basis of our political ideals seems to make him a very Holmesian kind of pragmatist democrat.

Rorty, however, calls his political ideals a *Deweyan* kind of pragmatist democracy, and here, I think, he is on shaky ground. By contrast to Holmes, Dewey constantly stressed the connection between democracy on the one hand, and organized intelligence, the idea of society as a continuing educational enterprise animated by the scientific spirit, on the other. He said that "[m]ajority rule, just as majority rule, is as foolish as its critics charge it with being"; the essence of democracy for him was not counting heads, but the fact that "counting heads compels prior recourse to methods of discussion, consultation, and persuasion."[73]

"[T]he future of democracy," he wrote, "is allied with spread of the scientific attitude."[74] As he described it, this attitude involved "willingness to hold belief in suspense, ability to doubt until evidence is obtained; willingness to go where evidence points . . .; enjoyment of new fields for inquiry and of new problems." An undemocratic society, for Dewey, was one which "internally and externally sets up barriers to free intercourse and communication of experience."[76] While solidarity was essential to democracy, ethnocentricity or local prejudice played no part in it. Democracy would have its consummation only with the birth of what Dewey called "the Great Community," a social order in which "free social inquiry is indissolubly wedded to the art of full and moving communication." To be successfully democratic, the public had to get smart as well as get together.

Like Holmes, Dewey regarded his own commitment to democracy as a form of faith. He described it, significantly, not as "a soldier's faith," but as "a common faith."[78] The object of Dewey's faith was not rooted prerationally in the experience of each individual, as Holmes saw human attachments to places and people, barberry bushes and granite rocks. Rather, Dewey's faith was in the natural goods, things common to human experience—"the values of art in all its forms, of knowledge, of effort and of rest after striving, of education and fellowship, of friendship and love, of growth in mind and body." Above all, the object of faith was "intelligence," conceived not in individual or narrowly cognitive terms, but as the passionate, yet critical, cooperative quest for a common human life that maximized human potential. The virtues of criticism,

73. JOHN DEWEY, THE PUBLIC AND ITS PROBLEMS 207 (Gateway Books 1946) (1927).

74. JOHN DEWEY, FREEDOM AND CULTURE 148 (1939).

76. JOHN DEWEY, DEMOCRACY AND EDUCATION (1916), *reprinted in* 9 JOHN DEWEY: THE MIDDLE WORKS 1899–1924, at 1, 105 (Jo Ann Boydston ed., Southern Ill. Univ. Press 1980).

78. JOHN DEWEY, A COMMON FAITH (1934), *reprinted in* 9 JOHN DEWEY: THE LATER WORKS 1925–1953, at 1, 35 (Jo Ann Boydston ed., Southern Ill. Univ. Press 1986).

respect for evidence, and open mindedness were built into Dewey's conception of secular faith, and thus into his conception of democracy. In contrast, Holmes's existentialist "leap of faith," his soldier's commitment that was adorable precisely because it was blind, had no place in Dewey's ideal.

Holmes and Dewey both spoke of democracy as an *experiment,* but not with the same resonance. Holmes conceived of some impersonal force, History, Chance, or Fate, as running the experiment. For him, human beings were just the experimental subjects; the (somewhat more intelligent) rats in the cage.

Dewey, while likewise stressing the precarious and contingent character of the human situation, was more inclined to see a democratic citizenry as an aspiring community of political scientists, striving to set up and run the experiment of their collective life themselves. As the term "experiment" connotes, success was not guaranteed in either case, but Dewey, much more than Holmes, thought the outcome would turn on the progress or failure of education, science, and organized intelligence.

The contrast in the defenses of free speech offered by these two men further marks their difference. Dewey saw free discussion as a positive tool of social progress, which he conceived as similar to the progress of science under conditions of free inquiry. Holmes more stressed the skeptical case against justifying repression of deviant views—no one could prove them false or harmful with the requisite certainty.

LOUIS MENAND, THE METAPHYSICAL CLUB
(2001).

The lesson Holmes took from the war can be put in a sentence. It is that certitude leads to violence. This is a proposition that has an easy application and a difficult one. The easy application is to ideologues, dogmatists, and bullies—people who think that their rightness justifies them in imposing on anyone who does not happen to subscribe to their particular ideology, dogma, or notion of turf. If the conviction of rightness is powerful enough, resistance to it will be met, sooner or later, by force. There are people like this in every sphere of life, and it is natural to feel that the world would be a better place without them.

But this is not quite what Holmes felt. He did have an intense dislike of people who presented themselves as instruments of some higher power. "I detest a man who knows that he knows," as he wrote, late in life, to his friend Harold Laski. And he had a knee-jerk suspicion of causes. He regarded them as attempts to compel one group of human beings to conform to some other group's idea of the good, and he could see no authority for such attempts greater than the other group's certainty that it knew what was best. "'some kind of despotism is at the bottom of seeking for change," he wrote to Laski. "I don't care to boss my neighbors and to require them to want something different from what they do—even when, as frequently, I think their wishes more or less suicidal."

His standard example in criticizing the reformist mentality was the abolitionists. "The abolitionists had a stock phrase that a man was either a knave or a fool who did not act as they (the abolitionists) *knew* to be right," he wrote to another old friend, the British jurist Frederick Pollock, in 1929. "so Calvin thought of the Catholics and the Catholics of Calvin. So I don't doubt do the more convinced prohibitionists think of their opponents today. When you know that you know persecution comes easy. It is as well that some of us don't know that we know anything." Holmes acknowledged that there were skeptics among the abolitionists he had known in Boston before the war (he was thinking of his mother and, possibly, of Emerson), and that his own skepticism was learned partly from them. But abolitionism came to stand in his thought for the kind of superior certitude that drives men (frequently men other than the ones who are certain) to kill one another.

Still, Holmes did not think that the world would be better off without people like this, because he thought that *everyone* was like this—and this is the difficult part of his belief about certitude and violence. It is easy to condemn unwarranted certainty in others; we are always confident that people we disagree with would be improved by a little self-doubt. We even remind ourselves, in our better moments, to be skeptical of our own convictions. In the end, though, there just are some things that we are certain about. We have beliefs we cannot help feeling are valid—the belief, for instance, that slavery is wrong. And when push comes to shove over those beliefs, we are prepared to shove back.

Holmes admitted that he, too, was capable of taking up arms in the name of what he thought was right. When that day came, nothing could save him from the resort to violence, not even the knowledge that what he was fighting for was, in the end, just his preference. "You respect the rights of man—," he wrote to Laski. "I don't, except those things a given crowd will fight for—which vary from religion to the price of a glass of beer. I also would fight for some things—but instead of saying that they ought to be I merely say they are part of the kind of world that I like—or should like."

"Men to a great extent believe what they want to," Holmes wrote in 1918, when he had been sitting on the Supreme Court for sixteen years. But he did not think that the absence of a higher authority made it pointless to talk of beliefs as good or bad, true or false, right or wrong. He only thought that rightness and wrongness are functions of the circumstances in which our lives happen to be embedded. Since we cannot (except at the margin) change the circumstances, it makes sense for us to talk of right and wrong without mental quotation marks. In the long view of human affairs custom and habit may be contingent, but in the short view they are often as good as necessity. "Man is like any other organism, shaping himself to his environment so wholly that after he has taken the shape if you try to change it you alter his life," Holmes told

Einstein. "All of which is all right and fully justifies us in doing what we can't help doing and trying to make the world into the kind of world that we think we should like; but it hardly warrants our talking much about absolute truth." Truth, Holmes said many times, is just the name for what it is impossible for a person to doubt. "All I mean by truth is the path I have to travel," as he explained to his friend Alice Green.

The key to Holmes's civil liberties opinions is the key to all his jurisprudence: it is that he thought only in terms of aggregate social forces; he had no concern for the individual. The spectacle of individuals falling victim to dominant political or economic tendencies, when those tendencies had been instantiated in duly enacted laws, gave him a kind of chilly satisfaction. It struck him as analogous to the death of soldiers in a battlefield victory, and justified on the same grounds—that for the group to move ahead, some people must inevitably fall by the wayside. "Every society rests on the death of men," he liked to provoke his friends by saying. He had, consequently, virtually no faith in the notion of individual human agency. On his view, successful people, like Morgan and Rockefeller, just had a better grasp of social tendencies than unsuccessful people did. Everyone is simply riding the wave chance has put them on. Some people know how to surf; some people drown.

Holmes's defense of civil liberties had nothing to do, in other words, with the notion that such liberties were owed to people merely by the fact of their being human—a belief he held in conspicuous contempt. He could defend the right of socialists and pacifists to express their views on grounds that those views represented a legitimate social interest, and at the same time exhibit indifference to the suffering of for example, Southern blacks victimized by de facto discrimination. In his most notorious opinion, in the case of *Buck v. Bell* (1927), he voted, in language evoking the Civil War, to uphold a Virginia law permitting the involuntary sterilization of mentally incompetent persons. "We have seen more than once that the public welfare may call upon the best citizens for their lives," he wrote. "It would be strange if it could not call upon those who already sap the strength of the State for these lesser sacrifices." He disliked the self-righteous, but he had no sympathy for the weak. He reversed, in effect, the priorities of his youth: he took the Constitution for his text and rejected the Declaration of Independence.

When Holmes emerged as a consistent judicial defender of economic reform and of free speech, he became a hero to progressives and civil libertarians—to people like Louis Brandeis, Learned Hand, Walter Lippmann, and Herbert Croly. Holmes did not share the politics of these people, but he did not think it was his business as a judge to have a politics, and he did nothing to discourage their admiration. It suited his conception of heroic disinterestedness to serve as their Abbot—privately denouncing the stupidity of the views he strove, often boldly and alone, to defend. "It has given me great pleasure to sustain the Constitutionality of laws that I believe to be as bad as possible, because I thereby helped to mark the difference between what I would forbid and what the Constitution permits," as he explained to his cousin John T. Morse.

Holmes did not defend the interests of labor because he wished to see those interests prevail. He defended them because he believed that every social interest should have its chance. He believed in experiment. He knew what the alternative was.

* * *

In 1932, after he had retired from the Court and was nearing the end, Holmes tried to read aloud to Marion Frankfurter, Felix Frankfurter's wife, a poem he liked about the Civil War, but he broke down in tears before he could finish it. They were not tears for the war. They were tears for what the war had destroyed. Holmes had grown up in a highly cultivated, homogeneous world, a world of which he was, in many ways, the consummate product: idealistic, artistic, and socially committed. And then he had watched that world bleed to death at Fredericksburg and Antietam, in a war that learning and brilliance had been powerless to prevent. When he returned, Boston had changed, and so had American life. Holmes had changed too, but he never forgot what he had lost. "He told me," Einstein reported, "that after the Civil War the world never seemed quite right again."

Additional Readings

Holmes's life and work

Albert W. Alschuler, Without Values: The Life, Work, and Legacy of Justice Holmes (2000)

Robert Gordon, Holmes's *Common Law* as Legal and Social Science, 10 Hofstra L. Rev. 719 (1982)

Oliver Wendell Holmes, Jr., Collected Legal Papers (1920)

David Luban, Justice Holmes and the Metaphysics of Judicial Restraint, 44 Duke L.J. 449 (1994)

Yosal Rogat, The Judge as Spectator, 31 U. Chi. L. Rev. 213 (1964)

G. Edward White, Justice Oliver Wendell Holmes: Law and the Inner Self (1993)

Edmund Wilson, Patriotic Gore: Studies in the Literature of the American Civil War (1962)

Philip P. Wiener, Evolution and the Founders of Pragmatism (1942)

Morton White, Social Thought in America: The Revolt Against Formalism (1957)

Holmes's free speech opinions

Edward J. Bloustein, Holmes: His First Amendment Theory and His Pragmatist Bent, 40 Rutgers L. Rev. 283 (1988)

David S. Bogan, The Free Speech Metamorphosis of Mr. Justice Holmes, 11 Hofstra L. Rev. 97 (1982)

Lee C. Bollinger, The Tolerant Society, ch. 5 (1986)

H.L. Pohlman, Justice Oliver Wendell Holmes: Free Speech and the Living Constitution (1991)

Richard A. Posner, The Speech Market and the Legacy of *Schenck*, in Eternally Vigilant: Free Speech in the Modern Era (Lee C. Bollinger and Geoffrey R. Stone ed. 2002)

Yosal Rogat & James O'Fallon, Mr. Justice Holmes: A Dissenting Opinion—The Speech Cases, 36 Stan. L. Rev. 1349 (1984)

G. Edward White, Justice Holmes and the Modernization of Free Speech Jurisprudence: The Human Dimension, 80 Calif. L. Rev. 391 (1992)

John H. Wigmore, Abrams v. U.S.: Freedom of Speech and Freedom of Thuggery in War–Time and Peace–Time, 14 U. Ill. L. Rev. 539 (1920)

The marketplace metaphor

Ronald W. Adelman, The First Amendment and the Metaphor of Free Trade, 38 Ariz. L. Rev. 1125 (1996)

R.H. Coase, The Market for Goods and the Market for Ideas, 64 Amer. Econ. Rev: Papers & Proc 384 (1974)

David Cole, Agon at Agora: Creative Misreadings in the First Amendment Tradition, 95 Yale L.J. 857 (1986)

Alvin I. Goldman & James C. Cox, Speech, Truth, and the Free Market for Ideas, 2 Legal Theory 1 (1996)

Stanley Ingber, The Marketplace of Ideas: A Legitimizing Myth, 1984 Duke L.J. 1

Red Lion and Tornillo

Jerome A. Barron, Access to the Press—A New First Amendment Right, 80 Harv. L. Rev. 1641 (1967)

Lee C. Bollinger, Freedom of the Press and Public Access: Toward a Theory of Partial Regulation of Mass Media, 75 Mich. L. Rev. 1 (1976)

Thomas G. Krattenmaker and Lucas A. Powe, Jr., Regulating Broadcast Programming (1994)

Lucas A. Powe, Jr., Tornillo, 1987 Supreme Court Review 345

Jonathan Weinberg, Broadcasting and Speech, 81 Calif. L. Rev. 1101 (1993)

Finley

Randall P. Bezanson, The Government Speech Forum: *Forbes* and *Finley* and Government Speech Selection Judgments, 83 Iowa L. Rev. 953 (1998)

Steven J. Heyman, State–Supported Speech, 1999 Wisc. L. Rev. 1119

Robert C. Post, Subsidized Speech, 106 Yale L. J. 151 (1996)

Chapter Seven

LOUIS BRANDEIS

ERIC FONER, THE STORY OF AMERICAN FREEDOM

(1999).

In 1924, the social scientist Horace Kallen remarked that the United States had just passed through "one of the most critical ten-year periods" in its history. Among the changes was the disintegration of Progressivism as a political movement and body of thought. The wartime belief in the conscious creation of a new world order died in Paris, and the government's success in whipping up mass hysteria and xenophobic hatreds seemed to undermine the very foundation of democratic thought—the idea of the self-directed citizen. By the 1920s, the idea of "the people" as a rational collective entity, invented during the American Revolution, appeared to have been rendered obsolete. Freudians emphasized the unconscious, instinctual motivations of human behavior; scientists pointed to wartime IQ tests allegedly demonstrating that large numbers of Americans were mentally unfit for self-government. "The great bulk of people are stupid," one advertising executive commented, explaining why ads played on the emotions rather than providing actual information.

During the 1920s, Walter Lippmann published two of the most penetrating indictments of democracy ever written, *Public Opinion* and *The Phantom Public,* valedictories to Progressive hopes for the application of "intelligence" to social problems via mass democracy. Instead of acting out of careful consideration of the issues or even individual or collective self-interest, the American voter, Lippmann claimed, was ill-informed, myopic, and prone to fits of enthusiasm. Not only were modern problems beyond the understanding of ordinary men and women (a sentiment that had earlier led Lippmann to favor administration by experts), but in an age of mass communications the independent citizen was nothing but a myth. The government, like advertising copywriters and journalists, had perfected the art of creating and manipulating public opinion—a process Lippmann called the "manufacture of consent"— while at the same time consumerism was sapping Americans' concern for public issues. Dewey, who struggled to defend the idea of an engaged citizenry as the basis of social betterment, ceded ground before Lippmann's critique. "The public," Dewey wrote, "seems to be lost; it is certainly bewildered."

Another casualty of the war and its aftermath was Progressivism's blithe faith in the federal government as the embodiment of national purpose. Not only wartime repression but the constitutional amendment prohibiting the manufacture and sale of intoxicating liquors, passed by Congress in 1917 and ratified two years later, offered to many urban Progressives and Greenwich Village bohemians a notable illustration of how public power, in the wrong hands, could go grievously awry. Building on prewar struggles for freedom of expression by labor, socialists, and birth control advocates, some Progressives now acquired a new appreciation for civil liberties—rights an individual may assert against government—as essential elements of American freedom. In effect, they rediscovered Madison's warning that democratic government itself could endanger freedom. The result was the beginning of a subtle shift from the language of majority rule and effective democracy to a discourse of rights, checks on state power, and individual autonomy. In the name of a "new freedom for the individual," the 1920s saw the birth of a coherent concept of civil liberties, and with it the beginnings of meaningful legal protection for freedom of speech against the actions of the state.

PHILIPPA STRUM, BRANDEIS: BEYOND PROGRESSIVISM

(1993).

Like other political thinkers and politicians, [Louis Dembitz Brandeis] cared about power. Unlike many, he emphasized not means but goals, and the purpose most important to him was the establishment, by the government and other institutions, of policies that would best enhance individual fulfillment. Indeed, the only justification for any political, economic, or social institution was its contribution to that overarching goal. Although he believed that the human need for emotional and intellectual interaction necessarily resulted in the creation of community, and although he pointed out the concomitant responsibility of the individual to the community and its well-being, he never forgot that the legitimacy of government—that most formal expression of community—depended upon its serving as the extension of individuals.

His individualism was far from selfish. The individual had always to be treated as subject, never as object; and to whatever extent the state affected the individual, it was justified in doing so only if it extended the individual's freedom. This view, he believed, was what the Founding Fathers had in mind.

Brandeis's emphasis on individual freedom did not imply approval of the self-centered capitalist of the late nineteenth and early twentieth centuries or of the worker whose only interests were private. Crucial to individual fulfillment was a participation in the political process that both contributed to the enhancement of freedom and became an element of individual fulfillment. Brandeis would have agreed with Rousseau that a human being's faculties can be fully exercised and developed only in a civil state, where citizens enjoy the freedom that comes from "obedience to the law one has prescribed for oneself." Similarly, he paralleled John Stuart Mill in viewing fulfillment of "public duty" as aiding in the development of character and of a government that "can fully satisfy all the exigencies of the social state."

Brandeis repeatedly emphasized that human beings had not only rights but responsibilities. The citizen who had adequate time and knowledge to participate in the political process and did not do so was reprehensible, for he or she was guilty of taking without giving. Brandeis became known as "the people's attorney" because of his devotion to public causes—a devotion for which he refused to accept remuneration and in fact spent substantial amounts of his own money as well as his time and energy. He did so out of a conviction that individuals who possessed talents that might help others had an obligation to use them and that involvement in public policymaking was one of the highest forms of civilized behavior. Leaving politics to the politicians was inexcusable. He considered it "obvious" that no democratic government could work well without citizen participation. "It is customary for people to berate politicians," he noted. "But after all, the politicians, even if their motives are not of the purest, come much nearer performing their duties as citizens than the so-called 'good' citizens who stay at home." Just as Mill declared that "the contented man, or the contented family, who have no ambition ... to promote the good of their country or their neighborhood ... excite in us neither admiration nor approval," so Brandeis argued that "public discussion is a political duty" and a nonparticipating citizenry was the "greatest menace to freedom."

His political thought, then, centered on such basic concepts as the individual, liberty, rights, responsibilities, power, justice, human possibilities, and human limitations. Most of these words have been used by a multiplicity of political theorists and politicians. Brandeis, however, combined them into a unique formulation of the ideal state that maximized individual involvement in both the political process and economic decisionmaking and that secured political and economic autonomy in the industrial age. He did not view the state as an entity that would do for others what they could not do for themselves; rather, it was to be both the expression of the cumulative will of individuals and the mechanism by which they would control their own lives.

These premises led to his opposition to bigness in both governmental and economic institutions. The basic unit of democracy is the individual; of capitalism, the dollar and the work unit. Two of the key questions with which Brandeis wrestled were how to reconcile the emphasis on individual dignity implicit in democracy with the emphasis on profits that is so central to capitalism and how to respond to the assertion that capitalism demanded the creation of ever-larger entities. He thought that overly large institutions inevitably lost their ability to think in terms of individuals and to respond to their needs. Worse, they tended to be beyond the intellectual understanding and control of any individual. This problem was as true in the political sphere as it was in the economic. A federal executive branch so big that it could not be comprehended, much less controlled, by the president was as undesirable and dangerous as a corporation whose chief executive officer did not know what the company's departments were doing. Bigness resulted not in the efficiency that often was claimed for it but in sloppiness, inattention to detail, and, ultimately, injustice either to the taxpayers who funded the public bureaucracies or to the workers within a private corporate entity. Perhaps Brandeis would not have agreed that "small is beautiful," but he would have joined Socrates in advocating moderation in all things, including institutional size.

His insistence upon institutions large enough to be efficient but small enough to be controllable was and continues to be misinterpreted by the leaders of the New Deal and their heirs as a sentimental and unsophisticated yearning for an earlier age that could and should not be replicated. Their scorn, coupled with Brandeis's preference for action and short speeches and articles rather than for political treatises, has led to his being ignored as an American political thinker with ideas well worth considering. Today's scholars remember him primarily for the opinions he wrote during his twenty-three years of service on the Supreme Court. Lawyers focus only on the opinions and on his contribution to sociological jurisprudence, which lay in his insistence that facts about society's needs were key in ascertaining whether particular legislation was constitutional.

This response is particularly unfortunate because Brandeis may have had some of the answers to the problems that continue to plague American society. It has become a commonplace for American politicians following in the footsteps of Jimmy Carter and Ronald Reagan to appeal to the electorate's inchoate sense that big government has somehow gotten out of hand; the government repeatedly expresses surprised dismay at the "necessity" to spend taxpayers' money to "bail out" huge corporations on the verge of economic collapse; General Motors, that exemplar of "bigger is better," is rethinking and retrenching; and neither big government nor big business has demonstrated the will or the knowledge to solve the problems of poverty, homelessness, inequality, individual financial insecurity, or unemployment. Perhaps it is time to revisit Brandeis.

It is conceivable that his ideas, and particularly his rejection of the popular belief that big, centrally managed corporations were not only the organic wave of the future but crucial to the nation's economic well-being, were wrong. The unwillingness of the New Deal to try them out rendered that speculation moot. Anyone who reads Brandeis, however, will find the accusation of naiveté itself naive. Brandeis understood quite well how the economy worked and the impact that his thinking, if implemented, would have on it. That fact can be demonstrated by explaining how his thought reflected his experiences and how experience was filtered through the stubborn insistence on human dignity that was a constant of his life. This book, therefore, is the story not only of his thought but also of the context in which it developed.

Brandeis was not a philosopher, nor, despite his continuous and eclectic reading, did he derive his ideas primarily from books. As a young man he had read Emerson and James, and his approach was both pragmatic and utilitarian, but he would have been puzzled if asked to what school of political thought he belonged. He had premises and first principles. He regularly addressed the question of how to make institutions work in keeping with those principles, but, consonant with both the American distaste for ideology and his view of himself as an activist, he had no interest in producing a treatise expounding his philosophy, nor did he employ the vocabulary of political theory common to the academy. "I have no rigid social philosophy. I have been too intense on concrete problems of practical justice," he maintained. "As a whole, I have not got as much from books as I have from tackling concrete problems," he added. "I have generally run up against a problem, have painfully tried to think it out, with a measure of success, and have then read a book and found to my surprise that some other chap was before me."

Brandeis did not use the theorist's phrase "political virtue," for example, and yet it is implicit in his discussion of civic responsibility. The focal point of his thinking, as that of William James, was the individual. Brandeis had copied passages from James into the notebooks he kept while in law school, and although there is no record of his ever having used the word "pragmatism," his approach to social problems surely can be given that name. The key mechanism he employed to bring the individual and society into harmony was experience. He considered experience filtered through intelligence to be the primary source of knowledge about almost everything, including the way the good state could best be achieved. In this view he paralleled not only James but John Dewey. Interestingly, John Dewey, reviewing Felix Frankfurter's *Mr. Justice Brandeis,* praised Brandeis's "strict adherence to this policy of reference to factual context" and added, "Nor can I imagine any sound social or ethical philosophy in which this idea is not fundamental." Dewey's philosophy of instrumentalism was based on experimentation. He had acknowledged that while there was "real uncertainty and contingency" in the universe and the world was "in some respect ... incomplete and in the making," there was "in things a grain against which we cannot successfully go." The coexistence of uncertainty and of something immutable required experimentation if truth was to be found: "We cannot even discover what that grain is except as we make this new experiment or that fresh effort ... in a world where discovery is genuine, error is an inevitable ingredient of reality." Human beings had to use error, "to turn it to account, to make it fruitful." Like Dewey, Brandeis viewed experience and experimentation as good in and of themselves because of the knowledge that could be derived from them. Certainly experience was central to his thought. He learned from it; he regarded speculation without experimentation as useless. His openness to new ideas was one aspect of an extraordinary mind and character; in this, he personified the approach to politics that he espoused. To see *how* his ideas developed may be to understand *why* they took the shape they did.

There were ways in which Brandeis's thought resembled that of late nineteenth-century English reform liberals, although there is no indication that he was familiar with their thinking. Rather, faced with similar problems, he came to many similar solutions. One historian has described the Fabian vision "of a society that was scientifically—which is to say, rationally—organized, in which all the parts were arranged, ordered, regulated, planned, so as to make for the most efficient and equitable whole;" it was a vision that Brandeis shared. He would not have agreed, however, with their desire to move power from the individual to the state or with their distrust of the average person. Instead, he would have seconded John Dewey's statement that "democratic equality may be construed as individuality"; individualism was fostered by political equality and, eventually, by economic equality as well.

There are two additional, unusual elements in Brandeis's thought that should be noted before turning to its evolution and the role that the times in which he lived played in its formulation. The first is the relationship between traditional civil liberties and economic rights; the second is the nature of citizenship.

Americans generally use the term "civil liberties" to connote the individual's right to be free from governmental action. They employ a separate category of "civil rights" to describe equal treatment of all citizens by the government and the government's assumption of responsibility to ensure equal treatment by various private bodies such as employers, places of public accommodation, and universities. Human rights as defined by such post-World War II documents as the Universal Declaration of Human Rights and the International Covenant on Economic, Social and Cultural Rights have included a category more usually found in European polities and generally given the rubric "economic rights": the right to an assured income, to adequate medical treatment, to education. American civil libertarians still are embroiled in the questions of the extent to which such economic rights should be part of national policy and the degree to which they can be subsumed under already existing sections of the Constitution.

Brandeis may have been one of the few major political figures in the twentieth century to adopt a peculiarly American approach that would reject the perceived dichotomy between civil liberties and economic rights. He did not speak of economic rights but of economic liberty, or, rather, of liberty in the economic sphere as part of an all-encompassing liberty that made life worth living. Brandeis used the words "rights" and "liberties" somewhat interchangeably, meaning both the moral demand of the individual to be free from governmental interference and the individual's claim on the government for provision of such services as education without which a citizen could not participate meaningfully in the political process. He viewed the Founding Fathers as sharing his belief that "Liberty ... [is] the secret of happiness," and in many ways his mature thought was an attempt to outline the roles that could be played by the national and state governments, law, and economic entities in ensuring individual liberty. "Liberty" meant as much control of one's fate as is humanly possible; economic liberty meant an extensive degree of control by the individual over his or her life in the economic sphere. Brandeis saw political and economic liberty as inextricably interrelated. A person deprived of economic liberty could not be a politically free and active citizen.

Because he postulated the necessity for both economic and political liberty, Brandeis went beyond progressivism. Most Progressives viewed the proper role of government as the creation and maintenance of a relatively even economic playing field, which required government to become the regulator of big business on behalf of the citizen. Brandeis ultimately rejected the idea of government regulation of big business in favor of the conviction that, like political democracy, economic democracy can best be guarded by individuals rather than by the state. His vision of economic liberty was similar to his picture of political liberty: a society in which members of an entity, whether citizens of a democratic political system or workers in a factory, make the decisions most important to their lives. One might in fact argue that Brandeis was a republican about politics but a democrat when it came to the economy. He accepted the necessity for representative government in the sprawling United States, although he preferred the pure democracy practiced by the Jewish communities in Palestine on their kibbutzim. His goal of worker-participation, although he never described it in detail, appears to have been closer to one of pure workplace democracy. He developed an economic counterpart to Mill's belief that as people know their own interests best, the only government that can be trusted to adopt policies in the people's best interest is one chosen by the people themselves; the only people who can articulate and create workplace policies that will be just are those who are most affected by them.

The second element of importance to Brandeis's thought is the nature of citizenship, or more specifically, civic duty and civic courage. To him, as to the Greek philosophers, civic virtue was involvement in public life. It was obvious to Brandeis that citizenship brought responsibilities as well as rights, for the whole premise of democracy is that the citizens will rule. Citizens were obliged to participate actively in the political process and not only because their failure to do so would prevent the political system from being truly democratic. Citizen responsibility was a means, but it was also a good in itself; it was a method by which human beings developed their full potential. "The development of the individual is ... both a necessary means and the end sought," Brandeis declared. "The great developer is responsibility." Human beings would grow as a result of fulfilling their democratic responsibilities in both the political system and the workplace. Here Brandeis went beyond Plato to concentrate on the beneficent effects of civic "virtue" not only on the "polis" but on the individual as well. Thus there was a psychological component to Brandeis's thought: Democracy was not only, as Winston Churchill is reputed to have said, "the worst political system ever invented except for all the others"; it was the system best designed to produce truly free, fully developed human beings.

The performance of civic duty depended upon adequate leisure. Without time to inform themselves, citizens could not participate intelligently in the political process. Here Brandeis, whose life-style and work habits tended toward the puritanical, departed from the Protestant work ethic. Puritans sought the measure of a person in his or her work. Brandeis found it, in good part, in the citizen's use of leisure time for participation in political life and other self-fulfilling activities. "Leisure does not imply idleness," according to Brandeis. "It means ability to work not less but more, ability to work at something besides breadwinning.... Leisure, so defined, is an essential of successful democracy." Leisure was a psychological as well as a physical necessity. He could "do twelve months' work in eleven months, but not in twelve," Brandeis said, and assumed the same was true of other people. The intelligent use of leisure was as good for the citizen as it was for the society. Any economic system that did not permit adequate leisure time therefore doomed both individual self-fulfillment and any hope of democracy.

To Brandeis, a major component of the free, developed person was courage. Personal courage was a theme of his life, and he demonstrated it on dozens of occasions. Perhaps one of the earliest examples occurred when his eyes gave out while he was a student at Harvard Law School and a number of doctors told him he would have to abandon his goal of becoming a lawyer. Brandeis ignored them and kept looking until he found a doctor who agreed that by minimizing his own reading and relying on fellow students to read most of the necessary material to him, he could continue in the law. The "only" requirement was that Brandeis develop a photographic memory, and so he did, going on to earn the highest grades of any student in the law school's history.

Civic courage was simply that sort of personal courage extended into the public arena. To Brandeis, personal liberty and courage in the civic sphere were inextricably linked. The Founding Fathers, he would write, not only "believed liberty to be the secret of happiness," but they also "believed ... courage to be the secret of liberty." Brandeis equated moral courage and civic virtue with freedom. It was only the good citizen who could truly be free, for the willingness to face the vicissitudes of public life was a prerequisite of liberty. Brandeis learned civic courage from the adults in his abolitionist family, whose abhorrence of slavery made them highly unpopular with their Kentucky neighbors. He needed it again as a Bostonian. During his student days at Harvard and his early years as a practicing attorney, he was "taken up" by Boston Brahmins, invited to their homes and their soirees. His experiences as a lawyer, however, convinced him that many of the ideas held by the welcoming Brahmins were wrong. He began to oppose their deeply held beliefs about the preponderant power employers should enjoy and their view of state legislatures as properly being little more than the instruments of the propertied classes. Brandeis came to believe in equal power for employees and employers, and he was shocked at the ability of capitalists to buy legislative votes. His popularity with many of his Brahmin acquaintances quickly disintegrated, but he was certain that as a citizen he had an obligation to speak for what was right. Repeatedly, throughout his life, in making opponents of the big banks and the money trust, Charles S. Mellen and the massive New Haven Railroad empire, J. P. Morgan and the steel trust, President Taft and the Morgan–Guggenheim syndicate in the Pinchot–Ballinger affair, Brandeis demonstrated his own civic courage. He expected no less of the people around him; moreover, he made it a part of his belief system and of his political thought. Involvement in public life was a challenge, and there was nothing Brandeis relished more. "Bear in mind," he told an admirer, "that in canoeing I have enjoyed not only floating down streams. Paddling up them was also a feature." He was known among his summer neighbors on Cape Cod as a man who would brave the wildest waters in his canoe. His canoeing might almost be a metaphor for his approach to the political process: "Floating down" was to be enjoyed, but "paddling up" was to be expected and was to be greeted with zest. Being a citizen in the contentious world of public policy was more than a responsibility; it was fun.

ALPHEUS THOMAS MASON, BRANDEIS: A FREE MAN'S LIFE

(1956).

"I know," Holmes himself said, "no way of finding the fit man so good as the fact of winning it [command] in the competition of the market." Industrial magnates whom Brandeis denounced as guilty of unconscionable social wrongs, Holmes admired as having triumphed in the life and death struggle of competition. "I regard a man like Hill [James J., the railroad giant] as representing one of the greatest forms of human power, an immense mastery of economic details, an equal grasp of general principles, and ability and courage to put his conclusions into practice with brilliant success. . . ."

Holmes was naturally unsympathetic toward any government interference with this struggle, this triumph of the fittest. Those government controls which Brandeis strove to win as essential to social justice, Holmes decried as humbug: "I don't disguise my belief that the Sherman Act is a humbug based on economic ignorance and incompetence, and my disbelief that the Interstate Commerce Commission is a fit body to be entrusted with rate-making, even in the qualified way in which it is entrusted."

Obviously to call two men "liberals" who held views so diametrically opposed is to empty this much abused word of all meaning. Holmes was a liberal primarily in the sense that he enforced (as he himself said) "whatever constitutional laws Congress or anybody else sees fit to pass—and do it in good faith to the best of my ability."

It was this tolerance of social change that constituted an important area of agreement. Both believed in freedom as the way to truth; both understood the essence of politics as involving an unending search for points of equilibrium, for balance between conflicting social forces. Both saw a more stable society resulting from struggle and change—an evolution no force on earth could stop. They agreed that the limits of conflicting social desires must ultimately be defined, and that this is the essence of government. They agreed also in holding that no mechanical rule can determine precisely where Aristotle's Golden Mean is to be found, that "government is not an exact science."

The dissenters parted company, however, as to the factors to be taken into account when confronted with a specific case. For Holmes the power factor—that is, legislative majorities—was usually decisive, not because the dictates of majorities were necessarily right, but because of the futility of opposing or arguing with a superior force. For him, "wise or not, the proximate test of a good government is that the dominant power has its way." Though Brandeis did not ignore the power factor, he did stress knowledge as an auxiliary measure. Nor was Holmes unmindful of the effectiveness of Brandeis's approach. There should be, he said, no "slackening in the eternal pursuit of the more exact. The growth of education is an increase in the knowledge of measure ... ; it is a substitution of quantitative for qualitative judgments." Although the "worth of the competing social ends ... cannot be reduced to number and accurately fixed," it is of "the essence of improvement that we should be as accurate as we can."

Despite such professions, Holmes himself showed no dominant inclination to shape economic forces constructively. His contributions to our liberalism are essentially negative. He not only detected the blindness of conservatives to the inevitability of change, but also exposed the illusions of reformers who believe that by changing property, or otherwise revolutionizing institutions, man can surely reach freedom's final goal. Holmes's liberalism must be measured primarily in terms of his own rare openmindedness when most judges were singularly obtuse. He failed to contribute constructively, not because he did not value facts, not because he was unaware of the path of progress as hit upon by Brandeis, but because he could not bring himself to undertake "the eternal pursuit of the more exact." For the factual studies in which Brandeis reveled, Holmes expressed "fastidious disrelish." His reaction, amounting almost to inertia, when Brandeis suggested that he spend a summer investigating the textile industry, is typical:

"Brandeis the other day drove a harpoon into my midriff with reference to my summer occupations," Holmes wrote Pollock, May 26, 1919. "He said 'you talk about improving your mind, you only exercise it on the subjects with which you are familiar. Why don't you try something new, study some domain of fact. Take up the textile industries in

Massachusetts and after reading the reports sufficiently you can go to Lawrence and get a human notion of how it really is.' I hate facts. I always say the chief end of man is to form general propositions, adding that no general proposition is worth a damn. Of course a general proposition is simply a string for the facts and I have little doubt that it would be good for my immortal soul to plunge into them, good also for the performance of my duties, but I shrink from the bore, or rather I hate to give up the chance to read this and that, that a gentleman should have read before he dies. . . ."

Brandeis read economics as well as Euripides; Holmes read and reread Plato. The results are clearly reflected in their judicial opinions. Holmes is the enlightened skeptic; Brandeis, the militant crusader.

HENRY J. FRIENDLY, MR. JUSTICE BRANDEIS: THE QUEST FOR REASON

108 U.Pa.L.Rev.985 (1960).

Judge Hand has spoken of the apocalyptic quality of Brandeis. So it is appropriate if, for my summation, I go to the great words in the Gospel according to John: "the truth shall make you free." Surely this was the essence of Brandeis' teaching. He was the authentic child of the Aufklärung; he had none of today's doubts as to whether the truth could be ascertained. He did not believe with the evangelist that this truth could be found by abiding in the Word or in becoming the disciple of any leader. Neither did he think it came from intuition or from speculation in metaphysics. He thought it could and would come only from the relentless, disinterested and critical study of facts.

LOUIS D. BRANDEIS, HOURS OF LABOR

Address to the Civic Federation of New England (1906).

We need leisure, among other reasons, because with us every man is of the ruling class. Our education and condition of life must be such as become a ruler. Our great beneficent experiment in democracy will fail unless the people, our rulers, are developed in character and intelligence.

* * *

To attain proper development of character, mind and body, a short working day is essential, and the eight-hour day is in most occupations and for most people not too short.

* * *

An extra hour of labor may render useless those other hours which might have been devoted to development, or to the performance of other duties, or to pleasure. The excess load is wasteful with man as well as with horses or vehicles or machinery. Whether the needed education of the citizens is to be given in classes or from the political platform, in the discussion of the lodges or in the trades unions, or is to be gained from the reading of papers, periodicals, or books, freshness of mind is imperative; and to the preservation of freshness of mind a short work day is for most people essential.

PHILIPPA STRUM, LOUIS D. BRANDEIS: JUSTICE FOR THE PEOPLE

(1984).

On February 19, 1903, the state of Oregon passed a law establishing a maximum of ten hours' work a day for women employed in manufacturing, mechanical establishments, and laundries. Joe Haselbock, overseer of Curt Muller's Grand Laundry in Portland, broke the law on September 4, 1905, by requiring Mrs. Elmer Gotcher to work more than ten hours. Muller was charged on September 18, found guilty of the misdemeanor, and fined ten dollars. (The statute provided that violators be fined no less than ten and no more than twenty-five dollars). Muller appealed to the Supreme Court of Oregon, which affirmed his conviction, and then to the Supreme Court of the United States.

When Florence Kelley, the secretary general of the National Consumers' League, and Josephine Goldmark, Brandeis's sister-in-law and Kelley's associate in the league, discovered that the case was to be argued before the United States Supreme Court, they were eager to ensure that the best possible case be made on behalf of maximum hours for women, a cause the league had long espoused. Mrs. Kelley had already decided that the best course of action would be to prove that overwork adversely affected the health and safety of women, and she hoped to present the Court with factual evidence to support that claim.

* * *

When Kelley and Goldmark approached Brandeis in Boston, he agreed to come into the case, provided that Oregon make him its official counsel, and that the league provide him within a fortnight with the kind of extensive documentation he felt he would require.

* * *

He needed a vast collection of facts about the effects of long working hours on women, because that would be the heart of his approach. Both Oregon and the league were pleased to meet his demands. Thus, as of November 14, 1907, Brandeis had a new *pro bono publico* case; Florence Kelley, Josephine Goldmark, her sister Pauline Goldmark (secretary of the New York City Consumers' League), and a few others had the job of combing the Columbia University and New York Public Libraries for every bit of material they could find.

* * *

For the first time, Brandeis devoted only two pages of his brief to legal precedents, almost all of them taken from *Lochner* itself. Instead of fighting *Lochner's* assertion of the liberty of contract as a constitutional right, Brandeis cited it as one of his authorities. He also, however, cited *Lochner* to affirm that the right could be abridged by a state in order to protect health, safety, morals, and the general welfare. He reminded the Court of its statement in *Lochner* that "when the validity of a statute is questioned, the burden of proof" is on the questioners, rather than on the state. In the Court's own words, unless it found "no 'fair ground, reasonable in and of itself, to say that there is material danger to the public health (or safety), or to the health (or safety) of the employees (or to the general welfare), if the hours of labor are not curtailed,' " it had to sustain the statute. In other words, unless the Court was ready to say that Oregon had no reasonable basis for concluding that there was danger to health, safety, and welfare unless hours were curtailed, the Court's own logic forced it to sustain the law as constitutional.

That was the sum of Brandeis's legal argumentation—two pages' worth. Then, to prove that Oregon was not alone in its conclusion, Brandeis added fifteen pages of excerpts from state and foreign laws limiting women's hours, noting that in "no instance has any such law been repealed." That completed the first part of the brief. The second, entitled "The World's Experience upon which the Legislation Limiting the Hours of Labor for Women is Based," was ninety-five pages long. It had numerous subtitles ranging from "The Dangers of Long Hours," to "The Reasonableness of the Ten–Hour Day" and "Laundries." Each subtitle introduced a collection of statistics on the point.

* * *

Describing his oral argument before the Court, which replicated the format of his brief, Josephine Goldmark wrote, "In hours of preparation beforehand, submerging himself first in the source material, he was determining the exclusion or inclusion of detail, the order, the selectiveness, the emphasis which marked his method. Once determined upon, it had all the spontaneity of a great address because he had so mastered the details that they fell into place, as it were, in a consummate whole." Brandeis let the "facts" speak for themselves.

The technique worked. The Court upheld the law and specifically credited Brandeis and his approach. It is rare for the Court to mention an advocate by name, but Justice Brewer, writing the majority opinion for the Court, commented, "It may not be amiss, in the present case, before examining the constitutional question, to notice the course of legislation as well as expressions of opinion from other than judicial sources. In the brief filed by Mr. Louis D. Brandeis . . . is a very copious collection of all these matters, an epitome of which is found in the margin."

NEW STATE ICE CO. v. LIEBMANN

Supreme Court of the United States, 1932.
285 U.S. 262, 52 S.Ct. 371, 76 L.Ed. 747.

* * *

Mr. JUSTICE BRANDEIS (dissenting).

Chapter 147 of the Session Laws of Oklahoma 1925, declares that the manufacture of ice for sale and distribution is "a public business"; confers upon the Corporation Commission in respect to it the powers of regulation customarily exercised over public utilities; and provides specifically for securing adequate service. The statute makes is a misdemeanor to engage in the business without a license from the commission; directs that the license shall not issue except pursuant to a prescribed written application, after a formal hearing upon adequate notice both to the community to be served and to the general public, and a showing upon competent evidence, of the necessity "at the place desired"; and it provides that the application may be denied, among other grounds, if "the facts proved at said hearing disclose that the facilities for the manufacture, sale and distribution of ice by some person, firm or corporation already licensed by said commission at said point, community or place, are sufficient to meet the public needs therein."

* * *

The people of the United States are now confronted with an emergency more serious than war. Misery is widespread, in a time, not of scarcity, but of overabundance. The long-continued depression has brought unprecedented unemployment, a catastrophic fall in commodity prices, and a volume of economic losses which threatens our financial institutions. Some people believe that the existing conditions threaten even the stability of the capitalistic system. Economists are searching for the causes of this disorder and are re-examining the basis of our industrial structure. Business men are seeking possible remedies. Most of them realize that failure to distribute widely the profits of industry has been a prime cause of our present plight. But rightly or wrongly, many persons think that one of the major contributing causes has been unbridled competition. Increasingly, doubt is expressed whether it is economically wise, or morally right, that men should be permitted to add to the producing facilities of an industry which is already suffering from overcapacity. In justification of that doubt, men point to the excess capacity of our productive facilities resulting from their vast expansion without corresponding increase in the consumptive capacity of the people. They assert that through improved methods of manufacture, made possible by advances in science and invention and vast accumulation of capital, our industries had become capable of producing from 30 to 100 per cent. more than was consumed even in days of vaunted prosperity; and that the present capacity will, for a long time, exceed the needs of business. All agree that irregularity in employment—the greatest of our evils—cannot be overcome unless production and consumption are more nearly balanced. Many insist there must be some form of economic control. There are plans for proration. There are many proposals for stabilization. And some thoughtful men of wide business experience insist that all projects for stabilization and proration must prove futile unless, in some way, the equivalent of the certificate of public convenience and necessity is made a prerequisite to embarking new capital in an industry in which the capacity already exceeds the production schedules.

Whether that view is sound nobody knows. The objections to the proposal are obvious and grave. The remedy might bring evils worse than the present disease. The obstacles to success seem insuperable. The economic and social sciences are largely uncharted seas. We have been none too successful in the modest essays in economic control already entered upon. The new proposal involves a vast extension of the area of control. Merely to acquire the knowledge essential as a basis for the exercise of this multitude of judgments would be a formidable task; and each of the thousands of these judgments would call for some measure of prophecy. Even more serious are the obstacles to success inherent in the demands which execution of the project would make upon human intelligence and upon the character of men. Man is weak and his judgment is at best fallible.

Yet the advances in the exact sciences and the achievements in invention remind us that the seemingly impossible sometimes happens. There are many men now living who were in the habit of using the age-old expression: "It is as impossible as flying." The discoveries in physical science, the triumphs in invention, attest the value of the process of trial and error. In large measure, these advances have been due to experimentation. In those fields experimentation has, for two centuries, been not only free but encouraged. Some people assert that our present plight is due, in part, to the limitations set by courts upon experimentation in the fields of social and economic science; and to the discouragement to which proposals for betterment there have been subjected otherwise. There must be power in the states and the nation to remould, through experimentation, our economic practices and institutions to meet changing social and economic needs. I cannot believe that the framers of the Fourteenth Amendment, or the states which ratified it, intended to deprive us of the power to correct the evils of technological unemployment and excess productive capacity which have attended progress in the useful arts.

To stay experimentation in things social and economic is a grave responsibility. Denial of the right to experiment may be fraught with serious consequences to the nation. It is one of the happy incidents of the federal system that a single courageous state may, if its citizens choose, serve as a laboratory; and try novel social and economic experiments without risk to the rest of the country. This Court has the power to prevent an experiment. We may strike down the statute which embodies it on the ground that, in our opinion, the measure is arbitrary, capricious, or unreasonable. We have power to do this, because the due process clause has been held by the Court applicable to matters of substantive law as well as to matters of procedure. But, in the exercise of this high power, we must be ever on our guard, lest we erect our prejudices into legal principles. If we would guide by the light of reason, we must let our minds be bold.

MR. JUSTICE STONE joins in this opinion.

LOUIS K. LIGGETT CO. v. LEE

Supreme Court of the United States, 1933.
288 U.S. 517, 53 S.Ct. 481, 77 L.Ed. 929.

Mr. JUSTICE BRANDEIS (dissenting in part).

In my opinion, the judgment of the Supreme Court of Florida should be affirmed.

Florida Laws 1931 (Ex. Sess.), chapter 15624, is legislation of the type popularly called Anti–Chain Store Laws. The statute provides for the licensing of retail stores by the state, the counties, and the municipalities—a system under which large revenues may be raised. But the raising of revenue is obviously not the main purpose of the legislation. Its chief aim is to protect the individual, independently-owned, retail stores from the competition of chain stores. The statute seeks to do this by subjecting the latter to financial handicaps which may conceivably compel their withdrawal from the state. An injunction against its enforcement is sought on the ground that the law violates rights guaranteed by the Federal Constitution.

* * *

There is a widespread belief that the existing unemployment is the result, in large part, of the gross inequality in the distribution of wealth and income which giant corporations have fostered; that by the control which the few have exerted through giant corporations individual initiative and effort are being paralyzed, creative power impaired and human happiness lessened; that the true prosperity of our past came not from big business, but through the courage, the energy, and the resourcefulness of small men; that only by releasing from corporate control the faculties of the unknown many, only by reopening to them the opportunities for leadership, can confidence in our future be restored and the existing misery be overcome; and that only through participation by the many in the responsibilities and determinations of business can Americans secure the moral and intellectual development which is essential to the maintenance of liberty. If the citizens of Florida share that belief, I know of nothing in the Federal Constitution which precludes the state from endeavoring to give it effect and prevent domination in intrastate commerce by subjecting corporate chains to discriminatory license fees.

To that extent, the citizens of each state are still masters of their destiny.

LOUIS D. BRANDEIS TO ROBERT W. BRUERE

Letter of February 25, 1922, summarizing at the latter's request informal remarks that Brandeis had delivered to the Federal Council of Churches.

Refuse to accept as inevitable any evil in business (e.g., irregularity of employment). Refuse to tolerate any immoral practice (e.g., espionage). But do not believe that you can find a universal remedy for evil conditions or immoral practices in effecting a fundamental change in society (as by State Socialism). And do not pin too much faith in legislation. Remedial institutions are apt to fall under the control of the enemy and to become instruments of oppression.

Seek for betterment within the broad lines of existing institutions. Do so by attacking evil *in situ;* and proceed from the individual to the general. Remember that progress is necessarily slow; that remedies are necessarily tentative; that because of varying conditions there must be much and constant enquiry into facts . . . and much experimentation; and that always and everywhere the intellectual, moral and spiritual development of those concerned will remain an essential—and the main factor—in real betterment.

This development of the individual is, thus, both a necessary means and the end sought. For our objective is the making of men and women who shall be free, self-respecting members of a democracy—and who shall be worthy of respect. Improvement in material conditions of the worker and ease are the incidents of better conditions—valuable mainly as they may ever increase opportunities for development.

The great developer is responsibility. Hence no remedy can be hopeful which does not devolve upon the workers participation in, responsibility for, the conduct of business; and their aim should be the eventual assumption of full responsibility—as in co-operative enterprises. This participation in, and eventual control of, industry is likewise an essential of obtaining justice in distributing the fruits of industry.

But democracy in any sphere is a serious undertaking. It substitutes self-restraint for external restraint. It is more difficult to maintain than to achieve. It demands continuous sacrifice by the individual and more exigent obedience to the moral law than any other form of government. Success in any democratic undertaking must proceed from the individual. It is possible only where the process of perfecting the individual is pursued. His development is attained mainly in the processes of common living. Hence the industrial struggle is essentially an affair of the Church and is its imperative task.

WHITNEY v. CALIFORNIA

Supreme Court of the United States, 1927.
274 U.S. 357, 47 S.Ct. 641, 71 L.Ed. 1095.

MR. JUSTICE SANFORD delivered the opinion of the Court.

By a criminal information filed in the Superior Court of Alameda County, California, the plaintiff in error was charged, in five counts, with violations of the Criminal Syndicalism Act of that State. She was tried, convicted on the first count, and sentenced to imprisonment. The judgment was affirmed by the District Court of Appeal. Her petition to have the case heard by the Supreme Court was denied. And the case was brought here on a writ of error which was allowed by the Presiding Justice of the Court of Appeal, the highest court of the State in which a decision could be had.

On the first hearing in this Court, the writ of error was dismissed for want of jurisdiction. Thereafter, a petition for rehearing was granted; and the case was again heard and reargued both as to the jurisdiction and the merits.

The pertinent provisions of the Criminal Syndicalism Act are:

"Section 1. The term 'criminal syndicalism' as used in this act is hereby defined as any doctrine or precept advocating, teaching or aiding and abetting the commission of crime, sabotage (which word is hereby defined as meaning willful and malicious physical damage or injury to physical property), or unlawful acts of force and violence or unlawful methods of terrorism as a means of accomplishing a change in industrial ownership or control or effecting any political change.

"Sec. 2. Any person who:. . . . Organizes or assists in organizing, or is or knowingly becomes a member of, any organization, society, group or assemblage of persons organized or assembled to advocate, teach or aid and abet criminal syndicalism;. . . .

"Is guilty of a felony and punishable by imprisonment."

* * *

The following facts, among many others, were established on the trial by undisputed evidence: The defendant, a resident of Oakland, in Alameda County, California, had been a member of the Local Oakland branch of the Socialist Party. This Local sent delegates to the national convention of the Socialist Party held in Chicago in 1919, which resulted in a split between the "radical" group and the old-wing Socialists. The "radicals"-to whom the Oakland delegates adhered-being ejected, went to another hall, and formed the Communist Labor Party of America. Its Constitution provided for the membership of persons subscribing to the principles of the Party and pledging themselves to be guided by its

Platform, and for the formation of state organizations conforming to its Platform as the supreme declaration of the Party. In its "Platform and Program" the Party declared that it was in full harmony with "the revolutionary working class parties of all countries" and adhered to the principles of Communism laid down in the Manifesto of the Third International at Moscow, and that its purpose was "to create a unified revolutionary working class movement in America," organizing the workers as a class, in a revolutionary class struggle to conquer the capitalist state, for the overthrow of capitalist rule, the conquest of political power and the establishment of a working class government, the Dictatorship of the Proletariat, in place of the state machinery of the capitalists, which should make and enforce the laws, reorganize society on the basis of Communism and bring about the Communist Commonwealth; advocated, as the most important means of capturing state power, the action of the masses, proceeding from the shops and factories, the use of the political machinery of the capitalist state being only secondary; the organization of the workers into "revolutionary industrial unions"; propaganda pointing out their revolutionary nature and possibilities; and great industrial battles showing the value of the strike as a political weapon; commended the propaganda and example of the Industrial Workers of the World and their struggles and sacrifices in the class war; pledged support and co-operation to "the revolutionary industrial proletariat of America" in their struggles against the capitalist class; cited the Seattle and Winnipeg strikes and the numerous strikes all over the country "proceeding without the authority of the old reactionary Trade Union officials," as manifestations of the new tendency; and recommended that strikes of national importance be supported and given a political character, and that propagandists and organizers be mobilized "who can not only teach, but actually help to put in practice the principles of revolutionary industrial unionism and Communism."

Shortly thereafter the Local Oakland withdrew from the Socialist Party, and sent accredited delegates, including the defendant, to a convention held in Oakland in November 1919, for the purpose of organizing a California branch of the Communist Labor Party. The defendant, after taking out a temporary membership in the Communist Labor Party, attended this convention as a delegate and took an active part in its proceedings. She was elected a member of the Credentials Committee, and, as its chairman, made a report to the convention upon which the delegates were seated. She was also appointed a member of the Resolutions Committee, and as such signed the following resolution in reference to political action, among others proposed by the Committee:

> "The C. L. P. of California fully recognizes the value of political action as a means of spreading communist propaganda; it insists that in proportion to the development of the economic strength of the working class, it, the working class, must also develop its political power. the C. L. P. of California proclaims and insists that the capture of political power, locally or nationally by the revolution-

> ary working class can be of tremendous assistance to the workers in their struggle of emancipation. Therefore, we again urge the workers who are possessed of the right of franchise to cast their votes for the party which represents their immediate and final interest—the C. L. P.—at all elections, being fully convinced of the utter futility of obtaining any real measure of justice or freedom under officials elected by parties owned and controlled by the capitalist class."

The minutes show that this resolution, with the others proposed by the committee, was read by its chairman to the convention before the Committee on the Constitution had submitted its report. According to the recollection of the defendant, however, she herself read this resolution. Thereafter, before the report of the Committee on the Constitution had been acted upon, the defendant was elected an alternate member of the State Executive Committee. The Constitution, as finally read, was then adopted. This provided that the organization should be named the Communist Labor Party of California; that it should be "affiliated with" the Communist Labor Party of America, and subscribe to its Program, Platform and Constitution, and "through this affiliation" be "joined with the Communist International of Moscow"; and that the qualifications for membership should be those prescribed in the National Constitution. The proposed resolutions were later taken up and all adopted, except that on political action, which caused a lengthy debate, resulting in its defeat and the acceptance of the National Program in its place. After this action, the defendant, without, so far as appears, making any protest, remained in the convention until it adjourned. She later attended as an alternate member one or two meetings of the State Executive Committee in San Jose and San Francisco, and stated, on the trial, that she was then a member of the Communist Labor Party. She also testified that it was not her intention that the Communist Labor Party of California should be an instrument of terrorism or violence, and that it was not her purpose or that of the Convention to violate any known law.

* * *

While it is not denied that the evidence warranted the jury in finding that the defendant became a member of and assisted in organizing the Communist Labor Party of California, and that this was organized to advocate, teach, aid or abet criminal syndicalism as defined by the Act, it is urged that the Act, as here construed and applied, deprived the defendant of her liberty without due process of law in that it has made her action in attending the Oakland convention unlawful by reason of "a subsequent event brought about against her will, by the agency of others," with no showing of a specific intent on her part to join in the forbidden purpose of the association, and merely because, by reason of a lack of "prophetic" understanding, she failed to foresee the quality that others would give to the convention. The argument is, in effect, that the character of the state organization could not be forecast when she attended the convention; that she had no purpose of helping to create an instrument of terrorism and violence; that she "took part in formulating and presenting to the convention a resolution which, if adopted, would have committed the new organization to a legitimate policy of political reform by the use of the ballot"; that it was not until after the majority of the convention turned out to be "contrary minded, and other less temperate policies prevailed" that the convention could have taken on the character of criminal syndicalism; and that as this was done over her protest, her mere presence in the convention, however, violent the opinions expressed therein, could not thereby become a crime. This contention, while advanced in the form of a constitutional objection to the Act, is in effect nothing more than an effort to review the weight of the evidence for the purpose of showing that the defendant did not join and assist in organizing the Communist Labor Party of California with a knowledge of its unlawful character and purpose. This question, which is foreclosed by the verdict of the jury—sustained by the Court of Appeal over the specific objection that it was not supported by the evidence—is one of fact merely which is not open to review in this Court, involving as it does no constitutional question whatever. And we may add that the argument entirely disregards the facts that the defendant had previously taken out a membership card in the National Party; that the resolution which she supported did not advocate the use of the ballot to the exclusion of violent and unlawful means of bringing about the desired changes in industrial and political conditions; and that, after the constitution of the California Party had been adopted, and this resolution had been voted down and the National Program accepted, she not only remained in the convention, without protest, until its close, but subsequently manifested her acquiescence by attending as an alternate member of the State Executive Committee and continuing as a member of the Communist Labor Party.

* * *

That the freedom of speech which is secured by the Constitution does not confer an absolute right to speak, without responsibility, whatever one may choose, or an unrestricted and unbridled license giving immunity for every possible use of language and preventing the punishment of those who abuse this freedom; and that a State in the exercise of its police power may punish those who abuse this freedom by utterances inimical to the public welfare, tending to incite to crime, disturb the public peace, or endanger the foundations of organized government and threaten its overthrow by unlawful means, is not open to question. *Gitlow v. New York*, 268 U. S. 652, 666, 668.

By enacting the provisions of the Syndicalism Act the State has declared, through its legislative body, that to knowingly be or become a member of or assist in organizing an association to advocate, teach or aid and abet the commission of crimes or unlawful acts of force, violence or terrorism as a means of accomplishing industrial or political changes, involves such danger to the public peace and the security of the State, that these acts should be penalized in the exercise of its police power. That determination must be given great weight. Every presumption is to be indulged in favor of the validity of the statute; and it may not be declared unconstitutional unless it is an arbitrary or unreasonable attempt to exercise the authority vested in the State in the public interest.

The essence of the offense denounced by the Act is the combining with others in an association for the accomplishment of the desired ends through the advocacy and use of criminal and unlawful methods. It partakes of the nature of a criminal conspiracy. That such united and joint action involves even greater danger to the public peace and security than the isolated utterances and acts of individuals is clear. We cannot hold that, as here applied, the Act is an unreasonable or arbitrary exercise of the police power of the State, unwarrantably infringing any right of free speech, assembly or association, or that those persons are protected from punishment by the due process clause who abuse such rights by joining and furthering an organization thus menacing the peace and welfare of the State.

We find no repugnancy in the Syndicalism Act as applied in this case to either the due process or equal protection clauses of the Fourteenth Amendment on any of the grounds upon which its validity has been here challenged.

The order dismissing the writ of error will be vacated and set aside, and the judgment of the Court of Appeal

Affirmed.

MR. JUSTICE BRANDEIS (concurring.)

Miss Whitney was convicted of the felony of assisting in organizing, in the year 1919, the Communist Labor Party of California, of being a member of it, and of assembling with it. These acts are held to constitute a crime, because the party was formed to teach criminal syndicalism. The statute which made these acts a crime restricted the right of free speech and of assembly theretofore existing. The claim is that the statute, as applied, denied to Miss Whitney the liberty guaranteed by the Fourteenth Amendment.

The felony which the statute created is a crime very unlike the old felony of conspiracy or the old misdemeanor of unlawful assembly. The mere act of assisting in forming a society for teaching syndicalism, of becoming a member of it, or assembling with others for that purpose is given the dynamic quality of crime. There is guilt although the society may not contemplate immediate promulgation of the doctrine. Thus the accused is to be punished, not for attempt, incitement or conspiracy, but for a step in preparation, which, if it threatens the public order at all, does so only remotely. The novelty in the prohibition introduced is that the statute aims, not at the practice of criminal syndicalism, nor even directly at the preaching of it, but at association with those who propose to preach it.

Despite arguments to the contrary which had seemed to me persuasive, it is settled that the due process clause of the Fourteenth Amendment applies to matters of substantive law as well as to matters of procedure. Thus all fundamental rights comprised within the term liberty are protected by the federal Constitution from invasion by the states. The right of free speech, the right to teach and the right of assembly are, of course, fundamental rights. See *Meyer v. Nebraska*, 262 U. S. 390; *Pierce v. Society of Sisters*, 268 U. S. 510; *Gitlow v. New York*, 268 U. S. 652, 666. These may not be denied or abridged. But, although the rights of free speech and assembly are fundamental, they are not in their nature absolute. Their exercise is subject to restriction, if the particular restriction proposed is required in order to protect the state from destruction or from serious injury, political, economic or moral. That the necessity which is essential to a valid restriction does not exist unless speech would produce, or is intended to produce, a clear and imminent danger of some substantive evil which the state constitutionally may seek to prevent has been settled. See *Schenck v. United States*, 249 U. S. 47, 52.

It is said to be the function of the Legislature to determine whether at a particular time and under the particular circumstances the formation of, or assembly with, a society organized to advocate criminal syndicalism constitutes a clear and present danger of substantive evil; and that by enacting the law here in question the Legislature of California determined that question in the affirmative. Compare *Gitlow v. New York*, 268 U. S. 652, 668, 671. The Legislature must obviously decide, in the first instance, whether a danger exists which calls for a particular protective measure. But where a statute is valid only in case certain condition exist, the enactment of the statute cannot alone establish the facts which are essential to its validity. Prohibitory legislation has repeatedly been held invalid, because unnecessary, where the denial of liberty involved was that of engaging in a particular business. The powers of the courts to strike down an offending law are no less when the interests involved are not property rights, but the fundamental personal rights of free speech and assembly.

This court has not yet fixed the standard by which to determine when a danger shall be deemed clear; how remote the danger may be and yet be deemed present; and what degree of evil shall be deemed sufficiently substantial to justify resort to abridgment of free speech and assembly as the means of protection. To reach sound conclusions on these matters, we must bear in mind why a state is, ordinarily, denied the power to prohibit dissemination of social, economic and political doctrine which a vast majority of its citizens believes to be false and fraught with evil consequence.

Those who won our independence believed that the final end of the state was to make men free to develop their faculties, and that in its government the deliberative forces should prevail over the arbitrary. They valued liberty both as an end and as a means. They believed liberty to the secret of happiness and courage to be the secret of liberty. They believed that freedom to think as you will and to speak as you think are means indispensable to the discovery and spread of political truth; that without free speech and assembly discussion would be futile; that with them, discussion affords ordinarily adequate protection against the dissemination of noxious doctrine; that the greatest menace to freedom is an inert people; that public discussion is a political duty; and that this should be a fundamental principle of the American government.[2] They recognized the risks to which all human institutions are subject. But they knew that order cannot be secured merely through fear of punishment for its infraction; that it is hazardous to discourage thought, hope and imagination; that fear breeds repression; that repression breeds hate; that hate menaces stable government; that the path of safety lies in the opportunity to discuss freely supposed grievances and proposed remedies; and that the fitting remedy for evil counsels is good ones. Believing in the power of reason as applied through public discussion, they eschewed silence coerced by law—the argument of force in its worst form. Recognizing the occasional tyrannies of governing majorities, they amended the Constitution so that free speech and assembly should be guaranteed.

Fear of serious injury cannot alone justify suppression of free speech and assembly. Men feared witches and burnt women. It is the function of speech to free men from the bondage of irrational fears. To justify suppression of free speech there must be reasonable ground to fear that serious evil will result if free speech is practiced. There must be reasonable ground to believe that the danger apprehended is imminent. There must be reasonable ground to believe that the evil to be prevented is a serious one. Every denunciation of existing law tends in some measure to increase the probability that there will be violation of it.[3] Condonation of a breach enhances the probability. Expressions of approval add to the probability. Propagation of the criminal state of mind by teaching syndicalism increases it. Advocacy of lawbreaking heightens it still further. But even advocacy of violation, however reprehensible morally, is not a justification for denying free speech where the advocacy falls short of incitement and there is nothing to indicate that the advocacy would be immediately acted on. The wide difference between advocacy and incitement, between preparation and attempt, between assembling and conspiracy, must be borne in mind. In order to support a finding of clear and present danger it must be shown either that immediate serious violence was to be expected or was advocated, or that the past conduct furnished reason to believe that such advocacy was then contemplated.

Those who won our independence by revolution were not cowards. They did not fear political change. They did not exalt order at the cost of

2. Compare Thomas Jefferson: "We have nothing to fear from the demoralizing reasonings of some, if others are left free to demonstrate their errors and especially when the law stands ready to punish the first criminal act produced by the false reasonings; these are safer corrections than the conscience of the judge." Also in first Inaugural Address: "If there be any among us who would wish to dissolve this union or change its republican form, let them stand undisturbed as monuments of the safety with which error of opinion may be tolerated where reason is left free to combat it."

3. Compare Judge Learned Hand in Masses Publishing Co. v. Patten (D. C.) 244 F. 535, 540.

liberty. To courageous, self-reliant men, with confidence in the power of free and fearless reasoning applied through the processes of popular government, no danger flowing from speech can be deemed clear and present, unless the incidence of the evil apprehended is so imminent that it may befall before there is opportunity for full discussion. If there be time to expose through discussion the falsehood and fallacies, to avert the evil by the processes of education, the remedy to be applied is more speech, not enforced silence. Only an emergency can justify repression. Such must be the rule if authority is to be reconciled with freedom. Such, in my opinion, is the command of the Constitution. It is therefore always open to Americans to challenge a law abridging free speech and assembly by showing that there was no emergency justifying it.

Moreover, even imminent danger cannot justify resort to prohibition of these functions essential to effective democracy, unless the evil apprehended is relatively serious. Prohibition of free speech and assembly is a measure so stringent that it would be inappropriate as the means for averting a relatively trivial harm to society. A police measure may be unconstitutional merely because the remedy, although effective as means of protection, is unduly harsh or oppressive. Thus, a state might, in the exercise of its police power, make any trespass upon the land of another a crime, regardless of the results or of the intent or purpose of the trespasser. It might, also, punish an attempt, a conspiracy, or an incitement to commit the trespass. But it is hardly conceivable that this court would hold constitutional a statute which punished as a felony the mere voluntary assembly with a society formed to teach that pedestrians had the moral right to cross uninclosed, unposted, waste lands and to advocate their doing so, even if there was imminent danger that advocacy would lead to a trespass. The fact that speech is likely to result in some violence or in destruction of property is not enough to justify its suppression. There must be the probability of serious injury to the State. Among free men, the deterrents ordinarily to be applied to prevent crime are education and punishment for violations of the law, not abridgment of the rights of free speech and assembly.

The California Syndicalism Act recites in section 4:

> "Inasmuch as this act concerns and is necessary to the immediate preservation of the public peace and safety, for the reason that at the present time large numbers of persons are going from place to place in this state advocating, teaching, and practicing criminal syndicalism, this act shall take effect upon approval by the Governor."

This legislative declaration satisfies the requirement of the Constitution of the state concerning emergency legislation. But it does not preclude inquiry into the question whether, at the time and under the circumstances, the conditions existed which are essential to validity under the federal Constitution. As a statute, even if not void on its face, may be challenged because invalid as applied, the result of such an inquiry may depend upon the specific facts of the particular case.

Whenever the fundamental rights of free speech and assembly are alleged to have been invaded, it must remain open to a defendant to present the issue whether there actually did exist at the time a clear danger, whether the danger, if any, was imminent, and whether the evil apprehended was one so substantial as to justify the stringent restriction interposed by the Legislature. The legislative declaration, like the fact that the statute was passed and was sustained by the highest court of the State, creates merely a rebuttable presumption that these conditions have been satisfied.

Whether in 1919, when Miss Whitney did the things complained of, there was in California such clear and present danger of serious evil, might have been made the important issue in the case. She might have required that the issue be determined either by the court or the jury. She claimed below that the statute as applied to her violated the federal Constitution; but she did not claim that it was void because there was no clear and present danger of serious evil, nor did she request that the existence of these conditions of a valid measure thus restricting the rights of free speech and assembly be passed upon by the court of a jury. On the other hand, there was evidence on which the court or jury might have found that such danger existed. I am unable to assent to the suggestion in the opinion of the court that assembling with a political party, formed to advocate the desirability of a proletarian revolution by mass action at some date necessarily far in the future, is not a right within the protection of the Fourteenth Amendment. In the present case, however, there was other testimony which tended to establish the existence of a conspiracy, on the part of members of the International Workers of the World, to commit present serious crimes, and likewise to show that such a conspiracy would be furthered by the activity of the society of which Miss Whitney was a member. Under these circumstances the judgment of the State court cannot be disturbed.

Our power of review in this case is limited not only to the question whether a right guaranteed by the federal Constitution was denied, but to the particular claims duly made below, and denied. We lack here the power occasionally exercised on review of judgments of lower federal courts to correct in criminal cases vital errors, although the objection was not taken in the trial court. This is a writ of error to a state court. Because we may not inquire into the errors now alleged I concur in affirming the judgment of the state court.

Mr. Justice Holmes joins in this opinion.

Questions

1) What kind of an argument is Brandeis making? Does his invocation of the views of "those who won our independence by revolution" suggest an argument from *authority*? Does his declension from "fear breeds repression" to "hate menaces stable government" indicate an argument from *consequences*? Or does all his talk about "courageous, self-reliant men" and the menace of "an inert people" signal an argument from *character?*

Or does his opening premise "the final end of the state [is] to make men free to develop their faculties" introduce an argument from *autonomy*?

2) How does Brandeis's argument compare with Holmes's in terms of (a) the view of human nature on which it is based and (b) the value it ascribes to dissenting speech?

3) Both Brandeis and Madison (along with Hand) emphasize the role that free speech plays in democratic governance. How do Brandeis and Madison differ regarding exactly what they take that role to be?

4) Does Brandeis view free speech as a collective benefit or an individual entitlement? How does his understanding of the relationship between individual freedom and societal well-being and progress compare with that of Milton? That of Mill?

5) Is Brandeis too optimistic about the capacity of refutation and education ("more speech" "good counsels") to contain and/or correct the harms caused by free speech? How much does his argument depend on (blind?) faith in that capacity?

6) How does the imminence requirement relate to Brandeis's underlying theory? Is the time frame within which the feared harm is expected to materialize important to him for the same reason that it is important to Holmes?

7) Judge Hand stated in *Masses* that the freedom of speech derives from democratic theory and that democratic theory does not justify the protection of a speaker who tells his audience that it is their duty or in their interest to violate the law. Brandeis also rests his interpretation of the freedom of speech on democratic theory. He cites Hand's *Masses* opinion in his *Whitney* concurrence. Why was Brandeis not persuaded by Hand's point regarding the implications of democratic theory for speakers who engage in the direct advocacy of law violation?

8) Brandeis states that speech can be regulated "in order to protect the State from destruction or from serious injury, political, economic, or moral"? Later he says: "[I]t must be shown either that immediate serious violence was to be expected or was advocated, or that past conduct furnished reason to believe that such advocacy was then contemplated." Finally, he says: "The fact that speech is likely to result in some violence or in destruction of property is not enough. There must be the probability of serious injury to the State." Is there an important difference in these various formulations of the danger that must be clear and imminent? Which formulation is most consistent with his discussion of the value of free speech?

9) Why didn't Brandeis rule in favor of Anita Whitney on the ground that the First Amendment embodies a principle against guilt by association? Recall that Ms. Whitney was convicted on the basis of the dangerousness of views regarding the necessity for violent revolution that at her trial she denied holding, and that the prosecution never attempted to prove that she held; her conviction was for associating with persons who held such views. Shouldn't the philosophy of free speech that Brandeis articulates in his concurrence generate a strong principle against guilt by association?

10) Does Brandeis offer any reason to protect flag burners? To protect persons such as the schoolchildren in *Gobitis* and *Barnette* who objected to pledging allegiance to the flag?

PERICLES, FUNERAL ORATION

in Thucydides, History of the Peloponnesian War (ca. 404 B.C.).

[W]e alone think that a man who does not take part in public affairs is good for nothing, while others only say he is "minding his own business." We are the ones who develop policy, or at least decide what is to be done; for we believe that what spoils action is not speeches, but going into action without first being instructed through speeches. In this too we excel over others: ours is the bravery of people who think through what they will take in hand, and discuss it thoroughly; with other men, ignorance makes them brave and thinking makes them cowards. But the people who most deserve to be judged tough-minded are those who know exactly what terrors or pleasures lie ahead, and are not turned away from danger by that knowledge.

* * *

In sum, I say that our city as a whole is a lesson for Greece, and that each of us presents himself as a self-sufficient individual, disposed to the widest possible diversity of actions, with every grace and great versatility. This is not merely a boast in words for the occasion, but the truth in fact, as the power of this city, which we have obtained by having this character, makes evident.

* * *

Try to be like these men, therefore: realize that happiness lies in liberty, and liberty in valor, and do not hold back from the dangers of war. Miserable men, who have no hope of prosperity, do not have a just reason to be generous with their lives; no, it is rather those who face the danger of a complete reversal of fortune for whom defeat would make the biggest difference: they are the ones who should risk their lives. Any man of intelligence will hold that death, when it comes unperceived to a man at full strength and with hope for his country, is not so bitter as miserable defeat for a man grown soft.

ASHUTOSH A. BHAGWAT, THE STORY OF *WHITNEY v. CALIFORNIA*: THE POWER OF IDEAS

in Constitutional Law Stories (M. Dorf ed. 2004).

Charlotte Anita Whitney was born on July 7, 1867 in San Francisco, California. Among her ancestors were five members of the Mayflower complement, an early governor of Massachusetts Colony, and several veterans of the Revolutionary War. Her father was a successful attorney who later served as a State Senator in California. On her mother's side of the family, one of her uncles (by marriage) was Stephen J. Field, Associate Justice of the United States Supreme Court. Whitney attended Wellesley College and graduated in 1889 with a Bachelor of Science degree. After graduation, she undertook a six month tour of Europe, before returning to her hometown of Oakland, California. In short, Anita Whitney was very much a member of the cultural and economic elite of the late-nineteenth century United States, seemingly destined for the typical life of women of that stratum. As it turned out, however, Whitney's life took quite a different course, culminating in her appearance before the United States Supreme Court as a criminal defendant.

Whitney's transformation from a life of upper-class privilege to that of a social activist appears to have begun during a trip to the east coast in 1893, when she first seriously took up charitable work. Upon returning to Oakland, Whitney became actively involved in local charitable endeavors, and in 1901 was named the secretary of the Associated Charities of Alameda County. In 1903 she was appointed the first (unpaid) juvenile probation officer for Alameda County. And in 1906 Whitney heavily participated in relief efforts in Oakland following the San Francisco earthquake and fire, assisting in the care of thousands of refugees who fled San Francisco for Oakland. After the crisis created by the great earthquake had eased, Whitney spent several years working with charitable organizations in Boston and New York City, until in 1911, worn out and disillusioned, she returned once again to Oakland.

In the following years, Whitney's interests gradually evolved from social work to politics. Contemporary press accounts of her trial and conviction describe Whitney as a "club woman," a member of the sorts of women's social clubs that were frequented by the upper middle class, educated elite, and which during this period were transforming into vehicles for women's involvement in politics. Whitney began her own political career by joining the Prohibition movement, and then the Women's Suffrage movement. She served as a leader of the effort to extend the right to vote to women in California, which end was accomplished in 1911, and then as the first president of the California Civic League (while simultaneously assisting with suffrage movements in Oregon and Nevada). During this period (the early to mid nineteen-teens), Whitney was for the first time brought into contact with the workers' movement in the United States. The growing power of, and attacks against one part of that movement, the Industrial Workers of the World ("IWW"), had a profound influence on Whitney's own developing radicalism.

The IWW, better known as the "Wobblies," was founded in 1905. The stated aim of the organization, which exists to this day, albeit with less influence, was, and is, to create "One Big Union," and its statement of purpose begins with the declaration that "[t]he working class and the employing class have nothing in common." The form of radicalism represented by the Wobblies was new and unusual in the United States, and the IWW was, rightly or wrongly, accused of fomenting violence during strikes. As a consequence, the Wobblies were unsurprisingly met by great hostility from "the employing class." During the first decade of the Wobblies" existence, their organizers, leaders, and members faced constant harassment and violence from the authorities, but also developed substantial support among workers, especially in the western United States. Public opinion was divided regarding the IWW's treatment by the authorities. Interestingly (and in retrospect ironically), the Wobblies played a pivotal role during this period in the development of a true, modern free speech movement, though their interest in free speech was more as a tool to fight for workers" causes than as a general right.

The Wobblies' activities during the first two decades of the twentieth century, particularly their "free speech fights" and their militant organizing of destitute and socially powerless workers (among them migrant workers) elicited a great deal of support and admiration in progressive circles, including from Anita Whitney. With the entry of the United States into World War I in the spring of 1917, however, the tide of public opinion turned decisively against the IWW and other left-wing organizations. The IWW and other leftist organizations such as the Socialist Party were firmly opposed to America's entry into the war, which they viewed as being waged on behalf of capitalist and colonialist interests at the expense of workers. Such opposition, however, was widely viewed as treasonous in the highly patriotic atmosphere of 1917 to 1919. In addition, the Bolshevik Revolution in November of 1917 fed widespread fears of a violent, workers' revolution in the United States and western Europe. The immediate product of wartime hysteria and the post-war Red Scare was the enactment of a series of laws essentially outlawing opposition to the war or support of violent revolution. The most important of these laws was the federal Espionage Act of 1917, which was used to initiate a wave of prosecutions against opponents of the war, including most famously the prosecution and imprisonment of Eugene Debs, the leader of the Socialist Party. In addition, many states adopted "criminal syndicalism" statutes forbidding the advocacy of criminal or violent action as a means of industrial reform. These state statutes were directed specifically at the Wobblies, and were used to imprison much of the IWW leadership. California's Criminal Syndicalism statute, which came into effect on April 30, 1919, was typical, inasmuch as it was wielded primarily against the Wobblies. In late 1919, however, the statute ensnared a most unusual and unexpected victim: Anita Whitney.

During the years following Whitney's successful work in the women's suffrage movement, she was exposed to radical activists in the workers' rights movement. By 1914, observing the brutal treatment accorded IWW organizers and increasingly convinced that changes in industrial organization were essential if any serious progress was to be made in addressing poverty and its related ills, Whitney joined the Socialist Party of Eugene Debs. Her radicalism increased over the next several years. This process culminated in the summer of 1919, when as a result of the Bolshevik Revolution in Russia, the Socialist Party split over the question of whether it should join the Communist International. At a convention in Chicago, the more radical elements (who supported the Soviet Union) were expelled from the Socialist Party, and formed the rival Communist Labor Party. While Whitney was not present in Chicago, upon hearing of the split she helped to organize the Communist Labor Party of California, leading the local Oakland chapter of the Socialist Party into the newly organized party and serving on the credentials and resolutions committee at the Communist Labor Party's organizing convention. At the convention Whitney personally supported a relatively moderate platform advocating only an electoral strategy; but her position was defeated, and the California party adopted the national party's more radical platform, which among other things, explicitly endorsed the activities and "example" of the IWW. Whitney made no protest against this result, and remained active in the party, serving as a member of the party's state executive committee. During this same period, though she never joined the IWW, Whitney provided substantial support to the IWW defense committee and committed most of her personal fortune to providing bail for jailed Wobblies. It was Whitney's support of the Wobblies, along with her membership in the Communist Labor Party, which led to her criminal prosecution and ultimately the Supreme Court's decision in *Whitney v. California.*

In late November of 1919, Anita Whitney delivered a speech in Oakland to the California Civic League (of which she had been a founding member) on the subject of "The Negro Problem," speaking out against recent lynchings and race riots. Because of Whitney's political activities the talk was controversial, but the membership of the organization voted to proceed nonetheless. At the end of her address, Whitney was placed under arrest by Inspector Fenton Thompson of the Oakland police department, an active red-baiter. In arresting Whitney, Thompson acted against the wishes of his immediate superior, Oakland chief of police Walter Peterson (who later supported a pardon for Whitney), but with the support of other, more senior officers.

Three months later, Whitney's trial began. Whitney was represented at trial by Thomas H. O'Connor, a well-respected criminal defense attorney. O'Connor, however, only became involved in the case on the eve of trial, and was refused a continuance to better prepare by the trial judge, James G. Quinn of the Superior Court, even though O'Connor's daughter was suffering from influenza at the time. Despite the defense's best efforts, the beliefs and actions of Whitney herself received little attention during the trial. In the prosecution's view (which was favorably received by the judge), such matters were irrelevant because the California Criminal Syndicalism statute forbade not only syndicalism itself (defined as "advocating . . . the commission of crime, sabotage . . ., or unlawful acts of force and violence or unlawful methods of terrorism as a means of accomplishing a change in industrial ownership"), but also mere *membership* in any organization "organized or assembled to advocate, teach or aid and abet criminal syndicalism." Because of this expansive definition of the offense, the prosecution was able to enter into evidence sensational and damaging (and occasionally perjured) testimony regarding the credo and positions of the Communist Labor Party, and by extension of the Communist International and the IWW. As a consequence, Whitney's trial devolved into another part of the larger national campaign during the Red Scare to eviscerate these organizations, notwithstanding the reality that Anita Whitney herself had never engaged in, nor even directly advocated the use of violence.

Two days into the trial, O'Connor contracted influenza. Once again, however, Judge Quinn refused a continuance, requiring O'Connor to proceed despite his fever. A few days later O'Connor fell into a delirium, and died soon after. Once again, a continuance was denied, and Whitney had to proceed with new, unprepared counsel (one Nathan C. Coghlan). After several more weeks of testimony, Whitney was convicted on one count of criminal syndicalism based on her membership in the Communist Labor Party, and sentenced to serve one to fourteen years in the San Quentin penitentiary.

Reaction to Whitney's conviction was mixed. There was predictable criticism from the Left—*The Nation,* for example, published a scathing description of her arrest and trial—but prosecutions under state syndicalism acts continued across the country with wide public support. Whitney seemed headed for prison when her request for bail was denied, and did in fact serve several days in the county jail before the judge relented and granted bail pending appeal because of concerns about the effects of imprisonment upon her health (Whitney was already fifty-two years old at the time of her conviction). Whitney did not have the funds to cover her bail because most of her fortune was tied up in providing bail for convicted Wobblies; as a result, friends raised the necessary funds on her behalf and Whitney remained a free woman.

* * *

On hearing the news of the Supreme Court's decision Whitney announced she would not request a pardon from the Governor because she "had done nothing to be pardoned for," and that she was ready to serve her sentence. It was not, however, to be. Immediately after Whitney's conviction was finally affirmed, her lawyers requested a pardon on her behalf from the new Governor of California, C. C. Young, and a massive new state-wide writing campaign on her behalf was initiated, as a result of which thousands of letters and telegrams were sent to the Governor's office. Whitney's supporters at this stage included prominent businessmen, clergymen, the legislator who originally drafted the California Syndicalism statute, and the Mayor of Oakland. On June 20, Governor Young issued a lengthy statement granting Whitney a full pardon. The Governor explained that the Syndicalism Act had never been intended to apply to people like Whitney, but was instead targeted at the violent Wobblies, that her conviction was a product of post-war hysteria and of a deeply flawed trial, and that to send Whitney to prison given the circumstances was "an action absolutely unthinkable." So Anita Whitney went free to fight more battles.

* * *

Anita Whitney's collision with the California Syndicalism Act by no means ended her brushes with the law or her political activism. She experienced several legal difficulties during the decade following her pardon, including a conviction in the 1930s for allegedly falsifying attesting signatures to an election petition on behalf of the Communist Party, for which she avoided jail time only because her nephew chose to pay her $600 fine. In 1934 Whitney ran for State Treasurer on the Communist Party ticket and earned 100,000 votes—a sufficient number to secure the party's position on the ballot. She repeated that performance running for State Comptroller in 1938, and then for the United States Senate in 1940. Whitney also served as state chair of the Communist Party from 1936 to 1944, and during the later years of this period served as a member of the party's national committee. In addition to her electoral activities, throughout the period from the late 1920s through the 1940s Whitney also supported various organizations (including the famous Brotherhood of Sleeping Car Porters) active in anti-segregation/civil rights causes and worked on behalf of farm workers in central California, many of whom were racial minorities—all at a time when civil rights issues were almost entirely ignored by the mainstream of American politics. Whitney's life remained to its end an exemplar of the sort of active, participatory citizen of a democracy which Justice Brandeis extolled in the Supreme Court case bearing her name.

NEAR v. MINNESOTA

Oral Argument

January 30, 1930

In *Near v. Minnesota* (1931) the Supreme Court invalidated as a prior restraint an injunction, authorized by a special state nuisance law, forbidding the continued publication of a viciously anti-semitic newspaper that repeatedly had accused Minneapolis city officials of being controlled by a Jewish Mafia. The following passage, quoted in Justice Butler's dissenting opinion, conveys the flavor of the publication:

> "Practically every vendor of vile hooch, every owner of a moonshine still, every snake-faced gangster and embryonic yegg in the Twin Cities is a JEW.

"Having these examples before me, I feel that I am justified in my refusal to take orders from a Jew who boasts that he is a 'bosom friend' of Mr. Olson.

"I find in the mail at least twice per week, letters from gentlemen of Jewish faith who advise me against 'launching an attack on the Jewish people.' These gentlemen have the cart before the horse. I am launching, nor is Mr. Guilford, no attack against any race, BUT:

"When I find men of a certain race banding themselves together for the purpose of preying upon Gentile or Jew; gunmen, KILLERS, roaming our streets shooting down men against whom they have no personal grudge (or happen to have); defying OUR laws; corrupting OUR officials; assaulting business men; beating up unarmed citizens; spreading a reign of terror through every walk of life, then I say to you in all sincerity, that I refuse to back up a single step from that 'issue'—if they choose to make it so:

"If the people of Jewish faith in Minneapolis wish to avoid criticism of these vermin whom I rightfully call 'Jews' they can easily do so BY THEMSELVES CLEANING HOUSE.

"I'm not out to cleanse Israel of the filth that clings to Israel's skirts. I'm out to 'hew to the line, let the chips fly where they may.'

"I simply state a fact when I say that ninety per cent. of the crimes committed against society in this city are committed by Jew gangsters.

"It was a Jew who employed JEWS to shoot down Mr. Guilford. It was a Jew who employed a Jew to intimidate Mr. Shapiro and a Jew who employed JEWS to assault that gentleman when he refused to yield to their threats. It was a JEW who wheedled or employed Jews to manipulate the election records and returns in the Third ward in flagrant violation of law. It was a Jew who left two hundred dollars with another Jew to pay to our chief of police just before the last municipal election, and:

"It is Jew, Jew, Jew, as long as one cares to comb over the records.

"I am launching no attack against the Jewish people AS A RACE. I am merely calling attention to a FACT. And if the people of that race and faith wish to rid themselves of the odium and stigma THE RODENTS OF THEIR OWN RACE HAVE BROUGHT UPON THEM, they need only to step to the front and help the decent citizens of Minneapolis rid the city of these criminal Jews.

The lawyer representing the state, James E. Markham, hoped to appeal to Justice Brandeis's experience as a frequent victim of anti-semitic prejudice. At oral argument, the following exchange took place, as recounted by Fred Friendly in his book about the case, *Minnesota Rag*.

When Justice Brandeis began to speak, his quiet authority created an expectancy which commanded the attention of everyone in the courtroom. Now the first and—at that time—only Jew on the Court was about to deliver his homily. The Justice directed his hard questions not to Near's attorney, who was defending a newspaper which had attacked "the entire Jewish race," but to the lawyer for the State of Minnesota.

"Mr. Markham," the gentle catechism from Brandeis began, "in these articles, [in the *Saturday Press*] the editors state that they seek to expose combinations between criminals and public officials in conducting and profiting from gambling halls. They name the chief of police and other officials." Brandeis glanced alternately at his notes and Markham. "They [Near and Guilford] state that they have been threatened with being, to use their own words, "bumped off." They state that shortly after commencing publication, Guilford was set upon by thugs and shot in the abdomen.

"We do not know whether these allegations are true or false," Brandeis went on, "but we do know that just such criminal combinations exist to the shame of some of our cities. What these men did seems like an effort to expose such a combination. Now, is that not a privileged communication if there ever was one? How else can a community secure protection from that sort of thing if people are not allowed to engage in free discussion of such matters?"

Brandeis' voice did not seem to increase by a decibel but his level of intensity rose with his lesson. "Of course, there was defamation; you cannot disclose evil without naming the doers of evil. It is difficult to see how one can have a free press and the protection it affords in the democratic community without the privilege this act seems to limit. You are dealing here not with a sort of a scandal too often appearing in the press, and which ought not to appear to the interest of anyone, but with a matter of prime interest to every American citizen. What sort of matter could be more privileged?"

"Assuming it to be true," Markham countered. He hoped that Brandeis and his fellow Justices would not accept everything in the *Saturday Press* as gospel.

"No!" Brandeis snapped back, meaning that even if it wasn't true, a malicious and scandalous statement could not be restrained before publication. "A newspaper cannot always wait until it gets the judgment of a court. These men set out on a campaign to rid the city of certain evils."

"So they say," Markham interposed again.

"Yes, of course, so they say," Brandeis echoed, sounding more like an editor than the Boston lawyer who thirty-seven years earlier had lectured the press on privacy. Near and Guilford, he continued, "went forward with a definite program, and certainly they acted with great courage. They invited suit for criminal libel if what they said was not true. Now, if that campaign was not privileged, if that is not one of the things for which the press chiefly exists, then for what does it exist?"

In the dramatic pause that followed, Markham could find no words. Brandeis was being patient, for he understood Minnesota's position even though he found it unacceptable. "As for such defamatory matter being issued regularly or customarily, how can such a campaign be conducted except by persistence and continued iteration?"

HARRY KALVEN, JR., A WORTHY TRADITION
(1988).

Justice Holmes's dissent in *Gitlow*, like his *Abrams* peroration, is extraordinary prose to find in a judicial opinion, and I suspect it has contributed beyond measure to the charisma of the First Amendment. But it also carries the disturbing suggestion that the defendants' speech is to be protected precisely because it is harmless and unimportant. It smacks, as will the later protections of Jehovah's Witnesses, of a luxury civil liberty.

The full counter-argument, which the dissenters failed to make in *Gitlow*, is entered by Justice Brandeis in *Whitney v. California* two years later. Indeed, *Whitney* is close enough to *Gitlow* in its statute and on its facts that Brandeis's opinion can properly be read as though he were responding directly to the Sanford opinion in *Gitlow*. Although his opinion has no immediate impact on the majority view, it marks a considerable further evolution of the dissenters' principle, which has now passed through three distinct stages: the original statement in *Schenck;* the philosophic peroration by Justice Holmes in *Abrams;* and the extensive and eloquent gloss now added by Justice Brandeis in *Whitney*.

The statute under which Miss Whitney was convicted made it a felony to organize, assist in organizing, or knowingly become a member of "any organization, society, group or assemblage of persons organized or assembled to advocate, teach or aid and abet criminal syndicalism." It defined "criminal syndicalism" as "the commission of crime, sabotage ... or unlawful acts of force and violence or unlawful methods of terrorism as a means of accomplishing a change in industrial ownership or control or effecting any political change."

Like *Gitlow*, *Whitney* arose out of the splintering of the American Socialist Party. Miss Whitney, who had joined the more "radical" Communist Labor Party, attended a meeting at which a California branch of the party was organized. Considerable ambiguity attaches to her role at the meeting. She sponsored a resolution favoring use of the ballot which was defeated, and she denied at trial that it was her purpose that the "new" party use terrorism. The Court, however, declined to look into this issue, arguing that it was foreclosed by the jury verdict affirmed by the Court of Appeals below, and that, in any event, she had remained at the meeting after the defeat of her resolution without protesting. Thus, *Whitney* put into issue the constitutionality of using criminal sanctions to penalize advocacy of terrorism despite the fact that it was far from clear that Miss Whitney had so advocated.

Gitlow had been indicted for what he had done personally, that is, for participating directly in the publication of the "Manifesto." Miss Whitney was indicted for participating in organizing a group to teach criminal syndicalism. At this juncture we reach a major transition in the nature of the speech problem, from one of regulating the content of speech to one of regulating what are best called "political conspiracies." This is the form in which the legion of anti-Communist cases will come to the Court in the next decades, and we shall devote considerable attention to it in later chapters. For the moment, it need not distract us, though we should note that Justice Brandeis remarks on the "novelty" of the statute at the start of his opinion.

The majority, relying on *Gitlow*, requires only a page and a half to dispose of the free speech issue. The opinion by Justice Sanford indicates once again how little the clear and present danger test means to the majority at this time. Sanford does not refer to it; he relies on a strong presumption of the constitutionality of the statute; and he refers to utterances which tend "to incite to crime" and to "endanger the foundations of organized government." Although there is no proof in the record that the advocacy with which Miss Whitney was charged created a high degree of danger, the majority dismisses such a consideration as immaterial. In its view, advocating the syndicalist doctrine of selective violence is enough.

Justice Brandeis, in an opinion joined by Justice Holmes, launches an eloquent protest against the bland analysis of the majority opinion. In durable rhetoric he explores the policy basis of our commitment to free speech and analyzes with care when, in light of that policy, a danger can be said to be imminent enough and serious enough to warrant restriction.

Although *Whitney* marks the sixth consecutive decision in which the majority has either ignored the clear and present danger test or found it inapplicable, Justice Brandeis asserts at the outset:

> That the necessity which is essential to a valid restriction does not exist unless speech would produce, or is intended to produce, a clear and imminent danger of some substantive evil which the State constitutionally may seek to prevent has been settled. See *Schenck v. United States.*

The stamina and tactics of these classic dissents are remarkable. In professional lawyering terms, the performance of Justices Holmes and Brandeis is outrageous. They keep insisting that they are adhering to the Court's true rule adopted in *Schenck.* They have been told by the majority that clear and present danger is not now and never was the general test and that it is applicable only in cases where speech is punished under statutes aimed at acts. They have conveniently forgotten *Debs*, and, in the face of the majority's skepticism, they have never paused to explain how *Schenck* itself comported with the test. Yet we are all deeply in their debt for their outrageous behavior. They have kept alive a counter-tension in the tradition, and their towering prestige has invested the slogan with almost mesmerizing force. Like twin Moses come down from Mount Sinai bearing the true Commandment, they see little need to argue that the formula is rightly derived from the First Amendment, merely that it is.

Although possibly a mite less eloquent than Justice Holmes, Justice Brandeis constructs his argument in a much more lawyer-like fashion. In response to the majority's deference to the legislative judgment as to the danger of criminal syndicalist advocacy, he argues that in constitutional law the legislature cannot pull itself up by its own bootstraps:

> The legislature must obviously decide, in the first instance, whether a danger exists which calls for a particular protective measure. But where a statute is valid only in case certain conditions exist, the enactment of the statute cannot alone establish the facts which are essential to its validity.

This answer is powerful. If the legislature could make conclusive findings of constitutional facts, the function of judicial review of legislation on First Amendment grounds would virtually disappear. But Justice Sanford in *Gitlow* had not eschewed all judicial review of the application of pure speech statutes; rather, he had said that in cases involving such statutes the appropriate standard of review was substantive due process, and he had confined the clear and present danger test to *Schenck*-like cases, where the statute proscribes acts, not words. Thus, Brandeis does not fully meet Sanford's argument. He does not explain why we must read *Schenck* as having launched a principle so much broader than the facts required. Yet when he has finished his full argument, it will be apparent that he has not begged the question but has dealt seriously with all aspects of it.

Brandeis begins his exegesis of the clear and present danger standard by posing a series of question:

> This Court has not yet fixed the standard by which to determine when a danger shall be deemed clear; how remote the danger may be and yet be deemed present; and what degree of evil shall be deemed sufficiently substantial to justify resort to abridgement of free speech and assembly as the means of protection.

The agenda is to prove a splendid one. But how extraordinary to say that the Court has "not yet" attended to resolving ambiguities in the test, when the Court has so steadfastly refused to grant the test the status Holmes and Brandeis claim for it. It is the two dissenters who have not yet determined these features of their formula.

Before answering his three questions about the test, Justice Brandeis pauses to examine the underlying policy which dictates such stringent control over the regulation of speech. The passage is quite wonderful and provides, among other things, a rejoinder to Sanford's query as to why the state must leave alone speech which advocates in general terms tactics of force, terrorism, and sabotage:

> Those who won our independence believed that the final end of the State was to make men free to develop their faculties; and that in its government the deliberative forces should prevail over the arbitrary. They valued liberty both as an end and as a means. They believed liberty to be the secret of happiness and courage to be the secret of liberty. They believed that freedom to think as you will and to speak as you think are means indispensable to the discovery and spread of political truth; that without free speech and assembly discussion would be futile; that with them, discussion affords ordinarily adequate protection against the dissemination of noxious doctrine; that the greatest menace to freedom is an inert people; that public discussion is a political duty; and that this should be a fundamental principle of the American government.

To intrude for a moment: Here at last is an effort to work the test back to the Constitution itself. Justice Brandeis supplies the statement that was so noticeably lacking in *Schenck.* The basic American premise, embodied in the basic document of government, is that "freedom to think what you will and to speak what you think are means indispensible to the discovery and spread of political truth." He continues:

> They recognized the risks to which all human institutions are subject. But they knew that order cannot be secured merely through fear of punishment for its infraction; that it is hazardous to discourage thought, hope and imagination; that fear breeds repression; that repression breeds hate; that hate menaces stable government; that the path of safety lies in the opportunity to discuss freely supposed grievances and proposed remedies; and that the fitting remedy for evil counsels is good ones. Believing in the power of reason as applied through public discussion, they eschewed silence coerced by law—the argument of force in its worst form. Recognizing the occasional tyrannies of governing majorities, they amended the Constitution so that free speech and assembly should be guaranteed.

This passage serves to correct the ill-fitting private crime analogy Justice Holmes automatically reached for. What is at stake is not the false shouting of "fire" in a theater or the counselling of murder; rather, it is a matter of providing maximum opportunity for "the power of reason as applied through public discussion." And what is to be guarded against, in Brandeis's memorable phrase, is the ugliness of "silence coerced by law." With these grand premises made explicit, Justice Brandeis turns to the question of how *clear* and *present* the danger must be:

> Fear of serious injury cannot alone justify suppression of free speech and assembly. Men feared witches and burnt women. It is the function of speech to free men from the bondage of irrational fears. To justify suppression of free speech there must be reasonable ground to fear that serious evil will result if free speech is practiced. There must be reasonable ground to believe that the danger appre-

> hended is imminent. There must be reasonable ground to believe that the evil to be prevented is a serious one.

Again we intrude. There is plausibility to the clear and present danger test as Justice Brandeis derives it from the basic architecture of American values. The point is simple: Freedom of speech is so essential to the American way of life and thought, and confidence in its power is so deep, that only an extraordinary threat to the safety of the community justifies departing from those expectations by employing the law to coerce silence.

Being the careful lawyer, Justice Brandeis now turns to the practical task of distinguishing among admittedly risky forms of speech. At this point his opinion bears an arresting resemblance to Judge Hand's opinion in *Masses*, which he cites. Both seek to locate words which are "triggers of action." One talks in terms of "incitement"; the other in terms of "clear and present danger." As I see it, despite the differences in idiom, both are making the same point:

> Every denunciation of existing law tends in some measure to increase the probability that there will be violation of it. Condonation of a breach enhances the probability. Expressions of approval add to the probability. Propagation of the criminal state of mind by teaching syndicalism increases it.

Note that in this last sentence Justice Brandeis fully acknowledges the common sense of Justice Sanford's view in *Gitlow*. He is, however, firmly convinced that we cannot stop there:

> Advocacy of law-breaking heightens it still further. But even advocacy of violation, however reprehensible morally, is not a justification for denying free speech where the advocacy falls short of incitement and there is nothing to indicate that the advocacy would be immediately acted on. The wide difference between advocacy and incitement, between preparation and attempt, between assembling and conspiracy, must be borne in mind. In order to support a finding of clear and present danger it must be shown either that immediate serious violence was to be expected or was advocated, or that the past conduct furnished reason to believe that such advocacy was then contemplated.

As in Hand's opinion, the analytic device is to array categories of dangerous speech, and the effort is to locate the last term in the series, whatever the precise label given to it. It would seem to matter little whether we talk of "clear and present danger" or of "incitement." What is sought is concrete advocacy of direct and immediate criminal action; and what is to be guarded against is censorship of "denunciation," "condonation," "expressions of approval," "teaching of radical doctrine." In Brandeis's terms, which recall *Masses* and anticipate *Brandenburg*, what is to be guarded against is censorship "where advocacy falls short of incitement."

Justice Brandeis goes on to underscore with zest another strand of the argument for free speech: the efficacy of counter-speech as the remedy for evil speech. In the case of speech harms there is a distinctive self-help remedy that makes the intervention of law less urgent than in the case of physical harms—more speech:

> Those who won our independence by revolution were not cowards. They did not fear political change. They did not exalt order at the cost of liberty. To courageous, self-reliant men, with confidence in the power of free and fearless reasoning applied through the processes of popular government, no danger flowing from speech can be deemed clear and present, unless the incidence of the evil apprehended is so imminent that it may befall before there is opportunity for full discussion. If there be time to expose through discussion the falsehood and fallacies, to avert the evil by the processes of education, the remedy to be applied is more speech, not enforced silence. Only an emergency can justify repression. Such must be the rule if authority is to be reconciled with freedom. Such, in my opinion, is the command of the Constitution. It is therefore always open to Americans to challenge a law abridging free speech and assembly by showing that there was no emergency justifying it.

One might hope that the splendid admonition of this last sentence, although uttered in the spirit of dissent, has served to expunge from the memory of the society, if not from the records of the Court, the nastiness of Justice McKenna's dictum about the defendant's challenge in *Gilbert:* "It would be a travesty on the constitutional protection he invokes to assign him its protection."

Justice Brandeis was seventy-one years old when he wrote this remarkable opinion; Justice Holmes was seventy-nine years old when he wrote his eloquent peroration in *Abrams;* Alexander Meiklejohn was seventy-eight years old when he wrote his stirring essay on free speech. It is the mark of the topic that it recruits such distilled wisdom from the concerned elders of the society, and it is the special blessing of the American heritage that it has had such elders to rise and speak.

ROBERT M. COVER, THE LEFT, THE RIGHT, AND THE FIRST AMENDMENT, 1918–1928

40 Md. L. Rev. 349 (1981).

The development of Brandeis's thought was very different from that of Holmes. By 1923 Brandeis had come to regret that he had not written separately in the 1919 cases. His 1923 remarks to Felix Frankfurter reveal a great deal about the early opinions:

> I have never been quite happy about my concurrence in *Debs* and *Schenck* cases. I had not then thought the issues of freedom of speech out—thought at the subject, not through it. Not until I came to write the *Pierce* and *Schaefer* cases did I understand it. I would have placed the *Debs* case on the war power—instead of taking

Holmes's line about "clear and present danger." Put it frankly on war power—like Hamilton case [*Hamilton v. Kentucky Distilleries & Warehouse Co.,* 251 U.S. 146 (1919)]—and then the scope of the espionage legislation would be confined to war. [In the *Hamilton* opinion, written by Mr. Justice Brandeis, the Court upheld the War-time Prohibition Act, ch. 212, 40 Stat. 1045, 1046 (1918), on the ground that it was a reasonable exercise of Congress's power to make all laws "necessary and proper" for carrying into execution its express war powers.] But in peace the protection against restrictions of freedom of speech would be unabated. You might as well recognize that during a war—

FF: All bets are off.

LDB: Yes, all bets are off. But we would have a clear line to go on. I didn"t know enough in the early cases to put it on that ground. Of course you must also remember that when Holmes writes, he doesn't give a fellow a chance—he shoots so quickly.

But in *Schaefer* and *Pierce* cases I made up my mind I would put it all out, let the future know what weren't allowed to say in the days of the war and following.[87]

* * *

Brandeis's *Whitney* concurrence[119] started out as a dissent in the case of *Ruthenberg v. Michigan.*[120] Virtually every bit of the free speech theory and rhetoric in the opinion was crafted to its present form and fitted to the facts of *Ruthenberg,* but it was rendered moot when the defendant in that case died.[121] Brandeis then grafted the long free speech essay to what had started as a very short, page-and-a-half concurrence in *Whitney.* It is of some relevance to know this because it removes at least one red herring from an understanding of how far Brandeis intended to go. Within the Communist labor party, Anita Whitney herself had stood with the so-called "political faction" which argued for continuation of participation by the party in some forms of conventional politics. She was a most sympathetic, goodhearted former social worker of impeccable family. Ruthenberg, however, had been the first national secretary of the Communist Party. After his arrest in 1922, he had remained a major figure on the national level in the Communist Party and had attended the "Bridgman Convention" as a member of the central executive committee. Although not an advocate of immediate revolution, Ruthenberg had personally authored statements calling for "extra-parliamentary means of achieving power." In his own words, "this includes the use

87. Brandeis-Frankfurter Conversations, Brandeis Papers (Harvard Law School Library).

119. Whitney v. California, 274 U.S. 357, 372 (1927) (concurring opinion).

120. 273 U.S. 782 (1927). *See Whitney v. California* files, Brandeis Papers, Files 44–5 through 44–9 (Harvard Law School Library) (containing drafts of a *Ruthenberg v. Michigan* opinion which develop verbatim the rhetoric which finally emerged in the *Whitney* opinion).

121. 273 U.S. 782 (1927).

of armed force."[124] Brandeis's concurrence in *Whitney* was authored as a dissent for the *Ruthenberg* case, and it must be understood as applicable to the facts of that case: to the conviction of a hard-core, national leader of the Party, apprehended while attempting to cover the retreat of a secret convention at which the first official envoy of the Comintern was attempting to dictate party unity on the basis of a plan which included a secret, extra-legal party apparatus. Early drafts of Brandeis's Ruthenberg opinion included a paragraph characterizing the Communist Party as a conspiracy to train cadres for infiltration. Brandeis concluded, however, that this character was insufficient to justify repression without evidence of the immediate danger of illegal acts resulting therefrom.

The most striking new element in Brandeis's thought that is revealed by the *Whitney* concurrence is the shift from a focus upon legislative process to a more inclusive public politics. The essay on free speech begins by characterizing the essential choice of political modes as being one between the "deliberative" and the "arbitrary." The commitment to the "deliberative" mode is then historically validated as the act of the Founders to which an ongoing commitment is eternally necessary. Brandeis's research for the *Whitney/Ruthenberg* opinion suggests some of the principal problems that this commitment entailed. What is the role of the call to disorderly, non-deliberative change in politics? Brandeis had James Landis, his clerk in 1925–1926, prepare a memorandum on calls to resistance of the Fugitive Slave Law and resistance to Prohibition. It is likely that from such research there emerged the language in the opinion: "Every denunciation of existing law tends in some measure to increase the probability that there will be violation of it."

Brandeis did not deny the danger, but required the commitment to liberty in the face of it as an act of courage demanded by the structure of our politics. This understanding of liberty of expression deepens the sense that "clear and present danger" is to be understood as applicable only to those emergencies in which the deliberative mode has insufficient time to operate. Brandeis had come to believe that the great dichotomy was between the deliberative and the arbitrary, between reason and force in politics. Law mediates that dichotomy and becomes justifiably arbitrary and coercive *only* by remaining the *product* of as purely deliberative a process as possible. Scrawled in Brandeis's hand across the back of Landis's memorandum on calls to resist the Fugitive Slave Law and Prohibition is the first approximation, and then the final language, of the sentence in *Whitney* which identifies the force of law itself with the arbitrary in the public space of politics.

First there is written: "Believers in the force of reason they rejected silencing by law as the argument of force." Then underneath that sentence is scrawled: "As I interpret their acts—Believing in the power of reason as applied through public discussion, they eschewed silence coerced by law—the argument of force in the worst form."[129]

124. *See* People v. Ruthenberg, 229 Mich. 315, 339, 201 N.W. 358, 365 (1924).

129. Brandeis Papers, File 44–6 (Harvard Law School Library). The last quoted sentence appears almost verbatim in 274 U.S. at 375.

THORNHILL v. STATE OF ALABAMA

Supreme Court of the United States, 1940.
310 U.S. 88, 60 S.Ct. 736, 84 L.Ed. 1093.

* * *

MR. JUSTICE MURPHY delivered the opinion of the Court.

Petitioner, Byron Thornhill, was convicted in the Circuit Court of Tuscaloosa County, Alabama, of the violation of Section 3448 of the State Code of 1923. The Code Section reads as follows: "Loitering or picketing forbidden.—Any person or persons, who, without a just cause or legal excuse therefor, go near to or loiter about the premises or place of business of any other person, firm, corporation, or association of people, engaged in a lawful business, for the purpose, or with intent of influencing, or inducing other persons not to trade with, buy from, sell to, have business dealings with, or be employed by such persons, firm, corporation, or association, or who picket the works or place of business of such other persons, firms, corporations, or associations of persons, for the purpose of hindering, delaying, or interfering with or injuring any lawful business or enterprise of another, shall be guilty of a misdemeanor; but nothing herein shall prevent any person from soliciting trade or business for a competitive business."

* * *

Those who won our independence had confidence in the power of free and fearless reasoning and communication of ideas to discover and spread political and economic truth. Noxious doctrines in those fields may be refuted and their evil averted by the courageous exercise of the right of free discussion. Abridgment of freedom of speech and of the press, however, impairs those opportunities for public education that are essential to effective exercise of the power of correcting error through the processes of popular government.

* * *

Section 3448 has been applied by the State courts so as to prohibit a single individual from walking slowly and peacefully back and forth on the public sidewalk in front of the premises of an employer, without speaking to anyone, carrying a sign or placard on a staff above his head stating only the fact that the employer did not employ union men affiliated with the American Federation of Labor; the purpose of the described activity was concededly to advise customers and prospective customers of the relationship existing between the employer and its employees and thereby to induce such customers not to patronize the employer. *O'Rourke v. City of Birmingham*, 27 Ala.App. 133, 168 So. 206. The statute as thus authoritatively construed and applied leaves room for no exceptions based upon either the number of persons engaged in the proscribed activity, the peaceful character of their demeanor, the nature of their dispute with an employer, or the restrained character and the accurateness of the terminology used in notifying the public of the facts of the dispute.

* * *

In the circumstances of our times the dissemination of information concerning the facts of a labor dispute must be regarded as within that area of free discussion that is guaranteed by the Constitution. It is recognized now that satisfactory hours and wages and working conditions in industry and a bargaining position which makes these possible have an importance which is not less than the interests of those in the business or industry directly concerned. The health of the present generation and of those as yet unborn may depend on these matters, and the practices in a single factory may have economic repercussions upon a whole region and affect widespread systems of marketing. The merest glance at State and Federal legislation on the subject demonstrates the force of the argument that labor relations are not matters of mere local or private concern. Free discussion concerning the conditions in industry and the causes of labor disputes appears to us indispensable to the effective and intelligent use of the processes of popular government to shape the destiny of modern industrial society. The issues raised by regulations, such as are challenged here, infringing upon the right of employees effectively to inform the public of the facts of a labor dispute are part of this larger problem. We concur in the observation of Mr. Justice Brandeis, speaking for the Court in *Senn*'s case (301 U.S. at page 478): "Members of a union might, without special statutory authorization by a state, make known the facts of a labor dispute, for freedom of speech is guaranteed by the Federal Constitution."

It is true that the rights of employers and employees to conduct their economic affairs and to compete with others for a share in the products of industry are subject to modification or qualification in the interests of the society in which they exist. This is but an instance of the power of the State to set the limits of permissible contest open to industrial combatants. See Mr. Justice Brandeis in *Duplex Printing Press Co. v. Deering*, 254 U.S. 443, 488. It does not follow that the State in dealing with the evils arising from industrial disputes may impair the effective exercise of the right to discuss freely industrial relations which are matters of public concern. A contrary conclusion could be used to support abridgment of freedom of speech and of the press concerning almost every matter of importance to society.

The range of activities proscribed by Section 3448, whether characterized as picketing or loitering or otherwise, embraces nearly every practicable, effective means whereby those interested—including the employees directly affected—may enlighten the public on the nature and causes of a labor dispute. The safeguarding of these means is essential to the securing of an informed and educated public opinion with respect to a matter which is of public concern. It may be that effective exercise of the means of advancing public knowledge may persuade some of those reached to refrain from entering into advantageous relations with the business establishment which is the scene of the dispute. Every expression of opinion on matters that are important has the potentiality of inducing action in the interests of one rather than another group in society. But the group in power at any moment may not impose penal sanctions on peaceful and truthful discussion of matters of public interest merely on a showing that others may thereby be persuaded to take action inconsistent with its interests. Abridgment of the liberty of such discussion can be justified only where the clear danger of substantive evils arises under circumstances affording no opportunity to test the merits of ideas by competition for acceptance in the market of public opinion. We hold that the danger of injury to an industrial concern is neither so serious nor so imminent as to justify the sweeping proscription of freedom of discussion embodied in Section 3448.

VIRGINIA STATE BOARD OF PHARMACY v. VIRGINIA CITIZENS CONSUMER COUNCIL, INC.

Supreme Court of the United States, 1976.
425 U.S. 748, 96 S.Ct. 1817, 48 L.Ed.2d 346.

MR. JUSTICE BLACKMUN delivered the opinion of the Court.

The plaintiff-appellees in this case attack, as violative of the First and Fourteenth Amendments, that portion of § 54–524.35 of Va. Code Ann. (1974), which provides that a pharmacist licensed in Virginia is guilty of unprofessional conduct if he "(3) publishes, advertises or promotes, directly or indirectly, in any manner whatsoever, any amount, price, fee, premium, discount, rebate or credit terms . . . for any drugs which may be dispensed only by prescription."

* * *

Price advertising, it is argued, will place in jeopardy the pharmacist's expertise and, with it, the customer's health. It is claimed that the aggressive price competition that will result from unlimited advertising will make it impossible for the pharmacist to supply professional services in the compounding, handling, and dispensing of prescription drugs. Such services are time consuming and expensive; if competitors who economize by eliminating them are permitted to advertise their resulting lower prices, the more painstaking and conscientious pharmacist will be forced either to follow suit or to go out of business. It is also claimed that prices might not necessarily fall as a result of advertising. If one pharmacist advertises, others must, and the resulting expense will inflate the cost of drugs. It is further claimed that advertising will lead people to shop for their prescription drugs among the various pharmacists who offer the lowest prices, and the loss of stable pharmacist-customer relationships will make individual attention and certainly the practice of monitoring impossible. Finally, it is argued that damage will be done to the professional image of the pharmacist. This image, that of a skilled and specialized craftsman, attracts talent to the profession and reinforces the better habits of those who are in it. Price advertising, it is said, will reduce the pharmacist's status to that of a mere retailer.

* * *

The challenge now made, however, is based on the First Amendment. This casts the Board's justifications in a different light, for on close inspection it is seen that the State's protectiveness of its citizens rests in large measure on the advantages of their being kept in ignorance. The advertising ban does not directly affect professional standards one way or the other. It affects them only through the reactions it is assumed people will have to the free flow of drug price information. There is no claim that the advertising ban in any way prevents the cutting of corners by the pharmacist who is so inclined. That pharmacist is likely to cut corners in any event. The only effect the advertising ban has on him is to insulate him from price competition and to open the way for him to make a substantial, and perhaps even excessive, profit in addition to providing an inferior service. The more painstaking pharmacist is also protected but, again, it is a protection based in large part on public ignorance.

It appears to be feared that if the pharmacist who wishes to provide low cost, and assertedly low quality, services is permitted to advertise, he will be taken up on his offer by too many unwitting customers. They will choose the low-cost, low-quality service and drive the "professional" pharmacist out of business. They will respond only to costly and excessive advertising, and end up paying the price. They will go from one pharmacist to another, following the discount, and destroy the pharmacist-customer relationship. They will lose respect for the profession because it advertises. All this is not in their best interests, and all this can be avoided if they are not permitted to know who is charging what.

There is, of course, an alternative to this highly paternalistic approach. That alternative is to assume that this information is not in itself harmful, that people will perceive their own best interests if only they are well enough informed, and that the best means to that end is to open the channels of communication rather than to close them. If they are truly open, nothing prevents the "professional" pharmacist from marketing his own assertedly superior product, and contrasting it with that of the low-cost, high-volume prescription drug retailer. But the choice among these alternative approaches is not ours to make or the Virginia General Assembly's. It is precisely this kind of choice, between the dangers of suppressing information, and the dangers of its misuse if it is freely available, that the First Amendment makes for us. Virginia is free to require whatever professional standards it wishes of its pharmacists; it may subsidize them or protect them from competition in other ways. But it may not do so by keeping the public in ignorance of the entirely lawful terms that competing pharmacists are offering. In this sense, the justifications Virginia has offered for suppressing the flow of prescription drug price information, far from persuading us that the flow is not protected by the First Amendment, have reinforced our view that it is. We so hold.

[A dissenting opinion by JUSTICE REHNQUIST is omitted.]

CENTRAL HUDSON GAS & ELECTRIC CORP. v. PUBLIC SERVICE COMMISSION OF NEW YORK.

Supreme Court of the United States, 1980.
447 U.S. 557, 100 S.Ct. 2343, 65 L.Ed.2d 341.

* * *

MR. JUSTICE REHNQUIST, dissenting.

The Court today invalidates an order issued by the New York Public Service Commission designed to promote a policy that has been declared to be of critical national concern. The order was issued by the Commission in 1973 in response to the Mideastern oil embargo crisis. It prohibits electric corporations "from *promoting* the use of electricity through the use of advertising, subsidy payments . . . , or employee incentives." Although the immediate crisis created by the oil embargo has subsided, the ban on promotional advertising remains in effect.

* * *

The plethora of opinions filed in this case highlights the doctrinal difficulties that emerge from this Court's decisions granting First Amendment protection to commercial speech. My Brother Stevens, quoting Mr. Justice Brandeis in *Whitney v. California*, 274 U.S. 357, 376–377 (1927), includes Mr. Justice Brandeis' statement that "[t]hose who won our independence by revolution were not cowards. They did not fear political change. They did not exalt order at the cost of liberty." Mr. Justice Blackmun, in his separate opinion, joins only in the Court's judgment because he believes that the Court's opinion "does not provide adequate protection for truthful, nonmisleading, noncoercive commercial speech." Both Mr. Justice Stevens and Mr. Justice Blackmun would apply the following formulation by Mr. Justice Brandeis of the clear-and-present-danger test to the regulation of speech at issue in this case:

> "If there be time to expose through discussion the falsehood and fallacies, to avert the evil by the processes of education, the remedy to be applied is more speech, not enforced silence. Only an emergency can justify repression." *Whitney v. California, supra*, at 377 (concurring opinion).

Although the Court today does not go so far as to adopt this position, its reasons for invalidating New York's ban on promotional advertising make it quite difficult for a legislature to draft a statute regulating promotional advertising that will satisfy the First Amendment requirements established by the Court in this context.

Two ideas are here at war with one another, and their resolution, although it be on a judicial battlefield, will be a very difficult one. The sort of "advocacy" of which Mr. Justice Brandeis spoke was not the advocacy on the part of a utility to use more of its product. Nor do I think those who won our independence, while declining to "exalt order at the cost of liberty," would have viewed a merchant's unfettered freedom to advertise in hawking his wares as a "liberty" not subject to extensive regulation in light of the government's substantial interest in attaining "order" in the economic sphere.

Questions

1) Notice that the Court asserts in *Thornhill v. Alabama* that Justice Brandeis's understanding of the First Amendment entails substantial constitutional protection for labor picketing on the ground that "free discussion concerning the conditions in industry and the causes of labor disputes" is "indispensable to the effective and intelligent use of the processes of popular government to shape the destiny of modern industrial society." Can this argument be used to justify the protection of commercial advertising as well? Might political opinions about regulation of the drug industry be informed by awareness of disparities in prescription drug prices? Is advertising by attorneys analogous to labor picketing?

2) Justice Blackmun's majority opinion in *Virginia Board of Pharmacy* is based on the proposition that the First Amendment enacts a powerful antipaternalism principle regarding the regulation of ideas and information. About the state's prohibition of price advertising for prescription drugs, the opinion says: "There is, of course, an alternative to this highly paternalistic approach. That alternative is to assume that this information is not itself harmful, that people will perceive their own best interests if only they are well enough informed, and that the best means to that end is to open the channels of communication rather than to close them." Is such a rejection of "paternalistic" justifications for regulation also an important feature of Brandeis's *Whitney* opinion? Recall his statements "the fitting remedy for evil counsels is good ones" and "the remedy to be applied is more speech, not enforced silence." Notice that Justice Blackmun makes a Brandeisian "more speech" argument in *Virginia Board of Pharmacy*: "nothing prevents the 'professional' pharmacist from marketing his own assertedly superior product, and contrasting it with that of the low-cost, high-volume prescription drug retailer." Would Brandeis have joined Justice Blackmun's opinion?

3) Is the prohibition on prescription drug advertising truly paternalistic? Can it be characterized, not as an effort to restrict the choices available to consumers for their own good, but rather as an effort to save the small, service-oriented pharmacist so as to *expand* the choices available to consumers and opportunities available to would-be entrepreneurs? Recall

Justice Brandeis's dissenting opinion in *Liggett Co. v. Lee* (p. 674). Which regulation is more paternalistic: *Virginia Board's* ban on drug advertising or the law at issue in *Central Hudson*, which prohibited in the interest of conservation all advertising by public utilities that promoted the use of electricity?

4) What exactly is the source of the principle that paternalistic reasons for regulating speech are especially problematic under the First Amendment? Which of the principal authors we have studied thus far provides the most support for such an antipaternalism principle?

ROBERT H. BORK, NEUTRAL PRINCIPLES AND SOME FIRST AMENDMENT PROBLEMS

47 Ind. L. J. 1 (1971).

The law has settled upon no tenable, internally consistent theory of the scope of the constitutional guarantee of free speech. Nor have many such theories been urged upon the courts by lawyers or academicians. Professor Harry Kalven, Jr., one whose work is informed by a search for theory, has expressed wonder that we should feel the need for theory in the area of free speech when we tolerate inconsistencies in other areas of the law so calmly.[45] He answers himself:

> If my puzzle as to the First Amendment is not a true puzzle, it can only be for the congenial reason that free speech is so close to the heart of democratic organization that if we do not have an appropriate theory for our law here, we feel we really do not understand the society in which we live.[46]

Kalven is certainly correct in assigning the first amendment a central place in our society, and he is also right in attributing that centrality to the importance of speech to democratic organization. Since I share this common ground with Professor Kalven, I find it interestng that my conclusions differ so widely from his.

I am led by the logic of the requirement that judges be principled to the following suggestions. Constitutional protection should be accorded only to speech that is explicitly political. There is no basis for judicial intervention to protect any other form of expression, be it scientific, literary or that variety of expression we call obscene or pornographic. Moreover, within that category of speech we ordinarily call political, there should be no constitutional obstruction to laws making criminal any speech that advocates forcible overthrow of the government or the violation of any law.

I am, of course, aware that this theory departs drastically from existing Court-made law, from the views of most academic specialists in the field and that it may strike a chill into the hearts of some civil libertarians. But I would insist at the outset that constitutional law,

45. H. Kalven, The Negro and the First Amendment 4–5 (1966).

46. *Id.* at 6.

viewed as the set of rules a judge may properly derive from the document and its history, is not an expression of our political sympathies or of our judgments about what expediency and prudence require. When decision making its principled it has nothing to say about the speech we like or the speech we hate; it has a great deal to say about how far democratic discretion can govern without endangering the basis of democratic government. Nothing in my argument goes to the question of what laws should be enacted. I like the freedoms of the individual as well as most, and I would be appalled by many statutes that I am compelled to think would be constitutional if enacted. But I am also persuaded that my generally libertarian commitments have nothing to do with the behavior proper to the Supreme Court.

In framing a theory of free speech the first obstacle is the insistence of many very intelligent people that the "first amendment is an absolute." Devotees of this position insist, with a literal respect they do not accord other parts of the Constitution, that the Framers commanded complete freedom of expression without governmental regulation of any kind. The first amendment states: "Congress shall make no law ... abridging the freedom of speech...." Those who take that as an absolute must be reading "speech" to mean any form of verbal communication and "freedom" to mean total absence of governmental restraint.

Any such reading is, of course, impossible. Since it purports to be an absolute position we are entitled to test it with extreme hypotheticals. Is Congress forbidden to prohibit incitement to mutiny aboard a naval vessel engaged in action against an enemy, to prohibit shouted harangues from the visitors' gallery during its own deliberations or to provide any rules for decorum in federal courtrooms? Are the states forbidden, by the incorporation of the first amendment in the fourteenth, to punish the shouting of obscenities in the streets?

No one, not the most obsessed absolutist, takes any such position, but if one does not, the absolute position is abandoned, revealed as a play on words. Government cannot function if anyone can say anything anywhere at any time. And so we quickly come to the conclusion that lines must be drawn, differentiations made. Nor does that in any way involve us in a conflict with the wording of the first amendment. Laymen may perhaps be forgiven for thinking that the literal words of the amendment command complete absence of governmental inhibition upon verbal activity, but what can one say of lawyers who believe any such thing? Anyone skilled in reading language should know that the words are not necessarily absolute. "Freedom of speech" may very well be a term referring to a defined or assumed scope of liberty, and it may be this area of liberty that is not to be "abridged."

If we turn to history, we discover that our suspicions about the wording are correct, except that matters are even worse. The framers seem to have had no coherent theory of free speech and appear not to have been overly concerned with the subject. Professor Leonard Levy's, work, *Legacy of Suppression,* demonstrates that the men who adopted the first amendment did not display a strong libertarian stance with respect to speech. Any such position would have been strikingly at odds with the American political tradition. Our forefathers were men accustomed to drawing a line, to us often invisible, between freedom and licentiousness. In colonial times and during and after the Revolution they displayed a determination to punish speech thought dangerous to government, much of it expression that we would think harmless and well within the bounds of legitimate discourse. Jeffersonians, threatened by the Federalist Sedition Act of 1798, undertook the first American elaboration of a libertarian position in an effort to stay out of jail. Professor Walter Berns offers evidence that even then the position was not widely held. When Jefferson came to power it developed that he read the first amendment only to limit Congress and he believed suppression to be a proper function of the state governments. He appears to have instigated state prosecutions against Federalists for seditious libel. But these later developments do not tell us what the men who adopted the first amendment intended, and their discussions tell us very little either. The disagreements that certainly existed were not debated and resolved. The first amendment, like the rest of the Bill of Rights, appears to have been a hastily drafted document upon which little thought was expended. One reason, as Levy shows, is that the Anti–Federalists complained of the absence of a Bill of Rights less because they cared for individual freedoms than as a tactic to defeat the Constitution. The Federalists promised to submit one in order to get the Constitution ratified. The Bill of Rights was then drafted by Federalists, who had opposed it from the beginning; the Anti–Federalists, who were really more interested in preserving the rights of state governments against federal power, had by that time lost interest in the subject.

We are, then, forced to construct our own theory of the constitutional protection of speech. We cannot solve our problems simply by reference to the text or to its history. But we are not without materials for building. The first amendment indicates that there is something special about speech. We would know that much even without a first amendment, for the entire structure of the Constitution creates a representative democracy, a form of government that would be meaningless without freedom to discuss government and its policies. Freedom for political speech could and should be inferred even if there were no first amendment. Further guidance can be gained from the fact that we are looking for a theory fit for enforcement by judges. The principles we seek must, therefore, be neutral in all three meanings of the word: they must be neutrally derived, defined and applied.

The law of free speech we know today grows out of the Supreme Court decisions following World War I—*Schenck v. United States, Abrams v. United States, Gitlow v. New York, Whitney v. California*—not out of the majority positions but rather from the opinions, mostly dissents or concurrences that were really dissents, of Justices Holmes and Brandeis. Professor Kalven remarks upon "the almost uncanny power" of these dissents. And it is uncanny, for they have prevailed despite the considerable handicap of being deficient in logic and analysis as well as in history. The great Smith Act cases of the 1950's, *Dennis v. United States,*[54] as modified by *Yates v. United States,*[55] and, more recently, in 1969, *Brandenburg v. Ohio*[56] (voiding the Ohio criminal syndicalism statute), mark the triumph of Holmes and Brandeis. And other cases, culminating perhaps in a modified version of *Roth v. United States,*[57] have pushed the protections of the first amendment outward from political speech all the way to the fields of literature, entertainment and what can only be called pornography. Because my concern is general theory I shall not attempt a comprehensive survey of the cases nor engage in theological disputation over current doctrinal niceties. I intend to take the position that the law should have been built on Justice Sanford's majority opinions in *Gitlow* and *Whitney.* These days such an argument has at least the charm of complete novelty, but I think it has other merits as well.

Before coming to the specific issues in *Gitlow* and *Whitney,* I wish to begin the general discussion of first amendment theory with consideration of a passage from Justice Brandeis' concurring opinion in the latter case. His *Whitney* concurrence was Brandeis' first attempt to articulate a comprehensive theory of the constitutional protection of speech, and in that attempt he laid down premises which seem to me correct. But those premises seem also to lead to conclusions which Justice Brandeis would have disowned.

As a starting point Brandeis went to fundamentals and attempted to answer the question why speech is protected at all from governmental regulation. If we overlook his highly romanticized version of history and ignore merely rhetorical flourishes, we shall find Brandeis quite provocative.

> Those who won our independence believed that the final end of the state was to make men free to develop their faculties; and that in its government the deliberative forces should prevail over the arbitrary. They valued liberty both as an end and as a means. They believed liberty to be the secret of happiness and courage to be the secret of liberty. The belief that freedom to think as you will and to speak as you think are means indispensable to the discovery and spread of political truth; that without free speech and assembly discussion would be futile; that with them, discussion affords ordinarily adequate protection against, the dissemination of noxious doctrine.... They recognized the risks to which all human institutions are subject. But they knew ... that it is hazardous to discourage thought, hope and imagination; that fear breeds repression; that repression breeds hate; that hate menaces stable government; that the path of safety lies in the opportunity to discuss freely supposed

54. 341 U.S. 494 (1951).

55. 354 U.S. 298 (1957).

56. 395 U.S. 444 (1969).

57. 354 U.S. 476 (1957).

> grievances and proposed remedies; and that the fitting remedy for evil counsels is good ones.[58]

We begin to see why the dissents of Brandeis and Holmes possessed the power to which Professor Kalven referred. They were rhetoricians of extraordinary potency, and their rhetoric retains the power, almost half a century latter, to swamp analysis, to persuade, almost to command assent.

But there is structure beneath the rhetoric, and Brandeis is asserting, though he attributes it all to the Founding Fathers, that there are four benefits to be derived from speech. These are:

1. The development of the faculties of the individual;
2. The happiness to be derived from engaging in the activity;
3. The provision of a safety value for society; and,
4. The discovery and spread of political truth.

We may accept these claims as true and as satisfactorily inclusive. When we come to analyze these benefits, however, we discover that in terms of constitutional law they are very different things.

The first two benefits—development of individual faculties and the achievement of pleasure—are or may be found, for both speaker and hearer, in all varieties of speech, from political discourse to shop talk to salacious literature. But the important point is that these benefits do not distinguish speech from any other human activity. An individual may develop his faculties or derive pleasure from trading on the stock market, following his profession as a river port pilot, working as a barmaid, engaging in sexual activity, playing tennis, rigging prices or in any of thousands of other endeavors. Speech with only the first two benefits can be preferred to other activities only by ranking forms of personal gratification. These functions or benefits of speech are, therefore, to the principled judge, indistinguishable from the functions or benefits of all other human activity. He cannot, on neutral grounds, choose to protect speech that has only these functions more than he protects any other claimed freedom.

The third benefit of speech mentioned by Brandeis—its safety valve function—is different from the first two. It relates not to the gratification of the individual, at least not directly, but to the welfare of society. The safety valve function raises only issues of expediency or prudence, and, therefore, raises issues to be determined solely by the legislature or, in some cases, by the executive. The legislature may decide not to repress speech advocating the forcible overthrow of the government in some classes of cases because it thinks repression would cause more trouble than it would prevent. Prosecuting attorneys, who must in any event pick and choose among cases, given their limited resources, may similarly decide that some such speech is trivial or that ignoring it would be wisest. But these decisions, involving only the issue of the expedient

58. 274 U.S. at 375.

course, are indistinguishable from thousands of other managerial judgments governments must make daily, though in the extreme case the decision may involve the safety of the society just as surely as a decision whether or not to take a foreign policy stand that risks war. It seems plain that decisions involving only judgments of expediency are for the political branches and not for the judiciary.

This leaves the fourth function of speech—the "discovery and spread of political truth." This function of speech, its ability to deal explicitly, specifically and directly with politics and government, is different from any other form of human activity. But the difference exists only with respect to one kind of speech: explicitly and predominantly political speech. This seems to me the only form of speech that a principled judge can prefer to other claimed freedoms. All other forms of speech raise only issues of human gratification and their protection against legislative regulation involves the judge in making decisions of the sort made in *Griswold v. Connecticut.*

It is here that I begin to part company with Professor Kalven. Kalven argues that no society in which seditious libel, the criticism of public officials, is a crime can call itself free and democratic. I agree, even though the framers of the first amendment probably had no clear view of that proposition. Yet they indicated a value when they said that speech in some sense was special and when they wrote a Constitution providing for representative democracy, a form of government that is meaningless without open and vigorous debate about officials and their policies. It is for this reason, the relation of speech to democratic organization, that Professor Alexander Meiklejohn seems correct when he says:

> The First Amendment does not protect a "freedom to speak." It protects the freedom of those activities of thought and communication by which we "govern." It is concerned, not with a private right, but with a public power, a governmental responsibility.[60]

But both Kalven and Meiklejohn go further and would extend the protection of the first amendment beyond speech that is explicitly political. Meiklejohn argues that the amendment protects:

> Forms of thought and expression within the range of human communications from which the voter derives the knowledge, intelligence, sensitivity to human values: the capacity for sane and objective judgment which, so far as possible, a ballot should express.
>
> He lists four such thoughts and expressions:
>
> 1. Education, in all its phases.... 2. The achievements of philosophy and the sciences.... 3. Literature and the arts.... 4. Public discussions of public issues....[61]

60. Meiklejohn, *The First Amendment Is an Absolute*, 1961 Sup. Ct. Rev. 245, 255.

61. *Id.* at 256–57.

Kalven, following a similar line, states: "[T]he invitation to follow a dialectic progression from public official to government policy to public policy to matters in the public domain, like art, seems to me to be overwhelming."[62] It is an invitation, I wish to suggest, the principled judge must decline. A dialectic progression I take to be a progression by analogy from one case to the next, an indispensable but perilous method of legal reasoning. The length to which analogy is carried defines the principle, but neutral definition requires that, in terms of the rationale in play, those cases within the principle be more like each other than they are like cases left outside. The dialectical progression must have a principled stopping point. I agree that there is an analogy between criticism of official behavior and the publication of a novel like *Ulysses,* for the latter may form attitudes that ultimately affect politics. But it is an analogy, not an identity. Other human activities and experiences also form personality, teach and create attitudes just as much as does the novel, but no one would on that account, I take it, suggest that the first amendment strikes down regulations of economic activity, control of entry into a trade, laws about sexual behavior, marriage and the like. Yet these activities, in their capacity to create attitudes that ultimately impinge upon the political process, are more like literature and science than literature and science are like political speech. If the dialectical progression is not to become an analogical stampede, the protection of the first amendment amendment must be cut off when it reaches the outer limits of political speech.

Two types of problems may be supposed to arise with respect to this solution. The first is the difficulty of drawing a line between political and non-political speech. The second is that such a line will leave unprotected much speech that is essential to the life of a civilized community. Neither of these problems seems to me to raise crippling difficulties.

The category of protected speech should consist of speech concerned with governmental behavior, policy or personnel, whether the governmental unit involved is executive, legislative, judicial or administrative. Explicitly political speech is speech about how we are governed, and the category therefore includes a wide range of evaluation, criticism, electioneering and propaganda. It does not cover scientific, educational, commercial or literary expressions as such. A novel may have impact upon attitudes that affect politics, but it would not for that reason receive judicial protection. This is not anomalous, I have tried to suggest, since the rationale of the first amendment cannot be the protection of all things or activities that influence political attitudes. Any speech may do that, and we have seen that it is impossible to leave all speech unregulated. Moreover, any conduct may affect political attitudes as much as a novel, and we cannot view the first amendment as a broad denial of the power of government to regulate conduct. The line drawn must, therefore, lie between the explicitly political and all else. Not too much should be made of the undeniable fact that there will be hard cases. Any theory

62. Kalven, *The New York Times Case: A Note on "The Central Meaning of the First Amendment,"* 1964 SUP. CT. REV. 191, 221.

of the first amendment that does not accord absolute protection for all verbal expression, which is to say any theory worth discussing, will require that a spectrum be cut and the location of the cut will always be, arguably, arbitrary. The question is whether the general location of the cut is justified. The existence of close cases is not a reason to refuse to draw a line and so deny majorities the power to govern in areas where their power is legitimate.

The other objection—that the political-nonpolitical distinction will leave much valuable speech without constitutional protection—is no more troublesome. The notion that all valuable types of speech must be protected by the first amendment confuses the constitutionality of laws with their wisdom. Freedom of non-political speech rests, as does freedom for other valuable forms of behavior, upon the enlightenment of society and its elected representatives. That is hardly a terrible fate. At least a society like ours ought not to think it so.

The practical effect of confining constitutional protection to political speech would probably go no further than to introduce regulation or prohibition of pornography. The Court would be freed of the stultifying obligation to apply its self-inflicted criteria: whether "(a) the dominant theme of the material taken as a whole appeals to a prurient interest in sex; (b) the material is patently offensive because it affronts contemporary community standards relating to the description or representation of sexual matters; and (c) the material is utterly without redeeming social value."[63] To take only the last criterion, the determination of "social value" cannot be made in a principled way. Anything some people want has, to that degree, social value, but that cannot be the basis for constitutional protection since it would deny regulation of any human activity. The concept of social value necessarily incorporates a judgment about the net effect upon society. There is always the problem that what some people want some other people do not want, or wish actively to banish. A judgment about social value, whether the judges realize it or not, always involves a comparison of competing values and gratifications as well as competing predictions of the effects of the activity. Determination of "social value" is the same thing as determination of what human interests should be classed as "fundamental" and, therefore, cannot be principled or neutral.

To revert to a previous example, pornography is increasingly seen as a problem of pollution of the moral and aesthetic atmosphere precisely analogous to smoke pollution. A majority of the community may foresee that continued availability of pornography to those who want it will inevitably affect the quality of life for those who do not want it, altering, for example, attitudes toward love and sex, the tone of private and public discourse and views of social institutions such as marriage and the family. Such a majority surely has as much control over the moral and

63. A Book Named "John Clelend's Memoirs of a Woman of Pleasure" v. Attorney General, 383 U.S. 413, 418 (1966).

aesthetic environment as it does over the physical, for such matters may even more severely impinge upon their gratifications. That is why, constitutionally, art and pornography are on a par with industry and smoke pollution. As Professor Walter Berns says "[A] thoughtful judge is likely to ask how an artistic judgment that is wholly idiosyncratic can be capable of supporting an objection to the law. The objection, "I like it," is sufficiently rebutted by "*we* don't."[64]

We must now return to the core of the first amendment, speech that is explicitly political. I mean by that criticisms of public officials and policies, proposals for the adoption or repeal of legislation or constitutional provisions and speech addressed to the conduct of any governmental unit in the country.

A qualification is required, however. Political speech is not any speech that concerns government and law, for there is a category of such speech that must be excluded. This category consists of speech advocating forcible overthrow of the government or violation of law. The reason becomes clear when we return to Brandeis' discussion of the reasons for according constitutional protection to speech.

The fourth function of speech, the one that defines and sets apart political speech, is the "discovery and spread of political truth." To understand what the Court should protect, therefore, we must define "political truth." There seem to me three possible meanings to that term:

1. An absolute set of truths that exist independently of Constitution or statute.

2. A set of values that are protected by constitutional provision from the reach of legislative majorities.

3. Within that area of life which the majority is permitted to govern in accordance with the Madisonian model of representative government, whatever result the majority reaches and maintains at the moment.

The judge can have nothing to do with any absolute set of truths existing independently and depending upon God or the nature of the universe. If a judge should claim to have access to such a body of truths, to possess a volume of the annotated natural law, we would, quite justifiably, suspect that the source of the revelation was really no more exalted than the judge's viscera. In our system there is no absolute set of truths, to which the term "political truth" can refer.

Values protected by the Constitution are one type of political truth. They are, in fact, the highest type since they are placed beyond the reach of simple legislative majorities. They are primarily truths about the way government must operate, that is, procedural truths. But speech aimed at the discovery and spread of political truth is concerned with more

64. Berns, *Pornography vs. Democracy: The Case for Censorship,* THE PUB. INTEREST, Winter, 1971, at 23.

than the desirability of constitutional provisions or the manner in which they should be interpreted.

The third meaning of "political truth" extends the category of protected speech. Truth is what the majority thinks it is at any given moment precisely because the majority is permitted to govern and to redefine its values constantly. "Political truth" in this sense must, therefore, be a term of art, a concept defined entirely from a consideration of the system of government which the judge is commissioned to operate and maintain. It has no unchanging content but refers to the temporary outcomes of the democratic process. Political truth is what the majority decides it wants today. It may be something entirely different tomorrow, as truth is rediscovered and the new concept spread.

Speech advocating forcible overthrow of the government contemplates a group less than a majority seizing control of the monopoly power of the state when it cannot gain its ends through speech and political activity. Speech advocating violent overthrow is thus not "political speech" as that term must be defined by a Madisonian system of government. It is not political speech because it violates constitutional truths about processes and because it is not aimed at a new definition of political truth by a legislative majority. Violent overthrow of government breaks the premises of our system concerning the ways in which truth is defined, and yet those premises are the only reasons for protecting political speech. It follows that there is no constitutional reason to protect speech advocating forcible overthrow.

A similar analysis suggests that advocacy of law violation does not qualify as political speech any more than advocacy of forcible overthrow of the government. Advocacy of law violation is a call to set aside the results that political speech has produced. The process of the "discovery and spread of political truth" is damaged or destroyed if the outcome is defeated by a minority that makes law enforcement, and hence the putting of political truth into practice, impossible or less effective. There should, therefore, be no constitutional protection for any speech advocating the violation of law.

I believe these are the only results that can be reached by a neutral judge who takes his values from the Constitution. If we take Brandeis' description of the benefits and functions of speech as our premise, logic and principle appear to drive us to the conclusion that Sanford rather than Brandeis or Holmes was correct in *Gitlow* and *Whitney*.

Benjamin Gitlow was convicted under New York's criminal anarchy statute which made criminal advocacy of the doctrine that organized government should be overthrown by force, violence or any unlawful means. Gitlow, a member of the Left Wing section of the Socialist party, had arranged the printing and distribution of a "Manifesto" deemed to call for violent action and revolution. "There was," Justice Sanford's opinion noted, "no evidence of any effect resulting from the publication and circulation of the Manifesto." Anita Whitney was convicted under California's criminal syndicalism statute, which forbade advocacy of the commission of crime, sabotage, acts of force or violence or terrorism "as a means of accomplishing a change in industrial ownership or control, or effecting any political change." Also made illegal were certain connections with groups advocating such doctrines. Miss Whitney was convicted of assisting in organizing the Communist Labor Party of California, of being a member of it and of assembling with it. The evidence appears to have been meager, but our current concern is doctrinal.

Justice Sanford's opinions for the majorities in *Gitlow* and *Whitney* held essentially that the Court's function in speech cases was the limited but crucial one of determining whether the legislature had defined a category of forbidden speech which might constitutionally be suppressed. The category might be defined by the nature of the speech and need not be limited in other ways. If the category was defined in a permissible way and the defendant's speech or publication fell within the definition, the Court had, it would appear, no other issues to face in order to uphold the conviction. Questions of the fairness of the trial and the sufficiency of the evidence aside, this would appear to be the correct conclusion. The legislatures had struck at speech not aimed at the discovery and spread of political truth but aimed rather at destroying the premises of our political system and the means by which we define political truth. There is no value that judges can independently give such speech in opposition to a legislative determination.

Justice Holmes'' dissent in *Gitlow* and Justice Brandeis' concurrence in *Whitney* insisted the Court must also find that, as Brandeis put it, the "speech would produce, or is intended to produce, a clear and imminent danger of some substantive evil which the state constitutionally may seek to prevent." Neither of them explained why the danger must be "clear and imminent" or, as Holmes had put it in *Schenck,* "clear and present" before a particular instance of speech could be punished. Neither of them made any attempt to answer Justice Sanford's argument on the point:

> [T]he immediate danger [created by advocacy of overthrow of the government] is none the less real and substantial, because the effect of a given utterance cannot be accurately foreseen. The state cannot reasonably be required to measure the danger from every such utterance in the nice balance of a jeweler's scale. A single revolutionary spark may kindle a fire that, smoldering for a time, may burst into a sweeping and destructive conflagration. It cannot be said that the state is acting arbitrarily or unreasonably when in the exercise of its judgment as to the measures necessary to protect the public peace and safety, it seeks to extinguish the spark without waiting until it has enkindled the flame or blazed into conflagration. It cannot reasonably be required to defer the adoption of measures for its own peace and safety until the revolutionary utterances lead to actual disturbances of the public peace or imminent and immediate danger of its own destruction; but it may, in the exercise of its

> judgment, suppress the threatened danger in its incipiency....[70]

To his point that proof of the effect of speech is inherently unavailable and yet its impact may be real and dangerous, Sanford might have added that the legislature is not confined to consideration of a single instance of speech or a single speaker. It fashions a rule to dampen thousands of instances of forcible overthrow advocacy. Cumulatively these may have enormous influence, and yet it may well be impossible to show any effect from any single example. The "clear and present danger" requirement, which has had a long and uneven career in our law, is improper not, as many commentators have thought, because it provides a subjective and an inadequate safeguard against the regulation of speech, but rather because it erects a barrier to legislative rule where none should exist. The speech concerned has no political value within a republican system of government. Whether or not it is prudent to ban advocacy of forcible overthrow and law violation is a different question although. Because the judgment is tactical, implicating the safety of the nation, it resembles very closely the judgment that Congress and the President must make about the expediency of waging war, an issue that the Court has wisely thought not fit for judicial determination.

The legislature and the executive might find it wise to permit some rhetoric about law violation and forcible overthrow. I am certain that they would and that they should. Certain of the factors weighted in determining the constitutionality of the Smith Act prosecutions in *Dennis* would, for example, make intelligible statutory, though not constitutional, criteria: the high degree of organization of the Communist party, the rigid discipline of its members and the party's ideological affinity to foreign powers.

Similar objections apply to the other restrictions Brandeis attempted to impose upon government. I will mention but one more of these restrictions. Justice Brandeis argued that:

> Even imminent danger cannot justify resort to prohibition of these functions essential to effective democracy, unless the evil apprehended is relatively serious.... Thus, a state might, in the exercise of its police power, make any trespass upon the land of another a crime, regardless of the results or of the intent or purpose of the trespasser. It might, also, punish an attempt, a conspiracy, or an incitement to commit the trespass. But it is hardly conceivable that this court would hold constitutional a statute which punished as a felony the mere voluntary assembly with a society formed to teach that pedestrians had the moral right to cross unenclosed, unposted, waste lands and to advocate their doing so, even if there was imminent danger that advocacy would lead to a trespass. The fact that speech is likely to result in some violence or in destruction of property is not enough to justify its suppression. There must be the probability of serious injury to the state.[72]

70. 268 U.S. at 669.

72. 274 U.S. at 377–78.

It is difficult to see how a constitutional court could properly draw the distinction proposed. Brandeis offered no analysis to show that advocacy of law violation merited protection by the Court. Worse, the criterion he advanced is the importance, in the judge's eyes, of the law whose violation is urged.

Modern law has followed the general line and the spirit of Brandeis and Holmes rather than of Sanford, and it has become increasingly severe in its limitation of legislative power. *Brandenburg v. Ohio,* a 1969 per curiam decision by the Supreme Court, struck down the Ohio criminal syndicalism statute because it punished advocacy of violence, the opinion stating:

> ... *Whitney* [the majority opinion] has been thoroughly discredited by later decisions.... These later decisions have fashioned the principle that the constitutional guarantees of free speech and free press do not permit a State to forbid or proscribe advocacy of the use of force or of law violation except where such advocacy is directed to inciting or producing imminent lawless action and is likely to incite or produce such action.

It is certainly true that Justice Sanford's position in *Whitney* and in *Gitlow* has been completely undercut, or rather abandoned, by later cases, but it is not true that his position has been discredited, or even met, on intellectual grounds. Justice Brandeis failed to accomplish that, and later Justices have not mounted a theoretical case comparable to Brandeis.

Questions

1) Does Brandeis's rationale for free speech justify the protection of "non-political" speech such as literature, scientific research findings, labor picketing, or commercial advertising? When he was nominated for a seat on the Supreme Court in 1987, at his confirmation hearing Judge Bork was skewered for believing that the First Amendment does not protect literary and artistic expression. But how, if at all, could Brandeis justify protecting this kind of speech—or other forms of non-political speech—on the basis of the argument he sets forth in *Whitney*?

2) What could Brandeis say in response to Bork's argument?

3) What does Brandeis mean when he refers to "political truth?" A view of truth similar to that of Mill? Of Holmes? Something captured by Bork's three alternatives?

ROBERT C. POST, THE CONSTITUTIONAL CONCEPT OF PUBLIC DISCOURSE: OUTRAGEOUS OPINION, DEMOCRATIC DELIBERATION, AND HUSTLER MAGAZINE v. FALWELL

103 Harv. L. Rev. 603 (1990).

Certain speech, of course, is clearly and obviously recognizable as substantively relevant to democratic self-government. Most speech about public officials falls into this category. But it does not follow from this fact that speech less easily recognizable can with confidence be ruled out as irrelevant to matters of public concern. Robert Bork, for example, once proposed limiting constitutionally protected speech to that "concerned with governmental behavior, policy or personnel."[338] Bork's proposal was attractive because it seemed to follow so directly from the logic of democratic self-governance, and to offer a clean and precise definition of speech about matters of public concern.

On closer inspection, however, Bork's proposal proved inadequate, because it missed the fundamental point that the first amendment safeguards public discourse not merely because it informs government decisionmaking, but also because it enables a culturally heterogeneous society to forge a common democratic will. The formation of this will depends upon the ability of public discourse to sustain deliberation about our identity as a people, as well as about what specifically we want our government to do. That is why most would unquestionably consider as public discourse the public discussion of such issues as the proper role of motherhood, the disaffection of the young, and the meaning of American citizenship, even if this discussion did not occur within the specific context of any proposed or actual government action.

The public realm, as Hanna Pitkin has eloquently remarked, is where the "people determine what they will collectively do, settle how they will live together, and decide their future, to whatever extent that is within human power."[340] To decide these things, however, is to engage in a process of "collective self-definition," of determining "who we shall be, for what we shall stand." To classify speech as public discourse is, in effect, to deem it relevant to this collective process of self-definition and decisionmaking. There is obviously no theoretically neutral way in which this can be done. Speech can be deemed irrelevant for national self-definition only in the name of a particular, substantive vision of national identity. If this is done with the authority of the law, possible options for democratic development will be foreclosed.

338. Bork, Neutral Principles and Some First Amendment Problems, 47 IND. L.J. 1, 27 (1971).

340. Pitkin, Justice: On Relating Private and Public, 9 Pol. Theory 327, 343 (1981).

The problem can be illustrated by Samuel Warren's and Louis Brandeis' famous article The Right to Privacy,[342] published in 1890, which virtually created the common law tort of invasion of privacy. The origins of the article were said to lie in the outrage which Warren, a genuine Boston Brahmin, felt at newspaper reports of his private entertainments. Warren and Brandeis argued that such gossip was not of public concern and that it usurped "the space available for matters of real interest to the community." Yet, in retrospect, public fascination with the doings of the rich and the aristocratic at the turn of the century may have played an integral part in the general movement toward the creation of the welfare state, with its progressive tax and other instruments of wealth redistribution. Although reports of Samuel Warren's particular dinner parties may well have lacked significance, they formed part of this much larger process by which the people, as a public, came to alter their vision of the nation. In retrospect, therefore, Warren's and Brandeis' dismissal of such gossip as merely "idle" and as the bearer only of "triviality," has come to seem an unattractive example of self-serving class prejudice.

The fundamental theoretical difficulty faced by writers like Warren and Brandeis, who would place limits on what ought to be pertinent to the formation of a common democratic will, is that any effort substantively to circumscribe public discourse is necessarily self-defeating, for it displaces the very democratic processes it seeks to facilitate.

VINCENT BLASI, THE FIRST AMENDMENT AND THE IDEAL OF CIVIC COURAGE: THE BRANDEIS OPINION IN WHITNEY v. CALIFORNIA

29 Wm & Mary L. Rev. 653 (1988).

Brandeis was not the first person to think about free speech in terms of its impact on the character traits of the citizenry. Nor was Brandeis the first person to equate tolerance with courage and censorship with cowardice. Why then should we consider the *Whitney* opinion one of the turning points in the history of first amendment adjudication?

There are two bases for skepticism here, and I would like to address them one at a time. First, the connection between civic courage and contemporary doctrine is not entirely recondite; surely some probative value attaches to the fact that the Court has invoked the ideal of civic courage at critical junctures in the doctrine-building experience. In addition, the adjudicative significance of the idea of civic courage is partly a function of the inability of other free speech rationales to account fully for the doctrinal pattern that has developed over the past sixty years. I am convinced that several features of contemporary first amendment doctrine could not have evolved as they have without the push they received from the ideal of engaged, confident, innovative citizenship around which Brandeis constructed his opinion in *Whitney*.

Take, for example, the proposition that no idea, whatever its message and whatever its history, can be considered as a general matter to

342. Warren & Brandeis, The Right to Privacy, 4 Harv. L. Rev. 193 (1890).

be too evil or too dangerous to be voiced freely in public debate. It is straining to defend this proposition by claiming that the harms that ensue when receptive listeners are persuaded by certain messages are inevitably outweighed by the benefits those messages bestow. Perhaps the harms caused by predictable abuses of the authority to censor might justify an unqualified principle against prohibitions of ideas, but one wonders if the slope is really so slippery that all ideas must be immune from censorship. The ideal of civic courage provides much-needed reinforcement for the principle that no idea can be banished from public debate. As Meiklejohn put it, in language that seems to echo the *Whitney opinion*: "To be afraid of ideas, any idea, is to be unfit for self-government." The experience of contending openly against truly evil and dangerous ideas makes us a stronger, more vital political community. The potential benefits of that experience justify the risk, not always negligible, that the evil ideas may for a time cause harm.

Another core proposition of modern first amendment doctrine is that speech on public issues cannot be regulated solely because of its intemperate, misleading, or unfair quality. The Supreme Court has gone so far as to legitimate exaggeration and vilification.[135] The arguments for this proposition that rest on a balancing of consequences and a fear of government overreaching are convincing to a degree, but the ideal of civic courage provides the strongest justification for the principle that individual listeners, not the state, must determine the boundaries of communicative acceptability. That allocation of authority, in the words of Justice Harlan, "will ultimately produce a more capable citizenry."[136]

A third example of the resolving power of the ideal of civic courage is the doctrine of prior restraint. There are, of course, functional reasons why the regulation of speech prior to its initial dissemination may be viewed as especially problematic. But the functional argument against prior restraint has been challenged. The most powerful critique of prior restraint remains that of John Milton, and he emphasized how regulation in advance reflects a cautious, cowardly, unimaginative mentality. It is an affirmation of civic courage to permit a communication to proceed that may eventually be ruled illegal, to accept the risk of its interim consequences until legal sanctions can be applied on the basis of actual events rather than anxious predictions.

The illustrations could be proliferated but the point should be clear. Character provides a benchmark for interpretation that can supplement constitutional analysis based on consequences, historical commitments, or notions of conceptual coherence. We think differently about free speech issues than we otherwise would because of the ideal of civic courage.

* * *

135. Cantwell v. Connecticut, 310 U.S. 296, 310 (1940).

136. Cohen v. California, 403 U.S. 15, 24 (1971).

The very fact, however, that the ideal of civic courage occupies a distinctive place in the first amendment tradition underscores the second reservation one might have regarding the significance of the opinion. Is it not likely that an idea with such deep roots in Western political thought would somehow have worked its way into the doctrinal fabric without the contribution of Brandeis? If the character ideal of civic courage was not a novel idea when he wrote, why is Justice Brandeis's opinion so important? The answer, I believe, can be captured in two words: conviction and credibility. As befits the work of a consummate lawyer, it is the opinion's persuasiveness, not its originality, that accounts for its stature.

Others before Brandeis may have expressed the view that fear threatens democracy far more than subversion. Predecessors may have alluded to the notion of civic courage. But no one, not even Milton, had managed to convey so forcefully the conviction that the essential character of a political community is both revealed and defined by how it responds to the challenge of threatening ideas. And no one previously had expounded the ideal of civic courage in a way that integrates such seemingly divergent virtues as confidence, humility, ingenuity, historical perspective, love of country, distrust of government, concern for the common good, and self-reliance. That Brandeis was able to do so convincingly in a short space is a tribute not only to his eloquence but also to the fact that civic courage meant so much to him.

The eloquence of the *Whitney* opinion is of a special sort. In the apt characterization of one experienced observer, the opinion contains "what may well be the most powerful judicial rhetoric of this century, emanating from a Justice not given to flights of eloquence."[145] Brandeis's prose does not display the lyrical grace that Holmes commanded, or the dazzling word selection that Cardozo employed. "Men feared witches and burnt women" is a sentence that speaks volumes and certainly sticks in the mind, but not because of the flow or lilt of its language. What makes Brandeis's writing eloquent is its simplicity. His crisp, unadorned cadence bespeaks a depth of conviction seldom encountered in legal discourse. The *Whitney* opinion is not so much an argument as a testament.

It is a credible testament because it comes from a man whose idealism had nothing whatever to do with escapism, ignorance, or inexperience. Here was a man who had spent most of his long professional life in the trench warfare of reform politics, a man who had read voraciously and with a critical intelligence that was legendary. And still, in an opinion that can only be described as a profoundly personal statement, he affirms a belief in the possibility of democracy and in the positive value of the freedom of speech. He considers civic courage an ideal worth pursuing even in the modern age.

145. [Louis H. Pollak, Advocating Civil Liberties: A Young Lawyer Before the Old Court, 17 Harv. C.R.-C.L. L. Rev. 1, 8–9 (1982).]

Questions

1) Is it appropriate to build an interpretation of the First Amendment around a character ideal such as civic courage? Is such a referent too imprecise or too controversial to constitute a doctrinal building block?

2) What exactly does civic courage mean? Civic engagement generally? Willingness to innovate? Willingness to exercise independent judgment? To take unpopular stands? To adapt to a changing civic environment? To persevere in the face of opposition and mistreatment? Not to lose faith in the value of democratic participation? To commit oneself in some sort of civic capacity?

3) What does Brandeis's philosophy of free speech imply about the constitutionality of campaign spending limits? Does civic courage require that we not fear the power of high-spending candidates to "buy" elections because an independent, engaged citizenry can always resist their messages no matter how often they are broadcast? Or is the modern practice of saturation attack advertising regulable under the First Amendment on the theory that it contributes to political cynicism and disengagement?

Additional Readings

Brandeis's life and thought

Stephen W. Baskerville, Of Laws and Limitations: An Intellectual Portrait of Lewis Dembitz Brandeis (1994)

Louis D. Brandeis, The Curse of Bigness (1934)

Louis D. Brandeis and Samuel D. Warren, The Right to Privacy, 4 Harv. L. Rev. 193 (1890)

Robert A. Burt, Two Jewish Justices: Outcasts in the Promised Land (1988)

Allon Gal, Brandeis of Boston (1980)

Thomas K. McCraw, Prophets of Regulation (1984)

Bruce Alan Murphy, The Brandeis/Frankfurter Connection (1982)

Lewis J. Paper, Brandeis: An Intimate Biography of One of America's Truly Great Supreme Court Justices (1983)

A. L. Todd, Justice on Trial: The Case of Louis D. Brandeis (1964)

Clyde Spillenger, Elusive Advocate: Reconsidering Brandeis as People's Lawyer, 105 Yale L. J. 1445 (1996)

Philippa Strum ed., Brandeis on Democracy (1995)

Melvin I. Urofsky, Louis D. Brandeis and the Progressive Tradition (1981)

Labor picketing and the First Amendment

James Gray Pope, Labor and the Constitution: From Abolition to Deindustrialization, 65 Tex. L. Rev. 1071 (1987)

Virginia Board of Pharmacy

Thomas Jackson and John C. Jeffries, Jr., Commercial Speech: Economic Due Process and the First Amendment, 65 Va. L. Rev. 1 (1979)

Daniel Lowenstein, "Too Much Puff": Persuasion, Paternalism, and Commercial Speech, 56 U. Cinc. L. Rev. 1205 (1988)

Commercial advertising and the First Amendment

C. Edwin Baker, Commercial Speech: A Problem in the Theory of Freedom, 62 Iowa L. Rev. 1 (1976)

Robert C. Post, The Constitutional Status of Commercial Speech, 48 UCLA L. Rev. 1 (2000)

Martin H. Redish, The First Amendment in the Marketplace: Commercial Speech and the Values of Free Expression, 39 Geo. Wash. L. Rev. 429 (1971)

Martin H. Redish, Tobacco Advertising and the First Amendment, 81 Iowa L. Rev. 589 (1996)

Steven Shiffrin, The First Amendment and Economic Regulation: Away From a General Theory of the First Amendment, 78 Nw. U. L. Rev. 1212 (1983)

William W. Van Alstyne, Remembering Melville Nimmer, Some Cautionary Notes on Commercial Speech, 43 UCLA L. Rev. 1635 (1996)

Chapter Eight

ALEXANDER MEIKLEJOHN

JOHN PATRICK DIGGINS, THE PROUD DECADES: AMERICA IN WAR AND PEACE 1941–1960

(1988).

Rumors of covert communist activity first surfaced in spring 1945 when federal agents raided the office of *Amerasia,* a radical journal of Asian affairs, and found classified documents that had been taken from the State Department. No evidence could be found that the editors intended to pass on the documents to a foreign power. But the following year the Canadian government announced the arrest of twenty-two persons charged with illegally passing information to Soviet officials and the probability that the NKVD had established espionage rings in Britain and the United States. Meanwhile, Congress's House Un–American Activities Committee (HUAC) had stepped up its investigation of subversive infiltration into government, industry, organized labor, the movie industry, and the universities. HUAC's interrogations created bitter controversy and divided Hollywood and the academic intellectuals.

The Truman administration, fearing that the Republicans would exploit the growing anticommunist scare, issued a loyalty order in March 1947, requiring FBI checks on all government workers. Sixteen thousand employees were investigated. Not one was found to be disloyal or a card-carrying communist. But two were dismissed as security risks; 202 who resigned were regarded as unsuitable for such "personal" reasons as homosexuality; and about one hundred others lost their jobs because of "reasonable grounds" to suspect possible disloyalty. Often the employees had no opportunity to confront their accusers or even to be informed of the nature of the accusations. Such trial by innuendo had a devastating effect upon the morale of government employees, especially in the State Department, where foreign affairs specialists were intimidated into acquiescing to cold war orthodoxy.

While the innocent felt pressured into conforming, the guilty felt pressured into informing. In the summer of 1948 Elizabeth Bentley and Whittaker Chambers testified before congressional committees that they had engaged in espionage for Soviet agents and that they were quite willing to name others who had done so.

* * *

Chambers testified to HUAC that Alger Hiss, a former State Department officer present at the Yalta Conference, had been a member of the CP during the Popular Front era of the 1930s. Instead of admitting that like many students in the 1930s, he had flirted with communism, Hiss denied the charges and sued Chambers for libel. The denial did not impress Congressman Richard M. Nixon, who sensed that if Hiss functioned as an implanted agent, as Chambers suggested, he need not have been a known CP member. Nixon offered his prosecutorial services to Chambers. He then surprised everyone by charging not merely that Hiss had been a party member but that he had been a communist spy and had copied State Department documents that Chambers had passed to the Russians. At first such charges seemed incredible to many Democrats. Truman and Acheson defended Hiss and dismissed the hearings as a "red herring." Liberals also tended to believe in Hiss's innocence and claimed that Chambers, Nixon, and the FBI were merely Red-baiting. Yet Chambers dramatically produced—from of all places, a pumpkin on his farm—secret documents, some of which bore Hiss's handwriting and others copied from a typewriter that once belonged to Hiss. When this evidence emerged, a federal grand jury issued a perjury indictment against Hiss for denying Chambers' allegations. The first trial resulted in a hung jury; the second, in January 1950, in a conviction.

With the accusations and denials headlined daily in the press, the Hiss trial became one of the most sensational American political controversies of the twentieth century. The two figures stood as symbols of a cold war morality play. Chambers was a tortured ex-communist full of guilt and suicidal despair, but with a newly discovered religiosity that made him all too ready to atone for the sins of a whole generation. Hiss, the embodiment of the Ivy League, had offered his talents to the Roosevelt administration: composed, articulate, well-dressed, well-mannered, well-connected, and bookish. Most HUAC members, including Nixon, Karl Mundt, and Chairman J. Parnell Thomas, were anti-New Deal avengers out to discredit the whole program of liberalism. Before long the seed of suspicion had been planted: Hiss, the Harvard Law School graduate groomed for national leadership, the epitome of the new elite ruling class, had been seduced to spying by a foreign power. How many more Hisses were there among the wise and famous?

Probably not many, but the question haunted Americans in late 1949 and throughout the spring and summer of the following year. During that period America experienced a series of shocking events and revelations: the fall of China; the uncovering of a spy ring in England headed by Klaus Fuchs, a scientist who had worked on the Los Alamos Project; the alarming news that the Soviet Union had exploded an atom bomb; the conviction of communist leaders under the Smith Act; and the arrest of Ethel and Julius Rosenberg on espionage charges. All of these events lay ready for someone audacious enough to link together into a vast conspiratorial scheme, even if the scheme had to be invented.

When Joseph McCarthy made his now-famous speech to the Republican Women's Club in Wheeling, West Virginia, on February 9, 1950, the gnawing impression that there were communists in high places in government had been bandied about for some time. But McCarthy was the first to cite names and numbers. Not only Hiss but Dean Acheson, the "pompous diplomat in striped pants, with a phony British accent." They were all of a type, "the bright young men who are born with silver spoons in their mouths." It was not that our enemy is so powerful, McCarthy emphasized in explaining America's setbacks abroad, it was the "traitorous actions of those who have been treated so well by this Nation." McCarthy then told the startled ladies that while he did not have the time to go through all the names of CP members in the State Department, he had in his hand a list of 205. The whole show of waving a paper in his hand was an impulsive bluff. When the news soon blared through the press, reporters quizzed him on the precise number. McCarthy scaled it down from 205 to fifty-seven and then, two evenings later in Nevada, he screamed in a drunken stupor that newsmen had stolen the document with the figures.

* * *

McCarthy never turned up a single communist not known to the FBI or other intelligence agencies. But from 1950 to 1954 he became a powerful force of intimidation and terror in American political life. In the Senate he had the support of Taft, Kenneth Wherry, and Styles Bridges. When a Senate committee headed by the Maryland Democrat Millard Tydings reported that McCarthy's accusations were unfounded, McCarthy circulated faked photos showing Tydings whispering to the head of the CP. Whether or not such tactics accounted for Tydings' failure to be reelected in 1950, other members of the Senate and House would think twice before speaking out against McCarthy. A consummate demagogue, McCarthy played upon cold war emotions and made charges so fantastic that frightened people believed the worst; for any accusation so sensational makes the truth seem a dull anticlimax. He was a master of the "pseudo-event," press conferences where he announced another round of charges with a mass of documents which, upon close inspection, turned out to prove little, but by then the news of who was named had made the headlines.

* * *

In 1948 congressmen Richard Nixon and Karl Mundt sponsored a bill in the House requiring communists to register with the government. Two years later they supported Pat McCarran, a conservative Democratic senator from Nevada, in passing the Internal Security Act, better known as the McCarran Act. Voted into law shortly after the outbreak of the Korean War, the McCarran Act required that communist and communist-front organizations register with the Subversive Activities Control Board, which in addition would investigate any group reported to be ideologically suspect. It also empowered the federal government to order the arrest of persons suspected of subversive activity in times of national emergency. Truman and several congressmen denounced the McCarran Act as unconstitutional.

* * *

Truman's veto of the bill was easily overridden in the House, 286 to 48, and in the Senate, 57 to 10. The McCarran Act represented, Truman protested in his veto message, "the greatest danger to freedom of press, speech, and assembly since the Sedition Act of 1798."

In 1952 Truman also attacked another bill cosponsored by McCarran, the Immigration and Nationality Act. Designed in part to establish immigration quotas, the bill set up complicated screening procedures to keep out "subversives" and aliens who had been associated with totalitarian states. In addition, it authorized the attorney general to deport immigrants affiliated with communist organizations even if they had received citizenship. The bill extended to the State Department's Passport Office nearly arbitrary power of deciding who could enter and leave the United States. This second "McCarran Act" proved even more embarrassing than the first. It denied Supreme Court Justice William O. Douglas permission to travel to China. Even more ironical, America soon discovered that those who fled totalitarian governments did so not to spread communism but to escape it. Truman predicted this in his veto message when he described the bill as an "absurdity" that reflected an iron-curtain mentality similar to the Soviet Union's. Once again Congress overrode the veto.

Truman's opposition to the McCarran Act, to HUAC, and to McCarthyism in general was courageous. Many politicians, even some liberal Democrats, feared taking on McCarthy. Truman did so fearlessly. Even in states like Massachusetts, where McCarthy had a strong following among Catholics, Truman lashed out at the shameless tactics of the Wisconsin demagogue. "The President of the United States," wrote columnist Murray Kempton, "is gambling that McCarthy is an overrated punk." While Republicans ducked the issue, the scrappy Truman defied his own Democratic advisors and kept up the counterattack. "Not even for campaign purposes would Harry Truman blanch or quail," Kempton continued. "Yesterday in Cumberland, Maryland, where McCarthy is generally credited with deciding the 1950 Senate election, the President called Joe 'a political gangster,' a denizen of the 'political underworld,' a dealer of the 'big lie.' His audience listened open-mouthed and then applauded."

* * *

Eisenhower chose to remain aloof of the anticommunist controversy, believing it would demean the office of the presidency to engage McCarthy in the game of gutter politics, "to get into a pissing contest with a skunk," as he remarked privately in language that Truman would have used publicly. Such a stance displayed more wisdom than courage. Eisenhower said nothing when McCarthy told General Ralph Zwicker, the president's old friend who had been wounded and decorated in the D–Day landing, that he was not fit to wear a uniform. As did so many other politicians, Eisenhower feared McCarthy, especially the prospect that the senator would turn on the Republican administration as he had on the Democratic.

* * *

He would indeed. In McCarthy's feverish imagination every American institution had become a hotbed of radicalism. Government, schools, churches, even the CIA was "infiltrated" by communists, and the Atomic Energy Commission was about to be unless Eisenhower allowed McCarthy's subcommittee to investigate it. Serving on the subcommittee were Roy M. Cohn and G. David Schine, smart young lawyers who loved the power of subpoena and the glare of publicity while enjoying the illusion of invulnerability. Even Edward R. Murrow's exposure of McCarthy, watched by millions of Americans on CBS's "See It Now," resulted in the courageous broadcaster receiving bundles of hate mail. But when Schine was notified, in November 1953, that he had been drafted into the army, one of the most remarkable dramas in American political history began: the Army–McCarthy Hearings.

McCarthy had already been tangling with the army when stories began to spread in the press that Cohn had put pressure on officers at Fort Dix to make life easier for Private Schine. McCarthy reacted by claiming that the army was trying to force him to call off his exposure of communists in the military service. The Senate, embarrassed by the accusations of its fellow member, aware of McCarthy's drinking problem, and perhaps sensing that he was, at last, expendable, decided to hold public meetings carried live on national television. The army appointed as its special counsel Joseph Welch, a gentle, folksy sixty-three-year-old attorney with a devotion to fairness and civility. The hearings opened amid a barrage of television cameras and cables in the Senate Caucus Room on April 22, 1954. The television audience, estimated to be as high as twenty million, watched the proceedings for thirty-five days.

During the first several weeks McCarthy seemed invincible, holding forth faked documents and calling out, "Mr. Chairman, a point of order," to interrupt any testimony that might turn against him. Then the hearings developed into a tense personal duel when Welch asked McCarthy questions he refused to answer, leaving the impression that the Senator was as duplicitous as communists who hid behind the Fifth Amendment. The audience began to warm to Welch's dignified manner and wit. Desperate, McCarthy played his last card. He informed the room that Welch's law firm had been employing a former member of the Communist party, a man named Fisher. The shaken Welch, trying to control his rage, calmly replied to McCarthy before the hushed audience. "Until this moment, Senator, I think I never really gauged your cruelty or your recklessness. Fred Fisher is a young man who went to the

Harvard Law School and came into my firm and is starting what looks to be a brilliant career with us." He then told the television audience that he and others in the firm knew that Fisher had once belonged to the Lawyers Guild and had left it when he became aware of its procommunist politics. Welch knew that Cohn was aware of Fisher's background, so why was McCarthy bringing it up now? "Little did I dream," Welch continued staring McCarthy in the face,

> you could be so reckless and so cruel as to do an injury to that lad. It is true he is still with Hale and Dorr. It is true that he will continue to be with Hale and Dorr. It is, I regret to say, equally true that I fear he shall always bear a scar needlessly inflicted by you. If it were in my power to forgive you for your reckless cruelty I would do so. I like to think that I am a gentle man, but your forgiveness will have to come from someone other than me.

Reeling from the moving rebuke, McCarthy grumbled that Welch had no right to mention cruelty since he had "been baiting Cohn here for hours." "Senator, may we not drop this?" Welch pleaded.

> We know he belonged to the Lawyers Guild, and Mr. Cohn nods his head at me. I did you, I think, no personal injury, Mr. Cohn.

Cohn, biting his lips and trembling, whispered back, "No, sir."

> I meant to do you no personal injury, and if I did, I beg your pardon.

Cohn again nodded, and McCarthy, now in panic, tried again to bring up the subject of Fisher.

> Let us not assassinate this lad further, Senator. You have done enough. Have you no sense of decency, sir, at long last? Have you left no sense of decency?

The audience broke into applause and then hurried to leave the hearing room. "I was sick to my stomach," recalled one of the few remaining McCarthy supporters who stayed in his seat. Staggering back to his table, McCarthy turned his palms up and shrugged his shoulders, asking "What did I do?" The next day newspapers across the country provided the answer with headlines celebrating the defeat of "Cruelty" by "Decency."

Shortly after the hearings ended Eisenhower met privately with Welch and congratulated him for his handling of the army's case.

* * *

In November 1954, McCarthy was finally censured, by a vote of 64 to 23. It took the Senate almost three years to condemn a fellow member who had made a mockery out of civil liberties and had turned anticommunism into a farce.

GEOFFREY R. STONE, PERILOUS TIMES: FREE SPEECH IN WARTIME

(2004).

How many government employees were affected by the federal loyalty program? During the Truman era (1947–53), more than 4.7 million individuals were investigated. Approximately 1 percent of these investigations unearthed enough "derogatory" information to trigger full-field investigations by the FBI, which conducted roughly 40,000 such investigations. Approximately 8,000 (or 20 percent) of these investigations led to the filing of formal charges before a departmental or agency loyalty board. These boards cleared more than 90 percent of the individuals investigated, finding no reasonable basis to doubt their loyalty. They thus ordered the discharge of approximately 500 individuals. On appeal, the Civil Service Commission's Loyalty Review Board overturned about a third of these findings of disloyalty.

Thus, from 1947 to 1953, roughly 350 federal employees were discharged because of doubts about their loyalty. In addition, approximately 2,200 federal employees, upon learning they were under investigation, "voluntarily" resigned rather than allow the process to continue.

At first glance, one might muse that these numbers don't look so bad. After all, the FBI cleared 80 percent of the individuals on whom it conducted full-field investigations, the agency and departmental loyalty boards exonerated 90 percent of those who were formally accused of disloyalty, and the Civil Service Commission's Loyalty Review Board reversed a third of these findings on appeal. In the end, only about .00007 of all federal civilian employees (roughly one in 13,000) who were subjected to investigation in the Truman era were discharged for disloyalty.

But this misses the point. Even setting aside the question whether these individuals actually posed a threat to the United States or "deserved" to be discharged, we need to step back to grasp the true impact of this program. Suppose more than 90 percent of all criminal defendants were found "not guilty" at trial. We would know immediately that something was terribly amiss in our criminal justice system. Although a loyalty hearing is not a criminal trial, the experience of an individual subjected to such a proceeding was often terrifying, humiliating, and grievously harmful to his reputation, even if he was ultimately "cleared" by the tribunal. Even those exonerated of disloyalty suffered severe and long lasting hardship.

Moreover, the harm was not limited to those dragged before a loyalty board. Because of the ambiguity of the very concept of "disloyalty," and the highly secretive nature of the process, no federal employee—or *prospective* federal employee—could consider herself exempt from the danger of investigation. Any slip of the tongue, any unguarded statement, any criticism of official policy, any "suspicious" friendship, or any "questionable" reading matter could lead to her undoing.

The loyalty program created a pervasive sense of being "watched." It was as if a noxious cloud had engulfed the nation, and numbers alone cannot capture how corrosive the policy had become. Almost every federal agency employed its own "security officers," whose job it was to unearth information about agency employees. These officers scrutinized and recorded the conduct, sentiments, associations, relationships, conversations, and personal lives of employees. They compiled secret dossiers on "suspect" individuals and shared them with the FBI, the Civil Service Commission, and HUAC. They rewarded "tips" and encouraged employees to report on one another. To keep things simple, they often proposed "deals" to employees against whom they harbored "suspicions"—if the employee would resign, the security officer would suspend the inquiry. The pressure on honest, law-abiding, loyal employees to yield to the whims, prejudices, and abuse of security officers was often insurmountable.

The FBI's insistence on shielding the identity of informers exacerbated the danger. In only 6 percent of the loyalty hearings did the accused learn the identity of her accuser. In those few cases in which the informer's identity came to light, the stupidity or venality of the accusation was often shocking, adding to the sense of vulnerability. In one case, for instance, the informer testified that she had reported the accused because he had a mustache and never wore his tie home at the end of the day. The informer explained that she had "heard people say that ... those are indications that he is not a capitalist." In another case, the informer revealed at the hearing that he had accused the employee of disloyalty because the employee "thought the colored should be entitled to as much as anybody else," a view the informer associated with communism. The anonymity of informers left every federal employee open to the vagaries of crackpots, schemers, scandalmongers, and personal enemies.

As John Lord O'Brian observed at the time, secret investigations foster "suspicion, distrust ... and a general undermining of morale." It was *essential* to avoid suspicion. The cost of being ensnared in a loyalty investigation was fearsome. As one lawyer commented, those dismissed from government employment "cannot find jobs; the FBI hounds them; their social standing in the community is ruined; they receive crank mail; their friends desert them." Abe Fortas, who represented many individuals before loyalty boards, noted that even those cleared of disloyalty suffered "heartaches and personal disasters."

The only sensible approach was to keep one's head down. Prudence was the order of the day. One government employee remarked, "If Communists like apple pie and I do, I see no reason why I should stop eating it. But I would." It was dangerous to be seen speaking with the wrong person or reading the wrong journal. One federal employee discovered a collection of the *New Masses* when he moved into a house. To avoid the risk that someone might think he read such material, he burned it. It was always safer not to join an organization. One could never know who else might be a member. In this era, the fragility of free expression—the capacity to frighten individuals into remaining silent rather than risk harm to themselves and their families—was powerfully demonstrated and exploited.

The loyalty program first promulgated in 1947 evolved over time. [I]n 1951 President Truman amended the program to *expand* the standard of "disloyalty." In May 1953, President Eisenhower announced a further revision. Executive Order no. 10450 established a new and even more expansive standard of disloyalty—"any behavior, activities or associations which *tend to show* that the individual is not reliable or trustworthy" would henceforth be sufficient for dismissal. In October, Eisenhower amended Executive Order no. 10450 to add a new basis for automatic dismissal—invocation of the Fifth Amendment privilege against compelled self-incrimination before a congressional committee in an inquiry involving alleged disloyalty.

The Eisenhower administration boasted in late 1953 that 1,456 employees had left the government under its new loyalty program. Shortly before the 1954 congressional elections, Vice President Nixon trumpeted that seven thousand federal employees had been dismissed or resigned as a result of the Eisenhower program and that the administration was "kicking the communists and fellow travelers ... out of government...by the thousands." Between 1947 and 1956, approximately 2,700 federal civil service employees were dismissed and another 12,000 "voluntarily" resigned as a result of the government's loyalty program.

It was never quite clear precisely what this program was intended to accomplish. It was certainly not well calculated to catch spies. No spy would have been so naïve as to join a "listed" organization or so clumsy as to be discovered by the largely unprofessional federal security officers. Rather, the program was intended, at best, to identify and exclude from federal employment those American citizens who might be tempted to assist foreign agents or otherwise fail to perform their responsibilities faithfully. In theory, of course, this goal is perfectly legitimate. In practice, however, it was a train wreck. In their investigations of more than four million federal civilian employees, the government's two hundred loyalty boards did not uncover a *single* instance of actual espionage or subversive malfeasance.

Most critics of the federal loyalty program have focused on the procedural unfairness of the hearings. The lack of specificity in the charges, the anonymity and unreliability of informers, the inability to confront and cross-examine one's accusers, the wide discretion of the loyalty boards, and the absence of factual findings combined to create a sense that these were "star-chamber" proceedings devoid of the most fundamental guarantees of due process.

But there was an even deeper difficulty. The government's inability to define "disloyalty," its focus on beliefs and associations rather than overt acts, and its effort to predict future criminal behavior on the basis of an individual's past or present disagreement with government policy doomed the program from the start. The very concept of "loyalty" is painfully elusive. It is defined entirely by a state of mind. Does it mean "my country, right or wrong"? Can a citizen oppose government policies—including a war—and still be "loyal"?

The negative impact on "loyal" Americans—those who were wrongfully discharged, those who resigned rather than submit to the process, those who were chilled in their political expression and activities, those who were degraded and humiliated in their everyday lives—far outweighed any *legitimate* benefit the government derived from the program. The loyalty program stifled meaningful debate, demanded conformity, and discouraged Americans from thinking, reading, talking, or acting in any way that was out of the "mainstream" of contemporary political, cultural, or social thought.

Perhaps most important, it reversed the essential relationship between the citizen and the state in a democratic society. As Madison, Gallatin, Jefferson, and others came to understand during the controversy over the Sedition Act of 1798, the citizens of a self-governing society must be free to think and talk openly and critically about issues of governance. Under the loyalty program, however, it was the *government* that defined which thoughts and ideas would be permitted. Dissenting views, nonconforming opinions, were deemed "disloyal." This reflected an utter lack of confidence in the American people. Nothing "so dangerously corrupts" the integrity of a democracy "as a loss of faith" in its own citizens.

UNITED STATES v. DENNIS

United States Court of Appeals Second Circuit, 1950.
183 F.2d 201.

L. HAND, CIRCUIT JUDGE.

The defendants Dennis and others appeal from a judgment of conviction upon an indictment for violation of Section 3 of the "Smith Act," that is, for "wilfully and knowingly" conspiring to organize the Communist Party of the United States as a group to "teach and advocate the overthrow and destruction" of the government "by force and violence," and "knowingly and wilfully to advocate and teach the duty and necessity of overthrowing and destroying" the government by "force and violence."

* * *

From this wearisome analysis of the decisions of the Supreme Court it has appeared, as we indicated at the outset, that to deprive an utterance of the protection of the Amendment it is not always enough that the purpose of the utterer may include stirring up his hearers to illegal conduct—at least, when the utterance is political. The same utterance may be unprotected, if it be a bare appeal to action, which the Amendment will cover, if it be accompanied by, or incorporated into, utterances addressed to the understanding and seeking to persuade. The phrase, "clear and present danger," has come to be used as a shorthand statement of those among such mixed or compounded utterances which the Amendment does not protect. Yet it is not a *vade mecum;* indeed, from its very words it could not be. It is a way to describe a penumbra of occasions, even the outskirts of which are indefinable, but within which, as is so often the case, the courts must find their way as they can. In each case they must ask whether the gravity of the "evil," discounted by its improbability, justifies such invasion of free speech as is necessary to avoid the danger. We have purposely substituted "improbability" for "remoteness," because that must be the right interpretation. Given the same probability, it would be wholly irrational to condone future evils which we should prevent if they were immediate; that could be reconciled only by an indifference to those who come after us. It is only because a substantial intervening period between the utterance and its realization may check its effect and change its importance, that its immediacy is important; and that, as we have said, was the rationale of the concurrence in *Whitney v. People of State of California, supra*. We can never forecast with certainty; all prophecy is a guess, but the reliability of a guess decreases with the length of the future which it seeks to penetrate. In application of such a standard courts may strike a wrong balance; they may tolerate "incitements" which they should forbid; they may repress utterances they should allow; but that is a responsibility that they cannot avoid. Abdication is as much a failure of duty, as indifference is a failure to protect primal rights.

In the case at bar the defence seems to us to kick the beam. One may reasonably think it wiser in the long run to let an unhappy, bitter outcast vent his venom before any crowds he can muster and in any terms that he wishes, be they as ferocious as he will; one may trust that his patent impotence will be a foil to anything he may propose. Indeed, it is a measure of the confidence of a society in its own stability that it suffers such fustian to go unchecked. Here we are faced with something very different. The American Communist Party, of which the defendants are the controlling spirits, is a highly articulated, well contrived, far spread organization, numbering thousands of adherents, rigidly and ruthlessly disciplined, many of whom are infused with a passionate Utopian faith that is to redeem mankind. It has its Founder, its apostles, its sacred texts—perhaps even its martyrs. It seeks converts far and wide by an extensive system of schooling, demanding of all an inflexible doctrinal orthodoxy. The violent capture of all existing governments is one article of the creed of that faith, which abjures the possibility of success by lawful means. That article, which is a common-place among initiates, is a part of the homiletics for novitiates, although, so far as conveniently it can be, it is covered by an innocent terminology, designed to prevent its disclosure. Our democracy, like any other, must meet that faith and that creed on the merits, or it will perish; and we must not flinch at the challenge. Nevertheless, we may insist that the rules of the game be observed, and the rules confine the conflict to weapons drawn from the universe of discourse. The advocacy of violence may, or may not, fail; but in neither case can there be any "right" to use it.

Revolutions are often "right," but a "right of revolution" is a contradiction in terms, for a society which acknowledged it, could not stop at tolerating conspiracies to overthrow it, but must include their execution. The question before us, and the only one, is how long a government, having discovered such a conspiracy, must wait. When does the conspiracy become a "present danger"? The jury has found that the conspirators will strike as soon as success seems possible, and obviously, no one in his senses would strike sooner. Meanwhile they claim the constitutional privilege of going on indoctrinating their pupils, preparing increasing numbers to pledge themselves to the crusade, and awaiting the moment when we may be so far extended by foreign engagements, so far divided in counsel, or so far in industrial or financial straits, that the chance seems worth trying. That position presupposes that the Amendment assures them freedom for all preparatory steps and in the end the choice of initiative, dependent upon that moment when they believe us, who must await the blow, to be worst prepared to receive it.

We need not say that even so thoroughly planned and so extensive a confederation would be a "present danger" at all times and in all circumstances; the question is how imminent: that is, how probable of execution—it was in the summer of 1948, when the indictment was found. We must not close our eyes to our position in the world at that time. By far the most powerful of all the European nations had been a convert to Communism for over thirty years; its leaders were the most devoted and potent proponents of the faith; no such movement in Europe of East to West had arisen since Islam. Moreover in most of West Europe there were important political Communist factions, always agitating to increase their power; and the defendants were acting in close concert with the movement. The *status quo,* hastily contrived in 1945, was showing strains and tensions, not originally expected. Save for the unexpected success of the airlift, Britain, France and ourselves would have been forced out of Berlin, contrary to our understanding of the convention by which we were there. We had become the object of invective upon invective; we were continuously charged with aggressive designs against other nations; our efforts to reestablish their economic stability were repeatedly set down as a scheme to enslave them; we had been singled out as the chief enemy of the faith; we were the eventually doomed, but the still formidable, protagonist of that decadent system which it was to supplant. Any border fray, any diplomatic incident, any difference in construction of the *modus vivendi*—such as the Berlin blockade we have just mentioned—might prove a spark in the tinder-box, and lead to war. We do not understand how one could ask for a more probable danger, unless we must wait till the actual eve of hostilities. The only justification which can be suggested is that in spite of their efforts to mask their purposes, so far as they can do so consistently with the spread of the gospel, discussion and publicity may so weaken their power that it will have ceased to be dangerous when the moment may come. That may be a proper enough antidote in ordinary times and for less redoubtable combinations; but certainly it does not apply to this one.

Corruptio optimi pessima. True, we must not forget our own faith; we must be sensitive to the dangers that lurk in any choice; but choose we must, and we shall be silly dupes if we forget that again and again in the past thirty years, just such preparations in other conntries have aided to supplant existing governments, when the time was ripe. Nothing short of a revived doctrine of *laissez faire,* which would have amazed even the Manchester School at its apogee, can fail to realize that such a conspiracy creates a danger of the utmost gravity and of enough probability to justify its suppression. We hold that it is a danger "clear and present."

MARTIN H. REDISH, UNLAWFUL ADVOCACY AND FREE SPEECH THEORY: RETHINKING THE LESSONS OF THE MCCARTHY ERA

73 U.Cin.L.Rev. 9 (2004).

To historians, the Cold War in recent years has become quite hot. More than twenty years after the historical book on the so-called "McCarthy era" of the late 1940s and early 1950s in the United States appeared to have been irrevocably sealed, startling revelations in the 1990s of previously secret documents—documents whose very existence was unknown except to a very few—appeared dramatically to alter well accepted understandings of historians about this troubled period in American history. During that era, when the nation first began to grasp the gravity of the threat posed by the Soviet Union and the Eastern Bloc nations to our national security, both the government and private institutions imposed extensive and severe punishment on American Communists, and often on any American who at one time had been a Communist or even suspected of being a Communist and failed to repudiate those connections.

Once the McCarthy era ended, historians vigorously debated whether such suppression was ever justified by anything other than the nation's naked ideological repugnance for Communism. Many concluded that, whatever dangers the Soviet Union and its allies may have presented, American Communists caused no real threat to our internal security. Rather, the expression of national security concerns was merely a subterfuge, strategically designed to justify the persecution of those who held repugnant political views. Others, however, continued to see American Communists as nothing more than a tool of Joseph Stalin and the Soviet Union. In the words of a respected group of historians, "[t]o their admirers and defenders, American Communists [were] usually . . . seen as idealistic and committed radical populists. They built unions, fought for racial and social equality, and battled fascism, often prodding their reluctant fellow citizens to live up to America's democratic ideals." However, "[t]o their enemies, American Communists were 'soldiers of Stalin,' committed to a totalitarian philosophy and willing to alter their political stance whenever it suited the foreign policy needs of the Soviet Union."

By the early 1970s, the view that American Communists had presented no real threat became the dominant position among American historians. The fears of the dangers presented by American Communists that had dominated American society during the period in question were generally "dismissed as the product of paranoid fears created by third-rate spy novels." Certainly, those scholars who adopted this so-called "revisionist" view argued, whatever minimal threat to which the Communist Party of the United States of America (CPUSA) actually gave rise failed to justify the widespread suppression of American Communists that took place during the period in question. The true rationale for the suppression of American Communists, according to the revisionists, was not really a threat to national security, but rather the ideological offensiveness of the views expressed by American Communists.

* * *

For much of the latter part of the twentieth century, this view was so widely accepted that few scholars bothered to challenge it seriously. As the last decade of the century dawned, this well accepted view was about to change dramatically. It was the revelation of two sets of previously unavailable documents, one in the United States and one in the former Soviet Union, that jolted the relatively peaceful world of mid-twentieth century American political history. While "[t]he revisionists . . . either denied or downplayed arguments about what others have described as the dark side of American communism," these documents, according to the historians who initially reviewed them, "provide[d] a powerful challenge to the revisionist perspective."

The first set of documents to be made known to the world in the 1990s were the so-called Comintern documents, named after the entity in the Soviet Union that for many years had supervised Communist parties throughout the world. The documents were made available, in a limited manner, to selected American historians by the Russian government following the fall of the Soviet Union. After the revelations of Comintern were made known, "[i]t [was] no longer possible to maintain that the Soviet Union did not fund the American party, that the CPUSA did not maintain a covert apparatus, and that key leaders and cadres were innocent of connection with Soviet espionage."[13] These documents established that the CPUSA had never functioned as an independent political organization. Indeed, according to the historians who reviewed the documents, apparently "there was never a time when the CPUSA made its decisions autonomously, without being obliged to answer to or—more precisely—without wishing to answer to Soviet authority."

An even more startling historical jolt came in 1995, with the declassification of the highly secret Venona documents. These were previously unknown decryptions of cable messages sent by agents of the Soviet intelligence service, the KGB, in America back to officials in Moscow. The United States had originally begun the secret decryption

13. [Harvey Klehr et al., The Soviet World of American Communism 18 (1998).]

program in 1943, in order to determine whether the Soviet Union was seriously pursuing a separate peace with Nazi Germany. By the time that American intelligence officials had deciphered the first messages in 1946, the war was over and the program's initial goal therefore rendered superfluous. What the United States agents learned, however, proved far more important than an answer to the original inquiry. In the words of historians Haynes and Klehr, "[e]spionage, not diplomacy, was the subject of these cables."[15] The United States discovered that since 1942, the nation had been targeted by an intense and widespread Soviet espionage program that had utilized numerous professional Soviet agents and hundreds of Americans, often taken from the ranks of the CPUSA's so-called "secret apparatus"-cadres of specially recruited and American Communists who were fiercely loyal to the Party and its goals.

The revelation of the Comintern documents and the release of the Venona documents dramatically altered the historical topography of the McCarthy period. Anti–Communist scholars have now begun a revisionist effort of their own, defending the persecution of the CPUSA and, in some instances, attempting to resurrect Senator McCarthy's tattered reputation. No longer could liberal historians reasonably maintain that governmental oppression of American Communists lacked any basis in reality. The Comintern documents demonstrated that since its inception, the Communist Party in America had been heavily influenced, if not totally controlled, by the Soviet Union. While certain left-leaning hard liners remain unconvinced, for the most part scholars have conceded that the Venona documents establish that American Communists had engaged in substantial espionage activity, passing on secret or classified information to Soviet agents and facilitating Soviet espionage in other ways throughout much of the 1930s and 1940s.

* * *

One may reasonably wonder why, if the American Communist leaders were vulnerable to prosecutions for espionage, the government instead chose to prosecute them for the constitutionally far more questionable Smith Act violations. While there appears to be no clear answer to this question, several possibilities readily come to mind. Initially, one may speculate that the FBI was concerned that bringing numerous prosecutions for espionage would have required exposure of relevant Venona documents and thereby threatened the secrecy of the decryption program. Even if this were true, however, the fact does not justify sweeping violations of First Amendment rights through resort to alternative prosecutions.

Another possible explanation is that espionage prosecutions would not have taken the FBI from point A to its intended point B. [FBI Director J. Edgar] Hoover's goal was clearly "to establish the illegal status of the Communist Party of the United States of America." While

15. [John Earl Haynes & Harvey Klehr, Venona: Decoding Soviet Espionage in America 9 (1999).]

individualized prosecutions for espionage or the facilitation of espionage would no doubt have caused serious political harm to the party, they would not necessarily have had the practical impact of outlawing its very existence. Though the Smith Act prosecutions did not have that effect as a technical matter, they clearly came far closer than espionage prosecutions would have.

Finally, it is important not to ignore the implicit message sent to the public at large by the very fact of the Smith Act prosecutions. As already noted, those prosecutions sought to punish neither espionage, attempted overthrow, nor even the beginnings of an organized effort to make preparations for an attempted overthrow. Rather, they punished those who had organized a group that engaged in and dispensed unpopular political thought, and may have contemplated the abstract possibility of violent overthrow. The message to the nation, though never stated explicitly, seems to have been quite clear: "Engage in unpopular political thought at your own risk." This was a strategic benefit that Hoover never could have hoped for from prosecutions for far more extreme behavior, such as espionage, in which most Americans would never even consider engaging.

PALLAVI GUNIGANTI, ALEXANDER MEIKLEJOHN: TEACHER AND CITIZEN

Alexander Meiklejohn was born in Rochdale, England on February 3, 1872, the youngest of eight sons and the only one not to have been born in Scotland, a disability for which his brothers teased him incessantly. His parents, James and Elizabeth Meiklejohn, had moved from Dunipace, Scotland so that his father, a textile worker, could be close to the new technologies in his industry. Rochdale provided an early model for the kind of community Alexander Meiklejohn later would seek to create: a workers' cooperative in which membership was open, each household had one equal vote regardless of how many shares it held, and all profits were redistributed in proportion to shares held. The Rochdale Society of Equitable Pioneers' motto was "All who contribute to the realization of wealth ought to participate in its distribution." There was a great deal of social interaction and political discussion, and no religious discrimination.

Despite his enthusiasm for the cooperative, James Meiklejohn decided that in order to provide a better life for his large family, they should move to New England and take advantage of the post-Civil War demand there for experienced textile workers. They sailed for America in 1880, and spent four years in Appanoag, Rhode Island before settling in Pawtucket. There the Clan Fraser and Congregational Church served as the Meiklejohns' Scottish community, a substitute for the Rochdale cooperative. The family flourished economically. Alexander played sports enthusiastically. However, as Scottish tradition designated the youngest son of a family to be the scholar, he also excelled in his schoolwork while his older brothers went to work. His high school valedictorian speech, defending Pawtucket's prohibition of alcohol, evidenced an early belief that a democratic society can limit certain behavioral liberties in the interests of social welfare.

The whole family pooled its resources to send Alexander to Brown University, where he continued as a student-athlete. His 1889–1893 matriculation put him in the middle of the school's transition from a required "classical" curriculum that emphasized the humanities and character development to the science-heavy elective system, a fashion that was sweeping the Ivy League. Meiklejohn thought the new curriculum was too anarchic, disjointed and confusing. He found refuge in Brown's philosophy department, which at the time held Kant in particularly high esteem. He was valedictorian of his college class as well. His May 1893 commencement oration delved into Goethe's *Faust* and concluded, "The Christian creed does tell us of God's love, but so does every form of faith reveal to its worshippers the eternal truths ... The Christian faith is true, but it is not and cannot be the Truth."

Meiklejohn remained at Brown to get his master's degree in philosophy on the advice of the school's president, Elisha Benjamin Andrews. The reasons for this recommendation were not as flattering as might be supposed. President Andrews told his prize student: "A Scot has to love either whiskey or philosophy. Since you don't love whiskey, your decision is made for you." Meiklejohn transferred his graduate work to Cornell when his favorite professor, James Seth, took an appointment there. He continued to play sports, and helped to bring Canadian ice hockey to the United States. Meiklejohn's Ph.D. dissertation was entitled "Kant's Theory of Substance." President Andrews hired him back to Brown's philosophy department in the fall of 1897, where he eschewed lectures in favor of teaching by means of Socratic dialogue. He moved back into his parents' house, contributing most of his income to the family. He won election to the local school board seat that his father had once held. In the fall of 1901, at the age of 29, Meiklejohn accepted the position of Dean of Men at Brown. The next June, he married a young woman he had met at Cornell, Nannine La Villa. During the next several years, the couple had three sons. Meiklejohn later joked that he had better luck in teaching hockey to his sons than philosophy to his students.

As dean until 1912, he was involved with admissions, discipline, athletics and social life. He strove to help young men from working-class backgrounds—like his own—find the resources to attend college. Meiklejohn considered their representation in the student body necessary to a democratic college community. He believed in strict and fair discipline, in order to shape students into men capable of self-government. He always listened to a misbehaver's side of the story before punishing him. Meiklejohn's interests in athletics and ethics converged when Brown revoked its rule against having students who had played professional sports play on its amateur teams. He wrote an article for Harper's Weekly about how athletics was beginning to commercialize universities, and how the win-at-all-costs attitude was detrimental to student-athletes' character. His bold cure for the corruption was to turn athletics over to the students themselves. He called a college meeting, modeled on New England town meetings, in which he strove to persuade the students of his view. They agreed to retain the amateur rule for the current year, but disappointed Meiklejohn by voting to permit "summer ball" for college athletes the next year. He considered this a democratically made decision that repudiated the democratic integrity of the school.

Still, he continued to push for democratic education. His spring 1908 article, "College Education and the Moral Ideal," invoked philosophy in determining what progressive teachers should do. "If Kant is right, then the function of the college is not to do what it is told, but to study deeply into the art of living, to see what is needed in human experience, and to send men out instructed and inspired by the possession of the best things of which our human nature is capable." At this time, the major controversy at Brown was student-owned and run fraternities, which Meiklejohn thought—despite having been a member of the academically-oriented Theta Delta Chi— tended to isolate members from the rest of the student body and thus impede the sense of unity and democracy. The fraternities also often kept their members from pursuing any serious intellectual goals due to the demands of social life and contempt for academics, as Meiklejohn revealed by publishing their academic rankings. These reforms attracted attention, and as a result the trustees at Amherst College offered Meiklejohn the presidency there. He left Brown with a parting admonition that students must remember the real purpose of their education: "don't be afraid to think and to think hard."

Meiklejohn was inaugurated as Amherst's eighth president on October 16, 1912. He was popular with many of the students for instituting a student council and an open feedback system which he used to make changes to the curriculum. Students also enjoyed his progressive sermons, which generally were inspired by texts other than the Bible. In January 1914, he announced a new core curriculum, "(1) to put an end to the mere 'smattering' of elective courses" and "(2) to unite all the students in the general task of getting a unified knowledge of human life and experience." His plan for the study of Social and Economic Institutions was revised by the older faculty into an elective freshman survey. A student described the shift that had occurred in just a few years thus: "Before Meiklejohn, we sat on the porch at Psi Upsilon, put our feet up on the rail, drank, and talked about fraternities, dates, and sports. When Meiklejohn had been around for a while, we sat on the Psi U porch, drank and talked about fraternities, dates, sports, Epictetus, labor unions, and the problems of the liberal college."

Meiklejohn's daughter was born in December 1916 amid growing apprehension that the U.S. would join the war raging in Europe. He objected to seeing the college turned into an instrument of the developing military machinery. Even after the declaration of war in 1917, Meiklejohn urged his students not to forget their obligation to think, even as they obeyed the law and answered the call of military duty. The War Department demanded his help in rooting out "subversive and seditious activities," including any disapproved political beliefs among the faculty, which were to be reported to the National Security League, a nongovernmental agency. Meiklejohn was outraged at this and at Columbia University's firing of two professors for participating in antiwar activities. During the postwar recession and labor unrest, he opposed the use of students as strikebreakers. In the fall of 1920 he helped to open a new school for workers, at which they studied texts that included Marx and Lenin among many other thinkers, and discussed topics like "Protective Legislation."

Ten years into his presidency, in June of 1923, the Amherst faculty passed a resolution calling for Meiklejohn's resignation. He had lost the support of his faculty for a variety of reasons: his innovative ideas regarding curriculum and teaching methods, his opposition to the emphasis on athletics, his recruitment of younger faculty members whose views and methods troubled the senior faculty, and his extravagance in running the president's residence with six servants. The college's trustees asked Meiklejohn to resign, which he did. To protest his dismissal, thirteen graduating seniors refused their diplomas at that year's commencement; eight faculty members resigned. Upon leaving Amherst, Meiklejohn commenced a career as a writer and public speaker living in New York City. A few years later, in 1925, his wife Nannine died of cancer.

The next year, Meiklejohn became a philosophy professor at the University of Wisconsin. In his first class, he told the undergraduates, "I abominate lectures. The only way to really learn this subject is by having you talk; and if you won't discuss, we'll just have to wait until somebody does talk." His plan for an Experimental College received nationwide media attention, and the Wisconsin state legislature guaranteed it two years of financial support. In June 1926, Meiklejohn married Helen Everett, the daughter of a former Brown colleague, who had a doctorate in labor policy and had investigated WWI factory conditions by working in them herself. The Experimental College admitted its first class in the fall of 1927, with its first year curriculum focusing textually on the civilization of ancient Athens as an early democratic community, but with the discussion focusing on questions that were equally applicable to modern America. The College was considered a success in educational circles, but the radicalism of some of its students created tensions in Wisconsin. Combined with the budget cuts necessitated by the Depression, this led the University of Wisconsin to close the Experimental College in May 1932.

Meiklejohn continued to hold an appointment at Wisconsin until 1938, but he took a sabbatical from teaching in 1933 to move to Berkeley and begin working in adult education there, a project for which he was granted an additional two semesters' leave. It was his first role as an educator wholly outside academia; as Time Magazine put it, "Dr. Meiklejohn will help radicals, businessmen, teachers, artists, laborers, preachers and scientists in scrutinizing contemporary civilization and its problems." The San Francisco School of Social Studies became part of the adult education movement of the 1930s, as the demand for inexpensive and self-improving leisure activity boomed due to the high level of unemployment. The only entrance requirements were affirmative answers to Helen Everett–Meiklejohn's queries: "Do you have the inclination to study? Can you come regularly to group meetings? Will you participate in the discussion?"

Meiklejohn helped to establish a chapter of the American Civil Liberties Union in Northern California in the winter of 1934. The following summer, he submitted an article to *Harper's Magazine* entitled, "Liberty—For What?" In it, he declared that the freedom to manage one's property without interference had taken precedence in America over the principles of "liberty, equality and fraternity [that] were essential to the spirit of liberal democracy." His book *What Does America Mean?* discussed the theme of the article in greater depth. Justice Louis Brandeis praised the work, observing that Meiklejohn had "said to Americans the things they most need to hear." However, Meiklejohn and the San Francisco School began falling under ideological suspicion; the American Legion's spies who participated in adult discussion groups decided that the school was "a breeding ground for Communists." In 1938 a new era began when the United States House of Representatives created the House Un–American Activities Committee. Meiklejohn criticized the committee as a threat to free speech. He asked, "What do we, as Americans, propose to do about opinions which many of us deeply and passionately condemn?" He concluded, "So far as minds are concerned, the art of democracy is the art of thinking independently together."

In June 1940, Congress took a step further by passing the Smith Act, which prohibited advocating the violent overthrow of the U.S. government, and required all citizens who joined certain organizations to register with a federal agency. Meiklejohn, along with John Dewey, Felix Frankfurter and Norman Thomas, sat on the national board of the American Civil Liberties Union. When the organization attempted to comply with the Smith Act by kicking out Communists, he was the only one among them to protest. His petition stated, "The heart of democracy is civil liberty for everybody without distinction up to the point of unlawful activities, committed or attempted." In October 1940, UC–Berkeley terminated the contract of a professor who supported and discussed the Communist Party in his classes. Meiklejohn considered the firing a hypocritical betrayal of the University's mission, which he deemed to be "preaching and teaching democratic freedom."

By 1945, Meiklejohn's radical reputation had been rehabilitated sufficiently that the Assistant Secretary of State asked him to be a delegate to the United Nations Educational, Scientific and Cultural Organization (UNESCO). However, he still insisted on challenging orthodoxies. In his Walgreen Lectures, delivered at the University of Chicago, Yale, and St. John's College, Meiklejohn argued that the First Amendment requires absolute freedom to express opinions. He criticized Justice Holmes's clear-and-present-danger test as untrue to that fundamental principle. The lectures were published in 1948 as *Free Speech and its Relation to Self–Government.* That book, together with several articles about the First Amendment that Meiklejohn wrote in its wake, has had a lasting impact on the development of modern First Amendment thought. Throughout the McCarthy Era, Meiklejohn fought for his beliefs about free speech on a variety of issues and in numerous public forums. He came to the defense of the Hollywood Ten, writing an amicus brief that claimed films were a medium of public education and thus should be protected from congressional investigation.

In November of 1954 the United States Senate condemned Senator Joseph McCarthy. In the spring of 1955, the Senate Judiciary Committee's Subcommittee on Constitutional Rights began investigating the abuses of HUAC. Meiklejohn, along with Professor Chafee and other leading First Amendment scholars, testified before that subcommittee on November 14, 1955. In his testimony, Meiklejohn spelled out before the senators his view that the First Amendment provides for absolute protection to express opinions. Meiklejohn joined the National Campaign to Abolish the House Un–American Activities Committee. His efforts received a setback in 1959 when by a vote of 5–4 the Supreme Court ruled in *Barenblatt v. United States* that HUAC could compel a man to answer whether he had ever been a member of the Communist Party. Meiklejohn published his scathing criticism of the decision in the University of Chicago Law Review. His scholarly protest had no effect on the Court majority, however: one year later, the Justices upheld the contempt conviction of Meiklejohn's friend, Frank Wilkinson, for refusing to answer HUAC's questions.

Meiklejohn was honored by lectureships named for him at Brown and at the University of Wisconsin. He was able to travel to Brown to hear Justice William O. Douglas deliver the inaugural Meiklejohn Lecture. The American Association of University Professors established the annual Alexander Meiklejohn Freedom Award in 1958. On December 6, 1963, Meiklejohn received from President Lyndon B. Johnson the Presidential Medal of Freedom, an honor for which he had been selected by President John F. Kennedy.

Alexander Meiklejohn died in Berkeley, California, on December 17, 1964, at the age of 92. Among the many memorial tributes was this from Harry Kalven, Jr.:

> I have always suspected that Socrates, however wise and admirable, would have made a trying and difficult companion. "Alec" was a Socrates who wore well, a Socrates it was fun to be with, a Socrates for all seasons.

ALEXANDER MEIKLEJOHN, FREE SPEECH AND ITS RELATION TO SELF–GOVERNMENT

(1948).

We Americans think of ourselves as politically free. We believe in self-government. If men are to be governed, we say, then that governing must be done, not by others, but by themselves. So far, therefore, as our own affairs are concerned, we refuse to submit to alien control. That refusal, if need be, we will carry to the point of rebellion, of revolution. And if other men, within the jurisdiction of our laws, are denied their right to political freedom, we will, in the same spirit, rise to their defense. Governments, we insist, derive their just powers from the consent of the governed. If that consent be lacking, governments have no just powers.

* * *

Now, this political program of ours, though passionately advocated by us, is not—as we all recognize—fully worked out in practice. Over one hundred and seventy years have gone by since the Declaration of Independence was written. But, to an unforgivable degree, citizens of the United States are still subjected to decisions in the making of which they have had no effective share. So far as that is true, we are not self-governed; we are not politically free. We are governed by others. And, perhaps worse, we are, without their consent, the governors of others.

* * *

What, then, is the difference between a political system in which men do govern themselves and a political system in which men, without their consent, are governed by others? Unless we can make clear that distinction, discussion of freedom of speech or of any other freedom is meaningless and futile.

Alien government, we have said, is simple in idea. It is easy to understand. When one man or some self-chosen group holds control, without consent, over others, the relation between them is one of force and counterforce, of compulsion on the one hand and submission or resistance on the other. That relation is external and mechanical. It can be expressed in numbers—numbers of guns or planes or dollars or machines or policemen. The only basic fact is that one group "has the power" and the other group has not. In such a despotism, a ruler, by some excess of strength or guile or both, without the consent of his subjects, forces them into obedience. And in order to understand what he does, what they do, we need only measure the strength or weakness of the control and the strength or weakness of the resistance to it.

But government by consent—self-government—is not thus simple.

* * *

And the crux of the difficulty lies in the fact that, in such a society, the governors and the governed are not two distinct groups of persons. There is only one group—the self-governing people. Rulers and ruled are the same individuals. We, the People, are our own masters, our own subjects. But that inner relationship of men to themselves is utterly different in kind from the external relationship of one man to another. It cannot be expressed in terms of forces and compulsions. If we attempt to think about the political procedures of self-government by means of the ideas which are useful in describing the external control of a hammer over a nail or of a master over his slaves, the meaning slips through the fingers of our minds. For thinking which is done merely in terms of forces, political freedom does not exist.

* * *

Political freedom does not mean freedom from control. It means self-control. If, for example, a nation becomes involved in war, the government must decide who shall be drafted to leave his family and home, to risk his life, his health, his sanity, upon the battlefield. The government must also levy and collect and expend taxes. In general, it must determine how far and in what ways the customs and privileges of peace are to be swept aside. In all these cases it may be taken for granted that, in a self-governing society, minorities will disagree with the decisions which are made. May a minority man, then, by appeal to the principle of "consent," refuse to submit to military control? May he evade payment of taxes which he thinks unwise or unjust? May he say, "I did not approve of this measure; therefore, as a self-governing man, I claim the right to disobey it"?

Certainly not! At the bottom of every plan of self-government is a basic agreement, in which all the citizens have joined, that all matters of public policy shall be decided by corporate action, that such decisions shall be equally binding on all citizens, whether they agree with them or not, and that, if need be, they shall, by due legal procedure, be enforced upon anyone who refuses to conform to them. The man who rejects that agreement is not objecting to tyranny or despotism. He is objecting to political freedom.

* * *

I have been saying that, under the plan of political freedom, we maintain by common consent a government which, being stronger than any one of us, than any group of us, can take control over all of us. But the word "control" strikes terror into the hearts of many "free" men, especially if they are mechanically minded about their freedom. Out of that fear there arises the passionate demand that the government which controls us must itself be controlled. By whom, and in what ways?

In abstract principle, that question is easy to answer. A government of free men can properly be controlled only by itself. Who else could be trusted by us to hold our political institutions in check? Shall any single individual or any special group be allowed to take domination over the agencies of control? There is only one situation in which free men can answer "yes" to that question. If the government, as an institution, has broken down, if the basic agreement has collapsed, then both the right and the duty of rebellion are thrust upon the individual citizens. In that chaotic and desperate situation they must, for the sake of a new order, revolt and destroy, as the American colonies in 1776 revolted and destroyed. But, short of such violent lawlessness in the interest of a new law, there can be no doubt that a free government must be its own master. If We, the People are to be controlled, then We, the People must do the controlling. As a corporate body, we must exercise control over our separate members. That principle is a flat denial of the suggestion that we, acting as an unorganized and irresponsible mob, may drive into submission ourselves acting as an organized government. What it means is that the body politic, organized as a nation, must recognize its own limitations of wisdom and of temper and of circumstance, and must, therefore, make adequate provision for self-criticism and self-restraint. The government itself must limit the government, must determine what it may and may not do. It must make sure that its attempts to make men free do not result in making them slaves.

* * *

As we proceed now to reflect upon the relations of a thinking and speaking individual to the government which guards his freedom, we may do well to turn back for a few moments to the analysis of those relations given by Plato. The Athenian philosopher of the fourth century B.C. was himself caught in our paradox. He saw the connection between self-government and intelligence with a clarity and wisdom and wit which have never been excelled. In his two short dialogues, the *Apology* and the *Crito,* he grapples with the problem which we are facing.

In both dialogues, Plato is considering the right which a government has to demand obedience from its citizens. And in both dialogues, Socrates, a thinker and teacher who had aroused Plato from dogmatic slumber, is the citizen whose relations are discussed. The question is whether or not Socrates is in duty bound to obey the government. In the *Apology* the answer is "No." In the *Crito* the answer is "Yes." Plato is obviously using one of the favorite devices of the teacher. He is seeming to contradict himself. He is thereby demanding of his pupils that they save themselves and him from contradiction by making clear a basic and elusive distinction.

In the *Apology,* Socrates is on trial for his life. The charge against him is that in his teaching he has "corrupted the youth" and has "denied the Gods." On the evidence presented by a kind of un-Athenian Subversive Activities Committee he is found guilty. His judges do not wish to put him to death, but they warn him that, unless he will agree to stop his teaching or to change its tenor, they must order his execution. And to this demand for obedience to a decree abridging his freedom of speech, Socrates replies with a flat and unequivocal declaration of disobedient independence. My teaching, he says, is not, in that sense, under the abridging control of the government. Athens is a free city. No official, no judge, he declares, may tell me what I shall, or shall not, teach or think. He recognizes that the government has the power and the legal right to put him to death. But so far as the content of his teaching is concerned, he claims unqualified independence. "Congress shall make no law abridging the freedom of speech," he seems to be saying. Present-day Americans who wish to understand the meaning, the human intention, expressed by the First Amendment, would do well to read and to ponder again Plato's *Apology,* written in Athens twenty-four centuries ago. It may well be argued that if the *Apology* had not been written—by Plato or by someone else—the First Amendment would not have been written. The relation here is one of trunk and branch.

But the argument of the *Crito* seems, at least, to contradict that of the *Apology.* Here Socrates, having been condemned to death, is in prison awaiting the carrying out of the sentence. His friend Crito urges him to escape, to evade the punishment. This he refuses to do. He has no right, he says, to disobey the decision of the government that he must drink the hemlock. That government has legal authority over the life and death of its citizens. Even though it is mistaken, and, therefore, unjust, they must, in this field, conform to its decisions. For Socrates, obedience to the laws which would abridge his life is here quite as imperative as was disobedience to laws which would abridge his belief and the expression of it. In passages of amazing beauty and insight, Socrates explains that duty to Crito. He represents himself as conversing with The Laws of Athens about the compact into which they and he have entered. The Laws, he says, remind him that for seventy years, he has "consented" to them, has accepted from them all the rights and privileges of an Athenian citizen. Will he now, they ask, because his own life is threatened, withdraw his consent, annul the compact? To do that would be a shameful thing, unworthy of a citizen of Athens.

Plato is too great a teacher to formulate for us, or for his more immediate pupils, the distinction which he is here drawing. He demands of us that we make it for ourselves. But that there is a distinction and that the understanding of it is essential for the practice of freedom, he asserts passionately and without equivocation. If the government attempts to limit the freedom of a man's opinions, he tells us, that man, and his fellows with him, has both the right and the duty of disobedience. But if, on the other hand, by regular legal procedure, his life or his property is required of him, he must submit; he must let them go willingly. In one phase of man's activities, the government may exercise control over him. In another phase, it may not. What, then, are those two phases? Only as we see clearly the distinction between them, Plato is saying, do we know what government by consent of the governed means.

The difficulties of the paradox of freedom as applied to speech may perhaps be lessened if we now examine the procedure of the traditional American town meeting. That institution is commonly, and rightly, regarded as a model by which free political procedures may be measured. It is self-government in its simplest, most obvious form.

In the town meeting the people of a community assemble to discuss and to act upon matters of public interest—roads, schools, poorhouses, health, external defense, and the like. Every man is free to come. They meet as political equals. Each has a right and a duty to think his own thoughts, to express them, and to listen to the arguments of others. The basic principle is that the freedom of speech shall be unabridged. And yet the meeting cannot even be opened unless, by common consent, speech is abridged. A chairman or moderator is, or has been, chosen. He "calls the meeting to order." And the hush which follows that call is a clear indication that restrictions upon speech have been set up. The moderator assumes, or arranges, that in the conduct of the business, certain rules of order will be observed. Except as he is overruled by the meeting as a whole, he will enforce those rules. His business on its negative side is to abridge speech. For example, it is usually agreed that no one shall speak unless "recognized by the chair." Also, debaters must confine their remarks to "the question before the house." If one man "has the floor," no one else may interrupt him except as provided by the rules. The meeting has assembled, not primarily to talk, but primarily by means of talking to get business done. And the talking must be regulated and abridged as the doing of the business under actual conditions may require. If a speaker wanders from the point at issue, if he is abusive or in other ways threatens to defeat the purpose of the meeting, he may be and should be declared "out of order." He must then stop speaking, at least in that way. And if he persists in breaking the rules, he may be "denied the floor" or, in the last resort, "thrown out" of the meeting. The town meeting, as it seeks for freedom of public discussion of public problems, would be wholly ineffectual unless speech were thus abridged. It is not a Hyde Park. It is a parliament or congress. It is a group of free and equal men, cooperating in a common enterprise, and using for that enterprise responsible and regulated discussion. It is not a dialectical free-for-all. It is self-government.

These speech-abridging activities of the town meeting indicate what the First Amendment to the Constitution does not forbid. When self-governing men demand freedom of speech they are not saying that every individual has an unalienable right to speak whenever, wherever, however he chooses. They do not declare that any man may talk as he pleases, when he pleases, about what he pleases, about whom he pleases, to whom he pleases. The common sense of any reasonable society would deny the existence of that unqualified right. No one, for example, may, without consent of nurse or doctor, rise up in a sickroom to argue for his principles or his candidate. In the sickroom, that question is not "before the house." The discussion is, therefore, "out of order." To you who now listen to my words, it is allowable to differ with me, but it is not allowable for you to state that difference in words until I have finished my reading. Anyone who would thus irresponsibly interrupt the activities of a lecture, a hospital, a concert hall, a church, a machine shop, a classroom, a football field, or a home, does not thereby exhibit his freedom. Rather, he shows himself to be a boor, a public nuisance, who must be abated, by force if necessary.

What, then, does the First Amendment forbid? Here again the town meeting suggests an answer. That meeting is called to discuss and, on the basis of such discussion, to decide matters of public policy. For example, shall there be a school? Where shall it be located? Who shall teach? What shall be taught? The community has agreed that such questions as these shall be freely discussed and that, when the discussion is ended, decision upon them will be made by vote of the citizens. Now, in that method of political self-government, the point of ultimate interest is not the words of the speakers, but the minds of the hearers. The final aim of the meeting is the voting of wise decisions. The voters, therefore, must be made as wise as possible. The welfare of the community requires that those who decide issues shall understand them. They must know what they are voting about. And this, in turn, requires that so far as time allows, all facts and interests relevant to the problem shall be fully and fairly presented to the meeting. Both facts and interests must be given in such a way that all the alternative lines of action can be wisely measured in relation to one another. As the self-governing community seeks, by the method of voting, to gain wisdom in action, it can find it only in the minds of its individual citizens. If they fail, it fails. That is why freedom of discussion for those minds may not be abridged.

The First Amendment, then, is not the guardian of unregulated talkativeness. It does not require that, on every occasion, every citizen shall take part in public debate. Nor can it even give assurance that everyone shall have opportunity to do so. If, for example, at a town meeting, twenty like-minded citizens have become a "party," and if one of them has read to the meeting an argument which they have all approved, it would be ludicrously out of order for each of the others to insist on reading it again. No competent moderator would tolerate that wasting of the time available for free discussion. What is essential is not that everyone shall speak, but that everything worth saying shall be said. To this end, for example, it may be arranged that each of the known conflicting points of view shall have, and shall be limited to, an assigned share of the time available. But however it be arranged, the vital point, as stated negatively, is that no suggestion of policy shall be denied a hearing because it is on one side of the issue rather than another. And this means that though citizens may, on other grounds, be barred from speaking, they may not be barred because their views are thought to be false or dangerous. No plan of action shall be outlawed because someone in control thinks it unwise, unfair, un-American. No speaker may be declared "out of order" because we disagree with what he intends to say. And the reason for this equality of status in the field of ideas lies deep in the very foundations of the self-governing process. When men govern themselves, it is they—and no one else—who must pass judgment upon unwisdom and unfairness and danger. And that means that unwise ideas must have a hearing as well as wise ones, unfair as well as fair, dangerous as well as safe, un-American as well as American. Just so far as, at any point, the citizens who are to decide an issue are denied acquaintance with information or opinion or doubt or disbelief or criticism which is relevant to that issue, just so far the result must be ill-considered, ill-balanced planning for the general good. *It is that mutilation of the thinking process of the community against which the First Amendment to the Constitution is directed.* The principle of the freedom of speech springs from the necessities of the program of self-government. It is not a Law of Nature or of Reason in the abstract. It is a deduction from the basic American agreement that public issues shall be decided by universal suffrage.

* * *

By the relevant clause of the Fifth Amendment we are told that no person within the jurisdiction of the laws of the United States may be "deprived of life, liberty, or property, without due process of law." And, whatever may have been the original reference of the term "liberty," as used in that sentence when it was written, it has been, in recent times, construed by the Supreme Court to include "the liberty of speech." The Fifth Amendment is, then, saying that the people of the United States have a civil liberty of speech which, by due legal process, the government may limit or suppress. But this means that, under the Bill of Rights, there are two freedoms, or liberties, of speech, rather than only one. There is a "freedom of speech" which the First Amendment declares to be non-abridgable. But there is also a "liberty of speech" which the Fifth Amendment declares to be abridgable. And for the inquiry in which we are engaged, the distinction between these two, the fact that there are two, is of fundamental importance. The Fifth Amendment, it appears, has to do with a class of utterances concerning which the legislature may, legitimately, raise the question, "Shall they be endured?" The First Amendment, on the other hand, has to do with a class of utterances concerning which that question may never legitimately be raised. And if that be true, then the problem which Mr. Holmes has suggested—that of separating two classes of utterances—becomes the problem of defining the difference between, and the relation between, the First and Fifth amendments, so far as they deal with matters of speech.

The nature of this difference comes to light if we note that the "liberty" of speech which is subject to abridgment is correlated, in the Fifth Amendment, with our rights to "life" and "property." These are private rights. They are individual possessions. And there can be no doubt that among the many forms of individual action and possession which are protected by the Constitution—not from regulation, but from undue regulation—the right to speak one's mind as one chooses is esteemed by us as one of our most highly cherished private possessions. Individuals have, then, a private right of speech which may on occasion be denied or limited, though such limitations may not be imposed unnecessarily or unequally. So says the Fifth Amendment. But this limited guarantee of the freedom of a man's wish to speak is radically different in intent from the unlimited guarantee of the freedom of public discussion, which is given by the First Amendment. The latter, correlating the freedom of speech in which it is interested with the freedom of religion, of press, of assembly, of petition for redress of grievances, places all these alike beyond the reach of legislative limitation, beyond even the due process of law. With regard to them, Congress has no negative powers whatever. There are, then, in the theory of the Constitution, two radically different kinds of utterances. The constitutional status of a merchant advertising his wares, of a paid lobbyist fighting for the advantage of his client, is utterly different from that of a citizen who is planning for the general welfare. And from this it follows that the Constitution provides differently for two different kinds of "freedom of speech."

* * *

The felt need of an individual to speak on a given occasion may be contrary to the common good. And, in that case, the private need, under proper safeguards, must give way. But the First Amendment, as noted in our first lecture, is not saying that any man may talk whenever and wherever he chooses. It is not dealing with that private issue. It is saying that, as interests, the integrity of public discussion and the care for the public safety are identical. We Americans, in choosing our form of government, have made, at this point, a momentous decision. We have decided to be self-governed. We have measured the dangers and the values of the suppression of the freedom of public inquiry and debate. And, on the basis of that measurement, having regard for the public safety, we have decided that the destruction of freedom is always unwise, that freedom is always expedient. The conviction recorded by that decision is not a sentimental vagary about the "natural rights" of individuals. It is a reasoned and sober judgment as to the best available method of guarding the public safety. We, the People, as we plan for the general welfare, do not choose to be "protected" from the "search for truth." On the contrary, we have adopted it as our "way of life," our method of doing the work of governing for which, as citizens, we are responsible. Shall we, then, as practitioners of freedom, listen to ideas which, being opposed to our own, might destroy confidence in our form of government? Shall we give a hearing to those who hate and despise freedom, to those who, if they had the power, would destroy our institutions? Certainly, yes! Our action must be guided, not by their principles, but by ours. We listen, not because they desire to speak, but because we need to hear. If there are arguments against our theory of government, our policies in war or in peace, we the citizens, the rulers, must hear and consider them for ourselves. That is the way of public safety. It is the program of self-government.

* * *

When men decide to be self-governed, to take control of their behavior, the search for truth is not merely one of a number of interests which may be "balanced," on equal terms, against one another. In that enterprise, the attempt to know and to understand has a unique status, a unique authority, to which all other activities are subordinated.

* * *

Political self-government comes into being only insofar as the common judgment, the available intelligence, of the community takes control over all interests, only insofar as its authority over them is recognized and is effective.

And it is that authority of these truth-seeking activities which the First Amendment recognizes as uniquely significant when it says that the freedom of public discussion shall never be abridged.

ALEXANDER MEIKLEJOHN TO THE HEAD OF THE SAN FRANCISCO OFFICE OF THE FEDERAL BUREAU OF INVESTIGATION

December 20, 1951.

Dear Sir,

A week or two ago one of your agents called to ask me about a person whom I have known for forty years as pupil, colleague, and friend, and whom I would gladly recommend for any appointment he is willing to take.

When the issue of "Loyalty" was raised, I explained to your agent that the questions he was asking were of two kinds, one of which I am glad to answer, while the others are such that, as a believer in the Constitution, I find it necessary to refuse to answer them. This was the same attitude which I had expressed to another of your agents, about three years ago. The two young men, especially the later one, found it hard, apparently, to understand the grounds of my decision. It seems desirable, therefore, that I state them, as directly as possible, to you, so that you may have them for reference. If, at any point, the statement is unclear, I shall be very glad to talk it over with you.

1. On the one hand, I am glad to give information concerning a person's abilities, training, character, and, in general, his fitness for the office in question. And if Loyalty be given its proper meaning of "unqualified devotion to the best interests of the nation, as one sees them," I feel both willing and obliged to speak freely about that.

2. But the term "Loyalty" is sometimes used as referring to a man's opinions about our form of government or our national policies, the assumption being that if a man disagrees with prevailing beliefs on these matters, he is "disloyal." When questions seem to imply this constitutionally false and misleading use of terms, I feel bound, under the First Amendment, to refuse to answer them. I cannot, therefore, give information about a man's beliefs, or party affiliations, or organizational connections. To do so seems to me a serious violation of the most significant principle of our form of government.

It is not easy to make, and to hold fast to, such a decision as this, but the other decision is, for me, impossible.

Please let me know if I can be of service in any way.

Yours,

/s/ Alexander Meiklejohn

ALEXANDER MEIKLEJOHN, WHAT DOES THE FIRST AMENDMENT MEAN?

20 U. Chi. L. Rev. 461, 465–68 (1953).

It is the purpose of this paper to ask whether, under the strains of world war and domestic conflict, recent opinions of the Court have cleared away confusion and error about our freedom or have increased those evils. And, as a representative instance under that general inquiry, we will examine specifically the concurring opinion of Mr. Justice Frankfurter in *Dennis v. United States.*

* * *

[T]he *Dennis* case brought before the Court the specific question, "Has Congress authority to restrict the freedom of the 'advocacy of revolution?' " The federal legislature had claimed that authority when, in the words of the Smith Act, it had said:

> It shall be unlawful for any person . . . (3) to organize or help to organize any society, group, or assembly of persons who teach, advocate, or encourage the overthrow or destruction of any government in the United States by force or violence, or to be or to become a member of, or affiliate with, any such society, group, or assembly of persons, knowing the purposes thereof.

The opinion which we are to discuss supports that claim. It notes the fact that the claim seems, at least, to violate the First Amendment, if that amendment be read literally. But the Amendment, it insists, should not be read literally. To this effect, it says:

> The language of the First Amendment is to be read, not as barren words found in a dictionary but as symbols of historic experience illumined by the presuppositions of those who employed them. Not what words did Madison and Hamilton use but what was in their minds which they conveyed. Free speech is subject to prohibition of those abuses of expression which a civilized society may forbid.[8]

With the first of those three statements it would be hard to quarrel. Words, as found one by one in a dictionary, make sense. But they do not make sentences. And the First Amendment is a sentence. The second statement is, also, clearly valid, though it makes the questionable suggestion that Madison and Hamilton, as they explained the Constitution, did not succeed in saying what was "in their minds." The last statement is, I think, hopelessly vitiated by its use of the phrase "Free Speech" to indicate the scope of the First Amendment. It is clearly true that many "abuses of expression" may be suppressed without violation of the religious or political freedom of the speaker. But that statement is irrelevant for our argument unless it is shown that the advocacy of revolution is one of those abuses. Can that be shown? The opinion contends that it can. This article will contend that it cannot.

8. Dennis v.United States, 341 U.S. 494, 523 (1951) (Frankfurter, J. concurring).

The thesis that the legislature has the authority to abridge the freedom of the advocacy of revolution is phrased by the opinion in the form of a question and answer, as follows:

> The right of a man to think what he pleases, to write what he thinks, and to have his thoughts made available for others to hear or read has an engaging ring of universality. The Smith Act and this conviction under it no doubt restrict the exercise of free speech and assembly. Does that, without more, dispose of the matter?[9]

The opinion's answer to that question is a decided, "No." The notion that the people of the United States are assured of unlimited political freedom is, we are told, an "engaging" one. But, for the sober purposes of the law, it cannot be maintained. Congress is empowered, on occasions to be determined at its own discretion, to abridge such freedoms as those of speech and of assembly, to "make exceptions" to the First Amendment. The answer of this article to the same question is an equally decided, "Yes." The First Amendment, we shall argue, is not "open to exceptions." And to say that a given act of the legislature restricts any one of the freedoms over which the Amendment stands guard does "dispose of the matter." Such an act is unconstitutional.

With the field of conflict thus outlined, we may now proceed to consider specific issues within it, one by one. The *Dennis* case, it should be noted, does not raise questions of religious freedom. Our argument, therefore, will deal only with political problems.

"Not what words did Madison and Hamilton use, but what was in their minds which they conveyed." In that sentence, the opinion summons, to support its thesis, the two chief writers of that interpretation of the Constitution which is given by the "Federalist." My own reading of that interpretation, however, seems to show that, at the two essential points, Madison and Hamilton are witnesses *against* the opinion, rather than *for* it. We must now argue that case.

First of all, what are the two conflicting views concerning the "political right" of the people of the United States to "advocate the overthrow of the government by force and violence?" The opinion says:

> Of course, no government can recognize a "right" of revolution or a "right" to incite revolution if the incitement has no other purpose or effect.[10]

What considerations or arguments are "in the mind" of the writer of that sentence, covered by the phrase, "of course," we are not told. It stands as an unexplained assertion.

The "Federalist," on the other hand, is equally insistent, but more explanatory, on the opposite side of the issue. It finds, as basic features of our American plan of government, not only the right to "advocate revolution," but also, the right of "revolution" itself. This second assertion is not relevant to our present argument, but since it throws light on

9. Ibid., at 520–21.

10. Ibid., at 549.

the right of advocacy, we must briefly note what Madison and Hamilton say about it.

By contrast with the "of course" of the opinion, they staunchly support the assertion of the Declaration of Independence when it says:

> [W]henever any form of government becomes destructive of these ends (for which it was instituted) it is the right of the people to alter or to abolish it and to institute new government, laying its foundations on such principles and organizing its powers in such form, as to them shall most likely to effect their safety and happiness.

In a number of passages, that right of revolt is reasserted by the Federalist debaters. And in one of these, Hamilton goes so far as to declare that it is an important advantage of the proposed federal union that it provides an easier and more secure road for revolutionary action than is available in the smaller units of the separate states. His plea reads, in part, as follows:

> If the representatives of the people betray their constituents, there is no resource left but in the exertion of that original right of self-defence which is paramount to all positive forms of government, and which against the usurpations of their national rulers, may be exerted with infinitely better prospect of success than against those of the rulers of an individual State.... The smaller the extent of the territory, the more difficult will it be for the people to form a regular or systematic plan of opposition, and the more easy will it be to defeat their early efforts.... How wise will it be in them by cherishing the union to preserve to themselves *an advantage which can never be too highly prized.*[11]

As Hamilton thus advises the people to treasure and maintain that "right" of revolution "which can never be too highly prized," what was "in his mind"? There can be little doubt that he would agree with the opinion's declaration that the right to revolt is not "political," that no government can "recognize" it. We shall not find that right established either by constitutional provision or by legislative enactment. But that the right exists and is a basic feature of our plan of government, Hamilton is equally certain and emphatic. What he is here saying is that, if a government exists by the consent of its citizens, there is implicit in it an "original" and "prepolitical" right without which the structure of consent would be meaningless. The Declaration of Independence is, for him, valid. If the grounds of consent are destroyed, the obligations of consent are destroyed with them. The opinion is, therefore, wrong. At this point its witnesses give evidence, not for it, but against it. It must be added to round out the picture, however, that whenever citizens abandon "political" methods and resort to force, the government which they attack has an equally original and valid "right" to repel the attack by use of its own force.

11. Hamilton, Madison, and Jay, The Federalist or the New Constitution, XXVIII, 135–36 (Everyman's Library, 1911). (Emphasis added.)

But, second, Madison and Hamilton are both convinced that the right to advocate revolution, as contrasted with the right to actively engage in it, is clearly "political," and gives expression to a valid constitutional principle upon which the structure of political freedom rests. That principle which, in the judgment of the "Federalist," runs through the Constitution, is explicitly stated by the First Amendment. What it says is that a government is maintained by the free consent of its citizens only so long as the choice whether or not it shall be maintained is recognized as an open choice, which the people may debate and decide, with conflicting advocacies, whenever they may choose. If the time or the occasion should ever come—as by the decisions of our courts it seems now to have come—when the people of this nation are prevented by their subordinate agencies from considering and advocating and deciding whether or not to maintain the present form of our government, then, in the opinion of the "Federalist," that form of government has already ceased to exist. In that case, we have come to the absurdity of declaring that a man who believes that fundamental constitutional change is needed for the sake of the general welfare is, thereby, shown to be disloyal to the nation. As Madison and Hamilton wrote their "Federalist" arguments, they were meeting the onslaughts of critics who passionately condemned the proposed Constitution and were doing everything in their power to defeat it. And as against those onslaughts, though they themselves had many objections to the new plan, they fought back with equally spirited counter-advocacy. And that method of counter-advocacy is still available to our government as it meets the attacks of those who would seek to destroy its present form and put another in its place. But to make the advocacy of revolution a criminal offense, as the Smith Act does, is to violate the basic principle of political freedom which the "Federalist" explains and defends. At this point, neither in written words nor in the ideas underlying those words, do Madison and Hamilton give support to the opinion which has summoned them to testify in its behalf.

ALEXANDER MEIKLEJOHN, TESTIMONY PRESENTED BEFORE THE SUBCOMMITTEE ON CONSTITUTIONAL RIGHTS, UNITED STATES SENATE COMMITTEE ON THE JUDICIARY

Eighty-fourth Congress, First Session, November 14, 1955.

Mr. Chairman and Members of the Committee:

I deeply appreciate your courtesy in asking me to join with you in an attempt to define the meaning of the words, "Congress shall make no law . . . abridging the freedom of speech, or of the press; or the right of the people peaceably to assemble, and to petition the government for a redress of grievances." Whatever those words may mean, they go directly to the heart of our American plan of government. If we can understand them we can know what, as a self-governing nation, we are trying to be and to do. Insofar as we do not understand them, we are in grave danger of blocking our own purposes, of denying our own beliefs.

1

It may clarify my own part in our conference if I tell you at once my opinion concerning this much-debated subject. The First Amendment seems to me to be a very uncompromising statement. It admits of no exceptions. It tells us that the Congress and, by implication, all other agencies of the government are denied any authority whatever to limit the political freedom of the citizens of the United States. It declares that with respect to political belief, political discussion, political advocacy, political planning, our citizens are sovereign, and the Congress is their subordinate agent. That agent is authorized, under strong safeguards against the abuse of its power, to limit the freedom of men as they go about the management of their private, their non-political, affairs. But the same men, as they endeavor to meet the public responsibilities of citizenship in a free society, are in a vital sense, which is not easy to define, beyond the reach of legislative control. Our common task, as we talk together today, is to determine what that sense is.

Mr. Chairman, in view of your courtesy to me, I hope you will not find me discourteous when I suggest that the Congress is a subordinate branch of the government of the United States. In saying this I am simply repeating in less passionate words what was said by the writers of the *Federalist* papers when, a century and three-quarters ago, they explained the meaning of the proposed Constitution to a body politic which seemed very reluctant to adopt it. Over and over again the writers of those papers declared that the Constitutional Convention had given to the people adequate protection against a much-feared tyranny of the legislature. In one of the most brilliant statements ever written about the Constitution, the *Federalist* says—

> It is one thing to be subject to the laws, and another to be dependent on the legislative body. The first comports with, the last violates, the fundamental principles of good government, and, whatever may be the forms of the Constitution, unites all power in the same hands. (No. 71)

It is chiefly the legislature, the *Federalist* insists, which threatens to usurp the governing powers of the people. In words which unfortunately have some relevance today, it declares that "it is against the enterprising ambition of this department that the people ought to indulge their jealousy and exhaust all their precautions." And, further, the hesitant people were assured that the Convention, having recognized this danger, had devised adequate protections against it. The representatives, it was provided, would be elected by vote of the people. Elections would be for terms brief enough to ensure active and continuous popular control. The legislature would have no law-making authority other than those limited powers specifically delegated to it. A general legislative power to act for the security and welfare of the nation was denied on the ground that it would destroy the basic postulate of popular self-government on which the Constitution rests.

As the *Federalist* thus describes, with insight and accuracy, the Constitutional defenses of the freedom of the people against legislative invasion, it is not speaking of that freedom as an "individual right" which is bestowed upon the citizens by action of the legislature. Nor is the principle of the freedom of speech derived from a law of Nature or of Reason in the abstract. As it stands in the Constitution, it is an expression of the basic American political agreement that, in the last resort, the people of the United States shall govern themselves. To find its meaning, therefore, we must dig down to the very foundations of the self-governing process. And what we shall there find is the fact that when men govern themselves, it is they—and no one else—who must pass judgment upon public policies. And that means that in our popular discussions, unwise ideas must have a hearing as well as wise ones, dangerous ideas as well as safe, un-American as well as American. Just so far as, at any point, the citizens who are to decide issues are denied acquaintance with information or opinion or doubt or disbelief or criticism which is relevant to those issues, just so far the result must be ill-considered, ill-balanced planning for the general good. It is that mutilation of the thinking process of the community against which the First Amendment is directed. That provision neither the Legislature, nor the Executive, nor the Judiciary, nor all of them acting together, has authority to nullify. We Americans have, together, decided to be politically free.

2

Mr. Chairman, I have now stated for your consideration the thesis that the First Amendment is not "open to exceptions"; that our American "freedom of speech" is not, on any grounds whatever, subject to abridgment by the representatives of the people. May I next try to answer two arguments which are commonly brought against that thesis in the courts and in the wider circle of popular discussion?

The first objection rests upon the supposition that freedom of speech may on occasion threaten the security of the nation. And when these two legitimate national interests are in conflict, the government, it is said, must strike a balance between them. And that means that the First Amendment must at times yield ground. The freedom of speech must be abridged in order that the national order and safety may be secured.

In the courts of the United States, many diverse opinions have asserted that "balancing" doctrine. One of these, often quoted, reads as follows:

> To preserve its independence, and give security against foreign aggression and encroachment, is the highest duty of every nation, and to attain these ends nearly all other considerations are to be subordinated. It matters not in what form such aggression comes.... The government, possessing the powers which are to be exercised for protection and security, is clothed with authority to determine the occasion on which the powers shall be brought forth.

That opinion tells us that the "government" of the United States has unlimited authority to provide for the security of the nation, as it may seem necessary and wise. It tells us, therefore, that constitutionally, the government which has created the defenses of political freedom may break down those defenses. We, the people, who have enacted the First Amendment, may by agreed-upon procedure modify or annul that amendment. And, since we are, as a government, a sovereign nation, I do not see how any of these assertions can be doubted or denied. We Americans, as a body-politic, may destroy or limit our freedom whenever we choose. But what bearing has that statement upon the authority of Congress to interfere with the provisions of the First Amendment? Congress is not the government. It is only one of four branches to each of which the people have denied specific and limited powers as well as delegated such powers. And in the case before us, the words, "Congress shall make no law ... abridging the freedom of speech," give plain evidence that, so far as Congress is concerned, the power to limit our political freedom has been explicitly denied.

There is, I am sure, a radical error in the theory that the task of "balancing" the conflicting claims of security and freedom has been delegated to Congress. It is the failure to recognize that the balancing in question was carefully done when, one hundred seventy years ago, the Constitution was adopted and quickly amended. The men who wrote the text of that Constitution knew, quite as well as we do, that the program of political freedom is a dangerous one. They could foresee that, as the nation traveled the ways of self-government, the freedom of speech would often be used irresponsibly and unwisely, especially in times of war or near-war, and that such talking might have serious consequences for the national safety.

They knew, too, that a large section of the voting population was hostile to the forms of government which were then being adopted. And, further, they had every reason to expect that in a changing world, new dissatisfactions would arise and might in times of stress break out into open and passionate disaffection. All these considerations, I am saying, were as clearly and as disturbingly present to their minds as they are to our minds today. And because of them, the First Amendment might have been written, not as it is, but as the Courts of the United States have re-written it in the war-maddened years since 1919. The Amendment might have said, "Except in times and situations involving 'clear and present danger' to the national security, Congress shall make no law abridging the freedom of speech." Or it might have read, "Only when, in the judgment of the legislature, the interests of order and security render such action advisable shall Congress abridge the freedom of speech." But the writers of the Amendment did not adopt either of these phrasings or anything like them. Perhaps a minor reason for their decision was the practical certainty that the Constitution, if presented in that form, would have failed of adoption. But more important than such questionable historical speculation are two reasons which are as valid today as they were when the Amendment was decreed.

First, our doctrine of political freedom is not a visionary abstraction. It is a belief which is based in long and bitter experience, which is thought out by shrewd intelligence. It is the sober conviction that, in a society pledged to self-government, it is never true that, in the long run, the security of the nation is endangered by the freedom of the people. Whatever may be the immediate gains and losses, the dangers to our safety arising from political suppression are always greater than the dangers to that safety arising from political freedom. Suppression is always foolish. Freedom is always wise. That is the faith, the experimental faith, by which we Americans have undertaken to live. If we, the citizens of today, cannot shake ourselves free from the hysteria which blinds us to that faith, there is little hope for peace and security, either at home or abroad.

Second, the re-writing of the First Amendment which authorizes the legislature to balance security against freedom denies not merely some minor phase of the amendment but its essential purpose and meaning. Whenever, in our Western civilization, "inquisitors" have sought to justify their acts of suppression, they have given plausibility to their claims only by appealing to the necessity of guarding the public safety. It is that appeal which the First Amendment intended, and intends, to outlaw. Speaking to the legislature, it says, "When times of danger come upon the nation, you will be strongly tempted, and urged by popular pressure, to resort to practices of suppression such as those allowed by societies unlike our own in which men do not govern themselves. You are hereby forbidden to do so. This nation of ours intends to be free. 'Congress shall make no law ... abridging the freedom of speech.' "

The second objection which must be met by one who asserts the unconditional freedom of speech rests upon the well-known fact that there are countless human situations in which, under the Constitution, this or that kind of speaking may be limited or forbidden by legislative action. Some of these cases have been listed by the courts in vague and varying ways. Thus libels, blasphemies, attacks upon public morals or private reputation have been held punishable. So too, we are told that "counselling a murder" may be a criminal act, or "falsely shouting fire in a theatre, and causing a panic." "Offensive" or "provocative" speech has been denied legislative immunity. "Contempt of court," shown by the use of speech or by refusal to speak, may give basis for prosecution. Utterances which cause a riot or which "incite" to it may be subject to the same legal condemnation. And this listing of legitimate legislative abridgments of speech could be continued indefinitely. Their number is legion.

In view of these undoubted facts, the objection which we must now try to meet can be simply stated. In all these cases, it says, inasmuch as speaking is abridged, "exceptions" are made to the First Amendment. The Amendment is thus shown to be, in general, "open to exceptions." And from this it follows that there is no reason why a legislature which has authority to guard the public safety should be debarred from making an "exception" when faced by the threat of national danger.

Now the validity of that argument rests upon the assumed major premise that whenever, in any way, limits are set to the speaking of an individual, an "exception" is made to the First Amendment. But that premise is clearly false. It could be justified only if it were shown that the Amendment intends to forbid every form of governmental control over the act of speaking. Is that its intention? Nothing could be further from the truth. May I draw an example from our own present activities in this room? You and I are here talking about freedom within limits defined by the Senate. I am allowed to speak only because you have invited me to do so. And just now everyone else is denied that privilege. But further, you have assigned me a topic to which my remarks must be relevant. Your schedule, too, acting with generosity, fixes a time within which my remarks must be made. In a word, my speaking, though "free" in the First Amendment sense, is abridged in many ways. But your speaking, too, is controlled by rules of procedure. You may, of course, differ in opinion from what I am saying. To that freedom there are no limits. But unless the chairman intervenes, you are not allowed to express that difference by open speech until I have finished my reading. In a word, both you and I are under control as to what we may say and when and how we may say it. Shall we say, then, that this conference, which studies the principle of free speech, is itself making "exceptions" to that principle? I do not think so. Speech, as a form of human action, is subject to regulation in exactly the same sense as is walking, or lighting a fire, or shooting a gun. To interpret the First Amendment as forbidding such regulation is to so misconceive its meaning as to reduce it to nonsense.

The principle here at issue was effectively, though not clearly, stated by Mr. Justice Holmes when, in the *Frohwerk* case, he said—

> The First Amendment, while prohibiting legislation against free speech as such, cannot have been, and obviously was not, intended to give immunity to every form of language.... We venture to believe that neither Hamilton nor Madison, nor any other competent person, ever supposed that to make criminal the counselling of a murder would be an unconstitutional interference with free speech.

Those words of the great Justice, by denying that the First Amendment intends to forbid such abridgments of speech as the punishing of incitement to murder, seem to me to nullify completely the supposed evidence that the amendment is "open to exceptions." They show conclusively the falsity of the "exception" theory which has been used by the courts to give basis for the "danger" theory of legislative authority to abridge our political freedom. If, then, the "danger" theory is to stand it must stand on its own feet. And those feet, if my earlier argument is valid, seem to be made of clay.

3

Mr. Chairman, in the first section of this paper I spoke of the negative fact that the First Amendment forbids the legislature to limit the political freedom of the people. May I now, surveying the same ground from its positive side, discuss with you the active powers and responsibilities of free citizens, as these are described or taken for granted in the general structure of the Constitution as a whole? If I am not mistaken, we shall find here the reasons why the words of the great proclamation are so absolute, so uncompromising, so resistant of modification or exception.

The purpose of the Constitution is, as we all know, to define and allocate powers for the governing of the nation. To that end, three special governing agencies are set up, and to each of them are delegated such specific powers as are needed for doing its part of the work.

Now that program rests upon a clear distinction between the political body which delegates powers and the political bodies—Legislative, Executive, and Judicial—to which powers are delegated. It presupposes, on the one hand, a supreme governing agency to which, originally, all authority belongs. It specifies, on the other hand, subordinate agencies to which partial delegations of authority are made. What, then, is the working relation between the supreme agency and its subordinates? Only as we answer that question shall we find the positive meaning of the First Amendment.

First of all, then, what is the supreme governing agency of this nation? In its opening statement the Constitution answers that question. "We, the People of the United States," it declares, "do ordain and establish this Constitution ... " Those are revolutionary words which define the freedom which is guaranteed by the First Amendment. They mark off our government from every form of despotic polity. The legal powers of the people of the United States are not granted to them by some one else—by kings or barons or priests, by legislators or executives or judges. All political authority, whether delegated or not, belongs, constitutionally, to us. If any one else has political authority, we are lending it to him. We, the people, are supreme in our own right. We are governed, directly or indirectly, only by ourselves.

But now what have we, the people, in our establishing of the Constitution, done with the powers which thus inhere in us? Some of them we have delegated. But there is one power, at least, which we have not delegated, which we have kept in our own hands, for our own direct exercise. Article 1, (2), authorizes the people, in their capacity as "electors," to choose their representatives. And that means that we, the people, in a vital sense, do actively govern those who, by other delegated powers, govern us. In the midst of all our assigning of powers to legislative, executive, and judicial bodies, we have jealously kept for ourselves the most fundamental of all powers. It is the power of voting, of choosing by joint action, those representatives to whom certain of our powers are entrusted. In the view of the Constitution, then, we the people are not only the supreme agency. We are also, politically, an active electorate—a Fourth, or perhaps better, a First Branch which, through its reserved power, governs at the polls. That is the essential meaning of the statement that we Americans are, in actual practice, politically a free people. Our First Amendment freedom is not merely an aspiration. It is an arrangement made by women and men who vote freely and, by voting, govern the nation. That is the responsibility, the opportunity, which the Constitution assigns to us, however slackly and negligently we may at times have exercised our power.

It follows from what has just been said that under the Constitution, we Americans are politically free only insofar as our voting is free. But to get the full meaning of that statement we must examine more closely what men are doing when they vote, and how they do it.

The most obvious feature of activity at the polls is the choosing among candidates for office. But under our election procedures, with their party platforms and public meetings, with the turmoil and passion of partisan debate, the voters are also considering and deciding about issues of public policy. They are thinking. As we vote we do more than elect men to represent us. We also judge the wisdom or folly of suggested measures. We plan for the welfare of the nation. Now it is these "judging" activities of the governing people which the First Amendment protects by its guarantees of freedom from legislative interference. Because, as self-governing women and men, we the people have work to do for the general welfare, we make two demands. First, our judging of public issues, whether done separately or in groups, must be free and independent—must be our own. It must be done by us and by no one else. And second, we must be equally free and independent in expressing, at the polls, the conclusions, the beliefs, to which our judging has brought us. Censorship over our thinking, duress over our voting; are alike forbidden by the First Amendment. A legislative body, or any other body which, in any way, practices such censorship or duress, stands in "contempt" of the sovereign people of the United States.

But, further, what more specifically are the judging activities with which censorship and duress attempt to interfere? What are the intellectual processes by which free men govern a nation, which therefore must be protected from any external interference? They seem to be of three kinds.

First, as we try to "make up our minds" on issues which affect the general welfare, we commonly—though not commonly enough—read the printed records of the thinking and believing which other men have done in relation to those issues. Those records are found in documents and newspapers, in works of art of many kinds. And all this vast array of idea and fact, of science and fiction, of poetry and prose, of belief and doubt, of appreciation and purpose, of information and argument, the voter may find ready to help him in making up his mind.

Second, we electors do our thinking, not only by individual reading and reflection, but also in the active associations of private or public discussion. We think together, as well as apart. And in this field, by the group action of congenial minds, by the controversies of opposing minds, we form parties, adopt platforms, conduct campaigns, hold meetings, in order that this or that set of ideas may prevail, in order that that measure or this may be defeated.

And third, when election day finally comes, the voter, having presumably made up his mind, must now express it by his ballot. Behind the canvas curtain, alone and independent, he renders his decision. He acts as sovereign, one of the governors of his country. However slack may be our practice, that, in theory, is our freedom.

What, then, as seen against this Constitutional background, is the purpose of the First Amendment, as it stands guard over our freedom? That purpose is to see to it that in none of these three activities of judging shall the voter be robbed, by action of other, subordinate branches of the government, of the responsibility, the power, the authority, which are his under the Constitution. What shall be read? What he himself decides to read. With whom shall he associate in political advocacy? With those with whom he chooses to associate. Whom shall he oppose? Those with whom he disagrees. Shall any branch of the government attempt to control his opinions or his vote, to drive him by duress or intimidation into believing or voting this way or that? To do this is to violate the Constitution at its very source. We, the people of the United States, are self-governing. That is what our freedom means.

4

Mr. Chairman, this interpretation of the First Amendment which I have tried to give is, of necessity, very abstract. May I, therefore, give some more specific examples of its meaning at this point or that?

First, when we speak of the Amendment as guarding the freedom to hear and to read, the principle applies not only to the speaking or writing of our own citizens but also to the writing or speaking of every one whom a citizen, at his own discretion, may choose to hear or to read. And this means that unhindered expression must be open to non-citizens, to resident aliens, to writers and speakers of other nations, to anyone, past or present, who has something to say which may have significance for a citizen who is thinking of the welfare of this nation. The Bible, the Koran, Plato, Adam Smith, Joseph Stalin, Gandhi, may be published and read in the United States, not because they have, or had, a right to be published here, but because we, the citizen-voters, have authority, have legal power, to decide what we will read, what we will think about. With the exercise of that "reserved" power, all "delegated" powers are, by the Constitution, forbidden to interfere.

Second, in the field of public discussion, when citizens and their fellow thinkers "peaceably assemble" to listen to a speaker, whether he be American or foreign, conservative or radical, safe or dangerous, the First Amendment is not, in the first instance, concerned with the "right" of the speaker to say this or that. It is concerned with the authority of the hearers to meet together, to discuss, and to hear discussed by speakers of their own choice, whatever they may deem worthy of their consideration.

Third, the same freedom from attempts at duress is guaranteed to every citizen as he makes up his mind, chooses his party, and finally casts his vote. During that process, no governing body may use force upon him, may try to drive him or lure him toward this decision or that, or away from this decision or that. And for that reason, no subordinate agency of the government has authority to ask, under compulsion to answer, what a citizen's political commitments are. The question, "Are you a Republican?" or "Are you a Communist?", when accompanied by the threat of harmful or degrading consequences if an answer is refused, or if the answer is this rather than that, is an intolerable invasion of the "reserved powers" of the governing people. And the freedom thus protected does not rest upon the Fifth Amendment "right" of one who is governed to avoid self-incrimination. It expresses the constitutional authority, the legal power, of one who governs to make up his own mind without fear or favor, with the independence and freedom in which self-government consists.

And fourth, for the same reason, our First Amendment freedom forbids that any citizen be required under threat of penalty to take an oath, or make an affirmation as to beliefs which he holds or rejects. Every citizen, it is true, may be required, and should be required, to pledge loyalty, and to practice loyalty, to the nation. He must agree to support the Constitution. But he may never be required to *believe* in the Constitution. His loyalty may never be tested on grounds of adherence to, or rejection of, any *belief.* Loyalty does not imply conformity of opinion. Every citizen of the United States has Constitutional authority to approve or to condemn any laws enacted by the Legislature, any actions taken by the Executive, any decisions rendered by the Judiciary, any principles established by the Constitution. All these enactments which, as men who are governed, we must obey, are subject to our approval or disapproval, as we govern. With respect to all of them, we, who are free men, are sovereign. We are "The People." We govern the United States.

5

Mr. Chairman, I have tried to state and defend the assertion that the Constitutional guarantee of political freedom is not "open to exceptions." Judgment upon the theoretical validity of that position I now leave in your hands.

But as between conflicting views of the First Amendment, there is also a practical question of efficiency. May I, in closing, speaking with the tentativeness becoming to a non-lawyer, offer three suggestions as to the working basis on which decisions about political freedom should rest?

First, the experience of the courts since 1919 seems to me to show that, as a procedural device for distinguishing forms of speech and writing and assembly which the Amendment does protect from those which it does not protect, the "clear and present danger" test has failed to work. Its basic practical defect is that no one has been able to give it dependable, or even assignable, meaning. Case by case, opinion by opinion, it has shifted back and forth with a variability of meaning which reveals its complete lack of Constitutional basis. In his opinion confirming the conviction of Eugene Dennis and others for violation of the Smith Act, Judge Learned Hand reviewed the long series of judicial attempts to give to the words "clear and present" a usable meaning. His conclusion reads, in part, as follows:

> The phrase "clear and present danger" . . . is a way to describe a penumbra of occasions, even the outskirts of which are indefinable, but within which, as is so often the case, the courts must find their way as they can. In each case they must ask whether the gravity of the "evil," discounted by its improbability, justifies such an invasion of free speech as is necessary to avoid the danger.

And to this bewildering interpretation of the words, "clear and present," he adds:

> That is a test in whose application the utmost differences of opinion have constantly arisen, even in the Supreme Court. Obviously it would be impossible to draft a statute which should attempt to prescribe a rule for each occasion; and it follows, as we have said, either that the Act is definite enough as it stands, or that it is practically impossible to deal with such conduct in general terms.

Those words, coming from the penetrating and powerful mind of Learned Hand, show how intolerable it is that the most precious, most fundamental, value in the American plan of government should depend, for its defense, upon a phrase which not only has no warrant in the Constitution but has no dependable meaning, either for a man accused of crime or for the attorneys who prosecute or defend him or for the courts which judge him. That phrase does not do its work. We need to make a fresh start in our interpreting of the words which protect our political freedom.

Second, as we seek for a better test, it is of course true that no legal device can transform the making of decisions about freedom into a merely routine application of an abstract principle. Self-government is a complicated business. And yet, the "no-exception" view which I have offered seems to me to promise a more stable and understandable basis for judicial decision than does the 1919 doctrine which the courts have been trying to follow. For example, the most troublesome issue which now confronts our courts and our people is that of the speech and writing and assembling of persons who find, or think they find, radical defects in our form of government, and who devise and advocate plans by means of which another form might be substituted for it. And the practical question is, "How far, and in what respects, are such revolutionary planning and advocacy protected by the First Amendment?"

It is, of course, understood that if such persons or groups proceed to forceful or violent action, or even to overt preparation for such action, against the government, the First Amendment offers them, in that respect, no protection. Its interest is limited to the freedom of judgment-making—of inquiry and belief and conference and persuasion and planning and advocacy. It does not protect either overt action or incitement to such action. It is concerned only with those political activities by which, under the Constitution, free men govern themselves.

From what has just been said it follows that, so far as speech and writing are concerned, the distinction upon which the application of the First Amendment rests is that between "advocacy of action" and "incitement to action." To advocacy the amendment guarantees freedom, no matter what may be advocated. To incitement, on the other hand, the amendment guarantees nothing whatever.

This distinction was sharply drawn by Justice Brandeis when, in the *Whitney* case, he said—

> Every denunciation of existing law tends in some measure to increase the probability that there will be violations of it. Condonation of a breach enhances the probability. Propagation of the criminal state of mind by teaching syndicalism increases it. Advocacy of lawbreaking heightens it still further. But even advocacy of violation, however reprehensible morally, is not a justification for denying free speech where the advocacy falls short of incitement and there is nothing to indicate that the advocacy would be immediately acted on.

Those words, I think, point the way which decisions about our political freedom can, and should, follow. An incitement, I take it, is an utterance so related to a specific overt act that it may be regarded and treated as a part of the doing of the act itself, if the act is done. Its control, therefore, falls within the jurisdiction of the legislature. An advocacy, on the other hand, even up to the limit of arguing and planning for the violent overthrow of the existing form of government, is one of those opinion-forming, judgment-making expressions which free men need to utter and to hear as citizens responsible for the governing of the nation. If men are not free to ask and to answer the question, "Shall the present form of our government be maintained or changed?"; if, when that question is asked, the two sides of the issue are not equally open for consideration, for advocacy, and for adoption, then it is impossible to speak of our government as established by the free choice of a self-governing people. It is not enough to say that the people of the United States were free one hundred seventy years ago. The First Amendment requires, simply and without equivocation, that they be free now.

Third, and finally, if we say, as this paper has urged, that in many situations, speech and writing and assembly may be controlled by legislative action, we must also say that such control may never be based on the ground of disagreement with opinions held or expressed. No belief or advocacy may be denied freedom if, in the same situation, opposing beliefs or advocacies are granted that freedom.

If then, on any occasion in the United States, it is allowable to say that the Constitution is a good document, it is equally allowable, in that situation, to say that the Constitution is a bad document. If a public building may be used in which to say, in time of war, that the war is justified, then the same building may be used in which to say that it is not justified. If it be publicly argued that conscription for armed service is moral and necessary, it may be likewise publicly argued that it is immoral and unnecessary. If it may be said that American political institutions are superior to those of England or Russia or Germany, it may, with equal freedom, be said that those of England or Russia or Germany are superior to ours. These conflicting views may be expressed, must be expressed, not because they are valid, but because they are relevant. If they are responsibly entertained by anyone, we, the voters, need to hear them. When a question of policy is "before the house," free men choose to meet it, not with their eyes shut, but with their eyes open. To be afraid of any idea is to be unfit for self-government. Any such suppression of ideas about the common good, the First Amendment condemns with its absolute disapproval. The freedom of ideas shall not be abridged.

ALEXANDER MEIKLEJOHN, THE FIRST AMENDMENT IS AN ABSOLUTE

1961 Supreme Court Review 245.

What I have said is that the First Amendment, as seen in its constitutional setting, forbids Congress to abridge the freedom of a citizen's speech, press, peaceable assembly, or petition, whenever those activities are utilized for the governing of the nation. In these respects, the Constitution gives to all "the people" the same protection of freedom which, in Article I, Section 6(1), it provides for their legislative agents: "and for any speech or debate in either House, they shall not be questioned in any other place." Just as our agents must be free in their use of their delegated powers, so the people must be free in the exercise of their reserved powers.

What other activities, then, in addition to speech, press, assembly, and petition, must be included within the scope of the First Amendment? First of all, the freedom to "vote," the official expression of a self-governing man's judgment on issues of public policy, must be absolutely protected. None of his subordinate agencies may bring pressure upon him to drive his balloting this way or that. None of them may require him to tell how he has voted; none may inquire by compulsory process into his political beliefs or associations. In that area, the citizen has constitutional authority and his agents have not.

Second, there are many forms of thought and expression within the range of human communications from which the voter derives the knowledge, intelligence, sensitivity to human values: the capacity for sane and objective judgment which, so far as possible, a ballot should express. These, too, must suffer no abridgment of their freedom. I list four of them below.

1. Education, in all its phases, is the attempt to so inform and cultivate the mind and will of a citizen that he shall have the

wisdom, the independence, and, therefore, the dignity of a governing citizen. Freedom of education is, thus, as we all recognize, a basic postulate in the planning of a free society.

2. The achievements of philosophy and the sciences in creating knowledge and understanding of men and their world must be made available, without abridgment, to every citizen.

3. Literature and the arts must be protected by the First Amendment. They lead the way toward sensitive and informed appreciation and response to the values out of which the riches of the general welfare are created.

4. Public discussions of public issues, together with the spreading of information and opinion bearing on those issues, must have a freedom unabridged by our agents. Though they govern us, we, in a deeper sense, govern them. Over our governing, they have no power. Over their governing we have sovereign power.

A Paradox

Out of the argument thus far stated, two apparently contradictory statements emerge. Congress may, in ways carefully limited, "regulate" the activities by which the citizens govern the nation. But no regulation may abridge the freedom of those governing activities. I am sure that the two statements are not contradictory. But their combination is, to say the least, paradoxical. It is that paradox that I must now face as I try to respond to Professor Kalven's challenge.[28] As a non-lawyer, I shall not discuss in detail the difficulties and puzzlements with which the courts must deal. I can only suggest that, here and there, seeming contradictions are not real.

First. A distinction must be drawn between belief and communication in their relations to Congressional authority. A citizen may be told when and where and in what manner he may or may not speak, write, assemble, and so on. On the other hand, he may not be told what he shall or shall not believe. In that realm each citizen is sovereign. He exercises powers that the body politic reserves for its own members. In 1953, testifying before the Senate Committee on Constitutional Rights, I said:

> . . . our First Amendment freedom forbids that any citizen be required, under threat of penalty, to take an oath, or make an affirmation, as to beliefs which he holds or rejects. Every citizen, it is true, may be required and should be required, to pledge loyalty, and to practice loyalty, to the nation. He must agree to support the

28. The writing of this paper is largely due to the friendly insistence of Professor Harry Kalven, Jr., of the Law School of the University of Chicago. He and I have had, in recent years, a continuing exchange of ideas. Professor Kalven tells me that he is not sure that my interpretation of the First Amendment can stand the test of lawyer-like application to the many specific situations which the courts must handle. In response to that challenge, I cannot presume to offer fully specific answers to specific problems. I can only suggest principles, bringing them as near as I can to the actual issues with which the courts deal.

> Constitution. But he may never be required to *believe* in the Constitution. His loyalty may never be tested on grounds of adherence to, or rejection of, any *belief*. Loyalty does not imply conformity of opinion. Every citizen of the United States has Constitutional authority to approve or to condemn any laws enacted by the Legislature, any actions taken by the Executive, any judgments rendered by the judiciary, any principles established by the Constitution. All these enactments which, as men who are governed, we must obey, are subject to our approval or disapproval, as we govern. With respect to all of them we, who are free men, are sovereign. We are "The People." We govern the United States.

However far our practice falls short of the intention expressed by those words, they provide the standard by which our practice must be justified or condemned.

Second. We must recognize that there are many forms of communication which, since they are not being used as activities of governing, are wholly outside the scope of the First Amendment. Mr. Justice Holmes has told us about these, giving such vivid illustrations as "persuasion to murder"[30] and "falsely shouting fire in a theatre and causing a panic."[31] And Mr. Justice Harlan, referring to Holmes and following his lead, gave a more extensive list:[32] "libel, slander, misrepresentation, obscenity, perjury, false advertising, solicitation of crime, complicity by encouragement, conspiracy...." Why are these communications not protected by the First Amendment? Mr. Justice Holmes suggested an explanation when he said of the First Amendment in *Schenck:*[33] "It does not even protect a man from an injunction against uttering words that may have all the effect of force."

Now it may be agreed that the uttering of words cannot be forbidden by legislation, nor punished on conviction, unless damage has been done by them to some individual or to the wider society. But that statement does not justify the imputation that all "words that may have all the effect of force" are denied the First Amendment's protection. The man who falsely shouts "Fire!" in a theatre is subject to prosecution under validly enacted legislation. But the army officer who, in command of a firing squad, shouts "Fire!" and thus ends a life, cannot be prosecuted for murder. He acts as an agent of the government. And, in fact, all governing communications are intended to have, more or less directly, "the effect of force." When a voter casts his ballot for a tax levy, he intends that someone shall be deprived of property. But his voting is not therefore outside the scope of the First Amendment. His voting must be free.

The principle here at stake can be seen in our libel laws. In cases of private defamation, one individual does damage to another by tongue or

30. Abrams v. United States, 250 U.S. 616, 627 (1919).

31. Schenck v. United States, 249 U.S. 47, 52 (1919).

32. 366 U.S. at 49 n. 10.

33. 249 U.S. at 52.

pen; the person so injured in reputation or property may sue for damages. But, in that case, the First Amendment gives no protection to the person sued. His verbal attack has no relation to the business of governing. If, however, the same verbal attack is made in order to show the unfitness of a candidate for governmental office, the act is properly regarded as a citizen's participation in government. It is, therefore, protected by the First Amendment. And the same principle holds good if a citizen attacks, by words of disapproval and condemnation, the policies of the government, or even the structure of the Constitution. These are "public" issues concerning which, under our form of government, he has authority, and is assumed to have competence, to judge. Though private libel is subject to legislative control, political or seditious libel is not.

Third. In discussions of the First Amendment too little attention has been given to the regulatory word "peaceable" in relation to "assembly." It suggests principles of limitation which apply also to speech, press, petition, and to the other forms of communication which support them. This limitation is significant in demonstrating that a citizen's governing is often both "regulated" and "free."

Peaceableness in governing may serve either one or both of two purposes. It provides protection for an assembly against external violation of rules of public order. It also seeks to ensure that relations within the assembly shall succeed in serving the governing function which warrants its protection by the First Amendment. The first of these purposes has to do with relations between the assembly and "outsiders" who, disagreeing with its ideas and intentions, may seek to disrupt the discussion and, in various ways, to render it ineffectual. In this situation, both the local authorities which have authority to "regulate" and the police who seek to apply the regulations are held responsible by the intention of the First and Fourteenth Amendments. No ordinance may be based upon disapproval of policies to be discussed or decreed by the assembly. And the police must, to the limit of their power, defend the meeting from interruption or interference by its enemies. But basically more important are the conditions of peaceableness within an assembly itself. It is, of course, impossible that everyone should be allowed to express his point of view whenever and however he chooses. In a meeting for discussion, as contrasted with a lecture, however, no one may be "denied the floor" on the ground of disapproval of what he is saying or would say. And, if the interests of a self-governing society are to be served, vituperation which fixes attention on the defects of an opponent's character or intelligence and thereby distracts attention from the question of policy under discussion may be forbidden as a deadly enemy of peaceable assembly. Anyone who persists in it should be expelled from the meeting, and, if need be, the police should give help in getting it done.

I cannot, however, leave those words on record without noting how inadequate, to the degree of non-existence, are our public provisions for active discussions among the members of our self-governing society. As we try to create and enlarge freedom, such universal discussion is imperative. In every village, in every district of every town or city, there should be established at public expense cultural centers inviting all citizens, as they may choose, to meet together for the consideration of public policy. And conditions must be provided under which such meetings could be happily and successfully conducted. I am not thinking of such lunatic-fringe activities as those in Hyde Park in London. I am thinking of a self-governing body politic, whose freedom of individual expression should be cultivated, not merely because it serves to prevent outbursts of violence which would result from suppression, but for the positive purpose of bringing every citizen into active and intelligent sharing in the government of his country.

Fourth. Largely because of our failure to make adequate provision for free and unhindered public discussion, the courts are called upon to judge the constitutionality of local ordinances which forbid or limit the holding of public meetings in public places. Such ordinances come into effect when individuals or groups assemble in such a way as to interfere with other interests of the community or of its members. The most striking and perplexing cases of this kind occur when meetings are held on the public streets or in parks whose primary use is, in the opinion of the authorities, blocked or hindered to a degree demanding action. Now if such ordinances are based upon official disapproval of the ideas to be presented at the meeting, they clearly violate the First Amendment. But if no such abridgment of freedom is expressed or implied, regulation or prohibition on other grounds may be enacted and enforced.

It must not be assumed that every governmental regulation of a public meeting is, under current conditions, destructive of political freedom. Conditions of traffic on a city street are very different from those in the relatively open spaces of a country village. Parks may be needed for rest, quiet, and release from excitement and strain. Just as an individual, seeking to advocate some public policy may not do so, without consent, by interrupting a church service, or a classroom, or a sickroom, or a session of Congress or of the Supreme Court, or by ringing a doorbell and demanding to be heard, so meetings must conform to the necessities of the community, with respect to time, place, circumstance, and manner of procedure. And, unless those considerations are dishonestly used as a cover for unconstitutional discrimination against this idea or that, there is no First Amendment complaint against the ordinances which express them. The Amendment, I repeat, does not establish an "unlimited right to talk."

It must further be noted that in "emergency" situations, when something must be said and no other time, place, circumstance, or manner of speech will serve for the saying of it, a citizen may be justified in "taking the law into his own hands." In the famous example of Mr. Justice Holmes, a man is not allowed to shout "Fire!" *falsely* in a theatre. But, if, during a performance in a theatre, a person sees a fire which threatens to spread, he is not only allowed, he is duty-bound, to try to find some way of informing others so that a panic may not ensue with its disastrous consequences. The distinction between "falsely" and "truly" is here fundamental to an understanding of what freedom is.

Fifth. In the current discussions as to whether or not "obscenity" in literature and the arts is protected by the First Amendment, the basic principle is, I think, that literature and the arts are protected because they have a "social importance" which I have called a "governing" importance. For example, the novel is at present a powerful determinative of our views of what human beings are, how they can be influenced, in what directions they should be influenced by many forces, including, especially, their own judgments and appreciations. But the novel, like all the other creations of literature and the arts, may be produced wisely or unwisely, sensitively or coarsely, for the building up of a way of life which we treasure or for tearing it down. Shall the government establish a censorship to distinguish between "good" novels and "bad" ones? And, more specifically, shall it forbid the publication of novels which portray sexual experiences with a frankness that, to the prevailing conventions of our society, seems "obscene"?

The First Amendment seems to me to answer that question with an unequivocal "no." Here, as elsewhere, the authority of citizens to decide what they shall write and, more fundamental, what they shall read and see, has not been delegated to any of the subordinate branches of government. It is "reserved to the people," each deciding for himself to whom he will listen, whom he will read, what portrayal of the human scene he finds worthy of his attention. And at this point I feel compelled to disagree with Professor Kalven's interpretation of what I have tried to say. In his recent article on obscenity, he wrote:[34]

> The classic defense of John Stuart Mill and the modern defense of Alexander Meiklejohn do not help much when the question is why the novel, the poem, the painting, the drama, or the piece of sculpture falls within the protection of the First Amendment. Nor do the famous opinions of Hand, Holmes, and Brandeis. The emphasis is all on truth winning out in a fair fight between competing ideas. The emphasis is clearest in Meiklejohn's argument that free speech is indispensable to the informed citizenry required to make democratic self-government work. The people need free speech because they vote. As a result his argument distinguishes sharply between public and private speech. Not all communications are relevant to the political process. The people do not need novels or dramas or paintings or poems because they will be called upon to vote. Art and belles-lettres do not deal in such ideas—at least not good art or belles-lettres....

In reply to that friendly interpretation, I must, at two points, record a friendly disavowal. I have never been able to share the Miltonian faith that in a fair fight between truth and error, truth is sure to win. And if one had that faith, it would be hard to reconcile it with the sheer stupidity of the policies of this nation—and of other nations—now

34. Kalven, *Metaphysics of the Law of Obscenity*, 1960 Sup. Ct. Rev. 1, 15–16.

driving humanity to the very edge of final destruction. In my view, "the people need free speech" because they have decided, in adopting, maintaining and interpreting their Constitution, to govern themselves rather than to be governed by others. And, in order to make that self-government a reality rather than an illusion, in order that it may become as wise and efficient as its responsibilities require, the judgment-making of the people must be self-educated in the ways of freedom. That is, I think, the positive purpose to which the negative words of the First Amendment gave a constitutional expression. Moreover, as against Professor Kalven's interpretation, I believe, as a teacher, that the people do need novels and dramas and paintings and poems, "because they will be called upon to vote." The primary social fact which blocks and hinders the success of our experiment in self-government is that our citizens are not educated for self-government. We are terrified by ideas, rather than challenged and stimulated by them. Our dominant mood is not the courage of people who dare to think. It is the timidity of those who fear and hate whenever conventions are questioned.

Questions

1) What kind of an argument is Meiklejohn making? Which thinker whom we have studied previously comes closest to making the *type* of argument that Meiklejohn is making?

2) The self-government rationale for free speech is often contrasted with two other leading rationales, truth-seeking and autonomy. Yet Meiklejohn seems to embrace notions of autonomy and truth-seeking. So what exactly is the relationship Meiklejohn envisions between these ideas?

3) Meiklejohn asserts that Socrates's positions in the *Apology* and the *Crito* are reconcilable. He says: "For Socrates, obedience to the laws which would abridge his life is here quite as imperative as was disobedience to laws which would abridge his belief and the expression of it." Why exactly is that? How, if at all, does Meiklejohn's view of self-government help us to understand why Socrates must both speak his mind and die for it?

4) Does Meiklejohn's analogy to the town meeting do much to advance his argument? Exactly how? Can principles and procedures appropriate for a town meeting tell us anything about how speech should or should not be regulated in mass society?

5) Meiklejohn differentiates the "private right of speech" from the "freedom of public discussion" and asserts that only the latter is absolutely protected under the First Amendment. He says: "The constitutional status of a merchant advertising his wares, of a paid lobbyist fighting for the advantage of his client, is utterly different form that of a citizen who is planning for the general welfare." Is this distinction defensible in theory? In practice? Can someone who believes that in their actual political

behavior most citizens put self-interest ahead of the public good nevertheless embrace Meiklejohn's basic understanding of the First Amendment? How can we tell whether a speaker urging a controversial position is "planning for the general welfare?"

6) In his testimony before the Senate subcommittee, Meiklejohn expresses criticism of First Amendment opinions written by Justice Holmes and Judge Hand, and praise for Justice Brandeis's *Whitney* opinion. What is it about the Brandeis opinion that leads Meiklejohn to believe that it is consistent with his own "absolutist" view of the First Amendment? Do Brandeis and Meiklejohn share a similar understanding of democratic theory? Does Meiklejohn assert or imply that the final end of the State is to make men free to develop their faculties? Does he value liberty both as an end and as a means? Does he believe that the First Amendment was designed to promote the ideal of civic courage?

7) Meiklejohn asserts that the freedom of speech is primarily for the benefit of listeners rather than speakers. Is this a necessary implication of his theory of self-government? A permissible inference from that theory?How might the protection of a listener-oriented First Amendment differ from those of a speaker-oriented First Amendment?

8) What does Meiklejohn mean when he says that the First Amendment guarantees "equality of status in the field of ideas (p. 753)?" Does his theory of self-government provide a rationale for the principle that the legal regulation of speech cannot be based on viewpoint discrimination, i.e., a government preference for some ideas over others? Exactly how might that principle, which has come to play a central role in contemporary First Amendment doctrine, follow from Meiklejohn's conception of self-government?

9) Like Meiklejohn, Learned Hand derived his understanding of the freedom of speech from the American agreement to be self-governed. Like Meiklejohn, Hand believed that the commitment to self-government deprives government officials of the authority to forbid or punish the dissemination of any idea simply because those officials believe the idea to be evil, dangerous, or likely to mislead. However, Hand believed that the one idea that is not left beyond government control is the idea that it is in the interest or is the duty of citizens to violate the law; he thought that the commitment to self-government entails a concomitant commitment to the rule of law. This probably explains his opinion in the *Dennis* case. Why does Meiklejohn believe that the commitment to self-government implies the opposite principle: that persons who advocate the violation of law, such as Communists calling for violent revolution, are entitled under the First Amendment to disseminate their message no matter how "un-American" or dangerous officials believe that idea to be? Who better understands the implications of the commitment to self-government, Hand or Meiklejohn?

10) Does Meiklejohn's theory provide any basis for extending First Amendment protection to literature? To scientific claims? To "private" expressions of social attitudes in the workplace?

LEARNED HAND, SOURCES OF TOLERANCE

79 U. Pa. L. Rev. 1 (1930).

While there lingers in political platforms and other declamatory compositions the notion that each man, if only he could be disabused of false doctrine, would act and vote with an enlightened eye to the public weal, few really believe it. We know well that an objective calculus of human values is impossible, and if it were available, would be so thin and speculative that men would not accept it. For any times that can count in human endeavor, we must be content with compromises in which the more powerful combination will prevail. The most we can hope is that if the maladjustment becomes too obvious, or the means too offensive to our conventions, the balance can be re-established without dissolution, a cost greater than almost any interests can justify. The method of Hamilton has had its way; so far as we can see must always have its way; in government, as in marriage, in the end the more insistent will prevails.

FRANK H. EASTERBROOK, THE STATE OF MADISON'S VISION OF THE STATE: A PUBLIC CHOICE PERSPECTIVE

107 Harv.L.Rev. 1328 (1994).

* * *

The core of Madisonian resistance—the common weal to be found and implemented by virtuous legislators—turns out to be empty. It is not simply that Rousseau's concept of general will is hollow.[37] It is that there is no virtuous way to aggregate private wills into collective decisions. People of good will have no common ground around which to rally! They have their own conceptions of the public interest but no way to insist that the collective choice necessarily reflect their views. We are doomed by the logic of majority voting to aggregate private preferences rather than to find a common public good.

ROBERT POST, MEIKLEJOHN'S MISTAKE: INDIVIDUAL AUTONOMY AND THE REFORM OF PUBLIC DISCOURSE

64 U. Colo. L. Rev. 1109 (1993).

His paradigm of the town meeting specifically presupposes that the function of American democracy is to achieve an orderly, efficient, and

37. See JEAN-JACQUES ROSSEAU, THE SOCIAL CONTRACT 72–74 (Maurice Cranston trans., Penguin Paperback 1968) (1762).

rational dispatch of common business, and it consequently implies that aspects of public discourse incompatible with that function are constitutionally expendable. To the extent public discourse is thus truncated, a particular concept of national identity is placed beyond the reach of the communicative processes of self-determination.

The difficulty with Meiklejohn's analysis, therefore, is that it reflects an insufficiently radical conception of the reach of self-determination, which encompasses not merely the substance of collective decisions, but also the larger framework of function within which such collective decisionmaking is necessarily conceived as taking place. It is precisely because he is certain about the nature of that framework that Meiklejohn can, for example, unproblematically appeal to the authority of a moderator. But Kenneth Karst noted long ago that in fact the "state lacks 'moderators' who can be trusted to know when 'everything worth saying' has been said."[34] The state lacks such moderators because the very standards necessary to distinguish "relevant" from "irrelevant" speech (or "original" from "repetitious" speech, or "orderly" from "disorderly" speech, or even "rational" from "irrational" speech) are themselves matters of potential dispute. We can settle disputes about the nature of these standards only by appealing to particular conceptions of the larger framework of function that gives collective decisionmaking its telos. Conflicts about the nature of these standards ought therefore to be a matter for debate within public discourse. To use a particular version of these standards to censor public discourse would be, *pro tanto*, heteronomously to foreclose the open-ended search for collective self-definition.

The same point can be made with respect to the agenda-setting mechanisms of a town meeting. Public control over the presentation and characterization of issues within a town meeting seems unproblematic because of a shared agreement concerning efficient institutional function and procedure. But within democratic life generally such agreement cannot be assumed without concomitantly diminishing the arena for self-determination. This is because "[p]olitical conflict is not like an intercollegiate debate in which the opponents agree in advance on the definition of the issues":

> As a matter of fact, *the definition of the alternatives is the supreme instrument of power*.... He who determines what politics is about runs the country, because the definition of the alternatives is the choice of conflicts, and the choice of conflicts allocates power.[36]

The state ought not to be empowered to control the agenda of public discourse, or the presentation and characterization of issues within public discourse, because such control would necessarily circumscribe the potential for collective self-determination.

34. Kenneth Karst, *Equality and the First Amendment*, 43 U. CHI. L. REV. 20, 40 (1975).

36. ELMER E. SCHATTSCHNEIDER, THE SEMISOVEREIGN PEOPLE: A REALIST'S VIEW OF DEMOCRACY IN AMERICA 66 (2d ed. 1975).

These elementary examples can be given general theoretical formulation. Managerial structures necessarily presuppose objectives that are unproblematic and hence that can be used instrumentally to regulate domains of social life. The enterprise of public discourse, by contrast, rests on the value of autonomy, which requires that all possible objectives, all possible versions of national identity, be rendered problematic and open to inquiry. No particular objective can justify the coercive censorship of public discourse without simultaneously contradicting the very enterprise of self-determination. As a consequence public discourse always appears intolerably formless and incoherent to those who care about the instrumental accomplishment of particular purposes, whether they be the voting of wise decisions or the maintenance of rational debate. Public discourse seems to them to consist merely of "a Hyde Park" filled with "unregulated talkativeness."

Justice Harlan captured this aspect of public discourse in *Cohen v. California*.[38] He observed that democratic dialogue "may often appear to be only verbal tumult, discord, and even offensive utterance." But Harlan understood that this disorder, this "verbal cacophony," is merely a "necessary side effect[]" of the fact that, "in a society as diverse and populous as ours," public discourse is organized not to accomplish anything in particular, but instead to serve as a medium within which heterogeneous versions of collective identity can be free continuously to collide and reconcile.

Self-determination, we might say, is something that *happens* within public discourse; there is no external Archimedean point from which it can be compelled or its outcome anticipated. We can decide, within public discourse, to form and set in motion specific organizations of order and instrumental rationality, like town meetings. But it would be a grave mistake to confuse these discrete institutions with the sea of tumult and discord that is public discourse itself.

BERNARD WILLIAMS, TRUTH AND TRUTHFULNESS: AN ESSAY IN GENEALOGY

(2002).

Within United States jurisprudence, other approaches to First Amendment doctrine, co-existing uneasily with the marketplace tradition, have explained the significance of free speech in terms of democratic participation. One of them, particularly influenced by Alexander Meiklejohn, understands the rules governing free speech in political connections in terms of their contribution to the conditions for fruitful and orderly democratic debate. Meiklejohn took as his model a town meeting, in which speech is regulated by a chairman in order to facilitate informed and reasonable deliberation; as he put it in a famous formulation, "What is essential is not that everyone shall speak, but that

38. 403 U.S. 15 (1971).

everything worth saying shall be said." This approach, which has powerful contemporary support, naturally leads to allowing more interventionist policies, favouring such things as constraints on campaign finance, requirements of balanced discussion on TV networks, and the withdrawal of protection from racist and other kinds of prejudicial speech. It could also encourage positive initiatives in support of public service broadcasting and so on. To some extent, the proposals that would naturally go with this approach overlap with what might be needed for a closer approximation to an idealized market in truth: this is hardly surprising, granted that one requirement for orderly and fruitful democratic debate is accurate information.

However, the Meiklejohnian theory itself has been criticized from the point of view of democratic legitimacy, as relying on an impoverished notion of participation. On this view, the model of the "orderly conduct of business" wrongly takes for granted a consensus about what the business is, and does not allow for the fact that one aim and effect of political intervention can precisely be to change the agenda. A function of the town chairman is to exclude disorderly and offensive expression, but speech in that style is certainly part of the political process and has traditionally been defended by the United States courts as such. Other democratic societies take various views of these issues of principle and their practical implications. Unlike Americans, they do not have the questionable advantage of discussing them in terms of First Amendment jurisprudence, but they are all faced with similar conflicts. It is not simply that the marketplace theory of free speech is deceptive because it elides the huge differences between a commercial and an idealized market. Even if we give up the idea that a literal market in communication approximates to an idealized market of ideas, there will still be serious conflicts between the demands of truth transmission, on the one hand, and some implications of democratic legitimacy on the other. What the conflicts will be, and how extensive, depends on the prevailing conception of democratic legitimacy and how it interprets ideas such as participation. No liberal democracy can afford to be too discouraging of expressive, disorderly, and even prejudicial speech, or too fussy about who publishes it or how, and it cannot force people to think about public or political matters. At the same time, the basic rights of liberal society and democratic freedoms themselves depend on the development and protection of methods for discovering and transmitting the truth, and this requires that public debate embody in some form an approximation to an idealized market. Squaring this circle must be a prime aim of institutional invention in liberal states.

SHARON ACHINSTEIN, MILTON AND THE REVOLUTIONARY READER

(1994).

By merging radical Protestantism with classical precedent, the printing press, and the pulpit, Milton appealed to an idea of a public sphere that matched the political needs of the English Revolution. Speaking freely is a precondition of *Areopagitica*, but Milton's tract is not merely a free speech; it is also a question directed at parliamentary readers to make a decision about the kind of citizens they imagine the English to be. The choice Milton offered his audience was whether they thought ordinary English citizens were capable of participating in politics or not. Milton posited that difference most clearly in the following words: "consider what Nation it is whereof ye are, and whereof ye are the governours: a nation not slow and dull, but of a quick, ingenious, and piercing spirit." The contrast between these two conceptions is repeatedly stressed throughout the pamphlet, as Milton suggests that Parliament's decision on the matter would expose its attitude toward English citizens. If English citizens were thought to be "slow and dull," then "the whiff of every new pamphlet should stagger them out of their catechism." Milton jokes here, knowing that his beloved fellow Englishmen were nothing of that sort. As a "quick, ingenious" nation, rather, the English public is "musing, searching, revolving new notions and ideas wherewith to present.... Others [are] as fast reading, trying all things, assenting to the force of reason and convincement." These two conceptions about audience capabilities—slow and dull or quick and ingenious—can be seen to operate as competing theories of readers in the public sphere, and in presenting these two contrasting images, Milton exposes the assumptions behind censorship he wished to challenge. In Milton's line of thinking, English citizens were qualified as readers, worthy to exercise their reasoning abilities amid a barrage of conflicting opinions.

Questions

1) If "an objective calculus of human values is impossible" such that "we must be content with compromises in which the more powerful combination will prevail" (Judge Hand), if "[w]e are doomed by the logic of majority voting to aggregate private preferences rather than to find a common good" (Judge Easterbrook), does Meiklejohn's conception of self-government and his interpretation of the First Amendment fall apart?

2) Robert Post claims that "Meiklejohn's mistake" is to fail to realize that the regime of self-government ultimately rests on the value of individual autonomy "which requires that all possible objectives, all possible versions of national identity, be rendered problematic and open to inquiry." Post criticizes Meiklejohn for his desire that public deliberation aspire to the orderliness and businesslike discharge of an agreed-upon agenda that is evoked by the popular image of a town meeting. Is Post persuasive, both in the way he reads Meiklejohn and in the claims he makes regarding the role of self-government in First Amendment theory?

3) Sharon Achinstein claims that in *Areopagitica* Milton rested his argument on a controversial conception of the capabilities of audiences in the public sphere. Does Meiklejohn make this move as well? Is his conception of the public sphere and of the capabilities of audiences similar to Milton's?

WILLIAM J. BRENNAN, JR., THE SUPREME COURT AND THE MEIKLEJOHN INTERPRETATION OF THE FIRST AMENDMENT

79 Harv. L. Rev. 1 (1965).

I especially prize the honor of the invitation to deliver the Alexander Meiklejohn Lecture. Dr. Meiklejohn's rich legacy to American education may be seen on virtually every college campus in this land. General acceptance of the educational ideas and practices of this militant champion of freedom may not have been won easily or very soon, but none will deny that his fight over nearly half a century brought substantial victory. None more richly deserved the Medal of Freedom, the nation's highest civilian honor, presented by President Johnson to Dr. Meiklejohn a year ago last December.

The interests of this scholar, philosopher, and man of learning ranged, of course, far beyond his own field of education. He was not a lawyer, yet his views on the first amendment are a significant contribution to the debate over the limits that great keystone of our freedom places on governmental regulation of expression. It is those views and their relevance to the Supreme Court's views of the first amendment that I have made the subject of this lecture.

* * *

Dr. Meiklejohn's position, unlike Justice Black's absolute view, would have allowed distinctions among libel laws by virtue of the principle of "governing importance." He said:[44]

> The principle here at stake can be seen in our libel laws. In cases of private defamation, one individual does damage to another by tongue or pen; the person so injured in reputation or property may sue for damages. But, in that case, the First Amendment gives no protection to the person sued. His verbal attack has no relation to the business of governing. If, however, the same verbal attack is made in order to show unfitness of a candidate for governmental office, the act is properly regarded as a citizen's participation in government. It is, therefore, protected by the First Amendment. And the same principle holds good if a citizen attacks, by words of disapproval and condemnation, the policies of the government, or even the structure of the Constitution. These are "public" issues concerning which, under our form of government, he has authority,

44. [Alexander Meiklejohn, The First Amendment Is an Absolute, 1961 Supreme Court Rev. 245, 259.]

and is assumed to have competence, to judge. Though private libel is subject to legislative control, political or seditious libel is not.

This brings me back to *New York Times v. Sullivan.* Some of the statements in the advertisement were not true. The first amendment question was whether its protections nevertheless limit a state's power to apply traditional libel law principles, since the statements were made in criticism of the official conduct of a public servant. In other words, the case presented a classic example of an activity that Dr. Meiklejohn called an activity of "governing importance" within the powers reserved to the people and made invulnerable to sanctions imposed by their agency-governments. The Court held that Alabama's use of its civil libel law in this context violated the constitutional guarantees. Professor Kalven suggests that the result might have been based on the "clear and present danger," "redeeming social value," or "balancing" tests;[46] however, he correctly points out that the opinion relied on none of these tests. Instead, the Court examined history to discern the central meaning of the first amendment, and concluded that that meaning was revealed in Madison's statement "that the censorial power is in the people over the Government, and not in the Government over the people."[47] This, the Court said, was the lesson taught by the great controversy over the Sedition Act of 1798. That act created a crime, punishable by a $5,000 fine or five years in prison:

> . . . if any person shall write, print, utter or publish . . . any false, scandalous and malicious writing or writings against the government of the United States, or either house of the Congress . . . or the President . . . , with intent to defame . . . or to bring them, or either of them, into contempt or disrepute; or to excite against them, or either or any of them, the hatred of the good people of the United States. . . .

That act expired by its terms in 1801, and no case testing its constitutionality was brought to the Supreme Court. It had been roundly condemned, however, as patently unconstitutional in a broadside attack joined in by Jefferson and Madison. The attack was founded upon their claim that the Government established by the Constitution was powerless to impose sanctions for criticism of Government and Government officials. *The New York Times* opinion concludes that this view carried the day in the court of history. The opinion gives particular attention to Madison's views forcefully expressed in the Virginia Resolutions of 1798. The Court states:

> Madison prepared the Report in support of the protest. His premise was that the Constitution created a form of government under which "The people, not the government, possess the absolute sovereignty." The structure of the government dispersed power in reflec-

46. [Harry Kalven, Jr., The New York Times Case: A Note on the "Central Meaning of the First Amendment," 1964 Supreme Court Rev. 191, 208, 209, 213–18.]

47. 4 ANNALS OF CONGRESS 934 (1794).

> tion of the people's distrust of concentrated power, and of power itself at all levels. This form of government was "altogether different" from the British form, under which the Crown was sovereign and the people were subjects. "Is it not natural and necessary, under such different circumstances," he asked, "that a different degree of freedom in the use of the press should be contemplated?" ... Earlier, in a debate in the House of Representatives, Madison had said: "If we avert to the nature of Republican Government, we shall find that the censorial power is in the people over the Government, and not in the Government over the people." 4 Annals of Congress, p. 934 (1794). Of the exercise of that power by the press, his Report said: "In every state, probably, in the Union, the press has exerted a freedom in canvassing the merits and measures of public men, of every description, which has not been confined to the strict limits of the common law. On this footing the freedom of the press has stood; on this foundation it yet stands...." 4 Elliot's Debates, *supra*, p. 570. The right of free public discussion of the stewardship of public officials was thus, in Madison's view, a fundamental principle of the American form of government.

Professor Kalven's appraisal of the opinion is this:

> The Court did not simply, in the face of an awkward history, definitively put to rest the status of the Sedition Act. More important, it found in the controversy over seditious libel the clue to "the central meaning of the First Amendment." The choice of language was unusually apt. The Amendment has a "central meaning"—a core of protection of speech without which democracy cannot function, without which, in Madison's phrase, "the censorial power" would be in the Government over the people and not "in the people over the Government." This is not the whole meaning of the Amendment. There are other freedoms protected by it. But at the center there is no doubt what speech is being protected and no doubt why it is being protected. The theory of the freedom of speech clause was put right side up for the first time.

Then, in capsule form, Professor Kalven says the opinion held that "the central meaning of the Amendment is that seditious libel cannot be made the subject of government sanction. The Alabama rule on fair comment is closely akin to making seditious libel an offense. The Alabama rule therefore violated the central meaning of the Amendment."

The Court also buttressed the decision by reference to a case, *Barr v. Matteo*,[53] which created an absolute privilege barring libel suits against high-ranking government officials for statements, even if defamatory, made in their official capacity. Of this, Professor Kalven says:

> There is the analogy to *Barr v. Matteo* and the privilege of the high-ranking government executive. The rationale in *Barr* was that the

53. 360 U.S. 564 (1959).

threat of damage suits would dampen the ardor of the official for the performance of his duties. "Analogous considerations support the privilege for the citizen-critic of government. It is as much his duty to criticize as it is the official's duty to administer." It is now not only the citizen's privilege to criticize his government, it is his duty. At this point in its rhetoric and sweep, the opinion almost literally incorporated Alexander Meiklejohn's thesis that in a democracy the citizen as ruler is our most important public official.

But Professor Kalven was also mindful of my earlier caveat that courts are chary of sudden fundamental changes in doctrine, for he says:

> The closing question, of course, is whether the treatment of seditious libel as the key concept for development of appropriate constitutional doctrine will prove germinal. It is not easy to predict what the Court will see in the *Times* opinion as the years roll by. It may regard the opinion as covering simply one pocket of cases, those dealing with libel of public officials, and not destructive of the earlier notions that are inconsistent only with the larger reading of the Court's action. But the invitation to follow a dialectic progression from public official to government policy to public policy to matters in the public domain, like art, seems to me to be overwhelming. If the Court accepts the invitation, it will slowly work out for itself the theory of free speech that Alexander Meiklejohn has been offering us for some fifteen years now.

HARRY KALVEN, JR., THE NEW YORK TIMES CASE: A NOTE ON THE "CENTRAL MEANING OF THE FIRST AMENDMENT"

1964 Sup. Ct. Rev. 191.

It is perhaps a fitting postscript to say that I had occasion this summer to discuss the *Times* case with Mr. Meiklejohn. Before I had disclosed my own views, I asked him for his judgment of the *Times* case. "It is," he said, "an occasion for dancing in the streets."

KEYISHIAN v. BOARD OF REGENTS OF THE UNIVERSITY OF THE STATE OF NEW YORK

Supreme Court of the United States, 1967.
385 U.S. 589, 87 S.Ct. 675, 17 L.Ed.2d 629.

MR. JUSTICE BRENNAN delivered the opinion of the Court.

Appellants were members of the faculty of the privately owned and operated University of Buffalo, and became state employees when the University was merged in 1962 into the State University of New York, an institution of higher education owned and operated by the State of New York. As faculty members of the State University their continued employment was conditioned upon their compliance with a New York plan, formulated partly in statutes and partly in administrative regulations, which the State utilizes to prevent the appointment or retention of "subversive" persons in state employment.

Appellants Hochfield and Maud were Assistant Professors of English, appellant Keyishian an instructor in English, and appellant Garver, a lecturer in Philosophy. Each of them refused to sign, as regulations then in effect required, a certificate that he was not a Communist, and that if he had ever been a Communist, he had communicated that fact to the President of the State University of New York. Each was notified that his failure to sign the certificate would require his dismissal. Keyishian's one-year-term contract was not renewed because of his failure to sign the certificate. Hochfield and Garver, whose contracts still had time to run, continue to teach, but subject to proceedings for their dismissal if the constitutionality of the New York plan is sustained. Maud has voluntarily resigned and therefore no longer has standing in this suit.

Appellant Starbuck was a nonfaculty library employee and part-time lecturer in English. Personnel in that classification were not required to sign a certificate but were required to answer in writing under oath the question, "Have you ever advised or taught or were you ever a member of any society or group of persons which taught or advocated the doctrine that the Government of the United States or of any political subdivisions thereof should be overthrown or overturned by force, violence or any unlawful means?" Starbuck refused to answer the question and as a result was dismissed.

* * *

Appellants have also challenged the constitutionality of the discrete provisions of subdivision 1(c) of § 105 and subdivision 2 of the Feinberg Law, which make Communist Party membership, as such, prima facie evidence of disqualification. The provision was added to subdivision 1(c) of § 105 in 1958 after the Board of Regents, following notice and hearing, listed the Communist Party of the United States and the Communist Party of the State of New York as "subversive" organizations. Subdivision 2 of the Feinberg Law was, however, before the Court in Adler and its constitutionality was sustained. But constitutional doctrine which has emerged since that decision has rejected its major premise. That premise was that public employment, including academic employment, may be conditioned upon the surrender of constitutional rights which could not be abridged by direct government action. Teachers, the Court said in *Adler*, "may work for the school system upon the reasonable terms laid down by the proper authorities of New York. If they do not choose to work on such terms, they are at liberty to retain their beliefs and associations and go elsewhere." 342 U.S., at 492. The Court also stated that a teacher denied employment because of membership in a listed organization "is not thereby denied the right of free speech and assembly. His freedom of choice between membership in the organization and employment in the school system might be limited, but not his freedom of speech or assembly, except in the remote sense that limitation is inherent in every choice."

However, the Court of Appeals for the Second Circuit correctly said in an earlier stage of this case, "the theory that public employment which may be denied altogether may be subjected to any conditions, regardless of how unreasonable, has been uniformly rejected." *Keyishian v. Board of Regents*, 345 F.2d 236, 239. Indeed, that theory was expressly rejected in a series of decisions following *Adler*. In *Sherbert v. Verner*, 374 U.S. 398, 404, we said: "It is too late in the day to doubt that the liberties of religion and expression may be infringed by the denial of or placing of conditions upon a benefit or privilege."

We proceed then to the question of the validity of the provisions of subdivision 1 of § 105 and subdivision 2 of § 3022, barring employment to members of listed organizations. Here again constitutional doctrine has developed since *Adler*. Mere knowing membership without a specific intent to further the unlawful aims of an organization is not a constitutionally adequate basis for exclusion from such positions as those held by appellants.

In *Elfbrandt v. Russell*, 384 U.S. 11, we said, "Those who join an organization but do not share its unlawful purposes and who do not participate in its unlawful activities surely pose no threat, either as citizens or as public employees." We there struck down a statutorily required oath binding the state employee not to become a member of the Communist Party with knowledge of its unlawful purpose, on threat of discharge and perjury prosecution if the oath were violated. We found that "(a)ny lingering doubt that proscription of mere knowing membership, without any showing of 'specific intent,' would run afoul of the Constitution was set at rest by our decision in *Aptheker v. Secretary of State*, 378 U.S. 500." In *Aptheker* we held that Party membership, without knowledge of the Party's unlawful purposes and specific intent to further its unlawful aims, could not constitutionally warrant deprivation of the right to travel abroad. As we said in *Schneiderman v. United States*, 320 U.S. 118, 136, "(U)nder our traditions beliefs are personal and not a matter of mere association, and ... men in adhering to a political party or other organization ... do not subscribe unqualifiedly to all of its platforms or asserted principles." "A law which applies to membership without the 'specific intent' to further the illegal aims of the organization infringes unnecessarily on protected freedoms. It rests on the doctrine of 'guilt by association' which has no place here." Thus mere Party membership, even with knowledge of the Party's unlawful goals, cannot suffice to justify criminal punishment, see *Scales v. United States*, 367 U.S. 203, nor may it warrant a finding of moral unfitness justifying disbarment. *Schware v. Board of Bar Examiners*, 353 U.S. 232.

These limitations clearly apply to a provision, like § 105, subd. 1(c), which blankets all state employees, regardless of the "sensitivity" of their positions. But even the Feinberg Law provision, applicable primarily to activities of teachers, who have captive audiences of young minds, are subject to these limitations in favor of freedom of expression and association; the stifling effect on the academic mind from curtailing freedom of association in such manner is manifest, and has been documented in recent studies. *Elfbrandt* and *Aptheker* state the governing standard: legislation which sanctions membership unaccompanied by specific intent to further the unlawful goals of the organization or which is not active membership violates constitutional limitations.

* * *

MR. JUSTICE CLARK, with whom MR. JUSTICE HARLAN, MR. JUSTICE STEWART and MR. JUSTICE WHITE join, dissenting.

* * *

The majority says that the Feinberg Law is bad because it has an "overbroad sweep." I regret to say—and I do so with deference—that the majority has by its broadside swept away one of our most precious rights, namely, the right of self-preservation. Our public educational system is the genius of our democracy. The minds of our youth are developed there and the character of that development will determine the future of our land. Indeed, our very existence depends upon it. The issue here is a very narrow one. It is not freedom of speech, freedom of thought, freedom of press, freedom of assembly, or of association, even in the Communist Party. It is simply this: May the State provide that one who, after a hearing with full judicial review, is found to have wilfully and deliberately advocated, advised, or taught that our Government should be overthrown by force or violence or other unlawful means; or to have wilfully and deliberately printed, published, etc., any book or paper that so advocated and to have personally advocated such doctrine himself; or to have willfully and deliberately become a member of an organization that advocates such doctrine, is prima facie disqualified from teaching in its university? My answer, in keeping with all of our cases up until today, is "Yes"!

I dissent.

OWEN M. FISS, FREE SPEECH AND SOCIAL STRUCTURE

71 Iowa L. Rev. 1405 (1986).

For the most part, the Free Speech Tradition can be understood as a protection of the street corner speaker. An individual mounts a soapbox on a corner in some large city, starts to criticize governmental policy, and then is arrested for breach of the peace. In this setting the first amendment is conceived of as a shield, as a means of protecting the individual speaker from being silenced by the state.

First amendment litigation first began to occupy the Supreme Court's attention during World War I, a time when the constitutional shield was rather weak. The street corner speaker could be arrested on the slightest provocation. Those early decisions were openly criticized, most notably in the dissents of Brandeis and Holmes, but that criticism—eloquent and at times heroic—stayed within the established framework and sought only to expand the frontiers of freedom incrementally; it sought to place more restrictions on the policeman and to give more and more protection to the street corner speaker. In this incremental quality, the criticism took on the character of the progressive movement in general, and also shared its fate. The progressive critique achieved its first successes during the thirties, at the hands of the Hughes Court, but its final vindication awaited the Warren Court: It was only then that the shield around the speaker became worthy of a democracy.

* * *

I would be the first to acknowledge that there has been something noble and inspiring about the fifty year journey from [the World War I cases] in 1919 to *Brandenburg* in 1969. A body of doctrine that fully protects the street corner speaker is of course an accomplishment of some note; the battles to secure that protection were hard fought and their outcome was far from certain. *Brandenburg* is one of the blessings of our liberty. The problem, however, is that today there are no street corners, and the doctrinal edifice that seems to someone like Kalven so glorious when we have the street corner speaker in mind is largely unresponsive to the conditions of modern society.

Under the Traditional extolled by Kalven, the freedom of speech guaranteed by the first amendment amounts to a protection of autonomy—it is the shield around the speaker. The theory that animates this protection, and that inspired Kalven, and before him Meiklejohn, and that now dominates the field, casts the underlying purpose of the first amendment in social or political terms: The purpose of free speech is not individual self-actualization, but rather the preservation of democracy, and the right of a people, as a people, to decide what kind of life it wishes to live. Autonomy is protected not because of its intrinsic value, as a Kantian might insist, but rather as a means or instrument of collective self-determination. We allow people to speak so others can vote. Speech allows people to vote intelligently and freely, aware of all the options and in possession of all the relevant information.

The crucial assumption in this theory is that the protection of autonomy will produce a public debate that will be, to use the talismanic phrase once again, "uninhibited, robust, and wide-open." The Tradition assumes that by leaving individuals alone, free from the menacing arm of the policeman, a full and fair consideration of all the issues will emerge. The premise is that autonomy will lead to rich public debate. From the perspective of the street corner, that assumption might seem plausible enough. But when our perspective shifts, as I insist it must, from the street corner to, say, CBS, this assumption becomes highly problematic. Autonomy and rich public debate—the two free speech values—might diverge and become antagonistic. Under CBS, autonomy may be insufficient to insure a rich public debate. Oddly enough, it might even become destructive of that goal.

* * *

We can thus see that the key to fulfilling the ultimate purposes of the first amendment is not autonomy, which has a most uncertain or double-edged relationship to public debate, but rather the actual effect of a broadcast: On the whole does it enrich public debate? Speech is protected when (and only when) it does, and precisely because it does, not because it is an exercise of autonomy. In fact, autonomy adds nothing and if need be, might have to be sacrificed, to make certain that public debate is sufficiently rich to permit true collective self-determination. What the phrase "the freedom of speech" in the first amendment refers to is a social state of affairs, not the action of an individual or institution.

The risk posed to freedom of speech by autonomy is not confined to situations when it is exercised by CBS, or by the other media, but occurs whenever speech takes place under conditions of scarcity, that is,whenever the opportunity for communication is limited. In such situations one utterance will necessarily displace another. With the street corner, the element of scarcity tends to be masked; when we think of the street corner we ordinarily assume that every speaker will have his or her turn, and that the attention of the audience is virtually unlimited. Indeed, that is why it is such an appealing story. But in politics, scarcity is the rule rather than the exception. The opportunities for speech tend to be limited, either by the time or space available for communicating or by our capacity to digest or process information. This is clear and obvious in the case of the mass media, which play a decisive role in determining which issues are debated, and how, but it is true in other contexts as well. In a referendum or election, for example, there is every reason to be concerned with the advertising campaign mounted by the rich or powerful, because the resources at their disposal enable them to fill all the available space for public discourse with their message. Playing Muzak on the public address system of a shopping mall fills the minds of those who congregate there. Or consider the purchase of books by a library, or the design of a school curriculum. The decision to acquire one book or to include one course necessarily entails the exclusion of another.

* * *

Classical liberalism presupposes a sharp dichotomy between state and citizen. It teaches us to be wary of the state and equates liberty with limited government. The Free Speech Tradition builds on this view of the world when it reduces free speech to autonomy and defines autonomy to mean the absence of government interference. Liberalism's distrust of the state is represented by the antagonism between the policeman and soapbox orator and by the assumption that the policeman is the enemy of speech. Under the received Tradition, free speech becomes one strand—perhaps the only left—of a more general plea for limited government. Its appeals has been greatly enhanced by our historical commitment to liberalism.

Nothing I have said is meant to destroy the distinction presupposed by classical liberalism between state and citizen, or between the public and private. Rather, in asking that we shift our focus from the street corner to CBS, I mean to suggest that we are not dealing with hermetically sealed spheres.

* * *

No longer can we identify the policeman with evil and the citizen with good. The state of affairs protected by the first amendment can just as easily be threatened by a private citizen as by an agency of the state. A corporation operating on private capital can be as much a threat to the richness of public debate as a government agency, for each is subject to constraints that limit what it says or what it will allow others to say. The state has a monopoly on the legitimate use of violence, but this peculiar kind of power is not needed to curb and restrict public debate. A program manager need not arrest someone (lawfully or otherwise) to have this effect, but only choose one program over another, and although that choice is not wholly free, but constrained by the market, that does not limit the threat that it poses to the integrity of public debate. Rather, it is the source of the problem. All the so-called private media operate within the same structure of constraint, the market, which tends to restrict and confine the issues that are publicly aired.

Just as it is no longer possible to assume that the private sector is all freedom, we can no longer assume that the state is all censorship. That too is one of the lessons of the shift from the street corner orator to CBS. It reminds us that in the modern world the state can enrich as much as it constricts public debate: The state can do this, in part, through the provision of subsidies and other benefits. Here I am thinking not just of the government's role in licensing CBS, but also and more significantly of government appropriations to public television and radio, public and private universities, public libraries, and public educational systems. These institutions bring before the public issues and perspectives otherwise likely to be ignored or slighted by institutions that are privately owned and constrained by the market. They make an enormous contribution to public discourse, and should enjoy the very same privileges that we afford those institutions that rest on private capital (and, of course, should be subject to the same limitations).

We can also look beyond the provision of subsidies, and consider whether the state might enrich public debate by regulating in a manner similar to the policeman. CBS teaches that this kind of governmental action—once again based on content—might be needed to protect our freedom. The power of the media to decide what it broadcasts must be regulated because, as we saw through an understanding of the dynamic of displacement, this power always has a double edge: It subtracts from public debate at the very moment that it adds to it. Similarly, expenditures of political actors might have to be curbed to make certain all views are heard. To date we have ambivalently recognized the value of state regulation of this character on behalf of speech—we have a fairness doctrine for the broadcast media and limited campaign financing laws. But these regulatory measures are today embattled, and in any event, more, not less, is needed. There should also be laws requiring the owners of the new public arenas—the shopping centers—to allow access for political pamphleteers. A commitment to rich public debate will allow, and sometimes even require the state to act in these ways, however elemental and repressive they might at first seem. Autonomy will be sacrificed, and content regulation sometimes allowed, but only on the assumption that public debate might be enriched and our capacity for collective self-determination enhanced. The risks of this approach cannot be ignored, and at moments they seem alarming, but we can only begin to evaluate them when we weigh in the balance the hidden costs of an unrestricted regime of autonomy.

LILLIAN R. BEVIER, REHABILITATING PUBLIC FORUM DOCTRINE: IN DEFENSE OF CATEGORIES

1992 Supreme Court Review 79.

In the companion cases of *International Society for Krishna Consciousness v Lee* and *Lee v International Society for Krishna Consciousness*, the Supreme Court finessed an important opportunity to chart a clear future course for public forum doctrine. Instead of clarifying the law, shifting majorities of justices aligned themselves behind two seemingly inconsistent results, as the Court sustained an airport authority's ban on solicitation of money and invalidated its ban on distribution of literature. The opinions reveal that the Court is deeply divided and that it is mired in substantive and methodological confusion. A doctrinal consensus that once seemed to be emerging has now dissolved, and uncertainties abound on the crucial question of how intensively the Court will review regulations of speech on public property.

* * *

From the point of view of those who advocate a broad public forum right, the law governing the First Amendment constraints on government's power to regulate speech in publicly owned property had an inauspicious beginning. In *Davis v Massachusetts*, the Supreme Court sustained the criminal conviction of a defendant for speaking on the Boston Common without a permit, in violation of an ordinance prohibiting such activity. Echoing the rationale of the Massachusetts Supreme Judicial Court, Chief Justice White analogized the state's rights as owner to those of a private owner. Thus, the Court held that "[t]he right to absolutely exclude all right to use, necessarily includes the authority to determine under what circumstances such use may be availed of, as the greater power contains the lesser."

The *Davis* rule that state ownership entailed unreviewable state power to control speech in public places did not survive. Some thirty years later it yielded to the combined pressures of the modern activist state and the perseverance of civil liberties claimants. The case that effectively overruled *Davis* was *Hague v CIO*, in which the Court voided an ordinance requiring permits for the holding of meetings "in or upon the public streets, highways, public parks or public buildings of Jersey City." In a plurality opinion, Justice Roberts uttered the famous dictum that has become the paradigm of rhetoric supportive of speech rights in public places. Ironically, the dictum also contained the latent ambiguities that continue to plague public forum doctrine to this day:

> Wherever the title of streets and parks may rest, they have immemorially been held in trust for the use of the public and, time out of mind, have been used for purposes of assembly, communicating thoughts between citizens, and discussing public questions. Such use of the streets and public places has, from ancient times, been part of the privileges, immunities, rights, and liberties of citizens. The privilege of a citizen of the United States to use the streets and parks for communication of views on national questions may be regulated in the interest of all; it is not absolute, but relative, and must be exercised in subordination to the general comfort and convenience, and in consonance with peace and good order; but it must not, in the guise of regulation, be abridged or denied.

Justice Roberts's words, which rejected the notion that ownership alone could provide a predicate for unreviewable state power to exclude speech from public places, took on the *rhetorical* "aura of a large democratic principle" of guaranteed access to public places. The passage also points in a quite different direction, however, for in its own terms it applies only to streets and parks. Moreover, the Roberts dictum does not specify the principle's lineage: was it born of constitutional command or was it simply a by-product of entrenched historical practice? Finally, the dictum provided no *analytical* guidance on the criteria for determining the appropriate application of the principle in the future. This analytical gap remains unfilled.

* * *

Apart from establishing the vagueness constraint, the cases decided between 1939 and the early 1960s did little to resolve the substantive ambiguities that were latent in the *Hague* dictum. That there were many unanswered questions became evident when the civil rights movement took to the streets in the mid–1960s, and a variety of local attempts to curb public protests in the South reached the Court for review. In 1965, Harry Kalven wrote for this journal his classic article on the public forum in which he became the first expressly to propose

> that in an open democratic society the streets, the parks, and other public places are an important facility for public discussion and political process. They are in brief a *public forum* that the citizen

> can commandeer ... [a]nd ... what is required is in effect a set of Robert's Rules of Order for the new uses of the public forum.

Kalven's article did more than coin the phrase that has defined for a generation a central First Amendment issue. It also gave shape and content to the *Hague* dictum and poured substance into the concept of a First Amendment right of access to at least some public places—streets and parks.

During the decade or so following Kalven's article, commentators and Court decisions probed the limits and the rationale of this right. Citizens claimed, and sometimes the Court appeared to grant, a First Amendment right to protest in public places that had little in common with streets and parks. Commentators suggested that a presumptive First Amendment right of access to public places (where citizens otherwise have a "right to be") ought to be the baseline against which any governmental decision to exclude must be justified on a case-by-case basis.

* * *

In 1972, the Court in *Grayned v City of Rockford* sustained an ordinance that prohibited any noise near a school that "disturbs ... the peace and good order of such school." Although the Court upheld the ordinance, the opinion appeared to contemporary observers to endorse the activist approach. *Grayned* appeared to offer "a comprehensive, intelligible approach" to the public forum right, for it suggested in dictum that the Court must decide *in every case* "whether the manner of expression is basically incompatible with the normal activity of the particular place at the particular time." The implication was that the government would have to satisfy the Court in every case that its decision to exclude was justified by such a showing of incompatibility.

This implication was short-lived. In *Lehman v City of Shaker Heights*, a political candidate challenged the constitutionality of the city of Shaker Heights' refusal to sell him car card space in the city's buses for his campaign ads. In the face of the city's policy of displaying only commercial advertisements, Lehman argued that the car cards "constitute a public forum protected by the First Amendment, and that there is a guarantee of nondiscriminatory access to such publicly owned and controlled areas of communication." The argument looked like a winner. Because the car cards were already devoted to communicative purposes, Lehman's proposed use could hardly be called "basically incompatible" with them. Nonetheless, Justice Blackmun's plurality opinion declared that "[n]o First Amendment forum is here to be found," and it deferred to the city's decision to deny access.

Public forum jurisprudence since *Grayned* and *Lehman* has reflected a struggle to strike a sensible balance between *Grayned*'s call for judicial review of every denial of First Amendment access and *Lehman*'s call for deference to the decisions of forum managers.

* * *

The cacophony of opinions in *Lee* testifies to deep division among the Justices about the underlying purpose of public forum doctrine. One way to understand the division is to see it as reflecting tension between two models of the First Amendment which have competed since *Hague* to supply the underlying premise of the public forum right.

First, there is the Enhancement model, which is concerned with how much speech takes place in society and with the overall quality of public debate. It is visionary in character. It envisions the First Amendment as embodying an ideal of democratic discourse in a self-governing society. The Enhancement model is committed to the view that First Amendment rules can and ought to be effective tools for augmenting both the quality and quantity of public debate, and accepts the corollary proposition that the Amendment sometimes imposes affirmative duties on government to maximize the opportunities for expression. It focuses almost exclusively on the substantive merits of particular claims. It takes as given that judicial review is an appropriate legal device for the realization of its ideals and seldom displays misgivings about the possibility that it might entail untoward institutional implications.

The Enhancement model derives in large part from the implications of Justice Brennan's opinion in *New York Times v Sullivan.* In particular, it takes its cue from Brennan's affirmation of a "profound national commitment to the principle that debate on public issues should be uninhibited, robust and wide-open." According to the Enhancement model, this commitment has both substantive and strategic dimensions. Substantively, it presupposes that the core mission of the First Amendment is to promote an idealized vision of the democratic process by promoting speech about public and, in particular, political issues. Strategically, it presupposes a judicial mandate to interpret the First Amendment aggressively so as to promote and facilitate "uninhibited, robust and wide-open" debate. In its strategic dimension, this model assumes that " . . . the widest possible dissemination of information from diverse and antagonistic sources is essential to the welfare of the public," and that individuals have a constitutionally protected interest in *effective* self-expression. It ascribes to the Court the responsibility of devising legal rules that will make these assumptions a reality. The Enhancement model assumes that legal doctrine can transform public debate both qualitatively and quantitatively.

On the other hand is the Distortion model. This model shares with the Enhancement model the premise that the central mission of the First Amendment is to protect speech about government and political issues, broadly defined. The Distortion model differs from the Enhancement model, however, in its strategic dimension and its much less idealized vision of public debate. The Distortion model sets a less ambitious agenda for First Amendment doctrine. Instead of conceiving the Amendment as authorizing the Court affirmatively to enhance the quality of public debate or to prime the pump of quantity, the Distortion model portrays the First Amendment as embodying nothing more than a set of constraints upon government actors. It adopts no norm or idealized vision of quality or quantity of public debate except that which results from a rigidly enforced official government neutrality. This model regards the First Amendment as a source of negative rights (freedoms from) rather than as a source of positive entitlements (freedoms to). In contrast to the ambitious agenda of the Enhancement model, the Distortion model entails a modest notion of what First Amendment rules can and ought to do. According to the Distortion model, the essential task of First Amendment rules is to restrain government from deliberately manipulating the content or outcome of public debate and to prohibit it from censoring, punishing, or selectively denying speech opportunities to disfavored views.

The Enhancement and Distortion models have strikingly different implications for judicial review. Under the Enhancement model, the Court's responsibility is to ensure that speech is not unduly curtailed and to devise rules that will maximize the opportunities for expression. Under the Distortion model, the Court's responsibility is only to determine whether the challenged government practice reflects deliberate governmental discrimination against disfavored viewpoints. When the Court adopts a categorical approach under this model, it does so, not with a view to promoting "more speech," but with a view to minimizing the risk of governmental abuse.

CASS SUNSTEIN, REPUBLIC.COM

(2001).

As of this writing, many newspapers, including the *Wall Street Journal*, allow readers to create "personalized" electronic editions, containing exactly what they want, and excluding what they do not want. If you are interested in getting help with the design of an entirely personalized paper, you can consult an ever-growing number of Websites, including individual.com (helpfully named!) and crayon.com (a less helpful name, but evocative in its own way).

In reality, we are not so very far from complete personalization of the system of communications. Consider just a few examples.

- Broadcast.com has "compiled hundreds of thousands of programs so you can find the one that suits your fancy.... For example, if you want to see all the latest fashions from France twenty-four hours of the day you can get them. If you're from Baltimore living in Dallas and you want to listen to WBAL, your hometown station, you can hear it."
- Sonicnet.com allows you to create your own musical universe, consisting of what it calls "Me Music." Me Music is a "place where you can listen to the music you love on the radio station YOU create ... A place where you can watch videos of your favorite artists and new artists."
- Zatso.com allows users to produce "a personal newscast." Its intention is to create a place "where you decide what's news."

Your task is to tell "what TV news stories you're interested in," and Zatso.com turns that information into a specifically designed newscast. From the main "This is the News I Want" menu, you can choose stories with particular words and phrases, or you can select topics, such as sports, weather, crime, health, government/politics, and much more.

- Info Xtra offers "news and entertainment that's important to you," and it allows you to find this "without hunting through newspapers, radio and websites." Personalized news, local weather, and "even your daily horoscope or winning lottery number" will be delivered to you once you specify what you want and when you want it.
- TiVo, a television recording system, is designed, in the words of its Website, to give "you the ultimate control over your TV viewing." It does this by putting "you at the center of your own TV network, so you'll always have access to whatever you want, whenever you want." TiVo "will automatically find and digitally record your favorite programs every time they air" and will help you create "your personal TV line-up." It will also learn your tastes, so that it can "suggest other shows that you may want to record and watch based on your preferences."
- Intertainer, Inc. provides "home entertainment services on demand," not limited to television but also including music, movies, and shopping. Intertainer is intended for people who want "total control" and "personalized experiences." It is "a new way to get whatever movies, music, and television you want anytime you want on your PC or TV."
- George Bell, the chief executive officer of the search engine Excite, exclaims, "We are looking for ways to be able to lift chunks of content off other areas of our service and paste them onto your personal page so you can constantly refresh and update that "newspaper of me." About 43 percent of our entire user data base has personalized their experience on Excite."

If you put the words "personalized news" in any search engine, you will find vivid evidence of what is happening. And that is only the tip of the iceberg. Thus MIT technology specialist Nicholas Negroponte prophecies the emergence of "the Daily Me"—a communications package that is personally designed, with each component fully chosen in advance.

Many of us are applauding these developments, which obviously increase individual convenience and entertainment. But in the midst of the applause, we should insist on asking some questions. How will the increasing power of private control affect democracy? How will the Internet, the new forms of television, and the explosion of communications options alter the capacity of citizens to govern themselves? What are the social preconditions for a well-functioning system of democratic deliberation, or for individual freedom itself?

* * *

For countless people, the Internet is producing a substantial decrease in unanticipated, unchosen interactions with others. Many of us telecommute rather than going to work; this is a rapidly growing trend. Rather than visiting the local bookstore, where we are likely to see a number of diverse people, many of us shop for books on Amazon.com. Others avoid the video store or the grocery because Kosmo.com is entirely delighted to deliver *Citizen Kane* and a pizza. Because of MP3 technology, a visit to the local music store may well seem a hopeless waste of time. Thus communications specialist Ken Auletta enthuses, "I can sample music on my computer, then click and order. I don't have to go to a store. I don't have to get in a car. I don't have to move. God, that's heaven."

If you are interested in anything at all—from computers to linens to diamonds to cars—Buy.com, or MySimon.com, or Bloomingdales.com, or productopia.com, or pricecan.com, or any one of hundreds of others, will be happy to assist you. Indeed, if you would like to attend college, or even to get a graduate degree, you may be able to avoid the campus. College education is already being offered on line. A recent advertisement for New York University invites people to attend "the Virtual College at NYU" and emphasizes that with virtual education, you can take a seat "anywhere" in the class—and even sit alone.

It would be foolish to claim that this is bad, or a loss, in general or on balance. On the contrary, the dramatic increase in convenience is a wonderful blessing for consumers. Driving around in search of gifts, for example, can be a real bother. (Can you remember what this used to be like? Is it still like that for you?) For many of us, the chance to point-and-click is an extraordinary improvement. And many people, both rich and poor, take advantage of new technologies to "go" to places that they could not in any sense have visited before—South Africa, Germany, Iran, stores and more stores everywhere, an immense variety of specialized doctors' offices (with some entertaining surprises as you search; for example, lungcancer.com is a law firm's Website, helping you to sue, rather than a doctor's site, helping you to get better). But it is far from foolish to worry that for millions of people, the consequence of this increased convenience is to decrease the set of chance encounters with diverse others—and also to be concerned about the consequence of the decrease for democracy and citizenship.

Or consider the concept of *collaborative filtering*—an intriguing feature on a number of sites, and one that is rapidly becoming routine. Once you order a book from Amazon.com, for example, Amazon.com is in a position to tell you the choices of other people who like that particular book. Once you have ordered a number of books, Amazon.com knows, and will tell you, what other books—and compact discs and movies—you are likely to like based on what people like you have liked. Other

Websites, such as Qrate.com and Movielens, are prepared to tell you which new movies you'll enjoy and which you won't—simply by asking you to rate certain movies, then matching your ratings to those of other people, and then finding out what people like you think about movies that you haven't seen. Collaborative filtering is used by CDnow, Moviefinder.com, Firefly, and increasingly many others. We have seen that TiVo, the television recording system, is prepared to tell you what other shows you'll like, based on what shows you now like.

Collaborative filtering is only the beginning. "Personalized shopping" is becoming easily available, and it is intended, in the words of a typical account, to "match the interests and buying habits of its customers, from fabric preferences to room designs to wish lists." Or consider the suggestion that before long we will "have virtual celebrities.... They'll look terrific. In fact, they'll look so terrific that their faces will be exactly what *you* think is beautiful and not necessarily what your neighbor thinks, because they'll be customized for each home." (Is it surprising to hear that at least one Website provides personalized romance stories? That it asks you for information about "your fantasy lover," and then it designs a story to suit your tastes?)

In many ways what is happening is quite wonderful, and some of the recommendations from Amazon.com and analogous services are miraculously good, even uncanny. (Thousands of people have discovered new favorite authors through this route.) But it might well be disturbing if the consequence is to encourage people to narrow their horizons, or to cater to their existing tastes rather than to form new ones. Suppose, for example, that people with a certain political conviction find themselves learning about more and more authors with the same view, and thus strengthening their existing judgments, only because most of what they are encouraged to read says the same thing. In a democratic society, might this not be troubling?

E Pluribus Unum, and Jefferson vs. Madison

Any heterogeneous society faces a risk of fragmentation. This risk has been serious in many periods in American history, most notably during the Civil War, but often in the twentieth century as well. The institutions of the Constitution were intended to diminish the danger, partly by producing a good mix of local and national rule, partly through the system of checks and balances, and partly through the symbol of the Constitution itself. Thus the idea of *e pluribus unum* (from many, one) can be found on ordinary currency, in a brief, frequent reminder of a central constitutional goal.

Consider in this regard the instructive debate between Thomas Jefferson and James Madison about the value of a bill of rights. In the founding era, Madison, the most important force behind the Constitution itself, sharply opposed such a bill, on the ground that it was unnecessary and was likely to sow confusion. Jefferson thought otherwise, and insisted that a bill of rights, enforced by courts, could be a bulwark of liberty. Madison was eventually convinced of this point, but he emphasized a very different consideration: the unifying and educative functions of a bill of rights.

In a letter to Jefferson on October 17, 1788, Madison asked, "What use, then, it may be asked, can a bill of rights serve in popular Government?" His basic answer was that the "political truths declared in that solemn manner acquire by, degrees the character of fundamental maxims of free Government, and as they become incorporated with the National sentiment, counteract the impulses of interest and passion." In Madison's view, the Bill of Rights, along with the Constitution itself, would eventually become a source of shared understandings and commitments among extremely diverse people. The example illustrates the founders' belief that for a diverse people to be self-governing, it was essential to provide a range of common experiences.

Two Conceptions Of Sovereignty, and Holmes vs. Brandeis

We are now in a position to distinguish between two conceptions of sovereignty. The first involves consumer sovereignty, the idea behind free markets. The second involves political sovereignty, the idea behind free nations. The notion of consumer sovereignty underlies enthusiasm for the "Daily Me"; it is the underpinning of any utopian vision of the unlimited power to filter. Writing in 1995, Bill Gates cheerfully predicted, "Customized information is a natural extension.... For your own daily dose of news, you might subscribe to several review services and let a software agent or a human one pick and choose from them to compile your completely customized 'newspaper.' These subscription services, whether human or electronic, will gather information that conforms to a particular philosophy and set of interests." Or recall the first epigraph to this book, Gates's celebratory words in 1999: "When you turn on DirectTV and you step through every channel—well, there's three minutes of your life. When you walk into your living room six years from now, you'll be able to just say what you're interested in, and have the screen help you pick out a video that you care about. It's not going to be 'Let's look at channels 4, 5, and 7.' " This is the principle of consumer sovereignty in action.

The notion of political sovereignty underlies the democratic alternative, which poses a challenge to Gates's vision on the ground that it may well undermine both self-government and freedom, properly conceived. Recall here John Dewey's words: "Majority rule, just as majority rule, is as foolish as its critics charge it with being. But it never is *merely* majority rule.... The important consideration is that opportunity be given ideas to speak and to become the possession of the multitude. The essential need is the improvement of the methods and constitution of debate, discussion and persuasion. That is *the* problem of the public."

Consumer sovereignty means that individual consumers are permitted to choose as they wish, subject to the constraints provided by the price system, and also by their current holdings and requirements. This idea plays a significant role in thinking not only about economic markets, but also about both politics and communications. When we talk as if politicians are "selling" a message, and even themselves, we are treating the political domain as a kind of market, subject to the forces of supply and demand. And when we act as if the purpose of a system of communications is to ensure that people can see exactly what they "want," the notion of consumer sovereignty is very much at work.

The idea of political sovereignty stands on different foundations. It does not take individual tastes as fixed or given. It prizes democratic self-government, understood as a requirement of "government by discussion," accompanied by reasongiving in the public domain. Political sovereignty comes with its own distinctive preconditions, and these are violated if government power is not backed by justifications, and represents instead the product of force or simple majority will.

Of course the two conceptions of sovereignty are in potential tension. A commitment to consumer sovereignty may well compromise political sovereignty if, for example, free consumer choices result in insufficient understanding of public problems, or if they make it difficult to have anything like a shared or deliberative culture. We will create serious problems if we confound consumer sovereignty with political sovereignty. If the latter is our governing ideal, for example, we will evaluate the system of free expression partly by seeing whether it promotes democratic goals. If we care only about consumer sovereignty, the only question is whether consumers are getting what they want. The distinction matters for policy as well. If the government takes steps to increase the level of substantive debate on television or in public culture, it might well be undermining consumer sovereignty at the same time that it is promoting democratic self-government.

With respect to the system of freedom of speech, the conflict between consumer sovereignty and political sovereignty can be found in an unexpected place: the great constitutional dissents of Supreme Court Justices Oliver Wendell Holmes and Louis Brandeis. In the early part of the twentieth century, Holmes and Brandeis were the twin heroes of freedom of speech, dissenting, usually together, from Supreme Court decisions allowing the government to regulate political dissent. Sometimes Holmes wrote for the two dissenters; sometimes the author was Brandeis. But the two spoke in quite different terms. Holmes wrote of "free trade in ideas," and treated speech as part of a great political market, with which government could not legitimately interfere. Consider a passage from Holmes' greatest free speech opinion.

> When men have realized that time has upset many fighting faiths, they may come to believe even more than they believe the very foundations of their own conduct that the ultimate good desired is better reached by free trade in ideas—that the best test of truth is the power of the thought to get itself accepted in the competition of the market, and that truth is the only ground upon which their

> wishes safely can be carried out. That at any rate is the theory of our Constitution.

Brandeis's language, in his greatest free speech opinion, was quite different.

> Those who won our independence believed that the final end of the state was to make men free to develop their faculties; and that in its government the deliberative forces should prevail over the arbitrary.... They believed that ... without free speech and assembly discussion would be futile; ... that the greatest menace to freedom is an inert people; that public discussion is a political duty; and that this should be a fundamental principle of the American government.

Note Brandeis's suggestion that the greatest threat to freedom is an "inert people," and his insistence, altogether foreign to Holmes, that public discussion is not only a right but "a political duty." Brandeis sees self-government as something dramatically different from an exercise in consumer sovereignty. On Brandeis's self-consciously republican conception of free speech, unrestricted consumer choice is not an appropriate foundation for policy in a context where the very formation of preferences, and the organizing processes of the democratic order, are at stake.

In fact Brandeis can be taken to have offered a conception of the social role of the idealized citizen. For such a citizen, active engagement in politics, at least some of the time, is an obligation, not just an entitlement. If citizens are "inert," freedom itself is at risk. This does not mean that people have to be thinking about public affairs all or most of the time. But it does mean that each of us has rights and duties as citizens, not simply as consumers. As we will see, active citizen engagement is necessary to promote not only democracy but social well-being too. And in the modern era, one of the most pressing obligations of a citizenry that is not inert is to ensure that "deliberative forces should prevail over the arbitrary." For this to happen, it is indispensable to ensure that the system of communications promotes democratic goals. Those goals emphatically require both unchosen exposures and shared experiences.

Republicanism Without Nostalgia

These are abstractions; it is time to be more concrete. I will identify three problems in the hypothesized world of perfect filtering. These difficulties would beset any system in which individuals had complete control over their communications universe and exercised that control so as to decrease *shared communications experiences* and *exposure to materials that would not have been chosen in advance but that nonetheless are beneficial*, both to the person who is exposed to them and to society at large.

The first difficulty involves fragmentation. The problem here comes from the creation of diverse speech communities, whose members make significantly different communications choices. A possible consequence is considerable difficulty in mutual understanding. When society is fragmented in this way, diverse groups will tend to polarize, in a way that can breed extremism and even hatred and violence. New technologies, emphatically including the Internet, are dramatically increasing people's ability to hear echoes of their own voices and to wall themselves off from others. An important result is the existence of *cybercascades*—processes of information exchange in which a certain fact or point of view becomes widespread, simply because so many people seem to believe it.

The second difficulty involves a distinctive characteristic of information. Information is a public good in the technical sense that once some person knows something, other people are likely to benefit as well. If you learn about crime in the neighborhood or about the problem of global warming, you will probably tell other people, and they will benefit from what you have learned. In a system in which each person can "customize" his own communications universe, there is a risk that people will make choices that generate too little information, at least to the extent that individual choices are not made with reference to their social benefits. An advantage of a system with general interest intermediaries and with public forums—with broad access by speakers to diverse publics—is that it ensures a kind of social spreading of information. At the same time, an individually filtered speech universe is likely to underproduce what I will call *solidarity goods*—goods whose value increases with the number of people who are consuming them. A presidential debate is a classic example of a solidarity good.

The third and final difficulty has to do with the proper understanding of freedom and the relationship between consumers and citizens. If we believe in consumer sovereignty, and if we celebrate the power to filter, we are likely to think that freedom consists in the satisfaction of private preferences—in an absence of restrictions on individual choices. This is a widely held view about freedom. Indeed, it is a view that underlies much current thinking about free speech. But it is badly misconceived. Freedom consists not simply in preference satisfaction but also in the chance to have preferences and beliefs formed under decent conditions—in the ability to have preferences formed after exposure to a sufficient amount of information, and also to an appropriately wide and diverse range of options. There can be no assurance of freedom in a system committed to the "Daily Me."

"Must Carry": Constitutional Debates

Some of the most interesting developments in the law of speech involve "access rights" or "must carry" rules. In fact the public forum doctrine creates a kind of "must carry" rule for streets and parks. These sites must be opened up for speech. You and I are entitled to have access to them. Is there any place for "must carry" rules on the Internet, or in the current technological environment? Could Congress say that Websites must carry certain links?

To answer these questions, and as preface for discussion of policy options, it is necessary to have some sense of the legal background. In the 1970s, the Supreme Court held that government has the authority to subject television and radio broadcasters to a kind of "must carry" rule, in the form of the old fairness doctrine, requiring attention to public issues and an opportunity for diverse views to speak. At the same time, the Court rejected the idea that private newspapers may be treated as public forums and subject to "must carry" rules. The apparent difference between broadcasters and newspapers—fragile in the 1970s, and still more fragile today—is that the former are "scarce," largely for technological reasons, and hence are more properly subject to governmental controls.

Now that the scarcity rationale has weakened, the continued viability of the fairness doctrine remains an open question. If the FCC tried to reinstate the doctrine, the Court might strike it down. But the Court has nonetheless upheld legislation that imposes "must carry" rules on cable television providers. The relevant legislation, still on the books, requires cable providers to set aside a number of their channels for both "local commercial television stations" and "noncommercial educational television stations." Congress defended these requirements as a way of ensuring the economic viability of broadcasters, on whom many millions of Americans continue to rely (about 30% as of 2000). In finding the "must carry" requirements constitutional, the Court said, "assuring that the public has access to a multiplicity of information sources is a governmental purpose of the highest order, for it promotes values central to the First Amendment." The Court also emphasized the "potential for abuse of ... private power over a central avenue of communication," and stressed that the Constitution "does not disable the government from taking steps to ensure that private interests not restrict, through physical control of a critical pathway of communication, the free flow of information and ideas."

In so saying, the Court was recalling Justice Brandeis' emphatically republican conception of the First Amendment. Indeed, Justice Breyer, in a separate opinion, made the link with Justice Brandeis explicit: The statute's "policy, in turn, seeks to facilitate the public discussion and informed deliberation, which, as Justice Brandeis pointed out many years ago, democratic government presupposes and the First Amendment seeks to achieve." Here, then, is an unambiguous endorsement of the idea that government has the power to regulate communications technologies to promote goals associated with deliberative democracy.

So far, so good. But for those interested in thinking about the implications of the Court's decision for the Internet and other technologies, there is considerable ambiguity in the case. How crucial was it, to the Court's reasoning, that the cable provider controlled access to cable stations? Suppose that a speaker seeks a right of access to a particular Website, and complains that he is excluded by private power (made possible of course by law). Might "private power" also be a problem if, as with the Internet, there are countless other available Websites, and indeed if speakers seeking access to one particular Website are permitted to create Websites of their own? The Court does not say. The constitutional status of other sorts of "must carry" rules, and other rights of access, is unclear.

Links, Hyperlinks, and the Scarce Commodity of Attention

A central issue for the future will involve the use of links and hyperlinks, designed to heighten or to decrease the risk of fragmentation. To understand that issue, return to the fact that one of the most important of all commodities, in the current situation, is people's attention. This is what companies are endlessly competing to obtain. Much activity on the Internet, by those interested in profits and other goods, is designed to produce greater attention, even if only for a moment. If a company or a political candidate can get attention from ten thousand people for as little as two seconds, it will have accomplished a great deal.

Almost everyone has noticed that many Websites do not, and need not, charge a fee for users. If you want to go to WashingtonPost.com, or NewYorkTimes.com, or NewRepublic.com, you can do so for free, and hence you can get the content of countless magazines and newspapers without paying a penny. Nor is the phenomenon limited to magazines and newspapers. If you want to learn about cancer, for example, you can find out a great deal from oncology.com, entirely free of charge. Why is this? It is because advertisers are willing to foot the bill. What advertisers are buying is access, and usually brief access at that, to people's eyes—a small period of attention.

Here again we can see that those who use Websites are commodities at least as much as they are consumers; they are what Websites are selling to advertisers for a fee, sometimes a large one. Targeting and customization are playing a large role here, as advertisers come to learn, with some precision, how many people, and which people, visit from which advertisements. Of course advertisements cannot guarantee sales. Most people who see an icon for Bloomingdale's or Amazon.com will simply ignore it. But some will not; they will be curious and see what there is to see. Or they will file it away in some part of their minds for future use.

If we combine an understanding of access rights and "must carry" rules with an appreciation of the crucial role of attention, we might enlist advertisers' practices in the service of public interest goals. In other words, people in the private and public sector, knowing that attention is valuable, might think of ways to capture that attention, not to coerce people, but to trigger their interest in material that might produce individual and social benefits. Links among sites are the obvious strategy here. Ideally, such links would be provided voluntarily. It might also be worthwhile to consider legislation designed to ensure more in the way of links and hyperlinks, on a viewpoint-neutral basis.

Linked Sites

In the context of the Internet, the point of "carrying," or "must carry," is to get people's attention, however fleetingly. Consider in this light a proposal: Providers of material with a certain point of view might also provide access to sites with a very different point of view. Townhall.com, a site featuring conservative opinions, might agree to provide icons for liberal sites, in return for an agreement, from those sites, to provide icons for sites carried on Townhall.com. The icon itself would not require anyone to read anything. It would merely provide a signal, to the viewer, that there is a place where a different point of view might be consulted. Of the thousands or millions of people who choose any particular site, not most, but undoubtedly a few, would be sufficiently interested to look further. Best of all, this form of "carriage" would replicate many features of the public street and the general interest intermediary. It would alert people to the existence of materials other than those they read. We have seen that some sites do this already. The problem is that the practice remains unusual.

We could even imagine a situation in which many partisan sites offer a links page saying something like, "We have a clear point of view, and we hope that more people will come to believe what we do. But we are also committed to democratic debate and to discussion among people who think differently. To that end we are providing links to other sites, in the interest of providing genuine debate on these issues." If many sites would agree to do this, the problem of fragmentation might be substantially reduced.

There is another possibility. Especially popular Websites could provide links to a random draw of sites designed to educate people and to promote attention to public issues. The random draw of links might change every month, or every week, or even every day. All that would be required would be the display of an icon. It would be up to you to decide whether to visit the site. We could easily imagine a situation in which (say) the twenty-five most popular sites, in any two-month period, provided icons for a random draw of many other sites dealing with public questions. Of course this is only a sketch; the details could be filled in various different ways.

Hyperlinks

For those who object to intrusions on the siteowner's control over the site itself, other approaches might be imagined. The simplest would be to increase the use of hyperlinks. Consider the fact that when you use LEXIS, the legal research tool, and call up any judicial opinion, you will see, in that opinion, references to other judicial opinions and occasionally academic writing; those references are hyperlinks, enabling you to click on them and thus to get immediate access to the document in question. Many sites now offer a similar feature. In some cases, for example, a book title given in a review or discussion will operate as a hyperlink; if you click on it, you will immediately go to a site from which you can purchase the book in question.

We might easily imagine a situation in which textual references to organizations or institutions are hyperlinks, so that if, for example, a conservative magazine such as the *National Review* refers to the World Wildlife Fund or Environmental Defense, it also allows readers instant access to their sites. As compared with links in the form of advertisements, the advantage of the hyperlink approach is that it is less costly to the siteowner and less intrusive on its prerogatives—indeed, it is barely an intrusion at all. The disadvantage is that a hyperlink is generally less attention-grabbing than an advertisement. Here as elsewhere, the ideal would be for sites to do this on their own, not through government mandates. In chapter 3 we saw that it is common for political sites to offer links to like-minded sites, but quite uncommon for them to offer links to those with opposed views. We could easily imagine the emergence of a new and good democratic custom: Sites would generally ensure that references to other organizations are hyperlinks too.

To the extent that sites do not do this, voluntary self-regulation through cooperative agreements might do the job. If these routes do not work, it would be worthwhile considering content-neutral regulation, designed to ensure more in the way of both links and hyperlinks. To be sure, free speech problems could be raised here—especially in light of the danger that a requirement of hyperlinks might discourage references to opposing groups in the first instance. What is most important is that we could easily imagine a situation in which links or hyperlinks were the ordinary practice, used in a way that would promote goals of both consumers and citizens, without compromising the legitimate interest of site owners.

There are other possible approaches, more and less radical. For example, those who choose to visit certain sites—say, especially popular ones or ones with distinctive political views—might automatically be connected, at certain times, to sites maintained by those seeking access. Drawing on the public forum analogy, law and technology specialist Noah Zatz has suggested that through this route, "sidewalks" might be created in cyberspace, allowing speakers to have "specific access" to certain users, subject to reasonable time, place, and manner restrictions. An obvious objection is that many people would find this intrusive. Attempting to have access to the Website of *Time* magazine, they might find themselves opening a page to Citizens for Control of Nuclear Power as well. This is indeed an intrusion. But is it much different from daily life on a street or in a park? Is it much different from reading the newspaper or a general interest magazine? Because it is so easy to close a Webpage, any intrusion on Internet users seems far more trivial than those introduced via public forums and general interest intermediaries, intrusions that produce many benefits. What is important about Zatz's proposal is not the relatively complex details, which I do not mean to endorse, but the effort to adapt technology to the service of goals associated with the public forum doctrine.

* * *

Much of what I have argued here is captured in some passages from two great theorists of freedom and democracy, John Stuart Mill and John Dewey. First Mill:

> It is hardly possible to overstate the value, in the present state of human improvement, of placing human beings in contact with other persons dissimilar to themselves, and with modes of thought and action unlike those with which they are familiar.... Such communication has always been, and is peculiarly in the present age, one of the primary-sources of progress.

And now Dewey:

> The belief that thought and its communication are now free simply because legal restrictions which once obtained have been done away is absurd. Its currency perpetuates the infantile state of social knowledge. For it blurs recognition of our central need to possess conceptions which are used as tools of directed inquiry and which are tested, rectified and caused to grow in actual use. No man and no mind was ever emancipated merely by being left alone.

With these ideas in view, I have stressed the severe problems, for individuals and societies alike, that are likely to be created by the practice of self-insulation—by a situation in which many of us wall ourselves off from the concerns and opinions of our fellow citizens. The ideal of consumer sovereignty, well-represented in the supposedly utopian vision of complete "personalization," could produce severe risks for a democracy. Rather than a utopian vision, it is best understood as a kind of nightmare, the stuff of science fiction, carrying large lessons about some neglected requirements of democratic self-government.

Questions

1) Based on the vision of self-government that he elaborates, should Meiklejohn be as concerned about "The Daily Me" as Sunstein is? Who among Milton, Madison, Mill, Hand, Holmes, and Brandeis ought to be especially troubled by "The Daily Me"?

2) Does Sunstein overestimate the degree to which persons using the Internet are able to filter out unwanted ideas and information? If studies were to show *both* that the Internet leads most people to customize their intake of information and opinion more than was common in the pre-digital era *and* that most people who use the Internet nevertheless are exposed to a wider range as well as a greater volume of information and opinion due to the efficiencies of the medium, does Sunstein's argument fall apart?

3) Is it appropriate to alter our understanding of the meaning of the First Amendment based on the perceived social effects of technological developments? If so, should such alterations await the perception that the social effects are well documented and stable?

4) Does Sunstein undervalue the contribution to democracy, and to the values of the First Amendment, that the Internet makes by empowering persons with unorthodox views to find like-minded confederates and to mobilize for political action?

UNITED STATES v. AMERICAN LIBRARY ASSOCIATION

Supreme Court of the United States, 2003.
539 U.S. 194, 123 S.Ct. 2297, 156 L.Ed.2d 221.

CHIEF JUSTICE REHNQUIST announced the judgment of the Court and delivered an opinion, in which JUSTICE O'CONNOR, JUSTICE SCALIA, and JUSTICE THOMAS joined.

To address the problems associated with the availability of Internet pornography in public libraries, Congress enacted the Children's Internet Protection Act (CIPA). Under CIPA, a public library may not receive federal assistance to provide Internet access unless it installs software to block images that constitute obscenity or child pornography, and to prevent minors from obtaining access to material that is harmful to them. The District Court held these provisions facially invalid on the ground that they induce public libraries to violate patrons' First Amendment rights. We now reverse.

To help public libraries provide their patrons with Internet access, Congress offers two forms of federal assistance. First, the E-rate program established by the Telecommunications Act of 1996 entitles qualifying libraries to buy Internet access at a discount. In the year ending June 30, 2002, libraries received $58.5 million in such discounts. Second, pursuant to the Library Services and Technology Act (LSTA), as amended, the Institute of Museum and Library Services makes grants to state library administrative agencies to "electronically lin[k] libraries with educational, social, or information services," "assis[t] libraries in accessing information through electronic networks," and "pa[y] costs for libraries to acquire or share computer systems and telecommunications technologies." In fiscal year 2002, Congress appropriated more than $149 million in LSTA grants. These programs have succeeded greatly in bringing Internet access to public libraries: By 2000, 95% of the Nation's libraries provided public Internet access.

By connecting to the Internet, public libraries provide patrons with a vast amount of valuable information. But there is also an enormous amount of pornography on the Internet, much of which is easily obtained. The accessibility of this material has created serious problems for libraries, which have found that patrons of all ages, including minors, regularly search for online pornography. Some patrons also expose others to pornographic images by leaving them displayed on Internet terminals or printed at library printers.

Upon discovering these problems, Congress became concerned that the E-rate and LSTA programs were facilitating access to illegal and harmful pornography. Congress learned that adults "us[e] library computers to access pornography that is then exposed to staff, passersby, and children," and that "minors acces[s] child and adult pornography in libraries."

But Congress also learned that filtering software that blocks access to pornographic Web sites could provide a reasonably effective way to prevent such uses of library resources. By 2000, before Congress enacted CIPA, almost 17% of public libraries used such software on at least some of their Internet terminals, and 7% had filters on all of them. A library can set such software to block categories of material, such as "Pornography" or "Violence." When a patron tries to view a site that falls within such a category, a screen appears indicating that the site is blocked. But a filter set to block pornography may sometimes block other sites that present neither obscene nor pornographic material, but that nevertheless trigger the filter. To minimize this problem, a library can set its software to prevent the blocking of material that falls into categories like "Education," "History," and "Medical." A library may also add or delete specific sites from a blocking category, and anyone can ask companies that furnish filtering software to unblock particular sites.

Responding to this information, Congress enacted CIPA. It provides that a library may not receive E-rate or LSTA assistance unless it has "a policy of Internet safety for minors that includes the operation of a technology protection measure ... that protects against access" by all persons to "visual depictions" that constitute "obscen[ity]" or "child pornography," and that protects against access by minors to "visual depictions" that are "harmful to minors." The statute defines a "[t]echnology protection measure" as "a specific technology that blocks or filters Internet access to material covered by" CIPA. CIPA also permits the library to "disable" the filter "to enable access for bona fide research or other lawful purposes." Under the E-rate program, disabling is permitted "during use by an adult." Under the LSTA program, disabling is permitted during use by any person.

Appellees are a group of libraries, library associations, library patrons, and Web site publishers, including the American Library Association (ALA) and the Multnomah County Public Library in Portland, Oregon (Multnomah). They sued the United States and the Government agencies and officials responsible for administering the E-rate and LSTA programs in District Court, challenging the constitutionality of CIPA's filtering provisions. A three-judge District Court convened pursuant to § 1741(a) of CIPA.

After a trial, the District Court ruled that CIPA was facially unconstitutional and enjoined the relevant agencies and officials from withholding federal assistance for failure to comply with CIPA. The District Court held that Congress had exceeded its authority under the Spending Clause, U.S. Const., Art. I, § 8, cl. 1, because, in the court's view, "any public library that complies with CIPA's conditions will necessarily violate the First Amendment." The court acknowledged that "generally the First Amendment subjects libraries' content-based decisions about which print materials to acquire for their collections to only rational [basis] review. But it distinguished libraries' decisions to make certain Internet material inaccessible. "The central difference," the court stated, "is that by providing patrons with even filtered Internet access, the library permits patrons to receive speech on a virtually unlimited number of topics, from a virtually unlimited number of speakers, without attempting to restrict patrons' access to speech that the library, in the exercise of its professional judgment, determines to be particularly valuable." Reasoning that "the provision of Internet access within a public library . . . is for use by the public . . . for expressive activity," the court analyzed such access as a "designated public forum." The District Court also likened Internet access in libraries to "traditional public fora . . . such as sidewalks and parks" because it "promotes First Amendment values in an analogous manner."

Based on both of these grounds, the court held that the filtering software contemplated by CIPA was a content-based restriction on access to a public forum, and was therefore subject to strict scrutiny. Applying this standard, the District Court held that, although the Government has a compelling interest "in preventing the dissemination of obscenity, child pornography, or, in the case of minors, material harmful to minors," the use of software filters is not narrowly tailored to further those interests. We noted probable jurisdiction, 537 U.S. 1017, and now reverse.

Congress has wide latitude to attach conditions to the receipt of federal assistance in order to further its policy objectives. *South Dakota v. Dole,* 483 U.S. 203, 206 (1987). But Congress may not "induce" the recipient "to engage in activities that would themselves be unconstitutional. To determine whether libraries would violate the First Amendment by employing the filtering software that CIPA requires,[2] we must first examine the role of libraries in our society."

Public libraries pursue the worthy missions of facilitating learning and cultural enrichment. Appellee ALA's Library Bill of Rights states that libraries should provide "[b]ooks and other . . . resources . . . for the interest, information, and enlightenment of all people of the community the library serves." To fulfill their traditional missions, public libraries

2. Justice Stevens misapprehends the analysis we must perform to determine whether CIPA exceeds Congress' authority under the Spending Clause. He asks and answers whether it is constitutional for Congress to "impose [CIPA's filtering] requirement" on public libraries, instead of "allowing local decisionmakers to tailor their responses to local problems." But under our well-established Spending Clause precedent, that is not the proper inquiry. Rather, as the District Court correctly recognized, we must ask whether the condition that Congress requires "would . . . be unconstitutional" if performed by the library itself.

CIPA does not directly regulate private conduct; rather, Congress has exercised its Spending Power by specifying conditions on the receipt of federal funds. Therefore, *Dole* provides the appropriate framework for assessing CIPA's constitutionality.

must have broad discretion to decide what material to provide to their patrons. Although they seek to provide a wide array of information, their goal has never been to provide "universal coverage." Instead, public libraries seek to provide materials "that would be of the greatest direct benefit or interest to the community." To this end, libraries collect only those materials deemed to have "requisite and appropriate quality." See W. Katz, Collection Development: The Selection of Materials for Libraries 6 (1980) ("The librarian's responsibility ... is to separate out the gold from the garbage, not to preserve everything").

We have held in two analogous contexts that the government has broad discretion to make content-based judgments in deciding what private speech to make available to the public. In *Arkansas Ed. Television Comm'n v. Forbes,* 523 U.S. 666, 672–673 (1998), we held that public forum principles do not generally apply to a public television station's editorial judgments regarding the private speech it presents to its viewers. "[B]road rights of access for outside speakers would be antithetical, as a general rule, to the discretion that stations and their editorial staff must exercise to fulfill their journalistic purpose and statutory obligations." Recognizing a broad right of public access "would [also] risk implicating the courts in judgments that should be left to the exercise of journalistic discretion."

Similarly, in *National Endowment for Arts v. Finley,* 524 U.S. 569, 585, 586 (1998), we upheld an art funding program that required the National Endowment for the Arts (NEA) to use content-based criteria in making funding decisions. We explained that "[a]ny content-based considerations that may be taken into account in the grant-making process are a consequence of the nature of arts funding." In particular, "[t]he very assumption of the NEA is that grants will be awarded according to the 'artistic worth of competing applicants,' and absolute neutrality is simply inconceivable." We expressly declined to apply forum analysis, reasoning that it would conflict with "NEA's mandate ... to make esthetic judgments, and the inherently content-based 'excellence' threshold for NEA support."

The principles underlying *Forbes* and *Finley* also apply to a public library's exercise of judgment in selecting the material it provides to its patrons. Just as forum analysis and heightened judicial scrutiny are incompatible with the role of public television stations and the role of the NEA, they are also incompatible with the discretion that public libraries must have to fulfill their traditional missions. Public library staffs necessarily consider content in making collection decisions and enjoy broad discretion in making them.

The public forum principles on which the District Court relied, 201 F.Supp.2d, at 457–470, are out of place in the context of this case. Internet access in public libraries is neither a "traditional" nor a "designated" public forum. See *Cornelius v. NAACP Legal Defense & Ed. Fund, Inc.,* 473 U.S. 788, 802 (1985) (describing types of forums). First, this resource—which did not exist until quite recently—has not "immemorially been held in trust for the use of the public and, time out of mind, ... been used for purposes of assembly, communication of thoughts between citizens, and discussing public questions." *International Soc. for Krishna Consciousness, Inc. v. Lee,* 505 U.S. 672, 679 (1992). We have "rejected the view that traditional public forum status extends beyond its historic confines." *Forbes, supra,* at 678. The doctrines surrounding traditional public forums may not be extended to situations where such history is lacking.

Nor does Internet access in a public library satisfy our definition of a "designated public forum." To create such a forum, the government must make an affirmative choice to open up its property for use as a public forum. "The government does not create a public forum by inaction or by permitting limited discourse, but only by intentionally opening a non-traditional forum for public discourse." *Cornelius, supra,* at 802. The District Court likened public libraries' Internet terminals to the forum at issue in *Rosenberger v. Rector and Visitors of Univ. of Va.,* 515 U.S. 819 (1995). In *Rosenberger,* we considered the "Student Activity Fund" established by the University of Virginia that subsidized all manner of student publications except those based on religion. We held that the fund had created a limited public forum by giving public money to student groups who wished to publish, and therefore could not discriminate on the basis of viewpoint.

The situation here is very different. A public library does not acquire Internet terminals in order to create a public forum for Web publishers to express themselves, any more than it collects books in order to provide a public forum for the authors of books to speak. It provides Internet access, not to "encourage a diversity of views from private speakers," *Rosenberger, supra,* at 834, but for the same reasons it offers other library resources: to facilitate research, learning, and recreational pursuits by furnishing materials of requisite and appropriate quality. As Congress recognized, "[t]he Internet is simply another method for making information available in a school or library." It is "no more than a technological extension of the book stack."[3]

3. Even if appellees had proffered more persuasive evidence that public libraries intended to create a forum for speech by connecting to the Internet, we would hesitate to import "the public forum doctrine ... wholesale into" the context of the Internet. *Denver Area Ed. Telecommunications Consortium, Inc. v. FCC,* 518 U.S. 727, 749 (1996) (opinion of BREYER, J.). "[W]e are wary of the notion that a partial analogy in one context, for which we have developed doctrines, can compel a full range of decisions in such a new and changing area."

The dissents agree with the District Court that less restrictive alternatives to filtering software would suffice to meet Congress' goals. But we require the Government to employ the least restrictive means only when the forum is a public one and strict scrutiny applies. For the reasons stated above, such is not the case here. In deciding not to collect pornographic material from the Internet, a public library need not satisfy a court that it has pursued the least restrictive means of implementing that decision.

In any case, the suggested alternatives have their own drawbacks. Close monitoring of computer users would be far more intrusive than the use of filtering software, and would risk transforming the role of a librarian from a professional to whom patrons turn for assistance into a compliance officer whom many patrons might wish to avoid. Moving terminals to places where

The District Court disagreed because, whereas a library reviews and affirmatively chooses to acquire every book in its collection, it does not review every Web site that it makes available. Based on this distinction, the court reasoned that a public library enjoys less discretion in deciding which Internet materials to make available than in making book selections. We do not find this distinction constitutionally relevant. A library's failure to make quality-based judgments about all the material it furnishes from the Web does not somehow taint the judgments it does make. A library's need to exercise judgment in making collection decisions depends on its traditional role in identifying suitable and worthwhile material; it is no less entitled to play that role when it collects material from the Internet than when it collects material from any other source. Most libraries already exclude pornography from their print collections because they deem it inappropriate for inclusion. We do not subject these decisions to heightened scrutiny; it would make little sense to treat libraries' judgments to block online pornography any differently, when these judgments are made for just the same reason.

Moreover, because of the vast quantity of material on the Internet and the rapid pace at which it changes, libraries cannot possibly segregate, item by item, all the Internet material that is appropriate for inclusion from all that is not. While a library could limit its Internet collection to just those sites it found worthwhile, it could do so only at the cost of excluding an enormous amount of valuable information that it lacks the capacity to review. Given that tradeoff, it is entirely reasonable for public libraries to reject that approach and instead exclude certain categories of content, without making individualized judgments that everything they do make available has requisite and appropriate quality.

* * *

Within broad limits, "when the Government appropriates public funds to establish a program it is entitled to define the limits of that program." *Rust v. Sullivan,* 500 U.S. 173, 194. In *Rust,* Congress had appropriated federal funding for family planning services and forbidden the use of such funds in programs that provided abortion counseling. Recipients of these funds challenged this restriction, arguing that it impermissibly conditioned the receipt of a benefit on the relinquishment of their constitutional right to engage in abortion counseling. We rejected that claim, recognizing that "the Government [was] not denying a benefit to anyone, but [was] instead simply insisting that public funds be spent for the purposes for which they were authorized."

The same is true here. The E-rate and LSTA programs were intended to help public libraries fulfill their traditional role of obtaining material of requisite and appropriate quality for educational and infor-

their displays cannot easily be seen by other patrons, or installing privacy screens or recessed monitors, would not address a library's interest in preventing patrons from deliberately using its computers to view online pornography. To the contrary, these alternatives would make it *easier* for patrons to do so.

mational purposes. Congress may certainly insist that these "public funds be spent for the purposes for which they were authorized." Especially because public libraries have traditionally excluded pornographic material from their other collections, Congress could reasonably impose a parallel limitation on its Internet assistance programs. As the use of filtering software helps to carry out these programs, it is a permissible condition under *Rust.*

JUSTICE STEVENS asserts the premise that "[a] federal statute penalizing a library for failing to install filtering software on every one of its Internet-accessible computers would unquestionably violate [the First] Amendment." But—assuming again that public libraries have First Amendment rights—CIPA does not "penalize" libraries that choose not to install such software, or deny them the right to provide their patrons with unfiltered Internet access. Rather, CIPA simply reflects Congress' decision not to subsidize their doing so. To the extent that libraries wish to offer unfiltered access, they are free to do so without federal assistance. "A refusal to fund protected activity, without more, cannot be equated with the imposition of a 'penalty' on that activity." *Rust, supra,* at 193. "[A] legislature's decision not to subsidize the exercise of a fundamental right does not infringe the right." *Id.*[6]

Appellees mistakenly contend, in reliance on *Legal Services Corporation v. Velazquez,* 531 U.S. 533 (2001), that CIPA's filtering conditions "[d]istor[t] the [u]sual [f]unctioning of [p]ublic [l]ibraries." In *Velazquez,* the Court concluded that a Government program of furnishing legal aid to the indigent differed from the program in *Rust* "[i]n th[e] vital respect" that the role of lawyers who represent clients in welfare disputes is to advocate *against* the Government, and there was thus an assumption that counsel would be free of state control. The Court concluded that the restriction on advocacy in such welfare disputes would distort the usual functioning of the legal profession and the federal and state courts before which the lawyers appeared. Public libraries, by contrast, have no comparable role that pits them against the Government, and there is no comparable assumption that they must be free of any conditions that their benefactors might attach to the use of donated funds or other assistance.[7]

6. These holdings, which Justice Stevens ignores, also make clear that his reliance on *Rutan v. Republican Party of Ill.,* 497 U.S. 62 (1990), *Elrod v. Burns,* 427 U.S. 347 (1976), and *Wieman v. Updegraff,* 344 U.S. 183 (1952) is misplaced. See *post,* at 2316. The invalidated state action in those cases involved true penalties, such as denial of a promotion or outright discharge from employment, not nonsubsidies.

7. Relying on *Velazquez,* Justice STEVENS argues mistakenly that *Rust* is inapposite because that case "only involved and only applies to ... situations in which the government seeks to communicate a specific message," and unlike the Title X program in *Rust,* the E-rate and LSTA programs "are not designed to foster or transmit any particular governmental message." But he misreads our cases discussing *Rust,* and again misapprehends the purpose of providing Internet terminals in public libraries. *Velazquez* held only that viewpoint-based restrictions are improper " 'when the [government] does not itself speak or subsidize transmittal of a message it favors *but instead expends funds to encourage a diversity of views from private speakers.*' "531 U.S., at 542. As we have stated above, public libraries do not install Internet terminals to provide a forum for Web publishers to express themselves, but rather to provide patrons with online material of requisite and appropriate quality.

Because public libraries' use of Internet filtering software does not violate their patrons' First Amendment rights, CIPA does not induce libraries to violate the Constitution, and is a valid exercise of Congress' spending power. Nor does CIPA impose an unconstitutional condition on public libraries. Therefore, the judgment of the District Court for the Eastern District of Pennsylvania is

Reversed.

JUSTICE KENNEDY, concurring in the judgment.

If some libraries do not have the capacity to unblock specific Web sites or to disable the filter or if it is shown that an adult user's election to view constitutionally protected Internet material is burdened in some other substantial way, that would be the subject for an as-applied challenge, not the facial challenge made in this case.

JUSTICE BREYER, concurring in the judgment.

The Act does impose upon the patron the burden of making this request. But it is difficult to see how that burden (or any delay associated with compliance) could prove more onerous than traditional library practices associated with segregating library materials in, say, closed stacks, or with interlibrary lending practices that require patrons to make requests that are not anonymous and to wait while the librarian obtains the desired materials from elsewhere. Perhaps local library rules or practices could further restrict the ability of patrons to obtain "overblocked" Internet material. But we are not now considering any such local practices. We here consider only a facial challenge to the Act itself.

Given the comparatively small burden that the Act imposes upon the library patron seeking legitimate Internet materials, I cannot say that any speech-related harm that the Act may cause is disproportionate when considered in relation to the Act's legitimate objectives. I therefore agree with the plurality that the statute does not violate the First Amendment, and I concur in the judgment.

JUSTICE SOUTER, with whom JUSTICE GINSBURG joins, dissenting.

I

Like the other Members of the Court, I have no doubt about the legitimacy of governmental efforts to put a barrier between child patrons of public libraries and the raw offerings on the Internet otherwise available to them there, and if the only First Amendment interests raised here were those of children, I would uphold application of the Act. We have said that the governmental interest in "shielding" children from exposure to indecent material is "compelling," *Reno v. American Civil Liberties Union,* 521 U.S. 844, 869–870 (1997), and I do not think that the awkwardness a child might feel on asking for an unblocked terminal is any such burden as to affect constitutionality.

Nor would I dissent if I agreed with the majority of my colleagues that an adult library patron could, consistently with the Act, obtain an unblocked terminal simply for the asking. I realize the Solicitor General represented this to be the Government's policy, and if that policy were communicated to every affected library as unequivocally as it was stated to us at argument, local librarians might be able to indulge the unblocking requests of adult patrons to the point of taking the curse off the statute for all practical purposes. But the Federal Communications Commission, in its order implementing the Act, pointedly declined to set a federal policy on when unblocking by local libraries would be appropriate under the statute. Moreover, the District Court expressly found that "unblocking may take days, and may be unavailable, especially in branch libraries, which are often less well staffed than main libraries."

In any event, we are here to review a statute, and the unblocking provisions simply cannot be construed, even for constitutional avoidance purposes, to say that a library must unblock upon adult request, no conditions imposed and no questions asked. First, the statute says only that a library "may" unblock, not that it must. In addition, it allows unblocking only for a "bona fide research or other lawful purposes," and if the "lawful purposes" criterion means anything that would not subsume and render the "bona fide research" criterion superfluous, it must impose some limit on eligibility for unblocking. There is therefore necessarily some restriction, which is surely made more onerous by the uncertainty of its terms and the generosity of its discretion to library staffs in deciding who gets complete Internet access and who does not. We therefore have to take the statute on the understanding that adults will be denied access to a substantial amount of nonobscene material harmful to children but lawful for adult examination, and a substantial quantity of text and pictures harmful to no one. As the plurality concedes, this is the inevitable consequence of the indiscriminate behavior of current filtering mechanisms, which screen out material to an extent known only by the manufacturers of the blocking software, see 201 F.Supp.2d, at 408 ("The category lists maintained by the blocking programs are considered to be proprietary information, and hence are unavailable to customers or the general public for review, so that public libraries that select categories when implementing filtering software do not really know what they are blocking").

We likewise have to examine the statute on the understanding that the restrictions on adult Internet access have no justification in the object of protecting children. Children could be restricted to blocked terminals, leaving other unblocked terminals in areas restricted to adults and screened from casual glances. And of course the statute could simply have provided for unblocking at adult request, with no questions asked. The statute could, in other words, have protected children without blocking access for adults or subjecting adults to anything more than minimal inconvenience, just the way (the record shows) many librarians had been dealing with obscenity and indecency before imposition of the federal conditions. Instead, the Government's funding conditions engage in overkill to a degree illustrated by their refusal to trust even a library's staff with an unblocked terminal, one to which the adult public itself has no access.

The question for me, then, is whether a local library could itself constitutionally impose these restrictions on the content otherwise available to an adult patron through an Internet connection, at a library terminal provided for public use. The answer is no. A library that chose to block an adult's Internet access to material harmful to children (and whatever else the undiscriminating filter might interrupt) would be imposing a content-based restriction on communication of material in the library's control that an adult could otherwise lawfully see. This would simply be censorship. True, the censorship would not necessarily extend to every adult, for an intending Internet user might convince a librarian that he was a true researcher or had a "lawful purpose" to obtain everything the library's terminal could provide. But as to those who did not qualify for discretionary unblocking, the censorship would be complete and, like all censorship by an agency of the Government, presumptively invalid owing to strict scrutiny in implementing the Free Speech Clause of the First Amendment. "The policy of the First Amendment favors dissemination of information and opinion, and the guarantees of freedom of speech and press were not designed to prevent the censorship of the press merely, but any action of the government by means of which it might prevent such free and general discussion of public matters as seems absolutely essential." *Bigelow v. Virginia,* 421 U.S. 809, 829 (1975).

II

The Court's plurality does not treat blocking affecting adults as censorship, but chooses to describe a library's act in filtering content as simply an instance of the kind of selection from available material that every library (save, perhaps, the Library of Congress) must perform. ("A library's need to exercise judgment in making collection decisions depends on its traditional role in identifying suitable and worthwhile material; it is no less entitled to play that role when it collects material from the Internet than when it collects material from any other source"). But this position does not hold up.[2]

A

Public libraries are indeed selective in what they acquire to place in their stacks, as they must be. There is only so much money and so much

2. Among other things, the plurality's reasoning ignores the widespread utilization of interlibrary loan systems. With interlibrary loan, virtually any book, say, is effectively made available to a library's patrons. If, therefore, a librarian refused to get a book from interlibrary loan for an adult patron on the ground that the patron's "purpose" in seeking the book was not acceptable, the librarian could find no justification in the fact that libraries have traditionally "collect[ed] only those materials deemed to have 'requisite and appropriate quality.' In any event, in the ensuing analysis, I assume for the sake of argument that we are in a world without interlibrary loan."

shelf space, and the necessity to choose some material and reject the rest justifies the effort to be selective with an eye to demand, quality, and the object of maintaining the library as a place of civilized enquiry by widely different sorts of people. Selectivity is thus necessary and complex, and these two characteristics explain why review of a library's selection decisions must be limited: the decisions are made all the time, and only in extreme cases could one expect particular choices to reveal impermissible reasons (reasons even the plurality would consider to be illegitimate), like excluding books because their authors are Democrats or their critiques of organized Christianity are unsympathetic. See *Board of Ed., Island Trees Union Free School Dist. No. 26 v. Pico,* 457 U.S. 853, 870–871 (1982) (plurality opinion). Review for rational basis is probably the most that any court could conduct, owing to the myriad particular selections that might be attacked by someone, and the difficulty of untangling the play of factors behind a particular decision.

At every significant point, however, the Internet blocking here defies comparison to the process of acquisition. Whereas traditional scarcity of money and space require a library to make choices about what to acquire, and the choice to be made is whether or not to spend the money to acquire something, blocking is the subject of a choice made after the money for Internet access has been spent or committed. Since it makes no difference to the cost of Internet access whether an adult calls up material harmful for children or the Articles of Confederation, blocking (on facts like these) is not necessitated by scarcity of either money or space.[3] In the instance of the Internet, what the library acquires is electronic access, and the choice to block is a choice to limit access that has already been acquired. Thus, deciding against buying a book means there is no book (unless a loan can be obtained), but blocking the Internet is merely blocking access purchased in its entirety and subject to unblocking if the librarian agrees. The proper analogy therefore is not to passing up a book that might have been bought; it is either to buying a book and then keeping it from adults lacking an acceptable "purpose," or to buying an encyclopedia and then cutting out pages with anything thought to be unsuitable for all adults.

B

The plurality claims to find support for its conclusions in the "traditional missio[n]" of the public library. The plurality thus argues, in effect, that the traditional responsibility of public libraries has called for denying adult access to certain books, or bowdlerizing the content of what the libraries let adults see. But, in fact, the plurality's conception of a public library's mission has been rejected by the libraries themselves. And no library that chose to block adult access in the way mandated by the Act could claim that the history of public library practice in this

3. Of course, a library that allowed its patrons to use computers for any purposes might feel the need to purchase more computers to satisfy what would presumably be greater demand, but the answer to that problem would be to limit the number of unblocked terminals or the hours in which they could be used. In any event, the rationale for blocking has no reference whatever to scarcity.

country furnished an implicit gloss on First Amendment standards, allowing for blocking out anything unsuitable for adults.

Institutional history of public libraries in America discloses an evolution toward a general rule, now firmly rooted, that any adult entitled to use the library has access to any of its holdings.[4] To be sure, this freedom of choice was apparently not within the inspiration for the mid–19th century development of public libraries, see J. Shera, Foundations of the Public Library: The Origins of the Public Library Movement in New England, 1629–1855, p. 107 (1949), and in the infancy of their development a "[m]oral censorship" of reading material was assumed, E. Geller, Forbidden Books in American Public Libraries, 1876–1939, p. 12 (1984). But even in the early 20th century, the legitimacy of the librarian's authority as moral arbiter was coming into question. And the practices of European fascism fueled the reaction against library censorship. See M. Harris, History of Libraries in the Western World 248 (4th ed.1995). The upshot was a growing understanding that a librarian's job was to guarantee that "all people had access to all ideas," and by the end of the 1930s, librarians' "basic position in opposition to censorship [had] emerged," Krug & Harvey, ALA and Intellectual Freedom: A Historical Overview, in Intellectual Freedom Manual, pp. xi, xv (American Library Association 1974).

By the time McCarthyism began its assaults, appellee American Library Association had developed a Library Bill of Rights against censorship and an Intellectual Freedom Committee to maintain the position that beyond enforcing existing laws against obscenity, "there is no place in our society for extra-legal efforts to coerce the taste of others, to confine adults to the reading matter deemed suitable for adolescents, or to inhibit the efforts of writers to achieve artistic expression." So far as I have been able to tell, this statement expressed the prevailing ideal in public library administration after World War II, and it seems fair to say as a general rule that libraries by then had ceased to deny requesting adults access to any materials in their collections. The adult might, indeed, have had to make a specific request, for the literature and published surveys from the period show a variety of restrictions on the circulation of library holdings, including placement of materials apart from open stacks, and availability only upon specific request. But aside from the isolated suggestion, I have not been able to find from this period any record of a library barring access to materials in its collection on a basis other than a reader's age. It seems to have been out of the question for a library to refuse a book in its collection to a requesting adult patron, or to presume to evaluate the basis for a particular request.

* * *

4. That is, libraries do not refuse materials to adult patrons on account of their content. Of course, libraries commonly limit access on content-neutral grounds to, say, rare or especially valuable materials. Such practices raise no First Amendment concerns, because they have nothing to do with suppressing ideas.

C

Thus, there is no preacquisition scarcity rationale to save library Internet blocking from treatment as censorship, and no support for it in the historical development of library practice. To these two reasons to treat blocking differently from a decision declining to buy a book, a third must be added. Quite simply, we can smell a rat when a library blocks material already in its control, just as we do when a library removes books from its shelves for reasons having nothing to do with wear and tear, obsolescence, or lack of demand. Content-based blocking and removal tell us something that mere absence from the shelves does not.

I have already spoken about two features of acquisition decisions that make them poor candidates for effective judicial review. The first is their complexity, the number of legitimate considerations that may go into them, not all pointing one way, providing cover for any illegitimate reason that managed to sneak in. A librarian should consider likely demand, scholarly or esthetic quality, alternative purchases, relative cost, and so on. The second reason the judiciary must by shy about reviewing acquisition decisions is the sheer volume of them, and thus the number that might draw fire. Courts cannot review the administration of every library with a constituent disgruntled that the library fails to buy exactly what he wants to read.

After a library has acquired material in the first place, however, the variety of possible reasons that might legitimately support an initial rejection are no longer in play. Removal of books or selective blocking by controversial subject matter is not a function of limited resources and less likely than a selection decision to reflect an assessment of esthetic or scholarly merit. Removal (and blocking) decisions being so often obviously correlated with content, they tend to show up for just what they are, and because such decisions tend to be few, courts can examine them without facing a deluge. The difference between choices to keep out and choices to throw out is thus enormous, a perception that underlay the good sense of the plurality's conclusion in *Board of Ed., Island Trees Union Free School Dist. No. 26 v. Pico,* 457 U.S. 853 (1982), that removing classics from a school library in response to pressure from parents and school board members violates the Speech Clause.

III

There is no good reason, then, to treat blocking of adult enquiry as anything different from the censorship it presumptively is. For this reason, I would hold in accordance with conventional strict scrutiny that a library's practice of blocking would violate an adult patron's First and Fourteenth Amendment right to be free of Internet censorship, when unjustified (as here) by any legitimate interest in screening children from harmful material.[8] On that ground, the Act's blocking requirement

8. I assume, although there is no occasion here to decide, that the originators of the material blocked by the Internet filters could object to the wall between them and any adult audience they might attract, although they would be unlikely plaintiffs,

in its current breadth calls for unconstitutional action by a library recipient, and is itself unconstitutional.

[A dissenting opinion by Justice STEVENS is omitted.]

LILLIAN R. BEVIER, UNITED STATES v. AMERICAN LIBRARY ASSOCIATION: WHITHER FIRST AMENDMENT DOCTRINE

2003 Supreme Court Review 163.

Begin by considering the rights of library patrons, authors, even libraries themselves with respect to libraries' collections of print materials. All members of the Court agreed, as a matter of First Amendment law and practical necessity, that libraries must have substantial discretion over what materials to acquire and that rational basis review of their content-based acquisition decisions is therefore appropriate. This consensus is not surprising, since no court decision has ever "considered a First Amendment challenge to a library's decision not to purchase a book or to accept one as a donation."[100] Indeed, a "central, if not the principal, responsibility of libraries is making managerial, not ministerial, selection decisions."[101] It follows that, in their roles as providers and selectors of content, libraries are neither traditional nor designated public forums. This makes sense because libraries' acquisition decisions do not present a systematic discernible risk that government will deliberately manipulate the content of public debate, or attempt to distort its outcome, or censor, punish, or selectively deny speech opportunities to disfavored views.

Consider what this implies about whether public library patrons can in any meaningful sense be said to have First Amendment rights of access to particular works, or whether authors can be said to have First Amendment rights of access to library shelves. The conclusion that there are no rights of access to or for obscenity or child pornography is wholly unsurprising, as such materials are unprotected even from government

given that their private audience would be unaffected by the library's action, and many of them might have no more idea that a library is blocking their work than the library does. It is for this reason that I rely on the First and Fourteenth Amendment rights of adult library patrons, who would experience the more acute injury by being denied a look at anything the software identified as apt to harm a child (and whatever else got blocked along with it). In practical terms, if libraries and the National Government are going to be kept from engaging in unjustifiable adult censorship, there is no alternative to recognizing a viewer's or reader's right to be free of paternalistic censorship as at least an adjunct of the core right of the speaker. The plurality in *Board of Ed., Island Trees Union Free School Dist. No. 26 v. Pico,* 457 U.S. 853 (1982), saw this and recognized the right of students using a school library to object to the removal of disfavored books from the shelves. By the same token, we should recognize an analogous right on the part of a library's adult Internet users, who may be among the 10% of American Internet users whose access comes solely through library terminals. There should therefore be no question that censorship by blocking produces real injury sufficient to support a suit for redress by patrons whose access is denied.

100. [Mark S. Nadel, The First Amendment's Limitation on the Use of Internet Filtering in Public and School Libraries: What Content Can Librarians Exclude? 78 Tex L Rev 1117, 1134 (2000)]

101. *Id.* at 1134.

punishment. Equally unsurprising, however, is the conclusion that there would be no rights of access to wholly protected speech, even to or for wholly protected speech of immense social or educational value.[102]

Another way to phrase the point is to say that citizens—whether library patrons or authors—have no right to require courts to scrutinize libraries' content-based acquisition decisions. It is important to note that this conclusion does not assume that the quantity of protected speech that libraries exclude is minimal. To the contrary, no library could possibly collect or even make available to its patrons every constitutionally protected work. Nor does the conclusion assume that libraries' content-based decisions would survive strict scrutiny. Rather it reflects a judgment about comparative institutional advantage. Libraries' content-based acquisition decisions are a product of a complex interaction of professional judgments, patron preferences, and resource constraints that courts are ill-equipped to disentangle. It is worth remembering that the First Amendment is about negative rights. A library's decision not to purchase any particular material does not put at risk or threaten to punish any citizen for exercising First Amendment rights, nor does it require any citizen to forgo or to perform any action that the First Amendment protects from government interference.

* * *

Of course, even in nonpublic forums, government's decisions must be "reasonable and not an effort to suppress expression merely because public officials oppose the speaker's view."[108] A fair reading of CIPA and the context in which it was enacted does not support the inference that Congress intended to manipulate public discourse or to handicap particular points of view—except to protect adults and minors from exposure to unprotected obscenity and child pornography and to protect minors from exposure to sexually explicit speech harmful to them. CIPA induces libraries to install Internet filters pursuant to a transparent, constitutionally permissible, policy to protect adults from unprotected speech and minors from speech unprotected for them, and no reason exists to doubt the legislature's good faith in pursuing that policy. In addition, Congress attempted to minimize the extent to which overblocking would deny patrons access to protected speech. Though it is easy to question its one-size-fits-all approach as a matter of policy, it is hard to find in that approach any evidence of discrimination against particular points of view. In terms of their restrictiveness and effectiveness, the means

102. The single possible exception to this conclusion would arise in a case where a patron could prove that a library failed to purchase particular works because of disagreement with the viewpoint expressed therein. There are no such reported cases, however. Courts have occasionally been willing to consider and even to overrule libraries' removal decisions when they find them to be viewpoint discriminatory. It is plausible to conclude that they have done so, however, only because they feel confident that they can identify impermissible viewpoint discrimination in that context, but "when librarians decide what books to acquire, there is generally no way to know why any particular book was not selected."

108. Cornelius v. NAACP Legal Education and Defense Fund, 473 U.S. 788, 800 (1985).

Congress adopted to achieve its compelling interests and the means that the district judge and the dissenters endorsed were different only in degree, and assessing them required the kind of judgments about which judges possess no comparative advantage and reasonable minds could plainly differ. Moreover, implementation of the filter requirement "chills" no speech—protected or unprotected—because CIPA neither punishes nor directly regulates speech. Finally, CIPA "suppresses" speech only to the same extent that any library's inability to make some material instantly available to its patrons suppresses speech.

Questions

1) Is it a necessary implication of Meiklejohn's argument that the government has an affirmative responsibility under the First Amendment to manage the public airwaves in a manner that promotes balanced treatment of controversial issues of public concern? A responsibility to regulate the Internet to that end? A responsibility to make public resources available to private speakers so as to enhance the quality and quantity of public debate? A responsibility to subsidize private speech? Are there aspects of Meiklejohn's analysis that someone who believes that government has none of these responsibilities might embrace?

2) Does Meiklejohn's argument have any bearing on the Court's decision in *United States v. American Liberty Association?* Do the civic responsibilities of self-governing citizens require that they have unfiltered access to the Internet at public expense? Does Meiklejohn's claim that content regulation is inconsistent with self-government apply to the regulation at issue in that case?

LEE C. BOLLINGER, THE TOLERANT SOCIETY

(1986).

Doubts about the magnitude of Meiklejohn's achievement. . . . go far beyond questions about his originality and skill in conventional legal analysis. They go to the fundamental issue of whether what he had to say has any real meaning or message for the world we actually inhabit. Here there are two fundamental problems with the analysis, as described so far, both of which we discussed in earlier chapters. The first is whether the theory has anything to say about speech restrictions that are the *product* of the democratic system, and not simply the imposition of censorship by a government acting outside of democratic procedures. The second is whether the theory has anything to say about why in particular we should protect speech that seeks to undermine the system itself—for example, by advocating the violation of concededly legitimate laws. To read the essay with these questions in mind leads us to a deeper structure in Meiklejohn's argument.

Meiklejohn was clearly aware of the reality of democratic intolerance and clearly intended the protection to extend to subversive speech. He was writing in the immediate post-World War II years, at the beginning of the Cold War. The period bore a close parallel to the climate of severe intolerance during and immediately after World War I, when Holmes first dealt with the subject of free speech. At the very beginning of the essay, in the preface, Meiklejohn spoke to this reality of intolerance, noting that an extensive system of internal security had been devised, with widespread public support, to uncover "un-American" and "disloyal" activities and agents. Referring to Federal Bureau of Investigation activities, he said:

> And that procedure reveals an attitude toward freedom of speech which is widely held in the United States. Many of us are now convinced that, under the Constitution, the government is justified in bringing pressure to bear against the holding or expressing of beliefs which are labeled dangerous. Congress, we think, may rightly abridge the freedom of such beliefs.

These were "wretched days of postwar and, it may be, of prewar, hysterical brutality." The question to be answered, then, was should the society refrain from employing legal coercion against these subversive ideas, against those who would say that "the Constitution is a bad document," "that [war] is not justified," "that [conscription] is immoral and unnecessary," "that the [political systems] of England or Russia or Germany are superior to ours." Even more pointedly, he asks, "Shall we listen to ideas which ... might destroy confidence in our form of government," from those who "hate and despise freedom to those who, if they had the power, would destroy our institutions?" Should we permit the publication of Hitler's *Mein Kampf*, of Lenin's *The State and the Revolution*, or of Engels and Marx's *Communist Manifesto*?

Thus, given this assumed reality, Meiklejohn would ultimately have to confront not only the general question "What do you do when the public has restricted speech through the democratic process?" but also the further question "Why protect this particular brand of speech?" At the time Meiklejohn wrote, not only was there a form of self-government actually at work, though perhaps not the one Meiklejohn would have wanted, but the type of speech being excluded from the system was that which allegedly directly challenged, or sought to undermine, the system itself. His paradigm of the traditional town meeting gave him no obvious solution to these difficulties, for it was not the "chair" alone that was seeking to silence opinion; and it was not obvious why a community could not decide that speech that sought to undermine the system established for the resolution of disputes should not be tolerated.

Why should a theory of free speech, which envisions its purpose as serving the system of self-government, lead to the conclusion that a self-governing society cannot choose to prohibit speech that advocates the end of self-government itself? This was the central challenge put by Wigmore in 1920 and more recently by Bork:

> Speech advocating forcible overthrow of the government contemplates a group less than a majority seizing control of the monopoly power of the state when it cannot gain its ends through speech and

political activity. Speech advocating violent overthrow is thus not "political speech" as that term must be defined by a Madisonian system of government. It is not political speech because it violates constitutional truths about processes and because it is not aimed at a new definition of political truth by a legislative majority. Violent overthrow of government breaks the premises of our system concerning the ways in which truth is defined, and yet those premises are the only reasons for protecting political speech. It follows that there is no constitutional reason to protect speech advocating forcible overthrow.

Quite clearly, Meiklejohn was of the view that the only interest cognizable under the principle of free speech was the public, or collective, interest and not any individual interest of the speaker. What that collective interest consists of, especially in cases involving extremist speech (such as the advocacy of a dictatorship), is far from clear if approached in conventional First Amendment terms.

It is either inaccurate or too simple to suggest that Meiklejohn, like Mill, believed the advantage would be a new truth or a livelier appreciation of a received truth. Despite his frequent claim that his was a practical, businesslike orientation to the First Amendment, Meiklejohn never really said what important information would be the payoff for the act of tolerance. Plausible arguments might, of course, be imagined. It might be thought useful to know what everyone is thinking within the society, especially those segments that are most likely to act destructively. [S]uch data could conceivably be helpful in organizing the society, distributing benefits, or identifying and correcting problems. Or, as we also saw earlier, a more limited argument might be that the society has, through the act of suppression, effectively rendered itself incapable of engaging in self-government because it no longer has the minimally necessary information to make intelligent decisions.

But Meiklejohn never advanced such arguments. Despite his early, rather vague comments that the function of free speech is to help the society get its business done, by ensuring the acquisition of information, the real theme of the essay turns out to be much larger. As the discussion progresses, we find that free speech provides the occasion for making a general assessment of the intellectual character of the society, as revealed by the act of speech suppression, and the opportunity to make a recommendation for an equally general remedy. It is here that the essay's power rests: not in its logic or its abstract concepts, but in its characterization of the meaning of the act of tolerance and its counterpart of intolerance. The "theory" of free speech is not really theory in the usual sense of the word (an abstract description of the world as it is or ought to be), but part of an overall rhetorical effort to persuade us to become the sort of people Meiklejohn would like us to be.

Additional Readings

McCarthyism

David Caute, The Great Fear: The Anti–Communist Purge Under Truman and Eisenhower (1978)

Larry Ceplair and Steven Englund, The Inquisition in Hollywood: Politics in the Film Community 1930–1960 (1979)

Harvey Klehr, John Earl Haynes & Fridrikh Igorevich Firsiv, The Secret World of American Communism (1995)

David M. Oshinsky, A Conspiracy So Immense: The World of Joe McCarthy (1983)

Michael Paul Rogin, The Intellectuals and McCarthy: The Radical Specter (1967)

Ellen Schrecker, No Ivory Tower: McCarthyism and the Universities (1986)

William M. Wiecek, The Legal Foundations of Domestic Anticommunism: The Background of Dennis v. United States, 2001 Supreme Court Review 375

Meiklejohn's life and thought

Adam R. Nelson, Education and Democracy: The Meaning of Alexander Meiklejohn 1872–1964 (2001)

Cynthia Stokes Brown, ed., Alexander Meiklejohn: Teacher of Freedom (1981)

Alexander Meiklejohn, What Does America Mean? (1935)

Alexander Meiklejohn, The Experimental College (1932)

Arthur Upham Pope, Alexander Meiklejohn, The American Scholar, Autumn, 1965, p. 644

Keyishian v. Board of Regents

Harry Kalven, Jr., A Worthy Tradition, ch. 27 (1988)

The public forum doctrine

Daniel Farber & John Nowak, The Misleading Nature of Public Forum Analysis: Content and Context in First Amendment Adjudication, 50 Va. L. Rev. 1219 (1984)

Harry Kalven, Jr., The Concept of the Public Forum, 1965 Supreme Court Review 1

Robert C. Post, Between Governance and Management: The History and Theory of the Public Forum, 34 UCLA L. Rev. 1713 (1987)

Geoffrey R. Stone, Fora Americana: Speech in Public Places, 1974 Supreme Court Review 233

United States v. American Library Association

Jim Chen, Mastering Eliot's Paradox: Fostering Cultural Memory in an Age of Illusion and Allusion, 89 Minn. L. Rev. 1361 (2005)

Felix Wu, United States v. American Library Ass'n: The Children's Internet Protection Act, Library Filtering, and Institutional Roles, 19 Berkeley Tech. L. J. 555 (2004)

The Internet and the freedom of speech

Lawrence Lessig, The Future of Ideas: The Fate of the Commons in a Connected World (2001)

Dawn C. Nunziato, The Death of the Public Forum in Cyberspace, 20 Berkeley Tech. L. J. 1115 (2005)

Eugene Volokh, Freedom of Speech, Shielding Children, and Transcending Balancing, 1997 Supreme Court Review 141

Eugene Volokh, Freedom of Speech, Permissible Tailoring, and Transcending Strict Scrutiny, 144 U. Pa. L.Rev. 2427 (1996)

Sunstein's Republic.com

Anupam Chandler, Whose Republic? 69 U. Chi. L. Rev. 1479 (2002)

Dan Hunter, Philippic.com, 90 Calif. L. Rev. 611 (2002)

Mark S. Nadel, Customized News Services and Extremist Enclaves in Republic.com, 54 Stan. L. Rev. 831 (2002)

Chapter Nine

THE CONTEMPORARY TURN TOWARD INDIVIDUAL–CENTERED THEORIES

No one since Meiklejohn has produced writing about the freedom of speech that has achieved—or is ever likely to achieve—the canonical status of the essays and judicial opinions around which this book is organized. Nevertheless, contemporary thought on the subject is not wholly lacking in "value added." In particular, the last few decades have witnessed an uncoordinated effort by scholars and judges of widely differing values and temperaments to uncover reasons to accord free speech a high priority that do not depend at bottom on the claim that the collective social and political benefits of unregulated speech outweigh its costs. Possibly the move away from breezy utilitarian generalizations is due to the perception that any claim of net collective benefits is hard to verify across the broad range of First Amendment issues generated by modern technologies and intensified cultural antipathies. Possibly an increased awareness of the social costs of speech—costs of intrusion and mobilization for wrongdoing exacerbated by new technological capacities—has contributed to the de-emphasis of cost-benefit arguments. In any event, the thrust of recent work on the First Amendment has been individual-centered, focused on such concepts as autonomy, individual flourishing, political consent, and personal character. Even arguments that are instrumental in form tend to invoke asserted causal relationships between free speech and certain capacities of individuals that in turn help those individuals to serve the collective good. In these respects, there has been a contemporary turn toward individual-centered theories of free speech.

A good way to study the materials that comprise this chapter is to catalogue the various types of individual-centered arguments and to evaluate those arguments by contrasting them with each other and with the more "collectivist" arguments of the preceding chapters. In addition, the arguments in this chapter may help you to identify aspects of the thought of Milton, Madison, Mill, Hand, Holmes, Brandeis, and Meiklejohn that are "individual-centered" in their own distinctive way, even while being embedded in bold assertions about collective benefits.

JACK M. BALKIN, DIGITAL SPEECH AND DEMOCRATIC CULTURE: A THEORY OF FREEDOM OF EXPRESSION FOR THE INFORMATION SOCIETY

79 N.Y.U. L. Rev. 1 (2004).

Probably the most important theoretical approach to freedom of speech in the twentieth century has argued that freedom of speech is valuable because it preserves and promotes democracy and democratic self-government. The notion that there is an important connection between freedom of speech and democracy is hardly new—people have understood the connection for as long as democracies have been around. But the twentieth century produced a special emphasis on that connection, and during the course of the twentieth century, many thinkers claimed that the very purpose of freedom of speech was not so much to promote individual autonomy or personal fulfillment as to promote democratic deliberation about public issues. We can find the beginnings of this idea in Progressive Era thinkers in the first two decades of the twentieth century. The most famous statement is by the philosopher of education Alexander Meiklejohn, and his approach has greatly influenced later theorists.

As a shorthand, I will call the democracy-based approach of Meiklejohn and his followers the "republican" or "progressivist" approach. That is because a focus on democratic deliberation rather than individual autonomy is characteristic of republican political theory, and it is also characteristic of much thinking in the Progressive Era in the United States. Progressivism is a sensibility, an attitude about what democracy is and what wise government can do. The progressive has faith in government's ability to promote the public interest through rational deliberation, works to structure government and public decisionmaking to promote deliberation and consensus about important public policy issues, worships expertise, and views popular attitudes and popular culture with suspicion because they tend to be emotional, parochial, irrational, untutored, and in need of channeling, refinement, and education.

I think it is no accident that the progressivist/republican approach to free speech arose in the twentieth century, for this was also the century of mass media. People who endorse democratic theories of free speech understand that although mass media can greatly benefit democracy, there is also a serious potential conflict between mass media and democratic self-governance. The reason is that mass media are held by a comparatively few people, and their ownership gives this relatively small group enormous power to shape public discourse and public debate.

* * *

Nevertheless, the paradigm case that motivates the progressivist agenda—the case of few speakers broadcasting to a largely inactive mass audience—no longer describes the world we live in. Even if, as I have argued, the new digital technologies do not displace mass media, they exist alongside it and build on top of it. Digital technologies give lots of people, more than ever before, a chance to participate in the creation and development of public culture. Technological changes in how speech is transmitted, and in who gets to participate in that transmission, change the focus of free speech theory.

* * *

Let me begin by pointing to five characteristics of Internet speech that I believe are exemplary of freedom of speech generally. These characteristics are hardly new to the Internet; rather, my point is that the Internet makes them particularly salient. That salience, I shall argue, reshapes our conception of the free speech principle.

First, speech on the Internet ranges over every possible subject and mode of expression, including the serious, the frivolous, the gossipy, the erotic, the scatological, and the profound. The Internet reflects popular tastes, popular culture, and popular enthusiasms.

Second, the Internet, taken as a whole, is full of innovation. The tremendous growth of the Internet in a relatively short period of time shows how enormously creative ordinary people can be if given the chance to express themselves. And it demonstrates what ordinary people can do when they are allowed to be active producers rather than passive recipients of their cultural world.

Third, much of the source of that creativity is the ability to build on something else. This is particularly true of the World Wide Web. As originally conceived, the very structure of HTML code encourages copying, imitation, and linking. The continual innovation and transformation we see in digital media stems directly from their ability to use the old to make the new. Digital media allow lots of people to comment, absorb, appropriate, and innovate—to add a wrinkle here, a criticism there. Internet speech continually develops through linkage, collage, annotation, mixture, and through what I have called routing around and glomming on. Internet speech, like all speech, appropriates and transforms. It imitates, copies, builds upon and mixes.

Fourth, Internet speech is participatory and interactive. People don't merely watch (or listen to) the Internet as if it were television or radio. Rather, they surf through it, they program on it, they publish to it, they write comments and continually add things to it. Internet speech is a social activity that involves exchange, give and take. The roles of reader and writer, producer and consumer of information are blurred and often effectively merge.

Fifth, and finally, because Internet speech is a social activity, a matter of interactivity, of give and take, it is not surprising that Internet speech creates new communities, cultures and subcultures. In this way, it exemplifies an important general feature of freedom of speech: Freedom of speech allows us, each of us, to participate in the growth and development of the cultures and subcultures that, in turn, help constitute us as individuals. Freedom of speech is part of an interactive cycle of social exchange, social participation, and self-formation. We speak and we listen, we send out and we take in. As we do this, we change, we grow, we become something other than we were before, and we make something new out of what existed before.

To sum up, the Internet makes particularly salient five facts about free speech: Speech ranges over a wide variety of subjects, including not only politics but also popular culture. The speech of ordinary people is full of innovation and creativity. That creativity comes from building on what has come before. Speech is participatory and interactive as opposed to mere receipt of information. It merges the activities of reading and writing, of production and consumption. Finally, speech involves cultural participation and self-formation. The Internet reminds us how central and important these features are to speech generally. It reveals to us in a new way what has always been the case.

And this brings me to a central point: The populist nature of freedom of speech, its creativity, its interactivity, its importance for community and self-formation, all suggest that a theory of freedom of speech centered around government and democratic deliberation about public issues is far too limited. The free speech principle has always been about something larger than democracy in the narrow sense of voting and elections, something larger even than democracy in the sense of public deliberation about issues of public concern. If free speech is about democracy, it is about democracy in the widest possible sense, not merely at the level of governance, or at the level of deliberation, but at the level of culture. The Internet teaches us that the free speech principle is about, and always has been about, the promotion and development of a democratic culture.

Democracy is far more than a set of procedures for resolving disputes. It is a feature of social life and a form of social organization. Democratic ideals require a further commitment to democratic forms of social structure and social organization, a commitment to social as well as political equality. And the forces of democratization operate not only through regular elections, but through changes in institutions, practices, customs, mannerisms, speech, and dress. A "democratic" culture, then, means much more than democracy as a form of self-governance. It means democracy as a form of social life in which unjust barriers of rank and privilege are dissolved, and in which ordinary people gain a greater say over the institutions and practices that shape them and their futures.

What makes a culture democratic, then, is not democratic governance but democratic participation. A democratic culture includes the institutions of representative democracy, but it also exists beyond them, and, indeed undergirds them. A democratic culture is the culture of a democratized society; a democratic culture is a participatory culture.

If the purpose of freedom of speech is to realize a democratic culture, why is democratic cultural participation important? First, culture is a source of the self. Human beings are made out of culture. A democratic culture is valuable because it gives ordinary people a fair opportunity to participate in the creation and evolution of the processes of meaning-making that shape them and become part of them; a democratic culture is valuable because it gives ordinary people a say in the progress and development of the cultural forces that in turn produce them.

Second, participation in culture has a constitutive or performative value: When people are creative, when they make new things out of old things, when they become producers of their culture, they exercise and perform their freedom and become the sort of people who are free. That freedom is something more than just choosing which cultural products to purchase and consume; the freedom to create is an active engagement with the world.

By "culture" I mean the collective processes of meaning-making in a society. The realm of culture, however, is much broader than the concern of the First Amendment or the free speech principle. Armaments and shampoo are part of culture; so too are murder and robbery. And all of these things can affect people's lives and shape who they are. The realm of culture for purposes of the free speech principle is a subset of what anthropologists study as forms of culture. It refers to a set of historically contingent and historically produced social practices and media that human beings employ to exchange ideas and share opinions. These are the methods, practices, and technologies through which dialogue occurs and public opinion is formed. For example, today people generally regard art as a social practice for the exchange of ideas, and they regard motion pictures as a medium of expression.[58] These practices and media of social communication construct the realm that we regard as "speech" for purposes of the free speech principle.[59] We cannot give an exhaustive list

58. It was not always thus. See Post, Recuperating First Amendment Doctrine, *supra* note 57, at 1252–53 (discussing Mutual Film Corp. v. Industrial Comm., 236 U.S. 230, 243–45 (1915), in which Supreme Court originally held that motion pictures were not "organs of public opinion"). By 1952, the Supreme Court had come around, stating that "it cannot be doubted that motion pictures are a significant medium for the communication of ideas." Joseph Burstyn, Inc. v. Wilson, 343 U.S. 495, 501 (1952). The difference between the Court's statements in 1915 and 1952 reflects important changes in American society to which the Court's First Amendment doctrines eventually responded. The scope of the free speech principle always grows out of a normatively inflected recognition of sociological realities.

59. The free speech principle also applies to regulations of conduct that do not involve a generally recognized medium for the communication of ideas when the government regulates conduct because it disagrees with or desires to suppress the ideas it believes the conduct expresses. See United States v. O'Brien, 391 U.S. 367, 377–78 (1968) (holding that reasons for regulation of conduct must be unrelated to suppression of free expression). Thus, when government effectively treats conduct as a medium for the communication of ideas and punishes it on that basis, the free speech principle is also implicated.

of these practices and media precisely because the social conventions and technologies that define them are always evolving; even so, it seems clear enough that the Internet and other digital technologies are media for the communication of ideas, and an increasingly important way for people to express their ideas and form their opinions. They are central—and I would say crucial—media for the realization of a democratic culture.

Culture has always been produced through popular participation. Digital technology simply makes this aspect of democratic life more obvious, more salient. Radio and television are technologies of mass cultural reception, where a few speakers can reach audiences of indefinite size. But the Internet is a technology of mass cultural participation in which audiences can give as well as receive, broadcast as well as absorb, create and contribute as well as consume. Digital technology makes the values of a democratic culture salient to us because it offers the technological possibility of widespread cultural participation.

What is the difference between grounding freedom of speech on the promotion of democracy and grounding it on the promotion of a democratic culture? What is at stake in the move to culture?

There are three important differences, I think, and each stems from the weaknesses of the progressivist/republican model: They concern the status of nonpolitical expression, the role of popular culture, and the importance of individual participation and individual liberty.

A. Nonpolitical Expression

A serious difficulty with the progressivist/republican model has always been that a wide variety of activities, of which art and social commentary are only the most salient examples, have always fit poorly into a democratic theory of free expression. Lots of speech is not overtly political. Nevertheless, it gets protected under the progressivist/republican model because it is useful for political discussion, because it may become enmeshed in political controversies (and thus threatened or suppressed for political reasons), or because it is very hard to draw lines separating what is political from what is not. In like fashion, lots of activities cannot easily be classified as deliberation—like singing, shouting, protesting, gossiping, making fun of people, or just annoying them or getting them angry. Nevertheless, these activities are protected because we can think of them as raw materials for further democratic deliberation or because we cannot easily draw lines separating them from the social practice of deliberation. In both cases, then, we have kinds of speech that are at the periphery rather than the core; we protect them in aid of something more central and precious. In short, the progressivist vision sees democratic deliberation about public issues at the core of constitutional concern and other subjects and other forms of expression as peripheral or supplementary.

I have never been satisfied with this approach. I think something is missing here, and the notion of democratic culture helps us understand why. The point of democracy, as its name implies, is to put power in the hands of the people, to give ordinary people some measure of control over the forces that shape their lives and some degree of say about how the world around them develops. But law and governance are only parts of this world. Culture is an even larger part, and in some ways it has an even more capacious role in structuring our lives. The various processes of communication and cultural exchange are the sources of the self and its development over time. Our ideas, our habits, our thoughts, our very selves are produced through constant communication and exchange with others. The influence is reciprocal: Through this continuous communication and exchange, we shape culture and are shaped by it in turn. We absorb it, we inhabit it, we make it new. We send it out into the world, we make it part of us.

Culture is more than governance, more than politics, more than law. And if democracy is giving power to the people, then true democracy means allowing people not only to have a say about who represents them in a legislature, or what laws are passed, but also to have a say about the shape and growth of the culture that they live in and that is inevitably part of them. Power to the people—democracy—in its broadest, thickest sense, must include our relationship not simply to the state but to culture as a whole, to the processes of meaning-making that constitute us as individuals. Those processes of meaning-making include both the ability to distribute those meanings and the ability to receive them.

Culture is an essential ingredient of the self, and so freedom of speech means participation in the forces of culture that shape the self. We participate in the growth and development of culture through interaction, through communicating to others and receiving ideas from others. Cultural democracy is mimetic democracy, the continuous distribution, circulation, and exchange of bits of culture from mind to mind. This vision of culture is not democratic because people are voting on what is in their culture. It is democratic because they get to participate in the meaning-making processes that form and reproduce culture. They do this through communicating with and interacting with others. Moreover, democratic culture is not democratic because people are participating in processes of deliberation about governance, or even public issues. Rather it is democratic because it is participation in the creation and shaping of culture, which is, at the same time, participation in the growth and development of the self.

B. Popular Culture

The second basic problem with the work of Meiklejohn and his heirs has been its relative neglect and suspicion of popular culture. Popular culture is often seen as mass culture controlled by corporations, which demobilizes the citizenry; as sensationalism or dumbed-down speech, which adds little of importance to democratic deliberation; or as mere entertainment, which distracts people from serious discussion of public issues. But from the perspective of democratic culture, popular culture and entertainment should not be merely peripheral or a distraction. They should be a central part of what freedom of speech is about.

In an age of unidirectional mass media, popular culture was, to a very large extent, mass culture—a set of commodities manufactured and sent out to be consumed by a mass audience. But the Internet allows mass culture to be appropriated by ordinary citizens and become, more than ever before, a truly popular culture, because it allows what I have called routing around and glomming on.

We can understand the controversies over intellectual property in this light. Media corporations are turning to digital rights management to avoid digital piracy. But much of what traditional mass media most fears and resents is not piracy but cultural appropriation—individual riffs on mass media digital products shared with others—and the ability of consumers to route around a controlled advertising and marketing environment. Shifting our focus from democracy to democratic culture helps us see that the problem in the digital age is not just deliberation about public issues. It is also the importance of letting ordinary people engage in appropriation and innovation rather than mere consumption; it is the value of ordinary people being able to "rip, mix, and burn," to route around traditional media gatekeepers and glom onto existing media products.

In a democratic culture, we are interested in protecting not only speech about public issues, but also speech that concerns popular expression in art, as well as cultural concerns such as gossip, mores, fashions, and popular music. The progressivist/republican approach has tended to valorize high culture and high quality programming as aids to democratic deliberation (often conflating the two in the process), with "low" culture protected only as a peripheral concern. But if freedom of speech is concerned with the promotion of a truly democratic culture, popular culture is every bit as important as so-called high culture. In fact, in a democratic culture, the distinction between high culture and low culture begins to blur and the difference between them becomes increasingly difficult to maintain. High culture continually borrows from popular culture; moreover, as culture becomes increasingly democratized, the popular culture of today often turns out to be the high culture of tomorrow.

C. Individual Participation

A third problem with the progressivist/republican model has been its tendency to seek to manage discourse and structure public debate. This desire is hardly surprising: In a world dominated by mass media controlled by a relative handful of very wealthy corporations, it seems important to make sure that dissenting views get a word in edgewise, that serious issues are not driven out by the media's never-ending quest for profits, and that audiences are not stultified and demobilized by an endless stream of increasingly vapid entertainment. As a result, the progressivist model has downplayed individual liberty and instead played up the protection of democratic processes, including robust debate on public issues and the creation of an informed citizenry. Earlier, I noted Meiklejohn's famous statement that the point of freedom of speech is not that everyone shall speak, but that everything worth saying shall be said. Meiklejohn even analogized the system of free expression to a town meeting. The purpose of the town meeting was to shape a public agenda for discussion of serious issues; there would be time for only some people to speak. The important point was that the participants in the meeting be informed and stick to the agenda because everyone would decide what to do on the basis of the information presented. Although Meiklejohn's town meeting seems quite distant from the electronic mass media, it had many of the same features: scarcity of time, the need for a public agenda, and the importance of an informed citizenry. Hence the need for regulation was very much the same.

Democratic culture, by contrast, is not solely concerned with people's ability to be informed about a particular agenda. It is concerned with participation, interaction, and the ability of people to create, to innovate, to borrow ideas and make new ones. Meiklejohn remarked that his ideal town meeting was "self-government," not a "dialectical free-for-all." That opposition may hold true for a particular form of democracy. But in a democratic culture, and especially the culture of the Internet, freedom of expression is a dialectical free-for-all, a continuous process of interactivity and innovation, in which culture and discussion move and grow in any number of different directions.

Here again a shift in focus from democracy to democratic culture responds to the sorts of freedoms that digital technologies make possible. Digital technologies and telecommunications networks mean that people are no longer forced into the role of mere spectators and consumers; they can be active participants, creating, commenting, and broadcasting their own ideas to a larger public. And in a world in which active participation in the creation and distribution of culture becomes possible for so many, liberty is an important good to be prized, valued, and nourished.

The progressivist/republican conception of free speech arose in the twentieth century because ordinary people were shut out of the most pervasive and important forms of speech and were reduced to the roles of spectators, consumers, and recipients. In that world, protecting the liberty of a favored few who owned the means of communication from regulation was less important than producing discussion on public issues and promoting a robust agenda of diverse and antagonistic sources so that the citizenry could be well-informed and engaged with the great public issues of the day. But new technologies make it possible for vast numbers of people to participate, innovate, and create, to route around and glom on to the traditional mass media and their products. This has increased enormously the practical liberty of the ordinary citizen to speak, and to reach a vast audience. When technology makes liberty possible, liberty once again must return to the forefront of concern.[74]

74. Indeed, the standard progressivist/republican arguments for regulation of broadcast, cable, and satellite can and should be rearticulated in terms of the more populist perspective of promoting democratic culture. The key point is that the United States has adopted a hybrid system: Instead of separating the functions

The twentieth-century concern with speech as a method of democratic deliberation privileges the delivery of information about issues of public concern to the public, who receive this information through asymmetric and unidirectional mass media. I do not wish to deny the importance of that conception; I merely want to insist that it is only a partial conception, inadequate to deal with the features of speech that the new digital technologies bring to the foreground of our concern. The values behind freedom of speech are about production as much as reception, about creativity as much as deliberation, about the work of ordinary individuals as much as the mass media.

of editor and distributor, and treating all distribution networks as common carriers like telephone companies, it has allowed a small number of editors/speakers to own powerful distribution networks not open to all in return for accepting various public service obligations and regulations. Thus the hybrid system is based on the model of a contract or a quid pro quo.

Although the hybrid system denies the vast majority of people free access to key distribution networks, it may nevertheless have been justified in the past by its economic advantages. Arguably it offers necessary incentives for broadcasters, cable companies, and owners of satellite systems to invest in, produce, and deliver a wide variety of diverse programming for viewers and listeners that will enrich public debate and public culture. Thus, it provides considerable grist for the mill of a democratic culture.

Nevertheless, a hybrid system is hardly perfect. Heavy reliance on advertising tends to create a significant mismatch between what broadcasters deliver and what viewers want, in part because advertisers seek content that appeals to the common tastes of certain valued demographic groups (whose preferences may otherwise be quite heterogenous) rather than content that crosscuts demographic groups or appeals to groups with comparatively little disposable income or comparatively unmanipulable consumption patterns. Advertisers will also tend to push for content that helps induce greater consumption instead of content that appeals to and fulfils other values that viewers might have. For example, viewers may value many kinds of content that are not strongly tied to shopping, purchasing, and consumption. They may value content that educates them or inspires them to change their lives, rethink their values, or make use of their creative powers. Finally, market forces also will, almost by definition, underproduce content that has high positive externalities (like educational content, or balanced and informative coverage of news) because the value of that content to society cannot be captured by market forces, and, all other things being equal, the greater the positive externalities, the more underproduction there will be.

The hybrid model of media regulation is not constitutionally required. Rather, it is a quid pro quo or contractual arrangement, and it is constitutional to the extent that it promotes the values of a democratic culture. To be sure, regulatory quid pro quos can violate free speech rights if they impose an unconstitutional condition on free speech. However, structural regulations of the mass media that seek to counteract the limitations of mass media markets should be constitutional if there is a clear nexus between the goals of the regulation and the purposes behind the choice of a hybrid system. To the extent that structural regulations and public interest obligations of mass media compensate for the limitations of a hybrid model, they are tied to the very justifications for issuing broadcast licenses and cable franchises in the first place: They help further the goal of promoting a rich public sphere and a vibrant, participatory, and democratic culture. If government can make a sufficiently good case that the regulations will have this effect, the regulations should not be regarded as unconstitutional conditions on a media company's First Amendment rights. Likewise, public broadcasting that supplements existing markets with content that government reasonably believes to be valuable (like children's programming) should also be constitutionally permissible.

STEVEN H. SHIFFRIN, THE FIRST AMENDMENT, DEMOCRACY, AND ROMANCE

(1990).

I want to argue that Ralph Waldo Emerson and Walt Whitman understood more about the relationship of freedom of speech to American democracy than did Oliver Wendell Holmes or Alexander Meiklejohn, that their insights are closer to prevailing conceptions of American democracy than those currently prevailing in the legal commentary, and that if their insights were taken seriously, the impetus to repress speech on public or private issues would be substantially diminished.

In establishing these claims, I will use the little-noticed case of *Connick v. Myers.* It exhibits the impoverished character of legal discourse about freedom of speech as well as any case I know. Sheila Myers was an Assistant District Attorney in New Orleans for five-and-a-half years. As the Court put it, "She served at the pleasure of ... Harry Connick, the District Attorney for Orleans Parish." Sometime in 1980 Connick decided to transfer Myers to a different section of the criminal court. Myers objected to the transfer and to a number of other aspects about the managerial policies of the office. She expressed her concerns to Dennis Waldron, one of the First Assistant District Attorneys, who apparently countered that her views were not shared by others in the office. Apparently in response to that comment, Myers prepared a questionnaire soliciting the views of her co-workers, fifteen district attorneys, "concerning office transfer policy, office morale, the need for a grievance committee, the level of confidence in supervisors, and whether employees felt pressured to work in political campaigns."

Upon learning of the questionnaire, Waldron phoned Connick at home and told him Myers was creating a ' "mini-insurrection' " within the office. Connick returned to the office and informed Myers soon thereafter that her distribution of the questionnaire was "an act of insubordination." Connick fired Myers, and after litigation over the issue, the District Court found that he fired her because she had distributed the questionnaire. Myers argued that her discharge was unconstitutional. She argued that her distribution of the questionnaire was a protected exercise of free speech.

The federal district court in the Eastern District of Louisiana agreed with Myers; so did the United States Court of Appeals for the Fifth Circuit. But the Supreme Court agreed with Connick. By a 5–4 vote, it upheld the firing of Myers. In approaching the question for the majority, Justice White concentrated on whether Myers's speech was political in character. After parading a series of quotations about the importance of political speech and self-government, Justice White concentrated on whether Myers's speech addressed a "matter of public concern." The general inquiry was said to be grounded on the issue of whether the subject matter was one upon which ' "free and open debate is vital to informed decisionmaking by the electorate.' " The Court stated that if the speech was not of public concern, there was no first amendment protection against dismissal.

The Court found that most of the questions on Myers's questionnaire did not relate to a matter of public concern. Questions involving office morale, the possibility of a grievance committee, the transfer policies of the office, and the processes by which they were implemented were all deemed to be outside the scope of public concern. The Court did find that one of Myers's questions touched upon a question of public concern. The question (number 11 of 14) asked whether Myers's co-workers felt pressured to work in political campaigns on behalf of candidates supported by the District Attorney's Office. Nonetheless, the Court concluded that the government interests outweighed the first amendment interests. Connick, it was said, did not need to "tolerate action which he reasonably believed would disrupt the office, undermine his authority, and destroy close working relationships." At the same time, the Court observed that different fact situations involving public employees might support a constitutional claim: "Although today the balance is struck for the government, this is no defeat for the First Amendment."

In dissent, Justice Brennan complained that "the public will be deprived of valuable information with which to evaluate the performance of elected officials." He thought that Myers's entire questionnaire addressed issues of public concern "because it discussed subjects that could reasonably be expected to be of interest to persons seeking to develop informed opinions about the manner in which the Orleans Parish District Attorney, an elected official charged with managing a vital governmental agency, discharges his responsibilities." As to whether Myers's critical comments had so far interfered with the operation of a government office as to warrant dismissal, Brennan concluded that the Court's deference to Connick's fears about the impact of Myers's statements was excessive. He saw no reason to overturn the lower court's finding that ' "[I]t cannot be said that the defendant's interest in promoting the efficiency of the public services performed through his employees was either adversely affected or substantially impeded by plaintiff's distribution of the questionnaire.' "

In assessing these opinions, we might recognize at the outset that the government has a substantial interest in the character of working relationships in a district attorney's office, that these relationships could be disrupted by a single obstreperous "bad actor," and that federal judges might have a difficult time discerning, after the fact, what the true interpersonal state of affairs might have been at the time of a dismissal. One can at least understand why some members of the Court might want to stay out of disputes of this kind. Nonetheless, I insist that *Connick v. Myers* is indeed a defeat for the first amendment. And the most substantial aspect of the loss is that no one on the Court, not even Justice Brennan, seemed to appreciate the character of the values at stake.

There is nothing very complex about the values involved. I suspect they would be the first resort of anyone who had not been exposed to the reigning judicial precedents. We might imagine how Sheila Myers might have thought about the case before she saw a lawyer. Myers, of course, *is* a lawyer; so that background might have infected her capacity to see the situation clearly. Her vision, too, might have been clouded by the existing community of legal discourse with its paeans to democracy and self-government. If not, I suspect her first reaction would have nothing to do with public issues or private issues. Her assumption might well be that the first amendment guaranteed the right to speak about any subject and that it most especially guaranteed the right to dissent against existing customs, habits, conventions, processes, and institutions. It is possible that Myers was gathering evidence so that she could go to the voters with her information. But she may have had more "modest" goals in mind. She might simply have wanted to speak out against the management of the office. She presumably wanted to stimulate others in the office to begin discussing office policies and management. For all we know, Myers's questionnaire might have spelled the beginning of a union organizing campaign.

In any event, we do know that Sheila Myers had a view of employer-employee relationships different from Dennis Waldron's or Harry Connick's. Waldron thought the distribution of the questionnaire constituted a "mini-insurrection"; Connick called it "insubordination." Myers, on the other hand, thought that employer-employee relationships included the possibility of vigorous dissent.

So understood, Myers's claim stands in a great first amendment tradition. It was a tradition well understood by Ralph Waldo Emerson and Walt Whitman. For them, and I would argue for most Americans, the point of Myers's claim has little to do with whether there were voters out there combing the pages of the local *Times-Picayune* to learn about office morale in the District Attorney's office. For them, American democracy meant that Americans could speak out against any of the existing institutions, habits, customs, and traditions. Emerson and Whitman may have celebrated a mythical American, but they celebrated an American who was not wedded to the comforts of the present nor tied by the bonds of the past. They celebrated the courage of the nonconformist, the iconoclast, the dissenter. In urging self-reliance and independence of thought, in praising the heroism of those willing to speak out against the tide, they sided with the romantics—those willing to break out of classical forms. Their conception of democracy had little to do with voting and everything to do with the American spirit. They sided with John Stuart Mill, in recognizing the ease of conformity. And, with Mill, they sponsored nonconformity.

In so doing, they struck a responsive chord. Emerson spoke at a special time in American history. It was a period when there was substantial discussion of the failure of Americans to produce a genuinely independent literature, a period when Tocqueville and others were observing that the abstract American commitment to freedom and civil liberties was not matched by the spirit of its people. Indeed Tocqueville, reacting to his concern about the tyranny of the majority and of public opinion, had insisted that "I know no country in which, speaking generally, there is less independence of mind and true freedom of discussion than in America." For whatever complicated reasons, as

Barbara Packer observes. Emerson's recurrent pleas against the fear of speaking out "came to seem, to a whole generation, [as] an agent of liberation." Arthur Schlesinger has come to call Emerson the "quintessential American" and Walt Whitman is called America's greatest poet. For my purposes, however, no one need think that Emerson is the quintessential American. One might grant such a title to Washington, Lincoln, Jefferson, or, even better, one could rail against the very concept of a quintessential American. Indeed, for present purposes, it is perfectly satisfactory if one rejects (or accepts) Emerson's idealism, his stance toward evil, his glorification of intuition, the character of his individualism, his views about the relationship between the one and the many, or his rendition of the relationship of humanity to nature. It is enough to recognize that Emerson and Whitman eloquently express an important part of the American tradition—the part that encourages an independent spirit.

It is that tradition to which I appeal. Anyone who takes that tradition seriously must flinch at the Court's mindless observation in *Myers* that, "This is no defeat for the First Amendment." The *Myers* case tells public employees everywhere to shut up or get fired. The loss is not merely that voters will lose information. The loss is the failure to appreciate that the protection of dissent and its nurturance is a major American value.

One can only speculate what the outcome of *Connick v. Myers* might have been if a different rhetoric had animated first amendment decision-making from *Schenck* onward. The usual range of first amendment metaphors did not serve Myers's needs. The self-government-town-hall perspective, of course, led down a path to fantasyland. Even the often-used metaphor of the marketplace of ideas was not difficult for the Court to sidestep. The Court was able to portray the Connick–Myers dispute not as a contest for Truth emerging in the Marketplace of Ideas, but as an everyday squabble in the workplace, something best left outside the federal courts. If the first amendment were regularly conceived as specially prizing dissent, however, Myers's claim could have been articulated in terms that placed her in the center of first amendment traditions, not at its periphery.

The *Myers* case is not uniformly regarded as a first amendment outrage. Some believe that the government interest is substantial in public employment contexts and that the litigation process is likely to exacerbate difficulties in the workplace. Even if that view were accepted, it would be a mistake to indulge the comforting delusion that free speech values are not at stake. If workers are not free to speak out in the workplace, if they are habituated to knuckle silently under authority, their speech is not free. Perhaps most Americans or the Court believes that workplaces can not be run effectively if workers are free to criticize their bosses, but anyone who believes that should be forced to recognize that free speech values have been compromised; one ought not be able to pretend that those values are not involved.

It might be argued that the Court's treatment of first amendment values in *Myers* is merely an aberrational and undeliberative reflection of its desire to avoid involvement in particular employment disputes. But the Court's failure to recognize the first amendment value of dissent is not confined to employment disputes. There are many other important cases, and these cases are the inevitable reflections of the Court's general approach to first amendment questions. Some of these cases have been sharply criticized by the commentators. What gives these criticisms particular energy and sting, I would argue, has been the Court's failure to protect dissent.

A striking example is the case of *FCC v. Pacifica Foundation.* There the Court upheld the imposition of sanctions against a radio station for broadcasting a George Carlin monologue called "Filthy Words." Carlin's humorous monologue was a satire against societal verbal taboos. In a "variety of colloquialisms," he repeated over and over the words that "will curve your spine, grow hair on your hands and [laughter] maybe, even bring us, God help us, peace without honor [laughter], um, and a bourbon," namely, "shit, piss, fuck, cunt, cocksucker, motherfucker, and tits." The monologue evoked frequent laughter from a live studio audience, but the FCC was not amused. It moved against the radio station for broadcasting "indecent" language, and the Supreme Court upheld the FCC's action. The words were considered too vulgar and too offensive for the radio, at least in the early afternoon and in the manner presented by Carlin. The Court observed that "[a]dults who *feel the need* may purchase tapes and records or go to theaters and nightclubs *to hear these words.*"

Most people with any first amendment bones in their bodies are troubled by the *Pacifica* case. But the nub of the first amendment insult has little to do with self-government or with the marketplace of ideas. The concern does not flow from a worry that voters will be deprived of valuable information. Concern that the truth about vulgar language might not emerge in the marketplace of ideas may be well placed, but it is not a sufficient concern to explain the widespread outrage against the decision. Again, the decision is an affront to a notion of content-neutrality, but there are many of those. The *Pacifica* case produces heat precisely because Carlin's speech is considered by many to be precisely what the first amendment is *supposed* to protect. Carlin is attacking conventions; assaulting the prescribed orthodoxy; mocking the stuffed shirts; Carlin *is* the prototypical dissenter.

GLICKMAN v. WILEMAN BROTHERS & ELLIOTT, INC.

Supreme Court of the United States, 1997.
521 U.S. 457, 117 S.Ct. 2130, 138 L.Ed.2d 585.

JUSTICE THOMAS, with whom JUSTICE SCALIA joins as to Part II, dissenting.

* * *

Although the Constitution may not "enact Mr. Herbert Spencer's Social Statics," *Lochner v. New York,* 198 U.S. 45, 75 (1905) (Holmes, J., dissenting), and thus the Government has a considerable range of authority in regulating the Nation's economic structure, part of the Constitution—the First Amendment—does enact a distinctly individualistic notion of "the freedom of speech," and Congress may not simply collectivize that aspect of our society, regardless of what it may do elsewhere.

FREDERICK SCHAUER, FREE SPEECH: A PHILOSOPHICAL ENQUIRY

(1982).

Chapter 4

Free speech and the good life

Must Free Speech Be Instrumental?

The arguments discussed in the preceding chapters hold in common a consequentialist approach to freedom of speech. Both the argument from truth and the argument from democracy treat free speech not as an end but as a means. In the former argument free speech is a means of increasing knowledge, discovering error, and identifying truth; in the latter it is a means of ensuring the proper functioning of a state based on the principles of self-government. Each of these arguments values open communication for what it does, not for what it is.

The argument from truth and the argument from democracy also have a common emphasis on the interests of society at large rather than on the interests of the individual. Freedom of speech is most commonly conceived to be an individual interest; but there are two types of individual interests, and they must be distinguished. Some individual interests are valuable by virtue of the benefits derived by the persons exercising the interests. Other individual interests are recognized not primarily because of their ultimate value for the individual, but because the value to the person exercising them is instrumental to the value that accrues to society from the widespread exercise of individual interests. Both the argument from truth and the argument from democracy are examples of this latter variety of individual interests. The individual rights they generate are but a mediate step towards maximizing the goals of society at large.

* * *

In contrast to this social side of individual interests, both this chapter and the next focus on freedom of speech as an individual interest in a narrower (and stronger) sense. Here the ultimate point of reference is the individual, not the state, or society at large. Although society may benefit from the satisfaction of individual interests, the arguments discussed here treat such benefits as incidental to a primary focus on individual well-being. An individual interest in this strong sense remains important even if society might in some way, or on balance, be worse off for recognizing it. Here individual well-being is an end in itself.

The arguments discussed in this and the next chapter are interrelated, and the division is neither wholly distinct nor wholly satisfactory. But individual autonomy and choice is sufficiently important that it seems right to treat it as separate from a discussion of individual development. The latter will be treated now; the former is the subject of the next chapter.

* * *

The question is whether free speech is a component of the 'good life'. Is free speech an integral part of human nature, or self-realization? The emphasis is on free speech as an autonomous value, not a value instrumental to some social objective. Free speech has at times been suggested to be a good in itself, without need of further justification. This hypothesis is the point of departure for this chapter.

Some would find it sufficient to stop at this point, contending that freedom to say what you wish is of course good, not needing further argument or analysis. These people claim to intuit the intrinsic goodness of free speech. But recognition of a Free Speech Principle requires more. There may be value in intuitionist thinking in social and political philosophy, but almost any activity with which governments normally interfere can be maintained under some theory to be inherently good. To say merely that free speech is inherently good is insufficient to establish a Free Speech Principle, because it does not distinguish speech from a wide range of other voluntary actions. Here intuitions are insufficient. A Free Speech Principle requires that speech be treated differently, and only if a reason for such differential treatment exists can we say there is a Free Speech Principle.

The view of freedom of speech as an intrinsic good is most commonly articulated in terms of a particular perception of human nature, and a particular perception of the ideal aspirations of mankind. This approach sees man as continually striving for improvement and self-development, and it sees free communication as an integral part of this objective.

But this argument is fundamentally misguided. Equating freedom of speech with happiness, or holding it essential to pleasure, is simply false. Many people indeed believe that freedom to express their opinions is a primary component of their happiness. But others are as likely to be satisfied with other freedoms, or prefer the security or intellectual anaesthesia that accompanies rigid controls on expression. The warning of the Grand Inquisitor in *The Brothers Karamazov* demands respect. It is not a necessary truth that people equate happiness with freedom in a broad sense. To equate happiness with a particular type of freedom is even less warranted. Moreover, there are numerous interests to consider—the interests of speakers, the interests of listeners, and the interests of third parties affected by the consequences of speech. An attempt to justify free speech purely in terms of happiness is met by the often-conflicting pleasures involved, as well as by the argument's tenuous empirical assumptions.

Aristotelian conceptions of happiness present a stronger argument for freedom of speech as an intrinsic good. The argument is then grounded not so much on what man is as on what man ought to be. This conception of the rich life is derived from ideas of personal growth, self-fulfilment, and development of the rational faculties. Under this conception, one who is enjoying the good life may be neither content nor euphoric in the ordinary sense. He may not even be happy in the ordinary sense, for his happiness resides not in, for example, sensual satisfaction, but in knowing that he has maximally developed all the *potential* that distinguishes man *qua* man from all other creatures. He should feel satisfied in the knowledge that he is realizing his full potential. If it is the power of reason that distinguishes man from other forms of animal life, then only by fully exploiting this power can one be said to enjoy a full life. Because the basis of this conception of the full life is complete use and development of the mind and thinking process, speech is said to be an integral component of self-fulfilment, the one being inseparable from the other. Free speech is thus said to be justified not because it provides a benefit to society, but because it is a primary good.

* * *

If there is a natural right to communicate, apart from any natural right to general liberty, it is most sensibly derived from the idea of freedom of thought. Freedom of thought (or its synonyms freedom of belief and freedom of conscience) seems particularly amenable to a naturalistic justification, because few things can more easily be perceived as inherently good than the independent use of one's mind to come to such conclusions as it wishes. However, the very value of freedom of thought points up the futility of considering freedom of thought to be an important principle of political theory. We can think silently. It is not necessary to speak or write in order to think. And when we think silently, our thoughts are beyond the reach of government sanction. Obviously thoughts can be *influenced* by government. Propaganda is an example, and so is a system of explicit or implicit rewards. But a silent thought *qua* thought is immune from punishment, and to that extent is discretely different from outward expression or communication. Prisoners in some of the Nazi concentration camps supposedly sang a song entitled 'Meine Gedänke Sind Frei' (My Thoughts Are Free). The intended meaning is particularly relevant—whatever you may do to me, whatever you may physically compel me to do *or say,* my thoughts are still free because they remain beyond the reach of your powers.

Government sanctions may penalize belief to the extent of driving it deeply underground. Punishing those known to hold certain beliefs, compelling the affirmation of belief, requiring the disclosure of belief, and precluding people with certain beliefs from holding government positions are all restrictions on freedom of thought. But they are restrictions only on *expressed* thought. These restrictions operate against overt manifestations of thought, and against those who are unwilling to lie for their beliefs, but this is not the same as punishing the thought alone. The largely internal nature of what we ordinarily call a thought puts that thought to a great extent beyond the power of governmental punishment.

Thoughts and beliefs, however, are not static. They develop, they change, they are embellished or combined, and at times they are rejected. The argument for a natural right to free speech is premised on the assumption that this process operates effectively only when there is communication. Reading, writing, speaking and exchanging ideas with others is perceived to be of critical importance if thoughts are to develop and grow in the human mind. The theory aims to protect not *a* thought, but the process of thinking.

Here it is important to remember that language is not only the medium of communication, it is also the medium of thinking. We think not in complete abstractions, but (most commonly) in words. Our ability to think creatively, therefore, is to a great degree dependent upon our language. If communication is stifled, the development of language is restricted. To the extent, therefore, that we curtail the development of linguistic tools, we chill the thought process that utilizes those very same tools. Although Waismann and others have emphasized that language must follow our thoughts, it is in many respects equally true that thoughts follow our language. Each is a cutting edge for the further development of the other.

The theory that communication and personal relationships are central features of human development has roots in the writings of Aristotle. If man is a political and social animal, then communication and the use of language are vital components of humanity, because we relate to other people predominantly by linguistic communication. This argument is not that communication facilitates certain types of relationships (although of course it does). Rather it is that communication is an integral part of human nature, at least when human beings are viewed in this social and political way. If communication is that basic to mankind, it is argued, then its special protection is easily justified.

At the heart of this argument, whether characterized in terms of individual values or in terms of social and political values, is the concept of self-development. The argument is based on the proposition that a person who uses his faculties to their fullest extent, who is all that it is possible to be, is in some sense better off, and in an Aristotelian sense happier, than those whose development is stultified. And because it is thinking, reasoning, rationality, and complex interrelationships with others that distinguish humanity from other forms of animal life, then it is the faculties of reason and thinking that are at the core of self-development. What is seen as the ultimate goal for man is the fullest use of the capacity to think, the greatest degree of mental exertion, the exploration of the limits of the mind.

But minds do not grow in a vacuum. Intellectual isolationism is almost wholly inconsistent with intellectual development. The image of the mountaintop guru, developing great ideas in a sublime and isolated existence, is far more myth than reality. For one thing, we learn to think as we are taught language. Further intellectual self-development comes from communication of our ideas to others. Our thoughts are refined when we communicate them. Often we have an idea in some amorphous and incipient stage, but see it develop or see its weaknesses for the first time when the idea must be specifically articulated in a form intelligible to some other person.

Seen in this light, communication is an integral part of the self-development of the speaker, because it enables him to clarify and better understand his own thoughts. Communication may also be inseparable from the self-realization of the hearers, the recipients of communication. Mill (whose disclaimer of making appeals to natural rights should not be taken too seriously) was concerned both with the development of the mind and with the values of choice and diversity. He saw reason and intellect as faculties that improved with exercise, and in his view the greatest practice came from exercising the powers of choice, of intellectual discrimination. Communication makes an individual aware of choices he may not be able to imagine or formulate alone, and thereby furthers the self-development of the recipient of a wide variety of different ideas and opinions. As we hear more ideas, then we have more ideas to evaluate. And as we are compelled to evaluate more ideas, then we have more opportunity to practise the important skill of evaluating and choosing among ideas.

If we accept the premise that mental self-fulfilment is a primary good, then the way in which the communication of ideas is related to intellectual development provides an apparently sound argument for a special freedom to communicate, and a correlative freedom to be the object of communication. But the superior (compared to other forms of animal life) rationality of human beings does not necessarily lead to the conclusion that the development of this particular faculty is more important than the development or satisfaction of other desires or needs less peculiarly human. Other characteristics not exclusive to humanity also profit from development and fulfilment. Our physical well-being, our non-intellectual pleasures, our need for food and shelter, and our desire for security are also important, although these are wants we share with the rest of the animal world. Because any governmental or private action to restrict communication is usually justified in the name of one of these or other similar wants of all or part of humanity, a particular protection of communication under this version of a natural rights theory must assume that communication is *prima facie* more important than these other interests. This priority is often justified by reference to the unique characteristics of the species *homo sapiens*. But it is equally plausible to conclude that the needs and wants that man *shares* with other animals are, for that reason, more basic and therefore more important.

Those sympathetic towards natural rights arguments in moral and political philosophy will find the argument for freedom to communicate appealing because that argument attempts to demonstrate that communication is indeed an important interest. But the argument does not demonstrate why freedom to communicate is more important than other well-recognized interests, and thus it does not show why freedom to communicate should be an independent principle of political philosophy.

The argument from self-fulfilment underscores the importance of communication, but the argument can be deployed with equal force in reference to most human needs or desires. If an argument from inherent goodness supports a right to free speech, so too can it support a right to eat, a right to sleep, a right to shelter, a right to a decent wage, a right to interesting employment, a right to sexual satisfaction, and so on *ad infinitum.* But when a list of rights becomes coextensive with the list of wants, or even with the list of fundamental needs, we lose any strong sense of having a right. Because governmental action of any kind almost always is directed towards satisfaction of some important need or want of the population, a right to free speech that rests on the same footing can no longer sensibly operate as a side constraint against such action in furtherance of the public interest. The Free Speech Principle, if it exists, operates as a side constraint, or trump. But if all of the suits are trumps, we are in effect playing at no trumps.

Freedom or Freedom of Speech?

The argument from self-fulfilment suffers from a failure to distinguish intellectual self-fulfilment from other wants and needs, and thus fails to support a distinct principle of free speech. But the same conclusion follows even if we accept the primacy of intellectual self-fulfilment. For the sake of argument, let us assume that there is something special about the power of reason that commends the development of its particular faculties to special treatment. Let us assume further that intellectual development occurs primarily, as many have argued, through a process of mental exploration, a process by which a range of alternatives gives the mind room in which to expand and the challenge with which to develop.

Under these assumptions, communication does seem rather important. Communication informs us of the choices and hypotheses made or suggested by others while also allowing us to refine our own thoughts through the necessity of articulating them. But once again the connexion between communication and the realization of human potential is, although seductively appealing at first glance, still logically incapable of generating a true Free Speech Principle. The fact that *A* may cause *B,* or even that *A* must cause *B,* does not entail the proposition that only *A* can cause *B.* There is no reason *X, Y* or *Z* cannot also cause *B.* Even if communication is a sufficient condition for intellectual self-fulfilment, it does not follow that it is a necessary condition. The fact that communication will produce the desired result does not mean that that same result cannot also be produced by *experiences*. It seems as likely that intellectual self-realization can be fostered by world travel, by keen observation, or by changing employment every year, to give just a few examples. These and many other experiences can open one's eyes, triggering deeper thought and consequent development of the intellect. There is nothing in the argument that shows communication to be necessarily better than any of these other methods of mental development.

Moreover, even if communication is a necessary condition for intellectual advancement, that does not make it a sufficient condition. The value of communication in the process of intellectual development is of necessity limited by the range of experiences that are the subjects of the communication. F. A. Hayek, in *The Constitution of Liberty,* argues that we over-estimate the importance of freedom of thought and ideas at the expense of underestimating the value of actually *doing* things. He argues that speech follows experience, and therefore that freedom of speech is meaningful only when there is freedom of action, because new ideas spring from new environments and additional experiences. Hayek's argument is not without flaws, but it is particularly apt here. If we are concerned with the development of the mind, then choice, diversity, individuality and novelty are every bit as important in the entire range of human conduct as in the particular segment of man's activities that we call 'communication'. If we take Hayek's point that the value of communication is dependent upon what it is that can be communicated, then the other forms of conduct are logically prior to and therefore possibly more important than communication.

I do not mean to be taken as saying that communication is not valuable. I am only arguing that it is but one aspect of an Aristotelian argument for an extremely wide-ranging freedom to engage in multitudinous varieties of conduct. The argument from self-fulfilment can be a powerful argument for freedom in a very broad sense, but it tells us nothing in particular about freedom of speech. Freedom of speech under such a theory is merely a component part (or an instance) of that general Good that we often call 'freedom' or 'liberty'. Therefore, to the extent that we support or provide for freedom in this general sense, we find that freedom of speech is included *pro tanto*. Conversely, and more significantly, to the extent that a given society or government has for some reason elected to limit individual liberty in the broad sense, there remains no reason freedom of speech should not be subject to equivalent limitations.

CHAPTER 5

INDIVIDUALITY AND FREE SPEECH

The Liberal Ideology

Freedom of speech is commonly thought of as a liberal doctrine. Freedom of speech, freedom of religion and some freedom in personal way of life are usually considered to be among the primary components of that amorphous credo that is commonly called 'liberalism'. Liberalism is frequently characterized by a particular preoccupation with individualism and individual rights, especially as against the state or against the majority. Liberalism places great stock in personal choice, personal freedom, and the value of variety, or diversity. It is concerned with the interests of the individual, and is often accused of being less aware of and less concerned with social interaction and communal values.

The arguments I have discussed in this book, particularly the arguments in chapters 2 and 3, in large part belie this reflexive association of freedom of speech with liberalism. Upon closer analysis both the argument from truth and the argument from democracy emerged in a form that does not look especially liberal. I do not mean that anything presented so far is necessarily inconsistent with liberalism. Rather, the arguments have not been notably concerned with the individualism and choice that constitute the foundations of liberal ideology. The values underlying the arguments from truth and democracy are more social than individual. In the previous chapter, however, the liberal flavour of the concept of free speech began to appear. Yet in the context of the specific purpose here, the result was a dead end. The arguments from self-fulfilment appeared under critical scrutiny to be little more than arguments for general liberty. We learned little in particular about free speech except that free speech can be subsumed under some broad notions of personal freedom. The arguments provided scant assistance in justifying a Free Speech Principle.

When we speak of liberalism, or for that matter when we speak of liberty, we suggest principles based on individuality. Although we may argue that respect for individuals is the keystone of the best society, our primary concern is less for social benefits than it is for the good of individuals *qua* individuals, and not individuals *qua* members of a social group. Liberalism embodies a profound respect for individual differences, and as a consequence places great emphasis on individual choice. By respecting freedom as choice, liberalism recognizes (as it must) that freedom is hardly a worthwhile topic of consideration if everyone's freedom is directed toward the same desires, the same choices and the same actions. Freedom that does not produce diversity when that freedom is exercised is psychologically unrealistic as well as fundamentally inconsistent with the liberal creed. Diversity of action is not merely a result of liberalism. It lies at the core of liberalism. A theory of government represented by a presumption in favour of freedom is grounded on the disutility of conformity, or at least on the conscious refusal to regard conformity or uniformity as important primary goods. By encouraging diversity and individual choice, and by raising barriers to governmental or social interference with those goals, liberalism sees itself as especially concerned with human dignity, a dignity that is insulted when there is insufficient respect for personal choice.

* * *

The Argument from Autonomy

In the *Crito* Socrates acknowledges the 'right' of the state to punish him, and therefore refuses to escape to the safe shores of Thessaly. Yet in the *Apology* he has just said 'that I shall never alter my ways, not even if I have to die many times'. On the face of it the two dialogues present an inconsistency. If there is a duty of obedience to the state, then why does Socrates refuse to change his ways? One answer, suggested in the *Apology* itself, is that although the state may legitimately exercise power within its domain, there is an area of choice that belongs to Socrates himself. Perhaps, then, Socrates is asserting a claim of sovereignty, or autonomy, over his own mind, an autonomy that leaves to him the final choice on any matter, even if by choosing one alternative rather than another he must accept some physical punishment inflicted by the state. This notion of individual sovereignty, or individual autonomy, now associated with Kant, provides the foundation for a theory of freedom of speech premised on the ultimate sanctity of individual choice.

My earlier treatment of freedom of conscience is relevant here. When we refer to freedom of conscience, we ordinarily mean some sort of private domain of the mind, some area that is under the exclusive control of the individual. This domain is off limits to the state, not only as a matter of moral right, but also as a matter of necessity. If I say that I am following my conscience, I mean that I am retreating into that portion of my personality that is an exclusive preserve against governmental interference. Similarly, references to freedom of thought mark off an area of exclusive control by the individual, an area that simultaneously sets the outer boundaries of permissible (and practical) state intrusion. The concept is not altogether unlike the distinction between self-regarding and other-regarding actions, or Dworkin's distinction between personal and external preferences, or the arguments of those who seek to limit governmental power by resort to appeals to notions of personal dignity. Human dignity or human personality may be perceived as inherently personal. It is *mine,* intrinsically and morally beyond the force of government coercion. The argument I am outlining here makes an analogous distinction. The distinction is easier to accept, however, because it employs a much narrower conception of the area that is under exclusive individual control. Because thought may be inherently as well as morally beyond the reach of state power, it is plausible to suggest that the province of thought and individual decision-making is an area, or the only area, in which the individual is truly autonomous. As a narrower conception of the range of autonomy, this formulation is largely immune from many of the attacks on theories that postulate substantially larger areas of self-regarding actions.

From this conception of individual autonomy Thomas Scanlon, in a very important article, constructs an impressive argument for freedom of expression. Beginning with the premise that the 'powers of the state are limited to those that citizens could recognize while still regarding themselves as equal, autonomous, rational agents', Scanlon seizes on the autonomy component of that premise to argue that 'a person must see himself as sovereign in deciding what to believe and in weighing competing reasons for action'. '[A]n autonomous person cannot accept without independent consideration the judgment of others as to what he should believe or what he should do'. Thus Scanlon's argument hinges on the fact that the ultimate choice as to any question, whether of belief or of action, rests with the individual. Even when an act is prohibited by law, even properly, the autonomous individual retains the choice whether to obey the law or to violate the law and take the consequences. These are decisions that government cannot and must not make, as they are wholly within the boundaries of individual sovereignty.

Scanlon derives the substance of his argument for freedom of speech from this notion of absolute individual sovereignty in matters of choice. If the final decision is properly for the individual, then that individual's decision ought to be as informed and intelligent as possible. Thus the information material to this individual decision ought not to be restricted. Scanlon's argument touches Meiklejohn's point that the government cannot pre-select the information available to the sovereign electorate. Scanlon makes essentially the same argument, but he sees the issue from the perspective of individual rather than electoral sovereignty. Thus Scanlon argues that no government has the authority to distort the individual's ultimate choice by preventing him from hearing any argument solely because it is on one side of an issue rather than another. He focuses not so much on what is restricted but on the reasons for the restriction. 'Those justifications [for restricting speech] are illegitimate which appeal to the fact that it would be a bad thing if the view communicated by certain acts of expression were to become generally believed.' Scanlon's theory, therefore, is best characterized not as a right to speech, but rather as a right to receive information and, more importantly, a right to be free from governmental intrusion into the ultimate process of individual choice. It is a right to be free from an assault on what Felix Frankfurter called the 'citadel of the person'.

Scanlon's argument, although couched in the style of Kant and of the *Apology,* also has a strong contractarian basis. Individual autonomy is closely related to the concept of a state with limited powers. Indeed, they are opposite sides of the same coin. The individual is sovereign and autonomous because, quite simply, this area of ultimate choice has not been ceded to the state. Writing in a more recent article, Scanlon associates his theory with the writings of Rawls, designating the argument for freedom of speech as the Principle of Limited Authority. Because the state has no authority ultimately 'to decide matters of moral, religious or philosophic doctrine (or of scientific truth)', because those in the Original Position would not grant that authority, the state therefore has no mandate to limit the information upon which this choice may be made by the individual for the individual. In this form the argument is hardly novel. Locke, in the *Letter Concerning Toleration,* grounds much of his argument on the premise that solely the individual is authorized to decide questions of faith. 'The care of souls is not committed to the civil magistrate, any more than to other men'. Even earlier Spinoza drew the connexion between mental autonomy and freedom of speech in his *Tractatus Theologico-Politicus.* These are all variations on the theme that places reliance on a division of authority between state and individual, a division that may be based on notions of inherent autonomy, or on the terms of a social contract, or, as suggested by Charles Fried, on ideas of comparative institutional competence.

In any form, the argument is not without flaws. The so-called 'right' of civil disobedience is to a great extent the foundation of the theory, because the right of access to persuasion (whether from factual information or normative arguments) is in turn grounded on a right to disobey even those laws that are just and that are in the interests of society. Perhaps the individual does retain this degree of autonomy. And probably an individual who chose to act autonomously in the most informed and intelligent manner would, if rational, seek out many opinions before making a decision. But there is a difference between what the rational individual would do and what the state should do. A limitation on the state's power to interfere with the information available makes sense only if the state must recognize the right of civil disobedience. The argument from autonomy is plausible only if the state can be deemed to say, 'You can obey, or you can pay the penalty; it makes no difference to us.' But this seems odd. It seems more reasonable to hold that if a law is indeed just, then the state is politically and morally authorized to enforce compliance, not merely collect penalties for non-compliance. We do not expect the state, having enacted a law, to be neutral on the issue of whether it is obeyed. The conclusion from this is not that there is no such thing as individual autonomy or individual sovereignty. Rather it is that it would be anomalous for the state to recognize that autonomy, at least in respect to areas in which the state validly may regulate. Personal moral philosophy cannot always be congruent with political philosophy. If a law is just, then a state is neither morally nor politically precluded from attempting to ensure compliance. Limiting that information that might produce non-compliance is not the only means at the state's disposal in attempting to ensure compliance, but there is no reason given in the argument from autonomy that compels us to prohibit the state from using this tool.

Moreover, because the argument from autonomy 'rests on a limitation of the authority of states to command their subjects rather than on a right of individuals', it is much more adaptable to governments on the authoritarian model than a democratically conceived society. For if it is applied to the democratic model, then presumably the people could change the rules of the game, a fact that Scanlon himself recognizes. But this seems to be what takes place in any case of suppression. Suppression in a democratic society is most commonly suppression in the name of the people. The suppression is never based on unanimous consent of the population, but neither is any other governmental action. In order for the argument from autonomy to hold up, it must be rooted in social contract theory, in some original position of unanimity. But if this is the case, the argument fails to tell us why the state's authority is more limited in dealing with speech than it is in dealing with other forms of conduct. It is circular to answer that individual autonomy supplies the reason, because what is missing is some reason why a group of individuals in the original position would choose to recognize some sort of 'right' to disobey just laws.

These difficulties notwithstanding, the argument from autonomy represents a significant contribution to free speech theory. It shares a natural rights foundation with some of the other ideas discussed in this and the preceding chapters, and like other arguments it relies on concepts of individuality and dignity. The value of the argument from autonomy is that it is an argument that is directed at *speech,* rather than at the entire range of interests that might with some minimal plausibility be designated 'individual'. The argument from autonomy stresses the motives of those who would suppress *arguments,* not the motives of those who suppress individuality. It is an argument for freedom of communication in a limited sense, and that is its greatest strength. As an argument for freedom of speech, rather than merely a particularized application of an argument for freedom in a broad and abstract sense, the argument from autonomy employs broadly liberal principles to address specifically the problem of free speech.

The natural rights underpinnings of the argument from autonomy are not universally appealing. But even from a positivist or utilitarian perspective the argument from autonomy is important because it emphasizes freedom of speech as a principle embedded in a line of demarcation between the individual and government. That line may neither be straight, distinct or easy to locate, but it represents a division nevertheless. In relying on this separation between the individual and the organization of government, the argument from autonomy shares numerous characteristics with the most valuable features of both the argument from truth and the argument from democracy.

Questions

1) Professor Schauer distinguishes between arguments for free speech that view individual flourishing or well-being as an end in itself and those that view benefits to individuals as instrumental to various collective goods. Do all of the arguments that we have studied so far fall into the latter camp? Who among Milton, Madison, Mill, Hand, Holmes, Brandeis, and Meiklejohn comes closest to making an argument that treats individual flourishing or well-being as an end in itself?

2) Schauer says: "Many people indeed believe that freedom to express their opinions is a primary component of their happiness. But others are as likely to be satisfied with other freedoms, or prefer the security of intellectual anaesthesia that accompanies rigid controls on expression. The warning of the Grand Inquisitor in *The Brothers Karamazov* demands respect ... An attempt to justify free speech purely in terms of happiness is met by the often-conflicting pleasures involved, as well as by

the argument's tenuous empirical assumptions." Is Schauer right about this? Is the claim that the overwhelming majority of persons equate freedom of thought and freedom of expression with personal happiness sustainable as an empirical matter in Western democracies, if not in all political cultures? If so, is that enough to make the case, or does an argument for free speech that is based on individual well-being necessarily depend on plausible claims about a universal human nature?

COHEN v. CALIFORNIA

Supreme Court of the United States, 1971.
403 U.S. 15, 91 S.Ct. 1780, 29 L.Ed.2d 284.

MR. JUSTICE HARLAN delivered the opinion of the Court.

This case may seem at first blush too inconsequential to find its way into our books, but the issue it presents is of no small constitutional significance.

Appellant Paul Robert Cohen was convicted in the Los Angeles Municipal Court of violating that part of California Penal Code § 415 which prohibits "maliciously and willfully disturb(ing) the peace or quiet of any neighborhood or person * * * by * * * offensive conduct * * *." He was given 30 days' imprisonment. The facts upon which his conviction rests are detailed in the opinion of the Court of Appeal of California, Second Appellate District, as follows:

> "On April 26, 1968, the defendant was observed in the Los Angeles County Courthouse in the corridor outside of division 20 of the municipal court wearing a jacket bearing the words 'Fuck the Draft' which were plainly visible. There were women and children present in the corridor. The defendant was arrested. The defendant testified that he wore the jacket knowing that the words were on the jacket as a means of informing the public of the depth of his feelings against the Vietnam War and the draft.

"The defendant did not engage in, nor threaten to engage in, nor did anyone as the result of his conduct in fact commit or threaten to commit any act of violence. The defendant did not make any loud or unusual noise, nor was there any evidence that he uttered any sound prior to his arrest."

In affirming the conviction the Court of Appeal held that "offensive conduct" means "behavior which has a tendency to provoke others to acts of violence or to in turn disturb the peace," and that the State had proved this element because, on the facts of this case, "(i)t was certainly reasonably foreseeable that such conduct might cause others to rise up to commit a violent act against the person of the defendant or attempt to forceably remove his jacket." The California Supreme Court declined review by a divided vote. We brought the case here, postponing the consideration of the question of our jurisdiction over this appeal to a hearing of the case on the merits. We now reverse.

* * *

I

In order to lay hands on the precise issue which this case involves, it is useful first to canvass various matters which this record does not present.

The conviction quite clearly rests upon the asserted offensiveness of the words Cohen used to convey his message to the public. The only "conduct" which the State sought to punish is the fact of communication. Thus, we deal here with a conviction resting solely upon "speech," not upon any separately identifiable conduct which allegedly was intended by Cohen to be perceived by others as expressive of particular views but which, on its face, does not necessarily convey any message and hence arguably could be regulated without effectively repressing Cohen's ability to express himself. Further, the State certainly lacks power to punish Cohen for the underlying content of the message the inscription conveyed. At least so long as there is no showing of an intent to incite disobedience to or disruption of the draft, Cohen could not, consistently with the First and Fourteenth Amendments, be punished for asserting the evident position on the inutility or immorality of the draft his jacket reflected.

Appellant's conviction, then, rests squarely upon his exercise of the "freedom of speech" protected from arbitrary governmental interference by the Constitution and can be justified, if at all, only as a valid regulation of the manner in which he exercised that freedom, not as a permissible prohibition on the substantive message it conveys. This does not end the inquiry, of course, for the First and Fourteenth Amendments have never been thought to give absolute protection to every individual to speak whenever or wherever he pleases or to use any form of address in any circumstances that he chooses. In this vein, too, however, we think it important to note that several issues typically associated with such problems are not presented here.

In the first place, Cohen was tried under a statute applicable throughout the entire State. Any attempt to support this conviction on the ground that the statute seeks to preserve an appropriately decorous atmosphere in the courthouse where Cohen was arrested must fail in the absence of any language in the statute that would have put appellant on notice that certain kinds of otherwise permissible speech or conduct would nevertheless, under California law, not be tolerated in certain places. No fair reading of the phrase "offensive conduct" can be said sufficiently to inform the ordinary person that distinctions between certain locations are thereby created.[3]

In the second place, as it comes to us, this case cannot be said to fall within those relatively few categories of instances where prior decisions

3. It is illuminating to note what transpired when Cohen entered a courtroom in the building. He removed his jacket and stood with it folder over his arm. Meanwhile, a policeman sent the presiding judge a note suggesting that Cohen be held in contempt of court. The judge declined to do so and Cohen was arrested by the officer only after he emerged from the courtroom.

have established the power of government to deal more comprehensively with certain forms of individual expression simply upon a showing that such a form was employed. This is not, for example, an obscenity case. Whatever else may be necessary to give rise to the States' broader power to prohibit obscene expression, such expression must be, in some significant way, erotic. It cannot plausibly be maintained that this vulgar allusion to the Selective Service System would conjure up such psychic stimulation in anyone likely to be confronted with Cohen's crudely defaced jacket.

This Court has also held that the States are free to ban the simple use, without a demonstration of additional justifying circumstances, of so-called "fighting words," those personally abusive epithets which, when addressed to the ordinary citizen, are, as a matter of common knowledge, inherently likely to provoke violent reaction. *Chaplinsky v. New Hampshire*, 315 U.S. 568 (1942). While the four-letter word displayed by Cohen in relation to the draft is not uncommonly employed in a personally provocative fashion, in this instance it was clearly not "directed to the person of the hearer." *Cantwell v. Connecticut*, 310 U.S. 296, 309 (1940). No individual actually or likely to be present could reasonably have regarded the words on appellant's jacket as a direct personal insult. Nor do we have here an instance of the exercise of the State's police power to prevent a speaker from intentionally provoking a given group to hostile reaction. There is, as noted above, no showing that anyone who saw Cohen was in fact violently aroused or that appellant intended such a result.

Finally, in arguments before this Court much has been made of the claim that Cohen's distasteful mode of expression was thrust upon unwilling or unsuspecting viewers, and that the State might therefore legitimately act as it did in order to protect the sensitive from otherwise unavoidable exposure to appellant's crude form of protest. Of course, the mere presumed presence of unwitting listeners or viewers does not serve automatically to justify curtailing all speech capable of giving offense. While this Court has recognized that government may properly act in many situations to prohibit intrusion into the privacy of the home of unwelcome views and ideas which cannot be totally banned from the public dialogue, we have at the same time consistently stressed that "we are often 'captives' outside the sanctuary of the home and subject to objectionable speech." The ability of government, consonant with the Constitution, to shut off discourse solely to protect others from hearing it is, in other words, dependent upon a showing that substantial privacy interests are being invaded in an essentially intolerable manner. Any broader view of this authority would effectively empower a majority to silence dissidents simply as a matter of personal predilections.

In this regard, persons confronted with Cohen's jacket were in a quite different posture than, say, those subjected to the raucous emissions of sound trucks blaring outside their residences. Those in the Los Angeles courthouse could effectively avoid further bombardment of their sensibilities simply by averting their eyes. And, while it may be that one has a more substantial claim to a recognizable privacy interest when walking through a courthouse corridor than, for example, strolling through Central Park, surely it is nothing like the interest in being free from unwanted expression in the confines of one's own home. Given the subtlety and complexity of the factors involved, if Cohen's "speech" was otherwise entitled to constitutional protection, we do not think the fact that some unwilling "listeners" in a public building may have been briefly exposed to it can serve to justify this breach of the peace conviction where, as here, there was no evidence that persons powerless to avoid appellant's conduct did in fact object to it, and where that portion of the statute upon which Cohen's conviction rests evinces no concern, either on its face or as construed by the California courts, with the special plight of the captive auditor, but, instead, indiscriminately sweeps within its prohibitions all "offensive conduct" that disturbs "any neighborhood or person."

II

Against this background, the issue flushed by this case stands out in bold relief. It is whether California can excise, as "offensive conduct," one particular scurrilous epithet from the public discourse, either upon the theory of the court below that its use is inherently likely to cause violent reaction or upon a more general assertion that the States, acting as guardians of public morality, may properly remove this offensive word from the public vocabulary.

The rationale of the California court is plainly untenable. At most it reflects an "undifferentiated fear or apprehension of disturbance (which) is not enough to overcome the right to freedom of expression." *Tinker v. Des Moines Indep. Community School Dist.*, 393 U.S. 503, 508 (1969). We have been shown no evidence that substantial numbers of citizens are standing ready to strike out physically at whoever may assault their sensibilities with execrations like that uttered by Cohen. There may be some persons about with such lawless and violent proclivities, but that is an insufficient base upon which to erect, consistently with constitutional values, a governmental power to force persons who wish to ventilate their dissident views into avoiding particular forms of expression. The argument amounts to little more than the self-defeating proposition that to avoid physical censorship of one who has not sought to provoke such a response by a hypothetical coterie of the violent and lawless, the States may more appropriately effectuate that censorship themselves.

Admittedly, it is not so obvious that the First and Fourteenth Amendments must be taken to disable the States from punishing public utterance of this unseemly expletive in order to maintain what they regard as a suitable level of discourse within the body politic. We think, however, that examination and reflection will reveal the shortcomings of a contrary viewpoint.

At the outset, we cannot overemphasize that, in our judgment, most situations where the State has a justifiable interest in regulating speech will fall within one or more of the various established exceptions, discussed above but not applicable here, to the usual rule that governmental bodies may not prescribe the form or content of individual expression. Equally important to our conclusion is the constitutional backdrop against which our decision must be made. The constitutional right of free expression is powerful medicine in a society as diverse and populous as ours. It is designed and intended to remove governmental restraints from the arena of public discussion, putting the decision as to what views shall be voiced largely into the hands of each of us, in the hope that use of such freedom will ultimately produce a more capable citizenry and more perfect polity and in the belief that no other approach would comport with the premise of individual dignity and choice upon which our political system rests. See *Whitney v. California*, 274 U.S. 357, 375—377 (1927) (Brandeis, J., concurring).

To many, the immediate consequence of this freedom may often appear to be only verbal tumult, discord, and even offensive utterance. These are, however, within established limits, in truth necessary side effects of the broader enduring values which the process of open debate permits us to achieve. That the air may at times seem filled with verbal cacophony is, in this sense not a sign of weakness but of strength. We cannot lose sight of the fact that, in what otherwise might seem a trifling and annoying instance of individual distasteful abuse of a privilege, these fundamental societal values are truly implicated. That is why "(w)holly neutral futilities * * * come under the protection of free speech as fully as do Keats' poems or Donne's sermons," *Winters v. New York*, 333 U.S. 507, 528 (1948) (Frankfurter, J., dissenting), and why "so long as the means are peaceful, the communication need not meet standards of acceptability," *Organization for a Better Austin v. Keefe*, 402 U.S. 415 (1971).

Against this perception of the constitutional policies involved, we discern certain more particularized considerations that peculiarly call for reversal of this conviction. First, the principle contended for by the State seems inherently boundless. How is one to distinguish this from any other offensive word? Surely the State has no right to cleanse public debate to the point where it is grammatically palatable to the most squeamish among us. Yet no readily ascertainable general principle exists for stopping short of that result were we to affirm the judgment below. For, while the particular four-letter word being litigated here is perhaps more distasteful than most others of its genre, it is nevertheless often true that one man's vulgarity is another's lyric. Indeed, we think it is largely because governmental officials cannot make principled distinctions in this area that the Constitution leaves matters of taste and style so largely to the individual.

Additionally, we cannot overlook the fact, because it is well illustrated by the episode involved here, that much linguistic expression serves a dual communicative function: it conveys not only ideas capable of relatively precise, detached explication, but otherwise inexpressible emotions as well. In fact, words are often chosen as much for their emotive as their cognitive force. We cannot sanction the view that the Constitution, while solicitous of the cognitive content of individual speech has little or no regard for that emotive function which practically speaking, may often be the more important element of the overall message sought to be communicated. Indeed, as Mr. Justice Frankfurter has said, "(o)ne of the prerogatives of American citizenship is the right to criticize public men and measures—and that means not only informed and responsible criticism but the freedom to speak foolishly and without moderation." *Baumgartner v. United States*, 322 U.S. 665, 673–674 (1944).

Finally, and in the same vein, we cannot indulge the facile assumption that one can forbid particular words without also running a substantial risk of suppressing ideas in the process. Indeed, governments might soon seize upon the censorship of particular words as a convenient guise for banning the expression of unpopular views. We have been able, as noted above, to discern little social benefit that might result from running the risk of opening the door to such grave results.

It is, in sum, our judgment that, absent a more particularized and compelling reason for its actions, the State may not, consistently with the First and Fourteenth Amendments, make the simple public display here involved of this single four-letter expletive a criminal offense. Because that is the only arguably sustainable rationale for the conviction here at issue, the judgment below must be reversed.

Reversed.

MR. JUSTICE BLACKMUN, with whom THE CHIEF JUSTICE and MR. JUSTICE BLACK join.

I dissent, and I do so for two reasons:

1. Cohen's absurd and immature antic, in my view, was mainly conduct and little speech. The California Court of Appeal appears so to have described it, 1 Cal.App.3d 94, 100, 81 Cal.Rptr. 503, 507, and I cannot characterize it otherwise. Further, the case appears to me to be well within the sphere of *Chaplinsky v. New Hampshire*, 315 U.S. 568 (1942), where Mr. Justice Murphy, a known champion of First Amendment freedoms, wrote for a unanimous bench. As a consequence, this Court's agonizing over First Amendment values seems misplaced and unnecessary.

2. I am not at all certain that the California Court of Appeal's construction of § 415 is now the authoritative California construction.

ROBERT H. BORK, THE TEMPTING OF AMERICA

(1990).

Moral relativism became explicit in the cases dealing with obscenity and pornography. *Cohen v. California* threw first amendment protection around the behavior of a man who wore into a courthouse a jacket bearing words which suggested that the reader perform an act of extreme anatomical implausibility (copulation, to put it euphemistically) with the Selective Service System. Justice Harlan, writing for a majority of the Court, said the state could not ban such obscenity in public. "[T]he principle contended for by the State seems inherently boundless. How is one to distinguish this from any other offensive word?" From the perspective of moral relativism all words are the same. To take Harlan's line, one might as well say that the negligence standard of tort law is invalid because it is inherently boundless. How is one to distinguish the reckless driver from the safe one? The answer in both cases is by the standards of the community, applied through the common sense of the jury. Almost all judgments in law, as in life, are ones of degree. As Holmes said:

> [T]he law is full of instances where a man's fate depends on his estimating rightly, that is, as the jury subsequently estimates it, some matter of degree. If his judgment is wrong, not only may he incur a fine or short imprisonment, as here; he may incur the penalty of death. "An act causing death may be murder, manslaughter, or misadventure according to the degree of danger attending it" by common experience in the circumstances known to the actor.

The law has never flinched from such judgments except when, as in the case of morals, judges seriously doubt the community's right to make moral judgments. But Harlan made it even clearer that moral relativism was the basis for the decision when he observed, and apparently thought the observation decisive: "[O]ne man's vulgarity is another's lyric." If the statement that one man's moral judgment is as good as another's were taken seriously, it would be impossible to see how law on any subject could be permitted to exist. After all, one man's larceny is another's just distribution of goods.

Almost unlimited personal autonomy in these areas is defended with the shopworn slogan that the individual should be free to do as he sees fit so long as he does no harm to others. The formula is empty. The question is what the community is entitled to define as harm to others. It is difficult to know the origin of the peculiar notion that what the community thinks to be moral harm may not be legislated against. That notion has been given powerful impetus in our culture, as Gertrude Himmelfarb has shown, by John Stuart Mill's book, *On Liberty*. As she demonstrates, Mill himself usually knew better than this. It is, in any event, an idea that tends to dissolve social bonds. As Lord Devlin said, "What makes a society is a community of ideas, not political ideas alone but also ideas about the way its members should behave and govern their lives." A change in moral environment—in social attitudes toward sex, marriage, duties toward children, and the like—may surely be felt to be as harmful as the possibility of physical violence or the absence of proportional representation of ethnic groups in the work force. The Court has never explained, nor has anyone else, why what the community feels to be harm may not be counted as one.

These are not negligible matters. Any healthy society needs a view of itself as a political and moral community. The fact that laws about such matters are invalidated may be less important than the moral lesson taught. Traditional views of morality are under attack from many quarters. Attempts to change morality are constitutionally protected, but defiance of laws based upon morality should not be. In the arena of symbolism, which is how a culture defines itself, it hurts badly that the Justices, whom Eugene Rostow, former dean of the Yale law school, called "inevitably teachers in a vital national seminar," should teach the lesson that Americans' attempt to define their communities politically and morally through law is suspect, and probably pernicious.

Questions

1) In *Cohen v. California*, Justice Harlan for the majority and Justice Blackmun for the dissenters offer sharply contrasting interpretations of the Supreme Court's 1942 precedent, *Chaplinsky v. New Hampshire.* Which interpretation is most true to what the Court actually said in *Chaplinsky* (p. 7)? Notice that one member of the *Cohen* majority (Justice Douglas) and one member of the *Cohen* dissent (Justice Black) were members of the Court that unanimously decided *Chaplinsky.*

2) Does the argument from autonomy that Schauer describes and concludes "represents a significant contribution to free speech theory" support the right to utter profanity in public that was recognized in *Cohen v. California*? Do the autonomy-based constraints on what reasons government can invoke for limiting the choices available to its citizens preclude all efforts to prevent the coarsening or degradation of public discourse?

3) Recall that Justice Harlan says in *Cohen* that the First Amendment "is designed and intended to remove governmental restraints from the arena of public discussion, putting the decision as to what views shall be voiced largely in the hands of each of us, in the hope that use of such freedom will ultimately produce a more capable citizenry and more perfect polity and in the belief that no other approach would comport with the premise of individual dignity and choice upon which our political system rests." Is this an argument from autonomy? An argument similar to that made by Professor Thomas Scanlon, as described by Schauer? How do the Harlan and Scanlon arguments differ?

4) Does Judge Bork's argument in reference to *Cohen v. California* that moral harms can be a legitimate basis for regulating speech suggest that he agrees with the positions taken by Charles Lawrence (p. 431) regarding racially derogatory speech and Catharine MacKinnon (p. 400) regarding sexually subordinating speech? Should local democratic majorities be free under the First Amendment to enforce a morality of public discussion concerning those subjects? Does Bork's call for the recognition of moral harms reject the points made by Judge Easterbrook in *Hudnut* (p. 395) regarding the impropriety of viewpoint regulation? The argument of Jeremy Waldron (p. 405) regarding the social value of moral distress?

5) Does the Court's decision in *Cohen v. California* depend on the assumption that a speaker who believed that domestic dissent was undermining troop morale would not have been prosecuted for wearing a jacket that said "Fuck the war protestors"? Should a universally enforced ban on displaying written profanity in public places where it is likely to be seen by unwilling audiences be considered viewpoint discrimination?

6) Suppose Cohen had worn his jacket in the courtroom while the court was in session and been convicted for displaying profanity in that specific setting. Same result?

7) Justice Harlan was often considered the preeminent "conservative" jurist of the mid-twentieth-century Supreme Court. Justice Black was often considered the preeminent "liberal" jurist of that period. Toward the end of their tenure, they became close friends despite their jurisprudential differences. Within four months of the *Cohen* decision, both Justices were forced by failing health to resign; both died (in the same wing of the Bethesda Naval Hospital) shortly thereafter. *Cohen* was the second-to-last free speech case on which these great Justices ruled. The last was the Pentagon Papers case, *New York Times v. United States*, involving a different form of criticism of the Vietnam War. Justice Black voted to protect the publishing of classified information but not Cohen's "absurd and immature antic." Justice Harlan, the reverse. Of the authors we have studied, whose argument supports the view that Cohen's form of criticism of government has the stronger claim to protection? Whose supports the view that the *New York Times*'s claim is the stronger?

CHARLES FRIED, THE NEW FIRST AMENDMENT JURISPRUDENCE: A THREAT TO LIBERTY

59 U.Chi.L.Rev. 225 (1992).

Freedom of expression is properly based on autonomy: the Kantian right of each individual to be treated as an end in himself, an equal sovereign citizen of the kingdom of ends with a right to the greatest liberty compatible with the like liberties of all others.[40] Autonomy is the foundation of all basic liberties, including liberty of expression. There are famous difficulties in defining these spheres of liberty against encroachment by the actions of others—one man's liberty is another's constraint—and many have despaired of deriving any practical conclusions from this principle as it relates to laws bearing on conduct. But the way is much clearer with respect to thought, expression and persuasion. There the claim to liberty runs directly to the foundational. Our ability to deliberate, to reach conclusions about our good, and to act on those conclusions is the foundation of our status as free and rational persons. No conviction forced upon us can really be ours at all. Limits may be put

40. See Immanuel Kant, Foundations of the Metaphysics of Morals (Bobbs-Merrill, 1959); Immanuel Kant, The Metaphysical Elements of Justice (Bobbs-Merrill, 1965).

on my actions insofar as my actions impinge on others, but my status as a rational sovereign requires that I be free to judge for myself what is good and how I shall arrange my life in the sphere of liberty that the similar spheres of others leave me.[41] I cede authority to the state to draw the necessary concrete boundaries between our respective spheres of action. But no such necessity requires, indeed self-respect forbids, that I cede to the state the authority to limit my use of my rational powers. That is why lying, while not the most damaging offense to another's moral right, is one of the clearest. It is also why the state has no claim to dominion over our minds: what we believe, what we are persuaded to believe, and (derivatively) what others may try to persuade us to believe.

The realization of these foundational rights in the First Amendment law of free expression illustrates the relation of institutions to foundations. The First Amendment does not protect a person from lies or imposition by private individuals. Rather the First Amendment protects against impositions by government—"Congress shall make no law ... abridging the freedom of speech," "nor shall any state deprive any person ... of his free speech liberties." The Constitution is hardly concerned with the government lying, and few have argued that you have a constitutional right to have the government refrain from lying to you. Rather, the pressing problems center around government restrictions on speech by others. Indeed, some of the cases in which government might be seen as acting on the Kantian principle—punishing false or misleading speech, or speech designed to circumvent rational evaluation—are just those in which free speech objections to government interference are typically made, though not always successfully. The paradigmatic free speech case is one in which government prevents a person from speaking or punishes him for having spoken-presumably to deter such speech in the future.

The Constitution is concerned only with limits on government, even though a person's autonomy may be assaulted as much if an employer, a neighbor or a family member silences him or stops his access to speech. Other legal norms take care of non-governmental offenses. The background system of private rights goes a long way toward vindicating free speech rights against private actors. John may not interfere with Jane's decision to publish Bill's letter in her newspaper. But neither may Bill complain if Jane decides she does not want to publish that letter. It is her newspaper. I may say what I want at a gathering in my own home, but I have no right to invade your home in order to give a speech there. Free speech values are preserved in this process because of the neutrality of these ordinary background systems of tort, property and criminal law. Perhaps this is why for a long time no one thought to apply constitutional free speech analysis to the law of defamation—unlike

41. We should not confuse this Kantian definition of autonomy with a completely different notion: the subjectivity of the good. To claim, as Kantians do, that the moral value of the good depends on its being freely chosen and that therefore the capacity to choose is primary, does not imply at all that there are no objective criteria of the good, or that the good is whatever is chosen, nor yet some thesis about the subjectivity of values.

criminal libel, where the First Amendment always was thought to apply—until the misuse of that cause of action by the Alabama state police forced latent problems into the open.[48] This is also why commentators have not drawn into question laws against fraud and assault: they protect private rights, and often at the instance of a private party, not the state.

* * *

The Constitution protects primarily against state silencing of private speech because silencing is distinctive. Silencing invokes the power of the state against both speaker and audience. It stops both mouth and ears. It prevents a transaction between citizens. Classic free speech law privileges speech transactions between citizens as none of the state's business. We acknowledge the state's authority over us in all sorts of situations, but by silencing, the state is asking us to acquiesce in sovereignty over our minds, our rational capacities. That is a deeper kind of subordination than one which at least leaves us free to judge that what the state has done is wrong.

In the case in which the audience does not care to receive the communication, the offense to autonomy is harder to identify. At its limit, where no injury is done to others by the unwanted speech, silencing offends a pure autonomy interest: a right to act (here, speak) where there is no harm to others. But cannot the frustration of the audience's wish that the speaker be silent constitute a kind of harm to it? Perhaps, but not one that should be cognizable in law. It is central to the idea of a fundamental right to liberty that no one should curtail (or ask the state to curtail) the liberty of another when the only reason is disagreement about another's conception of the good. State regulation of unwelcome expression is the punishment of pure ideas or beliefs—the outlawing of having ideas or beliefs, or of letting people know that you have them. This injustice is related, but not identical, to that done in the communicative case. We derive them both from the notion that in a free, just society (a liberal society) no one may be compelled to adopt or to deny any particular theory of the good (although he may be compelled to act on such a theory when communal action is otherwise warranted). This concept of justice limits what we may do to punish unilateral expression and what we may do to forbid communications that may convince an audience to modify its conception of the good.

Private impositions and limitations differ fundamentally from state impositions. First, they issue from the limiting person's own exercise of liberty: the newspaper does not wish to carry my op-ed piece, the private university does not wish to include my intellectual system in its course of study. Second, these limitations derive from other private rights that the limiter might have: rights to privacy, or more commonly, rights to property. A liberal society acknowledges private domains in part to allow the development of individual conceptions of the good. If another individual can invoke the power of the state to override that dominion it is

48. New York Times v. Sullivan, 376 U.S. 254, 268 (1964).

likely to be an illiberal claim of authority by the state to adjudicate between two persons' conceptions of the good. Even a judgment by the state that it would be good for you to hear a speech you do not agree with while you are in your own private space is an illiberal assertion of authority. By contrast, time, place, and manner regulations, which are content-neutral, are not an illiberal assertion of authority, but rather a good faith attempt by the liberal state to adjust zones of privacy without regard to what will be pursued within those zones.

CHRISTINA E. WELLS, REINVIGORATING AUTONOMY: FREEDOM AND RESPONSIBILITY IN THE SUPREME COURT'S FIRST AMENDMENT JURISPRUDENCE

32 Harv.Civ.Rt.-Civ.Lib. L. Rev. 159 (1997).

Introduction

Several influential scholars agree that individual autonomy—the concept of people as rational, self-deliberating actors—has been a driving force behind the Supreme Court's protection of speech and expression.[1] A lively debate has arisen, however, as to whether autonomy should underlie free speech jurisprudence. Some commentators favor the Court's approach, arguing that freedom from government censorship is critical to our development as individuals and our capacity for self-governance.[2] In contrast, other scholars contend that First Amendment jurisprudence should focus less on protecting individual autonomy. They argue that the Court should occasionally uphold government regulation of speech, especially regulation designed to remedy distortions in the current "marketplace of ideas"[3] or to otherwise "insure the richness of public debate."[4]

The autonomy debate has raged in First Amendment scholarship in recent years, both generally and in specific contexts such as hate speech, broadcast regulation, and campaign finance reform, and the debate is far from resolution. The intractability of the two sides is largely due to the impoverished notion of autonomy that dominates the debate. By grounding the Court's autonomy rationale in its antipathy toward content discrimination of speech, the debate posits autonomy as personified by isolated and self-interested individuals acting with little or no regard for

1. See, e.g., CASS R. SUNSTEIN, DEMOCRACY AND THE PROBLEM OF FREE SPEECH 141 (1993); Owen M. Fiss, Free Speech and Social Structure, 71 IOWA L. REV. 1405, 1409–10 (1986); Charles Fried, The New First Amendment Jurisprudence: A Threat to Liberty, 59 U. CHI. L. REV. 225, 233–34 (1992); Robert C. Post, Racist Speech, Democracy, and the First Amendment, 32 WM. & MARY L. REV. 267, 279–80 (1991); David A. Strauss, Persuasion, Autonomy, and Freedom of Expression, 91 COLUM. L. REV. 334, 353–55 (1991). But see Geoffrey R. Stone, Autonomy and Distrust, 64 U. COLO. L. REV. 1171, 1172 (1993).

2. See, e.g., Fried, *supra* note 1, at 233; Post, *supra* note 1, at 282.

3. See SUNSTEIN, *supra* note 1, at 28–43; Owen M. Fiss, Why the State?, 100 HARV. L. REV. 781, 788 (1987).

4. Fiss, Why the State?, *supra* note 3, at 791; see also Cass R. Sunstein, Free Speech Now, 59 U. CHI. L. REV. 255, 267 (1992).

their community or the welfare of other individuals. The debate thus pits a rather unsympathetic version of autonomy against the needs of the community and the welfare of its citizens in a manner that is largely irresolvable.

A closer examination of the structure of the Court's free speech jurisprudence, however, reveals that it reflects a far richer and more complex concept of autonomy—one based on the rights and responsibilities of personhood that is generally associated with Immanuel Kant. Autonomy in this sense is not about atomistic individuals but about social creatures entitled to respect for their dignity. In turn, members of society are responsible for respecting the dignity of others. As such, Kantian autonomy attempts to reconcile, rather than divorce, individuality and community. With this understanding of autonomy, we can reexamine the scholarly debate.... An analysis of free speech cases in light of Kantian autonomy refutes the assumption that the Court has elevated the speech rights of individuals over the needs of the community. On the contrary, the Court's jurisprudence attempts to reconcile individuality and community.

* * *

I. THE CONCEPTION OF AUTONOMY EMERGING FROM THE SCHOLARLY DEBATE

A central issue in the autonomy debate has been whether the government's regulation of speech can improve the quality of public discourse. Scholars on both sides of the issue agree that the Court is antipathetic toward such regulation, and emphasizes that its current jurisprudence is particularly hostile toward government suppression of speech based upon its content. Thus, the debate's focus is whether the Court's approach is defensible.

Scholars who generally favor the Court's approach point out that our "status as rational sovereign[s] requires that [we] be free to judge for [ourselves] what is good and how [we] shall arrange [our] li[ves]...."[14] Thus, the Court's hostility toward government suppression of speech is essential to preserve public discourse and, ultimately, our capacity for self-governance.[15] In contrast, scholars criticizing the Court's unrelenting antipathy toward government regulation of speech agree that it stems from a desire to protect autonomy,[16] but view the consequences negatively. According to these commentators, the Court's desire to erect a "shield around the speaker"[17] actually distorts public debate and undermines democracy, primarily by ignoring the fact that the State is not the only threat to speech.[18] They argue that in today's era of huge media corporations and social inequality, it is far too easy for politically or economically powerful speakers to corner the speech market, thereby

14. Fried, *supra* note 1, at 233.

15. See, e.g., *id.* at 233; Post, *supra* note 12, at 1116; Strauss, *supra* note 1, at 356.

16. See, e.g., Fiss, Free Speech and Social Structure, *supra* note 1, at 1409–10.

17. *Id.* at 1409.

18. See, e.g., SUNSTEIN, *supra* note 1, at xix, 93; Fiss, Free Speech and Social Structure, *supra* note 1, at 1409–13.

distorting debate as much or more than any government regulation. Instead of focusing on autonomy, which exalts the speaker's rights and is consistently hostile to government regulations, these scholars conclude that we should view "the state not only as an enemy but also as a friend of speech.... When the state acts to enhance the quality of public debate, we should recognize its actions as consistent with the first amendment."[21]

One of the most striking aspects of the debate is the conception of autonomy that underlies it. Both sides assume that the Court's hostility toward content discrimination is the best example of its concern for protection of autonomy. Autonomy in this sense translates into individual freedom from government interference. Moreover, once conceived of as a negative liberty, autonomy becomes closely associated with speakers; as the debate is framed, autonomy in the Court's free speech jurisprudence means freedom of the speaker to say whatever she wants. It is this characterization of autonomy that makes the debate so intractable. Labeling autonomy solely as the right of the speaker conjures up images of atomistic individuals saying whatever they wish with little regard for the needs of others. Scholars thus associate autonomy with the lone speaker defending her right to shout racial epithets or the large corporation defending its right to donate huge sums of money to political candidates. Both invoke the label "freedom of speech" while ignoring the substantial emotional harm and distortion of public debate such speech can cause. Under the terms of the debate, one is forced to choose between being either pro-autonomy or pro-community. Society, and more importantly the Supreme Court, apparently cannot value both ideals.

But does the debate accurately portray the concept of autonomy reflected in the Court's free speech jurisprudence? Scholars are at least partially correct in locating an autonomy rationale in the Court's hostility toward government censorship. Their mistake, however, is focusing only on that aspect of the Court's jurisprudence. In order to fully understand the Supreme Court's conception of autonomy, one must examine the overall structure of the Court's jurisprudence, which encompasses not only the Court's principle against content discrimination but also its treatment of low-value speech. That examination reveals a richer and more complex notion of autonomy, one that focuses not only on freedom from government interference but also on private citizens' relationships with each other. This conception of autonomy is far removed from atomistic individualism. Instead, it recognizes that we are social beings with rights and responsibilities. This critical insight may provide a middle ground to the debate's otherwise rigid division between autonomy and community.

II. Autonomy in Kant's Moral and Political Theory

The conception of autonomy underlying the Court's free speech jurisprudence derives primarily from Immanuel Kant's moral and politi-

21. Fiss, Free Speech and Social Structure, *supra* note 1, at 1416; see also SUNSTEIN, *supra* note 1, at xix.

cal philosophy. I rely on Kant not only because he was "arguably the most important moral philosopher of the modern period"[25] but also because his "extraordinarily powerful [theory] ... still seems to many thoughtful people to be an essentially correct view."[26] This Part discusses the major themes of Kant's philosophy and its general implications for a system of free expression. Part III then discusses the Court's actual free speech jurisprudence and its relation to Kantian philosophy.

A. *Kantian Theory*

In the Kantian ethic, "every rational being exists as an end in himself."[28] Thus, Kant equates autonomy and personhood. Scholars interpret autonomy, in this sense, as less a right than a capacity of persons to "make and act on their own decisions."[29] Significantly, our innate autonomy (or freedom or dignity) does not leave us entirely free to act to satisfy our desires. Rather, each individual's autonomy implies an obligation to respect the freedom of others and imposes responsibility when we fail to do so. Kantian autonomy is considered to be a foundation for moral precepts—in other words, what we ought to do given the innate dignity of all persons. Nevertheless, autonomy is not a concept limited to the moral realm. Instead, Kant's notion of autonomy has a significant place in his political theory, defining not only the role of the State but also the legal rights and obligations of citizens toward each other.

According to Kant, the ultimate justification of the State is to protect the autonomy of its citizens. As an initial matter, our innate autonomy surely limits the powers of the State against us; a government recognizing the autonomy of its citizens necessarily derives its authority from the rational consent of the governed.[34] Thus, the State has no power to coerce us to act consistently with its independent conception of what is right or good. Rather, its laws must respect our ability to deliberate and our capacity to choose. Viewed in isolation, this aspect of Kantian theory seems to support the concept of autonomy emerging in the scholarly debate, which embodies only the right of individuals

25. ROGER J. SULLIVAN, IMMANUEL KANT'S MORAL THEORY xiii (1989).

26. *Id.*

28. IMMANUEL KANT, FOUNDATIONS OF THE METAPHYSICS OF MORALS 46 (Lewis W. Beck trans., Bobbs-Merrill 1959).

29. Richard H. Fallon, Jr., Two Senses of Autonomy, 46 STAN. L. REV. 875, 878 (1994) [hereinafter Fallon, Autonomy]; see also JEFFRIE G. MURPHY, KANT: THE PHILOSOPHY OF RIGHT 80 (1970) (noting that in Kantian theory "[t]he worth of a rational being, and thus the worth of man, consists ... in his autonomy from the course of mere phenomenal nature. For his dignity consists in his being a self-legislative member in a realm of ends."); SULLIVAN, *supra* note 25, at 235 (defining Kantian autonomy as "the ability and obligation of a person to act on rational principles of his or her own adoption").

34. See, e.g., IMMANUEL KANT, THE METAPHYSICS OF MORALS (1797), reprinted in KANT: POLITICAL WRITINGS, *supra* note 33, at 131, 139, 163 [[hereinafter KANT, METAPHYSICS OF MORALS] ("[T]he Supreme power originally rests with the people.... [Each citizen has the] lawful freedom to obey no law other than that to which he has given his consent."). Not surprisingly, Kant believed that the only moral government—the only government recognizing the autonomy of its citizens—was a republic. *Id.* at 163.

against the government. But Kant's political philosophy is not so one-sided.

Recognizing that the actions of autonomous individuals operating in a society can clash, Kant believed that the State could bring its coercive power to bear against its citizens and thereby limit their freedom, in one, and only one, circumstance—when some citizens' actions infringe upon the freedom of others, and coercion is necessary to preserve the others' autonomy.[37] Such coercive action by the State preserves the dignity of its citizens by ensuring that individuals act in a manner that respects the freedom of others. Thus, the capacity for autonomy creates a moral entitlement that imposes an obligation, enforceable by the State, to respect the autonomy of other persons.

There is, however, a significant limitation on the State's ability to enforce this obligation. The State may protect our freedom from infringement by others, but only with respect to external actions and not with respect to the motives for such actions.[39] As Professor Roger Sullivan explains, the State may "constrain the citizens from violating the respect due others, but it cannot insist that they do so because they respect them."[40] This limitation is important because it implies a distinction between acceptable and unacceptable State uses of coercion. State coercion designed to preserve each citizen's autonomy from unwarranted interference comports with a general respect for the autonomy of all citizens. But coercion designed to bring internal motives in line with respect for such freedom imposes the State's view of what is right or good on its citizens. Thus, our obligations to each other, while legally enforceable, are still tempered with the ability to believe what we wish.

Viewing Kantian political theory as a whole, one sees a different view of autonomy than that which has emerged in the autonomy debate. Rather than focusing on autonomy as a right to be free from interfer-

37. See KANT, METAPHYSICS OF MORALS, *supra* note 34, at 134. Kant notes:

> [I]f a certain use to which freedom is put is itself a hindrance to freedom in accordance with universal laws (i.e., if it is contrary to right), any coercion which is used against it will be a hindrance to a hindrance of freedom, and will thus be consonant with freedom in accordance with universal laws—that is, it will be right. It thus follows by the law of contradiction that right entails the authority to apply coercion to anyone who infringes it.

Id. Importantly, only the State is entitled to use coercion to preserve freedom. Individuals are not so entitled. See, e.g., KANT, THEORY & PRACTICE, *supra* note 33, at 75 ("[N]o-one can coerce anyone else other than through the public law and its executor, the head of the state....").

39. Kant made clear that "[t]he concept of right ... applies only to those relationships between one person and another which are both external and practical." KANT, METAPHYSICS OF MORALS, *supra* note 34, at 132–33. Thus,

> although [the] law imposes an obligation on me, it does not mean that I am in any way expected, far less required, to restrict my freedom myself to these conditions purely for the sake of this obligation. On the contrary, reason merely says that individual freedom is restricted in this way by virtue of the idea behind it....
>
> If it is not our intention to teach virtue, but only to state what is right, we may not and should not ourselves represent this law of right as a possible motive for actions.

Id. at 133–34. In this sense, Kant's Principle of Right is a slightly restricted version of his moral law which does concern itself with the motives for our actions.

40. ROGER J. SULLIVAN, AN INTRODUCTION TO KANT'S ETHICS 24 (1994).

ence, Kant sees autonomy as an innate capacity of each person, which imposes obligations on us as members of an organized society. As such, Kantian autonomy is not the right of atomistic individuals working toward their own personal goals. Rather, autonomy recognizes that people are "inherently social being[s who] . . . live and move and have their being in a public forum."[42]

B. Implications for a System of Free Expression

What would a system of laws designed to facilitate free expression look like if based upon a Kantian conception of autonomy? While Part III discusses many of the nuances of such a system as it exists in the Supreme Court's jurisprudence, a broad sketch of some of the more significant aspects of that system is appropriate here for a better understanding of its overall foundation.

As an initial matter, such a system would not focus on the rights of the speaker qua speaker but on the integrity of our thought processes as individuals and members of a community. Our thought processes are integral to our capacity for deliberation and self-governance. Ensuring their integrity is thus a necessary aspect of any system of laws built upon Kantian autonomy. Given that we develop our thought processes by communicating with others, and thereby develop our capacity for self-governance, protecting public expression is especially important. As Kant asks, "[H]ow much and how accurately would we think if we did not think, so to speak, in community with others to whom we communicate our thoughts and who communicate their thoughts to us[?]"[43] Thus, we should protect those who publicly express themselves because of their contributions to the development of the rational capacities of both the speaker and her audience.[44]

Obviously, protection from overreaching state censorship is essential to the public exercise of our rational faculties. A system of free expression based on Kantian autonomy, however, would not merely concern itself with protection against government suppression. Because the State's purpose is to preserve the dignity of its citizens, such a system would also ensure that citizens use speech consistently with autonomy. The State can and should regulate speech that, by attempting to override the thought processes of other individuals, disrespects their rational capacities.[46] Such speech does not facilitate, but rather detracts from, the

42. [Ernest J. Weinrib, Law as Idea of Reason, in ESSAYS ON KANT'S POLITICAL PHILOSOPHY 15, 41 (Howard L. Williams ed., 1992)]; see also SULLIVAN, *supra* note 25, at 260; Jeremy Waldron, Kant's Legal Positivism, 109 HARV. L. REV. 1535, 1566 (1996).

43. IMMANUEL KANT, WHAT IS ORIENTATION IN THINKING, reprinted in KANT: POLITICAL WRITINGS, *supra* note 33, at 237, 247; see also IMMANUEL KANT, AN ANSWER TO THE QUESTION: "WHAT IS ENLIGHTENMENT?," reprinted in KANT: POLITICAL WRITINGS, (*supra* note 33, at 54, 55); HANNAH ARENDT, LECTURES ON KANT'S POLITICAL PHILOSOPHY 40 (Ronald Beiner ed., 1982).

44. See ARENDT, *supra* note 43, at 39.

46. I base this argument on Kant's moral and political theory, but it is, to some extent, my extension of his principles. Kant clearly argued against government suppression of speech, but his views on regulation of private coercive speech are less devel-

public exercise of reason and is therefore the proper subject of the State's coercive powers.

Determining when speech is coercive is no easy task. The task is made more difficult by the fact that the State must walk a fine line between regulating the external and internal aspects of speech. The State must regulate speech because of the coercive impact it has on our thought processes, not because of any particular idea that is expressed. The ability to test ideas through public communication is a necessary aspect of autonomy; we cannot relinquish it to the State or any other person. Deeming speech coercive because the government or its citizens dislikes or finds harmful the ideas expressed imposes an orthodoxy and cuts off debate in an impermissible manner.

In sum, a system of free expression based on a Kantian notion of autonomy involves more than the freedom of the speaker to speak as she wishes. Rather, it involves the ability and responsibility of individuals, as part of a community, to engage in dialogue in order to develop their rational capacities.

III. AUTONOMY AS REFLECTED IN THE STRUCTURE OF THE SUPREME COURT'S FREE SPEECH JURISPRUDENCE

My argument that the Court's jurisprudence reflects an autonomy rationale is subject to a few important caveats. First, I do not offer Kantian autonomy as a universal rationale explaining all of the Court's free speech jurisprudence. Indeed, there are so many intricacies to free speech doctrine that identifying a completely unifying principle may be impossible. Kantian autonomy, however, largely explains at least two of the major "organizing principles" of the Court's jurisprudence: the Court's review of regulations for content discrimination and its designation of certain speech as low-value. Moreover, Kantian autonomy can illuminate those areas of jurisprudence on which the scholarly debate has concentrated.

Second, I do not assert that the Court has explicitly adopted Kantian autonomy as the basis of its doctrinal organizing principles. Other than Justice Brandeis's famous statement that "the final end of the State [is] to make men free to develop their faculties,"[50] few Justices have explicitly invoked such a concept. Indeed, other factors arguably contradict my argument. For example, several Justices have eschewed a jurisprudence based on Kantian autonomy.[52] In addition, to the extent the Court has

oped. Nevertheless, Kant's philosophy, especially his belief that laws permitting lying would make a just State impossible, supports regulation of such speech. See IMMANUEL KANT, ON A SUPPOSED RIGHT TO LIE FROM ALTRUISTIC MOTIVES, reprinted in CRITIQUE OF PRACTICAL REASON AND OTHER WRITINGS ON MORAL PHILOSOPHY 346 (Lewis W. Beck trans., Univ. of Chicago Press 1949).

50. Whitney v. California, 274 U.S. 357, 375 (1927) (Brandeis, J., concurring).

52. Justice Holmes, for example, was no fan of Kant's political theory, instead arguing that the law should recognize that people act on "justifiable self-preference." OLIVER WENDELL HOLMES, THE COMMON LAW 41, 41–44 (1923); see also David M. Rabban, The Emergence of Modern First Amendment Doctrine, 50 U. CHI. L. REV. 1205, 1267–83 (1983) (discussing

adopted an autonomy rationale, it has been hopelessly inconsistent, sometimes viewing the First Amendment as protecting speakers' rights and sometimes as protecting listeners' rights.

But the Court's manifestation of Kantian autonomy does not lie in the Court's rhetoric or in the beliefs of independent Justices. My argument is that the Court's overall structural approach and reasoning when resolving free speech issues is remarkably consistent with a Kantian ideal. Moreover, explicit recognition of a relationship between Kantian autonomy and the Court's free speech jurisprudence might alleviate some of the Court's doctrinal and rhetorical inconsistencies. The remainder of this Part outlines the most critical aspects of free speech doctrine insofar as they relate to Kantian autonomy.

A. *The Court's Distinction Between Content–Based and Content–Neutral Regulations of Speech*

The Court's approach to content-based and content-neutral regulations of speech distinguishes between government regulations that "limit communication because of the message it conveys" (content-based regulations) and government regulations that affect speech but are not aimed at its content (content-neutral regulations). The Court heavily disfavors content-based regulations, striking them down unless the government can show that the law is narrowly drawn to meet a compelling state interest. In contrast, the Court reviews content-neutral regulations under the more lenient standard of intermediate scrutiny, upholding the regulations as long as they "are justified without reference to the content of the regulated speech, ... are narrowly tailored to serve a significant governmental interest, and ... leave open ample alternative channels for communication of the information." The differing treatment of content-neutral and content-based regulations and the differing standards applied to each reflect that aspect of Kantian autonomy that requires the State to respect our thought processes.

The fact that content-based laws violate Kantian autonomy is best reflected in the purposes for which so many of those laws are enacted. For example, the government often regulates speech because it does not trust individuals to make correct decisions if exposed to certain information.[60] Distrust of the ability of citizens to make decisions is antithetical

Justice Holmes's jurisprudence and his "disdain" of a Kantian rationale for the law). Indeed, Justice Holmes's reference to speakers as "poor and puny anonymities," even in his opinions arguing for protection of speech, implies far less respect for human dignity than a Kantian rationale. See Abrams v. United States, 250 U.S. 616, 629 (1919) (Holmes, J., dissenting).

Of the current Court, Chief Justice Rehnquist is the most obvious anti-Kantian candidate. His willingness to uphold even the most paternalistic regulations of speech, see, e.g., Rust v. Sullivan, 500 U.S. 173 (1991) (Rehnquist, C.J.) (upholding government regulation banning recipients of federal funds from counseling about the availability of abortion as a method of family planning); Posadas de P. R. Assocs. v. Tourism Co., 478 U.S. 328 (1986) (Rehnquist, C.J.) (upholding Puerto Rico statute banning casino advertising aimed at its citizens), is clearly inconsistent with a Kantian rationale.

60. See, e.g., Virginia State Bd. of Pharmacy v. Virginia Citizen's Consumer Council, 425 U.S. 748, 768 (1976) (dealing with State fear that information regarding drug

to autonomy, and the Court has invalidated numerous content-based laws that have such paternalistic justifications. Also, government officials often justify content-based restrictions by arguing that they protect citizens from offensive speech, under the premise that citizens ought not to have to deal with unpleasant or abhorrent words and ideas. Attempts to protect citizens from disagreeable speech treat adults as children and deny their capabilities to withstand or counter unpleasant events. Further, they allow those holding a dominant viewpoint in society to silence or restrict the dissemination of views with which they disagree, thereby making the government a vehicle for private citizens' disrespect for the thought processes of others. Not surprisingly, the Court has also found this justification wanting. Finally, the government may enact content-based restrictions simply because it disapproves of the speaker's point of view. Such restrictions amount to governmental attempts to substitute its thoughts for those of its citizens, in effect determining for us which views are right and wrong. Again, the Court has recognized that such justifications are illegitimate. Thus, by protecting against the improper motivations generally underlying content-based regulations of speech, the Court's doctrine reflects a consciousness of our inalienable dignity and a desire to protect this dignity from coercive government incursions.

The Court's more lenient approach to content-neutral standards similarly fits within a Kantian autonomy rationale, as such restrictions do not usually impinge upon our innate dignity in the same manner as content-based limitations. Improper government motivation is less of a danger with content-neutral restrictions because, by definition, these regulations must be justified without reference to the content of expression. In the context of a law regulating the decibel levels of sound trucks, for example, such a justification might be that trucks blaring their messages in private residential neighborhoods are significant invasions of privacy. That justification is relatively neutral, applies to all speech regardless of its message, and leaves open other opportunities of expression. Thus, the government does not appear to be regulating speech in a manner designed to coerce our thought processes. Of course, ostensibly impartial justifications for content-neutral regulations can be pretextual: the government's real motive behind the law could be disapproval of the speaker's viewpoint. Nevertheless, much of the time, the government's neutral justifications are legitimate efforts to balance expression with other important concerns, such as order or privacy. Furthermore, the Court does not merely rubber stamp content-neutral laws but applies intermediate scrutiny in order to ensure that content-neutral laws do not suppress speech inappropriately. To the extent that content-neutral regulations have a severe impact on viewpoints or speakers, the Court has been willing to strike down such regulations.

Thus, the Court's approach to content discrimination is consistent with the Kantian desire to ensure the integrity of thought processes

prices might adversely influence consumer decision making); Whitney v. California, 274 U.S. 357, 371 (1927) (dealing with State fear that advocacy of communism would prompt people to attempt to overthrow the government).

integral to our capacity for autonomy. The Court's approach to content-based and content-neutral regulations, however, reflects only one aspect of Kantian autonomy—protection from State interference with our thought processes. One sees the other aspect of Kantian autonomy—regulating private citizens' attempted coercion of our thought processes—in the Court's approach to low-value speech.

B. *The Court's Approach to Low–Value Speech*

Although its First Amendment jurisprudence is generally protective of speech, the Court has never assumed that all speech is of equal value. Instead, the Court has created certain categories of low-value speech that it believes deserve less protection than other speech. Examples of such low-value speech are: speech that incites unlawful activity; fighting words; obscenity; and, to some extent, commercial speech and libel. Unfortunately, the Court has provided little guidance with respect to what speech should be considered low-value. Its only consistent statement is that low-value speech is "no essential part of any exposition of ideas and is of such slight social value as a step to the truth that any benefit that may be derived from it is clearly outweighed by the social interest in order and morality."[73] That statement, although explaining why the Court has created categories of low-value speech, does not explain when speech falls into those categories. Not surprisingly, scholars have widely criticized the Court for creating low-value categories which many believe have no place in First Amendment jurisprudence. In addition, the Court's failure to define specifically when speech becomes low-value has engendered much debate over the salient characteristics of such speech.

Despite scholars' concerns, there is a unifying principle to the Court's low-value speech analysis that also illuminates its legitimate place in free speech jurisprudence. A close examination of the Court's approach to the various categories of low-value speech reveals that it is consistent with a Kantian notion of autonomy. Specifically, the Court has attempted to carve out as low-value speech that disrespects other citizens' thought processes, thus making it a proper subject for State regulation. Furthermore, and consistent with Kantian autonomy, the Court has made a strong effort to limit State regulation only to speech that invades rather than appeals to our rationality. The remainder of this Part examines the Court's doctrine in five specific areas of low-value speech: incitement of illegal action; fighting words; obscenity; libel; and commercial speech.

73. Chaplinsky v. New Hampshire, 315 U.S. 568, 572 (1948). The Court's description of speech as having no social value first appeared with respect to its fighting words doctrine. However, the Chaplinsky language, or variants thereof, has appeared in almost all of the low-value speech cases. See, e.g., Roth v. United States, 354 U.S. 476, 484 (1957) ("[I]mplicit in the history of the First Amendment is the rejection of obscenity as utterly without redeeming social importance."); Beauharnais v. Illinois, 343 U.S. 250, 256–57 (1952) ("[L]ibelous ... utterances are no essential part of any exposition of ideas."); Valentine v. Chrestenson, 316 U.S. 52, 54 (1942) (noting that "purely commercial advertising" does not amount to the "exercise ... of communicating information and disseminating opinion").

1. *Incitement of Illegal Action*

The Court's doctrine regarding incitement provides an excellent illustration of the autonomy rationale in its low-value speech jurisprudence. According to the Court, the government can suppress speech advocating unlawful conduct only if "it is directed to inciting or producing imminent lawless action and is likely to incite or produce such action";[77] mere "abstract teaching" of the moral necessity of such action will not sustain punishment. For example, the State may punish speech designed to whip an angry mob into a violent and destructive frenzy, but it may not punish a political rally in which the speaker advocates violence as a tool for revolution.

The Court's requirement of imminent lawless action is easily justified as based upon concern for autonomy. Speech designed to incite immediate violence or lawless action does not appeal to our thought processes. Rather, it disrespects our rationality and is designed to elicit an unthinking, animalistic response. Thus, the Court's test protects our collective thought processes and imposes consequences on speakers who violate the freedom of citizens to think rationally. Acceptable state action, however, does not include punishing mere advocacy of unlawful action. Speech designed to persuade people to violate the law is not coercive in the same sense as speech designed to incite imminent lawlessness; the former contributes to rather than detracts from our deliberative processes, even if the idea advocated is perceived as undesirable. Punishment of such speech is an unreasonable impediment to our public exercise of reason, as the Court has recognized numerous times. Thus, the Court's incitement doctrine maintains a narrow line to protect our rationality from both private and state interference.

2. *Fighting Words*

One can view the Court's approach to fighting words—"those which by their very utterance inflict injury or tend to incite an immediate breach of the peace"[82]—in the same vein. In the Court's eyes, such words do "not in any proper sense communicat[e] ... information or opinion";[83] rather, they are more akin to physical assaults. As such, fighting words do not appeal to our rational or deliberative capacities. They are instead designed to induce us to react violently and without thinking, much as a punch in the mouth induces the victim to respond in an unthinking manner.

The fact that the Court refuses to consider offensive speech as being low in value further bolsters the autonomy rationale argument. In order to qualify as fighting words, speech must "have a direct tendency to cause acts of violence by the person to whom, individually, the remark is addressed."[85] The State cannot ban speech that does not rise to this level

77. Brandenburg v. Ohio, 395 U.S. 444, 447–48 (1969).

82. Chaplinsky v. New Hampshire, 315 U.S. 568, 572 (1942).

83. *Id.* (quoting Cantwell v. Connecticut, 310 U.S. 296, 309–10 (1940)).

85. Gooding v. Wilson, 405 U.S. 518, 523 (1972).

simply because people are offended or angered by the ideas expressed. Distasteful or abhorrent speech, while often unpleasant or even painful, does not coerce or manipulate others to react in an immediately violent or irrational manner. In fact, offensive speech often expresses emotions that persuade others regarding the speaker's point of view or at least invite debate. Thus, as with its incitement doctrine, the Court has attempted to distinguish between speech that invades the dignity of others, for which the speaker must bear the consequences, and speech that must be free from state interference in order to protect our thought processes from state coercion.

3. *Obscenity*

The Court's obscenity doctrine is also consistent with Kantian autonomy. In *Roth v. United States*,[89] the Court held that obscenity did not enjoy First Amendment protection because it is "utterly without redeeming social importance."[90] In so holding, the Court defined obscenity as "material which deals with sex in a manner appealing to prurient interest."[91] Significantly, the *Roth* Court took great pains to distinguish obscenity from portrayals of sex expressing "ideas having even the slightest redeeming social importance,"[92] including unorthodox, controversial, or hateful ideas, which the Court believed should enjoy full constitutional protection. By requiring that obscene material have a "prurient" appeal, the Court's jurisprudence targets expression that is intended to appeal to our physical rather than our mental capacities, just as fighting words are like a physical assault rather than speech. The Court's attempt to distinguish speech that disrespects our thought processes from sexually oriented speech that nevertheless appeals to our rational nature is analogous to the Court's line drawing with incitement and fighting words. Both distinctions allow the State to protect against and punish private interference with our deliberative capacities while still maintaining unfettered dialogue, even on topics that some might find uncomfortable.

Claiming that the Court's approach to obscenity is consistent with Kantian autonomy is not without controversy. Three potential counter-arguments are especially important in that respect. First, many scholars contend that the Court's determination that obscenity has no value actually violates our autonomy by imposing a dominant viewpoint regarding acceptable lifestyles.[94] Like these scholars, I find troubling the notion that obscenity is worthless, but the debate over obscenity's actual

89. 354 U.S. 476 (1957).

90. *Id.* at 484.

91. *Id.* at 487. The Court has since refined the Roth standard. Currently, it defines obscenity as that material which appeals to a prurient interest, depicts sexual conduct in a patently offensive manner, and lacks serious, redeeming social value. See Miller v. California, 413 U.S. 15, 24 (1973).

92. Roth, 354 U.S. at 484.

94. See, e.g., Steven G. Gey, The Apologetics of Suppression: The Regulation of Pornography as Act and Idea, 86 MICH. L. REV. 1564, 1565 (1988); Michael J. Perry, Freedom of Expression: An Essay on Theory and Doctrine, 78 NW. U. L. REV. 1137, 1182 (1983); David A.J. Richards, Free Speech and Obscenity Law: Toward a Moral Theory of the First Amendment, 123 U. PA. L. REV. 45, 82 (1974).

value is beyond the scope of this Article. The important fact is that the Court has attempted to carve out only a small portion of material for suppression based upon its belief that such information invades our thought processes. Most sexually oriented speech remains untouched. In fact, the Court has gone out of its way to protect such speech when it believes the government to be engaging in unreasonable censorship.[95] Thus, regardless of whether obscenity actually is valueless, the Court's reasoning is consistent with a Kantian notion of autonomy.

Second, one could argue that the Court's current standard for judging obscenity belies my argument regarding Kantian autonomy. While the *Roth* standard characterized obscenity as without social value, current doctrine defines obscenity as that material which appeals to a "prurient" interest and that merely lacks "serious" social value. Thus, one could conclude that the Court's current obscenity jurisprudence is not limited to speech which invades our thought processes. While the Court appears to have relaxed its standard regarding social value, its maintenance of the "prurient" interest requirement in both definitions nevertheless suggests that it is at least trying to limit state regulation to speech that in some way coerces or disrespects our rationality.

Finally, one could argue that the Court's heavy reliance on history and accepted social practice in formulating its obscenity doctrine is inconsistent with an autonomy rationale. To be sure, history played a large role in the Court's decision not to accord obscenity First Amendment protection. But the Court's modern definition clearly deviates from historical definitions of obscenity, which encompassed far more literature, art, and other useful information than the Court's current definition. Thus, the Court's attempt to narrow the definition of obscenity to that which has a "prurient" appeal, although influenced by history, is at least partly compatible with autonomy concerns.

4. Libel

Although the Court originally maintained that "libelous ... utterances are no essential part of any exposition of ideas,"[100] it currently gives substantial protection to false statements of fact regarding public officials and public figures.[101] The Court's extension of First Amendment protection to such statements, however, had little to do with a belief that they have any value as speech. Indeed, the Court has explicitly stated that such statements have little, if any, First Amendment value.[102] Rather, the desire to avoid chilling potential speakers by building a protective wall around speech on public issues, especially criticism of the

95. American Booksellers Ass'n v. Hudnut, 771 F.2d 323, 332 (7th Cir. 1985), aff'd mem., 475 U.S. 1001 (1986) (striking down as viewpoint discrimination an antipornography ordinance banning graphic and sexually explicit portrayals of women as inferiors or subordinates).

100. Beauharnais v. Illinois, 343 U.S. 250, 256–57 (1952).

101. See New York Times v. Sullivan, 376 U.S. 254, 280 (1964); Gertz v. Robert Welch, Inc., 418 U.S. 323, 342–43 (1974).

102. See, e.g., Hustler Magazine, Inc. v. Falwell, 485 U.S. 46, 52 (1988) ("False statements of fact are particularly valueless...."); Gertz, 418 U.S. at 340 ("[T]here is no constitutional value in false statements of fact.").

government, largely drove the Court's decisions.[103] Such reasoning is consistent with a Kantian view of autonomy.

The Court's decision that libelous utterances are valueless protects our thought processes from private coercion. As Professor Strauss has noted:

> Lying is the clearest case of . . . coercion-like, autonomy-invading manipulation. . . . When a speaker tells a lie in order to influence the listener's behavior, the metaphor of commandeering the listener's mind, and making it serve the speaker's ends instead of the listener's, seems especially appropriate. The speaker really does inject her own false information into the thought processes of the listener for the purpose of making those processes produce the outcome that the speaker desires.[104]

In other words, false statements of fact are designed not to persuade or appeal to our rational senses but to override them and unreasonably damage the libeled person's reputation as a result. Consequently, we can hold persons making those statements responsible for such invasions.

Some might argue, however, that the Court's refusal to extend protection of defamation law to public figures and officials except in extreme circumstances argues against an autonomy rationale. After all, if lies invade our thought processes, why should lies about public officials and figures be any different? The answer rests in the issue of seditious libel that played an important role in *Sullivan*. In that case, an Alabama official used libel law not to protect a personal reputation but to shut down criticism of the government by members of the civil rights movement. In such a circumstance, libel law did not protect autonomy from invasion by private citizens but became a tool of the government to suppress speech that it disliked. Recognizing the dangers of such misuse and its chilling effect on speech, the Court established its requirement that public officials show actual malice before recovering damages. Thus, one can view the actual malice standard as the Court's attempt to walk the same fine line it has walked in other low-value speech areas. It attempts to preserve our deliberative capacities from invasive lies by imposing liability for such lies but also seeks to keep the government from suppressing disagreeable speech.

5. Commercial Speech

As with libel, commercial speech was once thought to have no value but now enjoys substantial First Amendment protection.[114] Insofar as Kantian autonomy is concerned, the Court's decisions are directly aimed at State coercion of our thought processes. Indeed, antipathy toward State paternalism has been a central focus of the Court's commercial

103. See Hustler, 485 U.S. at 52 (noting that the Court's actual malice rule provides "breathing space" for free expression); Sullivan, 376 U.S. at 279 (discussing the fear that strict libel laws would deter true speech as well as false statements of fact).

104. Strauss, *supra* note 1, at 366.

114. See Virginia Citizens Consumer Council, 425 U.S. at 762.

speech decisions.[115] Yet there is also an element of protecting our thought processes from private coercion. The Court has made it clear that States are free to regulate false, misleading, and deceptive advertising, stressing that "[u]ntruthful speech, commercial or otherwise has never been protected for its own sake."[116] As with libelous statements, the Court's pronouncement reflects a desire to protect against invasive lies and deception that attempt to override rather than appeal to our thought processes. As with other areas of low-value speech, however, the Court has drawn a line between acceptable government regulation of lies and unacceptable attempts to regulate thoughts.

C. Kantian Autonomy and the Court's Free Speech Jurisprudence

Thus far, I have argued that the structure of the Court's First Amendment jurisprudence is consistent with a Kantian autonomy rationale, although not in the narrow sense espoused by many scholars. Although the Court's doctrine clearly presumes a sphere of liberty from state regulation, the focus of most scholars' autonomy arguments, its doctrine regarding low-value speech shows that the right to say what we wish is not the only aspect of autonomy encompassed in the First Amendment. Instead, notions of autonomy impose upon all of us an enforceable responsibility not to invade the thought processes of others by using speech in a coercive manner.

What conclusions can we draw regarding the fact that the Court's decisions are consistent with Kant's theory of autonomy? First, thinking of autonomy as encompassing liberty and responsibility reveals that the Court's First Amendment jurisprudence is about dialogue. Autonomy is not about atomistic, selfish individuals but about people with different ideas and strong disagreements coming together as members of a community to discuss issues. That discussion need not be passionless, but it must not be coercive if we are to maintain our status as autonomous individuals in a civilized society.

Second, the Court's jurisprudence acknowledges that some issues are better left to a sphere of moral obligations. The idea that the First Amendment has something to do with moral obligations might seem odd given that, textually, its concerns are clearly legal—i.e., it is specifically directed toward determining the acceptability of laws regulating speech. However, the Court's attempt to walk the fine line of protecting society from coercive private speech without allowing government censorship involves an element of moral rather than legal obligation. For example,

115. The Virginia Citizens Consumer Council Court soundly rejected the State's argument that consumers might act against their interests if given drug price information, noting that "[i]t is precisely this kind of choice, between the dangers of suppressing information, and the dangers of its misuse if it is freely available, that the First Amendment makes for us." Virginia Citizens Consumer Council, 425 U.S. at 770. Just this year, the Court reaffirmed its anti-paternalism sentiment in the commercial speech context. See Liquormart, Inc. v. Rhode Island, 116 S. Ct. 1495, 1508 (1996) ("The First Amendment directs us to be especially skeptical of regulations that seek to keep people in the dark for what the government perceives to be their own good.").

116. Virginia Citizens Consumer Council, 425 U.S. at 771–72.

while the Court is willing to allow criminal punishment of fighting words, it will not punish speech merely because we are offended by it. Fighting words may be offensive but that is not why the State may regulate them. Instead, it may regulate fighting words because they go beyond being offensive ideas and invade our thought processes by instigating an unthinking, physical response. Such words are appropriate for legal regulation. But offensive speech, although we may disagree with it, conveys an idea. To allow the State to suppress it is to abdicate our moral responsibility to discuss our disagreements and try to resolve them. Only individuals living in a community can come to a determination of what is right and wrong. In this sense, although the First Amendment (and the rhetoric of the Court's opinions) is couched in terms of law, it does recognize an element of moral obligation with respect to speech.

GEOFFREY R. STONE, AUTONOMY AND DISTRUST

64 U. Colo. L. Rev. 1171 (1993).

If we were to ask ourselves what First Amendment doctrine would have to look like if the Court actually had embraced the pure autonomy model, we would predict that the central issue in every case would be whether the challenged law unduly limits the opportunities of individuals for free expression.

This is not, however, our actual First Amendment doctrine. To the contrary, current First Amendment doctrine is much richer and more complex than the autonomy model would suggest. Consider, for example, the content-based/content-neutral distinction, which plays a central role in the Court's First Amendment jurisprudence and which, as I shall explain, has nothing to do with autonomy.

In general, and to vastly oversimplify, the Court gives its highest scrutiny to viewpoint-based restrictions of speech, such as a law providing that "no person may criticize the war"; it gives something akin to intermediate scrutiny to subject-matter restrictions, such as a law providing that "no one may make political speeches on a military base"; and, it employs a form of ad hoc balancing to content-neutral restrictions, such as a law that restricts leafleting in public buildings.

Although the Court's analysis of content-neutral restrictions focuses largely on the protection of autonomy, its analysis of content-based restrictions derives in large part from the Court's quite distinct concerns with impermissible government motivation and distortion of public debate.

As the Court has long recognized, it is a central precept of our First Amendment jurisprudence that government may not restrict the expression of an idea merely because it disapproves of the idea and fears that citizens may unwisely adopt it in the course of political debate. This precept drives much of our free speech doctrine and lies at the very heart of the content-based/content-neutral distinction.

This is so because even when government offers an explanation for restricting speech other than its mere disapproval of the idea expressed—for example—"listeners may be persuaded to act unlawfully if they hear the speech"—there is always the risk that this explanation is a mere pretext and that the government's real motivation is to suppress the offending point of view. The content-based/content-neutral distinction tracks this concern, for viewpoint-based restrictions are most likely to be the product of such motivations, content-neutral restrictions are least likely to be the product of such motivations, and subject-matter restrictions fall somewhere in between.

The concern over distortion of public debate works in much the same manner. That is, one factor the Court considers in evaluating the constitutionality of particular restrictions on speech is the extent to which the restriction not only limits the opportunities for free expression, but does so in a content-differential manner so as to alter what would be the distribution of views without the restriction.

I want to emphasize that the Court's concern here is not with preserving some ideal distribution of views that perfectly captures what we might think to be "quality" public debate. Rather, the baseline that is sought to be preserved is the actual distribution of views that exists in the real world, and that is not the product of intentional government intervention. The reason for this concern is not a naive belief that this actual distribution is necessarily ideal but, rather, a distrust of government efforts that have the purpose or effect of altering that distribution.

Like the concern with impermissible government motivation, the concern with distortion of public debate helps drive the Court's content-based/content-neutral distinction, for viewpoint-based restrictions are most likely to distort public debate in this manner, content-neutral restrictions are least likely to distort public debate in this manner, and subject matter restrictions fall somewhere in between.

Now, the key point in all of this is that none of it is responsive to the pure autonomy model of the First Amendment. It is the Court's concern, both implicitly and explicitly, with impermissible motivation and distortion of public debate that belies the claim that we can sensibly understand our Free Speech Tradition in terms of the pure autonomy model; for whatever doctrines such an approach would yield, they surely would look nothing like our contemporary First Amendment jurisprudence.

Why does any of this matter? Well, suppose our Free Speech Tradition really was premised on the pure autonomy model. We know, of course, that under that Tradition the right of the individual to speak is not absolute. To the contrary, individual autonomy may be restricted in order to further a broad range of competing government interests. In appropriate circumstances, for example, speech may be limited because it is too noisy, or too disruptive, or too dangerous.

Under a pure autonomy model, one would simply weigh the extent to which any particular restriction of speech limits the opportunities for free expression against such competing government interests. Against such a background, the collectivist claim might seem quite sensible. After all, if we can legitimately restrict speech to promote quiet and order, surely we can restrict it to promote quality public debate as well.

What this masks, however, is the direct conflict between the collectivist agenda and the Court's traditional—and in my view healthy—distrust of government efforts to regulate public debate. Even though collectivism may seem to be merely one more reason for regulating speech when we understand First Amendment doctrine entirely in terms of autonomy, it looks quite different when we see it through the lens of distrust. It is for this reason that we must understand the central role that distrust, as well as autonomy, plays in our Free Speech Tradition.

Questions

1) Charles Fried and Christina Wells both interpret the First Amendment with reference to the Kantian conception of autonomy. Fried concedes that a person's autonomy can be assaulted by private actors as well as by government. But he asserts that the "background system of private rights goes a long way toward vindicating free speech rights against private actors." Does Professor Wells disagree? Does her extended demonstration of an autonomy-based rationale for according diminished protection under the First Amendment to "low-value" speech imply that government has a duty to regulate such speech so as to protect the autonomy of persons who might be injured by it? How would that government responsibility apply to the issue of racial hate speech? On-site abortion protests?

2) Does Professor Stone's point that distrust of government is a major factor explaining many particulars of First Amendment doctrine suggest that Professor Wells reads too much into the doctrinal pattern which she claims demonstrates a strong judicial regard for autonomy? Or is the principle of distrust itself autonomy driven?

VINCENT BLASI, SIX CONSERVATIVES IN SEARCH OF THE FIRST AMENDMENT: THE REVEALING CASE OF NUDE DANCING

33 Wm & Mary L. Rev. 611 (1992).

Indiana's public indecency statute makes it a misdemeanor to appear in a public place knowingly or intentionally "in a state of nudity." The statute contains a detailed definition of "nudity":

> "Nudity" means the showing of the human male or female genitals, pubic area, or buttocks with less than a fully opaque covering, the showing of the female breast with less than a fully opaque covering of any part of the nipple, or the showing of covered male genitals in a discernibly turgid state.

The law forbids not only common forms of public indecency such as streaking, mooning, and lewd exhibitionism, but also by its terms appears to prohibit a woman from appearing in public in a see-through blouse. Neither the statute nor the Indiana case law specifies what a fully clothed male must do to avoid criminal liability should his genitals become discernibly turgid in a public place. Would he satisfy the mens rea element of the crime by remaining in the public place, or would it be a defense that he tried his best to forestall, and indeed was distressed by, his physiological reaction?

The Indiana Supreme Court declined several opportunities to construe the statute narrowly to avoid possible constitutional problems. *State v. Baysinger*[13] reversed a lower court determination that the public indecency statute was unconstitutionally vague and overbroad. Explicitly rejecting the course taken by its counterparts in Arizona and Oregon, the Indiana Supreme Court refused to define public place "to exclude places where persons willingly enter." Instead, the court interpreted the prohibition on public nudity to extend to "any place where the public is invited and are free to go upon special or implied invitation—a place available to all or a certain segment of the public."

* * *

The *Glen Theatre* litigation caused judges at all levels of the federal judiciary to grapple with the various First Amendment issues raised by Indiana's prohibition of nude dancing.

* * *

In the Seventh Circuit, Judges Richard Posner and Frank Easterbrook, longtime colleagues on the University of Chicago Law School faculty and leading lights of the law-and-economics movement, engaged in a debate of a quality one rarely encounters in the pages of the law reports. Posner and Easterbrook share much more than an institutional affiliation and a taste for economic analysis. Both judges command forensic skills of the first order. In addition, judging by the erudition displayed in their opinions in the topless dancing case, both men are deeply interested in and knowledgeable about the performing and visual arts. Despite their many affinities, the two judges sharply and passionately disagreed over whether striptease dancing is "speech" within the meaning of the First Amendment.

Judge Posner focused his analysis on the claim, accepted by the district court,[69] that a striptease dance is "conduct" rather than "expressive activity" and hence outside the ambit of First Amendment concern. Posner called this conclusion "indefensible and a threat to artistic freedom." Perhaps reflecting the conservative economist's unwillingness to employ external criteria to ascribe differential value to personal

13. 397 N.E.2d 580 (Ind. 1979).

69. See Glen Theatre, Inc. v. Civil City of S. Bend, 695 F.Supp. 414, 419 (N.D. Ind. 1988), rev'd sub nom. Miller v. Civil City of S. Bend, 887 F.2d 826 (7th Cir.1989), rev'd, 904 F.2d 1081 (7th Cir.1990) (en banc), rev'd sub nom. Barnes v. Glen Theatre, Inc., 111 S.Ct. 2456 (1991).

preferences, Posner was at pains in his opinion to avoid letting class bias or aesthetic evaluation influence his assessment of the legal status of the dancing at issue. He equated for constitutional purposes Darlene Miller's nude dancing in the Kitty Kat Lounge in South Bend with the nude (under Indiana's definition) performance of the Dance of the Seven Veils in a recent production of the opera *Salome* at the Chicago Lyric Opera.

One might suppose that a defining feature of legal conservatism would be the willingness to notice some of the contextual differences between nude dancing in bars and in classical ballet performances. Conservatives pride themselves on their sensitivity to social context and their distrust of abstractions that lump together divergent, distinctive phenomena.[73] Judge Posner duly noted the elements of barroom striptease that might cast doubt on its claim to First Amendment protection:

> Because the dancers at the Kitty Kat Lounge are not professional dancers, because three of the four dances were not choreographed, because the music to which they dance is canned, and because the dancers sell drinks to the customers afterward, it is tempting to suppose that the "expressive" elements of their "performance" are phony—that the dance and the music are figleaves to conceal the absence of figleaves.[74]

But he was not persuaded. He recounted the long and varied history of striptease dancing from the satyr plays of ancient Greece to the scandalous performances of Sally Rand, Gypsy Rose Lee, and Isadora Duncan. He found in this history a refutation of the claim that striptease has more the quality of sexual encounter than artistic statement:

> The striptease was not invented in order to place a cultural patina on displays of naked women. Of course, there would be no female stripteases without a prurient interest in the female body; but that is just to say that there would be no erotic art without Eros. Though there is no striptease without some stripping—in today's moral climate, without a great deal of stripping—the dancing and the music are not distractions from the main theme, patched on to fool the censor; they are what make a given female body expressive of a specifically sexual emotion. The striptease is the ensemble of the music, the dance, the disrobing, and the nude end state; it is more erotic than any of its components; and what makes it more erotic than the body itself, or the disrobing itself, is, precisely, that it is expressive of erotic emotion.

Judge Posner specified what striptease dancing expresses that mere nudity does not:

> [N]udity and disrobing are not invariably associated with sex. The goal of the striptease—a goal to which the dancing is indispens-

73. See, e.g., EDMUND BURKE, REFLECTIONS ON THE REVOLUTION IN FRANCE 52–55 (J.G.A. Pocock ed., 1987) (1790); FRIEDRICH A. HAYEK, THE CONSTITUTION OF LIBERTY 54–70 (1960); MICHAEL OAKESHOTT, On Being Conservative, in RATIONALISM IN POLITICS AND OTHER ESSAYS 168–96 (1967).

74. Miller, 904 F.2d at 1091 (Posner, J., concurring).

> able—is to enforce the association: to make plain that the performer is not removing her clothes because she is about to take a bath or change into another set of clothes or undergo a medical examination; to insinuate that she is removing them because she is preparing for, thinking about, and desiring sex.

Having established to his satisfaction that striptease makes a statement, Posner considered the argument that such dancing "is not the type of expression that the First Amendment protects, because it is not the expression of ideas or opinions." He concluded that such a limitation on the scope of the First Amendment would have disturbing implications for the arts:

> If the striptease dancing at the Kitty Kat Lounge is not expression, Mozart's piano concertos and Balanchine's most famous ballets are not expression. This is not to suggest that striptease dancing is indistinguishable from these other forms of expression. But they cannot be distinguished on the ground that a piano concerto and a (nonpantomimic) ballet express ideas and a striptease expresses emotion. If the concert and the ballet have meaning—and I do not doubt that there is a meaningful sense in which they do—so has the striptease.

Judge Posner reinforced the point with a detailed analysis of Titian's painting of a voluptuous nude, *Venus with a Mirror*, on permanent display in the National Gallery of Art:

> We might try to close the gap between the intellectual and the emotional by saying that the painting expresses a concept of beauty, of opulence, of balance, and so forth. But among the "so forth" are feminine sexuality and desirability, and if these are "concepts" in *Venus with a Mirror* they are "concepts" in a striptease (or in a Playboy pin-up) in just the same sense. The striptease version is coarse, unsubtle, "artless," even degraded, but the two works are "conceptual" to the same degree.

But even if a limiting principle based on the difference between intellectual and emotional appeal might seem troubling on close analysis, the nagging objection remains that the First Amendment is somehow debased when interpreted to protect the raw sexuality of the barroom striptease. Judge Posner confronted this objection head-on:

> One can argue from the text and background of the First Amendment that the constitutional protection of freedom of speech is limited to the discursive and the didactic, that non-didactic art should be totally excluded, or at the very least that low-grade erotic entertainment should be—the Founding Fathers would writhe in their graves if they knew that the nude dancers of the Kitty Kat Lounge could enwrap themselves with the First Amendment.

For Judge Posner, however, the difficult task of elaborating a nondiscriminatory First Amendment could not be avoided by resort to originalism, especially not by employing a standard so unprincipled as whether the framers "would writhe in their graves":

> [O]ne can reply that such arguments merely demonstrate the inadequacy of original understanding as a guide to constitutional interpretation; that they would if accepted change the Constitution from a living document into a petrified reminder of the limits of human foresight; that a conception of free speech which privileges the burning of the American flag but permits government to ban performances of twelve-tone music is more absurd than one that protects flag burning, twelve-tone music, and striptease; and that if the purpose and scope of the First Amendment's speech and press clauses are exhausted in the protection of political speech, because freedom of political speech is all that is necessary to preserve our democratic political system, this implies the exclusion from the amendment's protections not only of all art (other than the political) but also of science. For one can have democracy without science, just as one can have democracy without art.

To fail in the effort to place striptease dancing outside the ambit of First Amendment concern is not necessarily to conclude that such dancing is constitutionally immune from regulation. The State of Indiana argued that even if the striptease is speech in the First Amendment sense, it can be regulated under the state's power to enforce morality. Judge Posner rejected this contention. His analysis reveals why he had viewed as the central issue in the case, and had explored at such length, the question whether nude dancing is the type of expression with which the First Amendment is concerned at all.

Posner rejected the proposition that as a general matter the Constitution forbids government from attempting to enforce morality. He put the point forcefully:

> I do not argue that legislation, to be valid, must have some empirical basis or serve some utilitarian end. The modern state is not forbidden to interfere with transactions between consenting, competent adults merely because it is unable to show that third parties are harmed. The state is free to embody in legislation the moral opinions of its dominant groups, or for that matter of any group influential with the legislature—is free, therefore, to make hostility to nonmarital sex, disgust at public displays of nudity, revulsion at vulgar erotic entertainment, and embarrassment at public displays of nudity premises of state action even though it is difficult to ground these moralistic emotions in pragmatic social concerns.

Just as the Fourteenth Amendment (or the Ninth Amendment) does not enact Herbert Spencer's *Social Statics*,[85] neither does it enact John Stuart Mill's *On Liberty* or H.L.A. Hart's *Law, Liberty, and Morality.*

85. See Lochner v. New York, 198 U.S. 45, 75 (1905) (Holmes, J., dissenting).

In Judge Posner's view, however, the balance between individual freedom and state authority shifts once the First Amendment becomes implicated:

> [T]he state is free to act upon the moral preferences of the majority only up to the limits set by the federal Constitution. Those limits are not the sky when the activity restricted by state legislation is expressive activity in a sense that I believe encompasses erotic dance performances in general and the striptease in particular.

Posner did not deny Indiana all power to regulate nude dancing. He surmised that special social harms might be associated with the barroom setting, as well as special regulatory authority under the Twenty–First Amendment. But he read the First Amendment to prohibit a state from enforcing in the name of morality a comprehensive prohibition on striptease dancing without regard to setting or proven material harm.

Judge Posner did not explain why he considered the enforcement of morality an insufficient basis for limiting First Amendment rights. In contrast to his patient exploration of the proper scope of First Amendment concern, his rejection of the claim that speech can be regulated in order to serve moral values was conclusory. He did not say whether he considered moral justifications for limiting speech too inherently expansive to be reconciled with the purposes of the First Amendment, or whether he saw in the freedom of speech a commitment to open-ended moral as well as political evolution. It is a weakness of his long, erudite, and thoughtful opinion that he did not treat Indiana's claim to enforce its morality even against First Amendment activities with the same care that he treated the state's claim that nude dancing is not speech in the First Amendment sense.

* * *

Possibly provoked by Judge Posner's analysis, Judge Frank Easterbrook devoted most of his opinion to a call for precisely the kind of line drawing that Posner argued is illegitimate. Easterbrook saw differences of constitutional significance between barroom striptease and nude ballet. He considered the First Amendment to be concerned exclusively with the expression of "ideas," "thoughts," and "messages," not "emotions" as such. He disputed Judge Posner's contention that the striptease dances at issue conveyed a message of eroticism to barroom and peep show audiences in a manner comparable to the way such a message might be communicated by serious works of art:

> Sophisticates go to the museum and see Renoir's *Olympia* or to the opera and see a soprano strip during the Dance of the Seven Veils in Strauss' *Salome*. If the First Amendment protects these expressions, the argument goes, Joe Sixpack is entitled to see naked women gyrate in the pub. Why does this follow? That a dance in *Salome* expresses something does not imply that a dance in JR's Kitty Kat Lounge expresses something, any more than the fact that Tolstoy's *Anna Karenina* was a stinging attack on the Russian social order

implies that the scratching of an illiterate is likely to undermine the Tsar.

In defense of his refusal to draw lines between various forms of entertainment, Judge Posner had made much of the point that abstract art and nonprogrammatic music have less of an articulable message than a striptease. Posner labelled as "philistine" the "notion that all art worthy of the name has a 'message.' " He could not believe that under the First Amendment "Beethoven's string quartets are entitled to less protection than Peter and the Wolf." Drawing on his own considerable knowledge of the fine arts, Judge Easterbrook responded that for all serious works of art, those in which narrative does not predominate as well those in which it does, there is a message in the sense required by the First Amendment:

> Bach's *Mass in B Minor*, Beethoven's *Pastoral (Sixth) Symphony*, Wagner's *Parsifal*, Mahler's *Resurrection (Second) Symphony*, the Beatles' *Sergeant Pepper's Lonely Hearts Club Band*, like other vocal, religious, and program music, tell stories—sometimes sexually explicit ones, as in Orff's *Carmina Burana*, which, if it were not sung in Latin, could not be put on the airwaves. People may fairly dispute whether absolute music, such as LaMonte Young's *Well-Tuned Piano*, communicates thoughts, but surely it embodies them (the right place for the major third, etc.); all that we call music is the product of rational human thought and appeals at least in part to the same faculties in others. . . .
>
> Like mimes, ballets tell stories, often erotic stories, and clothing (or lack of it) may help the tale unfold. No one can miss the sensual message in Stravinsky's *Le Sacre Du Printemps* or the fairy tale in Tchaikovsky's *Nutcracker*. Ballet rarely approaches absolute music in abstraction. Even Balanchine's choreography to Stravinsky's *Agon*, a model of spare movement, does not suppress the contest to which the title refers. People objected to Nijinsky and Isadora Duncan because of the message rather than the medium.[104]

Easterbrook found no real message in striptease: "Barroom displays are to ballet as white noise is to music."

In contrast to Judge Posner's near hypersensitivity concerning the perils of cultural elitism, Judge Easterbrook seemed almost to relish the opportunity to draw lines, "to distinguish serious art from swill." One might be tempted to read into the Easterbrook opinion a judicial embrace of what some conservatives would call standards of excellence. The opinion is more complicated than that. Judge Easterbrook's ambitious effort to distinguish art from entertainment was at least as much the product of his concern about excessive judicial power as any view he may have about popular culture. He did, in fact, say that he would find the nude scene in the musical *Hair* to fall within the protection of the First Amendment.

104. 904 F.2d at 1125 (Easterbrook, J., dissenting).

For Judge Easterbrook, the obligation to interpret the First Amendment requires of a judge the willingness to draw lines, and to do so via the medium of categorical rules. Unless the ambit of First Amendment concern is demarcated with relative clarity, and demarcated in a way that excludes the all-embracing phenomenon of entertainment, courts would wind up evaluating the reasonableness of all legislative attempts to regulate entertainment. That would be substantive due process reincarnate. Judges can best prevent its recurrence "by insisting on categorical rules." With characteristic certitude, Judge Easterbrook explained his categorical understanding of the First Amendment: " 'Conduct' and 'speech' are the principal categories, and observing that distinction is essential if we wish to maintain the boundary between legislative and judicial roles in a democratic society."

No doubt referring to the speech-conduct distinction among others, Judge Posner had described the case as presenting "a symphony of sterile dichotomies." Judge Easterbrook, however, offered an unapologetic, and indeed both sophisticated and spirited, defense of his dichotomy:

> Any sentient being knows that categories are imperfect. Lawyers are trained to disparage line-drawing by showing that no matter where the line goes you can frame essentially indistinguishable cases on either side. Such a line is nonsensical!, comes the coupe de grace. The exercise is child's play in the domain of art and entertainment, for "what is art?" is a question unanswered for centuries ..... Judges who see the many facets of a subject, who know that just as a line cannot bisect a sphere so no one-dimensional rule can partition a multi-dimensional world, also must understand the role lines play in governance and the allocation of functions.

Easterbrook invoked Holmes in support of this point, and even produced a good imitation of a Holmesian aphorism: "Complex reality mocks rules, yet we must deny ourselves the comfort of requiring the law to match the universe."

BARNES v. GLEN THEATRE, INC.

Supreme Court of the United States, 1991.
501 U.S. 560, 111 S.Ct. 2456, 115 L.Ed.2d 504.

CHIEF JUSTICE REHNQUIST delivered the opinion of the Court.

Respondents are two establishments in South Bend, Indiana, that wish to provide totally nude dancing as entertainment, and individual dancers who are employed at these establishments. They claim that the First Amendment's guarantee of freedom of expression prevents the State of Indiana from enforcing its public indecency law to prevent this form of dancing. We reject their claim.

* * *

Several of our cases contain language suggesting that nude dancing of the kind involved here is expressive conduct protected by the First

Amendment. In *Doran v. Salem Inn, Inc.,* 422 U.S. 922, 932 (1975), we said: "[A]lthough the customary 'barroom' type of nude dancing may involve only the barest minimum of protected expression, we recognized in *California v. LaRue,* 409 U.S. 109, 118 (1972), that this form of entertainment might be entitled to First and Fourteenth Amendment protection under some circumstances." In *Schad v. Mount Ephraim,* 452 U.S. 61, 66 (1981), we said that "[f]urthermore, as the state courts in this case recognized, nude dancing is not without its First Amendment protections from official regulation." These statements support the conclusion of the Court of Appeals that nude dancing of the kind sought to be performed here is expressive conduct within the outer perimeters of the First Amendment, though we view it as only marginally so. This, of course, does not end our inquiry. We must determine the level of protection to be afforded to the expressive conduct at issue, and must determine whether the Indiana statute is an impermissible infringement of that protected activity.

Indiana, of course, has not banned nude dancing as such, but has proscribed public nudity across the board. The Supreme Court of Indiana has construed the Indiana statute to preclude nudity in what are essentially places of public accommodation such as the Glen Theatre and the Kitty Kat Lounge. In such places, respondents point out, minors are excluded and there are no nonconsenting viewers. Respondents contend that while the State may license establishments such as the ones involved here, and limit the geographical area in which they do business, it may not in any way limit the performance of the dances within them without violating the First Amendment.

* * *

This and other public indecency statutes were designed to protect morals and public order. The traditional police power of the States is defined as the authority to provide for the public health, safety, and morals, and we have upheld such a basis for legislation. In *Paris Adult Theatre I v. Slaton,* 413 U.S. 49, 61 (1973), we said:

> "In deciding *Roth* [*v. United States,* 354 U.S. 476 (1957)], this Court implicitly accepted that a legislature could legitimately act on such a conclusion to protect 'the social interest in order and morality.' "

And in *Bowers v. Hardwick,* 478 U.S. 186, 196 (1986), we said:

> "The law, however, is constantly based on notions of morality, and if all laws representing essentially moral choices are to be invalidated under the Due Process Clause, the courts will be very busy indeed."

Thus, the public indecency statute furthers a substantial government interest in protecting order and morality.

This interest is unrelated to the suppression of free expression. Some may view restricting nudity on moral grounds as necessarily related to expression. We disagree. It can be argued, of course, that almost limitless types of conduct—including appearing in the nude in public—are "expressive," and in one sense of the word this is true. People who go about in the nude in public may be expressing something about themselves by so doing. But the court rejected this expansive notion of "expressive conduct" in *O'Brien,* saying:

> "We cannot accept the view that an apparently limitless variety of conduct can be labeled 'speech' whenever the person engaging in the conduct intends thereby to express an idea."

And in *Dallas v. Stanglin,* 490 U.S. 19 (1989), we further observed:

> "It is possible to find some kernel of expression in almost every activity a person undertakes—for example, walking down the street or meeting one's friends at a shopping mall—but such a kernel is not sufficient to bring the activity within the protection of the First Amendment. We think the activity of these dance-hall patrons coming together to engage in recreational dancing—is not protected by the First Amendment."
>
> *Id.,* at 25.

Respondents contend that even though prohibiting nudity in public generally may not be related to suppressing expression, prohibiting the performance of nude dancing is related to expression because the State seeks to prevent its erotic message. Therefore, they reason that the application of the Indiana statute to the nude dancing in this case violates the First Amendment, because it fails the third part of the *O'Brien* test, viz: the governmental interest must be unrelated to the suppression of free expression.

But we do not think that when Indiana applies its statute to the nude dancing in these nightclubs it is proscribing nudity because of the erotic message conveyed by the dancers. Presumably numerous other erotic performances are presented at these establishments and similar clubs without any interference from the State, so long as the performers wear a scant amount of clothing. Likewise, the requirement that the dancers don pasties and G-strings does not deprive the dance of whatever erotic message it conveys; it simply makes the message slightly less graphic. The perceived evil that Indiana seeks to address is not erotic dancing, but public nudity. The appearance of people of all shapes, sizes and ages in the nude at a beach, for example, would convey little if any erotic message, yet the State still seeks to prevent it. Public nudity is the evil the State seeks to prevent, whether or not it is combined with expressive activity.

This conclusion is buttressed by a reference to the facts of *O'Brien.* An Act of Congress provided that anyone who knowingly destroyed a Selective Service registration certificate committed an offense. O'Brien burned his certificate on the steps of the South Boston Courthouse to influence others to adopt his antiwar beliefs. This Court upheld his conviction, reasoning that the continued availability of issued certificates served a legitimate and substantial purpose in the administration of the Selective Service System. O'Brien's deliberate destruction of his certificate frustrated this purpose and "[f]or this noncommunicative impact of his conduct, and for nothing else, he was convicted." It was assumed that O'Brien's act in burning the certificate had a communicative element in it sufficient to bring into play the First Amendment, but it was for the noncommunicative element that he was prosecuted. So here with the Indiana statute; while the dancing to which it was applied had a communicative element, it was not the dancing that was prohibited, but simply its being done in the nude.

The fourth part of the *O'Brien* test requires that the incidental restriction on First Amendment freedom be no greater than is essential to the furtherance of the governmental interest. As indicated in the discussion above, the governmental interest served by the text of the prohibition is societal disapproval of nudity in public places and among strangers. The statutory prohibition is not a means to some greater end, but an end in itself. It is without cavil that the public indecency statute is "narrowly tailored"; Indiana's requirement that the dancers wear at least pasties and G-strings is modest, and the bare minimum necessary to achieve the State's purpose.

The judgment of the Court of Appeals accordingly is

Reversed.

JUSTICE SCALIA, concurring in the judgment.

I agree that the judgment of the Court of Appeals must be reversed. In my view, however, the challenged regulation must be upheld, not because it survives some lower level of First Amendment scrutiny, but because, as a general law regulating conduct and not specifically directed at expression, it is not subject to First Amendment scrutiny at all.

[A concurring opinion by JUSTICE SOUTER and a dissenting opinion by JUSTICE WHITE, joined by JUSTICES MARSHALL, BLACKMUN, and STEVENS, are omitted.]

CITY OF ERIE v. PAP'S A.M. TDBA "KANDYLAND"

Supreme Court of the United States, 2000.
529 U.S. 277, 120 S.Ct. 1382, 146 L.Ed.2d 265.

* * *

JUSTICE SCALIA, with whom JUSTICE THOMAS joins, concurring in the judgment.

* * *

The city of Erie self-consciously modeled its ordinance on the public nudity statute we upheld against constitutional challenge in *Barnes v. Glen Theatre, Inc.,* 501 U.S. 560 (1991), calculating (one would have supposed reasonably) that the courts of Pennsylvania would consider themselves bound by our judgment on a question of federal constitutional law. In *Barnes,* I voted to uphold the challenged Indiana statute "not because it survives some lower level of First Amendment scrutiny, but because, as a general law regulating conduct and not specifically directed at expression, it is not subject to First Amendment scrutiny at all." Erie's ordinance, too, by its terms prohibits not merely nude dancing, but the act—irrespective of whether it is engaged in for expressive purposes—of going nude in public. The facts that a preamble to the ordinance explains that its purpose, in part, is to "limi[t] a recent increase in nude live entertainment," that city councilmembers in supporting the ordinance commented to that effect, and that the ordinance includes in the definition of nudity the exposure of devices simulating that condition, neither make the law any less general in its reach nor demonstrate that what the municipal authorities *really* find objectionable is expression rather than public nakedness. As far as appears (and as seems overwhelmingly likely), the preamble, the councilmembers' comments, and the chosen definition of the prohibited conduct simply reflect the fact that Erie had recently been having a public nudity problem not with streakers, sunbathers or hot dog vendors but with lap dancers.

There is no basis for the contention that the ordinance does not apply to nudity in theatrical productions such as Equus or Hair. Its text contains no such limitation. It was stipulated in the trial court that no effort was made to enforce the ordinance against a production of Equus involving nudity that was being staged in Erie at the time the ordinance became effective. Notwithstanding Justice STEVENS' assertion to the contrary, however, neither in the stipulation, nor elsewhere in the record, does it appear that the city was aware of the nudity—and before this Court counsel for the city attributed nonenforcement not to a general exception for theatrical productions, but to the fact that no one had complained. One instance of nonenforcement—against a play already in production that prosecutorial discretion might reasonably have "grandfathered"—does not render this ordinance discriminatory on its face.

* * *

Moreover, even were I to conclude that the city of Erie had specifically singled out the activity of nude dancing, I still would not find that this regulation violated the First Amendment unless I could be persuaded (as on this record I cannot) that it was the communicative character of nude dancing that prompted the ban. When conduct other than speech itself is regulated, it is my view that the First Amendment is violated only "[w]here the government prohibits conduct precisely because of its communicative attributes." *Barnes,* 501 U.S., at 577. Here, even if one hypothesizes that the city's object was to suppress only nude dancing, that would not establish an intent to suppress what (if anything) nude dancing communicates. I do not feel the need, as the Court does, to identify some "secondary effects" associated with nude dancing that the city could properly seek to eliminate. (I am highly skeptical, to tell the truth, that the addition of pasties and G-strings will at all reduce the tendency of establishments such as Kandyland to attract crime and prostitution, and hence to foster sexually transmitted disease.) The traditional power of government to foster good morals (*bonos mores*), and the acceptability of the traditional judgment (if Erie wishes to endorse it) that nude public dancing *itself* is immoral, have not been repealed by the First Amendment.

* * *

Questions

1) Based on his opinions in *Barnes v. Glen Theatre* and *Erie v. Paps A.M.*, how should Justice Scalia think about *Cohen v. California*? The flag burning decision, *Texas v. Johnson* (notice that he joined Justice Brennan's majority opinion)? Could the attempted regulations in *Cohen* and *Texas v. Johnson* be justified as efforts to enforce a "morality" of language use and flag treatment? Or are those cases in which the activity in question was regulated "precisely because of its communicative attributes?" In this respect, how is a taboo on public nudity different from a language taboo?

2) Under the Kantian analysis developed by Professor Wells, should nude dancing in an enclosed environment before a willing audience be considered low-value speech subject to regulation on the ground that its portrayal of impersonal, commercialized, objectivized female sexuality diminishes the autonomy of all women?

3) Notice that in both *Barnes* and *City of Erie*, Justice Scalia invokes his "general law" theory of the First Amendment. He states that a general prohibition of public nudity that applies to nude dancing but also to many forms of non-expressive nudity "must be upheld, not because it survives some lower level of First Amendment scrutiny, but because, as a general law regulating conduct and not specifically directed at expression, it is not subject to First Amendment scrutiny at all." Would the Espionage Act of 1917, at issue in *Masses*, *Schenck*, and *Debs*, qualify as such a general law in that it prohibited obstructing the recruiting service by physical acts as well as advocacy? Should Justice Scalia apply this principle to a law that limited total campaign spending if it imposed a cap on the full range of campaign expenses—polling, travel, office space, etc.—not just expenses for communicative activities? Do any of the arguments of Milton, Madison, Mill, Hand, Holmes, Brandeis, or Meiklejohn provide support for this "general law" theory? Which comes closest?

JOSEPH RAZ, LIBERALISM, SKEPTICISM, AND DEMOCRACY

74 Iowa L. Rev. 761 (1989).

Fear of uniformity and of the denial of individual autonomy has led many liberal writers to insist that the state should have nothing to do with the promotion of ideals of the good life. This in turn has led to the impoverishment of their understanding of human flourishing and of the relations between individual well-being and a common culture. Instead, one should denounce the rejection of autonomy and the embracing of uniformity as misguided conceptions of individual well-being. Only through a conception of well-being based on autonomy and value pluralism can we restore the true perspective of the role of morality in politics. Let me explain.

"Pluralism" is often used to indicate a position according to which different ways of life and different conceptions of the good should be tolerated regardless of their moral value. "Value pluralism" as used here marks a different and competing idea. It represents the view that there are many different and incompatible valuable ways of life. Different occupations (the physician, the politician, the miner, the police officer, the artist, the athlete, the academic) and different styles of life (that of the single person, of a member of a large family, of the lover of the open country or of metropolitan cities) call forth different qualities, develop different aspects of people's personalities and suppress others. Some people have such distinctive abilities and disabilities that they can find fulfillment in one way only. But most of us have it in us, at least when we are still young, to develop in different directions, to become different persons. The point I am anxious to stress is one which I hope is implicitly generally recognized. It is that many of the routes open to us in our lives are both incompatible and valuable. They are valuable in that each style of life, each pursuit is good and contributes to the well-being of the persons engaged in it. They are incompatible in that no person can combine all of them in one single life, as they call on different qualities and require the relative neglect or even suppression of other qualities which are good in themselves. It is this value multiplicity, this incompatibility of much that is valuable, that I mean by value pluralism.

Value pluralism is intimately associated with autonomy. The latter has two major aspects. The first is that of self-definition. It is the thought that what we are is, in significant respects, what we become through successive choices during our lives, that our lives are a continuous process of self-creation. This is not the rather repugnant thought of people having and pursuing life-plans. It does not presuppose, though it is compatible with, a reflective attitude to one's life as a whole, or the setting to oneself of life-long targets, or of considering and evaluating one's course in life in a very reflective, intellectual way. Some people are like that. Most are not. The idea of self-definition is none the less crucial in understanding their lives and its meaning. They make themselves into what they finally turn out to be through successive small and medium-size decisions, through drifting as much as through steering a course for themselves. Self-definition tells of a view of individual well-being which emphasizes the importance of activity in judging the success of a life, and rejects a sharp separation of the goodness of a person and the goodness of that person's life. One is what one is making oneself into through the conduct of one's life. Or, at least, this is so to a significant degree.

The second aspect of the idea of autonomy goes well beyond self-definition. It is that autonomy is valuable only if one steers a course for one's life through significant choices among diverse and valuable options. The underlying idea is that autonomous people had a variety of incompatible opportunities available to them which would have enabled them to develop their lives in different directions. Their lives are what they are because of the choices made in situations where they were free to go various different ways. The emphasis here is on the range of options available to the agent. This points to a connection between autonomy and pluralism. A pluralistic society, we may say, not only recognizes the existence of a multiplicity of values but also makes their pursuit a real option available to its members. But it is not merely that autonomy and pluralism require the availability of a wide range of options. They are also at one in requiring that those be valuable options.

We value autonomy to the extent that it adds to the well-being of the autonomous person. We regard the fact that a life was autonomous as adding value to it. We think of our own lives and the lives of others as better for having been developed autonomously. But we value autonomous choices only if they are choices of what is valuable and worthy of choice. Those who freely choose the immoral, ignoble, or worthless we judge more harshly precisely because their choice was free. If a person drifts into a wasteful, self-degrading way of life because he knows no better, because he never had the chance to develop differently, we judge his life for what it is worth, but mitigate our judgment of him because he had no choice. No such mitigation is available to those who freely and deliberately choose the same immoral, ignoble, or worthless life, having had opportunities to choose otherwise. This shows that autonomy does not always lead to the well-being of the autonomous person. It can make his life worse if it leads him to embrace immoral or ignoble pursuits. Autonomy contributes to one's well-being only if it leads one to engage in valuable activities and pursuits.

A conception of individual well-being which combines autonomy and value pluralism meets the liberal question of how a political pursuit of ideals of the good can be combined with an attitude of toleration and respect for individual freedom. Perfectionist liberalism has firm moral foundations. On the one hand, on this conception governments' function is to protect and promote, within the bounds of their competence, the well-being of people. On the other hand, we claimed that people prosper through a life of self-definition consisting of free choices among a plurality of incompatible but valuable activities, pursuits, and relationships, i.e. a plurality of valuable and incompatible styles and forms of life. This value pluralism, and not scepticism, or value neutrality, is the liberal bulwark against uniformity, against a society imposing through its government or otherwise a uniform vision of the ideal form of life on its population. Furthermore, given that the flourishing life is the self-created life, i.e. a life engaged in freely chosen valuable activities and pursuits, it is not a life which governments or anyone else can give to people, let alone impose on them. Autonomy speaks of an active life freely engaged in by the agent. It is incompatible with any vision of morality being thrust down people's throats.

Hence a government dedicated to pluralism and autonomy cannot make people good. To be autonomous, they have to choose their own lives for themselves. Governments, and other people generally, can help people flourish, but only by creating the conditions for autonomous life, primarily by guaranteeing that an adequate range of diverse and valuable options shall be available to all. Beyond that they must leave individuals free to make of their lives what they will.

The Importance of the Common Good

So far I have tried to draw a picture of perfectionist liberalism which bases the liberal respect for freedom on a political concern for the well-being of individuals. One of the virtues of this form of liberalism is that its doctrine of freedom is moored in a wider conception of the good person and the good society, rather than being cut off from them as is the case with liberal doctrines of moral neutrality and others. This is the clue to the way to rid liberalism of its association with self-centred individualism.

The clue is in the dependence of autonomy on the environment. The life of the autonomous person is distinctive not by what it is, but by how it came to be what it is. It is marked by the fact that it could have been otherwise and became what it is through the choices of that person. It is marked by the fact that the autonomous agent had many options which he rejected. To show that a person had an autonomous life, we have to look not only at him but also at his environment. One is autonomous only if one lives in an environment rich with possibilities. Concern with autonomy is concern with the environment.

The environment determines whether one has the conditions of autonomy, and it is the conditions of autonomy which are, up to a point, the charge of political institutions. Governments cannot make people have a flourishing autonomous life. That is up to each one to see to himself. But governments can help put people in conditions where they are able to have that kind of life by protecting and promoting the creation of the environment which makes such a life a possibility. Toleration as respect for individual freedom not only is consistent with, it in fact requires concern for and involvement with others.

It is important to see that this is not merely a moral requirement of concern for all. It is also, to a degree, a precondition of having the required environment oneself. The availability of options depends in part on private goods such as money. But options also depend on public goods, which are available to all and which serve all. Public goods lie at the foundations of most options. Options are to a considerable degree socially defined. A British coalminer is someone engaged in extracting coal. But he is also someone whose job involves certain patterns of relations with colleagues and bosses, certain patterns of work routines and leisure times, etc. And beyond all that he is someone whose fortunes are affected by the public images and myths of coalmining, the images of physical hard work, dirt and blackness, courage and danger, camaraderie, and a long tradition of loyalty and struggle, of belonging to the aristocracy of the working class, etc. Those for whom there is a real option of becoming a coalminer or of leaving the mines have a choice whose meaning is partly determined by a public culture which contributes to making mining what it is.

It is much the same not only for all occupations but also for all leisure activities, such as stamp-collecting, train-spotting, jazz music, and amateur photography, which are all recognized forms of social activity with their attendant rewards, traditions, and public images determining their social status and thus their meaning for individuals who may or may not choose to engage in them. The same is true of personal relations. Marriage, friendships, parenthood, and the others are all moulded and patterned by the common culture which determines to a very considerable degree the bounds of possible options available to individuals.

The conditions of autonomy require an environment rich in possibilities. In that they require an appropriate public culture, for it is the public culture which to a considerable degree determines the nature and quality of the opportunities available in a society. But to the extent that the conditions of autonomy require a suitable public culture, they depend on the common good, that is, on a good which if available to one is available to all and whose benefits can be had by all without competition or conflict.

We should not, of course, underestimate the degree to which our society involves competition for resources. Nor should we underestimate the severity of the distributional problems which a morality of personal autonomy gives rise to, with its requirement that an adequate range of diverse and valuable options be within the reach of all. It is important, however, to see clearly the crucial role of a suitable common culture sustaining and defining the options available in a society. Recognition of the importance of such a common culture leads to the rejection of moral individualism. It also dispels any impression that an autonomy-based morality encourages self-centred and socially indifferent attitudes, or that it regards social relations as based on negotiated agreements.

An autonomy-sustaining common culture is a presupposition of the freedom of one and all. People concerned with their own autonomy must be concerned with the flourishing of the common culture. They must be concerned with the existence of one major condition for the autonomy of all.

JOSEPH RAZ, FREE EXPRESSION AND PERSONAL IDENTIFICATION

11 Oxford J. of Legal Studies 303 (1991).

THE PUZZLE

Freedom of expression is a liberal puzzle.[1] Liberals are all convinced of its vital importance, yet why it deserves this importance is a mystery. The source of the problem is simple. While a person's right to freedom of expression is given high priority, and is protected (or, in political morality, is held to deserve protection) to a far greater degree than a person's interest in having employment, or in not running a risk of an accident when driving along public roads, it is evident that most people value these interests, and many others which do not enjoy special legal protection, much more than they value their right to free expression. Worse still, there can be little doubt that most people are right not to value their right to free expression highly. With few exceptions, people's interest in their right to free expression is rather small.

The right of freedom of expression protects people's freedom to communicate in public. "Communication" is to be understood broadly to include much more than the communication of propositional information. It includes any act of symbolic expression undertaken with the intention that it be understood to be such an act by the public or part of the public. Thus communication here covers not only all the forms of language-dependent communication but also pictorial and musical communication, and a whole range of symbolic acts such as picketing, displaying banners, wearing uniform. It does not cover acts of expression which are not convention-based symbolic expression, such as blushing, or expressing anger at one's competitor's success by setting fire to his shop.[2] Furthermore, to be protected communication has to be public, i.e. addressed to or made available to the public or any section of the public. It is essentially a right actively to participate in and contribute to the public culture.[3]

Given this understanding of the scope of the right the liberal puzzle is apparent. Rights protect interests and it is natural to expect the importance or stringency of the rights to reflect the importance to the right-holder of the interest that they protect.[4] But most people participate in public expression rarely if at all. For most of them, participation is confined to addressing local communities about local matters (for

1. In this essay "Liberalism" refers to a political culture which dominates in some societies, or subcultures, and not to any particular philosophical doctrine.

2. Many acts which carry a symbolic meaning also have some other standard consequences, e.g. pickets impede traffic. This may affect "balancing tests" but does not exclude them from protection.

3. Freedom of expression includes the passive freedom to listen and the corresponding negative freedoms, i.e. the freedom not to communicate and not to listen.

4. For a discussion of rights in general, see my *The Morality of Freedom*, ch. 5. Constitutional rights are discussed in ch. 8. The discussion in this essay relies on, and further develops, the framework discussed there.

example, concern with the maintenance of street lights in one's neighbourhood expressed in a local paper or a local meeting). While that interest is important to a large number of people, it can be protected by a much weaker right than the one the liberal doctrine of free expression upholds. It is true that we have an interest in the freedom to engage in activities we are unlikely to engage in, but, other things being equal, that interest is proportionate to the likelihood, and for most people it is very small indeed.

I should be careful not to underestimate the interest people may have in the freedom to engage in public speech. It is not part of my case that most people have no interest in the freedom of public expression. All I am arguing is that many other interests most people have are much more valuable to them than their interest in this freedom. Yet it is the freedom to express oneself publicly, rather than the more valuable interests, which enjoys special protection.

The responses to the puzzle are numerous. Most of them fall into five categories. First is the contention that appearances are misleading and that people have a great interest in their own freedom of expression. It lies at the heart of their humanity, is a requirement of personhood or rationality, etc.

Second comes the contention that, while people's interest in their own freedom of expression may be small there is absolutely no reason, or only minuscule ones, for curtailing it. At least there can be no legitimate reason for curtailing it, since its possession and its exercise do no one any harm. Words do not kill. To the counter-argument that they do, the reply can be to redefine the right so that, where words infringe other people's interests (as in libel or invasion of privacy), there one's freedom does not stretch, or at least there it has to be balanced against other interests. A sophisticated version of this argument regards the right to free expression as a right against its curtailment for certain reasons, e.g. that what is expressed is false, or an abomination or repugnant. This allows one to restrict the freedom, provided this is done for other reasons.

Third comes the contention that, while people's interest may be small, the risk that curtailment will be unjustified is particularly great in this area. This could be because governments are worse judges of the justification of public expression than they are of welfare and other matters, or because they have an institutional interest in restricting expression unjustifiably (it threatens their power), etc.

Fourth are the arguments which suggest that, while the likely harm to the right-holders in cases of curtailed freedom of public expression is not particularly great, the wrong done to them is great. The wrong done to them, according to this argument, is not to be measured in consequentialist terms. The very act of censorship insults the censored, denies their rationality, treats them as means rather than ends in themselves, etc.

Fifth come the arguments that a person's right to free expression is protected not in order to protect him, but in order to protect a public good, a benefit which respect for the right of free expression brings to all those who live in the society in which it is respected, even those who have no personal interest in their own freedom.

Of course these different avenues are not mutually exclusive, and quite a number of writers have buttressed their defence of the right to freedom of expression by combining arguments from different categories. In this article I will examine just one idea which leads to two arguments which belong respectively to the fifth and fourth types; both arguments regard free expression as a public good.

It is not my purpose to propose a comprehensive account of freedom of expression. The considerations I will put forward are insufficient in several respects to justify the right of free expression as it is practiced in some Western democracies and advocated by some political theorists. One possible conclusion is that the liberal emphasis on free expression is overdone. Another is that there are other important considerations in support of the right which I will not consider. The second conclusion is certainly warranted, and possibly there is something in the first conclusion as well. All this will remain unexplored here.

* * *

The Core Case: Validating Forms of Life

Much public expression, in books, newspapers, television, cinema, etc., portrays and expresses aspects of styles or forms of life. Views and opinions, activities, emotions, etc., expressed or portrayed, are an aspect of a wider net of opinions, sensibilities, habits of action or dressing, attitudes, etc., which, taken together, form a distinctive style or form of life.[17] An important case for the importance of freedom of expression[18] arises out of the fact that public portrayal and expression of forms of life validate the styles of life portrayed, and that censoring expression normally expresses authoritative condemnation not merely of the views or opinions censored but of the whole style of life of which they are a part.

The fact that much public expression expresses or portrays aspects of ways of life is often either overlooked or taken for granted as a trivial and irrelevant point. It is overlooked because often writers on freedom of expression focus attention on types of speech of which this is not true, or

17. Though naturally any single act of expression can be an element of, or fit in with, various forms of life. The only point is that it does not fit with all. Note that nowhere do I define 'forms of life'. For the purpose of this argument the precise understanding of the term is immaterial. The only material points are that different aspects of activities, tastes, styles, and attitudes are seen to belong together, in the ordinary way in which we can distinguish the yuppy, or the middle class, or the "Sloane Ranger", etc. Whatever other aspects of styles or forms of life are material to the argument will emerge as the argument of the essay develops.

18. i.e. a situation in which freedom of expression occurs, not of a right to free expression.

at least not true in any straightforward way. For example, claims about the relative merit of high interest rates versus high taxation as a means of dampening consumer spending do not express any way of life. The same goes for publication of an academic article about the origin of galaxies, etc. Discussion of such cases normally focuses on the importance of the information conveyed and of being free to convey it. But these cases have an additional aspect. Engaging in such speech is part of the normal activities of economists, politicians, journalists, or scientists. Prohibiting or censoring such speech distorts and impedes these activities, and if such measures are they render those activities impossible and can constitute their public condemnation. This is true of interference with much free expression. It points to the fact that public expression is itself an element of several styles of life.

Of course, this fact in itself is no argument for the *special* protection of free expression. Many non-speech activities are integral to many different styles of life. One should be aware of this factor whenever the state criminalizes or otherwise impedes various activities. It would be wrong, however, to dismiss this consideration just on the ground that it is not unique to acts of expression. Even though it applies to other cases too, it may justify greater protection of free expression than of freedom to engage in other activities, if only for the reason that the justification of each freedom involves comparing good and ill, merits and demerits; and the demerits, the disadvantages of engaging in various activities, are not the same. Prayer may be part of a religion which involves ritual bodily mutilation of young children. Respect for this religious style of life may weigh equally in favour of tolerating both prayer and mutilation. But the arguments against tolerating the two practices are far from equal, and the result need not be the same.

The argument that I wish to explore covers cases in which the very act of expression is an element of a way of life as a special case. It covers also speech by people who do not share the style of life about aspects of which they express themselves. That is why I refer to portrayals or descriptions of ways of life as the paradigmatic, though not the only, case to which my argument applies. These include cases in which the concern is not with the interest of the speaker and the way his speech is an aspect of his life, but the way it reflects, expresses, or describes the life of others.

A typical example of this is a portrayal of a family in a television sitcom. Let us say, a husband and wife have two children, an adolescent girl, romantic and full of dreams about poetry, her boyfriend, her studies, her tennis, and a younger boy, continuously quarrelling with the neighbours' children, making his first steps as a computer hack, teasing his older sister to tears. While such portrayals are typical of the kind of expression I am concerned with, they are not the only ones. The argument extends to discussion and comments on activities, beliefs, attitudes, and of responses to them. It also, and most importantly, extends to pornography, to prayer-books, and to much else which, while only sometimes portraying ways of life, are always meant to be used as part of certain ways of life.

The reason to focus on acts of expression of this type is that they fulfil important functions in contemporary societies.[19] Three are of prime concern to my argument:

1. They serve to familiarize the public at large with ways of life common in certain segments of the public.

2. They serve to reassure those whose ways of life are being portrayed that they are not alone, that their problems are common problems, their experiences known to others.

3. Finally, they serve as validation of the relevant ways of life. They give them the stamp of public acceptability.

I shall talk of portrayal in the public media as validating the experience or way of life portrayed or expressed, as a shorthand to refer to all three functions of such expression. The use of the term "validation" suggests the direction of the argument.

That public portrayal has an important validating function is a contingent fact of human nature. But, although contingent, it is deeply rooted and of great importance to the preservation of any culture. Even traditional homogeneous societies, in which individuals find themselves enmeshed in close-knit social networks, depend for the legitimation of their culture and its transmission and renewal on its expression and portrayal in the public arena. The difference is that contemporary pluralistic societies place a high value on recognizing the existence of a plurality of valuable ways of life, and of the possibility of change and the generation of novel, valuable forms of life. Furthermore, we depend more than ever before on a culture which saturates us with images and messages through the public media, which have acquired a great power both to encourage and to stifle and marginalize activities, attitudes, and the like.

To a large extent the validating functions of public expression acquire their contemporary importance from two much-discussed aspects of contemporary societies, their urban anonymity, and their cultural and ethical pluralism. These mean that people depend more than ever on public communication to establish a common understanding of the ways of life, range of experiences, attitudes, and thinking which are common and acceptable in their society. They also depend on finding themselves reflected in the public media for a sense of their own legitimacy, for a feeling that their problems and experiences are not freak deviations.[20]

19. By "contemporary societies" I mean societies like ours. Many past societies shared these features, and some contemporary ones lack them. But it seems to me important to start from the here and now, and not from an abstract enumeration of relevant features.

20. For the existence of the problem consider the proliferation of support groups for people who are drug-abusers, smokers, teenage mothers, fat, thin, etc.

THE FIRST ARGUMENT: TOLERATING AND ENCOURAGING VALIDATION

Freedom of expression touches on the validation of ways of life in two ways, yielding two distinct arguments for it. First, while it exists and inasmuch as it is exercised, ways of life which are portrayed and expressed are validated through their portrayal and expression. People get the reassurance that others know of their problems, experiences, attitudes, etc., and that they are acceptable in the society. Second, because of this significance of expression, censorship and criminalization acquire a wider negative significance. They express not merely disapproval of the particular act of expression which is censored. They express disapproval of the whole way of life (of all the ways of life) of which it is a part. In contemporary societies, public portrayal validates ways of life, whereas censorship is authoritative public condemnation of the way of life. The first argument for freedom of expression arising out of these considerations asserts that freedom of expression renders a great service to people's well-being. This service takes three forms.

First, validation of a way of life through its public expression is of crucial importance for the well-being of individuals whose way of life it is. It helps their identification with their way of life, their sense of its worth, and their sense that their way of life facilitates rather than hinders their integration into their society.

Second, such validation is important for making ways of life a real option for people. Absence of validation makes them suspect, and unattractive, and jeopardizes the chances that people will choose them.

Third, public validation is an essential element in the process of cultural transmission, preservation, and renewal. It is one of the central arenas for the assertion of traditions, and for challenging traditions and experimenting with new forms of relationships, attitudes, and styles of life.

This argument shows freedom of expression to be a public good, a constitutive element of a public culture. It points to a strong, positive case for free expression. It points to the importance not only of the absence of censorship but of providing access to the means of public expression to those who portray various ways of life, and express different points of view.[21] At the same time the argument supports only a weak, overridable right. Like all public-good arguments, it is weak on setting boundaries. No major difficulty arises if one allows, say private television stations to deny access to certain views, so long as those views can find other avenues of expression. No major problem arises from restricting the areas in towns in which demonstrations can be held, so

21. At its most abstract level, the argument does not distinguish between privately owned and publicly owned means of expression (such as land, newspapers, public halls, or television stations). It establishes a reason for all those who control means of public expression to allow access to them. But in establishing the ways such abstract reasons are to receive institutional support and become enforceable by law, it may be reasonable to distinguish between privately owned and publicly owned means of expression and to impose lesser duties on the former. Such matters cannot be determined in the abstract.

long as the areas available provide for a reasonably effective way of expressing views and displaying the intensity with which they are felt.

THE SECOND ARGUMENT: CENSORSHIP AS INSULT

To a certain extent the issue of boundaries is helped by a second argument. It derives from the evil of censorship and criminalization, which extends a good deal beyond denying people the benefits of a culture in which expression is free. Because of the validating function of public expression, pure content-based censorship[22] has acquired a symbolic meaning. It expresses official, authoritative disapproval and condemnation of the style of life of which the censored communication is a part.[23]

People's relations with the society in which they live is a major component in their personal well-being. It is normally vital for personal prosperity that one should be able to identify with one's society, should not be alienated from it, should feel a full member of it. The importance of this factor derives from two concerns. First, a significant part of the activities and pursuits through which people prosper (or fail to prosper) involves engagement with larger groups (their workplace or trade association, their city, sports or other leisure association, a variety of civic activities, in support of the home-less, single mothers, war veterans, etc.). Full membership in the society is essential for free participation in the activities of such groups (except in those which are dedicated to achieving full membership for certain subgroups—membership of such subgroups sometimes presupposes absence of full membership in one's country's society). Second, the very ability to identify with one's society is an independent background good, and feeling alienated from it is a significant handicap. They have a considerable, often imperceptible impact on people's ability to engage in activities involving relations with other people, or contributions to their well-being or to the common good. Official denunciation or condemnation of one's way of life is a major obstacle to identification with one's society, and this is a powerful argument against it.

22. "Pure" content-based censorship is marked by the reasons for the censorship. Censorship is pure content-based if the reason for it is the disapproval of the content of the act of expression, rather than merely an attempt to avoid undesirable consequences of its publication. Prohibition of the publication of military secrets is content-based but not "purely" content-based. "Content" is meant to include style: expressing a view by the use of violent language or gesture has, for the purposes of this discussion, a different content from its expression in polite academic language. This follows from the fact that attitudes, emotions. etc., and not merely a cognitive content, are covered by "expression". Pure content-based censorship can take the form of prior restraint, criminalization, or regulation. But the last is characteristically based on desire to minimize the consequences of the act of expression, and is only very rarely purely content-based. Criminalization and prior restraint can be either purely content-based or based on a perceived reason to avoid or mitigate the consequences of the speech.

23. I use this expression to indicate both acts of expression which are themselves a part of a form of life and those which portray, describe, discuss, etc., aspects of forms of life. Both are covered by the arguments advanced here.

Just like the first argument, the second rests on a public-good case for free expression. The evil to be avoided is not a specific harm to the interests of the right-holder caused by denying him free expression. It is a harm to the common interest of all, and especially of those whose interests are served by the condemned way of life and its prosperity. Because this is the meaning of *every* act of content-based censorship, and of *every* content-based criminalization of acts of symbolic public expression, the second argument solves many of the boundary problems which the first argument generates.

In some ways this second argument is the more powerful of the two. Content-based censorship and criminalization are a public and authoritative condemnation. Their repudiation of ways of life which they reject is insulting and hurtful, and their negative meaning is a stronger reason against censorship and criminalization than the reason for free expression deriving from the value of the validation of styles of life through their public portrayal. In a culture in which expression is free, validation is provided by people exercising their freedom. They provide validation and not the state, not society using its authoritative voice. Society's official attitude welcomes and facilitates such validation, but it is given only where members of that society wish to give it through their exercise of freedom of expression. Content-based censorship and criminalization not only deny individuals the opportunity to provide validation but constitute official condemnation of the way of life aspects of which are censored or criminalized.

The symbolic meaning of content-based censorship and criminalization gives the second argument considerable weight where it applies. But its range is limited compared with the first argument. The symbolic meaning of condemnation of the style of life to which the expression belongs is a feature of pure content-based prohibitions. It is not typical of other restrictions on free expression, such as banning demonstrations from the vicinity of churches during the high holidays, out of respect for the feelings of worshippers, or banning them on certain highways during the rush hour, in order to facilitate commuters' journeys home. Similarly, the interest of would-be speakers in having access to the public has to be reconciled with the interest of the public not to be made a captive audience, a reconciliation which requires many pragmatic compromises between speakers who wish to address people where they are likely to be and members of the public who wish to be able to use public arenas without being subjected to acts of expression which they regard as odious.[24] The second argument does not extend to such cases, and while the first argument does it establishes only a weak right, which is subject to compromises when it clashes with such legitimate concerns.

24. Of course, members of the public also have an interest in easy access to information which they wish to receive. The conflict I am alluding to is not between speakers and the public. It is between speakers and the sections of the public who wish to have easy access to them and other sections of the public who wish to be free of their intrusion.

The weight and scope differences between the two arguments should not be exaggerated. Limited acts of prior restraint by a minor official, even though content-based, do not carry the message of official condemnation to the same degree as major legislation extensively criminalizing the portrayal of a group's way of life. Even pure content-based censorship is a matter of degree, though this is normally relevant to the degree of wrongness of the act rather than to its justification. Justification is, however, at stake in mixed cases. Often criminalization or prior restraint[25] is based both on pure content-based reasons and on a perceived reason to avoid the consequences of acts of expression. Furthermore, given that the underlying reasons for such criminalization and prior restraint are so commonly mixed, almost every content-based criminalization or prior restraint is perceived as expressing in part official condemnation of the content of expression.[26] Since the evil is in the public perception, almost every content-based criminalization and prior restraint is subject to the considerations of my second argument.

These observations presuppose that the public meanings of permitting and prohibiting are not contraries. Whereas prohibition (i.e. censorship and criminalization) condemns the prohibited conduct, permission does not endorse what is permitted, it merely tolerates it. How should facilitating actions be judged? How should one judge state subsidies to science? Does their denial to astrology amount to its condemnation? How should access to the media be judged? Does the provision of television time to Muslims and its non-provision to Buddhists constitute condemnation of the latter and endorsement of the former? The main point to bear in mind is that the issue is factual, not logical. It is not to be resolved by arguing, say, that subsidies are a positive interference, like censorship, and not merely a non-interference, like permissions, and that therefore they are an endorsement, whereas a refusal to facilitate is no condemnation. Nor would it do to argue that, since no effective access is likely to be possible to some ideas or ways of life (since they have no rich supporters), it follows that refusal to facilitate is condemnation. The only issue is what is the public meaning of certain acts, and the same act can have different meanings in different societies.[27] The meaning may depend on considerations of the kind mentioned, and on many others (the reasons for lack of facilitation being obvious ones,[28] as are the normal expectations in that society). I am assuming that, generally, providing access to the public media in our society does not speak of approval but of toleration. And that its denial does not amount to condemnation by the society. Therefore, the second argument does not support a positive

25. I have in mind all content-based criminalization and prior restraint, pure or impure, i.e. excluding only those which are designed merely to enforce regulatory measures rather than to stop all expression of a certain content.

26. The exceptions are instances where the importance of the non-content-based reasons is clear, as with vital military secrets.

27. More awkwardly for setting the boundaries of the right, it may have different meanings to different groups in the same society.

28. Compare denying subsidies to Buddhists on the ground that there are none in the country with their denial on the ground that Buddhism is repugnant, or morally corrupting.

right of access to the means of public expression. The state's failure to give philosophers an assured access to the means of expression does not amount to an authoritative condemnation of philosophy by the state, whereas censorship and criminalization of philosophical publications are such a condemnation.

Broadly speaking, the position is this. Regulatory restrictions are subject to the first argument only. In general, content-based criminalization and prior restraint are subject to the second argument, for in most cases they express condemnation of the way of life portrayed or expressed. Where the restriction is pure content-based, the argument is normally decisive. Where the restriction is based also on good reasons to avoid certain consequences of the act of expression, the need for such restriction has to be assessed against the reasons against it adumbrated above.

Finally, neither of the two arguments protects most acts of expression about particular individuals. Similarly, the democratic argument for free expression does not concern, with some obvious exceptions, speech regarding identifiable ordinary persons. Naturally, it does protect many comments regarding individuals who are holders of or candidates for public office, or who are otherwise involved in politics. Similarly, the arguments I am considering here do protect speech about individuals who become symbols of certain cultures, or ideologies, or who have acquired a status of paradigmatic representatives of styles of life, cultures, etc. But, with these exceptions, the right to freedom of expression does not conflict with the law of libel and right of privacy.

Protecting Bad Speech

Any doctrine of freedom of expression must face the question: why should society respect people's freedom to express false, worthless, degrading, depraved, etc., views and opinions? It is an essential aspect of any doctrine of free expression that it purports to justify the freedom to what we can generically call bad speech (by which I do not mean that it must justify the freedom to express anything, however bad). Does my argument do that? Does it not depend on the value of the protected speech? This objection misunderstands the nature of my argument. It does indeed depend on the value to be found in the ways of life of which protected speech is a part. But bad speech is often a part[29] of a good way of life, or at any rate one which should not be condemned by society through its official organs. This point is important not only for the justification of freedom of expression but for any doctrine of toleration.

* * *

So the arguments I am advancing provide reasons to protect much bad speech. But they do not protect all bad speech. To be protected by these arguments, it has to be an expression or portrayal of something

29. Either in being strictly speaking a part of, or in portraying something which is part of, a bad style of life.

which is a part of a valuable way of life. Some ways of life are without redeeming features. Some of their aspects have no place in any worthwhile way of life, and their expression or portrayal is not protected by the arguments advanced here.

This is not the place to discuss in detail what makes a way of life totally unacceptable. This is one of the central questions of ethics. But it is worth noting that the task is not straightforward. Moral philosophy tends to concentrate on single items: which acts are wrong or right, which character traits are admirable and which are not. The character of a way of life depends on evaluating a much broader canvas, of practices, character traits, attitudes, beliefs, and so on. It raises questions rarely discussed by theorists. Some tests seek perfection, and would disallow any but forms of life without any blemish. They are based on a misunderstanding of the task. It is not to imagine perfect or saintly lives, but good and worthwhile ones. Other tests, while sensible in their motivation, may be deemed too lenient. For example, it may be suggested that any form of life which may enhance the quality of life of a person, while not involving him in any major sin, is acceptable. By this test, which is admittedly too vague to be accepted without much further development, even Nazism is acceptable. Many youngsters were rescued from a life of drifting and petty criminality, were transported into organized, spirited activities in Nazi youth clubs, enjoyed camaraderie and a sense of proud membership in their nation, partaking of its culture and traditions, as well as a sense of purpose in their life, while being lucky enough never to have become involved in Nazi crimes. Such cases raise difficult issues which I will leave on one side.[34] One sufficient condition for the unacceptability of a style of life is that the activities essential and distinctive to its pursuit are rightly forbidden by law. But this test is incomplete, and in any case merely defers the question. For it all depends on what is rightly forbidden by law.

* * *

Needless to say, my arguments do not establish a universal moral right to freedom of expression. Nor do they establish that the value of freedom of expression is universal to all human societies. The core considerations on which the arguments rest apply to most familiar societies. But even they are not universal, and certainly the ramifications of the arguments depend on cultural features which vary from country to country. Finally, while the arguments of this essay do not cover all aspects of the conventional liberal doctrine of free expression, their implications are not confined to freedom of expression. They may have special force in cases of expression, but they can be applied to condemn some forms of moral paternalism, such as forcing people to refrain from sexual activities which are, let us assume, immoral.

34. One response, suggested to me by Anthony Duff, is to distinguish between morally mistaken and morally evil beliefs. The latter can perhaps be said to diminish the quality of one's life, as well as one's character, even if one does not act wrongly as a result of such beliefs.

All that being said, the arguments do point to the great importance of free expression. They turn on the fundamental need for public validation of one's way of life, and on the need for public recognition as a way of transmitting, preserving, and developing ways of life. In the circumstances of contemporary life these considerations touch the very foundations of pluralistic societies. In this respect, the argument I have adumbrated joins three other arguments to form the foundation of a liberal doctrine of free expression. The other three are: (1) freedom of expression as a prerequisite of a democratic government; (2) freedom of expression as vital for the prosperity of a pluralistic culture; (3) freedom of expression as a crucial element in controlling possible abuses and corruption of power. All four arguments point to the need to make freedom of expression a foundational part of the political and civic culture of pluralistic democracies.

HURLEY v. IRISH-AMERICAN GAY, LESBIAN AND BISEXUAL GROUP OF BOSTON

Supreme Court of the United States, 1995.
515 U.S. 557, 115 S.Ct. 2338, 132 L.Ed.2d 487.

JUSTICE SOUTER delivered the opinion of the Court.

The issue in this case is whether Massachusetts may require private citizens who organize a parade to include among the marchers a group imparting a message the organizers do not wish to convey. We hold that such a mandate violates the First Amendment.

I

March 17 is set aside for two celebrations in South Boston. As early as 1737, some people in Boston observed the feast of the apostle to Ireland, and since 1776 the day has marked the evacuation of royal troops and Loyalists from the city, prompted by the guns captured at Ticonderoga and set up on Dorchester Heights under General Washington's command. Washington himself reportedly drew on the earlier tradition in choosing "St. Patrick" as the response to "Boston," the password used in the colonial lines on evacuation day. Although the General Court of Massachusetts did not officially designate March 17 as Evacuation Day until 1938, the City Council of Boston had previously sponsored public celebrations of Evacuation Day, including notable commemorations on the centennial in 1876, and on the 125th anniversary in 1901, with its parade, salute, concert, and fireworks display.

The tradition of formal sponsorship by the city came to an end in 1947, however, when Mayor James Michael Curley himself granted authority to organize and conduct the St. Patrick's Day–Evacuation Day Parade to the petitioner South Boston Allied War Veterans Council, an unincorporated association of individuals elected from various South Boston veterans groups. Every year since that time, the Council has applied for and received a permit for the parade, which at times has included as many as 20,000 marchers and drawn up to 1 million watchers. No other applicant has ever applied for that permit. Through 1992, the city allowed the Council to use the city's official seal, and provided printing services as well as direct funding.

In 1992, a number of gay, lesbian, and bisexual descendants of the Irish immigrants joined together with other supporters to form the respondent organization, GLIB, to march in the parade as a way to express pride in their Irish heritage as openly gay, lesbian, and bisexual individuals, to demonstrate that there are such men and women among those so descended, and to express their solidarity with like individuals who sought to march in New York's St. Patrick's Day Parade. Although the Council denied GLIB's application to take part in the 1992 parade, GLIB obtained a state-court order to include its contingent, which marched "uneventfully" among that year's 10,000 participants and 750,000 spectators.

In 1993, after the Council had again refused to admit GLIB to the upcoming parade, the organization and some of its members filed this suit against the Council, the individual petitioner John J. "Wacko" Hurley, and the city of Boston, alleging violations of the State and Federal Constitutions and of the state public accommodations law, which prohibits "any distinction, discrimination or restriction on account of ... sexual orientation ... relative to the admission of any person to, or treatment in any place of public accommodation, resort or amusement."

* * *

The court held that because the statute did not mandate inclusion of GLIB but only prohibited discrimination based on sexual orientation, any infringement on the Council's right to expressive association was only "incidental" and "no greater than necessary to accomplish the statute's legitimate purpose" of eradicating discrimination. Accordingly, it ruled that "GLIB is entitled to participate in the Parade on the same terms and conditions as other participants."

The Supreme Judicial Court of Massachusetts affirmed, seeing nothing clearly erroneous in the trial judge's findings that GLIB was excluded from the parade based on the sexual orientation of its members, that it was impossible to detect an expressive purpose in the parade, that there was no state action, and that the parade was a public accommodation within the meaning of § 272:92A. Turning to petitioners' First Amendment claim that application of the public accommodations law to the parade violated their freedom of speech (as distinguished from their right to expressive association, raised in the trial court), the court's majority held that it need not decide on the particular First Amendment theory involved "because, as the [trial] judge found, it is 'impossible to discern any specific expressive purpose entitling the Parade to protection under the First Amendment.' "

* * *

If there were no reason for a group of people to march from here to there except to reach a destination, they could make the trip without expressing any message beyond the fact of the march itself. Some people might call such a procession a parade, but it would not be much of one. Real "[p]arades are public dramas of social relations, and in them performers define who can be a social actor and what subjects and ideas are available for communication and consideration." S. Davis, Parades and Power: Street Theatre in Nineteenth-Century Philadelphia 6 (1986). Hence, we use the word "parade" to indicate marchers who are making some sort of collective point, not just to each other but to bystanders along the way. Indeed, a parade's dependence on watchers is so extreme that nowadays, as with Bishop Berkeley's celebrated tree, "if a parade or demonstration receives no media coverage, it may as well not have happened." Parades are thus a form of expression, not just motion, and the inherent expressiveness of marching to make a point explains our cases involving protest marches. In *Gregory v. Chicago,* 394 U.S. 111, 112 (1969), for example, petitioners had taken part in a procession to express their grievances to the city government, and we held that such a "march, if peaceful and orderly, falls well within the sphere of conduct protected by the First Amendment." Similarly, in *Edwards v. South Carolina, supra,* 372 U.S., at 235, where petitioners had joined in a march of protest and pride, carrying placards and singing The Star Spangled Banner, we held that the activities "reflect an exercise of these basic constitutional rights in their most pristine and classic form."

The protected expression that inheres in a parade is not limited to its banners and songs, however, for the Constitution looks beyond written or spoken words as mediums of expression. Noting that "[s]ymbolism is a primitive but effective way of communicating ideas," *West Virginia Bd. of Ed. v. Barnette,* 319 U.S. 624, 632 (1943), our cases have recognized that the First Amendment shields such acts as saluting a flag (and refusing to do so), *id.,* at 632, 642, wearing an armband to protest a war, *Tinker v. Des Moines Independent Community School Dist.,* 393 U.S. 503, 505–506 (1969), displaying a red flag, *Stromberg v. California,* 283 U.S. 359, 369 (1931), and even "[m]arching, walking or parading" in uniforms displaying the swastika, *National Socialist Party of America v. Skokie,* 432 U.S. 43 (1977). As some of these examples show, a narrow, succinctly articulable message is not a condition of constitutional protection, which if confined to expressions conveying a "particularized message," cf. *Spence v. Washington,* 418 U.S. 405, 411 (1974), would never reach the unquestionably shielded painting of Jackson Pollock, music of Arnold Schöenberg, or Jabberwocky verse of Lewis Carroll.

Not many marches, then, are beyond the realm of expressive parades, and the South Boston celebration is not one of them. Spectators line the streets; people march in costumes and uniforms, carrying flags and banners with all sorts of messages (*e.g.,* "England get out of Ireland," "Say no to drugs"); marching bands and pipers play; floats are pulled along; and the whole show is broadcast over Boston television. To be sure, we agree with the state courts that in spite of excluding some applicants, the Council is rather lenient in admitting participants. But a private speaker does not forfeit constitutional protection simply by combining multifarious voices, or by failing to edit their themes to isolate an exact message as the exclusive subject matter of the speech. Nor, under our precedent, does First Amendment protection require a speaker to generate, as an original matter, each item featured in the communication. Cable operators, for example, are engaged in protected speech activities even when they only select programming originally produced by others. *Turner Broadcasting System, Inc. v. FCC,* 512 U.S. 622, 636 (1994) ("Cable programmers and cable operators engage in and transmit speech, and they are entitled to the protection of the speech and press provisions of the First Amendment"). For that matter, the presentation of an edited compilation of speech generated by other persons is a staple of most newspapers' opinion pages, which, of course, fall squarely within the core of First Amendment security, *Miami Herald Publishing Co. v. Tornillo,* 418 U.S. 241, 258 (1974), as does even the simple selection of a paid noncommercial advertisement for inclusion in a daily paper, see *New York Times v. Sullivan,* 376 U.S. 254, 265–266. The selection of contingents to make a parade is entitled to similar protection.

Respondents' participation as a unit in the parade was equally expressive. GLIB was formed for the very purpose of marching in it, as the trial court found, in order to celebrate its members' identity as openly gay, lesbian, and bisexual descendants of the Irish immigrants, to show that there are such individuals in the community, and to support the like men and women who sought to march in the New York parade. The organization distributed a fact sheet describing the members' intentions, App. A51, and the record otherwise corroborates the expressive nature of GLIB's participation. In 1993, members of GLIB marched behind a shamrock-strewn banner with the simple inscription "Irish American Gay, Lesbian and Bisexual Group of Boston." GLIB understandably seeks to communicate its ideas as part of the existing parade, rather than staging one of its own.

* * *

Since every participating unit affects the message conveyed by the private organizers, the state courts' application of the statute produced an order essentially requiring petitioners to alter the expressive content of their parade. Although the state courts spoke of the parade as a place of public accommodation, once the expressive character of both the parade and the marching GLIB contingent is understood, it becomes apparent that the state courts' application of the statute had the effect of declaring the sponsors' speech itself to be the public accommodation. Under this approach any contingent of protected individuals with a message would have the right to participate in petitioners' speech, so that the communication produced by the private organizers would be shaped by all those protected by the law who wished to join in with some expressive demonstration of their own. But this use of the State's power violates the fundamental rule of protection under the First Amendment, that a speaker has the autonomy to choose the content of his own message.

"Since *all* speech inherently involves choices of what to say and what to leave unsaid," *Pacific Gas & Electric Co. v. Public Utilities Comm'n of Cal.,* 475 U.S. 1, 11 (1986), one important manifestation of the principle of free speech is that one who chooses to speak may also decide "what not to say." Although the State may at times "prescribe what shall be orthodox in commercial advertising" by requiring the dissemination of "purely factual and uncontroversial information," *Zauderer v. Office of Disciplinary Counsel of Supreme Court of Ohio,* 471 U.S. 626, 651 (1985), outside that context it may not compel affirmance of a belief with which the speaker disagrees, see *Barnette,* 319 U.S., at 642. Indeed this general rule, that the speaker has the right to tailor the speech, applies not only to expressions of value, opinion, or endorsement, but equally to statements of fact the speaker would rather avoid, subject, perhaps, to the permissive law of defamation. Nor is the rule's benefit restricted to the press, being enjoyed by business corporations generally and by ordinary people engaged in unsophisticated expression as well as by professional publishers. Its point is simply the point of all speech protection, which is to shield just those choices of content that in someone's eyes are misguided, or even hurtful.

Petitioners' claim to the benefit of this principle of autonomy to control one's own speech is as sound as the South Boston parade is expressive. Rather like a composer, the Council selects the expressive units of the parade from potential participants, and though the score may not produce a particularized message, each contingent's expression in the Council's eyes comports with what merits celebration on that day. Even if this view gives the Council credit for a more considered judgment than it actively made, the Council clearly decided to exclude a message it did not like from the communication it chose to make, and that is enough to invoke its right as a private speaker to shape its expression by speaking on one subject while remaining silent on another. The message it disfavored is not difficult to identify. Although GLIB's point (like the Council's) is not wholly articulate, a contingent marching behind the organization's banner would at least bear witness to the fact that some Irish are gay, lesbian, or bisexual, and the presence of the organized marchers would suggest their view that people of their sexual orientations have as much claim to unqualified social acceptance as heterosexuals and indeed as members of parade units organized around other identifying characteristics. The parade's organizers may not believe these facts about Irish sexuality to be so, or they may object to unqualified social acceptance of gays and lesbians or have some other reason for wishing to keep GLIB's message out of the parade. But whatever the reason, it boils down to the choice of a speaker not to propound a particular point of view, and that choice is presumed to lie beyond the government's power to control.

* * *

The statute is a piece of protective legislation that announces no purpose beyond the object both expressed and apparent in its provisions, which is to prevent any denial of access to (or discriminatory treatment in) public accommodations on proscribed grounds, including sexual orientation. On its face, the object of the law is to ensure by statute for gays and lesbians desiring to make use of public accommodations what the old common law promised to any member of the public wanting a meal at the inn, that accepting the usual terms of service, they will not be turned away merely on the proprietor's exercise of personal preference. When the law is applied to expressive activity in the way it was done here, its apparent object is simply to require speakers to modify the content of their expression to whatever extent beneficiaries of the law choose to alter it with messages of their own. But in the absence of some further, legitimate end, this object is merely to allow exactly what the general rule of speaker's autonomy forbids.

It might, of course, have been argued that a broader objective is apparent: that the ultimate point of forbidding acts of discrimination toward certain classes is to produce a society free of the corresponding biases. Requiring access to a speaker's message would thus be not an end in itself, but a means to produce speakers free of the biases, whose expressive conduct would be at least neutral toward the particular classes, obviating any future need for correction. But if this indeed is the point of applying the state law to expressive conduct, it is a decidedly fatal objective. Having availed itself of the public thoroughfares "for purposes of assembly [and] communicating thoughts between citizens," the Council is engaged in a use of the streets that has "from ancient times, been a part of the privileges, immunities, rights, and liberties of citizens." *Hague v. Committee for Industrial Organization,* 307 U.S. 496, 515. Our tradition of free speech commands that a speaker who takes to the street corner to express his views in this way should be free from interference by the State based on the content of what he says. The very idea that a noncommercial speech restriction be used to produce thoughts and statements acceptable to some groups or, indeed, all people, grates on the First Amendment, for it amounts to nothing less than a proposal to limit speech in the service of orthodox expression. The Speech Clause has no more certain antithesis. See, *e.g., Barnette,* 319 U.S., at 642. While the law is free to promote all sorts of conduct in place of harmful behavior, it is not free to interfere with speech for no better reason than promoting an approved message or discouraging a disfavored one, however enlightened either purpose may strike the government.

* * *

Our holding today rests not on any particular view about the Council's message but on the Nation's commitment to protect freedom of speech. Disapproval of a private speaker's statement does not legitimize use of the Commonwealth's power to compel the speaker to alter the message by including one more acceptable to others. Accordingly, the judgment of the Supreme Judicial Court is reversed, and the case is remanded for proceedings not inconsistent with this opinion.

It is so ordered.

BOY SCOUTS OF AMERICA v. DALE

Supreme Court of the United States, 2000.
530 U.S. 640, 120 S.Ct. 2446, 147 L.Ed.2d 554.

CHIEF JUSTICE REHNQUIST delivered the opinion of the Court.

Petitioners are the Boy Scouts of America and the Monmouth Council, a division of the Boy Scouts of America (collectively, Boy Scouts). The Boy Scouts is a private, not-for-profit organization engaged in instilling its system of values in young people. The Boy Scouts asserts that homosexual conduct is inconsistent with the values it seeks to instill. Respondent is James Dale, a former Eagle Scout whose adult membership in the Boy Scouts was revoked when the Boy Scouts learned that he is an avowed homosexual and gay rights activist. The New Jersey Supreme Court held that New Jersey's public accommodations law requires that the Boy Scouts readmit Dale. This case presents the question whether applying New Jersey's public accommodations law in this way violates the Boy Scouts' First Amendment right of expressive association. We hold that it does.

* * *

In *Roberts v. United States Jaycees,* 468 U.S. 609, 622 (1984), we observed that "implicit in the right to engage in activities protected by the First Amendment" is "a corresponding right to associate with others in pursuit of a wide variety of political, social, economic, educational, religious, and cultural ends." This right is crucial in preventing the majority from imposing its views on groups that would rather express other, perhaps unpopular, ideas. See *ibid.* (stating that protection of the right to expressive association is "especially important in preserving political and cultural diversity and in shielding dissident expression from suppression by the majority"). Government actions that may unconstitutionally burden this freedom may take many forms, one of which is "intrusion into the internal structure or affairs of an association" like a "regulation that forces the group to accept members it does not desire." Forcing a group to accept certain members may impair the ability of the group to express those views, and only those views, that it intends to express. Thus, "[f]reedom of association ... plainly presupposes a freedom not to associate."

The forced inclusion of an unwanted person in a group infringes the group's freedom of expressive association if the presence of that person affects in a significant way the group's ability to advocate public or private viewpoints. *New York State Club Assn., Inc. v. City of New York,* 487 U.S. 1, 13 (1988). But the freedom of expressive association, like many freedoms, is not absolute. We have held that the freedom could be overridden "by regulations adopted to serve compelling state interests, unrelated to the suppression of ideas, that cannot be achieved through means significantly less restrictive of associational freedoms." *Roberts, supra,* at 623.

To determine whether a group is protected by the First Amendment's expressive associational right, we must determine whether the group engages in "expressive association." The First Amendment's protection of expressive association is not reserved for advocacy groups. But to come within its ambit, a group must engage in some form of expression, whether it be public or private.

Because this is a First Amendment case where the ultimate conclusions of law are virtually inseparable from findings of fact, we are obligated to independently review the factual record to ensure that the state court's judgment does not unlawfully intrude on free expression. The record reveals the following. The Boy Scouts is a private, nonprofit organization. According to its mission statement:

> "It is the mission of the Boy Scouts of America to serve others by helping to instill values in young people and, in other ways, to prepare them to make ethical choices over their lifetime in achieving their full potential.
>
> "The values we strive to instill are based on those found in the Scout Oath and Law:
>
> "Scout Oath
>
> "On my honor I will do my best
"To do my duty to God and my country
"and to obey the Scout Law;
"To help other people at all times;
"To keep myself physically strong,
"mentally awake, and morally straight.
>
> "Scout Law
>
> "A Scout is:
"Trustworthy Obedient
"Loyal Cheerful
"Helpful Thrifty
"Friendly Brave
"Courteous Clean
"Kind Reverent."

Thus, the general mission of the Boy Scouts is clear: "[T]o instill values in young people." *Ibid.* The Boy Scouts seeks to instill these values by having its adult leaders spend time with the youth members, instructing and engaging them in activities like camping, archery, and fishing. During the time spent with the youth members, the scoutmasters and assistant scoutmasters inculcate them with the Boy Scouts' values—both expressly and by example. It seems indisputable that an association that seeks to transmit such a system of values engages in expressive activity. See *Roberts, supra,* at 636 (O'CONNOR, J., concurring) ("Even the training of outdoor survival skills or participation in community service might become expressive when the activity is intended to develop good morals, reverence, patriotism, and a desire for self-improvement").

Given that the Boy Scouts engages in expressive activity, we must determine whether the forced inclusion of Dale as an assistant scoutmaster would significantly affect the Boy Scouts' ability to advocate public or private viewpoints. This inquiry necessarily requires us first to explore, to a limited extent, the nature of the Boy Scouts' view of homosexuality.

The values the Boy Scouts seeks to instill are "based on" those listed in the Scout Oath and Law. The Boy Scouts explains that the Scout Oath and Law provide "a positive moral code for living; they are a list of 'do's' rather than 'don'ts.' " The Boy Scouts asserts that homosexual conduct is inconsistent with the values embodied in the Scout Oath and Law, particularly with the values represented by the terms "morally straight" and "clean."

Obviously, the Scout Oath and Law do not expressly mention sexuality or sexual orientation. And the terms "morally straight" and "clean" are by no means self-defining. Different people would attribute to those terms very different meanings. For example, some people may believe that engaging in homosexual conduct is not at odds with being "morally straight" and "clean." And others may believe that engaging in homosexual conduct is contrary to being "morally straight" and "clean." The Boy Scouts says it falls within the latter category.

* * *

The Boy Scouts publicly expressed its views with respect to homosexual conduct by its assertions in prior litigation. For example, throughout a California case with similar facts filed in the early 1980's, the Boy Scouts consistently asserted the same position with respect to homosexuality that it asserts today. See *Curran v. Mount Diablo Council of Boy Scouts of America,* 72 Cal.Rptr.2d 410, 952 P.2d 218 (1998). We cannot doubt that the Boy Scouts sincerely holds this view.

We must then determine whether Dale's presence as an assistant scoutmaster would significantly burden the Boy Scouts' desire to not "promote homosexual conduct as a legitimate form of behavior." As we give deference to an association's assertions regarding the nature of its expression, we must also give deference to an association's view of what would impair its expression. That is not to say that an expressive association can erect a shield against antidiscrimination laws simply by asserting that mere acceptance of a member from a particular group would impair its message. But here Dale, by his own admission, is one of a group of gay Scouts who have "become leaders in their community and are open and honest about their sexual orientation." Dale was the copresident of a gay and lesbian organization at college and remains a gay rights activist. Dale's presence in the Boy Scouts would, at the very least, force the organization to send a message, both to the youth members and the world, that the Boy Scouts accepts homosexual conduct as a legitimate form of behavior.

Hurley is illustrative on this point. There we considered whether the application of Massachusetts' public accommodations law to require the organizers of a private St. Patrick's Day parade to include among the marchers an Irish–American gay, lesbian, and bisexual group, GLIB, violated the parade organizers' First Amendment rights. We noted that the parade organizers did not wish to exclude the GLIB members because of their sexual orientations, but because they wanted to march behind a GLIB banner. We observed:

> "[A] contingent marching behind the organization's banner would at least bear witness to the fact that some Irish are gay, lesbian, or bisexual, and the presence of the organized marchers would suggest their view that people of their sexual orientations have as much claim to unqualified social acceptance as heterosexuals.... The parade's organizers may not believe these facts about Irish sexuality to be so, or they may object to unqualified social acceptance of gays and lesbians or have some other reason for wishing to keep GLIB's message out of the parade. But whatever the reason, it boils down to the choice of a speaker not to propound a particular point of view, and that choice is presumed to lie beyond the government's power to control."

Here, we have found that the Boy Scouts believes that homosexual conduct is inconsistent with the values it seeks to instill in its youth members; it will not "promote homosexual conduct as a legitimate form of behavior. As the presence of GLIB in Boston's St. Patrick's Day parade would have interfered with the parade organizers' choice not to propound a particular point of view, the presence of Dale as an assistant scoutmaster would just as surely interfere with the Boy Scouts' choice not to propound a point of view contrary to its beliefs.

* * *

JUSTICE STEVENS' dissent makes much of its observation that the public perception of homosexuality in this country has changed. Indeed, it appears that homosexuality has gained greater societal acceptance. But this is scarcely an argument for denying First Amendment protection to those who refuse to accept these views. The First Amendment protects expression, be it of the popular variety or not. See, *e.g., Texas v. Johnson,* 491 U.S. 397 (1989) (holding that Johnson's conviction for burning the American flag violates the First Amendment); *Brandenburg v. Ohio,* 395 U.S. 444 (1969) (holding that a Ku Klux Klan leader's conviction for advocating unlawfulness as a means of political reform violates the First Amendment). And the fact that an idea may be embraced and advocated by increasing numbers of people is all the more reason to protect the First Amendment rights of those who wish to voice a different view.

JUSTICE STEVENS' extolling of JUSTICE BRANDEIS' comments in *New State Ice Co. v. Liebmann,* 285 U.S. 262, 311 (1932), confuses two entirely different principles. In *New State Ice,* the Court struck down an Oklahoma regulation prohibiting the manufacture, sale, and distribution of ice without a license. Justice Brandeis, a champion of state experimentation in the economic realm, dissented. But Justice Brandeis was never a champion of state experimentation in the suppression of free speech. To the contrary, his First Amendment commentary provides compelling support for the Court's opinion in this case. In speaking of the Founders of this Nation, Justice Brandeis emphasized that they "believed that freedom to think as you will and to speak as you think are means indispensable to the discovery and spread of political truth." *Whitney v. California,* 274 U.S. 357, 375. He continued:

> "Believing in the power of reason as applied through public discussion, they eschewed silence coerced by law—the argument of force in its worst form. Recognizing the occasional tyrannies of governing majorities, they amended the Constitution so that free speech and assembly should be guaranteed."

We are not, as we must not be, guided by our views of whether the Boy Scouts' teachings with respect to homosexual conduct are right or wrong; public or judicial disapproval of a tenet of an organization's expression does not justify the State's effort to compel the organization to accept members where such acceptance would derogate from the organization's expressive message. "While the law is free to promote all sorts of conduct in place of harmful behavior, it is not free to interfere with speech for no better reason than promoting an approved message or discouraging a disfavored one, however enlightened either purpose may strike the government." *Hurley,* 515 U.S., at 579.

The judgment of the New Jersey Supreme Court is reversed, and the case is remanded for further proceedings not inconsistent with this opinion.

It is so ordered.

JUSTICE STEVENS, with whom JUSTICE SOUTER, JUSTICE GINSBURG, and JUSTICE BREYER join, dissenting.

New Jersey "prides itself on judging each individual by his or her merits" and on being "in the vanguard in the fight to eradicate the cancer of unlawful discrimination of all types from our society." *Peper v. Princeton Univ. Bd. of Trustees,* 389 A.2d 465, 478 (1978). Since 1945, it has had a law against discrimination. The law broadly protects the opportunity of all persons to obtain the advantages and privileges "of any place of public accommodation." The New Jersey Supreme Court's construction of the statutory definition of a "place of public accommodation" has given its statute a more expansive coverage than most similar state statutes. And as amended in 1991, the law prohibits discrimination on the basis of nine different traits including an individual's "sexual orientation." The question in this case is whether that expansive construction trenches on the federal constitutional rights of the Boy Scouts of America (BSA).

Because every state law prohibiting discrimination is designed to replace prejudice with principle, Justice Brandeis' comment on the States' right to experiment with "things social" is directly applicable to this case.

> "To stay experimentation in things social and economic is a grave responsibility. Denial of the right to experiment may be fraught with serious consequences to the Nation. It is one of the happy incidents of the federal system that a single courageous State may, if its citizens choose, serve as a laboratory; and try novel social and economic experiments without risk to the rest of the country. This Court has the power to prevent an experiment. We may strike down the statute which embodies it on the ground that, in our opinion, the measure is arbitrary, capricious or unreasonable. We have power to do this, because the due process clause has been held by the Court applicable to matters of substantive law as well as to matters of procedure. But in the exercise of this high power, we must be ever on our guard, lest we erect our prejudices into legal principles. If we would guide by the light of reason, we must let our minds be bold." *New State Ice Co. v. Liebmann,* 285 U.S. 262, 311 (1932).

In its "exercise of this high power" today, the Court does not accord this "courageous State" the respect that is its due.

The majority holds that New Jersey's law violates BSA's right to associate and its right to free speech. But that law does not "impos[e] any serious burdens" on BSA's "collective effort on behalf of [its] shared goals," *Roberts v. United States Jaycees,* 468 U.S. 609, 622, 626–627 (1984), nor does it force BSA to communicate any message that it does not wish to endorse. New Jersey's law, therefore, abridges no constitutional right of BSA.

* * *

Several principles are made perfectly clear by *Jaycees* and *Rotary Club.* First, to prevail on a claim of expressive association in the face of a State's antidiscrimination law, it is not enough simply to engage in *some kind* of expressive activity. Both the Jaycees and the Rotary Club engaged in expressive activity protected by the First Amendment,[14] yet that fact was not dispositive. Second, it is not enough to adopt an openly avowed exclusionary membership policy. Both the Jaycees and the Rotary Club did that as well. Third, it is not sufficient merely to articulate *some* connection between the group's expressive activities and its exclusionary policy. The Rotary Club, for example, justified its male-only

14. See *Roberts v. United States Jaycees,* 468 U.S. 609, 626–627 (1984) ("[T]he organization [has] taken public positions on a number of diverse issues . . . worthy of constitutional protection under the First Amendment"); *Board of Directors of Rotary Int'l v. Rotary Club of Duarte,* 481 U.S. 537, 548 (1987) ("To be sure, Rotary Clubs engage in a variety of commendable service activities that are protected by the First Amendment").

membership policy by pointing to the " 'aspect of fellowship ... that is enjoyed by the [exclusively] male membership' "and by claiming that only with an exclusively male membership could it "operate effectively" in foreign countries.

Rather, in *Jaycees,* we asked whether Minnesota's Human Rights Law requiring the admission of women "impose[d] any *serious burdens* 'on the group's "collective effort on behalf of [its] *shared goals.*' " Notwithstanding the group's obvious publicly stated exclusionary policy, we did not view the inclusion of women as a "serious burden" on the Jaycees' ability to engage in the protected speech of its choice. Similarly, in *Rotary Club,* we asked whether California's law would "affect in any *significant way* the existing members' ability" to engage in their protected speech, or whether the law would require the clubs "to abandon their basic goals." The relevant question is whether the mere inclusion of the person at issue would "impose any serious burden," "affect in any significant way," or be "a substantial restraint upon" the organization's "shared goals," "basic goals," or "collective effort to foster beliefs." Accordingly, it is necessary to examine what, exactly, are BSA's shared goals and the degree to which its expressive activities would be burdened, affected, or restrained by including homosexuals.

The evidence before this Court makes it exceptionally clear that BSA has, at most, simply adopted an exclusionary membership policy and has no shared goal of disapproving of homosexuality. BSA's mission statement and federal charter say nothing on the matter; its official membership policy is silent; its Scout Oath and Law—and accompanying definitions—are devoid of any view on the topic; its guidance for Scouts and Scoutmasters on sexuality declare that such matters are "not construed to be Scouting's proper area," but are the province of a Scout's parents and pastor; and BSA's posture respecting religion tolerates a wide variety of views on the issue of homosexuality. Moreover, there is simply no evidence that BSA otherwise teaches anything in this area, or that it instructs Scouts on matters involving homosexuality in ways not conveyed in the Boy Scout or Scoutmaster Handbooks. In short, Boy Scouts of America is simply silent on homosexuality. There is no shared goal or collective effort to foster a belief about homosexuality at all—let alone one that is significantly burdened by admitting homosexuals.

* * *

Dale's inclusion in the Boy Scouts is nothing like the case in *Hurley.* His participation sends no cognizable message to the Scouts or to the world. Unlike GLIB, Dale did not carry a banner or a sign; he did not distribute any factsheet; and he expressed no intent to send any message. If there is any kind of message being sent, then, it is by the mere act of joining the Boy Scouts. Such an act does not constitute an instance of symbolic speech under the First Amendment.[21]

21. The majority might have argued (but it did not) that Dale had become so publicly and pervasively identified with a position advocating the moral legitimacy of

It is true, of course, that some acts are so imbued with symbolic meaning that they qualify as "speech" under the First Amendment. See *United States v. O'Brien,* 391 U.S. 367, 376 (1968). At the same time, however, "[w]e cannot accept the view that an apparently limitless variety of conduct can be labeled 'speech' whenever the person engaging in the conduct intends thereby to express an idea." *Ibid.* Though participating in the Scouts could itself conceivably send a message on some level, it is not the kind of act that we have recognized as speech.[22] Indeed, if merely joining a group did constitute symbolic speech; and such speech were attributable to the group being joined; and that group has the right to exclude that speech (and hence, the right to exclude that person from joining), then the right of free speech effectively becomes a limitless right to exclude for every organization, whether or not it engages in *any* expressive activities. That cannot be, and never has been, the law.

* * *

[A dissenting opinion by JUSTICE SOUTER, joined by JUSTICE GINSBURG and JUSTICE BREYER, is omitted.]

Questions

1) Joseph Raz develops the argument that free expression is valuable in part for its role in validating various ways of life. He says: "In a culture in which expression is free, validation is provided by people exercising their freedom. They provide validation and not the state, not society using its authoritative voice." What is the source of the preference for the former procedure of validation over the latter? Does Raz have an answer to the critic who claims the authority to regulate speech precisely to prevent the insidious"validation" by means of public expression of ways of life that the majority of persons consider unworthy of validation even if undeserving of persecution?

2) Which side of the dispute in *Hurley v. Irish–American Gay, Lesbian, and Bisexual Group of Boston*, if either, gains support from Raz's argument for free expression as a source of personal identification? Does Raz's argument support the right to expressive association that was recognized in *Boy Scouts of America v. Dale*?

homosexuality (as opposed to just being an individual who openly stated he is gay) that his leadership position in BSA would necessarily amount to using the organization as a conduit for publicizing his position. But as already noted, when BSA expelled Dale, it had nothing to go on beyond the one newspaper article quoted above, and one newspaper article does not convert Dale into a public symbol for a message. BSA simply has not provided a record that establishes the factual premise for this argument.

22. This is not to say that Scouts do not engage in expressive activity. It is only to say that the simple act of joining the Scouts—unlike joining a parade—is not inherently expressive.

VINCENT BLASI, FREE SPEECH AND GOOD CHARACTER: FROM MILTON TO BRANDEIS TO THE PRESENT

in Eternally Vigilant: Free Speech in the Modern Era (Lee C. Bollinger and Geoffrey R. Stone eds. 2002).

INTRODUCTION

When pressed to defend the extraordinary priority accorded the freedom of speech in the United States—a priority not really replicated in other liberal democracies—First Amendment devotees typically invoke one or more of three basic rationales. First, the liberty to express one's thoughts and to form them by unrestricted reading and listening is an essential attribute, it is said, of human autonomy, of what it means to be a self-directed person possessed of human dignity. Second, free speech is the foundational mechanism of the search for truth, at both the individual and the societal levels. In this view, a free "marketplace of ideas" produces a more accurate, probing, and richly textured understanding of fact and value than can any prescribed orthodoxy. Third, for a society committed to the project of self-government, in which ultimate political responsibility rests with the mass of ordinary citizens, free speech is invaluable as a means of civic education and participation.[1]

This trilogy of rationales is venerable, and there is much to be said for each of them. But there are problems. Yes, we all like to think of ourselves as autonomous, but how many of us possess even a rudimentary understanding of this profound, elusive Kantian notion? And if we did, would we necessarily embrace its strong assumptions regarding human agency and also conclude that speech is special among the liberties that sustain the self? Yes, truth is important, but truth-seeking is such a different activity for the votary, the pragmatist, and the skeptic as to confound any effort to generalize regarding the priority to be accorded truth-seeking, the role free speech plays in facilitating it, and the significance of the many "market failures" that distort the flow of ideas and information. Yes, self-government is a noble ideal and one with a textual mooring in the Constitution, but what it means for citizens to give meaningful consent or to engage in meaningful participation are the very questions that fuel the clash of modern political philosophies. This phenomenon of radical disagreement emerging from the shared commitment to self-government appears also at the level of First Amendment doctrine. Consider the issue of campaign spending limits. Must a self-governing voter be free to hear as much speech about an election as private resources can produce? Or do the risks of corruption, plutocratic bias, citizen alienation, and the diversion of energies to fund-raising justify the imposition of spending limits as a means of preserving the self-governing capacities of voters? Moreover, the justification for free speech from self-government fails to provide a reason to protect literature or scientific inquiry, an unsettling prospect even for minimalists

1. For excellent critical summaries of the traditional rationales for the freedom of speech, *see* FREDERICK SCHAUER, FREE SPEECH: A PHILOSOPHICAL ENQUIRY 15–72 (1982); Kent Greenawalt. *Free Speech Justifications*, 89 COLUM. L. REV. 119 (1989).

who can live with the exclusion of commercial advertising, workplace harassment, and hard-core pornography from the ambit of First Amendment concern. In brief, the tired trilogy of conventional free-speech justifications is at best incomplete, and at worst so abstract and protean as to be of limited intellectual or practical utility.

In light of these difficulties, it is odd that a somewhat different, and to my mind less problematic, rationale for the freedom of speech has not received more attention in recent times, particularly since it figured prominently during the first three hundred years of systematic writing in defense of toleration. This is a special kind of argument from character that builds from the claim that a culture that prizes and protects expressive liberty nurtures in its members certain character traits such as inquisitiveness, distrust of authority, willingness to take initiative, and the courage to confront evil. Such character traits are valuable, so the argument goes, not for their intrinsic virtue but for their instrumental contribution to collective well-being, social as well as political. This claim plausibly can be said to form the spine of each of the renowned defenses of free speech produced by John Milton,[2] John Stuart Mill,[3] Oliver Wendell Holmes,[4] and Louis Brandeis.[5] Yet today we pick up on other features of those classic writings, usually by finding some way to enlist their observations in the service of the familiar arguments for free speech from autonomy, truth-seeking, and self-government.

In this essay I trace how two of the master builders of the free-speech tradition, John Milton and Louis Brandeis, emphasized character in their arguments against the regulation of speech. Milton and Brandeis did not value the strengthening of character for identical reasons, nor did they seek to nurture precisely the same character traits. Nevertheless, they have in common the view that character is important in large part because it is instrumental to the pursuit of collective objectives. Moreover, despite the nearly three centuries that separate their inquiries, Milton and Brandeis overlap to a striking degree in the character traits they value most and in the connections they perceive between the freedom of speech and the flourishing of those traits. After examining in context exactly what they say about character, I elaborate the basic insights of Milton and Brandeis with attention to how their observations and ideals fit contemporary conditions. In the process I seek to identify how a robust principle of freedom of speech might even today serve a number of collective goals by means of its impact on the character of the populace.

Two introductory caveats are in order. I do not mean to suggest that the argument from character ought completely to displace the rationales for free speech that have held sway in the modern era. I aim merely to redress an imbalance in the way the principle of freedom of speech is

2. JOHN MILTON, *Areopagitica[1644], in* COMPLETE POEMS AND MAJOR PROSE 716 (Merritt Hughes ed., 1957).

3. JOHN STUART MILL, ON LIBERTY[1859] (Stefan Collini ed., 1989).

4. Abrams v. United States, 250 U.S. 616 (1919) (Holmes, J., dissenting).

5. Whitney v. California, 274 U.S. 357 (1927) (Brandeis, J., concurring).

justified and thereby appreciated. Nor do I claim that greater attention to character would directly yield better First Amendment doctrines. Doctrine building is a complex endeavor that, when done well, takes into account a host of practical and institutional considerations in addition to underlying justifications. No doctrine-generating algorithm is offered or intimated here. My ambition is not to solve specific problems so much as to shore up the flagging conviction that the freedom of speech, as a general matter and as conventionally understood, really is worth the heavy costs it sometimes imposes.

Milton

Like Machiavelli before him, Milton was preoccupied with the question of political energy. He saw individual character as the key to collective energy. He valued strength of will, acuteness of perception, ingenuity, self-discipline, engagement, breadth of vision, perseverance; he detested rigidity, stasis, withdrawal, timidity, small-mindedness, indecision, laziness, deference to authority. In the *Areopagitica*, his extended polemic of 1644 against the licensing of books and pamphlets, Milton emphasizes the connection between free speech and good character. "I cannot praise," he says, "a fugitive and cloistered virtue, unexercised and unbreathed, that never sallies out and sees her adversary...."

Responding to his own adversaries who were asserting the need for more order, more standards, more authority, more closure in the realm of religious inquiry, Milton scornfully describes the "fruits which a dull ease and cessation of our knowledge will bring forth among the people." "How goodly and how to be wished were such an obedient unanimity as this, what a fine conformity would it starch us all into! Doubtless a staunch and solid piece of framework as any January could freeze together." "[F]aith and knowledge," he asserts, "thrives by exercise.... " Truth he likens "to a streaming fountain; if her waters flow not in a perpetual progression, they sicken into a muddy pool of conformity and tradition."

Milton's regard for the active life was not just a cultural preference. He saw the stakes as greater than that, involving nothing less than the control of evil. Political energy, he realized, is a sometime source of progress but also a frequent cause of strife and oppression. His crucial move was to conclude that harm, even the harm that flows from malignant political energy, can best be contained and repaired by a citizenry that is energized in a countervailing way: intellectually independent, morally engaged, politically resilient, not afraid to speak out or to stand up. His views in this matter were shaped by his lifelong study of the problem of evil. As the creator of Satan in *Paradise Lost*, probably the most brilliant and destructive demagogue in the whole of English literature, Milton can hardly be accused of failing to appreciate how words can do harm. He did not believe, however, that the discovery of evil justifies the regulation of speech. In fact, Milton thought evil so pervasive, insidious, and perdurable a force in human affairs as to demand in response something more than the blunt instruments and formal gestures of the law.[13] Evil can be combatted, he was convinced, only from within: by the vigilance of a population accustomed to challenging authority; by the ingenuity and integrity that a licensing regime is bound to discourage; by the hard work of discerning, confronting, refuting, and choosing that censors seek to disburden citizens from having to undertake.

This emphasis on character is at once the most distinctive and the most pervasive feature of Milton's argument for the liberty of printing. However, proponents of the regulation of speech frequently invoke concerns relating to character on their side of the debate.[15] In Milton's day as in ours, the claim that liberty improves character was, if not patently implausible, at best controversial. We must, therefore, look more closely at Milton's conception of character and explore what he took to be the relationship between character and censorship.

When he turns to the "manifest hurt" that licensing will cause, Milton's choice of terms is revealing. He describes censorship as a "discouragement," an "affront," a "dishonour and derogation to the author," a "servitude," a "disparagement," a "reproach," a "thraldom," "a particular disesteem," an "undervaluing and vilifying of the whole nation." He objects that every author is "mistrusted and suspected," made to "trudge to his leave-giver," and then, if all goes well, to "appear in print like a puny with his guardian," displaying "his censor's hand on the back of his title to be his bail and surety that he is no idiot or seducer. . . ." No doubt Milton spoke from personal experience regarding the indignity of asking for official approval to publish. An author of his skill and dedication must have felt particular umbrage at having to submit to "the fearfulness or the presumptuous rashness of a perfunctory licenser." Whatever the role personal pique might have played in provoking Milton's challenge to the parliamentary licensing scheme, there can be little question that he considered censorship to be genuinely corrosive of character.

Exactly how, we might ask, is character threatened by the fact that a political regime distrusts its citizens and requires them to behave as supplicants? To Milton's mind, censorship undermines character by encouraging individuals to shirk their civic and religious responsibilities. The imagery of childhood is employed repeatedly in the *Areopagitica*. A writer forced to run the censor's gauntlet must thereby appear to his readers "a pupil teacher," an instructor "under the wardship of an overseeing fist." For a community to maintain its tenets and taboos by

13. Milton worried a lot about excessive reliance on law. In *Areopagitica* he states: "[H]ere the great art lies to discern in what the law is to bid restraint and punishment, and in what things persuasion only is to work. If every action which is good or evil in man at ripe years were to be under pittance, and prescription and compulsion, what were virtue but a name . . . ?"

15. *See, e.g.*, WALTER BERNS, THE FIRST AMENDMENT AND THE FUTURE OF AMERICAN DEMOCRACT (1976); FRANCIS CANAVAN, FREEDOM OF EXPRESSION: PURPOSE AS LIMIT (1984); HARRY CLOR, OBSCENITY AND PUBLIC MORALITY (1969); Willmoore Kendall, *The "Open Society" and Its Fallacies*, 54 AM. POL. SCI. REV. 972 (1960); Henry J. McCloskey, *Liberty of Expression: Its Grounds and Limits*, 13 INQUIRY 219 (1970).

means of "law and compulsion" rather than "exhortation" is "to captivate under a perpetual childhood of prescription. . . ." "What advantage is it," Milton asks, "to be a man over it is to be a boy at school" if "serious and elaborate writings" are examined like "the theme of a grammar-lad under his pedagogue . . . " Citizens who are treated like children will behave like children, he implies, and one thing we know children do surpassingly well is to let adults take on the unpleasant chores.

In an age so notable for its polemics, as well as for its exhilarating scientific and philosophical formulations, can it be that inquiry and disputation were seen as burdensome chores that many persons might seek to evade? Milton certainly thought so. Consider the case of religion. Perhaps the most extended figure in the whole tract is that of the man who "finds religion to be a traffic so entangled, and of so many piddling accounts," that he "resolves to give over toiling, and to find himself out some factor to whose care and credit he may commit the whole managing of his religious affairs." To this surrogate the shirking principal "resigns the whole warehouse of his religion, with all the locks and keys, into his custody; and indeed makes the very person of that man his religion. . . ." With such a delegation, "his religion is now no more within himself, but is become a dividual moveable, and goes and comes near him according as that good man frequents the house." Milton is unsparing in his satire of this evasion of religious responsibility: "He entertains him, gives him gifts, feasts him, lodges him; his religion comes home at night, prays, is liberally supped and sumptuously laid to sleep; rises, is saluted. . . . [H]is religion walks abroad at eight, and leaves his kind entertainer in the shop trading all day without his religion."

Preachers too are at risk of shirking their duties, living off old notes, "the gatherings and savings of a sober graduateship." By means of "forming and transforming, joining and disjoining variously, a little bookcraft and two hours meditation" the "easily inclinable" clergyman can cobble together a passable sermon, assisted as he might also be by "interlinearies, breviaries, synopses, and other loitering gear." However, "if his back door be not secured by the rigid licenser," if "a bold book may now and then issue forth and give the assault to some of his old collections in their trenches," such a preacher may have to do his own work, if only to "set good guards and sentinels about his received opinions." Even this would represent progress, according to Milton. "God send," he says, "that the fear of this diligence which must then be used do not make us affect the laziness of a licensing church."

Milton opposed censorship in large part because he placed legal regulation in the same category as reliance on factors and cribs: an effort to free ordinary citizens and ordinary worshippers from the salutary if onerous duty of cease-less personal inquiry. Because character played so large a role in his thought, these various delegations of responsibility assumed for him a special significance. "[I]f the men be erroneous who appear to be the leading schismatics," he says, "what withholds us but our sloth, our self-will, and distrust in the right cause, that we do not give them gentle meetings and gentle dismissions, that we debate not and examine the matter thoroughly with liberal and frequent audience; if not for their sakes yet for our own?"

Laziness, stubbornness, lack of trust, lack of confidence—these are some of the character flaws that, according to Milton, are nurtured by restrictions on free printing. Another is "precipitant zeal," the impulse to rush to judgment. We "make no distinction," he complains, when encountering persons whom we fear "come with new and dangerous opinions." We "forejudge them ere we understand them. . . ." No other sentence in the *Areopagitica* has so much the quality of a personal plea: Milton's own unconventional opinions on divorce—he believed incompatibility to be a legitimate ground even in the absence of infidelity—were forejudged, badly mischaracterized, and used to hold him up to ridicule in important public forums. Being treated most unfairly as a licentious and irresponsible radical was very likely a formative experience for this exceptionally serious and disciplined young man. On the subject of forejudgment, he knew of what he spoke.

Licensing, indeed all legal regulation of speech, must employ forejudgment to some degree. It must proceed by categorization and incomplete characterization. Problems of proof distort judgment further. Speakers, moreover, have mixed and easily misunderstood motives. Ideas have layers and textures that resist legal classification. They have the capacity to breed but also a vulnerability to misappropriation, qualities that bedevil even well-intentioned efforts to predict their consequences. All of these features make the regulation of speech a particularly imprecise endeavor. In his pragmatist mode, Milton argues that the indiscriminate nature of licensing invites partisan abuse. But he was troubled by the indiscriminate nature of licensing at least as much for its embodiment of forejudgment, a character defect he often devoted his art to exposing.

Because the regulation of printing typically is imbued with imprecision and futility, the act of licensing also has the character of a formal gesture, a regulatory show. Central to Milton's thought in several domains—religion, poetry, politics, education, marriage—was his disdain for reliance on forms. Those who would regulate writings judge them superficially for several reasons, but important among them is the fact that most of the time the censorship of ideas is not really meant to be a discriminating gesture. It is intended rather to be a formal discharge of regulatory responsibility or a public affirmation of conventional forms of authority and thought. This was Milton's understanding of the true nature of licensing and a major source of his contempt for the practice.

He saw formalism as a means of avoiding the challenges of a complex, changing, often deceiving and dispiriting world. If obeisance were an adequate means of coping and of seeking salvation, the avoidance implicit in formalism might not be a matter of the highest concern. Milton, however, believed that both survival and salvation require of humankind active choice. False appearances abound in life. Taken at face value, they will mislead. They are most likely to mislead a people not experienced at getting beneath formal surfaces and exercising the capacity for critical choice. Milton's poetry repeatedly forces the reader to make hard choices and tempts her to make wrong choices. Famously signaling his break with Calvinism, he asserts in *Areopagitica:* "Many there be that complain of divine Providence for suffering Adam to transgress. Foolish tongues! When God gave him reason, he gave him freedom to choose, for reason is but choosing. . . ."

That Milton built his argument for free printing around the importance of choice does not mean that he held an exalted view of the power of human reason. In 1644 the world seemed to him more complicated and inscrutable than he had previously appreciated. Apparently, he was experiencing disillusionment during this period as a result of his own poor judgment in choosing a marriage partner, the harsh response to his divorce tracts, and more generally the dashing of his hopes for a swift, decisive Reformation. Abandoning the apocalyptic tone of his earlier antiprelatical pamphlets, Milton states in *Areopagitica:* "It is not the unfrocking of a priest, the unmitring of a bishop and the removing him from off the presbyterian shoulders, that will make us a happy nation." Much more than such changes of form will be required, he now realizes. Only sustained effort, the determination to persevere amid the temptation to despair, the courage to choose and the strength to choose wisely and continually, will advance "the slow-moving reformation which we labour under. . . ." In the penultimate book of *Paradise Lost,* the archangel Michael explains to Adam why fallen man must endure so much suffering and injustice:

. . . good with bad
Expect to hear, supernal grace contending
With sinfulness of men, thereby to learn
True patience. . . .[55]

Milton considered licensing a policy driven by impatience, and as such a threat to the character of the English people. He embraced the freedom of speech so that his fellow citizens might hear "good with bad . . . thereby to learn true patience."

The virtue of patience belongs disproportionately to those who are capable of thinking in historical terms, as Milton most assuredly was. One of the reasons for valuing the freedom of speech is that it nurtures a nation's sense of history. When permitted a hearing and a place in the historical record, dissenting currents of thought can shape the future. When exposed to independent scrutiny in the court of history, even the most powerful rulers do not have a free hand. History, of course, will exist with or without the freedom of speech. But how a nation understands and uses its history is a vital dimension of the historical process itself. Milton thought censorship threatened the historical process pri-

55. Milton, *Paradise Lost,* bk. XI, II. 358–61, *in* Complete Poems and Major Prose, *supra* note 2, at 441.

marily by its impact on character. A people afraid of new ideas, trustful of censors and hostile to bold thinkers, will be left behind, he suggests, by the sweep of history. Such a people will lack both vision and the ability to learn from experience. Patriot (and historian) that he was, he did not want this to be the fate of the English nation, as he thought it had been in the fourteenth century when the nascent reformation offered by John Wycliffe was thwarted by the deadly combination of timidity, ignorance, and censorship.

Perhaps the most important aspect of Milton's historical imagination is his emphasis on the process of renewal. With his command of ancient, patristic, and medieval sources, he viewed both the Reformation and the parliamentary challenge to Stuart tyranny as efforts to recover forgotten wisdom and dissipated energy. The *Areopagitica* is replete with images of decay and reinvigoration. The process of renewal feeds, Milton believed, off the sense of purpose and possibility that "much arguing, much writing, many opinions" can help to engender. In this view, free speech is not primarily a mechanism for deliberation and persuasion so much as a phenomenon shaping the character and aspirations of the population. Contrary to the common scholarly assumption, *Areopagitica* may not have been written with the ambition, seemingly quixotic, of persuading the Long Parliament to abolish the practice of licensing. Milton knew the reigning Presbyterian faction to be intransigent on the issue of censorship and ill disposed to his person because of his views on divorce. The tract may instead have been aimed primarily at the Cromwellian Independents in Parliament and the army, in the hope that future agents of renewal would not lose their enthusiasm for toleration once they gained the reins of power.

Although in 1644 Milton already might have seen himself as writing for a more propitious future time, it was not until 1660 that events tested to the utmost his resolve to embrace the historical perspective. In none of his writings does he better express his belief in the importance of speech than in the closing words of *The Ready and Easy Way To Establish a Free Commonwealth*, a pamphlet written in anguish to protest the headlong rush of the strife-weary English people to restore the Stuart monarchy. Blind, betrayed by his countrymen and even by his erstwhile hero Cromwell, eligible for execution on account of his polemics in defense of the regicide, his great epic poem nowhere near finished, Milton remained unbowed. Risking his freedom and possibly his life, he challenged the ascendant royalists by issuing an uncompromising indictment of monarchical government. As other republicans were busy trimming to protect their positions against the impending Restoration, Milton defiantly reaffirmed his commitment to the Good Old Cause, finding succor in the prospect of eventual political renewal:

> Thus much I should perhaps have said though I were sure I should have spoken only to trees and stones, and had none to cry to, but with the prophet, "O earth, earth, earth!" to tell the very soil itself what her perverse inhabitants are deaf to. Nay, though what I have spoke should happen . . . to be the last words of our expiring liberty.

> But I trust I shall have spoken persuasion to abundance of sensible and ingenuous men, to some perhaps, whom God may raise of these stones to become children of reviving liberty. . . .[61]

Whether speaking of responsibility, forejudgment, the worship of form, perseverance, the courage to choose, impatience, or renewal, Milton emphasizes the inner person. Censorship, he says, leads only to "the forced and outward union of cold and neutral, and inwardly divided minds." More than the ideas lost or the causes squelched, such minds were for him the chief casualty of licensing.

BRANDEIS

Notwithstanding the magisterial articulations of Justices Holmes,[63] Roberts,[64] Jackson,[65] Black,[66] Harlan,[67] and Brennan[68] among others, if there is a single passage in the United States Reports that best captures why the freedom of speech might be considered the linchpin of the American constitutional regime, it is the following paragraph from Justice Brandeis's concurring opinion in *Whitney v. California:*

> Those who won our independence believed that the final end of the State was to make men free to develop their faculties; and that in its government the deliberative forces should prevail over the arbitrary. They valued liberty both as an end and as a means. They believed liberty to be the secret of happiness and courage to be the secret of liberty. They believed that freedom to think as you will and to speak as you think are means indispensable to the discovery and spread of political truth; that without free speech and assembly discussion would be futile; that with them discussion affords ordinarily adequate protection against the dissemination of noxious doctrine; that the greatest menace to freedom is an inert people; that public discussion is a political duty; and that this should be a fundamental principle of the American government. They recognized the risks to which all human institutions are subject. But they knew that order cannot be secured merely through fear of punishment for its infraction; that it is hazardous to discourage thought, hope and imagination; that fear breeds repression; that repression breeds hate; that hate menaces stable government; that the path of safety lies in the opportunity to discuss freely supposed grievances and proposed remedies; and that the fitting remedy for evil counsels is good ones.

61. MILTON, *The Ready and Easy Way to Establish a Free Commonwealth* (1660), *in* COMPLETE POEMS AND MAJOR PROSE, *supra* note 2, at 880, 898.

63. *See, e.g.,* Abrams v. United States, 250 U.S. 616 (1919) (Holmes, J., dissenting).

64. *See, e.g.,* Cantwell v. Connecticut, 310 U.S. 296 (1940); Hague v. C.I.O., 307 U.S. 496 (1939).

65. *See, e.g.,* West Va. State Bd. of Educ. v. Barnette, 319 U.S. 624 (1943).

66. *See, e.g.,* New York Times v. United States, 403 U.S. 713 (1971) (Black, J. concurring); Bridges v. California, 314 U.S. 252 (1941).

67. *See, e.g.,* Cohen v. California, 403 U.S. 15 (1971).

68. *See, e.g.,* New York Times v. Sullivan, 376 U.S. 254 (1964); Texas v. Johnson, 491 U.S. 397 (1989).

> Believing in the power of reason as applied through public discussion, they eschewed silence coerced by law—the argument of force in its worst form. Recognizing the occasional tyrannies of governing majorities, they amended the Constitution so that free speech and assembly should be guaranteed.[69]

This statement contains a list of propositions, succinctly stated and Delphic in tone, that do not obviously add up to a coherent philosophy. One might suspect Brandeis, the consummate lawyer, of pleading in the alternative in this paragraph. That view is wrong, I believe. There is one idea here, not many, and it represents Brandeis's distinctive contribution to the history of First Amendment thought. Permit me to parse this pregnant text.

> *Those who won our independence believed that the final end of the State was to make men free to develop their faculties....*

Whatever may have been the beliefs of "[t]hose who won our independence," we can be certain that Brandeis considered the purpose of government to be "to make men free to develop their faculties." Some might see in this an endorsement of the view that freedom of speech is designed to promote self-development of a highly personal and subjective sort, what my colleague Henry Monaghan likes to call the "feel-good theory of the First Amendment." In light of what follows, however, it is better to read Brandeis here as affirming the principle of self-government, specifically the premise that the state exists solely by the sufferance of, through the efforts of, and for the benefit of the individuals who comprise it. The focus is on the relationship between the individual and the state.

> *[T]he deliberative forces should prevail over the arbitrary.*

This is the first of several passages that might lead one to accuse Brandeis of too rationalistic a view of the process of opinion formation. But in erecting this model of contending forces, Brandeis need not have entertained a naive faith in the wisdom and fairness of collective deliberation to prefer that process to the alternative of unilateral decree by an unaccountable sovereign. From this perspective, freedom of speech is most important for what it implies about sovereignty. Again, the foundational principle is self-government.

> *They valued liberty both as an end and as a means. They believed liberty to be the secret of happiness and courage to be the secret of liberty.*

These sentences embrace what philosophers call a strong theory of the person. A particular kind of citizen is described: one concerned with personal happiness, to be sure, but not the private, self-regarding creature celebrated by some libertarian philosophies. The happiness Brandeis considers the legitimate aspiration of humankind is gained by struggle, by drawing on the demanding virtue of courage. Liberty is valuable as an end because the often difficult experience of exercising a measure of

69. 274 U.S. 357, 375–76 (1927).

control over one's commitments and paths of development, of choosing what to believe and how to interact with others, is personally fulfilling. Liberty is valuable as a means because persons who have made themselves what they are through the exercise of their own initiative make the best citizens; such persons achieve the most for their societies.

> *They believed that freedom to think as you will and to speak as you think are means indispensable to the discovery and spread of political truth . . . .*

This is as close as Brandeis gets to the claim that unregulated discussion yields truth. Notice that, in contrast to Holmes, Brandeis never tells us what is "the best test of truth."[72] He never employs the metaphor of the marketplace. He speaks only of "political truth," and he uses the phrase "means indispensable" to link activities described in highly personal terms—"think as you will," "speak as you think"—with the collective goal of "political truth." His emphasis in this passage is on the attitudes and atmosphere that must prevail if the ideals of self-government and happiness-through-courage are to be realized. Brandeis is sketching a good society here, but not an all-conquering dialectic.

> *[D]iscussion affords ordinarily adequate protection against the dissemination of noxious doctrine . . . .*

This is a thought Brandeis twice repeats within the space of three paragraphs. He says, a few lines after the passage quoted, "the fitting remedy for evil counsels is good ones." And two pages after that: "If there be time to expose through discussion the falsehood and fallacies, to avert the evil by the processes of education, the remedy to be applied is more speech, not enforced silence." Did he really believe this? Do we believe it today?

Brandeis was no ingenue on the subject of public opinion. He knew from his sometimes bitterly fought reform battles in Massachusetts how often the triumph of even a very good idea depends on the hard work, money, savvy, and perseverance of its proponents.

He was a close student of Walter Lippmann, who was commenting at the time on how the phenomenon of mass culture was making public opinion dangerously manipulable.[74]

It is noteworthy that Brandeis never speaks of noxious doctrine being refuted or eliminated or defeated. He talks of societal self-protection and the fitting remedy. He warns us not to underestimate the value of discussion, education, good counsels. His point is that noxious doctrine is most likely to flourish when its opponents lack the personal qualities of wisdom, creativity, and confidence. And those qualities, he suggests, are best developed by discussion and education, not by lazy and impatient reliance on the coercive authority of the state. To those who would justify censorship on the ground that purveyors of evil ideas can manipu-

72. *Compare* Abrams v. United States, 250 U.S. 616, 630 (1919) (Holmes, J., dissenting).

74. *See* Robert M. Cover, *The Left, the Right, and the First Amendment: 1918–1928,* 40 Md. L. Rev. 349, 363–69 (1981).

late public opinion, Brandeis almost surely would answer that it is incumbent upon the defenders of good ideas to learn how to influence public opinion even more skillfully.

> *[T]he greatest menace to freedom is an inert people; ... public discussion is a political duty.... They recognized the risks to which all human institutions are subject.*

The juxtaposition of these observations is revealing. Brandeis was an idealist, but he was not a perfectionist. When he speaks of the benefits of political participation, his major concern is with the preservation of freedom. He does not claim that participatory democracy produces the wisest policies on a day-to-day basis. Nor does he assert, though he may well have believed, that regular and active political participation is a necessary feature of a personally fulfilling life. To Brandeis, public discussion is a "duty." It is a duty because political liberty is a fragile condition, easily lost when its institutions and traditions fall into the hands of inert people.

> *[T]hey knew that order cannot be secured merely through fear of punishment ... ; that it is hazardous to discourage thought, hope and imagination; that fear breeds repression; that repression breeds hate; that hate menaces stable government....*

Here is the counsel of a conservative, addressing the question of how best to secure order and keep government stable. To some, the passage may sound like the "safety valve" rationale for freedom of speech: dissidents will do less mischief if they are permitted to let off steam. The problem with this argument is that it is too tactical in inspiration, and perhaps too condescending, to serve as the basis for a constitutional principle. Moreover, it seems a crude generalization to say that most dissidents will consider the opportunity to speak a fair substitute for the redress of their substantive discontents.

Why did Brandeis want to encourage "thought, hope and imagination" in persons whose views are unlikely to win majoritarian approval? If such persons take their thoughts and hopes too seriously, are they not likely to be all the more frustrated when their ideas and their bids for power are rejected?

I do not think Brandeis wanted hopeful, vital, imaginative dissidents because he thought they could be mollified by civil liberties. Rather, he believed that in a political community personal qualities such as hope and imagination tend to be contagious and reciprocal. If the marginal, powerless members of the community retain some semblance of spirit, the mainstream is more likely to sustain its own vitality. And when dissidents become gripped by fear and hate, so too does the majority. The phrase "repression breeds hate" can be read as a double entendre: it is not just the hate experienced by the dissidents that concerns Brandeis, but also the hate that is felt by those who possess the power to punish dissent. The passage is not primarily about consequences or tactics; it is about character.

> *Believing in the power of reason as applied through public discussion, they eschewed silence coerced by law—the argument of force in its worst form.*

This sentence, more than any other in the *Whitney* opinion, has led many to view Brandeis's argument as dated. Perhaps an Enlightenment figure such as Jefferson could believe in the power of reason. Perhaps a Progressive like Brandeis could. But how often today do we hear experienced, observant people proclaim their faith in the power of reason?

There can be little doubt that Brandeis was sincere in asserting that power, not just wisdom or happiness, attaches to reasoning capacity. In his own life he had parlayed his extraordinary facility at reasoning into a considerable amount of personal power. He had used that power and drawn on that reasoning facility to help many people. It would be a mistake, however, to read into this passage the naive claim—naive in 1927 as well as today—that reason will almost always triumph, at least in the long run. I do not detect in Brandeis's language the echo of Milton's famous rhetorical question: "Who ever knew truth put to the worse in a free and open encounter?" From personal experience, Brandeis knew plenty about vested interests, market distortions, and the siren songs of demagogues.

It is essential to read the sentence as a whole. His belief in the power of reason should be seen as a commitment inspired by his emphatic distaste for the alternative: "silence coerced by law—the argument of force in its worst form." How much power reason really exerts is an enduring and intriguing question. I agree with Robert Cover's conclusion that Brandeis did not resolve this question for himself by disinterested observation and reflection.[78] He resolved the question by saying, in effect, that we simply *have* to believe in the power of reason in order to preserve a system of government in which the coercive power of the state does not swamp the individual. If we abandon the faith that reason matters, we are left with a society governed exclusively by force. The First Amendment is meant to serve as a counterweight, Brandeis seems to say, to the natural tendency of all citizens, those in the majority as well as those in the minority, to lose confidence in reason and pursue their goals through force.

The importance of confidence is a theme that permeates the succeeding paragraphs of the opinion:

> *Fear of serious injury cannot alone justify the suppression of free speech and assembly. Men feared witches and burnt women. It is the function of speech to free men from the bondage of irrational fears. . . .*
>
> *Those who won our independence by revolution were not cowards. They did not fear political change. They did not exalt order at the cost of liberty.*

78. *See* COVER, *supra* note 74, at 387–88.

Brandeis presents his stringent standard for regulating speech as appropriate for a nation of "courageous, self-reliant men, with confidence in the power of free and fearless reasoning...." These resonant sentences add up to a celebration of the virtue of courage. They are in tune with the conclusion that emerges from a close, contextual reading of the earlier paragraph: Brandeis valued a strong doctrine of free speech largely for its contribution to the character of the political community, particularly the character of those who possess the power to regulate.

Why was he so concerned with character? Why was he convinced that courage is the paramount virtue in a democracy? In her excellent biography of Brandeis, Philippa Strum suggests an answer. She describes the intensive reading program Brandeis undertook during the summer of 1914 after the leaders of the Zionist movement had recruited him to their cause. She lists the several books on Judaism that he read, but notes:

> The most important book Brandeis read, and one he quoted throughout his life and made certain that all the members of his extended family read, was not about Zionism: it was Alfred Zimmern's *The Greek Commonwealth*....
>
> Zimmern's political views paralleled those of Brandeis, and the idea of the Greek city-state matched the possibilities of Palestine. Zimmern may have been the catalyst for the ideas already circulating in Brandeis's mind, or he may have offered Brandeis a new way of looking at Zionism. Whatever the case, the book was one of the few that Brandeis considered central to his life....[79]

Strum reports that Brandeis was so impressed by the book that he arranged for Professor Zimmern to accompany him a few years later on a trip to the Middle East. She continues:

> In order to understand the importance of Zimmern for Brandeis, one must first appreciate the high esteem in which Brandeis held the Greeks of fifth-century Athens. The highest tribute that Brandeis could give his uncle Dembitz was that "he reminded one of the Athenians." Brandeis also compared the Founding Fathers to the Athenians in his most eloquent defense of free speech ..., [his opinion] in *Whitney v. California*. He wrote, in part, "They believed liberty to be the secret of happiness and courage to be the secret of liberty." Paul Freund, who was first Brandeis's law clerk and then his lifelong friend, has identified the sentence as coming from Pericles's "Funeral Oration." Zimmern shared Brandeis's high regard for the "Funeral Oration"; the premise of his book is that the oration reflects the greatest heights ever reached by democracy.

79. PHILIPPA STRUM, LOUIS D. BRANDEIS: JUSTICE FOR THE PEOPLE 237 (1984). On the importance of Zimmern's book to Brandeis, *see also* DEAN ACHESON, MORNING AND NOON 50 (1965) ("[T]wo interacting themes seem to have dominated [Brandeis's] talk—the Greek Genius ... and the curse of Bigness."); Paul A. Freund, *Mr. Justice Brandeis: A Centennial Memoir,* 70 HARV. L. REV. 769, 789–90 (1957) (Zimmern's *The Greek Commonwealth* "was the book most likely to be recommended by Brandeis to friends in his later years.").

Professor Strum offers further evidence of where Brandeis acquired his regard for the virtues of courage and civic commitment:

> Other indications of Brandeis's interest in ancient Greece include the comment of the reporter who followed Brandeis around for two days in 1916 and wrote wryly, "Euripides, I now judge, after having interviewed Brandeis on many subjects, said the last word on most of them." Jacob de Haas noted, "Greek and Roman history are as clear to him as though they were part of the morning's news." His favorite and most often quoted poem was from Euripides' The Bacchae; he clearly felt it expressed his view of citizenship and public service. In short, to discover how the model political human being would function in the model political society, Brandeis turned to the Athenians.

To Brandeis, as to Jefferson whom he studied and admired, the project of democratic governance depends on nothing so much as the vitality, the daring, the inventiveness, the steadfastness of individual citizens. It is revealing that among the many books on ancient Greece that Brandeis read, the one that had the most profound effect on him was that by Alfred Zimmern. This is a book about government that has as its centerpiece not the discourses of Plato and Aristotle, not the tragedies of Aeschylus and Sophocles, but the Funeral Oration of Pericles, as rendered by Thucydides.

The Funeral Oration enumerates the virtues of Athenian citizens that account for the greatness of the city. The character traits mentioned by Pericles have a noteworthy emphasis when viewed in the context of the virtues one commonly associates with the literature and political philosophy of classical Greece. In the Funeral Oration there is little talk of discipline, balance, obedience, acceptance of role, respect for the gods, subordination of self, avoidance of pride, or search for the mean. There is instead talk of "free liberality," "exceptional versatility," and "adventurous spirit." If Pericles can be said to have a dominant theme, it is that Athenian citizens achieve so much for their city-state because their civic commitment is not coerced but rather flows freely out of the vital and variegated quality of life the city makes possible. In pointed contrast to other city-states, says Pericles, "we do not think that there is an incompatibility between words and deeds...." To the contrary, Athenian civic courage depends on the cultivation of intellectual independence:

> Others are brave out of ignorance; and, when they stop to think, they begin to fear. But the man who can most truly be accounted brave is he who best knows the meaning of what is sweet in life and what is terrible, and then goes out undeterred to meet what is to come.

Perhaps the passage from Thucydides that best captures what Brandeis esteemed in the Athenians comes not from the Funeral Oration but from a speech of the Corinthians warning the Spartans "what sort of people these Athenians are against whom you will have to fight."

> An Athenian is always an innovator, quick to form a resolution and quick at carrying it out. You, on the other hand, are good at keeping things as they are; you never originate an idea, and your action tends to stop short of its aim. Then again, Athenian daring will outrun its own resources; they will take risks against their better judgment, and still, in the midst of danger, remain confident. But your nature is always to do less than you could have done, to mistrust your own judgment, however sound it may be, and to assume that dangers will last forever.

It is this quality of initiative—the willingness to take chances, to persist against the odds, to embark on novel ventures in the face of scorn and risk, to commit oneself—that provides the essential connection between Brandeis's regard for Athenian democracy and his emphasis in the *Whitney* opinion on the virtue of civic courage.

The importance Brandeis attached to initiative can hardly be overstated. During his career as a progressive reformer he devised and fought to implement a remarkable number of creative solutions to seemingly entrenched problems. One of his favorite essays was "Self-Reliance" by Ralph Waldo Emerson, which consists largely of a plea for individual initiative. The political creed for which Brandeis is best known is well encapsulated by the title of one of his books, *The Curse of Bigness.* All his life he railed against and resisted the modern trend toward larger units of business and governmental organization. His major concern was that bureaucracy breeds caution and stifles initiative. It is no wonder he found special meaning in those writings that emphasize the innovative quality of Athenian civic life.

Read against this background, two sentences of the *Whitney* opinion emerge as particularly important: "Those who won our independence by revolution were not cowards. They did not fear political change." To Brandeis, the measure of courage in the civic realm is the capacity to experience change—even rapid and fundamental change—without losing perspective or confidence. Assessments of the benefits and risks of unregulated discussion are certain to be affected by what general disposition the decisionmaker has toward the phenomenon of change. The courageous attitude, Brandeis asserts, is that of receptivity to new arrangements and new ways of thinking. Progress, the value literally at the root of the Progressive philosophy, depends on receptivity to change. And while speech no doubt contributes directly to change by ventilating grievances and reform proposals, the freedom of speech may be most valuable for its indirect effect, profound even if subtle, on societal attitudes toward change. Those attitudes largely determine how the political community responds to the grievances and reforms that are brought to public attention. Not just judges but all of us need to be emancipated from "the bondage of irrational fears" as we encounter unsettling proposals for change. The essence of Brandeis's ideal of civic courage is a healthy mentality regarding change. The character conducive to the maintenance of that mentality is what he considered the principal benefit of a robust freedom of speech.

WHAT ABOUT NOW?

It may seem that the eloquence and brilliance of Milton and Brandeis can only be dishonored by a mundane attempt to elaborate their ideas in systematic form and contemporary argot. That, however, is the task I undertake. I hope to demonstrate that their insights about character constitute a resource to be exploited in resolving the First Amendment disputes of today.

What then are the character traits that, in light of contemporary conditions, we might believe are especially valuable and likely to be promoted by according free speech an extremely high priority? From our study of Milton and Brandeis, several traits come to mind: inquisitiveness, independence of judgment, distrust of authority, willingness to take initiative, perseverance, courage to confront evil, aversion to simplistic accounts and solutions, capacity to act on one's convictions even in the face of doubt and criticism, self-awareness, imagination, intellectual and cultural empathy, resilience, temperamental receptivity to change, tendency to view problems and events in a broad perspective, and respect for evidence. This is a long list, yet still incomplete. Nevertheless, the character profile it generates is anything but vacuous, and certainly not to be taken for granted.

But how is character affected by a constitutional commitment? Is the key what such a commitment says, or what it does? The passions evoked by constitutional controversies often have a lot to do with what the disputants take to be the symbolic stakes. To understand the impact of a vital First Amendment culture, however, we do better to focus on material considerations. A legal system influences character not so much by preaching or teaching tolerance as by exerting coercive authority to protect dissenters.[98] The resulting environment, in which dissent is both an option and an inescapable reality, is the principal source of the effect upon character, or so I maintain. It would be wrong to discount entirely the prospect of hortatory influence, but the environmental impact of free speech deserves the greater emphasis.

The most important environmental consequence of protecting free speech is the intellectual and moral pluralism, and thus disorder in a

98. In this respect, among others, the argument advanced here differs from the most important recent effort to integrate a concern about character into First Amendment analysis, that developed by Lee Bollinger. *See* LEE C. BOLLINGER, THE TOLERANT SOCIETY (1986). Bollinger's argument is limited to one crucial character trait, the capacity to control the intolerance one necessarily must feel toward persons whose speech or conduct manifests beliefs that threaten individual or community identity. Bollinger views the protection of free speech as a commitment that can teach us how to understand and manage this pervasive, natural, morally worthy (in proportion) but often overflowing and self-destructive impulse. The character traits that I believe are nurtured by a free-speech culture are numerous and various, extending far beyond the capacity to control the impulse to intolerance. Those traits are nurtured, moreover, primarily by the experience of living in a vibrant, dynamic, contentious society rather than by the pedagogic contribution of a legal norm of toleration. Despite these differences, the debt my treatment of the subject owes to Bollinger's pathbreaking resurrection of the concern about character is considerable.

sense, thereby engendered. In matters of belief, conventional structures of authority are weakened, rebellion is facilitated, closure is impaired. Persons who live in a free-speech regime are forced to cope with persistent, and frequently intractable, differences of understanding. For most of us that is a painful challenge, at least in the realms that matter to us most. Being made to take account of such differences shapes our character.

For example, a person who cannot ignore the existence of understandings antithetical to her own must find some way to come to terms with her views. Such a coming to terms can take a variety of forms: blindly digging in, angry denigration of persons with different notions, self-doubt, a deepening of conviction and enhanced awareness of the grounds for one's beliefs, curiosity about the sources of disagreement, confusion, a redoubling of proselytizing zeal, or a grudging and gradual weakening of certitude that may lead eventually to a change of mind. Faced with perdurable difference, many persons will run a gamut of responses over time. What is less likely to ensue the more difference is salient is complacency about one's beliefs and the stasis that complacency engenders. Simply by energizing the experience of belief formation, a free-speech regime's legitimation of difference can nurture many of the positive character traits outlined above.

In addition to forcing persons to confront their differences of understanding, free speech influences character by altering the complex process by which authority is constituted. Few if any of us can do without authority. By requiring us to do without *inherited* authority, *unquestioned* authority, *unaccountable* authority, *unitary* authority, a free-speech regime creates a salutary void. We fill that void by creating other authoritative structures in our lives, ranging from institutions founded on collective (and revocable) consent, to social norms enforced by social sanctions, to precommitments and other sources of self-discipline. Perhaps one could label this process the exercise of autonomy, but it matters, in terms of the instrumental function of character, that the emphasis is on the role of choice in the creation of authority rather than the experience of choice as an essential attribute of personhood. Collectively and individually, we are different people, more capable of certain initiatives and sacrifices, for having helped to determine the authorities that constrain and guide us.

A third way that a free-speech regime helps to mold character is by emboldening persons for whom orthodox understandings do not ring true. In most societies, even those that celebrate free speech, despair is the common lot of the dissenter. No doubt it can be intoxicating to act out differences: rebellion has intelligible psychological roots and a whiff of romance as well. That should not obscure the point that for most of us, most of the time, it is a discomforting and often threatening experience to be out on a limb. Despite the real satisfactions of forbidden inquiry and unvarnished self-expression, the path of pleasure more frequently lies in the direction of going along. Despite the widespread perception that in modern society too many people flaunt and exaggerate their differences, the more common response still is to bury them. In many circumstances that is surely the socially desirable outcome; it is hard to imagine a functional society that was not replete with reticence and trimming. Precisely because the burying of differences is such a pervasive and necessary practice, however, the capacity to pursue differences when occasion demands serves a most important social function.

A culture that protects and celebrates free speech can help to nurture that capacity in several ways. The legitimation of dissent can reduce the degree to which persons with unorthodox ideas are viewed as deserving of ostracism or retaliation. Also, rallies, meetings, and publications can inform dissenters that they are not so isolated, not so far on the margin, as they might have assumed. Facilitating various experiences of solidarity is one of the most consequential, because most energizing, functions of a free-speech regime. In addition, the spectacle of some persons standing up to authority or convention or corruption or evil or mediocrity can enhance in others the sense of duty to take enough responsibility for their convictions to act on them.

Finally, a regime of free speech can help to develop character by requiring those who would beat back bad ideas and contain evil demagogues to pursue those worthy objectives in the most arduous, and thereby most enduring, way: engagement rather than prohibition. The claim here is not that truth and justice will always prevail in a fair marketplace of ideas. We will never have such a marketplace, and truth and justice would not always prevail even if we did. Rather, the notion is that the *experience* of confronting falsehood and evil profoundly shapes the character of a person or a society, and that such an experience is short-circuited by censorship. In this view, the most dangerous ideas can only be defeated by strong persons, not by repressive laws. The two are not, of course, mutually exclusive, but the disturbing tendency, illustrated by our recent efforts to control racism on college campuses, is to think the day's work is done when the self-congratulatory code is enacted. The passage of laws too often has the quality of a moral shortcut, and too often diverts what could be honest, if stressful, exchanges that might actually affect beliefs into shallow forensic contests over legal coverage. In denying the moral shortcut, a free-speech regime strengthens the character of its citizens.

These are some of the ways that the protection of free speech can promote certain character traits under contemporary conditions. We must next inquire why the flourishing of those character traits might be thought to serve collective well-being.

One benefit of free speech is its contribution to a system of checks and balances. Broadly conceived, such a system includes not only the efforts of different branches of the same government to keep each other in line, but also intergovernmental checks on the abuse of authority in a federal system (states checking the federal government and vice versa) and checking by private citizens via elections and less formal manifestations of public sentiment. To do their work, all the various checking agents depend on information concerning what the potential abusers of authority are doing. Often such checking agents rely heavily on the power of communication to mobilize resistance to any discovered abuses. In this regard, the freedom of speech is a mechanism that facilitates the system of checks and balances.

That is not my concern here. Particularly for a process that entails opposition to abuses by powerful actors, mechanisms and procedures cannot be efficacious if the persons who must employ them lack certain demanding personal qualities. Independence of mind is one of those qualities because abuses usually can be rationalized, excused, or ignored by observers who are temperamentally inclined not to question their inertia-driven perceptions of regularity and good faith. For the same reason, general distrust of authority is a functional attitude in this sphere. Another character trait of particular significance for the checking process is perseverance. Miscreant officials seldom go quietly once their transgressions are brought to light. Checking is work for persons who can endure counterattacks and speak truth to power not once or twice but like a broken record. By the same token, a populace accustomed to judging on grounds of evidence and argument rather than preconception or loyalty is more likely to heed the whistleblower, as is a populace not easily discouraged by complexity or delay. To the extent that the experience of living in a contentious, unruly free-speech culture nurtures these traits, the First Amendment has instrumental value for the checking process quite apart from the mechanisms of communication it provides.

Character serves collective well-being in many ways other than by helping to control abuses of power. One is by facilitating compromise. Institutions ranging from marriages to democratic governments flourish or fail depending on how skillful participants are at the difficult art of compromise. To a large degree, the capacity to compromise depends on character. A free-speech culture can help to foster some of the attitudes, skills, and even norms that successful compromise requires. This is important because when persons negotiate their differences poorly, becoming in the event manipulative or resentful or disengaged, collective well-being is not advanced. In addition to the costly side effects of such attitudes, compromises struck in their shadow are likely to be unstable.

Persons who live in a society suffused with conflicting opinions ought on that account to be more skillful at compromise. No doubt overheated rhetoric can fuel resentments and foster political greed, but not so much, I would argue, as censorship can with the fantasies of purification and domination it encourages. Frustration with the blind, stubborn resistance of those who refuse to see matters our way will always be a major source of human unhappiness. The more that frustration is chronic, endemic to the very texture of social life, the better chance we have of learning to function in the face of it.

Free speech engenders fears but also hopes, and compromise is built on hopes. It is easier to stay engaged, to find value in that half a loaf, if tomorrow may bring change for the better. Similarly, the capacity to compromise frequently depends on the self-confidence and sense of perspective of those who are asked to settle for less. Persons whose identities have been forged by experiences of doubt, challenge, and choice are more likely to possess the self-awareness and perspective that compromise demands.

Probably the single most important way that free speech serves collective well-being is by helping persons and institutions adapt to a changing world. As with checking, adaptation depends on mechanisms of communication but even more on the character of the populace. And as various forces such as technological advances and demographic developments cause the pace of change to accelerate, this process of adaptation looms larger and larger as an ingredient of well-being.

Adaptation begins with awareness. When prevailing ideas and arrangements cease to work well in an altered environment, the common tendency is to ignore or minimize the phenomenon. A society that encourages questioning, auditing, experimenting, and revising is more likely to notice problems generated by changing conditions.

At least as crucial to the process of adaptation is a temperamental receptivity to change. A free-speech culture weakens attachments to existing patterns by ventilating alternatives and increasing public awareness of changes that are already afoot. The sheer proliferation of perspectives in play all but forces individuals caught in the maelstrom to adopt a dynamic frame of reference.

Awareness of change, even receptivity to it, does not necessarily engender productive adaptation, however. Good judgment is required for a person or institution to determine how to thrive in uncharted terrain. Heavy reliance on tradition or authority is maladaptive in a rapidly changing environment. What is needed is perceptiveness, boldness, independence of mind, the willingness to experiment, flexibility—in short the capacity to make choices. Passivity and avoidance are the vices to be feared.

Whatever else the freedom of speech does or does not do, it asks its practitioners, speakers and listeners alike, continuously to choose: what to say, how to say it, whom to address, which speakers and messages to hear, what to believe. The more experienced persons are at making choices of this sort, the better their choices ought to be.

Unless, of course, too much choosing leads to decisional anomie. Successful adaptation requires not just the willingness to choose but the discipline to care about the wisdom of one's choices. Critics of what they take to be the ascendant consumerist culture of ideas worry that the celebration of free speech ends up being a celebration of destructively casual attitudes toward knowledge and belief. Surely there is something to this critique. Persons who feel overwhelmed by the choices with which they are confronted cannot be expected to stay engaged and retain perspective. Under such conditions, impulses will reign and adaptation will suffer.

The crucial question is whether a strong constitutional commitment to free speech fosters or forestalls this dangerous phenomenon of disorientation in the face of choice. Were it possible effectively to shield persons from the riot of choices produced by the conditions of modern life, were it possible to legislate simplicity and stability, we might well conclude that censorship is the cure for disorientation. But such shielding is *not* possible, at least not in a political community as large, demographically diverse and mobile, and economically dynamic as the present-day United States. The complexity of the choices we face transcends any particular policy regarding free speech. And if we cannot help but choose, far better that we be shielded from susceptibility to simplistic perceptions and expectations. Although demagogues enabled by toleration can and do peddle simpleminded nostrums, the net effect of a robust free-speech tradition, I submit, is to make audiences more familiar and comfortable with complexity and thereby more skeptical of such nostrums. To the extent that is true, the supremely important objective of productive adaptation is served.

In addition to receptivity to change and good judgment regarding how to cope with it, an adaptive society needs creative ideas. Admittedly, the wellsprings of creativity are elusive; geniuses certainly have emerged in repressive regimes. Nevertheless, by tolerating unorthodox opinions and inquiries a community encourages creativity, both by valuing it and by enabling creative persons to achieve visibility and interact. A free-speech tradition appears to matter especially at what might be termed the second level of original thought, not that of rare geniuses with gifts and wills so profound as to overwhelm their environments, but among the foot soldiers of creative adaptation, the persons who diagnose and tinker and test and guess and implement. Such persons shape a culture and are in turn shaped by it. A vibrant culture of ideas can nurture the talents of such persons.

Checking, compromise, and adaptation are collective endeavors that contribute to well-being across a wide spectrum of political arrangements. When sovereignty resides in the people, however, as in a representative democracy, additional capacities that can be developed and sustained by free speech assume special importance. Among the most significant are the willingness of ordinary citizens to participate in collective projects, to assume some measure of responsibility for social outcomes, and more generally to maintain collective energy, resilience, and aspiration.

One way that a free-speech tradition fosters such capacities is by instituting an ethic of distrust and critique of all institutions, not least of government. Critique presupposes responsibility and concern. An effective critic participates in civic life and provokes others to do so. A high level of accountability can energize both the sources and the targets of critical scrutiny.

As with adaptation, however, the social psychology of civic participation is complicated, contestable, and resistant to meaningful empirical verification. Promiscuous distrust and critique could lead to cynical disengagement from collective endeavors, the postmodern equivalent of medieval quietism. Why should we believe that pervasive and telling criticism of established institutions engenders more engagement than withdrawal? It is those very institutions, after all, that serve for most persons as the predominant forums for civic participation. Loyalty to and trust in civic institutions may provide a necessary foundation for personal commitment.

Given our current point in the cycles of the public mood, we naturally tend to associate free speech with rampant negativism, if not nihilism. And surely in any age disenchantment is one of the consequences of the unremitting scrutiny of institutions. But systematic critique carries also an implicit message of hope: hope that standards of performance continue to obtain, hope that reform is possible. Otherwise, why bother? Institutions, like persons, are respected more when much is demanded of them than when they are indulged or ignored, and that holds true even when the demands are in some sense unreasonable. Moreover, the very act of participating in the practice of institutional critique, if only as a listener, connects the ordinary citizen with the collective endeavors that constitute public life. That connection is both contingent and crucial to individual and collective well-being. Loyalty and trust, the preconditions for civic engagement, flow more from connectedness than innocence.

Connectedness, responsibility, hope—these are vital ingredients of civic participation that a commitment to free speech can help sustain. At least as important to the maintenance of political energy are two virtues that typically do not receive the emphasis they deserve: perseverance and resilience. To bring about reforms, almost always it is necessary to keep knocking on the door, over and over again, refusing to take no for an answer. To preserve hard-won gains, almost always it is necessary to ride out storms of defeated expectations and consequent disillusionment. Staying power is the linchpin of efficacious civic participation. This is all the more true in a culture buffeted by multifarious forces that serve to shorten the individual and institutional attention span.

The relationship between free speech and the civic virtues of perseverance and resilience is as difficult to pin down as it is significant. On the one hand, we might fear that too much free thinking and toleration contributes to the erosion of shared standards of judgment. If so, the capacity to stay committed may be adversely affected. Citizens fighting only for their "preferences" may not be as fiercely determined and thereby as capable of enduring the slings and arrows of outrageous resistance as persons whose civic participation is motivated by notions of honor, fundamental justice, or divinely ordained (or natural) entitlement. In this view, free speech complicates perceptions, complexity sows the seeds of doubt, and doubt weakens the will, all to the detriment of staying power.

On the other hand, one might believe, as I do, that naivete is the most important characteristic of quitters. Persons who have scant experience negotiating ideological and cultural differences, who manage to insulate themselves from all but kindred spirits, are the civic actors most likely to harbor unrealistic expectations and to wilt when those expectations are defeated. In this view, perseverance flows from experience and perspective. Whatever its relationship to autonomy, truth-seeking, or fair representation, a free-speech tradition cannot help but broaden horizons and reduce naivete. If perseverance and resilience are as integral to civic well-being as I think they are, that effect should count heavily in any assessment of the benefits of free expression.

So far I have concentrated on the affirmative side of the equation. I have examined the various ways that the protection of free speech can serve collective well-being via characterological effects. A skeptic could grant the claims I have put forward in this regard and still conclude that, on balance, a robust free-speech principle disserves collective well-being precisely because of its impact on character. For a culture of free speech may be thought to foster self-indulgence and excess. The capacity to define and enforce limits is a major element of well-being, at the societal level no less than the personal. Even when free speech promotes checking, compromise, adaptation, and engagement in the ways specified above, the individual traits that help to generate those social benefits may simultaneously undercut the project of setting limits. In nurturing such traits as exuberance, independence, and savvy, free speech sharpens a double-edged sword.

Must freedom cause its practitioners to devalue and defy bounds? The assertedly natural progression from liberty to license has always figured prominently in the rhetoric of opposition to free speech. Thoughtful proponents of toleration concede the point. "Some degree of abuse is inseparable from the proper use of everything," said Madison in what is the foundational essay on the meaning of the First Amendment, "and in no instance is this more true than in that of the press."[99] Madison thought such abuses were a price worth paying, but his observations regarding the wisdom of enduring inevitable excesses were not directed specifically to effects on character. Licentiousness might be considered especially subversive when character is the concern.

Consider, for example, the Supreme Court's much heralded decision in *New York Times v. Sullivan.*[100] To encourage vigorous criticism of government and thwart efforts by the targets of such criticism to use libel law to achieve political objectives, the Court construed the First Amendment to permit recovery by a public official only upon proof that his critic published the offending statement with knowledge of its falsity or reckless disregard for the truth. Perhaps, although there is much dispute about this, the balance struck by the Court can be justified by a

99. James Madison, *Report on the Virginia Resolutions Concerning the Alien and Sedition Laws, in* The Mind of the Founder 299, 332 (Marvin Meyers ed., 1958).

100. 376 U.S. 254 (1964).

utilitarian calculation regarding which stories critical of officials ought to reach the public and which injuries caused thereby warrant legal redress. But the *Sullivan* doctrine does more than strike a balance in these terms: it nurtures a journalistic ethic. Factual inaccuracy is excused and thereby destigmatized; holding a story for further sourcing is discouraged. What is glorified by the Court is "uninhibited, robust, and wide-open" reporting. Over time, we might fear, the immunity from liability established by *Sullivan* will adversely affect the character of journalists, weakening their resolve to get the details of a story right. In this environment, even the consumers of critical stories about public officials might come to care less whether an exposé is strictly accurate in its particulars.

The dilemma is apparent. We do need energetic, irreverent, adroit reporters who are not seduced by the trappings of office or cowed by the threat of a lawsuit. But we also need reporters who cherish the truth and appreciate their own fallibility in finding it—reporters, that is, who understand limits. In fostering journalistic aggressiveness and independence, does *Sullivan* exact too high a price in the currency of limits? The same question could be asked about a host of other icons in the First Amendment pantheon, for example Justice Harlan's magnanimous opinion for the Court in *Cohen v. California*,[101] establishing the right to employ profane words in public settings.

As occurs at other junctures in the case for toleration, judgment on this point depends heavily on one's faith (or lack of it) in corrective dynamics. In my experience, among engaged people excesses beget reactions. The spectacle of a person or cause or profession losing all sense of balance and decency tends to bring home to others the need to reinvigorate the moral and social order, not least by attending to the character demands of that order. There are ways to deal with overzealous reporting and breaches of public decorum other than by invoking the heavy, slow-moving, clumsy artillery of the law. Informal, nonofficial sanctions and judgments, Milton recognized, will always provide the most important "bonds and ligaments" that hold a society together. Reporters who take liberties with the truth will be corrected far more by demanding editors and readers than by libel judgments. Protesters who assault the sensibilities of the public will be reigned in when their tactics cause audiences to recoil and their opponents to succeed in discrediting them. Such informal limits are a function of social vitality. They depend on dimensions of character that are blunted in repressive regimes.

It might be argued that the forces of nonofficial correction gain vitality from regulatory backup. Newspaper editors, for example, could be inspired to develop rigorous internal standards for fact-checking if losing a libel suit were a more common experience. In theory, there is no reason why the legal and informal limits on speech cannot be synergetic. In operation, however, that phenomenon is more likely to be the exception than the rule. The content of laws regulating speech cannot help but

101. 403 U.S. 15 (1971).

be affected, in the direction of weakening the scope and strength of the limits imposed, by some severe institutional constraints: the risk of ideological bias by judges, juries, and law enforcement officials; the peculiar difficulty of describing instances of communication in the categories of legal language; the contingencies that thwart the effort to predict or measure the consequences of particular acts of expression. Because of those constraints, legal sanctions can do only a small fraction of the work of setting limits. The informal sanctions on speech need to be much more substantial, pervasive, finely calibrated, and subtle than their formal counterparts could ever be. In this regard, the watered-down limits imposed by the institutionally constrained legal regime can actually impair the development of informal limits by establishing either a low benchmark or a false perception that meaningful limits are already in place. As a rule, the most effective limits on speech originate and derive their sustenance from sources other than formal laws.

In part this is so because the limits must themselves be dynamic and adaptive. The forces of excess do not follow set patterns. The transgressions of investigative reporters assume new forms as technological capacities expand, competitive pressures intensify, and audiences change. The advent of cyber-space necessitates the construction of a wholly new type of public decorum. The accelerating commercialization of American life, not excluding the life of the mind, raises issues of limits we have barely begun to address. Limits are not fixed essences to be found and enforced. They are ongoing judgments, made in response to the novel mix of threats, needs and aspirations of a particular time and place. If a free-speech tradition does indeed help citizens to confront problems, retain perspective, and exercise judgment in a changing environment, in no project are those skills more valuable than that of enforcing the tacit, uncodified standards of behavior that make for a resilient social order.

In the last analysis, behind this concern about limits lies the primordial fear of anarchy. It would be foolish to underestimate the role this fear has played—and continues to play—in disputes over free speech. No one with even a passing acquaintance with Hobbes can dismiss the threat of anarchy out of hand, or cabin it in the seventeenth century. The veneer of civilization may be just that.

Anarchy can flow from self-indulgence or zeal but so too can it flow from the failure to check, or compromise, or adapt, or take responsibility for social outcomes, or confront evil. What provoked countless persons over the centuries to fight and sometimes die for the principle of freedom of speech was, more often than not, a particular form of disorder, something we might with Locke call anarchy: the unrestrained use of the coercive apparatus of the state to stamp out difference and hold on to power. The limits that keep in check the anarchic impulse to wreak vengeance on persons who challenge the reigning orthodoxy are among the essential "bonds and ligaments" of a civilized society. Those limits depend on constitutional structures but even more on strength of character.

"[T]he greatest menace to freedom," said Brandeis, "is an inert people."[105] He added, echoing Milton,[106] that such a people is also the greatest menace to order.[107] That is why, for all its costs and excesses, free speech, the archenemy of inertia, is so important.

Questions

1) In a liberal democracy is it the legitimate business of the state to promote good character? Is it more appropriate—or less dangerous—for "the state" to promote good character by recognizing the individual right to free speech as a constitutional matter than by enforcing morals by means of legal sanctions?

2) Who among Madison, Mill, Hand, Holmes, and Meiklejohn comes closest to making an argument from character?

ROBERT POST, RECONCILING THEORY AND DOCTRINE IN FIRST AMENDMENT JURISPRUDENCE

88 Calif. L. Rev. 2353 (2000).

INTRODUCTION

The simple and absolute words of the First Amendment float atop a tumultuous doctrinal sea. The free-speech jurisprudence of the First Amendment is notorious for its flagrantly proliferating and contradictory rules, its profoundly chaotic collection of methods and theories. Yet, strange to say, those fluent in the law of free speech can predict with reasonable accuracy the outcomes of most constitutional cases. It seems that what is amiss with First Amendment doctrine is not so much the absence of common ground about how communication within our society ought constitutionally to be ordered, as our inability to formulate clear explanations and coherent rules capable of elucidating and charting the contours of this ground.

First Amendment doctrine veers between theory and the exigencies of specific cases. The function of doctrine is both to implement the objectives attributed by theory to the Constitution and to offer principled grounds of justification for particular decisions. Doctrine becomes confused when the requirements of theory make little sense in the actual circumstances of concrete cases, or when doctrine is required to articu-

105. *See* Whitney v. California, 274 U.S. 357, 375 (1927) (Brandeis, J., concurring).

106. *See* MILTON, *supra* note 2, at 742:

> There be who perpetually complain of schisms and sects, and make it such a calamity that any man dissents from their maxims. It is their own pride and ignorance which causes the disturbing, who neither will hear with meekness nor can convince, yet all must be suppressed which is not found in their syntagma. They are the troublers, they are the dividers of unity, who neglect and permit not others to unite those disservered pieces which are yet wanting to the body of Truth.

107. 274 U.S. at 375: "[I]t is hazardous to discourage thought, hope and imagination.... [F]ear breeds repression ... repression breeds hate ... hate menaces stable government...."

late the implications of inconsistent theories. First Amendment doctrine has unfortunately suffered from both these difficulties.

In a remarkable series of opinions in 1919, Justice Oliver Wendell Holmes virtually invented both First Amendment theory and First Amendment doctrine. He advanced the theory of the marketplace of ideas, and he demonstrated how doctrine would have to evolve to implement this new theory. But soon thereafter the Court articulated a competing and in some respects inconsistent theory, which focused on the practice of democratic self-government. In this essay I examine each of these two theories of the First Amendment to illustrate the complex ways in which theory, doctrine, and common sense interact in First Amendment jurisprudence. My objective is to explore the sources of the current disarray of First Amendment doctrine and to assess the kinds of clarification that we may reasonably anticipate from an analytically rigorous First Amendment jurisprudence.

* * *

The First Amendment and the Marketplace of Ideas

The theory of the marketplace of ideas focuses on "the truth-seeking function" of the First Amendment. It extends the shelter of constitutional protection to speech so that we can better understand the world in which we live. It would follow from the theory, therefore, that at a minimum the Constitution ought to be concerned with all communication conveying ideas relevant to our understanding the world, whether or not these ideas are political in nature. This does not mean, of course, that the Constitution would prohibit all regulation of such communication. But it does imply that regulation of such communication ought to be evaluated according to the constitutional standards of the theory.

This is in fact the way that contemporary First Amendment doctrine defines the range of communication that triggers First Amendment scrutiny. The so-called *Spence* test, for example, holds that the First Amendment will come "into play" whenever "an intent to convey a particularized message [is] present," and, given the context, "the likelihood [is] great that the message would be understood by those who viewed it."[35] This broad doctrinal rule uses the potential communication of ideas to define what will count as "speech" for purposes of the First Amendment. It thus crisply expresses the principle that the regulation of any communication capable of increasing understanding must be subjected to constitutional review.

While this principle follows more or less directly from the theory of the marketplace of ideas, it does not in fact correspond to the common sense of judges, as expressed in the resolution of actual cases. Much behavior that passes the *Spence* test because it successfully communicates a particularized message is not regarded as bringing the First

35. Texas v. Johnson, 491 U.S. 397, 403–4 (1989) (quoting Spence v. Washington, 418 U.S. 405, 410–11 (1974)).

Amendment into play. Such conduct ranges from terrorist bombings to written warnings on consumer products. It is not that regulation of this conduct is affirmatively permitted by the First Amendment; it is rather that courts do not even subject such regulation to First Amendment scrutiny. When measured by the actual shape of the law, therefore, it is immediately apparent that the *Spence* test, which defines speech in a manner that follows from the theory of the marketplace of ideas, simply cannot stand.

First Amendment jurisprudence is filled with analogous disparities between actual decisions and doctrinal rules that would appear to follow from the theory of the marketplace of ideas. For example, it is black-letter law that the First Amendment applies "the most exacting scrutiny to regulations that suppress, disadvantage, or impose differential burdens upon speech because of its content."[38] Such a rule would seem to express the requirement that the state remain neutral within the marketplace of ideas, for it is formulated in such a way as to apply not merely to political speech, but to the entire range of "speech" as defined by the *Spence* test. Yet content-based regulation of speech is routinely enforced without special constitutional scrutiny, as for example when lawyers or doctors are held liable in professional malpractice for the communication of irresponsible opinions. Or consider the black-letter rule that "[t]he First Amendment recognizes no such thing as a 'false' idea." This rule also seems to express a central value of the marketplace of ideas, and it is accordingly also said to apply generally to "speech," and not merely to political speech. Yet "false" ideas can be regulated not only in the context of professional malpractice, but also in the context of commercial speech, where speakers can be sanctioned if they communicate in ways that are "misleading."

There is thus a disturbingly large gap between the actual shape of our constitutional law and doctrinal rules that seem to express the theory of the marketplace of ideas. This gap suggests either that we do not believe in the theory of the marketplace of ideas, or that our doctrine has somehow misconstrued the actual implications of the theory. The latter alternative seems to me the more plausible. Although First Amendment doctrine presently understands "the truth-seeking function" of the marketplace of ideas to flow directly from the communicative properties of speech, in fact truth-seeking requires much more. It requires an important set of shared social practices: the capacity to listen and to engage in self-evaluation, as well as a commitment to the conventions of reason, which in turn entail aspirations toward objectivity, disinterest, civility, and mutual respect. Thus John Dewey once remarked that rational deliberation depends upon "the possibility of conducting disputes, controversies and conflicts as cooperative undertakings in which both parties learn by giving the other a chance to express itself," and that this cooperation is inconsistent with one party conquering another "by forceful suppression . . . a suppression which is none the

38. Turner Broadcasting Sys. v. FCC, 512 U.S. 622, 642 (1994).

less one of violence when it takes place by psychological means of ridicule, abuse, intimidation, instead of by overt imprisonment or in concentration camps."[42]

The social practices necessary for a marketplace of ideas to serve a truth-seeking function are perhaps most explicitly embodied in the culture of scholarship inculcated in universities and professional academic disciplines. Certainly this culture is what Charles Sanders Peirce had in mind when he advocated "the method of science" as a preferred avenue toward truth, a method that he explicitly contrasted with the "method of authority" which employs the "organized force" of the state to suppress "liberty of speech."[43] In this limited sense there is deep insight in the Court's often repeated observation that "[t]he college classroom with its surrounding environs is peculiarly the 'marketplace of ideas."[44] The augmentation of knowledge within professional academic disciplines does not flow merely from the fact that ideas are formally free from official censorship, but rather from the fact that this freedom is embedded within what John Stuart Mill once called a "real morality of public discussion." In the absence of such a morality, it is merely tautological to presume that truth is what most people come to believe after open discussion.

It is thus inaccurate to infer that the theory of the marketplace of ideas requires that the First Amendment protect all speech that communicates ideas. Instead, the theory requires the protection only of speech that communicates ideas and that is embedded in the kinds of social practices that produce truth. The Court's failure to offer doctrinal articulation of the social prerequisites of truth-seeking is a significant source of the gap between doctrinal rules attempting to embody the theory of the marketplace of ideas and the actual shape of our First Amendment law.

Society consists of myriad forms of social practices, and speech is constitutive of almost all of these practices. The number of these practices that can plausibly be rendered consistent with the truth-seeking function of a marketplace of ideas is relatively small. It makes no sense, for example, to locate a truth-seeking function in the speech between lawyers or doctors and their clients, or in the communication contained in product warning labels. Judges recognize this distinction; their common sense rebels against applying to such situations doctrinal rules based upon completely incompatible social presuppositions. That is why First Amendment doctrine differs from the actual shape of our law.

42. John Dewey, *Creative Democracy—The Task Before Us, reprinted in* CLASSIC AMERICAN PHILOSOPHERS 389, 393 (Max H. Fisch ed., 1951).

43. Charles S. Peirce, *The Fixation of Belief, in* VALUES IN A UNIVERSE OF CHANCE 91, 110–11 (Philip P. Wiener ed., 1958). It is likely that Holmes was exposed to this essay while he was a member of the Metaphysical Club at Harvard. See David S. Bogen, *The Free Speech Metamorphosis of Mr. Justice Holmes,* 11 HOFSTRA L. REV. 97, 120 (1982).

44. Healy v. James, 408 U.S. 169, 180 (1972).

To implement accurately the theory of the marketplace of ideas, therefore, doctrinal rules would have to confine the scope of their application to those domains of social life where the prerequisite forms of social organization for a functioning marketplace of ideas either were present or could constitutionally be conjured into existence. Exactly where the theory could appropriately be applied, of course, would be highly debatable, but I suspect that under any fair construction the scope of its application would be quite narrow.

The First Amendment and Democratic Self-Government

If the theory of the marketplace of ideas tends to efface the social practices by which it is in fact sustained, thereby inducing a free-floating image of pure communication, the democratic theory has not suffered any such liability. It has never been subject to the same mystification as has the marketplace of ideas. We instantly recognize self-government as a discrete and embodied social practice, and for this reason courts applying democratic theory have been clear that the First Amendment protects only speech pertinent to self-determination. Thus, for example, in the important early decision of *Thornhill v. Alabama*[48] the Court asserted that because freedom of speech was essential to "the maintenance of democratic institutions," it embraced "the liberty to discuss publicly and truthfully all matters of public concern" so that "members of society" could "cope with the exigencies of their period."

Democratic theory, however, has been subject to its own ambiguities. The constitutional meaning of self-government has proved intensely controversial. It is of course generally agreed that democracy subsists in the people governing themselves, but historically there have been two competing accounts of the practice of self-determination, each with different implications for First Amendment doctrine.

One account, associated with the work of Alexander Meiklejohn, views democracy as a process of "the voting of wise decisions."[50] The First Amendment is understood to protect the communicative processes necessary to disseminate the information and ideas required for citizens to vote in a fully informed and intelligent way. Meiklejohn analogizes democracy to a town meeting; the state is imagined as a moderator, regulating and abridging speech "as the doing of the business under actual conditions may require." For this reason "abusive" speech, or speech otherwise inconsistent with "responsible and regulated discussion," can and should be suppressed. From the Meiklejohnian perspective, "the point of ultimate interest is not the words of the speakers, but the minds of the hearers," so that the First Amendment is seen as safeguarding collective processes of decisionmaking rather than individual rights. Meiklejohn summarizes this theory in a much-quoted and influential aphorism: "What is essential is not that everyone shall speak, but that everything worth saying shall be said."

48. 310 U.S. 88 (1940).

50. Alexander Meiklejohn, Political Freedom: The Constitutional Power of the People 26 (1965).

The alternative account of democracy, which I shall call the "participatory" theory, does not locate self-governance in mechanisms of decisionmaking, but rather in the processes through which citizens come to identify a government as their own. According to this theory, democracy requires that citizens experience their state as an example of authentic self-determination. How such an experience can be sustained presents something of a puzzle, because citizens can expect to disagree with many of the specific actions of their government. The solution to this puzzle must be that citizens in a democracy experience their authorship of the state in ways that are anterior to the making of particular decisions. The participatory account postulates that it is a necessary precondition for this experience that a state be structured so as to subordinate its actions to public opinion, and that a state be constitutionally prohibited from preventing its citizens from participating in the communicative processes relevant to the formation of democratic public opinion.

If, following the usage of the Court, we term these communicative processes "public discourse," then the participatory approach views the function of the First Amendment to be the safeguarding of public discourse from regulations that are inconsistent with democratic legitimacy. State restrictions on public discourse can be inconsistent with democratic legitimacy in two distinct ways. To the extent that the state cuts off particular citizens from participation in public discourse, it *pro tanto* negates its claim to democratic legitimacy with respect to such citizens. To the extent that the state regulates public discourse so as to reflect the values and priorities of some vision of collective identity, it preempts the very democratic process by which collective identity is to be determined.

Although both the Meiklejohnian and participatory perspectives share the common problem of specifying which communication is necessary for self-government and hence worthy of constitutional protection, they differ in at least two fundamental respects. First, the Meiklejohnian approach interprets the First Amendment primarily as a shield against the "mutilation of the thinking process of the community," whereas the participatory approach understands the First Amendment instead as safeguarding the ability of individual citizens to participate in the formation of public opinion. The Meiklejohnian theory thus stresses the quality of public debate, whereas the participatory perspective emphasizes the autonomy of individual citizens.

Second, the Meiklejohnian perspective imagines the state within the arena of public discourse as occupying the position of a neutral moderator, capable of saving public discourse from "mutilation" by distinguishing between relevant and irrelevant speech, abusive and nonabusive speech, "high" and "low" value speech, and so forth. It specifically repudiates the notion that public discourse is "a Hyde Park," filled with "unregulated talkativeness." The participatory approach, in contrast, denies that there can be any possible neutral position within public discourse, because public discourse is precisely the site of political contention about the nature of collective identity, and it is only by reference to some vision of collective identity that speech can be categorized as relevant or irrelevant, abusive or not abusive, of "high" or "low" value. The participatory theory understands national identity to be endlessly controversial, so that national identity cannot without contradiction provide grounds for the censorship of public discourse itself.

In both of these respects the Meiklejohnian perspective is structurally quite analogous to the theory of the marketplace of ideas. Both theories focus primarily on maintaining the integrity of processes of collective thinking. The Meiklejohnian approach seeks to safeguard the dialogue necessary for voting wise decisions; the theory of the marketplace of ideas seeks to protect the dialogue necessary for advancing truth. Just as Holmes in his *Abrams* dissent stressed that in proposing the theory of the marketplace of ideas he was "speaking only of expressions of opinion and exhortations," so contemporary Meiklejohnians seek to distinguish "between cognitive and noncognitive aspects of speech" and to award "less constitutional protection" to the latter. Both theories are keenly aware of the prerequisites for constructive thinking. Just as Dewey viewed "ridicule, abuse, [and] intimidation" as incompatible with rational discussion, so Meiklejohn viewed "abusive" speech as incompatible with a well-ordered town meeting.

Reconciling First Amendment Theory and Doctrine

It is particularly significant that our First Amendment tradition decisively rejects these critical components of both the Meiklejohnian perspective and the theory of the marketplace of ideas. American courts have consistently opted to protect individual autonomy against regulations of public discourse designed to maintain the integrity of collective thinking processes. In the area of campaign finance reform, for example, the Supreme Court has forcefully asserted that "the concept that government may restrict the speech of some elements of our society in order to enhance the relative voice of others" should be repudiated as "wholly foreign to the First Amendment."[64] In contexts ranging from restrictions on pornography and hate speech to "right-of-reply" statutes applicable to newspapers, contemporary advocates of the Meiklejohnian position have sharply and frequently complained of the tendency of courts to extend constitutional protection to individual rights even when the exercise of such rights "distorts" public discussion by perpetuating imbalances of social and economic power.

This commitment to individual rights is one of the hallmarks of our distinctively American free-speech jurisprudence. The one notable exception to this commitment has been the Court's approval of federal regulations of the broadcast media. These regulations, which were designed to promote a balanced and well-ordered national dialogue on public issues, were clearly inspired by Meiklejohnian principles. Before adjudging such regulations constitutional, however, the Supreme Court

64. Buckley v. Valeo, 424 U.S. 1, 48–49 (1976).

took extraordinary care to characterize broadcast licensees as trustees for the speech of others, rather than as themselves direct participants in the conduct of self-governance. This characterization enabled the Court to regard the imposition of broadcast regulations as not infringing on autonomous participants in the process of self-determination, and hence as compatible with the participatory approach.

American free-speech jurisprudence is also unique in its refusal to permit governments to exclude from public discourse irrational or abusive speech, or speech otherwise deemed incompatible with rational dialogue. Beginning with cases like *Cantwell v. Connecticut*[67] and *Terminiello v. Chicago,*[68] First Amendment decisions have stood foursquare for the proposition that constitutional protection should be extended to speech within public discourse that is "outrageous"[69] or "offensive";[70] that is filled with "exaggeration" or "vilification";[71] that is "indecent";[72] that ruptures the "dignity" of its recipient;[73] or that is perceived as an instrument of "aggression and personal assault."[74] According to both the Meiklejohnian tradition and the theory of the marketplace of ideas, there is little constitutional reason to protect such speech, because it runs so directly contrary to the prerequisites of constructive thinking.

The participatory approach, by contrast, explains both why such speech is protected and why this protection is limited. The participatory approach does not focus on the cognitive cogency of speech, but rather on its facilitation of democratic participation. Even irrational and abusive speech can, within particular circumstances, serve as a vehicle for the construction of democratic legitimacy. When irrational and abusive speech serves this function, which is to say when it is deemed within public discourse, its regulation would both compromise the neutrality of the state and the autonomy of those participating within public discourse. But when such speech does not serve this function, which is to say when it is deemed not within public discourse, it can be and commonly is regulated. The upshot is a uniquely American jurisprudence that displays an overriding constitutional conviction to interpret the First Amendment "to ensure that the individual citizen can effectively participate in and contribute to our republican system of self-government."[77]

This analysis suggests that where the doctrinal implications of different prominent theories of the First Amendment collide, courts will tend to give priority to the participatory theory of democracy. But this does not mean that other theories do not continue to have weight and consequence when they are not inconsistent with the participatory

67. 310 U.S. 296 (1940).

68. 337 U.S. 1 (1949).

69. Hustler Magazine v. Falwell, 485 U.S. 46, 53 (1988).

70. Cohen v. California, 403 U.S. 15, 22 (1971).

71. *Cantwell,* 310 U.S. at 310.

72. Reno v. ACLU, 521 U.S. 844, 869 (1997).

73. Boos v. Barry, 485 U.S. 312, 322 (1988).

74. Time, Inc. v. Hill, 385 U.S. 374, 412 (1967) (Fortas, J., dissenting).

77. Globe Newspaper Co. v. Superior Court, 457 U.S. 596, 604 (1982).

theory. Just as the marketplace of ideas continues to inform constitutional understandings of academic freedom, so the Meiklejohnian perspective continues to structure the regulation of speakers like the broadcast media, who are not understood to be participants in public discourse.

The full force of the participatory theory is most strikingly revealed when its requirements are contrasted with a regime of speech governed by a competing theory, like the Meiklejohnian approach. Consider, for example, the area of "commercial speech." The Court has never intimated that commercial speech should receive constitutional protection because participation in such speech facilitates democratic legitimacy. Instead the Court has explained that commercial speech merits First Amendment concern because it serves an "informational function."[78] "The free flow of commercial information," the Court has argued, is "indispensable to the formation of intelligent opinions" necessary for enlightened "public decisionmaking in a democracy."[79]

This reasoning represents a classic explication of the Meiklejohnian tradition. It stresses the cognitive contribution of speech to democratic decisionmaking, rather than the legitimation producing effects of speech understood as a vehicle of participation. The pattern of constitutional protection which the Court has extended to commercial speech thus follows a distinctly different pattern than that afforded to public discourse. The Court has allowed regulations of commercial speech that are necessary to preserve the integrity of its informational function, and hence it has accorded to commercial speech a "lesser protection."[80] Commercial speech can be suppressed if it is "misleading"[81] or "overreaching"[82] or "intrusive" and invasive of "privacy."[83] Yet because commercial speech is not understood as a vehicle for participation in the creation of democratic legitimacy, such regulation is not inconsistent with the participatory approach.

The example of commercial speech suggests that First Amendment jurisprudence contains several operational and legitimate theories of freedom of speech, so that it is quite implausible to aspire to clarify First Amendment doctrine by abandoning all but one of these theories. In this short essay I have been able to discuss only the most important theories of the First Amendment, but there are certainly others. Many prominent academics, for example, have argued that the First Amendment should be interpreted so as to protect a value known variously as "individual self-realization,"[85] "individual self-fulfillment,"[86] or "human liberty,"[87]

78. Central Hudson Gas & Elec. v. Public Serv. Comm'n, 447 U.S. 557, 563 (1980).

79. Virginia State Bd. of Pharmacy v. Virginia Citizens Consumer Council, 425 U.S. 748, 765 (1976).

80. United States v. Edge Broadcasting Co., 509 U.S. 418, 426 (1993).

81. *Central Hudson,* 447 U.S. at 566.

82. Ohralik v. Ohio State Bar Ass'n, 436 U.S. 447, 461 (1978).

83. Florida Bar v. Went For It, Inc., 515 U.S. 618, 624 (1995).

85. Martin H. Redish, *The Value of Free Speech,* 130 U. Pa. L. Rev. 591, 593 (1982).

86. Thomas I. Emerson, The System of Freedom of Expression 6 (1970).

87. C. Edwin Baker, Human Liberty and Freedom of Speech (1989).

and occasionally there have been court decisions that appear to be inexplicable except by reference to some such theory of "individual liberty."[88] But there are not many such decisions, and so the theory does not seem to be very powerful.

Sometimes diverse First Amendment theories converge on similar doctrinal rules. The "clear and present danger" test formulated by Holmes may well be an example of such an overdetermined rule. But sometimes diverse First Amendment theories will require inconsistent doctrinal regimes, and when this occurs courts must decide which theory is to be given priority. I have argued in this essay that on the whole courts tend to give priority to the participatory theory of democracy, so that courts will not implement the doctrinal implications of other theories when they are inconsistent with the participatory approach.

The example of commercial speech, however, indicates that courts will nevertheless feel free to impose the doctrinal implications of other theories of the First Amendment when they are not inconsistent with the requirements of the participatory theory. We might generalize this insight by observing that theories of the First Amendment can be arranged according to a lexical priority. When theories conflict with each other, courts must decide the order in which theories should take precedence. To say, therefore, that a theory like "individual self-fulfillment" or even the marketplace of ideas is not powerful is to say that it ranks low in this lexical order, and that it cannot explain many decisions whose outcomes are not also required by lexically prior theories.

This way of conceptualizing the relationship of doctrine to theory accepts that we shall always have inconsistent regimes of First Amendment doctrine. But it also promises that this inconsistency can itself display a certain kind of order. The rules of the participatory theory will be imposed when required by that theory; the rules of the Meiklejohnian perspective will be imposed when required by that perspective and not incompatible with the participatory theory; the rules of the theory of the marketplace of ideas will be imposed when required by that theory and not incompatible with the participatory and Meiklejohnian approaches; and so forth.

The nature of this lexical ordering has been obscured by the tendency of courts to speak of First Amendment rules as applying to speech generally, thus systematically effacing the domains of speech actually implicated by different First Amendment theories. For example, in describing the First Amendment regime imposed upon commercial speech, the Supreme Court will remark that "[o]ur jurisprudence has emphasized that 'commercial speech [enjoys] a limited measure of protection, commensurate with its subordinate position in the scale of First Amendment values'; and is subject to 'modes of regulation that might be impermissible in the realm of noncommercial expression.' "[89] By charac-

88. *See, e.g.,* Stanley v. Georgia, 394 U.S. 557, 565 (1969).

89. Board of Trustees of the State Univ. v. Fox, 492 U.S. 469, 477 (1989) (quoting *Ohralik,* 436 U.S. at 456).

terizing commercial speech as subordinate to "noncommercial expression," the Court propagates a patent falsehood. There are many areas of noncommercial expression that receive no First Amendment protection at all, as the example of consumer product warnings illustrates. Thus the Court should instead have said that commercial speech receives less protection than "public discourse," thereby making clear that what is really at stake is the priority between the participatory and the Meiklejohnian theories of the First Amendment.

CONCLUSION

By perennially speaking as though speech were itself the object of First Amendment doctrine, the Court has promulgated a confusing regime of conflicting doctrinal rules that cannot possibly mean what they say. This is the underlying cause of what is now generally acknowledged to be the sorry state of First Amendment doctrine. If, as I have suggested, the plurality of legitimate First Amendment theories limits the kind of doctrinal simplicity and clarity that is constitutionally obtainable, we can nevertheless expect courts to specify the lexical priority among First Amendment theories, as well as to be clear about the domain of speech pertinent to each theory. If courts can follow these simple prescriptions, we will have come a long way toward calming the tumultuous sea of First Amendment doctrine.

Questions

1) Professor Post proposes an individual-centered "participatory theory" which locates self-governance "in the processes through which citizens come to identify a government as their own" so that "citizens experience their state as an example of authentic self-determination." How does this rationale for free speech protection compare with the individual-centered theories described by Balkin, Shiffrin, Schauer, Fried, Wells, Raz, and Blasi? Which theory has the strongest foundation in liberal tradition and constitutional text and history? Which promises best to advance the project of First Amendment doctrinal elaboration? Need these theories be mutually exclusive?

2) Professor Post believes that his individual-centered participatory theory supports the Supreme Court's assertion (p. 279) in *Buckley v. Valeo*, the case that invalidated campaign spending limits, that "the concept that government may restrict the speech of some elements of our society in order to enhance the relative voice of others" is "wholly foreign to the First Amendment." Does the participatory theory also support the Court's specific rulings in *Buckley* that every candidate for political office has a right to spend unlimited sums of money from personal resources in conducting her campaign, and that every member of the political community has a right to spend unlimited sums of money to pay for political advertising aimed at influencing the outcome of an election so long as those expenditures are not co-ordinated with the candidate's campaign? Do all of the other individual-centered theories that we have studied in

this chapter carry such implications? Which individual-centered theory is most consistent with the claim that some limits on campaign spending can be reconciled with the First Amendment?

3) Does Post's participatory theory offer resources for justifying the Supreme Court's decision in *West Virginia State Board of Education v. Barnette*? More so than Meiklejohn's theory? More so than the other individual-centered theories we have studied in this chapter?

Additional Readings

Autonomy and free speech

C. Edwin Baker, Human Liberty and Freedom of Speech (1989)

Gerald Dworkin, The Theory and Practice of Autonomy (1988)

Richard Fallon, Two Senses of Autonomy, 46 Stan. L. Rev. 875 (1994)

Kent Greenawalt, Free Speech Justifications, 89 Colum. L. Rev. 119 (1989)

Diana T. Meyers, Self, Society, and Personal Choice (1989)

Brian C. Murchison, Speech and the Self–Realization Value, 33 Harv. C.R.-C.L. L. Rev. 443 (1998)

Martin H. Redish, The Value of Free Speech, 130 U. Pa. L. Rev. 591 (1982)

David A. J. Richards, Toleration and the Constitution (1986)

David Strauss, Persuasion, Autonomy, and Freedom of Expression, 91 Colum. L. Rev. 334 (1991)

Susan H. Williams, Truth, Autonomy, and Speech: Feminist Theory and the First Amendment (2004)

Cohen v. California

William Cohen, A Look Back at *Cohen v. California*, 34 UCLA L. Rev. 1595 (1987)

Daniel Farber, Civilizing Public Discourse: An Essay on Professor Bickel, Justice Harlan, and the Enduring Significance of *Cohen v. California*, 1980 Duke L. J. 283

Ronald J. Krotoszynski, Jr., *Cohen v. California*: "Inconsequential Cases" and Larger Principles, 74 Tex. L. Rev. 1251 (1996)

Barnes v. Glen Theatre and Erie v. Pap's A.M.

Christopher Thomas Leahy, Comment, The First Amendment Gone Awry: *City of Erie v. Pap's A.M.*, Ailing Analytical Structures, and the Suppression of Protected Expression, 150 U. Pa. L. Rev. 1021 (2002)

Robert C. Post, Recuperating First Amendment Doctrine, 47 Stan. L. Rev. 1249 (1995)

Hurley

Darren Lenard Hutchinson, Accommodating Outness: *Hurley*, Free Speech, and Gay and Lesbian Equality, 1 U. Pa. J. Const. L. 85 (1998)

Madhavi Sunder, Note, Authorship and Autonomy As Rites of Exclusion: The Intellectual Propertization of Free Speech in *Hurley v. Irish–American Gay, Lesbian and Bisexual Group of Boston*, 49 Stan. L. Rev. 143 (1996)

Gretchen Van Ness, Parades & Prejudice: The Incredible True Story of Boston's St. Patrick's Day Parade & The U.S. Supreme Court, 30 New Eng. L. Rev. 625 (1996)

Boy Scouts of America v. Dale

Erwin Chemerinsky & Catherine Fisk, The Expressive Interests of Associations, 9 Wm. & Mary Bill Rts. J. 595 (2001)

Daniel A. Farber, Speaking in the First Person Plural: Expressive Association and the First Amendment, 85 Minn. L. Rev. 1483 (2001)

David McGowan, Making Sense of *Dale,* 18 Const. Commentary 121 (2001)

Seana Valentine Shiffrin, What Is Really Wrong With Compelled Association? 99 Nw. U. L. Rev. 839 (2005)

*

Index

References are to Pages

References are to Pages

References are to Pages

References are to Pages

References are to Pages

References are to Pages

†